T0181772

Requirements Engineering

Klaus Pohl

Requirements Engineering

Fundamentals, Principles, and Techniques

Prof. Dr. Klaus Pohl
University of Duisburg-Essen
Paluno - The Ruhr Institute for Software Technology
Gerlingstraße 16
45127 Essen
Germany
klaus.pohl@paluno.uni-due.de

ISBN 978-3-662-51888-5 ISBN 978-3-642-12578-2 (eBook)
DOI 10.1007/978-3-642-12578-2
Springer Heidelberg Dordrecht London New York

ACM Computing Classification (1998): D.2, K.6

Cover design: KuenkelLopka GmbH, Heidelberg

Printed on acid-free paper

Springer is part of Springer Science+Business Media (www.springer.com)

Preface

I chose requirements engineering as a research area in the early 1990s. The experience I gained in several industrial projects indicated that insufficient requirements engineering causes inconsistent, incomplete, and incorrect requirements specifications and is responsible for a significant number of the problems encountered in development projects. It hence became my desire and conviction to sustainably improve the way requirements are elicited, documented, and used in system development.

Current situation in practice

Since the early 1990s, the area of requirements engineering has evolved considerably. Researchers have developed, validated, and transferred into practice innovative solutions for numerous requirements engineering problems. Many companies have recognised the importance of requirements engineering and, as a consequence, started to put more emphasis on the early "phase" of system development. Universities have also started teaching dedicated requirements engineering courses to both undergraduate and graduate students.

Nevertheless, my industrial collaboration with practitioners, as well as presentations at national and international conferences, indicates that requirements engineering is still performed in an insufficient, inefficient, and ad hoc manner in many cases. Frequently, essential aspects of requirements engineering are still neglected. Even the stakeholders responsible for the development process in an organisation typically have only insufficient, partial knowledge about requirements engineering.

Yet Another Book on Requirements Engineering?

Lack of a comprehensive textbook

Is there really a need for yet another book on requirements engineering? An analysis of existing German and English requirements engineering books revealed that most of the existing books provide excellent contributions to requirements engineering from different perspectives. However, a comprehensive, well-structured, and easy-to-understand textbook or compendium did not exist.

Aim of This Book

Fundamentals, principles, and techniques

This book aims to provide a comprehensive, well-structured introduction to the fundamentals, principles, and techniques of requirements engineering based on knowledge and experience gained in research and on industrial projects. The various aspects of requirements engineering described in this book are illustrated with numerous examples. In addition, checklists and guidelines are provided to support the application of the requirements engineering principles and techniques described in this book in practice. For each topic, annotated literature recommendations point to selected further reading.

Textbook and compendium

Briefly, this book is a comprehensive requirements engineering textbook and compendium.

Target Audience

Professionals, students, and lecturers

This book is aimed at professionals, students, and lecturers in the area of software and systems engineering as well as business information systems. Professionals involved in or affected by requirements engineering such as project managers, business and systems analysts, architects, developers and testers, and requirements engineers will find in their daily work that this book is a valuable compendium and source of important requirements engineering fundamentals, principles, and practicable techniques. My personal motivation for writing this book was also to provide my undergraduate and graduate students with a textbook which will accompany them throughout their studies and their professional career. Lecturers who want to use this textbook in their courses can find reference courses, accompanying lab exercises, as well as teaching slides on the book's website www.requirements-book.com (see "Teaching a Requirements Engineering Course" below).

Content of This Book

Part I of the book provides a comprehensive introduction to the fundamentals of requirements engineering and briefly characterises the evolution of requirements engineering from an early, informal phase in the software development process to a continuous, project-spanning and cross-product activity. At the end of Part I, the requirements engineering framework which serves as the backbone of this book is presented. The framework consists of four building blocks:

Structure for the system context

- *Four context facets*: Each software-intensive system is embedded in a given context. An adequate consideration of the system context during requirements engineering is essential for each successful system development. Back in 1993, Matthias Jarke and myself therefore defined the main aim of requirements engineering as "establishing a vision in context" [Jarke and Pohl 1993].

  Part II of the book outlines the separation between the system and its context, and proposes a structure for the system context to facilitate its consideration in all requirements engineering activities.

Goals, scenarios, and solution-oriented requirements

- *Three kinds of requirements artefacts*: The documented (specified) system requirements are the key results of a requirements engineering process. Our requirements engineering framework differentiates three kinds of requirements (artefacts): *goals*, which document (abstract) intentions concerning the system; *scenarios*, which describe concrete examples of achieving or failing to achieve the goals and are used, among other things, to document the usage view of the system; *solution-oriented requirements* such as data, functional, and behavioural models, which document the requirements for the system in detail and are primarily used to support the subsequent system development activities and thus the correct realisation of the system.

Part III of the book outlines the characteristics of the three kinds of requirements and describes commonly used types of goals, scenarios, and solution-oriented requirements. Moreover, the role of goals and scenarios in all core and cross-sectional activities of requirements engineering is briefly discussed (see below). Details about the use of goals and scenarios in all requirements engineering activities are described in those parts of the book describing the activities.

Documentation, elicitation, and negotiation

- *Three core activities*: We differentiate three core requirements engineering activities: *elicitation*, *documentation* (specification) and *negotiation*. These three activities are derived from the three dimensions of requirements engineering: the content dimension, the documentation dimension, and the agreement dimension (see [Pohl 1994; Pohl 1997]).

  The three core activities are elaborated upon in Part IV of the book. For the documentation activity, different documentation languages (including natural language and model-based requirements documentation) are described and hints and guidelines for applying the different documentation languages and techniques during requirements engineering are provided. For the elicitation and negotiation activities, established techniques that are frequently used in requirements engineering are described.

Validation and management

- *Two cross-sectional activities*: Besides the three core activities, two cross-sectional activities are essential for the success of requirements engineering: the validation activity and the management activity. The main aim of the validation activity is threefold: it validates whether the context has been adequately considered during requirements engineering, it validates the documented requirements, and it validates whether the requirements engineering activities have been performed consistently with the process guidelines. We consider (requirements) management as a part of requirements engineering. The management activity consists of three key sub-activities, namely ensuring requirements traceability, prioritising requirements, and managing requirements changes.

  Part V of the book describes the techniques for supporting the validation activity. Part VI elaborates on the management activity and its sub-activities.

Part VII of the book presents our goal- and scenario-based requirements engineering method COSMOD-RE. COSMOD-RE supports the intertwined development of requirements and architectural artefacts for software-intensive (embedded) systems. It employs a hierarchy of four abstraction layers and defines requirements artefacts (goals, scenarios, and solution-oriented requirements) and architectural artefacts for each abstraction layer. It further structures the development process of these artefacts into three co-design processes: the system-level co-design process, the function-level co-design process, and the hardware/software-level co-design process. The co-development of requirements and architectural artefacts with COSMOD-RE is illustrated using a simplified driver assistance system.

Part VIII of the book elaborates on the relationships between requirements engineering and requirements-based testing and sketches the key differences between requirements engineering in single-system engineering and requirements engineering in software product line engineering.

Teaching a Requirements Engineering Course?

References to different basic level, advanced level, and special-purpose courses can be found on the book's website (www.requirements-book.com). The courses range from a 14-week course with 2 h of lectures per week to 4 h lessons on specific topics, as well as overview lessons on fundamental aspects of requirements engineering. Each course unit refers to the relevant parts of the book. The teaching goals for each unit are explicitly stated, and exercises and practical training to accompany the course units are sketched out.

Experiences and Feedback

No book is perfect. Despite diligence and thorough proofreading, this book may contain errors or parts that deserve improvement. If you have detected a mistake, if you miss a topic, or if you have any constructive suggestions for improvement, please do not hesitate to send an email to:

feedback@requirements-book.com

or to provide your feedback on the book's website:

www.requirements-book.com

I look forward to receiving your valuable suggestions for improvement.

History of This Book

This book is based on a German requirements engineering textbook published first in 2007 (first edition) and then in 2008 (second edition). Without the German textbook, this book would never have been possible.

However, this book is not just a translation of the second German edition. During the writing of this book several parts have been significantly reworked and new material has been added, especially regarding documentation of solution-oriented requirements, the COSMOD-RE method, and requirements engineering for product lines. The third German edition will be based on the English version of our textbook.

Acknowledgements

German textbook

First, I want to thank my PhD students and post-docs for many fruitful discussions, constructive suggestions for improvement, and their commitment which made the German textbook possible, especially Kim Lauenroth, Ernst Sikora, and Thorsten Weyer for their contributions to Parts I to VII and Andreas Metzger, Günter Halmans, and Andreas Froese for their contributions to Part VIII. I am indebted to Lero (the Irish Software Engineering Research Centre) for supporting several book meetings and especially to Kevin Ryan who successfully encouraged me to finalise the German book project.

English textbook

Second, I want to thank the people who supported me in writing the English textbook for their extensive assistance in the translation from German into English as well as for their contributions to the significantly reworked parts of this book and the numerous improvements and extensions throughout the entire book:

Ernst Sikora
Nelufar Ulfat-Bunyadi

In addition, I would like to thank all the other people from my research group for their valuable proofreading and numerous constructive suggestions for improvement, especially Marian Daun, André Heuer, Kim Lauenroth, Mark Rzepka, Bastian Tenbergen, and Thorsten Weyer.

Furthermore, I would like to thank my students, industrial partners, and the people attending our tutorials and trainings for continuously asking critical questions — a valuable source for many improvements. I also want to thank Ralf Gerstner, Colin Marsh, and Ulrike Stricker from Springer for their support in publishing this book.

My deepest thanks go to my wife Bärbel and to my children Timo and Ella for their incomparable patience, support, and understanding.

Klaus Pohl
Essen, 2010

Table of Contents

Part I
Fundamentals and Framework

Overview Part I – Fundamentals and Framework

Requirements engineering is a critical success factor for each software development project. This part of the book elaborates on:

- *The term "requirement"*
- *The differentiation between functional requirements, quality requirements, and constraints*
- *The embedding of requirements engineering in the organisational context*
- *The development of requirements engineering from an initial software development phase to a continuous project- and product-spanning activity*
- *The difference between problem definition and solution description*

In addition, our framework for requirements engineering is described in this part of the book. The framework consists of the following building blocks:

- *The four context facets: the subject, the usage, the IT (information technology) system, and the development facet*
- *The three core activities: elicitation, documentation, and negotiation*
- *Two cross-sectional activities: validation and management*
- *Three kinds of requirements artefacts: goals, scenarios, and solution-oriented requirements*

The framework serves as the backbone of this book. The structure of this book is explained in more detail at the end of this part.

Classification Part I Fundamentals and Framework	Basic	Advanced
1 Motivation		
1.1 Software-Intensive Systems	✓	
1.2 Importance of Requirements Engineering	✓	
1.3 Embedding of Requirements Engineering in the Organisational Context	✓	
2 Requirements		
2.1 The Term "Requirement"	✓	
2.2 Requirement Types	✓	
2.3 Problem vs. Solution	✓	
3 Continuous Requirements Engineering		
3.1 Traditional Systems Analysis	✓	
3.2 Essential Systems Analysis		✓
3.3 Requirements Engineering as an Early Development Phase	✓	
3.4 Shortcomings of Systems Analysis and Phase-Oriented Requirements Engineering	✓	
3.5 Continuous Requirements Engineering	✓	
4 The Requirements Engineering Framework		
4.1 Goal of Requirements Engineering: Establishing a Vision in Context	✓	
4.2 Overview of the Framework	✓	
4.3 Four Context Facets	✓	
4.4 Three Core Activities	✓	
4.5 Two Cross-Sectional Activities	✓	
4.6 The Three Kinds of Requirements Artefacts	✓	
4.7 Overview of the Book	✓	

Chapter 1
Motivation

In this chapter, we outline:

- *The main challenges faced when developing software-intensive systems*
- *The importance of requirements engineering for the development of software-intensive systems*
- *The embedding of requirements engineering into the organisational context and the relationships of requirements engineering to other processes within the organisation*

1.1 Software-Intensive Systems

Two kinds of software-intensive systems

Nowadays, software is pervasive in most industrial sectors such as the automobile industry, mechanical engineering, financial services, consumer electronics, or medical devices and is a key technology for product innovation. We call a system a "software-intensive system" if essential parts of its functionality and/or its qualities are realised by software. We differentiate between two kinds of software-intensive systems:

Mainly software

- *Information systems*: An information system collects, stores, transforms, transmits, and/or processes information or data. The goal of an information system is to provide users (persons or other systems) with the information they need, at the right time and in the right place. An example of an information system is a bank accounting system which informs customers about the balance of their accounts or the processing of their payments and bank transfers. An information system consists mainly of software running on general-purpose computers.

Software and hardware closely integrated

- *Embedded software-intensive systems*: In contrast to information systems, software is only one part of an embedded software-intensive system, albeit an important part which often enables innovative functionality and qualities. In an embedded software-intensive system, the software is closely integrated with hardware, i.e. often complex interactions between the hardware and the software parts of the system need to be realised. A typical example of an embedded software-intensive system is an anti-lock braking system (ABS) of a car. The software of the ABS control unit interacts closely with the hardware (e.g. wheel sensors, break system, engine control system, etc.) to prevent wheel lock-up even if the driver steps on the brake pedal firmly and the road is slippery. ABS thus ensures, among other things, that the vehicle can still be steered even under such conditions.

1.1.1 Example: Importance of Embedded Systems in the Automotive Industry

Importance of software in the automotive industry

The automotive industry provides a prominent example of the increasing importance of embedded software-intensive systems in many domains. Evidence for the increasing importance of software in the automotive domain is provided by many studies. For example, a survey conducted by the McKinsey consulting company has forecast a shift in the relation between the electronics and the mechanics of a car towards the former causing an increase in the cost of the electronics from 11% to 24% of the total cost of a car (see [VDA 2003]).

Market volume of software increases dramatically

Another study conducted by Mercer Management Consulting, Fraunhofer-Gesellschaft, and Robert Bosch GmbH in 2004 forecasts a strong increase in the market volume of software in the automotive industry. The forecast for the market volume of technological components, i.e. electrical and electronic systems, sensors, integrated circuits (ICs), and software, is based on interviews with decision-makers of the automotive manufacturers and subcontractors. As illustrated in Fig. 1-1, the interviewees predicted a growth in the market volume for technological components in the automotive sector from 127 billion euros in 2002 to 316 billion euros in 2015

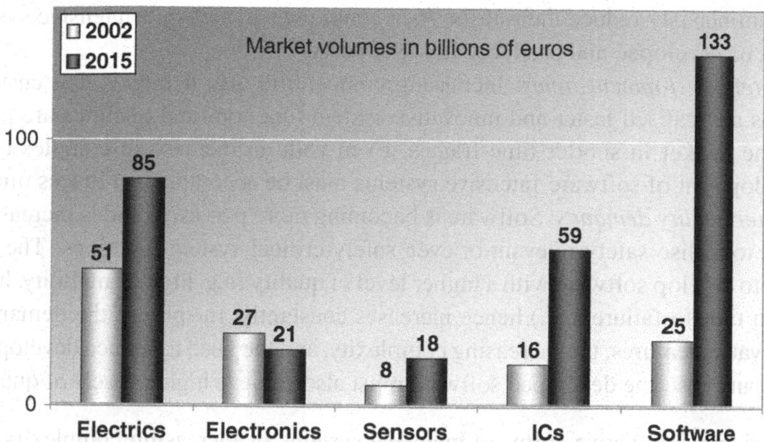

Fig. 1-1 *Market volume of software in the automotive sector for the year 2002 and forecast for the year 2015 (according to [Honsig 2005])*

(see [FAST 2004]). The market volume of software is predicted to grow from 25 billion euros in 2003 to 133 billion euros in 2015 (see [Honsig 2005]). The overall predicted increase in market volume for software is thus approximately 530% overall and, on average, approximately 15% per year over 12 years. The anticipated growth rate of software hence exceeds the anticipated growth rate for electricity, electronics, integrated circuitry, and sensors.

1.1.2 Challenges in the Development of Software-Intensive Systems

Today, the development of software-intensive systems (both embedded systems as well as information systems) faces a number of challenges which can be characterised as follows:

- *Software-based innovations*: Customers increasingly demand innovative features. Companies are hence put under pressure to offer innovative features even in mid-range products. Software is the key technology for realising innovative product features. Software therefore plays an increasingly crucial role in system development and becomes a (if not the) crucial factor for the success of a product.

Software as a driver for innovation

- *Increasing complexity*: The complexity of a software-intensive system significantly increases, for example, due to the increasing number of functions realised by software, the increasing integration between different systems, and the increasing number of system variants provided in order to fulfil customer needs. This trend poses new challenges for the development of such systems. For example, it demands new development methods which systematically support developers in dealing with this increasing complexity.

Need for new approaches

- *Pressure to reduce costs*: Stagnating markets, increasing competition, and customers' demands for lower product prices put many companies under pressure

Pressure to reduce costs

to continuously reduce their costs. As a consequence, software-intensive systems must be developed and produced at lower costs.

Increasing time pressure

- *Shorter development times*: Increasing competition also demands that customer needs are realised faster and innovative system functions and qualities are placed on the market in shorter time frames. Even with an increase in complexity, the development of software-intensive systems must be accomplished in less time.

Increasing quality demands

- *Higher quality demands*: Software is becoming more pervasive and is increasingly used to realise safety-relevant or even safety-critical system functions. The pressure to develop software with a higher level of quality (e.g. high availability, higher mean time to failure, etc.) hence increases constantly. In spite of the demand for innovative features, the increasing complexity, and the need to reduce development time and cost, the developed software must also achieve higher levels of quality.

Summarising, innovative software-intensive systems of increasing complexity must be developed with a higher level of quality, in a shorter time frame, and at lower costs — a significant challenge for the development of software-intensive systems.

Requirements engineering is already essential for successful system development today (see Section 1.2). Requirements engineering is also a key factor for dealing with the challenges outlined above. As explained in Section 3.5, overcoming these challenges necessitates establishing requirements engineering as a continuous, project-spanning and cross-product activity.

1.2 Importance of Requirements Engineering

1.2.1 Impact on Project Success

Project success rates

Various studies of the Standish Group state that inappropriate requirements engineering is one of the most important reasons for project failures. The frequently cited *Standish Group Report* from 1995 [The Standish Group 1995] reports that only 52.7% of the projects analysed in the study were finished, but they exceeded the estimated budget by up to 189%.[1] Moreover, on average only 42% of the planned system functions were implemented.[2] Of the projects 16.1% were finished on time, within budget, and realised all the planned system functions.[3] Of all projects 31.1% were cancelled and did not deliver the desired results.

Comparison of the years 1994–2004

Figure 1-2 provides an overview of the project success rates from 1994 to 2009 taken from the *CHAOS studies* of the Standish Group. The figure shows that the percentage of successfully finished projects in 2009 was significantly higher than in 1994. However, the value has been stagnating since 1996 at a rate around 30%. In all the studies summarised in Fig. 1-2, at least 65% of the projects failed or finished

[1] More recent studies reveal that, in the year 2000, only 45% of the projects were finished (see [The Standish Group 2002]).

[2] The numbers mentioned hold for large US companies. In the case of small companies, 78.4% of the projects were successfully finished and, on average, 74.2% of the planned system functions were realised (see [The Standish Group 1995]).

[3] This value is a mean value which takes large companies as well as small and medium-sized companies into account. In the case of large companies only 9% of the projects were finished on time and within budget.

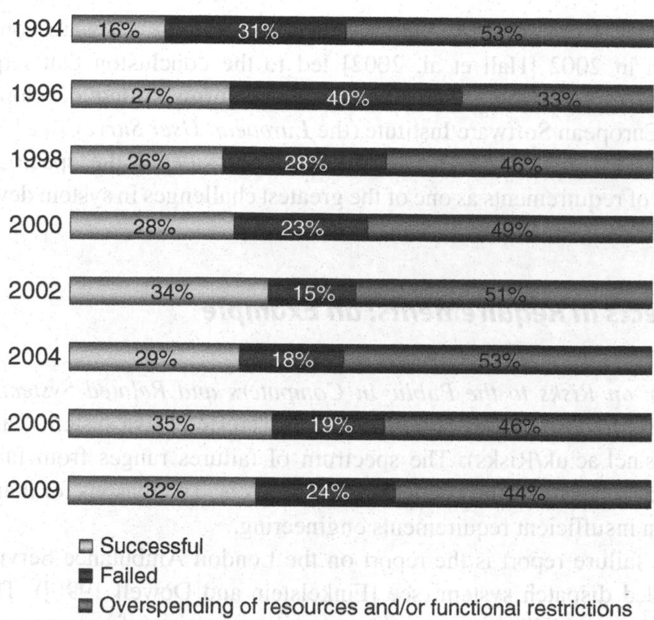

Fig. 1-2 *Project success rates from 1994 to 2009 taken from the Standish Group (CHAOS) studies [The Standish Group 2009]*

with an overspend above the estimated resources and/or with restricted implemented functionality. Thus the situation has not changed significantly since 1996.

Of failures 48% are due to inadequate requirements engineering

The reasons why projects finished with an overspend above the estimated resources and/or restricted implemented functionality have been elicited (see e.g. [The Standish Group 1995]). Figure 1-3 depicts the different reasons and the percentage of each reason stated by the project participants. Reasons that are definitely related to insufficient and poor requirements engineering are highlighted in dark grey in Fig. 1-3. Together, they sum up to 48%.

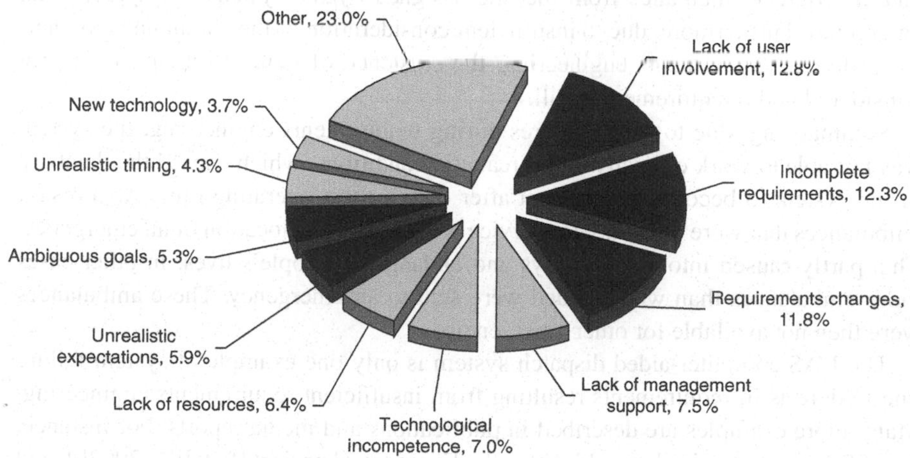

Fig. 1-3 *Reasons for resource overspend and/or functional restrictions (based on data from [The Standish Group 1995])*

Confirmation by further studies

Other studies reveal similar results. Interviews with 12 software companies in Great Britain in 2002 [Hall et al. 2002] led to the conclusion that requirements defects caused approximately 50% of the problems during system development. In a study of the European Software Institute (the *European User Survey Analysis Report*, [ESI 1996]), 50% of the companies consulted considered the specification and management of requirements as one of the greatest challenges in system development.

1.2.2 Defects in Requirements: an Example

In the *Forum on Risks to the Public in Computers and Related Systems* by Peter Neumann, several descriptions of failures in software-intensive systems can be found (http://catless.ncl.ac.uk/Risks). The spectrum of failures ranges from failures with minor consequences to failures with disastrous effects. The reasons for many of these failures lay in insufficient requirements engineering.

London Ambulance Service (LAS)

A famous failure report is the report on the London Ambulance Services (LAS) computer-aided dispatch system (see [Finkelstein and Dowell 1996]). This system was designed to partially automate the manual processing of emergency calls. An emergency call should be answered by an employee of the LAS, who should ask for the location of the emergency. Based on this information, the system should determine the ambulances which were close to the location of the emergency. An ambulance close to the emergency location and ready for service should be dispatched to the emergency.

Consequences of deficient requirements

However, the requirements engineering process for the LAS computer-aided dispatch system was rather poor. For instance, ambulance crews were insufficiently involved in the requirements engineering process. This led, among other things, to inappropriate user interfaces for the communication devices in the ambulances. As a consequence, information about emergencies that was given to the ambulance crews via these devices was partly incorrect or insufficient. In addition, the crews had difficulties in operating the devices correctly and hence became frustrated in using the system. Also, the requirements did not account for the case in which a crew might take a different ambulance from the one assigned by the system to respond to an emergency. Furthermore, due to insufficient consideration of the communication network during requirements engineering, the existence of radio black spots was not considered in the requirements at all.

Failure of the system in operation

Summarising, due to many failures during requirements engineering, the system was not able to work correctly under realistic conditions, which caused the database of the system to become inconsistent after only a short operating time. As a result, ambulances that were not ready for service were sent to the location of an emergency. This partly caused intolerable delays and endangered people's lives. In other cases more ambulances than were needed were sent to an emergency. These ambulances were then not available for other emergencies.

Other examples

The LAS computer-aided dispatch system is only one example of system failure due to defects in requirements resulting from insufficient requirements engineering. Many more examples are described in publications and media reports. For instance, Sutcliffe reports on similar problems in the Eurocontrol project [Sutcliffe 2002b], and Potts reports on requirements-related problems in projects of the US Department of Defense [Potts 1999].

1.2.3 Defects in Requirements Cause High Costs

Specification defects

The importance of requirements engineering is often underestimated. Consequently, requirements specifications often have serious defects. Requirements are, for example, overlooked and thus neglected or are specified ambiguously, incompletely, or even contradict each other.

Of the failures in source code 50% can be traced to requirements defects

Often, requirements defects are uncovered during later system development phases. From experience, nearly 50% of the failures found in program source code can be traced back to requirements defects. At the same time, the cost of removing defects in requirements increases the later the defects are detected during the development process [Möller 1996].

Detect requirements defects and gaps as early as possible

If a requirements defect is detected during programming, the cost to fix the defect is approximately 20 times higher than the effort required to detect and fix the defect during requirements engineering. If the requirements defect is not detected until acceptance testing, the effort required can be up to 100 times greater (see [Boehm and Basili 2001]). The aim should thus be to detect and remove requirements defects as early as possible in system development. In other words, one should ensure that the requirements specification has no serious defects or gaps during requirements engineering.

!

Hint 1-1: *Increasing importance of requirements engineering*

Reasons for the increasing importance of requirements engineering in practice include:

- ❑ The failure of projects due to requirements defects
- ❑ The significantly higher costs to remove requirements defects during later system development phases
- ❑ The challenge to develop innovative, individual, and complex software-intensive systems faster, with a higher level of quality, and with lower costs
- ❑ The increasing importance of software-intensive systems in many industrial sectors
- ❑ The significantly higher number of system functions, the tighter integration with other systems, and a more differentiated usage

1.3 Embedding of Requirements Engineering in the Organisational Context

Interfaces between requirements engineering and other processes

Requirements engineering is always embedded within a specific organisational context (see e.g. [Damian and Chisan 2006]). In the organisational context, other processes and workflows are executed which interface with the requirements engineering process. The requirements engineering process receives information through these interfaces and provides information via these interfaces to the other processes.

Examples of such organisational processes are marketing, product management, customer relationship management, and project management. We sketch the interrelations with these processes in Section 1.3.1.

In addition, requirements engineering is also embedded within the development processes established in an organisation (see [Sommerville 2007] for a description of different development processes). In Section 1.3.2, we outline the main interrelations of requirements engineering with other software development phases.

Involving stakeholders from other processes

In general, relevant stakeholders from other organisational processes, as well as stakeholders from other development phases such as design, test, or maintenance, should be involved in requirements engineering in order to ensure that their needs are considered during requirements engineering.

These stakeholders have different interests and different backgrounds. During requirements engineering, they form a team responsible for eliciting, negotiating, and documenting the requirements for the system and the desired quality. If the right stakeholders are involved at the right times in requirements engineering, requirements defects and expensive rework are significantly reduced or even totally avoided.

!

Hint 1-2: *Stakeholder*

Stakeholders are persons or organisations that have an interest in the system to be developed (see Definition 6-1 on Page 79 as well as Section 6.2.1).

1.3.1 Interrelations with Other Organisational Processes

Mutual influences between requirements engineering and other organisational processes

Requirements engineering is always embedded within an organisation and thus is influenced by other organisational processes and vice versa. For example, if a dedicated product management process is established within an organisation, requirements engineering has to interface with this process. Requirements engineering, for example, obtains product strategies, information about competing products, or key success requirements from the product management process. Conversely, requirements engineering passes new, innovative requirements to product management (see Chapter 9 in [Pohl et al. 2005] and Chapter 4 in [Ebert 2008]).

Embedding RE within an organisational context may vary

The way in which requirements engineering (RE) is embedded within an organisation can vary significantly. The embedding is influenced, for example, by the structure of the existing organisational processes. If the organisation changes, the setting for and the practice of requirements engineering can likewise change. The embedding is also influenced by the way in which requirements engineering is employed. For example, whether requirements engineering is understood as a software development phase (see Section 3.4) or viewed as a continuous activity (see Section 3.5).

Nevertheless, there are typical interactions between requirements engineering and other organisational processes which we briefly describe below (see Fig. 1-4).

RE and product management

- *Interrelation with product management*: Product management defines and manages the product portfolio of an organisation. Product management typically defines a product roadmap as well as a product strategy for each product. The product roadmap mainly defines at which point in time which version of a system will be brought to the market and with which features. Key requirements for a new system or the next system release are thus often defined by product management in cooperation with requirements engineering. This obviously requires

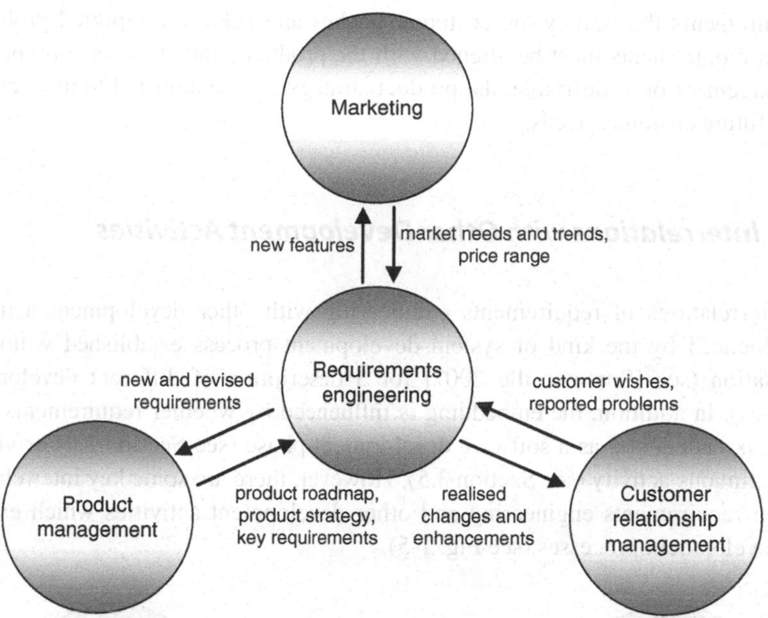

Fig. 1-4 *Interrelations between requirements engineering and other processes in the organisation*

that an agreement about the system features be achieved between product management and requirements engineering. Typically, product management suggests key requirements which are refined and (if required or desired) revised by requirements engineering to establish a complete requirements specification. In addition, requirements engineering typically suggests newly elicited or newly invented system features to product management. These are considered while planning subsequent products or product releases, or even for revising the features to be realised in the current system release. A strong mutual interdependency therefore typically exists between requirements engineering and product management.

RE and marketing

- *Interrelation with marketing*: Marketing aims to increase the market share of an organisation and to secure its current share. Marketing thus often represents the "sales perspective" when defining the key features for a new system or system release. Marketing is involved, for instance, in determining the pricing policy of the organisation and can thus define a price range within which the system to be developed must be sold. When defining the requirements for the system, this price range must obviously be considered. In addition, marketing contributes information such as market needs and trends as well as knowledge about competitors' products and future development plans to the requirements engineering process. Vice versa, requirements engineering informs marketing about new features which might be of interest to attract new customers to the organisation or which might even facilitate entering a new market segment.

RE and customer relationship management

- *Interrelation with customer relationship management*: Customer relationship management collects suggestions for improvement, needs, and problem reports from current customers. This information is obviously valuable input for requirements engineering. Requirements engineering can address the wishes, problems, and improvements suggested by current customers and develop these into a set of requirements that satisfy the customer wishes and solve the reported problems. Such requirements must be aligned with the product strategy defined by product management or, if desirable, the product strategy can be adjusted to meet current and future customer needs.

1.3.2 Interrelations with Other Development Activities

Influence of RE on other development activities

The interrelations of requirements engineering with other development activities are influenced by the kind of system development process established within the organisation (see [Sommerville 2007] for a description of different development processes). In addition, the embedding is influenced by whether requirements engineering is understood as a software development phase (see Section 3.4) or viewed as a continuous activity (see Section 3.5). However, there are some key interrelations between requirements engineering and other development activities which exist in most development processes (see Fig. 1-5).

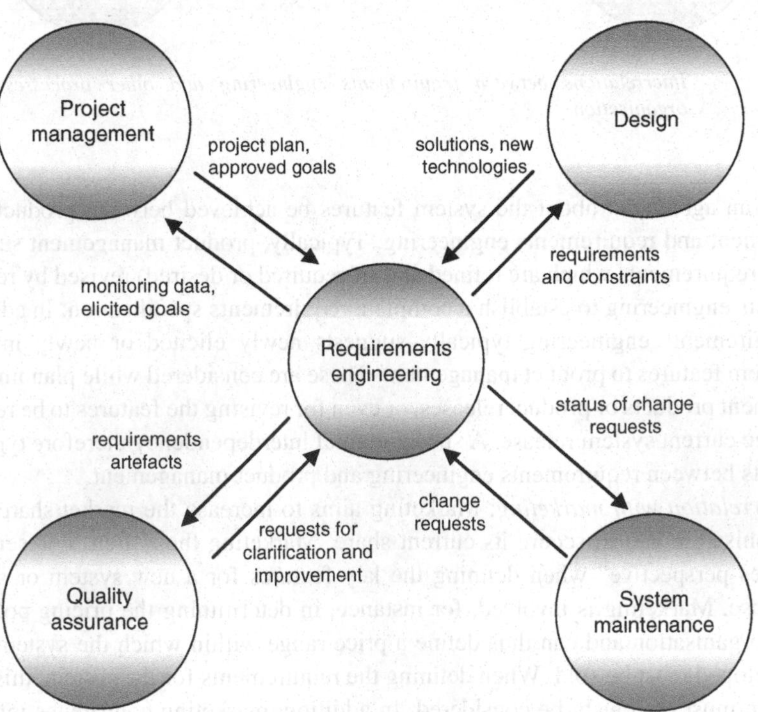

Fig. 1-5 *Interrelations between requirements engineering and other development activities*

The interrelations with the development activities depicted in Fig. 1-5 can be characterised as follows:

RE and project management

- *Interrelation with project management*: Project management is responsible for defining and maintaining an overall system development plan. Therein, it considers the goals set by other organisational processes or units, such as product management or strategic management, and has to inspect and approve the system goals elicited during requirements engineering. In consideration of the cost, resource, and time restrictions, project management plans the different development phases and defines milestones for the development of the system, including milestones for requirements engineering. In planning and monitoring the development process, project management interacts closely with the requirements management activities outlined in Part VI.

- *Interrelation with design*: The design process of a system comprises different activities such as the design of system interfaces, the design of the system architecture, and the detailed design of system components. Requirements engineering is responsible for defining the relevant requirements for all these design activities. Design process responsibilities include activities for checking whether the defined requirements can be realised under the given resource and risk constraints defined for the project. Based on the defined requirements, the design process makes suggestions for solution concepts to be discussed with the relevant stakeholders. In addition, the design process informs requirements engineering about new technologies enabling new and innovative requirements. The interrelations between requirements engineering and design (or between the problem definition and the solution description) are elaborated further in Section 2.3. Our requirements engineering method COSMOD-RE tightly integrates requirements and design activities (while still separating requirements and design artefacts) as outlined in Part VII.

RE and design

- *Interrelation with quality assurance*: Quality assurance is responsible for ensuring that the system is developed with the desired functionality and quality. For instance, system testing (a part of quality assurance) is responsible for detecting deviations between the implementation of the system and the specified requirements. Requirements engineering provides quality and functional requirements to the quality assurance and the test activities, based upon which test artefacts such as test cases are derived. Quality assurance, in turn, requests requirements engineering to resolve requirements defects detected during quality assurance activities and, if necessary, to clarify requirements to enable the specification of adequate test artefacts. We elaborate on the interrelations between requirements engineering and testing, especially the derivation of test artefacts based on the specified requirements, in Chapter 37.

RE and quality assurance

- *Interrelation with system maintenance*: After the system is put into operation or made available on the market, system maintenance is responsible for the correction of defects detected during system operation and the integration of required extensions into the system. During maintenance, the requirements specified for the system are used to determine whether a reported defect or a requested extension demands the definition of new requirements, or whether already defined but incorrectly implemented requirements caused the defect or led to the suggested extension. In general, corrections and extensions that affect the specified requirements have to pass the change management process for requirements (see Chapter 33). In order to keep the system specifications up to date, changes and extensions realised during system maintenance activities must be documented.

RE and system maintenance

Chapter 2
Requirements

In this chapter, we explain:

- *The difference between functional requirements, quality requirements, and development constraints*
- *The difficulties caused by declaring requirements as "non-functional"*
- *The differentiation between the problem ("what?") and the solution ("how?") with regard to the different phases of the development process*
- *The influence of design decisions on requirements*

2.1 The Term "Requirement"

The IEEE 610.12-1990 standard defines the term "requirement" as follows:

Definition 2-1: *Requirement*

(1) A condition or capability needed by a user to solve a problem or achieve an objective.
(2) A condition or capability that must be met or possessed by a system or system component to satisfy a contract, standard, specification, or other formally imposed documents.
(3) A documented representation of a condition or capability as in (1) or (2).

[IEEE Std 610.12-1990]

User needs and required properties

According to Definition 2-1, requirements define both (1) needs and goals of users, and (2) conditions and properties of the system to be developed that result, for example, from organisational needs, laws, or standards.

Requirement vs. requirements artefact

According to point (3) in Definition 2-1, both documented as well as undocumented conditions and capabilities are called requirements. In this book, however, we use the term "requirements artefact" to refer to a documented requirement.

Definition 2-2: *Requirements artefact*

A requirements artefact is a documented requirement.

Different kinds of requirements

The documented requirements define the foundation for executing all other development activities and are therefore essential for every development project. Therein, the term "requirement" refers to different aspects of the system as well as the development process. In Example 2-1, requirements R2 and R3 describe functionality, i.e. services to be provided by the new system. R1 and R5 define qualities the system should provide with respect to certain functionality. Requirement R4 defines a constraint (restriction) for the system development process.

Example 2-1: Requirements for a house information system[4]

R1 The system shall offer a user-friendly interface.
R2 The house information system shall generate a monthly report containing all granted and denied admittances to the house.
R3 If the PIN (personal identification number) the user enters at the keypad is correct, the system shall open the door and record the granted access, i.e. it should record the date and time, and the name of the PIN owner.

(to be continued)

4 For reasons of simplicity we use very generic "requirements" in the example. If the requirements were to be included in a requirements specification, the requirements stated in the example would have to be refined. For example, for requirement R1 the exact meaning of "user-friendly" would have to be defined.

Example 2-1 *(continued)*

R4 The system shall be available on the market by 1 May 2006.

R5 The unlocking of the door shall happen within 0.8 s after the PIN has been entered correctly.

2.2 Requirement Types

Three main types of requirements

In the literature and many requirements engineering standards, although sometimes named slightly differently, the following three main types of requirements are differentiated (see e.g. [IEEE 830-1998; Lauesen 2002; Robertson and Robertson 2006; Sommerville 2007; Wiegers 2003]):

- Functional requirements (see Section 2.2.1)
- Quality requirements (see Section 2.2.2)
- Constraints (see Section 2.2.3)

In the following sub-sections, we explain each of these three requirement types. Furthermore, in our framework for requirements engineering, we consider goals and scenarios as essential types of requirements artefacts in addition to the three requirement types stated above (see Section 4.6).

2.2.1 Functional Requirements

Functionality for the users

Functional requirements specify the functionality the system shall provide to its users (persons or other systems; see Definition 2-3).

Definition 2-3: *Functional requirements*

"These [functional requirements] are statements of services the system should provide, how the system should react to particular inputs and how the system should behave in particular situations. In some cases, the functional requirements may also state what the system should not do. [...]

[...] When expressed as user requirements, the requirements are usually described in a fairly abstract way. However, functional system requirements describe the system function in detail, its inputs and outputs, exceptions, and so on."

[Sommerville 2007]

Example 2-2 depicts a functional requirement defined for a security system of a building.

Example 2-2: Functional requirement

R31 If a sensor detects that a glass pane is damaged or broken, the system shall inform the security company.

Three perspectives: data, function, and behaviour

Traditionally, functional requirements are documented using three complementary, but partially overlapping, perspectives: the data perspective, the functional perspective, and the behavioural perspective. We elaborate on the three perspectives in Part III.c.

The requirements defining the data, functions, and behaviour of the system are, in most cases, solution-oriented requirements since they are defined in a way that mainly supports the realisation of the system (see Section 4.6 and Chapter 13, respectively, for a detailed explanation). In contrast to this, goals are defined in a solution-neutral way (see Section 4.6.1).

2.2.2 Quality Requirements

Quality properties of the system to be developed

Quality requirements define quality properties of the system to be developed, e.g. the performance of the system, its reliability, or its stability. Often, a quality requirement defines a quality which affects the entire system. However, a quality requirement may also define quality properties for a particular service, function, or system component. Quality requirements are often architectural drivers, i.e. they influence the architecture of the system significantly (see [Bass et al. 2003; Clements et al. 2002; Starke 2008]). We define quality requirements as follows:

Definition 2-4: *Quality requirement*

A quality requirement defines a quality property of the entire system or of a system component, service, or function.

Types of Quality Requirements

There are many different types of quality requirements and various taxonomies for quality requirements (see, e.g. [Chung et al. 2000; Lauesen 2002; McCall et al. 1977; Wiegers 2003]). Figure 2-1 depicts the taxonomy of quality requirements defined in [Wiegers 2003].

Quality properties of a system

As indicated in Fig. 2-1, a requirements specification contains quality requirements that are primarily important to users as well as quality requirements that are primarily important to developers. The individual quality properties are briefly explained in

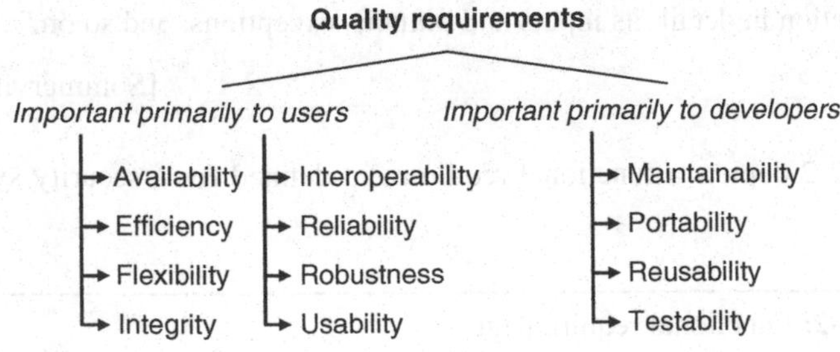

Fig. 2-1 *A quality requirements taxonomy, as defined in [Wiegers 2003]*

Tab. 2-1. A detailed description of the quality properties can be found in [Wiegers 2003]. This taxonomy is, however, not exhaustive, i.e. there are also other types of quality requirements that may be important for a project, such as performance or safety requirements. When defining quality requirements, the relationships among the different types of quality requirements must be considered. For instance, efficiency requirements are often in conflict with other requirements such as flexibility and portability requirements.

Tab. 2-1 *Quality properties of a system as defined in [Wiegers 2003]*

Quality property	Short description
Availability	Availability refers to the percentage of time during which the system is actually available for use and fully operational.
Efficiency	Efficiency is a measure of how well the system utilises hardware resources such as processor time, memory, or communication bandwidth.
Flexibility	Flexibility indicates how much effort is needed to extend the system with new capabilities.
Integrity	Integrity denotes how well the system is protected against unauthorised access, violations of data privacy, information loss, and infections through maleficent software.
Interoperability	Interoperability indicates how easily the system can exchange data or services with other systems.
Reliability	Reliability is the probability of the system executing without failure for a specific period of time.
Robustness	Robustness is the degree to which a system or component continues to function correctly when confronted with invalid inputs, defects in connected systems or components, or unexpected operating conditions.
Usability	Usability measures the effort the user requires to prepare input for, operate, and interpret the output of the system.
Maintainability	Maintainability indicates how easy it is to correct a defect or make a change in the system.
Portability	Portability relates to the effort it takes to migrate a system or component from one operating environment to another.
Reusability	Reusability indicates the extent to which a component can be used in systems other than the one for which it was initially developed.
Testability	Testability refers to the ease with which the software components or integrated system can be tested to find defects.

Non-functional Requirements

Quality requirement vs. non-functional requirement

Traditionally, many authors differentiate between functional and non-functional requirements (see e.g. [Gause und Weinberg 1989; Davis 1993; Chung et al. 1999; Kotonya and Sommerville 1997]). Also in practice, this differentiation is commonly used in requirements specifications. As explained below, non-functional requirements and quality requirements are not the same thing.

Avoid the term "non-functional" requirement

We strongly recommend not using the term "non-functional requirement" for several reasons. Most non-functional requirements described in the literature, as well as most requirements categorised as non-functional in requirements specifications, in practice are in fact underspecified requirements. When looking at so-called non-functional requirements more carefully, two types of non-functional requirements can be identified:

- *Underspecified functional requirements*: Quite often a non-functional requirement documents an underspecified functional requirement. In such a case, we strongly recommend refining the underspecified functional requirement, i.e. defining it in more detail as a (set of) functional requirement(s) and, if required, with additional quality requirements.
- *Quality requirements*: Besides the underspecified functional requirements, the so-called non-functional requirements also document quality requirements. In other words, the requirements which remain after separating out the underspecified functional requirements are quality requirements. As explained above, quality requirements define required quality properties of the entire system or of system components, services, or functions (see Definition 2-4).

Summarising, a non-functional requirement is either an underspecified functional requirement or a quality requirement (see Fig. 2-2).

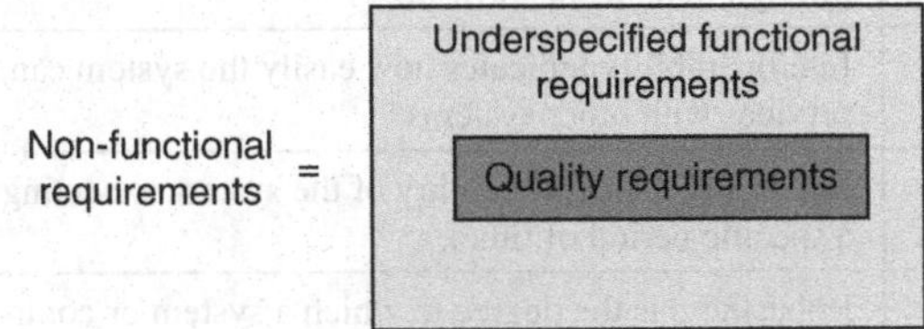

Fig. 2-2 *Separation of "non-functional" requirements into underspecified functional requirements and quality requirements*

Underspecification causes ambiguity

Non-functional requirements that conceal underspecified functional requirements unfortunately allow many different interpretations concerning the desired system properties. The requirement R12 used in Example 2-3 is often used as an example of non-functional requirements. Obviously, this requirement documents an underspecified functional requirement.

Example 2-3: Non-functional requirement/underspecified functional requirement

R12 The system shall be secure.

On looking at requirement R12 from Example 2-3 in slightly more detail, several questions arise due to the underspecification of this requirement, such as:

- What does the adjective "secure" mean?
- Which properties shall the system provide in order to be "secure"?
- How can one check whether the implemented system is "secure"?

Consequences of underspecified requirements

If such an underspecified requirement is not refined and detailed during requirements engineering, there is a very high risk that different stakeholders will interpret the requirement in entirely different ways. For example, each stakeholder could interpret the term "secure" of Example 2-3 in a fairly different way and therefore the realisation of the system will most likely never meet the stakeholders' expectations. Moreover, there is no way to objectively prove or check whether requirement R12 is realised correctly in the final system.

Refinement of non-functional requirements

Non-functional requirements that conceal underspecified functional requirements should therefore be refined. For example, the underspecified requirement R12 in Example 2-3 could be refined into the set of requirements listed in Example 2-4. By refining the original, underspecified requirement, the functionality and quality expected from the system are clearly defined.

Example 2-4: Refinement of the underspecified requirement from Example 2-3 – "R12: The system shall be secure."

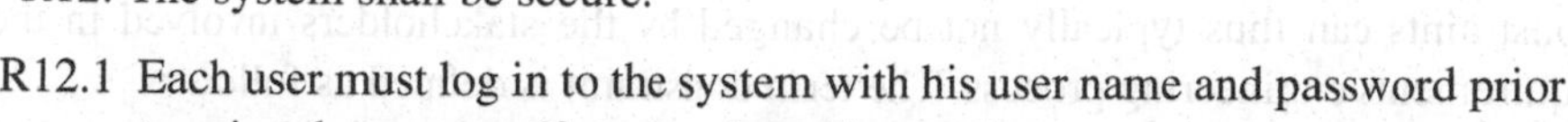

R12.1 Each user must log in to the system with his user name and password prior to using the system. (*functional requirement*)

R12.2 The system shall remind the user every four weeks to change the password. (*functional requirement*)

R12.3 When the user changes his password, the system shall validate that the new password is at least eight characters long and contains alphanumeric characters. (*functional requirement*)

R12.4 The user passwords stored in the system must be protected against password theft. (*quality requirement - integrity*)

Non-functional requirements are often not further refined

Practical experience indicates that underspecified requirements, declared as "non-functional" requirements, are rarely refined and elaborated in more detail during requirements engineering. Thereby, underspecified requirements become part of the final requirements specification and are eventually released for subsequent development activities. We thus strongly recommend avoiding the category of "non-functional" requirements when writing specifications. Where a requirement is declared as "non-functional" in a specification, we recommend carefully checking this requirement (see also Hint 2-1).

Hint 2-1: *How to deal with "non-functional" requirements*

- Avoid the category "non-functional" requirements in the requirements specification.
- Instead, differentiate between functional requirements and (specific types of) quality requirements (see Fig. 2-1).
- "Non-functional" requirements often conceal underspecified functional requirements.
- Only a few of the so-called non-functional requirements are actually quality requirements.
- For each "non-functional" requirement, check whether it represents an underspecified functional requirement and, if so, refine it adequately.

Refinement of quality requirements

If a "non-functional" requirement represents a quality requirement, also the quality requirement can be underspecified. In this case, the underspecified quality requirement needs to be refined as well.

2.2.3 Constraints

Constraints are rarely changeable

Besides defining the functional and quality requirements for the system, constraints are also documented during requirements engineering. Constraints either restrict the development process or the properties of the system to be developed. Constraints are typically superimposed by other organisational processes (e.g. time or resource constraints from project management) or by the environment or context in which the system shall operate (see Part II for a detailed description of the system context). Constraints can thus typically not be changed by the stakeholders involved in the requirements engineering process. The term constraint is defined as follows:

> **Definition 2-5:** *Constraint*
>
> A constraint is an organisational or technological requirement that restricts the way in which the system shall be developed.
>
> based on [Robertson and Robertson 2006]

Types of Constraints

Constraints can be differentiated by their origin. For instance, one can distinguish cultural constraints (i.e. constraints originating from the cultural background of the system users), legal constraints (i.e. constraints originating from laws and standards), organisational constraints, physical constraints, project constraints, etc.

Constraints on the system and the development process

Another way of distinguishing constraints is to consider the subject affected by a constraint. A constraint can affect the system itself (e.g. it may demand or restrict a system function) or the development process of the system (e.g. the process model to be used). Example 2-5 presents constraints that affect the system itself. A constraint affecting the development process can apply, for instance, to the requirements engineering process, the architectural design process, the implementation process, the test process, or several of these processes. Example 2-6 presents some constraints that affect the development process.

More detailed descriptions of different types of constraints can be found, for instance, in [Schienmann 2002; Kotonya and Sommerville 1997].

> **Example 2-5:** Constraints affecting the system
>
> C1 Due to current conditions defined by the insurance company, only the security technician is allowed to deactivate the control function of the system.
>
> C2 A fire protection requirement demands that the terminals in the sales rooms do not exceed the size 120 cm (height) × 90 cm (width) × 20 cm (depth).

Example 2-6: Constraints affecting the development process

C3 The effort for the development of the system must not exceed 480 person-months.

C4 The system must be developed using the Rational Unified Process.

The Restricting Effect of Constraints

Restrictions on requirements

In principle, each constraint defines a restriction on the realisation of functional and quality requirements of the system (see [Gause 2005]). Constraints hence restrict the range of alternatives available for realising the requirements and, thus, also the range of alternatives for realising the entire system. Two extreme situations can occur with respect to the restricting effect of constraints: On one extreme, a constraint might not restrict the realisation of any requirement at all. On the other extreme, a constraint could prohibit a requirement or a set of requirements from being realised, i.e. the restriction defined by the constraint can eliminate all possible realisation options.

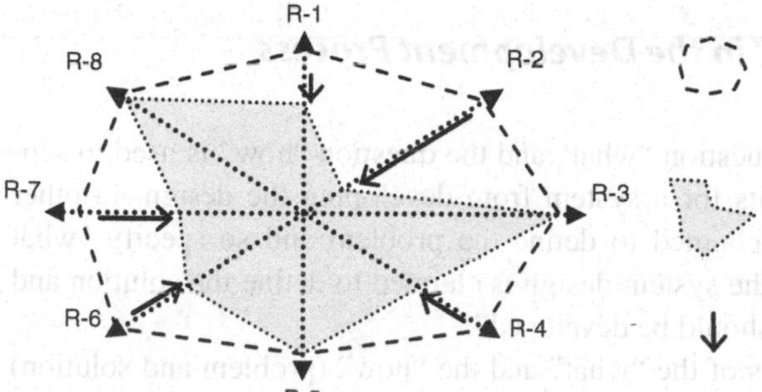

Fig. 2-3 *Restrictions imposed by constraints*

Figure 2-3 shows, schematically, the range of realisation alternatives for requirements without considering constraints (Fig. 2-3, area enclosed by dashed lines). The restrictions on the potential solutions imposed by the constraints are illustrated for each requirement by the black arrows. The shaded area represents the remaining range of realisation alternatives with consideration of the constraints.

Constraints as a source of requirements

Besides their restricting effect, constraints may also lead to the change of requirements or the definition of new requirements. Example 2-7 illustrates this case.

Example 2-7: Impact of constraints

The following requirement has been defined for the security system of a building based on a stakeholder interview:

R-F-17: A personal password shall be used for the authentication of each person at the access control system.

(to be continued)

Example 2-7 (*continued*)

During an interview, the director of a security firm mentions that according to a governmental law the access control for such buildings must comply with the standard 77/12/EG. On reading the standard, the requirements engineer recognises that the standard forbids the authentication with a personal password for such buildings. Instead, the standard requires authentication with a fingerprint sensor and with an accuracy of at least 60 minutiae.[5]

This newly identified constraint leads to a change of the requirement R-F-17 as well as to the new requirement R-Q-4.

R-F-17: A fingerprint sensor has to be used for the authentication of each person at the access control system.

R-Q-4: The authentication must be performed with an accuracy of at least 60 minutiae.

2.3 Problem vs. Solution

2.3.1 "What" vs. "How" in the Development Process

Simplified characterisation of "what" and "how"

The distinction between the question "what" and the question "how" is used to separate defining the requirements for a system from developing the design. In other words, the requirements are claimed to define the problem and so specify "what should be developed", while the system design is claimed to define the solution and so specifies "how the system should be developed".

"What" and "how" depends on stakeholders' viewpoints

The above characterisations of the "what" and the "how" (problem and solution) depend on the perspective from which one looks at the system to be developed. For the system architects, the system requirements in fact define the "what" and the resulting system architecture defines the "how". In contrast, for the requirements engineer, the overall system vision (see Section 4.1) defines the "what" and the specified requirements define the "how". In other words, different stakeholders in the development process have different views about the "what" and the "how" of their development tasks (see e.g. [Davis 1993]). The interpretation that requirements define the "what" and the design defines the "how" is thus by far too simplistic. The development artefacts associated with the "what" and the "how" heavily depend on the stakeholders' perspectives.

What–how pairs

Figure 2-4 depicts several what–how pairs that can be identified in a development process. Each pair denotes a problem definition and a corresponding solution description. Therein, each solution description to a problem imposed by a higher level of abstraction defines, at the same time, the problem for the next abstraction level. Therefore, the different what–how pairs depicted in Fig. 2-4 overlap.

Vision (what) and system requirements (how)

The what–how pairs shown in Fig. 2-4 can be characterised as follows. Typically, the initial problem of a development project is defined by a vision that shall be established in a given context (see Section 4.1). Based on this problem definition, the

[5] Minutiae denote characteristic details of a fingerprint. Simple approaches conclude that two compared fingerprints are identical when about 12 identical minutiae are found.

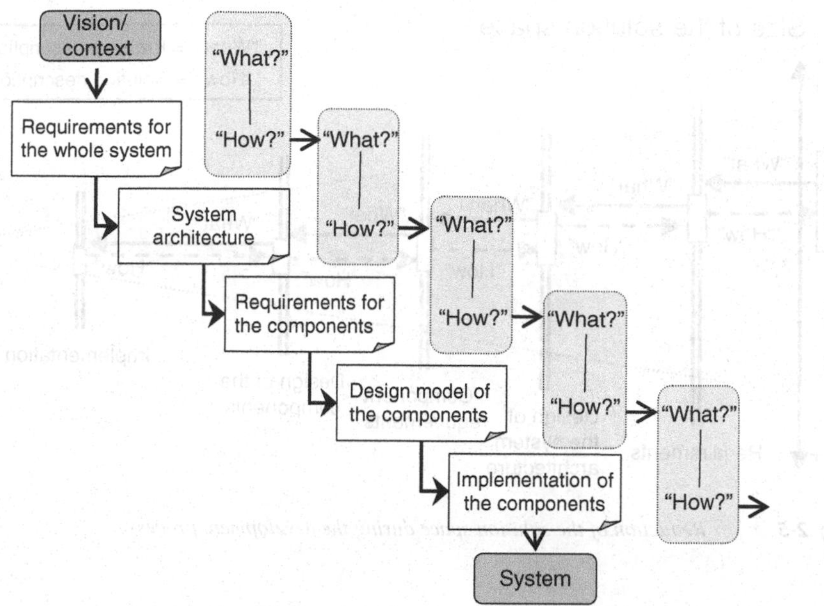

Fig. 2-4 *"What?" versus "how?" in the system development process*

requirements engineers (together with other stakeholders) develop the system requirements. The system requirements hence define a solution for realising the vision in the existing context. In other words, the system requirements define a possible solution to the initial problem of the development project.

System requirements (what) and system architecture (how)

At the same time, the system requirements define the problem to be solved in the next development stage. Based on this problem definition (i.e. the system requirements), the system architects define the system architecture. Therein the system architecture defines a possible solution to the initial problem of this development stage (i.e. the system requirements).

System architecture (what) and component requirements (how)

The system architecture defines, together with the associated system requirements, the problem for the next development stage. At this stage, the component requirements specifications (one specification for each component) define the solution to the initial problem of this development stage.

Component requirements (what) and component design (how)

The requirements defined for a specific component define the problem for the design of this component. The component designer develops a design specification of the component based on the component requirements and the overall system architecture. The resulting component design defines a solution for realising the component requirements (in compliance with the system architecture).

Problem and solution from the perspective of a programmer

The above consideration may be continued down to the implementation level. From the perspective of the programmer, the design model of a specific component along with the associated component requirements defines the problem, and the developed source code defines a possible solution to this problem.

Reduction of the solution space

What all the what–how pairs have in common is that, for the given problem (what), many different solutions (how) exist. By iterating between problem definition and solution description in each phase of the development process, the number of possible solutions is successively reduced. Fig. 2-5 illustrates the successive reduction of the solution space during the development process.

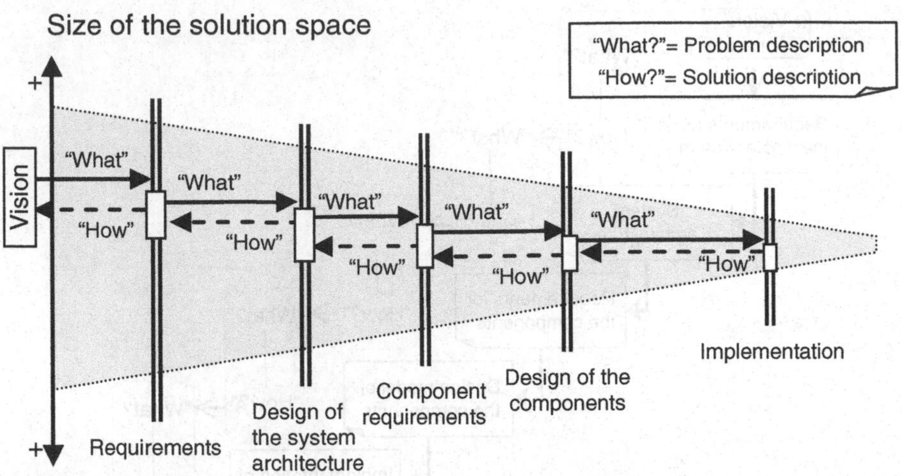

Fig. 2-5 *Reduction of the solution space during the development process*

2.3.2 "What" vs. "How" during Requirements Engineering

"What?" vs. "how?" within a development phase

The differentiation between "what" and "how" also occurs within a single development phase. For example, during requirements engineering a high-level requirement can define the "what" to be "realised" by a set of more detailed requirements which, in this case, define the "how" for realising the more abstract requirement.

In Example 2-8, the underspecified requirement R12 from Example 2-3 is refined by the three functional requirements R12.1–R12.3. Requirement R-12 describes the "what", at an abstract level, whereas requirements R12.1–R12.3 define "how" R12 shall be realised.

Example 2-8: Problem definition and solution description

Problem definition – "What?"

R-12: The navigation system shall allow the driver to enter the destination of the trip conveniently.

Solution description – "How?"

R12.1: When the driver starts a new trip, the navigation system shall display a roadmap of the area centred on the current position.

R12.2: The navigation system shall allow the driver to scroll and zoom into the roadmap.

R12.3: After the driver has selected a destination on the roadmap, the system shall allow the driver to edit the destination details (city, street, and house number).

2.3.3 Interactions between "What" and "How"

An important observation in system development is that the process of defining the problem (the "what") and the process of developing a solution (the "how") are tightly intertwined. In other words, contrary to what is often stated in the literature and sometimes also assumed by practitioners, the problem definition is typically not independent of the solution definition. In other words, problem definition and solution development are not performed as a sequential, one-way process. In fact, complex interactions between defining the "what" and developing the "how" exist. This can be illustrated by considering the interactions between requirements engineering and architectural design.

Architecture influences requirements

Requirements serve as the basis for the design of the system architecture. Conversely, findings made during architectural design also influence the requirements; requirements can be enabled or constrained by architectural decisions (see [Miller et al. 2008]). Architectural decisions can thereby initiate the modification, the refinement, or the removal of documented requirements (see, e.g. [Bass et al. 2003]). Furthermore, during the development process, requirements can be defined that are not elicited from customers or users but are initiated by architectural decisions (see e.g. [Hatley et al. 2000]).

Twin-peaks model

The twin-peaks model (proposed by [Nuseibeh 2001] based on ideas of [Ward and Mellor 1985]) illustrates the two-way interactions between defining requirements and designing the architecture (see Fig. 2-6).

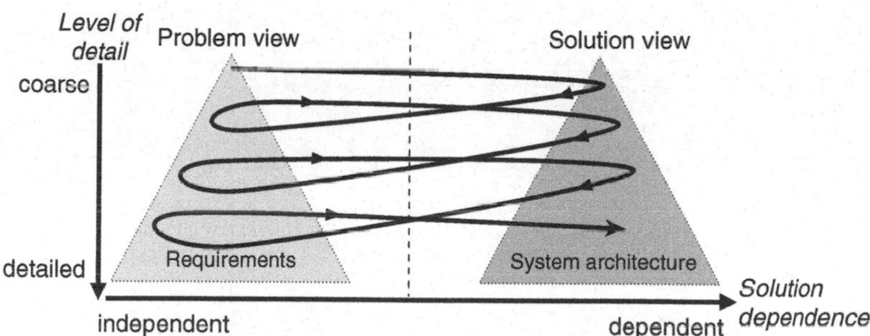

Fig. 2-6 *Interactions between requirements engineering and architectural design (based on [Nuseibeh 2001] and [Ward and Mellor 1985])*

Influence of architectural decisions on requirements

The twin-peaks model represents the interactions between requirements engineering and architectural design as a spiral that alternates between requirements and architecture and, at the same time, proceeds from coarse-grained artefacts to artefacts defined at a detailed level. At the beginning of the process, requirements artefacts at a high abstraction level are used to define the initial system architecture. Architectural design decisions lead to the modification and refinement of the initial, coarse-grained requirements. This, in turn, leads to the modification and refinement of the system architecture, and so on.

An important conclusion directly results from the twin-peaks model: A large proportion of requirements are specified with a (preliminary) solution in mind.

Hierarchy of abstraction layers

The approach depicted in Fig. 2-6 can be elaborated further by distinguishing between discrete levels of abstraction, i.e. by dividing the vertical axis of Fig. 2-6 in distinct areas, so-called abstraction layers.

The COSMOD-RE method (Part VII)

In Part VII, we introduce a hierarchy of four abstraction layers for software-intensive systems and describe our goal- and scenario-based method COSMOD-RE which supports the co-development of requirements and architectural artefacts across the four abstraction layers.

Chapter 3
Continuous Requirements Engineering

In this chapter, we:

- *Provide an overview on traditional systems analysis*
- *Explain the difference between the essence and incarnation of a system*
- *Discuss the shortcomings of implementing requirements engineering as an early development phase of a development process*
- *Elaborate on the principles and advantages of implementing requirements engineering as a continuous, project-spanning, and cross-product activity*

K. Pohl, *Requirements Engineering*,

3.1 Traditional Systems Analysis

Systems analysis considers existing systems

The term "systems analysis" subsumes different approaches that define requirements for a new (release of a) system based on the analysis of an existing system or process. During systems analysis, existing systems or processes are analysed so as to define requirements for the system to be developed. Typically, the new system (partly) automates and thereby (partly) replaces existing systems and processes.

Analysis of functions, data, and behaviour

Traditional systems analysis defines the desired functional aspects of a system in terms of functions, data, and behaviour. As outlined in Section 2.2.1, functions, data, and behaviour are three complementary and partly overlapping perspectives for defining functional requirements. The three perspectives, along with the corresponding modelling languages such as data flow diagrams, entity-relationship models, and behavioural models are described in detail in Part III.c.

Structured Analysis

A (and maybe the most) famous method for systems analysis is Structured Analysis (SA) proposed by DeMarco [DeMarco 1978]. Structured Analysis served as the basis for numerous enhancements such as Essential Systems Analysis [McMenamin and Palmer 1988] or Modern Structured Analysis [Yourdon 1989]. In Structured Analysis, data flow diagrams are used to document the system functions and the input and output data flows of each function.

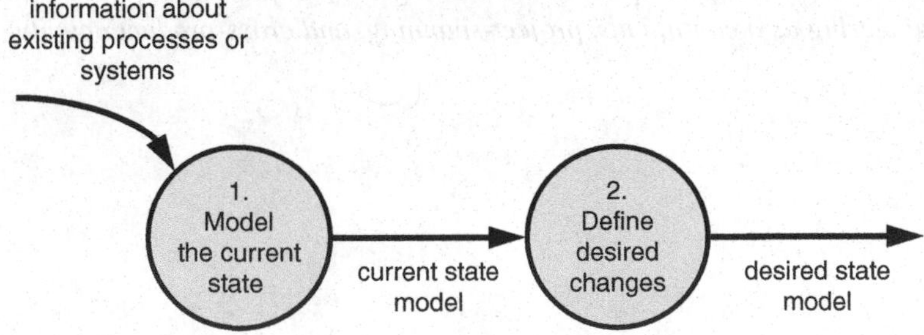

Fig. 3-1 *Current-state and desired-state models in systems analysis*

Current state and desired state

Figure 3-1 provides a very coarse model of the Structured Analysis approach. As depicted, Structured Analysis suggests documenting the current state in the current-state model based on the analysis of existing systems and/or processes. The desired changes are then integrated into the current-state model, thereby defining the desired-state model.

The distinction between current-state analysis and the definition of the desired state can be found in DeMarco's Structured Analysis as well as in other Structured Analysis methods (see e.g. [Ross and Schoman 1977; Gane and Sarson 1977; Weinberg 1978; McMenamin and Palmer 1988; Yourdon 1989]):

The current-state model documents the current systems/processes

- *Analysis of the current state:* During the analysis of the current state, existing systems and processes are analysed, and the identified and collected requirements are documented in a current-state model. The current-state model thus defines the current realisation of the system and thus reflects the current situation. The analysis of the current state thus ensures that requirements are documented which are already realised in the existing systems and processes, known by the involved stakeholders, and/or recorded in documents such as error reports. In addition, information about the context in which the system is embedded is elicited and documented, for example, information about the interfaces between the system and its environment (see "Eliciting Existing Requirements" in Section 21.5 and "System Context" in Part II). Both the documented requirements and the documented context information are essential for developing the new system.

- *Definition of the desired state*: The stakeholders analyse the current-state model and identify potential improvements to be realised by the new system. These improvements are integrated into the current-state model (i.e. the current-state model is adapted to reflect the improvements), thereby creating the desired-state model. The desired-state model thus defines the requirements for the system to be developed and forms the basis for the realisation of the new system.

The desired-state model defines the requirements for the new system

Figure 3-2 illustrates the definition of the current-state and the desired-state models as well as their relationships.

Embedding of the new system into the existing context

The realisation of the desired-state model results in a new system that (partly) replaces the existing system and/or processes in the real world. Consequently, the new system must be integrated into the existing environment. In order to ensure that the embedding of the system into the existing context (reality) is successful, the embedding into the existing context has to be considered during the change definition as well as during the development of the new system. This is indicated in Fig. 3-2 by the arrow pointing from the existing system to the new system and by the dashed arrow pointing to the arrow labelled "change definition".

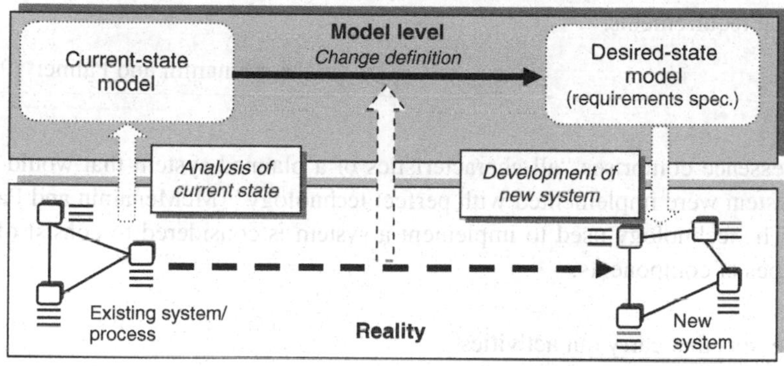

Fig. 3-2 *Current-state and desired-state models (based on [Haumer et al. 1998])*

Physical vs. logical models

As stated above, the desired-state model specifies the requirements that the system to be developed must fulfil. Clearly, a requirements model should not be biased by technological or implementation considerations (e.g. of the existing system or process). Therefore, Structured Analysis approaches typically distinguish between a physical and a logical model. First, a physical current-state model is developed. This physical current-state model is then pruned of physical characteristics, which results in a logical current-state model. To define the requirements for the system, the desired changes are integrated into the logical current-state model, thereby defining the logical desired-state model. However, the Structured Analysis approaches such as in [DeMarco 1978] did not provide methodological guidelines for deriving a logical model. This led to considerable confusion about what should be defined in a logical model and what should not. This gap was closed by the Essential Systems Analysis method (see Section 3.2).

3.2 Essential Systems Analysis

Differentiation between essence and incarnation

Essential Systems Analysis was proposed by McMenamin and Palmer [McMenamin and Palmer 1984]. Essential Systems Analysis extends and improves the Structured Analysis (SA) method of DeMarco. The basic idea behind the Essential Systems Analysis method is to differentiate between the essence and the incarnation of a system. The essence of a system subsumes all the true requirements for the system. A true requirement is a property or capability that the system must have regardless of the way in which the system is implemented, i.e. regardless of a particular technology used and the restrictions resulting therefrom (e.g. limited memory space).

3.2.1 Essence vs. Incarnation

The term "essence" is defined as follows:

Definition 3-1: *Essence of a system*

"A true requirement is a feature or capability that a system must possess in order to fulfil its purpose, regardless of how the system is implemented. We call the complete set of true requirements for a system the essence of the system or the essential requirements."

[McMenamin and Palmer 1984]

Essence: perfect technology

The essence comprises "all characteristics of a planned system that would exist if the system were implemented with perfect technology" [McMenamin and Palmer 1984]. The technology used to implement a system is considered to consist of two basic types of components:

- Processors that carry out activities
- Containers that store data in order to provide it to processors

Perfect technology assumption

A system implemented using perfect technology consists of perfect processors and perfect containers [McMenamin and Palmer 1984]:

- *Perfect processor*: "A perfect processor would be able to do anything and everything instantly; this is, it would have infinite capabilities and infinite workload capacity. It would cost nothing, consume no energy, take no space, generate no heat, never make a mistake, and never break down."
- *Perfect container*: "A perfect container would have many of the same virtues. It wouldn't cost anything, and it would be able to hold an infinite amount of data. Any processor would be able to access conveniently the data it carried."

Essential models

An essential model is a model that defines the essence of a system. An essential model can be defined for an existing system as well as for a system to be developed.

An essential model of a system to be developed defines the requirements for this system under the assumption that perfect technology is used for realising the system.

Incarnation: imperfect technology

In contrast to the essence, the incarnation of a system is defined under the assumption of using real, imperfect technology for its realisation. Incarnation models are therefore often called physical models or implementation models.[6] McMenamin and Palmer define the incarnation of a system as follows:

Definition 3-2: *Incarnation of a system*

"The sum of people, wires, paper clips, carbon paper, pencils, typewriters, computer terminals, office furniture, file cabinets, offices, telephones, CPUs, and so forth that are used to implement the essential activities and memory of a system are what we call its incarnation."

[McMenamin and Palmer 1984]

3.2.2 Approach

Modelling the incarnation of the current system

Similarly to Structured Analysis, Essential Systems Analysis differentiates between current- and desired-state models. However, in Essential Systems Analysis, the current-state model is transferred into an essential model (see Fig. 3-3: "2. Derive essence") by means of well-defined rules, and the desired changes are defined based on the essential current-state model (in Fig. 3-3: "3. Define desired changes"). By defining the changes, the essential desired-state model is created. Then, the intended

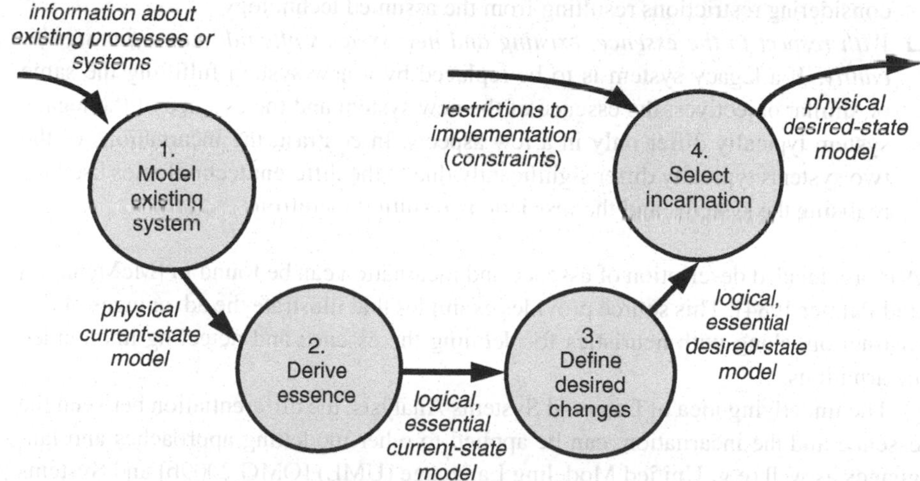

Fig. 3-3 Current and desired-state models in Essential Systems Analysis (based on [McMenamin and Palmer 1984])

[6] The differentiation between essence and incarnation in Essential Systems Analysis has many commonalities with the differentiation between logical (conceptual) and physical schemata in database design (e.g. [Tsichritzis and Klug 1978]).

incarnation, i.e. concrete technologies to be used for realising the system, are selected (in Fig. 3-3: "4. Select incarnation"). Based on the selected incarnation and the resulting restrictions for the implementation, the so-called physical desired-state model is defined. A physical desired-state model thus defines the incarnation of the system to be developed.

3.2.3 Advantages of Essential Systems Analysis

The strict separation of essence and incarnation facilitates considering solely the system functions without intermingling technology realisation details. When compared with physical models, essential models thus offer several advantages:

Not affected by technology changes

- *Essential models are more stable*: The perfect technology assumption makes essential models independent of any technological changes. Moreover, the essential system functions change rarely (in general) when compared with changes in technology. Essential models are thus far more stable than physical models.

Less complexity

- *Essential models are significantly smaller*: Essential models are generally much smaller (approximately by a factor of 5–10) than the corresponding physical models. The essential models are thus easier to understand than the more complex physical models. Moreover, for adapting essential models, less effort is required compared with the adaptation of the more complex physical models.

No implicit design decisions

- *No design restrictions*: Essential models prevent unintentional, implicit design decisions since they do not define any technology. Essential models are thus neutral with respect to the technology used for realising the system. Physical models often manifest (unintended or intended) design restrictions or even design decisions by specifying technology details, making technology assumptions, and/or considering restrictions resulting from the assumed technology.

Essence of legacy systems is retained to a large extent

- *With respect to the essence, existing and new systems often do not differ significantly:* If a legacy system is to be replaced by a new system fulfilling the same or similar objectives, the essence of the new system and the essence of the legacy system typically differ only in a few aspects. In contrast, the incarnations of the two systems typically differ significantly due to the different technologies used for realising the systems and the restrictions resulting therefrom.

A more detailed description of essence and incarnation can be found in [McMenamin and Palmer 1984]. This source provides examples that illustrate the advantages of this distinction, along with heuristics for defining the essence and detecting unintended incarnations.

Applying the principle of essence and incarnation to other development models

The underlying idea of Essential Systems Analysis, the differentiation between the essence and the incarnation, can be applied to other modelling approaches and languages as well (e.g. Unified Modeling Language (UML) [OMG 2009b] and Systems Modeling Language (SysML) [OMG 2008a]). For example, essential behavioural models, data models, goal models, or essential scenarios can be defined. In fact, although often called different things, several modelling approaches differentiate between an "essential" and an "incarnation" model.

Applying essence and incarnation in development processes

Moreover, the principle of separating the essence and the incarnation of a system is independent of the development process or approach used for developing a system and can thus be applied in common development processes and approaches such as the V-Model [V-Modell 2006], the V-Model XT [Rausch and Broy 2007; V-Modell 2009], agile methods [Highsmith 1999; Stapleton 1997; Cockburn 2006], or the Rational Unified Process (RUP) [Kruchten 2003].

3.3 Requirements Engineering as an Early Development Phase

In many lifecycle and process models, such as the waterfall model [Royce 1987] or the V-Model [V-Modell 2006], requirements engineering (RE) is regarded as a single phase of the software development process which has a defined start and end time. This is illustrated in Fig. 3-4. The task of this requirements engineering phase is to develop the requirements specification for the system. After the requirements for the system have been elicited and specified, the system is developed.

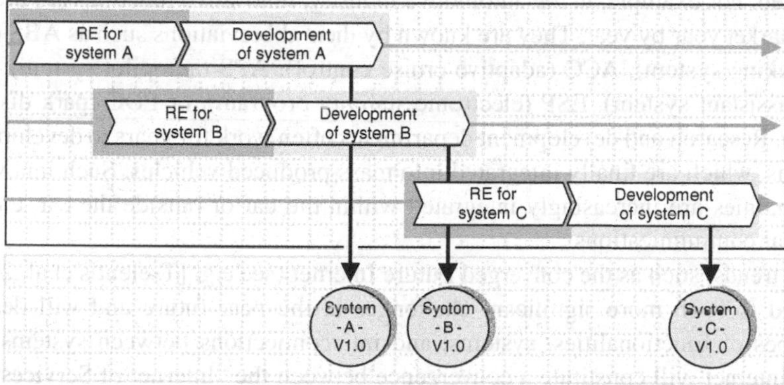

Fig. 3-4 *Requirements engineering as an early phase in development projects*

Specification of requirements at the beginning of a project

As depicted in Fig. 3-4, requirements engineering is thus performed for each project (e.g. for system A) at the beginning of the development process. The elicited requirements are documented in a project-specific requirements specification that then serves as a reference document for the following development phases.

Independent elicitation in each project

For each project, the requirements are elicited independently from any other project. Performing requirements engineering as an early, project-specific development phase is thus very similar to the approaches applied in Structured Analysis and Essential Systems Analysis.

3.4 Shortcomings of Systems Analysis and Phase-Oriented Requirements Engineering

The essence of a system was typically well understood

Structured Systems Analysis and the understanding of requirements engineering as an early development phase were developed at a time when the key focus of developing new software applications was on (partly) automating established and well-understood processes and systems. Typical examples of such software applications are information systems such as book-keeping systems or the partial automation of manufacturing processes. When realising such systems, the processes and workflows were typically optimised and partially adapted. In summary, Structured Analysis and requirements engineering as an early development phase were mainly applied to analyse processes and systems which had already been established for a long period of time, for which at least one incarnation existed and whose essence was, in principle, well understood.

Change in the types of systems to be developed

In recent years, this situation has changed. Software-intensive information and embedded systems realise increasingly innovative functionality which did not exist before. In contrast to most of the applications developed in the 1980s and early 1990s, the essence is not so well understood for such systems. In the case of information systems, for example, new technologies such as the Internet and web-based applications enable the development of totally new types of organisational processes, and new applications supporting new types of interactions which would not be feasible at all without this technology.

Similarly, new technologies also revolutionise the types of embedded systems to be developed. For example, in the automotive industry, innovative functions are brought to the market year by year. They are known by their abbreviations such as ABS (anti-lock braking system), ACC (adaptive cruise control), APS (autopilot system), BAS (brake assistant system), ESP (electronic stability program), or PDC (park distance control). Research and development departments often work for years to develop such functions, which are finally integrated into mass-produced vehicles. Such innovative functionalities are increasingly integrated within the car or outside the car, e.g. via car-to-car communications.

Challenges in the Future Internet

New trends, such as the converged Future Internet (see e.g. [Tselentis et al. 2009]) will lead to even more significant challenges in the near future and will demand new types of functionalities, systems, and interconnections between systems. The Future Internet will constitute a convergence between the "Internet of Services", the "Internet of Things", and the "Internet of Content":

- *Internet of Services*: The Internet of Services relates to the provision, discovery, composition, and consumption of (software) services via the Internet.
- *Internet of Things*: The Internet of Things relates to embedded systems, sensors, and actuators that collect and carry information about real-world objects which can be accessed online due to their (future) interconnection via the Internet.
- *Internet of Content (and Media)*: The Internet of Content (and Media) relates to the discovery, distribution, combination, and consumption of all kinds of media objects (such as text, image, 3D graphics, audio, and video) which carry meta-information about their content, are interconnected, and can be accessed via the Internet.

Convergence of embedded and information systems

The converged Future Internet will thus incorporate a wide range of technologies from the embedded, media, and information systems domains. For example, software-intensive embedded systems will be empowered to offer their functionality to the "world" as well as to use a large variety of existing services to fulfil their own purpose. Future software-intensive systems will exploit the converged Future Internet, will constantly be adjusted to incorporate new services, and will offer even more innovative functionality.

Insufficient methodical support

The goal of requirements engineering has thus changed significantly in recent years and will change even more so in the future. Nowadays, the stakeholders involved in requirements engineering face the problem of developing and eliciting requirements for new and innovative system functionalities and qualities, in contrast to the definition of requirements based on an analysis of already existing functionalities realised by an existing system.

Requirements engineering as an early development phase and traditional Structured Systems Analysis are not able to meet the challenges outlined above, nor the challenges facing the development of software-intensive systems described in Section 1.1.2. Moreover, implementing requirements engineering as an early development phase has further significant shortcomings, such as:

Lack of requirements updates

- *No continuity*: Requirements engineering is only performed for a particular time period. This has several disadvantages. For example, changes that occur later in the development process are not reflected in the requirements, i.e. the requirements artefacts are not updated. As a consequence, the requirements specification does not document the realised requirements and thus cannot be used, for example, during software maintenance or in another development project.

Analysing the current state is time consuming

- *Requirement for an analysis of the current state*: When developing the next system release, an outdated requirements specification is only available if the requirements are not continuously updated. In most cases, it is not even known which parts of the specification reflect the implemented requirements and which parts are out of date. Therefore, for each development project, a new time-consuming and costly analysis of the current state is required, which leads to delayed market entry.

Only ad hoc reuse of requirements

- *No systematic requirements reuse*: The reuse of requirements across project and product boundaries is not systematically supported. Even if a large set of requirements are relevant for more than just one product (or project), the requirements generally have to be developed from scratch for each product. In such settings, requirements reuse happens, if at all, in an ad hoc manner. For example, this may happen where the same person is involved in several development projects and is therefore able to detect similarities and suggest the reuse of requirements.

Relevant information is ignored

- *Narrow focus*: In phase-oriented requirements engineering, the focus of requirements engineering is typically restricted to the system under development. In other words, the requirements engineers focus on realising the goals of the specific project on time and within budget. However, for this reason, in the phase-oriented approach, new ideas and solutions that are not immediately relevant for the specific system under development are not taken into account and hence not documented as requirements (e.g. for some other system and project) In this way, important opportunities for product innovation are lost. This is illustrated in Example 3-1.

E

Example 3-1: Narrow product focus

During requirements engineering for a video recorder, the requirements engineer gets to know that satellite operators and broadcasting corporations plan, in the near future, to transfer via satellite additional information about the program and movies shown (such as production company, film category, prices obtained, actors

(to be continued)

> **Example 3-1** (*continued*)
>
> involved, etc.) along with the picture data. Since the current technology used for the video recorder does not allow for the recording of additional program information, the requirements engineer does not define a requirement for recording and displaying the additional program data.
>
> The company develops, in parallel, a digital hard-disk recorder for which this information would have been highly relevant, since the software for the hard-disk recorder could easily be designed in a way that it records the program information on hard disk and displays this information to the user.

Mitigation of the shortcomings

Due to the need to develop and define requirements for innovative software functionality and qualities, and the shortcomings of implementing requirements engineering as an early development phase, we proposed considering requirements engineering as a continuous activity in 1994; requirements engineering should continuously elicit and document relevant changes in the real world at a conceptual level and involve all relevant stakeholders (see [Jarke and Pohl 1994]).

3.5 Continuous Requirements Engineering

Requirements engineering as a cross-lifecycle and cross-project activity

Both Structured Analysis and those approaches that regard requirements engineering as an early development phase consider requirements engineering as an activity that is executed at the beginning of a development project. In contrast, continuous requirements engineering is an activity which spans the entire system lifecycle and even extends across projects and products (see e.g. [Jarke and Pohl 1993; Pohl 1999]).

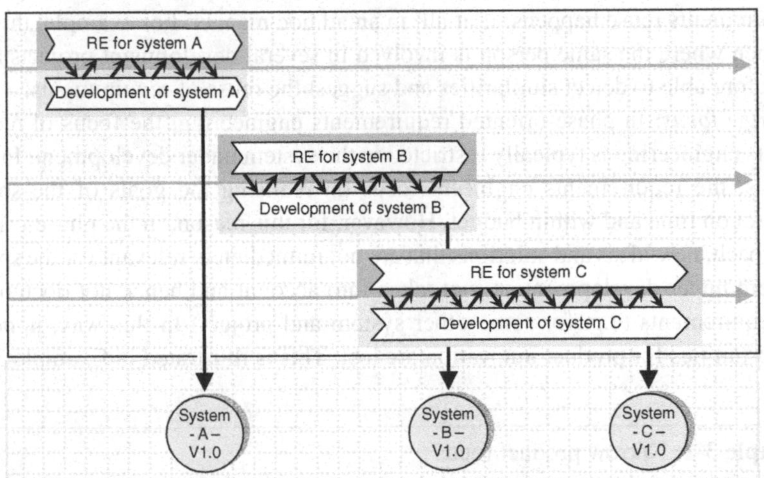

Fig. 3-5 *Requirements engineering as a cross-lifecycle activity*

Two kinds of continuous requirements engineering

Meanwhile, the idea of continuous requirements engineering has found its way into numerous process and lifecycle models such as the Rational Unified Process [Kruchten 2003], and various agile methods (e.g. Extreme Programming [Beck and

Andres 2004] and Scrum [Schwaber and Beedle 2001]). In all these process and lifecycle models, requirements engineering activities are performed to a different extent depending on the actual project status and project situation.

We differentiate two quality levels of continuous requirements engineering:

Requirements engineering as cross-lifecycle activity

- *Requirements engineering as a cross-lifecycle activity*: Requirements engineering as a cross-lifecycle activity is performed throughout the entire development process. The requirements engineering activity ensures for the consistent and traceable elicitation and management of requirements (see Fig. 3-5) during the entire system lifecycle. Requirements engineering interacts with all other development activities. For example, proposals for requirements changes detected and suggested during the architectural design are passed on to the requirements engineering activity. In addition, changes in the system context are identified and analysed during the entire development process and, if required, passed on to the actual development activities. Required changes can thus be immediately considered in the system release currently being developed.

Requirements engineering as a cross-project and cross-product activity

- *Requirements engineering as a cross-project and cross-product activity*: Requirements engineering as a cross-project and cross-product activity extends the scope of requirements engineering to comprise the continuous elicitation and management of requirements across different projects and products. Requirements engineering activities are no longer associated with an individual system development process and thus an individual project (see Fig. 3-6). In contrast, requirements engineering is viewed as an independent activity executed across multiple project and product developments. Elicited requirements are documented and recorded independently of a concrete system development in a dedicated requirements base. Whenever a new system or system release is to be developed, a coherent set of requirements to be realised is selected from the current requirements base (see Fig. 3-6). The packaging of the requirements for a specific system (release) can be performed at any time. In addition, feedback from the individual development projects is continuously evaluated and integrated into the requirements base. The same holds for changes that occur in the system context.

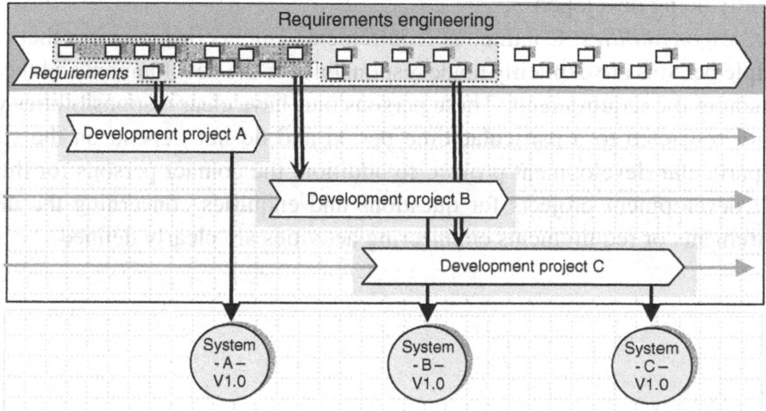

Fig. 3-6 *Requirements engineering as a cross-project and cross-product activity*

Advantages for short product lifecycles

We recommend to understand and implement requirements engineering as a cross-project activity if products have to be placed on the market in short time intervals or if the projects of an organisation typically share a common subject domain. Managing requirements across project boundaries leads to several advantages for the organisation. For example, if requirements are elicited and documented across projects, the requirements engineering process becomes more effective and efficient. On the other hand, cross-project requirements engineering may increase the required amount of coordination and communication across project boundaries and might lead to higher initial costs. However, according to our experience, the advantages by far outweigh the additional effort which might be required. The significant advantages obtained from cross-project and cross-product requirements engineering include:

Established requirements base

- *Systematic learning process*: Continuous cross-project requirements engineering establishes an institutionalised learning process in which the involved stakeholders continuously extend and improve their understanding of the most recent requirements for the products. This facilitates the exchange and sharing of requirements across projects and provides an up-to-date requirements base which provides a valuable input for all future development projects.

Up-to-date requirements

- *Requirements are always up to date*: Continuous requirements engineering ensures that changes caused by the system context (e.g. changes in market needs or laws), as well as requirements changes caused during system development, are integrated into the documented requirements, i.e. it ensures that the requirements base is up to date.

Reduction of development times

- *Shorter product development times*: Since the documented requirements are always up to date, a time-consuming analysis of the current state at the beginning of each development project is no longer needed. Thus, a new system release (or system) can be developed in less time.

Reuse of requirements and software artefacts across projects

- *Reuse across projects*: Requirements engineering as a cross-project activity supports the reuse of requirements artefacts and related software artefacts, such as components or test cases, across project boundaries. If a set of requirements which have been defined and realised for a previous system is reused for the system under development, the development artefacts created for the previous system (and associated with the reused requirements) can be retrieved. Subsequently, the stakeholders can analyse whether the retrieved artefacts can be reused for the system currently being developed.

Clear responsibilities

- *Clear responsibilities*: Continuous requirements engineering requires that one or multiple persons are explicitly made responsible for the development and the management of the requirements. These persons thus have clear responsibilities which are not restricted to a particular time period and do not depend on the staffing of a particular development project. In addition, the contact persons for the staff of all development projects for questions and enquiries concerning the defined requirements or requirements engineering activities are clearly defined.

Chapter 4
The Requirements Engineering Framework

This chapter provides an overview of our requirements engineering framework. The framework defines:

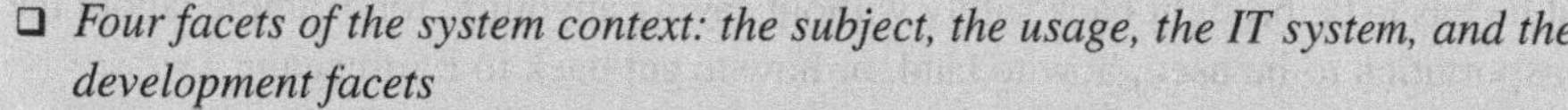

- *Four facets of the system context: the subject, the usage, the IT system, and the development facets*
- *Three core requirements engineering activities: documentation, elicitation, and negotiation*
- *Two cross-sectional activities: validation and management*
- *Three kinds of requirements artefacts: goals, scenarios, and solution-oriented requirements*

The structure of this book is derived from the requirements engineering framework and is briefly described at the end of this chapter.

4.1 Goal of Requirements Engineering: Establishing a Vision in Context

Vision defines intended change

Each requirement engineering process starts with an aim to change the current reality. Regardless of the complexity of the project, the essence of the desired change should be defined briefly and precisely. We call this definition of the envisioned change the system "vision". A prominent example is the vision expressed by John F. Kennedy in 1961 when he said: "First, I believe that this nation should commit itself to achieving the goal, before this decade is out, of landing a man on the moon and returning him safely to the earth" (speech of J.F. Kennedy in 1961 [Dudley 2000]).

A vision states a goal and not how the goal should be achieved

A vision may also express a small change to the current reality, such as the integration of a new functionality into a multimedia system, or the increase of the level of security of an online banking system. A vision defines only what should be changed without stating how the change should be implemented. In other words, the vision defines a goal but does not state how this goal should be achieved. In the example of John F. Kennedy, the vision defines that a man has to be sent to the moon and that he has to be brought back safely without saying anything, for example, about the transportation to be used, how to land, or how to get back to Earth again.

Vision as guidance

A vision does not express an unachievable illusion. Rather, it describes a goal that is clearly defined and verifiable, and often also associated with a particular point in time when it should be achieved. The vision serves, for all stakeholders involved in the development process, as guidance throughout the entire development process. The stakeholders align their activities with the defined vision. The information expressed in the vision is not sufficient to define all the requirements for the system at the required level of detail. The additional information needed to define the requirements fully must thus be elicited from other requirement sources such as stakeholders (e.g. customers, system users, domain experts), existing documents (e.g. laws, guidelines, standards), and existing systems (e.g. legacy systems, competitors' systems); see Part IV.b.

The system context

Each software-intensive system is embedded within a given context (the "system context"; see Glossary) that contains the requirement sources and strongly influences the definition of the system requirements. We elaborate on the system context and its influence on the system requirements in Part II.

Establishing a vision in context

The vision and the system context are thus the two essential inputs for the requirements engineering process. Whereas the vision is typically clearly defined, the system context is often not fully known and understood at the beginning of the requirements engineering process. The main goal of requirements engineering is thus to "establish a vision within an existing context" (see, e.g. [Jarke and Pohl 1993; Pohl 1997]).

4.2 Overview of the Framework

Our requirements engineering framework (see Fig. 4-1) defines the major structural elements of a requirements engineering process required for establishing a vision within an existing context. The framework consolidates various research results which have been developed based on problem statements elicited from industrial practice and which have been successfully validated and transferred to industry.

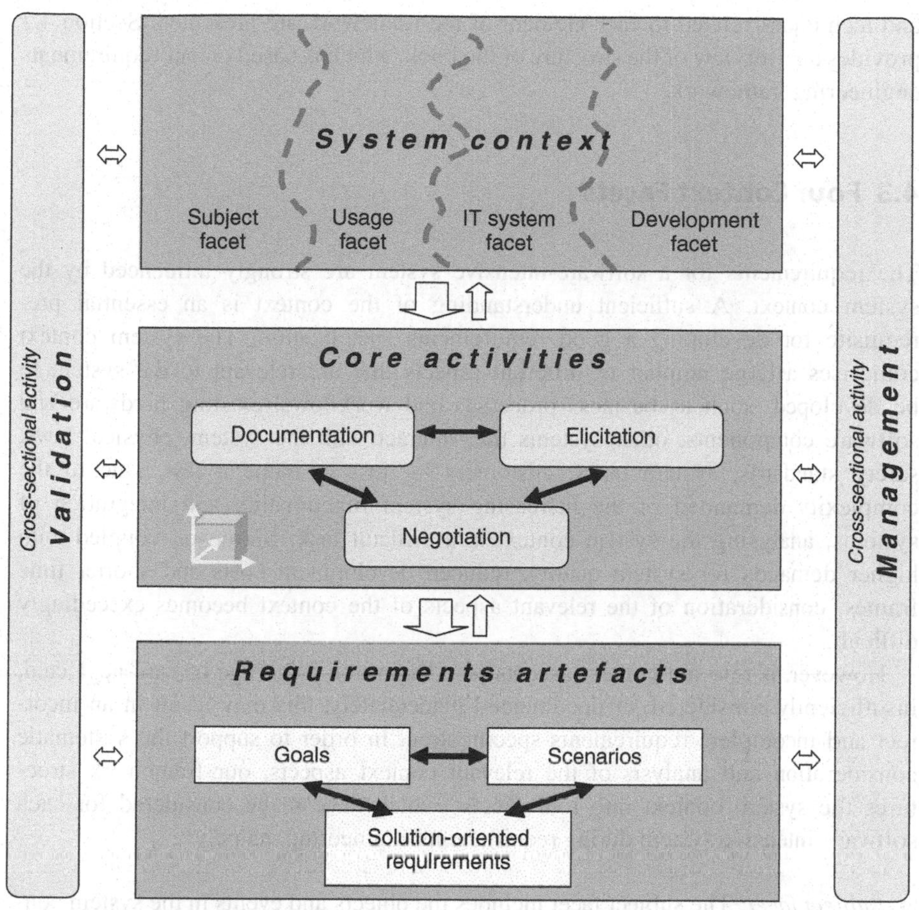

Fig. 4-1 *The requirements engineering framework*

Our framework has been successfully introduced in a number of organisations and companies which use the framework as a reference for structuring their requirements engineering processes, as a reference for the training of managers, requirements engineers, and developers, and for analysing the strengths and weaknesses of their requirements engineering processes. The framework consists of the following main building blocks:

Our framework has been adopted in several organisations

- *System context*: The framework structures the system context into four parts: the subject, the usage, the IT system, and the development facet.

Four context facets

- *Three core requirements engineering activities*: The three core requirements engineering activities (elicitation, documentation, and negotiation) are performed iteratively in order to establish the vision within the existing context.

Documentation, elicitation and negotiation

- *Two cross-sectional activities*: The two cross-sectional activities of validation and management support the core activities and secure the results of requirements engineering.

Validation and management

- *Requirements artefacts*: Our framework distinguishes three essential types of requirements artefacts: goals, scenarios, and solution-oriented requirements.

Three types of requirements artefacts

In Sections 4.3–4.6, the elements of our framework and the relationships between these elements are described in more detail. In Parts II–VI, fundamentals, principles,

Details of the framework

and techniques related to each element of the framework are presented. Section 4.7 provides an overview of the structure of the book, which is based on our requirements engineering framework.

4.3 Four Context Facets

Elicitation and consideration of all context aspects

The requirements for a software-intensive system are strongly influenced by the system context. A sufficient understanding of the context is an essential prerequisite for developing a good requirements specification. The system context comprises a large number of different aspects that are relevant to the system to be developed, such as business processes and workflows, existing hardware and software components, other systems that interact with the system, physical laws, safety standards, system users, customers — just to name a few. Due to the complexity demanded of the increasing system functionality and integration of systems, analysing the system context is a difficult task. Moreover, coupled with higher demands for system quality, reduced development costs and shorter time frames, consideration of the relevant aspects of the context becomes exceedingly difficult.

Insufficient consideration of context aspects leads to requirements defects

However, if relevant context aspects (see Definition 5-2, Page 65) are neglected, insufficiently considered, or documented inadequately, this may result in an incorrect and incomplete requirements specification. In order to support the systematic consideration and analysis of the relevant context aspects, our framework structures the system context into four facets[7] which have to be considered for each software-intensive system during requirements engineering, namely:

Objects and events relevant for the system

- *Subject facet*: The subject facet includes the objects and events in the system context that are relevant for the system. This includes, for example, objects and events that the system must store or process information about. In other words, information about the objects and events in the subject facet must be represented in the system. The objects of interest can be tangible as well as intangible objects. For instance, a software component that measures the speed of a vehicle requires a representation of the intangible object "speed" within the component. The subject facet also includes aspects that influence the representation of information about the objects and the events in the system, such as laws that forbid or regulate the recording of certain types of data within a software-intensive system, or laws which restrict the accuracy of the recorded data or the frequency of updating the data.

System usage

- *Usage facet*: A software-intensive system is used by people or other software-intensive systems in order to achieve a goal or to accomplish a certain task. The usage facet comprises all aspects concerning the system usage by people and other systems. This includes, for example, the various usage goals which exist, desired workflows, different user groups with specific characteristics, different interaction models with different associated interfaces as well as laws and standards restricting or influencing the system usage.

[7] The four facets are based on the four worlds of requirements engineering proposed in [Mylopoulos et al. 1990; Jarke and Pohl 1993].

- *IT system facet*: The system to be developed is eventually deployed into an existing IT infrastructure, which typically comprises existing software-intensive systems as well as existing hardware and software platforms, communication network(s), peripheral devices, and other hardware and software components used. The IT system facet comprises all aspects of the operational and technical environment including policies and strategies defining restrictions or guidelines for the use of any type of technology or operational environment. All these aspects of the technical and operational environment, as well as the constraints resulting from them, influence the definition of the system requirements. For example, the IT strategy might prescribe the communication protocol to be used, which obviously influences the communication requirements defined for the system, or the software platform might predefine a set of supported operating systems which in turn influences the defined requirements.

IT system environment

- *Development facet*: The development facet comprises all aspects of the context concerning the development process of the system. This includes process guidelines and constraints, development tools, quality assurance methods, maturity models, quality certifications, and other means or techniques for ensuring the quality (e.g. safety or security) of a software-intensive system. Each aspect of the development facet may be restricted by the client or by certain laws and standards. For instance, the client may demand that only certified tools are used during system development, or a standard might require that the system fulfils certain test criteria.

Aspects of the development process

4.3.1 Relationships between the Four Context Facets

The relationships between the four context facets can be illustrated by means of a very simple, logical model of a software-intensive system.

Relationship between subject facet and IT system facet

Each software-intensive system requires a representation of information about real-world objects (residing in the subject facet) such as the speed of a car or the name of a customer. The system represents the information about these real-world objects in a digital format using the available technology (residing in the IT system facet). The representation of the information about the real-world objects in the system constitutes a relationship between the subject facet and the IT system facet (see the black arrow labelled "Representation" in Fig. 4-2).

Relationship between IT system facet and usage facet

The system processes the represented information according to the defined functionality. The processing of the information takes place within the IT system facet. However, the system presents the results of the processing to its users (a person or another system) using an appropriate user interface. The presentation of the results to the user by means of some interface device constitutes a relationship between the IT system facet and the usage facet (see the black arrow labelled "Presentation" in Fig. 4-2).

Relationship between usage facet and subject facet

The system user interprets the output of the system obtained and associates it with real-world objects of the subject facet. This constitutes a relationship between the usage facet and the subject facet (see the black arrow labelled "Association" in Fig. 4-2).

Role of the development facet

The software-intensive system itself is a product of a development process which takes place in the development facet. The task of the development process is to consider, besides the relevant aspects of the development facet, the relevant aspects of the other three context facets and their relationships. Hence the development facet is related to each of the other three facets (as indicated by the three grey arrows in Fig. 4-2).

The four context facets and their relationships are discussed in detail in Part II.

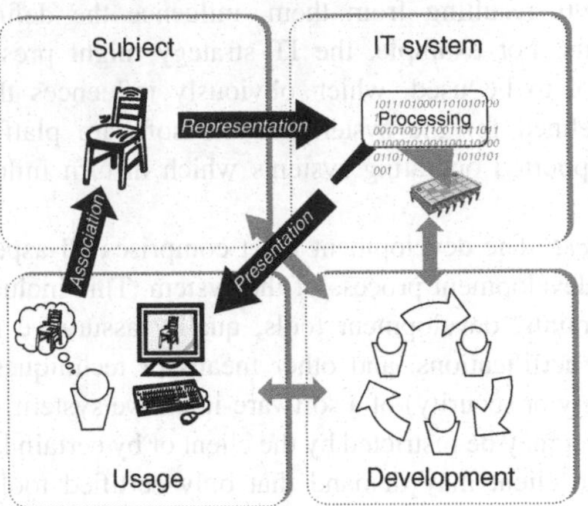

Fig. 4-2 *Logical relationships between the four context facets*

4.3.2 Use of the Four Context Facets

Improved quality of requirements documents

Structuring the system context into the four facets is a heuristic that has proven useful during, among other things, requirements elicitation, negotiation, and validation. Structuring the context into four facets supports a systematic consideration of the system context during requirements engineering. By considering each of the four facets, as well as their relationships, relevant context aspects can be identified more easily and, for example, the risk of neglecting an entire facet is reduced. Hence the completeness and the correctness of the specified requirements are significantly improved. According to our experience, the definition and use of simple checklists for each context facet, and for the relationships between the facets, facilitates a more systematic consideration of the system context and thus leads to requirements specifications of higher quality.

4.4 Three Core Activities

The requirements engineering process takes place in the development facet. The main goals of requirements engineering are characterised by the three dimensions of requirements engineering, as explained in Section 4.4.1 (see [Pohl 1993; Pohl 1994]).

From the three dimensions of requirements engineering, the three core activities of requirements engineering (documentation, elicitation, and negotiation) can be derived (see Section 4.4.2).

4.4.1 The Three Dimensions of Requirements Engineering

Figure 4-3 illustrates the three dimensions of requirements engineering, which can be characterised as follows:

- *Content dimension*: The content dimension deals with the understanding of the system requirements attained. At the beginning of the requirements engineering process, besides the system vision, only a few system requirements are known. The understanding of these requirements is typically vague, and the detailed requirements are mostly unknown. In contrast, at the end of the process, all the requirements are known and understood, preferably at the required level of detail. During the requirements engineering process, requirements must thus be elicited, including the development of new and innovative requirements. Consequently, the first essential goal of the requirements engineering process can be defined as: "All relevant requirements shall be explicitly known and understood at the required level of detail."

All requirements are known and understood in detail

- *Agreement dimension*: The agreement dimension deals with the level of agreement achieved between the relevant stakeholders about the known requirements. Different stakeholders can have different opinions about a system requirement. Conflicts between the stakeholders about system requirements thus have to be detected as early as possible. The detected conflicts should be resolved, either by achieving consensus or by making (well-founded) decisions. If requirements are defined without consolidating the stakeholders' different opinions, the unresolved conflicts will inevitably surface during or after the deployment of the new system. Unresolved conflicts put the acceptance of the system at risk and thereby endanger the realisation of the system vision. Consequently, the second goal of the requirements engineering process can be defined as: "To establish a sufficient agreement about the system requirements between the involved stakeholders."

Establish sufficient stakeholder agreement

- *Documentation dimension*: The documentation dimension deals with documenting and specifying the system requirements using different documentation/specification formats. Usually, information that is elicited during requirements engineering is first documented informally, either as a note, sketch, statement in a minute, or hand drawing, for example. Later, the requirements are documented and specified according to the documentation and specification formats and rules defined for the project. Such formats and rules can define the modelling language or a template to be used for documenting or specifying a particular type of requirement. The rules may also include other criteria for ensuring high quality of the requirements documentation and specification, such as consistency rules for requirements expressed in different formats. The third essential goal of the requirements engineering process can be defined as: "All requirements shall be documented/specified in compliance with the relevant documentation/specification formats and rules."

Documentation/specification of requirements in compliance with the defined formats and rules

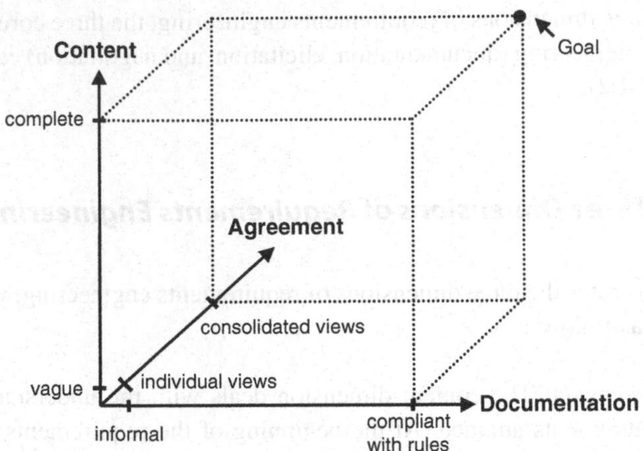

Fig. 4-3 *The three dimensions of requirements engineering (based on [Pohl 1994])*

The three essential goals of requirements engineering can thus be defined as follows:

D

Definition 4-1: *Goals of requirements engineering*

Requirements engineering is a cooperative, iterative, and incremental process which aims at ensuring that:

(1) All relevant requirements are explicitly known and understood at the required level of detail.

(2) A sufficient agreement about the system requirements is achieved between the stakeholders involved.

(3) All requirements are documented and specified in compliance with the relevant documentation/specification formats and rules.

4.4.2 The Core Activities

Derivation of the core activities from the three dimensions

From the three dimensions of requirements engineering, the three core activities of requirements engineering can be derived. Each core activity significantly contributes to the achievement of one of the three sub-goals of requirements engineering. We explain the three core activities below. The interactions between the core activities, as well as between the core activities and the cross-sectional activities, are explained in Section 4.5.1.

Documentation

Compliance with documentation and specification rules

The focus of the documentation activity is the documentation and specification of the elicited requirements according to the defined documentation and specification rules. In addition, other important types of information such as rationale or decisions must be documented (see Section 15.1). The documentation activity thus distinguishes the following sets of rules:

- *General documentation rules*: These rules apply to all kinds of information to be documented such as interview and meeting protocols, information about the context or decisions and rationale. These rules define, for instance, the document layout, required document headers, and required document management information such as authors or a version history.
- *Documentation rules*: These rules apply to each requirement documented at different stages of the requirements engineering process. The rules aim to ensure a sufficient quality of the documentation of the requirements mainly for use in other requirements engineering activities (e.g. negotiation or validation) while at the same time keeping the documentation effort low. Documentation rules may, for instance, prescribe a specific template to be used for documenting the requirements.
- *Specification rules*: These rules apply to all requirements which are included in the requirements specification. The specification rules aim to ensure high quality of the specified requirements which are used in the subsequent development activities as key input or might be part of contracts. The specification rules may prescribe, for instance, the use of syntactic requirements patterns or a requirements specification language (see Definition 17-6).

In general, specification rules are typically more restrictive than documentation rules.

Use of different formats

Depending on the intended use of a requirements artefact, different documentation and specification formats can be used. For example, a requirement might be documented using natural language to facilitate communication with a typical end user, while at the same time be specified using a formal requirements language to support the system architect in defining the system architecture. In general, different stakeholders prefer different documentation/specification formats. Hence a requirements artefact may have to be translated from one format into another one. The issue becomes keeping the documentation/specification of a requirement held in different formats consistent across formats when undertaking any change. The documentation activity is discussed in more detail in Part IV.a.

Elicitation

Progress in the content dimension

The goal of the elicitation activity is to improve the understanding of the requirements, i.e. to achieve progress in the content dimension. During the elicitation activity, requirements are elicited from stakeholders and other requirement sources. In addition, new and innovative requirements are collaboratively developed.

Eliciting requirements and jointly developing innovative requirements

The requirement sources relevant for the system are not always known at the beginning of the process. An essential task of the elicitation activity is therefore the systematic identification of relevant requirement sources. Relevant requirement sources include the stakeholders involved in the process, existing documentation, and existing predecessor systems. Requirements are elicited, for example, by interviewing the stakeholders or by analysing existing documents and systems. In addition, innovative requirements (which can typically not simply be elicited from a requirement source) are developed in a collaborative and creative process. The development of innovative requirements can, for example, be supported by applying creativity techniques such as brainstorming. The elicitation activity is described in more detail in Part IV.b.

Negotiation

Individual, conflicting stakeholder opinions

The system has to fulfil the needs and wishes of different stakeholders. Obviously, the needs and wishes of the different stakeholders can vary. Each stakeholder has his/her own view about the system to be developed. The different opinions of the stakeholders can be in conflict with one another.

Resolution of all existing conflicts

The goal of the negotiation activity is therefore twofold: First, all conflicts between the viewpoints of the different stakeholders have to be detected and made explicit. Second, the identified conflicts should be resolved (as far as possible). Depending on the cause of the conflict, different strategies can be applied for resolving it. At the beginning of the requirements engineering process, typically the viewpoints of the different stakeholders differ significantly. Ideally, at the end of the requirements engineering process, the negotiation activity has identified and resolved all conflicts which exist between the different stakeholders involved. The negotiation activity is described in more detail in Part IV.c.

4.5 Two Cross-Sectional Activities

Besides the three requirements engineering core activities, two cross-sectional activities significantly influence the requirements engineering process. The cross-sectional activities support the three core activities and secure the results of requirements engineering. The two cross-sectional activities are described in the following sub-sections.

Validation

The validation activity is a cross-sectional activity which consists of three sub-activities:

Validation of the artefacts

- *Validation of the requirements artefacts:* The validation of the requirements artefacts aims at detecting defects in the requirements. Only requirements with high quality provide a sound basis for the architectural design, the implementation of the system, and the development of test artefacts. Defects in requirements entail defects in the architecture, in the implementation, and in test artefacts. Requirements defects are rarely caused only by insufficient or inappropriate requirements documentation. In many cases, defects can be attributed to the non-fulfilment of one or more goals in each of the three dimensions (see Section 4.4.2). Validation thus has the key aim of validating the artefacts with regard to the content, the documentation, and the agreement dimensions. A requirement should only be used as a reference for the further development process or as part of a (legal) contract if it has been successfully validated under the consideration of all three validation aspects (content, documentation, and agreement).

Validation of the activities

- *Validation of the core activities:* The validation of the core activities (documentation, elicitation, and negotiation) has the goal of checking the compliance between the activities performed and the process and/or activity specifications. For example, one should validate whether the steps defined for an activity and the defined follow-up activities have been performed.

- *Validation of the consideration of the system context:* The validation of the consideration of the system context aims at validating whether the system context has been considered in the intended way during requirements engineering. In other words, this sub-activity aims at validating whether all relevant stakeholders have been involved in the process at the right time and whether the relevant context aspects of all four context facets have been considered during the requirements engineering process. For example, with respect to the usage facet, one should validate whether all required interactions between the system and its actors (users and other systems) have been elicited.

Validation of context consideration

The goals, principles, and techniques of the validation activity are described in detail in Part V.

Management

The management activity can be subdivided into the following three essential sub-activities:

- *Management of the requirements artefacts:* This activity comprises the management of the requirements artefacts throughout the system lifecycle. The management of the requirements artefacts includes the prioritisation of requirements, the persistent recording of requirements (e.g. by storing them in a database), the configuration management and the change management of the requirements as well as maintaining requirements traceability.

Management of the artefacts

- *Management of the activities:* This activity comprises the planning and control of the requirements engineering activities in order to ensure an efficient and effective overall requirements engineering process. If necessary, the planned workflow of the activities can be aligned to accommodate the current project situation.

Management of the activities

- *Observation of the system context:* The observation of the system context aims at identifying changes in the system context that are relevant for the system. A relevant context change typically requires the execution of one or more requirements engineering activities or a re-scheduling of activities. For example, it might require the execution of an elicitation activity and a documentation activity in order to document the new requirements caused by this change, or the execution of a change management activity to adjust existing requirements accordingly.

Management of changes to the context

The three essential requirements management activities are described in detail in Part VI.

4.5.1 Interrelations between the Five Activities

There are obvious interactions between the activities defined in our requirements engineering framework, i.e. the three core activities and the two cross-sectional activities. For example, the execution of one core activity (and thus progress mainly in one of the three dimensions) may lead to a decrease in the progress established in one of the other dimensions, and thus require the execution of additional activities. In other words, performing one requirements engineering activity typically causes the execution of additional requirements engineering activities. We illustrate the interactions between the three core and two cross-sectional activities in Examples 4-1 to 4-3.

Example 4-1: Elicitation of additional requirements

During an interview (i.e. the execution of an elicitation activity), new requirements are identified and documented in the interview minutes. The identification of the new requirements obviously leads to progress in the content dimension. However, the documentation of the new requirements in the interview minutes is not in compliance with the project-specific documentation rules. Thus an additional task for the documentation dimension is created, namely the documentation of the new requirements so as to be in compliance with the defined rules. In addition, the new requirements should be agreed between the stakeholders involved. Thus, a new validation activity is performed to check whether the stakeholders agree with the new requirement. During the validation of the agreement, conflicts about the requirement between the involved stakeholders might be identified. If so, these conflicts need to be resolved and the outcome of the conflict resolution must be documented and comply with the documentation rules, etc.

Example 4-2: Detection of a missing requirement

While reviewing a set of requirement artefacts (i.e. during the execution of a validation activity), the stakeholders detect that an important requirement has been omitted. The stakeholders briefly sketch the omitted requirement. Obviously, the new requirement is not yet documented in compliance with the defined documentation rules. Moreover, the documentation of the new (previously omitted) requirement does not contain all the required information, and not all the stakeholders have yet agreed to the new requirement. The identification of a new requirement during the validation activity (progress in the content dimension) thus might lead to the execution of additional elicitation, documentation, and negotiation activities.

Example 4-3: Removal of a requirement from the specification

Negotiations between customers and system users result in the removal of a requirement from the specification. The elimination of this requirement requires an evaluation of whether other requirements artefacts are affected by this change. The related requirements artefacts thus have to be analysed. In this example, the resolution of a conflict (progress in the agreement dimension) leads to the execution of additional activities in the content and documentation dimensions in order to check for inconsistencies resulting from the removal of the requirement and to adjust the documented artefacts accordingly, if required.

4.6 The Three Kinds of Requirements Artefacts

Goals, scenarios, and solution-oriented requirements

We use the term "requirements artefact" to refer to a documented requirement (see Definition 2-2 on Page 16). A requirements artefact thus documents a requirement using a specific documentation format. Different documentation formats which might be used to document a requirement are discussed in detail in Part III. In our framework, we differentiate three kinds of requirement artefacts, namely goals, scenarios, and solution-oriented requirements, which are also described in detail in Part III.

4.6.1 Goals

Stakeholder intentions

Requirements engineers need to understand the stakeholders' intentions with regard to the system to be developed. In requirements engineering, the stakeholders' intentions are documented as goals. Antón states in [Antón 1996] that goals "are high-level objectives of the business, organisation, or system". According to [Van Lamsweerde 2001], a goal is "an objective the system under consideration should achieve". We define a goal (in requirements engineering) as follows:

Definition 4-2: *Goal*

A goal is an intention with regard to the objectives, properties, or use of the system.

Prescriptive statements

Goals have a prescriptive nature, i.e. a goal states what is expected or required from the system. Thereby, goals differ from descriptive statements such as statements about the domain of the system (e.g. the description of a physical law). Example 4-4 depicts two goals for a navigation system.

Example 4-4: Goals for the car navigation system example

G_1: The system shall guide the driver to a desired destination automatically.

G_2: The response times of the system shall be 20% lower compared with the predecessor system.

Intentions of stakeholders

Goals (see Chapter 7) document the intentions of the stakeholders and abstract from system usage as well as from the realisation of the system. Goals refine the system vision into objectives to be fulfilled by the system.

A goal should be solution free, i.e. it should not predefine a specific solution. Hence, the stakeholders typically have many different alternatives for satisfying a goal, where each alternative may lead to different requirements.

Benefit of goals

The explicit definition of goals (stakeholder intentions) supports conflict resolution, leads to a better understanding of the system, and increases the acceptance of the system.

In Part III, we elaborate on different types of goals, the documentation of goals, and their usage in requirements engineering.

4.6.2 Scenarios

Examples of system usage

A scenario typically documents a concrete example of system usage. It thus illustrates the fulfilment (or non-fulfilment) of a goal (or set of goals). Thus, a scenario describes a concrete example of either how the system satisfies a goal or how it fails to satisfy a goal. A scenario may define an interaction sequence at different levels of abstraction. For example, a scenario can describe the interactions in detail and thus very close to reality or only document the essential interactions (and thereby abstract from the incarnation). We define a scenario as follows:

Definition 4-3: *Scenario*

A scenario describes a concrete example of satisfying or failing to satisfy a goal (or set of goals). It thereby provides more detail about one or several goals. A scenario typically defines a sequence of interaction steps executed to satisfy the goal and relates these interaction steps to the system context.

Scenarios illustrate goal satisfaction

Example 4-5 presents a scenario that documents a sequence of interactions between a driver and a driver assistance system. The scenario describes how the goal "facilitate automatic braking manoeuvres" can be achieved. In principle, goals and scenarios are complementary. For example, goals stimulate the elicitation of scenarios and vice versa.

In Part III.b, we elaborate on the characteristics of scenarios, different types of scenarios, their documentation, their usage in requirements engineering as well as their interrelations with goals.

Example 4-5: Scenario "Automatic braking manoeuvre"

Carl drives his car on the motorway at a speed of 50 mph. Peter, the driver of the car ahead of Carl, steps on the brake pedal firmly. After recognising that the car in front is braking, Carl pushes on the brake pedal as well. The on-board computer of Carl's vehicle detects that the safety distance to Peter's car is no longer maintained and issues a warning to the driver. The distance between the two cars continuously decreases. In order to support the driver, the on-board computer initiates an automated full braking. The computer informs Carl about the automatic braking manoeuvre. After the distance between the two cars stops decreasing, the on-board computer terminates the full braking manoeuvre. The on-board computer continues controlling the speed of Carl's car until the safety distance to Peter's car is maintained and informs Carl about the end of this "manoeuvre".

4.6.3 Solution-Oriented Requirements

Data, functions, behaviour, quality, and constraints

Solution-oriented requirements define the data perspective, the functional perspective, and the behavioural perspective on a software-intensive system (see

Section 2.2.1). Furthermore, solution-oriented requirements comprise (solution-oriented) quality requirements (see Section 2.2.2) and (solution-oriented) constraints (see Section 2.2.3).

Conceptual solution

In contrast to goals and scenarios, which should be defined fairly independently from a specific and intended solution, the definition of solution-oriented requirements often implies a conceptual (or logical) solution for the system (see Chapter 13). Data models, for instance, define entities, attributes, and relationships between entities (see Section 14.1).[8] Data models determine which data shall be represented in the system and, to some extent, how these data shall be represented. A behavioural model defines the states of the system and the externally visible behaviour with respect to these states (see Section 14.3). Thereby, it partially defines the intended solution. Solution-oriented requirements models thus often define a (partial) solution or even the basis for generating a solution from the requirements models (see Section 13.1).

In Part III.c, we present requirements models for documenting the data perspective, the functional perspective, and the behavioural perspective.

4.6.4 Use of the Three Kinds of Requirements Artefacts

The three artefact types are complementary

The three different kinds of requirements artefacts (goals, scenarios, and solution-oriented requirements) are used complementarily during requirements engineering. Using all three types of artefacts offers several advantages, as outlined throughout this book. For example, developing goals and scenarios prior to or along with solution-oriented requirements is an established principle for developing detailed system requirements based on a system vision (see e.g. [Jarke and Pohl 1993; Van Lamsweerde 2001; Antón 1996; Antón and Potts 1998; Yu 1997]). Applying a goal- and scenario-based approach typically leads to a significant improvement of the quality of the requirements specification. It improves, for example, the completeness of the specification (see amongst others [Antón and Potts 1998] as well as Section 7.1).

Moreover, scenarios put requirements into context and thus provide a good basis for deriving and developing detailed, solution-oriented requirements. For instance, scenarios explicitly document which stakeholders use the system as well as, via the goals associated with a scenario, the stakeholders' intentions for using the system (see Part III.b for more details). Moreover, goals and scenarios support the refinement of the requirements across different layers of abstraction, which is exploited by our goal- and scenario-based requirements engineering method COSMOD-RE (see Part VII).

4.6.5 The Term "Requirements" as Used in This Book

When we use the term "requirements" in this book, we refer to the three types of requirements outlined above (goals, scenarios, and solution-oriented requirements), as described in detail in Part III. For example, when we talk about requirements

[8] More precisely, a data model defines entity *types* and relationship *types* between the entity types (see Section 14.1).

elicitation we refer to the elicitation of goals, scenarios, and solution-oriented requirements. Therein, the term "solution-oriented requirements" refers to data, functional, and behavioural requirements as well as (solution-oriented) quality requirements and constraints.

D

Definition 4-4: *Requirements (as used in this book)*

When we use the term "requirements", we refer to goals, scenarios, and solution-oriented requirements (i.e. data, functional, and behavioural requirements, and solution-oriented quality requirements and constraints).

By defining more fine-grained types of requirements, a requirements classification scheme can be established which fits the needs of a particular domain, company, or project (see e.g. [Pohl 1996a; Young 2004]).

4.7 Overview of the Book

The structure of the book is derived from our requirements engineering framework. Fig. 4-4 illustrates which parts of the book discuss and describe which parts of the framework in detail.

Part II

- The structuring of the system context into four context facets is outlined in detail in Part II.

Part III

- The three kinds of requirements artefacts, their documentation, and their use are explained in detail in Part III. Part III is divided into three sub-parts. Part III.a focuses on goals, Part III.b on scenarios, and Part III.c on solution-oriented requirements.

Part IV

- The three requirements engineering core activities are explained in detail in Part IV. Part IV is divided into three sub-parts. Part IV.a outlines the documentation activity, Part IV.b the elicitation activity, and Part IV.c the negotiation activity.

Parts V and VI

- The two cross-sectional activities are explained in Part V (validation) and Part VI (management).

Parts VII and VIII

In addition to the detailed description of all aspects of our requirements engineering framework, we present our goal- and scenario-based requirements engineering method COSMOD-RE which integrates most of the aspects presented in this book (Part VII).

In Part VIII of this book, we outline the main challenges faced when applying our requirements engineering framework in a software product line setting and elaborate on the benefits of deriving test artefacts from requirements.

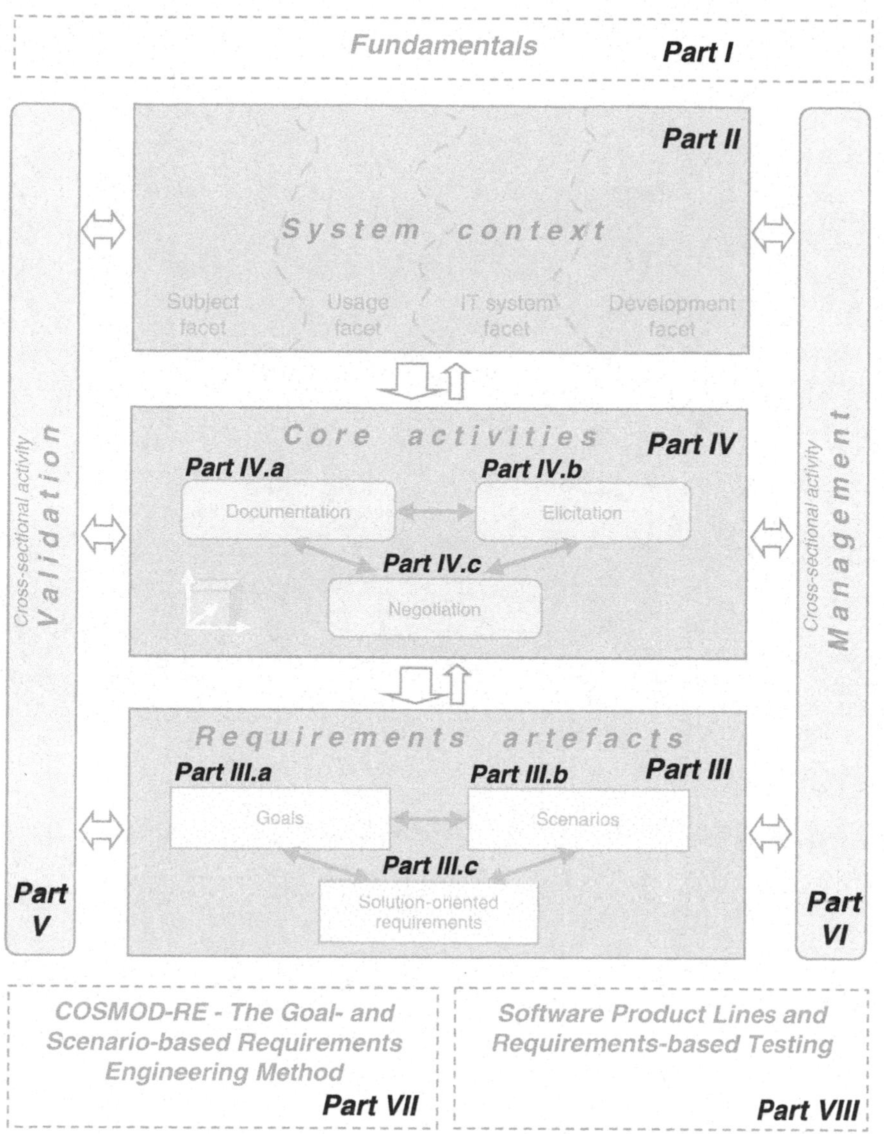

Fig. 4-4 *Structure of this book illustrated using the framework*

Part II
System Context

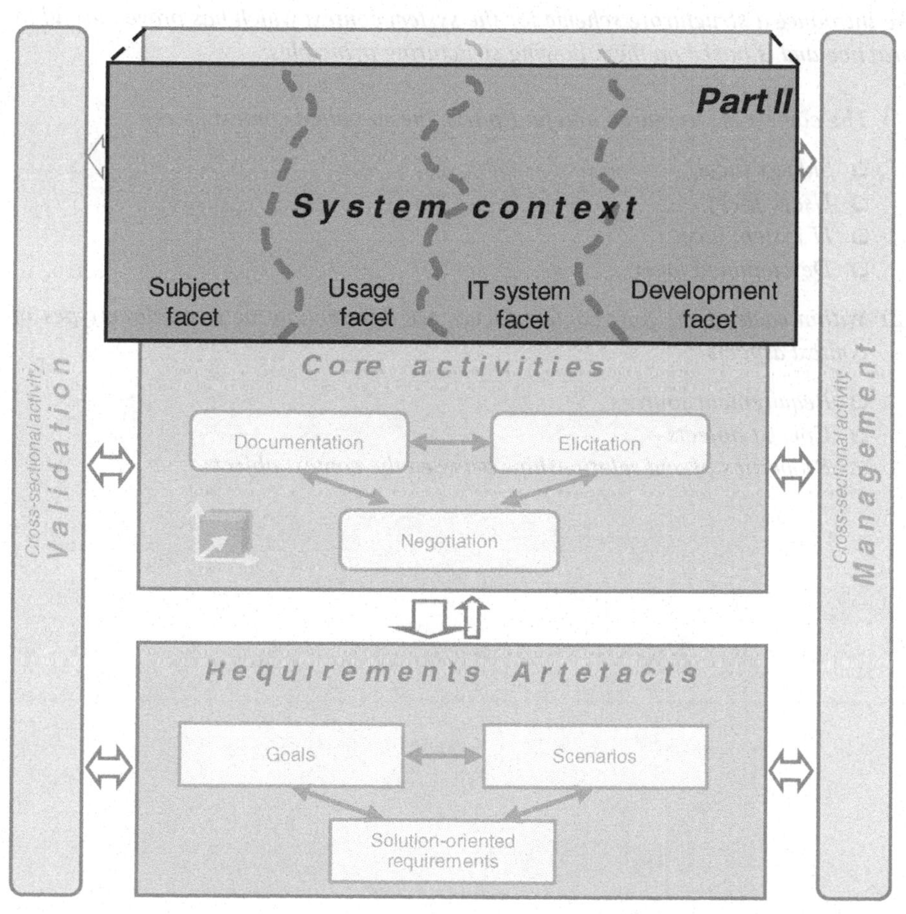

Overview Part II – System Context

This part of the book deals with the system context and its role in requirements engineering. We define two boundaries, the system boundary and the context boundary, to define the system context and separate the system context from the system and from the environment:

- *System boundary: This boundary separates the system from its context. The system boundary hence defines which material and immaterial objects belong to the system and can be changed during system development.*
- *Context boundary: This boundary separates the irrelevant part of the environment from the system context. The system context contains the material and immaterial objects to be considered when defining the requirements for the system.*

We introduce a structuring scheme for the system context which has proven useful in practice and is based on the following structuring principles:

(1) The context is structured into four parts, the so-called context facets:

- *Subject facet*
- *Usage facet*
- *IT system facet*
- *Development facet*

(2) Within each of the four context facets, we differentiate between three types of context aspects:

- *Requirement sources*
- *Context objects*
- *Properties of and relationships between the context objects*

Classification Part II System Context	Basic	Advanced
5 System and Context Boundaries		
5.1 The Term “Context”	✓	
5.2 System Boundary	✓	
5.3 Context Boundary	✓	
5.4 Need to Document	✓	
6 Structuring the System Context		
6.1 Structuring Principles		✓
6.2 Four Context Facets and Three Types of Context Aspects		✓
6.3 Relevant Context Aspects		✓
6.4 Different Roles of a Context Aspect		✓

Chapter 5
System and Context Boundaries

In this chapter, we explain:

- *The role of the system context during requirements engineering*
- *The system boundary, which separates the system from its context*
- *The context boundary, which separates the system context from the irrelevant environment*

5.1 The Term "Context"

Each system is embedded in an environment

A software-intensive system is always embedded in an environment. Requirements for the system can be neither studied nor defined without a proper consideration of the environment in which the system is embedded. The environment comprises a large variety of material and immaterial objects such as technical or non-technical systems, people, technologies, business processes, laws, sensors and actuators, existing software components, or physical laws.

The context influences the definition of requirements

The system environment significantly influences the definition of the requirements for the system. In principle, a system requirement cannot be properly defined, understood, or interpreted without considering the relevant parts and aspects of the environment in which the system is embedded (see e.g. [McMenamin and Palmer 1984; Davis 1993; Jarke and Pohl 1993; Hammond et al. 2001]). Ignoring, overlooking, or misconceiving important aspects of the system environment will most likely result in serious defects in the requirements specification. For example, a wrong assumption about the behaviour of an external system will most likely lead to an incorrect definition of the requirements specifying the interactions with the external system.

D

Definition 5-1: *System context*

The system context is the part of the system environment relevant for defining, understanding, and interpreting the system requirements. The system context consists of the four context facets: the subject facet, the usage facet, the IT system facet, and the development facet.

System context

The part of the system environment that has to be considered during system development is called the system context.[1] To separate the system context from the

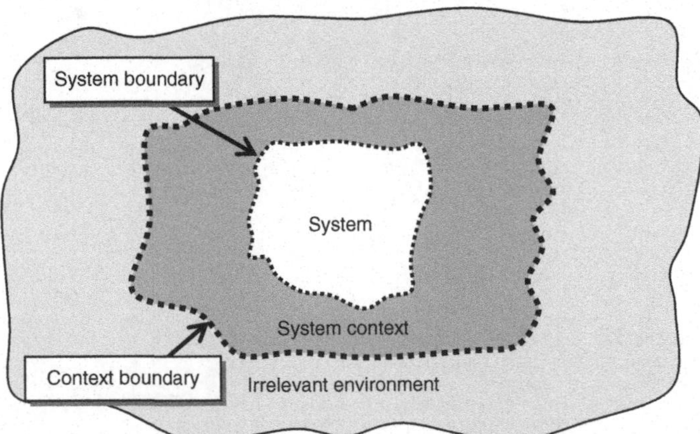

Fig. 5-1 *System boundary and context boundary separating the system, the context, and the irrelevant environment*

[1] In this book, we use the terms "system context" and "context" as synonyms.

system itself as well as from the irrelevant environment, we define two boundaries (see Fig. 5-1):

Changeable vs. stable artefacts

- *The system boundary*: By defining the system boundary, the stakeholders separate the aspects that belong to the system from the aspects that are part of the system context or the irrelevant environment, i.e. from aspects which do not belong to the system itself. Material and immaterial objects which belong to the system (i.e. artefacts that are within the system boundary) can be changed during system development. Artefacts outside the system boundary (i.e. artefacts that belong to the system context or the irrelevant environment) cannot be changed during the development process and are hence considered to be stable.

Relevant system context

- *The context boundary*: The context boundary separates the system context from the part of the environment that is considered to be irrelevant for the system development. In other words, the context boundary separates the irrelevant part of the environment from the relevant part and thus reduces the aspects of the environment to be considered during requirements engineering.

Requirements only exist in a context

A requirement only exists with respect to a given system context. A clear definition of the system context (i.e. a clear definition of the system and the context boundaries) is therefore a prerequisite for the correct definition of the system requirements. Only if the system context is properly taken into account, can the requirements for the system be defined, understood, and interpreted correctly.

Definition 5-2: *Context aspect*

Context aspects are material and immaterial objects of the system context such as people, technical and non-technical systems, processes, or physical laws.

We refer to the different objects (e.g. people, systems, processes, physical laws, etc.) that belong to the system context as context aspects (see Definition 5-2). Each context aspect has its specific relationships to the system. For example, some context aspects interact directly with the system and thus influence the definition of the system requirements, whereas other context aspects do not interact with the system at all but nevertheless influence the requirements for the system in some way (see Example 5-1).

Example 5-1: Examples of relationships between context aspects and the system

Example of a context aspect having a direct interaction relationship with the system:

- The bank customer uses the ATM (automated teller machine) to withdraw money from his account. When defining the requirements for the ATM, the specifics of the different customers of a bank must hence be taken into account (for instance, if the ATM is used by international customers, the user interface must support different languages).

Example of a context aspect having no interaction relationship with the system but still influencing the requirements for the system:

- A law requires that sensitive data items entered into a banking system and used within the system are encrypted using a certain encryption standard.

We elaborate on the system boundary in Section 5.2 and the context boundary in Section 5.3. In Section 5.4, we sketch the influence of the system context on the system requirements and discuss the need for documenting context aspects in more detail.

5.2 System Boundary

Changeable and unchangeable aspects

The system boundary separates the system to be developed from its environment. Everything within the system boundary is considered to be changeable during system development. For example, the system boundary can define that hardware and software parts, a business process, people, organisational structures, and/or an IT infrastructure belong to a system and can thus be changed. If, for instance, a business process of an organisation is part of the system, the business process can be changed and hence be redesigned during system development. In contrast, if the business process belongs to the system context it cannot be changed and hence cannot be redesigned during system development.

Definition 5-3: *System boundary*

The system boundary separates the system to be developed from the system context. The system boundary separates the parts that belong to the system and can hence be changed during the development process from the parts of the system context that cannot be changed during the development process.

Sources and sinks

In order to separate a system from the system context, for example, the sources and sinks of the system can be considered (see e.g. [DeMarco 1978]). Sources provide inputs to the system. Sinks receive output from the system. Examples of sources and sinks are:

- People
- Other technical or non-technical systems
- Sensors and actuators

System interfaces

Sources and sinks interact with the system via system interfaces. A system typically offers different types of interfaces such as human–machine interfaces, software interfaces, and hardware interfaces. The system provides its functionality or services to the environment, monitors the environment, influences environmental variables, and controls processes in the environment via the system interfaces. In other words, all interactions between the system and its environment take place via the system interfaces. Figure 5-2 sketches a system with four distinct interfaces.

Grey zone between the system and the system context

During requirements engineering, the system boundary as well as the interfaces are typically unstable, i.e. they change quite frequently. Only when the requirements are sufficiently well understood and documented (i.e. at the end of the requirements engineering process), do the system boundary and the system interfaces tend to become stable. For example, during requirements engineering some interfaces may not be

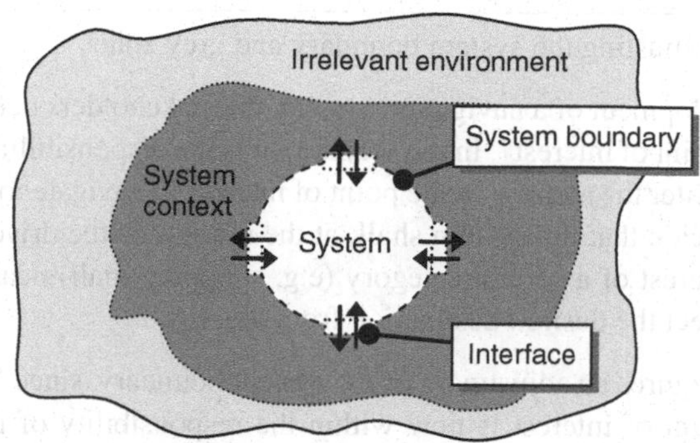

Fig. 5-2 *System boundary and system interfaces*

described in detail or may even be unknown. If some system functions are not known yet, the interfaces required for these functions are also unknown and therefore not yet defined. One may also encounter that parts of the system context which were assumed to be stable so far must be changed and therefore the system boundary has to be adjusted.

Due to an (initially) vague separation of the system and its context (i.e. a "blurred" definition of the system boundary) typically there is a so-called grey zone between the system and its context. The grey zone denotes, at a given point in time, the range of the potential system boundaries, as illustrated in Fig. 5-3.

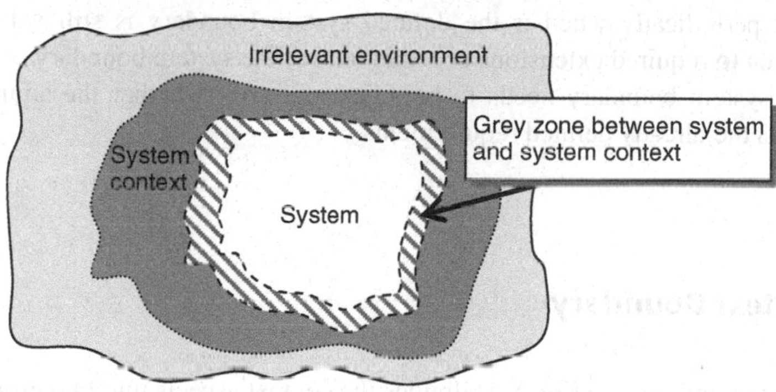

Fig. 5-3 *Grey zone between the system and the context*

Adjustment of the system boundary

In addition to a possible adjustment of the system boundary within the grey zone, the grey zone itself may also be adjusted during requirements engineering. For example, such an adjustment is required if material or immaterial objects which are currently part of the system context have to be changed. In this case, the grey zone is extended to cover these objects or, alternatively, the objects directly become part of the system. In the latter case, the grey zone is adjusted too, since these objects become part of the system and are thus located inside the system boundary. The adjustment of the system boundary and the adjustment of the grey zone are illustrated in Example 5-2.

Example 5-2: Adjusting the system boundary and grey zone

During the development of a navigation system, the stakeholders define a scenario "navigate to a point of interest". In the scenario, it is the responsibility of the driver to look up and enter the address of the point of interest to navigate to. Later on, the stakeholders decide that the system shall, at the request of the driver, display the 15 points of interest of a certain category (e.g. shopping mall) nearby and allow the driver to select the desired destination from this list.

This decision requires an adjustment of the system boundary, since looking up the address of a point of interest is now within the responsibility of the system. In addition, the grey zone of the system boundary has to be adjusted. For example, the stakeholders have to decide later on whether the updating of the points of interest, their addresses, opening times etc. is managed by the system at all, and if so, how the system obtains the new data (e.g. via mobile connection or new DVDs).

!

Hint 5-1: *Pay attention to the system boundary*

- Determine explicitly which aspects belong to the system.
- Determine which aspects are outside the system boundary.
- When defining the system boundary involve all relevant stakeholders.
- Try to reach an agreement about the system boundary. In case you cannot decide whether some object belongs to the system or not, put it in the grey zone.
- Check periodically whether the defined system boundary is still valid. Pay attention to required extensions or reductions of the system boundary.
- If the system boundary needs to be adjusted, verify whether the adjustment impacts the already defined requirements.

5.3 Context Boundary

Defining the context boundary

The context boundary (see Fig. 5-1) divides the context aspects into two groups. The system context comprises the first group of context aspects, namely the aspects to be considered during system development. The irrelevant environment comprises the second group of context aspects, namely those aspects that do not need to be considered during system development.

Definition 5-4: *Context boundary*

The context boundary separates the relevant part of the system environment from the irrelevant part. In other words, it separates the system context from the irrelevant environment which contains all those aspects that do not need to be considered during system development.

Adjustment of the context boundary

At the beginning of requirements engineering, many (if not all) stakeholders only know a fraction of the system environment and its influence on the system. As a consequence, the context boundary is typically barely understood and thus only vaguely and incompletely defined. During requirements engineering, for instance, identified material and immaterial objects are assigned either to the context or to the irrelevant environment. Thereby, the understanding and definition of the context boundary is typically improved.

Just like the definition of the system boundary, also the definition of the context boundary typically changes during requirements engineering. For example, the stakeholders may detect that an aspect of the system context has no influence on the system at all. In this case, the stakeholders define this aspect as part of the irrelevant environment and adjust the context boundary accordingly. A typical example is a law that is considered as potentially relevant first, but eventually turns out to have no impact on the system (see Example 5-3).

E

Example 5-3: Context restriction

A new GPS-enabled (Global Positioning System) mobile phone has initially been designed with the goal of protecting user privacy according to the current laws of the European Union. Special focus was placed on the system's discretion with user data — no sensitive data about the user shall leak out, for instance, to GSM (Global System for Mobile Communications) service providers.

However, during requirements engineering it becomes obvious that the system does not transmit any user data to the GSM service provider or any other system/actor. Consequently, the European privacy laws no longer have to be considered and are thus defined as part of the irrelevant environment.

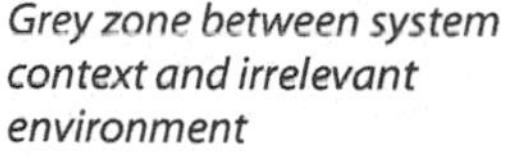

Similar to the grey zone between the system and the system context, there is a grey zone between the system context and the irrelevant environment (see Fig. 5-4). This grey zone contains context aspects that have been identified but not yet classified into aspects belonging to the system context and aspects belonging to the irrelevant environment. The grey zone thus contains aspects for which it is unclear whether they influence the definition of the system requirements or not.

During requirements engineering, an adjustment of the context boundary within the grey zone as well as an adjustment of the grey zone itself is typically required.

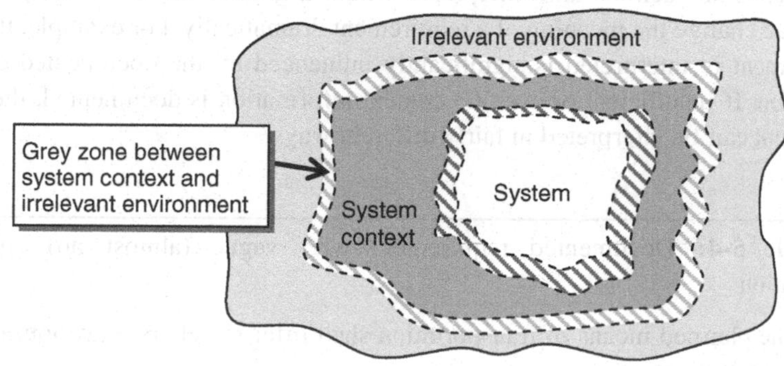

Fig. 5-4 *The grey zone between the system context and the irrelevant environment*

For example, if a context aspect within the grey zone is considered to be relevant for the definition of the system requirements and is thus added to the system context, the context boundary is changed, or if new context aspects are detected which potentially influence the definition of the requirements, these aspects are added to the grey zone. By adding context aspects to the grey zone or by removing context aspects from the grey zone, the grey zone is changed.

Since the context boundary separates the system context from the irrelevant environment (the rest of the universe), it is impossible to achieve a complete and precise definition of the context aspects which belong to the irrelevant environment.

!

Hint 5-2: *Defining the context boundary*

- ❑ Apply the structuring scheme of the four context facets explained in Chapter 6 in order to separate the system context, step by step, from the irrelevant environment.
- ❑ If you are unsure whether some context aspect impacts the system requirements or not, assign it to the grey zone.
- ❑ When you come to the conclusion that some context aspect is irrelevant for the system, document this aspect as a part of the irrelevant environment. This allows you to re-check the relevance of this aspect, for instance, when new system functionality is added.
- ❑ When defining new requirements (e.g. functions) check whether context aspects (e.g. a law) classified as irrelevant so far become relevant due to the new requirements.
- ❑ Use goals and scenarios to check whether specific aspects of the environment are relevant for the system or not. If an aspect is relevant, it should affect at least one goal or one scenario.
- ❑ Iterate these steps, since the system and context boundaries influence the definition of the goals and scenarios and vice versa (see COSMOD-RE Method; Part VII).

5.4 Need to Document Context Aspects

Requirements only exist in a given context

Requirements are defined and interpreted within a given context. A change in the context can change the meaning of a requirement dramatically. For example, the way a requirement is interpreted is significantly influenced by the documented context information. If insufficient or even no context information is documented, the same requirement can be interpreted in fairly different ways.

Example 5-4: Documented requirement with vague (almost no) context information

R23: The planned means of transportation shall offer travellers a fast journey to their destination.

Depending on the context information, the requirement shown in Example 5-4 has different interpretations. It is, for example, not clear whether the transport shall be performed by air, sea, land, or a combination of these. It is also unclear whether the requirement deals with a transport between the Earth and a space station. If the requirement was enriched with context information, misinterpretations could be avoided. For example, the context information "the system shall transport people from an island to the mainland, and there is no airstrip on the island" would reduce the potential interpretations of the requirement significantly (see [Gause and Weinberg 1989], p.14f, for some examples of misinterpreted requirements due to the lack of context information).

Restricting the Interpretations through Context Aspects

Context aspects (see Definition 5-2) restrict the possible interpretations of a requirement directly and indirectly. We illustrate this fact using the exemplary requirement R1 and its relationships depicted in Fig. 5-5:

Direct influence of context aspects

- *Direct influence*: As depicted in Fig. 5-5, requirement R1 has several relationships to context aspects. These relationships and the context aspects enrich the semantics of requirement R1 and thereby restrict possible interpretations. For example, if the requirement R23 from Example 5-4 was linked to the documented context information "The location is an island without an airstrip", this context information would restrict the possible interpretations of the requirement.[2]

Indirect influence of contextual aspects

- *Indirect influence*: In Fig. 5-5, requirement R1 has relationships to requirements R3, R5, and R8. These requirements are themselves related to context aspects. The context aspects related to the requirements R3, R5, and R8 also restrict the possible interpretations of the requirement R1.[3] For example, if the requirement R3 specifies that "Persons permanently living on the island should get a discount on car-ferry tickets" and this requirement is related to a context aspect (port with car-ferry facilities), this information also adds semantics to the requirement R1. This context aspect provides the information that one means of transportation should be a car-ferry which is facilitated by the existing harbour capabilities.

Need to Document Context Information

Documenting context information

Documenting the context aspects in an adequate way is essential for supporting the correct interpretation of requirements. Not surprisingly, requirements documents typically contain context information in addition to the documented requirements. However, the context information is often neither documented in a structured way nor elicited systematically.

Clear separation of context information and requirements

Furthermore, context information and requirements are frequently intermingled, which often makes a clear differentiation between context information and

[2] Note, the island and an airport cannot be changed by the system development process and thus they belong to the system context.

[3] Besides the context aspects, obviously, also requirements related to a given requirement add semantics and thereby restrict the possible interpretations of this requirement.

requirements impossible. Since context aspects cannot be changed during system development, this is already a significant problem itself. For example, if requirements and context information are intermingled, it is not obvious what can be changed during system development and what has to be considered as given, unchangeable constraints (i.e. what are the context aspects).

Avoiding redundant documentation of context information

Furthermore, the unsystematic documentation of context information often leads to redundancy because similar or identical context information is included in the definitions of multiple requirements. This causes additional problems. For instance, the documentation of similar or identical context information at different places in the documentation can lead to update anomalies (or, more precisely, to modification anomalies) and thus to inconsistencies.

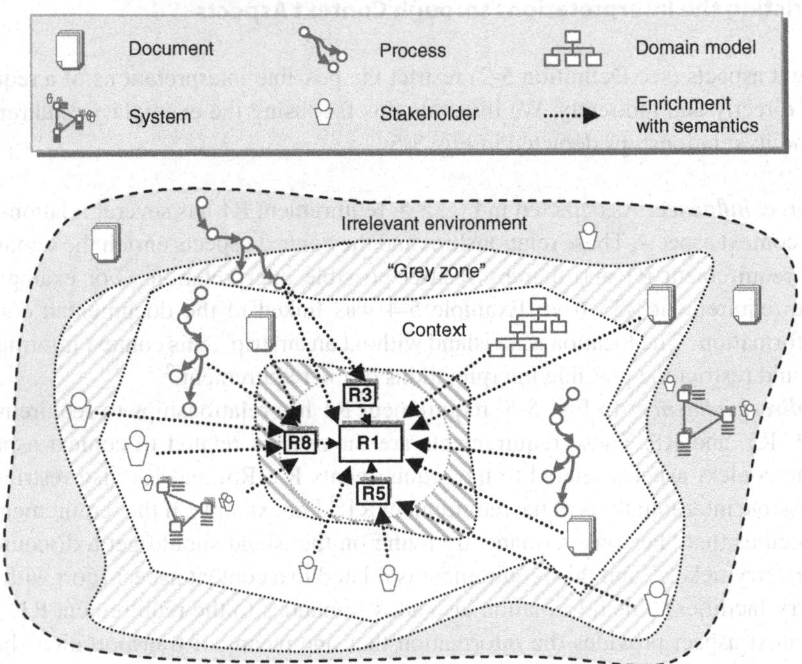

Fig. 5-5 *Context of a requirement*

Project-specific guidelines for documenting context information

To avoid such problems regarding the documentation of context information, we suggest defining project-specific guidelines for documenting context information. The guidelines should be project-specific since smaller projects typically require a smaller amount of documentation of context information than large projects in which several organisations, possibly residing in different countries, participate. The aim of the guidelines is to support the communication and consideration of context information during requirements engineering and system development. The guidelines should define, for example:

- The types of context aspects which should be considered and documented for the system to be developed
- The representation formats and the structure to be used for documenting context information

- ❑ The relationship types that shall be used to interrelate context information and requirements
- ❑ Responsibilities for documenting the context information

Structure of the system context

In Chapter 6, we present a coarse-grained structure for the system context that supports a systematic consideration of the context as well as a structured documentation of context information. The underlying structure can be used as a basis for defining project-specific guidelines for considering and documenting relevant context information.

Use project-specific checklists for context aspects

In order to support the systematic consideration of the context aspects, the project-specific guidelines should include checklists for each of the four context facets. The project-specific checklists can be defined based on the checklists presented in Sections 23.6 and 29.1.

Chapter 6
Structuring the System Context

In this chapter, we outline:

- *Two fundamental principles for structuring the system context*
- *The structuring of the system context into four context facets*
- *Three types of context aspects relevant within each context facet*
- *Examples of relevant context aspects within each of the four context facets*

Advantages of context structuring

Due to the variety of different context aspects that affect the system and thereby the system requirements, an elaborate structure for the system context is desirable. By dividing the context into distinct parts, the identification of relevant context aspects is supported. For example, relevant context aspects can be elicited separately for each part of the context. Likewise, the system and context boundaries can be defined for each part separately. In fact, a context structure facilitates focussing on specific context aspects during each requirements engineering activity and thus supports the core activities documentation, elicitation, and negotiation as well as the cross-sectional activities validation and management as outlined in Parts IV, V, and VI.

The context structuring in our requirements framework is based on two structuring principles, which are outlined in Section 6.1.

6.1 Structuring Principles

To structure the system context, we employ two structuring principles:

Differentiation between four context facets

- *Dividing the context into four context facets*: Firstly, dividing the context into different facets (see Fig. 6-1) supports the stakeholders during requirements engineering. For example, the stakeholders can initially focus on one context facet when eliciting the requirements, then perform a tailored elicitation of requirements for the second facet etc. Secondly, structuring the context into several distinct facets ensures that the stakeholders do not overlook an important facet during requirements engineering. For example, the stakeholders might only consider two out of three facets during requirements elicitation or only involve stakeholders from two of the three facets.

Classification of relevant aspects

- *Classification of context aspects*: In each context facet, we differentiate between different types of context aspects (see Fig. 6-2). Firstly, in each requirements engineering activity, each type of context facet can be addressed individually and systematically. For example, specific elicitation techniques could be applied for different types of context aspects. Secondly, the differentiation defines a standardised scheme for each facet which can be used, among other things, for explaining each facet in a standardised way. Third, different kinds of relationships can be defined between the context aspects as well as between the different context aspects and the requirements.

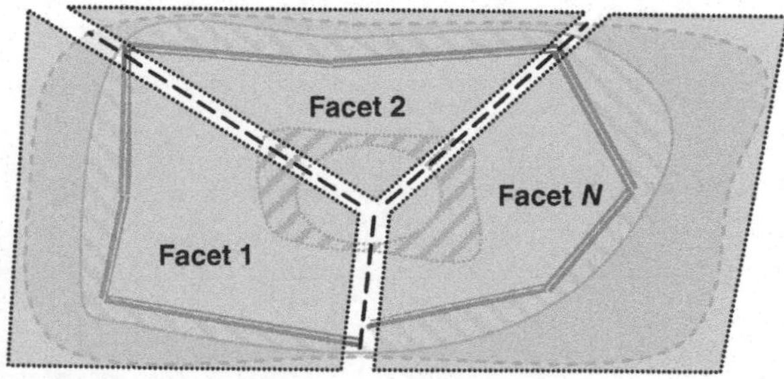

Fig. 6-1 *Structuring the context into facets*

In the following sections, we present a structure for the system context based on the two principles outlined above. In Section 6.2, we introduce three types of context aspects relevant for each context facet and for each software-intensive system. In Section 6.3, we introduce four context facets and explain the three context aspects for each of the four facets. Moreover, we illustrate the different aspects in each facet using examples.

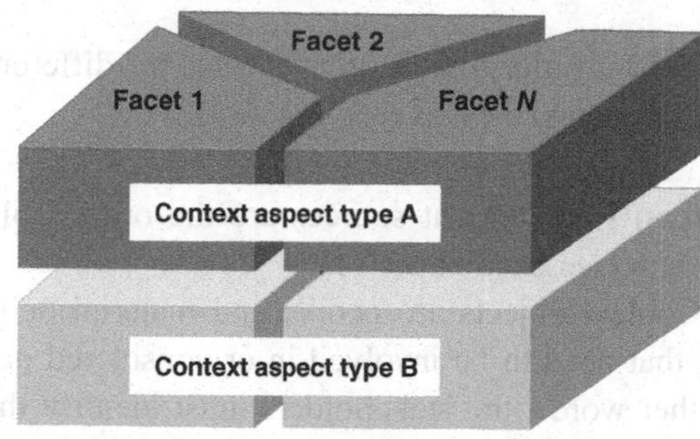

Fig. 6-2 *Classification of context aspects in each facet*

6.2 Four Context Facets and Three Types of Context Aspects

In Section 4.3, we proposed four context facets for structuring the system context:

- *Subject facet:* The subject facet comprises the objects and events in the context that are relevant for the system, for instance, because the system must store or process information about these objects and events. In other words, the objects and events in the subject facet must be represented in the system, e.g. by means of appropriate data structures. In addition, the subject facet comprises aspects that influence or constrain the representation of information in the system (e.g. data privacy laws disallowing the storage of certain types of data, or computational considerations demanding a certain accuracy of the data).

Objects and events to be represented in the system

- *Usage facet*: A software-intensive system is used by people or other software-intensive systems in order to achieve a goal or accomplish some task. The usage facet comprises all aspects concerning the usage of the system by people and other systems. These include, for instance, usage goals, desired usage workflows, different user groups with specific characteristics, different modes of interacting with the system through its user interface, etc.

System usage by external actors

- *IT system facet*: This facet comprises all aspects concerning the operational or technical environment in which the system is deployed. This environment comprises other software-intensive systems (existing systems and/or systems that are under development) as well as hardware and software components such as the underlying hardware and software platform, the communication network(s), peripheral devices, existing application software components, existing services, etc. In addition, the IT system facet deals with IT strategies and policies such as the policy to use only software components that have passed a specific certification.

Operational and technical environment

Development processes, methods, and tools

- *Development facet*: This facet comprises all aspects that influence the development of the system or, more specifically, all aspects in the context that are imposed, for instance, by law or by the client and relate to the development process of the system. Such aspects include, for example, process guidelines and constraints, development tools, development and quality assurance methods, maturity models, quality certifications, and other means or techniques for ensuring the quality of a software-intensive system.

Three types of context aspects

In addition to distinguishing the four context facets, we differentiate between the following three types of context aspects (see Fig. 6-3):

- *Requirement sources*: Requirement sources are the origins of the requirements defined for the system (see Section 6.2.1).
- *Context objects*: Context objects are people and material or immaterial objects in a context facet that need to be involved in or considered during requirements engineering. In other words, the stakeholders must identify the relevant context objects and elicit information about them (see Section 6.2.2).
- *Properties and relationships of context objects*: Properties and relationships represent additional information about the context objects and characterise a context object (person, material object, or immaterial object) within each context facet more precisely (see Section 6.2.3).

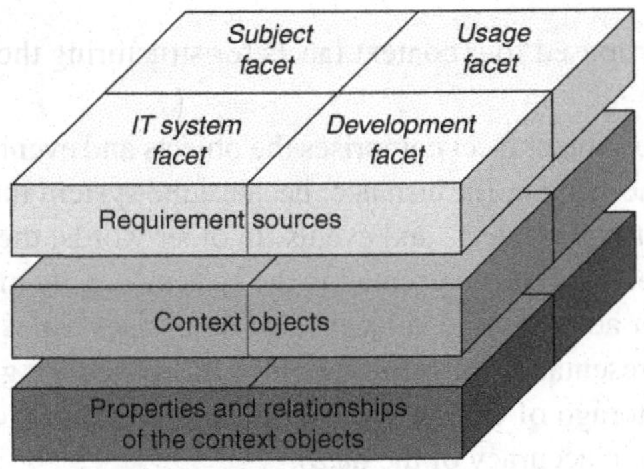

Fig. 6-3 *Three context aspects and four context facets*

6.2.1 Requirement Sources

Three types of requirement sources

We differentiate between three types of requirement sources: stakeholders, (existing) documents, and (existing) systems. In the following, we briefly characterise each type of requirement source.

Stakeholders

We define the term "stakeholder" in requirements engineering as follows:

D

Definition 6-1: *Stakeholder (in requirements engineering)*

A stakeholder is either a person or an organisation that has a potential interest in the system to be developed. A stakeholder typically has their own requirements for the system. A person can represent the interest of different stakeholders (people and/or organisations), i.e. a stakeholder can have more than one role and represent more than one stakeholder.

Based on [Robertson and Robertson 2006]

Typical stakeholders

A stakeholder typically has knowledge about one or multiple context aspects (requirement sources, context objects, properties/relationships) in one or multiple context facets (subject facet, usage facet, IT system facet, and development facet). Typical examples of stakeholders are customers, system developers, system users, architects, domain experts, software developers, testers, and maintenance staff. A stakeholder does not need to have an immediate interest in the development of the system himself.[4] He can represent general interests of a superior authority in the system development process which have influence on the definition of the requirements for the system. Typical examples of stakeholders representing the interests of higher authorities are data privacy officers, lawyers, patent agents, or work council members.

Existing Documentation

Importance of documents

The second kind of requirement source comprises existing documentation. Existing documents contain a significant amount of information required for defining the system requirements. Relevant documents include general-purpose documents (e.g. laws, standards), organisation specific documents (e.g. development guidelines, organisation-wide guidelines) or documents describing development artefacts of similar or predecessor systems (e.g. user manuals, system architecture documents, requirements specifications, test documentation, etc.).

Documents of predecessor systems

One example for the elicitation of requirements from documents is the reuse of requirements artefacts from a legacy system. Ideally, a complete, up-to-date requirements specification of a relevant legacy system exists which can just be reused. In practice, this is often not the case and thus requirements have to be elicited from different documentations of the legacy system (e.g. requirements documents, design documents, test documents, user manuals). The elicitation of requirements from existing documents can be supported by stakeholders who have been involved in the development of the legacy system. Hint 6-1 lists various document types to be considered during requirements elicitation.

[4] Throughout this book we have used "he/him" to refer to both genders.

!

Hint 6-1: *Examples of documents which could serve as valuable sources for requirements*

- ❑ Market analysis reports
- ❑ Letters of inquiry from clients
- ❑ Requirements documents of predecessor systems
- ❑ Requirements documents of legacy systems
- ❑ Architectural documents of legacy systems
- ❑ Source code of legacy systems
- ❑ Test documentation of legacy systems
- ❑ User manuals of legacy systems
- ❑ Business process documentation
- ❑ Descriptions of technical processes
- ❑ Descriptions of business processes
- ❑ Change request documentation of legacy systems
- ❑ Error reports for legacy systems
- ❑ Reported corrections of errors for legacy systems
- ❑ Laws
- ❑ Product specifications on websites
- ❑ Security guidelines
- ❑ Standards
- ❑ Usability test documents
- ❑ Etc.

Existing Systems

The third kind of requirement source comprises the existing systems themselves (as opposed to the documents related to these systems). We differentiate between three kinds of existing systems relevant for requirements engineering:

Three kinds of systems

- ❑ *Legacy and predecessor systems*: Legacy and predecessor systems are systems that serve a similar purpose as the system to be developed and that are available or in use in one of the organisations involved in the development.
- ❑ *Systems of competitors*: Systems of competitors which serve a similar purpose as the system to be developed belong to this category.
- ❑ *System analogy*: System analogies are systems that were developed for another domain but offer several characteristics that are important for the system to be developed (see Example 6-1).

Example 6-1: System analogy for a car safety system

The stakeholders defining the requirements for a car safety system search for some ideas for new and innovative requirements for the system. For this purpose, they participate in a demonstration of a collision prevention system from the aerospace domain and look for analogies which can inspire new ideas for the car safety system.

Elicitation of requirements

By analysing the existing system and experimenting with the system the stakeholders become aware of already implemented requirements for the system. Based on the experiences of using an existing system, stakeholders define requirements for the system to be developed. Thereby, they try to satisfy one or several of the following goals:

- Reproduction of properties of the existing system
- Enhancement of the properties of the existing system
- Avoidance of known deficiencies of the existing system
- Avoidance of errors that have already been fixed in the predecessor system

6.2.2 Context Objects

Persons, material and immaterial objects

Context objects are either immaterial or material objects or persons which exist in the system context and need to be considered when defining the requirements for the system. The stakeholders must thus identify and elicit information about the relevant context objects. Context objects are either:

- Persons such as users, clients, or administrators
- Legal bodies such as the organisations involved in the development project
- Material objects such as goods or constructional elements,
- Immaterial objects such as physical variables, mathematical functions, business processes, laws, or production processes

When considering the system context, it is important to identify, in each of the four context facets, all context objects which are relevant for the system to be developed.

Requirement source vs. context object

The following commonalities and differences exist between context objects and requirement sources. Each requirement source belongs to the system context and is either a person or an object. However, a requirement source is not necessarily a context object at the same time. For example, a domain expert who provides relevant information for the system to be developed is a relevant requirement source for the system. At the same time, the domain expert is typically not a context object since the system does not store or maintain information about the domain expert.

Multiple roles

However, a person can be a requirement source and a context object at the same time. For example, requirements can be elicited from a system user; thus the system user is a relevant requirement source. At the same time, the system user can be a context object, for example, if the system stores information about system users. The system might, for example, differentiate between different types of users (e.g. beginner, intermediate user and advanced user) in order to adjust the system functionality accordingly. However, even in this case, the role of the user as a requirement source can be clearly distinguished from the role of the user as a context object.

6.2.3 Properties and Relationships of Context Objects

Characterisation of context objects

The identification of a context object is generally not sufficient for deriving requirements for the system. To define the requirements typically more detailed information about the context objects is required. In other words, properties of the context objects and existing relationships between the context objects have to be elicited as well. Note that a relationship can exist among the context objects within one context facet, but also between context objects belonging to different context facets (see Section 6.3).

Properties and relationships

An example of a property of the context object "vehicle" is the current speed of the vehicle. Similarly, the context object "customer" typically has a property "name". An interaction scenario (see Definition 10-5) typically contains several relationships between context objects belonging to different context facets. For example, the user (a context object in the usage facet) enters data about a relevant object (a context object in the subject facet) into the system. Hence, the scenario documents relationships between objects belonging to different facets (the usage and subject facets in this case).

!

Hint 6-2: *Applying the proposed context structuring*

- Always create and maintain a glossary comprising the most important context objects as well as their properties and relationships. Alternatively, you may define a separate glossary for each of the four context facets.
- Document contextual knowledge or knowledge about the four context facets using appropriate documentation formats such as context models or templates for textual descriptions.
- When performing the requirements engineering activities, use checklists which support the consideration of all relevant context aspects (for all three types of aspects and within each of the four context facets).

6.3 Relevant Context Aspects within the Four Context Facets

In the following, we illustrate, for each of the four context facets, the different context aspects and provide hints for identifying the relevant context aspects, namely the relevant requirement sources, context objects, and their properties and relationships.

Vision determines which context aspects are relevant

The relevant requirement sources, context objects, and their properties and relationships to be considered within each context facet vary significantly depending on the system vision. For example, the requirement sources, the context objects, and properties and relationships to be considered for the system vision "Develop a system that calculates the tax on sales/purchases 20% faster" differ significantly from the ones to be considered for the system vision "Develop a car safety system that reduces the accident rate by 25%".

Different properties and relationships

Even if the same context objects are relevant for two systems, the properties and relationships of the objects to be considered may be completely different depending on the system vision. For example, the properties of the context object "vehicle" relevant for the vision "Develop a system that automatically calculates the motor vehicle tax" differ completely from the properties of the same context object relevant for the vision "Develop a car safety system". This does not only hold for the properties but also for the relationships which exist between context objects.

General types of context aspects

Despite the significant influence of the system vision on the relevant context aspects (requirement sources, context objects, and their properties and relationships), a set of generic types of context aspects for each context facet can be identified which are relevant for many software-intensive systems. In the following, we introduce generic types of requirement sources, context objects as well as their properties and relationships for each of the four context facets and illustrate them using examples.

6.3.1 Subject Facet

Requirement Sources in the Subject Facet

Domain experts

Domain experts are an important type of requirement source in the subject facet. They provide information about the subject domain of a system as well as the context objects about which the system must represent information. It may be necessary to involve different domain experts for different aspects of the subject facet or specific parts of the subject facet (see Example 6-2).

E

Example 6-2: Domain experts for a car safety system

The car safety system shall, for example, monitor the attention of the driver and take measures accordingly to prevent the driver from momentarily nodding off (microsleep) while driving. The driver is a central object of the system. The system must know about the current attention of the driver, hence this important property of the object "driver" must be represented in the system. In order to represent the property "attention" in the system, physicians and accident investigators are involved as domain experts, i.e. they serve as requirement sources. Furthermore, experts for braking systems and drive-train control systems are involved in order to specify the reaction of the car if an imminent microsleep of the driver is detected.

Thus, different domain experts for different aspects of the subject facet are considered during requirements engineering as important requirement sources.

Lawyers and data privacy officers

Other stakeholders who need to be involved as requirement sources for the subject facet are lawyers and data privacy officers. These stakeholders have expert knowledge about what kinds of data can be stored in the system, how the data must be stored (e.g. with respect to encryption), what kinds of data must be anonymised, how long specific kinds of data can or must be stored, and after how long certain types of data can or must be deleted.

Reference models of the subject domain

Relevant documents in the subject facet include, amongst others, reference models of the subject domain, often referred to as domain models. In a reference or domain model, one defines the context objects as well as their properties and relationships which might be relevant for the system to be developed and which can thus be reused.

Textbooks and laws

In addition, textbooks about the subject domain as well as laws that are relevant for the subject domain may also contain important information concerning relevant context objects for the system.

Existing systems

Furthermore, relevant information may be elicited from existing systems. The stakeholders may, for example, analyse the input and output masks on the user interface of an existing sales tax calculation system in order to identify relevant context objects for the system to be developed.

Context Objects in the Subject Facet

The relevant context objects in the subject facet strongly depend on the system vision and the desired system functionality. Types of context objects that are relevant for many systems include:

- Persons about which data is stored (e.g. customers, suppliers)
- Material objects (e.g. production goods, consumer goods)
- Immaterial objects (e.g. temperature, speed, mathematical functions)
- Processes (e.g. production or business processes that shall be supported or automated by the software-intensive system)

Example 6-3 lists some context objects relevant for a car safety system.

Example 6-3: Context objects in the subject facet

For a car safety system, among other things, the following context objects are relevant within the subject facet:

- The car itself as well as relevant parts of the car such as the engine, wheels, tyres, and brakes
- The occupants of the car such as the driver and the co-driver
- Other traffic participants such as cars driving ahead and pedestrians
- Environmental conditions outside the car such as air temperature, road conditions, etc.

Properties and Relationships in the Subject Facet

The properties to be considered in the subject facet are relevant properties of the identified context objects such as the property "attention" of the context object "driver" (Example 6-2), the property "pressure" of the context object "tyre", the property "distance" of the context object "car driving ahead" etc.

Properties of the mapping function

Besides the properties of the identified context objects, the mapping function to be applied to these objects plays an important role. The mapping function defines, for instance, the accuracy of the representation of the properties of the context objects in the system as well as the actuality of this representation. In addition, the mapping function must consider and respect existing laws that apply for the representation of the relevant properties such as data privacy laws.

Accuracy of the representation

The accuracy of the representation defines the precision of the representation of the properties of the real-world objects into properties of the objects in the system. The accuracy comprises the precision of the data as well as the abstraction from the real-world object. For instance, a navigation system may represent geographical information in the form of a two-dimensional or a three-dimensional model. These two models represent two different abstractions of the real world. Example 6-4 sketches restrictions with respect to the accuracy of the position of a car represented in a system.

> **Example 6-4:** Accuracy of the representation
>
> The system shall determine the position of the car via GPS (Global Positioning System) with an accuracy of 30 m (accuracy of data). Furthermore, determining the position within two dimensions is sufficient, i.e. the current altitude of the car does not have to be considered (abstraction of the representation).

Actuality of the representation

The actuality of the representation defines how the properties of real-world objects represented in the system are updated as well as in which time intervals the updates are performed. The update intervals are especially important for real-time systems (Example 6-5).

> **Example 6-5:** Actuality of the representation
>
> The system shall update the position of the car determined via GPS at least once per second in order to provide the driver with sufficient guidance in cities as well as on motorways.

Legal requirements

Legal requirements such as property and exploitation rights or privacy policies may restrict or even prescribe the representation as well as the actuality of context objects or their properties. Example 6-6 illustrates the prescription of the recording of data according to a given law.

> **Example 6-6:** Legal requirements for the representation
>
> A law prescribes that, for safety and control reasons, the current position and speed of each car have to be registered every 10 s and stored for a period of 2 months. The position shall be registered with a resolution between 50 and 100 m. The speed shall be registered with an accuracy of ± 3 km/h.

Relationship between objects of the subject and usage facets

Context objects of the subject facet are often associated with context objects of the usage facet. The relationships between context objects of the subject facet and context objects of the usage facet are explained in Section 6.3.2.

6.3.2 Usage Facet

Requirement Sources in the Usage Facet

Direct users and indirect users

Stakeholders in the usage facet are direct or indirect users of the system to be developed (see Example 6-7). Direct users have specific requirements for the user interface of the system. Indirect users are, amongst others, persons and systems with the following characteristics:

- The person or system does not use the system himself (itself) but is indirectly involved in the usage;
- The person or system influences the usage of the system;
- The person or system benefits from the usage indirectly.

For example, the head of a department is an indirect user of an information system if the employees of the department present cumulative reports generated by the information system to him.

A slightly more fine-grained differentiation of user types is described in [Eason 1988]: primary users, secondary users, and tertiary users. Primary users are the direct users of the system who may be full-time users. Secondary users are the occasional users or people who work directly with major outputs of the system. Tertiary users are affected by the operation of the system but are not direct users.

Example 6-7: Direct and indirect users of a car safety system

A direct user of a car safety system is the driver, since she or he controls the car and gets feedback from the car safety system concerning the current situation, e.g. the detection of a car driving ahead at a lower speed.

The co-driver is an indirect user of the system. Although the co-driver does not control the car actively, she or he may influence the driver's decisions, for example by directing the driver's attention to a warning signal.

Experts for user interfaces

Other important requirement sources are the experts for the user interface design. Such experts know existing standards and laws applicable to the user interface to be designed as well as common pitfalls and obstacles faced when developing user interfaces of a certain type. In addition, user interface experts can contribute significantly to the definition of usability tests.

In order to support the development of innovative requirements, experts of related application domains may be involved. For example, for the car safety system, experts from aircraft construction may be involved in order to gather new ideas for determining the distance to vehicles ahead.

Standards, laws, and regulations

Relevant documents in the usage facet include standards, laws, and regulations that define quality aspects of the user interface or permissible usage workflows (Example 6-8).

Example 6-8: Regulations for the design of the human–machine interface of a car

A regulation in the European catalogue of principles for the human – machine interface of a car defines: "The system has to be designed in such a way that it neither distracts the driver nor provides the driver with any type of visual entertainment".

Domain models

Domain models existing in the usage domain such as business process models are also important requirement sources. Such models determine, for instance, the allowed workflows and their embedding into the system context. By documenting the embedding of the usage workflows in the context, the domain models define how the system contributes to business processes.

System analogies

Existing systems that are used in the same or a similar way should also be considered as requirement sources for the system to be developed (see Example 6-9).

Example 6-9: System analogy for a car safety system

A working group is responsible for generating ideas for a new human– machine interface for cars produced in the year 2015. The human–machine interface shall be an in-car information system that comprises the car safety system along with other features. In order to support the generation of new ideas, the stakeholders of the car safety system participate in a simulation of the future cockpit of an airplane which realises new human–computer interfaces.

Context Objects of the Usage Facet

User groups

In the usage facet, user groups represent a typical context object. Knowledge about the desires and needs of different user groups is key for defining the usage requirements for a system. Different user groups may interact with the system in different ways. Therefore, it is essential to differentiate the relevant user groups of a system, as illustrated in Example 6-10.

Example 6-10: User groups of a car

For the development of the car safety system, the differentiation between sporty drivers and safety-oriented drivers is important. The system shall be able to adjust to these two types of drivers in order to avoid too many warnings for sporty drivers as well as too late system warnings and intervention for safety-oriented drivers.

Type of usage interface

Another important context object of the usage facet is the input modality of the user interface. For example, the type of user interface (e.g. haptic, acoustic, verbal, or visual) influences the design of the user interactions. Inputs made via touch-screen, keyboard, or speech recognition have intrinsically different impacts on user interaction. If particular interface types are common in the usage facet, they influence the requirements for the system to be developed (see Example 6-11). The same holds for established usage interfaces to other systems, for example, established interfaces for exchanging data with other systems such as BMEcat [BMEcat 2009].

Example 6-11: Human–machine interface of a car safety system

In the car series in which the car safety system shall be used, hints are provided to the driver via a classical display panel. A system for projecting the hints and warnings onto the windscreen is in the testing phase and shall go into production in the following year. The developers of the car safety system must consider both kinds of displays. This results in additional requirements such as the requirements for the system interface controlling the projection of hints onto the windscreen.

Usage workflows

The different usage workflows of the system constitute a core aspect of the usage facet. By embedding the system into usage workflows, the actual added value for the users (persons or systems) emerges. Besides the processes, the objects associated with the workflows such as roles, activities, and responsibilities are potential, relevant context objects. Furthermore, the expected added value of the usage is also a potential, relevant context object. A good understanding of the desired added value of the system facilitates an appropriate alignment of the usage workflows which guarantees that the intended added value is really achieved.

Interaction with other systems

Nearly all information systems and all embedded systems are not only used by humans but also by other systems. The added value of the system for other technical and software-intensive systems is therefore another important, relevant context object. From these context objects, requirements which address the interactions with other systems and their respective interfaces can be derived.

Properties and Relationships in the Usage Facet

Relationship between usage workflows

Context objects in the usage facet often have mutual relationships. One reason for these mutual relationships is the fact that a system function or service often directly or indirectly supports other functions or services. The requirements engineers need to understand such mutual relationships between the different usage workflows in order to define the requirements for supporting the different usage workflows correctly.

Relationship between user groups and usage workflows

The interaction with the system is often subject to restrictions that are determined by the affiliation of a user to a specific user group. For example, in an online course information system, a student may review a course and his grades, but only the faculty may review the course with all students' grades and make modifications where necessary. Furthermore, a user can also be maintenance personnel or other staff trusted with maintaining the system's integrity. The relationships between user groups and usage workflows constitute relevant context information of the usage facet from which often relevant requirements for the system can be derived.

Relationship to the IT system facet

Usage workflows are additionally influenced by the current operating status of the system. An important property of usage workflows is their allocation to different operation modes such as normal mode, energy-saving mode, or failure, recovery, and emergency modes (Example 6-12). The possible operation modes may be imposed by the IT system facet. If this is the case, a relationship between the usage and the IT system facet exists.

Example 6-12: Deactivation of a car safety system

An important aspect concerning the usage of the system is the possibility for the driver to deactivate the system. The interaction for deactivating the system is a context object of the usage facet. Another kind of deactivation of the system can be identified in the IT system facet, namely the automatic deactivation of the system due to a system failure.
The rules and conditions (e.g. defined by standards, laws, and regulations) already identified and documented in the IT system facet for the deactivation of the system also hold for the deactivation of the system by the driver. Hence, relationships between context objects (and their properties) of the usage and the IT system facet exist.

Relationship to the subject facet

Context objects and properties in the usage facet typically have relationships to context objects and properties of the subject facet. These relationships result from the fact that the system processes data about the context objects in the subject facet and their relationships and presents the results in a processed form (e.g. filtered, consolidated, or combined) to the system user (see Section 4.3). The system users (persons or other systems) must be able to interpret the output presented by the system correctly and to associate it with the corresponding context objects of the subject facet. A detailed explanation of the problem of representing information about a universe of discourse and interpreting the representation is given in Section 19.6.

Example 6-13: Association relationship with the subject facet

The driver must be able to intuitively associate the displayed warning with a concrete threat in the real world. The threat itself is typically related to a context object of the subject facet. For example, the threat "distance to the vehicle ahead is lower than the defined safety distance" is associated with the context object "vehicle ahead". The occurrence of the threat must be adequately represented in the system. In this way, a relationship is established between the usage facet and the subject facet.

6.3.3 IT System Facet

Requirement Sources in the IT System Facet

Stakeholders in the IT system facet

Relevant stakeholders in the IT system facet are all persons who deal with the planning, design, and operation of the IT system environment (e.g. persons who deal with systems interacting with the system to be developed). Examples of such persons are system architects, hardware developers, test specialists, maintenance specialists, or the chief technology officer, who is responsible for the company-wide IT strategy. Example 6-14 illustrates examples of stakeholders in the IT system facet for a car safety system.

Example 6-14: Stakeholders in the IT system facet

For a car safety system, an accurate interplay among all relevant electronic components (e.g. sensors, actuators, the brake control unit and the airbag control unit) is essential. Therefore, relevant stakeholders within the IT system facet to be involved in the requirements engineering process are, for example, developers of the brake control units, the airbag control units, the sensors and the actuators as well as experts for the communication protocols used in the car.

Technology consultants and suppliers

Additional stakeholders of the IT system facet to be involved in requirements engineering are experts with knowledge about market trends and strategies regarding relevant software and hardware components, such as technology consultants or suppliers of software and hardware components.

IT infrastructure documents

Typical examples of relevant documents of the IT system facet to be considered as requirement sources are the IT strategy document of the developing company, the IT strategy document of the customer, or documents describing the infrastructure and the relevant policies for system operation. If the system interacts with other existing systems, the documents defining the interfaces of these systems as well as the specifications of these systems are relevant requirement sources.

Reference architecture

Moreover, an existing reference architecture for the system and its environment is an important source for requirements within the IT system facet. Such an architecture defines, for instance, a common structure for an entire family of software-intensive systems.

Analysis of existing system designs

Relevant context information may also be gained by analysing existing systems in the IT system facet. For example, the structure of an existing system in the IT system facet can be analysed to determine requirements for the system to be developed (see Example 6-15).

Example 6-15: Analysing existing systems

To identify requirements for the operating system of a mobile communication end device, the stakeholders analyse the IT system architectures of existing communication end devices as well as the properties of the operating systems of these devices. The results are used to identify and define requirements for the system to be developed.

Context Objects in the IT System Facet

Relevant context objects in the IT system facet comprise:

- ❑ Hardware and software components that need to be considered during the development of the system (Example 6-16)
- ❑ The operation and maintenance of the system to be developed
- ❑ IT strategies of the involved companies

Example 6-16: Hardware and software components in a car

For the development of a car safety system, sensors and actuators installed in the car are relevant objects. Examples of such sensors and actuators are the wheel speed sensors or the acceleration sensors for the early detection of accidents.

In addition, bus systems installed in the car play a major role since the system has to support one or several of these bus systems in order to communicate with other systems in the car. Typical examples of bus systems used in the car are CAN (Computer Area Network [CAN 2009]), LIN (Local Interconnect Network [LIN 2009]), MOST (Media Oriented Systems Transport [MOST 2009]), and FlexRay ([FlexRay 2009]).

Another aspect of the IT system facet is the operating system to which the system is deployed. For example, in the car industry the operating system OSEK (*Offene Systeme und deren Schnittstellen für die Elektronik im Kraftfahrzeug* [OSEK/VDX 2009]; English: Open Systems and the Corresponding Interfaces for Automotive Electronics) is often used and thus represents a relevant aspect of the IT system facet.

In addition, for ensuring proper cooperation of the system with its IT system environment, the version numbers of the hardware components, software components, and the operating system with which the system must interact are relevant. The same holds for the version numbers of the protocols to be used for the interaction.

Influence on system operation

The IT environment to which the system has to be deployed may also determine, for instance, when and in which way data backups can or must be performed. For instance, the IT infrastructure may allow backup activities only within a specific time period such as during night time when no users are active or when the system is in stand by mode.

Influence of the IT strategy

Regarding the maintenance of the system, the IT strategy can prescribe, for example, that each system must provide remote maintenance functionalities. The IT strategy may also define which hardware and software components can be used, for example, by prescribing that only hardware and software components from specific manufacturers/producers shall be used. In addition, the IT strategy can also determine which technologies must currently be used, which old technologies have to be replaced by new ones and hence should not be used any longer as well as which technologies the company plans to employ in the future (Example 6-17). Such guidelines or prescriptions have different consequences for the system. For example, the interfaces and data types defined by the technologies to be used have to be considered.

Example 6-17: Use of FlexRay

Since the customers of the CarSoft company require more and more frequently that a FlexRay bus beinstalled in the cars, the IT strategy of CarSoft defines that all products of CarSoft have to support FlexRay as of 1 September 2009.

Development guidelines for processes and standards

The IT strategy can also impose that the system has to comply with specific standards (as described in Example 6-18) or that the system can only be developed by companies which have reached a specific maturity level with their development processes. The IT strategy of a provider of electronic financial services may impose, for example, that only software components developed at least with a CMMI (Capability Maturity Model Integration) maturity level of 3 may be used.

Example 6-18: Software architecture standard

The IT strategy imposes that all systems delivered after October 2009 have to conform to the AUTOSAR standard (Automotive Open System Architecture [AUTOSAR 2009]). The developers of the system must therefore consider the AUTOSAR architecture and adhere to the definitions in the AUTOSAR standard.

Properties and Relationships in the IT System Facet

Technical data of components

Relevant properties of context objects in the IT system facet are technical properties of hardware and software components such as performance characteristics or failure rates. Other relevant properties are cost or the availability and obligation to contractors and suppliers.

Operation profiles

Properties concerning the operation of the system are, for example, profiles of the expected processor and network load or tolerable response times of the system. Another essential property is the availability of the system. For example, if the system may be offline at most 3 h per year, this poses by far more challenges for the development of the system compared to the requirement that the system has to be available daily from 9:00 a.m. to 5:00 p.m.

Update policies

Furthermore, policies may define the exchange or update of hardware and software components in the IT system environment. Such policies also need to be considered already during the development of the system. A policy may demand, for example, that part of the system tests must be repeated each time that the operating system is updated.

6.3.4 Development Facet

Development process

The development process takes place in the development facet and clearly influences the way the system is developed. For example, the intensity of the quality assurance activities performed impacts the quality of the delivered system. Within the development facet also the consideration and adequate representation of the context aspects of the other three context facets as well as their relationships takes place (see Fig. 4-2, Page 46).

Requirement Sources in the Development Facet

Project-specific adaptation of development processes

Requirement sources in the development facet provide information for the development of the system. Such information (e.g. domain-specific experiences) is used, for example, to adjust the development process to the project-specific needs. Since the process quality essentially determines the quality of a product, the requirement sources of the development facet also influence the functionality and quality of the system.

Process stakeholders

In the development facet, stakeholders providing important information about all phases of the development process including maintenance and system replacement (such as information about development standards, organisation-specific guidelines, resource constraints, available personnel, programming standards, quality assurance standards etc.) represent a typical requirement source. These stakeholders can be divided into the following groups:

- Process engineers
- Process managers
- Process executors (e.g. requirements engineers, architects)

Guidelines for the development process

Obviously, also documents containing guidelines for or any other information about the development process are relevant requirement sources. Important documents are, for example:

- Development standards
- Development guidelines
- Method descriptions
- Best-practices documentation
- Project plans of previous projects

Context Objects, Properties, and Relationships in the Development Facet

Parts of the development process

The relevant context objects and their properties and relationships in the development facet concern all parts of the development process. Context objects include, among other things:

- Role definitions
- Artefact definitions
- Activity definitions
- Tools
- Resource availability and resource restrictions

Influence of resources

The available resources influence the development of the system significantly. For example, the number and the qualification of the developers available as well as the financial budget influence the extent to which certain requirements engineering activities are performed and obviously influence the decision of which requirements can be realised.

Tool environments and development languages

Another important context object is the tool environment to be used during the development process. The use of a specific set of tools may be imposed by the development facet. Moreover, the languages used for developing the system may be imposed, such as a specific formal specification language and an appropriate simulation environment, a specific, certified compiler for safety-critical systems, or specific configuration management tools. The characteristics of the tools as well as their relationships (interoperability and integration) obviously also influence the development process and must thus be considered.

Coordination of development processes

Complex systems are often not developed by a single organisation but are developed in different organisations in parallel; for example, components could be developed by different suppliers. If the system is developed by multiple organisations, the development processes of the companies involved need to be coordinated. The company-specific development processes and their coordination are thus important context objects of the development facet which have to be considered and understood properly.

Interfaces of development processes

Additional important context objects are the development process interfaces a component supplier must provide in order to integrate and align the different development processes. For example, such interfaces and their coordination are essential to ensure that a component producer provides the consumer with the right artefacts at the right time and with the required quality.

Process quality

The way software is developed (e.g. which development process is used, the maturity level achieved, etc.) is gaining increasing importance in the supplier–customer relationships. If the supplier can prove that his development process meets particular requirements (e.g. a certain maturity level), the trust of the customer in the quality of the created artefacts is typically increased. The customer may impose, for example, that the development process must follow a development standard such as SPICE (Software Process Improvement and Capability Determination) [Van Loon 2004; Hörmann et al. 2006], ISO 9000 (International Organization for Standardization) [ISO Std 9000], or CMMI [Chrissis et al. 2006].

Example 6-19: Development guidelines for a car safety system

For the development of the car safety system, a requirement imposes that the guidelines defined in the AUTOSAR standard have to be applied (see [AUTOSAR 2009]).

6.4 Different Roles of a Context Aspect

A specific context aspect may be relevant for more than one context facet. For instance, a requirement source may provide information that is relevant for the subject facet as well as the usage facet.

Support for the analysis of context aspects

If a context aspect is relevant for more than one facet, the differentiation between the four context facets is particularly helpful. The differentiation of four facets supports and even requires that for analysing and describing the context aspects all important aspects (defined in the four context facets) are considered. Due to individual preferences or incidental conditions, a stakeholder might analyse a context aspect (e.g. a requirement source) only with respect to system usage (i.e. the usage facet) and hence neglect, for example, the IT system facet. In such a case, the context structuring reminds the stakeholder to consider the subject facet, the IT system facet, and the development facet as well during the analysis and description of the context aspect. Thereby the likelihood that one context facet is preferred over the other ones or that a context facet is completely ignored is reduced.

Examples 6-20 and 6-21 illustrate the fact that a context aspect can be a requirement source in more than one facet.

E

Example 6-20: A user provides information about subject and usage facets

During the development of a software system for an insurance company, the requirements engineer interviews an insurance agent. The insurance agent explains typical workflows in his work environment. He provides details on customer data he enters into the system. Furthermore, he points out redundant steps in existing workflows that should be eliminated by the new software and mentions additional improvement possibilities in the workflows. The insurance agent thus provides information about the subject facet (e.g. the customer data) and the usage facet (e.g. the workflows).

E

Example 6-21: A user manual contains information about all four facets

The user manual of a predecessor system contains information about all four context facets:

- One chapter of the user manual describes the hardware and software environment of the predecessor system and thus contains information about the IT system facet.
- Another chapter provides details on the database schema of the system and thus contains information about the subject facet.
- In another chapter, restrictions which have to be considered during the development of user-defined extensions for the system are described such as the programming languages and compilers supported. This chapter thus contains information about the development facet.
- Yet another chapter describes the user interface in detail and thus contains information about the usage facet.

Classification by means of the context facets

Structuring the system context into the four facets supports the stakeholders in classifying and documenting the information that a requirement source contains or provides. Moreover, the requirement source may be analysed with respect to each of the four context facets separately (see Section 21.4). For example, when analysing the user manual of the predecessor system one stakeholder can focus on extracting relevant information about the IT system facet and disregard the other three facets, whereas other stakeholders can focus on other facets (see Section 22.8).

Not only the requirement sources, but also the other two types of context aspects (the context objects and their properties and relationships) may contain relevant information for several context facets. Example 6-22 illustrates this for the context object "sensor".

Example 6-22: A sensor as a context object in the subject and the IT system facets

A car safety system shall detect vibrations based on the data provided by a sensor. For this purpose, the interfaces and communication capabilities provided by the sensor have to be considered. Therefore, the sensor is a relevant context object in the IT system facet. Additionally, the car safety system shall check whether the sensor is working correctly. Therefore, certain properties of the sensor must be represented in the software and updated at regular time intervals. Thus, the sensor is also a relevant context object in the subject facet.

Within the two facets, the sensor has completely different roles. These roles should be analysed separately to avoid unintended intermingling of the properties and relationships of the sensor and thus incomplete consideration of its roles in the two facets.

Recommended Literature for Part II

Basic Reading

[Pohl 1993] introduces the four context facets as a structure for the system context and elaborates on the main goal of requirements engineering, namely establishing the system vision in context.

[Robertson and Robertson 2006] illustrate the importance of the system context using a system for the prediction and prevention of ice formation on streets. In Chapter 3, the authors provide details on different stakeholders. In Chapter 4, different kinds of systems that interact with the system to be developed are described.

Advanced Reading

[Gunter et al. 2000] present a formal reference model for the description of coherences between the system, its environment, and the interfaces between system and environment. The reference model defines five artefacts: W (World), R (Requirements), S (Specification), P (Program), and M (Machine), as well as their relationships using symbolic logic.

[McMenamin and Palmer 1984] explain, among other things, how the context of a system is modelled and how objects and events in the context are identified.

[Parnas and Madey 1995] describe the relationship between the system and the environment based on four formally specified variables that represent the inputs of the system, the outputs of the system, the environment variables that need to be monitored, and the variables that need to be controlled.

[Sutcliffe 2002a] proposes a method for modelling domain knowledge. Domain knowledge is documented using distinct modelling constructs such as agents, goals, objects, properties, states, and events.

Part III
Requirements Artefacts

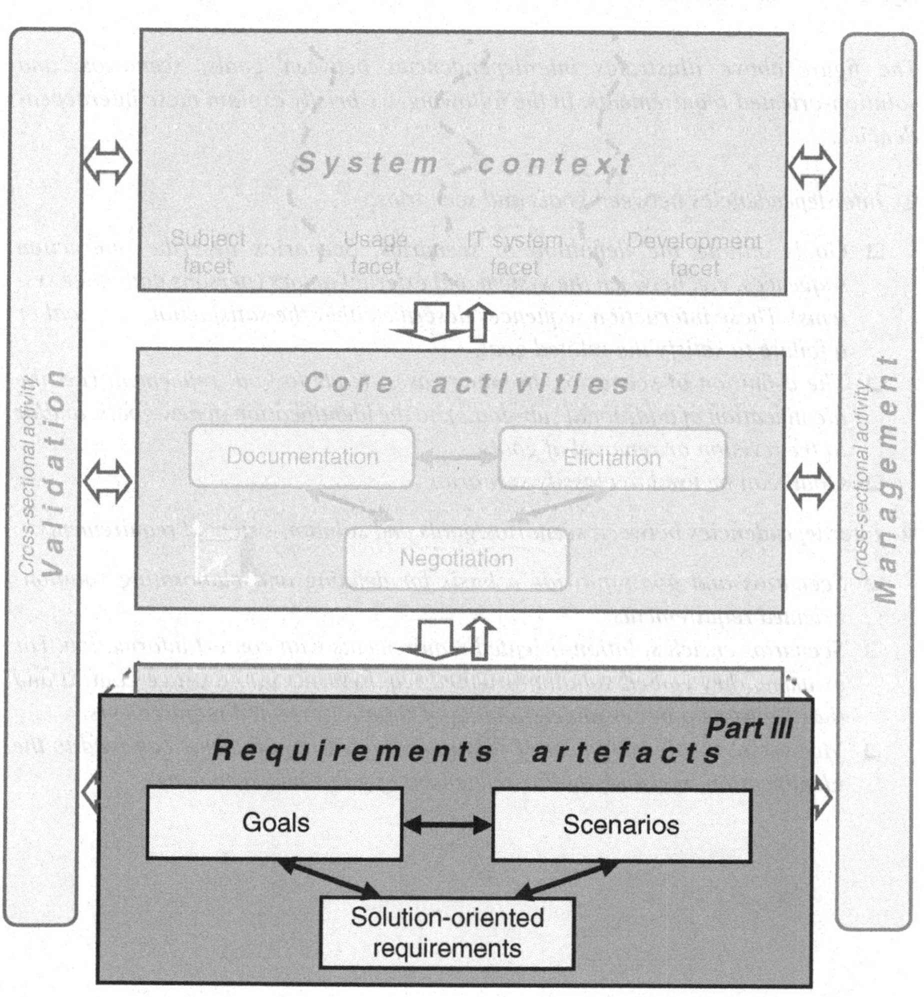

Interdependencies between Goals, Scenarios, and Solution-Oriented Requirements

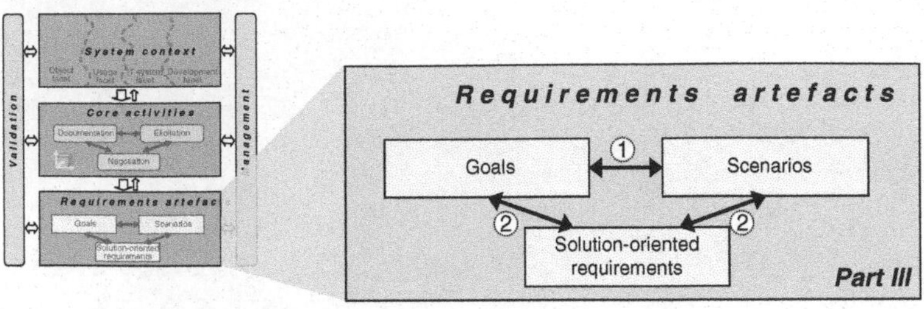

Fig. III-1 *Interdependencies between the three kinds of requirements artefacts*

The figure above illustrates interdependencies between goals, scenarios, and solution-oriented requirements. In the following, we briefly explain these interdependencies:

① *Interdependencies between goals and scenarios:*

- *Goals initiate the definition of scenarios. Scenarios describe interaction sequences, e.g. between the system and external actors (persons and other systems). These interaction sequences describe either the satisfaction of a goal or a failure to satisfy the related goal.*
- *The definition of scenarios, in many cases, leads to goal refinement (i.e. the identification of additional sub-goals), to the identification of new goals, and/or to the revision or removal of goals.*
- *Goals can be used to classify scenarios.*

② *Interdependencies between scenarios/goals and solution-oriented requirements:*

- *Scenarios and goals provide a basis for defining and elaborating solution-oriented requirements.*
- *Scenarios enrich solution-oriented requirements with context information. For example, they embed solution-oriented requirements into a usage-context and thus facilitate a better understanding of solution-oriented requirements.*
- *Vice versa, the development of solution-oriented requirements can lead to the identification, revision, and/or refinement of goals and scenarios.*

Overview Part III – Requirements Artefacts

Our framework differentiates between three types of requirements that complement each other:

- *Goals which document intentions of stakeholders*
- *Scenarios which document concrete examples of system usage*
- *Solution-oriented requirements which document conceptual solutions that satisfy the goals and scenarios and define the basis for realising the system*

In Part III, we elaborate on the three types of requirements:

- *In Part III.a, we outline the fundamentals of goal orientation in requirements engineering, introduce a reference template and rules for documenting goals in natural language, and define the concepts for documenting goals using (extended) AND/OR graphs. Moreover, we sketch two goal modelling frameworks: i* and KAOS.*
- *In Part III.b, we outline the fundamentals of using scenarios in requirements engineering. This part of the book provides an extensive overview of the different types of scenarios, presents reference templates for scenarios and use cases, and defines guidelines for documenting scenarios in natural language. Three techniques for modelling scenarios are introduced: use case diagrams, sequence diagrams, and activity diagrams. Furthermore, the benefits of goal-scenario-coupling are explained in this part.*
- *In Part III.c, we differentiate between three perspectives of solution-oriented requirements: data, function, and behaviour. This part of the book outlines the fundamentals of each perspective, sketches the documentation of solution-oriented requirements using natural language, and presents modelling techniques for each perspective, i.e. data modelling, function-oriented modelling, behavioural modelling as well as object-oriented modelling using UML and SysML. Therein, the integration of the three perspectives in UML and SysML is also outlined.*

Part III.a
Goals

Overview Part III.a – Goals

Goal orientation is essential for the success of the requirements engineering process. Goal models are well suited for explicitly documenting the intentions of different stakeholders as well as the dependencies existing between goals.

In Chapters 7 and 8, we outline:

- *The fundamentals of goal modelling in requirements engineering*
- *A reference template for documenting goals in natural language*
- *Rules for documenting goals*
- *The documentation of goals using (extended) AND/OR graphs*
- *The basic concepts of the two goal modelling frameworks i* and KAOS*

Classification Part III.a Goals	Basic	Advanced
7 Fundamentals of Goal Orientation		
7.1 Motivation	✓	
7.2 The Term "Goal"	✓	
7.3 AND/OR Goal Decomposition	✓	
7.4 Goal Dependencies		✓
7.5 Identifying Goal Dependencies		✓
8 Documenting Goals		
8.1 A Template for Documenting Goals	✓	
8.2 Seven Rules for Documenting Goals	✓	
8.3 Goal Modelling Languages and Methods	✓	
8.4 Documenting Goals Using AND/OR Trees and AND/OR Graphs	✓	
8.5 i* (i-Star)		✓
8.6 KAOS		✓
8.7 Deciding Which Goal Modelling Language to Use	✓	

Chapter 7
Fundamentals of Goal Orientation

In this chapter, we outline:

- *The motivation for goal-oriented requirements engineering*
- *The concept of AND/OR goal decomposition*
- *The different kinds of goal dependencies*

K. Pohl, *Requirements Engineering*,

7.1 Motivation

Goals document the intentions of stakeholders

Many established requirements engineering approaches explicitly consider the stakeholders' intentions during requirements engineering and make use of goal models for documenting these intentions (e.g. [Van Lamsweerde 2009; Yu 1993; Dardenne 1993; Antón 1996; Haumer et al. 1998; Pohl and Sikora 2005]). The effort required to consider and document goals in requirements engineering is, compared with the advantages gained, rather low. The explicit consideration and documentation of goals in requirements engineering exhibits, among other things, the following positive effects (see [Dardenne et al. 1991; Yue 1987; Van Lamsweerde 2001]):

Facilitate common understanding

- *Better understanding of the system*: Goals refine the overall system vision (see Section 4.1), clarify the value of the system for particular stakeholders and thereby provide the rationales for developing the system. The explicit documentation of goals typically results in a better common understanding of the purpose and objectives of the system.

Goal-driven requirements elicitation

- *Requirements elicitation*: Goals drive and guide the elicitation of requirements. For instance, for each goal, a set of requirements can be defined which must be fulfilled to satisfy the goal. Moreover, for each goal, scenarios can be defined to define typical interaction sequences which lead to goal satisfaction. Furthermore, defining scenarios in which a goal is not satisfied also contributes to a better understanding of the goal and supports requirements elicitation. Especially, goal–scenario–coupling has turned out to facilitate a systematic and successful requirements elicitation process (see Section 9.1.4).

Systematic identification of alternative realisations

- *Identification and evaluation of alternative realisations*: Typically, several possibilities exist to satisfy a goal. By decomposing goals into sub-goals, alternative realisations can be identified systematically. Moreover, goals are particularly well suited to evaluate alternative realisations and to choose the preferred one (see e.g. [Van Lamsweerde 2009]).

Identifying irrelevant requirements

- *Detection of irrelevant requirements*: The explicit consideration of goals supports the identification of irrelevant requirements. In order to identify irrelevant requirements, the stakeholders check for each requirement whether the requirement contributes to the satisfaction of a goal or not. If a requirement does not support the satisfaction of any defined goal, either the requirement is irrelevant for the system (see [Yue 1987]) or the defined goals are incomplete.

Rationales for requirements

- *Justification of requirements*: If a requirement contributes to the satisfaction of a goal, the goal documents a rationale for defining the requirement. Goals hence justify the definition of a requirement if the requirement must be realised in order to satisfy the goal (see [Ross and Schoman 1977; Dardenne et al. 1991]).

Proof of completeness

- *Completeness of requirements specifications*: The explicit documentation of the stakeholders' intentions as goals facilitates checking and proving the completeness of a requirements specification. With respect to the defined goals, a requirements specification is complete if, by implementing the defined requirements, all goals can be satisfied (see [Yue 1987]).

Identification and resolution of conflicts

- *Identification and resolution of conflicts*: Goal modelling further supports the resolution of conflicting requirements. Quite often, the origins of conflicting requirements are different stakeholder intentions (see [Nuseibeh et al. 1994]). Hence, conflict resolution should, at first, focus on resolving conflicting goals (which document the different stakeholder intentions) rather than on resolving the conflicting requirements that result from the different intentions.

- *Stability of goals*: Typically a goal can be satisfied in different ways. Depending on the alternative chosen, different functional and quality requirements are defined. If the alternative chosen to satisfy a specific goal changes in a project, the functional and quality requirements consequently have to be adapted as well. In contrast, the goal often remains unchanged (see [Antón et al. 1994]). Therefore, in comparison with functional or quality requirements, goal models are more stable.

Greater stability

7.2 The Term "Goal"

We already defined the term "goal" in Definition 4-2 on Page 53 as follows:

A goal is an intention with regard to the objectives, properties, or use of the system.

High-level goals and low-level goals

Goals can be defined at different levels of abstraction. High-level goals may define, for instance, objectives that are related to the company strategy or the product strategy. The successive decomposition (also called refinement) of these high-level goals into sub-goals (see Section 7.3) performed during the requirements engineering process results in more concrete goals which define the stakeholders' intention with regard to the use of the system and specific system properties. The refined goals may refer to both functional and quality properties of the system and its services.

7.3 AND/OR Goal Decomposition

Goals refine the vision

The system vision (see Section 4.1) typically defines the top-level goal for the system. All other goals should thus refine the system vision. The refinement of a goal is also called "goal decomposition". There are two kinds of goal decomposition (see e.g. [Bubenko et al. 1994; Dardenne et al. 1993; Mylopoulos et al. 1999]):

AND-decomposition

- *AND-decomposition of a goal*: The decomposition of a super-goal G into a set of sub-goals $G_1, \ldots, G_n$ with $n \geq 2$ is an AND-decomposition if and only if all sub-goals $G_1, \ldots, G_n$ must be satisfied in order to satisfy the super-goal G.

OR-decomposition

- *OR-decomposition of a goal*: The decomposition of a super-goal G into a set of sub-goals $G_1, \ldots, G_n$ with $n \geq 2$ is an OR-decomposition if and only if satisfying one of the sub-goals $G_1, \ldots, G_n$ is sufficient for satisfying the super-goal G.

Example 7-1 illustrates the decomposition of a goal G into three sub-goals by means of an AND-decomposition. According to the definition of the AND-decomposition, all sub-goals G_1, G_2, and G_3 must be satisfied in order to satisfy the goal G.

Example 7-1: AND-decomposition of a goal

The following goal G has been defined for a navigation system: "comfortable and fast navigation to the destination". The goal G is decomposed into the following three sub-goals by means of an AND-decomposition:

G_1: Easy entry of the destination
G_2: Automatic routing according to user-specific parameters
G_3: Displaying of traffic jams and automatic re-routing to avoid traffic jams

Documenting alternative solutions

Example 7-2 illustrates the decomposition of a goal G into two sub-goals by means of an OR-decomposition. According to the definition of the OR-decomposition, only one of the two sub-goals needs to be satisfied in order to satisfy the super-goal G. Hence, the OR-decomposition of a goal G is used to document alternative possibilities for satisfying a goal.

Example 7-2: OR-decomposition of a goal

The goal G "ability to localise the position of the car" is decomposed by an OR-decomposition into the following two sub-goals:

G_1: Localisation of the car via cell phone
G_2: Localisation of the car via GPS

7.4 Goal Dependencies

In addition to the AND-decomposition and OR-decomposition we define the following types of goal dependencies:

- "Requires" dependency (see Section 7.4.1)
- "Support" dependency (see Section 7.4.2)
- "Obstruction" dependency (see Section 7.4.3)
- "Conflict" dependency (see Section 7.4.4)
- Goal equivalence (see Section 7.4.5)

7.4.1 "Requires" Dependency between Goals

A goal G_1 is related to a goal G_2 by a "requires" dependency if the satisfaction of the goal G_2 is a prerequisite for satisfying goal G_1. However, the "requires" dependency does not imply that G_2 is a sub-goal of G_1. In other words, the "requires" dependency can exist between goals that are not in a decomposition relationship with each other. We define the "requires" dependency as follows:

Definition 7-1: *"Requires" dependency between goals*

A goal G_1 requires a goal G_2 if the satisfaction of G_2 is a prerequisite for satisfying G_1.

Example of a "requires" dependency

Example 7-3 presents a goal that is related to another goal by a "requires" dependency. The goal G_1 demands that the navigation system navigate around traffic congestions. The goal G_2 demands that the system be capable of receiving traffic messages. Since the capability of receiving traffic messages is a prerequisite for calculating a route around traffic congestions, a "requires" dependency exists between G_1 and G_2.

Example 7-3: "Requires" dependency

G_1: The system shall navigate the driver around traffic congestions.
G_2: The system shall be able to receive traffic messages.

"Requires" dependency: G_1 requires G_2.

7.4.2 "Support" Dependency between Goals

A goal support dependency exists between two goals G_1 and G_2 if (partially) satisfying the goal G_1 leads to a (partial) satisfaction of the goal G_2.

Definition 7-2: *Goal support dependency*

A goal G_1 supports a goal G_2 if the satisfaction of G_1 contributes positively to satisfying G_2.

Example of goal support

Example 7-4 describes two goals that are related by a "support" dependency. The "support" dependency between the goal G_1 "download map" and the goal G_2 "simple entry of destination" in the example can be explained as follows. If a destination is outside the maps that are available to the navigation system, the goal "simple entry of destination" cannot be satisfied. However, as expressed by the goal G_2, the system has the facility to download the needed electronic maps and then allow the driver to select the destination in the navigation system. Thus, the goal "download map" supports the goal "simple entry of destination".

Example 7-4: "Support" dependency

G_1: The navigation system shall be able to download electronic maps on demand.
G_2: The system shall allow simple entry of the destination for navigation.

"Support" dependency: G_1 supports G_2.

AND/OR-Decompositions

Note that each AND- or OR-decomposition implicitly represents a special type of "support" dependency. If, for example, G_2 is a sub-goal of G_1 and G_2 is related to G_1 by an AND-decomposition, the satisfaction of G_2 partially supports satisfying G_1. If G_2 is related to G_1 by means of an OR-decomposition, G_1 is satisfied whenever G_2 is satisfied. Hence G_2 strongly supports G_1.

7.4.3 "Obstruction" Dependency between Goals

Negative impact on goal satisfaction

An "obstruction" dependency exists between a goal G_1 and a goal G_2 if the (partial) satisfaction of G_1 hinders the satisfaction of G_2. An "obstruction" dependency can thus be understood as the opposite of a goal support dependency. An "obstruction" dependency cannot exist between goals that are part of an AND-decomposition. We define an "obstruction" dependency between two goals G_1 and G_2 as follows:

Definition 7-3: *Goal obstruction dependency*

A goal G_1 obstructs a goal G_2 if satisfying G_1 hinders the satisfaction of G_2.

Example of an "obstruction" dependency

Example 7-5 depicts an "obstruction" dependency between the goals G_1 and G_2. Satisfying the goal G_1 causes high data traffic and thus hinders the satisfaction of the goal G_2 "The data traffic shall be as low as possible".

Example 7-5: "Obstruction" dependency

G_1: The navigation system shall be able to download electronic maps via the GSM network on demand.

G_2: The data traffic over the GSM network caused by the navigation system shall be as low as possible.

"Obstruction" dependency: G_1 interferes with G_2.

7.4.4 "Conflict" Dependency between Goals

Goal conflicts are symmetric

A "conflict" dependency exists between two goals if the satisfaction of one goal entirely excludes the satisfaction of the other goal, and vice versa. A "conflict" dependency hence documents a very strong obstruction and is, in addition, symmetric. We define a "conflict" dependency between two goals as follows:

Definition 7-4: *Goal conflict dependency*

A conflict exists between a goal G_1 and a goal G_2 if

(1) Satisfying G_1 excludes the satisfaction of G_2, and
(2) Satisfying G_2 excludes the satisfaction of G_1.

A conflict between two goals exists, for example, if a stakeholder requires that a car can be localised via GPS (G_1 in Example 7-6), yet the privacy laws of a country forbid the localisation of vehicles (G_2 in Example 7-6). In this case, the goal of some stakeholder and the law of the country are clearly in conflict. Satisfying one of the two goals makes the satisfaction of the other goal impossible.

Example of a conflict between goals

Example 7-6: "Conflict" dependency

G_1: It shall be possible to localise the car via GPS.
G_2: The country-specific privacy laws shall be observed.
"Conflict" dependency: G_1 and G_2 are conflicting.

7.4.5 Goal Equivalence

An "equivalence" dependency exists between two goals if the satisfaction of one goal implies the satisfaction of the other goal. The "equivalence" dependency is thus symmetric in nature. Note that two goals can be equivalent with respect to goal satisfaction even if their definitions differ. We define the "equivalence" dependency between two goals G_1 and G_2 as follows:

Equivalence in goal satisfaction

Definition 7-5: *Goal equivalence dependency*

Two goals G_1 and G_2 are equivalent (with respect to goal satisfaction) if:

(1) Satisfying the goal G_1 leads to the satisfaction of the goal G_2, and
(2) Satisfying the goal G_2 leads to the satisfaction of the goal G_1.

For example, if the car safety regulations in country A are identical to the regulations in country B, the two goals presented in Example 7-7 are equivalent (with respect to goal satisfaction). Satisfying the goal G_1 implies the satisfaction of the goal G_2 and vice versa.

Example of goal equivalence

Example 7-7: Goal equivalence

G_1: The system shall comply with the car safety regulations of country A.
G_2: The system shall comply with the car safety regulations of country B.

The example illustrates that a goal equivalence relationship does not require that the two goal definitions be identical, i.e. goal equivalence should not be confused with the equality of goal definitions.

Goal equivalence ≠ equal goal definitions

7.5 Identifying Goal Dependencies

Goal dependencies are affected by context changes

The identification and the documentation of goal dependencies strongly depends on the stakeholders' knowledge about the system context (see Part II). For instance, the goal conflict dependency in Example 7-6 is based on the fact that the electronic localisation of cars is forbidden by law in a country in which the system shall be used. If the corresponding law in this country is changed, the conflict dependency between the two goals in Example 7-6 may no longer exist. Similarly, to identify the goal equivalence dependency in Example 7-7, the stakeholders must be familiar with the technical regulations in countries A and B, i.e. they must know that the two regulations are identical. However, if the regulations in one country change, the goal equivalence dependency may no longer exist.

The stakeholders must hence be aware that changes in the system context can invalidate goal dependencies which have been defined at an earlier point of time. Consequently, the stakeholders must constantly analyse whether changes in the context influence the defined goal dependencies or even the goals themselves.

Chapter 8
Documenting Goals

In this chapter, we introduce the most common techniques for documenting goals: the use of natural language and the use of dedicated goal modelling languages. With regard to the documentation of goals using natural language, we describe:

- *A template for documenting goals in natural language*
- *Seven rules for documenting goals*

For the model-based documentation of goals, we introduce:

- *AND/OR trees and AND/OR graphs*
- *The goal-oriented modelling framework i**
- *The KAOS framework for modelling and analysing goals*

K. Pohl, *Requirements Engineering*,

Goals can be documented using natural language or dedicated modelling languages

Goals and goal dependencies can be documented using natural language or a dedicated goal modelling language. Section 8.1 introduces a template for documenting goals in natural language. Section 8.2 defines seven rules for documenting goals. Section 8.3 provides a brief introduction to goal modelling languages and methods. Section 8.4 outlines the goal modelling using AND/OR trees and AND/OR graphs. Section 8.5 describes the basic concepts for modelling goals using the goal-oriented modelling framework i*, and Section 8.6 introduces the basic concepts for goal modelling using KAOS. Section 8.7 provides hints for choosing an appropriate goal modelling technique.

8.1 A Template for Documenting Goals

As described in Chapter 7, goals and goal dependencies can be documented using unstructured, natural language. Example 8-1 illustrates the documentation of a goal and its sub-goals in natural language.

Example 8-1: Documenting goals in natural language

G: Comfortable and fast navigation to the destination

The goal G is refined into the following three sub-goals (AND-decomposition):

G_1: Easy entry of the destination
G_2: Automatic routing according to user-specific parameters
G_3: Displaying of traffic jams and automatic re-routing to avoid traffic jams

Template for documenting goals

Compared with documentation of goals in unstructured, natural language, a template-based documentation of goals offers significant advantages (see Section 18.4.1). We hence introduce a template for documenting goals which comprises the following types of attributes (see Tab. 8-1):

- Attributes for uniquely identifying goals (Tab. 8-1, rows 1–2)[1]
- Management attributes (Tab. 8-1, rows 3–7)[2]
- Attributes for documenting references to the context (Tab. 8-1, rows 8–10)[3]
- Specific goal attributes (Tab. 8-1, rows 11–16), i.e. the goal level (Tab. 8-1, row 11), the description of the goal (Tab. 8-1, row 12), dependencies to other goals (Tab. 8-1, rows 13–15) as well as relationships to scenarios (Tab. 8-1, row 16)[4]
- An attribute for documenting any type of additional information (Tab. 8-1, row 17)

Table 8-2 depicts an example of a goal documented using the template introduced in Tab. 8-1.

[1] See Section 18.3.1 for an explanation of attributes facilitating the identification of requirements.

[2] See Section 18.3.7 for an explanation of management attributes.

[3] See Section 18.3.2 for an explanation of attributes documenting references to the context.

[4] The attributes in rows 13-16 refine the generic attribute "cross references" explained in Section 18.3.4.

Tab. 8-1 *Template for documenting goals*

Goal Template		
No.	**Section**	**Content / Explanation**
1	Identifier	Unique identifier of the goal
2	Name	Unique name for the goal
3	Authors	Names of the authors who have documented the goal
4	Version	Current version number of the documentation of the goal
5	Change history	List of the changes applied to the documentation of the goal including (for each change) the date of the change, the version number, the author, and, if necessary, the reason for and the subject of the change
6	Priority	Importance of the documented goal according to the specific prioritisation technique used
7	Criticality	Criticality of the goal, e.g. for the overall success of the system
8	Source	Name of the source (i.e. the stakeholder, document, or system) from which the goal originates
9	Responsible stakeholder	Name of the stakeholder who is responsible for the goal
10	Using stakeholders	Stakeholders who benefit from the satisfaction of the goal
11	Goal level	Identifier for the abstraction level at which the goal is defined
12	Goal description	Description of the goal according to the rules defined in Section 8.2
13	Super-goal	Reference to the super-goal including the type of decomposition (AND/OR)
14	Sub-goals	References to sub-goals including the type of decomposition (AND/OR)
15	Other goal dependencies	Further dependencies with other goals such as "requires", "conflict", etc.
16	Associated scenarios	References to scenarios that describe the satisfaction of the goal or a failure to satisfy the goal
17	Supplementary information	Additional information about this goal

!

Hint 8-1: *Systematic elicitation of goals and goal attributes*

- ❑ Try to elicit all relevant goals first
- ❑ Avoid capturing all goal attributes right at the beginning
- ❑ When defining attributes for a goal, define the basic attributes (identifier, name, source, responsible stakeholder, goal description) first
- ❑ Subsequently, define the attributes super-goal and sub-goals for each goal
- ❑ Validate whether the elicited goals are complete and the documented goal relationships are correct
- ❑ Complement missing goals and missing goal relationships and, if required, revise the defined goals and goal relationships
- ❑ Define scenarios in order to support the elicitation and validation of goals (see Section 12.3)
- ❑ Add missing information in all slots of the goal template

Note: If you elicit relevant information that does not fit in any of the predefined slots of the template, record this information in the slot "supplementary information" or define additional slots to document this information.

Tab. 8-2 *Example of template-based documentation of a goal*

Section	Content
Identifier	G-2-17
Name	Automatic navigation
Authors	Peter Miller, Dan Smith
Version	V.1.1
Change history	V.1.0 12.01.2009 Dan Smith V.1.1 14.02.2009 Peter Miller
Priority	High
Criticality	Medium
Source	William Garland (product manager)
Responsible stakeholder	Peter Miller
Using stakeholders	Driver of the car (usage facet)
Goal level	System level
Goal description	The system shall automatically direct the driver to the desired destination.
Super-goal	G-2-2: Comfortable and fast navigation to the destination
Sub-goals	G-2-25: Localisation of the car via GPS G-2-26: Download of electronic maps on demand
Other goal dependencies	Conflict with G-1-45: Reduce costs for cars Support of G-1-37: Technological leadership in the automotive segment of medium-sized vehicles
Associated scenarios	S-2-34: Navigate to destination
Supplementary information	The competing system SX-23-44 realises this goal.

8.2 Seven Rules for Documenting Goals

An easy-to-understand and precise documentation of goals increases the benefits of goal-oriented requirements engineering. In the following, seven rules for documenting goals in an understandable and precise manner are defined. We illustrate each rule using an example. Hint 8-3 summarises the seven rules.

Rule 1: concise documentation

Rule 1: document goals concisely. Document goals as concisely as possible (yet, not too briefly). Avoid unnecessary phrases, fillers, and repetition.

Example 8-2: Documenting a goal concisely

Goal G_1: Expert users as well as inexperienced users shall be able to use the system. Inexperienced users shall be able to use the system without having knowledge about the predecessor system. Furthermore, an inexperienced user shall be able to use the system without any training. For any user, it must be self-evident how to use the system. It must be possible to use the system even without knowledge of similar systems.

Improved definition of G_1:

The users shall be able to use the system without training and/or knowledge of the previous system.

Rule 2: active voice

Rule 2: use the active voice. Preferably use the active voice, when documenting goals. Avoid using the passive voice. Using the active voice enhances understandability and clearly names the actor.

E

Example 8-3: Using the active voice for documenting goals

Goal G_2: The duration of creating the quarterly reports shall be cut down by half compared with the predecessor system.

Improved definition of G_2:

The user shall be able to create quarterly reports in half of the time needed using the current system.

Rule 3: document the intention precisely

Rule 3: document the stakeholder's intention precisely. As far as possible, document the stakeholder's intention precisely. Ideally, it should be possible to check objectively (later on) whether the implemented system satisfies the goal or not. However, documenting goals in an objectively checkable way is not always desirable or possible (e.g. for softgoals as described in Sections 8.5 and 8.6).

E

Example 8-4: Documenting the intention precisely

Goal G_3: The system shall lead to an improved workflow in the company.

Improved definition of G_3:

The system shall speed up the workflow for order processing by at least 20%.

Rule 4: decompose high-level goals

Rule 4: decompose high-level goals into more concrete sub-goals. If a goal is very abstract, the stakeholders should decompose this goal during the requirements engineering process into more concrete sub-goals. The decomposition enables the stakeholders to check (later on) whether the system satisfies the sub-goals defined during the requirements engineering process.

Example 8-5: Decomposing a high-level goal

Goal G_4: Increase driving safety!

Improved definition of G_4:

The goal G_4 is decomposed into the following sub-goals by means of an AND-decomposition:

$G_{4,1}$: Reduce the braking distance on slippery roads by 20%.
$G_{4,2}$: Ensure that the vehicle remains steerable during braking manoeuvres.

Rule 5: state the value of the goal

Rule 5: state the additional value of the goal. Clearly describe the additional value that the goal offers to the stakeholders. Describe the intended additional value as precisely as possible.

Example 8-6: Clarifying the additional value of a goal

Goal G_5: The navigation system shall provide an intuitive way of entering the destination of a trip.

Improved definition of G_5:

The navigation system shall allow the driver to enter the desired destination without being distracted from driving.

Rule 6: rationales for a goal

Rule 6: document the reasons for introducing a goal. Provide a brief and precise description of the reasons for introducing the goal. Knowing the rationale for introducing a goal facilitates discussions about the goal itself and supports the identification of additional goals.

Example 8-7: Documenting the reasons for introducing a goal

Goal G_6: The system shall offer an intuitive user interface.

Improved definition of G_6:

The system shall offer an intuitive user interface, since 80% of its users use the system only once or twice a month.

Rule 7: avoiding unnecessary restrictions

Rule 7: avoid defining unnecessary restrictions. When documenting a goal, avoid defining unnecessary restrictions which constrain potential realisations of the system. Only define restrictions if they are super-imposed by law or a contractual document.

Example 8-8: Avoiding unnecessary restrictions in a goal definition

Goal G_7: The response times of the system shall be reduced by 10% by optimizing the time for data transfers.

Improved definition of G_7:

The response times of the system shall be reduced by 10%.

If restrictions are superimposed, e.g. by a client, the requirements engineers can try to weaken the restrictions and apply Hint 8-2.

!

Hint 8-2: *Dealing with stakeholders demanding a particular solution*

If a stakeholder (such as the client) demands a specific solution or expresses a specific constraint for the realisation of the system, apply the following steps:

- ❑ Elicit the actual, solution/constraint-free super-goal that is behind the required solution by asking "why" questions.
- ❑ Try to identify viable solution alternatives for the super-goal.
- ❑ Document the identified, alternative solutions as sub-goals of the solution-free super-goal using an OR-decomposition.

Consideration of the seven rules for documenting goals already during the elicitation of new goals is recommended in order to avoid eliciting inappropriate goals (e.g. goals which contain unnecessary restrictions) which might be difficult to correct afterwards.

Apply the rules already during elicitation

However, you should avoid putting too much emphasis on the enhancement of already elicited goals as this may hinder the elicitation of new goals. Instead, strive for achieving sufficient coverage of the stakeholders' intentions through the elicited goals. In addition, you should analyse the documented goals using the seven rules and the template (introduced in Section 8.1) later on and improve the documentation, if required.

!

Hint 8-3: *Seven rules for documenting goals*

Rule 1: Document goals concisely.
Rule 2: Use the active voice.
Rule 3: Document the stakeholder's intention precisely.
Rule 4: Decompose high-level goals into more concrete sub-goals.
Rule 5: State the additional value of the goal.
Rule 6: Document the reasons for introducing a goal.
Rule 7: Avoid defining unnecessary restrictions.

8.3 Goal Modelling Languages and Methods

The fundamentals of conceptual modelling languages and methods are described in detail in Chapter 19. In this section, we provide a brief overview on conceptual goal modelling languages. A goal modelling language supports the documentation of goals and their dependencies in a goal model. As explained in Section 19.5, a modelling language defines the syntax and semantics of the modelling constructs to be used when creating a model. Consequently, a goal modelling language defines the syntax and semantics of the modelling constructs to be used for creating a goal model.

Model-based and template-based documentation of goals complement each other

Conceptual goal models are particularly well suited to provide an overview of the goals and their dependencies. In a goal model, a goal is typically documented by a short label. In contrast, when using a goal template (see Section 8.1), typically, comprehensive information about a goal is documented. In particular, the goal itself is described in detail, and additional information about the goal such as its origin and its relationships to other artefacts are stated. Therefore, template-based goal documentation complements model-based goal documentation. Use of both kinds of documentation is therefore recommended (concerning the interrelation of textual and model-based requirements artefacts, see Chapter 20).

Advantages of model-based documentation

The use of a goal modelling language for documenting goals and their dependencies supports, among other things, the stakeholders' understanding of the goals and the stakeholders' communication about the goals. Furthermore, the advantages of using conceptual models instead of natural language documentation described in Section 20.1.1 are valid for goal models as well.

We define a goal model as follows:

Definition 8-1: *Goal model*

A goal model is a conceptual model that documents goals, their decomposition into sub-goals, and existing goal dependencies.

Common goal modelling languages

Common goal modelling languages include different dialects of AND/OR trees, the Goal-oriented Requirements Language (GRL) [GRL 2009], i* [Yu 1993], and KAOS [Van Lamsweerde 2009].

A goal modelling method is based on a goal modelling language and provides in addition:

Methods provide rules and guidelines for model creation

- *Rules and guidelines*: The rules and guidelines support the requirements engineers in the purposeful use of the modelling constructs of the goal modelling language for creating meaningful goal models. The rule and guidelines support the engineer in documenting known facts using the constructs defined by the goal modelling language. A simple example of a rule is: "If each goal in a set of goals represents an alternative way of realising a higher-level goal, relate this set of goals to the higher-level goal by an OR-decomposition." The rules and guidelines support the requirements engineer in mapping the given facts to expressions in a goal modelling language.

Methods provide management practices

- *Management practices*: Management practices support the stakeholders in planning and controlling the application of the method. They specify, for instance, which results need to be checked at which point of time. They also support the coordination of stakeholders as well as the management of the interfaces to other processes. Furthermore, management practices can provide support tailoring the method to project- and/or product-specific needs.

Methods for goal modelling

Common goal modelling methods include the Goal-Based Requirements Analysis Method (GBRAM) [Antón 1996], the Goal-Driven Change (GDC) method [Kavakli 1999], the i* framework [Yu 1993; Yu 1997], the KAOS framework [Dardenne et al. 1993] [Van Lamsweerde 2009], and the Non-Functional Requirements (NFR) framework [Chung et al. 1996].

8.4 Documenting Goals Using AND/OR Trees and AND/OR Graphs

Hierarchical goal decomposition

AND/OR trees and graphs (see e.g. [Antón 1996; Dardenne et al. 1993; GRL 2009]) are a popular modelling language for documenting goals, especially the hierarchical decomposition of goals. AND/OR trees and graphs are based on the AND/OR-decomposition of goals already described in Section 7.3. AND/OR trees have their roots in artificial intelligence (see [Simon 1996]). They have been introduced to document the decomposition of goals into mandatory and alternative sub-goals. AND/OR graphs extend AND/OR trees by allowing a sub-goal to be related to multiple super-goals.

8.4.1 Goal Modelling Using AND/OR Trees

Nodes represent goals; edges represent decomposition relationships

AND/OR trees consist of nodes which represent goals and directed edges which represent goal decompositions. A directed edge from a goal G_1 to a goal G_2 documents that G_2 is a sub-goal of G_1 and that G_1 is the super-goal of G_2. Each goal in an AND/OR goal tree is related to exactly one super-goal, except the root goal which is not related to a super-goal. Consequently, each goal can only contribute to one super-goal, i.e. a goal cannot be related to more than one super-goal. A goal in an AND/OR goal tree can thus have at most one incoming edge. Furthermore, the tree structure excludes the documentation of cyclic paths and thus a tree structure ensures that a goal cannot be directly or indirectly related to itself, i.e. a goal cannot be (transitively) defined as its own sub-goal.

D

Definition 8-2: *AND/OR tree (AND/OR goal tree)*

An AND/OR goal tree consists of nodes that represent goals and directed edges that represent AND-decomposition and OR-decomposition relationships between the goals. Each node (except the root note) is related to exactly one super-goal.

Graphical notation of AND/OR goal trees

The type of decomposition (AND-decomposition, OR-decomposition; see Section 7.3) is indicated by the graphical notation of the edges. A right-angled edge documents an AND-decomposition. A straight-lined edge documents an OR-decomposition. The graphical notation of the edge does not indicate the direction of the edge itself. Therefore it is commonly assumed that an AND/OR goal tree is depicted top-down, i.e. a root goal (depicted at the top of the tree) is decomposed into sub-goals (leaves) depicted below etc. The graphical notations used for an OR-decomposition and an AND-decomposition are depicted in Fig. 8-1.

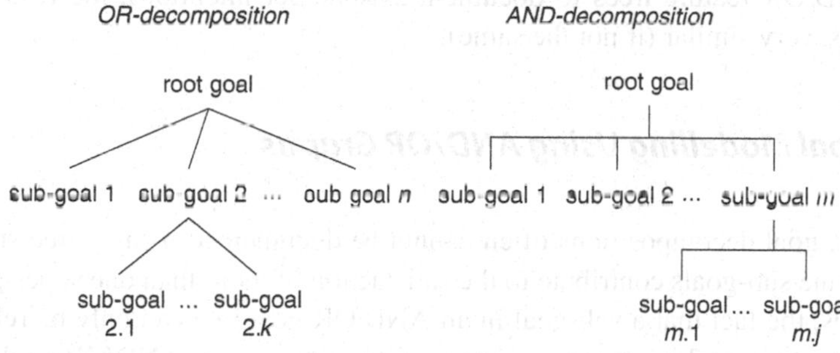

Fig. 8-1 *Notation of AND/OR goal trees*

Example of an AND/OR goal tree

Figure 8-2 shows an example of an AND/OR goal tree documenting the decomposition of the goal "comfortable and fast navigation to destination" into its sub-goals. The super-goal is refined by an AND-decomposition into three sub-goals. Thus, to satisfy the super-goal, all three sub-goals must be satisfied. The sub-goal "circumnavigating traffic jams" is again refined by an OR-decomposition into two sub-goals. Therein, the OR-decomposition documents that this goal can be satisfied either by satisfying the goal "manual entry of traffic jams in road traffic" or by satisfying the goal "autonomous update of traffic data", or by satisfying both goals.

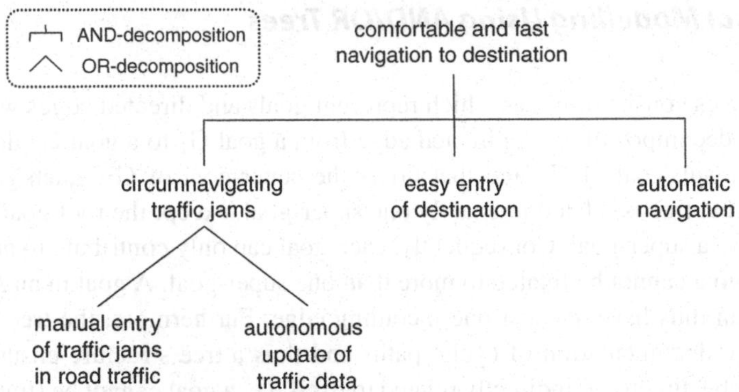

Fig. 8-2 *Example of goal modelling using AND/OR trees*

Goal trees vs. feature trees

In some domains, stakeholders prefer to use feature models in requirements engineering instead of goal models. Goal modelling was introduced in requirements engineering to document stakeholder intentions. In contrast, feature modelling has its roots in architectural design and was introduced to document AND/OR-decompositions of functional and quality properties of an architecture at an abstract, intentional level. The underlying modelling concepts of feature models (see e.g. [Kang et al. 1990; Batory 2005; Schobbens et al. 2006]) are thus very similar to AND/OR goal models. An example of a common feature modelling approach is FODA (Feature-Oriented Domain Analysis; see [Kang et al. 1990]).

Feature models as well as goal models mainly document hierarchical decompositions using AND/OR trees. Furthermore, quite often, stakeholder intentions pertain to properties that the architecture must realise. Hence, a large proportion of the goals identified during system development can also be documented as features, and vice versa.

In this book, we focus on goal modelling approaches. However, it is also possible to use AND/OR feature trees to document stakeholder intentions; the result is, in many cases, very similar (if not the same).

8.4.2 Goal Modelling Using AND/OR Graphs

One sub-goal, multiple super-goals

In practice, goal decompositions often cannot be documented using a tree structure because some sub-goals contribute to the satisfaction of more than one super-goal. In other words, the fact that a sub-goal in an AND/OR goal tree can only be related to exactly one super-goal is often too restrictive. For this reason, AND/OR goal graphs are typically used to document goal decompositions. In contrast to an AND/OR goal tree, an AND/OR goal graph allows a sub-goal to be related to multiple super-goals. Hence, in contrast to the nodes in AND/OR goal trees, a node in an AND/OR goal graph can have more than one incoming edge.

Definition 8-3: *AND/OR graph (AND/OR goal graph)*

An AND/OR goal graph is a directed, acyclic graph with nodes that represent goals and edges that represent AND-decomposition relationships and OR-decomposition relationships between the goals.

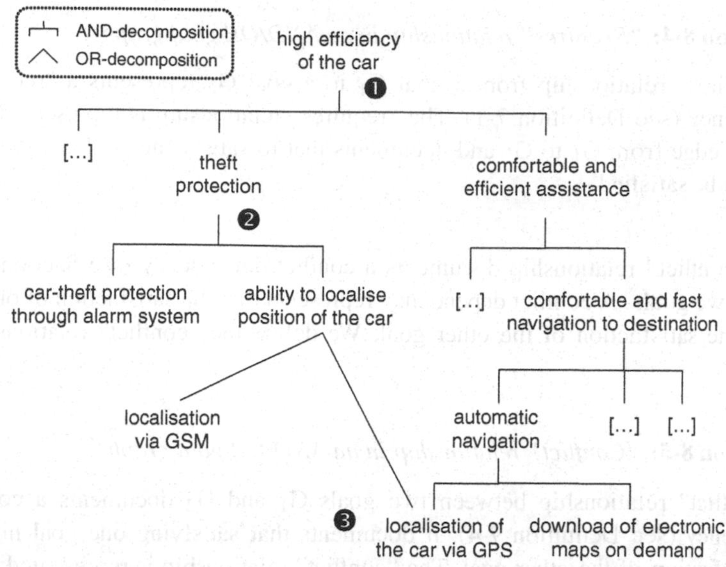

Fig. 8-3 *Example of a goal model documented using an AND/OR graph*

Example of an AND/OR graph

Figure 8-3 depicts a goal model documented using an AND/OR graph. Since the sub-goal "localisation of the car via GPS" contributes to two super-goals, the model shown in Fig. 8-3 cannot be documented using AND/OR trees.

Explanation of the example

The goal "high efficiency of the car" in Fig. 8-3 is decomposed into, amongst others, the goals "theft protection" and "comfortable and efficient assistance" (see ❶ in Fig. 8-3). To satisfy the root goal "high efficiency of the car", these two sub-goals as well as the sub-goals not shown in the figure must be satisfied. The goal "theft protection" is decomposed by an AND-decomposition into the two goals "car-theft protection through alarm system" and "ability to localise position of the car" (see ❷ in Fig. 8-3). The position of the car can be localised via GSM or via GPS. The goal "localisation of the car via GPS" is not only a sub-goal of the goal "ability to localise position of the car" but also a sub-goal of the goal "automatic navigation". The sub-goal "localisation of the car via GPS" is, thus, part of two goal decomposition relationships and consequently has two incoming edges (see ❸ in Fig. 8-3). Since the sub-goal "localisation of the car via GPS" has two incoming edges, the goal model is an AND/OR graph and not an AND/OR tree.

8.4.3 Additional Goal Dependencies in AND/OR Graphs

"Requires" relationship

AND/OR trees and AND/OR graphs facilitate documenting hierarchical goal decompositions in a clear and concise way. However, typically further goal dependencies exist (see Section 7.4) which have to be documented. We therefore extend AND/OR graphs by defining two additional types of edges representing the "requires" and the "conflict" dependencies. The "requires" relationship documents a "requires" dependency (see Section 7.4.1) between a goal G_1 and a goal G_2. A "requires" dependency defines that, to satisfy G_1, the goal G_2 must be satisfied. We define the "requires" relationship as follows:

D

Definition 8-4: *"Requires" relationship in an AND/OR goal graph*

A "requires" relationship from a goal G_1 to a goal G_2 represents a "requires" dependency (see Definition 7-1). The "requires" relationship is represented as a directed edge from G_1 to G_2 and documents that to satisfy the goal G_1, the goal G_2 must be satisfied.

"Conflict" relationship

The "conflict" relationship documents a conflict dependency (see Section 7.4.4) between two goals. A conflict dependency represents that the satisfaction of one goal hinders the satisfaction of the other goal. We define the "conflict" relationship as follows:

D

Definition 8-5: *"Conflict" relationship in an AND/OR goal graph*

A "conflict" relationship between two goals G_1 and G_2 documents a conflict dependency (see Definition 7-4). It documents that satisfying one goal hinders the satisfaction of the other goal. The "conflict" relationship is represented as an undirected edge between G_1 and G_2.

Figure 8-4 depicts an example of an extended AND/OR goal graph with a "requires" and a "conflict" relationship.

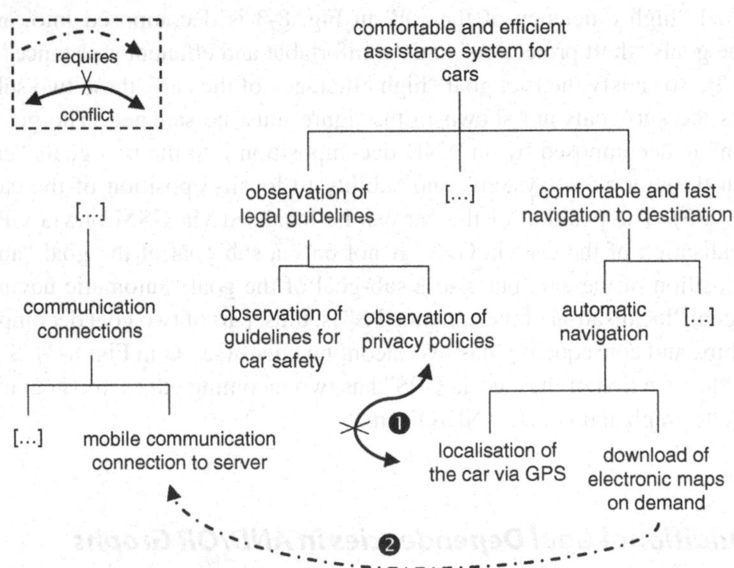

Fig. 8-4 *Example of goal modelling with extended AND/OR graphs*

Explanation of the example

The "conflict" relationship shown in Fig. 8-4 (❶) documents that the goal "observation of privacy policies" conflicts with the goal "localisation of the car via GPS". This means that, if one of the two goals is satisfied, the other goal cannot be satisfied any more. The "requires" relationship in Fig. 8-4 (❷) between the goal "download of electronic maps on demand" and the goal "mobile communication connection to server" documents that the goal "download of electronic maps on demand" can only be satisfied if the goal "mobile communication connection to server" is satisfied.

8.5 i* (i-Star)

Focus on dependencies between actors

The i* framework is a comprehensive approach for documenting and analysing goals and goal dependencies. i* is based on the idea that an actor depends on other actors in order to achieve its goals. The basic modelling constructs of i* are presented in Section 8.5.1. In i*, the actors and their dependencies are documented in the strategic dependency model (see Section 8.5.2). In addition, the goals, tasks, etc. of each actor are documented using the strategic rationale model (see Section 8.5.3).

8.5.1 Modelling Constructs of the i* Framework

*GRL and i**

i* is based on the modelling language GRL (Goal-oriented Requirements Language). GRL employs AND/OR trees for documenting goal decompositions. In addition, GRL provides modelling constructs for documenting quality (non-functional) aspects (see [GRL 2009]). In addition to the modelling constructs of GRL, i* provides guidance for creating and analysing i* models (see e.g. [Yu 1993; Yu 1997]).

*Basic concepts of i**

Figure 8-5 provides an overview of the basic modelling constructs offered in the i* framework. The modelling constructs of i* are divided into objects and relationships. Relationships are further subdivided into dependencies and links. In the following subsections, we briefly explain the basic modelling constructs of i* depicted in Fig. 8-5.

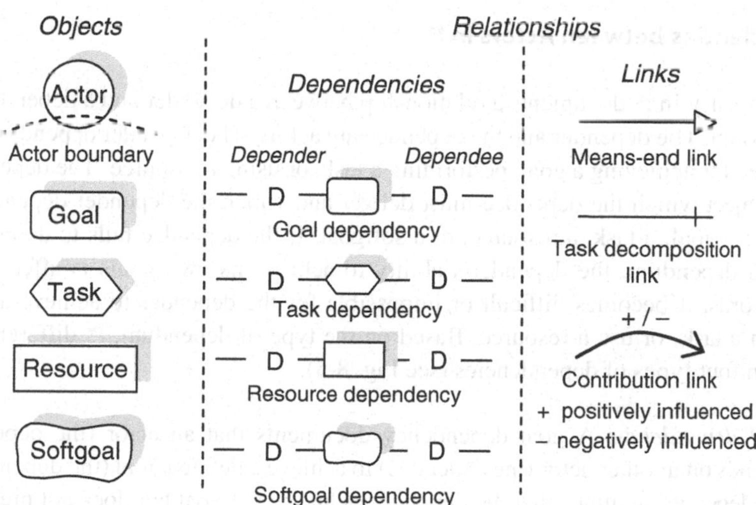

Fig. 8-5 *Notation of the modelling constructs in the i* framework*

Objects in i*

Five object types

i* offers five types of objects as shown on the left-hand side of Fig. 8-5:

- *Actor*: An actor is a person or a system that has a relationship to the system to be developed. i* refines the concept actor into three sub-concepts (not shown in Fig. 8-5; see [Yu 1993] for the graphical notation of these concepts):
  - *Agent*: An agent is an actor who has a concrete physical representation, e.g. a person or a system.
  - *Role*: A role defines the behaviour of an actor within a specific context. An actor can have several roles, and a role can be assigned to multiple actors.
  - *Position*: A position is a set of roles that can typically be played by one agent. An agent can occupy several positions.
- *Goal*: A goal answers "why?" questions. It describes a certain state in the world that an actor would like to achieve. However, a goal does not prescribe how it should be achieved.
- *Task*: A task specifies a particular way of doing something. Typically a task consists of a number of steps (or sub-tasks) that an actor must perform to execute the task.
- *Resource*: A resource is a (physical or informational) entity that the actor needs to achieve a goal or perform a task. The main concern about a resource is whether it is available and from whom.
- *Softgoal*: A softgoal is a condition in the world which the actor would like to achieve, but unlike the concept of (hard)goal, the criteria for the condition being achieved is not sharply defined [Yu 1995]. A softgoal is typically a quality attribute on one of the other elements, i.e. a goal, a task, or a resource. A softgoal is considered to be fulfilled if there is sufficient positive evidence for its fulfilment and little evidence against it (see [Mylopoulos 2001]).

Dependencies between Actors in i*

Relationships between a depender and a dependee on a dependum

A dependency in i* documents a relationship between a depender and a dependee for a dependum. The depender and the dependee are actors. The depender depends on the dependee for achieving a goal, performing a task, or using a resource. The dependum is the object which the dependee must deliver and which the depender depends on. It can be a goal, a task, a resource, or a softgoal. If the dependee fails to deliver the required dependum, the depender's ability to achieve its own goals is affected. In other words, it becomes difficult or impossible for the depender to achieve a goal, perform a task, or use a resource. Based on the type of dependum, i* differentiates between four types of dependencies (see Fig. 8-5):

Dependee must achieve a specified goal

- *Goal dependency*: A goal dependency documents that an actor (the depender) depends on another actor (the dependee) to achieve a defined goal (the dependum). The depender assumes that the dependee achieves the goal but does not prescribe how he/she should achieve the goal.

Dependee must perform a specified task

- *Task dependency*: A task dependency documents that an actor (the depender) depends on another actor (the dependee) to perform a task (the dependum) assigned to this actor (the dependee). A task dependency defines that the dependee must perform the assigned task to achieve a goal, without stating why the task needs to be performed.

- *Resource dependency*: A resource dependency expresses that an actor (the depender) depends on the availability of a physical or informational resource (the dependum) that is provided by another actor (the dependee).

Dependee must provide a resource

- *Softgoal dependency*: A softgoal dependency expresses that an actor (the depender) depends on another actor (the dependee) to perform a task that leads to the achievement of a softgoal (the dependum). The criteria for what constitutes achieving the softgoal are not clearly defined. Typically, the dependee offers several alternatives for achieving the softgoal, and the judgement of whether the softgoal is achieved or not is up to the depender.

Dependee must achieve a softgoal

Relationships between Objects in i*

The i* framework differentiates between three types of links that may exist between the four object types "goal", "task", "resource", and "softgoal" (see Fig. 8-5, right-hand side):

- *Means-end link*: A means-end link documents which softgoals, tasks, and/or resources contribute to achieving a goal. A means-end link thus documents why an actor wants to achieve a particular goal, perform a task, or use a particular resource. Means-end links also facilitate the documentation and evaluation of alternative ways to satisfy a goal, i.e. different decompositions of a goal into softgoals, tasks, and resources. Figure 8-6 illustrates means-end links between different object types.

Means for achieving a goal

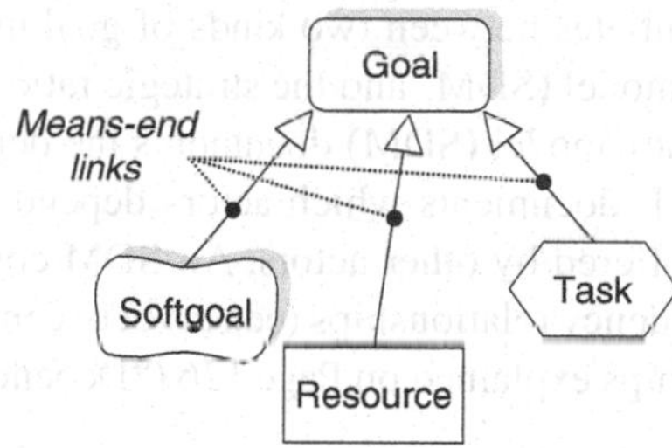

Fig. 8-6 *Means-end links in the i* framework*

- *Contribution link*: A contribution link documents a positive (+) or negative (–) influence on softgoals by tasks or other softgoals. A contribution link describes whether a task or a softgoal contributes to satisfying a softgoal positively or negatively. It does not define precisely which kind of support is offered or the extent of the support offered. Figure 8-7 shows contribution links between different object types.

Positive and negative contributions to a softgoal

- *Task decomposition link*: A task decomposition documents the essential elements of a task. A task decomposition link relates the task with its components, which can be any combination of sub-goals, sub-tasks, resources, or softgoals. The decomposition of a task can thus comprise sub-tasks that must be performed, sub-goals that

Refinement of a task

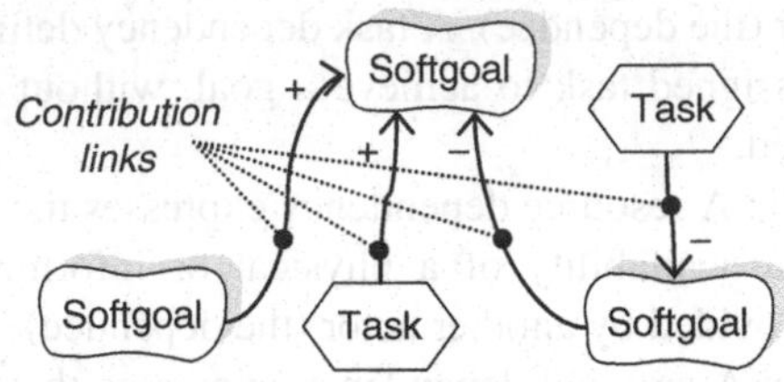

Fig. 8-7 *Contribution links in the i* framework*

must be achieved, resources that are needed, and softgoals that typically define quality goals for the task. Figure 8-8 depicts a set of task decomposition links between different object types.

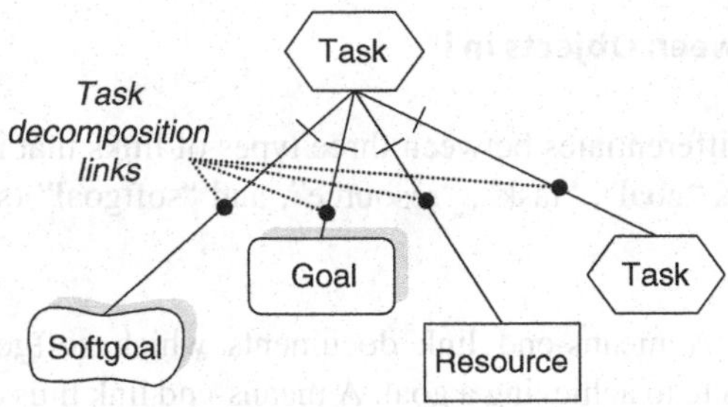

Fig. 8-8 *Task decomposition links in the i* framework*

8.5.2 Strategic Dependency Model (SDM)

Two i-models: SDM and SRM*

The i* framework differentiates between two kinds of goal models (see [Yu 1995]): the strategic dependency model (SDM) and the strategic rationale model (SRM).

SDM defines dependencies between actors

The strategic dependency model (SDM) documents the dependencies which exist between different actors. It documents which actors depend on which tasks, goals, softgoals, and resources offered by other actors. An SDM consists of a set of actors (nodes) and a set of dependency relationships (edges) between these actors. For creating an SDM, the relationships explained on Page 126 ("Dependencies between Actors in i*") are used.

Example of an SDM

Figure 8-9 depicts an excerpt of a strategic dependency model (SDM). This excerpt defines four dependencies between the actors "car driver" and "automotive manufacturer". The four dependencies are represented by four edges between the actor nodes. On each edge, the dependum of the type goal, resource, task, or softgoal is annotated. The reading direction is indicated by the orientation of the letter "D" that is annotated on the dependency links (for example, the dependency ❹ depicted in Fig. 8-9 has a different reading direction from the dependencies ❶-❸).

In the following, we explain the four dependencies depicted in Fig. 8-9:

Goal dependency

❶ This dependency is a goal dependency. It expresses that the "car driver" (depender) depends on the "automotive manufacturer" (dependee) for achieving the goal "avoiding accidents". Figure 8-10 depicts further details of this dependency in a strategic rationale model (SRM).

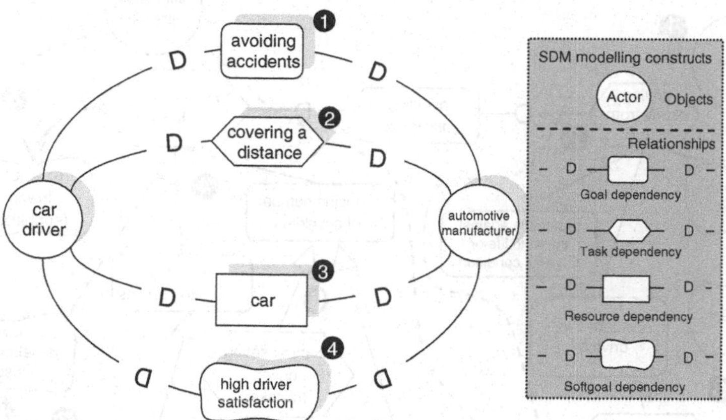

Fig. 8-9 *Example of a strategic dependency model in i**

❷ This task dependency documents that the "car driver" depends on the "automotive manufacturer" to execute the task "covering a distance". *Task dependency*

❸ The resource dependency documents that the "car driver" depends on "automotive manufacturer" to provide the resource "car". *Resource dependency*

❹ This softgoal dependency documents that the "automotive manufacturer" depends on the "car driver" to achieve the softgoal "high driver satisfaction". *Softgoal dependency*

8.5.3 Strategic Rationale Model (SRM)

The SRM justifies dependencies in the SDM

While the SDM provides an external view of the actors and their interdependencies, the strategic rationale model (SRM) details each actor and thereby supports reasoning about the actors, external relationships defined in the SDM. The SRM thus documents the internal rationale structure of each actor. The internal structure of an actor is defined in the SRM in terms of goals, tasks, resources, and softgoals as well as means-end, task decomposition, and contribution links between these objects. The SRM thus provides a way of modelling stakeholder interests and how they might be met (see [Yu 1997]).

Example of an SRM

Figure 8-10 depicts an SRM for a part of the SDM shown in Fig. 8-9. In the SRM, goals, tasks, resources, and softgoals are no longer represented as a dependum in a dependency relationship. They become structural elements of an actor which are hierarchically interrelated by means-end, task decomposition, and contribution links.

The SRM shown in Fig. 8-10 presents the internal structure of the two actors "driver" and "automotive manufacturer" for the goal dependency "avoiding accidents" of the SDM shown in Fig. 8-9. In the following, we explain the numbered relationships depicted in Fig. 8-10.

❶ The dashed line (actor boundary) defines the boundary of the internal rationale structure of the actor "driver". *Actor boundary*

❷ The task "driving safely from A to B" is decomposed by three task decomposition links into the softgoal "pleasure in driving" and the two goals "accident-free driving" and "protection against threat to life and physical condition". *Task decomposition link*

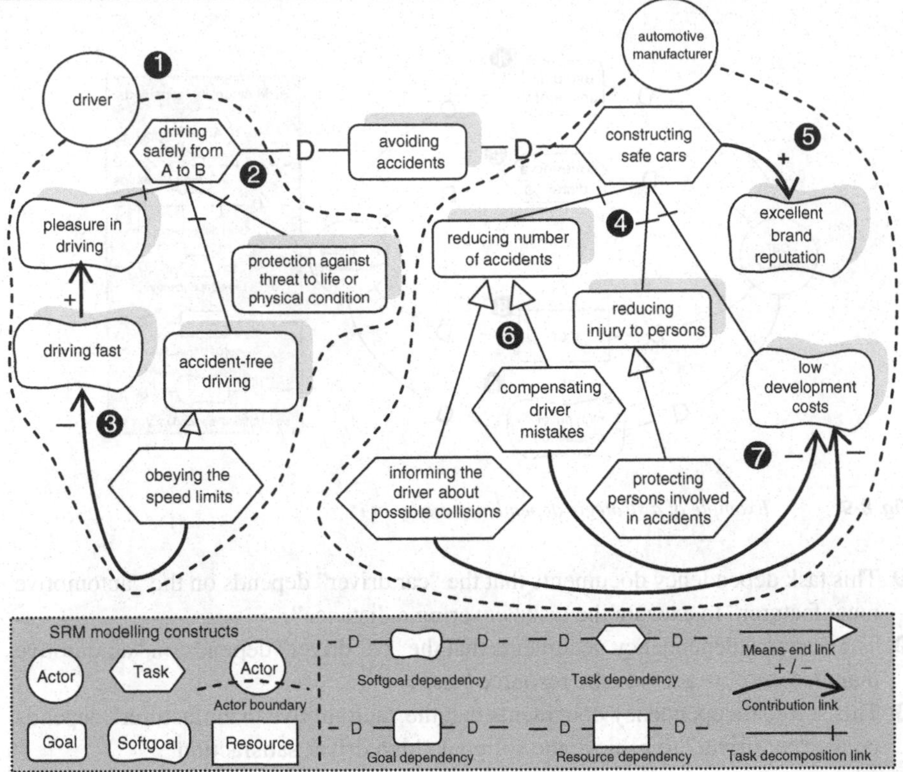

Fig. 8-10 *Example of a strategic rationale model in i**

Contribution link

❸ The contribution link between the task "obeying the speed limits" and the softgoal "driving fast" is annotated with a minus sign. This documents that the task "obeying the speed limits" has a negative influence on the satisfaction of the softgoal "driving fast".

Task decomposition link

❹ The task "constructing safe cars" of the actor "automotive manufacturer" is refined by task decomposition links into the goals "reducing number of accidents" and "reducing injury to persons" as well as the softgoal "low development costs".

Positive contribution link

❺ The automotive manufacturer has the softgoal "excellent brand reputation". The satisfaction of this softgoal is positively influenced by the task "constructing safe cars". The contribution link documents this positive influence.

Means-end link

❻ The tasks "informing the driver about possible collisions" and "compensating driver mistakes" are connected by two means-end links to the goal "reducing number of accidents". The two means-end links document that both tasks (the means) have the goal to reduce the number of accidents (the end). Often, means-end links from different tasks to the same goal document potential alternatives to satisfy the goal.

Negative contribution link

❼ The contribution links from the tasks "informing the driver about possible collisions" and "compensating driver mistakes" to the softgoal "low development costs" are annotated with a minus sign. This documents that both tasks have a negative influence on the satisfaction of the softgoal "low development costs".

8.6 KAOS

Six sub-models

The KAOS modelling language is part of the KAOS framework for eliciting, specifying, and analysing goals, requirements, scenarios, and responsibility assignments. A KAOS model comprises six complementary views or sub-models (see [Van Lamsweerde 2009]): the goal model, the obstacle model, the object model, the agent model, the operation model, and the behaviour model. All sub-models are interrelated via traceability links. In this section, we explain the goal sub-model and the assignment of goal responsibilities to agents within the KAOS framework.

8.6.1 Constructs for Goal Modelling in the KAOS Framework

Constructs for goal modelling

Figure 8-11 depicts the basic constructs for documenting goals and assigning goal responsibilities to agents provided by the KAOS framework (see [Van Lamsweerde 2009]). The constructs are explained below.

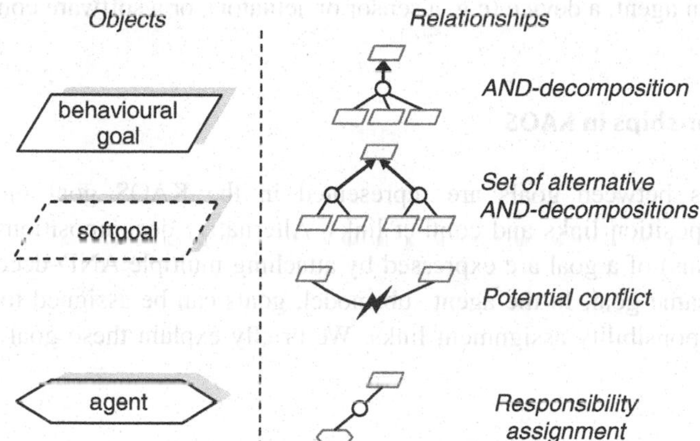

Fig. 8-11 *Basic constructs of the KAOS framework for modelling goals and assigning responsibilities for goals to agents*

Goals and Agents

Goals and agents

The object types "behavioural goal", "softgoal" and "agent" play a central role in the KAOS framework. In KAOS, a goal is either a behavioural goal or a softgoal and is defined as a prescriptive statement of intent that the system should satisfy through the cooperation of its agents (see [Van Lamsweerde 2009]). We briefly characterise behavioural goals, softgoals, and agents.

- *Behavioural goal*: A behavioural goal describes a set of admissible system behaviours. Behavioural goals can be defined in a clear-cut manner, i.e. one can verify whether the system satisfies a behavioural goal or not. A typical example of a behavioural goal is "The train doors shall remain closed while the train is moving". KOAS differentiates between two types of behavioural goals:

– *Achieve goal*: An "achieve goal" demands that the defined property must eventually hold.
– *Maintain goal*: A "maintain goal" requires that the defined property always holds (possibly under some condition).

In a KAOS goal model, the sub-type of a goal can be indicated as a prefix of the name of the goal.

- *Softgoal*: In KAOS, softgoals are used to document preferences among alternative system behaviours (see [Van Lamsweerde 2009]). An example of a softgoal is "The system shall minimise the travelling time". Like in i*, there is no clear-cut criterion for verifying the satisfaction of a softgoal. Softgoals are hence expected to be satisfied within acceptable limits rather than absolutely.
- *Agent*: While i* focusses primarily on agents within organisational structures, the agents defined in KAOS primarily relate to users and components of software-intensive systems. An agent is thus defined as an active system component which has a specific role for satisfying a goal (see [Van Lamsweerde 2009]). An agent can be a human agent, a device (e.g. a sensor or actuator), or a software component.

Goal Relationships in KAOS

Dependencies between goals are represented in the KAOS goal model using AND-decomposition links and conflict links. Alternative decompositions (i.e. OR-decompositions) of a goal are expressed by attaching multiple AND-decomposition links to the same goal. In the agent sub-model, goals can be assigned to agents by means of responsibility assignment links. We briefly explain these goal dependencies:

- *AND-decomposition*: An AND-decomposition link relates a super-goal to a set of sub-goals. An AND-decomposition link documents that the super-goal is satisfied if all sub-goals are satisfied (see Section 7.3).
- *Alternative decomposition*: OR-decompositions of a goal are documented in KAOS by assigning multiple AND-decompositions to the super-goal (see Fig. 8-11). Hence each alternative is represented as an AND-decomposition (which may also consist of just one sub-goal). The set of assigned AND-decompositions refines the super-goal into the different sets of sub-goals. The super-goal is satisfied if one of the alternatives (one AND-decomposition assigned to the super-goal) is satisfied.
- *Potential conflict*: Conflicts between goals are documented using potential conflict links. A potential conflict link documents that satisfying one goal may prevent the satisfaction of the other goal under certain conditions. This link does not hence correspond to the conflict dependency defined in Section 7.4.4, which documents that, when one goal is satisfied, the other goal cannot be satisfied.
- *Responsibility assignment*: Responsibility assignment links relate elements of the goal sub-model to elements of the agent sub-model. A responsibility assignment

link between a goal and an agent means that this agent is responsible for satisfying the goal. Only terminal goals can be assigned to an individual agent. If a goal is assigned to an individual agent it can thus not be further decomposed. In addition, alternative responsibility assignments can be defined, i.e. a goal can be related to multiple agents using a responsibility assignment relationship. When implementing the system, at least one of the alternative assignments needs to be chosen.

8.6.2 Modelling Goals in KAOS

The goal (sub-)model in KAOS documents goals, softgoals, and their dependencies (AND-decompositions, alternative decompositions, and potential conflicts). Figure 8-12 shows a simplified example of the decomposition of the goal "avoid traffic jams". This goal contributes to satisfying two softgoals, the softgoal "short travelling time" and the softgoal "low fuel consumption". A conflict link between the two softgoals indicates that it may not be possible to satisfy these two goals together (choosing a route with a shorter travelling time may increase the fuel consumption). The goal "avoid traffic jams" is decomposed into the two goals "detect traffic jams en route" and "recalculate route after detecting a traffic jam". The AND-decomposition link indicates that both sub-goals must be satisfied in order to satisfy the super-goal. The sub-goal "detect traffic jams en route" has two alternative decompositions. It can be satisfied either by satisfying the goal "allow driver to enter traffic jams" or by satisfying the goal "receive traffic messages".

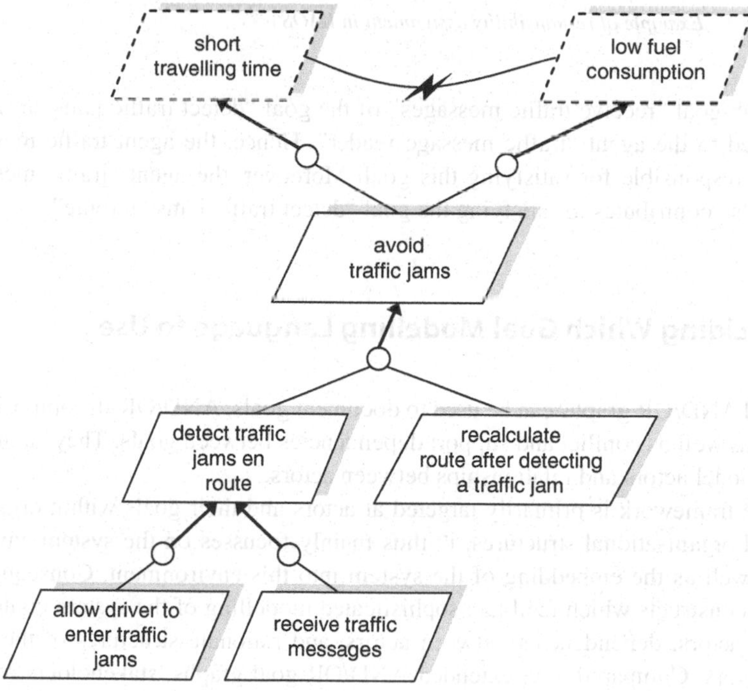

Fig. 8-12 *Example of a goal model in KAOS*

8.6.3 Modelling Responsibility Assignments in KAOS

Responsibility assignments are used in KAOS to interrelate goals defined in the goal sub-model and agents defined in the agent sub-model. A simplified example of such a responsibility assignment is shown in Fig. 8-13. The goal "allow driver to enter traffic jams" is related to the agent "user interface control" by a responsibility assignment link. This link expresses that the agent "user interface control" is responsible for satisfying the goal "allow driver to enter traffic jams". Hence, the agent "user interface control" also contributes to satisfying the super-goal "detect traffic jams en route".

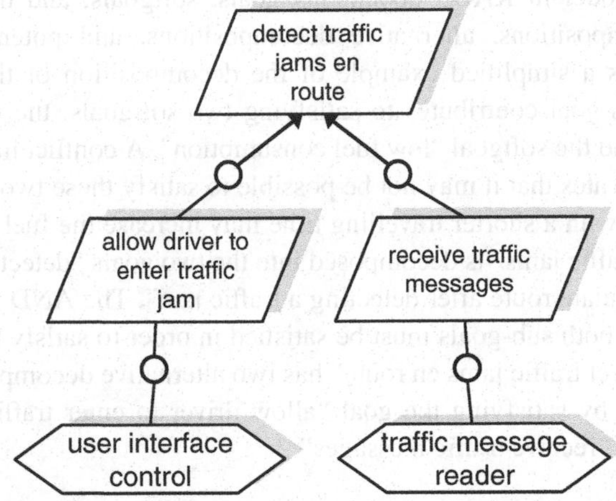

Fig. 8-13 *Example of responsibility assignment in KAOS*

The sub-goal "receive traffic messages" of the goal "detect traffic jams en route" is assigned to the agent "traffic message reader". Hence, the agent traffic message reader is responsible for satisfying this goal. Moreover, the agent "traffic message reader" also contributes to satisfying the goal "detect traffic jams en route".

8.7 Deciding Which Goal Modelling Language to Use

Extended AND/OR-graphs

Extended AND/OR graphs can be used to document goals, AND/OR-decompositions of goals as well as conflict and support dependencies between goals. They cannot be used to model actors and relationships between actors.

The i* framework is primarily targeted at actors and their goals within organisations and organisational structures. i* thus mainly focusses on the system environment as well as the embedding of the system into this environment. Consequently, i* offers constructs which facilitate sophisticated modelling of the system context in terms of actors, dependencies between actors, and rationale structures of the individual actors. Compared with extended AND/OR goal graphs, stakeholders require significantly more training to be able to create and to understand i* goal models. Compared with extended AND/OR goal graphs, creating i* goal models requires greater effort.

The KAOS framework is primarily targeted at agents that are users or components of software-intensive systems. The basic concepts for defining goals in the KAOS framework are very similar to extended AND/OR goal graphs. In addition, KAOS supports the modelling of (potential) conflicts and softgoals. Moreover, the goal model is supplemented with five other models: the obstacle model, the object model, the agent model, the operation model, and the behaviour model. Thus, KAOS also supports interrelating goal models with data, functional, and behavioural models. Compared with extended AND/OR goal graphs, the expressiveness of KAOS requires greater training effort and greater effort.

Hint 8-4: *Choosing a goal modelling language*

Consider the following when choosing a goal modelling language:

- Use extended AND/OR graphs if your main focus is the documentation of goals, their decompositions, and their dependencies.
- Use i* models if you aim to document and analyse the relationships between different actors in an organisation using an agent-oriented modelling paradigm.
- Use KAOS models if you aim to document the intended properties of the hardware and software components of a software-intensive system (especially an embedded system) using an agent-oriented modelling paradigm and if you aim to relate the defined goals with solution-oriented requirements models.

!

Tools supporting the creation of models exist for all three types of modelling notations. For i*, and especially for KAOS, the analytical capabilities of these tools typically go beyond the capabilities of modelling tools based on AND/OR graphs.

Hint 8-5: *Recommendations for documenting goals*

Documenting goals using templates as well as model-based techniques is recommended. To define a goal model you should:

- First, elicit the goals of the individual stakeholders.
- Second, describe each goal using the goal template. Consider the hints given in Section 8.1 when you define the goals using the goal template. For example, focus on the identification of sub-goals, decomposition relationships and goal dependencies first.
- Third, model the goals and the identified decompositions, and dependencies using (extended) AND/OR graphs.
- Fourth, validate the defined goals, decompositions, and dependencies.
- Fifth, complete the template for each goal (if possible).

In particular, for mission-critical, safety-critical, or other critical parts of the system, you should define KAOS or i* models in addition to (or even instead of) extended AND/OR graphs.

!

Recommended Literature for Part III.a

Basic Reading

[Rolland and Salinesi 2005] provide an overview on goal modelling in requirements engineering. The authors outline different approaches for goal modelling and report on experiences of using goal models in practice.

[Van Lamsweerde 2001] provides insight into general aspects of goal modelling and presents the different goal modelling approaches in a concise way. Furthermore, reasons for documenting goals in requirements engineering are given, and research challenges are discussed.

[Yu and Mylopoulos 1994] explain the use of i* models during the analysis, modelling, and design of software systems. The article provides valuable insights into the i* modelling concepts and illustrates the application of i*.

Advanced Reading

[Antón 1996] points out the importance of goal orientation in requirements engineering for the identification, organisation, and justification of requirements. She presents strategies for the identification and development of goals and the Goal-Based Requirements Analysis Method (GBRAM).

[Van Lamsweerde 2009] provides an in-depth description of the KAOS method. Among other things, the book provides a comprehensive description of the different sub-models of the KAOS framework, the KAOS method as well as the goal-based reasoning and analysis techniques which support the application of the KAOS method. Furthermore, the book elaborates on the development process from goal-oriented requirements via software specifications to software architectures.

Part III.b
Scenarios

Overview Part III.b – Scenarios

Goals document stakeholder intentions. Scenarios document sequences of interactions in which the system either satisfies some goals or fails to satisfy them. Hence, scenarios illustrate the stakeholders' intentions by means of positive and negative examples. Scenarios also illustrate the value of the system for its users in terms of sequences of interactions between the system and its actors (i.e. persons and systems interacting with the system). In addition, scenarios contain important context information. Use cases aggregate multiple scenarios that are associated with the same goal(s).

In this part of the book, we explain:

- *The fundamentals of scenarios in requirements engineering*
- *The main scenario types and their use in requirements engineering*
- *Reference templates for documenting scenarios and use cases in natural language*
- *Eleven rules for documenting scenarios*
- *The model-based documentation of scenarios by means of sequence diagrams and activity diagrams*
- *The model-based documentation of use cases and their relationships by means of use case diagrams*
- *The interdependencies between goals and scenarios in requirements engineering*
- *The advantages of using goals and scenarios in requirements engineering activities*

Classification **Part III.b Scenarios**	Basic	Advanced
9 Fundamentals of Scenarios		
9.1 Fundamentals of Scenarios	✓	
9.2 Scenarios as a Means for Putting Requirements in Context	✓	
9.3 Developing Scenarios for Each Context Facet	✓	
10 Scenario Types		
10.1 Current-State and Desired-State Scenarios	✓	
10.2 Positive and Negative Scenarios	✓	
10.3 Misuse Scenarios	✓	
10.4 Descriptive, Exploratory, and Explanatory Scenarios	✓	
10.5 Instance and Type Scenarios		✓
10.6 System-Internal, Interaction, and Context Scenarios		✓
10.7 Main Scenario, Alternative Scenarios, and Exception Scenarios	✓	
10.8 Use Cases: Grouping Scenarios	✓	
11 Documenting Scenarios		
11.1 Narrative Scenarios	✓	
11.2 Structured Scenarios	✓	
11.3 A Reference Template for Use Cases		✓
11.4 Eleven Rules for Documenting Scenarios	✓	
11.5 Sequence Diagrams		✓
11.6 Activity Diagrams		✓
11.7 Use Case Diagrams		✓
11.8 Use of the Different Scenario Types in the Requirements Engineering Process		✓
12 Benefits of Using Goals and Scenarios		
12.1 Benefits of Goal Orientation	✓	
12.2 Benefits of Using Scenarios	✓	
12.3 Benefits of Goal–Scenario–Coupling	✓	

Chapter 9
Fundamentals of Scenarios

In this chapter, we describe:

- *The motivation for using scenarios in requirements engineering*
- *The role of scenarios as a means for putting requirements in context*
- *The essential types of context information contained in scenarios*
- *The documentation of context information about each of the four context facets using scenarios*

When applying the first approaches for goal-oriented requirements engineering (e.g. [Van Lamsweerde et al. 1991; Dardenne et al. 1993; Yu 1993; Antón 1996; Chung et al. 1996]), it was recognised that goals alone do not sufficiently support, for instance, the elicitation of requirements (see [Potts 1997]). Goals are important means for documenting the stakeholders' intentions and thereby capturing the rationales for why the system is developed. However, stakeholders typically find it easier to communicate about requirements in terms of examples rather than in terms of abstract intentions. Scenarios are a natural way for stakeholders to explain what they want. Using scenarios, the stakeholder can do this by means of concrete, exemplary interaction sequences (see [Alexander and Maiden 2004]). In Definition 4-3 on Page 54, the term "scenario" is defined as follows:

> *A scenario describes a concrete example of satisfying or failing to satisfy a goal (or set of goals). It thereby provides more detail about one or several goals. A scenario typically defines a sequence of interaction steps executed to satisfy the goal and relates these interaction steps to the system context.*

Illustrating goal satisfaction

Hence a scenario illustrates how goals are satisfied (or not satisfied) by means of a concrete sequence of interactions between the system and its users. Scenarios can be used in all five requirements engineering activities. Section 12.2 provides an overview of the most important aspects of using scenarios in each requirements engineering activity.

Goal–scenario–coupling

Goal–scenario–coupling (see e.g. [Rolland et al. 1999]) means that goals and scenarios are developed together in a complementary way. Goal–scenario–coupling aims to bridge the gap between the stakeholders' intentions and the requirements for the system. The coupling of goals and scenarios has several advantages, especially for the elicitation and validation of requirements. We explain these advantages in Section 12.3.

9.1 Scenarios as Middle-Level Abstractions

Middle-level abstractions

In the 1950s, Mills pointed out that many established sciences had not managed to come to conclusions that were of immediate relevance for practice or that had an immediate relationship to the considered reality or universe of discourse [Mills 1959]. The main reason for this problem was seen in the fact that the considered universe of discourse was normally described only by abstract models. Mills suggested supplementing abstract models by other means of description that are more concrete than abstract models. These models should serve as intermediary abstractions between the abstract models and reality. Such intermediary models are called middle-level abstractions (see [Carroll 1995]).

Scenarios in requirements engineering

In requirements engineering, scenarios serve as such middle-level abstractions. Scenarios are more concrete than goals and conceptual models of function, data, and behaviour. Hence, they serve as intermediary abstractions between reality and abstract models (see [Carroll 1995; Potts 1997; Haumer et al. 1998]).

Figure 9-1 illustrates the use of scenarios as middle-level abstractions between conceptual models and reality. Due to the capability of scenarios to serve as middle-level abstractions, the development of scenarios has a strong positive impact on all requirements engineering activities.

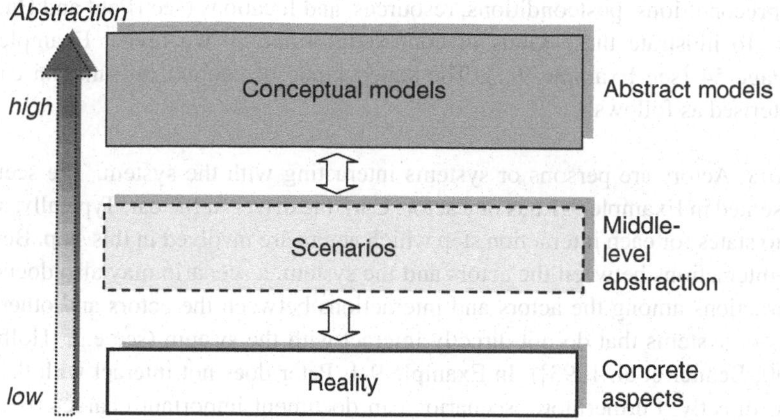

Fig. 9-1 *Scenarios as middle-level abstractions*

Abstraction levels of scenarios

The aspects documented in scenarios may have different abstraction levels. Hence, scenarios cover a certain range between low and high abstraction themselves. Scenarios may contain aspects that are very close to the considered fragment of reality (i.e. such scenarios abstract from reality only slightly). However, the abstraction level of scenarios may also come very close to the abstraction level of conceptual models.

Examples of scenarios with an abstraction level close to reality are multimedia scenarios such as video recordings of system usage (see e.g. [Haumer et al. 1998]) or the illustration of system usage by means of virtual reality. However, scenarios can also be fairly abstract. An example is the documentation of interactions with the system at the type level by means of sequence diagrams (see Section 11.5).

Flexible abstraction level of scenarios

The stakeholders can decide about the appropriate abstraction level of scenarios based on the intended use of the scenarios in the requirements engineering process. For example, in order to support model creation, several multimedia scenarios can be elicited first. Subsequently, a more abstract scenario can be developed that abstracts from the multimedia scenarios. Vice versa, in order to support communication with non-technical stakeholders, requirements engineers may decide to make an abstract scenario more concrete and hence define a set of scenarios at a lower abstraction level. In figurative sense, scenarios in requirements engineering serve as a mediator between the abstract and the concrete. If scenarios are documented in natural language, their abstraction level can be chosen almost arbitrarily depending on the situation.

9.2 Scenarios as a Means for Putting Requirements in Context

Context information in scenarios

Requirements only exist in a specfic context (see Section 5.4). Scenarios are particularly well suited for documenting information about the context (see e.g. [Benner et al. 1993; Potts et al. 1994; Carroll 1995; Cockburn 1997; Pohl and Haumer 1997]). Since scenarios document context information they establish a link between the requirements and the relevant context aspects (see Section 6.2). Typical pieces of information about the context that are documented in scenarios are actors, roles, goals, preconditions, postconditions, resources, and locations (see [Pohl and Haumer 1997]). To illustrate these kinds of context information, we revisit Example 4-5 from Page 54 (see Example 9-1). The stated kinds of context information can be characterised as follows:

Persons and systems interacting with the system to be developed

- *Actors*: Actors are persons or systems interacting with the system. The scenario presented in Example 9-1 has one actor: Carl, the driver of the car. Typically, a scenario states for each interaction step which actors are involved in this step. Besides the interactions between the actors and the system, a scenario may also document interactions among the actors and interactions between the actors and other persons or systems that do not directly interact with the system (see e.g. [Holbrook 1990; Benner et al. 1993]). In Example 9-1, Peter does not interact with the system, directly. Furthermore, scenarios can document important characteristics of the actors such as their intentions and roles.

Classification of actors

- *Roles*: A role characterises a specific class of actors. Hence roles can be used to classify the actors of a scenario. A role is defined in terms of the relationships and responsibilities that actors occupying this role have with regard to the system (see e.g. [Leite et al. 1997; Potts et al. 1994]). In Example 9-1, the actor "Carl" occupies the role of a driver.

Assignment of goals

- *Goals*: Scenarios illustrate the satisfaction of goals. For example, the scenario in Example 9-1 illustrates the satisfaction of the goal "maintain a safe following distance to the vehicle ahead". The corresponding goals are either assigned to the scenario itself (see [Leite et al. 1997]), to the actors (see [Regnell et al. 1996]), or to the individual scenario steps (see [Cockburn 1997; Haumer et al. 1998]).

Necessary conditions

- *Precondition*: Preconditions define conditions that must hold before executing the scenario in order to be able to execute the scenario. In Example 9-1 the condition "car drives at a speed of more than 50 mph" might be defined as a precondition for executing the scenario.

Success guarantees and minimal guarantees

- *Postcondition*: Postconditions define conditions that must hold, either within the system or in the system context, after executing the scenario (see e.g. [Regnell et al. 1996; Gough et al. 1995]). A postcondition for the scenario presented in Example 9-1 could define that no rear-end collision has occurred and that the safety distance to the vehicle ahead has been restored. The conditions that are met after a successful exectution of the scenario are called success guarantees. Conditions that are always met, independent of whether the execution was successful or not, are called minimal guarantees.

Required resources

- *Resources*: Resources are special preconditions that must hold so that a scenario can be executed. They refer to persons, information, temporal, financial, or other material resources that are needed for successful execution of the scenario. In Example 9-1, the accurate distance to the vehicle ahead is a critical resource that the system needs to execute the scenario successfully.

Execution environment

- *Location*: The location of a scenario can be a real or fictional place where the scenario is executed. A scenario can convey detailed information about this location and hence place the entire interaction sequence in a (real or fictional) context (see e.g. [Cockburn 1997; Carroll 1995]). In Example 9-1, the information "on the motorway" refers to the intended location where the scenario is executed. At a different location (e.g. in a city), the interaction sequence of the scenario might differ significantly. If the location is defined as a precondition, the scenario can only be executed at this location.

Furthermore we differentiate between system-internal scenarios, interaction scenarios, and context scenarios based on the extent of context information contained in a scenario (see Section 10.6).

Extent of context information in a scenario

Example 9-1: Context information in the scenario "Automatic braking manoeuvre"

Carl drives his car on the motorway at a speed of 50 mph. Peter, the driver of the car ahead of Carl, steps on the brake pedal firmly. After recognising that the car in front is braking, Carl pushes on the brake pedal as well. The on-board computer of Carl's vehicle detects that the safety distance to Peter's car is no longer maintained and issues a warning to the driver. The distance between the two cars continuously decreases. In order to support the driver, the on-board computer initiates an automated full braking. The computer informs Carl about the automatic braking manoeuvre. After the distance between the two cars stops decreasing, the on-board computer terminates the full braking manoeuvre. The on-board computer continues controlling the speed of Carl's car until the safety distance to Peter's car is maintained and informs Carl about the end of this "manoeuvre".

Examples of context information in the scenario:

- *Actor*: Carl
- *Role*: driver
- *Goal*: maintain safety distance
- *Precondition*: car drives at a speed of more than 50 mph (not stated in the scenario)
- *Postcondition*: no rear-end collision occurred and safety distance to vehicle ahead restored (not explicitly stated in the scenario)
- *Resource*: distance to Peter's car
- *Location*: on the motorway

9.3 Developing Scenarios for Each Context Facet

As explained in Section 6.2, the system context can be divided into four context facets: the subject facet, the usage facet, the IT system facet, and the development facet. A scenario can document information about just one or multiple context facets:

- *Subject facet*: In the subject facet, scenarios may be used to document, for example, the updating of information about relevant context objects represented in the system. For instance, a scenario "download electronic map" may be defined to describe the download of an electronic map required for calculating the route.
- *Usage facet*: In most cases, scenarios are used to specify usage workflows (see e.g. the scenario "navigate to destination" for the car assistance system presented in Tab. 11-3). Such scenarios mainly contain information about the usage facet. However, scenarios in the usage facet may also contain important information

about the other three facets. For instance, a usage scenario may also contain information about the objects that need to be represented in the system and the required level of detail of this representation.
- *IT system facet*: In the IT system facet, scenarios may be used in order to specify, for example, maintenance and backup procedures. For instance, a scenario "update firmware" may document the required interactions with the navigation system to update the firmware of the navigation system to a later version.
- *Development facet*: In the development facet, scenarios may be used for documenting sequences of interactions between the system and engineers who modify the system. A scenario in the development facet can describe, for instance, a sequence of interactions by which the route calculation algorithm of the navigation system is modified.

At present, the scenarios developed during requirements engineering are mainly usage scenarios. However, since the advantages of scenarios also apply to the other three context facets, the use of scenarios as middle-level abstractions should also be considered for the other three facets.

Chapter 10
Scenario Types

In this chapter, we explain different types of scenarios, namely:

- *Current-state and desired-state scenarios*
- *Positive and negative scenarios*
- *Misuse scenarios*
- *Descriptive, exploratory, and explanatory scenarios*
- *Instance and type scenarios*
- *System-internal scenarios, interaction scenarios, and context scenarios*
- *Main scenario, alternative scenarios, and exception scenarios*

Each scenario type is illustrated using examples. In addition, the grouping of main, alternative, and exception scenarios by means of use cases is explained.

Classification of scenarios

A scenario can be classified according to multiple different criteria such as its purpose, its contribution to goal satisfaction, or its abstraction level. In this chapter, we present different types of scenarios that result from applying different classification criteria. Note that, in many cases, it is possible to combine multiple classification criteria. Therefore, the presented scenario types are not mutually exclusive.

Current-state and desired-state scenarios

A scenario can document either the current state or the desired state of the system and its context. This leads to the distinction between current-state and desired-state scenarios (see Section 10.1).

Positive and negative scenarios

A scenario can be positive or negative. Positive scenarios document sequences of interactions that lead to the satisfaction of a specific goal or set of goals. Negative scenarios document sequences of interactions that result in the failure to satisfy a specific goal or set of goals. We explain positive and negative scenarios in Section 10.2.

Misuse scenarios

Misuse scenarios (also called misuse cases) document sequences of interactions in which a hostile actor uses the system against its purpose. We explain misuse scenarios in Section 10.3.

Descriptive, exploratory, and explanatory scenarios

The purpose of a scenario can be to describe, to explore, or to explain a sequence of interactions. A descriptive scenario presents a sequence of interactions in order to support the elicitation of requirements based on this sequence. An exploratory scenario documents alternative realisations and hence allows a set of different realisations to be explored. An explanatory scenario provides the background and rationales for particular interactions or interaction sequences. We explain descriptive, exploratory, and explanatory scenarios in Section 10.4.

Instance, type, and mixed scenarios

Based on the abstraction level of a scenario, we distinguish between instance scenarios, type scenarios, and mixed scenarios. Instance scenarios describe a sequence of concrete interactions between concrete actors. Type scenarios abstract from the concrete actors and interactions. Mixed scenarios contain both types of content: content at the instance level as well as content at the type level. Instance, type, and mixed scenarios are explained in Section 10.5.

System-internal, interaction, and context scenarios

With regard to the extent of context information contained in a scenario, we distinguish between system-internal scenarios (type A), interaction scenarios (type B), and context scenarios (type C). System-internal scenarios document interactions within the system. Interaction scenarios document interactions at the system boundary, i.e. interactions between the system and external actors (persons and systems). Context scenarios document interactions at the system boundary as well as additional information about the system context such as interactions among the external actors themselves. We explain these three types of scenarios in Section 10.6.

Main, alternative, and exception scenarios

The main scenario documents the normal way of satisfying a specific set of goals. Alternative scenarios describe alternative ways of satisfying this set of goals. Exception scenarios document how the system reacts to exceptional events in order to avoid a (critical) system failure. We explain these three types of scenarios in Section 10.7.

Use cases: grouping of main, alternative, and exception scenarios

In Section 10.8, we present use cases as a means for grouping a main scenario, a set of alternative scenarios, and a set of exception scenarios related to a specific set of goals.

10.1 Current-State and Desired-State Scenarios

Scenarios can be used to support both creating a conceptual model of an existing system in its context as well as creating a conceptual model of a desired system (see [Haumer et al. 1998]). Current-state scenarios support modelling an existing system in its context, whereas desired-state scenarios support modelling a desired system.

Current-State Scenarios

Indicative scenarios (current-state scenarios)

During the creation of a model of an existing system, scenarios are used, for instance, to document current system usage. Based on these usage scenarios, conceptual models of the current system are created (see Fig. 10-1). These models document specific aspects or perspectives of the reality described in the scenarios. For instance, a set of current-state scenarios can be used to support the definition of a functional model of the current system, i.e. a model documenting the functions of the current system, the data flows between the functions, and the data stores of the system (see Section 14.2 for more details about functional models). Scenarios that are used to support the modelling of the current state are called indicative scenarios (see [Jackson 1995; Haumer et al. 1998]) or current-state scenarios.

Desired-State Scenarios

Optative scenarios (desired-state scenarios)

In addition to using scenarios as indicative models, scenarios can also be used to describe desired system usage. Scenarios documenting desired system usage are called optative scenarios or desired-state scenarios since they describe a desired but not yet implemented reality (see [Jackson 1995]).

Scenarios as drivers for change

Indicative and optative scenarios are important drivers for change definition. Figure 10-1 depicts the relation between indicative and optative scenarios and their role in change definition.

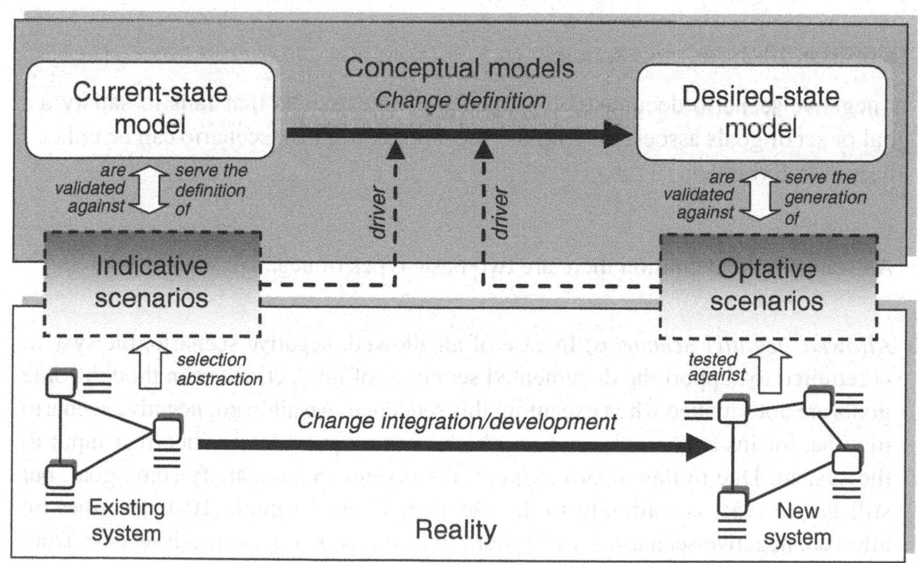

Fig. 10-1 *Indicative and optative scenarios (based on [Haumer et al. 1999])*

10.2 Positive and Negative Scenarios

Based on the mode of a scenario we differentiate positive and negative scenarios.

Positive Scenarios

Sequence of interactions to be supported by the system

A positive scenario documents a desired sequence of interactions leading to the satisfaction of a set of goals, i.e. stakeholder intentions, related to this scenario (if the scenario is executed successfully). An example of a positive scenario is the scenario "automatic braking manoeuvre" presented in Example 9-1. The execution of this scenario helps to avoid car accidents and hence reduces the danger for both the driver and the car. The system to be developed is required to support the sequence of interactions documented in a positive scenario, i.e. the system must be able to process the inputs and produce the outputs documented in the scenario. We define a positive scenario as follows:

Definition 10-1: *Positive scenario*

A positive scenario documents a sequence of interactions that satisfies a goal or set of goals associated with the scenario.

Negative Scenarios

Failure to satisfy goals

A negative scenario documents a sequence of interactions illustrating the failure to satisfy some goals specified for the system. We define the term negative scenario as follows:

Definition 10-2: *Negative scenario*

A negative scenario documents a sequence of interactions that fails to satisfy a goal or set of goals associated with the scenario. A negative scenario can be either allowed or forbidden.

Allowed and forbidden negative scenarios

As stated in the definition there are two basic types of negative scenarios:

- *Allowed, negative scenarios*: In case of an allowed, negative scenario, the system is required to support the documented sequence of interactions even though some goals are not satisfied when executing this sequence. An allowed, negative scenario may be, for instance, a scenario in which an actor provides an incorrect input to the system. Due to this incorrect input, the system cannot satisfy some goal, but still has to react accordingly to the incorrect input. Example 10-1 describes an allowed, negative scenario for the goal "Enable customers to withdraw cash from their account." In the example, the stated goal is not satisfied due to an insufficient account balance.

- *Forbidden, negative scenarios*: In case of a forbidden, negative scenario, the failure to satisfy the related goals cannot be tolerated, for instance, because the respective goals are critical for the system and/or its context. The execution of the sequence is regarded as a system failure. Such scenarios are also called failure scenarios. The stakeholders must take appropriate measures to prevent the execution of the sequence of interactions documented in a forbidden, negative scenario. They can, for instance, define allowed, negative scenarios that shall be executed when the event triggering the forbidden, negative scenario occurs. By executing the allowed, negative scenario the imminent system failure is prevented. Example 10-2 presents a forbidden, negative scenario for the goal "Enable customers to withdraw cash from their account". In the scenario, the customer's account is charged although the ATM dispenses no money. Clearly this behaviour of the ATM is not tolerable.

Example 10-1: Allowed, negative scenario

Chris inserts her bank card into the slot of the ATM (automated teller machine). Chris enters enters her personal identification number and the amount to withdraw. The ATM informs Chris that withdrawing the desired amount is not possible because the amount exceeds her balance.

Example 10-2: Forbidden, negative scenario

Jack inserts his bank card into the slot of the ATM. Jack enters enters his personal identification number and the amount to withdraw. The ATM charges the desired amount from Jack's account. When dispensing the money, the dispensing mechanism of the ATM fails.

Positive and negative scenarios complement each other

We recommend using positive as well as negative scenarios in requirements engineering. Negative scenarios can be used to delimit positive scenarios, i.e. to make clear which possible interaction sequences do not satisfy the specified goals. Additionally, in case of a negative scenario, the stakeholders must define whether the negative scenario is allowed or forbidden.

10.3 Misuse Scenarios

Intentional misuse of the system by a hostile actor

Abuse scenarios (see [McDermott and Fox 1999]) or misuse scenarios (see [Alexander 2003; Sindre and Opdahl 2001; Sindre and Opdahl 2005]) document the usage of a system against its purpose. In other words, a misuse scenario (sometimes also called a misuse case) describes a sequence of interactions in which a hostile actor uses the system against the stakeholders' intentions. The execution of a misuse scenario represents a threat for the system, the stakeholders, or other systems in the context. We define the term misuse scenario as follows:

Definition 10-3: *Misuse scenario (misuse case)*

A misuse scenario documents a sequence of interactions in which a hostile actor uses the system against the stakeholders' intention.

Example of a misuse scenario

Example 10-3 presents a misuse scenario that is related to the scenario shown in Example 9-1. In this misuse scenario, a hostile actor knowingly causes a dangerous situation and thereby misuses the car safety system.

Example 10-3: Misuse scenario for the car safety system

Tom, the driver of another car, intentionally cuts in right ahead of Carl in order to cause Carl's vehicle to perform a full braking. During this braking manoeuvre Carl is injured.

Eliciting safety and security requirements

Misuse scenarios are especially relevant when the system to be developed intrinsically deals with safety or security issues. Based on the elicited misuse scenarios, the requirements engineers can define safety and security requirements for such a system.

10.4 Descriptive, Exploratory, and Explanatory Scenarios

Purpose of the scenario

Based on the purpose of a scenario, we distinguish between descriptive, explanatory, and exploratory scenarios.

Descriptive Scenarios

Refinement of requirements and goals

A descriptive scenario describes a process or workflow for the purpose of understanding its operations, involved agents, triggering events etc. (see [Rolland et al. 1998a]). Descriptive scenarios are typically developed jointly by a group of stakeholders who thereby identify and capture required functions, relevant events, or new stakeholders. Descriptive scenarios primarily support the elicitation and refinement of goals and solution-oriented requirements (see [Rumbaugh et al. 1991; Jacobson et al. 1992]).

The scenario in Example 10-4 has been collaboratively developed by a group of stakeholders. It describes the required interactions between a driver and a navigation system for entering the destination. The development of the scenario initiated the identification of sub-goals and associated functions of which the stakeholders were not previously aware (for instance, the system shall offer a certain set of options when it cannot clearly recognise a destination entered by voice).

Example 10-4: Descriptive scenario "enter destination"

Carl wants to drive by car to Union Street in Plymouth. Carl uses the navigation system of the car to find the shortest route. He selects "enter destination". The navigation system displays "Please enter the desired destination either by

(*to be continued*)

Example 10-4 (*continued*)

voice input or manually". Carl decides to enter the destination by voice entry and says "Plymouth". Due to noise in the background and his poor pronunciation the system cannot recognise the destination clearly. The system displays the destination that it has recognised from the voice entry with the highest probability: "Portsmouth". The system also displays the message "Your entry could not be recognised unambiguously" as well as the following options:

(1) Accept destination (yes/no)
(2) New entry (new)
(3) Display similar locations (similar)
(4) Manual entry (press key "M")

Carl says "similar" and the system lists the locations "Portsmouth", "Plymouth", etc. Carl says "Plymouth" and the system selects Plymouth as the destination.

Exploratory Scenarios

Exploration and evaluation of possible, alternative solutions

An exploratory scenario is created to explore and evaluate possible, alternative solutions in order to support the selection of one alternative solution (see e.g. [Campbell 1992; Carroll 1995; Rolland et al. 1998a]). An exploratory scenario can be used, for instance, to explore and evaluate the effects of different solution-oriented requirements which represent alternative solutions for satisfying a specific goal. With exploratory scenarios, the stakeholders typically explore, at an early stage of requirements engineering, the effects of the possible, alternative solutions on system usage. To support the exploration and evaluation, exploratory scenarios should be related to the artefacts defining the requirements for the possible solutions (e.g. solution-oriented requirements models).

Example 10-5 presents a scenario that describes two different solutions for entering the starting point of a route. The scenario also documents the rationale for each possible realisation.

Example 10-5: Exploratory scenario "enter starting point"

Carl wants to drive to a destination using the navigation system of his car. The first question is whether the starting point of the journey is always the current position of the car or whether Carl can define the starting point himself. The automatic selection of the starting point avoids an additional user interaction and supports a quick navigation. Allowing entry of the starting point would facilitate the calculation of routes with starting points other than the current position. With this facility, the system could be used as a means for travel planning. Carl could find out, for instance, how far it is from Paris to Nice and how long it would take to get there independent of the current position of his car. A third possibility is to allow the user to choose between the function "navigation" (using the current position as starting point) and "navigation with entry of the starting point" in the user menu. Therein, the function "navigation" would be specified as the default setting.

Explanatory Scenarios

Justify and explain interactions

An explanatory scenario is created with the aim of explaining a goal, an alternative solution, or a sequence of interactions. An explanatory scenario typically includes rationales for the individual interactions as well as the sequence of interactions. In addition, an explanatory scenario can include alternative views of the different stakeholders (see [Nardi 1992; Wright 1992; Rolland et al. 1998a]).

An example of an explanatory scenario is presented in Example 10-6. This scenario does not only describe the sequence of interactions but also provides rationales for specific interaction steps (underlined in the example).

Example 10-6: Explanatory scenario "automatic braking manoeuvre"

As the distance between the two cars decreases rapidly, there is a high risk of a rear-end collision. A rapid change of lane might cause the car to skid or spin since the car is driving on the motorway at a high speed of more than 55 mph. Hence, prior to changing lane, the speed of the car must be reduced. Consequently, the on-board computer initiates an automatic emergency braking manoeuvre. As the antilock braking system ensures that the car remains steerable during a braking manoeuvre, Carl could safely change lane during the manoeuvre. In order to avoid the driver being startled by the automatic braking, the system informs Carl about the initiation of the emergency braking. After having restored a safe distance to the car driving ahead, the on-board computer passes control back to Carl. The system notifies Carl about the passing over of control in order to allow him to prepare to take over control.

!

Hint 10-1: *Descriptive, exploratory, and explanatory scenarios*

- ❑ Use descriptive scenarios to illustrate the meaning of goals and requirements, and in particular, to detail innovative ideas as well as innovative solutions.
- ❑ Use exploratory scenarios in order to support decision making. Especially when the decision criteria are unknown, exploratory scenarios help to find possible decision criteria. If different stakeholders document exploratory scenarios independently of each other, the stakeholders' different viewpoints become clear.
- ❑ Use explanatory scenarios to explain complex facts. Furthermore, use explanatory scenarios to explain the additional value of the system in detail to persons who are not involved in the development process.

10.5 Instance and Type Scenarios

Concrete vs. abstract content

The content of a scenario may be documented at different levels of abstraction. If the content of a scenario is at a concrete or instance level, the scenario is called an instance scenario. If a scenario is documented at an abstract or type level, it is called a type scenario (see [Carroll 1995]). The inputs and outputs of the interactions in a type scenario are types as well.

Instance Scenarios

Concrete instances of interactions

An instance scenario describes a concrete (existing or envisioned) sequence of interactions between concrete actors. The interactions of an instance scenario document concrete inputs and outputs, e.g. the input "Plymouth" which is entered as the destination of a route in Example 10-4. The actors of an instance scenario are concrete persons such as "Carl Miller" or concrete systems such as "the X1000 mail server installed in our company". Scenarios at the instance level are also referred to as "user stories" or "concrete scenarios" in the literature (see [Potts et al. 1994]).

Concrete inputs, outputs, and actors

An instance scenario does not have to define all its content, such as the context information at the instance level. It is sufficient to describe the actors and the interactions, i.e. the inputs and outputs, at the instance level.

Example 10-7 presents an excerpt of an instance scenario. This scenario documents actors as well as inputs and outputs at the instance level (e.g. a concrete driver, a concrete navigation system, and a concrete destination).

Example 10-7: Example of an instance scenario

Carl wants to drive to Union Street in Plymouth. Carl uses the navigation system of his VW Golf with licence number "E-IS-12". Carl selects "enter destination" in the main menu, enters the destination "Union Street in Plymouth", and presses the key "calculate route".

Type Scenarios

Abstraction from real sequences of interactions

A type scenario abstracts from the concrete actors, inputs, and outputs of a specific sequence of interactions. A type scenario refers to types of actors such as the role of a person (e.g. "driver"). Type scenarios describe interactions by means of types of inputs and types of outputs. Hence, the content of a type scenario abstracts from real processes, persons, and systems as well as specific inputs and outputs. A type scenario represents a set of instance scenarios in a similar way as a class in object-oriented analysis represents a set of objects with similar properties. By instantiating a type scenario with concrete persons, systems, functions, events, states, and conditions, instance scenarios are created (see [Rolland et al. 1998a]). Type scenarios are also called "abstract scenarios" or "conceptual scenarios" (see [Carroll 2000; Rolland et al. 1998a]).

Example of a type scenario

Example 10-8 presents an excerpt of a type scenario. This scenario documents actors as well as inputs and outputs at the type level (e.g. the driver, the navigation system, and the destination).

Example 10-8: Example of a type scenario

The driver wants to drive to a destination using the navigation system. He enters the destination. The system calculates the route from the current position of the car to the entered destination.

Mixed Scenarios

Mixed scenarios in practice

In practice, typically, mixed scenarios are used. Mixed or hybrid scenarios contain content at both the instance and the type level. For this reason, we prefer to speak of scenario content at the instance level or at the type level rather than speaking of instance and type scenarios. The reasons for the intermingling of different abstraction levels within a scenario include:

- Important content of the scenario shall be described in detail at the instance level, and less important content shall be described in an abstract way, i.e. at the type level.
- Content that is not completely understood is described at the instance level. By describing part of the content at the instance level, errors shall be avoided that might result from the early abstraction of poorly understood aspects of the scenario. The content of the scenario that is well understood is described at the type level.
- Conflicting or potentially conflicting content is described at the instance level in order to support communication among the stakeholders and conflict resolution.

Example 10-9 presents an excerpt of a mixed scenario. It contains content at both the instance and the type level. The system shall provide different possibilities to enter a destination. Therefore, these options are described in detail at the instance level. Other information is described at the type level (e.g. the driver and the system).

Example 10-9: Example of a mixed scenario

The driver activates the navigation system. The system asks the driver: "Please state your destination or press the 'enter destination' button on the main menu". The driver presses the "enter destination" button and enters the destination manually. After entering the destination the driver initiates the calculation of the route.

!

Hint 10-2: *Documenting the content of a scenario at the instance level*

To determine whether the content of a scenario should be documented at the instance level, check:

- whether a detailed consideration of the content is necessary because the content is not understood sufficiently well
- whether there is a potential conflict regarding the content
- whether the content is of particular importance

10.6 System-Internal, Interaction, and Context Scenarios

The scope of a scenario may be restricted to either the internals of a system or to the interactions between the system and its context, or it may also cover the interactions within the context. Depending on the scope of a scenario, we differentiate between system-internal scenarios, interaction scenarios, and context scenarios (see [Pohl and Haumer 1997]).

System-Internal Scenarios (Type A Scenarios)

Interaction of system components

System-internal scenarios (type A scenarios) focus exclusively on system-internal interactions, i.e. interactions that occur within the system boundaries. In other words, system-internal scenarios do not document any interactions between the system and the context. System-internal scenarios are used, for example, for specifying the collaboration of subsystems. We define the term system-internal scenario (type A scenario) as follows:

D

Definition 10-4: *System-internal scenario (type A scenario)*

A system-internal scenario documents only system-internal interactions, i.e. a sequence of interactions among different parts of a system.

Based on [Pohl and Haumer 1997]

Characterisation of a type A scenario

As illustrated in Fig. 10-2, type A scenarios are situated within the system boundaries. The figure schematically shows a system-internal scenario that documents the interactions between three system components. The scenario makes no reference to the system context (which is delimited from the system by a dashed line). Therefore, it is not obvious, for instance, why the interactions between the three components take place or how they contribute to the value the system offers its users.

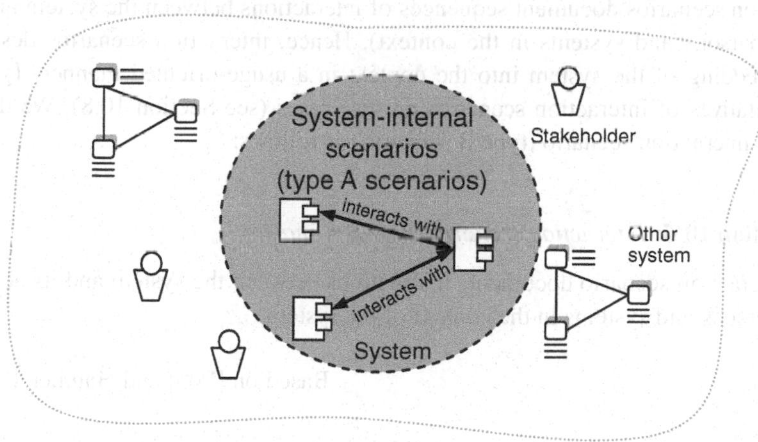

Fig. 10-2 System-internal scenarios (type A scenarios)

Example of system-internal scenario

Example 10-10 presents a system-internal scenario documented using natural language. This scenario documents a sequence of interactions between three components: "navigation control", "localisation", and "display control". Since the scenario makes no reference to the system context, it is difficult to conceive from the description of the scenario why these interactions take place. The stakeholders can only conjecture about the goals behind this sequence of interactions.

Example 10-10: System-internal scenario

The component "navigation control" requests the GPS coordinates from the "localisation" component. The "localisation" component provides the coordinates to the "navigation control". The component "navigation control" invokes the component "display control" and passes on the current position and the destination. The component "screen input" transmits the route parameters to the component "navigation control". Therewith, the "navigation control" component calculates the final route.

Relation to interaction scenario

When a system-internal scenario is related to an interaction scenario (type B scenario; see below), a relationship is established between the system-internal interactions and the interactions between the system and the context. A system-internal scenario or fragment thereof documents how the system realises some interaction with the context through a sequence of system-internal interactions. It thus shows how the system determines the reaction (output to the context) to an external event (input from the context) or a temporal event. Type A scenarios are typically used during architectural design. They are developed based upon type B and type C scenarios, which are explained in the following sections.

In our COSMOD-RE method (see Part VII), we explain the use of system-internal scenarios for refining interaction scenarios in order to support the development of requirements for the system components.

Interaction Scenarios (Type B Scenarios)

Interaction sequences between system and system users

Interaction scenarios document sequences of interactions between the system and its actors (persons and systems in the context). Hence, interaction scenarios describe the embedding of the system into the context in a usage-oriented manner. Typical representatives of interaction scenarios are use cases (see Section 10.8). We define the term interaction scenario (type B scenario) as follows:

Definition 10-5: *Interaction scenario (type B scenario)*

An interaction scenario documents interactions between the system and its actors (i.e. persons and systems in the context of the system).

Based on [Pohl and Haumer 1997]

Characterisation of a type B scenario

Figure 10-3 depicts schematically the interactions defined in a type B scenario, i.e. interactions between a system and its context. The dashed line in Fig. 10-3 represents the context boundary, i.e. the boundary between the relevant and the irrelevant context. A type B scenario describes the interactions with the context (in Fig. 10-3 four possible interactions with three persons and another system are shown). It does not describe the system-internal workflows.

Rationale for a type A scenario

As stated above, a type B scenario can be related to a type A scenario in order to document the reasons for the interactions in a type A scenario. The scenario described

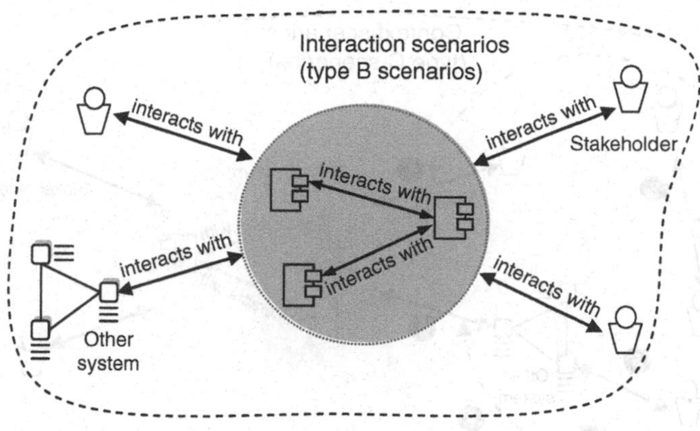

Fig. 10-3 *Interaction scenarios (type B scenarios)*

in Example 10-4 is a type B scenario, since it only considers interactions between the driver (user of the system) and the navigation system.

Context Scenarios (Type C Scenarios)

Additional context information

Context scenarios (type C scenarios) document, in addition to the direct interactions between the system and its context, also information about the context.

Indirect use of the system and its outputs

The additional context information may comprise, for example, interactions between system users and other persons who are not directly involved in the system usage or interactions between systems in the context of the system to be developed. A context scenario can also describe the influence of context aspects on the persons, systems, and interactions defined in the scenario. For example, the influence of business objectives, business processes, and organisational policies on the persons, systems, and their interactions may be documented. We define context scenario (type C scenario) as follows:

Definition 10-6: *Context scenario (type C scenario)*

A context scenario documents the direct interactions between the system and its actors as well as additional context information that is relevant for the system usage or the system itself, e.g. interactions among the actors as well as the indirect users of the system.

Based on [Pohl and Haumer 1997]

Figure 10-4 illustrates the possible range of context information documented in context scenarios (type C scenarios):

Rationale for interactions

- The interaction between the stakeholder and the system marked with ❶ takes place due to the interaction between two stakeholders in the context (see ❷ in Fig. 10-4). In a context scenario, both interactions can be documented.

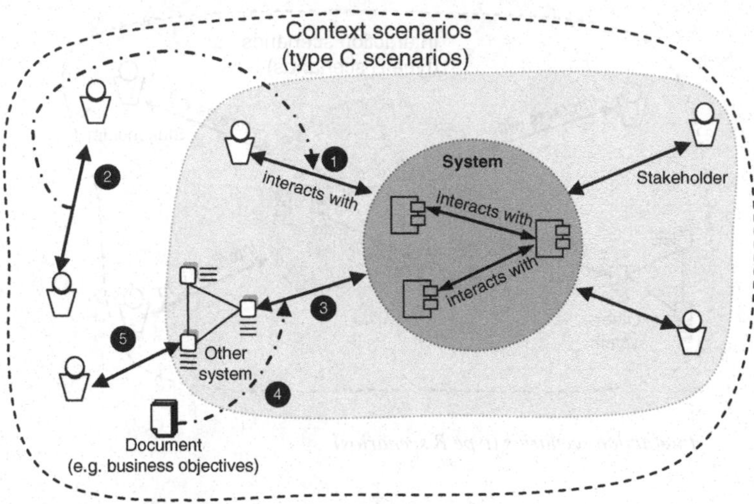

Fig. 10-4 *Context scenarios (type C scenarios)*

Usage of system outputs

- ❑ The interaction marked with ❸ between the system to be developed and some external system is required due to the business objectives defined in a document (see ❹ in Fig. 10-4). In addition, the external system informs another stakeholder about the result of the interaction (see ❺ in Fig. 10-4). The stated kinds of context information (❹ and ❺) can be documented in a context scenario along with the direct interaction ❸.

Example: source of system inputs

Example 10-11 contains a context scenario that documents the direct interactions between a driver and a navigation system as well as context information about the navigation system such as interactions in the context of the navigation system. It documents interactions between the driver's mobile phone and the route-planning system of the mobile network operator that are executed when the required maps are not available in the navigation system of the car.

Example 10-11: Context scenario (type C scenario) for the extended usage of a navigation system

The driver wants to drive to a destination located outside the maps that were shipped with the navigation system (the system). Since the navigation system cannot guide the driver without the maps, the driver decides to let the mobile network operator perform the routing.

The driver establishes a connection to the mobile network operator with his mobile phone and uses the online "route planning" service of the mobile network operator (the external system). The driver enters the starting point as well as the destination and the routing parameters (quickest route) in the user dialog of his mobile phone. The route-planning system calculates the route and transfers the route and the corresponding maps in a standardised format to the mobile phone.

The driver establishes a data connection to the navigation system of the car and transfers the received data. The navigation system of the car is now able to navigate to the destination.

!

Hint 10-3: *Type A, type B, and type C scenarios*

- ❑ Always use context scenarios (type C) in requirements engineering, if possible, i.e. enrich the scenarios with context information.
- ❑ Document the important context aspects in context scenarios and thereby relate the solution-oriented requirements to the context. Document, whenever required, relevant background information about the scenario and the individual interaction steps such as rationales of the scenario and the added value of the scenario.
- ❑ Derive system-internal scenarios (type A) from the context scenarios (type C) to support architectural design, i.e. to refine or detail the context scenarios through system-internal interactions.

10.7 Main Scenario, Alternative Scenarios, and Exception Scenarios

Classification of scenarios based on the associated goals

Typically, a goal can be satisfied in different ways. Hence, for a specific goal or set of goals, several scenarios exist, all of which satisfy these goals. With respect to a specific goal or set of goals, one can differentiate between the main scenario, alternative scenarios, and exception scenarios.

Main Scenario

Typical way of satisfying a set of goals

The main scenario documents the most common sequence of interactions for satisfying a goal. Hence, it documents the standard way of satisfying the goal. We define a "main scenario" as follows:

Definition 10-7: *Main scenario*

The main scenario documents the sequence of interactions that is normally executed in order to satisfy a specific set of goals.

Alternative Scenarios

Alternative ways of satisfying a set of goals

Alternative scenarios define alternative sequences of interactions for a main scenario, i.e. they document modified flows of interactions of the original scenario. An alternative scenario differs from the main scenario in one or multiple interaction steps and/or in the order of the interaction steps. However, the alternative scenarios of a specific main scenario still satisfy the goals that are associated with the main scenario.

Definition 10-8: *Alternative scenario*

An alternative scenario documents a sequence of interactions that can be executed instead of the main scenario and that results in the satisfaction of the goals that are associated with the main scenario.

Example 10-12 illustrates how an alternative scenario can be documented by defining an alternative interaction step for the main scenario:

Example 10-12: Definition of alternative interaction steps

Excerpt of the main scenario:
Step 11: ...
Step 12: The driver chooses a destination by pointing on an electronic map.
Step 13: ..
Excerpt of an alternative scenario:
Step 11: ...
Step 12a: The driver chooses a destination from a list of destinations.
Step 13: ...

Exception Scenarios

Reaction to known exceptions

During the execution of a scenario, exceptional events may occur, such as hardware failures, the breakdown of a network connection, or an illegal user input. An exception scenario documents how the system shall react to an exceptional event which occurs in some interaction step during the execution of another scenario. Due to the occurrence of the exceptional event it is impossible to satisfy the entire set of goals associated with this scenario. Hence, neither the normal course of interactions nor some alternative course can be performed. However, by executing the exception scenario, the system tries to satisfy the goals associated with the scenario to the extent that is achievable after the exceptional event has occured. Note that exception scenarios are still scenarios that the system must support (see Section 10.2). We define an exception scenario as follows:

Definition 10-9: *Exception scenario*

An exception scenario documents a sequence of interactions that is executed instead of the interactions documented in another scenario (main, alternative, or exception scenario) when an exceptional event occurs. As a consequence of the exceptional event, one or multiple goals associated with the original scenario cannot be satisfied.

Example 10-13 presents an exception scenario for the scenario "enter destination" of the navigation system.

Example 10-13: Exception scenario for the navigation system

Excerpt of the main scenario:
Step 12: ...
Step 13: The system confirms the successful entry of the destination.
Step 14: The system informs the driver about the successful calculation of the route to the destination.

(to be continued)

Example 10-13 *(continued)*

Step 15: ...
Excerpt of an exception scenario:
Step 13: ...
Step 14a: The navigation system detects that its power supply is about to break down.
Step 15a: The navigation system switches itself off.

Relating alternative and exception scenarios to the main scenario

Alternative scenarios and exception scenarios can be documented by replacing parts of a main scenario. Alternatively, a main or alternative scenario can be documented as a separate scenario. Independently of the choice of how alternative and exception scenarios are documented, we recommend relating each alternative and exceptional scenario to the corresponding main scenario. This can be achieved, for instance, by using the template for use cases presented in Section 11.3. Using the template ensures that the following information about the relationship between an alternative or exception scenario and the corresponding main scenario is documented:

- Which alternative and exception scenarios exist for the main scenario
- Which interaction sequence(s) in the main scenario are replaced by which interaction sequence(s) in the alternative or exception scenario
- When an alternative scenario should be executed and which event(s) result(s) in the execution of an exception scenario

Context information

By documenting alternative and exception scenarios, additional context information of a scenario (the main scenario) is documented. Moreover, comprehensive documentation of the different ways of satisfying the set of goals associated with the main scenario is provided. For this reason, we recommend grouping the main scenario, the alternative scenarios, and the exception scenarios related to a specific set of goals together in a use case (see Section 10.8).

!

Hint 10-4: *Main, alternative, and exception scenarios*

- For each main scenario, define the alternative scenarios that must be supported by the system.
- In addition, define known exception scenarios in order to account for known error conditions.
- Document which interaction steps in the main scenario are replaced by an alternative scenario.
- Document the conditions under which an exception scenario shall be executed.

10.8 Use Cases: Grouping Scenarios

Use cases were suggested in OOSE (Object-Oriented Software Engineering) [Jacobson et al. 1992] for the first time. Use cases group a main scenario with the corresponding alternative and exception scenarios (see e.g. [Salinesi 2004]). A "use case" is defined as follows:

Definition 10-10: *Use case*

The specification of sequences of actions, including variant sequences and error sequences, that a system, subsystem, or class can perform by interacting with outside objects to provide a service of value.

[Rumbaugh et al. 2005]

Constituents of a use case

A use case contains:

- *Context information*: The context information documented in a use case comprises, among other things, the stakeholders' goals with respect to this use case as well as preconditions and postconditions for the execution of the use case (see Section 9.2).
- *Main scenario*: Each use case has exactly one main scenario (see Section 10.7) that describes the typical sequence of interaction steps satisfying the goal or set of goals related to the use case.
- *Alternative scenarios*: A use case may have one or multiple alternative scenarios (see Section 10.7). An alternative scenario documents a sequence of alternative interaction steps that replace parts of or the entire main scenario.
- *Exception scenarios*: A use case may have one or multiple exception scenarios (see Section 10.7) that define how the system reacts to exceptions that occur during the execution of the main scenario, one of the alternative scenarios, or another exception scenario.

Relation between main, alternative, and exception scenarios

Figure 10-5 illustrates the relationship between a main scenario, two alternative scenarios (1 and 2) as well as one exception scenario (E1). Each alternative scenario is defined by one or several sequences of alternative interaction steps. The alternative scenario (1) consists of the sequences (1a) to (1b) and (1c) to (1d). The sequence (1a)

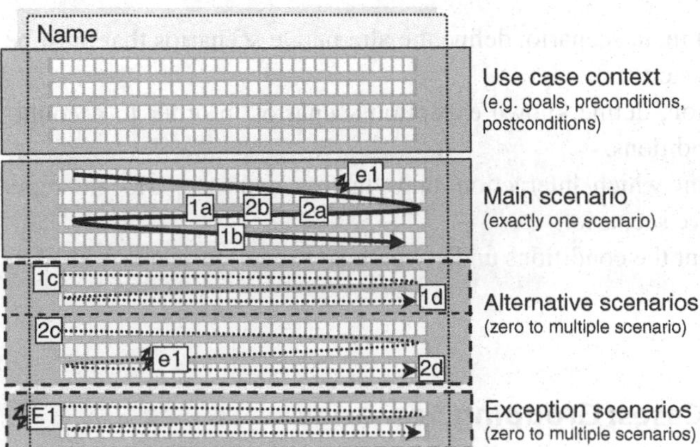

Fig. 10-5 *Constituents of a use case*

to (1b) replaces parts of the main scenario; the sequence (1c) to (1d) is executed in addition to the steps documented in the main scenario. If the event (e1) occurs, the interaction steps of the main scenario or the alternative scenario (2) are aborted in order to execute the exception scenario (E1).

Use Case Scenarios

Termination of a use case

If alternative and/or exception scenarios are defined for the main scenario of a use case, depending on the defined alternatives and exceptions, there are several possible, valid sequences of interactions. In addition, alternative scenarios that replace different parts of the main scenario may be combined with each other. Choosing different combinations of alternative scenarios generates further interaction sequences for a use case. We refer to the set of all interaction sequences that are defined explicitly or implicitly by a use case and that lead to a defined termination of the use case as the use case scenarios.

Definition 10-11: *Use case scenario*

A use case scenario is a valid sequence of interactions that results from the main, alternative, and exception scenarios defined for the use case and that leads to a defined termination of the use case. Therein, termination means that the use case scenario either leads to the satisfaction of the goals associated with the use case or to a defined abort.

Chapter 11
Documenting Scenarios

In this chapter, we describe different techniques for documenting scenarios and use cases, both using natural language as well as using models. With regard to the documentation of scenarios and use cases using natural language, we present:

- *Narrative scenarios, i.e. scenarios documented in natural language as short narrations*
- *The tabular description of the interaction sequences of scenarios*
- *A reference template for the structured documentation of scenarios*
- *A reference template for the structured documentation of use cases*

With regard to the model-based documentation of scenarios and use cases, we explain:

- *The utilisation of UML sequence diagrams for documenting interaction sequences of scenarios*
- *The utilisation of UML activity diagrams for documenting the control flows of scenarios and use cases*
- *Use case diagrams for documenting relationships between use cases and between use cases and actors*

K. Pohl, *Requirements Engineering*,

11.1 Narrative Scenarios

Documentation in natural language

A narrative scenario documents a sequence of interactions using natural language. It has the form of a short narration. The term "narrative" is rooted in psychology. Narrative psychology is a branch of psychology that deals with the way people work up and communicate their thoughts and experiences by means of stories (see [McAdams et al. 2006]).

Advantages of narrative scenarios

In requirements engineering, narrative scenarios are an important means for supporting the elicitation of knowledge about the system and its context. Due to the narrative form and the use of natural language, narrative scenarios are typically comprehensible to all stakeholders (see e.g. [Holbrook 1990; Erickson 1995]). Within narrative scenarios, information can be communicated at different abstraction levels. For instance, important aspects can be described in a more concrete way and less important aspects in a more abstract way (see Section 10.5). In a narrative scenario, descriptive, exploratory, and explanatory elements, as well as alternative and exceptional steps can be documented together with structural, functional, behavioural, and quality aspects. Example 11-1 presents a fragment of a narrative scenario that contains most of these aspects and elements (underlined in Example 11-1).

Example 11-1: Excerpt from a narrative scenario

The driver assistance system includes a (sub-)system for avoiding rear-end collisions. This system comprises (❶) distance sensors that (❷) permanently check the distance to the vehicle driving ahead (❸) in order to avoid an imminent rear-end collision. (❹) If the system detects that the distance falls below the safety distance yet is still outside the critical range, an acoustic warning signal sounds. (❺) Alternatively, a symbol or message may be displayed on the driver display in the cockpit of the car. If the driver has not reacted to the warning after 2 s and the distance between the two cars still decreases, (❻) the system reduces the speed of the car. (❼) If the distance (in metres) falls below one quarter of the driving speed (in km/h) at any time, the system initiates emergency braking.

Explanation:

(❶) Static/structural aspect
(❷) Functional aspect
(❸) Explanatory aspect
(❹) Behavioural aspect
(❺) Exploratory aspect
(❻) Step of an alternative scenario
(❼) Condition for an exception scenario

!

Hint 11-1: *Narrative scenarios*

Use narrative scenarios in order to:

- ❑ Elicit information about the context
- ❑ Elicit information about goals and requirements

Detail important aspects of narrative scenarios through structured textual scenarios and define, for example, alternative scenarios, exception scenarios, descriptive scenarios, and explanatory scenarios.

11.2 Structured Scenarios

The comprehensibility and readability of scenarios written in natural language can be significantly improved by documenting the interaction steps and/or the context information in a structured manner. The structured documentation of scenarios is described, e.g. in [Rumbaugh et al. 1991; Jacobson et al. 1992; Cockburn 2001].

11.2.1 Structured Documentation of Scenario Steps

Two approaches for the structured textual documentation of interaction sequences of a scenario have proven their worth:

- ❑ The enumeration of scenario steps
- ❑ The tabular documentation of interaction sequences

Sequential numbering of the interaction steps

Enumerating scenario steps means separating the individual interaction steps of the scenario from each other and numbering the scenario steps sequentially. The numbering of the steps indicates the sequential progression of the interaction steps of the scenario. The number of each step also represents a unique identifier within the scenario. This identifier can be used as a reference to a particular step. Furthermore, each step must state at least the name of the actor who initiates the interaction and a concise description of the interaction. Example 11-2 illustrates the structured documentation of the interaction steps of a scenario. The structured documentation of scenario steps using natural language is further supported by the rules presented in Section 11.4.

Example 11-2: Enumeration of scenario steps

(1) The driver activates the navigation system.
(2) The navigation system determines the current position of the car.
(3) The navigation system asks for the desired destination.
(4) The driver enters the destination.
(5) The navigation system identifies the relevant part of the map.
(6) The navigation system displays the map of the destination area.

(to be continued)

Example 11-2 *(continued)*

(7) The navigation system asks for the routing options.
(8) The driver selects the desired routing options.
(9) The navigation system calculates the route.
(10) The navigation system informs the driver that the route has been calculated.
(11) The navigation system creates a list of waypoints.
(12) The navigation system displays the next waypoint of the calculated route.

Tabular documentation of interaction steps

In the case of tabular documentation, the individual scenario steps are documented in separate cells of a table that contains one column for each actor involved in the scenario. The steps of the scenario are described separately, numbered line by line, and entered from top to bottom into the rows of the table according to the progression of the interactions (see the example in Tab. 11-1). Each scenario step is shown in the column corresponding to the actor who initiates the interaction. If necessary, several interactions may be listed in a row to document that these interactions are performed concurrently. In contrast to enumerated documentation of scenario steps, in tabular documentation the initiating actor of each interaction step is directly evident from the table (Example 11-2). Therefore, the actors do not need to be stated in the individual interaction steps of the scenario.

Tab. 11-1 *Tabular documentation of the interaction sequence of a scenario*

Scenario "Navigate to destination"	
Driver	**Navigation system**
1. Activates the navigation system.	
	2. Determines the current position.
	3. Asks for the destination.
4. Enters the destination.	
	5. Identifies the relevant part of the map.
	6. Displays a map of the target area.
	7. Asks for the routing options.
8. Enters the routing options.	
	9. Calculates the route.
	10. Displays that the route has been calculated.
	11. Creates a list of waypoints.
	12. Displays the next waypoint.

!

Hint 11-2: *Structured documentation of scenarios*

Use the tabular style for the final documentation of main, alternative, and exception scenarios. Number the individual interaction steps and enter them into the column corresponding to the actor who initiates the interaction or who is responsible for the interaction step.

Annotation: However, take care not to use the tabular style at a too early stage. Exploit the benefits of narrative scenarios, first, in order to elicit rich content such as solution-oriented requirements, goals, context information, and further interaction steps. Afterwards, define the interaction sequences of the scenarios more accurately by documenting them in the tabular style. The tabular documentation also simplifies the further use of the scenarios in the development process.

11.2.2 Reference Templates for Scenarios

Documentation of interaction sequences and context information

Reference templates support the structured documentation of the interaction sequence of a scenario (see Section 11.2.1) as well as the context information (see Section 9.2) and the management information (see Section 18.3) of the scenario. Table 11-2 shows a reference template for the structured documentation of a scenario.

Tab. 11-2 *Template for documenting a scenario in natural language*

Scenario Template		
No.	**Section**	**Content/Explanation**
1	Identifier	Unique identifier of the scenario
2	Name	Unique name of the scenario
3	Author	Names of the authors who have worked on the scenario description
4	Version	Current version number of the scenario
5	Change history	List of the changes applied to the scenario including, for each change, the date of the change, the version number, the author, and, if necessary, the reason for and the subject of the change
6	Priority	Indication of the importance of the described scenario according to the prioritisation technique used
7	Criticality	Criticality of the scenario, e.g. for the success of the system
8	Source	Denomination of the source ([stakeholder | document | system]) from which the scenario stems
9	Responsible stakeholder	The stakeholder responsible for the scenario
10	Short description	Concise description of the scenario (approximately 1/4 page)
11	Scenario type	Classification of the scenario based on the scenario types presented in Chapter 10, e.g. context, interaction, or system-internal scenario
12	Goal(s)	Goal(s) that shall be satisfied by executing the scenario including identifiers pointing to the associated goal definitions *Relevant rules* (see Section 11.4): ❑ Name the goal of the scenario explicitly (rule 10) ❑ Focus on the achievement of the goal (rule 11) *Rules for documenting goals* (see Section 8.2): ❑ Document goals concisely (rule 1) ❑ Use the active voice (rule 2) ❑ Document the stakeholder's intention precisely (rule 3) ❑ Decompose high-level goals into more concrete sub-goals (rule 4) ❑ State the additional value of the goal (rule 5) ❑ Document the reasons for introducing a goal (rule 6) ❑ Avoid defining unnecessary restrictions (rule 7)
13	Actors	Indication of the primary actor and other actors *Relevant rules* (see Section 11.4): ❑ Name the actors explicitly (rule 9)
14	Precondition	A list of necessary prerequisites that need to be fulfilled before the execution of the scenario can be initiated
15	Postcondition	A list of conditions that hold after execution of the scenario

Tab. 11-2 *(continued)*

Scenario Template		
No.	**Section**	**Content/Explanation**
16	Result	Description of the outputs that are created during execution of the scenario
17	Scenario steps	Detailed interaction sequence of the scenario: narrative/sequentially numbered/tabular *Relevant rules* (see Section 11.4): ❑ Use the present tense (rule 1) ❑ Use the active voice (rule 2) ❑ Use the subject–predicate–object (SPO) sentence structure (rule 3) ❑ Avoid modal verbs (rule 4) ❑ Only one interaction per sentence (rule 5) ❑ Number each scenario step (rule 6) ❑ Only one sequence of interactions per scenario (rule 7) ❑ Describe the scenario from the "view from afar" (rule 8) ❑ Explicitly name the actors (rule 9) ❑ Focus on illustrating the satisfaction of the goal (rule 11)
18	Qualities	Cross references to quality requirements
19	Relationships to other scenarios	Relationships of the scenario to other scenarios
20	Supplementary information	Additional information regarding this scenario

Specific and general attributes

The scenario attributes defined in this template comprise:[1]

- ❑ Attributes for the identification of scenarios (rows 1–2)
- ❑ Management attributes (rows 3–7)
- ❑ Attributes for documenting the reference to the system context (rows 8–9)
- ❑ Attributes for documenting general content aspects (rows 10 and 20)
- ❑ Specific scenario attributes (rows 11–19), i.e. the scenario type (row 11), the association to goals (row 12), the actors of the scenario (row 13), pre- and post-conditions (rows 14–15), the result of the scenario (row 16), the scenario steps (row 17), the reference to quality requirements (row 18) as well as the relationships to other scenarios (row 19)[2]

Table 11-3 illustrates the documentation of a scenario (including the associated context information) using the reference template shown in Tab. 11-2.

Business- or project-specific adaptation

Prior to documenting scenarios using the reference template, it may be necessary to adapt the template. For instance, the stakeholders may have to define additional slots (i.e. attributes) due to specific needs of the organisation or project such as project size, project risk, liability laws, or process standards. Additional attributes that may be relevant for documenting scenarios can be found in Section 18.2.

[1] See also the description of requirements attributes in Section 18.3.

[2] The attributes "goal(s)" (row 12), "qualities" (row 18), and "relationships of the scenario to other scenarios" (row 19) refine the general attribute "cross references" described in Section 18.3.4.

Tab. 11-3 *Example of the template-based documentation of a scenario*

Section	Content	
Identifier	S-2-34	
Name	Navigate to destination	
Author	Peter Miller	
Version	V.1.1	
Change history	V.1.0 12.01.2006 Dan Smith V.1.1 14.02.2006 Peter Miller	
Priority	Medium	
Criticality	High	
Source	William Garland (domain expert for navigation systems)	
Responsible stakeholder	Dan Smith	
Short description	After the driver has entered the destination, the navigation system calculates the route and directs the driver to the desired destination.	
Scenario type	Interaction scenario (type B scenario)	
Goal(s)	G-2-17: Automatic navigation to the destination	
Actors	Driver, navigation system	
Precondition	The navigation system is able to receive GPS signals from at least three GPS satellites.	
Postcondition	The driver has arrived at the desired destination.	
Result	Step-by-step route to the destination	
Scenario steps	1	Driver activates the navigation system.
	2	Navigation system determines the current position of the car.
	3	Navigation system asks for the desired destination.
	4	Driver enters the destination.
	5	Navigation system identifies the relevant part of the map.
	6	Navigation system displays the map of the target area.
	7	Navigation system asks for the routing options.
	8	Driver selects the routing options.
	9	Navigation system calculates the route.
	10	Navigation system informs the driver that the route has been calculated.
	11	Navigation system creates a list of waypoints.
	12	Navigation system directs the driver to the next waypoint.
Qualities	Q-7-42: The calculation of the route shall take at most 3.5 seconds.	
Relationships to other scenarios	S-2-24: Comfortable entry of the destination S-2-54: Navigate around traffic congestion S-3-12: Destination not contained in data base	
Supplementary information	The competing system SX-23-44 realises a similar scenario.	

!

Hint 11-3: *Systematic documentation of scenarios*

- ❑ Avoid filling in all attributes of a scenario right away.
- ❑ Elicit an initial set of basic scenarios, i.e. fill in only the basic attributes identifier, name, source, responsible stakeholder, short description, and scenario type.
- ❑ Relate each scenario with the goals that are satisfied by the scenario.
- ❑ Validate that all relevant scenarios have been elicited, e.g. by checking that each goal defined for the system is satisfied by some scenario.
- ❑ Document the missing scenarios as described in the second step.
- ❑ Complete the basic scenarios by filling in the remaining slots of the scenario template.

Note: When eliciting an initial set of scenarios, you may gather information about a scenario that is beyond the scope of a basic scenario. In this case, do not discard the information but document it for later use.

11.3 A Reference Template for Use Cases

Reference templates for the documentation of use cases

For documenting use cases, a reference template can be used in a similar way as for the documentation of individual scenarios. Reference templates for use cases are based on expert knowledge about the structured documentation of use cases in natural language. A reference template defines the different types of information that need to be documented for each use case. Furthermore, a reference template defines how to arrange or structure this information. In the following, we explain a comprehensive reference template for the documentation of use cases. Other examples of reference templates for use cases can be found, amongst others, in [Kulak and Guiney 2003; Cockburn 2001; Armour and Miller 2001; Larman 2004; Bittner and Spence 2003; Halmans and Pohl 2003].

!

Hint 11-4: *Use case templates*

- ❑ By using a reference template you leverage expert knowledge about the documentation of use cases, i.e. the types of information to be documented and the way of arranging and presenting this information. Hence, make sure that in the end each use case is specified based on a common reference template.
- ❑ Initially, employ a standard use case template such as the one presented in Tab. 11-4. However, as you gain experience in the application of use case templates, consider adapting the reference template according to the specific needs of your project or organisation.
- ❑ If you do not have the information you need for filling in some slot of the use case template, fill in "TBD" (to be determined) to document that this slot needs to be revisited at a later stage.

We suggest documenting use cases using the reference template presented in Tab. 11-4. This template is based on the template presented in [Halmans and Pohl 2003]). The template shown in Tab. 11-4 contains the following attributes:[3]

- ❑ Attributes for the unique identification of use cases (rows 1–2)
- ❑ Management attributes (rows 3–7)
- ❑ Attributes for documenting the reference to the context (rows 8–9)
- ❑ A short description of the use case (row 10)

Tab. 11-4 *Reference template for documenting use cases*

Use Case Template		
No.	**Section**	**Content/Explanation**
1	Identifier	Unique identifier of the use case
2	Name	Unique name for the use case
3	Author	Name of the authors who have worked on the use case description
4	Version	Current version number of the use case
5	Change history	List of the changes applied to the use case including, for each change, the date of the change, the version number, the author, and, if necessary, the reason for and the subject of the change
6	Priority	Importance of the use case according to the prioritisation technique used
7	Criticality	Criticality of the use case for the success of the system
8	Source	Denomination of the source ([stakeholder | document | system]) from which the use case stems
9	Responsible stakeholder	The stakeholder responsible for the use case
10	Short description	Concise description of the use case (approximately 1/4 page)
11	Use case level	Characterisation of the current level of detail of the use case, e.g. through the differentiation between: overview/user level/function group level
12	Goal(s)	Goal(s) that shall be satisfied by executing the use case scenarios including identifiers that point to the associated goal definitions *Relevant rules* (see Section 11.4): ❑ Name the goal of the scenario explicitly (rule 10) ❑ Focus on the achievement of the goal (rule 11) *Rules for documenting goals* (see Section 8.2): ❑ Document goals concisely (rule 1) ❑ Use the active voice (rule 2) ❑ Document the stakeholder's intention precisely (rule 3) ❑ Decompose high-level goals into more concrete sub-goals (rule 4) ❑ State the additional value of the goal (rule 5) ❑ Document the reasons for introducing a goal (rule 6) ❑ Avoid defining unnecessary restrictions (rule 7)
13	Primary actor	Indication of the primary actor (the actor who benefits the most from the execution of the use case). Typically, the primary actor initiates the execution of the use case. *Relevant rules* (see Section 11.4): ❑ Name the actors explicitly (rule 9)

[3] See also the description of requirements attributes in Section 18.3.

Tab. 11-4 *(continued)*

Use Case Template		
No.	**Section**	**Content/Explanation**
14	Other actors	Determination of all other actors involved in the use case *Relevant rules* (see Section 11.4): ❑ Name the actors explicitly (rule 9)
15	Precondition	A list of necessary prerequisites that need to be fulfilled before execution of the use case can be initiated
16	Postcondition	A list of conditions that hold after execution of the use case
17	Result	Description of the outputs that are created during execution of the use case
18	Main scenario	Description of the main scenario of a use case *Relevant rules* (see Section 11.4): ❑ Use the present tense (rule 1) ❑ Use the active voice (rule 2) ❑ Use the subject–predicate–object (SPO) sentence structure (rule 3) ❑ Avoid modal verbs (rule 4) ❑ Only one interaction per sentence (rule 5) ❑ Number each scenario step (rule 6) ❑ Only one sequence of interactions per scenario (rule 7) ❑ Describe the scenario from the "view from afar" (rule 8) ❑ Explicitly name the actors (rule 9) ❑ Focus on illustrating the satisfaction of the goal (rule 11)
19	Alternative scenarios	Description of alternative scenarios of the use case *Relevant rules* (see Section 11.4): ❑ see slot 18 – "Main scenario"
20	Exception scenarios	Description of exception scenarios of the use case *Relevant rules* (see Section 11.4): ❑ see slot 18 – "Main scenario"
21	Qualities	Cross references to quality requirements
22	Relationships to other use cases	Short description of the relationships of the use case (e.g. extend, include, or generalisation relationships) to other use cases
23	Supplementary information	Additional information for this use case

- ❑ Specific use case attributes (rows 11–22), i.e. the use case level (row 11), the goals of the use case or references to the definitions of the goals (row 12), the actors of the use case (rows 13 and 14), pre- and postconditions (rows 15–16), the result of the use case (row 17), the main scenario (row 18), alternative and exception scenarios (rows 19–20), references to quality requirements (row 21) as well as relationships to other use cases (row 22)[4]
- ❑ An attribute for documenting additional, relevant information about a use case (row 23)

Table 11-5 shows the documentation of the use case "navigate to destination" using the reference template presented in Tab. 11-4.

[4] The attributes "goal(s)" (row 12), "qualities" (row 21), and "relationships to other use cases" (row 22) refine the general attribute "cross references" described in Section 18.3.4.

Tab. 11-5 *Example of the template-based documentation of a use case*

Section	Content		
Identifier	UC-4-17		
Name	Navigate to destination		
Author	Peter Miller, Jane Smith		
Version	V.1.1		
Change history	V.1.0 P. Miller 13-4-2006 "Main scenario specified" V.1.1 J. Smith 27-5-2006 "Alternative and exception scenarios specified"		
Priority	Importance for success of the system "high"; technological risk "high"		
Criticality	High		
Source	L. White (domain expert for navigation systems)		
Responsible stakeholder	J. Smith		
Short description	The driver of the car enters the destination. The navigation system guides the driver to the desired destination.		
Use case level	User level		
Goal(s)	Entry of the destination, automatic navigation to destination		
Primary actor	Driver		
Other actors	Information server		
Precondition	TBD		
Postcondition	The driver has achieved his/her goal.		
Result	Route to the destination		
Main scenario	1	The driver activates the navigation system.	
	2	The navigation system determines the current position of the car.	
	3	The navigation system asks for the desired destination.	
	4	The driver enters the destination using the control panel of the navigation system.	
	5	The navigation system displays the map of the target area.	
	6	The navigation system asks for the routing options.	
	7	The driver selects the desired routing options.	
	8	The navigation system calculates the route.	
	9	The navigation system informs the driver that the route has been calculated.	
	10	The navigation system creates a list of waypoints.	
	11	The navigation system directs the driver to the next waypoint.	
Alternative scenarios	4a	The driver selects the destination by pointing on a map that the navigation system shows on its display.	
		4a1	The driver searches the destination in the electronic maps.
		4a2	The driver marks the destination in the electronic maps.
		4a3	The navigation system identifies the coordinates of the destination.
		4a4	The navigation system displays a detailed map of the destination.
		4a5	The navigation system asks the driver to mark the destination on the detailed map.
		4a6	The driver marks the destination of the navigation.
		4a7	The navigation system identifies the street and house number.
	Proceed with Step 6.		
Exception scenarios	5a	The navigation system cannot find the entered destination.	
		5a1	The navigation system informs the driver that the entered destination is not known.
		5a2	The navigation system asks the driver to choose another destination.
Qualities	Q-2-04 (Response time to user inputs) Q-2-06 (Ease of use)		
Relationships to other use cases	TBD		

!

Hint 11-5: *Systematic documentation of use cases*

- ❑ Avoid filling in all attributes of a use case right away.
- ❑ Start with eliciting an initial set of basic use cases. For these use cases, fill in the basic attributes such as name, source, responsible stakeholder, short description, goal, and primary actor.
- ❑ Define the relationships between the use cases as well as the relationships between the use cases and the goals specified for the system.
- ❑ Validate that the set of use cases is sufficiently complete, e.g. by exploiting the relationships between the use cases and the goals specified for the system.
- ❑ After the completing the set of use cases, define the main scenario, the result, and the "other actors" for each use case.
- ❑ Subsequently, identify alternative scenarios and exception scenarios.
- ❑ Eventually, complete the use cases by filling in the remaining slots.

Note: When eliciting basic use cases, you may gather information about a use case that is beyond the scope of a basic use case. In this case, do not discard the information but document it for later use.

11.4 Eleven Rules for Documenting Scenarios

Adhering to simple rules when documenting scenarios significantly increases the quality of the resulting scenarios. Thereby, the benefit of the scenarios for requirements engineering and the entire development process is increased. In the following, we present 11 rules that have proven useful in supporting the documentation of scenarios in natural language.[5] We subdivide the rules into:

- ❑ Rules concerning the language and grammar of scenarios
- ❑ Rules concerning the structure of scenarios
- ❑ Rules concerning the content of scenarios

Hint 11-6 at the end of this section provides a brief summary of the 11 rules for documenting scenarios.

Language and Grammar Rules

Rule 1: present tense

Rule 1: Use the present tense when documenting scenarios. Scenarios document exemplary courses of interactions. The description of the interactions is more vivid and comprehensible if the present tense is used.

[5] The 11 rules are based on our experiences with regard to the usage of scenarios and on the rules mentioned in [Cockburn 2001] and [Alexander and Maiden 2004].

Example 11-3: Scenarios in the present tense

The user entered his user name and password into the system. The system checked the correctness of the entered data.

Improved definition:

The user enters his user name and password into the system. The system checks the correctness of the entered data.

Rule 2: active voice

Rule 2: Use the active voice when documenting scenarios. Using the active voice makes clear who acts or initiates an interaction. Documenting scenario steps using the active voice guarantees that each scenario step clearly and unambiguously states the responsible actor. Thereby, the documented scenario assigns each action to the responsible person or system and hence avoids ambiguity concerning the initiator of an interaction.

Example 11-4: Scenarios in the active voice

The user name and password are entered and validated.

Improved definition:

The user enters his user name and password into the system. The system validates the correctness of the entered data.

Rule 3: SPO sentence structure

Rule 3: Use the subject–predicate–object (SPO) sentence structure. This simple sentence structure eases reading the scenario and supports focussing on the essential parts of the scenario.

Example 11-5: SPO sentence structure in scenarios

By means of the user database, the system validates the user data.

Improved definition:

The system validates the user data by means of the user database.

Rule 4: no modal verbs

Rule 4: Avoid modal verbs. Modal verbs express that an interaction is possible rather than that it happens. This contradicts the exemplary character of scenarios and should hence be avoided.

Example 11-6: Avoid modal verbs

The system should check the user data.

Improved definition:

The system checks the user data.

Structure Rules

Rule 5: each interaction in a separate sentence

Rule 5: Clearly separate each interaction from other interactions. Avoid describing several interactions within the same sentence. By adhering to this rule, the individual interactions can be numbered, identified, and referenced more easily.

Example 11-7: Each interaction in a separate sentence

The user submits a search query to the online shop, selects an item from the list of search results, and adds the item to the shopping cart.

Improved definition:

See Example 11-8

Rule 6: unique numbering

Rule 6: Number each scenario step. The unique numbering of the individual scenario steps improves the clarity of the scenario and facilitates referencing the scenario steps.

Example 11-8: Numbering scenario steps

(1) The user submits a query to the online shop.
(2) The system displays a list of search results.
(3) The user selects an item from the list.
(4) The user adds the item to his shopping cart.
(5) The user iterates steps 1 to 4 until he has finished shopping.

Content Rules

Rule 7: one interaction sequence per scenario

Rule 7: Only one interaction sequence per scenario. Describe only a single sequence of interactions in each scenario. Avoid merging a main scenario or an alternative scenario with other alternative or exception scenarios. Alternative and exceptional sequences should be described in separate scenarios.

Example 11-9: Only one sequence of interactions per scenario

[...]

(10) The user enters his user data into the system.
(11) The user data is correct → Continue with step (41).
(***incorrect user data***)
(11) System displays "incorrect user data, please retry".
(12) System asks the user to enter his data.
(13) The user enters his user data into the system.
(14) The user data is correct → Continue with step (41).
(***third attempt***)
(21) Perform steps (3) to (5).
(22) The user data is correct → Continue with step (41).
(***incorrect user data entered for the third time, therefore abort***)

(to be continued)

Example 11-9 (*continued*)

(31) System displays "incorrect user data – transaction cancelled".
(32) System returns credit card.
(***correct user data***)
(41) System displays "user data correct".
(42) System asks for the amount to be withdrawn.
[…]

Improved definition:

Main scenario:

[…]
(10) The user enters his user data into the system.
(11) System displays "user data correct".
(12) System asks the user for the amount of money to be withdrawn.
[…]

Alternative scenario: If step (10) is unsuccessful:

(11a.1) System displays "incorrect user data, please retry".
(11a.2) System asks the user for entering his data.
(11a.3) The user enters his user data into the system.

Exception scenario: In step (10), if user data entered incorrectly three times:

(11b.1) System displays "incorrect user data – transaction cancelled".
(11b.2) System returns credit card.

Rule 8: "view from afar"

Rule 8: Describe scenarios from the view of an outsider ("view from afar"). Avoid the description of details that are not necessary for a scenario. For example, abstain from detailed description of internal system workflows (i.e. type A scenarios, see Section 10.6), if the main task is to define the interactions between the user and the system.

Example 11-10: Right perspective for interaction scenarios

(1) The system receives the user name and password of the user.
(2) The system encrypts the user data.
(3) The system logs on to the user server.
(4) The system transfers the user data to the user server.
(5) The user server decrypts the user data.
(6) The user server checks the user data by means of the user database.
(7) The user server transmits that the user data is correct.
(8) The system logs off from the user server.
(9) The system informs the user that the login was successful.

Better wording:

(1) The user logs on with his user data.
(2) The system checks the data.
(3) The system informs the user about the successful login.

Rule 9: explicit actors

Rule 9: Explicitly name the actors involved. The actors involved in a scenario should be named explicitly in the scenario description. In this way, misunderstandings regarding the acting persons or systems are avoided. Sentences in the active voice support the explicit naming of actors in a scenario (see rule 2). The requirements engineers should also make clear which actor initiates the interaction and which actor is affected by the interaction. Adhering to rule 3 supports a clear distinction between the initiating and the affected actors in a scenario.

Example 11-11: Explicit actors

(1) The user logs on to the system.
(2) The system reports that there is no connection to the network.
(3) The system restarts.
(4) The connection to the network is re-established.
(5) The user logs on to the system.

Improved definition:

(1) The user logs on to the system.
(2) The system reports that there is no connection to the network.
(3) The user reboots the system.
(4) The system establishes the connection to the network.
(5) The user logs on to the system.

Rule 10: state the goal

Rule 10: Explicitly state the goal of the scenario. Scenarios describe the satisfaction or failure to satisfy a goal. Document for each scenario, which goal or goals are satisfied by executing the scenario (see Example 11-12).

Example 11-12: State the goal explicitly and focus on illustrating how the goal is satisfied

(1) An unauthorised user boots the system.
(2) The system displays status reports about the boot procedure.
(3) The system displays the successful boot on the screen.
(4) The system asks the user to enter his user name and password.
(5) The unauthorised user enters different, randomly chosen user names and passwords.
(6) After five unsuccessful login attempts, the system locks the login functionality for 30 min.

Improved definition:

Goal of the scenario: "Protecting the system against unauthorised access"

(1) An unauthorised user tries to log on to the system with a randomly chosen user name and password.
(2) After five unsuccessful login attempts, the system locks the login functionality for 30 min.

Rule 11: Focus on illustrating how the goal is satisfied by the scenario. Document how the scenario satisfies the goal that is related to this scenario (see rule 10) or fails to satisfy the goal. Avoid documenting unnecessary information, i.e. information that does not contribute to illustrating the satisfaction of the goal (see Example 11-12).

Rule 11: focus on the satisfaction of the goal

Hint 11-6: *Eleven rules for documenting scenarios*

!

Language and grammar of the scenario
Rule 1: Use the present tense.
Rule 2: Use the active voice.
Rule 3: Use the subject–predicate–object (SPO) sentence structure.
Rule 4: Avoid modal verbs.

Structure of the scenario:
Rule 5: Only one interaction per sentence.
Rule 6: Number each scenario step.

Content of the scenario
Rule 7: Only one sequence of interactions per scenario.
Rule 8: Describe the scenario from the "view from afar".
Rule 9: Explicitly name the actors.
Rule 10: Explicitly state the goal of the scenario.
Rule 11: Focus on illustrating the satisfaction of the goal.

11.5 Sequence Diagrams

Documenting requirements using models has several advantages over documenting requirements in natural language (see Section 20.1). A popular language for the model-based documentation of scenarios is the message sequence chart (MSC) language (see [ITU 1996; ITU 1998; ITU 1999]). Although MSCs were developed for the telecommunication domain, they are well suited for documenting different kinds of interactions such as the interactions between a system and its actors.

UML sequence diagrams

The Unified Modeling Language (UML) supports the documentation of sequences of interactions by means of sequence diagrams. UML sequence diagrams are based on the MSC language. Figure 11-1 shows the essential modelling constructs of UML sequence diagrams. Detailed information about the modelling constructs of sequence diagrams can be found in the UML specification [OMG 2009b] and in [Rumbaugh et al. 2005].

Modelling constructs of UML sequence diagrams

A sequence diagram documents a sequence of message exchanges between a set of roles (see e.g. [Rumbaugh et al. 2005]). A role in a UML sequence diagram can represent the system to be developed, a part of the system, or an external actor (i.e. a person or system interacting with the system to be developed). Each role is shown in the diagram as a lifeline, i.e. a vertical line representing the existence of the role over a period of time. A bar on the lifeline of a role indicates a period of time during which the role is active. A role is active, for instance, during the processing of a message received from another role. The activation of a role is shown in a sequence

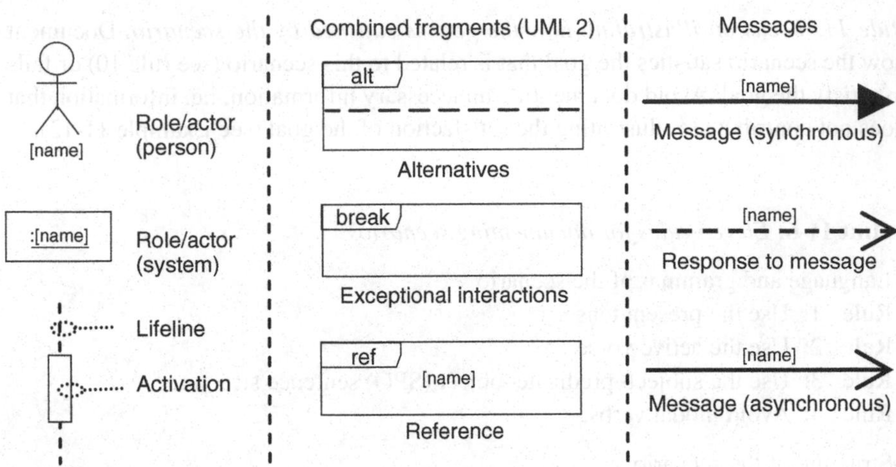

Fig. 11-1 *Essential modelling constructs of sequence diagrams*

diagram mainly for roles that represent technical entities such as (technical) systems or components.

Messages and interactions

Messages are modelled as horizontal arrows between lifelines. A message from one lifeline to another represents an interaction between the corresponding roles. UML differentiates between different types of messages, represented by different arrow styles (see [OMG 2009b]). In the case of a synchronous message (see Fig. 11-1), the sender of the message waits until he receives the response to this message. In contrast, in the case of an asynchronous message (see Fig. 11-1) the sender continues processing immediately after sending the message, i.e. the sender does not wait for the response.

Example

In the sequence diagram shown in Fig. 11-2, two roles are shown: the "driver" and the "navigationSystem" of the car. Since the role "driver" is occupied by a person and the role "navigationSystem" is occupied by a system, two different symbols are used for the two roles in the sequence diagram (corresponding to the notation shown in Fig. 11-1). The rectangular frame of the sequence diagram delimits the scenario. The name of the scenario is stated in the tab in the upper left corner of the frame.

Combined fragments

Combined fragments[6] support the grouping of messages and the assignment of a specific semantics to each group. In the following, we briefly explain the combined fragments "ref", "alt", and "break".

Reducing complexity using the "ref" fragment

The combined fragment "ref" refers to the interactions documented in another sequence diagram. The combined fragment "ref" means that the messages documented in the referenced sequence diagram are included in the sequence diagram

6 The specification of the Unified Modeling Language (UML) has been extended in version 2 with additional modelling constructs for sequence diagrams such as combined fragments (see [Rumbaugh et al. 2005]).

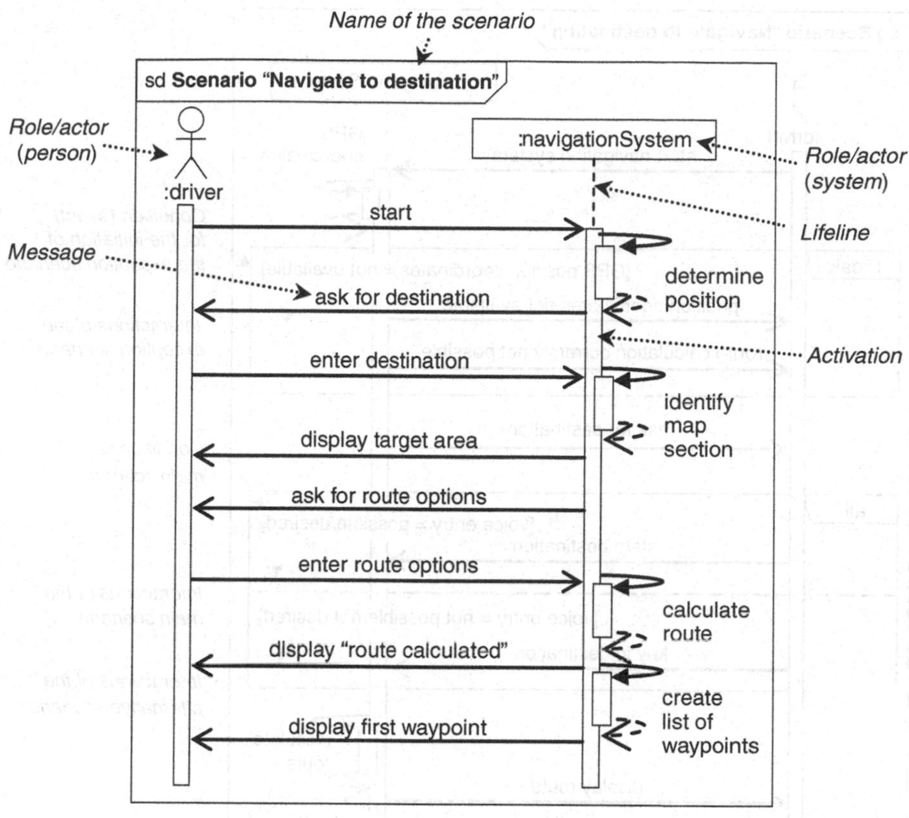

Fig. 11-2 *Documentation of a scenario in a sequence diagram*

containing the combined fragment "ref" at the position of the combined fragment. This type of combined fragment allows abstraction from the sequence of messages documented in the referenced sequence diagram and thus reduction of the complexity of the referring sequence diagram.

Exception scenario

The use of the combined fragments "break" and "alt" is illustrated in Fig. 11-3. The combined fragment "break" documents an exception scenario (see Section 10.7) The combined fragment "break" shown in Fig. 11-3 contains two messages: "position coordinates not available" and "route calculation currently not possible", which are sent only if the condition "GPS position coordinates = not available" evaluates to true. If this is the case, the execution of the scenario is aborted after the interactions documented in the "break" fragment have been executed.

Alternative scenario

The combined fragment "alt" documents an alternative scenario (see Section 10.7) that replaces the interaction step "state destination" in the main scenario. The alternative scenario is executed if voice entry is possible or desired, respectively. If voice entry is not possible or not desired, the destination can also be entered using the control panel. The message "key in destination", together with the other messages documented in the normal course of interactions, defines the alternative scenario.

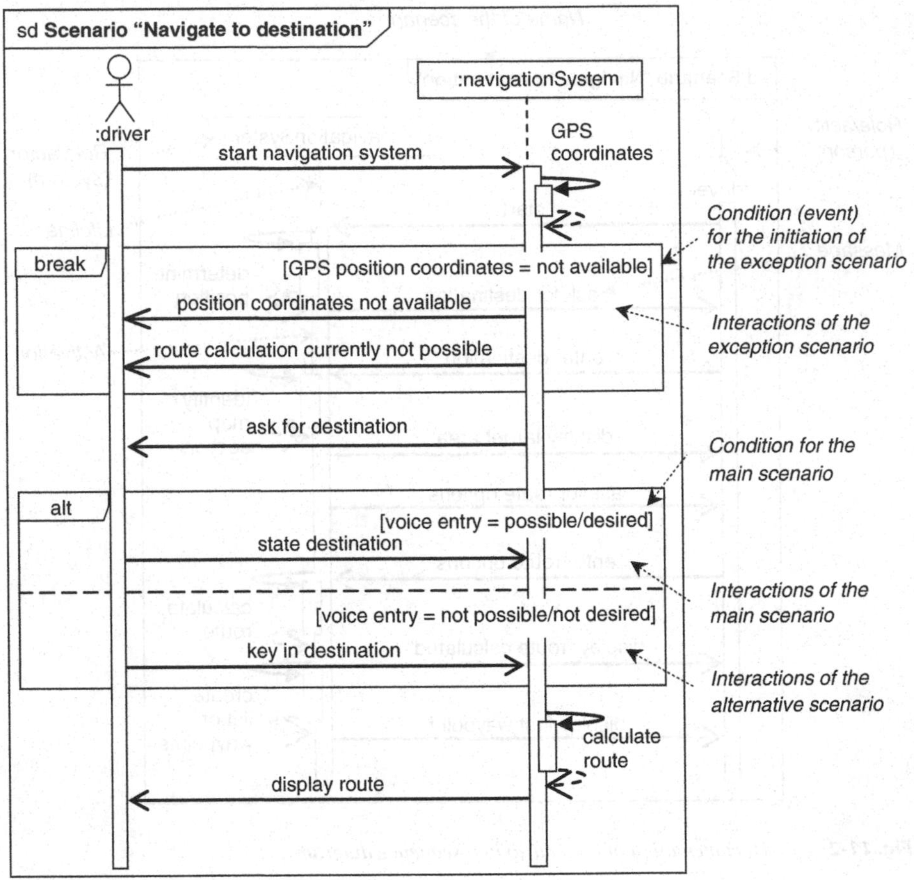

Fig. 11-3 *Alternative and exception scenarios in sequence diagrams*

!

Hint 11-7: *Documenting scenarios using sequence diagrams*

- ❑ Use sequence diagrams for the structured documentation of already well-understood main, alternative, and exception scenarios.
- ❑ Use characteristic names for the alternative and exception scenarios.
- ❑ Also in the case of sequence diagrams, focus on interactions that contribute to the satisfaction of the goal (or the goals); see rule 11 in Section 11.4.
- ❑ Avoid documenting interactions at a too detailed (e.g. algorithmic) level. Rather, take a view from afar, as recommended by rule 8 in Section 11.4.
- ❑ If the sequence diagram becomes too complex, use the combined fragment "ref" to divide the sequence diagram into multiple diagrams.
- ❑ Avoid extensive use of combined fragments such as "alt" or "break" as this violates the rule "Only one sequence of interactions per scenario" (rule 7 in Section 11.4).
- ❑ Deliberate use of comments eases the reading and understanding of sequence diagrams.

11.6 Activity Diagrams

Control flow of several scenarios

While UML sequence diagrams emphasise the sequence of interactions between the system and a set of actors over time, UML activity diagrams allow emphasis of the control flow between multiple scenarios such as the scenarios of a use case. In the following, we sketch the documentation of the control flow of scenarios in UML activity diagrams.

Control flow in the activity diagram

The main focus of an activity diagram is the control flow, i.e. the activities of the different actors and the possible orders of these activities. Figure 11-4 shows the most important modelling constructs of UML activity diagrams. More details on the modelling constructs can be found in [OMG 2009b; Rumbaugh et al. 2005].

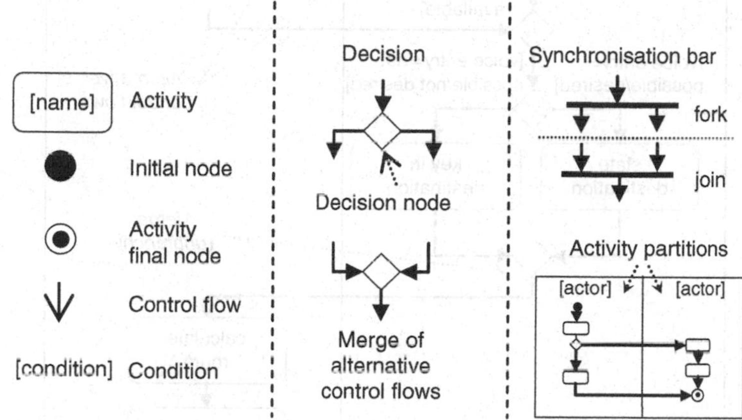

Fig. 11-4 *Important modelling constructs of UML activity diagrams*

Activity nodes

Activity diagrams are control flow graphs. The nodes of an activity diagram represent the execution of activities. The edges represent the flow of control from one activity to another. Activity diagrams have two special activity nodes with a predefined semantics: the initial node and the activity final node. The initial node represents an event that initiates the execution of the activity diagram. Activity final nodes represent the termination of the activity diagram.

Control flows and responsibilities

The representation of alternative control flows in activity diagrams is facilitated through decision nodes. At a decision node, the conditions for choosing one of the alternative control flows are annotated. Synchronisation bars represent concurrent control flows in activity diagrams. By using activity partitions, responsibilities of the system and the different actors for performing actions can be documented.

Main, alternative, and exception scenarios in activity diagrams

Activity diagrams are especially well suited for documenting the interrelations and execution conditions of main, alternative, and exception scenarios. Decision nodes represent the branching of the control flow between the main scenario and

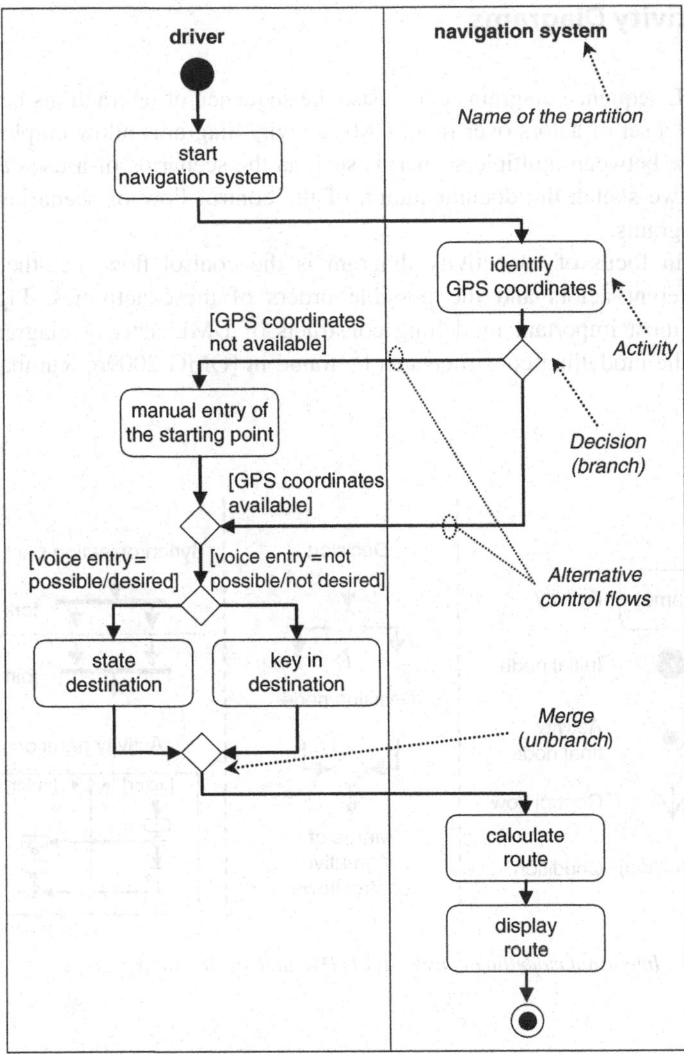

Fig. 11-5 *Documentation of the control flow of scenarios*

the alternative and exception scenarios. Figure 11-5 shows the activity diagram for the scenarios documented as a sequence diagram in Fig. 11-3.

Example with two activity partitions

The activity diagram shown in Fig. 11-5 is subdivided into two activity partitions. The first partition represents the responsibilities for activities and decisions of the actor "driver". The second partition represents the responsibilities of the navigation system. Alternative threads of control that document the alternative and exception scenarios start at the decision nodes.

!

Hint 11-8: *Documenting the control flow of several scenarios in an activity diagram*

- Use activity diagrams in order to document:
  - The control flow between multiple scenarios
  - The relationships between main, alternative, and exception scenarios
- Use activity diagrams especially if there are many alternative and/or exception scenarios, i.e. when many valid threads of execution exist.
- Avoid documenting the control flow of several scenarios in activity diagrams if:
  - The interaction sequence of the main scenario is not yet understood;
  - Alternative and exception scenarios are not sufficiently understood and/or their relationships to the main scenario are still unclear.

11.7 Use Case Diagrams

Relationships between use cases

Use case diagrams were suggested for the first time by [Jacobson et al. 1992] in order to support the analysis and documentation of the functionality of a system by means of simple models. Use case diagrams are not suited for documenting (sequences of) interactions between the system and the actors. However, they are well suited for documenting and visualising the relationships between the different use cases of a system as well as the relationships between the actors and the use cases.

Modelling constructs of use case diagrams

Figure 11-6 shows the most important modelling constructs of use case diagrams that are defined in the UML:

- *Actors (systems or persons)*: Actors represent systems or persons outside the system boundary that interact with the system to be developed. If the actor represents a person, the actor is drawn as a small stick figure (see Fig. 11-6). If the actor

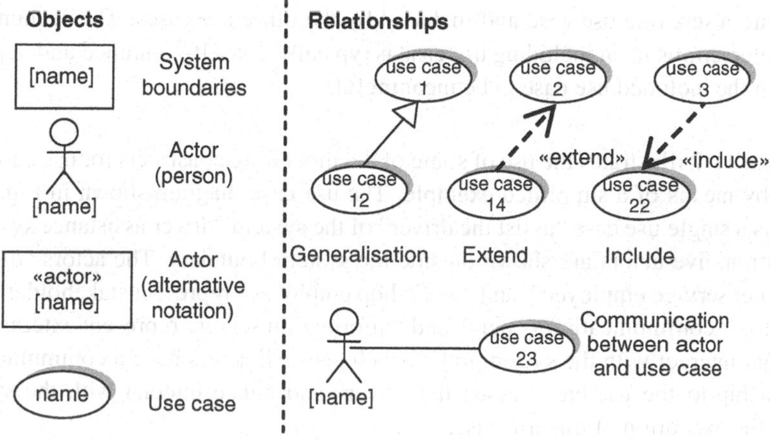

Fig. 11-6 *Important modelling constructs of a use case diagram*

represents a system, it is drawn as a box. Alternatively, a system actor can also be represented by a stick figure that is annotated with the stereotype *system.*

- *Use cases (see also* Definition 10-10*)*: A use case of the system to be developed is represented as an ellipse. The name of the use case is shown inside the ellipse.
- *System boundary*: The system boundary in a use case diagram (visually) delimits the system from its environment. The system boundary is drawn as a rectangle. The use cases for the system are placed within the system boundary. Optionally, the system boundary can be annotated with the name of the system.
- *Relationships between actors and use cases*: A relationship between an actor and a use case expresses that this actor interacts with the system during the execution of the use case. Relationships between actors and use cases are shown in a use case diagram as solid lines.
- *Relationships between use cases*: Use cases can be related to each other by means of the following three types of relationships:

  - *Generalisation relationship*: A generalisation relationship from a use case A to a use case B expresses that use case B is a generalisation of use case A. The specialised use case A inherits the interaction steps contained in the generalising use case B. In addition, the specialised use case A can extend interaction steps inherited from use case B with additional steps, if necessary (see [Rumbaugh et al. 2005]).
  - *Extend relationship*: An "extend" relationship from a use case A to a use case B expresses that the interaction sequence contained in use case A (the extending use case) extends the interaction sequence documented in use case B (the extended use case) at a defined location called the extension point. The extension is modal, i.e. it depends on the occurrence of a defined condition. The extended use case is defined independently of the extending use case and hence represents a meaningful use case event without the extending use case. The extending use case may or may not be meaningful by itself.
  - *Include relationship*: An "include" relationship from a use case A to a use case B expresses that use case A includes the interaction sequence documented in use case B. The "include" relationship is used if two or more use cases have a common part in their sequences of interactions. The common part is extracted into a separate use case and included by the other use cases. The sequence of interactions in an including use case is typically not self-contained and depends on the included use case to be meaningful.

Example illustrating the use of the modelling constructs

Figure 11-7 illustrates the use of some of the modelling constructs for use case diagrams by means of a simplified example. The use case diagram shown in Fig. 11-7 contains a single use case "assist the driver" of the system "driver assistance system". In addition, five actors are shown outside the system boundary. The actors "driver", "customer service employee", and "workshop employee" represent stakeholder roles. The actors "communication system" and "information server" represent external systems that interact with the system to be developed. All actors have a communication relationship to the use case "assist the driver" and hence interact with the system during the execution of this use case.

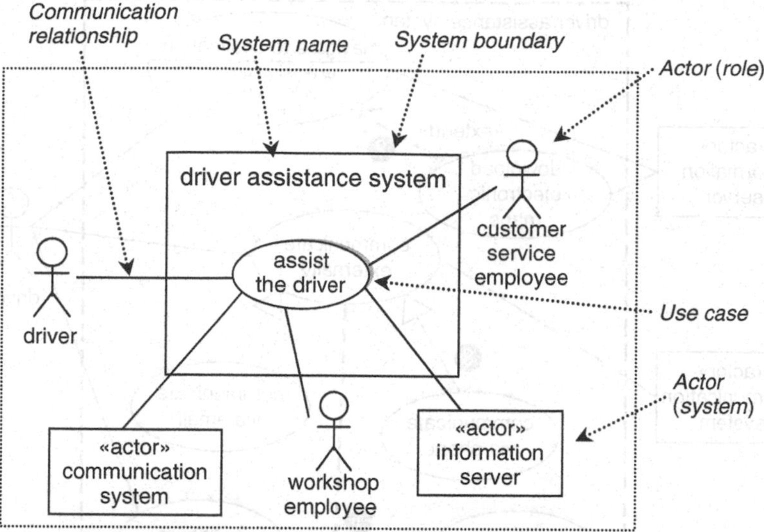

Fig. 11-7 *Modelling constructs of use case diagrams in an example*

!

Hint 11-9: *Size of a use case diagram*

A simple rule for developing use case diagrams is that they should contain about five to seven use cases. If a use case diagram contains fewer use cases (such as the example in Fig. 11-7), this may indicate that either the abstraction level of the use cases is too high or the system boundary has been defined too narrowly. If the system requires significantly more than five to seven use cases the system can be structured into logical components, and a use case diagram can be developed for each component. However, a large number of use cases may also indicate that the use cases are documented at a level of detail which is too low. To find out whether the use cases are documented at the right level of detail, the rules presented in Section 11.4 should be applied.

Refined example

In the following, we present a more complex example of a use case diagram that can be regarded as a refinement of the example shown in Fig. 11-7. The use case "assist the driver" is refined into the use cases "navigate to destination", "communicate externally", "configure car", and "support maintenance". The refined use cases are shown in Fig. 11-8. The relationships among these use cases are marked with the numbers ❶ to ❸ in Fig. 11-8.

These relationships can be explained as follows:

Include

❶ Each of the use cases "support maintenance", "communicate externally", and "configure car" is related to the use case "authenticate user" by means of an "include" relationship. This relationship expresses that the interaction steps documented in the use case "authenticate user" are also contained in each of the other three use cases.

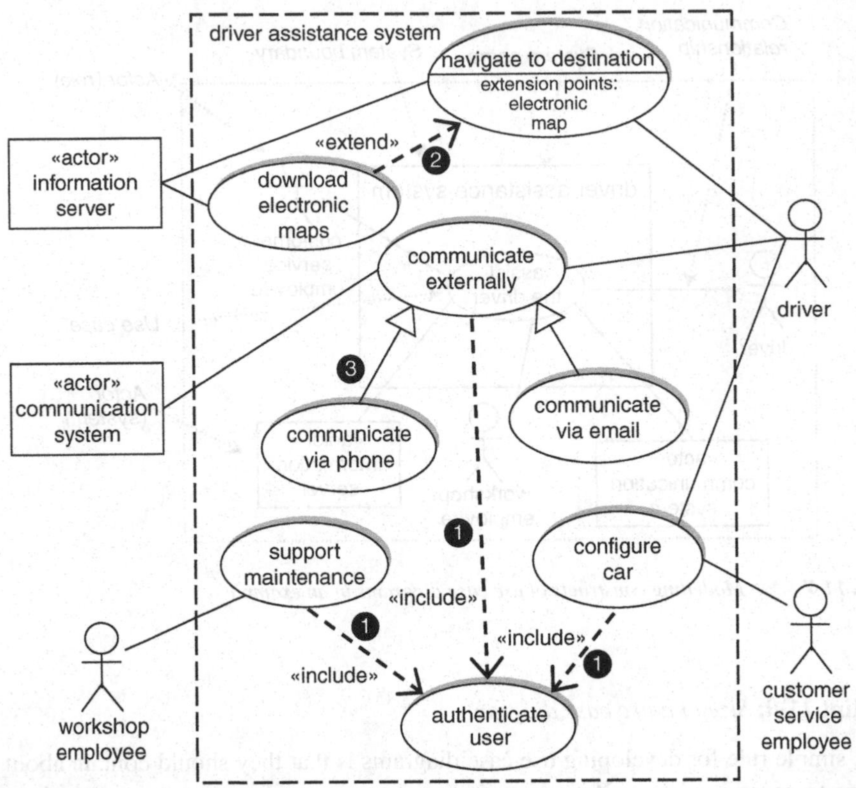

Fig. 11-8 *Refined use case diagram of the driver assistance system*

Extend

❷ The "extend" relationship between the use case "download electronic maps" and the use case "navigate to destination" expresses that the interaction steps documented in the former use case are part of the execution of the use case "navigate to destination" (when a defined event such as "required maps not available" occurs). The extension point "electronic map" shown inside the use case "navigate to destination" names the position in the use case at which the additional interaction steps for the download of electronic maps are executed.

Generalisation

❸ The generalisation relationship shown in Fig. 11-8 documents that the two use cases "communicate via phone" and "communicate via email" inherit the interaction steps documented in the generalising use case. The inherited interaction steps can be adapted, if necessary, in the specialised use cases and extended with additional steps.

Generalisation relationships between actors

The UML also provides a generalisation relationship among actors. A generalisation relationship from an actor A to an actor B expresses that actor A (the specialised actor) inherits the roles and relationships to use cases from actor B (the generalising actor; see e.g. [Rumbaugh et al. 2005]). In Fig. 11-8, the actors "workshop employee" and "customer service employee" could be generalised to an actor "employee". Then, the common aspects of the actors "workshop employee" and "customer service employee" would be assigned to the generalising actor "employee".

!

Hint 11-10: *Documentation of scenarios and use cases*

We recommend documenting use cases and scenarios using a combination of natural language documentation and model-based documantion:

- Document context information as well as the relationships of the main scenario to the alternative and exception scenarios by means of use case templates (see Section 11.3).
- Document interaction sequences of a use case within the use case templates using sequence diagrams, if possible (see Section 11.5). If sequence diagrams are not suited due to the stakeholders involved, use the tabular style for documenting the interaction sequences (see Section 11.2.1).
- Document relationships between well-understood main, alternative, and exception scenarios in activity diagrams (see Section 11.6). If this is not a viable option due to the stakeholders involved, use the tabular style instead (see Section 11.2.1).
- Employ use case diagrams in order to provide an overview of the relationships among use cases and the relationships between actors and use cases.

11.8 Use of the Different Scenario Types in the Requirements Engineering Process

In this section we evaluate the suitability of the different scenario types and the different representation formats of scenarios for two kinds of usage:

- *During the process*: Scenarios can be used during the requirements engineering process to support or even drive the elicitation, documentation, negotiation, and validation of requirements.
- *In the specification*: Scenarios can be included in the final requirements specification that is used as the basis for further development activities.

Table 11-6 shows the evaluation of each scenario type (see Chapter 10) and each representation format for these two kinds of usage. The evaluations ("–" not suited, "★" less suited, "★★" suited, "★★★" well suited) should be understood as rough estimations, since the suitability of a specific scenario type or representation format may differ according to the type of project and the specific situation in the requirements engineering process.

Tab. 11-6 *Suitability of the different scenario types and representation formats*

	Scenario type/ Representation format	Suitable for… Requirements engineering process	Requirements specification
Content	Narrative scenarios	★★★	–
	Current-state scenario	★★★	★
	Desired-state scenario	★★★	★★★
	Positive scenarios	★★★	★★★
	Negative scenarios	★★★	★★★
	Misuse scenarios	★★★	★★★
	Descriptive scenarios	★★	★★★
	Exploratory scenarios	★★★	–
	Explanatory scenarios	★★★	★
	Instance scenarios	★★	★
	Type scenarios	★	★★★
	Mixed scenarios	★★★	★★
	System-internal scenarios[7]	★	★★
	Interaction scenarios	★★	★★★
	Context scenarios	★★★	★★★
	Main scenarios	★★★	★★★
	Alternative scenarios	★★	★★★
	Exception scenarios	★★	★★★
	Use cases	★★★	★★★
Representation format	Textual (structured) scenarios	★★★	–
	Template-based scenarios and use cases	★★	★★★
	Sequence diagrams	★★	★★★
	Activity diagrams	–	★★
	Use case diagrams	★★	★★

[7] System-internal scenarios are used in requirements engineering for complex systems where requirements are specified for the system as well as for its sub-systems and components. We explain the use of system-internal scenarios in requirements engineering in Part VII.

Chapter 12
Benefits of Using Goals and Scenarios

In this chapter, we describe the main benefits of using goals and scenarios in requirements engineering. We outline:

- *The benefits of using goals and scenarios in each requirements engineering activity*
- *The benefits of goal–scenario–coupling*

K. Pohl, *Requirements Engineering*,

Use of goals and scenarios

This chapter explains the benefits of using goals (see Section 12.1) and scenarios (see Section 12.2) in the three core activities and the two cross-sectional activities of requirements engineering. Furthermore, the chapter describes the essential interdependencies between goals and scenarios. The positive effects of coupling goals and scenarios are illustrated by means of examples (see Section 12.3).

12.1 Benefits of Goal Orientation

The benefits of goal orientation in requirements engineering are presented, for instance, in [Loucopoulos 1994; Nuseibeh et al. 1994; Van Lamsweerde and Letier 2000; Rolland and Salinesi 2005]). In this section, we explain the essential benefits of using goals for each of the five requirements engineering activities outlined in Chapter 4.

12.1.1 Benefits for Documentation

Documentation in requirements engineering aims to document knowledge about the requirements and the context in an appropriate way (see Part IV.a).

Checking the requirements for completeness

During requirements documentation, goals can be used to check the completeness of the documented requirements or the requirements document. This aspect of goals was investigated by, amongst others [Yue 1987]. A set of requirements or a requirements document is complete according to Yue if the documented requirements suffice to satisfy the defined goals. Assuming that the goals are complete, the documented requirements can also be considered to be complete if this condition is met.

Avoiding irrelevant requirements

By explicitly considering goals, irrelevant requirements can be identified. An indication of the irrelevance of a requirement is that the requirement cannot be related to any goal as the requirement does not contribute to satisfying any of the defined goals. Hence, there is no justification for the existence of the requirement. Defining and implementing irrelevant requirements is also referred to as "gold plating".

Structuring of requirements documents

Goals can be used to structure requirements documents. The requirements document is then organised according to the decomposition structure of the goals. For instance, high-level goals can be used as section headings, and, for each high-level goal, the sub-goals decomposing this goal can be used as subsection headings. Eventually, each terminal goal, i.e. each goal that is not refined any further, can be used as the heading of the subsection that documents the requirements needed to satisfy that goal.

Definition of access paths to requirements

Each requirement in a requirements document contributes to the satisfaction of one or multiple goals. Goal models can be used to define logical access paths to the requirements in a requirements document. For this purpose, explicit relationships are defined between each goal and the requirements that contribute to the satisfaction of that goal. In this way, the goals provide access paths to the requirements document. In contrast to using goals for structuring a requirements document, the definition of logical access paths does not require structuring the requirements document according to the decomposition structure of the goals.

Detailed explanation in Part IV.a

The use of goals for documenting requirements is elaborated on in Part IV.a.

12.1.2 Benefits for Elicitation

Foundation for requirements elicitation

Goals document the stakeholders' intentions with respect to the system. Hence, stakeholders often make goals explicit in a conversation with the requirements engineer, e.g. by directly stating the goals. After some consolidation, the stakeholders' goals provide an initial basis for eliciting requirements that lead to the satisfaction of the goals (see [Dardenne et al. 1993; Van Lamsweerde 2001; Potts et al. 1994; Loucopoulos 1994]).

Goal-oriented requirements elicitation

If the goals for the system are known, the application of an elicitation technique can be aligned with a specific goal or set of goals, e.g. the goals documented in a specific branch of an AND/OR goal tree. Using goals for guiding requirements elicitation supports the systematic elicitation of requirements with a clear focus on satisfying the defined goals.

Identification and evaluation of alternative realisations

Furthermore, goal orientation supports the identification of potential alternative realisations. Therefor, a goal is first decomposed into a set of alternative sub-goals. Hence, satisfying one of the sub-goals is sufficient to satisfy the parent goal. In a second step, the stakeholders can sketch a possible realisation of each sub-goal (e.g. in terms of scenarios or solution-oriented requirements). Each such realisation is a possible realisation of the parent goal. The relevant scenarios or solution-oriented requirements identified for each sub-goal support the stakeholders in evaluating each possible realisation of the parent goal, e.g. with respect to cost and risk.

Refinement of the vision

Furthermore, the coupling of goals and scenarios has proven its worth for supporting requirements elicitation, and in particular the elcitation of new and innovative requirements (see Section 12.3). Requirements engineering is also a learning process for the stakeholders. Coupling goals and scenarios supports this learning process. Goals help to refine the system vision at an abstract level. Scenarios provide positive and negative examples of goal satisfaction.

Detailed explanation in Part IV.b

The use of goals during requirements elicitation is detailed in Part IV.b.

12.1.3 Benefits for Negotiation

Consolidation of different views

Stakeholders often have different views on the system to be developed. Due to the different views of the stakeholders, conflicts emerge among the stakeholders with regard to the requirements for the system (see [Nuseibeh et al. 1994]). The negotiation activity aims at consolidating the stakeholders' individual views in order to gain, preferably, a fully consolidated view on the requirements for the system.

Supporting conflict resolution

Conflicts in the solution-oriented requirements often result from conflicts between the intentions of the different stakeholders with regard to the system. Goal models can be used to identify and resolve conflicts between the different stakeholder intentions at an early stage of the requirements engineering process. Thereby, conflicts can be partly resolved before they creep into the solution-oriented requirements. However, requirements conflicts can never be fully avoided. Some conflicts may emerge only when detailed requirements are developed. In these cases, goals can (and should) still be used to support the resolution of conflicts. Requirements engineers should clarify whether the detected requirements conflicts are caused by a conflict in the stakeholders' intensions and goals (see e.g. [Van Lamsweerde and Letier 2000]). If this is the case, the conflicts can be resolved more easily by negotiating about the associated goals rather than by negotiating about a set of detailed requirements.

Detailed explanation in Part IV.c

In addition to supporting the identification and resolution of conflicts, goals can also be used to identify conflict types and select appropriate strategies for conflict resolution. The use of goals for attaining agreement about requirements is described in Part IV.c.

12.1.4 Benefits for Validation

Requirements validation (see Part V) aims at ensuring at an early stage that the right system is developed. The term "right" means, in this regard, that a system is developed that fulfils the consolidated set of wishes and expectations of all relevant stakeholders and meets all its constraints. The validation of requirements is supported by the explicit consideration of goals.

Validity of requirements with respect to a goal model

Based on the goals specified for a system, the requirements for the system can be validated. During the validation, for each goal and the set of requirements related to this goal, the stakeholders check whether the goal is satisfied if the system realises the requirements. If a goal cannot be satisfied by realising the associated requirements, the requirements may be incomplete or have some other type of defect. Note that, in the case of OR-decomposed goals, only one sub-goal needs to be satisfied in order to satisfy the parent goal. Hence the requirements specified for a system may be valid with respect to a goal model even if part of the sub-goals are not satisfied.

Detailed explanation in Part V

We describe the use of goals for supporting the validation of requirements in Part V.

12.1.5 Benefits for Management

Goals support the management activity in requirements engineering. Goals are particularly helpful for prioritising requirements and establishing requirements traceability.

Prioritisation of requirements

The explicit consideration of goals facilitates the prioritisation of requirements. In order to prioritise solution-oriented requirements, it is often possible to start with the prioritisation of the high-level goals specified for the system. The priorities of the goals are then "inherited" along the refinement relationships to the associated solution-oriented requirements (see Chapter 31).

Traceability of requirements

The explicit documentation of goals (together with the documentation of scenarios) helps to establish traceability in a project-specific way and supports the traceability of the requirement sources (see Chapter 30). By explicitly documenting goals, it is possible to establish traceability between the solution-oriented requirements and the stakeholders' wishes and expectations. Traceability is established by explicitly documenting the relationships between goals and the requirements that contribute to the satisfaction of these goals.

Detailed explanation in Part VI

The use of goals to support the management activity in requirements engineering is explained in Part VI.

12.2 Benefits of Using Scenarios

The benefits of using scenarios in requirements engineering are described, e.g. in [Alexander and Maiden 2004; Carroll 2000; Haumer et al. 1998; Haumer et al. 2000; Leite et al. 1997; Rolland et al. 1999; Sindre and Opdahl 2005; Weidenhaupt et al.

1998]. In this section, we sketch the main benefits of using scenarios in the five requirements engineering activities presented in Chapter 4.

12.2.1 Benefits for Documentation

Guiding requirements engineers by means of scenarios

Scenarios can be used to capture context information about the development facet (see Section 9.3). A scenario can describe, for instance, how a requirements engineer uses a specific template, checklist, or modelling language when documenting requirements, or how requirements artefacts of a specific type (e.g. goals) are used when creating requirements artefacts of a different type (e.g. solution-oriented requirements). In such a scenario, hints and instructions can be given, for instance, how to fill in the different slots of a use case template correctly. In this way, scenarios are specified for guiding requirements engineers during the documentation of requirements. In addition, requirements managers can derive from these scenarios, for instance, which attributes are needed for documenting requirements of a specific type.

Structuring requirements documents

Scenarios are also suited for structuring requirements documents. They can be used, for example, for defining views on a requirements document. If doing this, all requirements concerned with a specific scenario are associated with the scenario. This kind of structuring is especially advisable when the system is developed iteratively and a specific subset of scenarios or use cases is implemented in each iteration.

Providing rich context information for requirements

Scenarios facilitate illustrating or explaining solution-oriented requirements by means of examples. In addition, scenarios relate each requirement to relevant context aspects, to other solution-oriented requirements, and to goals. However, a prerequiste for this is that sencerios are interrelated with the corresponding solution-oriented requirements.

Embedding of requirements into a usage context

A scenario embeds requirements into a common usage context. By relating requirements to scenarios, each individual requirement can be traced to at least one scenario that places the requirement in a usage context and hence illustrates the additional value of the requirement for the stakeholders. Furthermore, if a requirement is related to multiple scenarios, stakeholders can obtain a better understanding of the requirement by considering the requirement in its different usage contexts.

Improvement of the comprehensibility of requirements

Since scenarios allow for relating requirements to each other and embedding them into the context, scenarios support not only requirements engineering but also the subsequent development activities as well as future change processes.

Detailed explanation in Part IV.a

The use of scenarios for requirements documentation is detailed in Part IV.a.

12.2.2 Benefits for Elicitation

The use of scenarios is an essential means for supporting the elicitation of requirements. Scenarios support the elicitation of knowledge and the understanding of the stakeholders' needs and intentions during requirements elicitation (see [Karat and Bennett 1991; Jacobson et al. 1992; Dardenne 1993; Potts et al. 1994; Rosson and Carroll 1993]).

Goal refinement

During the development of scenarios, typically, new goals are identified, existing goals are refined, and alternative ways of satisfying the known goals are identified (see Section 12.3).

Explanation of intentions

Scenarios provide an intuitive facility to communicate requirements for the system to be developed. A stakeholder can, for example, explain his or her intentions with the help of narrative scenarios (see Section 11.1). The resulting scenarios convey the goals for the system from the individual perspective of this stakeholder (see [Weidenhaupt et al. 1998; Carroll 2000]).

Communication support

By means of scenarios, poorly understood aspects of the system context can be explained and communicated easily. For example, the stakeholders may develop instance scenarios (see Section 10.5) that document concrete sequences of interactions in the system context of a driver assistance system.

Basis for the development of requirements

Furthermore, scenarios serve as a basis for the development of functional requirements for the system including the associated quality requirements.

Detailed explanation in Part IV.b

The use of scenarios for requirements elicitation is explained in Part IV.b.

12.2.3 Benefits for Negotiation

Scenarios are a simple means of communication and, according to experience, comprehensible to all stakeholders. Thus, scenarios can be used to analyse and resolve requirements conflicts.

Conflict analysis

During conflict analysis, the identification of conflicts, communication about conflicts, and resolution of conflicts can be supported by using scenarios to illustrate conflicts. Furthermore, the creation of scenarios during conflict analysis supports the detection of the actual cause of a conflict.

Conflict resolution

Scenarios can be used during conflict resolution for documenting alternative, possible realisations in a way that is comprehensible to all stakeholders. Hence scenarios contribute to achieving consensus more easily (see [Weidenhaupt et al. 1998]).

Detailed explanation in Part IV.c

The use of scenarios for attaining agreement about the requirements is described in Part IV.c.

12.2.4 Benefits for Validation

Scenarios document concrete examples of intended system usage. For this reason, they are well suited for involving different kinds of stakeholders in the validation of requirements artefacts. By means of scenarios, complex requirements can be presented to the stakeholders who validate the requirements in a comprehensible form.

Validating scenarios from different perspectives

Due to their good comprehensibility to technical and non-technical stakeholders, scenarios can be validated by a variety of stakeholders. Scenarios can be used, for example, to check whether the users of the system agree with the usage workflows. Architects can validate scenarios in order to check whether the scenarios convey sufficient information for developing an adequate architecture. Testers can validate scenarios in order to check whether sufficient information for developing test cases is available.

Scenarios can also be used to support the validation of other requirements artefacts. For instance, stakeholders can check solution-oriented requirements for completeness, correctness, and consistency with respect to the scenarios specified for the system. Incompleteness, incorrectness, and inconsistencies in the requirements can be detected by checking whether each positive scenario can be satisfied and each negative or misuse scenarios (see Section 10.1) can be prevented if the requirements are realised.

Validating other requirements artefacts using scenarios

Scenarios support, furthermore, the identification of irrelevant requirements in requirements documents. If a documented requirement is not related to a scenario, this is an indication of the irrelevance of the requirement.

Detecting irrelevant requirements

Since scenarios document context information, the scenarios related to the requirements can be used to incorporate additional context information during the validation of these requirements. This holds for the validation of solution-oriented requirements as well as goals and alternative realisation possibilities.

Including context information in the validation

Scenarios are used during validation preferably in combination with prototypes. By employing a prototype, the stakeholders can execute the scenarios interactively. Experimenting with the prototype or the scenarios realised in the prototype enables the stakeholders to detect additional errors, misunderstandings, and conflicts both in the prototypical realisation as well as in the underlying scenario definitions.

Combining prototypes and scenarios

The use of scenarios for supporting requirements validation is explained in Part V.

Detailed explanation in Part V

12.2.5 Benefits for Management

Within the management activity, scenarios support the prioritisation of requirements. For example, the stakeholders may determine the priorities of solution-oriented requirements based on the priorities that are assigned to the scenarios. For this purpose, the scenarios are prioritised, first. Subsequently, the priorities of the scenarios are used to prioritise the requirements related to the scenarios. According to experience, scenarios facilitate negotiation about the priorities of requirements even in very heterogeneous stakeholder groups.

Prioritisation support

Additionally, scenarios are well suited for determining what traceability information is needed in a project. For this purpose, scenarios describing the utilisation of the traceability information are developed. Based on these usage scenarios, requirements engineers determine which traceability relationships are needed to support these usage scenarios (see [Dömges and Pohl 1998; Pohl et al. 1997]).

Determining required traceability information

Scenarios support the management of solution-orientied requirements by acting as a bridge between solution-oriented requirements and goals. Scenarios illustrate goal satisfaction (or the failure to satisfy goals). Therefore, each scenario is related to one or multiple goals. In addition, scenarios put solution-oriented requirements into a usage context (see Section 12.2.1). Therefore, each scenario is also related to a set of solution-oriented requirements. Since scenarios are related to goals as well as to solution-oriented requirements, they also relate the stakeholders' goals and the solution-oriented requirements for the system to each other.

Link between goals and solution-oriented requirements

Scenarios support change management insofar as the context information contained in the scenarios supports an evaluation of the planned changes. Furthermore,

Support of change management

one can exploit the scenarios associated with a requirement that needs to be changed to assess which other requirements may be affected by the change as well.

Detailed explanation in Part VI

The use of scenarios for supporting the management activity in requirements engineering is explained in more detail in Part VI.

12.3 Benefits of Goal–Scenario–Coupling

Figure 12-1 illustrates the most important interdependencies between goals and scenarios. These interdependencies are the key motivation for coupling goals and scenarios in requirements engineering (see e.g. [Antón and Potts 1998; Antón et al. 2000; Haumer et al. 1998; Haumer et al. 1999; Potts 1995; Rolland et al. 1998b; Sutcliffe et al. 1998]). In the following sections, we explain each interdependency and illustrate by means of examples how the interdependencies can be exploited to support the requirements engineering activities.

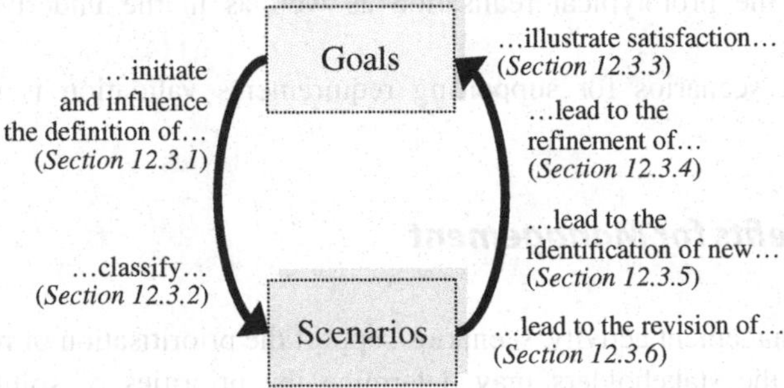

Fig. 12-1 *Interdependencies between goals and scenarios*

12.3.1 Goals Initiate the Definition of Scenarios

Better understanding of goals through scenarios

In order to improve the stakeholders' understanding of a goal, scenarios are developed for this goal. These scenarios describe exemplary interaction sequences that lead either to the satisfaction of the goal or to failure to satisfy the goal. Hence, a goal initiates the definition of scenarios (see Fig. 12-2).

Example of a goal initiating the definition of scenarios

The left-hand side of Fig. 12-2 shows an extract of a goal tree that documents the decomposition of the goal "high efficiency of the car". The sub-goal "protection against theft" is refined by the goals "car-theft protection through alarm system" and "ability to localise car position".

In order to gain additional knowledge about the goals "car-theft protection through alarm system" and "ability to localise car position", the stakeholders develop scenarios for these two goals. Thus, the two goals initiate the definition of new scenarios. The resulting scenarios describe exemplary workflows for the satisfaction of these goals (main and alternative scenarios) as well as sequences of interactions that are

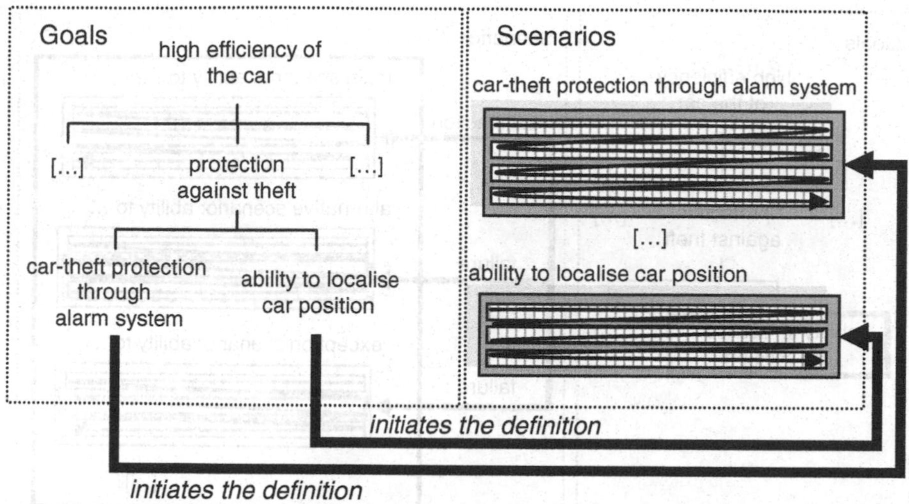

Fig. 12-2 *Goals initiate the definition of scenarios*

executed when defined exceptional events occur (exception scenarios). If goals in the goal model change, this leads to a change of the associated scenarios in the majority of cases.

12.3.2 Goals Classify Scenarios

Scenarios illustrate the satisfaction of goals or the failure to satisfy some goals. Hence, each scenario can be related to the goals that are (partly or fully) satisfied by the scenario. These goals can be used to classify the scenarios (see e.g. [Jacobson et al. 1992; Rolland et al. 1998b]). Based on the relationships between the goals and scenarios, the following classes of scenarios can be identified for each goal (see Section 10.7):

- *Scenarios documenting the satisfaction of the goal*: This set or class of scenarios can be determined by considering the scenarios of types "main" and "alternative" that are related to a specific goal. *Satisfaction of a goal*
- *Scenarios documenting the failure to satisfy the goal*: This set of scenarios can be determined by considering the scenarios of type "exception" that are related to a specific goal. *Failure to satisfy a goal*
- *Scenarios documenting system usage violating the goal*: This set of scenarios can be determined by considering the scenarios of type "misuse" that are related to a specific goal. *System usage to be prevented*

Figure 12-3 illustrates the classification by means of the goal "ability to localise car position". Three scenarios are associated with this goal: a main, an alternative, and an exception scenario.

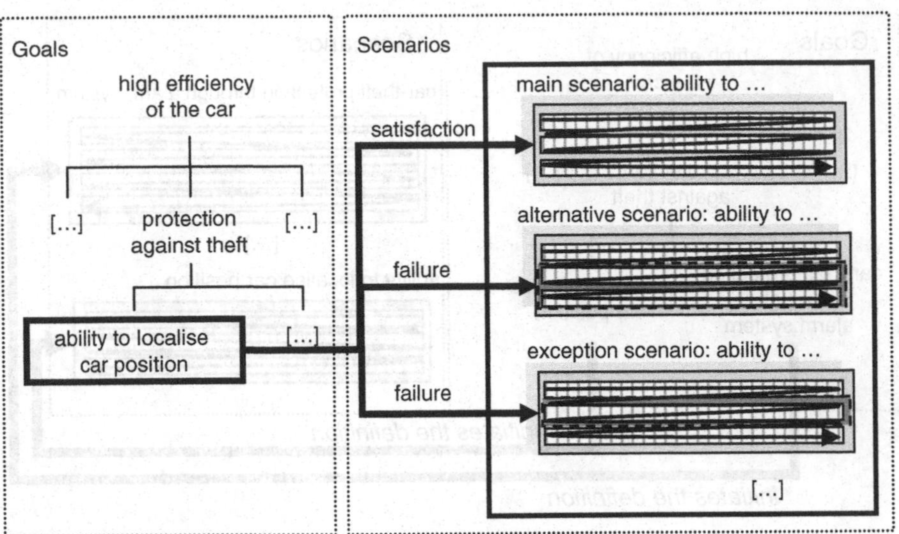

Fig. 12-3 *Classification of scenarios by means of goals*

12.3.3 Scenarios Illustrate Goal Satisfaction

Interaction sequences illustrate goal satisfaction

Scenarios illustrate the satisfaction of goals by means of exemplary interaction sequences. An exemplary interaction sequence provides additional information about a goal (see e.g. [Potts 1995; Pohl and Haumer 1997; Haumer et al. 1998]) such as:

- An example of satisifying the goal
- An example of failing to satisfy the goal
- An example of a purposeful violation of the goal, i.e. the misuse of the system (see Section 10.3)

Example of goal satisfaction

Figure 12-4 shows a main and an alternative scenario (right-hand side of Fig. 12-4) that illustrate the satisfaction of the goal "automatic navigation" (left-hand side of Fig. 12-4). The scenarios are represented using a sequence diagram with an "alt" fragment (see Section 11.5). Each of the two scenarios documents a sequence of interactions satisfying the associated goal.

12.3.4 Scenarios Initiate the Elaboration of Goals

Interplay between scenario definition and goal elaboration

Illustrating the satisfaction of goals by means of scenarios often leads to the elaboration of the goals. The elaboration of scenarios and the associated elaboration of goals support the stakeholders' learning process and improve the understanding of the requirements. By iterating between goal-oriented scenario definition and

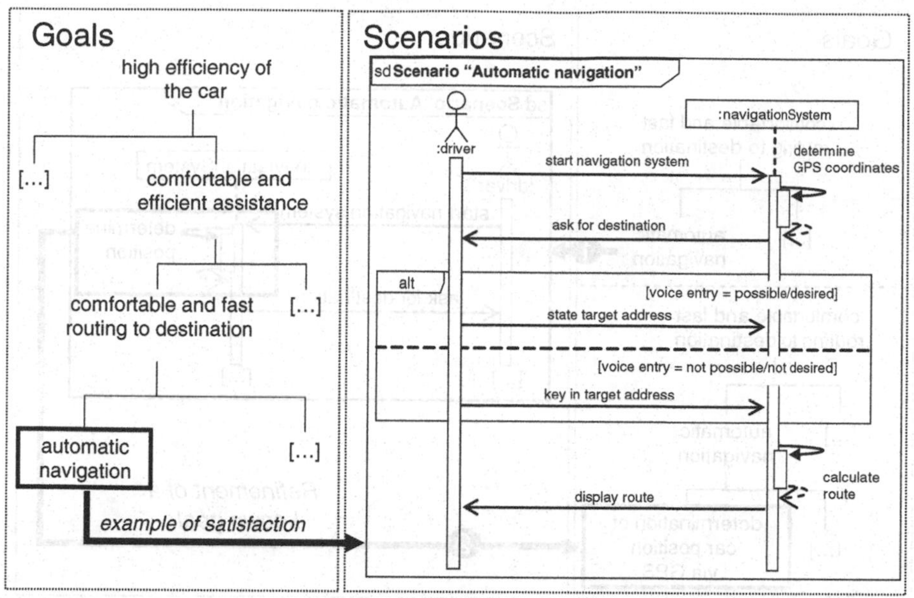

Fig. 12-4 *Scenarios illustrate goal satisfaction*

scenario-based goal elaboration, additional knowledge is successively gained about the stakeholders' goals and the intended ways of satisfying these goals. Thereby the understanding of the system to be developed is increased.

The elaboration of goals includes the following cases (see e.g. [Potts 1995; Haumer et al. 1998; Antón et al. 2000]):

- Goal decomposition, i.e. the identification of new sub-goals
- Identification of new, independent goals
- Revision or removal of existing goals

Goal Decomposition

A scenario initiates the definition of new sub-goals

When concretising a goal by means of a scenario, new sub-goals of this goal may be identified. Defining sub-goals for an existing goal is called goal decomposition (see Section 7.3).

Example of goal decomposition

Figure 12-5 shows an example of goal decomposition based on the development of a scenario. The satisfaction of the goal "automatic navigation" (left-hand side of Fig. 12-5) is illustrated by a scenario (right-hand side of Fig. 12-5). This step is marked with ❶ in Fig. 12-5. The first interaction in the presented scenario is the activation of the navigation system by the driver. The scenario documents that, in a second step, the navigation system determines the current position of the car. The definition of this interaction initiates the identification of a new sub-goal. The new sub-goal "determination of car position via GPS" of the goal "automatic navigation" is added to the goal model. This step is marked with ❷ in Fig. 12-5.

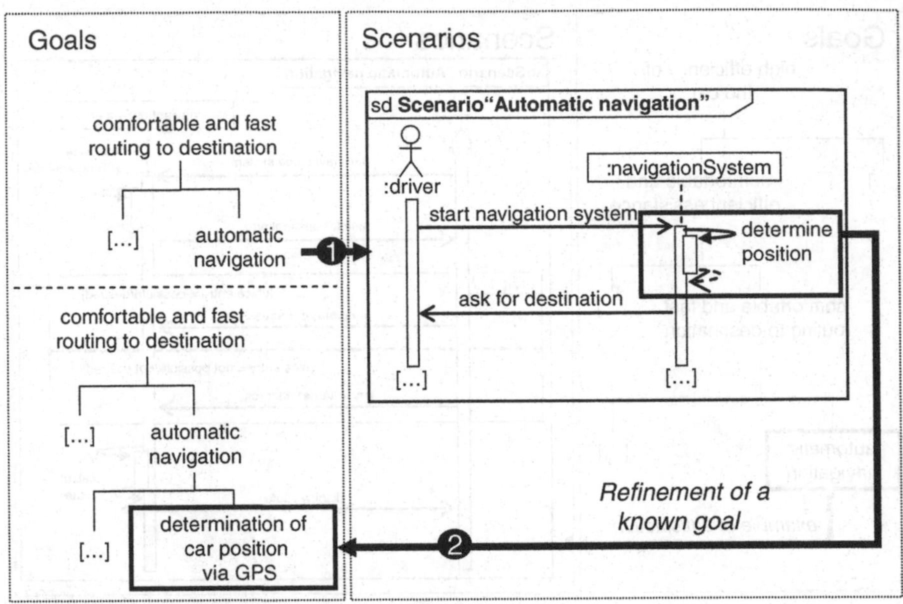

Fig. 12-5 *Decomposition of a goal initiated by a scenario*

Identification of New, Independent Goals

A scenario leads to the identification of independent goals

When the satisfaction of a goal is illustrated by a scenario, entirely new goals may be identified, i.e. goals that are independent goals, not sub-goals of some goal that is associated with the scenario (see [Antón et al. 2000; Haumer et al. 1998; Rolland et al. 1998b]).

Example of identifying new goals

Figure 12-6 illustrates the identification of a new goal with the help of a scenario. As shown in Fig. 12-6, first, the satisfaction of the goal "automatic navigation" is illustrated by a scenario (Fig. 12-6, ❶). The scenario documents that the driver of the

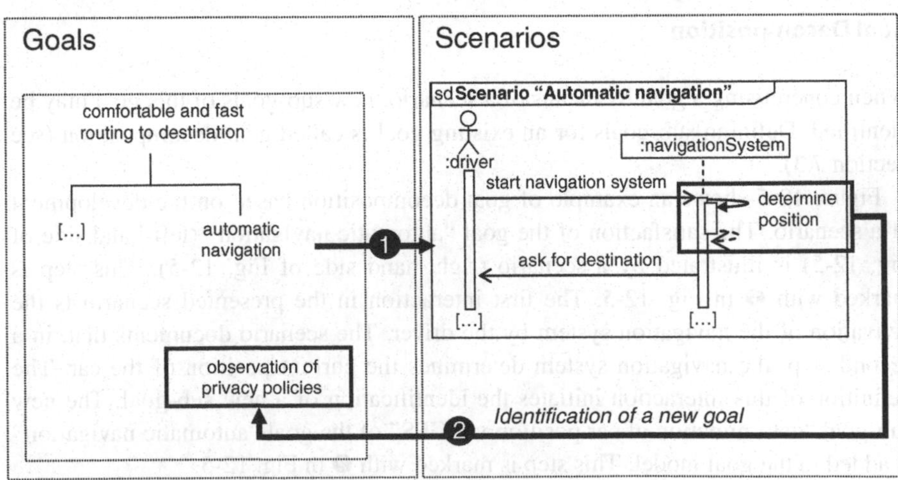

Fig. 12-6 *Identification of an independent goal initiated by a scenario*

car first activates the navigation system. Subsequently, the position of the car is determined automatically. With regard to the interaction step "determine position", the data security engineer remarks that all privacy policies definitely have to be adhered to when realising this functionality. Hence, a new goal "observation of privacy policies" is identified (Fig. 12-6, ❷) that has not been considered before. Unlike the goal identified in Section 12.3.4, this goal is not a sub-goal of some goal that is already associated with the scenario. Therefore, the new goal is specified as an independent goal.

Revision/Removal of Goals

A scenario initiates revision/removal of a goal

Concretising goals by means of scenarios can also lead to the revision or even the removal of goals associated with the scenario (see e.g. [Haumer et al. 1998; Haumer et al. 1999]). This interaction between goals and scenarios is especially important for the validation of goal models (see e.g. [Sutcliffe et al. 1998]).

Example of revising/ removing a goal

Figure 12-7 illustrates a revision of a goal that is initiated by a scenario. In the example, the satisfaction of the goal "manual entry of traffic blocks during the trip" is illustrated by a scenario (Fig. 12-7, ❶). In the scenario, the driver enters a traffic block manually during the trip by entering the number of the road and the blocked section of the present route. The validation of the goal reveals that the manual entry during the trip contradicts the legal regulations for driving safety (Fig. 12-7, ❷). Therefore, it is necessary to revise the goal "manual entry of traffic blocks during the trip" (Fig. 12-7, ❸). The revision of the goal can, for example, lead to the removal of the goal, i.e. the driver is not provided with the functionality to enter traffic blocks manually during the trip. Alternatively, the goal could be revised so that manual entry is only allowed for a stationary car or for a car driving at walking speed.

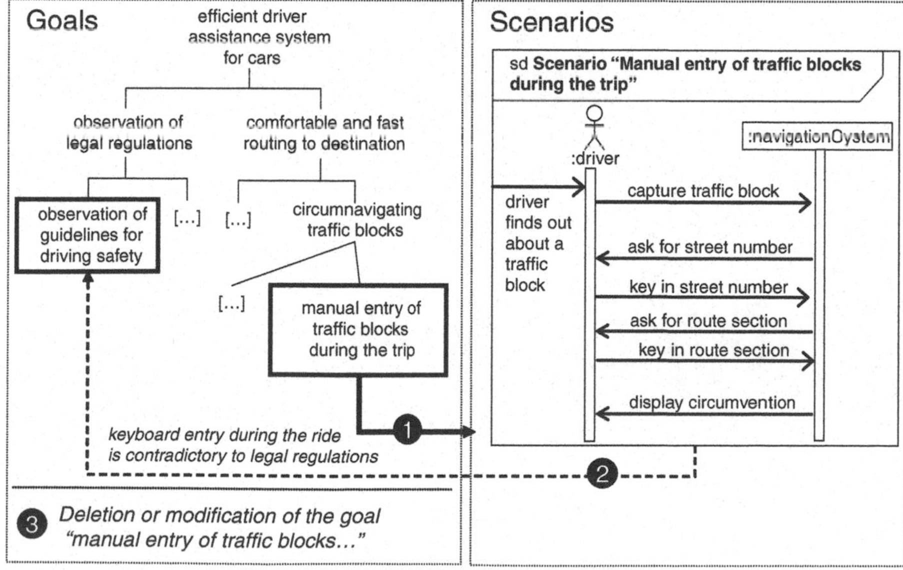

Fig. 12-7 *Revision of a goal initiated by a scenario*

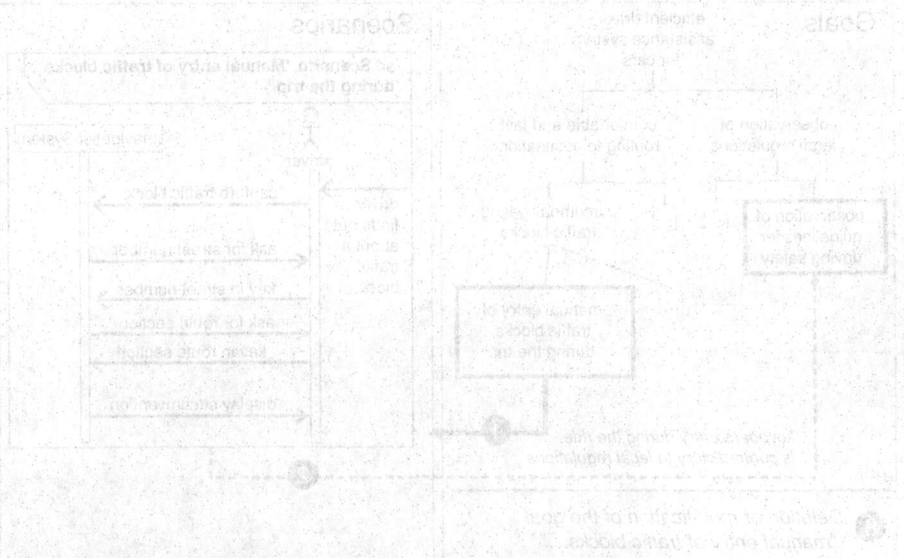

Recommended Literature for Part III.b

Basic Reading

[Carroll 2000] presents a scenario-based approach for analysing human–computer interactions. The book provides insight into the use of scenarios during system development.

In [Cockburn 2001], the main emphasis is put on the documentation of use cases in natural language. The book provides insight into the practice of writing use cases and offers a number of practical hints for the utilisation of use cases in projects.

Ivar Jacobson is one of the "fathers" of the Unified Modeling Language (UML). [Jacobson et al. 1992] provide an introduction to use case modelling and explain the importance of use cases as drivers of the entire development process.

[Weidenhaupt et al. 1998] provide an overview on the use of scenarios in requirements projects in practice. Besides the benefits of using scenarios, they also discuss the challenges of scenario usage in practice.

Advanced Reading

[Alexander and Maiden 2004] describe how to enhance system development by incorporating and analysing end-user scenarios. The use of scenarios is illustrated by means of case studies.

[Haumer et al. 1998] consider the elicitation and validation of requirements using scenarios. The authors explain the benefits of using scenarios for separating the system from its context and for embedding the requirements into a context.

[Rolland et al. 1998a] discuss the term "scenario" in detail and present a framework for the classification of scenarios.

In another article, [Rolland et al. 1998b] describe the complementary use of goals and scenarios in requirements engineering. Therein, the authors explain the relationships between goals and scenarios in requirements engineering.

[Sutcliffe et al. 1998] describe a method and a tool that support scenario-based requirements engineering. The application of the method and the tool are illustrated by means of a running example.

Part III.c
Solution-Oriented Requirements

Overview of Part III.c – Solution-Oriented Requirements

The goals and scenarios defined for the new system lay the foundation for deriving and developing solution-oriented requirements. Solution-oriented requirements specify, at the required level of detail, the desired properties and features of the system to be developed. Together with scenarios and goals, the solution-oriented requirements form the specification which provides the reference document for building the system.

In this part of the book, we outline:

- *The key differences and relationships between solution-oriented requirements and goals/scenarios*
- *The three traditional perspectives on solution-oriented requirements: the data, the functional, and the behavioural perspective*
- *Common conceptual modelling languages for documenting solution-oriented requirements*
- *The key concepts of the Unified Modeling Language (UML) for documenting and interrelating the three perspectives*
- *The interrelation of the three perspectives using the Systems Modeling Language (SysML)*

Classification Part III.c Solution-Oriented Requirements		Basic	Advanced
13	**Fundamentals**		
13.1	Three Perspectives on a Solution	✓	
13.2	Solution-Oriented Requirements, Goals, and Scenarios	✓	
14	**Documenting Solution-Oriented Requirements**		
14.1	Documenting Requirements in the Data Perspective	✓	
14.2	Documenting Requirements in the Functional Perspective	✓	
14.3	Documenting Requirements in the Behavioural Perspective	✓	
14.4	Documenting Quality Requirements in the Three Perspectives		✓
15	**Integration of the Three Perspectives**		
15.1	Extended Example	✓	
15.2	Relationships between the Perspectives	✓	
15.3	Integration Using UML 2		✓
15.4	Integration Using SysML		✓

Chapter 13
Fundamentals

In this chapter, we:

- *Introduce the three traditional perspectives on solution-oriented requirements*
- *Elaborate on the key differences between solution-oriented requirements, goals, and scenarios*
- *Describe the basic relationships between solution-oriented requirements, goals, and scenarios*

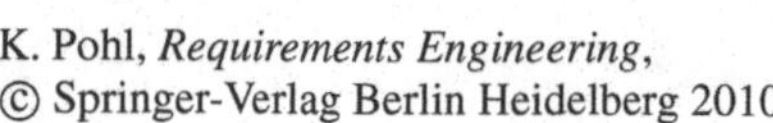

Solution-oriented requirements define the properties and features to be fulfilled by the system. Compared with goals and scenarios, solution-oriented requirements are defined in more detail. Goals and scenarios may document different views which are partly in conflict with each other, see e.g. conflicting goals (Section 7.4) and exploratory scenarios (Section 10.4). In contrast, solution-oriented requirements should document a single, consolidated view and be conflict free. In other words, any existing conflicts should be resolved prior to developing the system. Solution-oriented requirements, together with goals and scenarios, define the foundation for implementing the system. They jointly define the reference for the stakeholders (e.g. system architects, software engineers, quality assurance personnel) for developing the system. For example, based on the solution-oriented requirements, the system architecture as well as the test case designs are defined.

In the 1970s/1980s, three main perspectives for defining the solution-oriented requirements for a system were identified, and common modelling languages were established for documenting solution-oriented requirements in these perspectives. We outline these three perspectives in Section 13.1. In Section 13.2, we discuss the key differences between solution-oriented requirements, goals, and scenarios as well as the mutual relationships among them.

13.1 Three Perspectives on a Solution

Requirements for a software-intensive system should be defined in a way that facilitates the development of the system. Some development methods even support the generation of a software solution from a very detailed, formal requirements specification. Driven by the need to define requirements in a way that supports developing the software solution, three key perspectives on a software-intensive system were established during the 1970s and early 1980s. These perspectives are (still) commonly used in practice to define the requirements for software-intensive systems:

Data

- *Data perspective*: This perspective focusses on defining the data/information to be managed by the software-intensive system. In the data perspective, static aspects of the data are considered and defined such as the entities, relationships between entities, attributes, and attribute types relevant for the system. The manipulation of the data (the dynamic aspects of the data) is not considered in this perspective. Consequently, a specification focussing on the data perspective defines the requirements for the data and the data structures of the system. If the data of the system is defined at the required level of detail using a formal requirements specification language, the data structures for the software solution can even be generated. For example, entity–relationship models are commonly used to document the data and data structure of the system (see Section 14.1 for details). If the data is defined in an entity–relationship model at the required level of detail, relational database schemata for the software solution can be generated. An entity–relationship model thus partially predefines an intended solution at a conceptual level. We therefore call the requirements specified in entity–relationship models solution-oriented requirements.

- ❑ *Functional perspective*: The functional perspective typically defines the processes (functions) to be provided by the system, the manipulation of the data in each process, and the input–output relationships (information flows) among the processes. Traditionally, data flow diagrams are used to document the functional perspective of a system. By defining the processes, the interactions between the processes as well as the data stores to be implemented by the system (see Section 14.1.2 for details), data flow diagrams document requirements in a solution-oriented manner. Like for the data perspective, also for the functional perspective approaches have been proposed which even support the generation of a software solution (e.g. code fragments) based on a (formal and sufficiently detailed) functional requirements specification.

Function

- ❑ *Behavioural perspective*: The focus of the behavioural perspective is to define the overall behaviour of the system. Within this perspective, the external stimuli that the system receives and the reactions of the system as well as the relationship between stimuli and reactions are defined. In addition, the possible states (or modes) in which the system can be and the allowed transitions between the states (as reactions to stimuli) are defined. Hence this perspective focusses on the behavioural requirements for the system. Commonly, automata and statecharts are used for defining behaviour (see Section 14.3 for details). As for the other two perspectives, also for this perspective several approaches exist which support generating a software solution (e.g. design elements or source code) based on a formal, behavioural specification that is sufficiently detailed. For example, several approaches offer the possibility to generate executable code from statecharts.

Behaviour

We refer to the data, the functional, and the behavioural perspectives outlined above as the three traditional requirements perspectives. Each of these three perspectives represents a specific view on the software solution. Over the years, modelling languages have been developed to support the documentation of solution-oriented requirements within each perspective. We present some well-established modelling techniques for solution-oriented requirements in Chapter 14. A requirement defined within one of these perspectives (data, function, or behaviour) always partially defines an intended solution at a conceptual level. We therefore call such requirements solution-oriented requirements.

Relationships between the Three Perspectives

The three perspectives are related to each other

Although the three perspectives focus on different aspects of the intended solution, the modelling constructs defined for the languages of the three perspectives partly refer to the same subjects in the represented domain (universe of discourse). Thus the solution-oriented requirements defined in the three perspectives have some interrelationships. Examples of such relationships are:

Relationships due to data specifications

- ❑ *Specification of the data of the system in the data and functional perspectives*: The data requirements for the system are defined in the data perspective using, for instance, entity–relationship models (see Section 14.1). In addition, the data is also the subject of the requirements defined in the functional perspective. For example, a data flow model defines data flows (input and output data) between processes and data stores (see Section 14.2.1). Therein, the two perspectives focus on different aspects of the data. For instance, a functional specification does not define attributes, relationships between the data entities, cardinalities, and the like.

Relationships due to functional specifications

- *Specification of the system functions in the functional and behavioural perspectives*: A functional specification (e.g. a data flow model; see Section 14.2) is used to define the functions (processes) to be provided by the system. In addition, a behavioural specification specified using, for instance, statecharts (see Section 14.3) typically defines when specific functions shall be executed (e.g. it defines the states and/or the transitions at which a function shall be executed). Hence, both perspectives document information about the functions of the system and are therefore related to each other.

Integration of the perspectives

The representation of information about the same subjects in the universe of discourse in more than one perspective leads to overlaps of the documented information and thus requires alignment (integration) of the information represented in the three perspectives. Such an alignment helps, for instance, to detect inconsistencies between the perspectives. We illustrate the interrelation of the three perspectives in Section 15.1 using an example specification defined using the modelling languages for the three perspectives introduced in Chapter 14. Object-oriented modelling languages such as the UML (Unified Modeling Language) and languages for systems modelling such as the SysML (Systems Modeling Language) offer several means for integrating and aligning the requirements specified in the three perspectives as outlined in Chapter 15.

13.2 Solution-Oriented Requirements, Goals, and Scenarios

We outline the key differences between solution-oriented requirements and the goals and scenarios defined for the system in Section 13.2.1. In Section 13.2.2, we elaborate on the key relationships between solution-oriented requirements and goals and scenarios.

13.2.1 Key Differences

We characterise the key differences between solution-oriented requirements, goals, and scenarios based on five typical characteristics of these three artefact types:

Agreement about solution-oriented requirements

- *Agreement*: There is usually no complete agreement about goals. Goals document different viewpoints of the stakeholders and thus it may be the case that not all stakeholders agree with all goals (see Chapter 7). Similarly, not all stakeholders have to agree with all defined scenarios. For instance, some stakeholders may prefer one exploratory scenario, whereas other stakeholders prefer another one. In contrast, the solution-oriented requirements defined for the system should be agreed on by all stakeholders.

No requirements missing

- *Completeness*: Goals state the desired, essential properties of the system but do not define the details of each property. Scenarios typically do not define all possible sequences of interactions between the system and the context. They define exemplary, characteristic interaction sequences for satisfying the defined goals. In contrast, the solution-oriented requirements defined for a system should be as complete as possible. For example, a behavioural specification should define the overall behaviour of the system and not only parts of it like scenarios. Solution-oriented requirements must define all relevant details for implementing and testing the system.

- *Conflicts*: While goals typically contain conflicts (see Chapter 7), the solution-oriented requirements defined for the system should be free of conflicts. Thus, the stakeholders must resolve the conflicts that emerge during the requirements engineering process and decide which solution-oriented requirements are to be fulfilled by the system. Similar to goals, also scenarios can be in conflict with each other. For instance, scenarios may be defined that suggest entirely different ways of satisfying a specific goal.

Conflict free

- *Level of detail*: In contrast to goals and scenarios, solution-oriented requirements should be defined at a level of detail that facilitates the unambiguous realisation of the system. Compared with goals and scenarios, solution-oriented requirements thus contain far more detail.

Details specified

- *Intended solution*: Goals are defined independently of the intended solution, i.e. in a solution-neutral way. In contrast, solution-oriented requirements typically partly specify the intended solution and thus severely restrict the solution space. They facilitate the development and sometimes even the automatic generation of the software solution for a specific implementation platform. For example, from a data specification, a relational database schema used in the software solution can be generated. Moreover, solution-oriented requirements should not be neglected or ignored when developing (deriving) the software solution. In contrast, the scenarios defined during requirements engineering need not necessarily be realised by the system. For example, if a scenario has been defined to explore an alternative solution or illustrate possible user–system interactions, this scenario does not define an intended solution and hence does not need to be realised by the system.

Define intended solution

Figure 13-1 depicts the differences between goals, scenarios, and solution-oriented requirements along two dimensions: the level of agreement about the requirements

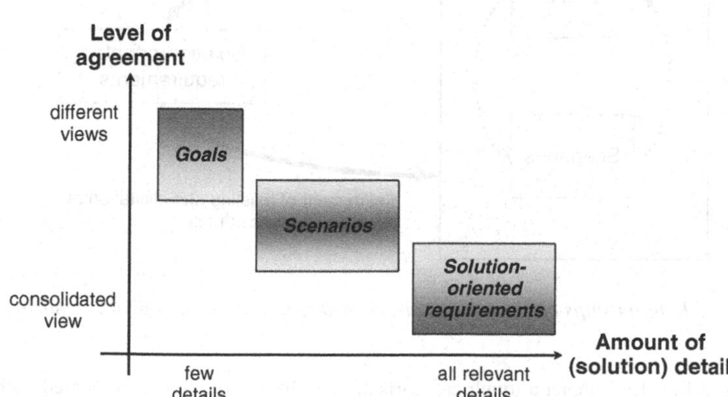

Fig. 13-1 *Coarse-grained characterisation of goals, scenarios and solution- oriented requirements*

and the amount of solution detail contained in the requirements artefacts.[1] As depicted in the figure, goals document different views of stakeholders (which may partly be in conflict with each other) and contain almost no details about the envisioned solution. Scenarios are more concrete than goals and, compared with goals, define more details about the envisioned solution. Prior to defining complete (detailed) scenarios, at least the high-level goals should be agreed on. Solution-oriented requirements, in contrast to goals, define more details about the envisioned solution. They restrict the potential software solutions more strongly than scenarios and thus define more solution details than scenarios. In addition, solution-oriented requirements should represent a consolidated view and be free of conflicts.

13.2.2 Key Relationships

Goals and scenarios are an excellent foundation for eliciting and validating solution-oriented requirements (see e.g. Van Lamsweerde and Willemet 1998; Van Lamsweerde 2009, Haumer et al. 1998]). Figure 13-2 depicts the key relationships between goals, scenarios, and solution-oriented requirements:[2]

Elicitation of requirements

- *Elicitation of solution-oriented requirements*: Solution-oriented requirements can be elicited from scenarios (and partially from goals) by analysing the scenarios and thereby identifying which particular solution-oriented requirement must be achieved to fulfil the scenarios.

Refinement of requirements

- *Refinement of solution-oriented requirements*: Scenarios and goals facilitate the refinement of solution-oriented requirements. For example, existing scenarios can be analysed to better understand an already documented solution-oriented requirement. The analysis of the scenario facilitates the elicitation of additional details and hence supports the refinement of the solution-oriented requirements.

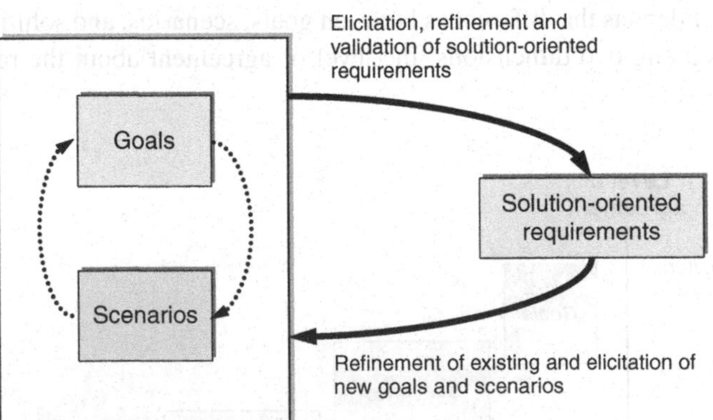

Fig. 13-2 *Relationships between solution-oriented requirements and goals/scenarios*

[1] The boxes in Fig. 13-1 depict a rough categorisation of the information documented with respect to the two dimensions. As indicated by the boxes, the level of agreement as well as the amount of solution details defined by each artefact type can vary.

[2] The interrelations between goals and scenarios are described in more detail in Section 12.3.

- *Validation of solution-oriented requirements*: Scenarios and goals facilitate the validation of solution-oriented requirements (see Section 27.7). For example, one can check whether each solution-oriented requirement contributes (positively or negatively) to a specific goal and thereby avoid "gold plating".[3] Furthermore, the stakeholders can check whether the solution-oriented requirement is in conflict with a defined scenario. For example, the defined overall system behaviour may forbid the execution of a (set of) scenario steps defined in the scenario.

Validation of requirements

- *Identification of new goals and scenarios*: Vice versa, the elicitation and definition of solution-oriented requirements (directly from stakeholders or other sources) can lead to the identification of new scenarios and/or goals which the system should fulfil as well as to a refinement of existing scenarios and goals.

Identification of scenarios and goals

Additional sources

As sketched above, scenarios and goals facilitate the elicitation of solution-oriented requirements (see [Van Lamsweerde und Willemet 1998; Van Lamsweerde 2009; Haumer et al. 1998]). However, solution-oriented requirements are also elicited from other sources (see Section 6.2).

Iterative process

Defining detailed solution-oriented requirements is typically achieved through an incremental process of eliciting solution-oriented requirements from various sources (including goals and scenarios), documenting, specifying, and validating the elicited solution-oriented requirements, and agreeing on the solution-oriented requirements to be fulfilled by the system. In addition to the elicitation, scenarios and goals also facilitate the validation of the solution-oriented requirements (see Section 27.7) as well as establishing agreement about the solution-oriented requirements (see Section 24.3).

[3] Gold plating refers to defining and implementing unnecessary features and requirements (see e.g. [Robertson and Robertson 2006]).

Chapter 14
Documenting Solution-Oriented Requirements

In this chapter, we describe common conceptual modelling languages for documenting solution-oriented requirements in the three perspectives:

- ❑ *Entity–relationship models and class diagrams for documenting requirements in the data perspective*
- ❑ *Data flow diagrams for documenting requirements in the functional perspective*
- ❑ *Automata, statecharts, and state machine diagrams for documenting requirements in the behavioural perspective*

Solution-oriented requirements can be documented using both conceptual modelling languages and natural language (see Chapters 17 and 18).

Documenting Solution-Oriented Requirements Using Natural Language

Intermingling of the perspectives

If solution-oriented requirements are documented using natural language, the three perspectives of data, function, and behaviour (see Section 13.1) are often intermingled. For example, the requirement documented in natural language in Example 14-1 defines data aspects ("glass break detector attached to entrance door"), functional aspects ("inform the security company") as well as behavioural aspects ("enter the alarm state") of the system.

> **Example 14-1:** Text-based documentation of a solution-oriented requirement
>
> R15: If a glass break detector attached to the entrance door detects that the entrance door has been damaged, the system shall enter the alarm state and inform the security company.

The documentation of requirements using natural language is described in detail in Chapters 17 and 18. Hence, in the following, we focus on the model-based documentation of solution-oriented requirements in the three perspectives.

Documenting Solution-Oriented Requirements Using Models

Documenting solution-oriented requirements using conceptual or formal models (also referred to as model-based requirements specification) allows a dedicated modelling language to be used for each perspective (data, function, and behaviour). A modelling language defines the essential concepts for documenting requirements in the respective perspective. The use of a modelling language therefore supports the stakeholders in focussing on a specific perspective when documenting solution-oriented requirements. Hence, in contrast to natural-language specification, model-based requirements help to avoid intermingling of the three perspectives (see e.g. [Davis 1993]). The separate documentation of requirements in the three perspectives using conceptual models is illustrated in Fig. 14-1:

- A data modelling language is used to document the data aspects such as the entities "entrance door" or "glass break detector" (see Example 14-1) and their mutual relationships (Fig. 14-1, top left).
- A behavioural modelling language is used to document the behavioural aspects such as "alarm state" or the event "entrance door damaged" (Fig. 14-1, top right).
- A functional modelling language is used to document the functional aspects such as the system function "inform security company" (Fig. 14-1, bottom).

Besides better separation of concerns (data, function, and behaviour), model-based requirements offer several other advantages over natural-language specification (see Section 20.1.1). In the following, we introduce modelling languages for documenting

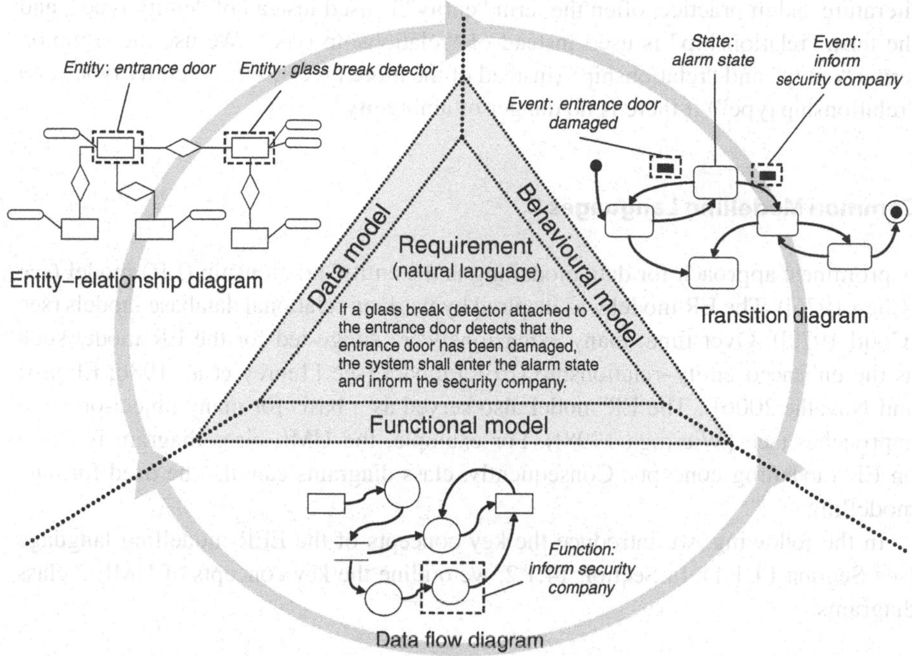

Fig. 14-1 *Model-based documentation of the three perspectives*

solution-oriented requirements in the three perspectives. For documenting requirements in the data perspective, we introduce the key concepts of the (enhanced) entity–relationship model and the UML 2[4] class diagram (see Section 14.1). For documenting requirements in the functional perspective, we introduce the key concepts of data flow diagrams (see Section 14.2). For documenting requirements in the behavioural perspective, we outline the key concepts of finite automata, statecharts, and UML 2 state machine diagrams (see Section 14.3). In addition, we refer to the relevant literature for more details about the modelling languages described in this chapter.

14.1 Documenting Requirements in the Data Perspective

Data models document data aspects such as entities and their relationships and attributes that are relevant for the system. Typically, the entities, attributes and relationships are identified by considering the subject facet (see Section 6.3). However, data aspects may also originate from considering other facets, i.e. the usage facet, the IT system facet, or the development facet.

Entity and relationship vs. entity type and relationship type

Data models are defined at the type level (or model level; see Section 19.5.2), i.e. they document entity types and relationship types. Concrete entities and relationships are instances of these entity types and relationship types. However, in the

[4] We use the term UML 2 in this book to denote versions 2.x of the Unified Modeling Language specified by the Object Management Group (OMG); see e.g. [OMG 2009b].

literature and in practice, often the term "entity" is used instead of "entity type", and the term "relationship" is used instead of "relationship type". We use the common terms "entity" and "relationship" (instead of the more precise terms "entity type" and "relationship type") if there is no danger of ambiguity.

Common Modelling Languages

From entity–relationship modelling to UML class diagrams

A prominent approach for data modelling is the entity–relationship (ER) model (see [Chen 1976]). The ER model was inspired by work on relational database models (see [Codd 1970]). Over time, many extensions were suggested for the ER model such as the enhanced entity–relationship (EER) model (see [Teorey et al. 1986; Elmasri and Navathe 2006]). The ER model also served as a basis for many object-oriented approaches (see [Wieringa 1998]). For example, the UML class diagram is based on ER modelling concepts. Consequently, class diagrams can also be used for data modelling.

In the following, we introduce the key concepts of the EER modelling language (see Section 14.1.1). In Section 14.1.2, we outline the key concepts of UML 2 class diagrams.

14.1.1 Enhanced Entity–Relationship Model

In the following, we briefly describe the key concepts of the enhanced entity–relationship (EER) model (which includes the elements of the standard ER model) according to [Elmasri and Navathe 2006].[5] Elements of the standard ER model are, e.g. entity types, relationship types, attributes, roles, and (simple) cardinality constraints. The EER model added concepts such as generalisation and specialisation relationships to the ER model. For a detailed introduction to the ER/EER model, we refer to [Elmasri and Navathe 2006].

Entity Type

Abstraction and classification of instances

An entity type (often also referred to as entity) represents a set of entities with similar properties. Therein, the entity type abstracts from the concrete entities (i.e. the instances). An entity can be a material or immaterial object in a domain of interest for the system. An entity type classifies the set of all entities into those entities that are instances of this entity type and those that are not. In the graphical notation of an ER model, an entity type is depicted as a rectangle (see Fig. 14-2).

Example of an entity type

The entity type "LIBRARY USER" depicted in Fig. 14-2 represents all library users. An instance of this entity type would be a specific library user, e.g. the library user "Carl".

[5] For simplicity, we use the term ER model for both, the standard entity-relationship model and the enhanced entity–relationship model in this book.

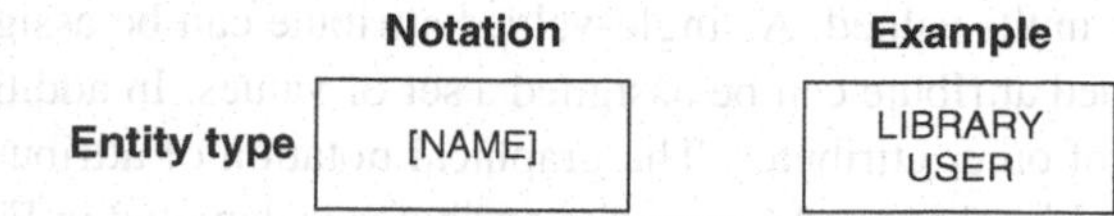

Fig. 14-2 *Graphical notation of an entity type*

Relationship Type

Abstraction from concrete relationships

A relationship type (often also referred to as relationship) relates two or multiple entity types. It represents a set of similar relationship instances that relate entities of the respective entity types and that are relevant for the system to be developed. Hence, a relationship type R between n entity types $E_1, \ldots, E_n$ defines a set of relationships between entities of the entity types $E_1, \ldots, E_n$. A relationship type classifies the relationships between a set of entities into relationships that are instances of this relationship type and those that are not. If exactly two entity types participate in a relationship (type), the relationship (type) is called a binary relationship (type). If three entity types participate in a relationship (type), the relationship (type) is called a ternary relationship (type).

Graphical notation

The graphical notation of a relationship type in an ER model is shown in Fig. 14-3. The relationship type shown in the figure represents a set of binary relationships.

Roles

An entity type that participates in a specific relationship type can be assigned a role which its entities take in a relationship of this relationship type. The role of a participating entity type is stated at the end of the relationship type. If the role is obvious, the role name can be omitted.

Example of a relationship type

Figure 14-3 depicts the relationship type "BORROWS" between the entity types "LIBRARY USER" and "BOOK". This relationship type represents the set of "BORROWS" relationships between concrete library users (such as "Mr. Miller") and concrete books (such as "Requirements engineering book with the signature SE-1213").

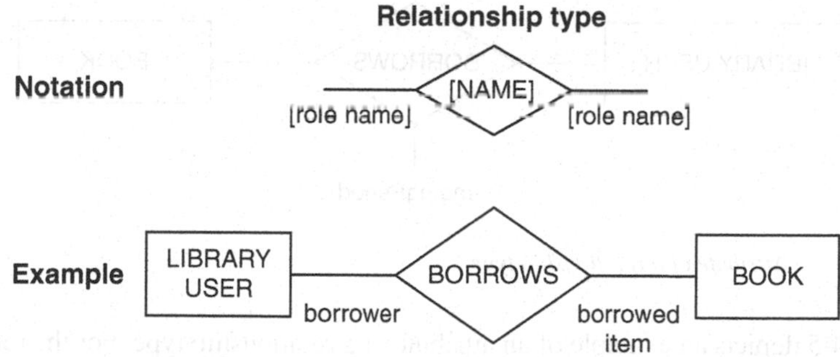

Fig. 14-3 *Graphical notation of a relationship type*

Attribute

Properties of entity/relationship types

An attribute defines a property that is relevant for the system. By defining an attribute for an entity type one defines the attributes of each entity of this type. An attribute can be either single- or multi-valued. A single-valued attribute can be assigned only one value. A multi-valued attribute can be assigned a set of values. In addition, attributes may be composed of other attributes. The graphical notation of attributes in an EER model including multi-valued and composite attributes is depicted in Fig. 14-4.

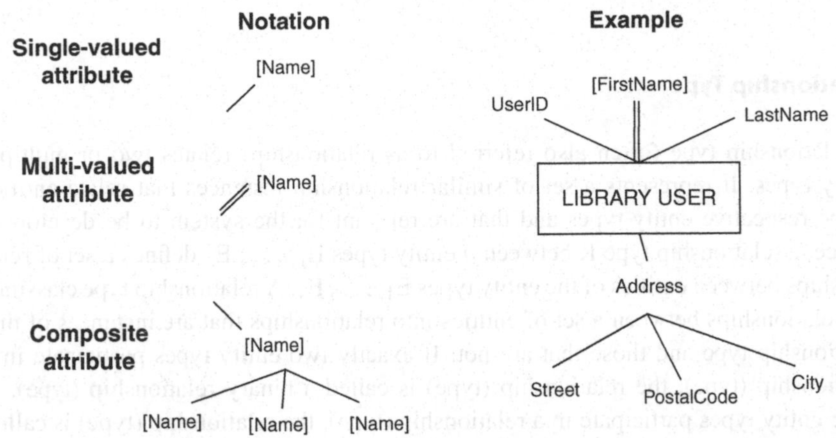

Fig. 14-4 *Graphical notation of attributes in an EER model*

Examples of attributes

The example depicted in Fig. 14-4 defines attributes for the entity type "LIBRARY USER". The attribute "FirstName" is defined as a multi-valued attribute, since a library user may have several given names. The attribute "Address" is a composite attribute that consists of the attributes "Street", "PostalCode", and "City".

Attributes of relationship types

Attributes can be defined for entity types and for relationship types. An attribute of a relationship type defines a property that belongs to the relationship type itself, i.e. a property that cannot be assigned to any of the entities that participate in the relationship type (see Fig. 14-5). The value of such an attribute characterises the relationship between the entities.

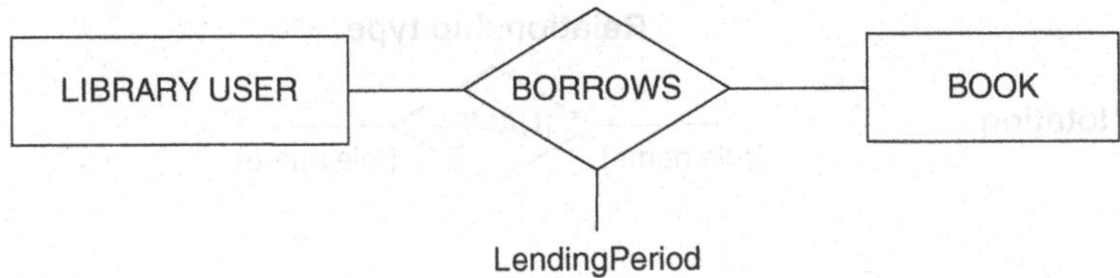

Fig. 14-5 *Attribute of a relationship type*

Fig. 14-5 depicts an example of an attribute of a relationship type. For the relationship type "BORROWS", the single attribute "LendingPeriod" is defined. The lending period cannot be modelled as an attribute of the entity type "LIBRARY USER" since a library user can borrow different books with different lending periods (e.g. short loans with a lending period of 1 week and regular loans with a lending period of 4 weeks). The lending period can also not be modelled as an attribute of the entity type "BOOK", since a concrete book can be borrowed by different users for different periods of time (e.g. 8 weeks by library employees and 4 weeks by other library users). Defining the lending period as an attribute of the relationship "BORROWS" allows for lending periods that are determined by the specific combination of library user and book.

Cardinality Constraint

Restricting instantiations

A cardinality constraint restricts the permissible number of entities that may participate in a defined relationship type. A cardinality constraint can be defined at each end of a relationship type. The (min, max) notation is used for defining cardinality constraints. A cardinality constraint (min, max) for an entity type *E* participating in a relationship type *R* means that each entity *e* of the entity type *E* must participate in at least *min* and at most *max* relationship instances of *R* at any point in time. The graphical notation for cardinality constraints is shown in Fig. 14-6.

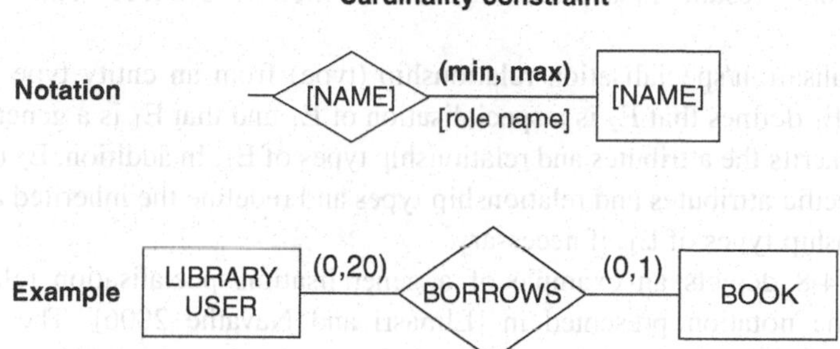

Fig. 14-6 *Graphical notation of a cardinality constraint in an EER model*

The cardinality constraints depicted in Fig. 14-7 express that a library user can borrow 0–20 books, while each book (i.e. each specific exemplar of a book) can be borrowed by at most one library user. At the bottom of Fig. 14-7, a valid instantiation of this model is illustrated, in which library user "1" borrows books "A" and "B", library user "2" borrows no book, and library user "3" borrows book "D".

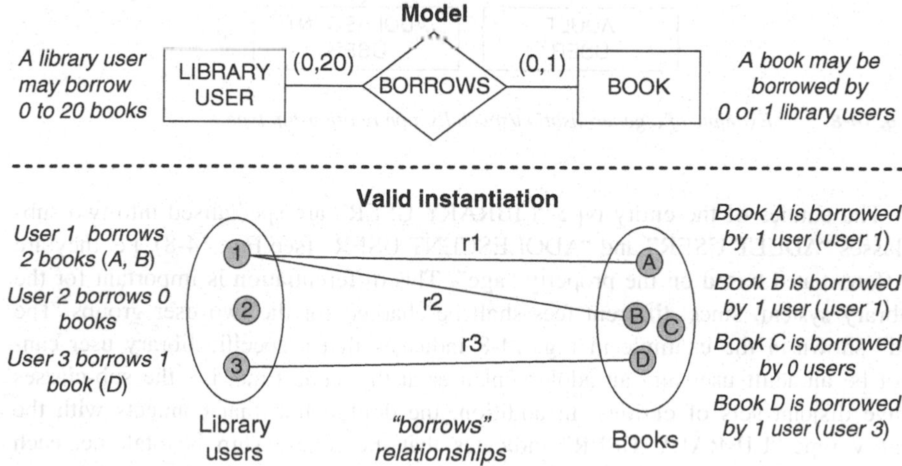

Fig. 14-7 *Cardinality constraints for a relationship type*

Generalisation and Specialisation

Super-class and sub-classes

The generalisation/specialisation relationship type is used to specialise a general entity type into a set of sub-classes or to generalise several specific entity types with common properties into a more general super-class. In other words, the generalisation/specialisation relationship (type) relates a super-class to a set of sub-classes.

Identifying sub-classes

By means of the generalisation/specialisation relationship, subsets of entities of the super-class are modelled that are relevant for the system to be developed and must therefore be defined explicitly. To define the sub-classes, a characteristic property is chosen that allows differentiation between the entities of the super-class. For instance, the property "type of binding" of the entity type "BOOK" results in sub-classes such as "PAPERBACK" and "HARDCOVER". Other properties result in different sets of sub-classes. For instance, the property "number of authors" results in sub-classes such as "MONOGRAPH" and "EDITED BOOK".

Inheritance of attributes and relationships

A generalisation/specialisation relationship (type) from an entity type E_2 to an entity type E_1 defines that E_2 is a specialisation of E_1 and that E_1 is a generalisation of E_2. E_2 inherits the attributes and relationship types of E_1. In addition, E_2 may have its own, specific attributes and relationship types and redefine the inherited attributes and relationship types of E_1, if necessary.

Example of a generalisation/ specialisation relationship

Figure 14-8 depicts an example of a generalisation/specialisation relationship based on the notation presented in [Elmasri and Navathe 2006]. The u-shaped subset symbol that is part of the notation indicates the direction of the generalisation/specialisation: the sets of entities of the sub-classes are subsets of the set of entities of the super-class.

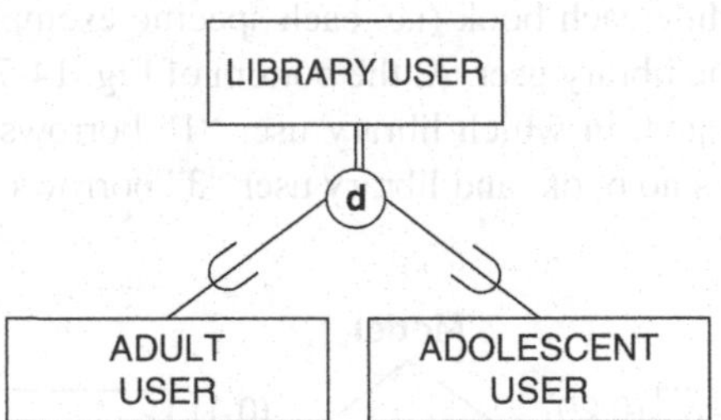

Fig. 14-8 *Example of a generalisation/specialisation relationship type*

The entities of the entity type "LIBRARY USER" are specialised into two sub-classes "ADULT USER" and "ADOLESCENT USER" (see Fig. 14-8), i.e. they are differentiated based on the property "age". This differentiation is important for the library system, since different fees shall be charged for the two user groups. The "d" shown in the example in Fig. 14-8 indicates that a specific library user cannot be an adult user and an adolescent user at the same time, i.e. the sub-classes have disjoint sets of entities. In addition, the double line that connects with the entity type "LIBRARY USER" indicates that the relationship is total, i.e. each entity of the entity type "LIBRARY USER" is either an adult user or an adolescent user.

Types of Generalisation Relationships

Generalisation relationships are classified according to the following characteristics:

- *Disjoint vs. overlapping*: A generalisation/specialisation relationship type can be overlapping or disjoint. If the relationship type is disjoint, entities of the super-class can belong to only one of the sub-classes. If the relationship is overlapping, entities of the super-class can belong to two or multiple sub-classes. *Disjoint vs. overlapping*
- *Total vs. partial*: A generalisation/specialisation relationship can be total or partial. If the relationship is total, each entity of the super-class must belong to at least one sub-class. If the relationship is partial, there may be entities of the super-class which do not belong to any of the sub-classes. *Total vs. partial*

In the following, we explain the four combinations that arise from the above characterisation of generalisation relationships.

Disjoint and total generalisation relationship

Figure 14-9 depicts a disjoint, total generalisation relationship. The circle with the "d" indicates that the entity sets of the sub-classes are disjoint. The double line connected to the super-class indicates that the generalisation relationship is total. Each entity of the super-class belongs to exactly one sub-class. For example, each library user is either an adult user or an adolescent user.

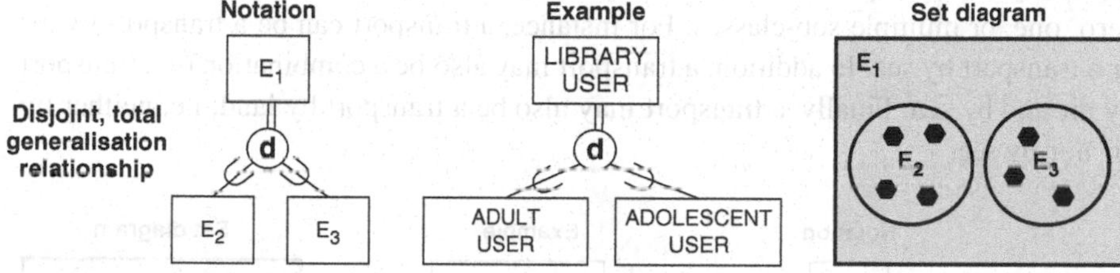

Fig. 14-9 *Disjoint, total generalisation relationship*

Disjoint and partial generalisation relationship

Figure 14-10 depicts a disjoint, partial generalisation relationship. The circle with the "d" indicates that the entity sets of the sub-classes are disjoint. The single line connecting the super-class indicates that the generalisation relationship is partial. Each entity of the super-class belongs to at most one sub-class. For instance, a vehicle can be a motorcycle, a passenger car, or some other type of vehicle. However, according to Fig. 14-10, no vehicle can be both, a motorcycle and a passenger car.

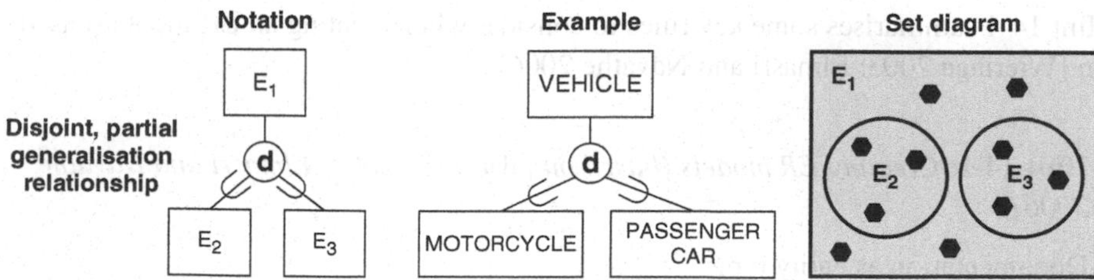

Fig. 14-10 *Disjoint, partial generalisation relationship*

Overlapping and total generalisation relationship

Figure 14-11 depicts an overlapping, total generalisation relationship. The circle with the "o" indicates that the entity sets of the sub-classes may overlap. The double line connecting the super-class indicates that the generalisation relationship is total. Each entity of the super-class belongs to at least one sub-class. For example, each book can be classified as a book that is written in English or a book that is written in a foreign language. In addition, there are books that are written in two languages, e.g. English and French, and hence belong to both sub-classes.

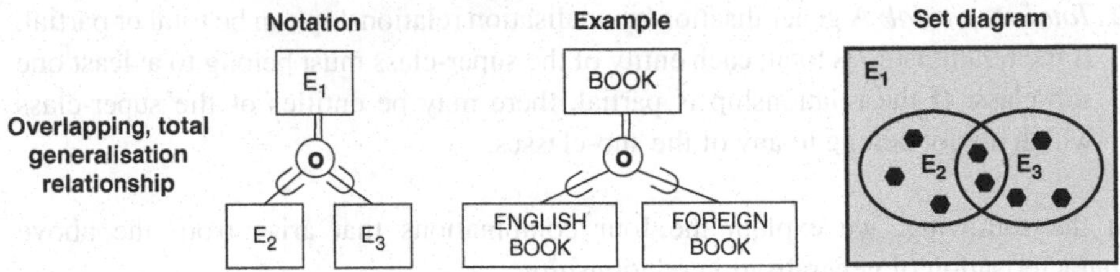

Fig. 14-11 *Overlapping, total generalisation relationship*

Overlapping and partial generalisation relationship

Figure 14-12 depicts an overlapping, partial generalisation relationship. The circle with the "o" indicates that the entity sets of the sub-classes may overlap. The single line connecting the super-class indicates that the generalisation relationship is partial. An entity of the super-class can belong to an arbitrary number of sub-classes, i.e. zero, one, or multiple sub-classes. For instance, a transport can be a transport by air or a transport by sea. In addition, a transport may also be a combination of a transport by air and by sea. Finally, a transport may also be a transport by land, i.e. neither by air nor by sea.

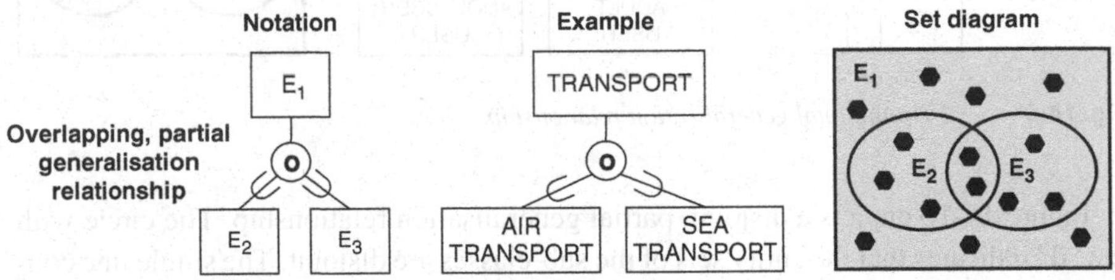

Fig. 14-12 *Overlapping, partial generalisation relationship*

Hints for Creating Entity–Relationship Models

Hint 14-1 summarises some key rules to consider when creating an ER model (based on [Wieringa 2003; Elmasri and Navathe 2006]).

!

Hint 14-1: *Creating ER models (based on [Wieringa 2003; Elmasri and Navathe 2006])*

Documentation as entity type:

- ❑ Objects of a specific type are modelled as an entity type if the system must send, receive, or persistently store information about these objects.

(to be continued)

Hint 14-1 *(continued)*

Documentation as attribute:

- Information about entity types that is relevant for the system (e.g. because the system must record this information) is documented using attributes.

Entity type versus attribute:

- An entity has an identity of its own. An attribute is only meaningful as a property of some entity (or relationship).
- If an entity type E_1 exists that has only one attribute and is only related to one other entity type E_2, you should consider modelling the entity type E_1 as an attribute of E_2.

Attribute versus relationship:

- If an attribute of an entity type E_1 is a reference to another entity type E_2, you should consider modelling this attribute as a relationship (type). This holds in particular if an attribute is defined for E_2 that is a reference to E_1.

Entity type versus relationship:

- While an entity has an identity of its own, a relationship draws its identity from the participating entities.

14.1.2 Class Diagrams

UML 2 class diagrams are used to document a system at different levels of abstraction. Class diagrams are created and refined during requirements engineering as well as during design and implementation. In this section, we focus on the use of class diagrams in requirements engineering. Class diagrams are used to document the static view of a system. In requirements engineering, class diagrams are used in a similar way to entity–relationship models (see Section 14.1.1), i.e. for documenting requirements in the data perspective. A class diagram consists of a set of classes and relationships between these classes.

In the following, we sketch the key concepts of UML 2 class diagrams used for documenting requirements in the data perspective. For a more detailed description of UML 2 class diagrams, we refer, for instance, to [Rumbaugh et al. 2005].

Class

Set of similar objects

A class describes a set of (material or immaterial) objects which have a similar structure, a similar behaviour, and similar relationships. Objects may define, for instance, specific orders, tasks, products, etc. Objects have a unique identity which means that two objects having the same attribute values are still distinguishable.

Compartments of a class

A class is typically depicted as a rectangle with three compartments (see Fig. 14-13). In the first compartment, the name of the class is defined. In the second compartment, the attributes are defined. The third compartment defines the operations provided by the class. Compartments may be suppressed (except the first one) or added as needed. The level of detail at which a class is defined depends on the modelling purpose.

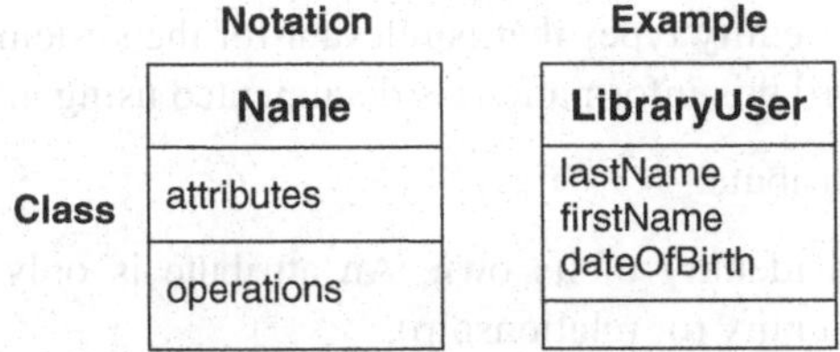

Fig. 14-13 *Graphical notation for classes*

Figure 14-13 depicts the class "LibraryUser". The class defines three attributes: "lastName", "firstName", and "dateOfBirth". Operations are not defined in the example, which is typical of an early requirements engineering stage. Hence the operations compartment of the class "LibraryUser" is empty. If a class defines a structural element of the system, the required functions of this element can be defined as operations in the operations compartment of the class.

Attribute

Defining details about an attribute

Attributes are defined as lines of text in the attribute compartment of a class. The notation for attributes is depicted in Fig. 14-14. Only the name is mandatory for defining an attribute. The concept of visibility is mostly used in detailed design. The type, multiplicity, and property string are used for defining details about an attribute in requirements engineering:

- *Type*: The type of the attribute is denoted by a classifier such as a class or a data type. The type restricts the values that can be assigned to the attribute.
- *Multiplicity*: The multiplicity consists of a lower bound and an upper bound. It indicates the permissible number of values that can be assigned to the attribute. An optional attribute has the lower bound "0". A mandatory attribute has the lower bound "1". A single-valued attribute has the upper bound "1". A multi-valued has an upper bound greater than one or "*" to denote that an arbitrary number of values can be assigned to this attribute. For instance, if an attribute is optional and can have at most four values (of the specified type), the multiplicity is defined as [0..4].
- *Property string*: Examples of property strings are {ordered}, {unique}, and {read only}. The property string {ordered} means that the values of this attribute are ordered according to some ordering criterion that is appropriate for the attribute type. The property string {unique} means that each value of a multi-valued attribute is unique, i.e. no two values are identical. The property string {read only} means that the value(s) of this attribute cannot be changed.

At the bottom of Fig. 14-14, several examples of attribute definitions are depicted. For instance, the attribute "lastName" has the type "String" and the multiplicity "[1..1]", i.e. the attribute is mandatory and single-valued. The default value for this attribute is "New user".

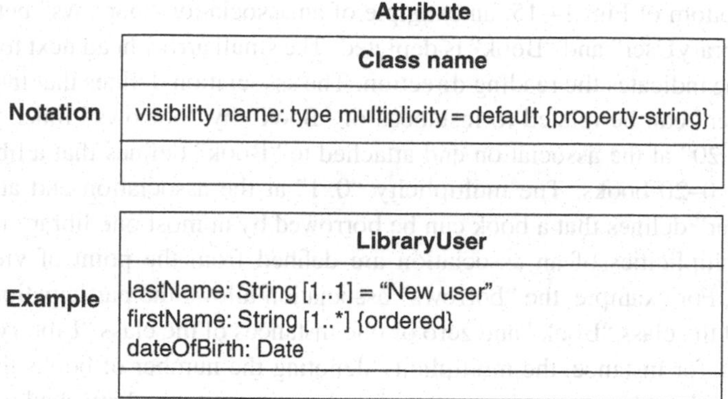

Fig. 14-14 *Attribute notation*

Association

Associations are used to relate classes to each other. An association A between two classes C_1 and C_2 represents a set of links between objects of the classes C_1 and C_2. An association that relates two classes (or a class to itself) is called a binary association. An association that relates n classes $C_1, \ldots, C_n$ is called an n-ary association. The notation of an association is depicted in Fig. 14-15. An association in a class diagram can optionally be annotated with the association name. At each end of an association, a role, a multiplicity, and a property string can be defined for the class attached at this end of the association:

- *Role*: The role name defines which role the class plays in this association.
- *Multiplicity*: The multiplicity defines how many instances of the class at the corresponding association end can participate in the association. The multiplicity at an association end is defined in the same way as the multiplicity of an attribute. Examples of valid multiplicities are "0..1", "0..*", and "1..*".
- *Property string*: The same property strings can be used for defining an association end as for defining an attribute. Examples of property strings are {ordered}, {unique}, and {read only}.

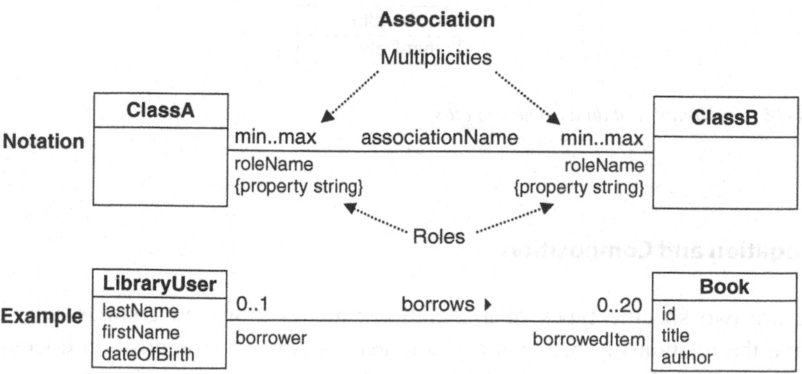

Fig. 14-15 *Graphical notation for associations*

Association ends

At the bottom of Fig. 14-15, an example of an association "borrows" between the classes "LibraryUser" and "Book" is depicted. The small arrow head next to the association name indicates the reading direction. The association defines that instances of "LibraryUser" can be related to instances of "Book" by "borrows" links. The multiplicity "0..20" at the association end attached to "Book" defines that a library user can borrow 0–20 books. The multiplicity "0..1" at the association end attached to "LibraryUser" defines that a book can be borrowed by at most one library user. Note that the multiplicities of an association are defined from the point of view of the association. For example, the "borrows" association allows the participation of 0–20 instances of the class "Book" and zero or one instances of the class "LibraryUser". In other words, for instance, the multiplicity denoting the number of books that can be associated with a library user is annotated at the association end attached to the class "Book".

Association classes

If the value of an attribute is not determined by a single class but depends on the relationship between multiple classes, this attribute can be defined as an attribute of an association class. An association class is both an association and a class at the same time. Therefore, an association class not only relates two or multiple classes but also defines attributes that characterise the relationships among these classes. The notation of an association class is depicted in Fig. 14-16. At the bottom of Fig. 14-16, the association class "Lending" is shown. This association class has an attribute "returnDate" that belongs to the association rather than to one of the participating classes.

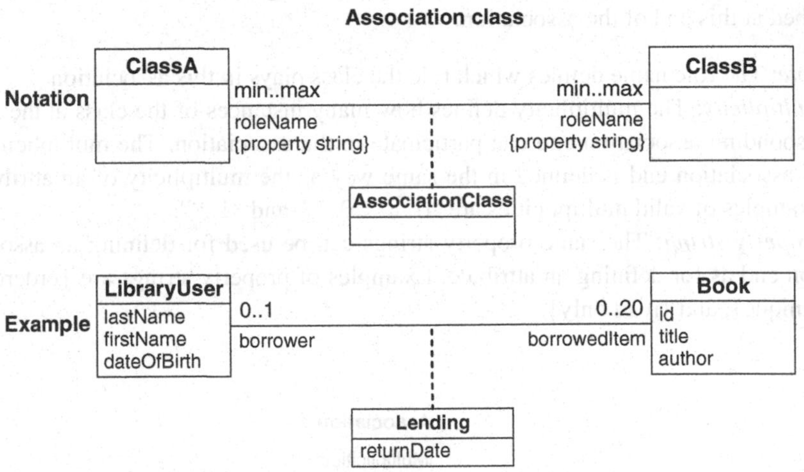

Fig. 14-16 *Notation of an association class*

Aggregation and Composition

There are two specific types of associations: aggregation and composition. Both describe the relationship between a whole and its parts. A composition documents a stronger form of whole–part relationship than an aggregation. In a composition relationship, each part may have only one owner, i.e. be part of only one composite.

Typically, a part of a composition cannot exist without the composite. If the composite is destroyed, all its parts are also destroyed. The graphical notation of aggregation and composition relationships is depicted in Fig. 14-17. A hollow diamond denotes an aggregation; a solid diamond denotes a composition. The diamond is drawn at the association end of the aggregate or composite class.

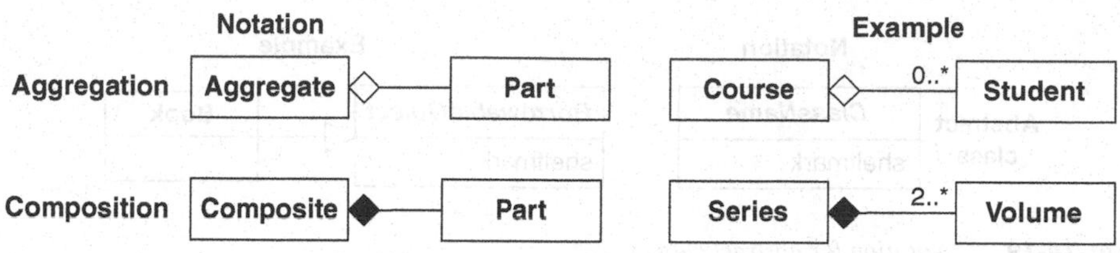

Fig. 14-17 Graphical notation for aggregation and composition

Example of aggregation and composition

The example depicted in Fig. 14-17 on the right defines that a student can be part of a course, and a volume can be part of a series. The aggregation relationship between "Course" and "Student" permits that a student can be part of multiple courses. In contrast, the composition relationship between "Series" and "Volume" demands that each volume be part of at most one series.

Generalisation

Relation between a sub-class and a super-class

A generalisation relationship relates a sub-class to a super-class. The instances of a sub-class are indirect instances of the super-class. A sub-class must be substitutable for its super-class. The sub-class inherits the attributes, operations, and relationships of the super-class. It may also define additional attributes, operations, and relationships and override the inherited attributes, operations, and relationships, if necessary. The graphical notation for generalisation relationships is depicted in Fig. 14-18.

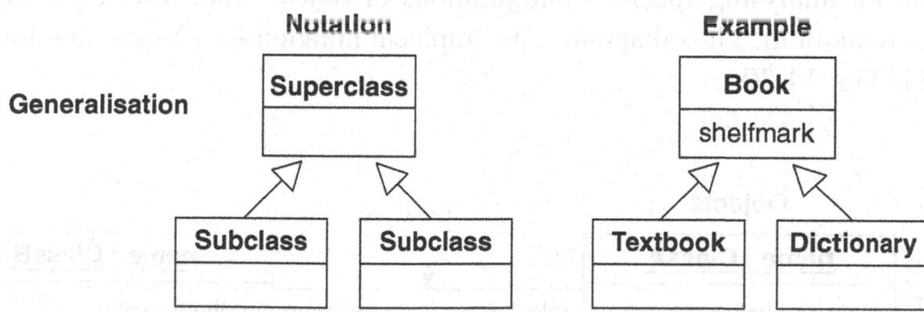

Fig. 14-18 Graphical notation for generalisation relationships

The example depicted in Fig. 14-18 defines two sub-classes of the class "Book": the class "Textbook" and the class "Dictionary". Since sub-classes inherit the attributes of the super-class, the classes "Textbook" and "Dictionary" also have the attribute "shelfmark".

Abstract Classes

No direct instances

An abstract class has no direct instances. Only the (non-abstract) sub-classes of the abstract class may have direct instances. The notation for abstract classes is depicted in Fig. 14-19. Abstract classes are defined like ordinary classes, yet the class name is written in italics.

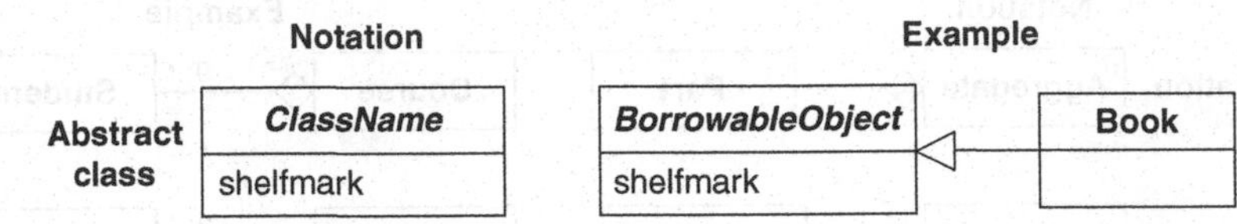

Fig. 14-19 *Notation for abstract classes*

Example of an abstract class

In the example depicted in Fig. 14-19, an abstract super-class "BorrowableObject" is defined to represent all types of media that can be borrowed from the library. This class defines the attributes that are shared by all types of media such as the attribute "shelfmark". Since "BorrowableObject" is abstract, it cannot have direct instances. However, the class "Book" defined as a sub-class of "BorrowableObject" is allowed to have direct instances.

Object

Class and object diagrams

An object is an instance of a class. It has concrete attribute values for each attribute defined by the class. Furthermore, an object is related to other objects by means of links. The links are instances of the associations of the class. Objects are usually not modelled in a class diagram. However, UML offers the object diagram for modelling objects and links between objects. An object diagram can be used to document the objects and object links in a system at a specific point of time, i.e. a kind of snapshot. Since objects instantiate classes and links instantiate associations an object diagram can be regarded as an instantiation of a class diagram. Creating object diagrams can be helpful for analysing specific configurations of objects and, from this, drawing conclusions about the class diagram. The graphical notation for objects (and links) is depicted in Fig. 14-20.

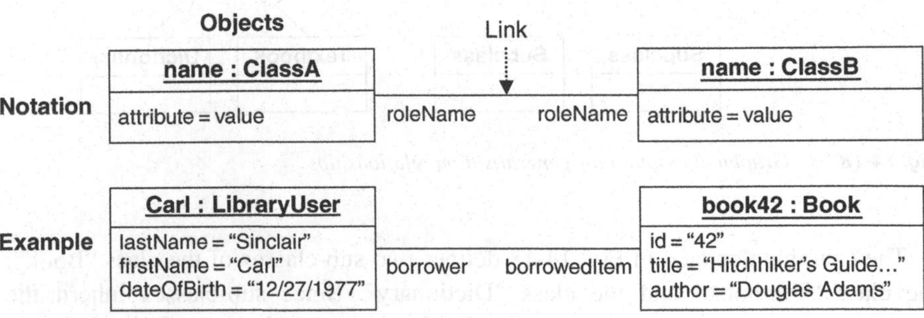

Fig. 14-20 *Graphical notation for objects*

Hints for Creating Class Diagrams

Since class diagrams are based on ER models, the rules presented in Hint 14-1 can also be applied to class diagrams. Additionally, the following rules (based on [Balzert 2001]) should be considered when creating class diagrams:

!

Hint 14-2: *Creating class diagrams*

Class:

- The name of a class should be a noun.
- The name of a class should be unique and comprehensive, i.e. it should, for example, not only describe the role of this class in a specific association with another class.

Association:

- The name of an association should be a verb.
- In case of reflexive associations (i.e. associations of a class to itself), role names must be annotated.
- If a class has multiple associations and plays different roles in the different associations, the role names should be annotated.
- If two classes are related by a whole–part relationship, a composition or aggregation relationship should be used instead of a general association. If a part can be owned by at most one composite at the same time and the composite is responsible for managing its parts (e.g. creation and destruction), a composition relationship should be used (solid diamond). To express that a part can belong to multiple aggregates at the same time, an aggregation relationship should be used (hollow diamond).

Attribute:

- The name of an attribute should be a noun.
- The name of an attribute should be unique.
- If it is not clear whether an attribute belongs to a class or to an association of the class, one should check whether the attribute still exists for each object of the class even if the association is removed. If it still exists, the attribute belongs to the class. Otherwise, it belongs to the association.

Class vs. attribute:

- The objects of a class exist independently of other objects. In contrast, an attribute only exists if the object with which the attribute is associated exists.

14.2 Documenting Requirements in the Functional Perspective

In the functional perspective, solution-oriented requirements are documented by means of functional models. A functional model of a system documents requirements for the system in terms of functions, data flows between the functions and data stores.

Functional Modelling Languages

Function modelling and Structured Analysis

Data flow models are the most popular representatives of functional models and are commonly used in function-oriented analysis methods. Prominent representatives of function-oriented analysis methods are, amongst others:

- Structured Analysis (SA) [DeMarco 1978; Weinberg 1978]
- Structured Analysis and Design Technique (SADT) [Ross and Schoman 1977]
- Structured Systems Analysis [Gane and Sarson 1977]
- Essential Systems Analysis [McMenamin and Palmer 1984]
- Modern Structured Analysis [Yourdon 1989; Yourdon 2006]

In Section 14.2.1, we introduce data flow diagrams based on [DeMarco 1978]. Section 14.2.2 discusses the key concepts of essential models (see Section 3.2) introduced by [McMenamin and Palmer 1984].

14.2.1 Data Flow Models

A data flow model consists of a set of data flow diagrams, a data dictionary, and so-called mini-specifications. In this section, we outline the key modelling constructs of data flow diagrams (DFDs) as well as the main concepts of data dictionaries and mini-specifications. For a detailed introduction to data flow models, we refer to [DeMarco 1978].

Process (Function)

Manipulation of data

A process or function represents a task or activity that the system shall provide or implement. A process consumes some input data, processes the data, and passes on the result (the output data) to another process, a data store (called a "file" in [DeMarco 1978]), or a sink. A process hence transforms inputs into outputs. Processes can be refined, i.e. a process can be described in more detail in a separate data flow diagram (DFD). We explain the concept of hierarchical decomposition on Page 243. The graphical notation of a process in a DFD is shown in Fig. 14-21.

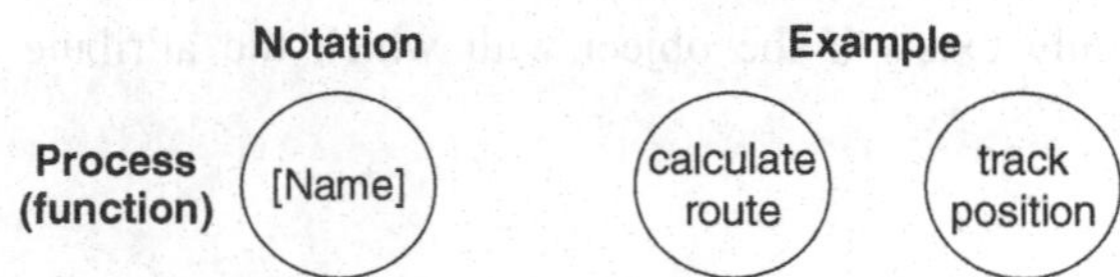

Fig. 14-21 *Graphical notation of a process in a DFD*

Examples of processes

Figure 14-21 depicts two processes (functions) of a navigation system. The process "calculate route" calculates a route from a source to a destination. The process "track position" keeps track of the current position of the car with respect to the calculated route.

Source/Sink

Sources and sinks are external objects (e.g. persons, groups of persons, departments, organisations, other systems) that communicate with the system through data flows.

External objects interacting with the system

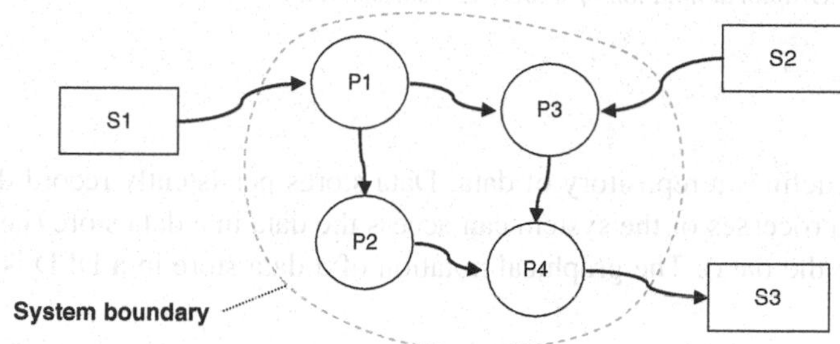

Fig. 14-22 *Sources and sinks are outside the system boundary*

System boundary

A source passes data on to the system or to the processes defined for the system. A sink receives data from the system or from the processes. As depicted in Fig. 14-22, sources and sinks are elements outside the system boundary, i.e. they reside in the context (see Chapter 5) and hence cannot be changed by the system development process.

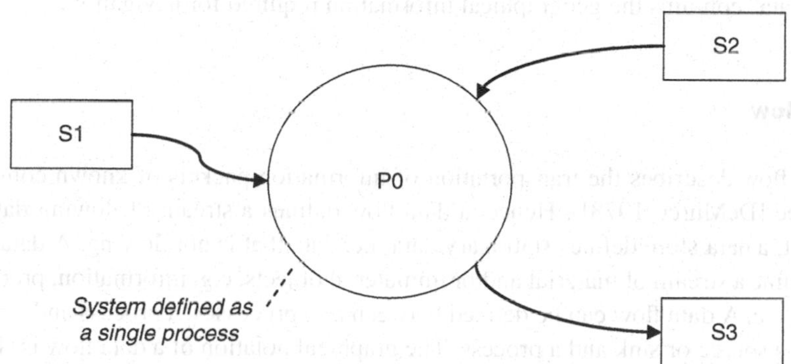

Fig. 14-23 *Context diagram*

System interfaces

The data flows between the system and the sources and sinks define the system interfaces. In Structured Analysis, the so-called context diagram (see [DeMarco 1978]) is used to define the system interfaces. In a context diagram, the system is defined as a single process that exchanges data with the sources and sinks (see Fig. 14-23). In more recent function-oriented approaches, the context diagram has been merged with the level 0 diagram; see Page 243f.

Persons, organisation structures etc. that reside within the system boundary are not modelled as sources and sinks. Figure 14-24 shows the graphical notation of sources/sinks in a DFD.

Examples of sources/sinks

Figure 14-24 depicts two examples of sources/sinks of a navigation system. The "Driver" is both a source and a sink since the navigation system receives input from the driver (e.g. the desired destination) and provides output to the driver (e.g. the directions). The "GPS device" is a source since it provides position coordinates to the system.

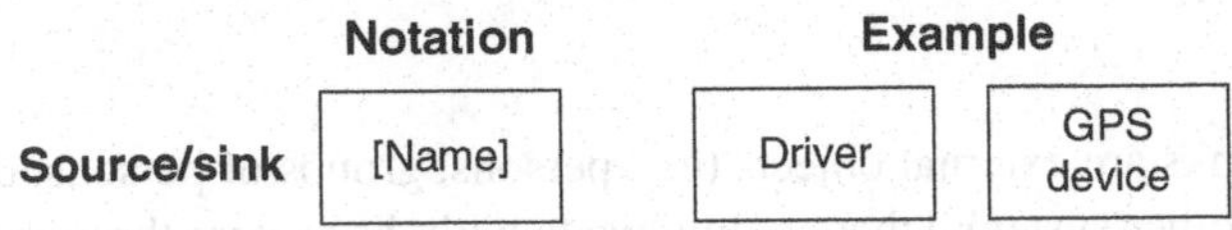

Fig. 14-24 Graphical notation of sources and sinks in a DFD

Data Store

Persistent data storage

A data store defines a repository of data. Data stores persistently record data in the system. The processes of the system can access the data in a data store (i.e. they can read or write the data). The graphical notation of a data store in a DFD is shown in Fig. 14-25.

	Notation	Example	
Data store	[Name]	route data	map data

Fig. 14-25 Graphical notation of data stores in a DFD

Figure 14-25 depicts two examples of data stores of a navigation system. The data store "route data" stores the current route after it has been calculated. The data store "map data" contains the geographical information required for navigation.

Data Flow

Moving data

A data flow describes the transportation of information packets of known composition (see [DeMarco 1978]). Hence, a data flow defines a stream of flowing data. In contrast, a data store defines stationary data, i.e. data that is not flowing. A data flow may define a stream of material and/or immaterial objects, e.g. information, products, energy, etc. A data flow can be defined between two processes, a process and a file as well as a source or sink and a process. The graphical notation of a data flow is shown in Fig. 14-26.

Examples of data flows

Figure 14-26 depicts several examples of data flows for a navigation system:

- The data flow "desired destination" from the source/sink "Driver" to the process "calculate route" (see "1" in Fig. 14-26) documents the flow of input data from the driver to the navigation system concerning the desired destination of the trip.
- The data flow "directions" from the process "determine directions" to the source/sink "Driver" (see "2" in Fig. 14-26) represents the flow of driving directions that the system provides to the driver.
- The data flow "deviation from route" from the process "track position" to the process "update route" (see "3" in Fig. 14-26) documents the flow of information about deviations from the calculated route between the process "track position" and the process "update route".
- The data flow from the data store "map data" to the process "calculate route" (see "4" in Fig. 14-26) documents flow of geographical data needed for calculating the route to the desired destination.

- The data flow "calculated route" from the process "calculate route" to the data store "route data" (see "5" in Fig. 14-26) documents the flow of route data to be stored in the data store.

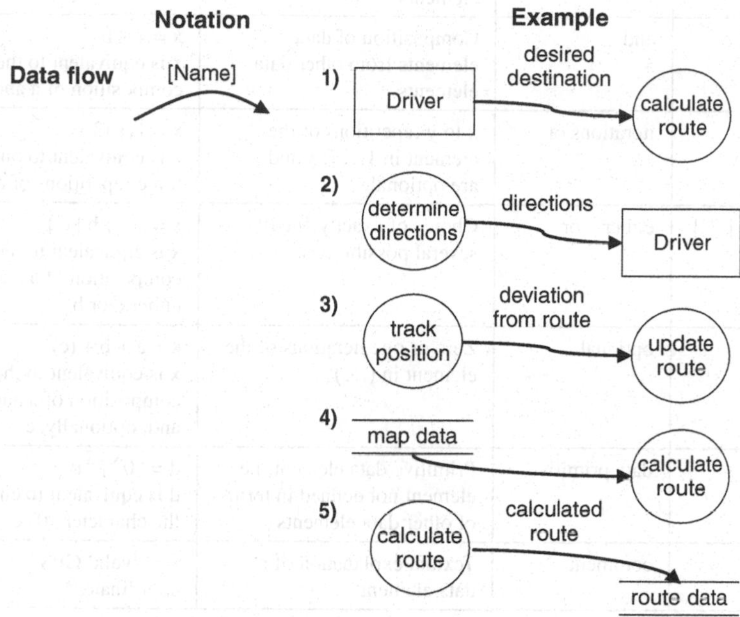

Fig. 14-26 *Graphical notation of a data flow in a DFD*

No control flow

It is important to note that DFDs are not used to define control flows. A DFD does not provide any information about the time when the processes are executed. DFDs merely show the data dependencies of the processes and document the input data required by the processes and the output data produced by the processes.

Extensions of DFDs

However, several extensions of the data flow diagram have been suggested to facilitate the definition of control flows (see e.g. [Hatley and Pirbhai 1988]).

Data Dictionary

The data dictionary contains the definitions of the data flows, data stores, and the components of data flows and data stores. The data dictionary is defined in parallel with data flow diagrams (DFDs). Without the data definitions contained in the data dictionary, the DFDs for a system are not well defined and hence cannot be interpreted unambiguously. In other words, each data flow and each data store documented in a DFD must be defined in the data dictionary. Table 14-1 describes the notation used for data definitions in the data dictionary (see [DeMarco 1978]).

Mini-Specification (Mini-Spec)

A mini-spec contains a concise description of a process. Each process defined in a DFD must be either defined by a mini-spec or refined by a lower-level DFD (see next

Tab. 14-1 *Notation for data definitions in the data dictionary*

Notation	Meaning	Explanation	Example
=	is equivalent to	Definition of a data element in terms of other data elements	x = y x is equivalent to y
+	and	Composition of data elements from other data elements	x = a + b x is equivalent to the composition of a and b
x{...}y	iterations of	x to y repetitions of the element in {...}; x and y are optional	x = 1{a}3 x is equivalent to one to three repetitions of a
[...|...|...]	either – or	Choice of exactly one of several possibilities.	x = a + [b | c] x is equivalent to the composition of a and either c or b
(...)	optional	Zero or one iterations of the element in (...)	x = a + b + (c) x is equivalent to the composition of a and b and, optionally, c
"..."	data primitive	Primitive data element, i.e. element not defined in terms of other data elements	d = "0" | "1" d is equivalent to either the character "0" or "1"
...	comment	Textual explanation of a data element	x = *valid GPS coordinates*

section). Without a mini-spec, a primitive process (i.e. a process that is not refined) has only a vaguely defined meaning. Consequently, the functional requirements documented by the set of DFDs containing this process are ambiguous.

Strategy for producing the required outputs of the process

A mini-spec describes briefly how a process produces its outputs based on its inputs. However, a mini-spec does not define an algorithm for producing the outputs but rather a strategy. A mini-spec can be defined, for instance, by means of structured text, i.e. a sequence of steps describing how the desired outputs are produced from the available inputs (see Example 14-2). The data elements to which a mini-spec refers must be defined in the data dictionary.

Example 14-2: Mini-spec of the process "calculate route"

Process "calculate route"

Each time the driver enters a new destination the system shall perform the following steps:

1. Write the "entered destination" into the data store "destinations"
2. Read the "routing preferences" from the data store "system settings"
3. Look up the current "position of the vehicle" and the "entered destination" in the data store "map data"
4. Determine the route from the current "position of the vehicle" to the "entered destination" according to the "routing preferences"
5. Store the "calculated route" in the data store "route data"
6. Display a "route overview" of the "calculated route" to the driver

Hierarchical Decomposition

Refinement of processes

A process that is defined in a DFD can be refined in another DFD. In this way, a hierarchy of DFDs at different levels is created. This hierarchy documents the functional requirements at different levels of detail (see Fig. 14-27).

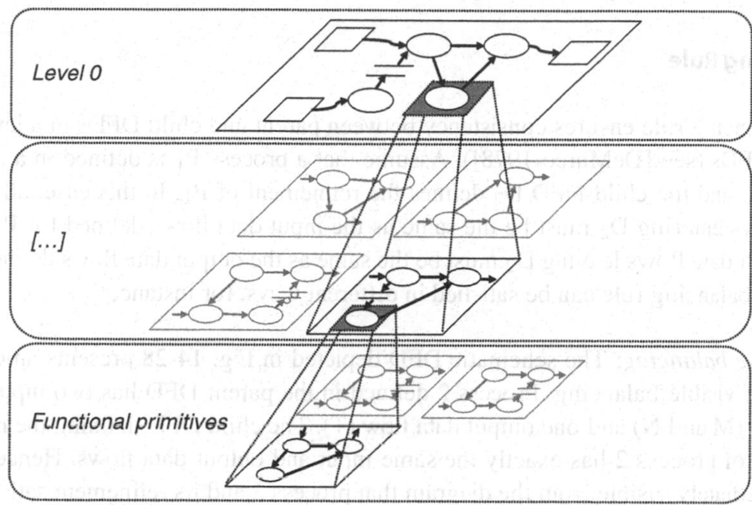

Fig. 14-27 *Data flow diagrams at multiple levels*

Level 0 diagram

The DFD at the highest level of the hierarchy (level 0; see Fig. 14-27) defines the overall functionality of the system with about five to seven processes and data stores. In the original approach, DeMarco differentiates between a context diagram, in which the sources and sinks and a single process representing the system are defined (see Page 239), and a level 0 diagram. In more recent approaches, the level 0 diagram and the context diagram have been merged into a single diagram. In addition, sources and sinks may also be defined in diagrams at lower levels, but only if they also exist at the higher level or if they define a refinement of a source or sink defined at a higher level.

DFDs at lower levels

The second level of the hierarchy (level 1; see Fig. 14-27) consists of several DFDs. Each DFD at level 1 refines a single process defined at level 0. Thereby, the processes defined in a DFD are hierarchically decomposed. The hierarchical decomposition of a process can span as many levels as needed.

Partial refinement of the processes defined at a higher level

In addition, a different number of decomposition levels can be defined for each process. The processes defined at the leaves of the decomposition hierarchy, i.e. processes which are not further refined, are called functional primitives (see Fig. 14-27). Note that functional primitives can be found at different levels of the decomposition hierarchy, since, typically, only part of the processes defined at the higher level are refined at the lower level.

Numbering scheme for parent/child processes

In order to ease the identification of child/parent processes of a specific process in a levelled set of DFDs, each process is numbered according to the following scheme:

- Level 0 processes are numbered 1, 2, 3 etc.
- Level 1 processes are numbered 1.X, 2.X, 3.X etc. For instance, the processes refining process 1 are numbered 1.1, 1.2, 1.3 etc.

- Level 2 processes are numbered 1.X.Y, 2.X.Y, 3.X.Y etc. For instance, the processes refining process 2.2 are numbered 2.2.1, 2.2.2, 2.2.3 etc.
- At lower hierarchy levels, the numbers can be abbreviated by assigning the number of the parent process (e.g. 2.2.3) to the child diagram, i.e. the DFD defining the refinement of the parent process. The processes in the child diagram are then numbered .1, .2, .3 etc. instead of 2.2.3.1, 2.2.3.2, 2.2.3.3 etc.

Balancing Rule

The balancing rule ensures consistency between parent and child DFDs in a levelled set of DFDs (see [DeMarco 1978]). Assume that a process P_1 is defined in a parent DFD D_1, and the child DFD D_2 defines the refinement of P_1. In this case, all input data flows entering D_2 must be the same as the input data flows defined for P_1, and all output data flows leaving D_2 must be the same as the output data flows defined for P_1. The balancing rule can be satisfied in different ways, for instance:

Same input/output data flows in parent and child DFD

- *Visible balancing*: The schematic DFD depicted in Fig. 14-28 presents an example of visible balancing. Process 2 defined in the parent DFD has two input data flows (M and N) and one output data flow (T). The child DFD defining the refinement of process 2 has exactly the same input and output data flows. Hence, it is immediately visible from the diagram that process 2 and its refinement satisfy the balancing rule since they have the same inputs (M and N) and the same outputs (T). The internal data flows P and Q defined in the child DFD do not affect the satisfaction of the balancing rule since they are not visible in the parent DFD.

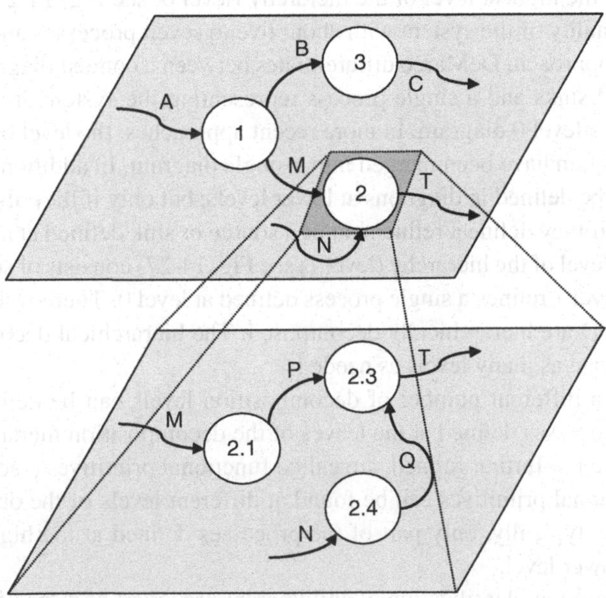

Fig. 14-28 *Example of visible balancing*

Decomposition of data flows

- *Dictionary balancing*: The schematic DFD depicted in Fig. 14-29 is an example of dictionary balancing. Process 2 defined in the parent DFD has two input data flows (M and N) and one output data flow (T), whereas the child DFD defining the refinement of process 2 has three input data flows (K, L, N) and one output data flow (T). Still, the balancing rule is satisfied since the data dictionary defines that data flow N is composed of data flows K and L.

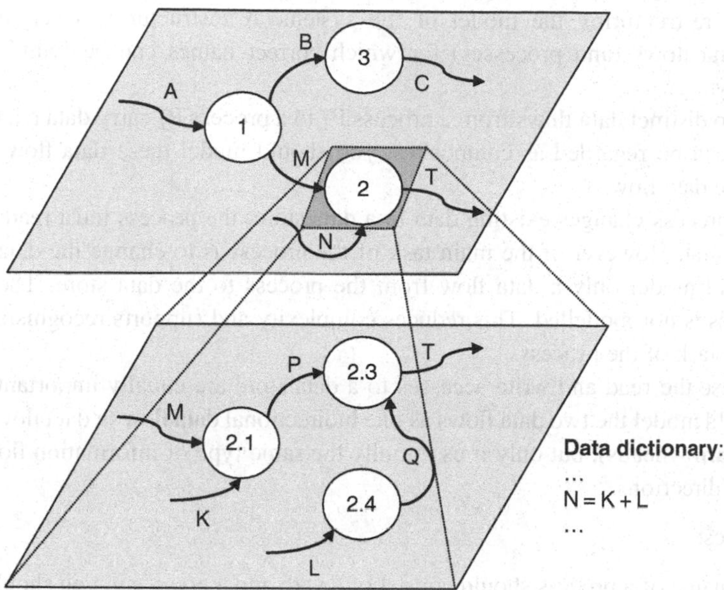

Fig. 14-29 *Example of dictionary balancing*

Hints for Creating Data Flow Diagrams

Hint 14-3 summarises some key rules to consider when creating a DFD (based on [DeMarco 1978]).

!

Hint 14-3: *Creating data flow diagrams*

Size of a DFD:

- ❑ Pay attention to keeping each DFD readable. A single DFD should not contain more than 7 ± 2 processes/data stores.

Data flows:

- ❑ Generally, each data flow must have a name that indicates the kind of data carried by this data flow. However, there is an exception to this rule. For better readability, the name of a data flow may be omitted if the data flow defines reading or writing access to a data store and the name of the data store already describes the data flow sufficiently.
- ❑ The name of a data flow should be comprehensible, i.e. it should characterise the information the data flow carries.
- ❑ The name of a data flow should also indicate key properties of the information (e.g. you should use “new route”, “alternative route”, or the like rather than just using “route” as name for the data flow).

(to be continued)

Hint 14-3 *(continued)*

- If it is difficult to find a good name for a data flow, the object considered might not actually be a data flow. In this case, you should consider restructuring the model of the system. A restructuring often results in data flows (and processes) for which correct names can be found more easily.
- If two distinct data flows from a process P_1 to a process P_2 carry data packages that can be regarded as composites, you should model these data flows as a single data flow.
- If a process changes existing data in a data store, the process must read these data first. However, if the main task of the process is to change the data, you should model only a data flow from the process to the data store. The read access is not modelled. This reduces complexity and supports recognising the main task of the process.
- In case the read and write accesses to a data store are equally important, you should model the two data flows as one bidirectional data flow (a data flow with two arrowheads), but only if essentially the same type of information flows in both directions.

Processes:

- The name of a process should consist of a verb and a noun, e.g. you should use "determine vehicle position" instead of just using "vehicle position".
- The name of a process should be comprehensible, i.e. it should fully characterise what the process does.
- If it is difficult to find the right name for a process, you should consider restructuring the model of the system. This often leads to new processes for which correct names can be found more easily.

Sources and sinks:

- Sources and sinks should be defined at the highest level of the hierarchy. If necessary, sources and sinks can be refined at lower levels.

Pay attention to avoiding the following errors:

- Avoid meaningless names for data flows such as "data" or "information".
- Avoid defining data flows that actually define control flows such as "get next record".
- Avoid data flows that define activation events (e.g. for a process) such as "start".
- Avoid meaningless names for processes such as "process data".
- Avoid defining processes which have only input data flows (i.e. produce no output) or which have only output data flows (i.e. create output independently of inputs).
- Avoid defining processes whose output data flows are identical to the input data flows (i.e. processes that do nothing).
- Avoid defining data stores with only outgoing data flows as well as data stores with only incoming data flows.
- Avoid defining data flows between data stores.
- Avoid defining data flows between sources and sinks.

14.2.2 Essential Models

Essential Systems Analysis is an enhancement of Structured Analysis. The main idea of Essential Systems Analysis is to differentiate between true (essential) requirements and false requirements. We have already described the essence and incarnation of a system as well as the overall approach of Essential System Analysis and its key advantages in Section 3.2. In this section, we describe the key elements of Essential Systems Analysis in more detail.

True vs. false requirements

Essential (true) requirements describe properties the system must offer regardless of the technology with which the system will be implemented (see Definition 3-1). False requirements are requirements that are biased by the technology. They define the incarnation of the system (see Definition 3-2).

Essential activities and memories

In an essential, functional system model, only the essential requirements are documented. The essence of a system comprises essential activities (processes) and essential memories (data stores). Essential activities are further differentiated into fundamental activities, custodial activities, and compound activities. We outline these elements of essential, functional models in the following sections.

For a detailed explanation of how to create essential models, see [McMenamin and Palmer 1984].

Fundamental Activity

Functions required to fulfil the system purpose

Fundamental activities are activities that justify the existence of the system. Each fundamental activity creates data flows that provide an output of the system, i.e. data flows from the system to the system context (sources and sinks). Figure 14-30 depicts a fundamental activity of a navigation system. The activity "determine directions" is a fundamental activity of a navigation system since the purpose of a navigation system is to provide driving directions to the driver during the trip.

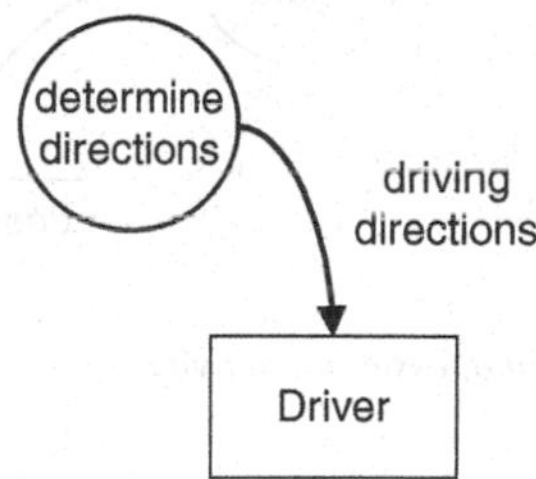

Fig. 14-30 *Example of a fundamental activity*

Custodial Activity

Storing and updating data in essential memories

Custodial activities create and maintain the essential memories of a system by obtaining and updating data the system needs for performing its fundamental activities. Hence, custodial activities create data flows towards essential memories. An example of a custodial activity is depicted in Fig. 14-31. The activity "update map" writes updated map data to the essential memory "map data" and thereby ensures that the geographic information stored in the navigation system is up to date.

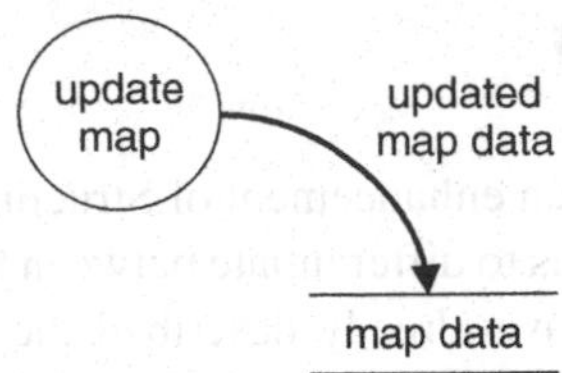

Fig. 14-31 *Example of a custodial activity*

Compound Essential Activity

Fundamental and custodial activity at the same time

Many essential activities are at the same time both fundamental as well as custodial activities, i.e. they provide output via data flows to the environment/context as well as updates of essential data via data flows to essential memories. Such activities are called compound essential activities. Figure 14-32 depicts an example of a compound essential activity. The activity "calculate route" offers an overview of the route to the driver via the data flow "route overview" and hence produces a data flow towards the context. In addition, "calculate route" also creates a data flow "new destination" towards an essential memory. Each new trip destination is stored in the essential memory "destinations" in order to be available when the driver wants to choose a destination from a list of previous destinations or for resuming navigation after a restart of the system. Hence, "calculate route" is a compound essential activity.

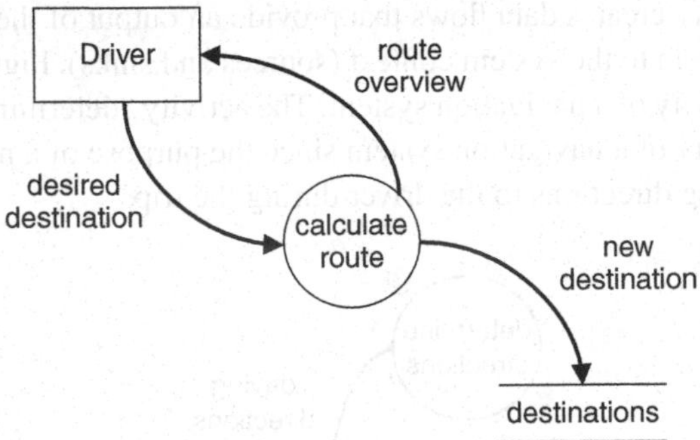

Fig. 14-32 *Example of a compound, essential activity*

Essential Memory

Data needed for fundamental activities

In Essential Systems Analysis, perfect technology is assumed inside the system boundaries. However, imperfect technology is assumed for the context of the system (see [McMenamin and Palmer 1984]). Therefore, if information (data) obtained from the context is not only required by the process receiving this information but is used by the system later on (e.g. trip destinations), it must be stored in the system in an essential memory. Essential memories hence store information/data obtained from the context of the system and needed by fundamental activities. Figure 14-33 depicts two essential memories of the navigation system. The essential memory "map data" stores geographic information obtained from the context and provides this information to the essential activity "calculate route". The essential memory "destinations" stores the trip destinations entered by the driver for later use such as generating a list of previous destinations for the driver or resuming navigation after the navigation system has been switched off and on again.

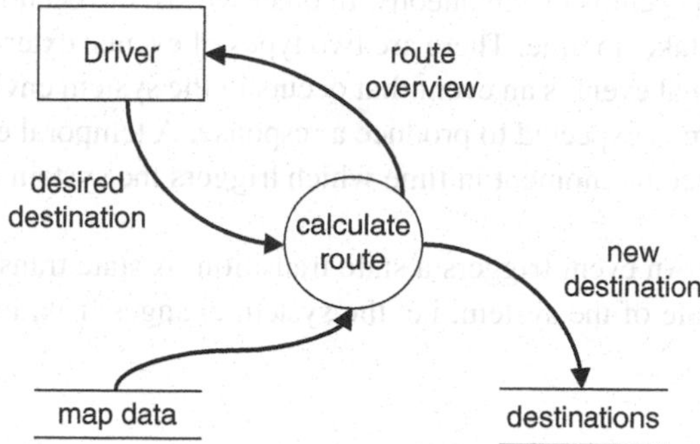

Fig. 14-33 *Examples of essential memories*

Hints for Creating Essential Models

McMenamin and Palmer propose four key principles that should be considered when creating essential models (see Hint 14-4).

Principles of essential modelling

!

Hint 14-4: *Principles of essential modelling (according to McMenamin and Palmer)*

The principle of technological neutrality:

- The essential model should not contain any information about the implementation of the system.

The principle of perfect internal technology:

- The technology within the system is perfect. However, the technology in the system context is not perfect.

The principle of the minimal essential model:

- When there is more than one way to specify an essential requirement, choose the simplest one.

The principle of the budget for complexity:

- No element of the model should be too complex for the reader to understand easily.

14.3 Documenting Requirements in the Behavioural Perspective

Behaviour models are used to document the reactive behaviour of a system. Typically, the dynamic behaviour of a system is defined using the following key concepts:

- *State*: A state defines a period of time in which the system behaves in a specific way and waits for the occurrence of a defined event that triggers a state transition.
- *Event*: An event is a discrete incident in the world (see [Wieringa 2003]). The occurrence of an event is instantaneous. In other words, the occurrence of an event is considered to take no time. There are two types of events: external and temporal events. An external event is an event that occurs in the system environment and for which the system is expected to produce a response. A temporal event is triggered by reaching a specific moment in time which triggers the system to perform some action.
- *State transition*: An event triggers a state transition. A state transition describes a change in the state of the system, i.e. the system changes from its current state to another state.

14.3.1 Behavioural Modelling Languages

Finite automata are often used to document the reactive behaviour of a system. The concept of finite automata is based on the work of [Hebb 1949] and [Huffman 1954]. In the following, we sketch the fundamentals of finite automata (Section 14.3.2) and of Mealy and Moore automata (Section 14.3.3). Furthermore, we sketch statecharts, a commonly used behavioural modelling language which is based on finite automata, in Section 14.3.4. An "extension" of statecharts, called state machine diagrams, is used in UML 2 [Rumbaugh et al. 2005] for defining system behaviour (Section 14.3.5).

14.3.2 Finite Automata

Deterministic vs. non-deterministic finite automata

The description of finite automata in this section is based on [Hopcroft et al. 2007]. A finite automaton consists of a finite set of states and a finite set of transitions. On the occurrence of an event, a state transition may take place. An automaton is called deterministic if, for each state and for each event, at most one state transition is defined. An automaton is called non-deterministic if for at least one state multiple transitions are defined for at least one event.

Deterministic Finite Automata (DFA)

Definition 14-1: *Deterministic finite automaton (DFA)*

A deterministic finite automaton is a five-tuple (Q, Σ, δ, q_0, F), where

- Q is a finite set of states.
- Σ is a finite set of input symbols (the input alphabet).
- δ is a transition function that takes as arguments a state *s* (from the set Q) and an input symbol *a* (from the set Σ) and returns a state *s′* (from the set Q).
- q_0 is the start or initial state. The state q_0 is one of the states in Q.
- F is the set of final or accepting states. The set F is a subset of Q.

based on [Hopcroft et al. 2007]

Transition diagram

Besides the mathematical definition as a five-tuple (see Definition 14-1), a deterministic finite automaton can be represented graphically as a directed graph. Such a graph is called a transition diagram. The graphical notations of the model elements are depicted in Fig. 14-34. As shown in Fig. 14-34, a state of the automaton is represented as a node of the graph. A transition is represented as a directed edge between two nodes and is labelled with the corresponding input symbol. The initial state of the automaton is indicated by an arrow with the label "Start". Final states are marked with a double circle line.

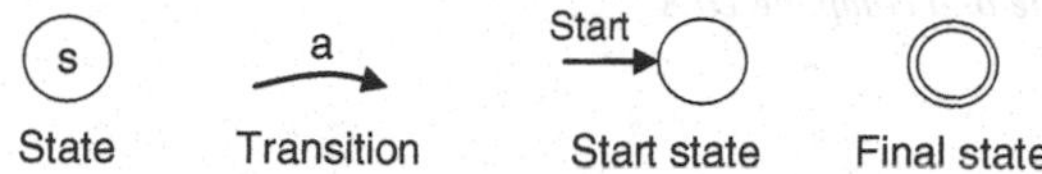

Fig. 14-34 *Graphical notation of the elements of an automaton*

Example of a DFA

Figure 14-35 depicts an example of a DFA which consists of four states. The initial state of the automaton is z_0. The automaton has one final state, namely the state z_3. If the DFA is in the initial state and receives the input symbol "h", it enters state z_1. If the DFA is in state z_1 and receives the input symbol "o" it enters state z_2. In state z_2, the DFA enters state z_1 when it receives "h" as input, or the final state z_3 when it receives "!" as input.

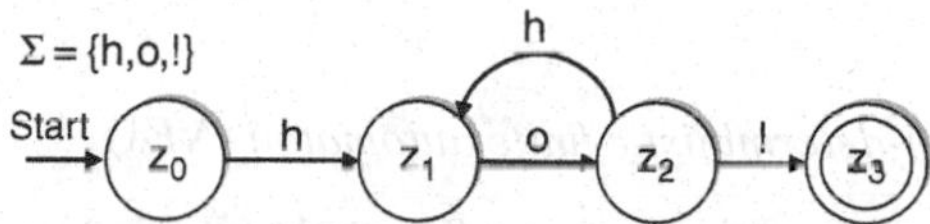

Fig. 14-35 *Example of a DFA*

Language accepted by a DFA

A deterministic finite automaton accepts a string x, if the sequence of transitions triggered by the symbols of x leads from the initial state to a final state of the DFA. The set of all strings accepted by a DFA is called the language of the DFA. The language of the DFA depicted in Fig. 14-35 is L(A) = ho(ho)*!, where "*" can be any number from 0 to n.

Complete vs. partial DFA

If a DFA defines for each state exactly one transition for each symbol of the input alphabet Σ, the DFA is called complete. If for at least one state no transition is defined for at least one input of the alphabet Σ, the automaton is called a partial DFA. According to this definition, the automaton in Fig. 14-35 is a partial DFA. A corresponding complete DFA is depicted in Fig. 14-36.

No ambiguities about possible behaviour

The complete automaton depicted in Fig. 14-36 defines an additional state z_4 and additional transitions to the state z_4 for each input symbol and each state for which the partial automaton depicted in Fig. 14-35 does not define a transition. Once the complete automaton has entered the state z_4, it remains in this state regardless of the inputs received, i.e. after entering the state z_4 the final state z_3 cannot be reached. Since z_4 itself is not defined as a final state, the complete automaton depicted in Fig. 14-36 accepts the same sequences of inputs as the partial automaton depicted in Fig. 14-35, i.e. the languages of both automata are identical: L(A) = ho(ho)*!. Since, in contrast to the partial DFA, the complete DFA

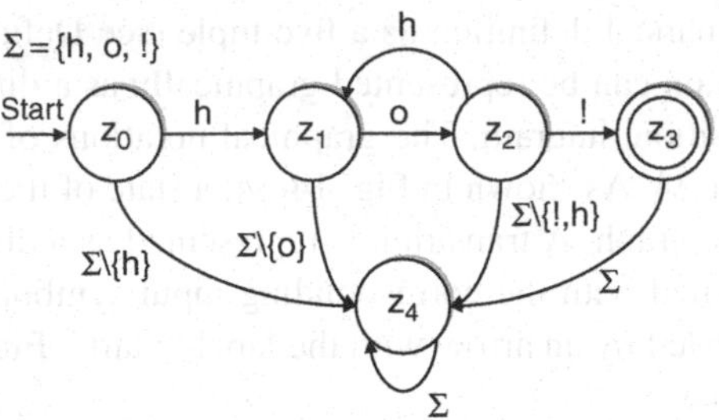

Fig. 14-36 *Example of a complete DFA*

defines, for each state, a transition for each possible input symbol, it completely defines the desired behaviours, i.e. it does not leave any ambiguity about the desired behaviour.

Non-deterministic Finite Automata (NFA)

A non-deterministic finite automaton (NFA) defines for at least one state and for at least one input symbol at least two transitions. In contrast to a DFA, the transition function of an NFA returns a set of states (see Definition 14-2).

D

Definition 14-2: *Non-deterministic finite automaton (NFA)*

A non-deterministic finite automaton is a five-tuple (Q, Σ, δ, q_0, F), where

- Q is a finite set of states.
- Σ is a finite set of input symbols (the input alphabet).
- δ is a transition function that takes as arguments a state *s* (from the set Q) and an input symbol *a* (from the set Σ) and returns **a subset** ***S*** of the states defined in Q.
- q_0 is the start or initial state. The state q_0 is one of the states in Q.
- F is the set of final or accepting states. The set F is a subset of Q.

based on [Hopcroft et al. 2007]

An NFA can be represented graphically in the same way as a DFA. In contrast to a DFA, a node of an NFA can have multiple outgoing edges labelled with the same input symbol. A state with two or more outgoing edges labelled with the same input symbol represents a fork in the execution path, as explained below.

Language of an NFA

After processing a sequence of input symbols, an NFA is typically not in one state but in a set of states *S* (which is a subset of the entire set of states Q defined for the automaton). If the NFA receives an input symbol *a*, the current set of states *S* is updated by applying the transition function to every state in the set *S*. If, for a state *x*of the set *S*, no transition is defined for the input symbol *a*, the corresponding execution path ends at state x (see Fig. 14-38). An NFA accepts an input sequence $a_1 a_2 \ldots a_n$ if the input sequence triggers a set of transitions leading from the initial state to a set of states that contains at least one final state.

Example of an NFA

Figure 14-37 depicts an example of an NFA. In the initial state z_0, the NFA performs a transition from z_0 to z_0 for any input (h,o,!) received. In addition, if in $z_0$the NFA receives the input "h" it enters two states, namely states z_0 and z_1 (see also Fig. 14-38). If the NFA is in state z_1 and receives input "o", it enters state z_2. If the input "!" is received in state z_2 a transition to the state z_3 is performed.

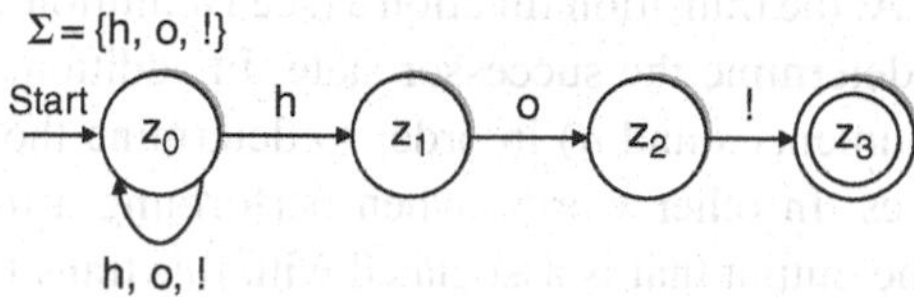

Fig. 14-37 *Example of an NFA*

The NFA depicted in Fig. 14-37 accepts any input sequence that ends with "ho!", i.e. the automaton has the language L(A) = (h+o+!)*ho! ("h+o+!" means "h" or "o" or "!").

Figure 14-38 illustrates the execution of the NFA depicted in Fig. 14-37 for the input sequence "hoho!". When the NFA receives input "h" in state z_0, the NFA performs two transitions and enters the states z_0 and z_1. The next input "o" causes a transition from z_0 to z_0 and from z_1 to z_2. For the next input symbol "h", no transition is defined for the state z_2. Therefore, the corresponding execution path ends in state z_2. Since, for the input symbol "h", two transitions are defined for the state z_0, the input symbol "h" leads to a transition from state z_0 to states z_1 and z_0. After receiving the next two input symbols "o" and "!", the NFA is finally in states z_0 and z_3 (see Fig. 14-38). Since z_3 is a final state, the automaton accepts the sequence "hoho!".

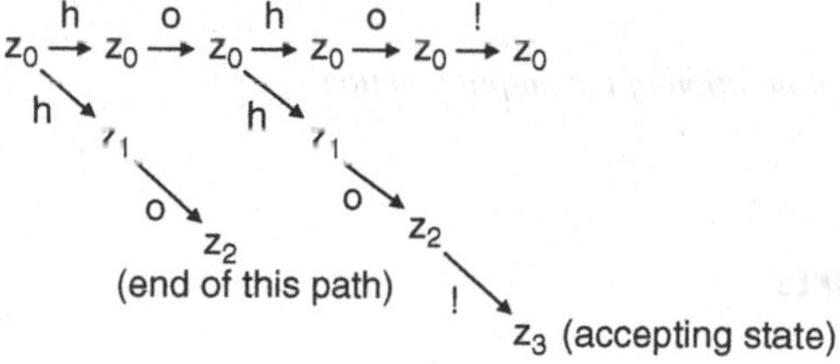

Fig. 14-38 *Sequences of states of the NFA for the input sequence "hoho!"*

14.3.3 Mealy and Moore Automata

Enhancements: output alphabet and output function

A finite state transducer (FST) is a special kind of finite automaton. In addition to the input alphabet and the transition function defined for a DFA, an FST defines a finite output alphabet Γ and an output function χ. Therefore, when processing a sequence of input symbols, an FST is able to produce a sequence of output symbols. In the context of modelling system behaviour, two special kinds of finite state transducers are considered: Mealy automata and Moore automata (see [Mealy 1955; Moore 1956]). A Mealy automaton differs from a Moore automaton in the way its output function is defined.[6]

Output function of a Mealy automaton

For a Mealy automaton, the output of the automaton depends on the current state and the input symbol, i.e. the output function has the current state and an input symbol as arguments. Consequently, the outputs of a Mealy automaton are associated with the defined transitions. When a Mealy automaton is in state s and receives an input symbol a, like for a DFA, the transition function δ (see Definition 14-1) is applied with arguments s and a to determine the successor state. In addition, the output function χ is applied (with arguments s and a) in order to determine the output symbol that the automaton produces. In other words, when performing a transition, the Mealy automaton produces the output that is associated with this transition.

Output function of a Mealy automaton

The output of a Moore automaton depends only on the current state. Consequently, the outputs of a Moore automaton are only associated with the states defined by the automaton. When a Moore automaton is in state s and receives an input symbol a, the transition function δ (see Definition 14-1) is applied with arguments s and a to determine the successor state s'. When entering the new state s', the output function χ is applied with a single argument s' in order to determine the output symbol that the automaton produces on entering state s'. In other words, when entering a state, the Moore automaton produces the output that is associated with this state.

Graphical notation

The graphical notation for defining the outputs of Mealy and Moore automata is depicted in Fig. 14-39. For a Mealy automaton, the output "o" is annotated at the transition (i.e. at an edge); for Moore automaton, the output is annotated at the state (i.e. inside a node).

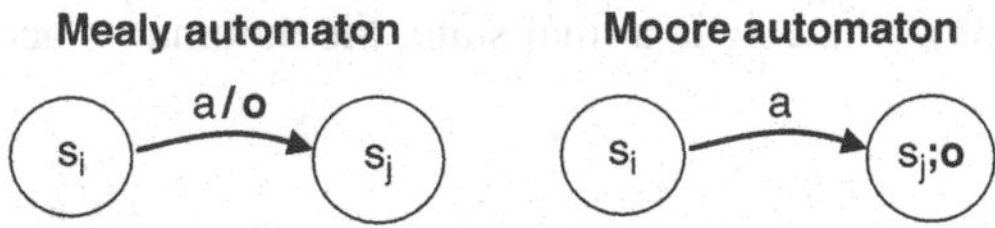

Fig. 14-39 *Graphical notation of the output function*

14.3.4 Statecharts

Enhancements of statecharts

To overcome some problems encountered when using finite automata for defining the behaviour of real software systems, Harel developed the statecharts modelling language (see [Harel 1987]). Statecharts extend finite automata by providing several enhancements which ease the modelling of system behaviour. In the following, we outline the key enhancements offered by statecharts (according to [Harel 1987]), namely:

[6] Note, however, that each Mealy automaton can be transformed into an equivalent Moore automaton, and vice versa (see [Hopcroft et al. 2007]).

- Defining actions for states and transitions
- Defining conditional transitions
- Hierarchical refinement of states
- Modelling concurrent behaviour

Defining Actions for States and Transitions

Actions in states and at transitions

Statecharts facilitate the definition of actions the system shall execute

- when performing a state transition (Mealy-like),
- on entering a specific state (Moore-like),
- while being in the state, or
- when leaving a state.

The graphical notation for actions (in states and transitions) is depicted in Fig. 14-40.

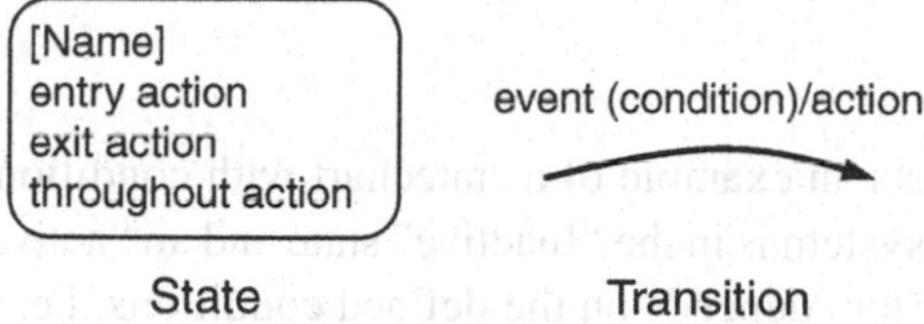

Fig. 14-40 *Graphical notations for states and transitions with actions*

Example of defining actions

Figure 14-41 depicts a fragment of a statechart defined for a navigation system which defines two states and one transition. In the state "Input of destination" the system allows the user to enter a destination for his trip. When entering this state, the system activates the input device for entering the destination (action "entry input device on"). While in this state the system processes the user input (action "throughout process input"). When leaving the state "Input of destination", the system deactivates the input device (action "exit input device off"). After the user has entered the destination (event "destination entered"), the system performs a transition to the state "Calculating route". On entering this state, the system deletes the current route (action "entry delete current route"). On leaving the state "Calculating route", i.e. when the calculation is finished, the system stores the calculated route (action "exit store route").

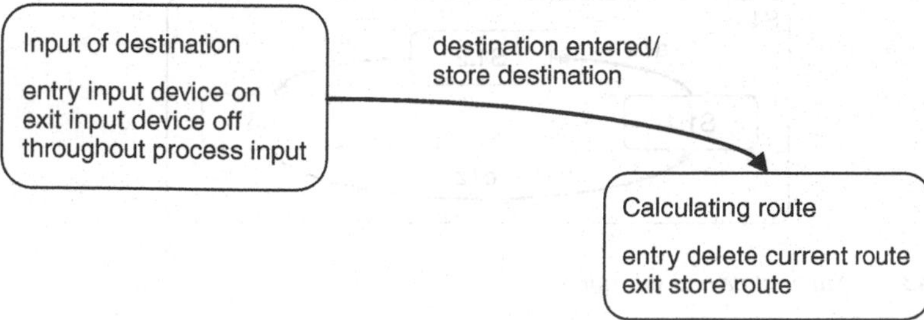

Fig. 14-41 *Defining actions in a statechart*

Conditional Transitions

Conditional state transition

Statecharts support the definition of conditional transitions. By adding a guarding condition to a transition, the transition is only performed when the corresponding event occurs and the condition is satisfied. The graphical notation for a conditional transition is depicted in Fig. 14-40. The condition is defined in brackets after the event that triggers the transition.

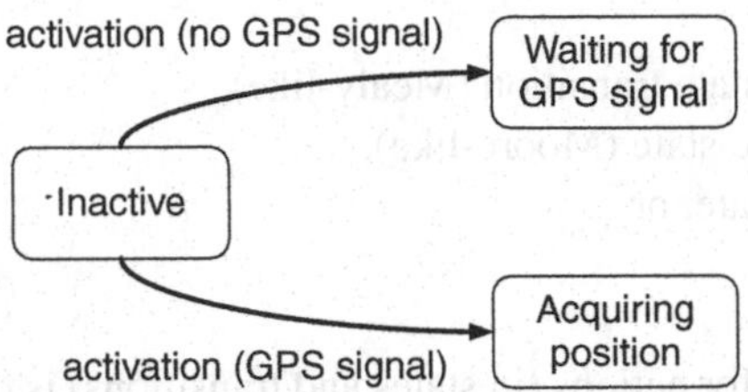

Fig. 14-42 *Example of defining conditional transitions in a statechart*

Figure 14-42 depicts an example of a statechart with conditional state transitions. When the navigation system is in the "Inactive" state and an "activation" event occurs, the reaction of the system depends on the defined conditions, i.e. whether the system performs a transition to the "Acquiring position" state or to the "Waiting for GPS signal" state. If the condition "GPS signal" is true, the system performs the transition to the "Acquiring position" state. If the condition "no GPS signal" is true, the system performs the transition to the "Waiting for GPS signal" state.

Hierarchical Refinement

Super-state and sub-states

Statecharts support the refinement of a state into a set of sub-states, or vice versa the "aggregation" of several states into a super-state. In other words, statecharts support the definition of hierarchies of states. A super-state encapsulates part of the system behaviour, i.e. the behaviour defined by the sub-states is encapsulated in the super-state (see Fig. 14-43).

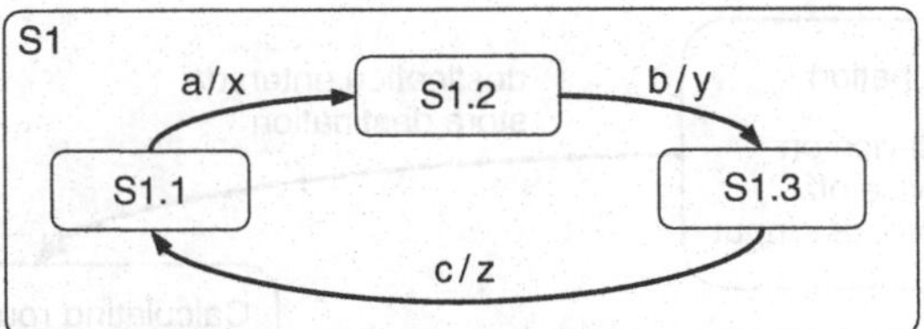

Fig. 14-43 *Super-state and sub-states*

Example of hierarchical state refinement

Figure 14-44 shows an example of state refinement. The state "Navigating" is decomposed into the three sub-states "Input of destination", "Calculating route", and "Tracking waypoints". The super-state "Navigating" is entered when the system is in the "Ready" state and the event "start navigation" occurs or when the system is in the "Acquiring position" state and the event "position acquired" occurs.

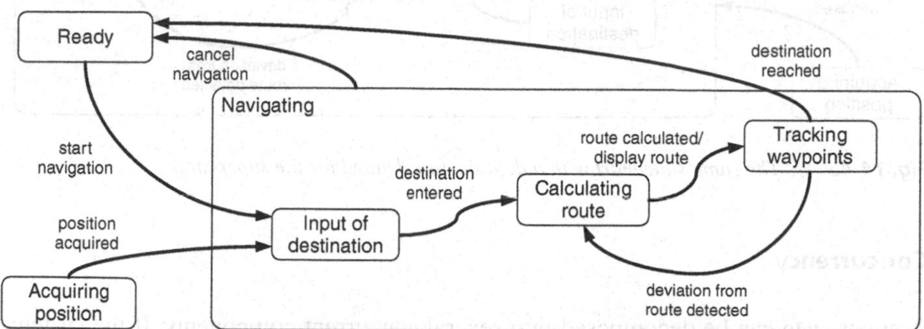

Fig. 14-44 *Refinement of a state (hierarchy)*

As depicted in Fig. 14-44, several transitions are defined between the three sub-states of the "Navigating" super-state. As long as these transitions are performed, the system remains in the super-state "Navigating". However, if the event "cancel navigation" occurs in any of the three sub-states or if the event "destination reached" occurs in the "Tracking waypoints" sub-state, the system leaves the "Navigating" state (as well as the corresponding sub-state) and enters the "Ready" state.

Default state

For each super-state, one sub-state can be defined as the default state. The default state is entered whenever a transition is performed which activates the super-state and, for this transition, the sub-state to be activated is not directly defined. The graphical notation for a default state is depicted in Fig. 14-45. The default state is denoted by a small arrow originating from a solid circle. When a default state is defined for a super-state, the transitions to the super-state can be defined without defining which sub-state should be entered.

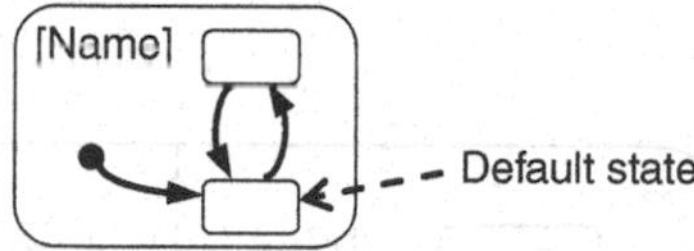

Fig. 14-45 *Graphical notation of a default state*

Example of a default state

Using a default state in the super-state "Navigating", the statechart shown in Fig. 14-44 can be defined as depicted in Fig. 14-46. The default state of the "Navigating" state is the state "Input of destination". The two transitions "start navigation" and "position acquired" end at the boundary of the super-state, i.e. they do not directly point to a sub-state. When one of the two transitions is performed, the system enters the default sub-state "Input of destination" as depicted in Fig. 14-46.

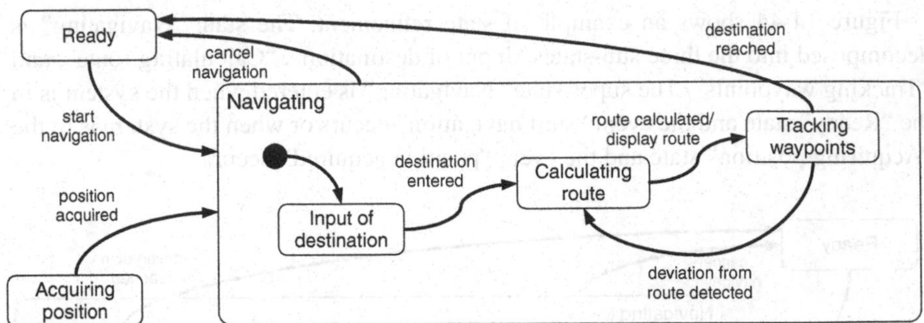

Fig. 14-46 *The same statechart with a default state defined for the super-state*

Concurrency

A super-state can be decomposed into several concurrent components. If the system enters a super-state for which concurrent components are defined, the system enters all components at the same time. A concurrent component can again be refined, i.e. for each concurrent component sub-states and transitions can be defined. The graphical notation for concurrent components is depicted in Fig. 14-47. The concurrent components of a super-state are separated from each other by a dashed line.

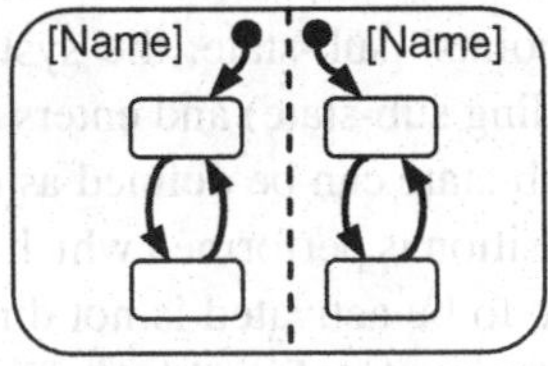

Fig. 14-47 *Graphical notation of concurrent components*

Example of concurrent sub-states

An example of a super-state with two concurrent components is shown in Fig. 14-48.

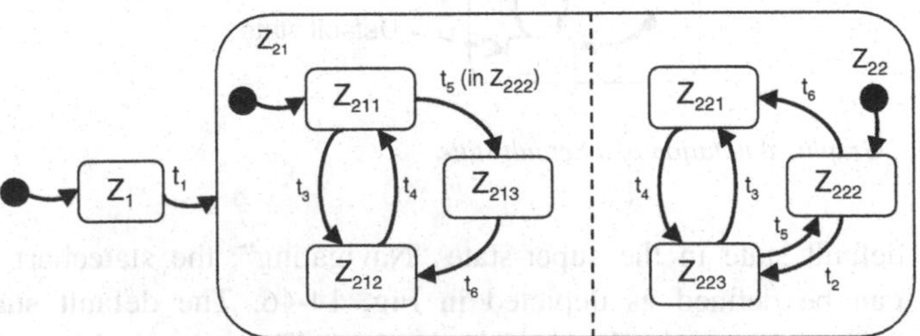

Fig. 14-48 *Decomposition of a super-state into concurrent components*

Synchronisation by means of conditions

It may be necessary to synchronise a set of concurrent components. For this purpose, conditions can be defined for the transitions defined in the components. An example of such a synchronisation is depicted in Fig. 14-48, where for the component Z_{21} the transition $t_5$is only performed if the component Z_{22} is in state Z_{222}.

Exemplary execution of the automaton

To illustrate the behaviour of an automaton with concurrent components (and synchronisation), we describe the reactions of the statechart depicted in Fig. 14-48 for the event sequence (t_1, t_2, t_3, t_4, t_5, t_6):

t_1: The system leaves the state Z_1 and enters the states Z_{211} and Z_{222}.
t_2: The system remains in state Z_{211} and enters the state Z_{223}.
t_3: The system enters the states Z_{212} and Z_{221}.
t_4: The system enters the states Z_{211} and Z_{223}.
t_5: The system remains in state Z_{211}, since the condition (in Z_{222}) is not true, and enters state Z_{222}.
t_6: The system remains in state Z_{211} and enters state Z_{221}.

Product construction

The overall behaviour of the super-state is defined by the orthogonal product of the behaviours of all its concurrent components. Therefore, the facility of defining concurrent components leads to statecharts which are easier to read and significantly less complex than an equivalent statechart defined without concurrent components would be. To illustrate this, Fig. 14-49 depicts a statechart defined without concurrent components which has the same behaviour as the statechart (defined using concurrent components) depicted in Fig. 14-48.

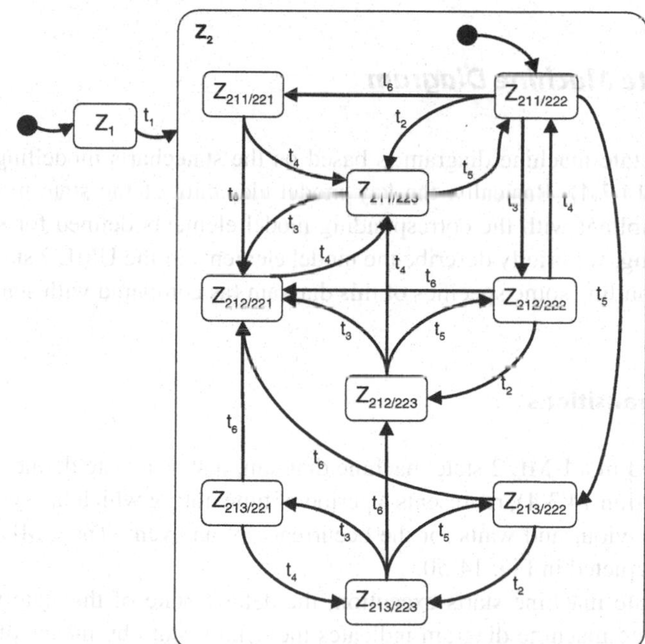

Fig. 14-49 *Equivalent statechart without concurrent components*

Hints for Creating Statecharts

When creating statecharts, the rules suggested in Hint 14-5 should be considered.

!

Hint 14-5: *Rules for creating statecharts (based on [Wieringa 2003])*

Identifying relevant states:

- Search for states in which the system does nothing else than wait for an event to occur.
- Search for states that represent behaviours which persist until they terminate themselves or until they are interrupted by an event with a higher priority.

Identifying relevant events:

- Search for two kinds of relevant events: external and temporal events. An event is relevant if the system is required to react to this event, i.e. when a state transition or the execution of an action (or both) is required.

Modelling hierarchies:

- Cluster multiple states into a super-state to document that these states have commonalities in their behaviour such as transitions to the same target state on the occurrence of a specific event.

14.3.5 State Machine Diagram

The UML 2 state machine diagram is based on the statecharts modelling language (see Section 14.3.4). Basically, the key model elements of the state machine diagram are compliant with the corresponding model elements defined for statecharts. In the following, we briefly describe the model elements of the UML 2 state machine diagram and outline some specifics of this diagram (as compared with statecharts).

States and Transitions

A state defined in a UML 2 state machine diagram, just as a state defined in a statechart (see Section 14.3.4), represents a period of time during which the system shows a specific behaviour and waits for the occurrence of an event. The UML 2 notation for states is depicted in Fig. 14-50.

Initial state

When a state machine starts execution, the default state of the state machine is entered. A state machine diagram indicates the default state by means of the initial

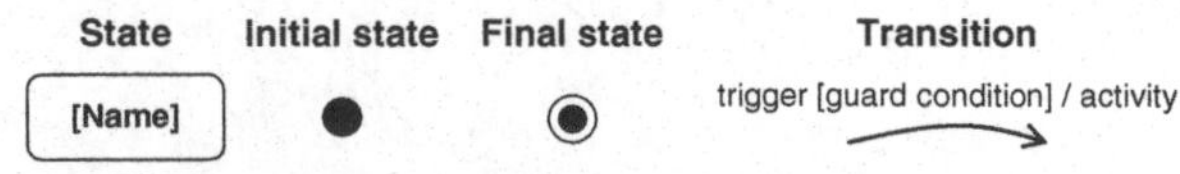

Fig. 14-50 *Notation for states and transitions*

state. The initial state is not an actual state of the system but rather a control element of the state machine. Hence, it is also called the "initial pseudostate". The initial pseudostate has a single transition leading to the default state of the state machine. Apart from this difference, the UML 2 notation for defining a default state is the same as in the statechart language (see Fig. 14-50). In addition to the initial pseudostate, UML 2 defines several other types of pseudostates. We refer to [Rumbaugh et al. 2005] for a description of pseudostates.

Transitions

A transition in a state machine diagram defines a change from one state to another. A transition is triggered by the occurrence of an event. In addition, a transition may be guarded by a guard condition. If a guard condition is defined for a transition, the transition is only taken if the guard condition evaluates to true (when the triggering event occurs). The UML 2 notation for transitions including triggering events and guard conditions is depicted in Fig. 14-50.

Event trigger

In UML 2, amongst others, the following event types can be used for defining the triggering event of a transition:

- *Change event*: A change event occurs if the evaluation of a Boolean condition defined by some expression (e.g. "A > B") changes from false to true after the value of a term of the Boolean expression has changed. The difference between a change event and a guard condition is that a guard condition is only evaluated once (when the triggering event of the transition occurs) whereas the Boolean condition of a change event is evaluated continuously.
- *Time event*: A time event occurs if a time expression is satisfied. A time expression may refer to absolute time (e.g. "at 8 p.m.") or to the elapsed time, for instance, since entering a specific state (e.g. "after 2 s").

Final state

The final state indicates that the state machine has completed its execution. A final state is not allowed to have outgoing, event-triggered transitions. Otherwise, it is an ordinary state and not a final state.

Activities

Entry, do, and exit activities

In a state machine diagram, activities to be performed by the system during a transition, on entering a state, on leaving a state, and while in a state can be defined, similarly to actions in a statechart. The notation for defining activities to be performed during a transition is depicted in Fig. 14-50. Figure 14-51 depicts the notation for activities to be performed on entering a state (entry), on leaving a state (exit), and while in a state (do).

Completion transition

A completion transition is a transition defined without a triggering event. A completion transition is enabled (or activated) as soon as all activities in the source state

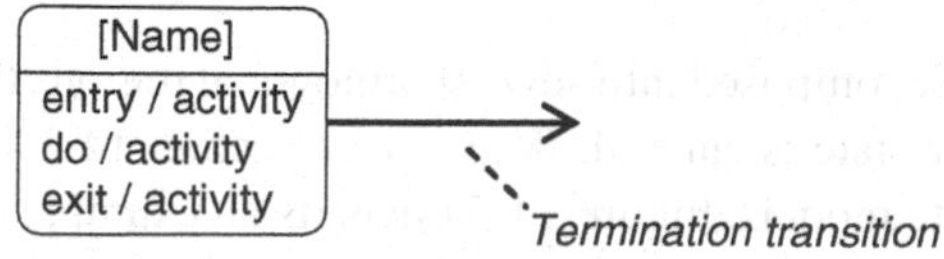

Fig. 14-51 *UML 2 notation for internal activities*

have been completed. If a completion transition is defined with a guard condition, the transition can only be taken if the guard condition is true. Several completion transitions with different guard conditions can be defined for a state.

Internal transition

By defining an internal transition for a state, it is possible to trigger an activity without a change of state. If the triggering event of the internal transition occurs while in the state, the activity defined for this transition is executed without exiting and re-entering the state. The notation for an internal transition is the same as the notation for entry, exit, and do activities (see Fig. 14-51). Figure 14-52 depicts an example of an internal transition. While the "Input of destination" state of the navigation system is active, each time that the event "help" occurs, the internal transition triggered by this event is performed, and the activity "display help" is executed. The entry and exit activities defined for the state are not executed when performing the internal transition.

Input of destination
entry / activate input device
exit / deactivate input device
help / display help

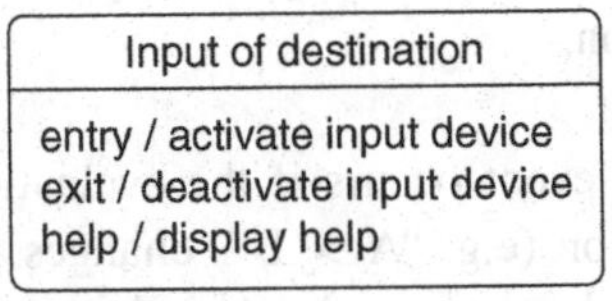

Fig. 14-52 *Example of an internal transition*

Hierarchical Refinement

As in statecharts, each state defined in a state machine diagram can be decomposed into a set of sub-states. Figure 14-53 depicts a super-state with a set of nested sub-states. As indicated in Fig. 14-53, initial states and final states can be used in combination with hierarchical refinement as mechanisms to support encapsulation of states, i.e. to separate the definition of behaviour within a state from the definition of behaviour outside the state. When the super-state is entered, the sub-state denoted by the initial pseudostate is entered. When the final state defined within the super-state is reached, the termination transition of the super-state is enabled.

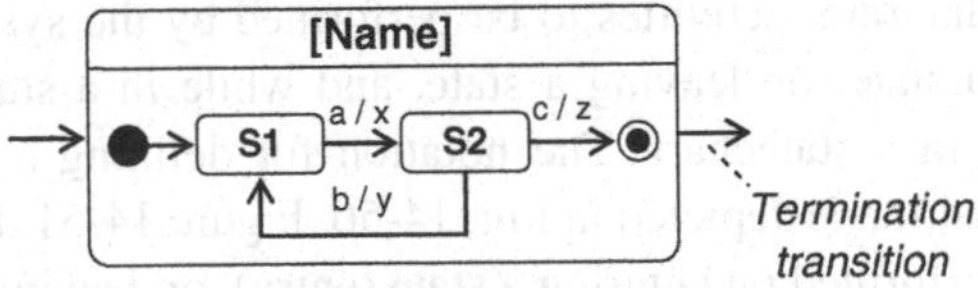

Fig. 14-53 *Super-state with nested sub-states*

Concurrency

A super-state can be decomposed into several orthogonal regions that execute concurrently when the super-state is entered. We refer to Section 14.3.4 for an explanation of concurrency in state models. Figure 14-54 depicts an example of a state in a UML 2 state machine diagram with two orthogonal regions. The termination transition of a state with orthogonal regions is enabled if each region has reached its final state.

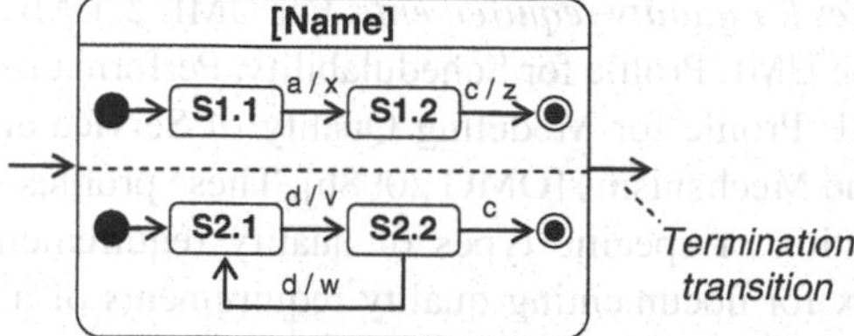

Fig. 14-54 *State with two orthogonal regions*

Submachine State

Referencing another state machine

A submachine state in a UML 2 state machine diagram is a state that references another state machine. The graphical notation for a submachine state is depicted in Fig. 14-55. The name of the submachine state is followed by a colon and the name of the referenced submachine. Entering the submachine state is equivalent to entering the default state of the submachine state machine (see Fig. 14-55). If the submachine state machine reaches its final state, the termination transition of the submachine state is enabled. The definition of submachine states facilitates the reuse of a state machine within other state machines.

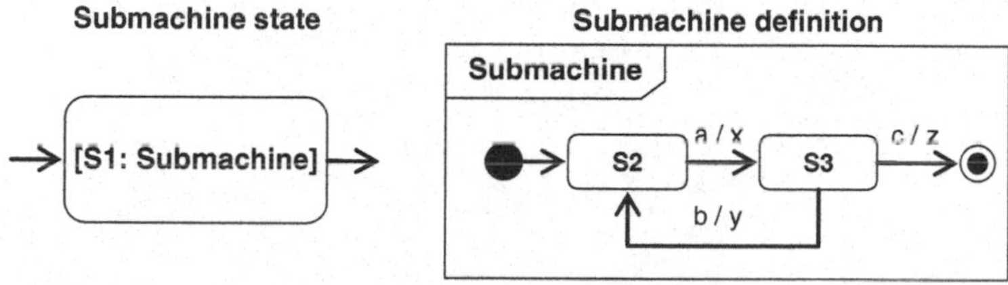

Fig. 14-55 *Submachine state and submachine state machine*

14.4 Documenting Quality Requirements in the Three Perspectives

Documentation of quality requirements

Quality requirements such as the accuracy or performance of a system function can be documented in all three perspectives. Quality requirements can be documented in the three perspectives, for example, by:

- *Using built-in language constructs*: Some modelling languages offer partial support for documenting specific types of quality requirements. For instance, some languages offer built-in support for documenting real-time requirements. The message sequence charts (MSC) language (see [ITU 2004]) provides constructs for timer setting, restart, stop, and time-out events. These constructs can be used for documenting real-time requirements. Some extensions of finite automata also support the documentation of real-time requirements. A well-known extension of finite automata is the timed automata model by [Alur and Dill 1994].

- *Using UML profiles for quality requirements*: For UML 2, UML profiles have been defined such as the UML Profile for Schedulability, Performance, and Time [OMG 2005] or the UML Profile for Modeling Quality of Service and Fault Tolerance Characteristics and Mechanisms [OMG 2008b]. These profiles support the model-based documentation of specific types of quality requirements. Such a profile defines the syntax for documenting quality requirements of a specific type such as performance requirements.
- *Using the SysML requirements diagram*: In SysML, quality requirements can be documented using the SysML requirements diagram. Each quality requirement can be defined as an individual model element (of the type "requirement"). Additionally, the corresponding model elements can be stereotyped as quality requirements (see Section 15.4). The defined quality requirements can be linked to other requirements or to model elements defined in other diagrams by means of requirements relationships.
- *Adding quality requirements as notes*: Quality requirements can also be documented by annotating the model elements using textual notes. For example, if a function shall provide results with a specific accuracy or within a specific time, these quality requirements can be annotated in a data flow diagram using textual notes. However, in contrast to the other possibilities for documenting quality requirements, these textual notes have no defined syntax and semantics. In other words, the quality requirements are documented as comments and not as dedicated model elements.

Chapter 15
Integration of the Three Perspectives

In this chapter, we describe:

- *The need for aligning the overlaps which exist between the three perspectives*
- *The interrelation of the three perspectives using Unified Modeling Language (UML)*
- *The interrelation of the three perspectives using Systems Modeling Language (SysML)*

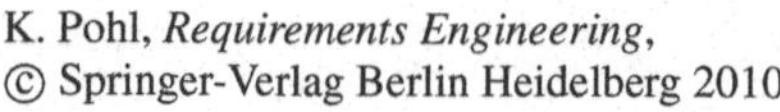

Each of the conceptual modelling approaches presented in Chapter 14 has been developed with primarily one specific perspective in mind (data, function, or behaviour). Today, requirements defined for a typical software-intensive system have to consider all three perspectives. Hence, data, behavioural and functional requirements models are typically defined for the software-intensive system.

As stated in Section 13.1, the corresponding models of the three perspectives are related to each other, as they partly refer to the same subjects in the universe of discourse. For instance, the data provided as input to the system is represented in both the data and the functional perspective. These interrelations between the three perspectives and the resulting requirements models can be used for checking the overall consistency of the requirements defined in the different perspectives. To facilitate consistency checks across the three perspectives, the corresponding models should be, to some degree, integrated. To achieve such integration typically the model elements of the three perspectives are interrelated by introducing explicit links between the different model elements.

In Section 15.1, we provide an example specification of solution-oriented requirements using conceptual models from each of the three perspectives. We use the example to illustrate the integration of the three perspectives (Section 15.2). Section 15.3 outlines the integration of the three perspectives using Unified Modeling Language (UML). Section 15.4 sketches additional means for supporting the integration of the three perspectives offered by Systems Modeling Language (SysML).

15.1 Extended Example

We illustrate the documentation of solution-oriented requirements in the three perspectives using a navigation system as an example. Assume that, initially, the following requirements are defined for the navigation system in natural language (Example 15-1).

Example 15-1: Requirements for the navigation system

Calculation of position and direction:

R1 The system shall determine the current position and direction of the car based on the GPS data, the wheel rotation, and the yaw rate.

Entry of destination:

R2 The system shall allow entry of an address to specify the destination of a trip.

R3 The system shall allow selection of a destination from a list of stored destinations.

Route calculation:

R4 The system shall calculate the fastest route from the current position of the car to the chosen destination.

R5 The system shall recalculate the route to the destination if the driver deviates from the calculated route.

Navigating to destination:

R6 During the trip, the system shall provide acoustic and visual driving directions.

In the following, we outline the detailed definition of these requirements in each of the three perspectives (data, function, and behaviour).

Data Perspective

The data requirements for the navigation system are defined in more detail using an entity–relationship (ER) model (see Section 14.1). The following entities are defined in the ER model (see Fig. 15-1):

Entities

- *Entity "DESTINATION"*: This entity represents destinations, for instance, entered by the driver as trip destinations (see R2) and stored in a list of destinations (see R3).
- *Entity "LOCATION"*: This entity denotes geographic positions with defined coordinates.
- *Entity "ROUTE"*: This entity represents routes to a destination calculated by the navigation system (see R4 and R5).
- *Entity "WAYPOINT"*: This entity represents a waypoint, i.e. a point on a route denoting a characteristic location such as a junction.
- *Entity "DIRECTION"*: This entity represents the acoustic and visual driving directions which the system provides to the driver e.g. when reaching a specific waypoint (see R6).
- *Entity "VEHICLE DATA"*: This entity represents the position and movement data of the vehicle at a specific point of time required by the navigation system such as position, speed, direction, yaw rate, or wheel rotation (see R1).
- *Entity "ROAD NETWORK"*: This entity represents the geographic information about a road network that is available to the navigation system for route calculation and navigation.
- *Entity "NETWORK FEATURE"*: This entity represents a feature in a road network. It is specialised by the entities (sub-classes) "ROAD" and "JUNCTION". The specialisation is partial since there may be other types of features such as "River", "Bridge", "Rail crossing" etc.
- *Entity "ROAD"*: This entity represents roads in a road network.
- *Entity "JUNCTION"*: This entity represents a junction in a road network.

Relationships

The entities depicted in Fig. 15-1 are related by the following relationships:

- *Relationship "HAS" between entities "ROUTE" and "DESTINATION"*: A route has exactly one destination, which is the destination entered by the driver.
- *Relationship "LOCATED AT" between entities "DESTINATION" and "LOCATION"*: To each destination one location is assigned. However, the location, i.e. the coordinates, of a destination may be (initially) unknown. Hence the cardinality is "(0,1)".
- *Relationship "CONSISTS OF" between entities "ROUTE" and "WAYPOINT"*: Each route consists of a set of waypoints denoting characteristic locations on the route such as junctions. Therein, a route must have at least two waypoints, the starting point of the route and the destination.

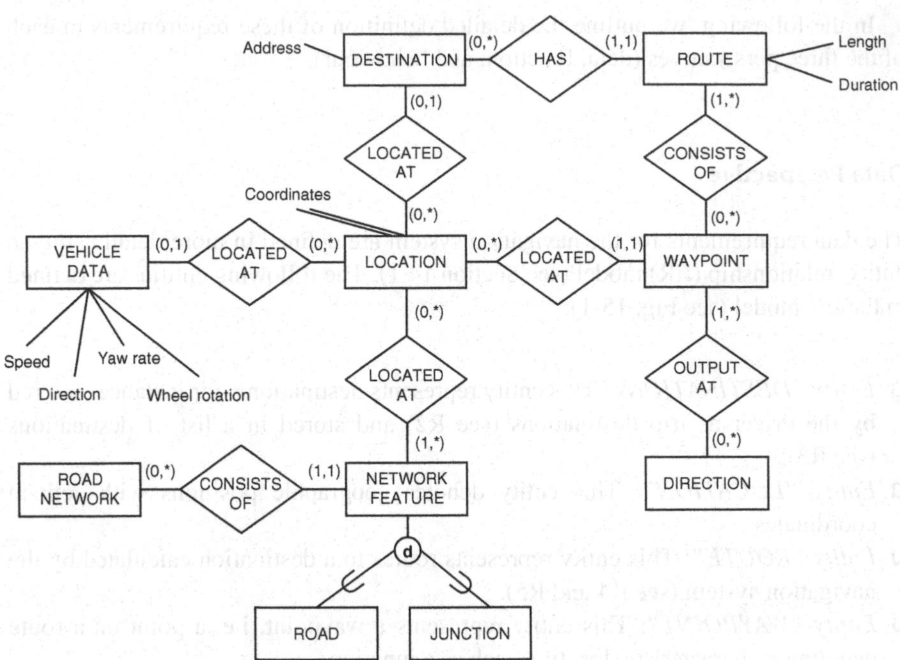

Fig. 15-1 *Entity–relationship model for the navigation system (data perspective)*

- *Relationship "OUTPUT AT" between entities "DIRECTION" and "WAYPOINT"*: This relationship relates a waypoint and the output, i.e. the directions the system provides to the driver at this waypoint.
- *Relationship "LOCATED AT" between entities "WAYPOINT" and "LOCATION"*: Each waypoint of a route must have exactly one location defining the coordinates of this waypoint.
- *Relationship "LOCATED AT" between entities "NETWORK FEATURE" and "LOCATION"*: A network feature has at least one location and may have an arbitrary number of locations, e.g. if the feature covers an area. A location can be assigned to an arbitrary number of features. If the location is outside the road network, no network feature is assigned to it. If the location is part of a junction, a junction feature and multiple road features are related to this location.
- *Relationship "CONSISTS OF" between entities "ROAD NETWORK" and "NETWORK FEATURE"*: A road network consists of an arbitrary number of network features.
- *Relationship "LOCATED AT" between entities "VEHICLE DATA" and "LOCATION"*: This relationship assigns a tuple of vehicle data to a location which denotes the position of the vehicle. Since the position may be unknown, the respective cardinality constraint is "(0,1)".

Functional Perspective

The functional aspects of the navigation system requirements are detailed using data flow diagrams (DFDs). The context diagram (see Fig. 15-2) defines a single function "navigate driver", the sources and sinks of the system ("Car sensors", "Driver", and "GPS satellites"), and the data flows between the system and its sources and sinks. Therein, "yaw rate", "wheel rotation", "GPS signal", and "desired destination" are flows directed towards the system, and "driving directions" is a flow directed towards the environment.

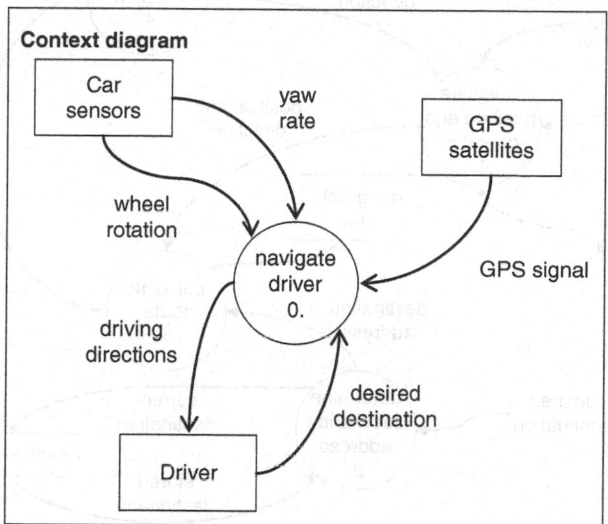

Fig. 15-2 *Context diagram of the navigation system (functional perspective)*

The level 0 DFD depicted in Fig. 15-3 details the single function defined in the context diagram into a network of functions and data stores connected by data flows.[7] The following data stores are defined in the diagram:

- *Data store "destinations"*: This data store maintains a list of destinations entered by the driver during past trips.
- *Data store "geographic data"*: This data store keeps the geographic information required for route calculation and navigation such as the road network of a specific country.

The function "navigate driver" defined in the context diagram (see Fig. 15-2) is refined into the following functions (see Fig. 15-3):

- *Function "calculate position and direction"*: This function calculates the position and direction of the vehicle (output flow "position and direction") based on sensor input (input flows "yaw rate", "wheel rotation", and "GPS signal").
- *Function "determine destination address"*: This function determines the destination address (output flow "destination address" and "current destination") based on the user input. The user can either enter the desired destination directly (input flow "desired destination") or choose a destination from a list of stored destinations (input flow "stored destination").

[7] As explained in Section 14.2 the context diagram and the level 0 diagram can be merged into a single diagram. We use separate diagrams here, for better readability.

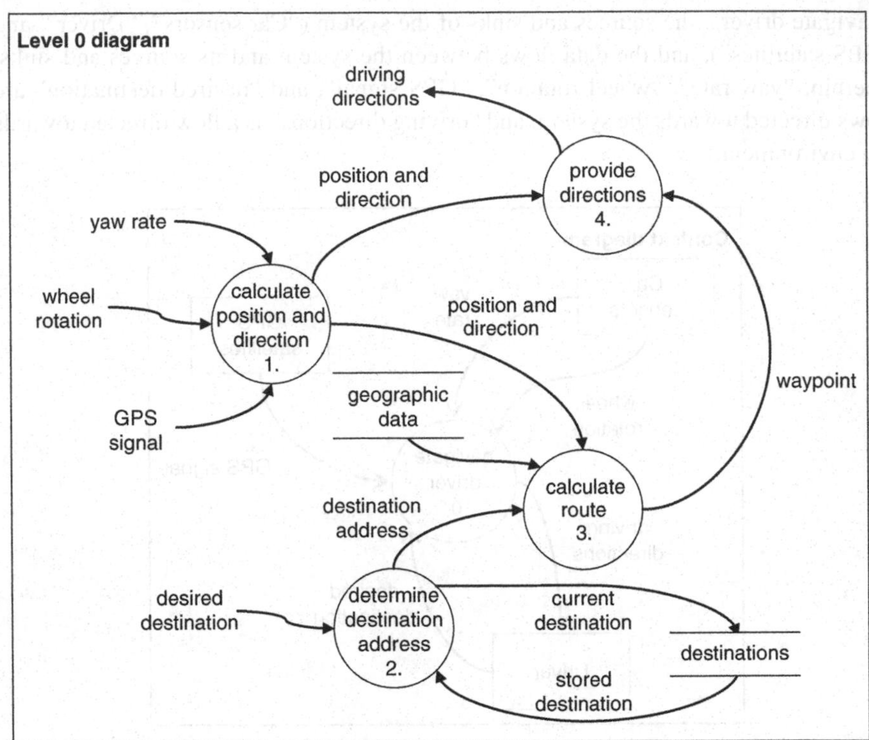

Fig. 15-3 *Level 0 data flow diagram for the navigation system (functional perspective)*[8]

- *Function "calculate route"*: This function calculates the route to the desired destination, i.e. a set of waypoints (output flow "waypoint"), based on the destination address (input flow "destination address"), the geographic data available to the system (input flow from data store "geographic data"), and the current position and direction of the vehicle (input flow "position and direction").
- *Function "provide directions"*: This function provides visual and acoustic driving directions (output flow "driving directions") based on the calculated route (input flow "waypoint") and the position and direction of the car (input flow "position and direction").

Behavioural Perspective

The behavioural requirements for the navigation system are detailed using the statechart modelling language (see Section 14.3) as depicted in Fig. 15-4.

At the top level, the state "Off" and the super-state "On" are defined:

- *State "Off"*: In this state, the navigation system is switched off.
- *State "On"*: In this state, the navigation system is switched on.

[8] Note that the level 0 DFD here is incomplete. It is, for example, not shown how data is entered into the data store "geographic data".

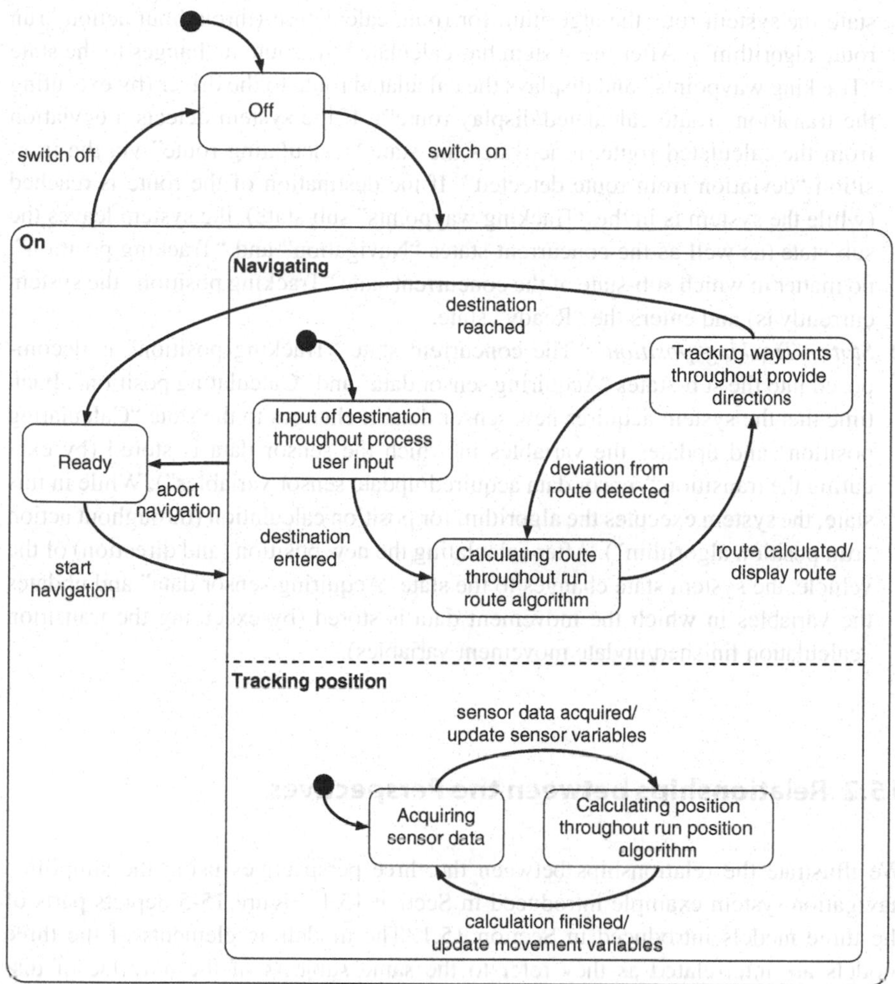

Fig. 15-4 *Statechart for the navigation system*

The super-state "On" has two sub-states, the state "Ready" and another state with the two concurrent states "Navigating" and "Tracking position":

- *State "Ready"*: In this sub-state, the navigation system does not provide any driving directions. When the user starts the navigation, the transition "start navigation" activates the concurrent states "Navigating" and "Tracking position". Via the transition "abort navigation", the driver can abort the navigation, no matter in which sub-states of the concurrent states "Navigating" and "Tracking position" the system currently is, i.e. the system leaves the concurrent states "Navigating" and "Tracking position" and enters the state "Ready".
- *State "Navigating"*: This concurrent sub-state is decomposed into three sub-states "Input of destination", "Calculating route", and "Tracking waypoints". "Input of destination" is the default state. The system changes from the state "Input of destination" to "Calculating route" when the driver has successfully entered the desired destination, i.e. when the transition "destination entered" is executed. While in this

state the system runs the algorithm for route calculation (throughout action "run route algorithm"). After the system has calculated the route it changes to the state "Tracking waypoints" and displays the calculated route to the driver (by executing the transition "route calculated/display route"). If the system detects a deviation from the calculated route, it activates the state "Calculating route" via the transition "deviation from route detected". If the destination of the route is reached (while the system is in the "Tracking waypoints" sub-state), the system leaves the sub-state (as well as the concurrent states "Navigation" and "Tracking position", no matter in which sub-state of the concurrent state "Tracking position" the system currently is) and enters the "Ready" state.

- *State "Tracking position"*: The concurrent state "Tracking position" is decomposed into the sub-states "Acquiring sensor data" and "Calculating position". Each time that the system acquires new sensor data, it changes to the state "Calculating position" and updates the variables in which the sensor data is stored (by executing the transition "sensor data acquired/update sensor variables"). While in this state, the system executes the algorithm for position calculation (throughout action "run position algorithm"). After calculating the new position (and direction) of the vehicle, the system state changes to the state "Acquiring sensor data" and updates the variables in which the movement data is stored (by executing the transition "calculation finished/update movement variables).

15.2 Relationships between the Perspectives

We illustrate the relationships between the three perspectives using the simplified navigation system example introduced in Section 15.1. Figure 15-5 depicts parts of the three models introduced in Section 15.1. The modelling elements of the three models are interrelated as they refer to the same subjects of the universe of discourse such as the same data items or the same functionality. For example, the data to be managed in the navigation system is defined in the data model (Fig. 15-5, top left). In addition, also the functional model (Fig. 15-5, bottom) refers to this data e.g. in terms of data flows and data stores. Likewise, the functional model defines the functions of the system. In addition, partial information about functions, e.g. when a specific function shall be executed, is contained in the behavioural model.

Documenting the relationships

Simple one-to-one relationships between model elements in different perspectives can be established by using the same names for the different elements which refer to the same subject in the universe of discourse. However, there is no guarantee that model elements with identical names in different perspectives really refer to the same subject in the universe of discourse. For example, different stakeholders may use the same term to refer to different subjects in the universe of discourse. In addition, the relationships themselves might be more complex and represent, for example, a one-to-many or a many-to-many relation (see Section 20.2). We thus recommend explicitly documenting the interrelations between the different perspectives by introducing explicit links between the different model elements defined in the perspectives.

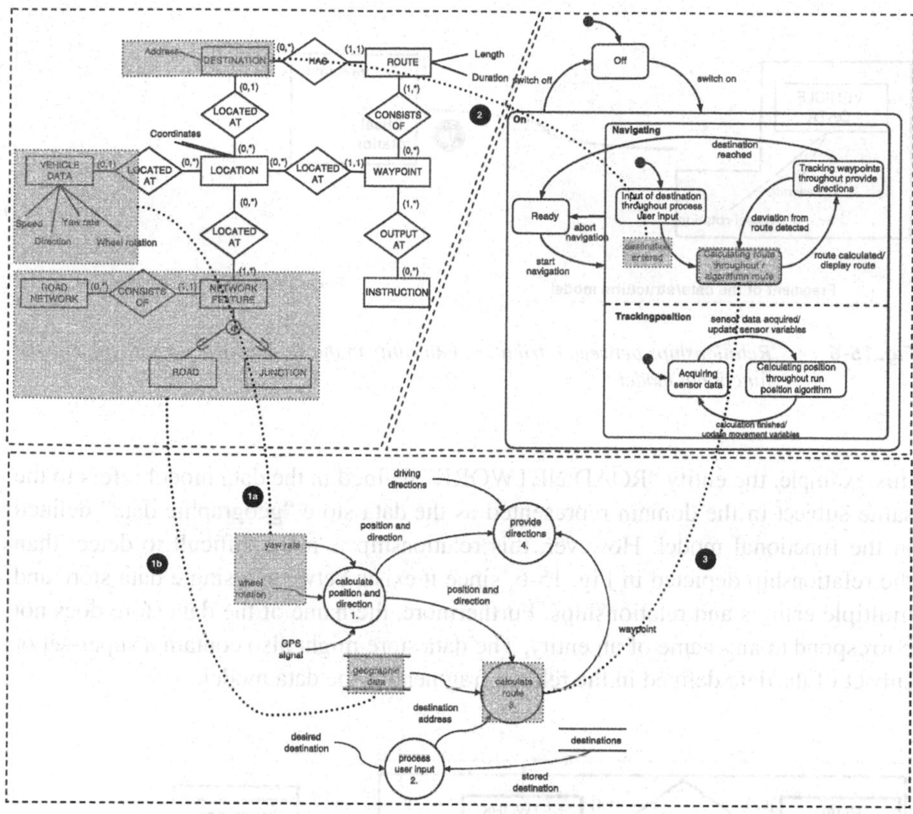

Fig. 15-5 *Examples of relationships between the three perspectives*

In the following, we explain the relationships depicted in Fig. 15-5 in more detail.

Relationships between the Data and the Functional Models

Figure 15-6 depicts an excerpt of the data model (see Fig. 15-1) and the functional model (see Fig. 15-3) defined for the system. These excerpts provide detailed information about the relationship labelled "1a" in Fig. 15-5. Both the attributes defined for the entity "VEHICLE DATA" as well as the data flows between the system context and the function "calculate position and direction" define information about the sensor data obtained by the system ("yaw rate" and "wheel rotation"), i.e. the definitions of the data in the data model and the data flows in the functional model are related to each other.

Note that the relationships are more difficult to detect if different names are used for attributes or data flows, or if the same names refer to different subjects represented by the attributes or data flows.

Another typical relationship between the functional model and the data model is depicted in Fig. 15-7 (which details the relationship labelled "1b" in Fig. 15-5). In

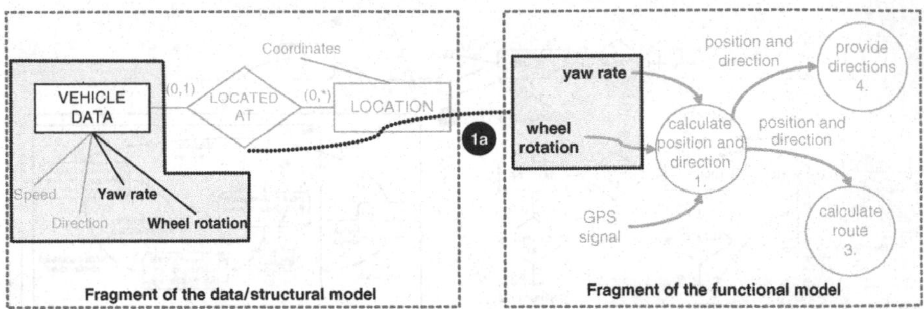

Fig. 15-6 *Relationships between attributes of an entity in the data model and data flows in the functional model*

this example, the entity "ROAD NETWORK" defined in the data model refers to the same subject in the domain represented as the data store "geographic data" defined in the functional model. However, this relationship is more difficult to detect than the relationship depicted in Fig. 15-6, since it exists between a single data store and multiple entities and relationships. Furthermore, the name of the data store does not correspond to any name of an entity. The data store might also contain a super-set or subset of the data defined in the related fragment of the data model.

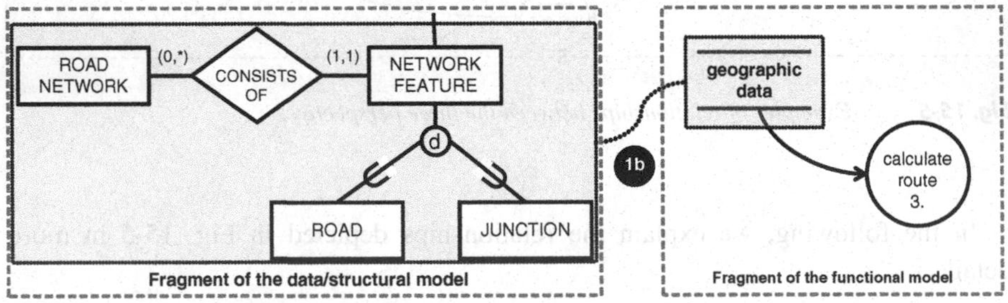

Fig. 15-7 *Relationship between a fragment of the data model and a data store in the functional model*

To keep the information defined in the two models consistent, typically consistency rules are defined between the two types of models. Such a consistency rule can require, for example, that "each data flow and data store defined in the functional model is interrelated with the entities and/or attributes of the data model which define the same information". Alternatively, to support recognition of the relationships, a consistency rule could be defined which requests that "identical names have to be used for the data elements defined in both models". The actual consistency rules applied in a project depend on the type and level of integration to be achieved.

Despite their relationships, the data model and the functional model focus on different aspects of the data. For example, the data model defines more details about the data such as attributes, data types, multiplicity as well as composition, aggregation, or generalisation relationships. Similarly, the functional model defines the functions consuming and producing the data.

Relationships between the Data and the Behavioural Models

Figure 15-8 depicts an excerpt of the data model and the behavioural model defined for the system. This excerpt provides detailed information about the relationship labelled "2" in Fig. 15-5. As depicted in the figure, both the entity "DESTINATION" defined in the data model and the event "destination entered" defined in the behavioural model document information about the destination, i.e. the definition of data in the data model is related to the definition of events in the behavioural model.

To keep the information documented in the two models consistent, consistency rules can be defined. Such a consistency rule can require, for example, that "each reference to a data element in the behavioural model is interrelated with the entities and/or attributes of the data model which define the same information". To support the recognition of relationships between the perspectives, a consistency rule could be defined which requests that "identical names have to be used for the data elements and the corresponding elements in the behavioural model".

The two models, i.e. the data model and the behavioural model, focus on different aspects of the data. For example, the data model defines more details about the data such as attributes, data types, multiplicity as well as composition, aggregation, or generalisation relationships. The behavioural model defines other kinds of additional information such as the transition triggered by a change of a certain data element or the specific values of the data elements in a given state.

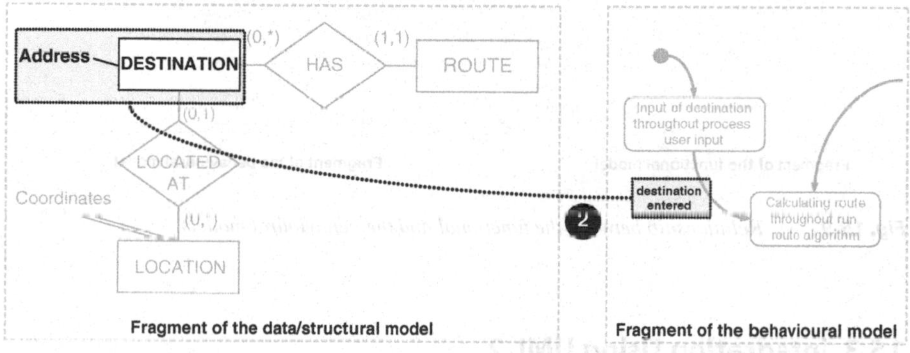

Fig. 15-8 *Relationship between a class in the data model and an event defined in the behavioural model*

Relationships between the Functional and the Behavioural Models

Figure 15-9 depicts an excerpt of the functional model and the behavioural model defined for the system. This excerpt provides detailed information about the relationship labelled "3" in Fig. 15-5. As depicted in the figure, the function "calculate route" defined in the functional model and the action "run route algorithm" referenced within the state "Calculating route" in the behavioural model define information about the calculation of a route. The behavioural model defines that the system shall perform the function "run route algorithm" while being in the state "Calculating route" and that the termination of the function (event "route calculated") causes a transition. The functional model defines the data produced and consumed by the function "calculate route".

To keep the information defined in both models consistent, a consistency rule such as "each function defined in the functional model must be referenced by at least one state and/or state transition in the behavioural model" can be defined to ensure that the behavioural model defines for each function when it shall be executed.

The two models focus on different aspects of the system functions. For example, the functional model defines the functions at different levels of detail (sub-process and super-processes) as well as the data flows consumed and produced by each function. In contrast, the behavioural model defines the events that initiate the execution of a function, the events that terminate the execution of a function, and the reaction of the system when the execution of a function is terminated.

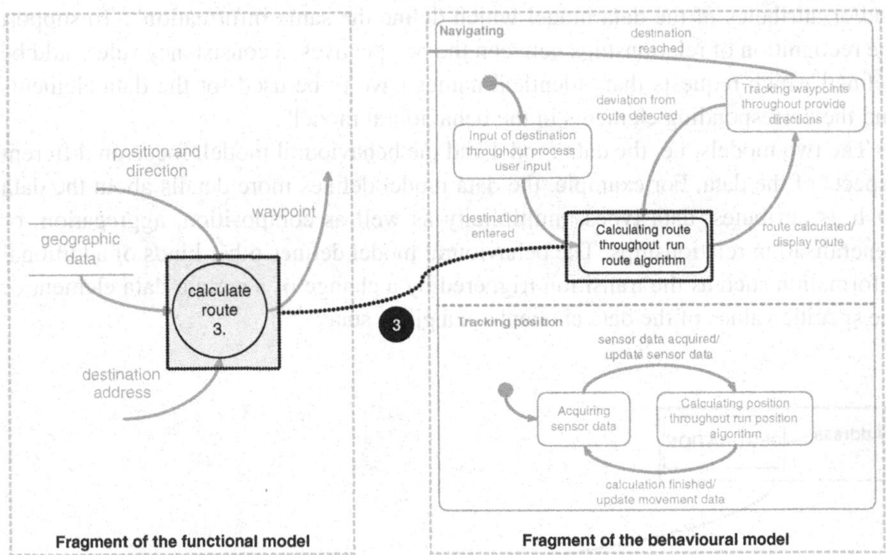

Fig. 15-9 *Relationship between the functional and the behavioural models*

15.3 Integration Using UML 2

Integration of the perspectives

Object-oriented modelling languages provide partial integration of the three perspectives (data, function, and behaviour) by defining modelling constructs that can be used to document requirements in two or all three perspectives. Object-oriented approaches focus on objects, or on classes whose instances are objects. A class or object combines definitions of data and the functions manipulating the data. Therein, the data elements of an object reflect the possible states of the object. The functions that operate on the data of an object are called operations. They determine the (state-dependent) behaviour of the object.

Roots of UML

At the beginning of the 1990s, numerous object-oriented modelling languages and object-oriented analysis methods were propagated. All of those approaches offered more or less sophisticated integration of the three traditional modelling perspectives. Three representatives of the object-oriented modelling approaches laid the foundation for the development of Unified Modeling Language (UML) at the end of the 1990s, namely: the Booch method [Booch 1994], OMT [Rumbaugh et al. 1991], and OOSE/Objectory [Jacobson et al. 1992].

By now, UML has become the de facto industrial standard for object-oriented modelling.

Overall, UML 2 offers 13 diagram types for documenting the requirements as well as the design of an object-oriented system. The following four diagrams are often used during the requirements engineering process:

- Activity diagrams (Section 11.6)
- Class diagrams (Section 14.1.2)
- Sequence diagrams (Section 11.5)
- State machine diagrams (Section 14.3.5)

Sequence diagrams and activity diagrams can be used for documenting scenarios in requirements engineering (see Chapter 11). Class diagrams can be used for documenting solution-oriented requirements in the data perspective, and state machine diagrams can be used for documenting solution-oriented requirements in the behavioural perspective.

Integration of the Perspectives

The support provided by UML 2 for partial integration of the three perspectives includes using common modelling constructs in different diagrams, the interrelation of elements defined in different diagrams, for instance, by means of the "trace dependency", and the assignment of entire diagrams to specific elements. Typical example of interrelating the perspectives are:

- *Relating a state machine to a class*: A state machine can be related (or attached) to a class. If a state machine is attached to a class, it defines the behaviour of the instances of this class. A state of the state machine corresponds to specific attribute values and links (i.e. instantiated relationships) of an object of this class. In requirements engineering, the behavioural requirements for the system can be defined using a state machine that is attached to a single class (defined in the data perspective) representing the system itself. This class is, however, often defined as an aggregation of many other classes which define the data elements of the system.
- *Relationship between a guard condition of an action (effect) and attributes of a class*: A guard condition defined for a transition in a state machine diagram can refer to the attributes of the class (defined in a class diagram) to which the state machine is attached.
- *Relating an action (effect) defined in a state machine diagram to an activity defined in an activity diagram*: An action defined in a state machine diagram (for a transition or a state) can be related to an activity defined in an activity diagram. In this case, the action defined in the state machine diagram defines the same functionality as the activity defined in the activity diagram.

A schematic example of partial integration between class diagrams (or their instances), state machine diagrams, and activity diagrams is depicted in Fig. 15-10.

Correspondences between the views

As depicted in Fig. 15-10, a state defined in the state machine diagram can correspond to a set of objects (i.e. instances of classes defined in a class diagram), links between objects (i.e. instances of associations between classes defined in a class diagram), and attribute values of the objects (Fig. 15-10, ❶). A Boolean expression that

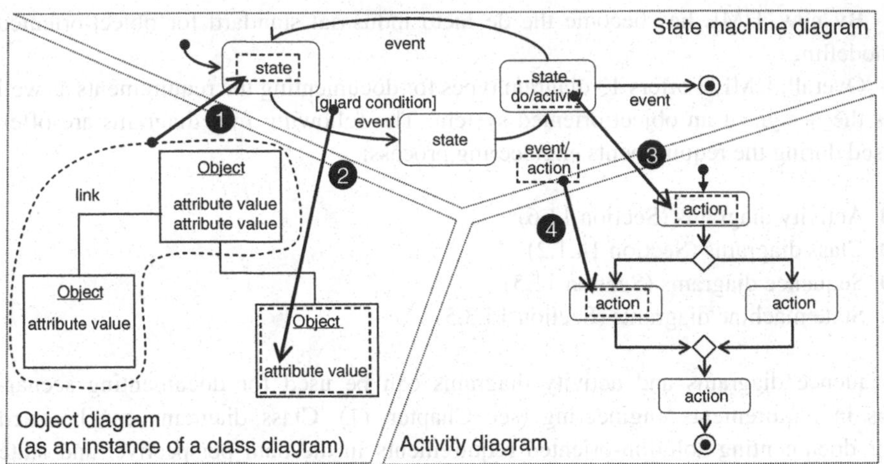

Fig. 15-10 *Interrelation of the three perspectives in UML 2*

is defined as a guard condition of a transition in a state machine diagram can refer to object attributes (Fig. 15-10, ❷). The activities that are defined for a state (entry, do, and exit activities; see Section 14.3.5) can correspond to the actions or activities defined in the activity diagram (Fig. 15-10, ❸). Likewise, actions that are defined for a transition in the state machine diagram can correspond to actions defined in the activity diagram (Fig. 15-10, ❹).

For a more detailed description of the interrelations between different UML 2 diagrams, see [Rumbaugh et al. 2005].

15.4 Integration Using SysML

Systems Modeling Language (SysML) [OMG 2008a] aims to support the specification, analysis, design, and verification of complex systems consisting of hardware, software, information, personnel, procedures, and organisations. Using the modelling constructs of SysML, requirements for such systems as well as the behaviour and structure of these systems can be documented. In contrast, UML was originally defined as a modelling language for software engineering. Since the specification of SysML is based on the specification of UML 2, the interrelation (and partial integration) of the three perspectives in SysML can be accomplished in the same way as in UML 2 (see Section 15.3).

Extensions

Besides reusing a subset of UML 2, SysML provides specific extensions for systems engineering. Among other things, SysML defines modelling constructs for documenting relationships between the elements of different models and thus provides additional means to support the interrelation of the three perspectives.

UML 2 and SysML

Some parts of UML 2 are not part of SysML. Figure 15-11 depicts an overview of the nine SysML diagram types and indicates which diagrams are the same as in UML 2, modified from UML 2, or new diagram types of SysML. A major difference between UML 2 and SysML is that SysML defines blocks as the building elements of a system instead of classes. Blocks and their relationships are defined in the block

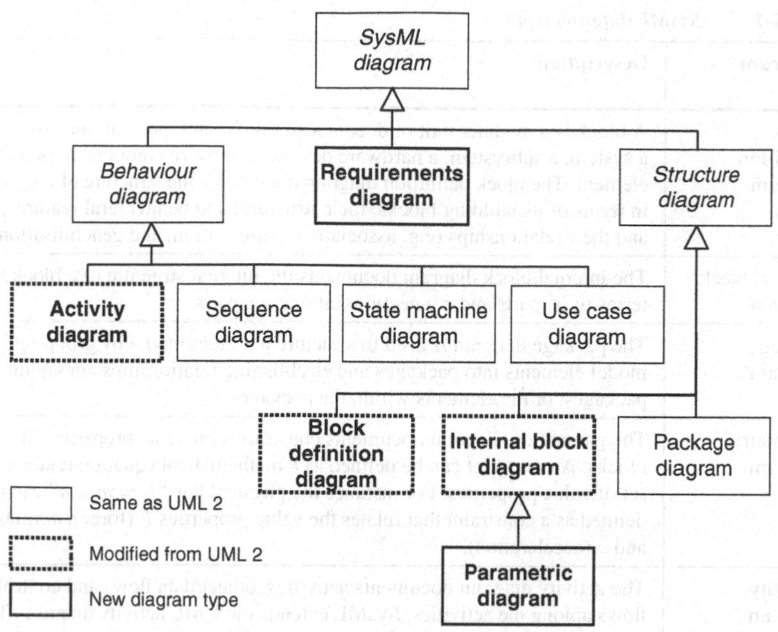

Fig. 15-11 *Overview of SysML diagram types (adapted from [OMG 2008a])*

definition diagram (which is based on the UML 2 class diagram). Section 15.4.1 briefly outlines the nine SysML diagram types.

15.4.1 SysML Diagram Types

The SysML diagram types are briefly characterised in Tab. 15-1.

Requirements diagram

The requirements diagram is a new diagram type defined by SysML (see Fig. 15-11). The requirements diagram facilitates interrelation of requirements with other views (diagrams) defined for the system. We first outline the modelling concepts of the requirements diagram (see Section 15.4.2). The use of SysML for documenting interrelations between requirements defined in the requirements diagram and other views defined for the system is described in Section 15.4.3.

15.4.2 Requirements Diagram

The requirements diagram comprises different modelling elements for documenting requirements and their mutual relationships as well as the relationships between the requirements and other elements of SysML diagrams. Figure 15-12 presents an overview of the key modelling elements of the SysML requirements diagram.

In SysML, a (textual) requirement is represented as a rectangle with the stereotype "requirement", as depicted in Fig. 15-12. A requirement in SysML has a unique identifier and a textual description (the describing text) which can also include a reference to an external document.

Tab. 15-1 *SysML diagram types*

Diagram Type	Description
Block definition diagram	A block is a modular unit of decomposition. It can represent, for instance, a system, a subsystem, a hardware device, a software component, or a data element. The block definition diagram documents the structure of a system in terms of its building blocks, their structural and behavioural features, and their relationships (e.g. association, composition, and generalisation).
Internal block diagram	The internal block diagram documents the internal structure of a block in terms of its parts and connections among the parts.
Package diagram	The package diagram is used to structure a system model by grouping model elements into packages and establishing relationships among the packages, or the elements within the packages.
Parametric diagram	The parametric diagram documents constraints on value properties of blocks. A constraint can be defined as a mathematical equation relating a set of value properties. For instance the physical law "$F = m \times a$" can be defined as a constraint that relates the value properties F (force), m (mass), and a (acceleration).
Activity diagram	The activity diagram documents activities, object/data flows and control flows among the activities. SysML extends the UML activity diagram. The extensions include, for instance, control operators which allow not only to enable but also to disable an activity, continuous object flows, and probabilities.
Sequence diagram	The sequence diagram documents interactions between actors and systems or between parts of a system (i.e. blocks).
State machine diagram	The state machine diagram documents the state transitions and activities or actions that a system or a part of a system performs as reactions to events.
Use case diagram	The use case diagram provides an overview of the scenarios documenting the usage of the system by its actors.
Requirements diagram	The requirements diagram documents requirements and their relationships such as hierarchical structure or refinement. In addition, it supports interrelation of requirements and other model elements which, for instance, satisfy or verify a requirement.

SysML itself does not predefine any specific requirements categories. However, just like UML 2, SysML supports the definition of stereotypes. Hence different types of requirements can be defined in SysML using stereotypes. For example, the following stereotypes can be defined (as sub-types of "requirement") and used for documenting different types of requirements for a system:

- ❑ Goal (stereotype *« goal »*)
- ❑ Scenario (stereotype *« scenario »*)
- ❑ Functional requirement (stereotype *« functionalRequirement »*)
- ❑ Quality requirement (stereotype *« qualityRequirement »*)
- ❑ Constraint (stereotype *« constraint »*)

Relationships between requirements and other model elements

SysML defines the following relationships among requirements, or relationships between requirements and other model elements:

- ❑ *Requirements containment relationship*: This relationship documents that a requirement (called a subrequirement) is part of another requirement (called a

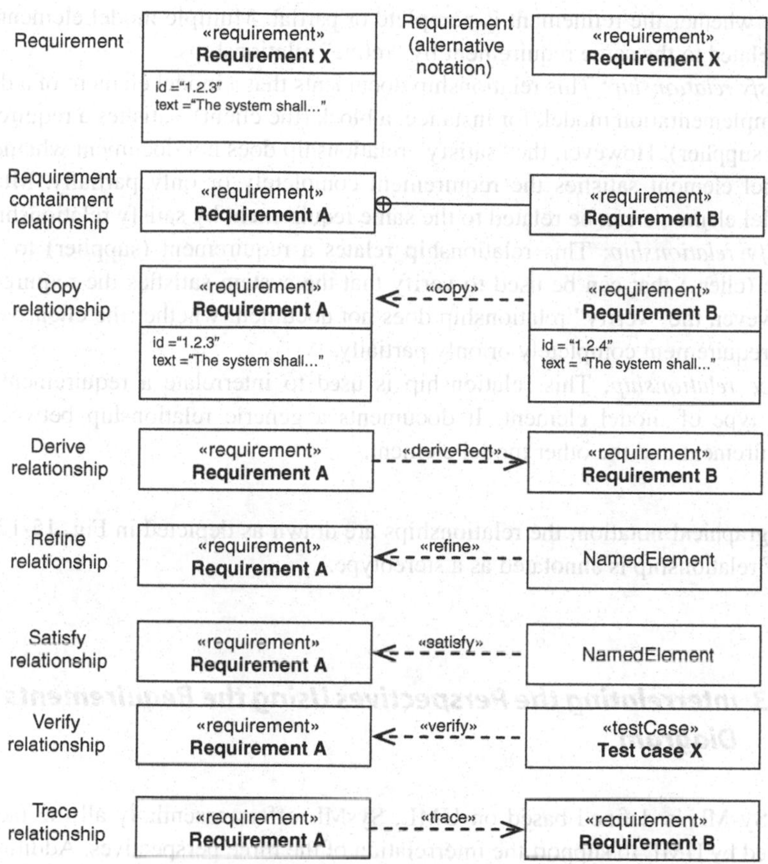

Fig. 15-12 *Modelling elements of the SysML requirements diagram*

compound requirement). A subrequirement can be part of at most one compound requirement at a time. If a requirement is decomposed into a (set of) subrequirement(s), the containment relationship defines that, to satisfy the compound requirement, all defined subrequirements must be satisfied.

- *Copy relationship*: This relationship documents that a requirement (called a client requirement) is a copy of another requirement (called a supplier requirement). The copy of a requirement is, for example, needed when a requirement is reused in another context (e.g. between different system versions or in product line development; see Chapter 38). The supplier requirement and the client requirement maintain a master–slave relationship which means that the name and the identifier of the client requirement are different from the original requirement, whereas the describing text is identical and cannot be edited. If the supplier requirement is decomposed into subrequirements, a copy of each subrequirement is made. Each subrequirement and its copy are associated by a copy relationship.
- *Derive relationship*: This relationship documents that a requirement (the client) can be derived from another requirement (the supplier). For instance, a functional requirement may be derived from a goal, or a subsystem requirement may be derived from a system requirement.
- *Refine relationship*: This relationship documents that a model element, for instance a use case, defines a requirement in more detail. The "refine" relationship does not

state whether the refinement is complete or partial. Multiple model elements can be related to the same requirement by "refine" relationships.

- *Satisfy relationship*: This relationship documents that a model element of a design or implementation model, for instance, a block (the client), satisfies a requirement (the supplier). However, the "satisfy" relationship does not document whether the model element satisfies the requirement completely or only partially. Multiple model elements can be related to the same requirement by satisfy relationships.
- *Verify relationship*: This relationship relates a requirement (supplier) to a test case (client) that can be used to verify that the system satisfies the requirement. However, the "verify" relationship does not document whether the client verifies the requirement completely or only partially.
- *Trace relationship*: This relationship is used to interrelate a requirement with any type of model element. It documents a generic relationship between the requirement and the other model element.

In the graphical notation, the relationships are drawn as depicted in Fig. 15-12. The type of relationship is annotated as a stereotype.

15.4.3 Interrelating the Perspectives Using the Requirements Diagram

Since SysML is defined based on UML, SysML offers essentially all the facilities provided by UML to support the interrelation of the three perspectives. Additionally, SysML provides relationships in its requirements diagram which can be used to support the interrelation of the three perspectives. Figure 15-13 depicts how the SysML requirements diagram can be used for interrelating different views of a system. In the middle of Fig. 15-13, a requirements diagram is depicted which, for reasons of illustration, consists of just one textual requirement. This requirement is related via "refine" links to different model elements, namely a block defined in a block diagram, an activity defined in an activity diagram, and a state defined in the state machine diagram. Each "refine" link documents that the modelling element related to the textual requirement defines (part of) the requirement in more detail. By relating the model elements of the different diagrams to a specific requirement, these model elements are, in addition, indirectly related to each other. To identify the model elements that have to be realised in order to fulfil the requirement, one simply has to follow all the "refine" links defined for the specific requirement. These elements can be checked, for instance, for consistency across the three perspectives.

Vice versa, the different model elements defined in the three perspectives can be traced to textual requirements by means of the "refine" links. Thereby, it is possible to check, for instance, whether each model element is related to a textual requirement and identify other modelling elements to which the element is related (by following the "refine" links and the other links from the requirement to the other model elements).

Separation and interrelation of the three perspectives

Summarising, UML and SysML both support separate documentation of data, function, and behaviour. In addition, UML and SysML offer facilities for interrelating the three perspectives. Interrelations are established, for instance, by:

- ❑ Attaching an entire diagram to an element defined in another diagram (e.g. a state machine to a class)
- ❑ Referring to an element defined in another diagram by its name (e.g. using the name of an attribute of a class in the definition of a guard condition
- ❑ Documenting explicit links between model elements (e.g. using the trace dependency)

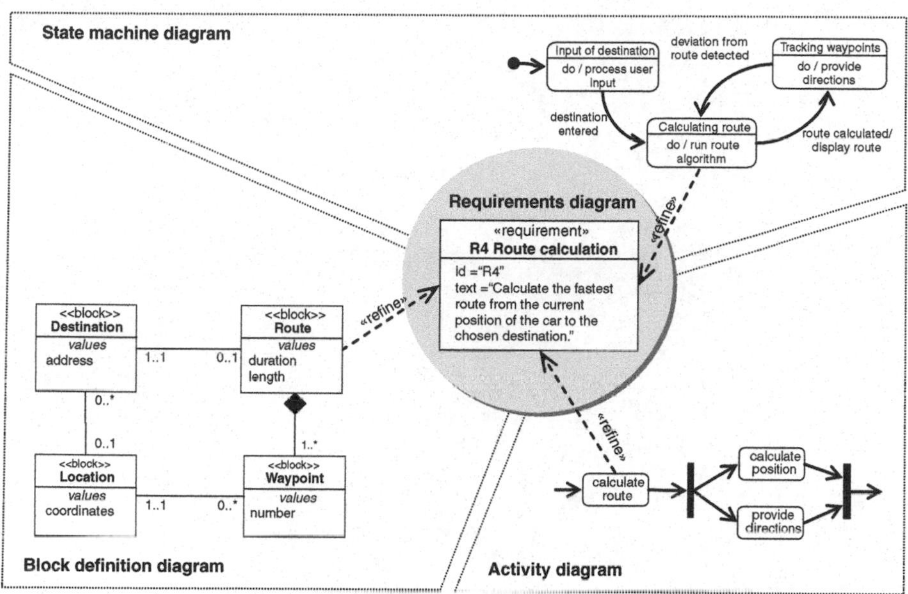

Fig. 15-13 *Interrelation of different perspectives via the requirements diagram*

Furthermore, SysML provides a new diagram type, the requirements diagram, which can be used for interrelating the three perspectives. A requirement documented in the requirements diagram can be related to elements of other diagrams, for instance, by means of "refine" relationships. Thereby, the three perspectives are still documented separately in the different diagrams (e.g. block definition, state machine, and activity diagrams) but are additionally interrelated via the textual requirements documented in the requirements diagram.

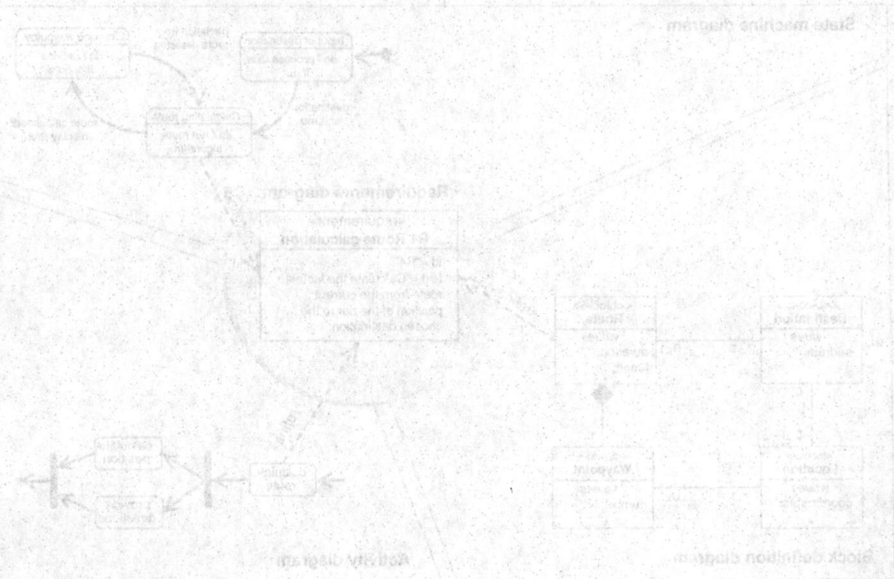

Recommended Literature for Part III.c

Data Modelling

Basic Reading

Inspired by the idea of the relational schema, Chen developed the entity–relationship (ER) modelling language. The ER modelling language is a conceptual language for documenting the data structure for a system. The most popular paper by Chen on the entity–relationship model is [Chen 1976].

Chapter 2 ("Problem Analysis") in [Davis 1993] explains the fundamentals of data-oriented problem analysis and presents well-established approaches and languages for data-oriented analysis such as entity–relationship modelling.

Advanced Reading

[Elmasri and Navathe 2006] explain data modelling and the design of relational and object-oriented databases. Furthermore, techniques and procedures for optimisation of databases are presented.

Martin 1989] provides an introduction to information engineering. In information engineering, company-wide information systems are analysed, planned, designed, and constructed with a focus on a company-wide data definition.

[Teorey et al. 1986] present an enhancement of the entity–relationship model introduced by Chen and describe a procedure for analysing and constructing data models.

[Vossen 2008] explains the use of entity–relationship models for constructing data models in database design. This textbook provides a comprehensive insight into relational database theory and into data modelling.

Function Modelling

Basic Reading

In Chapter 2 ("Problem Analysis"), [Davis 1993] provides an overview of different approaches for problem analysis and explains widespread approaches for function-oriented analysis such as data flow diagrams, Structured Analysis, and Modern Structured Analysis.

[DeMarco 1978] presents one of the most popular approaches for the analysis and modelling of the functional perspective: the data flow diagram. Data flow diagrams are enriched by data dictionaries and mini-specs which capture aspects of the data and behavioural perspective.

Advanced Reading

[Hatley and Pirbhai 1988] suggest a comprehensive enhancement of data flow diagrams by extending them with concepts for defining the control flows between functions. The focus of the extension is thus on real-time systems.

[McMenamin and Palmer 1984] describe Essential Systems Analysis. The authors explain, among other things, the differentiation between essence and incarnation as well as principles for creating essential models. They elaborate on the difference between the essence and the incarnation of a system using data flow diagrams. However, the principle ideas behind the differentiation of essence and incarnation can be applied to all other modelling techniques.

[Ross and Schoman 1977] describe Structured Analysis and Design Technique (SADT), and a modelling method for creating SADT diagrams.

[Yourdon 1989] describes an enhancement of Structured Analysis, called Modern Structured Analysis. Modern Structured Analysis is based on experiences made by applying Structured Analysis methods in practice.

Behaviour Modelling

Basic Reading

[Davis 1993] presents in Chapter 4 ("Specifying Behavioural Requirements") different approaches for modelling the behaviour of a system, including finite automata, Petri nets, and statecharts.

[Harel 1987] introduces statecharts, an enhancement of finite automata, and outlines the use of statecharts for modelling the reactive behaviour of a system. Statecharts belong to the most common used modelling languages for defining system behaviour.

Advanced Reading

[Baumgarten 1996] describes the formal fundamentals of Petri net theory and provides hints for modelling and creating Petri nets.

[Harel and Gery 1996] suggest a modelling language for defining the behaviour of object-oriented systems. The modelling language is based on statecharts.

[Hopcroft et al. 2007] is a standard textbook on theoretical computer science. The book describes the theory of formal languages and different kinds of automata such as deterministic and non-deterministic finite automata.

[Oberweis 1996] presents an approach for modelling workflows with Petri nets. The approach starts from an informal documentation of the workflows and supports its step-wise formalisation.

[Reisig 1986] provides an introduction to the theory of Petri nets which includes conditions/event nets, place/transition nets, and nets with arbitrary tokens.

In [Von der Beeck 1994], different kinds of semantics for statecharts are analysed and compared.

Modelling with UML and SysML

Basic Reading

[Friedenthal et al. 2008] provide a comprehensive introduction to systems modelling using the diagrams of the Systems Modeling Language (SysML).

[OMG 2008a] defines version 1.1 of SysML (Systems Modeling Language) released by the Object Management Group (OMG).

[OMG 2009b] documents version 2.2 of UML (Unified Modeling Language) superstructure released by the Object Management Group (OMG).

[Rumbaugh et al. 2005] provide a comprehensive description of Unified Modeling Language. The authors explain the syntax and semantics of all language elements of UML and its diagrams, including the elements of the class diagrams and activity diagrams.

Advanced Reading

[Wieringa 1998] provides insight into both structured as well as object-oriented analysis and design methods and compares the different methods.

Part IV
Core Activities

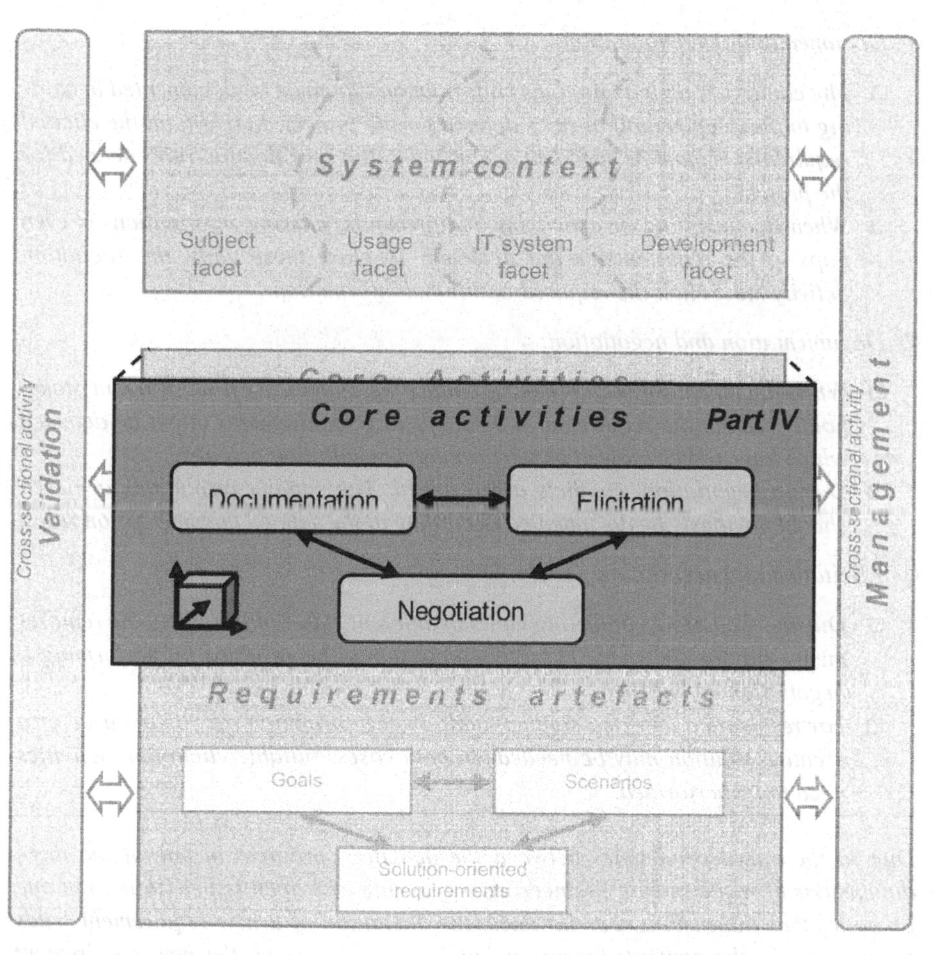

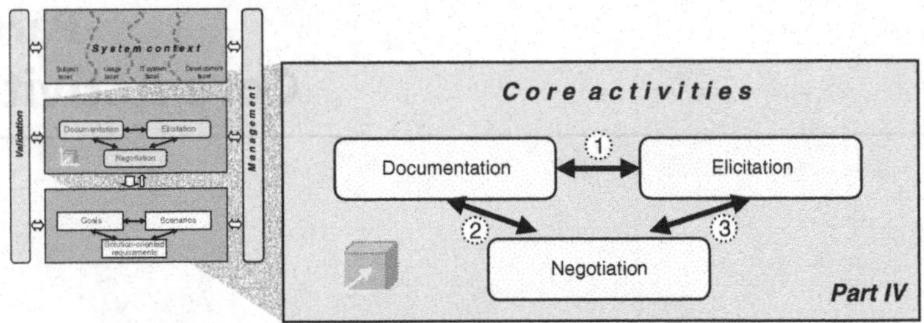

Fig. IV-1 *Interdependencies between the three core activities*

As depicted in Fig. IV-1, the three core requirements engineering activities are interrelated. In the following, we briefly characterise their key interdependencies:

① *Documentation and elicitation:*

- *The elicitation activity produces information that must be documented according to the documentation rules defined for the project. In addition, the elicited requirements must be specified according to the specification rules defined for the project.*
- *When documenting or specifying requirements, missing information or even gaps in the requirements are detected. To close these gaps, the elicitation activity must elicit the required additional information.*

② *Documentation and negotiation:*

- *When documenting requirements, conflicting statements from different stakeholders about the requirements or conflicting requirements might be detected which have to be resolved by performing a negotiation activity.*
- *During negotiation, conflicts are resolved. The conflict resolutions achieved should obviously be documented according to the defined documentation rules.*

③ *Elicitation and negotiation:*

- *During elicitation, conflicting views of different stakeholders about the requirements may be detected. These conflicts should be resolved by performing a negotiation activity.*
- *For resolving a detected conflict, additional information may be required or a creative solution may be needed. In both cases, suitable elicitation activities need to be performed.*

Due to the interdependencies between the activities, progress in one of the three dimensions of requirements engineering may create new open issues (to-dos) in one or both other dimensions. For instance, the elicitation of a new requirement leads to progress in the content dimension but, at the same time, the new requirement needs to be documented according to the documentation rules defined and thus a documentation task is created.

Overview Part IV – Core Activities

This part of the book is divided into three sub-parts. Each sub-part describes one of the three requirements engineering core activities in detail.

In Part IV.a, we discuss the documentation and specification of requirements including:

- *The difference between documentation and specification*
- *Techniques for the structured textual documentation and specification of requirements*
- *The fundamentals of conceptual modelling*
- *Fundamentals of and techniques for the model-based documentation and specification of requirements*

In Part IV.b, we discuss the elicitation of requirements including:

- *Techniques for identifying and prioritising requirement sources*
- *Techniques for eliciting existing requirements*
- *Techniques for developing new and innovative requirements*

In Part IV.c, we discuss requirements negotiation including:

- *Different types of conflicts*
- *Strategies for resolving conflicts*
- *Techniques for supporting conflict management*

Part IV.a
Documentation

Overview Part IV.a – Documentation

Information elicited during requirements engineering must be documented appropriately. In particular, the requirements for the system to be developed must be specified.

This part of the book mainly deals with the documentation and specification of requirements using natural language. In addition, it outlines the fundamentals of conceptual modelling and the use of conceptual models for specifying requirements. Specific conceptual models for documenting solution-oriented requirements as well as goals and scenarios are described in detail in Part III.

For documenting and specifying requirements using natural language, we outline:

- *The difference between documentation and specification*
- *Quality criteria for both individual requirements as well as requirements documents.*
- *Advantages and disadvantages of documenting requirements in natural language*
- *Techniques for reducing requirements ambiguity*
- *Reference structures for requirements documents*
- *Important requirements attributes, templates, and information models for the structured documentation of requirements*

For the model-based specification of requirements, we outline:

- *The fundamentals of conceptual modelling*
- *The principles of documenting conceptual modelling languages*

Furthermore, we sketch out the advantages of integrating model-based and textual requirements documentation.

Classification

Part IV.a
Documentation

		Basic	Advanced
16	**Fundamentals of Requirements Documentation**		
16.1	Motivation and Aims	✓	
16.2	Documentation vs. Specification	✓	
16.3	Quality Criteria for Requirements Artefacts		✓
16.4	Acceptance Criteria		✓
17	**Natural Language Documentation**		
17.1	Natural Language Requirement	✓	
17.2	Requirements Documents	✓	
17.3	Quality Criteria for Requirements Documents		✓
17.4	Use of Natural Language: Advantages and Disadvantages	✓	
17.5	Techniques for Avoiding Ambiguity		✓
18	**Structuring Natural Language Requirements**		
18.1	Reference Structures for Requirements Documents	✓	
18.2	Defining Attributes for Requirements		✓
18.3	Requirements	✓	
18.4	Templates and Information Models		✓
18.5	Establishing Views on Textual Requirements		✓
19	**Fundamentals of Conceptual Modelling**		
19.1	Physical vs. Conceptual Models	✓	
19.2	Model Properties	✓	
19.3	Semiotics of Conceptual Models	✓	
19.4	Quality of Conceptual Models	✓	
19.5	Modelling Languages		✓
19.6	Model Creation and Model Interpretation		✓
20	**Interrelation of Model-Based and Textual Requirements**		
20.1	Requirements Models		✓
20.2	Interrelating Requirements Models and Textual Requirements		✓
20.3	Traceability Meta-models		✓
20.4	Relationships between Conceptual Models and Textual Requirements		✓
20.5	Technical Realisation		✓

Chapter 16
Fundamentals of Requirements Documentation

In this chapter, we outline:

- *Why documentation is needed in requirements engineering and which kinds of information should be considered during documentation*
- *The difference between documentation and specification*
- *Quality criteria for the documentation of individual requirements*
- *The importance of documenting acceptance criteria for requirements*

16.1 Motivation and Aims

Goal of the documentation activity

The documentation activity aims to document important information elicited or developed when performing a core or cross-cutting requirements engineering activity, i.e. the information obtained from executing a documentation[1], elicitation, negotiation, validation, and/or management activity.

Importance of Documentation

Advantages of documentation

Documenting information during requirements engineering is indispensable for several reasons. The key advantages of good requirements documentation are (see e.g. [Sommerville and Sawyer 1997; Kovitz 1998]):

- *Persistence*: During a project, a large amount of different types of information are elicited and developed. Without proper documentation, the stakeholders involved can hardly memorise and reflect all this information.
- *Common reference*: By documenting the relevant information and making it available to all stakeholders, a common reference is provided that can be accessed by all project participants.
- *Promotes communication*: The common reference promotes discussions about the documented facts and thus supports communication among the stakeholders.
- *Promotes objectivity*: Unlike the verbal exchange of information, the exchange of information by means of documents is generally less amenable to unwanted alteration of the information, e.g. due to subjective interpretation.
- *Supports training of new employees*: If a new stakeholder joins the project, the documented information provides an excellent basis for becoming familiar with the project. The stakeholder can selectively access the relevant information needed in a particular situation or for performing a specific task.
- *Preserves expert knowledge*: Typically, not all project members know all relevant aspects of a system such as all relevant technologies or all relevant context aspects. Documenting such expert knowledge makes this knowledge available to all project participants and hence reduces the dependence on individual experts.
- *Helps to reflect on the problem*: When documenting information, the author is forced to structure the information in an appropriate way. Hence the author has to reflect on the information which often leads to the identification of gaps and inconsistencies.

Information to Be Documented

Examples of pieces of information to be documented

Each requirements engineering activity produces a multitude of different kinds of information. Part of this information must be made persistent by documenting it in an appropriate way. In the following, we provide some examples of relevant information that is elicited or created during the requirements engineering and needs to be documented as prescribed by the documentation rules of the project:

[1] The term "documentation" refers to the activity of documenting and not to a documented artefact that was created by the documentation activity.

- ❑ Agreement reached on requirements
- ❑ Alternative solutions for conflicts
- ❑ Brainstorming results
- ❑ Change requests
- ❑ Decision rationales
- ❑ Decisions about change requests
- ❑ Decisions regarding conflicts
- ❑ Deviations from documentation rules/guidelines
- ❑ Different stakeholder viewpoints
- ❑ Evolution of artefacts
- ❑ Identified contradictions
- ❑ Identified errors
- ❑ Identified gaps in documented requirements (goals, scenarios, and solution-oriented requirements)
- ❑ Identified requirements (goals, scenarios, and solution-oriented requirements)
- ❑ Information about context aspects
- ❑ Inspection results
- ❑ Interview results
- ❑ New and innovative requirements
- ❑ New context aspects
- ❑ New requirement sources
- ❑ Observation results
- ❑ Outcomes of workshops and group meetings
- ❑ Priorities
- ❑ Prioritisation of requirements
- ❑ Process information
- ❑ Responsible persons for activities
- ❑ Requirements documented in paper prototypes or sketches
- ❑ Results of prototype usage
- ❑ Results of walkthroughs
- ❑ Review results
- ❑ Risks
- ❑ Scenarios that possibly resolve a conflict
- ❑ Stakeholder arguments
- ❑ Stakeholder wishes and needs
- ❑ Utilised context aspects
- ❑ Utilised requirement sources
- ❑ Etc.

16.2 Documentation vs. Specification

Documenting information

Depending on the purpose of the documentation, the information resulting from the different requirements engineering activities are documented using different representation formats and at different levels of detail. For instance, an elicitation activity may produce requirements that are documented informally and in an unstructured manner, e.g. in the form of interview minutes, sketches, or audio recordings. The information resulting form the elicitation activity are analysed by the requirements engineers and/or other stakeholders in order to document the requirements contained in the documented elicitation results in compliance with the documentation rules and guidelines defined for the project. The documentation rules and guidelines support the requirements engineers in documenting the requirements in a proper way which facilitates, for example, the validation or verification of the requirements. These documentation rules and guidelines relate to the documentation dimension of requirements engineering (see Section 4.4).

Documentation vs. specification

The specification[2] of requirements is a specific kind of requirements documentation. Like the documentation, the specification aims to specify the requirements in compliance with the defined specification rules and guidelines. The difference between documentation and specification of information and requirements is depicted in Fig. 16-1.

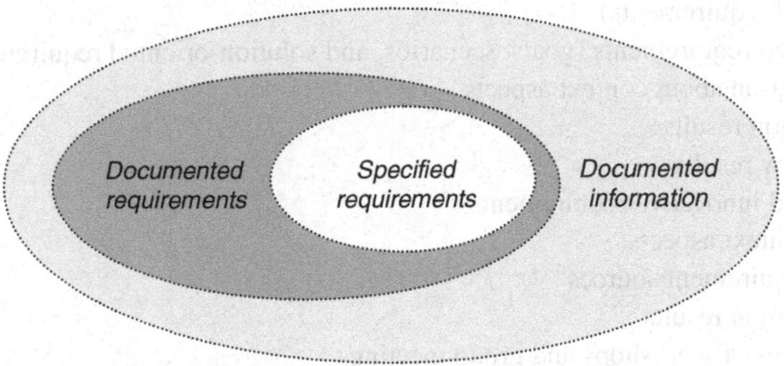

Fig. 16-1 *Documented vs. specified information and requirements*

Documentation of information vs. specification of requirements

As illustrated in Fig. 16-1 each specified requirement is also a documented requirement. However, a documented requirement is not necessarily a specified requirement. A documented requirement is a specified requirement only if the documentation of the requirement complies with the specification rules and guidelines defined for the project. As illustrated in Fig. 16-1, documented requirements are a subset of the documented information. Therefore, each documented requirement obviously represents documented information. The documented information contains all kinds of information documented during requirements engineering (such as minutes and change requests; see Page 296 for more examples) and thus does not only contain requirements. A documented piece of information only represents a documented requirement (a) if it documents information about a requirement and not any other type of information and (b) if the documentation complies with the documentation rules and guidelines defined for requirements.

Use of the terms documented vs. specified requirements throughout this book

Throughout the book, we mainly use the term "requirements documentation" to refer to documented and specified requirements. Moreover, we use the term "documented requirements" instead of "documented or specified requirements" to refer to requirements which are either documented or specified according to the defined documentation or the specification rules and guidelines, if not explicitly stated otherwise.

---

2 The term "specification" refers to the activity of specifying requirements and not to the result of this activity such as a specified requirement or a specification document.

As indicated in Section 4.4, we distinguish three kinds of rules and guidelines for documenting and/or specifying requirements:

Three kinds of rules/guidelines

- *General documentation rules and guidelines*: General documentation rules and guidelines include guidelines for structuring and creating minutes (e.g. interview minutes and inspection minutes), guidelines for the structure and content of change requests, guidelines for documenting conflicts and decisions, and documentation guidelines for ensuring the traceability of requirements artefacts as well as the overall progress in the process itself.
- *Documentation rules and guidelines for requirements*: The documentation rules and guidelines for the three types of requirements artefacts (goals, scenarios, and solution-oriented requirements) define how the requirements should be documented depending on the intended purpose of use of the documentation. Documentation rules and guidelines for requirements prescribe the documentation formats (e.g. natural language or model-based documentation), the abstraction level, the level of detail, and the level of formalisation the documented requirements should have. In addition, they define whether documented requirements may deviate from the rules and guidelines and to what extent, e.g. regarding the level of detail.
- *Specification rules and guidelines for requirements*: In most cases, the specification rules and guidelines impose additional restrictions in comparison with the documentation rules and guidelines. Like the documentation rules and guidelines, also the specification rules and guidelines define the required properties of the specified requirements of all three types of requirements (goals, scenarios, and solution-oriented requirements). Moreover, they define formats to be used to specify the requirements, the abstraction level, the level of detail, and the level of formalisation. Furthermore, specification rules and guidelines often define additional criteria such as quality criteria (e.g. correctness, consistency, and completeness) as well as traceability information to be recorded for the specified requirements.

We distinguish between the documentation of requirements defining the current state and the documentation of requirements defining the desired state. Information on the current state is elicited during the current-state analysis of existing systems and serve as a basis for the definition of the desired state, which defines the requirements for the system to be developed (see Section 3.1). We recommend using the same (or similar) documentation rules and guidelines for the documentation of requirements about the current state and the desired state.

Current-state documentation vs. desired-state documentation

16.3 Quality Criteria for Requirements Artefacts

Quality criteria define the expected quality of the requirements artefacts (i.e. the documented requirements; see Definition 2-2). The quality of a set of requirements artefacts depends on the quality of the individual requirements artefacts as well as the fulfilment of the quality criteria defined for the (set of) requirements artefacts. In this section, we present criteria for individual requirements artefacts. Quality criteria for sets of requirement artefacts and for entire requirements documents are described in Section 17.3.

Quality of individual requirements artefacts

Several sources (see e.g. [IEEE Std 830-1998; Robertson and Robertson 2006]) suggest similar quality criteria for requirements artefacts. These criteria apply to the documentation of requirements in natural language as well as to the model-based documentation of requirements. To ensure that all defined quality criteria are satisfied, typically several elicitation, documentation, validation, and management activities are performed, each of them focussing on one or few of the defined criteria.

In the following, we sketch out important, common quality criteria for requirements artefacts suggested in the literature. A requirements artefact should be:

No missing information

- *Complete*: A requirements artefact is complete if it adheres to the rules and guidelines defined for this type of requirements artefact and does not omit any piece of information that is relevant for some stakeholder (user, client, architect, tester, etc.). For example, a template for requirements artefacts of a specific type (see Section 18.4) can facilitate the validation of whether a requirements artefact of this type is complete (in the sense that no attribute is missing). For this purpose, the template defines the attributes to be documented for each requirements artefact of the specific type. In general, we differentiate between two kinds of completeness: the completeness of a single requirements artefact ("Has the requirement been captured completely?") as well as the completeness of a requirement document ("Does the requirements document include all necessary requirements?"). The completeness of requirements documents is discussed in Section 17.3.

Source, evolution, impact, and use

- *Traceable*: A requirements artefact is traceable if its source, its evolution as well as its impact and use in later development phases are traceable. Requirements traceability is discussed in detail in Chapter 31.

Confirmed by stakeholders

- *Correct*[3]: A requirements artefact is correct, if the relevant stakeholders confirm its correctness and demand that the system must realise the documented requirement completely. Hence, a documented requirement is incorrect, for instance, if it unnecessarily adds system functionality or quality properties (so-called gold plating).

Single valid interpretation

- *Unambiguous*: A requirements artefact is unambiguous, if its documentation permits only one valid interpretation. In contrast, an ambiguous requirement allows for different interpretations. The consequence of an ambiguous requirement may be that the requirement is not realised in the system as intended. The problem of ambiguity in natural language specification is discussed in detail in Section 17.4.2.

Example 16-1: Ambiguous requirement

R14-1: In order to authenticate himself, the driver enters an electronic card and a PIN. If invalid, the engine does not start.

Ambiguity: Does the "if invalid" refer to the card, the PIN, or both?

Easy to understand for the relevant stakeholders

- *Comprehensible*: A requirement is comprehensible if its content is easy to comprehend. The comprehensibility of a requirements artefact depends, among other

[3] The term "correctness" for requirements artefacts is somewhat problematic, since correctness in software development normally denotes the compliance of a program with its specification. However, in requirements engineering there is generally no documented reference against which the correctness of a requirement can be checked. Nevertheless, using validation techniques one can check whether the stakeholders agree with and demand the realisation of the requirements artefact.

things, on the documentation format chosen and the stakeholder(s) involved. Comprehensibility and unambiguousness are independent quality criteria. A requirement can be comprehensible but at the same time ambiguous (e.g. interpreted differently by different stakeholders). Vice versa, a requirement can be unambiguous but still incomprehensible. For instance, a requirements artefact documented in a formal language might not be understandable to many stakeholders, who can thus not detect a potential ambiguity.

- *Consistent*: A requirements artefact is consistent, if the statements within the artefact do not contradict each other. Besides the consistency of each single requirements artefact, especially the consistency of the entire set of requirements artefacts has to be taken into account during requirements documentation (see Section 17.3).

No contradictions

- *Verifiable*: A requirements artefact is verifiable, if the stakeholders can check whether the implemented system fulfils the documented requirement or not. For example, if a requirement is underspecified, it is not possible to decide objectively whether the requirement is realised as defined in the requirements artefact or not (see Example 16-2). To facilitate verifiability, typically acceptance criteria are defined (see Section 16.4).

Clear and objective acceptance criteria

Example 16-2: Verifiability of underspecified requirements

Verifiable: R1: The system must respond to event ES-2 in at least 80% of the cases within 2 s, and in all cases within 3 s at the latest for a system load between 80% and 90% of the maximum load as specified by constraint C14 (System load profile).

Unverifiable: R2: The normal response time of the system shall be less than 2 s.

R2 cannot be verified since it is unclear what the expression "normal response time" refers to, e.g. what type of response, which system load, and under what conditions the response time may be higher than 2 s.

- *Rated*: A requirements artefact is rated, if its relevance and/or its stability have been determined and documented.

Known relevance and stability

- *Up to date*: A requirements artefact is up to date, if it reflects the current status of the system and the system context, such as the current stakeholder wishes or current legal regulations.

Reflects current status of the system and its context

- *Atomic*: A requirements artefact is atomic, if it describes a single, coherent fact. A requirement is not atomic, if it describes multiple isolated or merely loosely coupled facts which can easily be divided into several requirements artefacts (see Example 16-3).

Single coherent fact

Example 16-3: Non-atomic requirement

R23: The user must log on to the system in order to be able to search for a particular order by order ID or by full-text search in the customer database.

Non-atomicity: The requirement R23 is not atomic because it describes user authentication as well as different ways of searching for orders.

In addition to the quality criteria suggested in the literature, we define further quality criteria for requirements artefacts and requirements documents which are derived from the three dimensions of requirements engineering in Section 27.3.

16.4 Acceptance Criteria

Acceptance test and acceptance criteria

An acceptance criterion defines a rule for checking a development artefact during a formal acceptance test of the system. In order to pass the acceptance test successfully, the considered artefact (e.g. the implemented system or a requirements artefact) must fulfil all defined acceptance criteria. If an artefact does not pass the acceptance test successfully (i.e. if it does not fulfil all required acceptance criteria) the artefact must be adapted accordingly and the acceptance test must be re-executed. Hence, acceptance criteria define the conditions for the acceptance of an artefact in such a verifiable, measurable way.

The requirements engineers should know the acceptance criteria for the requirements artefacts as early as possible in order to allow them to choose appropriate methods and tools for developing the artefacts in a way that they fulfil the acceptance criteria.

Objective verifiability

Acceptance criteria must facilitate an objective test of whether the criteria are fulfilled or not. This means that an acceptance criterion must not give leeway to misinterpretation or intentional manipulation. It should be possible to verify without doubt whether the checked artefact meets the acceptance criterion or not. Ideally, each acceptance criterion should be related to a set of measures (metrics) against which the fulfilment is checked. Whether a criterion is fulfilled or not should than be checked by comparing the actual values for the defined measures with the pre-defined target values.

Acceptance of requirements vs. acceptance of the system

We differentiate acceptance criteria for requirements artefacts from acceptance criteria for the implemented system. Both kinds of acceptance criteria, those for the acceptance of the requirements as well as those for the acceptance of the implemented system, have to be considered during requirements engineering. In Section 16.4.1, we outline acceptance criteria for individual requirements artefacts as well as for requirements documents. In Section 16.4.2, we outline acceptance criteria for the system, or its components.

16.4.1 Acceptance Criteria for Requirements Artefacts

Refinement of quality criteria

Acceptance criteria for requirements artefacts define which conditions a requirements artefact or the requirements document must fulfil for its successful acceptance. The acceptance criteria refine the documentation rules and guidelines (see Section 16.2) as well as the quality criteria for requirements artefacts (see Sections 16.3) and the requirements document (see Section 17.3). An acceptance criterion for the requirements document can define, for example, that the requirements document must not contain any contradictions, or that only 2% of the requirements are allowed to be underspecified.

Acceptance Criteria for Individual Requirements Artefacts

Inspection instructions for a requirements artefact

Acceptance criteria for individual requirements artefacts are used to verify the acceptance of an individual requirements artefact independently of any other requirements artefacts. Typically, such acceptance criteria refine quality criteria as well as documentation rules and guidelines by defining more detailed criteria, rules, and instructions for assessing whether a requirements artefact is accepted or not (Example 16-4).

E

> **Example 16-4:** Acceptance criteria for individual requirements
>
> - ❑ Each requirements artefact must have a valid identifier. The identifier of a requirement must be unique and structured according to the scheme <Category>-<Number>. Valid labels for categories are G (goal), S (scenario), and R (solution-oriented requirement). Valid numbers must have five digits. Numbers smaller than 10,000 must be filled to five digits with leading zeros.
> - ❑ For each requirements artefact, the realisation effort must be defined using one of the three values "high", "medium", or "low".
> - ❑ Each requirements artefact must be approved by the responsible project leader, the product manager, and the program manager. For each case, the date of approval and the signature have to be recorded.
> - ❑ For each requirement, the source from which the requirement originates must be unambiguously stated. The valid references to the requirement sources are listed in the document AQ-17-004.
> - ❑ For each system function, a trigger must be specified. Valid trigger types are "user action", "time event", and "system-internal event".

Checking the acceptance of a requirements artefact

To check the acceptance of a requirements artefact, the relevant acceptance criteria for this artefact should be listed in a checklist (see Section 29.1). This checklist should then be used to verify the fulfilment of the acceptance criteria. For example, the acceptance of a requirements artefact can be checked during an inspection (see Section 28.1). In such an inspection typically both the creators as well as the clients of the artefact participate. The decision regarding whether the requirements artefact is accepted is made based on the evaluation of the defined acceptance criteria as well as the identified shortcomings.

Acceptance Criteria for Requirements Documents

Quality criteria for the requirements document

Acceptance criteria for requirements documents are applied to the requirements document as a whole and not to individual requirements artefacts. Acceptance criteria for requirements documents refine the general documentation rules and guidelines as well as the quality criteria defined for requirements documents (see Section 17.3). They define measurable, quantitative rules, for instance, for checking the completeness of the document. The acceptance of the requirements document depends only on the fulfilment of the acceptance criteria defined for this document. Therein, an acceptance criterion for the document can include acceptance criteria defined for individual requirements artefacts. Example 16-5 lists some typical acceptance criteria for requirements documents.

Example 16-5: Exemplary acceptance criteria for requirements documents

- ❑ At most 3% of the textual goal descriptions documented according to template T-G-003, but excluding goals ranked as "high priority", may still contain gaps. (Note: The gaps must be filled later on in the development process.)
- ❑ For the acceptance of the requirements document, 98% of the functional requirements descriptions must have been successfully accepted according to the acceptance criteria for functional requirements (see document F-Acc-12-01).
- ❑ Each scenario contained in the requirements document must have been inspected at least one time under consideration of the acceptance criteria for scenarios (checklist CL-S-001). For each scenario for which a major defect or more than three minor defects were detected, a follow-up inspection must have been performed.

16.4.2 Acceptance Criteria for the System

Refinement of functional and quality requirements

Acceptance criteria define under which conditions the client will accept the implemented system or system component (see [IEEE Std 610.12-1990]). During the acceptance test, it is checked whether the system or the system component fulfils all the defined criteria or not. Acceptance criteria for the system specify requirements for the acceptance test and define, for instance:

Coverage criteria

- ❑ *Requirements for test case derivation*: In this case, the acceptance criterion defines which coverage criterion is used as well as the minimum coverage to be achieved (e.g. a coverage of 80%; see Chapter 37).

Input–output pairs

- ❑ *Definitions of inputs and outputs*: In this case, the acceptance criterion defines the inputs and outputs expected from the system or system component in the form of input–output pairs. Test cases must be created based on these criteria and executed during the acceptance test (see Chapter 37).

We differentiate acceptance criteria for verifying individual functional and quality requirements from acceptance criteria defined for the acceptance of the entire system or a system component.

Acceptance Criteria for Individual Functional and Quality Requirements

Acceptance criteria for individual functional and quality requirements define rules used to test whether the implemented system or component fulfils specific functional and quality requirements. These acceptance criteria are applied during the acceptance of the system or component. An example of an acceptance criterion for a functional requirement is presented in Example 16-6. Examples for acceptance criteria for a quality requirement are presented in Example 16-7.

Example 16-6: Acceptance criterion for a functional requirement

Requirement R1 specifies a functional property of an elevator control system:

- *R1*: "When the emergency stop button is pushed, the control system must stop the elevator within 1 s."

For this requirement, the following acceptance criterion A1 is defined:

- *Acceptance criterion A1*: The fulfilment of requirement R1 has to be proven by an acceptance test in the real operational environment. The acceptance test must be performed with the maximum payload allowed and at the maximum vertical speed. At least 30 test runs have to be performed. In at least 20 of the 30 test runs, the elevator must stop within 0.9 s. In at most 10 test runs, the system is allowed to take longer than 1 s to stop the evaluator, but not more than 1.5 s.

Example 16-7: Acceptance criteria for a quality requirement

The requirement R142 defines a performance requirement:

- *R142*: The system responds to a user input within 1 s.
- *Acceptance criterion A2.1*: The system shall respond to 98% of all requests within 1 s and to the remaining 2% within 5 s at an average load of 50 user requests per second.
- *Acceptance criterion A2.2*: When 1,000 users are logged on, the log-in process for another user must not take longer than 5 s.

Contribution to requirements validation

Defining acceptance criteria for requirements allows for an objective acceptance test. In addition, when defining acceptance criteria, typically defects in the requirements are uncovered (as during the creation of test artefacts; see Section 29.3). The acceptance criteria for stable, well-understood requirements should thus be defined already during requirements engineering. Besides the early detection of requirements defects, defining acceptance criteria during requirements engineering facilitates early development of test cases. Most importantly, only if the acceptance criteria are defined early can they be considered during system development. Defining acceptance criteria very late in the project, e.g. during acceptance testing, should thus be avoided.

However, a requirement has to be sufficiently understood and stable to justify spending the effort required to define concrete acceptance criteria.

Acceptance Criteria for the Entire System

Joint effect of a set of requirements

Acceptance criteria for the entire system address system properties that result from a set of or even all requirements specified for the system. The acceptance criteria for the entire system can refer to the acceptance criteria defined for individual functional and quality requirements. Example 16-8 describes three typical acceptance criteria.

Example 16-8: Acceptance criteria for the system

- For a successful acceptance test, 98% of all required test cases (see acceptance criteria A1 to A38) must be performed without serious deviations.
- The input–output pairs defined in the files IN-OUT-1 to IN-OUT-12 must be used during testing. The system has to produce the specified outputs in all cases.
- The acceptance test must be performed successfully in the environment defined in the document CONF-001 as well as in the environment defined in the document CONF-002.

Chapter 17
Natural Language Documentation

In this chapter, we describe:

- *Common types of requirements documents, especially two common types of requirements documents used in German-speaking countries called* Lastenheft *and* Pflichtenheft
- *Important quality criteria for requirements documents*
- *The advantages and disadvantages of documenting requirements in natural language*
- *The problem of ambiguity in natural language requirements documentation*
- *Three techniques to reduce the ambiguity of natural language requirement documentation*

Most common form of requirements documentation in practice

In practice, requirements are most commonly documented using natural language. In this chapter, we outline the fundamentals of documenting requirements using natural language and discuss its advantages and disadvantages. Moreover, to overcome the problems of natural language (textual) requirements specification, we recommend the (additional) use of requirements models (see Chapters 19 and 20) and compare natural language with model-based requirements documentations. Finally, we briefly sketch out the use of both natural language and model-based specifications to benefit from the advantages of both documentation approaches (see Chapter 20).

17.1 Natural Language Requirements

We use the term "natural language requirements" to refer to requirements that are documented using natural language such as English, French, German or the like. Throughout this book, we use the terms "natural language requirements" and "textual requirements" as synonyms and define the term "natural language requirement" (or, synonymously, textual requirement) as follows:

Definition 17-1: *Natural language requirement (textual requirement)*

A natural language requirement is a requirement that is documented using a natural language.

Intermingling of the three perspectives

If a functional requirement is documented using natural language, the three traditional perspectives of a functional requirement (data, function, and behaviour; see Definition 2-3 on Page 17) are often intermingled within a single, documented or specified requirement. For example, the requirement described in Example 17-1 contains data, functional, and behavioural elements. The three different perspectives are, however, not clearly identified in the documented requirement.

Example 17-1: Functional requirements in natural language

R2: If a glass break detector at the window detects that the pane has been damaged, the system shall inform the security service.

Structure: glass break detector, window, pane, system, security service

Function: detects, inform the security service

Behaviour: if [...] damaged, then inform [...]

Documentation of quality requirements in natural language

Moreover, if requirements are documented using natural language, even quality requirements (see Section 2.2) and functional properties may be intermingled. Example 17-2 shows the functional requirement of Example 17-1 extended by a quality property.

Example 17-2: Intermingling of function and quality

R2.1: If a glass break detector at the window detects that the pane has been damaged, the system shall inform the security service within 2 s at the latest.

Document functional and quality aspects separately

The obvious problem of such a requirements specification is that one or more parts of the specification can easily be overlooked. For example, the quality defined in requirement R 2.1 in Example 17-2 could easily be overlooked during testing. Functional and quality aspects should thus be documented separately even if the quality aspects are logically related to the functional aspects. Example 17-3 illustrates the separate documentation of the functional and quality aspects in two requirements.

Example 17-3: Separation of function and quality

Functional requirements:

R-F-17: The glass break detector at the window shall detect if the glass pane is damaged.

R-F-18: If the detector detects damage to the pane (see R-F-17), the system shall inform the security service.

Quality requirement:

R-Q-2: The system shall inform the security service (see R-F-18) within 2 s after detecting damage.

Advantages of separating function and quality

In general, the separate documentation of quality requirements and functional requirements avoids the risk that a requirement is overlooked. For example, for assessing the overall quality of the implemented system it can now be clearly defined that the requirement R-Q-2 of Example 16-3 has to be considered. The individual functional and quality requirements can be referenced in other artefacts more accurately. Moreover, if a quality requirement affects several functional requirements, the separate documentation avoids undesirable redundancy and thus the (update) problems associated with a redundant specification of the quality aspect in several requirements.

17.2 Requirements Documents

Traditional and generated requirements documents

The requirements for a system to be developed are traditionally defined in a requirements document. Typically a requirements document is structured following a common reference structure. Examples of typical requirements documents are the customer requirements specification and the system requirements specification. However, developing organisations increasingly employ database-supported tools for managing textual requirements. When using database-supported requirements management, a requirements document can, at each point in time, be generated from the requirements database (see Section 3.5 and Section 18.5). A requirements document can thus be regarded as a snapshot of (selected) requirements from a requirements database at a given point in time.

17.2.1 Types of Requirements Documents

Independently of whether requirements are managed in a document or in a database, it is often necessary to bundle selected requirements in a specific requirements document for a given purpose, such as defining the requirements which are the subject of a contract.

Purpose of creating a requirements document

A requirements document can be created, for example, for the following purposes:

- For facilitating communication between users, domain experts, requirements engineers, software developers, etc.
- As a reference model for creating an architectural design
- For negotiation in the case of commissioning development tasks
- As the contractual basis for a contract between the client and the contractor
- As the basis for deriving manuals such as user manuals or maintenance manuals
- As the basis for project planning, monitoring, and controlling

Due to their different purposes, the various requirements documents have different contents and differ in the level of detail with which the requirements are defined.

Recommendations regarding the content of requirements documents differ

Unfortunately, no consistent terminology for the different kinds of requirements documents exists. Moreover the recommendations given in the literature regarding which kinds of requirements documents are required in a development project and what these documents should contain differ significantly.

Requirements Documents in English-Speaking Countries

System requirements vs. software requirements specification

In English-speaking countries typically two kinds of requirements documents for software-intensive systems are distinguished:

- System requirements specification
- Software requirements specification

The system requirements specification defines the requirements for the system hardware and software as well as necessary relationships between hardware and software (see [IEEE Std 1233-1998]). The software requirements specification (see [IEEE Std 830-1998]) details the software requirements defined in the system requirements specification.

In Section 18.1, we discuss the use of a reference structure for requirements documents. As an example, we describe a detailed structure for a software requirements specification according to [IEEE Std 830-1998].

Requirements Documents in German-Speaking Countries

Lastenheft *and* Pflichtenheft

In German-speaking countries, two kinds of requirements documents are commonly differentiated:

- *Lastenheft* (see Section 17.2.2)
- *Pflichtenheft* (see Section 17.2.3)

The system requirements specification and the software requirements specification are both similar to the *Pflichtenheft* (see e.g. [Parnas and Madey 1995]).

System, hardware, and software requirements documents

For software-intensive systems, especially for embedded software-intensive systems, requirements documents are created not only for the system but also for each software and hardware component of the system. In this case, one differentiates between three types of requirements documents:

- *System requirements document*: This document defines the requirements for the entire system and thus for the hardware as well as for the software, including the interplay between the two parts. Typically, the requirements documented in the system requirements document need to be refined and assigned to individual hardware or software components.
- *Software component requirements document*: A software component requirements document defines the detailed requirements for a specific software component of the system.
- *Hardware component requirements document*: A hardware component requirements document defines the detailed requirements for a specific hardware component of the system.

This differentiation of requirements documents is orthogonal to the differentiation of *Lastenheft* and *Pflichtenheft*. For example, a *Pflichtenheft* is typically created for the entire system as well as for each individual software component and each individual hardware component.

17.2.2 The Lastenheft

Lastenheft *typically created by the client*

According to DIN 69901-5, the *Lastenheft* defines all requirements for the items and services the contractor must deliver [DIN 69901-5 2009]. In many cases, the *Lastenheft* additionally specifies the requirements from the user perspective, including all relevant constraints for the system and the development process. A *Lastenheft* is typically created by the client. We define the term *Lastenheft* as follows:

Definition 17-2: *Lastenheft*

The *Lastenheft* contains a definition of the system vision and a description of the essential system goals (functions and qualities), and names important context aspects (e.g. constraints) of the four context facets as well as their relationships to the vision and the defined system goals.

The system goals defined in the *Lastenheft* generally provide an abstract description of the desired functionalities and qualities the system should provide (see Example 17-4).

Example 17-4: Requirement defined in a *Lastenheft*

R-12: The safety system shall offer user and access management.

Context information

With regard to context aspects (see Section 6.2), a *Lastenheft* typically contains a list of the most relevant stakeholders, refers to relevant documents, legacy systems as well as competing systems, and defines central context objects as well as their properties.

The Lastenheft is the foundation for executing various tasks in the development process such as:

Basis for the Pflichtenheft

- *Creation of the* Pflichtenheft: The abstract requirements as well as the constraints and the relevant context aspects documented in the *Lastenheft* serve as the basis for creating the *Pflichtenheft* which defines the requirements in more detail (see Section 17.2.3).

Basis for contracts

- *Bidding and contract negotiation*: The *Lastenheft* serves as basis for an invitation for tender and, later on, for contract negotiations. Typically invitations for tenders are announced for the development of the *Pflichtenheft* based on the *Lastenheft* or even for the realisation of the system based on the *Lastenheft* in which case the creation of a *Pflichtenheft* is part of the tender.

Basis for the evaluation of alternatives

- *Evaluation of potential, alternative realisations*: The *Lastenheft* is used as a basis for effort estimation and calculation of the project duration. Based on this estimates, typically, the decision is made as to whether the system should be developed internally, a contract with an external company or other department to develop the system should be established, or instead of building a new system, existing systems should be purchased and adapted where necessary (make-or-buy decision).

Basis for risk assessment

- *Risk assessment*: The *Lastenheft* supports the risk assessment of the development project. Based on the *Lastenheft*, different feasibility studies can be performed in order to investigate and assess different risks associated with the development of the system such as technical risks, the risks of getting personnel with the required skills, or the risk of being able to commit the required resources in general.

17.2.3 *The* Pflichtenheft

According to DIN 69901-5, the *Pflichtenheft* describes the realisation of the *Lastenheft* and defines the detailed requirements for realising the system [DIN 69901-5 2009]. Thus, the *Pflichtenheft* details the requirements and constraints documented in the *Lastenheft*. Typically, the *Pflichtenheft* is created by the contractor whereas the *Lastenheft* is typically created by the client. We define the term *Pflichtenheft* as follows:

D

Definition 17-3: *Pflichtenheft*

The *Pflichtenheft* details the vision and the system goals (abstract functionalities and qualities) described in the *Lastenheft*. If required, it also details the constraints defined in the *Lastenheft* with regard to the intended technical realisation of the system.

The Lastenheft *is often part of the* Pflichtenheft

The requirements documented in the *Lastenheft* are typically defined in more detail and, if required, additional requirements are added during the creation of the

Pflichtenheft. The *Lastenheft* is thus often part of the *Pflichtenheft*. Example 17-5 illustrates the detailed definition of a requirement defined in the *Lastenheft* in the *Pflichtenheft*.

E

Example 17-5: Detailed requirements in the *Pflichtenheft*

The requirement as stated in the *Lastenheft*:

R-L-12: The safety system shall offer user and access management.

The requirements defined based on requirement R-L-12 contained in the *Pflichtenheft* (excerpt)

R-8: The safety system shall differentiate between the administrator and user of the system

…

R-14: The administrator shall be able to create new user accounts.

R-15: The system shall support the organisation of user accounts in user groups.

R-16: The administrator shall be able to assign and revoke access authorisations.

…

R-23: The user shall be able to change his/her personal access code.

…

Customer and system requirements specification: "What?" vs. "How?"

Whether artefacts in the development process relate to the definition of a problem ("What?") or to the description of a solution ("How?") depends on the specific perspective of the stakeholder (see Section 2.3). Figure 17-1 depicts the relation between the *Lastenheft* and the *Pflichtenheft* from the client's (creator of the *Lastenheft*) and from the contractor's perspectives. From the client's perspective, the vision defines the "What?" and the *Lastenheft* defines the solution, i.e. the "How?". From the contractor's perspective, the *Lastenheft* defines the "What?" and the *Pflichtenheft* defines the "How?".

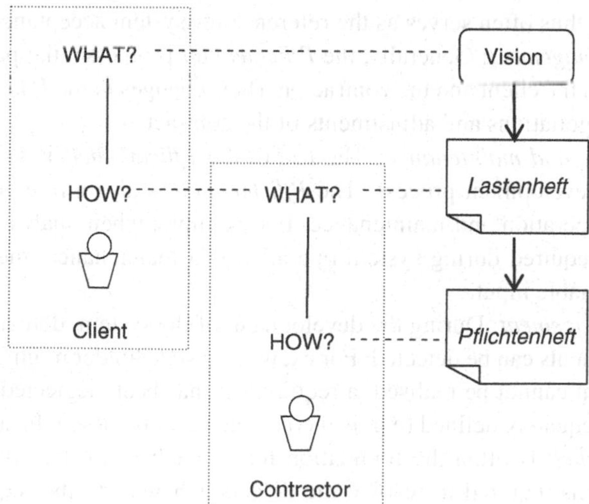

Fig. 17-1 *The* Lastenheft *and the* Pflichtenheft *– "what?" vs. "how?"*

Coarse-grained architecture

In many cases, the *Pflichtenheft* also contains an initial coarse-grained system architecture, defines the important system interfaces and contains an initial assignment of requirements to architectural components.

Real-time and safety requirements

The *Pflichtenheft* also defines real-time and safety requirements. With respect to the real-time and safety requirements, the *Pflichtenheft* also defines the risk associated with the operation of the system, as well as potential damages and their probability of occurrence. Furthermore, the *Pflichtenheft* defines for each potential damage whether its occurrence can be accepted and tolerated or not.

Role of the Pflichtenheft *in the development process*

The *Pflichtenheft* is thus essential for the development process. It is the key input for several development activities and serves as a reference throughout the entire development process. The *Pflichtenheft* is an essential input for the following system development activities:

Basis for project planning

- *Project planning*: During project planning, activities to be performed (such as design, coding or test activities), milestones and the resources required to perform the activities are defined based on the requirements and constraints defined in the *Pflichtenheft*.

Basis for design

- *Architectural design*: An adequate architecture can only be defined if detailed functional and quality requirements as well as design constraints are known (see e.g. [Maier and Rechtin 2009; Clements et al. 2002]). The *Pflichtenheft* is thus the cornerstone for creating an architectural design.

Information source for implementation

- *Implementation*: During high-level and detailed architectural design, the requirements assigned to the individual components and modules are typically not described in detail. Instead, the design documentation refers to the corresponding requirements defined in the *Pflichtenheft*. Consequently, the developers need access to the *Pflichtenheft* in order to be able to understand the requirements to be realised.

Basis for test case derivation

- *Tests*: The requirements and their associated acceptance criteria defined in the *Pflichtenheft* provide the foundation to define and derive test cases for the system to be developed.

Basis for system acceptance

- *System acceptance*: The *Pflichtenheft* typically defines the acceptance criteria (see Section 16.4.2) which have to be met by the implemented system. The *Pflichtenheft* thus often serves as the reference for system acceptance.

Contractual adaptations

- *Contract management*: Generally, the *Pflichtenheft* is an essential part of the contract between the client and the contractor. Thus, changes in the *Pflichtenheft* often lead to re-negotiations and adjustments of the contract.

System evolution

- *System usage and maintenance*: The use of the *Pflichtenheft* is not restricted to the system development process. The *Pflichtenheft* is also a reference document for system operation and maintenance. For example, when analysing the impact of changes required during system operation and maintenance, the *Pflichtenheft* provides valuable input.

Change impact evaluation and change integration

- *Change management*: During the development of the system, defects in the specified requirements can be detected. For example, a stakeholder might recognise that a requirement cannot be realised, a requirement has been neglected, or a requirement is inadequately defined (e.g. is incomplete or ambiguous). In such situations, the *Pflichtenheft* is often the foundation for an analysis of the impact of potential corrections required to resolve the defects. Changes to the requirement or a constraint should obviously be integrated in the *Pflichtenheft*.

17.3 Quality Criteria for Requirements Documents

Quality criteria for individual requirements and for documents

Quality criteria can be defined for each individual requirements artefact (see Section 16.3) as well as for an entire requirements document, or for specific sections in the document or a set of requirements defined in this document. A quality criterion for a requirements document can define, for instance, that there must be no inconsistencies between the functional requirements specified in the document. Like the quality criteria defined for the individual requirements, also the quality criteria defined for the entire (or part of the) requirements document can be used during the requirements engineering process in a constructive or analytic manner (see Section 27.2.1).

Three essential quality criteria

In the following, we explain three essential quality criteria that apply to the entire document: completeness, consistency, and modifiability and readability. In Section 27.3, we define additional quality criteria for requirements and requirements documents which are derived from the three dimensions of requirements engineering.

Completeness

No requirements overlooked

All requirements documented completely

There are two basic types of completeness: First, each requirement should be specified completely (see Page 299). Second, all relevant requirements have to be defined, i.e. no relevant requirement should be missing. A requirements document is thus considered to be complete if all relevant requirements are specified in the document and if each documented requirement is specified completely.

Completeness according to IEEE 830-1998

According to the IEEE standard 830-1998 [IEEE Std 830-1998] a requirements document which is based on the reference structure for software requirements specifications (SRS) is complete if it contains the elements described in Definition 17-4.

Definition 17-4: *Completeness of an SRS*

"An SRS is complete if, and only if, it includes the following elements:

a) All significant requirements, whether relating to functionality, performance, design constraints, attributes, or external interfaces. In particular any external requirements imposed by a system specification should be acknowledged and treated.
b) Definition of the responses of the software to all realisable classes of input data in all realisable classes of situations. Note that it is important to specify the responses to both valid and invalid input values.
c) Full labels and references to all figures, tables, and diagrams in the SRS and definition of all terms and units of measure."

[IEEE Std 830-1998]

!

Hint 17-1: *Identified gaps in a requirements document ("TBDs")*

(1) Document identified gaps in the documentation of a single requirement as well as missing requirements etc. in a requirements document by explicitly defining a "TBD" ("to be determined") for each gap.
(2) For each TBD, document the reason why the gap exists.
(3) For each TBD, define by when the TDB shall be resolved
(4) If possible, document how the TBD shall be resolved and the stakeholder responsible for resolving the TBD.

Consistency

No inconsistencies in the document or in the requirements

A requirements document is considered to be consistent if each individual requirement is (internally) consistently defined and if there exist no inconsistencies between the requirements defined in the requirements document.[4] The IEEE standard 830-1998 differentiates three types of inconsistencies in a requirements document:

Three types of inconsistencies

- *Inconsistent description of a real-world aspect/object*: At least two requirements describe the same real-world phenomenon with a different terminology (e.g. "enter the city you like to travel to" and "enter your destination").
- *Inconsistent properties of a real-world aspect/object:* The properties of a real-world phenomenon specified in at least two requirements contradict each other. For example, one requirement defines that the destination can only be entered via a touch screen while another requirement defines that the destination should only be entered by voice input in order to be compliant with legal regulations.
- *Inconsistent specification of actions:* There is a logical or temporal conflict between at least two actions specified in at least two requirements. For example, a requirement might define that a function X shall be executed before function Y is executed. At the same time, another requirement might define that Y shall be executed before B is executed, and a third requirement might define that B shall be executed before X is executed.

Modifiability and Readability

Structure and style

Modifiability and readability of a requirements document are influenced by the structure and style of the document. A requirements document is modifiable, if its structure and style support a simple, complete, and consistent modification of the requirements while still retaining the structure and style [IEEE Std 830-1998]. A requirements document is readable if the reader is able to extract and comprehend its contents easily.

[4] Note that there could be a conflict in a requirements document even if all requirements are unambiguously defined. In other words, the requirements document could be inconsistent even if all requirements contained in it are unambiguously defined.

To support the modifiability and readability of a requirements document the document should have a coherent structure (see Section 18.1), each individual requirement should have a unique identification (see Section 18.3.1), redundancies should be avoided, and the defined requirements should be atomic (see Section 16.3).

Modifiability and readability

!

Hint 17-2: *Avoid redundancy in requirements documents*

In case of changes, redundancies typically lead to defects in a specification since one or more redundant aspects may easily be overlooked when integrating the change. You should thus:

(1) Avoid redundancy in requirements documents as far as possible, for example, by employing a structure that reduces the redundancy/overlaps between the different sections of the document.
(2) Introduce cross references if redundancy cannot be avoided; cross-references support consistent change integration.

17.4 Use of Natural Language: Advantages and Disadvantages

The use of natural language for documenting requirements has several key advantages compared with using a formal specification language, but also some key disadvantages. For example, natural language allows the stakeholders to communicate and document nearly any kind of knowledge concerning the requirements for the system. The use of natural language in requirements engineering is thus essential to facilitate, for instance, the elicitation of requirements, the exchange of background information, or the development of new and innovative requirements. However, the use of natural language for documenting and communicating requirements also involves some key disadvantages, such as its inherent ambiguity, i.e. the use of natural language is not always the best choice for communicating and documenting requirements.

In Section 17.4.1, we briefly discuss the key advantages of using natural language for documenting requirements. In Section 17.4.2, we describe the key disadvantages of using natural language for documenting requirements. The advantages of using conceptual models for documenting requirements and the combined use of natural language and conceptual models for documenting requirements are outline in Section 20.1.

17.4.1 Key Advantages of Using Natural Language

The use of natural language requirements has three essential advantages [Kamsties 2001]:

Three main advantages

- *Universal*: The documentation of requirements in natural language is universal, since natural language can be used in any problem area or domain.
- *Flexible*: Natural language is flexible, since natural language allows arbitrary abstractions and refinements during requirements documentation.

- *Comprehensible*: Requirements documented in natural language are comprehensible to many stakeholders, since (assuming that the stakeholders know the language) no training or special tools are required.

17.4.2 Key Disadvantages of Using Natural Language

Significant disadvantage: ambiguity

The use of natural language for requirements documentation has some disadvantages: Natural language is inherently ambiguous. Ambiguously documented requirements have more than one valid interpretation and therefore suffer from the risk that different persons interpret a requirement differently.

A documented requirement is unambiguous, if all stakeholders with approximately the same knowledge about the system and its context interpret the requirement in the same way. A documented requirement is ambiguous, if different stakeholders with approximately the same knowledge about the system and its context interpret the requirement differently. There are two main reasons for different interpretations:

Defects of natural language

- *Underspecification*: If details about a requirement are not documented, different stakeholders can assume different details and thereby interpret the requirement in a different way. Thus, gaps or missing details are a common source of ambiguity. This type of ambiguity is mainly independent of the language used to document the requirement.

Four kinds of ambiguity

- *Defects of natural language*: In this case, the ambiguity is caused by the inherent ambiguity of natural language. Even if specified carefully, the inherent ambiguity of natural language often leads to different interpretations of a requirements artefact and is thus a significant problem in practice. [Berry et al. 2003] differentiate four kinds of ambiguity: lexical, syntactic, semantic, and referential ambiguity. Lexical, syntactic, and referential ambiguity entail semantic ambiguity. In addition, there are cases of semantic ambiguity that is not caused by lexical, syntactic, or referential ambiguity (see Example 17-8). This applies, for instance, to ambiguity caused by uncertainties about the binding strength of logical operators such as “and”, “or”, and “not”.

In the following, we elaborate on the four kinds of ambiguity (lexical, syntactic, semantic, and referential) and ambiguity caused by the use of vague terms in the documentation — another source of ambiguity. In Section 17.5, we present three techniques for reducing the ambiguity of requirements documented in natural language.

Lexical Ambiguity

Ambiguous terms

Lexical ambiguity has the following two major causes:

- *Synonyms*: A synonym is a word that has the same meaning as at least one other word. Examples of synonyms are “car/automobile”, “small/little”, and “sick/ill”.
- *Homonyms*: A homonym is a word that has different meanings in different contexts despite being spelled in the same way. An example of a homonym is the word “trunk”. In botany, this word typically refers to the stem of a tree, while in zoology the same word “trunk” refers to the nasal extension emerging from an elephant’s

face. Also, "trunk" is a typical description of a large, wooden chest, or luggage case, or, in American English, it can even refer to the rear cargo compartment of a motor vehicle. The term "homonym" merely refers to words with identical spelling and pronunciation. Words which merely sound identical but are spelled differently are called homophones. Examples of homophones are "right/rite" or "there/their/they're".

Synonyms and homonyms are thus a constant source of ambiguity in requirements engineering and are caused, for example, by different vocabulary used for technical terms in different companies, countries, or different departments within a large organisation.

Syntactic Ambiguity

Ambiguity due to syntactic structures

Syntactic ambiguity occurs if there are at least two valid syntax trees that can be assigned to the same sentence, and for each assignable syntax tree, the sentence has a different meaning (see e.g. [Hirst 1987]). Syntactic ambiguity is also referred to as structural ambiguity since a syntax tree denotes the grammatical structure of a sentence. Example 17-6 shows a textual requirement with syntactical ambiguity.

E

Example 17-6: Syntactic ambiguity of requirements

R2: The user enters the access card with the access code.

Two different syntax trees can be associated with the requirement R2 shown in Example 17-6. Figure 17-2 depicts these two syntax trees. The abbreviations used in the figure have the following meanings: S = sentence, NP = noun phrase, VP = verb phrase, PP = prepositional phrase, Det – definite article, N = noun, P = preposition, V = verb.

The requirement R2 can thus be interpreted in two ways:

- *Interpretation 1*: The user enters his access card and, in addition, his access code into some system.
- *Interpretation 2*: The user enters his access code by making use of his access card, i.e. the access card contains the access code.

Example 17-7 shows another example of a syntactically ambiguous requirement.

E

Example 17-7: Syntactic ambiguity of requirements

R21: The navigation system shall display the last five destinations and starting points.

The syntactic ambiguity of requirement R21 in Example 17-7 relates to the information the system shall display. A possible interpretation of requirement R21 is that the display of the navigation system shall display the last five items entered, may it

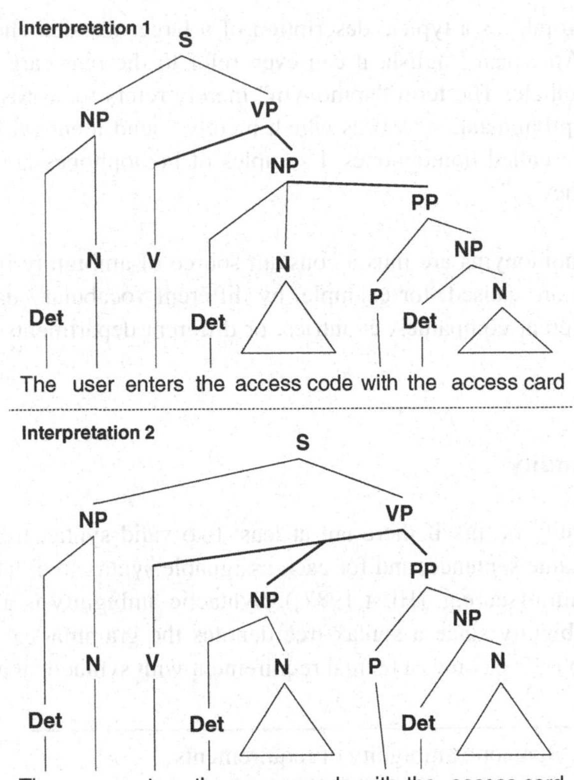

Fig. 17-2 *Two possible syntax trees for the requirement R2 stated in Example 17-6*

be destinations or starting points. Another possible interpretation is that the last five destinations and a set of starting points shall be displayed. In addition, another possible interpretation is that the system should display the last five destinations and the last five starting points.

A more detailed description of syntactic ambiguity of requirements documented in natural language can be found in [Berry et al. 2003].

Semantic Ambiguity

No unambiguous interpretability

Semantic ambiguity occurs when a sentence has more than one interpretation in the specific context, even if it contains no lexical or syntactic ambiguity. Example 17-8 contains a semantically ambiguous requirement.

Example 17-8: Semantic ambiguity of requirements

R24: If a window of the car is damaged and the interior surveillance of the car detects an intruder or a door of the car is opened without a car key, the safety system shall raise an alarm.

Example of semantic ambiguity

Due to the missing information regarding whether "and" binds stronger than "or", the requirement R24 of Example 17-8 can be interpreted differently. Example 17-9 depicts two possible interpretations of the requirement R24 of Example 17-8. The interpretations differ in the condition that leads to raising the alarm.

E

Example 17-9: Semantic ambiguity of requirements

Possible interpretation 1: "and" stronger than "or": [❶ and ❷] or ❸

If [❶ a window of the car is damaged and ❷ the interior surveillance of the car detects an intruder] or ❸ a door of the car is opened without a car key, the safety system raises an alarm.

Possible interpretation 2: "or" stronger than "and": ❶ and [❷ or ❸]

If ❶ a window of the car is damaged and [❷ the interior surveillance of the car detects an intruder or ❸ a door of the car is opened without a car key], the safety system raises an alarm.

According to interpretation 1 ("and" binds stronger than "or") shown in Example 17-9, opening a door of the car is sufficient to raise the alarm. In contrast, according to interpretation 2 ("or" binds stronger than "and"), a window of the car must have been damaged and, additionally, the interior surveillance system must detect an intruder or (alternatively) a door of the car must be opened without a car key to raise the alarm.

Lexical ambiguity leads to semantic ambiguity

Semantic ambiguity can be caused by the lexical ambiguity of individual words as well the syntactic ambiguity of a sentence. Each occurrence of lexical or syntactic ambiguity leads to semantic ambiguity. However, semantic ambiguity can also occur if the documented requirement has neither lexical nor syntactical ambiguity as illustrated by Example 17-8. The relationship between lexical/syntactic ambiguity and semantic ambiguity is depicted in Fig. 17-3.

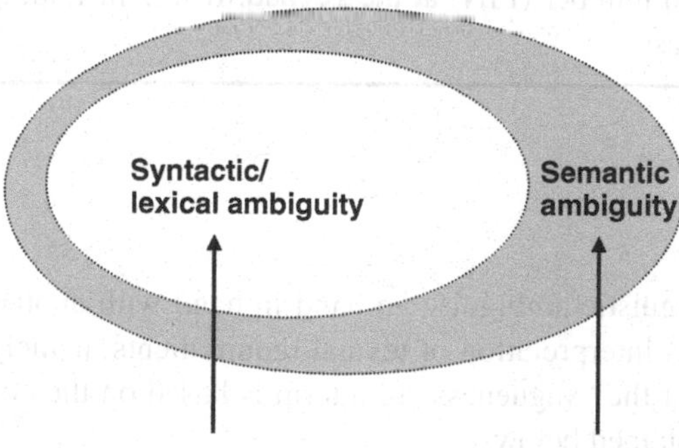

Fig. 17-3 *Relationship between syntactic and semantic ambiguity*

Referential Ambiguity

Several possibilities to resolve a reference

Referential ambiguity occurs if a word or phrase in a sentence refers to an object, and there are different interpretations regarding what this object is. The term "reference" can have two different meanings:

- The term "reference" can denote the relation between a symbol (or a word) and an object of the "real" world that is denominated by the symbol (see Section 19.3). With this interpretation of "reference", the referential ambiguity is caused by different "real"-world objects that are related to the same word or phrase.
- In linguistics the term "reference" denotes the relation between a word or phrase in a sentence and an expression (possibly in a different sentence) before or after this word or phrase.

In this section, we focus on the second meaning, i.e. the referential ambiguity caused by references between words and/or phrases.

Anaphor and cataphor

In linguistics, an anaphor is an expression in a sentence that refers back to a previous expression in the same sentence or in a previous sentence. The expression referred to by the anaphor is called the antecedent. A cataphor is similar to an anaphor but refers to an expression that appears in the text after the cataphor.

Referential ambiguity occurs when a person interpreting an anaphor or cataphor cannot unambiguously determine the associated antecedent of the anaphor or the expression referred to by the cataphor.

Example 17-10 depicts a requirement with referential ambiguity where the antecedent of the anaphor "it" in the second sentence cannot be determined unambiguously. For requirement R42 one cannot unambiguously determine whether the pronoun "it" refers to the access card or to the personal identification number. The person interpreting the requirement is in doubt under which condition the access is denied: If the access card is invalid or if the entered PIN is invalid?

Example 17-10: Referential ambiguity of requirements

R42: The customer inserts the access card into the card reader and enters a personal identification number (PIN) at the keypad. If it is invalid, the system shall deny the access.

Vagueness of Terms

The different types of linguistic ambiguity go hand in hand with another issue that hampers the unambiguous interpretation of textual requirements, namely vagueness of terms. The definition of the "vagueness" of a term is based on the concept of the "extension" of a term explained below.

Extension of a term

The extension of a term is the set of all objects that are denoted by this term. A term is considered vague if the extension is not known exactly or if at least one known borderline case exists. A borderline case exists, if there is an object for which it is impossible to determine whether the object belongs to the extension of the term or not.

Example 17-11: Vagueness due to a blurry definition of a term

All medium-sized vehicles shall be equipped with a navigation system.

Example of vagueness

The statement in Example 17-11 contains vagueness due to the expression "medium-sized vehicles". There are vehicles for which it is impossible to unambiguously determine whether the vehicle is a medium-sized vehicle or not. One person might allocate such a vehicle to the category of medium-sized vehicles while another person does not allocate the same vehicle to this category. In other words, the term "medium-sized vehicles" is not clearly defined. Note, that this issue is more relevant if requirements are interpreted by stakeholders from different cultures or backgrounds. For example, "medium-sized vehicle" refers to a concept which is understood similarly in a single country, but could have a different meaning in another country. For example, in Germany, different car types might be associated with "medium-sized vehicle" than in North America.

17.5 Techniques for Avoiding Ambiguity

We present three proven techniques for reducing the ambiguity of natural language requirements: glossaries, syntactic requirements patterns, and controlled languages. By applying these techniques, the risks related to the ambiguity of natural language requirements can be reduced.

17.5.1 Glossaries

Defining the meaning of terms

Lexical ambiguity is caused by homonyms (a word which has different meanings) and/or by synonyms (different words with the same meaning). This kind of ambiguity can be reduced or even totally avoided by explicitly defining the meaning of the different terms used in the specification in a glossary. A glossary is thus a collection of definitions of terms (see Definition 17-5).

Definition 17-5: *Glossary*

A glossary is a collection of technical terms that are part of a language (terminology). A glossary defines the specific meaning of each of these terms. A glossary can additionally contain references to related terms as well as examples that explain the terms.

Structure of glossary entries

The definitions of the terms in a glossary typically follow a predefined structure. Hint 17-3 suggests such a structure which consists of the parts "term", "definition", "synonyms", "related terms" (generalisations, specialisations, etc.), and "examples/counter-examples". In requirements engineering, examples and counter-examples can be provided, for example, by referring to scenarios where the term is used. Scenarios describe concrete examples of system usage and provide important context information which supports determining the correct interpretation of the terms (see [Weidenhaupt et al. 1998]).

!

Hint 17-3: *Structure of a glossary*

To define a term in the glossary you could use the following structure:

Term:	name of term
Definition:	definition text
Synonyms:	synonym-1; [...]
Related terms:	term-1; [...]
Examples/counter-examples:	references to examples/counter-examples

Example 17-12 shows a glossary entry using the structure suggested in Hint 17-3.

E

Example 17-12: Definition of a term using the structure suggested in Hint 17-3.

Term:	Route
Definition:	The specific instance of a direction from a starting point to a destination
Synonyms:	Itinerary
Related Terms:	Alternative route (specialisation)
Examples/Counter-examples:	[Link to a map showing an example route]

Benefits of glossaries

Explicitly defining important terms in a glossary helps to reduce or even avoids the following risks:

- The risk that some stakeholders do not know the meaning of a technical term and thus the technical term is interpreted differently
- The risk that different stakeholders interpret a technical term that is familiar to them differently
- The risk that different interpretations of a term exist but are not discovered; often different interpretations of a term surface during the definition of the term in the glossary
- The risk that the stakeholders use different terms for the same real-world object, i.e. synonyms
- The risk that stakeholders use the same term for several different real-world objects (possibly related to each other), i.e. homonyms

!

Hint 17-4: *Creating a glossary*

(1) Define a structure for the glossary entries to be used by all authors editing glossary entries.
(2) Check the structure of the glossary frequently.
(3) Ask stakeholders with different backgrounds to provide their own definition of a term and align the definitions obtained.

(to be continued)

Hint 17-4 (*continued*)

(4) If you question whether a term should be defined in the glossary, rather define the term than leave it out.
(5) Involve stakeholders with different backgrounds to review the glossary entries, comment on existing definitions, and identify missing ones.
(6) Make the glossary available online as hypertext, if possible.
(7) If possible, provide support for managing the glossary in the intra- or Internet, e.g. by establishing a wiki where stakeholders can comment on definitions and suggest new glossary entries (see e.g. [Stricker et al. 2009]).

17.5.2 Syntactic Requirements Patterns

Concrete syntactic structures

The use of syntactic patterns for documenting requirements aims, right from the beginning, at avoiding mistakes that frequently occur when defining textual requirements. An example of a frequent mistake is the use of the passive voice. Syntactic requirements patterns define concrete syntactic structures for documenting requirements. Such patterns are defined based on experience with syntactic structures for textual requirements and are applied to support the documentation of requirements (see also [Rolland and Proix 1992; Rupp and Goetz 2000; Schienmann 2002]). We define the term "syntactic requirements pattern" as follows:

D

Definition 17-6: *Syntactic requirements pattern*

A syntactic requirements pattern defines a syntactic structure for documenting requirements in natural language and defines the meaning of each part of the syntactic structure.

Syntactic requirements pattern

Figure 17-4 depicts an example of a syntactic pattern for documenting requirements in natural language, taken from [Rupp 2009].

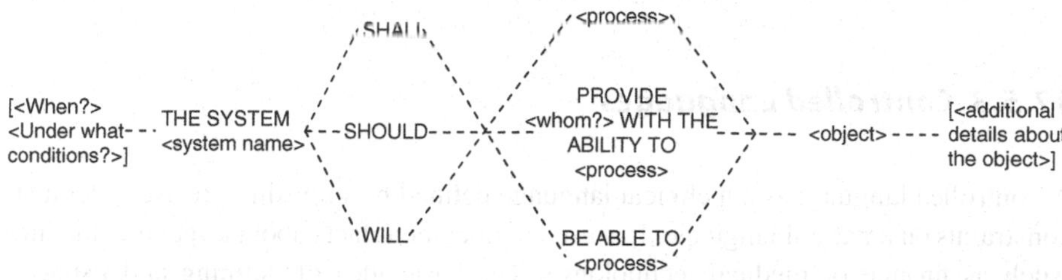

Fig. 17-4 *Syntactic requirements pattern for documenting requirements with a condition [Rupp 2009]*

The syntactic requirements pattern consists of the following structural elements (see [Rupp 2009]):

- *<When>*: This element of a requirement defines one or more logical or temporal conditions under which the function documented in the requirement shall be performed or provided.

- *<System name>*: This element defines the name of the system which shall provide the documented function. This system is the grammatical subject of the sentence.
- *"Shall/Should/... "*: This element indicates the importance of the requirement. For instance, the modal verb "shall" indicates a legally binding requirement, while "should" indicates a requirement that is highly recommended but would not make the system unacceptable if it is not implemented.
- *<Process>*: This element indicates the required functionality (called the "process" in [Rupp 2009]). This functionality is documented by a full verb such as "print" or "transfer". The syntactic pattern depicted in Fig. 17-4 distinguishes three types of functionality and suggests a different pattern for each type. The first pattern (<process>) applies to requirements that document functionality that the system shall offer independently of interactions with users. The second pattern (PROVIDE <whom?> WITH THE ABILITY TO <process>) applies to requirements that document functionality that the system shall provide to specific users. The third pattern (BE ABLE TO <process>) is suggested for documenting functionality that the system shall perform as reactions to trigger events from other systems (see [Rupp 2009]).
- *<Object>*: This element describes the object for which the functionality is required, such as the type of document to be printed (e.g. a tax form). The object as well as additional details about the object are documented after the process.

Example 17-3 shows a textual requirement defined using the syntactic requirements pattern depicted in Fig. 17-4.

Example 17-13: Documentation of requirements using a syntactic requirements pattern

R114: If the glass break detector detects the damaging of a window, the system shall inform the head office of the security service.

[<When>: If the glass break detector detects the damaging of a window] THE SYSTEM SHALL [<Process>: inform] [<Object>: the head office of the security service].

17.5.3 Controlled Languages

Controlled language for a domain

A controlled language is a technical language defined by imposing precisely defined constraints on a natural language. It is used to document facts about a specific domain (such as finance or medical technology). The basic idea of defining and using a controlled language stems from Lorenzen and Kamlah (see [Kamlah and Lorenzen 1996; Lorenzen 1973]). In computer science, Wedekind took up the idea of controlled languages in the domain of conceptual database design (see [Wedekind 1979]).

Restricted grammar and terminology

In contrast to traditional formal languages, controlled languages do not only define a formal grammar but also a vocabulary. By taking the domain for which the language is designed into account, a controlled language defines, in addition to the formal grammar, a set of permissible terms to be used in the expressions documented using this language. The meaning of each term is defined a priori and therefore does not need to be determined from the context of the phrase or sentence in which it is used (as is the case for expressions in natural languages). We define the term controlled language as follows:

Definition 17-7: *Controlled language*

A controlled language defines, for a specific domain, a restricted natural language grammar (syntax) and a set of terms (including the semantics of the terms) to be used within the restricted grammar to document statements about the domain.

Advantages of using a controlled language

Using a controlled language in requirements engineering has several advantages (see [Ortner 1997; Schienmann 2002]):

- Expressions documented in a controlled language are easy to understand, since they are similar to expressions in natural language.
- Expressions documented in a controlled language are less ambiguous than expressions in natural language, since they have a simplified underlying grammar and a predefined vocabulary with precise semantics.
- Expressions documented in a controlled language are semantically verifiable due to the formal grammar and the predefined terms.

Standardisation of requirements at the syntactic and the semantic level

In contrast to syntactic requirements patterns, which define the permissible syntactic structures of requirements, a controlled language thus also defines the semantics[5] of the statements. Controlled languages can thus be regarded as an extension of syntactic requirements patterns which, in addition to restricting the syntax (the grammatical structures), also precisely define the semantics of the resulting requirements.

In [Ortner 1997; Schienmann 2002], a four-step approach is suggested to develop a controlled language (see Fig. 17-5).

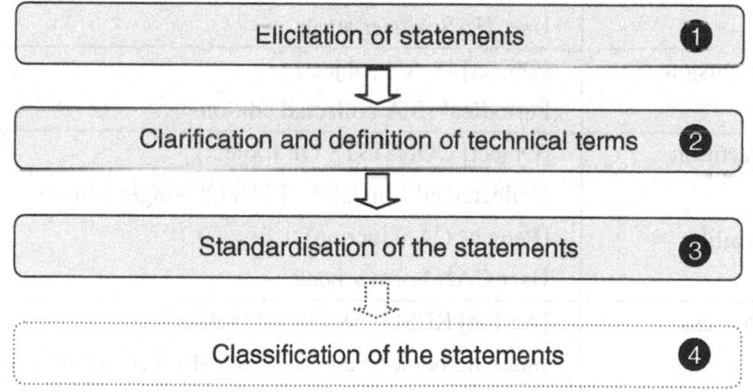

Fig. 17-5 *Four steps for defining a controlled language*

Elicitation of statements (Fig. 17-5, ❶)

During the elicitation of statements, technical experts elicit a list of fact-related, colloquial statements, e.g. by means of interviews (see Section 22.3).

[5] The term "semantics" is explained in detail in Section 19.3.

Clarification and definition of technical terms (Fig. 17-5, ❷)

During the clarification and definition of technical terms, the requirements engineer learns the correct use of the technical terms from the technical experts and defines formal usage rules for the technical terms. Example 17-14 depicts three typical usage rules for technical terms based on [Schienmann 2002].

Example 17-14: Usage rules in controlled language development

Subordination: $x \in \text{employee} \Rightarrow x \in \text{person}$
Equivalence: $x \in \text{library card} \Leftrightarrow x \in \text{user card}$
Contrariness: $x \in \text{periodical} \Rightarrow x \notin \text{serial}$

The subordination rule stated in Example 17-14 expresses that "employee" is a subtopic of "person". The equivalence rule defines that "library card" and "user card" are synonyms, and the contrariness rule states that a real-world object cannot be a "periodical" and a "serial" at the same time (since periodicals appear at regular intervals, but the parts of a serial generally appear at irregular intervals). In addition to the rules, the meaning of each predefined technical term is defined in a glossary.

Standardisation of statements (Fig. 17-5, ❸)

Finally, pattern types and sentence patterns for each pattern type are defined. The defined sentence patterns are used to document the requirements or, respectively, statements about the domain. Table 17-1 depicts different pattern types, sentence patterns for each pattern type, and examples of standardised requirements statements created using the sentence patterns.

Tab. 17-1 *Syntactic standardisation of requirements statements in a controlled language (based on [Schienmann 2002])*

Type of pattern	Pattern/example
Participation	[Object] HAS AN [object] User HAS A user status
Inclusion	[Object] IS AN [object] Periodical IS A collected edition
Partition	[Object] CONSISTS OF [object] Collected edition CONSISTS OF single editions
Ability	[Person] CAN [action] User CAN borrow book
Process	[Action] RESULTS FROM [action] Indexing book RESULTS FROM inventorying book
Rule	IF [event] AND [condition] THEN [action] IF book returned AND lending period exceeded THEN reminder charges

Classification of statements (Fig. 17-5, ❹)

Steps ❶, ❷, and ❸ are performed to define the meanings of statements and terms. In addition, to facilitate specifying the requirements in a model-based format, the standardised statements are classified in step ❹ according to their type (e.g. modelling construct).

Example 17-15 illustrates the classification of standardised statements using the patterns of the controlled language depicted in Tab. 17-1. The standardised expressions are "mapped" in Example 17-15 to static aspects of an object diagram (see [Schienmann 2002] for details).

Example 17-15: Classification of statements during the development of a controlled language

User HAS A user status ⇒ attribute
Periodical IS A collected edition ⇒ inheritance relationship
Collected edition CONSISTS OF single editions ⇒ aggregation
User CAN borrow book ⇒ method

E

Aim of defining and using a controlled language

The use of a controlled language improves communication between stakeholders, since ambiguities and misunderstandings about aspects of the underlying domain are avoided by use of a standardised terminology. Although a controlled language restricts the grammar and vocabulary of the natural language, the controlled language still seems familiar, since it merely regularises the use of habitual language constructs (see [Wedekind 1979]).

Due to the imposed restrictions, a controlled language is less expressive than natural language. In addition, stakeholders require extensive training to enable them to apply the controlled language. Furthermore, due to the constrained expressiveness and the necessity to observe the defined rules, a controlled language should not be used for eliciting requirements. However, a controlled language is well suited for specifying requirements (e.g. in system requirements specifications), especially when precisely delimited and well-understood domains are considered.

Chapter 18
Structuring Natural Language Requirements

In this chapter, we describe:

- *A reference structure for requirements documents*
- *Important attributes for requirements artefacts*
- *Template-based documentation of natural language requirements*
- *The use of information models to structure requirement artefacts*
- *The definition of views on natural language requirements*

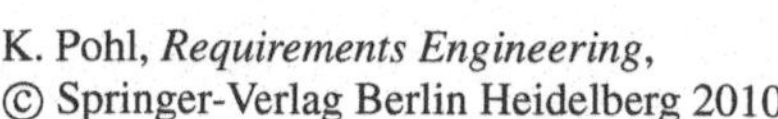

In this chapter, we deal with the structuring of requirements. This involves the structuring of entire requirements documents as well as the structuring of individual requirements artefacts. The structured documentation of requirements (as well as other kinds of information; see Section 16.1) supports all other requirements engineering activities, i.e. elicitation, negotiation, validation and management (see the respective parts of the book).

A requirements document typically comprises not only requirements artefacts (i.e. documented goals, scenarios, functional requirements, quality requirements, and constraints) but also important information about the system context (see Part II). We describe a common reference structure for requirements documents in Section 18.1.

In order to structure the information to be documented in the individual requirement artefacts, typically attributes are defined. Part of these attributes are common to all artefacts while others are specific to each artefact type. We outline the principles of assigning attributes to requirements artefacts in Section 18.2 and describe in detail common attributes which can be used for defining project-specific requirements attributes (Section 18.3). The attributes are organised into seven categories.

For structuring artefacts along with the assigned attributes, we suggest using templates and information models (Section 18.4). Due to the large amount of information that is typically documented in a requirements specification, selective access to the requirements artefacts is strongly desirable. In Section 18.5, we briefly outline the need for creating views on the requirements documentation and sketch out the creation of views on a requirements base.

18.1 Reference Structures for Requirements Documents

Proposed reference structures

Many recommendations for reference structures for requirements documents exist. Such recommendations are mainly defined by national and international standardisation organisations, business associations, individual companies, or even by individual divisions of companies. For example, in German-speaking countries, reference structures for the *Lastenheft* and the *Pflichtenheft* are defined by the VDI/VDE Standard 3694 [VDI/VDE 1991]. In English-speaking countries, the IEEE Standard 1233-1998 [IEEE Std 1233-1998] defines a reference structure for system requirements specifications (SyRS), and the IEEE Standard 830-1998 [IEEE Std 830-1998] defines a reference structure for software requirements specifications (SRS). The two reference structures defined by the IEEE as well as the ones defined by VDI/VDE are frequently used as basis for defining project- and domain-specific reference structures.

18.1.1 Advantages of a Reference Structure

Advantages of structuring

Using a reference structure for requirements documents improves the modifiability and readability of the document and facilitates checking of the requirements document for completeness and other quality criteria (for quality criteria for requirements documents, see Section 17.3). Hence, the use of a reference structure for structuring requirements documents offers several advantages:

- *Proven structure*: A reference structure is defined based on the experience of experts in the structuring of requirements documents. In other words, best practice experience is reflected in the reference structure. By using a reference structure, this expert and best practice knowledge is leveraged for the project.
- *Reference for completeness*: Reference structures facilitate checking whether the documented information is in compliance with the predefined structure. For example, the reference structure facilitates checking whether all aspects defined in the reference structure have been documented.
- *Focussing on the content*: Since a reference structure prescribes how the various pieces of information contained in a requirement document are structured, the requirements engineers can concentrate on the actual content of the specification rather than dealing with the structure of the document.
- *Same information at the same place*: A reference structure defines which information should be documented at which place within the document. Thus, even across projects, stakeholders always find the same kind of information at the same place. For example, requirements documents created using the same reference structure can be compared more easily in order to detect deviations, incompleteness, or inconsistencies.
- *Tool support*: Comprehensive tool support exists for creating a reference structure and using this structure to create a requirements document. For example, such tools provide editable templates for requirements documents as well as the possibility to generate a requirements document according to some standardised reference structure from the requirements stored in the requirements base (see Section 18.5).

18.1.2 Reference Structure According to IEEE Standard 830-1998

Applicable to Lastenheft *and* Pflichtenheft

According to our experience, the structure of many requirements documents in practice is defined based on the IEEE 1233-1998 (system requirements specification [IEEE Std 1233-1998]) or IEEE 830-1998 (software requirements specification [IEEE Std 830-1998]) standards. These two standards are, in many cases, the basis for the reference structures suggested for the *Lastenheft* and the *Pflichtenheft* (see Section 17.2).

Recommended structure of IEEE Std 830-1998

In the following, we describe the reference structure for software requirements specifications defined in the IEEE Standard 830-1998. The IEEE Standard 830-1998 structures a requirements document in three top-level parts (see Fig. 18-1). For the third part of a software requirements specification, "Specific Requirements", the IEEE standard defines several types of content to be included in this section and suggests several alternatives for organising this content. The different suggestions are outlined at the end of this section.

Table of Contents
1. Introduction
1.1 Purpose
1.2 Scope
1.3 Definitions, acronyms, and abbreviations
1.4 References
1.5 Overview
2. Overall Description
2.1 Product perspective
2.2 Product functions
2.3 User characteristics
2.4 Constraints
2.5 Assumptions and dependencies
3. Specific Requirements
Appendixes
Index

Fig. 18-1 *Standard structure for a software requirements specification according to [IEEE Std 830-1998]*

Part 1: Introduction

IEEE 830-1998: Introduction

Part one, "Introduction", consists of five sections:

- *Purpose*: In this section, the purpose of the specification and its intended audience (its intended use) are described.
- *Scope*: This section comprises the name of the software product to be developed, a description of what the software product will do (and, if appropriate, also what it will not do), and a description of the key aims of the software including its benefits, objectives, and goals.
- *Definitions, acronyms, and abbreviations*: In this section, important terms, acronyms as well as abbreviations which are required to properly understand the software requirements specification, are defined.
- *References*: This section comprises a list of all documents referenced in the requirements specification. For each referenced document, the version used and the source of the document are stated.
- *Overview*: This section provides an overview of the contents and the structure of the requirements document.

Part 2: Overall Description

IEEE 830-1998: Overall Description

Part two, "Overall Description", comprises five sections:

- *Product perspective*: In this section, the dependencies on other related products are described. If the software product is, for example, part of a larger system, this section relates requirements for the larger system to the functionality of the software and identifies interfaces between the larger system and the software as well as major constraints for the operation of the software (e.g. memory constraints and operation modes imposed by the surrounding system). The standard also recommends including a block diagram of the surrounding system showing its major components, interconnections, and external interfaces.

- *Product functions*: This section contains a condensed description of the major functions that the software will perform. In other words, this section provides a general overview of the functionality of the software product.
- *User characteristics*: In this section, the characteristics of the different users and user groups which influence the requirements for the software product are described (e.g. educational level, experience with similar systems, or technical expertise).
- *Constraints*: In this section, general constraints that limit the options during software development are defined such as regulatory policies, hardware limitations, interfaces to other applications, and safety and security considerations.
- *Assumptions and dependencies*: In this section, the assumptions on which the specification is based are explicitly documented, such as the assumption that a specific component will be available at a specific point in time. In addition, the requirements affected in case of a change of the assumptions are named.

Part 3: Specific Requirements

IEEE 830-1998: Specific Requirements

Part three, "Specific Requirements", is the largest part of a software requirements specification. The requirements in this part have to be defined at a level of detail that permits designing and implementing a software system that meets the defined requirements. In addition, the requirements documented in this part should support the test engineers in defining test artefacts and checking whether the system fulfils its requirements. Therefore, the recommendations included in Hint 18-1 for defining the specific requirements should be considered.

!

Hint 18-1: *Specification of Part 3: Specific Requirements*

Consider the following aspects when specifying a requirement:

(1) Each requirement shall have a unique identification.
(2) Each requirement shall fulfil the defined quality criteria (correctness, unambiguousness, completeness, consistency, verifiability, traceability, etc.).
(3) For each requirement, the acceptance criteria shall be defined.
(4) For each requirement, cross references to other parts of the specification or to earlier documents shall be documented, if applicable.
(5) The requirements shall be organised in a way that maximises readability and comprehensibility.

The part "Specific Requirements" contains the items depicted in Fig. 18-2. We first explain these items and then outline possible ways of organising the items.

- *External interfaces*: This section defines the interfaces described in part 2 of the SRS "Overall Description" in detail. It specifies all inputs and outputs of at the interfaces in detail. Among other things, the sources of inputs and destinations of outputs, relationships to other inputs/outputs, data and command formats to be used, and valid ranges and accuracy of inputs and outputs are specified.

3. Specific requirements
- External interfaces
  - User interfaces
  - Hardware interfaces
  - Software interfaces
  - Communications interfaces
- Functions
- Performance requirements
- Logical database requirements
- Design constraints
  - Standards compliance
  - Hardware limitations
  - [...]
- Software system attributes
  - Reliability
  - Availability
  - Security
  - Maintainability
  - Portability
  - [...]
- Other requirements

Fig. 18-2 *Possible contents of part 3 of an SRS according to [IEEE Std 830-1998]*

- *Functional requirements*: This section defines all functions that the software must perform in "accepting and processing the inputs and in processing and generating the outputs" [IEEE Std 830-1998]. These also include, for instance, validity checks on the inputs, and responses to exceptions. Furthermore the relationships of outputs to inputs must be defined.
- *Performance requirements*: This section defines all performance requirements for the software system. These include expected loads such as the number of simultaneous users or the number of transactions to be processed per time period. All performance requirements should be defined in a measurable way (see [IEEE Std 830-1998]).
- *Logical database requirements*: This section defines logical requirements for the information that shall be stored in a database including, for instance, data entities and their relationships, integrity constraints, and frequency of use.
- *Design constraints*: In this section, all constraints for the design of the system are defined. This includes constraints imposed by hardware limitations or by other standards.
- *Software system attributes*: In this section, additional quality requirements for the software system are defined. These include requirements with regard to reliability, availability, security, maintainability, and portability.
- *3.6 Other requirements*: In this section, additional requirements for the software system which cannot be allotted to one of the above-mentioned categories are defined.

Organising the Contents of Part 3 "Specific Requirements"

According to the IEEE Standard 830-1998, different classes of systems require different organisations of the requirements defined in part 3 "Specific Requirements" of the software requirements specification. Examples of such organisations are described in [IEEE Std 830-1998]. We briefly present two such structures:

- *System mode*: In this case, part 3 "Specific Requirements" of the SRS is structured according to the different operation modes of the system. This organisation is especially recommended for systems for which the system behaviour differs significantly depending on the current operation mode (e.g. training mode, normal mode, emergency mode). Such systems may even have different sets of functions for each mode. The suggested structure of part 3 "Specific Requirements" is depicted in Fig. 18-3 on the left-hand side.

- *User class*: In this case, part 3 "Specific Requirements" of the SRS is structured according to different user groups. This form of organisation is especially recommended for systems which provide different sets of functions to different user groups. In the case of a car safety system, for example, different functions exist for the driver and for maintenance staff. The suggested structure of part 3 "Specific Requirements" is depicted in Fig. 18-3 on the right-hand side.

3. Specific requirements 3.1 External interface requirements 3.1.1 User interfaces 3.1.2 Hardware interfaces 3.1.3 Software interfaces 3.1.4 Communications interfaces 3.2 Functional requirements 3.2.1 Mode 1 3.2.1.1 Functional requirement 1.1 ... 3.2.1.*n* Functional requirement 1.*n* 3.2.2 Mode 2 ... 3.2.*m* Mode *m* 3.2.*m*.1 Functional requirement *m*.1 ... 3.2.*m*.*n* Functional requirement *m*.*n* 3.3 Performance requirements 3.4 Design constraints 3.5 Software system attributes 3.6 Other requirements	3. Specific requirements 3.1 External interface requirements 3.1.1 User interfaces 3.1.2 Hardware interfaces 3.1.3 Software interfaces 3.1.4 Communications interfaces 3.2 Functional requirements 3.2.1 User class 1 3.2.1.1 Functional requirement 1.1 ... 3.2.1.*n* Functional requirement 1.*n* 3.2.2 User class 2 ... 3.2.*m* User class *m* 3.2.*m*.1 Functional requirement *m*.1 ... 3.2.*m*.*n* Functional requirement *m*.*n* 3.3 Performance requirements 3.4 Design constraints 3.5 Software system attributes 3.6 Other requirements

Fig. 18-3 *Organisation of part 3 of the SRS by mode (left-hand side) vs. organisation by user class (right hand side); see [IEEE Std 830-1998]*

The other structures for part 3 of the SRS suggested in [IEEE Std 830-1998] organise the requirements in this part according to:

- *Objects*: Organisation according to real-world aspects (context aspects) which the system represents, i.e. structuring the part according to entities of the subject facet.
- *Feature*: Organisation according to system features that are visible in the form of services at the different interfaces of the system.
- *Stimulus*: Organisation according to external stimuli that lead to the execution of specific system functions.
- *Response*: Organisation by describing all functions needed to generate a specific response.
- *Functional hierarchy*: Organisation of the requirements according to the decomposition of the system functionality into a hierarchy of functions (see Section 14.2).

18.2 Defining Attributes for Requirements

Information related to a requirement

During requirements engineering, a large amount of information accumulates for the requirements artefacts and should be documented in a structured way. Among other things, such information includes:

- Priority of a requirement
- Requirement type
- Status of the documentation of the requirement
- Status of the implementation of the requirement
- Stability of the requirement
- Source of the requirement
- Acceptance criteria for the requirement
- Conflicts that exist for the requirement
- Established agreement about the requirement

In this section, we outline the principles for structuring such information by means of attributes that are assigned to the different types of requirements artefacts.

Requirements Attributes

Structured documentation by assigning attributes

Assigning attributes to requirements is a well-established technique for structuring the information documented in requirements artefacts. Attributes can be assigned to a requirement artefact independently of the chosen documentation format. If a requirements artefact is documented using natural language, requirements templates are typically used, providing, for each attribute a corresponding slot in which the information is documented (see Section 18.4.1). If requirement artefacts are documented using conceptual models, the attributes are defined for the corresponding modelling constructs (see Section 18.4.2).

Definition of requirements attribute

The definition of a requirements attribute typically consists of at least an attribute name, the attribute semantics, the range of values of the attribute, and the semantics of the values.

We define the term "requirements attribute" as follows:

Definition 18-1: *Requirements attribute*

A requirements attribute is defined by the attribute name, the associated semantics of the attribute, the range of values defined for the attribute, and the semantics of these values.

Attribute Scheme

Attribute scheme for requirements

An attribute scheme defines the set of attributes for a particular requirement type such as a functional or quality requirement. We define the term "attribute scheme" as follows:

Definition 18-2: *Attribute scheme*

An attribute scheme defines the attributes for a particular requirement type. For each attribute, the attribute scheme defines a unique attribute name, the semantics of the attribute, its range of values, and the semantics of the values.

The definition of attribute schemes is typically domain-, project- and/or company-specific. The schemes for different types of requirements typically differ with respect to the attributes defined, the semantics of the attributes, the range of values, and/or the semantics of the values.

Example of an attribute scheme

Figure 18-4 depicts an exemplary attribute scheme for the requirement type "solution-oriented requirements". The attributes such as "identifier" or "stability" defined in this attribute scheme are depicted in the upper part of the figure. Each attribute of the attribute scheme is defined using a template which requires that, for each attribute, a unique name, its semantics, its range of values (i.e. the range of possible attribute values, e.g. sets of terms, discrete or continuous intervals), and the meanings of the values are defined. Figure 18-4 depicts the corresponding definitions for the attribute "stability".

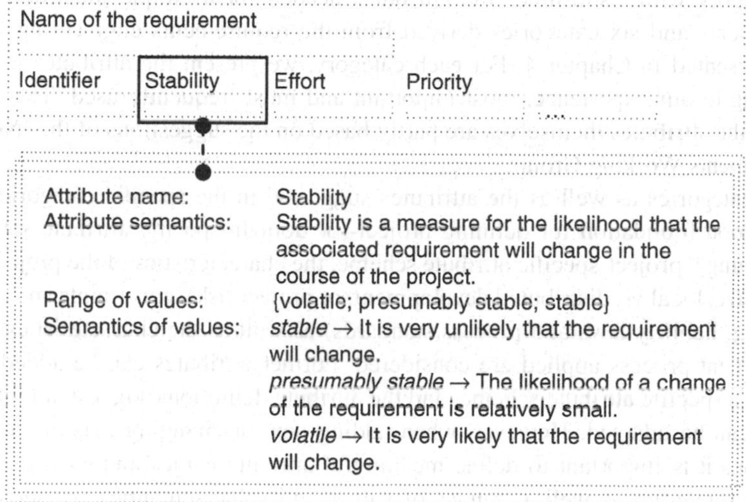

Fig. 18-4 *Example of an attribute scheme*

Exemplary assignment of values to attributes

During system development, values from the predefined range are assigned for each attribute. Figure 18-5 depicts the requirement "customer entry mask" for which attribute values have been assigned. In this example, the value "A-12-7" has been assigned to the attribute "identifier", the value "stable" to the attribute "stability", the value "20 person days" to the attribute "effort", and the value "medium" to the attribute "priority".

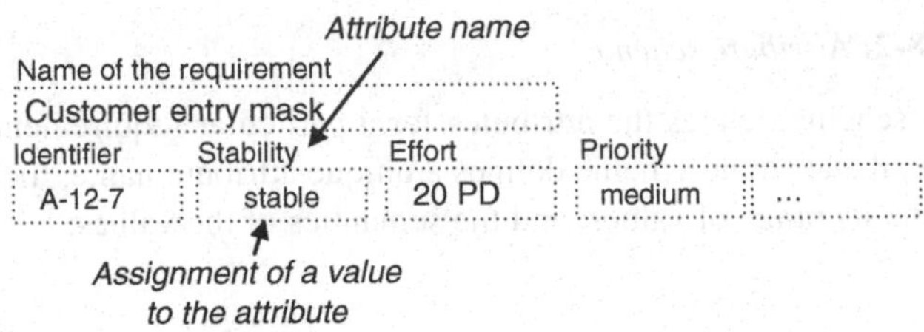

Fig. 18-5 *Example of the assignment of values to requirements attributes*

18.3 Requirements Attributes

A comprehensive collection of requirements attributes was assembled by the Requirements Working Group (RWG) of the International Council on Systems Engineering (INCOSE). Also, requirements management tools typically provide pre-defined attributes which can be assigned to the requirement types documented using the tool (see [Wiegers 1999]). Quasi-standard management attributes for the requirements such as a unique identifier, author, or date of change are typically assigned automatically by the management tools.

Seven categories of requirements attributes

In the following, we structure the requirements attributes into seven categories: one category which subsumes the attributes needed for a unique identification of requirements and six categories derived from the requirements engineering framework presented in Chapter 4. For each category, we present the attributes that are, according to our experience, most important and most frequently used. The definitions of the attributes themselves are partly based on the suggestions of the INCOSE Requirements Working Group.

Project-specific adaptation

The categories as well as the attributes suggested in the specific categories provide a good foundation for defining project- or domain-specific attribute schemes. For defining a project-specific attribute scheme, the characteristics of the project (e.g. project size, local vs. distributed development, or project risk), constraints and restrictions (e.g. liability laws and process standards) as well as the characteristics of the development process applied are considered. Further attributes can be added when defining a specific attribute scheme, and the attribute definitions suggested in the following can be adapted. However, when adding new or changing existing attribute definitions it is important to define meaningful attribute names and ensure that the attribute semantics as well as ranges of values and value semantics are adequately defined.

18.3.1 Identification (Category 1)

This category subsumes all attributes that ensure the unique identification of requirements. Typical examples of attributes for a unique identification are the identifier of a requirement and its name. The identifier of a requirement is typically a unique ID that unambiguously identifies the requirement. The name of a requirement should preferably characterise the content of the requirement and also be unique. Table 18-1 shows a simplified definition of these two attributes.

Tab. 18-1 *Attributes for the identification of requirements artefacts*

Attribute name	Semantics (outlined)	Range of values (outlined)	Semantics of values (outlined)
Identifier << unique >>	An ID which ensures the unique identification of a requirements artefact	Identifier = [G|S|R] "-" Category "-" Number Category = {Digit} Number = {Digit} Digit = [0|1|2|…|8|9]	*G* ≡ Requirements artefact is a goal *S* ≡ Requirements artefact is a scenario *R* ≡ Requirements artefact is a solution-oriented requirement *Category* ≡ Section where the artefact is defined *Number* ≡ Number of the requirement in the category
Name << unique >>	Unique name characterising the requirement	Sequence of characters	Equal to the meaning of the name in natural language

18.3.2 Context Relationships (Category 2)

Attributes for documenting relationships to the context

The second category comprises attributes that are used for documenting direct relationships of the requirements artefact to the context. Examples are the relationship(s) to the source(s) of the requirement (i.e. stakeholders, documents, or other systems) or to the context facet(s) having the greatest influence on the definition of the requirements artefact. In addition, a short justification for why the requirement exists should be given. The person currently responsible for the requirements artefact in the development process (from the development facet or any other context facet) should also be defined. Furthermore, the stakeholders who are affected by or use the requirements artefact are named in order to involve the right stakeholders, for instance, in the case of a requirements change. Table 18-2 shows the requirements attributes for documenting the relationships of a requirement to its context.

Tab. 18-2 *Attributes for documenting relationships between the requirement artefact and the context*

Attribute name	Semantics (outlined)	Range of values (outlined)	Semantics of values (outlined)
Source	Denominates the source or sources of the requirement	Stakeholders, documents, systems	Derived from the particular meaning of the context aspect (see Section 5.1)
Context facet	Denominates the facet(s) which mainly influenced the definition of the requirement	"Subject facet" "Usage facet" "IT system facet" "Development facet"	Derived from the particular meaning of the context aspect (see Section 5.1)
Reason	Denominates the reason why the requirement was defined	Document types (e.g. interview minutes, business plans)	Defined by the project- or company-specific document types
Responsible person	Denominates the stakeholder responsible for this requirement	Stakeholder from a context facet	Derived from the particular meaning of the context aspect (see Section 5.1)
Using stakeholders	Denominates the stakeholders who benefit from the requirement	Set of stakeholder identifiers	Derived from the stakeholder identifiers

18.3.3 Documentation Aspects (Category 3)

Attributes for capturing documentation aspects of the requirement

The third category comprises attributes for capturing information related to the documentation of the requirement. This includes the documentation and specification formats to be used for documenting the requirement, the documentation and specification rules to be considered as well as the status of validation of the documentation and specification aspects of the requirement (see Section 27.3). Table 18-3 depicts the template-based definition of the corresponding attributes that capture these aspects.

Tab. 18-3 *Attributes for defining documentation aspects*

Attribute name	**Semantics** (outlined)	**Range of values** (outlined)	**Semantics of values** (outlined)
Documentation formats	Denominates permissible formats for documenting this requirement	Natural language, UML or SysML models, scenario templates, goal templates	Derived from the meaning of the value assigned to the attribute
Documentation rules	Denominates the rules to be considered when documenting this requirement	References to the documentation rules	Denominates the artefact (e.g. file) in which the documentation rules are defined
Specification formats	Denominates permissible forms to be used for specifying this requirement	Natural language, UML or SysML models, scenario templates, goal templates	Derived from the respective meaning of the value assigned to the attribute
Specification rules	Denominates the rules to be considered when specifying this requirement	References to the specification rules	Denominates the artefact (e.g. file) in which the specification rules are defined
Validation status of the documentation	Denominates the current status of the validation of the documentation	"unchecked" "under examination" "partially checked" "checked" "in revision" "released"	*unchecked* ≡ the requirements artefact is not validated and it is not under examination *under examination* ≡ the requirement is currently being validated *partially checked* ≡ the requirement has been validated partially, but is currently not being checked *checked* ≡ the validation of the requirement has been finished *in revision* ≡ the requirements artefact is currently being revised *released* ≡ the requirements artefact has been checked. Revisions have been integrated and validated.

Tab. 18-3 *(continued)*

Attribute name	Semantics (outlined)	Range of values (outlined)	Semantics of values (outlined)
Validation status of the specification	Denominates the current status of the validation of the specification	"unchecked" "under examination" "partially checked" "checked" "in revision" "released"	See attribute "validation status of the documentation"

18.3.4 Content Aspects (Category 4)

Attributes for the documentation content aspects of a requirement

The fourth category of requirements attributes comprises attributes for documenting information related to the content of a requirements artefact. This information is mainly obtained from the elicitation activity (see Part IV.b). These attributes include the requirement type (e.g. goal, scenario, functional requirement, quality requirement, or constraint), a brief overview of the requirement, additional information provided by the creator, the status of the content (e.g. idea, rough content) as well as cross references to other development artefacts. For the requirement type we assume that detailed requirement types are predefined as values of this attribute. Those types are typically much more detailed than the requirement type used in the identifier (see Tab. 18-1, attribute "identifier"). The attribute "cross references" is used to document cross references to other requirements as well as to any other development artefacts. Since cross references can exist between any types of requirements, this attribute should be specialised by defining different types of cross references such as a cross reference between a super-goal and its sub-goals, or a cross reference between conflicting goals. Furthermore the content attributes include the status of the content (from the perspective of the creators) as well as the validation status of the content of the requirement (see Section 27.3). Table 18-4 defines the corresponding attributes for capturing the content aspects of a requirement.

Tab. 18-4 *Attributes for documenting content aspects*

Attribute name	Semantics (outlined)	Range of values (exemplarily outlined)	Semantics of values (exemplarily sketched)
Requirement type	Describes the type of the requirement with regard to the chosen requirements classification scheme	"Functional requirement" "Quality requirement" . . .	*Functional requirement* ≡ requirement describing functional system aspects *Quality requirement* ≡ requirement describing qualitative system aspects
Short description	Briefly summarises the content of the requirement	Text in natural language	Derived from the meaning of the text in natural language
Additional information	Contains additional information provided by the creator	Text in natural language	Derived from the meaning of the text in natural language

Tab. 18-4 *(continued)*

Attribute name	Semantics (outlined)	Range of values (exemplarily outlined)	Semantics of values (exemplarily sketched)
Cross references	Describes the relationships to other development artefacts	References to requirements artefacts (e.g. goals, scenarios, solution-oriented requirements), and to development artefacts (e.g. components, test cases)	Derived from the respective meaning of the values assigned to the attribute
Status of the content	Describes the completenes of the requirement content	"idea" "rough content" "detailed content"	*idea* ≡ content is sketchy and thus incomplete *rough content* ≡ essential content is there but details are missing *detailed content* ≡ the content is complete, including relevant details
Validation status of the content	Describes the current status of the validation of content aspects of the requirement	"unchecked" "under examination" "partially checked" "checked" "in revision" "released"	See Tab. 18-3, attribute "Validation status of the documentation"

18.3.5 Negotiation Aspects (Category 5)

Attributes for documenting negotiation aspects

This category comprises attributes for documenting information related to the negotiation about a requirements artefact. This information is mainly obtained from the negotiation activity (see Part IV.c). This includes the status of the stakeholders' negotiation about the requirement, the status of validation of the requirement from an agreement perspective (see Section 27.3), known conflicts about the requirement as well as decisions made during conflict resolution (see Section 25.4). Table 18-5 shows the corresponding requirements attributes and their definitions.

Tab. 18-5 *Attributes for documenting negotiation aspects*

Attribute name	Semantics (outlined)	Range of values (outlined)	Semantics of values (outlined)
Negotiation status	Describes the current level of agreement about the artefact	"unknown" "conflicting" "in agreement" "agreed"	*unknown* ≡ it is not known whether a conflict exists about this requirement *conflicting* ≡ there are known conflicts among the stakeholders with regard to this requirement *in agreement* ≡ the requirement is currently subject to agreement

Tab. 18-5 *(continued)*

Attribute name	Semantics (outlined)	Range of values (outlined)	Semantics of values (outlined)
			agreed ≡ the stakeholders have agreed upon the requirement
Validation status of the achieved agreement	Denominates the current status of validation of the achieved agreement	"unchecked" "under examination" "partially checked" "checked" "in revision" "released"	See Tab. 18-3, attribute "Validation status of the documentation"
Identified conflicts	Denominates identified conflicts about this requirement	Set of documented conflicts	Derived from the respective meaning of the values assigned to the attribute
Decisions	States the decisions that were made to attain agreement on this requirement	Set of documented decisions in the context of negotiation	Derived from the respective meaning of the values assigned to the attribute

18.3.6 Validation Aspects (Category 6)

Attributes for documenting validation aspects

The sixth category comprises requirements attributes for documenting information about the validation of a requirements artefact. This information is mainly obtained from the validation activity (see Part V). Requirements validation aims at checking the quality of a requirements artefact with regard to the three dimensions (content, documentation, and agreement). An essential kind of information is thus whether a requirements artefact fulfils the defined entry criteria for validation or not (see Section 28.1.7). Furthermore, this attribute category includes attributes for documenting the techniques to be used for validating the requirement (see Chapter 28), the step of the validation technique currently being executed as well as the overall status of the validation. Note that the status of validation of the documentation, content, and negotiation aspects of a requirement is already captured by attributes defined in the corresponding attribute categories (see Sections 18.3.3–18.3.5). Table 18-6 depicts the attributes in the validation category and their definitions.

Tab. 18-6 *Attributes for documenting validation aspects*

Attribute name	Semantics (outlined)	Range of values (outlined)	Semantics of values (outlined)
Compliance with entry criteria	Describes whether the artefact already complies with the defined entry criteria for validation	"compliant" "not compliant"	*compliant* ≡ the requirements artefact fulfils the defined entry criteria for validation *not compliant* ≡ the requirements artefact does not fulfil the defined entry criteria for validation

Tab. 18-6 *(continued)*

Attribute name	Semantics (outlined)	Range of values (outlined)	Semantics of values (outlined)
Validation techniques	Denominates the techniques to be used for validating the requirement	Names of validation techniques, including references to the descriptions of the techniques	Derived from the meaning of each name of a validation technique
Current validation step	Denominates the step of the validation technique currently being executed	Names of steps of the validation techniques	The denoted step is currently being executed to validate the requirement
Overall validation status	Denominates the current overall status of validation, determined based on the three validation states concerning documentation, content, and agreement	"unchecked" "under examination" "partially checked" "checked" "in revision" "released"	See Tab. 18-3, attribute "Validation status of the documentation"

18.3.7 Management Aspects (Category 7)

The seventh attribute category is used for documenting management information and the current management status of the requirements artefact. This information is mainly obtained from the management activity (see Part VI). We hence subdivide this category into:

- *Status attributes*: Requirements attributes that document the status of the requirements artefact
- *Management attributes*: Requirements attributes that document management information about the requirements artefact

Attributes for Documenting the Status

Risk, criticality, and priority

The requirements attributes risk, criticality, priority, and project status document different statuses about the requirement. For the attributes risk, criticality, and priority, different views can be documented; i.e. the semantics of the attribute has to be defined based on the actual view considered in the project. For example, the priority of a requirement can be defined with regard to its importance for the overall success of the system or its importance for satisfying a strategic business objective. In addition, depending on the prioritisation technique used, criticality and risk can also be considered when defining the priority of a requirement (see Chapter 32).

Stability, life-cycle phase, and status

The attribute "stability" documents the expected probability that the requirement will change. The life-cycle phase indicates the current part of the life cycle of the requirement. Table 18-7 depicts the different attributes for documenting the status of a requirement. For determining the status of a requirement the relevant attributes of the documentation (see Tab. 18-3), the content (see Tab. 18-4), and the agreement (see Tab. 18-5) might be considered.

Tab. 18-7 *Attributes for documenting the status information of a requirement*

Attribute name	Semantics (outlined)	Range of values (outlined)	Semantics of values (outlined)
Risk	Describes the risk associated with the requirement (e.g. regarding the schedule or the required resources) *Calculation: e.g. Risk = Probability of Occurrence × Impact*	"high" "medium" "low" "no"	For example, with regard to project planning: [*high* | *medium* | *low*] = the risk of this requirement in terms of meeting the deadlines defined in the project plan is high, medium, or low *no* ≡ this requirement causes no risk for meeting the deadlines defined in the project plan
Criticality	Criticality of the requirement, e.g. with regard to the risk of persons getting injured	"critical" "uncritical"	*critical* ≡ an error in the requirement (introduced e.g. during elicitation, documentation, or realisation) can result in a threat to the physical well-being of persons *uncritical* ≡ an error in the requirement does not endanger the physical well-being of persons
Priority	Describes, e.g. the importance of the requirement for achieving the overall goals defined for the system	"high" "medium" "low"	For example, for the success of the system: *high* ≡ realisation of the requirement is mandatory *medium* ≡ realisation of the requirement is important *low* ≡ realisation of the requirement is optional
Stability	Measure of the probability that the requirement changes in the course of the project	"stable" "probably stable" "volatile"	*stable* ≡ change probability is close to zero (<2%) *probably stable* ≡ change probability is low (<30%) *volatile* ≡ change probability is high (≥30%)
Life-cycle phase	Denominates the current phase in the life cycle of the requirement	"pre-concept" "specified" "development" "integration" "installation" "operation" "support"	*Pre-concept* ≡ requirement is not completely elicited/documented *specified* ≡ requirement is completely elicited and specified *development* ≡ requirement is the subject of design and implementation *integration* ≡ requirement is being integrated into the existing system *installation* ≡ requirement is being installed with the current system release *operation* ≡ system release of the requirement is currently in operation *support* ≡ requirement is currently subject of maintenance and support

Attributes for Documenting Management Information

Version, system release, estimated/ current effort, estimated/current cost

Besides the status attributes, additional management information has to be documented to support, for example, requirements management. Such information includes, for example, the authors of the requirement, the current version of the requirement, the change history as well as the system release in which the requirement shall be or has been implemented. Furthermore, the estimated effort and cost for implementing the requirement as well as the effort and cost already spent should be recorded. Table 18-8 summarises the corresponding attributes and their definitions.

Tab. 18-8 *Attributes for documenting general management information*

Attribute name	Semantics (outlined)	Range of values (outlined)	Semantics of values (outlined)
Authors	Denominates the authors of the requirements artefact	Set of identifiers which refer to the authors of the artefact (e.g. initials, personnel IDs)	Derived from the meaning of the identifiers
Version	Version of the requirement	Version = {Num} "." {Num} Num = [0|1|2|...|8|9]	The number before the separating dot is incremented, if milestones have been achieved or significant changes have been made. In the case of smaller changes, the number after the dot is incremented.
Change history	Lists the changes performed to the requirement	Set of textual descriptions	Derived from the meaning of the individual textual descriptions
System release	Denominates the release of the system in which this requirement is/will be realised	Set of system releases	The release number in which the requirement shall be realised or has been realised
Estimated effort	Effort for realising the requirement estimated e.g. by applying an effort estimation model	Positive integer in person days	The value represents the effort in person days estimated for realising the requirement
Current effort	Effort already spent for realising the requirement	Positive integer in person days	The value represents the effort in person days already spent on realising the requirement
Estimated cost	Estimated cost for realising the requirement estimated e.g. by applying a cost estimation model	Positive integer in EUR	The value represents the estimated effort in EUR for realising the requirement
Current cost	Amount already spent for realising the requirement	Positive integer in EUR	The value represents the expenses in a specific currency so far spent on realising the requirement

18.4 Templates and Information Models

Using the attributes for documentation

The requirements attributes presented in Section 18.3 can be used in different ways to support structured documentation of information about each requirement. In the following, we outline the use of attributes in template-based (Section 18.4.1) and information-model-based (Section 18.4.2) documentation of information about requirements.

18.4.1 Template-Based Documentation

Reference templates

By using templates, requirements and information about requirements can be documented easily and effectively in a structured manner. A template can be defined for each type of requirement (e.g. goal, scenario, functional requirement, quality requirement, constraint) by (selectively) reusing the attributes presented in Section 18.3. Furthermore, new attributes can be added and the reused ones can be adapted. Examples of templates for specific requirement types can, among others, be found in Part III, Pages 115, 171, and 175.

Templates for functional and quality requirements

In addition to goal, scenario, and use-case templates, also reference templates for functional requirements, quality requirements, and constraints can be defined. Besides the attributes defined in Section 18.3, further attributes for functional and quality requirements are defined in the Requirements Specification Model (RSM) [Pohl 1996a]. The attributes in the RSM have been defined based on an analysis of more than 20 requirements specification guidelines and standards. RSM defines specific attributes for different kinds of requirements; for instance, RSM defines approximately 30 attributes which can be used for documenting functional requirements.

Project-specific templates are mandatory

Due to the large amount of different kinds of information about requirements that can be documented, project-specific selection of the relevant attributes and thus a project-specific definition of the requirements templates is mandatory.

The advantages of applying reference templates for documenting requirements include:[6]

Use of templates has significant advantages

- *Determining the required information*: Reference templates support the documentation of requirements. They define which kinds of information shall be documented for each type of requirements. In addition, they define the permissible attribute values and the semantics of the attributes and values.
- *Detecting gaps*: If no values have been assigned to one or several attributes, the corresponding slots of the requirements in the template are empty. Template-based documentation thus facilitates detection of gaps in the documented requirements. Compared with an unstructured documentation, the detection of gaps requires significantly less effort.
- *Training employees*: The structuring of information and the definition of attributes facilitate the training of new employees. The employees can selectively search for information in a requirements document. In addition, the structure of the template indicates which information is important for a specific task.
- *Same information at the same place*: The same kind of information is always defined in the same place (assuming the templates are used correctly during documentation). For the individual requirements, a template-based specification offers the following advantages:

[6] The significant advantages of a template-based documentation of requirements are very similar to the advantages of using a reference structure for a requirements document (see Section 18.1.1). However the structure defined by the templates is, compared with the structure of a reference document, far more fine-grained. We thus recommend the use of both a reference structure for the documents as well as reference templates for the specification of the different requirement types.

- *Comparison of information*: Comparing different requirements of the same type becomes significantly easier, since similar information about the requirements can be found at the same place in each requirements artefact.
- *Selective access*: The reader can selectively access the documented information. An effort-intensive search for a specific piece of information in the entire requirements artefact or even the entire requirements document can thus be avoided.

Advantages for the other activities

In addition to the documentation activity, reference templates also support all other requirements engineering activities. The advantages obtained from a template-based documentation for the other activities correspond mainly to the advantages stated above. Moreover, a two-step procedure for the elicitation, negotiation, and validation of requirements can be established based on a simple categorisation of the attributes defined in the reference template. For this purpose, the attributes defined in the reference template are assigned to two categories:

- *Basic documentation:* This category subsumes all attributes that are indispensable even for an initial sketch of a requirement.
- *Detailed documentation:* This category subsumes all the additional attributes required for detailed documentation of the requirement.

For example, during requirements elicitation, the stakeholders can first focus on the elicitation of the basic attributes for a set of requirements. After the basic attributes for all the elicited requirements have been defined to a sufficient extent, the stakeholders focus on the attributes defined in the second category (detailed documentation). Similarly, during negotiation and validation, attributes of the first category (basic documentation) can be considered prior to attributes of the second category (detailed documentation).

18.4.2 Information Model-Based Documentation

Information models vs. templates

Similarly, as a reference template for documenting requirements, an information model defines attributes relevant for documenting a specific type of requirements artefact. Information-model-based documentation hence offers the same advantages as reference-template-based documentation of requirements (see Section 18.4.1).

However, unlike a reference template, an information model also defines relevant relationships between the attributes (and requirement types). Moreover, since the information model is defined using a modelling language, also consistency constraints and cardinalities of relationships can be defined and (automatically) checked. Information-model-based documentation of requirements thus offers additional advantages compared with the use of reference templates.

The information models depicted in this section are specified using Unified Modeling Language (UML; see Section 14.1.2).

Basis for tool support

The structuring of the requirements information in most requirements engineering tools is based on information models which define the types of requirements, their attributes, relationships, and consistency constraints. For example, the schemata for a relational database used to record and manage the information can be derived from the information models. Based on the information model, or the database schema derived from it, requirements management tools can, for example, generate views on the information recorded about the requirements (see Section 18.5).

Refinement of information models

Depending on the project, the information models can (or even have to) be further detailed by adding, for example, appropriate consistency constraints or rules, or by further refining the defined attributes. By detailing the information model, a more sophisticated structure and a higher level of formalisation of the recorded information can be achieved. Checking of the rules and constraints defined for the information model should be supported by the requirements engineering tool used for documenting the requirements.

Figure 18-6 shows an example of a coarse-grained information model that defines the relationships between three types of requirements artefacts: goals (see Part III.a), scenarios (see Part III.b), and solution-oriented requirements (see Part III.c).

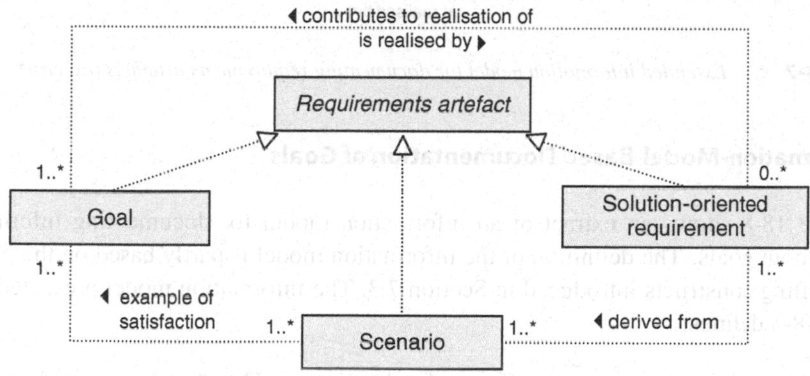

Fig. 18-6 *Simplified model of the relationships between the three types of requirements artefacts*

The abstract class "requirements artefact" is a generalisation of the artefact types "goal", "scenario", and "solution-oriented requirement". A scenario exemplifies the satisfaction of one or multiple goals, and the satisfaction of a goal is exemplified by one or multiple scenarios. In addition, the model defines that, from a scenario, one or multiple solution-oriented requirements can be derived and, conversely, each solution-oriented requirement shall be associated with one or multiple scenarios. Furthermore, a goal can be assigned to an arbitrary number of solution-oriented requirements that contribute to the realisation of this goal but does not have to be assigned to one. In contrast, each solution-oriented requirement must be associated with at least one goal. Concrete goals, scenarios, and solution-oriented requirements as well as their relationships are instances of the elements of the information model shown in Fig. 18-6.

Figure 18-7 shows a simple extension of the class "requirements artefact" introduced in Fig. 18-6. As depicted in Fig. 18-7, some attributes proposed in Section 18.3 have been defined as classes and assigned to the class "requirements artefact". According to this definition, a requirements artefact must be assigned exactly one identifier, one description, one criticality (class), one priority (class), and one risk (class).

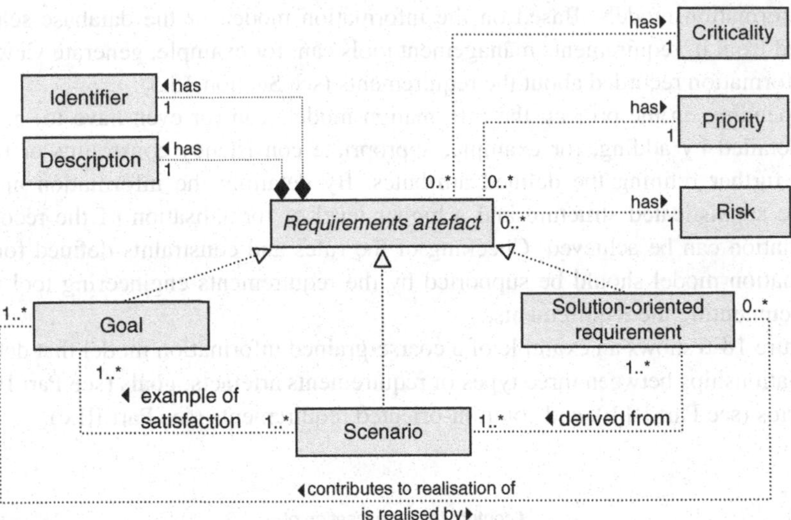

Fig. 18-7 *Extended information model for documenting requirements artefacts (excerpt)*

Information-Model-Based Documentation of Goals

Extract of an information model for goals

Figure 18-8 shows an extract of an information model for documenting information about goals. The definition of the information model is partly based on the goal modelling constructs introduced in Section 7.3. The information model presented in Fig. 18-8 defines:

❶ Each goal must have an identifier and a description. The identifier as well as the description of the goal must be unique.

❷ Each goal has at least one or multiple authors. Each stakeholder can be an author of an arbitrary number of goals (including zero).

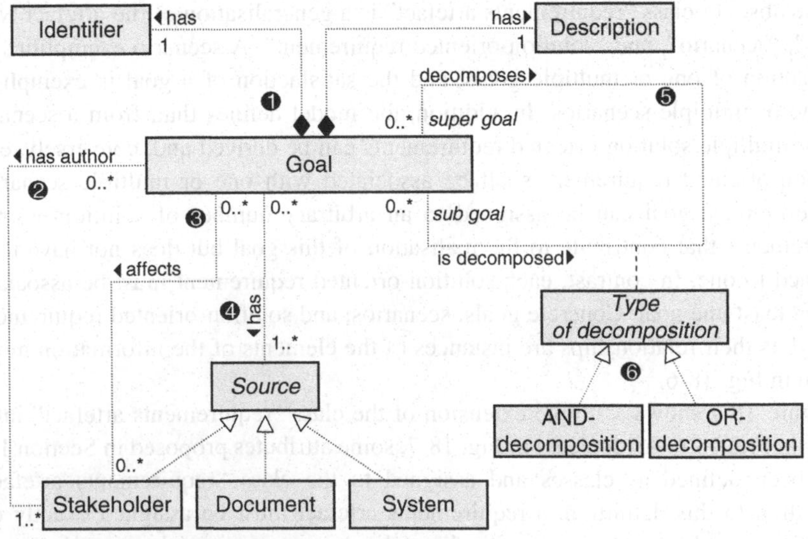

Fig. 18-8 *Information model for documenting goals (excerpt)*

❸ A goal may affect one or multiple stakeholders (but does not have to). A stakeholder can be affected by an arbitrary number of goals.
❹ A goal has at least one source and can have multiple sources. A source is either a stakeholder, a document, or a system. A source can be the origin of an arbitrary number of goals.
❺ A goal can be decomposed into an arbitrary number of sub-goals. At the same time, a goal can also be a sub-goal of an arbitrary number of super-goals. Hence, the information model permits the definition of goal graphs (see Section 8.4).
❻ A goal decomposition relationship is either of the type AND-decomposition or the type OR-decomposition (see Section 7.3).

Information-Model-Based Documentation of Scenarios

Figure 18-9 shows an extract of an information model for structuring the information to be documented about scenarios and the associated context (see Sections 5.4 and 9.2). The context information includes the embedding of the scenarios into the system context. The information model presented in the figure defines:

❶ Each scenario has a unique identifier and a unique name.
❷ For each scenario, one or multiple scenario steps of the type "interaction" have to be defined. The interaction steps of a scenario are ordered.
❸ For each scenario, arbitrary numbers of pre- and postconditions may be defined. Each pre- and postcondition must be assigned to at least one scenario.
❹ Exactly one scenario type is assigned to each scenario. A scenario type can be assigned to zero, one, or more scenarios.

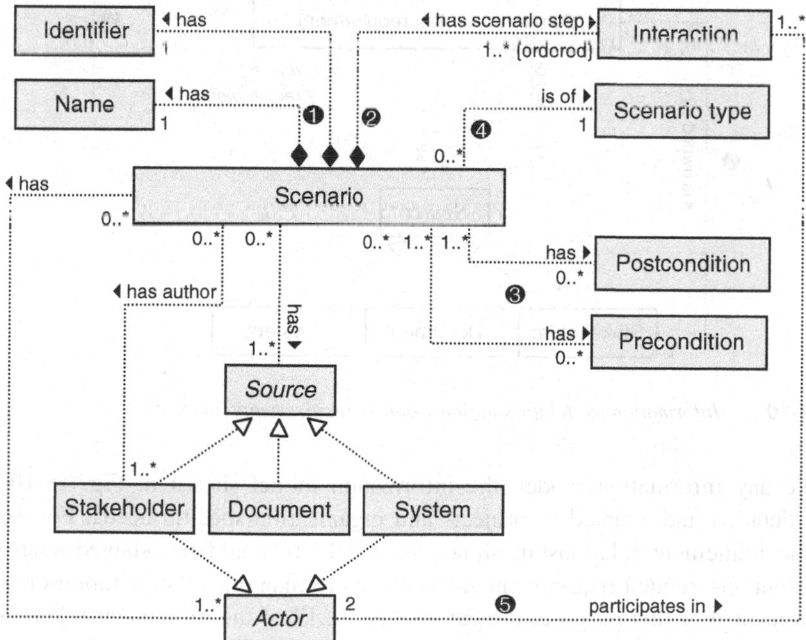

Fig. 18-9 *Information model for documenting scenarios (excerpt)*

❺ Exactly two actors participate in each interaction. Vice versa, each actor participates in at least one interaction. Moreover, each scenario has at least one actor assigned.

Note that the information model for documenting information about scenarios and the associated context contains far more context information than just that depicted in Fig. 18-9 (see, for example, the scenario templates defined in Chapter 11).

Information-Model-Based Documentation of Solution-Oriented Requirements

Figure 18-10 shows an extract of the information model for information about solution-oriented requirements. As for goals and scenarios, the source and the authors of the artefact are documented for solution-oriented requirements. In addition, the information model defines the following information:

❶ Each solution-oriented requirement has exactly one owner of the type "stakeholder" (at one point in time). A stakeholder does not have to own a solution-oriented requirement.

❷ A solution-oriented requirement can be detailed by an arbitrary number of solution-oriented requirements. Conversely, a solution-oriented requirement can detail at most one other solution-oriented requirement.

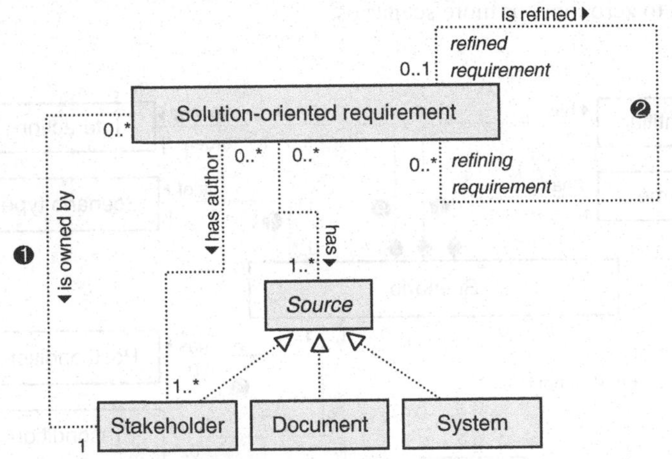

Fig. 18-10 *Information model for solution-oriented requirements (excerpt)*

Adapting the information model

Like any information model, the information model shown in Fig. 18-10 has to be detailed and adapted to project- and organisation-specific needs. For example, the refinement relationship shown in the figure could be adapted such that each solution-oriented requirement can refine more than one other solution-oriented requirement. For this purpose, the cardinality "0..1" of the refinement relationship (❷) must be replaced by the cardinality "0..*". Other possible kinds of adaptations of the information model according to project- and organisation-specific needs include distinguishing different types of solution-oriented requirements (data, function, and behaviour), defining additional attributes, and relating the model to conceptual modelling languages (see Chapter 14 for examples of conceptual modelling languages).

18.5 Establishing Views on Textual Requirements

The structuring of requirements artefacts through information models in combination with using database-supported requirements management tools facilitates selective access to the recorded requirements information, i.e. this kind of recording enables the creation of views on the recorded requirements information. Such views can be created, for example, using standardised query languages such as SQL 2003 (see [ISO/IEC Std 9075]) or the corresponding functionality provided by the requirements management tool. In contrast, in the case of unstructured, paper-based documentation, selective access to information and thus the creation of views on the documented requirements is close to impossible.

Necessity for establishing views

The number of requirements to be documented in development projects is continuously increasing. There are several reasons for this dramatic increase in requirements, such as the increasing amount of system functions or the increase in interactions with other systems, to name but two. Selective access to the documented requirements and the associated generation of specific views has thus become indispensable. Moreover, the need for selective access and the generation of views is enforced by the growing number of dependencies between requirements to be documented and relationships between requirements to be managed (see Chapter 31). A view represents a subset of the information recorded in the requirements base. In addition, it can also contain information which is derived (e.g. aggregated) from the requirements base.

Role-based view generation

In practice, views are often bound to specific roles. Ideally, for each role in the development project (e.g. product manager, project manager, developer), a specific view is defined which only contains the information needed for the specific tasks and responsibilities of this role and thereby avoids information overload. The views also provide the basis for establishing reading and (partial) writing restrictions for the requirements base.

In Section 18.5.1, we sketch out a procedure for generating views on a requirements base. In Section 18.5.2, we briefly describe the principles of generating a requirements document using views. We do not describe, in this book, the formalisation of views by means of a database query language such as SQL, which would, in addition, require the definition of a database schema based on the information models. For more information on transferring information models into database schemata and defining views on relational databases, we refer to [Elmasri and Navathe 2006]).

18.5.1 Generating Views on a Requirements Base

A requirements base records textual information about the requirements in a structured way. The structure for recording the information is defined using information models. From the users' perspective, an individual view on a requirements base is created by using the following basic operations:

Selection of artefact types

- *Selection of artefact types*: One possibility for generating a view is to select specific artefact types, attribute types, and/or relationship types to be included in the view. Requirements information of one or several selected artefact types is then included in the view. For each selected artefact type (source, goal, scenario, etc.), the information recorded for this artefact type is contained in the view, i.e. the information recorded for the selected types is not reduced by this operation. For example, based on the information model for documenting information about goals shown in Fig. 18-8, a view that includes the artefact types "identifier", "description", and "source" of a goal could be defineed. In this case, all recorded identifiers, descriptions, and sources defined for any kind of goal are included in the view.

Selection of instances of a type

- *Selection of instances of an information type*: The second kind of operation used for generating views reduces the artefacts of an artefact type and/or attribute contained in the view. For the selection of the instances, concrete values (or value ranges) can be defined for each artefact type (or its attributes). Only the instances matching the defined values (or value ranges) are then included in the view. For the information model shown in Fig. 18-8, for example, a view could be defined that includes only scenarios with the priority "essential".

Selection based on artefact relationships

- *Selection based on relationships*: In this case, the selection is performed based on recorded relationships of a specific relationship type. For example, if the relationship type "affects" defined between the artefact types "stakeholder" and "goal" is used as a selection criterion, only the instances of "goal" and "stakeholder" that are related via an instance of the "affects" relationship are included in the view.

Generation of artefacts

- *Generation of artefacts*: In this case, information to be included in the view is generated (derived) from the information recorded in the requirements base. For example, a new artefact "overall importance" can be defined in a view which is computed using a specific rating function. For this purpose, the rating function uses the attribute values for criticality, priority, and risk as inputs and generates, for each requirement, an attribute "rated importance" with one of the values "significant", "important", or "less important".

Combination of the selection criteria

Of course, the four basic operations outlined above can be combined to generate a view. Ideally, a view is defined such that it contains all the information required for the role(s) associated with the view and, conversely, does not contain information that is irrelevant for its associated role(s). In most cases, only a part of the requirements artefacts recorded in the requirements base are required in a particular view and, in addition, not all attributes of these artefacts are required. Therefore, the four basic operations are often combined in practical settings.

Example of view generation

Figure 18-11 schematically depicts the definition of a view based on the information model introduced in Fig. 18-7. The view provides an overview of scenarios defined for the goal "G-1-12" as well as solution-oriented requirements derived from the selected scenarios. The scenarios defined for the goal are selected based on the "example of satisfaction" relationship between the scenarios and the goal "G-1-12". The solution-oriented requirements are selected based on the "derived from" relationship between scenarios and solution-oriented requirements. In addition, a restriction is defined such that only requirements with the priority "high" should be included. Consequently, for selecting the artefacts to be included in the view, the definition of the view uses a set of different selection operations and criteria: it hides several artefact types (e.g. "source" and "criticality"), selects artefacts based on a specific

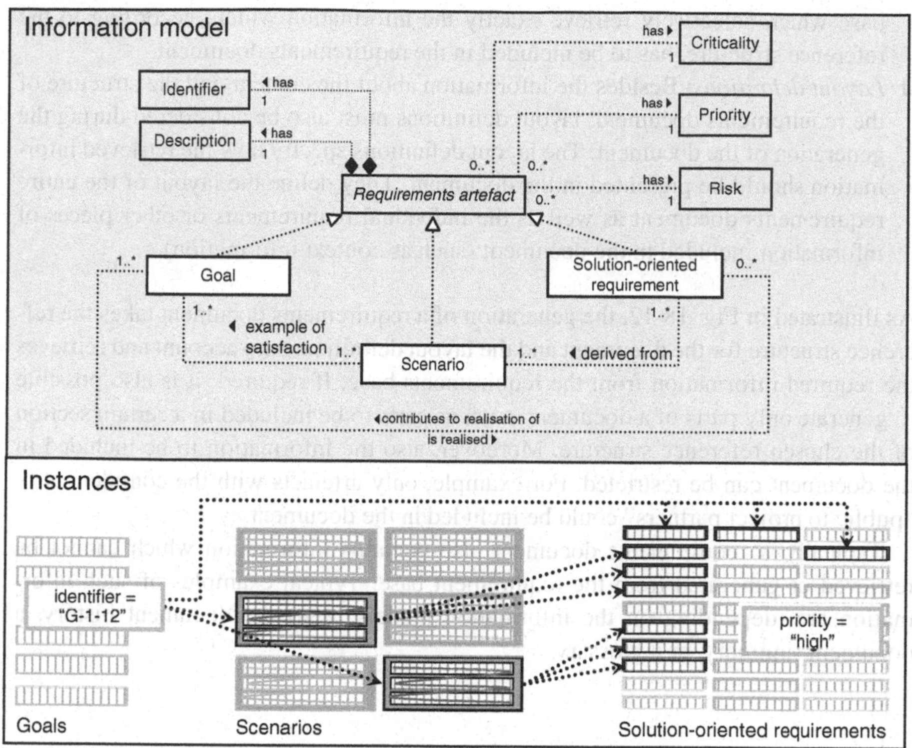

Fig. 18-11 *Illustration of the generation of a view*

value (identifier "G-1-12", priority "high") and considers relationships between different types of requirements (e.g. the "derived from" relationship between scenarios and solution-oriented requirements).

18.5.2 Generating the Requirements Document

Generating a requirements document

The mechanisms used for generating views can also be used to generate a requirements document automatically or semi-automatically. Figure 18-12 depicts, at an abstract level, the key concepts of generating requirements documents from the requirements base. In principle, the following information is used to generate a requirements document:

- *Requirements base and information models*: The information contained in the generated documented is retrieved from the requirements base using the structure defined by the information models (see the upper part of Fig. 18-12).
- *Reference structure for the requirements document*: The content of the requirements document is defined by a document reference structure. For instance, one of the reference structures outlined in Section 18.1 can be used. The reference structure for the requirements document to be generated can be defined e.g. as an XML schema definition (see [Van der Vlist 2002]). The definition of the reference structure is the key input for defining different views on the requirements

base which selectively retrieve exactly the information which, according to the reference structure, has to be included in the requirements document.

- *Layout definitions*: Besides the information about the content and the structure of the requirements document, layout definitions must also be considered during the generation of the document. The layout definitions specify how the retrieved information should be presented in the document. They define the layout of the entire requirements document as well as the individual requirements or other pieces of information included in the document (such as context information).

Generation of (partial) documents

As illustrated in Fig. 18-12, the generation of a requirements document takes the reference structure for the document and the layout definitions into account and retrieves the required information from the requirements base. If required, it is also possible to generate only parts of a document, such as parts to be included in a certain section of the chosen reference structure. Moreover, also the information to be included in the document can be restricted. For example, only artefacts with the confidentiality "public to project partners" could be included in the document.

Typically, a requirements document also contains information which cannot be retrieved or generated from the requirement base. Typical examples of such information are (depending on the information models used) the document history, a document summary, or a glossary.

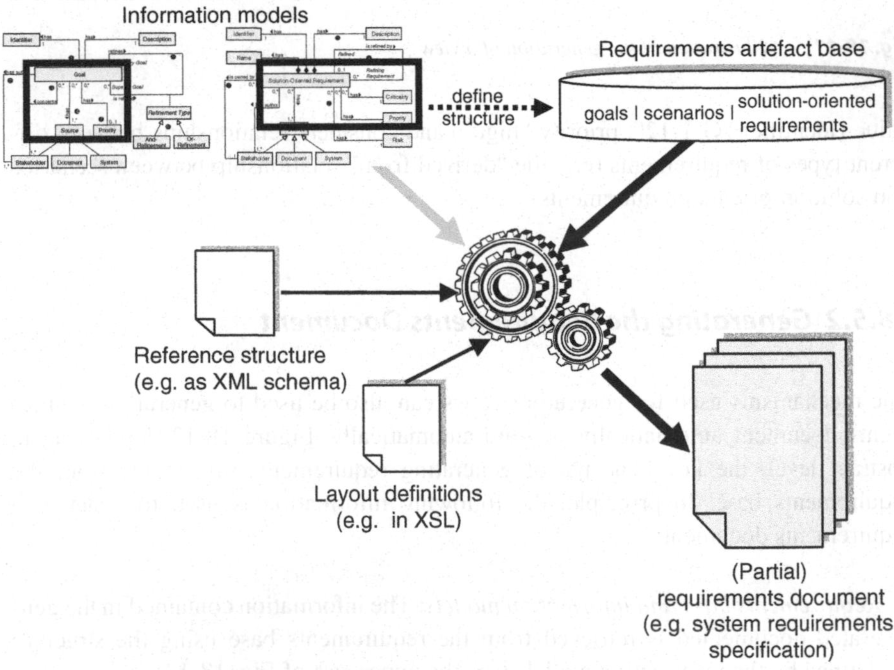

Fig. 18-12 *Generating a requirements document: a schematic, abstract overview*

Chapter 19
Fundamentals of Conceptual Modelling

In this chapter we describe:

- *The use of physical and conceptual models in engineering*
- *The essential properties of conceptual models*
- *The semiotics (syntax, semantics, and pragmatics) of conceptual models*
- *Quality aspects of conceptual models*
- *Definition of modelling languages and the role of meta-models in their definition*
- *Typical transformation effects that occur during model creation and model interpretation*

19.1 Physical vs. Conceptual Models

Different kinds of models

Models have been used for a long time with great success in many domains to support interpersonal communication and to specify systems and their properties. We distinguish two kinds of models:

- *Physical model*: In traditional engineering disciplines, a physical model of the system is created in order to better understand and analyse the properties of the system. For instance, in automotive engineering, a wind tunnel model is created to determine and to experimentally adjust the aerodynamics of a vehicle under construction. Or, for a new building, a smaller-scale physical model of the building is created to experience the building itself and its embedding in the environment.
- *Conceptual model*: In many domains, instead of physical models, symbolic models are created in order to better understand and analyse the properties of the system. Conceptual models are often documented using graphical symbols. Figure 19-1 depicts some examples of conceptual models from the domains of music (a score), architecture (a floor-plan of a building), and electrical engineering (a circuit diagram). Conceptual models especially support communication between different stakeholders and are far easier to comprehend than a natural language documentation of the same information.

A conceptual model is an abstract (partial) documentation of an existing or conceived (i.e. future) reality (see [Stachowiak 1973; Seidewitz 2003]). A model can represent information about material as well as immaterial things. The part of the existing or conceived reality which is represented in the model is often referred to as the "domain" or "the universe of discourse":

D

Definition 19-1: *Universe of discourse*

The universe of discourse comprises any part or aspect of the existing or conceived reality under consideration.

based on [Frisco 1998]

We define the term "model" as follows:

D

Definition 19-2: *Model*

A model is an abstract representation of the universe of discourse created for a specific purpose (use).

Conceptual models

Since software is an abstract (intangible) object, physical models such as a reproduction of the system at a reduced scale are generallynot used in software

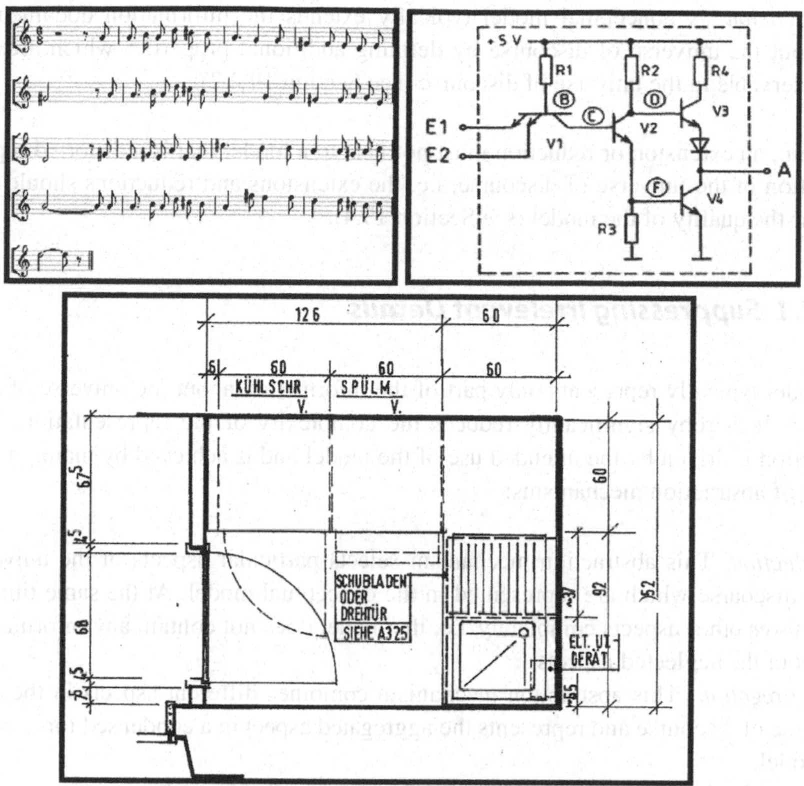

Fig. 19-1 *Examples of graphical models from different domains*

engineering. Instead, conceptual models are used to visualise specific aspects of the software-intensive system. Such conceptual models typically focus on a specific aspect of the system such as data, function, or behaviour.

19.2 Model Properties

Descriptive vs. prescriptive models

A conceptual model represents information about a specific universe of discourse. The information is documented using the modelling constructs defined in the modelling language used. Conceptual models can be descriptive and thus document information about the current state of the universe of discourse (see Section 3.1). A conceptual model can also be prescriptive. Prescriptive conceptual models represent an intended, future state of the universe of discourse. Desired-state models (see Section 3.1) are (typically) prescriptive models.

Both descriptive and prescriptive models have two central properties concerning the representation of the universe of discourse:

- *Reduction*: A conceptual model reduces the information documented about the universe of discourse (see Section 19.2.1).

- *Extension*: A conceptual model typically extends the information documented about the universe of discourse by defining additional properties which are not observable in the universe of discourse (see Section 19.2.2).

Therein, an extension or reduction must not lead to a model that is a distorted representation of the universe of discourse, i.e. the extensions and reductions should not impair the quality of the model (see Section 19.4).

19.2.1 Suppressing Irrelevant Details

Reduction

A model typically represents only part of the information about the universe of discourse. It thereby significantly reduces the complexity of the representation. The reduction is driven by the intended use of the model and is achieved by mainly three kinds of abstraction mechanisms:

- *Selection*: This abstraction mechanism selects particular aspects of the universe of discourse which are represented in the conceptual model. At the same time, it ignores other aspects completely, i.e. the model does not contain any information about the neglected aspects.
- *Aggregation*: This abstraction mechanism combines different aspects in the universe of discourse and represents the aggregated aspect in a condensed form in the model.
- *Classification/generalisation*: This abstraction mechanism identifies commonalities and suppresses differences between a set of aspects in the universe of discourse. The commonalities are then represented as generalised information in the model.

Example of selection and aggregation

During model creation, only information about the universe of discourse relevant for the intended use of the model is documented. For example, consider the creation of a map of the road network and the settlements in a specificcountry. In this

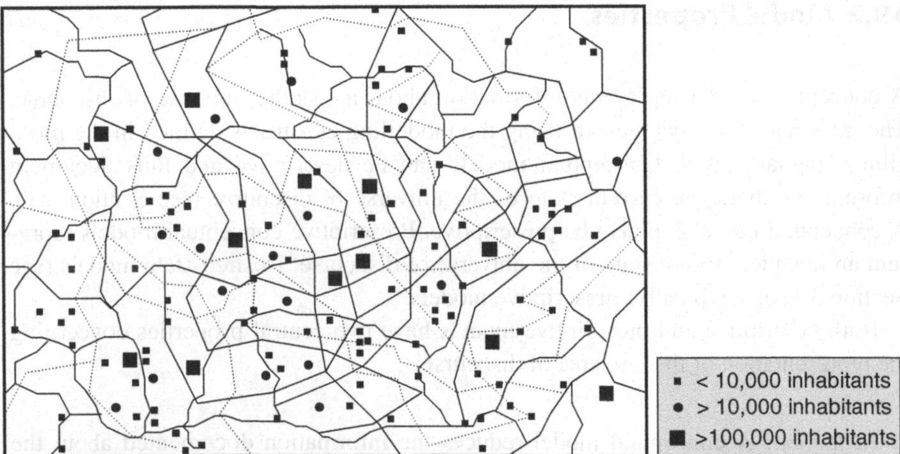

Fig. 19-2 *Reduction of information: only roads and settlements are represented*

case, only information about the roads and settlements in the universe of discourse is considered. The resulting model (the map) thus contains only information about the road network and the positions of settlements (see Fig. 19-2). Other information such as the colours, the shape of the surface, street names, railway connections, or the positions of hospitals is not represented in the conceptual model. Moreover, the resulting model aggregates information about the universe of discourse. For example, the model depicted in Fig. 19-2 aggregates information about the buildings of a settlement by representing a settlement as a single entity in the model.

The purpose of use determines whether a model is suitable or not

A model created for a specific purpose may be only partly suitable or not suitable at all for other purposes. If a user of the model depicted in Fig. 19-2 wants to identify the main roads which connect cities with more than 50,000 inhabitants, this model is not very well suited. The information documented in the model does not contain the main roads nor is it possible to detect which city has more than 50,000 inhabitants.

In contrast, the model depicted in Fig. 19-3 which represents information about the same universe of discourse is much better suited for this purpose, since the model only contains information about the main roads and cities with more than 50,000 inhabitants. Compared with the conceptual model depicted in Fig. 19-2, the model depicted in Fig. 19-3 disregards settlements having fewer than 50,000 inhabitants as well as smaller roads but contains the names of the streets and cities.

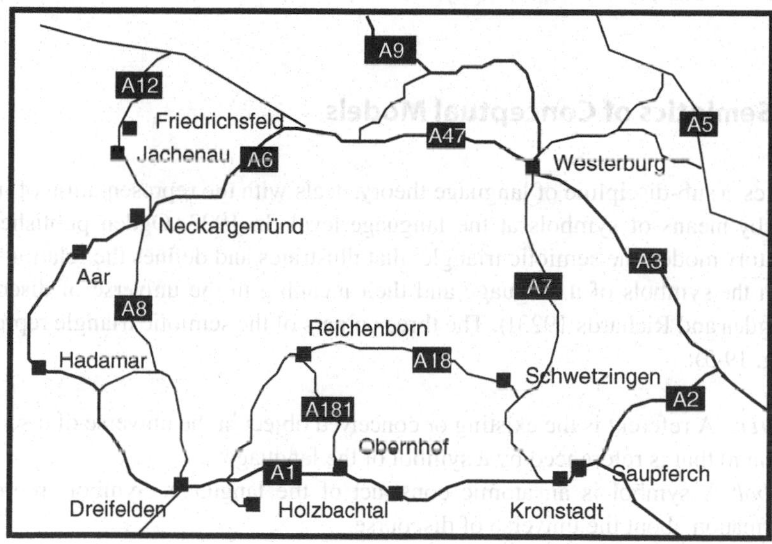

Fig. 19-3 *Reduction of information: only main roads and cities with more than 50,000 inhabitants are shown*

19.2.2 Defining Additional Properties

Extensions

Models may not only suppress information about the universe of discourse but also represent additional information that is not observable in the universe of discourse. A typical extension for maps is the definition of degrees of latitude and longitude.

The purpose of use determines the extension

Such additional properties are introduced to make models more comprehensible and manageable for the specific purpose of use. A possible extension of the map shown in Fig. 19-2 is the division of the model into quadrants to support the identification of cities represented in the map (see Fig. 19-4). With this additional information the location of a city can be specified, for example, as quadrant (3, E), which indicates that the city can be found in the third column and fifth row.

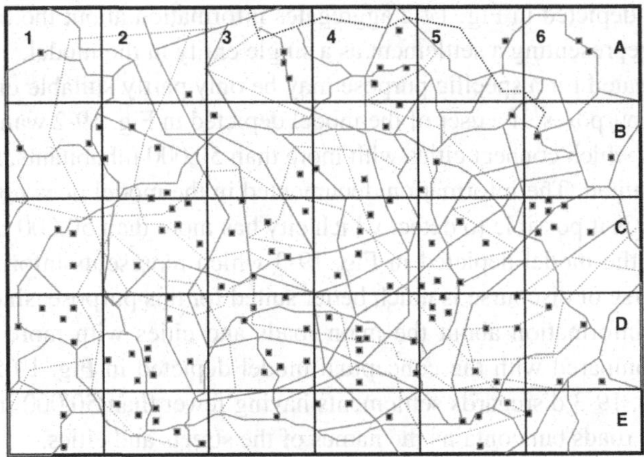

Fig. 19-4 *Example of an extension: definition of quadrants*

19.3 Semiotics of Conceptual Models

Semiotics, a sub-discipline of language theory, deals with the representation of information by means of symbols at the language level. In 1923, Ogden published an explanatory model, the semiotic triangle, that illustrates and defines the relationships between the symbols of a language and their meaning in the universe of discourse (see [Ogden and Richards 1923]). The three corners of the semiotic triangle represent (see Fig. 19-5):

- *Referent*: A referent is the existing or conceived object in the universe of discourse (domain) that is referenced by a symbol of the language.
- *Symbol*: A symbol is an atomic construct of the language. Symbols represent information about the universe of discourse.
- *Reference*: The reference (or thought) is the image a person has in mind about the referent and symbol.

Relations between symbol, referent, and reference

There is no direct relationship between a symbol ("representation") and a referent ("what is represented"). The relationship arises through the observer's conception ("reference"). During conception, the observer establishes a connection between a symbol and a referent. This connection establishes a meaning for the symbol for the observer. Semiotics constitutes the core of the model-theoretic fundamentals of conceptual models (see [Holmqvist et al. 1996]).

Explanation of the example

Figure 19-5 illustrates the relationships between referent, symbol, and reference. In the example, the considered aspect of the universe of discourse (the referent) is an existing, real frog. The symbol assigned to the reference ("frog") is the string

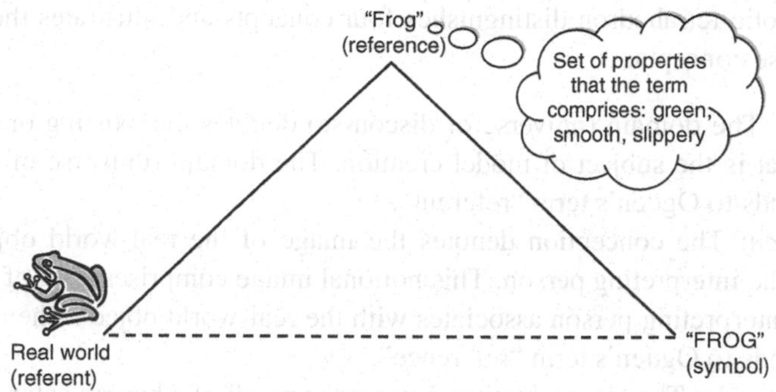

Fig. 19-5 *Example of the concepts of semiotics based on [Ogden and Richards 1923]*

"FROG". The reference is the "image" formed in the mind of the observer by the intensional properties of the referent such as "green", "smooth", or "slippery".

Semiotics according to Peirce

Unlike Ogden, who sees the conceptualisation as a central aspect, Peirce sees the role of the person interpreting the information during the conception as a central aspect. Peirce thus distinguishes four elementary aspects of semiotics (see [Hartshorne and Weiss 1931]):

- The physical representation (called the "symbol" in Ogden's model)
- The real-world object itself (called the "referent" in Ogden's model)
- The interpreting person (not explicitly present in Ogden's model)
- The conception of real-world objects and symbols formed by the interpreting person (similar to the "reference" in Ogden's model)

Semiotic Tetrahedron by FRISCO

The FRISCO report consolidates the two different definitions of semiotics by Ogden and Peirce [Falkenberg et al. 1998]. Figure 19-6 depicts the semiotic tetrahedron suggested in the FRISCO report to illustrate the semiotics of conceptual models

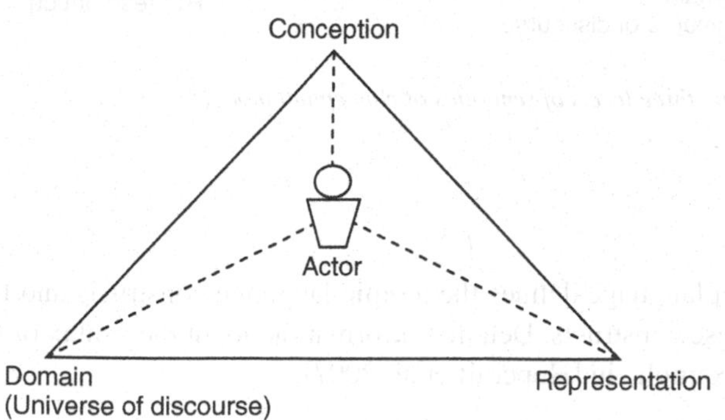

Fig. 19-6 *The semiotic tetrahedron according to FRISCO*

The semiotic tetrahedron distinguishes four concepts and illustrates the relations between these concepts:

Domain, conception, representation, and actor

- *Domain*[7]: The domain (universe of discourse) denotes the existing or conceived reality that is the subject of model creation. The domain (universe of discourse) corresponds to Ogden's term "referent".
- *Conception*: The conception denotes the image of the real-world object in the mind of the interpreting person. This notional image comprises a set of properties that the interpreting person associates with the real-world object. The conception corresponds to Ogden's term "reference".
- *Representation*: The representation denotes the result of a human actor describing his/her conceptions using a conceptual modelling language. The representation may be short and simple or large and complex. The representation corresponds to Ogden's term "symbol".
- *Actor*: The actor is depicted in the centre of the semiotic tetrahedron. The actor may either have the role of a "representer" or the role of an "interpreter". As a representer the actor conceptualises perceptions of the universe of discourse and represents them (using a conceptual modelling language) in order to communicate his/her conception of the universe of discourse appropriately. As an interpreter the actor interprets some representation (defined using a conceptual modelling language) and creates a conception of it in is his/her mind (see Section 19.6 for more details).

Using the semiotic tetrahedron, the three levels of semiotics suggested by [Morris 1946], syntax, semantics, and pragmatics, can be explained. Figure 19-7 depicts the three levels of semiotics within the semiotic tetrahedron (see [Falkenberg et al. 1998]).

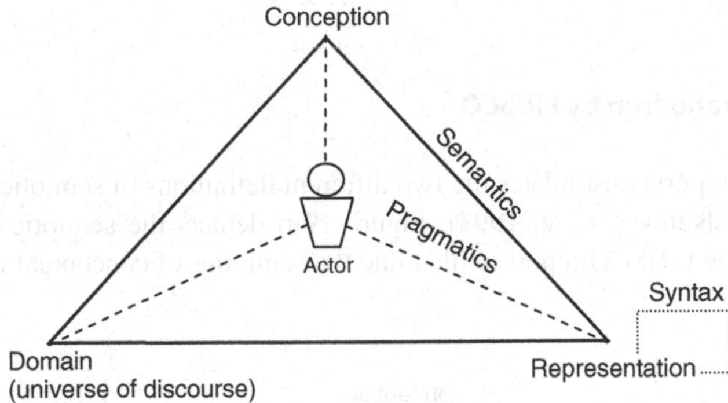

Fig. 19-7 *The three levels of semiotics of conceptual models*

Syntax

The syntax of a language defines the atomic language constructs and the valid combinations of these constructs. Detailed information about the syntax of languages can be found, for example, in [Hopcraft et al. 2007].

---

7 We prefer the term "universe of discourse" in this book rather than the term "domain" used in the FRISCO report (see Definition 19-1).

Semantics

The semantics defines the meaning of the language constructs (i.e. the meaning of the symbols and their combinations). The semantics is typically based on the defined syntactic rules. In the semiotic tetrahedron, the semantics of the language constructs is established through the assignment of the representations to the conceptions. The conceptions are formed by the actor according to his/her association with the referents in the universe of discourse.

Composition principle

The semantics of an arithmetic expression is composed of the semantics of the individual elements of the expression. Similarly, the semantics of a conceptual model results from the semantics of the constructs defined in the model. The logician and philosopher Gottlob Frege called this way of defining semantics the "composition principle" (see [Frege 1923]). The composition principle states that the semantics of a complex expression (e.g. a conceptual model) results from the semantics of its individual elements and the semantics of the composition of the elements (see also [Wittgenstein 1963]). The compositional semantics of a conceptual model is formed through the successive composition of partial models beginning with the atomic constructs. Thereby, the semantics of the model is composed step by step following the abstract syntactic structures of the language.

Pragmatics

Pragmatics of symbols/representations

The pragmatics deals with effects that the interpretation of the representation (symbol) has on the behaviour of the interpreting actor (see Fig. 19-7). Figure 19-8 illustrates the meaning of pragmatics within the semiotics. In the example, the pragmatics is, among other things, the reaction of the driver caused by perceiving and interpreting the traffic sign. The effect of the traffic sign on the driver of the car (the interpreting person) could be that the driver reduces the speed of the car in order to be able to observe the "right of way rules" when entering the roundabout.

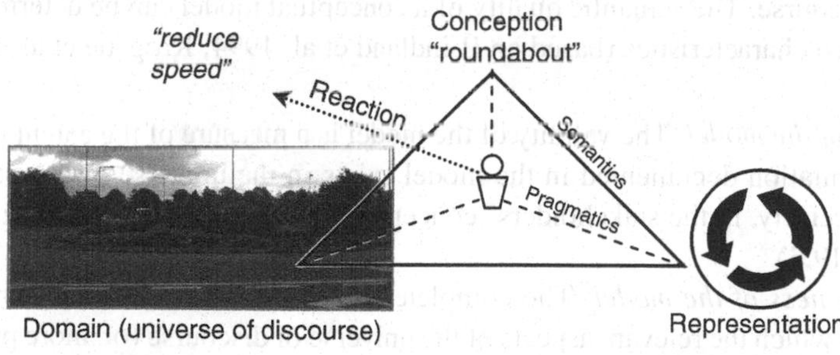

Fig. 19-8 *Example illustrating the pragmatics of a conceptual model*

19.4 Quality of Conceptual Models

Quality criteria

In order to assess the quality of conceptual models, the quality criteria defined for requirements artefacts can be used (see Section 16.3). The quality of a conceptual model can also be judged based on the semiotic tetrahedron presented inSection 19.3.

The quality s then assessed with respect to the three levels of semiotics: syntactic, semantic, and pragmatic quality (see [Lindland et al. 1994]).

Syntactic Quality ("Quality of the Form")

Adhering to syntactic rules

The syntactic quality of a conceptual model refers to the language constructs (representations) used in the model or, more precisely, to the adherence to syntactic rules. The syntactic quality of a conceptual model is thus a measure of compliance with the syntactic rules defined for the modelling language. Example 19-1 depicts some syntactic errors that might occur when creating a conceptual model. Those errors reduce the syntactic quality of a model. The detection and correction of syntactic errors is typically supported by modelling tools.

Example 19-1: Syntactic quality of conceptual models

Examples of syntactic errors in UML models:

- A use case in a UML use case diagram is represented as a triangle (instead of an ellipse).
- In a UML class diagram, a class is defined without a class name (which is mandatory according the syntactic rules).
- In a UML sequence diagram, the messages exchanged by the actors are drawn as plain lines without arrowheads.

Semantic Quality ("Quality of the Meaning")

Validity and completeness of the model

The semantic quality of a conceptual model states the extent to which the information documented in the conceptual model corresponds to the aspects that exist in the universe of discourse. The semantic quality of a conceptual model can be determined by means of two characteristics (based on [Lindland et al. 1994; Krogstie et al. 1995]):

- *Validity of the model*: The validity of the model is a measure of the extent to which the information documented in the model exists in the universe of discourse (or, more precisely, in the stakeholders' conceptions of the universe of discourse; see Section 19.3).
- *Completeness of the model*: The completeness of the model is a measure of the extent to which the relevant aspects of the universe of discourse (or, more precisely, the stakeholders' conceptions of the universe of discourse; see Section 19.3) are contained in the model.

Feasible validity and completeness

[Lindland et al. 1994] suggest that one should strive for feasible validity and completeness since, for all but the simplest problems, total validity and completeness cannot be achieved. Furthermore, when assessing the completeness of a model, the purpose of the model and hence the pragmatic quality must be taken into account (see below).

Example 19-2 illustrates some typical semantic errors in conceptual models.

Example 19-2: Semantic quality of conceptual models

Examples of errors in UML models that reduce the semantic quality of a conceptual model:

- ❑ A use case *A* depicted in a use case diagram has an "include" relationship to a use case *B*. However, in the universe of discourse the sequence of interactions documented in use case *A* does not include the sequence of interactions documented in use case *B*.
- ❑ A class "Person" documented in a class diagram has an attribute "date of birth" with multiplicity "0..*". This multiplicity is incorrect with respect to the represented universe of discourse, since every person has exactly one date of birth.
- ❑ In a class model that documents different products of an insurance company, there is no class "Life insurance", although the company offers life insurance. Hence, an important product from the underlying universe of discourse is not documented in the class diagram
- ❑ In a statechart which documents the current behaviour of a car safety system, a transition is defined for the input action "driver falls into a microsleep". However, the actual system does not have the facility to detect a microsleep of the driver. Hence, the documented transition has no referent in the represented universe of discourse.

Pragmatic Quality ("Quality of Usage")

Suitable for intended use

The pragmatic quality of a conceptual model describes the degree to which the model is suitable for its purpose (see [Price and Shanks 2005]). More precisely, the pragmatic quality describes how well the representation of information of the universe of discourse in the model is suited for the specific use. In order to determine the pragmatic quality of a conceptual model, it is necessary to determine the desired use of the considered model. Thus, the purpose for creating the model and the associated context of usage should be defined. Example 19-3 outlines some examples of low pragmatic quality of a model.

Example 19-3: Pragmatic quality of conceptual models

Examples of errors that decrease the pragmatic quality of a conceptual model:

- ❑ The requirements engineers have the task of creating a diagram to support communication of the (static) structure of a system to a customer. The requirements engineers decide to create a state diagram for this purpose. Although the created state diagram is syntactically and semantically correct, it has a low pragmatic quality since (due to the modelling constructs provided by a state diagram) it contains few static aspects.

(to be continued)

Example 19-3 (*continued*)

- A system architect creates sequence diagrams in order to support a discussion with a requirements engineer about usage aspects of the system. These sequence diagrams contain mostly system-internal interactions, i.e. interactions between system components, and only very few system–actor interactions (see Section 10.6). The sequence diagrams have a low pragmatic quality since the documented system-internal interactions are not suited to support the discussion about usage aspects of the system.

Interrelations between Syntactic, Semantic, and Pragmatic Quality

An error in a conceptual model often affects more than one quality aspect (syntactic, semantic, pragmatic quality) of a conceptual model:

- Syntactic errors often impair the semantic quality of a conceptual model since incorrect syntax frequently goes along with incorrect representation of aspects of the universe of discourse in the conceptual model.
- Semantic errors often impair the pragmatic quality of a model. If the model contains semantic errors, it conveys invalid or incomplete information about the universe of discourse. A model that is invalid or incomplete is often also not suitable for its purpose.
- Syntactic errors can also impair the pragmatic quality of the conceptual model. Models that contain syntactic errors are incomprehensible. This reduces the pragmatic quality because people cannot interpret the model correctly.

19.5 Modelling Languages

A modelling language is defined by its syntax and semantics (see Section 19.3). The syntax defines the permissible, atomic symbols (modelling constructs) and the rules for combining the symbols into language expressions (models or model fragments). The semantics defines the meaning of each individual symbol and the permissible combinations of symbols, where the semantics of a combination of symbols (i.e. a part of the model or the entire model) results from applying the composition principle.

19.5.1 Conceptual Modelling Languages

Abstract and concrete syntax

Languages for creating conceptual models are referred to as conceptual modelling languages (or, in short, modelling languages). With respect to the syntax of a conceptual modelling language, it is common to distinguish between the abstract syntax and the concrete syntax of the language:

- *Abstract syntax*: The abstract syntax defines the abstract language constructs of the modelling language and their permissible combinations without prescribing a specific notation for the constructs.

- *Concrete syntax*: The concrete syntax establishes a relationship between the language constructs defined by the abstract syntax and concrete representations of these constructs.

The concrete representations of an abstract language construct are called the notation of the language construct. The concrete syntax assigns at least one specific textual and/or graphical notation to each abstract language construct. The entire set of representations for all abstract language constructs is called the notation of the modelling language.

Notation of a modelling language

The separation of abstract and concrete syntax allows the assignment of different notations to the abstract syntax of a modelling language. For example, a textual notation, a graphical notation or even two different graphical notations can be defined for an abstract modelling construct. Figure 19-9 illustrates the assignment of different notations to an abstract language construct.

Several notations for language constructs

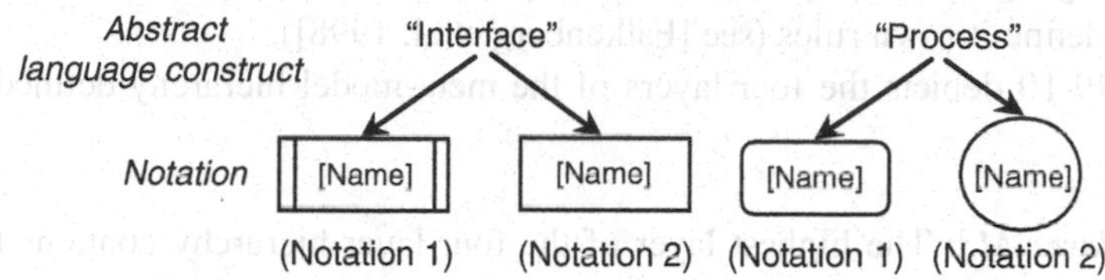

Fig. 19-9 *Abstract and concrete syntax of a modelling language*

The abstract syntax of a conceptual modelling language typically also contains well-formedness rules for the models or expressions created using the modelling language (see [Greenspan 1984; Borgida et al. 1985]). Although well-formedness rules are syntactic restrictions, in most cases the rules are derived from the semantics defined for the modelling language. Well formedness rules are thus also called "static semantics". Conceptual modelling languages typically include modelling constructs supporting abstraction such as classification, generalisation, or aggregation. The definition of the syntax and semantics of the abstraction constructs, including the well-formedness rules, can differ significantly from language to language.

Well-formedness rules

A modelling language is called a formal modelling language, if the syntax and the semantics of a conceptual modelling language are formally defined.

Formal modelling languages

Unified Modeling Language (UML; see [OMG 2009b]) is an example of a widely known and frequently used conceptual modelling language. More precisely, UML comprises a set of modelling languages. The syntax of UML is mainly formally specified. In contrast, most of the semantics is specified in natural language. UML is thus a semi-formal modelling language. An example of a formally defined modelling language is message sequence charts, for which the syntax and (to a large extent) also the semantics are formally defined (see [ITU 1996; ITU 1998]).

Unified Modeling Language (UML)

19.5.2 Meta-Modelling

A conceptual model can be used to define a conceptual modelling language. A conceptual model that defines a modelling language is called a "meta-model". The

Meta-Models and modelling languages

meta-model is an expression defined by means of a modelling language or, more precisely, by a meta-language. The "meta-language" itself can in turn be defined by a conceptual model. This model is called a "meta-meta-model" and the language used to define the meta-meta-model is called a "meta-meta-language".

This construction of meta-layers can be continued infinitely. A language defined at meta-layer $\mathcal{L}_n$ is used to define a language at meta-layer $\mathcal{L}_{n-1}$. The language defined at meta-layer $\mathcal{L}_n$ can be defined by a language defined at meta layer $\mathcal{L}_{n+1}$.

Hence, theoretically, the number of meta-layers of a conceptual modelling language is infinite. To avoid this problem, in practice, the meta-model hierarchy is closed at some layer. Often, four layers are sufficient (see [ISO/IEC Std 10027; OMG 2009a]). For instance, the Object Management Group (OMG) has suggested a four-layer meta-model hierarchy in the course of the standardisation efforts for UML. The meta-model hierarchy of UML 2 is closed by means of recursion at layer M3. The meta-model at layer M3 is defined using the MOF (Meta Object Facility), which is a meta-language defined by the OMG. The recursive closure at layer M3 means that the meta-language at this layer is self-descriptive, i.e. it is sufficiently expressive to be used to define its own rules (see [Falkenberg et al. 1998]).

Figure 19-10 depicts the four layers of the meta-model hierarchy defined by the OMG:

Meta-model layers

- *Model layer M3*: The highest layer of the four-layer hierarchy contains the definition of the MOF, which defines the language that can be used for defining meta-models at layer M2.
- *Model layer M2*: At layer M2, the UML meta-model is defined. The UML meta-model specifies the modelling constructs and the languages of UML. For example, the UML meta-model defines the constructs used to define class diagrams (such as class, association, generalisation) and the constructs used to define use case diagrams (such as actor, use case, extends).
- *Model layer M1*: At layer M1, concrete UML models for an application are defined using the modelling language defined at layer M2 by the UML meta-model. An example of a model defined at layer M1 is a concrete class diagram for a specific application (see Section 14.1.2).
- *Model layer M0*: Layer M0 at the bottom of the four-layer hierarchy comprises concrete instances of the models defined at layer M1. An example of such an instance is the employee "John Smith", who is an instance of the class "employee" defined in the class model at layer M1. The name "M0" shall indicate that this layer is, strictly speaking, not a model layer, since (according to our definition) there are no models defined at this layer but representatives which refer to concrete real-world instances of the model elements defined at layer M1.

Instantiations of a meta-model

Each model defined at one of the layers M3 to M1 defines a set of valid instantiations at the layer below. The specification of the OMG [OMG 2009b] of the UML class diagrams at layer M2 defines the set of all possible valid class diagrams which can be defined at layer M1. The class diagram itself is a valid instance of the UML meta-model defined at layer M2 if and only if it complies with all syntactic rules (the abstract syntax and the well-formedness rules) defined in the UML meta-model. Thus, the meta-model defined at layer M2 indirectly also constrains the set of valid instances at layer M0.

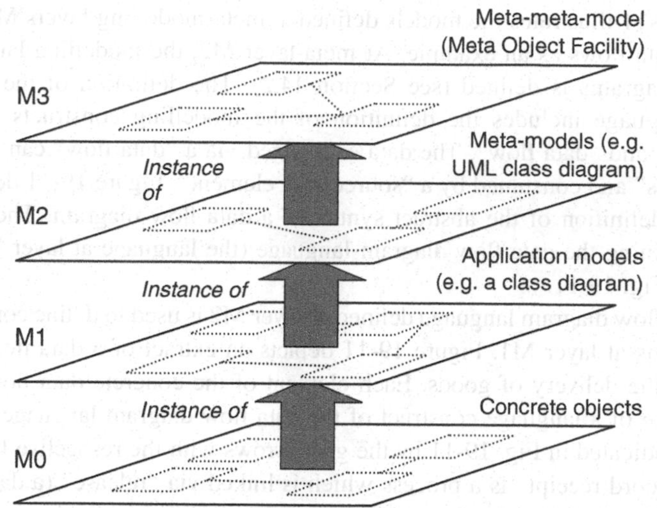

Fig. 19-10 *The four-layer meta-model hierarchy used by the OMG*

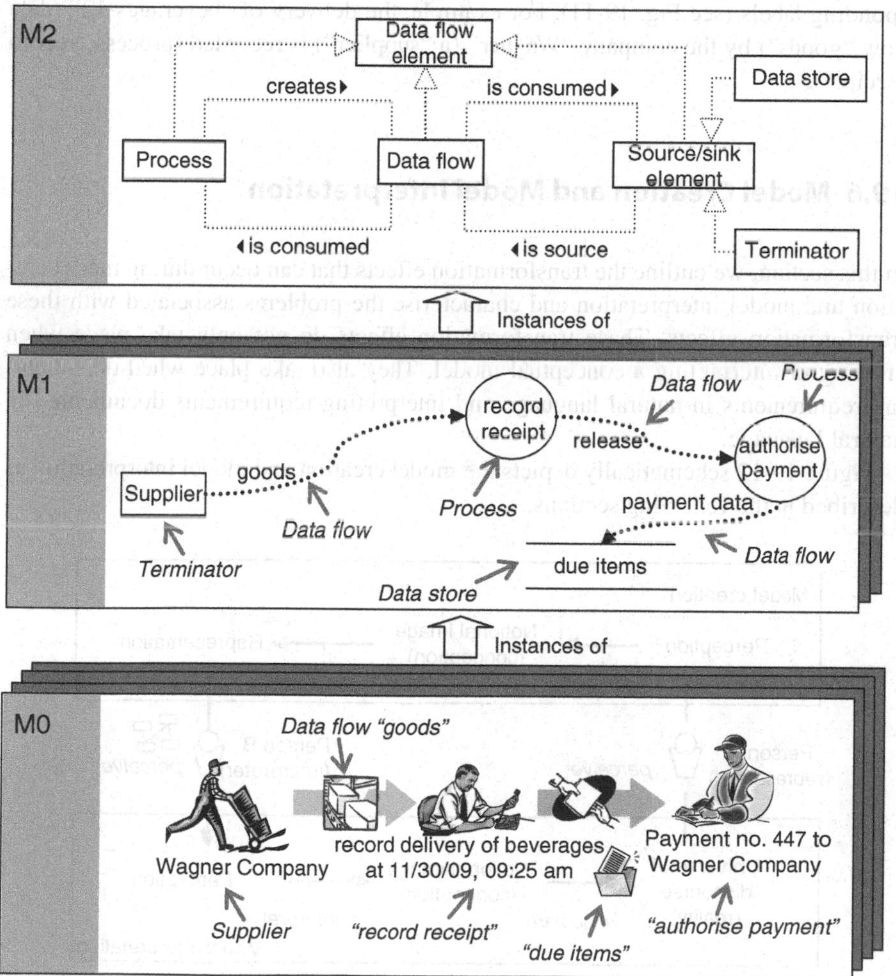

Fig. 19-11 *Meta-modelling example: data flow*

Meta-modelling example

Figure 19-11 illustrates the models defined at meta-modelling layers M2 through M0 using data flows as an example. At meta-layer M2, the modelling language for data flow diagrams is defined (see Section 14.2). The definition of the data flow diagram language includes the definition of the modelling constructs "process", "terminator" and "data flow". The data exchanged via a "data flow" can be created by a "process" and consumed by a "source/sink element". Figure 19-11 depicts only part of the definition of the abstract syntax of a data flow diagram. The language used for defining the data flow diagram language (the language at layer M3) is not depicted in Fig. 19-11.

The data flow diagram language defined at layer M2 is used to define concrete data flow diagrams at layer M1. Figure 19-11 depicts an extract of a data flow diagram defined for the delivery of goods. Each element of the concrete data flow diagram is an instance of a language construct of the data flow diagram language defined at M2 layer (indicated in Fig. 19-11 by the grey arrows with the respective labels). For example "record receipt" is a process which is linked via "release" (a data flow) to "authorise payment" (another process).

Each element at layer M0 is an instance of an element of the data flow diagram defined at layer M1. This is indicated at layer M0 by grey arrows with the corresponding labels (see Fig. 19-11). For example, the delivery of "beverages-12" (data flow "goods") by the company "Wagner" (a "supplier") is recorded (process "record receipt").

19.6 Model Creation and Model Interpretation

In this section, we outline the transformation effects that can occur during model creation and model interpretation and characterise the problems associated with these transformation effects. These transformation effects do not only take place when creating or interpreting a conceptual model. They also take place when documenting requirements in natural language and interpreting requirements documented in natural language.

Figure 19-12 schematically depicts the model creation and model interpretation as described in the following sections.

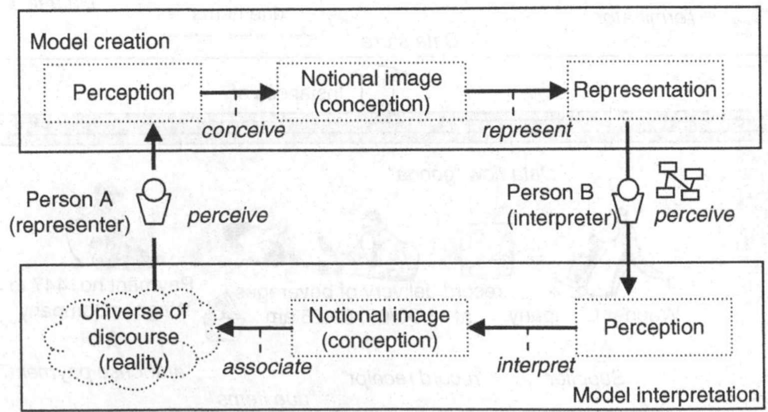

Fig. 19-12 *Transformation effects during model creation and model interpretation*

19.6.1 Model Creation

During model creation, the representer (i.e. the person creating the representation; "Person A" in Fig. 19-12) perceives the universe of discourse and forms a notional image (conception) of the considered part of the universe of discourse. The representer then expresses his conception of the universe of discourse in a representation using a modelling language ("represent" in Fig. 19-12). During the creation of the model, two transformations take place. Each transformation can cause an error (transformation effect) such as loss of information, incompleteness, or ambiguity:

Incomplete or distorted conception

- *Transformation during perception*: When the representer forms a notional image of the universe of discourse, the information about the universe of discourse is transformed unconsciously. This transformation can lead, for example, to an incomplete or distorted conception of the universe of discourse. The conception of the universe of discourse might comprise only specific details that can, in addition, also be distorted.
- *Transformation during representation*: This transformation occurs during the communication or documentation of the conception. It is based on the fact that notional images are documented differently depending on a person's knowledge, personal experiences, and the current situation. The transformation during representation can lead, for example, to an incomplete and/or distorted representation of a correct conceptualisation.

The transformation effects during representation can be resolved. For instance, the represented information can be analysed to detect missing details. In contrast the transformation effects during perception cannot be resolved. It is only possible to reduce these effects, for example, by involving multiple stakeholders to obtain a more objective view. The different types of transformation effects which can occur during representation (e.g. deletion, generalisation, and distortion, see [Bandler and Grinder 1975]) and hints for the mitigation of these effects using neuro-linguistic programming can be found in [Rupp 2009]).

Figure 19-13 depicts the transformation effects which occur during perception and during representation within the semiotic tetrahedron introduced in Section 19.3.

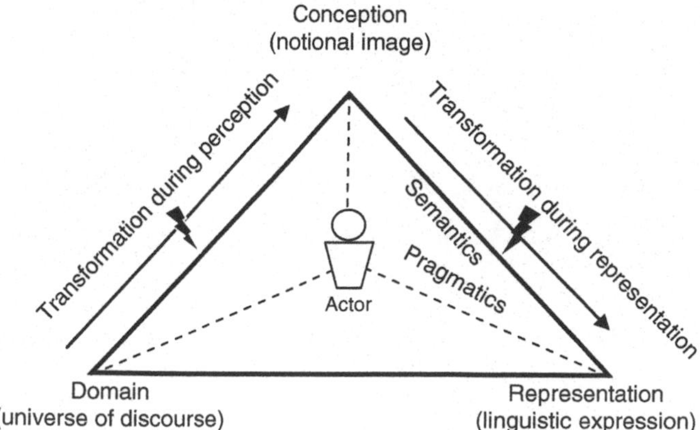

Fig. 19-13 *Transformation effects during perception and representation*

19.6.2 Model Interpretation

The interpreter ("Person B" in Fig. 19-12) interprets the representation (the model) and forms a notional image of the universe of discourse represented in the model. Therein the interpreter takes into account the semantics of the modelling constructs and the semantics of their composition. The meaning of the interpreted model and the model elements is defined by associating the notional images (conceptions) with the universe of discourse. Both transformation effects described in Section 19.6.1 can also occur during the interpretation of a model: During the interpretation of the model, unconscious transformation effects can occur leading, for instance, to a distorted conception of the model in the mind of the interpreter. In addition, transformation effects can occur while the interpreter creates associations between his/her notional image and the universe of discourse. Even if the interpreter's conceptualisation of the model is correct, these transformation effects can lead to a distorted association of model elements with the universe of discourse.

It is important that the interpreters of the representation (model) and the person creating the model share the same understanding of the constructs provided by the modelling language. The shared understanding of the modelling constructs is a prerequisite to enable the model interpreter to associate the information represented in the model with the same aspects of the universe of discourse that the modeller has documented in the representation (model). A formal definition of the syntax and semantics of the modelling language can reduce possible transformation effects but cannot completely avoid their occurrence.

Chapter 20
Interrelation of Model-Based and Textual Requirements

In this chapter, we describe:

- ❑ *The advantages of documenting requirements using models*
- ❑ *The complementary use of models and textual requirements*
- ❑ *Relationship types for interrelating textual and model-based requirements artefacts*

20.1 Requirements Models

Requirements artefacts can be documented using natural language or a conceptual modelling language (see Section 19.5.1). In this book, we refer to conceptual models that are used to document requirements as requirements models:

D

Definition 20-1: *Requirements model*

Requirements models are conceptual models that document requirements (goals, scenarios, or solution-oriented requirements) using a conceptual modelling language.

Knowledge of the modelling language required

The stakeholders who create a requirements model must know the modelling language in order to document the respective requirements correctly. Likewise, a stakeholder who interprets a requirements model must be familiar with the modelling language in order to interpret the model correctly. A stakeholder examining a data flow model must be aware of the notation used in the graphical model. For example, the stakeholder must be aware that a circle in a data flow model represents a system process and an arrow represents a data flow. Moreover, the stakeholder must be aware of the semantics associated with the concepts "data flow" and "process" (see Section 19.6 for details).

Requirements models described in this book

In different parts of the book, we describe conceptual modelling languages which facilitate the model-based documentation of goals, scenarios, and solution-oriented requirements. Table 20-1 provides an overview of the conceptual modelling languages introduced in the book. The requirement types associated with the modelling languages in Tab. 20-1 indicate a typical use of each modelling language. However, many conceptual modelling languages can be used to document requirements of different types. For instance, activity diagrams can be used for documenting scenarios as well as solution-oriented requirements such as functions or data flows.

Tab. 20-1 *Overview of conceptual modelling languages described in this book*

Kind of requirement	Type of model	Introduced in
Goals	AND/OR goal trees and graphs i* models KAOS goal model	Section 8.4 Section 8.5 Section 8.6
Scenarios	UML/SysML sequence diagram UML/SysML activity diagram UML/SysML use case diagram	Section 11.5 Section 11.6 Section 11.7
Solution-oriented requirements: data	Enhanced entity–relationship model UML class diagram	Section 14.1.1 Section 14.1.2
Solution-oriented requirements: function	Data flow diagram	Section 14.2.1/14.2.2
Solution-oriented requirements: behaviour	Finite automata Statecharts UML/SysML state machine diagram	Section 14.3.2/14.3.3 Section 14.3.4 Section 14.3.5

Advantages of Model-Based Requirements Documentation

Cognitive science: capturing and memorising pictorial information

Research in cognitive science has proven that humans capture and memorise information from pictures faster and better than information from texts (see [Glass and Holyoak 1986; Kosslyn 1988; Mietzel 2007]). These findings support the hypothesis that requirements models can be better understood and memorised than requirements documented using natural language.

Specific perspective

Several conceptual modelling languages were created specifically to support the modelling of requirements for a particular perspective of the universe of discourse. For instance, the entity–relationship language [Chen 1976] supports the documentation of the structural data aspects of the universe of discourse, whereas the documentation of aspects about the functions or the behaviour is not supported by the entity–relationship language. Similarly, the data flow diagram language [DeMarco 1978], statecharts [Harel 1987], and Unified Modeling Language [OMG 2009b]) support the documentation of requirements for a particular perspective of the universe of discourse.

Compared with natural language, a conceptual modelling language offers limited expressiveness. Modelling all aspects of the universe of discourse relevant for the system development thus typically requires the use of several conceptual modelling languages (see Part III.c).

Discrete levels of detail

Abstraction is an inherent property of a conceptual modelling language (see Section 19.2) which facilitates the creation of models of reduced complexity (compared with the complexity of the universe of discourse) and thus supports managing the complexity of the universe of discourse. Besides the abstraction achieved by focussing on a particular perspective of the universe of discourse, the built-in constructs of the conceptual modelling language for abstraction (such as classification, composition, or generalisation) support the reduction of complexity within the conceptual model itself.

Supporting problem understanding and problem solving

Especially when the universe of discourse and the system to be developed are very complex, the ability of conceptual models to support the stakeholders in focussing on specific aspects (perspectives) is useful. By offering predefined abstractions, conceptual modelling languages support the stakeholders in focussing on the relevant details of the universe of discourse and discarding insignificant details. Conceptual models are thus well suited for supporting problem understanding and the specification of the requirements for the system to be developed.

Support for quality assurance

Checking quality properties such as correctness, completeness, and consistency of a requirements specification documented in natural language is typically very time consuming and error prone. Conceptual modelling languages support the checking of certain quality properties of a specification. The tools used to define the conceptual models can, for example, check the syntactic quality of the model based on the defined syntax of the language. Moreover, checking certain semantic quality properties such as correctness or consistency can be supported. For example, inconsistencies can be (automatically) detected by checking the formally defined consistency rules. Checking the semantic quality is additionally supported by the explicit definition of relationships between the artefacts defined in the conceptual model. Moreover, relationships defined in a conceptual model are typically more evident and easier to comprehend than the relationships defined in a textual requirement document. Stakeholders reviewing requirements defined in a conceptual model are thus more likely to detect missing and incorrectly defined relationships than are stakeholders reviewing a textual requirements specification.

20.2 Interrelating Requirements Models and Textual Requirements

In practice, requirements are documented predominantly using natural language. Existing standards and reference structures for requirements documents (see Section 18.1) mainly deal with the documentation of requirements using natural language.

Advantages of combining textual requirements and requirements models

As outlined in Sections 17.4 and 20.1, the use of natural language as well as the use of conceptual modelling languages for documenting requirements have specific advantages and disadvantages. The advantages of the two documentation formats can be combined by using both formats for documenting requirements. In other words, a combination of both formats supports the elimination of specific disadvantages of each individual documentation format. For example, conceptual models can be used to visualise the relationships between textual requirements or to provide a more abstract view of the textual specifications. Models can also be used to detail requirements documented in natural language. For instance, a statechart could specify a set of textual requirements in more detail (see Fig. 20-1). Conversely, the requirements documented in a conceptual model can be enriched by annotating the model elements with textual requirements.

An Example

Figure 20-1 depicts a set of textual requirements, a statechart, and a relationship between the statechart and the textual requirements. This relationship documents that the statechart details the three requirements R12 to R14 defined in the textual specification. This simple relationship supports, for example, the validation of the textual requirements since it clearly indicates which statechart specifies which requirements in more detail (which might not be at all obvious if the requirements are spread throughout a specification containing several hundreds of requirements).

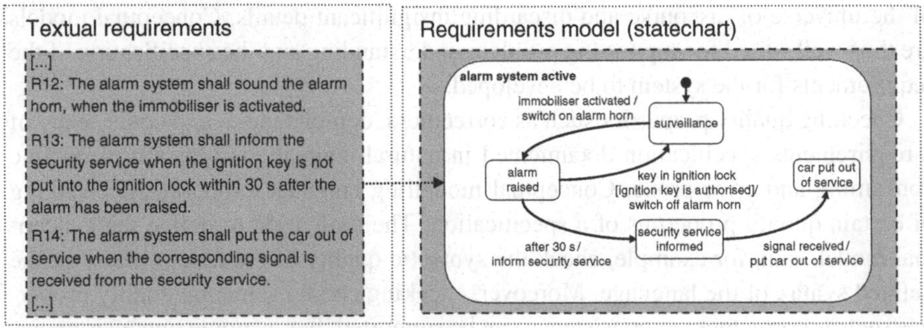

Fig. 20-1 *Simple example of a relationship between textual requirements and a requirements model*

Elimination of a defect in the textual requirements

A validation of the statechart depicted in Fig. 20-1 reveals that no transition is defined from the state "car put out of service". The detection of the missing transition indicates that the textual requirements are most likely incomplete. Without the relationship from the textual requirements to the requirements model this defect might not have been detected. To eliminate the defect, the model and the associated textual requirements are extended as illustrated in Fig. 20-2.

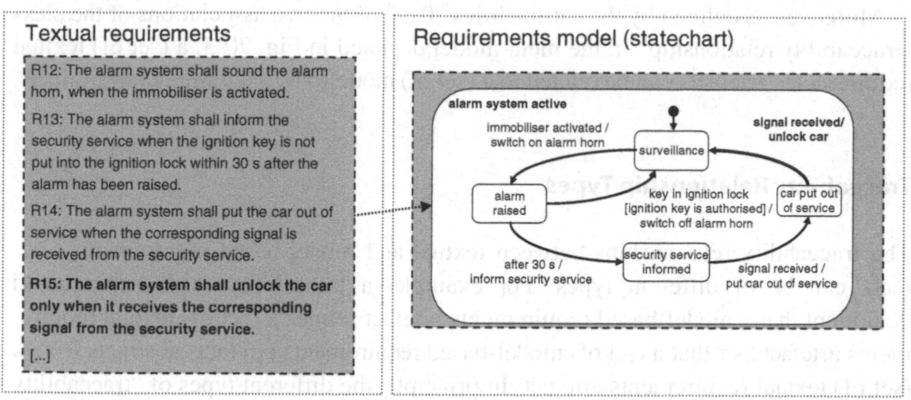

Fig. 20-2 *Corrected textual requirements and requirements model*

20.3 Traceability Meta-models

Relationships and relationship types

Figure 20-3 depicts a fragment of a meta-model defined for supporting the interrelation of textual and model-based requirements artefacts. According to the meta-model depicted in Fig. 20-3, an interrelation between textual and model-based requirements artefacts can be documented by traceability relationships. We elaborate on the documentation of traceability relationships and different traceability types in Chapter 31.

Traceability Relationships

Depending on the instantiation of the meta-model, the traceability relationships between traceable artefacts ("textual requirements artefact" and "model-based requirements artefact" as depicted in Fig. 20-3) can be defined at different levels of granularity. For example, if the class "model-based requirements artefact" is instantiated with an element which represents an entire model diagram, traceability relationships between the diagram and other artefact types can be defined. If the "model-based requirements artefact" is instantiated with an element referring

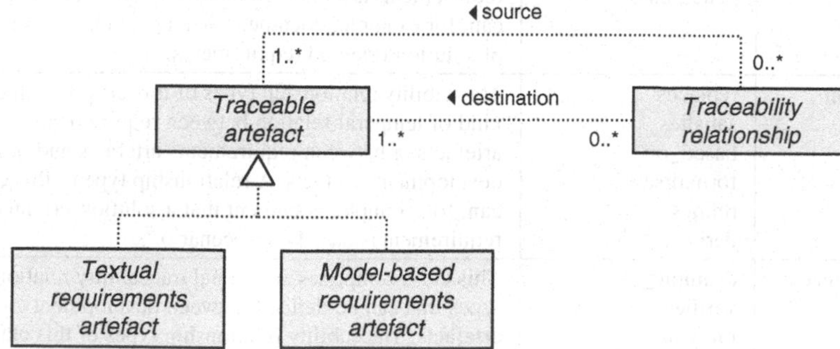

Fig. 20-3 *Fragment of a meta-model for documenting relationships between textual and model-based requirements artefacts*

to a class in a class diagram, traceability relationships between the class and other artefact types can be defined. In the latter case, the traceability relationships are more fine-grained than in the former case.

Cardinalities

Moreover, as defined by the cardinalities "0..*" of the two associations of the class "traceability relationship" in the meta-model depicted in Fig. 20-3, a (set of) textual requirements artefacts can be related to a (set of) model-based requirements artefacts.

Traceability Relationship Types

Defining traceability relationship types

The traceability relationships between textual and model-based requirements artefacts can be of different types. For example, a traceability relationship could document that a model-based requirements artefact refines a (set of) textual requirements artefacts, or that a (set of) model-based requirements artefacts abstracts from a (set of) textual requirements artefact. In principle, the different types of "traceability relationship" can be used to specify different traceability relationships in the model as sub-classes of the class "traceability relationship" are defined.

Common traceability relationship types

In the literature, numerous relationship types have been suggested for interrelating textual requirements and requirements models (see e.g. [Davis 1990; Pohl 1996a; Thayer and Dorfmann 2000]). Table 20-2 shows a selection of the relationship types that are suggested and described in detail in [Pohl 1996a]. The relationship

Tab. 20-2 *Traceability relationship types*

	Relationship type	Explanation
condition	constraint precondition	The traceability relationship types of this class document that a (requirements) artefact defines a restriction for another (requirements) artefact. For example, a goal can define a restriction for a scenario.
content	similar compares contradicts conflicts	Traceability relationship types of this class document dependencies between the content of the associated requirements artefacts or between requirements artefacts and other artefacts in the development process. A traceability relationship type of this class can be used, for example, to document a conflict relationship between two goals.
abstraction	classifies aggregates generalises	This class comprises traceability relationship types that represent abstraction dependencies between requirements artefacts. Relationship types of this class can, for example, document that a goal classifies a set of solution-oriented requirements.
evolution	replaces satisfies based_on formalises refines derived	Traceability relationship types of this class document a kind of temporal relation between requirements artefacts or between requirements artefacts and other development artefacts. A relationship type of this class can, for example, document that a solution-oriented requirement is based on a scenario.
miscellaneous	example_of verifies rationale responsible_for background comment	This class comprises additional traceability relationship types that can be defined between development artefacts. Traceability relationship types of this class document, for example, the fact that a scenario documents a concrete exemplary interaction sequence for a dynamic aspect of a set of solution-oriented requirements.

types are classified into five categories: condition, content, abstraction, evolution, and miscellaneous (see Section 30.3).

Traceability Relationship Examples

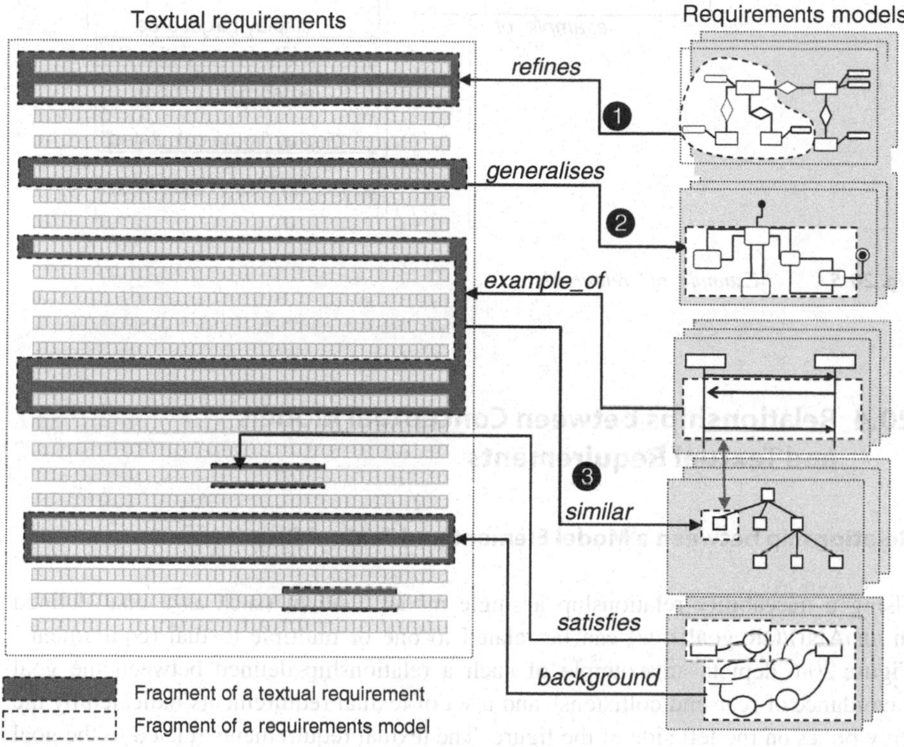

Fig. 20-4 *Relationships between requirements artefacts*

Figure 20-4 illustrates some relationships between textual requirements and requirements models (or model elements) defined using a subset of the relationship types shown in Tab. 20-2. The traceability relationships depicted in Fig. 20-4 document the following interrelations:

- ❶ The "refines" relationship between the fragment of the entity–relationship model and the associated textual requirements documents that the model fragment refines the associated textual requirements.
- ❷ The "generalises" relationship between the fragment of textual requirements and the statechart documents that the textual fragment represents a generalisation of the behavioural aspects defined in the statechart.
- ❸ The "similar" relationship between the set of textual requirements and a goal in the goal model expresses that the goal and the set of requirements document similar information.

Figure 20-5 depicts an "example_of" relationship between a scenario documented in a sequence diagram and the textual requirement which defines that the scenario represents an example of the realisation of the textual requirement.

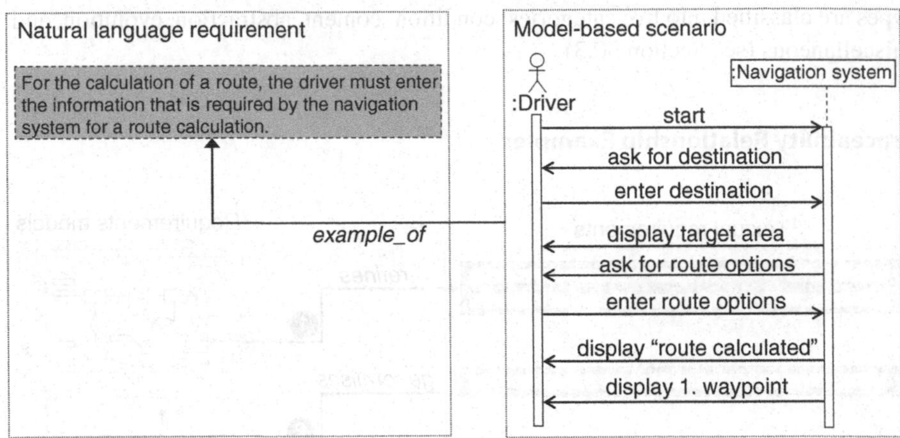

Fig. 20-5 *"Example_of" relationship*

20.4 Relationships between Conceptual Models and Textual Requirements

Relationship between a Model Element and Textual Requirements

Relationship between a goal and a set of textual requirements

Using a traceability relationship a single model element (such as a goal defined in an AND/OR goal tree) can be related to one or multiple textual requirements. Figure 20-6 depicts an example of such a relationship defined between the goal "avoidance of rear-end collisions" and a set of textual requirements indicated by the grey boxes on the left side of the figure. The textual requirements related to the goal could define the goal in more detail or document contextual information relevant for the goal (see Tab. 20-2).

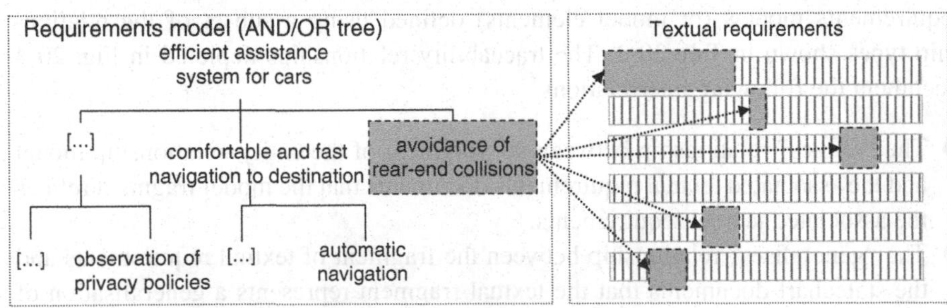

Fig. 20-6 *Relationship between a goal and a set of textual requirements*

By defining such traceability relationships, (parts of) the textual requirements can be associated to different requirements elements defined in the conceptual model, as depicted in Fig. 20-7.

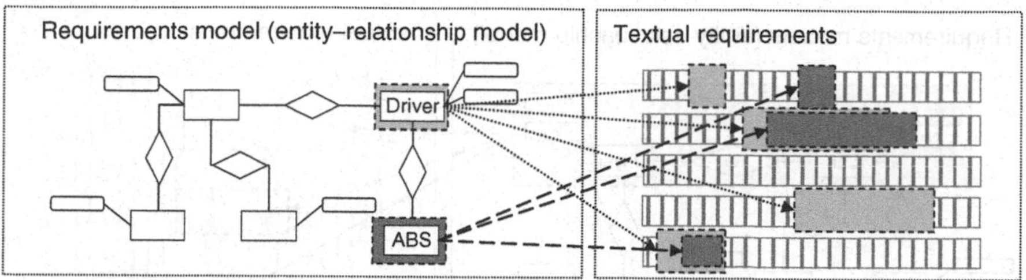

Fig. 20-7 *Relationship between entities and textual requirements*

Relationships to different model elements

As depicted in Fig. 20-7, each of the two entity types "driver" and "ABS" (anti-lock brakes) is related to a set of textual requirements. The textual requirements could, for example, define the entity types in more detail and/or define the usage of the entity types in a particular system function. Since different entity types could be used in a system function, the two sets of textual requirements related to the entities "driver" and "ABS" partly overlap, as depicted in Fig. 20-7.

Relationship between a Set of Model Elements and Textual Requirements

Interrelation of model parts and textual requirements

One or multiple textual requirements could be related to a part of the requirements model (or even a whole model). Figure 20-8 depicts an example of such an interrelation where part of a goal tree is associated with a set of textual requirements which might detail how the system satisfies the goals defined in the associated part of the goal model.

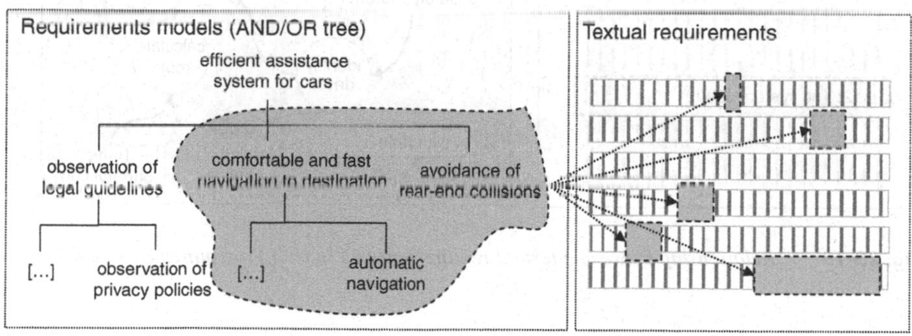

Fig. 20-8 *Relationship between a part of a goal model and textual requirements*

Figure 20-9 illustrates another example of a traceability relationship between a part of a conceptual model and a set of textual requirements. In this case, a part of an entity–relationship model is related to a set of textual requirements which might document details about the entities and attributes defined in the related part of the entity–relationship model.

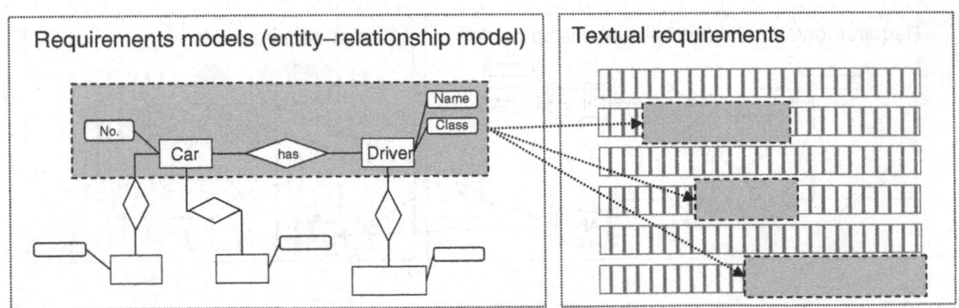

Fig. 20-9 Relationship between a part of an entity–relationship model and a set of textual requirements

Relationship between a Textual Requirement and Model Elements

Textual requirement and data flow diagram

Figure 20-10 depicts a traceability relationship defined between a textual requirement R12 and a requirements model, a data flow diagram. Depending on the type of the traceability relationship (see Tab. 20-2) this relationship may document that the textual requirements associated with the requirements model define the requirements documented in the model in more detail ("details" relationship). A textual requirement could obviously also be related to a single model element (such as the process "calculate route") or a part of a conceptual model.

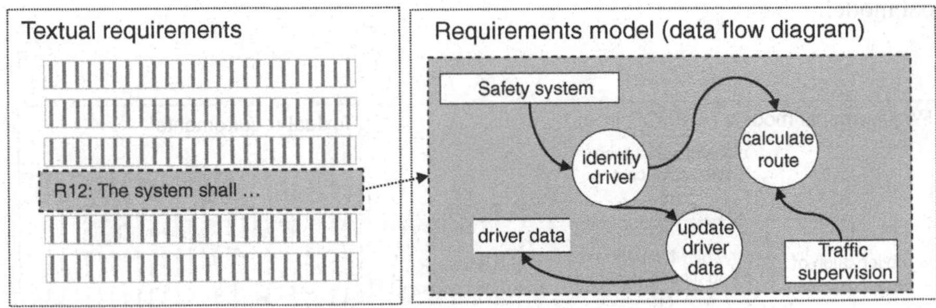

Fig. 20-10 Relationship between a textual requirement and (part of) a requirements model

Relationship between a Set of Textual Requirements and Model Elements

Textual requirements and goal model

Traceability relationships can also be used to interrelate a set of textual requirements with (part of) a requirements model or even with individual model elements. Figure 20-11 depicts a relationship from three textual requirements to two goals defined in a goal model. This relationship could, for example, document that the textual requirements contain the rationales for the two goals.

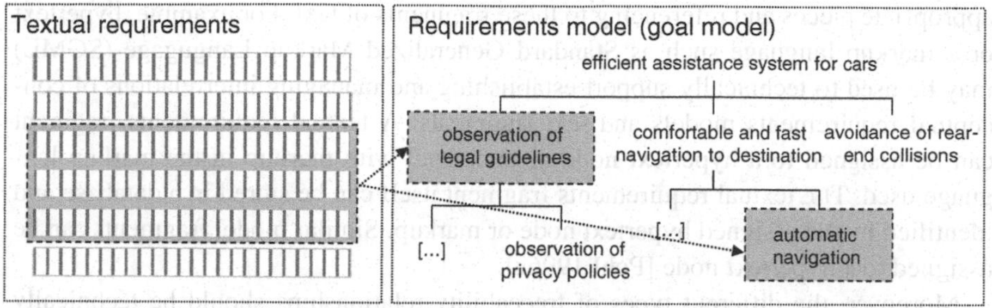

Fig. 20-11 *Relationship between textual requirements and requirements model elements*

Annotations of Model Elements

Explanation and additional details

An element of a conceptual model, parts of or a whole conceptual requirements model can be annotated with text by using a traceability relationship that interrelates the (part of the) conceptual model with a textual annotation. The annotation thereby enriches the model elements with additional information. The textual annotations can contain information which cannot be documented in the conceptual model itself.

Figure 20-12 illustrates the annotation of two goals documented in a goal model. The first annotation documents that an agreement about the goal "efficient assistance system for cars" has not yet been reached. The second annotation documents that the goal "comfortable and fast navigation to destination" will be discussed in the meeting on 23 May 2009.

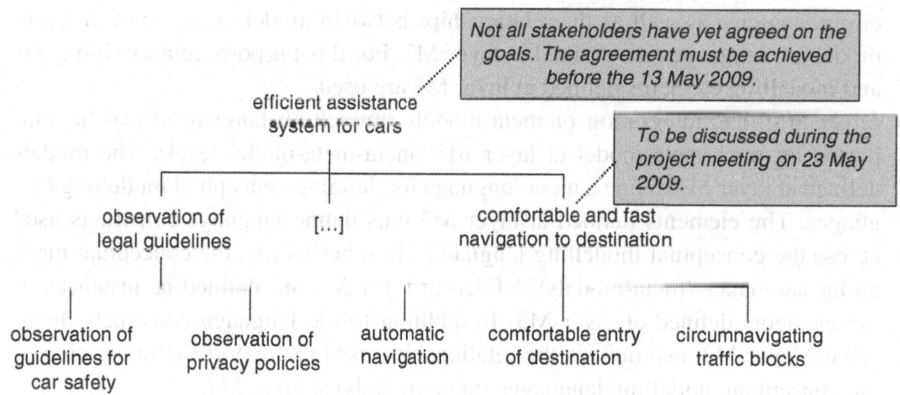

Fig. 20-12 *Annotation of model elements with natural language*

20.5 Technical Realisation

Fragmentation and referencing of textual requirements

Creating and managing traceability relationships between requirements artefacts requires appropriate tool support. For example, establishing relationships to fragments of textual requirements requires technical support for fragmenting text into appropriate pieces and referencing to these fragments of text. For example, hypertext or a markup language such as Standard Generalized Markup Langugage (SGML) may be used to technically support establishing and managing interrelations of conceptual requirements models and text fragments. A textual requirements fragment can be assigned to a hypertext node or annotated with markup in the markup language used. The textual requirements fragment itself can be stored in a database and identified by the assigned hypertext node or markup. Similar model fragments can be assigned to a hypertext node [Pohl 1996a].

Definition of appropriate models, meta-models, and meta-meta-models

Moreover, the different types of traceability relationships should be technically supported. For example, navigation in the requirements base using a specific traceability relationship type or set of types should be supported. A prerequisite for such support is the definition of the relationship types and the different requirements artefact types in a meta-model (see Section 20.3). The meta-model itself can be used to derive appropriate database schemata for managing the traceability relationships. For the technical realisation of tool support, the meta-model layers outlined in Section 19.5.2 play the following roles (see [Pohl 1996a] for a detailed description):

- *Layer M1*: The elements of the conceptual requirements models and the textual requirements are managed at layer M1. The requirements artefacts at layer M1 are defined using conceptual modelling languages (e.g. entity–relationship model, statechart, hypertext model). The modelling languages themselves are defined by the meta-models at layer M2. Therefore, each requirements artefact is recorded as an instance of an element of a meta-model (modelling language) defined at layer M2.
- *Layer M2*: At this layer, the modelling languages are defined by meta-models. Furthermore, the permissible relationships between the model elements of a modelling language as well as the relationships between model elements of different modelling languages are defined at layer M2. For this purpose, relationship types and modelling elements defined at layer M3 are used.
- *Layer M3*: The integration of meta-models (modelling languages) can be supported by meta-meta-model at layer M3 (meta-meta-model level). The models defined at layer M3 define a meta-language for defining conceptual modelling languages. The elements defined at layer M3 thus define language constructs used across the conceptual modelling languages. In other words, the conceptual modelling languages (meta-models) defined at layer M2 are defined as instances of the elements defined at layer M3. In addition to the language constructs themselves, layer M3 also defines the relationships used to support the integration of the conceptual modelling languages (meta-models) at layer M2.

The layer-based definition of the meta-language, the conceptual modelling languages, and the models which define the requirements artefacts as well as the traceability relationships between these artefacts provide a good basis for developing appropriate tool support. Without appropriate tool support, recording and managing the textual and model-based information, as well as the traceability relationships defined between them, is impossible. Appropriated tool support is thus a prerequisite for combining textual and model-based requirements documentations and leveraging the advantages of this combination as sketched in this section.

Recommended Literature for Part IV.a

Basic Reading

[IEEE Std 1233-1998] suggests a reference structure for system requirements specifications that can also be used as a reference structure for other specification documents.

[IEEE Std 830-1998] focuses on the creation of a software requirements specification in natural language. The standard defines quality criteria for specifications documented using natural language and suggests different reference structures for software requirements documents.

[Machado et al. 2005] discuss and explain the application of different modelling and specification techniques. They present a classification of meta-models for the model-based documentation of requirements and discuss features that modelling languages and modelling methods for requirements should have.

[Rupp 2009] explains, among other things, different aspects of textual requirements documentation and suggests a set of rules based on neuro-linguistic programming (NLP) for the detection and elimination of defects in textual requirements.

Advanced Reading

[Berry et al. 2003] provide a comprehensive insight into the ambiguity of textual requirements specifications. They describe different forms of ambiguity and provide helpful hints for detecting and avoiding ambiguities.

[Sag et al. 2003] provide a detailed introduction into syntactic theory. Syntactical issues, grammar generation, and other topics are discussed in detail for grammars of different languages. They provide a good explanation of syntactic ambiguity.

[Heim and Kratzer 1998] provide a comprehensive overview of semantics of languages and discuss the issues of semantic, lexical, and referential ambiguity in detail.

[Boman et al. 1997] consider the theoretical aspects of conceptual modelling. They deal, amongst other topics, with the meaning and structure of modelling languages. They also explain the fundamental abstraction concepts of conceptual modelling languages.

[Falkenberg et al. 1998] provide, in the FRISCO report, a comprehensive insight into the language-theoretic and model-theoretic fundamentals of conceptual modelling. They deal extensively with the different aspects of the semiotics of conceptual models (such as the syntax, the semantics, and the pragmatics).

[Pohl 1996a] presents an approach for the integration of text-based and model-based requirements artefacts. The integration of the artefacts is supported by meta-modelling and by the definition of a comprehensive set of traceability relationship types. A tool framework and environment for supporting requirements traceability is presented.

Part IV.b
Elicitation

Overview Part IV.b – Elicitation

Requirements elicitation is one of the three core requirements engineering activities. In this part of the book, we point out and characterise three main sub-activities of requirements elicitation, namely:

- *Identifying requirement sources*
- *Eliciting existing requirements*
- *Developing new requirements*

We further differentiate between elicitation techniques used within the three elicitation sub-activities and assistance techniques which are used to support the elicitation techniques. We describe six common elicitation techniques and five common assistance techniques, namely:

Elicitation techniques:

- *Interviews*
- *Workshops*
- *Focus groups*
- *Observation*
- *Questionnaires*
- *Perspective-based reading*

Assistance techniques:

- *Brainstorming*
- *Prototyping*
- *KJ method*
- *Mind mapping*
- *Elicitation checklists*

We characterise the suitability of these techniques for each elicitation sub-activity and provide a checklist with important hints for applying these techniques during requirements elicitation.

Classification

Part IV.b
Elicitation

		Basic	Advanced
21	**Fundamentals of Requirements Elicitation**		
21.1	Fundamentals of Requirements Elicitation	✓	
21.2	Requirements Elicitation: Definition	✓	
21.3	Use of Goals and Scenarios in Requirements Elicitation		✓
21.4	Sub-activity: Identifying Relevant Requirement Sources	✓	
21.5	Sub-activity: Eliciting Existing Requirements	✓	
21.6	Sub-activity: Developing New and Innovative Requirements	✓	
22	**Elicitation Techniques**		
22.1	Evaluation of the Techniques	✓	
22.2	Template for Describing the Techniques	✓	
22.3	Interview	✓	
22.4	Workshop	✓	
22.5	Focus Groups		✓
22.6	Observation	✓	
22.7	Questionnaires	✓	
22.8	Perspective-Based Reading		✓
23	**Assistance Techniques for Elicitation**		
23.1	Evaluation of the Techniques	✓	
23.2	Brainstorming	✓	
23.3	Prototyping		✓
23.4	KJ Method	✓	
23.5	Mind Mapping		✓
23.6	Elicitation Checklists	✓	

Chapter 21
Fundamentals of Requirements Elicitation

In this chapter, we outline:

- ❑ *The main goals of the requirements elicitation activity*
- ❑ *The use of goals and scenarios during requirements elicitation*
- ❑ *The three essential elicitation sub-activities*

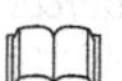

K. Pohl, *Requirements Engineering*,

21.1 Goal of Requirements Elicitation

Progress along the content dimension

Requirements elicitation is one of the three core activities of requirements engineering. The goal of requirements elicitation is to achieve progress in the content dimension (see Section 4.4) by eliciting new requirements as well as detailed information about existing requirements. The main goal of the elicitation activity is thus to elicit all requirements at the required level of detail for the system to be developed.

Diversity of requirement sources

Requirements exist in various forms, e.g. as ideas, intentions, or needs in the minds of stakeholders, as documented requirements typically in the form of text in natural language or requirements models, or in existing systems as implemented requirements. Hence, there are many diverse sources from which requirements need to be elicited.

Identification of relevant requirement sources

The different sources of requirements (e.g. stakeholders, documents, and existing systems) are typically not completely known at the beginning of the requirements engineering process. However, the consideration of all relevant sources of requirements during requirements elicitation is essential for the success of the requirements engineering process and hence the whole development process. Considering all relevant sources of requirements is not only important for eliciting all the requirements for the system, but also in order to support the acceptance of the system. Hence, the continuous search for relevant requirement sources is one of the three sub-activities of requirements elicitation (see Section 21.4).

Elicit existing requirements

Even if all relevant requirement sources are known, the requirements for the system must still be elicited from the identified sources. A main goal of the elicitation activity is hence to elicit existing requirements from known requirement sources. For eliciting requirements, the requirements engineers, among other things, conduct interviews with stakeholders, examine laws and documents such as market analyses or the development documentation of other systems, and/or analyse existing systems e.g. by experimenting with these systems (see, e.g., [Gause and Weinberg 1989]). The elicitation of existing requirements from identified sources is hence an important sub-activity of requirements elicitation (see Section 21.5). This sub-activity roughly corresponds to the analysis of the current state in Systems Analysis (see Section 3.1).

Develop new and innovative requirements

Nevertheless, requirements elicitation goes beyond the mere identification of requirements from different sources. In addition, new and innovative requirements should be developed as part of the requirements elicitation activity. New requirements can result, for instance, from applying creativity techniques, resolving conflicts, or discussion among the stakeholders. Obviously, new and innovative requirements for the system to be developed are typically not contained in or known by any requirement source. New and innovative requirements are often developed by combining individual views, opinions, and ideas of stakeholders with different backgrounds and experiences. The creation of new, innovative requirements is hence the third sub-activity of requirements elicitation (see Section 21.6).

Elicitation of goals, scenarios, functional and quality requirements, and constraints

When speaking of requirements elicitation, we mean the elicitation of all requirement types presented in Section 2.2. Consequently, the three sub-activities described in this chapter deal with the elicitation of goals, scenarios, functional requirements, quality requirements as well as constraints for the system to be developed. Furthermore, the elicitation techniques described in Chapter 22 (e.g. interviews) and the assistance techniques described in Chapter 23 (e.g. checklists) can be used for the elicitation and development of basically all types of requirements, i.e. goals, scenarios, functional requirements, quality requirements, and constraints. However, some specifics of goals and scenarios with respect to requirements elicitation are explained in Section 21.3.

21.2 Requirements Elicitation: Definition

Requirements elicitation

Following the characterisation of the requirements elicitation activity in Section 21.1, we define this core requirements engineering activity as follows:

D

Definition 21-1: *Requirements elicitation*

Requirements elicitation is one of the three core requirements engineering activities. The goal of the elicitation activity is to:

(1) Identify relevant requirement sources
(2) Elicit existing requirements from the identified sources
(3) Develop new and innovative requirements

The attainment of these three sub-goals is facilitated by the three sub-activities:

- Identifying relevant requirement sources (Section 21.4)
- Eliciting existing requirements (Section 21.5)
- Developing new and innovative requirements (Section 21.6)

21.3 Use of Goals and Scenarios in Requirements Elicitation

Goals and scenarios as well as their interrelations and their synergetic effects are described in detail in Parts III.a and III.b. As pointed out in Chapter 12, goals and scenarios are well suited to support requirements elicitation. Goals and scenarios are elicited using techniques for eliciting existing requirements and developing new and innovative requirements.

In the following, we briefly sketch the specifics of goals and scenarios and provide hints for using goals and scenarios in requirements elicitation.

Defining goals first

Goals enable the stakeholders to document their intentions for the system to be developed quickly and easily (see Part III.a). Stakeholders may refine goals (e.g. in a workshop) and document the goal refinement using, for instance, a graphical representation (see Chapter 8). In principle, goal models are well suited for documenting the purpose of the system at an abstract level.

Defining scenarios

Scenarios describe concrete system interactions and hence enable the stakeholders to describe concrete examples of satisfying the identified goals (see Part III.b). Moreover, scenarios put the requirements in context (see Section 9.2), which supports the stakeholders' understanding of the requirements. Scenarios are typically used to document concrete sequences of interactions between the system and its external actors, i.e. interactions between the system and its context (see, e.g. [Carroll

2000; Weidenhaupt et al. 1989]). However, there are various types of scenarios and ways of documenting scenarios (see Chapter 10) which can be used in requirements elicitation.

Iterative goal and scenario definition

Analysing documented scenarios often leads to the identification of new goals and/or adjustments of already documented goals. Conversely, the changes in the goal definitions typically lead to the elicitation of new scenarios and/or the revision of already documented scenarios (see Section 12.3).

Derivation of requirements from goals and scenarios

We highly recommend using goals and scenarios in requirements elicitation, especially to support the development of new and innovative requirements.

!

Hint 21-1: *Using goals and scenarios for eliciting detailed requirements*

- ❑ Elicit and develop goals jointly with the various stakeholders.
- ❑ Define scenarios for the identified goals by documenting concrete examples of goal satisfaction. Consider also scenarios in which the goals are not satisfied.
- ❑ Analyse the scenarios and identify possible new goals and/or goal refinements: Which goals does the scenario fulfil? Are these goals already known? Do these goals complement, contradict, or refine an already existing goal?
- ❑ Define scenarios for the newly identified and/or refined goals and thereby establish an iterative goal–scenario development cycle.
- ❑ Derive solution-oriented requirements (i.e. functional requirements, quality requirements, and constraints) from the defined goals and scenarios.
- ❑ Document solution-oriented requirements based on the identified goals and scenarios: Which properties must the system have in order to satisfy the goals as well as the scenarios?

21.4 Sub-activity: Identifying Relevant Requirement Sources

The goal of this sub-activity is to identify all relevant requirement sources in the system context (see Definition 5-1). In each requirements engineering process, there are obvious, well-known requirement sources such as the legacy system, various documents (e.g. a user requirements document or a vision document), or already identified stakeholders such as users or the vision holder. However, many relevant requirement sources are initially unknown and hence must be elicited.

Consequences of missing relevant requirement sources

If relevant requirement sources are not identified, they obviously cannot be considered during requirements elicitation. Failing to consider relevant requirement sources during requirements elicitation typically leads to an incomplete requirements specification. An incomplete requirements specification leads to low quality of the resulting system, for example, if important functions and quality properties are omitted. In addition, development cost and time are needed for implementing requirements that have not been identified in the first place due to incomplete consideration of the relevant requirement sources.

For identifying unknown but relevant requirement sources, we propose a two-step procedure (see Fig. 21-1). First, the requirements engineers identify potential requirement sources (see Section 21.4.1). Second, the requirements engineers assess the

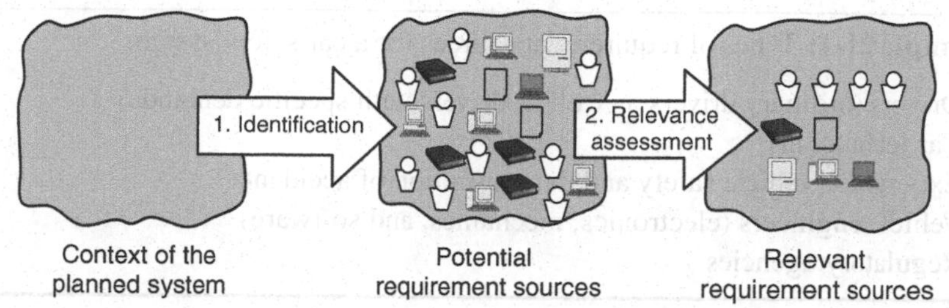

Fig. 21-1 *Identification of relevant requirement sources*

relevance of the identified sources. Based on this assessment, the relevant requirement sources to be considered during requirements elicitation are selected (see Section 21.4.2).

21.4.1 Identifying Potential Requirement Sources

The goal of this first step is to identify a large set of potential requirement sources. To identify potential requirement sources, we propose the following iterative procedure:

- ❑ Step 1: Identify additional, potential requirement sources (starting with the requirement sources already known) by
  - Asking already identified stakeholders for additional, potential requirement sources, e.g. by conducting interviews (see Section 22.3), workshops (see Section 22.4), or brainstorming sessions (see Section 23.2).
  - Checking already identified documents for additional, potential requirement sources, e.g. by analysing references to potential requirement sources contained in the documents or by means of perspective-based reading (see Section 22.8).
  - Analysing existing systems for additional potential requirement sources, e.g. by using a system with the goal in mind to identify and analyse the actors of this system (i.e. the roles of persons and other systems who interact with this system).
- ❑ Step 2: Record the newly identified, potential requirement sources in a list.
- ❑ Step 3: For each newly identified requirement source, perform "Step 1" again.

A general exit criterion for this procedure can hardly be defined. However, we suggest to iterate the steps until, in some iteration, the number of newly identified potential requirement sources becomes sufficiently low or even zero, i.e. until the set of identified requirement sources becomes (more or less) stable.

Checklists support identification

To support the identification of potential requirement sources, we suggest using checklists (see Section 23.6) which contain types of potentially relevant requirement sources (see Example 21-1 for examples of different types of requirement sources for a car safety system). For each type of requirement source, the context of the system should be analysed to identify potential instances of this type of requirement source.

Example 21-1: Types of requirement sources for a car safety system

- ❑ Drivers (ordinary drivers as well as drivers with specific demands)
- ❑ Car technicians
- ❑ Experts for vehicle safety and the prevention of accidents
- ❑ Vehicle engineers (electronics, mechanics, and software)
- ❑ Regulatory agencies

Consideration of all four context facets

In addition, we suggest defining a checklist for each context facet. Thus a checklist should be defined for each of the four facets containing important types of potential requirement sources. The stakeholders using such a checklist consider each type of requirement source to identify whether one or multiple instances of this type exist in the respective context facet.

Hint 21-2: *Consider all four context facets for identifying potential requirement sources:*

- ❑ Check the subject facet for potential requirement sources.
- ❑ Check the usage facet for potential requirement sources.
- ❑ Check the IT system facet for potential requirement sources.
- ❑ Check the development facet for potential requirement sources.

Comprehensive checklists

In Section 23.6, we provide comprehensive checklists for potential requirement sources. We provide a checklist for each of the four context facets as well as for the three types of requirement sources (stakeholders, documents, and existing systems). Example 21-2 shows an excerpt of a list of requirement sources for a car safety system. The list is structured according to the four context facets. In addition, the type of each requirement source is stated in parenthesis.

Example 21-2: Requirement sources for a car safety system

Subject facet:	IT system facet:
Bob Checker (accident assessor)	Betty Smith (car technician)
Chris Smith (physician)	Ute McDonald (car engineer)
	Peter Paul (sensor expert)
Usage facet:	Development facet:
Peter Miller (car driver)	Pit Mal (control unit expert)
Jim Wilde (professional driver)	John McNeel (engineer)
Manual V2.3	

Basic strategy for identifying potential requirement sources

Hint 21-3 summarises the basic strategy we recommend for identifying potential requirement sources. The strategy may be applied for each of the four context facet separately.

> **Hint 21-3:** *Iterative identification of potential requirement sources*
>
> (1) Ask already identified stakeholders for additional, potential requirement sources. Use checklists to support the interrogation of the stakeholders.
> (2) Search identified documents for additional, potential requirement sources by perspective-based reading (see Section 22.8).
> (3) Analyse existing systems for additional potential requirement sources, e.g. by examining the interactions with users and other systems.
> (4) For each newly identified requirement source, perform Step 1, 2, or 3 again.
>
> Stop the identification procedure if no or only very few (and potentially irrelevant) additional sources have been identified.

!

21.4.2 Selecting Relevant Sources

Not all identified sources can be considered

In principle, all identified potential requirement sources should be considered during requirements elicitation. In practice, the number of sources which can be considered is typically restricted by the resources (e.g. time, cost, availability of experts) that can be used for requirements elicitation. Therefore, only a subset of the identified, potential requirement sources can be considered during elicitation.

Assessing the relevance of a requirement source

The decision regarding whether an identified requirement source is considered or ignored during elicitation should be made based on the relative relevance of this requirement source. Ideally, assessing the relevance of each requirement source should be done objectively. However, an objective assessment of the relevance of each requirement source is time consuming and costly and thus almost not applicable in practice. We therefore recommend subjectively assessing the relevance of each requirement source.

Technique for Assessing the Relevance of Potential Requirement Sources

Technique to assess the relative relevance of requirement sources

The technique we suggest for assessing the relevance of the identified, potential requirement sources helps a group of stakeholders to assess the relevance of each source quickly and easily. The technique relies on the knowledge and intuition of the stakeholders involved and is based on a subjective relevance assessment technique known as the 100-dollar test (see [Gottesdiener 2002; Leffingwell and Widrig 2000]). The 100-dollar test allows a group of stakeholders to metaphorically spend money, 100 dollars, on the items to be assessed. Each stakeholder distributes the money on the different items. The average amount of money spent by the different stakeholders on a specific item denotes the relative weighting of that item.

Procedure for assessing relevance

We suggest determining the relative relevance of each identified, potential requirement source in a moderated group meeting by performing the following steps:

Assigning relevance points to stakeholders

1. Each stakeholder participating in the assessment of the relevance of the requirement sources gets a number of relevance points from the moderator. We recommend restricting the number of relevance points given to each stakeholder roughly by the number of potentially identified requirement sources divided by

three. For example, if 150 potential requirement sources have been identified, each stakeholder gets 50 relevance points.

Subjective, individual assessment of relevance

2. Each stakeholder subjectively assesses the relevance of each requirement source based on his/her knowledge and intuition. Based on their subjective assessment of relevance, each stakeholder distributes his/her relevance points on the requirement sources. Accumulation is not allowed, i.e. a stakeholder must not assign multiple relevance points to one requirement source.

   As a variation, one can allow the accumulation of up to three points per requirement source. In this case, the number of relevance points given to each stakeholder should roughly be the number of identified, potential requirement sources divided by two. For example, if 100 potential requirement sources have been identified, each stakeholder would get 50 relevance points, instead of 33 if no accumulation is allowed.

Sorting requirement sources based on relevance assessment

3. After the assignment of the relevance points by each stakeholder, the requirement sources are sorted according to the relevance points received. The sources with the highest numbers of relevance points are listed first.

Based on the list of requirement sources sorted according to the relevance assessment, the group (or the moderator) can now divide the sources into two subsets. The first subset contains the requirement sources to be considered during the elicitation. The second subset comprises the requirement sources for which (at least at this point in time) the decision has been made that these sources shall not be considered during requirements elicitation.

Selection of relevant requirement sources

The cut-off point for adding a requirement source to the subset of sources to be considered during elicitation can be chosen based on the result of the assessment. For example, the participants can decide that all requirement sources that have received at least one relevance point should be considered (if the number is not too large), or that all sources with at least three relevance points should be considered, or the top 50 ranked sources should be considered, etc.

Alternatively, the group may also decide to re-execute the assessment with a subset of the requirement sources (e.g. the ones with at least two relevance points), especially if the number of sources which have received at least one relevance point is still large.

Selection of sources is context sensitive

However, there is no general rule for the decision on how many requirement sources or which requirement sources should be considered during elicitation. The selection of the relevant sources as well as the definition of the upper bound of sources to be considered has to take into account the specific project, domain, type of system etc. Consequently, these decisions should be made by experienced requirements engineers and in cooperation with the other stakeholders.

Considering all Four Context Facets

Select requirement sources from all four context facets

Determining the relevance of requirement sources using the technique described above does not ensure an equal or adequate consideration of all four context facets (see Chapter 6). In other words, the selected relevant requirement sources might not adequately represent the four context facets. For example, requirement sources might be selected which mainly belong to the usage facet, or the IT system facet etc. If one (or even multiple) context facets are not adequately represented in the list of requirement sources to be considered during elicitation, there is a high chance that the elicited requirements will be incomplete.

When selecting the relevant requirement sources, the four context facets should hence be explicitly taken into account. For example, one of the following options can be chosen to explicitly consider the four context facets during the selection of requirement sources to be considered:

At least check whether all four facets are represented in the selected sources

- Check after the selection whether the selected requirement sources adequately represent the four context facets. If shortcomings are identified, re-execute the relevance assessment and/or select different requirement sources from the list of ranked, potentially relevant requirement sources (if not all sources with at least one relevance point have already been selected).

Execute the selection process for each context facet separately

- Classify the requirement sources according to the four facets and execute the technique for selecting the relevant sources for each facet separately (see Hint 21-4). Therein, different stakeholders can be involved in performing the assessment for each context facet. As a result, you obtain a list of relevant requirement sources for each context facet, i.e. four separate lists of relevant requirement sources. The final selection of the relevant requirement sources can either be made by all stakeholders or just by selecting the top ranks from each of the four context-facet-specific lists.

Project- and domain-specific aspects

If required, the presented technique can be further enhanced by taking additional, domain- and/or project-specific factors into account, such as particular laws, regulations, standards, mission-critical factors, etc.

!

Hint 21-4: *Assess the relevance of requirement sources for each context facet separately*

The assessment of the relevance of the identified, potential requirement sources should be performed separately for each context facet. Thereby, equal consideration of all four facets is guaranteed, which is an important prerequisite for equal consideration of the four facets during requirements elicitation.

In addition, when selecting the stakeholders who perform the assessment of the identified requirement sources, the four context facets should be taken into account in order to ensure that each of the four facets is adequately represented in the selection process.

21.5 Sub-activity: Eliciting Existing Requirements

In the following, we describe how existing requirements can be elicited from the relevant requirement sources, i.e. relevant stakeholders, relevant documents, and relevant existing systems (see Fig. 21-2).

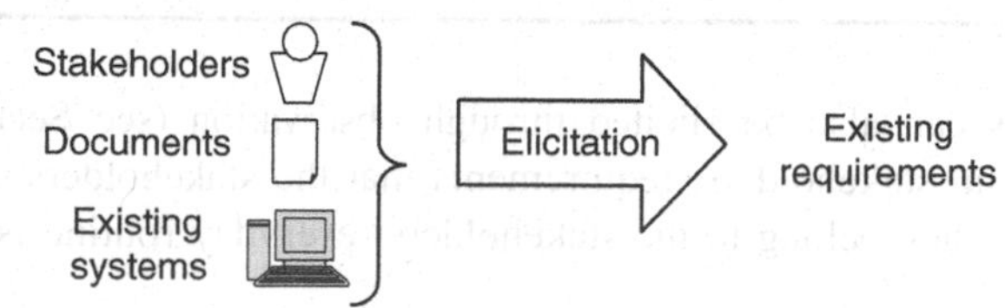

Fig. 21-2 *Sources of existing requirements*

21.5.1 Eliciting Existing Requirements from Stakeholders

Existing requirements can be elicited from stakeholders through conversations, questionnaires, or observation.

Elicitation through conversations

In a conversation, a stakeholder tells the requirements engineer his or her requirements. Conversations may take place within interviews (see Section 22.3) or during workshops (see Section 22.4). Example 21-3 illustrates how requirements are elicited in an interview.

Example 21-3: Requirements elicitation in an interview

Interviewer: "You have said that the car safety system shall keep a safe following distance. What do you mean by that? Could you draw a small sketch to clarify your requirement?"

Stakeholder: "I think of a situation in which the car drives at a high speed – let's say 65 mph – on the motorway. The distance to the car driving ahead becomes shorter. By a sensor, the car measures the distance to the car in front of it." (The stakeholder draws a sketch.) "If the distance is less than 300 feet, a yellow warning signal shall light up."

Interviewer: "What shall happen, if the driver does not react to this warning?"

Stakeholder: "If the distance decreases down to 200 feet, the warning signal shall turn from yellow to red and the driver's attention shall be called to the threat by an acoustic signal."

Elicitation by means of questionnaires

During the elicitation of requirements by means of questionnaires (see Section 22.7), the stakeholders write down their requirements themselves. Example 21-4 shows an excerpt from a questionnaire and the answers that were written down by a stakeholder.

Example 21-4: Requirements elicitation with questionnaires

Question 12: How can the safety of a car in the winter time be improved?

The safety system displays the safety status of the car to the driver at any time. The system displays, for example, a warning when the outside temperature is below 5°C and hence there is a high probability of icy roads.

Question 13: In your opinion, how can the risk of rear-end collisions be decreased?

The safety system checks the distance to cars driving ahead at regular intervals and warns the driver if the distance gets critically low.

Elicitation by means of observation

Requirements can also be elicited through observation (see Section 22.5). By observing relevant stakeholders, requirements that the stakeholders cannot express directly because they belong to the stakeholders' everyday routine (see e.g. [Beyer and Holzblatt 1998]) can be elicited particularly well. Example 21-5 illustrates how requirements for a car safety system can be elicited by means of observation.

Example 21-5: Requirements elicitation by observation

In order to elicit requirements for a car safety system, the requirements engineers observe different drivers (professional drivers, couriers, and chauffeurs) while driving a car and applying the brakes. The requirements engineers observe that many drivers apply the brakes already when the second or third car ahead brakes. Based on this observation, the requirements engineers define the requirement that the car safety system shall not only monitor the distance to the car driving directly ahead but also the distance to the second and, if possible, the third car ahead.

Acceptance criteria

When eliciting requirements from the relevant requirement sources, and in particular during interviews with clients, the requirements engineers should pay attention to potential acceptance criteria, i.e. measurable requirements that need to be demonstrably fulfilled in order to pass the system acceptance test (see Section 16.4). If the requirements engineers elicit a requirement that is a candidate for an acceptance criterion they should document this requirement and mark it as a potential acceptance criterion.

21.5.2 Eliciting Existing Requirements from Documents

In order to elicit existing requirements from documents, the requirements engineers have to read and analyse the relevant documents.

Example 21-6: Extract from a law for safety-critical systems in vehicles

All electronic systems in a vehicle that directly or indirectly influence the occupants' safety or the safety of other traffic participants must be designed in such a way that failure of the electronic system has no negative effects on safety.

The law from Example 21-6 must be considered during the design of the car safety system. As a result of analysing the law, the requirements engineers may define, for instance, the following two goals: "G1: The driver shall be able to override the actions of the system at any time" and "G2: The system must not disturb any other system even in the case of a system failure."

Techniques for reducing effort

Often, there is a large amount of written information such as specifications, standards, or laws that needs to be considered when developing a system. It is important, especially when faced with limited resources, to perform the elicitation of requirements from the relevant documents at an acceptable effort. For this purpose, perspective-based reading may be employed. Perspective-based reading (see Section 22.8) is a technique to support dealing with a large amount of written information.

21.5.3 Eliciting Existing Requirements from Existing Systems

Requirements that are implemented in an existing system can be elicited directly from the existing system, from stakeholders who are familiar with the system, or from documents about the existing system (such as user documentation or error reports).

Using or observing the system

The requirements engineers can elicit existing requirements that are implemented in a system by using the system or by observing the system (see Section 22.5). In the latter case, the requirements engineers either observe the behaviour of the system during its operation or by observing the system while it is used by some stakeholders.

Interviewing stakeholders of the system

In addition, existing requirements may be elicited by means of interviews with users or other stakeholders of the existing system (see Section 22.3). For example, requirements for the new system can be derived from the stakeholders' statements about necessary improvements of the existing system.

Analysing the documentation of existing systems

Finally, requirements may be elicited from documents about the existing system. In particular, the requirements engineers should analyse error reports as well as maintenance reports of legacy systems. By analysing these documents, the stakeholders can avoid making the same errors again during the development of the new system (see Example 21-7) or that the same defects occur in the new system, once again.

Example 21-7: Eliciting existing requirements from error reports

In an error report of a legacy system, the following error has been recorded:

Error FA-2003-1-10-F3: "The airstream cools the sensor that is responsible for measuring the outside temperature. Therefore, the displayed outside temperature is incorrect (too low), especially when driving at high speed."

Error Correction: Install a shielding to protect the temperature sensor from the airstream (see Correction Report K-B-2003-4-12-k5).

21.6 Sub-activity: Developing New and Innovative Requirements

New and innovative requirements cannot be elicited in the same way as existing requirements are elicited, i.e. by interviewing stakeholders, analysing documents, and observing existing systems. Rather, new and innovative requirements have to be developed in a creative process. The elicitation of new and innovative requirements can be supported to some extent by creativity techniques (see Fig. 21-3) such as brainstorming (see Section 23.2) or the Osborn checklist (see Section 23.6.4).

According to experience, innovative requirements emerge from bringing together different stakeholders with different views, from generating ideas (that may be very vague, initially), and even from requirements that appear to be conflicting but can be realised by means of a new, innovative solution. However, a prerequisite for successful creation of new and innovative requirements is successful cooperation of the different stakeholders. This is expressed, among other things, by [Gause and

Weinberg 1989],[1] who state that requirements engineering is a development process performed by a team of people. Unfortunately, the potential of creative requirements engineering is often underestimated in practice. For example, the requirements engineers are not provided with the degree of freedom needed for developing new and innovative requirements, and important creativity meetings such as requirements workshops are rarely held, e.g. due to time and cost constraints.

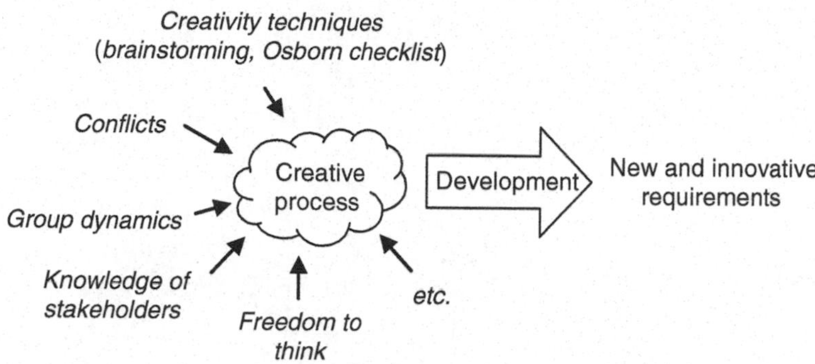

Fig. 21-3 *Elicitation of new and innovative requirements*

[1] [Gause and Weinberg 1989] describe the development of requirements as follows: "[...] developing requirements is actually a process of developing a team of people who
(1) understand the requirements,
(2) (mostly) stay together to work on the project,
(3) know how to work effectively as a team."

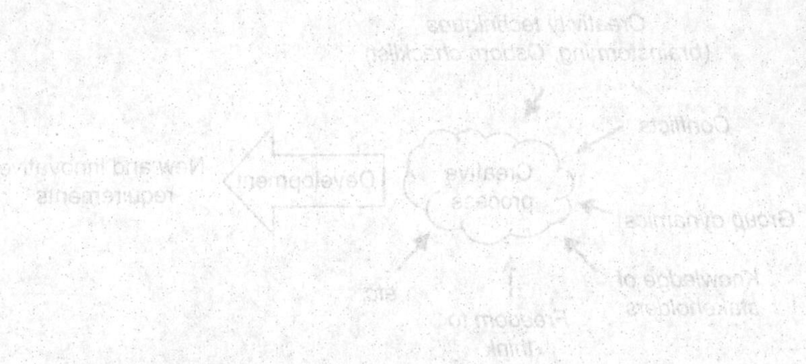

Chapter 22
Elicitation Techniques

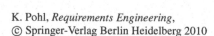

In this chapter, we explain:

- *Our template for the description of elicitation techniques*
- *Six techniques for requirements elicitation*

For each technique, we present:

- *Hints for preparation, execution, and follow-up work of the technique*
- *The benefits of the technique for the elicitation sub-activities*
- *An effort estimation for the technique*
- *Critical success factors of the technique*
- *A checklist with important hints for applying the technique*

22.1 Evaluation of the Techniques

In this chapter, we present the following six techniques for requirements elicitation:

- ❑ Interview (see Section 22.3)
- ❑ Workshop (see Section 22.4)
- ❑ Focus groups (see Section 22.5)
- ❑ Observation (see Section (22.6)
- ❑ Questionnaire (see Section 22.7)
- ❑ Perspective-based reading (see Section 22.8)

Effort and suitability for the three elicitation sub-activities

The six techniques differ with regard to the effort needed for applying each technique and their suitability for supporting the three sub-activities of requirements elicitation (see Chapter 21): identifying relevant requirement sources, eliciting existing requirements, and developing new and innovative requirements. Table 22-1 characterises the suitability of the individual techniques for each of the three sub-activities.

Tab. 22-1 *Suitability of the elicitation techniques for the three sub-activities*

Suitability of the technique for the sub-activities Technique	Effort	*Identifying requirement sources*	*Eliciting existing requirements*	*Developing new and innovative requirements*
Interview	Medium to high	✓	✓	✓
Workshop	High to very high	✓	✓	✓
Focus groups	Medium to high		✓	✓
Observation	High to very high		✓	
Questionnaire	Low to medium	✓	✓	
Perspective-based reading	Medium to high		✓	

22.2 Template for Describing the Techniques

We describe the elicitation techniques presented in this chapter and the assistance techniques in Chapter 23 as well as the techniques in Part V by means of a common template. The template eases access to these techniques and supports their comparison. The template consists of the following sections:

1. *Preparation*: This section describes the necessary actions for preparing the execution of a technique.
2. *Execution*: This section describes the essentials of performing the technique. If applicable, steps of the technique are presented and explained.

3. *Follow-up*: This section describes necessary actions to be executed after having performed the technique, such as required follow-up work.
4. *Checklist for applying the technique*: This section sums up the actions for the preparation, execution, and follow-up work of the technique in a comprehensive list.
5. *Benefit for the requirements engineering activity (e.g. requirements elicitation)*: This section describes in which way the technique supports the particular requirements engineering activity such as the requirements elicitation activity. In this chapter and Chapter 23, the suitability of the technique for each of the three sub-activities of requirements elicitation is explained.
6. *Effort*: In this section, a rough estimation of the effort for the application of the technique is given based on the effort categories presented in Fig. 22-1.
7. *Critical success factors*: This section describes critical factors that need to be considered for successful application of the technique (with respect to preparation, execution, and/or follow-up, as appropriate).

very high	high	medium	low	very low

Fig. 22-1 *Scheme for classifying the effort of the techniques and assistance techniques presented in this book*

22.3 Interview

Eliciting requirements and context information

The goal of conducting an interview in requirements engineering is to elicit requirements and context information for the system to be developed from a stakeholder or group of stakeholders. Basically, three kinds of interviews can be distinguished: standardised interviews, exploratory interviews, and unstructured interviews (see e.g. [Oppenheim 1999]).

Standardised interview

During a standardised interview, the interviewer asks the interviewee prepared questions concerning an issue of interest. Independently of the answers given, the interviewer does not deviate from the prepared questions. The standardised interview is appropriate when the opinions of many stakeholders concerning the same issue shall be canvassed. The results of standardised interviews are easier to compare due to the standardised list of questions.

Exploratory interview

An exploratory interview is a conversation by means of which the interviewer elicits information about the opinion or view of the interviewee with respect to some issue. The interview is based on a list of prepared questions that the interviewer poses to the interviewee. During an exploratory interview, the interviewer may deviate from the prepared questions, for instance, for a further enquiry regarding some answer given by the interviewee. The results of such an interview are qualitative. Hence, results of different exploratory interviews concerning the same issue are difficult to compare with each other.

Unstructured interview

Unstructured interviews typically do not make use of a prepared question catalogue. The interviewer freely asks broad questions and allows the interviewee to lead the conversation in a direction at his/her own discretion. The results of different unstructured interviews are very difficult, if not impossible, to compare. We hence recommend applying standardised or exploratory interviews for requirements elicitation.

Individual or group interviews

Furthermore, one can differentiate between individual and group interviews:

- *Individual interview*: During an individual interview, a single stakeholder answers the questions. The results of an individual interview hence reflect the opinion of one stakeholder.
- *Group interview*: During a group interview, a group of stakeholders answer the questions. The answers of different stakeholders to a question influence each other; they develop from the participants' conversation. The results of a group interview hence reflect the opinion of the group.

Influence of the particular kind of interview on the application of the technique

The preparation, execution, and follow-up actions of an interview are, in principle, the same regardless of the kind of interview (exploratory or standardised) and the number of participants (individual interviewee or group of interviewees). Hence, we describe preparation, execution, and follow-up actions of interviews in general and point out the differences with regard to the kind of interview and the number of participants where necessary.

22.3.1 Preparation

Defining the Goal of the Interview

Explicit definition of the goal

The definition of the goal of an interview should include the reason for performing the interview and indicate the expected results. The explicit definition of the goal of the interview supports the preparation and execution of the interview. We recommend, in addition, including in the definition of the goal the type(s) of requirements to be elicited during the interview, e.g. goals or scenarios (see Example 22-1).

Example 22-1: Goal of an interview

The goal of the interview is to refine the vision "accident-free driving". For this purpose, the intentions and ideas of the interviewees regarding the vision shall be elicited. The result of the interview shall be a set of goals which refine the vision. In addition, a few basic scenarios for accident-free driving shall be developed during the interview.

Selecting and Inviting Participants

Selection of the participants

Based on the goal of the interview, the participants for the interview are selected from the group of potential stakeholders (if applicable, by determining their relative importance using the technique presented in Section 21.4).

Timely invitation

The participants should be invited to the interview in due time (approximately 3 weeks in advance) in order to ensure the availability of the participants for the interview. The earlier the participants are invited, the higher the probability that they will be available for the interview.

In the context of the invitation, the participants should be informed about the goal of the interview. This motivates the participants and allows them to prepare for the interview and, if applicable, to provide the interviewer with relevant materials such as documents.

Communicating the goal of the interview

We recommend informing the participants additionally about the status and rationale of the system development as well as the planned use of the results of the interview. From this background information, the stakeholders can recognise what contributions to the system development process are expected from them.

Communicating the rationale in the invitation

Choosing the Interview Location

For conducting an interview, an undisturbed environment is needed, so that the interview participant(s) may concentrate completely on the interview. An interview at a participant's workplace has the advantage that documents can be easily accessed. However, conducting an interview at the participant's workplace should still be avoided because unplanned interruptions are very likely to occur.

Undisturbed environment

For group interviews, the location should offer sufficient space for all participants.

Defining the Interview Questions

Based on the goal of the interview, the requirements engineers have to develop appropriate questions that the interviewees shall answer. This especially holds for the standardised interview, where only predefined questions are posed. Example 22-2 shows an excerpt from a list of interview questions.

Working out a list of questions

Example 22-2: Excerpt from an interview questionnaire for the subject "car safety system"

- ❑ What does the term "safety in the car" mean for you?
- ❑ Which threats in traffic do you regard as critical?
- ❑ Which driver activities can be influenced by a car safety system?

Two basic kinds of interview questions can be distinguished:

- ❑ *Closed questions*: For each question, different response options are provided. The interviewee can choose one or multiple responses.
- ❑ *Open questions*: The interviewee is not provided with predefined response options. He answers the question in his own words.

Closed questions provide either a defined number of response options (alternative A, B, or C) or an interval within which the answers shall fall ("How old are you?" 1–99 years). Closed questions can be applied in order to investigate an issue that is well understood and where the possible answers are known in advance. A closed question is presented in Example 22-3. Since the available communication channels for the navigation system to be developed are known, the requirements engineers employ a closed question for the interview in this example.

Closed questions

Example 22-3: Closed question for requirements elicitation

The car navigation system shall be able to exchange data with other end devices such as mobile phones. Which means of communication shall be supported for the exchange of data with these devices?

- ❑ Serial interface
- ❑ Universal serial bus (USB) interface
- ❑ Infrared interface
- ❑ Bluetooth
- ❑ Wireless local area network (LAN)
- ❑ Memory cards (e.g. SD or CompactFlash cards)

Closed questions may be answered quickly and easily. The answers are directly comparable, since the interviewee can only choose between the given alternatives. This simplifies the analysis of the results. The disadvantage of closed questions is that no new answers or new ideas can be elicited.

Boolean question

A special type of closed question is a Boolean question. A Boolean question can be answered with "yes" or "no". Answers to these questions rarely allow deeper insight into the topic of the question. If the goal of the interview is to explore a topic in depth, it is important to minimise the use of Boolean questions. However, Boolean questions can be a useful tool to disambiguate answers of the interviewee. For instance, when the interviewee is asked a potentially uncomfortable question, he or she may answer evasively. Rephrasing the question in a way that requires a concrete answer (i.e. "yes" or "no") can help in this case.

Open questions

Open questions allow the interviewee to answer in his own words. Therefore, open questions are well suited for investigating issues that are not yet well understood. Open questions inspire the interviewee to express his opinion about an issue freely. However, the comparability of the answers given by different stakeholders to an open question is limited.

Example 22-4: Open question for requirements elicitation

Describe an ideal car safety system. How does the system recognise threats for the driver and how does it react to the detected threats?

Questions with a concrete context

Questions asked in an interview should be as concrete as possible so that the interviewee has a starting point for his answer. For example, the request, "Please tell us your aim for the system", is appropriate to elicit requirements for the system, but the elicited requirements will pertain to all aspects of the system. We recommend embedding the questions in a context that is as concrete as possible (e.g. usage context or system maintenance context). The four context facets (Part II) support finding an appropriate embedding. The question in Example 22-5 is targeted at eliciting information about the usage facet.

Example 22-5: Focussing interview questions through context facets

Could you name typical situations while driving a car in which motorists and cyclists are in danger?

A leading question is a question that suggests the interviewee's answer (see [Alexander and Stevens 2002]). Leading questions start, for example, with the expression "Don't you think that..." or "Isn't it true that...". Since leading questions suggest the answer, they are not suitable for eliciting information about the stakeholders' actual needs and views. Requirements engineers must therefore pay attention not to ask leading questions during an interview.

Avoid leading questions

Preparing for the Interviews

Before performing an interview, the interviewer should find out as much as possible about the interviewees. He should learn, for instance, about the personality of the interviewees, their position in the organisation, and their knowledge and responsibilities. The better the interviewer is prepared, the better he may influence the course of an open interview in a fruitful way. For example, retrieving background information about the interviewee can be done by asking the participants to fill out a pre-interview questionnaire in advance. Pre-interview questionnaires, also known as pre-test or pre-hoc questionnaires typically comprise demographics and very coarse questions concerning the topic of the interview.

Making oneself familiar with the participants

Each domain has its own terminology. Different terms often have different meanings for the interviewer and the interviewees. Due to these different meanings, misunderstandings emerge that influence the results of the interview negatively. Therefore, the interviewer and the interviewees need a common terminology, i.e. a terminology that is consistent for all participants. In general, this should be the terminology that is familiar to the stakeholders. The interviewer should therefore learn the stakeholders' terminology before performing the interviews and thereby avoid misunderstandings during the interview.

Knowing the participants' terminology

If a large number of stakeholders shall be interviewed in separate interviews, often, several interviewers conduct the interviews, e.g. in order to carry out the interviews within an acceptable time. In this case, the interviewers need to define a common approach so that all interviews proceed, as far as possible, in the same way. The interviewers should especially agree upon a common understanding of the interview questions and, if applicable, upon the given response options.

Agreement among the interviewers

22.3.2 Execution

We divide the execution of an interview into the phases opening, work element, and finalisation.

Opening

If the interview partners do not know each other, we recommend allowing at first a phase during which the partners get to know each other in an informal conversation.

During the opening of the interview, the interviewer explains the goal of the interview, provides information on the rationale for the interview, and explains how the results will be used. These explanations should briefly sum up the explanations contained in the invitation to the interview (see Section 22.3.1). However, the

Explaining the goal of the interview

stakeholder(s) should also be provided with some additional information. During the opening, the interviewer also answers the stakeholders' questions regarding the goal of the interview, the rationale, and the intended use of the interview results.

Introducing question

During an exploratory interview, the transition from the opening to the actual interview can be facilitated by a general question. The answers to a general question provide a good basis for the further conversation. An example of such a question for a vehicle safety system is given in Example 22-6.

Example 22-6: Beginning of an interview

Interviewer: How do you envisage a system that is able to keep a safe distance to the vehicle driving ahead?

Work Element

Providing feedback and asking questions

During the interview, the interviewer should always provide feedback to the interviewee on the elicited information. For this purpose, the interviewer may ask further questions concerning the elicited information (i.e. make enquiries) or briefly summarise the answers given by the interviewee. In this way, the interviewee is able to check whether the interviewer has understood the considered issue correctly. As a continuation of Example 22-6, Example 22-7 shows how an interviewer provides feedback ("measured by the sensors…") and, at the same time, continues the conversation ("…how shall the driver be warned?") by making an enquiry.

Example 22-7: Feedback in an interview

Interviewee: I think the car measures the distance to the vehicle driving ahead by means of sensors and warns the driver if the distance gets too low.

Interviewer: Let us assume that the distance measured by the sensors is too low. How shall the system warn the driver?

Making enquiries is especially important when the interviewer has not understood an issue completely or when he is not sure whether he has understood the issue correctly.

Creating simple models

Another way to provide immediate feedback to the interviewee about the elicited information is to document the stated facts using simple conceptual models (see e.g. [Alexander and Stevens 2002; Robertson and Robertson 2006]). The fundamentals of conceptual modelling are explained in Chapter 19. The interviewer may, for instance, document the system behaviour that is described in the interview in a simple behavioural model (see Section 14.3). In addition, sketching conceptual models during an interview supports the detection of aspects that are incomplete. If the interviewer detects such aspects he can investigate them further already during the interview itself.

Using scenarios

Another way to provide feedback and to handle the elicited knowledge is to document the information using scenarios. For instance, as explained in Section 9.3, aspects of system usage can be documented using scenarios. The creation of scenarios during an interview has the same positive effects as the creation of conceptual models, in general. In addition, scenarios are significantly easier to create than, for example, state models or data models. Furthermore, the risk of running off topic and focussing on the details of the model during the interview is reduced.

Paying attention to non-verbal communication

In addition to verbal communication, during an interview, also non-verbal communication plays an essential role. Gestures and tone of voice (see [Schulz von Thun 2005]) provide the interviewer with additional clues for interpreting the interviewee's answers. For instance, an aggressive tone in an answer indicates that the interviewer has addressed a subject that is inconvenient or embarrassing for the interviewee. In this case, the interviewer may either considerately and carefully investigate the subject by asking further questions, for instance, with the aim to identify conflicts concerning requirements (see Part IV.c). Alternatively, the interviewer may change the subject in order to frame it in a situation which is more suitable. Non-verbal reactions also indicate tacit knowledge (see [Polanyi 1958]) and implicit requirements. An answer from the interviewee conveying the message "That's obvious, why should we talk about this?" indicates that the interviewer has identified an implicit requirement. [Bray 2002] stresses the fact that good requirements engineers notice unexpected reactions to questions (e.g. when stakeholders knit their brows) and react accordingly.

Taking breaks

An interview is exhausting for all participants. Therefore, we recommend taking short breaks of about 5–10 min at regular intervals (approximately every 45 min). Short breaks improve the concentration of both the interviewee and the interviewer.

Focussing on the subject

During an interview, the conversation may run off topic and get stuck in details that may be interesting but are of little relevance to the goal of the interview. The interviewer is therefore responsible for ensuring that the conversation keeps to the point.

Documenting results

During the interview, the results must be documented in an appropriate way. This can be achieved, for example, by means of a written protocol, a video, or an audio record. We recommend that, especially during important interviews, an additional person should participate in the interview, being responsible for taking the minutes. This has the advantage that the interviewer can fully concentrate on the conversation with the interviewee. In addition, the interviewer does not have to interrupt the conversation to take notes.

Finalisation

Summing up

In order to finalise the interview, the interviewer briefly sums up the most important results of the interview for the interviewee. In this way, the interviewee can check again if his statements were understood correctly.

Providing positive feedback

During the summary, the interviewer should point out the most important conclusions that he has come to by conducting the interview. Thereby, the interviewer communicates to the interviewee that he has made an important contribution to the development of the system. An interview partner that is motivated in this way is more likely to be available for further interviews and for potential enquiries.

Expressing gratitude to the participants

At the end of the interview, the interviewer should explicitly thank the interviewee for his participation. If the interviewer shows his appreciation, this additionally motivates the interviewee to be available for enquiries or further interviews.

22.3.3 Follow-up

Analysing the results

After the interview, the interviewer analyses the results of the interview. During the follow-up phase of the interview, the final minutes are created, elicited requirements are documented, and created models and scenarios are validated. Identified gaps, contradictions, or inconsistencies are documented explicitly.

Asking the interviewees to confirm the results

We recommend sending the analysed results to the interviewees and asking them to check and confirm the results. If the amount of results from the interview is too large, we recommend asking the interviewees to check and confirm at least the elicited requirements. This kind of validation of the results of the interview by the interviewees reveals misunderstandings and, in addition, explicitly points out the interviewees' contribution.

22.3.4 Checklist for Applying the Technique

Hint 22-1 presents a checklist for the preparation, execution, and follow-up phases of an interview.

!

Hint 22-1: *Checklist for interviews*

Preparation – Interview goal:

- ❑ Explicitly define the goal of the interview.

Preparation – Interview participants:

- ❑ Choose the participants based on the goal of the interview.
- ❑ Invite all participants in due time.
- ❑ Communicate the goal and rationale of the interview to the participants.

Preparation – Interview location:

- ❑ Choose a location for the interview that provides an undisturbed environment and accommodates all participants.

Preparation – Interview questions:

- ❑ Use open as well as closed interview questions.
- ❑ Write all questions with as concrete a context as possible.
- ❑ Avoid leading questions.

Preparation – Preparation of the interviewer:

- ❑ Familiarise yourself with the interview partners.
- ❑ Learn the terminology of the participants.
- ❑ If several interviewers are involved, establish a common understanding of the interview questions among them.

(to be continued)

Hint 22-1 (*continued*)

Execution – Opening:

- ❑ At the beginning, sum up the goal and rationale of the interview for the interviewees.
- ❑ If possible, provide additional information beyond that provided in the invitation.
- ❑ Start the interview with an introductory question.

Execution – Work element:

- ❑ Ensure that the elicited information is correct by summing it up for the interviewee and clarifying unclear issues.
- ❑ Create models and/or scenarios during the interview in order to get immediate feedback from the interviewee.
- ❑ Pay attention to the non-verbal communication of the interviewees.
- ❑ Take regular breaks (approximately every 45 min).
- ❑ Do not run off topic.
- ❑ Document the results of the interview.

Execution – Finalisation:

- ❑ Sum up the elicited knowledge.
- ❑ Point out to the interviewees the importance of their contributions.
- ❑ Express your gratitude to the interviewees.

Follow-up:

- ❑ Finalise the interview minutes.
- ❑ Document the elicited requirements.
- ❑ Revise the created models and scenarios.
- ❑ Collect open issues in a to-do list.
- ❑ Distribute the results to the interviewees.
- ❑ Ask the interviewees to check and confirm the results.
- ❑ Identify requirements conflicts in the results of the interview and resolve them using the techniques presented in Part IV.c.

22.3.5 Benefit for Requirements Elicitation

Identifying Relevant Requirement Sources

Standardised interview with checklist

For identifying potential requirement sources, standardised interviews can be applied. Suitable interview questions for identifying requirement sources can be derived from the checklists presented in Section 23.6.4.

During the interview, the interviewer presents the questions or the checklist items to the interviewee. At the end of the interview, the interviewee should be asked to provide an estimation of the relevance of the stated requirement sources.

Eliciting Existing Requirements

Elicitation in a conversation

The stakeholders' requirements can be elicited directly during the interview without resorting to other means. The interviewer and the interviewee may, for example, develop goals and scenarios together and, subsequently, derive requirements from the goals and scenarios.

Developing requirements during interviews is especially advisable if the stakeholders' views differ significantly, if there are conflicts between different stakeholders or if the problem is very complex. In these cases, performing interviews first, and then discussing the results in workshops, has proven useful.

The following two examples present fragments of a fictional interview. In Example 22-8, the interviewer asks the interviewee to explain a previously stated goal by means of an example (a scenario). In order to continue the conversation, the interviewer further enquires regarding a part of the scenario described in Example 22-9. As a result, the interviewee refines the scenario.

Example 22-8: Asking the interviewee to explain a stated goal

Interviewer: You have said that you want to attain the goal "keeping a safe distance" with the car safety system. How do you imagine that? Could you explain it using an example?

Interviewee: I imagine a situation in which the car drives at high velocity – let's say 65 mph – on the motorway. The distance to the vehicle driving ahead is decreasing. The car measures the distance by means of a sensor. If the distance gets less than 330 feet (approximately 100 m), a yellow warning signal is displayed. The driver does not react. Thus, the distance decreases more and more.

At a distance of 250 feet (approximately 75 m) the warning signal turns from yellow to red. Additionally, the driver is pointed to the potential threat by an acoustic warning signal.

Example 22-9: Interviewee refines a scenario with regard to goal satisfaction

Interviewer: I wonder if the goal "keeping a safe distance" is actually attained in your example. What happens if the driver ignores the red warning signal?

Interviewee: At a distance of 170 feet (approximately 50 m) – I think this is the legal minimum distance for trucks – the system initiates an automatic breaking manoeuvre and hence ensures that the distance to the vehicle driving ahead does not fall below 170 feet (approximately 50 m).

Developing New and Innovative Requirements

Open interviews

Although an interview is not primarily intended for developing new and innovative requirements, innovative requirements may be obtained, especially during an open interview. The development of new and innovative requirements can be supported by skilful questions and by confronting the interviewee with early solution ideas. During group interviews, innovative requirements may result from discussions between the participants, or they may be elicited by inserting brainstorming sessions (see Section 23.2).

22.3.6 Effort

Effort for conducting the interviews

The effort involved in performing interviews depends essentially on the number of interviewees, the number and the types of questions asked (open or closed) as well as the way in which minutes are taken. If individual interviews as opposed to group interviews are performed, the interviews may absorb a lot of time. By performing group interviews, the time effort can generally be reduced to an acceptable level.

very high	high	medium	low	very low
	(✓)	✓		

Fig. 22-2 *Effort for interviews*

Analysis effort

Besides the execution of the interview, the follow-up work after the interview also takes some effort. Depending on the type of interview and the way of in which the minutes are taken, the effort required for the follow-up work may differ significantly. For instance, the analysis of audio recordings of stakeholders answering open questions requires, generally, a high effort, whereas the analysis of answers to closed questions requires little effort.

All in all, the effort required for an interview has to be rated as medium to high. In spite of this, interviews have proven useful for requirements elicitation and represent a standard technique for eliciting existing requirements.

22.3.7 Critical Success Factors

Communication skills

The quality of the results of an interview depends essentially on the communication skills of the interviewer. Experienced requirements engineers and those trained in communication are generally able to elicit more information from interviewees than inexperienced interviewers.

No leading questions

The interviewer should pose the interview questions without suggesting the interviewee's answers. Phrases like "Don't you think that..." indicate leading questions and hence should be avoided.

Clearly defined and communicated goal

A clear goal and a clear idea of the expected results are essential for a successful interview. In addition, expectations concerning the goal and the results of the interview must be communicated to the interviewees.

Terminology

The use of common terminology during the interview avoids misunderstandings. The interviewer should therefore familiarise himself with the terminology of the interviewees or of the interviewees' domain. During the interview, the interviewer is responsible for identifying and resolving ambiguities concerning the terminology.

Getting to know the interview partners

Prior to performing the interview, the interviewer should familiarise himself with the interview partners e.g. by learning about their tasks and their position in the organisation.

Avoiding the groupthink effect

In a group interview, the so-called groupthink effect (see [Janis 1982], cited in [Marakas 2002]) may occur. The groupthink effect refers to the tendency of less dominant participants to (prematurely) agree with more dominant participants' suggestions. If the requirements engineer expects that the groupthink effect might occur in the group of stakeholders to be interviewed, he should consider interviewing the less dominant stakeholders separately from the more dominant stakeholders, in order to elicit the requirements of both sub-groups.

22.4 Workshop

In a workshop, a group of stakeholders develops requirements for the system. In contrast to interviews, requirements are not canvassed from participants individually but are the results of group work. According to our experience, if a workshop is prepared and conducted well, it is a very successful technique for requirements elicitation. [Leffingwell and Widrig 2000] even refer to workshops as the most powerful technique for requirements elicitation.

22.4.1 *Preparation*

Defining the Workshop Goal

Explicit definition of the workshop goal

A concrete definition of the workshop goal positively affects the acceptance of the workshop by the participants. We recommend explicitly stating the types of requirements artefacts that are expected to be developed during the workshop when communicating the workshop goal (see Example 22-10).

Example 22-10: Workshop goal

The goal of the workshop is to develop goals and scenarios for the vision "accident-free driving".

Defining Work Results and a Work Procedure

Defining the work procedure

The work procedure defines how the workshop goal shall be attained and how the planned work results shall be produced. In the context of a workshop, typically different assistance techniques are used, such as:

- Brainstorming (see Section 23.2)
- KJ method (see Section 23.4)

- ❑ Iterative goal and scenario definition (see Chapter 12)
- ❑ Discussions
- ❑ Work in sub-groups and presentation of the results in the plenum

Creating an agenda

The planned work procedure for the workshop needs to be elaborated into an agenda that serves for orientation throughout the workshop (see Example 22-11). According to our experience, it is advisable to plan breaks of 5–10 min every 45 min during a workshop (or every 60–70 min during group work in sub-groups). These short breaks are typically not disclosed in the agenda.

Example 22-11: Agenda for a workshop

Day 1:

09:00 to 09:30	Welcome session and presentation of the goals of the workshop
09:30 to 10:00	Brainstorming: goals for the car safety system
10:00 to 10:45	Categorisation of the brainstorming results
10:45 to 11:15	Break
11:15 to 12:30	Grouping and refinement of the goals, assignment of goals to sub-groups
12:30 to 14:00	Lunch break
14:00 to 18:00	Work in sub-groups: scenario definition for the elicited goals
18:00 to 18:30	Presentation of the intermediate results by each sub-group
19:00 to 21:00	Joint dinner

Day 2: . . .

Choosing Participants, Inviting Participants, and Agreeing on the Goal

Selecting the participants

Any stakeholders who can contribute to attainment of the workshop goal(s) and hence the desired results should be invited to the workshop. If the number of potential workshop participants is too large, the technique for assessing the relevance of requirement sources presented in Section 21.4 can be applied in order to determine which participants are most important for attaining the workshop goals. We recommend inviting between 5 and 15 participants to a workshop.

Considering the context facets

Our requirements engineering framework can be used to support the selection of a representative set of stakeholders. To select a representative set of stakeholders, stakeholders from all four context facets should be invited to the workshop. In this way, it is ensured that no context facet is neglected during the workshop. Alternatively, workshops focussing on one or two facets may also be performed. For such workshops, participants are selected according to the chosen context facet(s).

Inviting stakeholders in due time

Inviting the stakeholders to the workshop in due time (approximately 4–6 weeks before the workshop) ensures that as many of the invited stakeholders as possible are available for the workshop. In contrast to rescheduling an interview, it is very difficult to change the date of a workshop because the number of participants involved is significantly higher. Therefore, participants should be invited as early as possible.

Communicating the goal to the participants

Along with receiving the invitation to the workshop the invited stakeholders should also be informed about the goal of the workshop. If possible, the workshop goal should be agreed upon by all participants. If necessary, this can also happen at the beginning of the workshop.

Communicating the rationale of the system development

We recommend to inform the participants additionally about the status and the rationale of the development of the system as well as the planned use of the workshop results.

Choosing the Workshop Location

Adequate room

A workshop requires a room that is large enough for the number of participants invited. The tables in the room should be arranged in a way that supports interaction among the participants, e.g. in an O- or U-shape. If the workshop agenda foresees work in sub-groups, additional rooms are required in order to avoid two or more sub-groups having to work in the same room and thereby disturbing each other.

Undisturbed room

Interruptions of the group work, for example, by mobile phone calls or by other persons diminish the participants' concentration, impair their motivation, and hence negatively affect the results. Therefore, interruptions should be avoided.

Technical equipment

Adequate (and fully functional) technical equipment in the workshop room is helpful for group work. At a minimum, a board for visualising facts should be available. We recommend an additional board or another medium to visualise results, e.g. of discussions about some issue. Additional visualisation media such as whiteboards, flipcharts, or overhead projectors serve as supporting media. Furthermore, the workshop organisers should check whether an internet connection, computers, or a printer are needed.

Appointing a Moderator

Responsibilities of the moderator

The moderator has the task of guiding the workshop. In particular, the moderator shall detect conflicts between the participants' views and support the participants in resolving these conflicts. Hence the moderator supports the participants in achieving consensus. In order to guide the workshop, the moderator has to know the workshop goal as well as the intended results. During the workshop, the moderator ensures that the activities of the group contribute to attaining the workshop goal. Activities which do not contribute to the workshop goal should be stopped by the moderator. However, this should be done with care, since too frequent or too early interventions by the moderator inhibit the participants' creativity.

Dealing with conflicts

Conflicts and contradictions that surface in a workshop should be regarded as opportunities for developing innovative ideas and solutions. Furthermore, by resolving conflicts and contradictions, a common understanding of the system is established. We deal with negotiating about requirements for the system and with conflict resolution in Part IV.c.

External moderator

For workshops where conflicts are very likely to occur it is recommended to appoint an external moderator. An external moderator is generally impartial towards the participants and neutral towards the workshop goal and results.

Accepted authority

In order to be able to guide a workshop successfully, the moderator must be accepted by all participants as an authority. In the case of external moderators, this is generally not a problem. If no external moderator is available, a workshop participant is appointed as the moderator. The moderator must be neutral. Hence he is not allowed to participate in the discussions about the requirements in order to be accepted as a neutral authority.

Appointing a Minute-Taker

Neutral minute-taker

It is recommended to invite an additional person (preferably someone with the necessary expert knowledge) to take the minutes during the workshop. If this is not possible, a workshop participant must be appointed as the minute-taker. Inviting an additional person to take the minutes has the advantage that the results are documented neutrally. In contrast, workshop participants tend to incorporate their own opinion into the minutes.

22.4.2 Execution

Opening

Presenting goals, intended results, and the agenda

During the opening, the moderator presents the workshop goal, the intended results, and the agenda to all participants. The participants have the opportunity to ask questions about the goal, the intended results, and the workshop agenda. If necessary, the agenda is adjusted.

Explaining the techniques

After the opening, the moderator briefly presents the techniques that shall be applied during the workshop. For example, if a brainstorming session shall be performed, the moderator briefly explains the brainstorming rules (see Section 23.2) in case some participants are not familiar with the technique.

Explicit conversation rules

Explicit behavioural rules should be defined. For example, it should be explicitly stated that interrupting other participants as they speak shall be avoided at all cost. After the moderator has laid out the workshop rules, the participants vote on each rule in order to determine whether the rule is binding for the workshop or not. The rules that have been approved should be made visible to all participants, e.g. by means of a poster, in order to support the participants and the moderator in ensuring that the rules are observed.

Dealing with breaches of the rules

An explicitly approved set of rules supports the moderator in guiding the group. In case of a breach of the rules, the moderator refers to the rules. By referring to the rules, the moderator invokes a concrete authority that has been approved by all participants.

Hint 22-2 presents the rules of theme-centred interaction according to [Cohn 2009]. All rules are written from the point of view of a participant, since they shall describe and influence their own behaviour.

!

Hint 22-2: *Rules of theme-centred interaction*

(1) First-person narrative: "Act for yourself in your statements; say 'I' instead of 'We' or 'One'."

(2) Reveal the motivation and rationale of your questions: "If you ask a question, say why you ask it and what it means to you."

(to be continued)

Hint 22-2 *(continued)*

(3) Preferably do not interpret: "Abstain from interpreting others as long as possible. Instead, express personal reactions."
(4) No generalisations: "Abstain from generalisations."
(5) Denote explicitly personal impressions: "If you talk about the behaviour or trait of another participant, say also what it means to you that he/she is the way he/she is (i.e. how you regard him/her)."
(6) Only one participant speaks at a time.
(7) If speeches of participants overlap, briefly collect the keywords.

Work Element

Moderator checks adherence to the agenda

During the workshop the moderator should take care that the agenda is adhered to. According to our experience, it is recommended to inform the participants in a neutral way about the time remaining when half of the time of an agenda item has passed, as well as 15 min before the time of the current agenda item runs out. The moderator may, for example, say: "Please note that half of the time planned for this agenda item has passed."

However, we advise against regarding the agenda as unchangeable. A productive and promising discussion can justify a change to the agenda. However, the change should only be made after all participants have agreed to it. If discussions are stopped due to the lack of time, we recommend using an idea repository (see Hint 22-3).

!

Hint 22-3: *Collect open issues in an idea repository*

You may collect open issues and questions that cannot be discussed further in an idea repository. An idea repository may be realised, for example, by means of a flipchart. Each open issue or question is written on the flipchart and is hence visible to everybody.

Moderator controls adherence to the conversation rules

The moderator is also responsible for reminding the participants to observe the conversation rules which have been agreed upon. A breach of the rules has to be addressed explicitly by the moderator. The moderator must indicate the breach of the rules in a neutral way by referring to the rule and without being offensive in any way.

Documentation of results

During the workshop, all relevant results should be documented (e.g. on a flipchart or whiteboard). The documentation should contain, besides the final results, also intermediate results. If no minute-taker was appointed during the preparation of the workshop, one of the participants must be asked to take the minutes. Especially in the latter case, it is important to advise the minute-taker to take the minutes in an objective way.

Documentation of decisions

In the course of the workshop, decisions are made, for example, about which goal should be discussed next or which of the discussed scenarios shall be implemented in the system. According to our experience, it is advisable to document decisions explicitly. Hint 22-4 describes aspects concerning a decision that need to be documented.

> **Hint 22-4:** *Explicit documentation of decisions*
>
> The following aspects of a decision should be documented:
>
> - Decision alternatives
> - Chosen alternative
> - Decision rationale
> - If applicable, the persons responsible for realising the decision

Documenting the rationales for decisions and, if applicable, defining a person who is responsible for realising the decision are especially important in order to ensure that the decisions are implemented. Particularly if implementing a decision is critical for the system and requires effort, it is important to designate the person responsible.

Finalisation

Collecting open issues

During a workshop many results are generated. This is especially the case when the workshop lasts for several days. Experience has shown that open issues, such as unconsidered items in the idea repository, often remain at the end of the workshop (see Hint 22-3). For each open issue, the participants should define a procedure for how the issue shall be dealt with further. For example, some participants of the group may agree to discuss open issues in interviews or make an appointment for another workshop. If open issues are not collected or if collected issues are not worked up, the participants' motivation for future workshops may decrease (see [Gottesdiener 2002]).

Retrospective/self-reflexion

At the end of a workshop, it is advisable to perform a retrospective on the workshop. During the retrospective, all participants have the opportunity to reflect upon their positive and negative experiences during the workshop. In order to perform the retrospective in a structured way, the KJ method can be used (see Section 23.2). Hint 22-5 suggests performing three separate enquiries using the KJ method to reflect on a workshop.

> **Hint 22-5:** *Workshop feedback by KJ method*
>
> *First round "What worked?"*: All participants are asked to write cards reflecting their positive impressions and experiences regarding the workshop. The participants might point out, for example, that good ideas for system requirements were developed during the workshop.
>
> *Second round "What did not work?"*: All participants record their negative impressions or experiences by writing cards. For example, the participants might criticise the organisation of the workshop or the techniques chosen.
>
> *Third round "What can be improved?"*: This kind of enquiry is especially important when several workshops are performed with the same participants. During this round, participants make suggestions for improving specific aspects of the
>
> *(to be continued)*

Hint 22-5 *(continued)*

workshop. A suggestion might be, for example, to make use of parallel work in sub-groups more extensively.

Remark: Note that the rules for theme-centric interaction stated in Hint 22-2 also apply to the feedback session of a workshop.

In the feedback session of a workshop, it is important to talk about positive aspects of the workshop first. People are more open to provide and accept criticism when positive aspects have been discussed first (see [Schulz von Thun 2005]).

Thanking the participants

In order to formally close the workshop, the moderator and the person responsible for the workshop should express their gratitude to the participants for their contributions and, by so doing, show their appreciation for the participants' commitment.

22.4.3 Follow-up

Pursuing open issues

After a workshop, the results of the workshop are worked up. Open issues, contradictions and gaps are identified (e.g. by checking the minutes) and resolved. If necessary, the relevant participants are involved in the follow-up work.

Approval of the minutes by all participants

The workshop minutes comprise all intermediate and final results of the workshop. If all workshop participants agree, the minutes are distributed among the participants. In this way the participants are able to check and approve the minutes. However, they can also propose changes to the minutes. Checking and approval of the minutes is important for resolving misunderstandings and amending the possibly subjective view of the minute-taker, if necessary.

22.4.4 Checklist for Applying the Technique

Hint 22-6 presents a checklist for the preparation, execution, and follow-up phases of a workshop.

!

Hint 22-6: *Checklist for workshops*

Preparation – Defining the workshop goal:

- ❑ Define the goal of the workshop explicitly.

Preparation – Defining expected results and a work procedure:

- ❑ Define the intended results explicitly.
- ❑ Define a procedure for attaining the workshop goal and producing the expected results.
- ❑ Sum up the work procedure in an agenda.
- ❑ Reserve time for regular breaks.

(to be continued)

Hint 22-6 *(continued)*

Preparation – Selecting and inviting the participants:

- ❑ Pay attention to the workshop goal when selecting participants.
- ❑ Ensure that the selection of participants is representative, e.g. with respect to the four context facets, each facet needs to be represented by some participant.
- ❑ Invite the participants in due time.
- ❑ Agree upon the workshop goal with the participants.

Preparation – Workshop location:

- ❑ Provide a suitable room that accommodates all participants and fosters communication.
- ❑ Provide an undisturbed working atmosphere.
- ❑ Provide appropriate technical equipment (whiteboard, projector, flipchart, etc.).

Preparation – Moderator and minute-taker:

- ❑ Invite an external moderator, if possible.
- ❑ Appoint an external minute-taker, if possible.

Execution – Opening:

- ❑ Present the workshop goal, the expected results, and the agenda at the beginning of the workshop.
- ❑ Allow for a discussion of the workshop goal, the expected results, and the agenda.
- ❑ Explain the techniques to be applied during the workshop.
- ❑ Define and present the conversation rules for the workshop.
- ❑ Let the participants vote on each rule.

Execution – Work element:

- ❑ The moderator takes care that the participants adhere to the agenda.
- ❑ The moderator takes care that the participants observe the conversation rules.
- ❑ The minute-taker is responsible for providing documentation of all intermediate and final results.
- ❑ Pay attention to documenting conflicts identified during the workshop.
- ❑ Try to resolve conflicts using the techniques described in Part IV.c (e.g. Win-Win approach).
- ❑ Take care that decisions are explicitly documented.

Execution – Finalisation:

- ❑ Ensure that all open issues have been documented.
- ❑ Define a procedure for resolving each open issue.
- ❑ Allow the participants to provide feedback on the workshop (positive, negative, improvements).
- ❑ Thank all participants for their contributions and commitment.

Follow-up:

- ❑ Consolidate the work results.
- ❑ Ask each participant to approve the workshop minutes.
- ❑ Let each participant approve the consolidated work results.

22.4.5 Benefit for Requirements Elicitation

Identifying Relevant Requirement Sources

Brainstorming and relevance assessment

During a workshop, brainstorming (see Section 23.2) can be performed in order to support the identification of requirement sources. After brainstorming, the group should determine the relevance of each identified, potential requirement source by means of the technique described in Section 21.4.

Considering the four context facets

Brainstorming sessions for identifying requirement sources during a workshop should consider all four context facets. This can be achieved either by performing a separate brainstorming session for each context facet (see Section 23.2.4) or, if the number of participants is large enough, by dividing the group into four sub-groups. Each sub-group then performs a brainstorming to identify requirements in a specific context facet. Subsequently, the results of the individual sub-groups are brought together to evaluate the results.

Eliciting Existing Requirements

Iterative goal and scenario definition

In order to elicit existing requirements during a workshop, iterative goal and scenario definition (see Chapter 12) can be applied. For this purpose, the group is divided into sub-groups of three to five participants. Each group is assigned a set of goals. Based on the assigned goals, the groups write up additional goals and scenarios iteratively. There are two different approaches for assigning the goals to the sub-groups:

1. *The same goals are assigned to each sub-group.* The advantage of this approach over the elicitation of goals and scenarios in a single, large group is that parallel work in sub-groups involves more participants actively. In addition, due to the group dynamics in each group, the sub-groups achieve different results. Bringing the results of the different sub-groups together and explaining the results to all participants generally leads to additional synergy effects. However, the disadvantage of this approach is the increased time required compared with the second approach.
2. *Each sub-group is assigned different goals.* The advantage of this approach is that the different sub-groups work on different sets of goals in parallel. Hence, in total, the group needs less time to deal with the entire set of goals. A disadvantage of this approach is that each goal is only elaborated on by one group. Therefore, fewer results are generated for each specific goal compared with the first approach.

After the work in sub-groups, the results of each group are presented and discussed in the plenum. During the discussion, all participants are allowed to express new ideas, suggest improvements, and, if applicable, express their disapproval of some of the results.

Developing New and Innovative Requirements

According to our experience, workshops are well suited for the collaborative and iterative development of ideas and hence for the development of new and innovative requirements. In addition, brainstorming can be applied in order to support the development of new and innovative requirements during a workshop. The use of brainstorming as an assistance technique for requirements elicitation is described in detail in Section 23.2.

22.4.6 Effort

Expenditure of resources

A workshop generally consumes a considerable amount of resources. To calculate the total effort required to conduct a workshop (e.g. in person-days), the duration of the workshop (in days) must be multiplied by the number of participants. In addition, some effort is required for the preparation and follow-up work for the workshop. All in all, we classify the effort for conducting a workshop as very high or, if the duration of the workshop is only a day or less, as high. However, according to our experience, the effort is often justified by the substantial results produced, its contribution to team-building, the consensus reached during the workshop, and the alignment of the expectations of the different participants with respect to the system.

very high	high	medium	low	very low
✓	(✓)			

Fig. 22-3 *Effort involved in conducting a workshop*

22.4.7 Critical Success Factors

Accepted goal

Participation in a workshop means investment of a large amount of resources for each participant. A crucial factor for a workshop to be successful is hence that all participants understand the workshop goal in the same way and accept it.

The "right" participants

Inviting the "right" participants to a workshop is also critical for the success of the workshop. The choice of the participants depends on the goal of the workshop and the system context. Based on our experience with workshops, we have defined the following heuristics for identifying the "right" participants:

!

Hint 22-7: *Identifying the "right" participants*

- *Expertise*: Participants must possess the right expertise with respect to the workshop goal.
- *Motivation*: Participants should be motivated to apply their knowledge and be interested in the workshop goals.
- *Decision-making authority*: During a workshop, decisions are made, amongst others, about requirements for the system. The participants should therefore have the authority to make decisions about the requirements for the system.
- *Soft skills*: A workshop always has a social component, which is especially reflected in the way in which the participants deal with each other, e.g. during discussions. Therefore, all participants should have good social skills.

Motivation of the participants

The participants' motivation is critical for the group work during a workshop and the results of this group work. Unmotivated participants contribute less to the workshop and may impair other participants' work, thereby demotivate these participants.

Moderator

As pointed out in Sections 22.4.1 and 22.4.2, the moderator plays an important role in a workshop. Appointing an experienced and well-trained moderator can considerably improve the results of a workshop. The moderator can guide the group in a more effective way, recognise strengths and weaknesses of individual participants, skilfully involve the participants, and thereby positively influence the results of the workshop.

Groupthink effect

As in a group interview, the groupthink effect may lead to less dominant participants accepting the more dominant participants' ideas and withholding their own opinions and ideas. The moderator should take care that all participants get the chance to voice their ideas and requirements, for instance, by encouraging the participants and by using techniques such as the KJ method. The moderator may also split the group into several sub-groups during the workshop to avoid the groupthink effect.

Undisturbed workshop location

The environment can play an important role in the success of a workshop. In particular, interruptions should be excluded as far as possible. This can be achieved, for instance, by choosing a workshop location outside the participants' workplace.

22.5 Focus Groups

Panel of stakeholders focus on a topic to identify requirements

The key concept of focus groups is that a panel of stakeholders focus on a chosen item to identify the requirements regarding this item (see e.g. [Sharp et al. 2007]). The focus item can be some topic of interest such as a work procedure in a company or a tangible item such as a given system. If the focus item is an existing system, the stakeholders can, for example, focus on the identification of problems with the current system and its use.

[Kuniasky 2003] distinguishes three types of focus groups:

Exploratory

- *Exploratory*: During an exploratory focus group session, the main goal is to elicit new requirements for the system. In this case, the focus item is typically rather vague.

Comparative

- *Comparative*: A comparative focus group session aims to elicit an initial set of requirement based on a competitor's product or a previous version of the system. The existing system and any available documentation can be used during the session.

Prioritisation

- *Prioritising*: A prioritising focus group session aims to prioritise already elicited requirements and to identify missing requirements.

22.5.1 Preparation

Defining the focus item and the goal

For each focus group session, the focus item as well as a clear goal must be defined. For instance, the focus can be on a competitor's system, with the goal of eliciting new requirements for the system to be developed.

Choosing the right participants

Based on the focus item and the goal the participants for the focus group meeting are identified. The participants should be representative stakeholders, ideally from all four context facets. However, if the focus of the session lies within one context facet, only stakeholders from this facet might be invited to the meeting. The number of stakeholder to be invited should be between three and ten (see [Sharp et al. 2007]).

Inviting the participants

The participants should be invited early enough, in order to enable thorough preparation of the focus group session. The invitation should include the time, location, and expected duration of the session. The invitation should also contain a brief description of the focus item and the goal of the session, the agenda, and sufficient information about the focus item (e.g. a product brochure of the competitor's system to be focussed on). A short explanation of the aim of a focus group might be helpful for the participants. In addition, the participants should be encouraged to prepare themselves for the focus group session with respect to the agenda, the goal, and the focus item.

Appointing a moderator and minute-taker

A moderator and a minute-taker must be appointed for the session. The moderator's task is to guide the session and to facilitate communication between the participants by making sure that every participant gets the chance to contribute. Also, the moderator needs to be able to calm the situation if conversation becomes too heated. The minute-taker shall record the key ideas and results of the session, paying attention to potential disagreement and discussions, as experiences show these to yield the most valuable information. Also complete agreement among the participants regarding a topic and a subject is a key finding that should thus be documented.

Suitable location

The room chosen for the focus group should be large enough to host all participants comfortably. Ideally, the room should have a set-up facilitating communication and creativity. The room should be equipped with flipcharts, pin-boards, and a projector.

22.5.2 Execution

When the moderator starts the focus group session, he should thank everyone for attending and briefly explain the agenda, the focus item and the goal of the meeting. He should also briefly explain how the session is supposed to be conducted and encourage everyone to share their thoughts and comments. The participants should be given the opportunity to ask initial questions before starting the session. At the beginning of the focus session itself, the moderator should again briefly introduce the focus item and point out its main features, open the discussion with a general question and encourage everyone to express their opinion, give a statement, or provide an answer.

Dealing with discussions that are too calm or overheated

During almost every focus group session, periods occur in which the discussion calms down or becomes excessively heated. Both situations are undesirable and require the moderator to intervene.

If the discussion calms down, the moderator can revive it with a summarising statement or a provocative or extreme statement. If the discussion becomes too heated, the moderator should intervene by summarising the discussion in an objective and neutral way, instructing the minute-taker to record the issues disagreed upon, and declaring that these issues will be resolved in another session. This is especially advisable when only a part of the group is involved in the discussion or if additional participants are needed to resolve the conflict. A short break may be helpful to calm down the discussion. Under no circumstances should the discussion escalate to a point where effective and creative group work is no longer possible.

A focus group session ends either when the allotted time is used up or all major issues have been discussed. The moderator shall thank the participants and offer insight into the minute-taker's protocol. This increases the participants' willingness to support the resolution of open issues during the follow-up phase.

22.5.3 Follow-up

Deriving requirements from protocols and transcripts

During the follow-up phase, the protocol and potential other recordings from the session are reviewed with respect to the requirements elicited during the session. The requirements as well as detected conflicts, conflict resolutions, and open issues are documented. The documented information and the requirements should be made available to all participants for validation and in order to increase their motivation for participating in further focus group sessions.

22.5.4 Checklist for Applying the Technique

Hint 22-8 contains a checklist for the preparation, execution, and follow-up phases of focus group sessions.

!

Hint 22-8: *Checklist for focus group sessions*

Preparation:

- ❑ Define the focus item and the goal of the session.
- ❑ Select appropriate participants and provide them with the required information.
- ❑ Find an appropriate room offering a creative and communicative work environment and the required equipment.
- ❑ Appoint an experienced moderator and a minute-taker.
- ❑ Invite the participants, communicating the focus item, goal, data, time, and location of the focus group session.

Execution:

- ❑ Welcome the participants and open the session with a brief introduction.
- ❑ Manage the discussion so that every participant contributes.
- ❑ Avoid discussions that are too heated and frequent periods of silence.
- ❑ At the end, thank the participants and invite them to review material provided later on.

Follow-up:

- ❑ Check the protocols and other recordings created for requirements, conflicts, conflict resolutions, and open issues.
- ❑ Let the participants validate the elicited requirements and information.

22.5.5 Benefit for Requirements Elicitation

Identifying Relevant Requirement Sources

Additional requirement sources

When conducting a focus group session, the involved stakeholders and the chosen focus item are the most important requirement sources (e.g. an existing system). In addition to the requirements, also new requirement sources can be identified during a focus group session. Nevertheless, the main goal of a focus group is not the identification of requirement sources. Due to the restricted focus defined by the focus item, focus groups are in general not very well suited to identify requirement sources.

Eliciting Existing Requirements

Suited but not main objective

Focus groups are well suited to eliciting existing requirements. For example, if the focus item is an existing system, the participants elicit requirements realised in this system. In other words, they make existing requirements in the system explicit. Nevertheless, eliciting existing requirements is typically not the main aim of a focus group meeting.

Developing New and Innovative Requirements

Actual value of focus groups: new and innovative requirements

When bringing together the right stakeholders with different knowledge and expertise to discuss the focus item, the identification of new ideas, concepts, new issues and solutions is almost guaranteed. The in-depth group discussions will lead to new insights, and thus new and innovative requirements will be elicited. Focus groups are thus very well suited to eliciting new ideas and requirements and to uncovering new issues and gaining new insights.

22.5.6 Effort

Low preparation effort

The preparation effort for a focus group is low to medium, depending on the number of stakeholders to be invited. The main effort is in preparing the material for the focus group, identifying the stakeholders to involve and fixing a date that suits all stakeholders.

The effort involved in a focus group session itself depends on the number of participants (including the moderator and the minute-taker) and the duration of the session (which is usually several hours). Overall, we estimate the effort for focus groups as medium and, if multiple focus group sessions are needed, as high. Still, the benefit for requirements engineering typically far outweighs the effort.

Since, due to its narrow focus, a focus group meeting is typically much shorter than a workshop (see Section 22.4), the effort required for a focus group meeting is typically much lower than for a workshop.

very high	high	medium	low	very low
	(✓)	✓		

Fig. 22-4 *Effort for focus groups*

22.5.7 Critical Success Factors

Participants' background and experience

Choosing the right participants is decisive for the success of a focus group session. The participants should have a strong interest in the focus item and sound knowledge and experience in the relevant area. The requirements engineers should take care to choose participants with different opinions and views on the focus items so that discussions are likely to occur.

Participant preparation and motivation

It is important for the success of a focus group session that the participants know the focus item and the goal of the session in advance and are motivated to prepare for the session. During the session, the participants' motivation to participate in the discussion is essential. Thus, the importance and the aim of the focus group session should be conveyed to the stakeholders when sending out the invitations as well as at the beginning of the session.

Experienced moderator to guide the discussions

An experienced moderator is required to keep the discussions at the right level of intensity. The moderator should be able to adequately deal with both overly calm as well as too heated discussions in order to avoid a negative impact on the outcome of the session.

Groupthink effect

The groupthink effect reported by [Marakas 2002] (see Section 22.3) also applies to focus groups (see [Kuniavsky 2003]). Dominant members of the group may suggest ideas that tempt other, less dominant participants to refrain from expressing their own ideas. In order to prevent relevant ideas and requirements from remaining unexpressed, the moderator should encourage less dominant participants to voice their ideas. Additionally, techniques such as the KJ method help to avoid the groupthink effect (see Section 23.4).

Comfortable, creative environment

Since it is important for the participants to feel comfortable during the session, a creative and undisturbed discussion environment is necessary, in which everyone may voice their opinion.

22.6 Observation

Observation means that an observer elicits requirements by observing stakeholders or existing systems. Eliciting requirements by means of observation has an important advantage compared with workshops or interviews. Stakeholders are able to provide better (e.g. more detailed) descriptions of their activities while they perform these activities than retrospectively, i.e. after having performed the activities (see [Beyer and Holtzblatt 1998]). This can be illustrated using a simple example: A person can describe how to tie one's shoes much easier while he ties his shoes.

Direct observation

We differentiate between direct and ethnographic observation. During direct observation (see [Bray 2002]), the observer watches the stakeholders while they perform a particular task, analyses their activities, and asks questions. Direct observation of an existing system means that the observer either watches some stakeholders using the system or how the system operates autonomously (if the system is able to do so).

Ethnographic observation

During ethnographic[2] observation (see [Kotonya and Sommerville 1997]), the observer spends a long period of time with the stakeholders to actively learn and understand their way of working and their working procedures. Therefore, the observer performs all the stakeholders' workflows himself/herself as far as possible. By performing the stakeholders' activities on his/her own, the observer obtains a profound understanding of these activities.

22.6.1 Preparation

Defining the Observation Goal

Goal-oriented observation

Performing the observation of persons or systems in a goal-oriented manner is recommended. Hence, for each observation a clear goal should be defined (see [Haumer et al. 1998]). During the observation, the observer acquires different impressions and different kinds of information. A clearly defined goal for performing the observation supports the observer in differentiating between relevant and irrelevant impressions. The observation goal should of course be chosen carefully to avoid precluding the observer from making (and recording) relevant observations.

Example 22-12: Exemplary observation goal

The goal of the observation is to elicit information about the behaviour of drivers in traffic with regard to braking.

Defining the Desired Results

When preparing an observation, the requirements engineers also define which requirements artefacts shall be created based on the results of the observation.

Defining planned results

Depending on the type of desired results, the observation is performed with a different focus. If the expected result is the definition of a goal graph (see Chapter 8), the requirements engineer focusses on the stakeholders' intentions, i.e. the requirements engineer interrogates the stakeholders about their intentions during the observation. In order to write up scenarios, the requirements engineer must focus on the stakeholders' interactions with each other as well as with existing systems.

[2] Ethnography is a method of ethnology and denotes participating observation (see [Hammersley and Atkinson 1995]).

Example 22-13: Desired result of an observation
During the observation of driver behaviour (with regard to the goal defined in Example 22-12) the requirements engineer shall elicit at least five scenarios that describe different behaviours of a driver during a braking manoeuvre.

Determining persons and/or systems to be observed

Furthermore, the persons and/or systems to be observed must be determined based on the observation goal. The persons and/or systems are typically selected from the set of identified requirement sources.

22.6.2 Execution

Each observation is an individual process. Therefore, it is not possible to define standardised instructions for performing observations [Hammersley and Atkinson 2007]. In the following, we present important guidelines for performing an observation as an elicitation technique as well as different ways of documenting observation results.

Observation Guidelines

Stakeholders are experts

Applying observation as a requirements elicitation technique is based on the assumption that the observed stakeholders are experts in performing their tasks (see [Kotonya and Sommerville 1997]). This assumption implies, for instance, that the observer should not put the observed activities into question.

Seeking the confidence of stakeholders

Stakeholders may perceive being observed by an unknown person as unpleasant. Therefore, we recommend informing the stakeholders about the goal and the rationale for the observation as a means of building trust. Trust is especially important for ethnographic observation, since the stakeholders shall train the observer to become familiar with the workflows etc. In this case, trust is the basis for the stakeholders to be willing to share their knowledge with the observer. The stakeholder's willingness to share his knowledge can be further improved by stressing that it is not him/her who is being observed, but the system he/she uses and/or the activities he/she performs.

Details are of value

Details about how the stakeholders perform their activities are very valuable for defining requirements. It is easier to capture these details by means of ethnographic observation than by means of direct observation. The reason is that, in order to be able to perform the activities himself, the observer must acquire detailed knowledge about these activities.

Documenting immediately

It quite easily happens that the observer forgets important details that he/she has obtained during the observation, or that the elicited information is displaced by new impressions. Therefore, the observer should document the elicited information immediately.

Being objective

The observation should be conducted in an objective or neutral way. However, observation results are always influenced by the subjective interpretation of the observer (see the description of "transformation during perception" in Section 19.6). Therefore, the observer should check, for each documented result, whether it has been obtained and documented objectively (see [Hammersley and Atkinson 2007]).

Asking the observee whether a specific, documented result can be concluded from a particular event during the observation can be helpful. Also, referring to audio and/or video tapes that have been recorded during the observation can aid in keeping the documented results objective (see below: "Documentation Formats").

Checking the authenticity of activities

When stakeholders know that they are being observed, they may change their behaviour and perform activities in a different way than usual. Therefore, the observer should check that his/her observations are authentic. This can be achieved for instance by discussing the results with a stakeholder who was not involved in the observation. The effect of changing one's behaviour when being observed can be reduced if the observee trusts the observer and is informed about the goal and rationale for the observation.

Supporting observation by inquiries

Frequently, observations do not lead to the results initially hoped for, because the observer does not get a clear enough insight into the stakeholder's activities or interactions with the system. This risk can be reduced by asking the stakeholder to talk out loud and verbally express his/her thoughts, plans, and internal processes. For instance, when observing the user interaction with a car navigation system, the observer may ask "What are you wondering about?" or "What would you like to do next?" after a few seconds have passed in which both the observer and the observee were silent. These kinds of inquiries are in fact essential in many cases.

Documentation Formats

A requirements engineer can choose among several means for documenting observation results (see [Kotonya and Sommerville 1997]).

Text

In the case of textual documentation of observation results, the observer takes minutes during the observation and documents his observations and findings. The disadvantage of textual documentation is that writing minutes distracts the observer from the events that take place around him/her.

Video

In the case of video documentation, the observer records the events using a video camera (see [Haumer et al. 1998]). One advantage of video documentation is the semantically rich conservation of the situation. In addition, the video recording can be watched as often as needed during the subsequent analysis. The disadvantage of video recordings is that stakeholders often perceive being recorded on video as unpleasant. Furthermore, the analysis of video recordings is very time consuming.

Audio

The observer can employ audio recording for documenting his/her comments about the observed situation. Audio recording serves as an alternative or a supplement to textual and video documentation.

22.6.3 Follow-up

Processing the records

Interpreting the documented observation results without having participated in the observation is very difficult (see [Kotonya and Sommerville 1997]). Hence, the information elicited during an observation must be processed in an appropriate way so that it becomes understandable for people who were not involved in the observation. For example, the requirements engineers can link the requirements that have been elicited during the observation to the recorded observations. Using appropriate tools, even sequences of video recordings can be linked to the requirements (see [Haumer et al. 1998]). Such links enrich the semantics of the requirements, serve as rationales for the requirements, and enhance the comprehensibility of the requirements.

Aligning documentation with stakeholders

We recommend aligning the observation results with the stakeholders who have been observed. Aligning the results with the stakeholders reduces the risk of working with incorrect interpretations of the observations. To align the results, the requirements engineers can, for instance, conduct interviews (see Section 22.3) or perform a workshop (see Section 22.4) with all observed stakeholders. Aligning the results with the observed stakeholders promotes a common understanding of the observed activities. In addition to improving the observer's understanding of the observed activities, the stakeholders' own understanding of their activities is improved as well (see [Beyer and Holtzblatt 1998]). This holds especially for activities that belong to the stakeholders' everyday routine and are hence not reflected on by the stakeholders during their work.

22.6.4 Checklist for Applying the Technique

Hint 22-9 presents a checklist for the preparation, execution, and follow-up phases of an observation.

!

Hint 22-9: *Checklist for observation*

Preparation:

- ❑ Define the observation goal.
- ❑ Define the aspects that shall be observed.
- ❑ Define the desired results.

Execution – Observation guidelines:

- ❑ Try to earn the trust of the stakeholders who are being observed.
- ❑ Pay attention to details of the stakeholders' activities.
- ❑ Document your impressions immediately.
- ❑ Check the objectivity of your results.
- ❑ Validate that your observations are authentic.

Execution – Documentation forms:

- ❑ Make suitable use of different documentation forms, i.e. textual documentation, video recordings, and audio recordings.

Follow-up:

- ❑ Process your recordings to make them understandable for other people.
- ❑ Link the elicited requirements to the respective recordings.
- ❑ Align the processed observation results with the stakeholders who have been observed.

22.6.5 Benefit for Requirements Elicitation

Identifying Relevant Requirement Sources

Not suitable

During observation, incidentally new, potential requirement sources may be identified as a by-product. However, observation is generally not recommended as a technique for goal-oriented identification of new requirement sources.

Eliciting Existing Requirements

Highly suitable

Both kinds of observation, i.e. direct observation as well as ethnographic observation, are suited for eliciting existing requirements. Ethnographic observation should be preferred if a lot of implicit knowledge needs to be elicited, for instance, because the observed activities belong to the stakeholders' daily routine. In any case, the observation needs to be focussed, i.e. a clear goal for the observation must be defined (see Section 22.6.1).

Developing New and Innovative Requirements

Indirectly suitable

Observation techniques are generally not suited for developing new and innovative requirements. However, the observer gains a deep understanding of the observed activities when performing ethnographic observation. This knowledge can support the development of new and innovative requirements in collaboration with other stakeholders.

22.6.6 Effort

Effort for execution

Requirements elicitation by means of observation generally needs a large amount of resources. The effort for ethnographic observation is higher than the effort for direct observation, since the observer is not just a passive spectator but spends a considerable time with the observed stakeholders, learns to perform their tasks, and thereby gains a deep understanding of these activities. Therefore, we recommend applying ethnographic observation only for selected aspects and only for systems which are critical to the success of the developing organisation. Direct observation is well suited for recurring activities, but less suited for exceptional activities, because it may take a long period of time for an exception to occur so that the exceptional activities can be observed.

Effort for analysis

The effort required for analysing the results of the observation depends mainly on how the results have been recorded. The analysis of textual documentation is less time consuming than the analysis of audio or video recordings (see [Kotonya and Sommerville 1997]).

All in all, we regard the effort for direct observation as high. However, if the focus is very narrow, the effort may also be medium to low. In case of ethnographic observation, we estimate the effort as very high, due to the need for the observer to spend a considerable time with the observed stakeholders.

	very high	high	medium	low	very low
Direct observation		✓			
Ethnographic observation	✓				

Fig. 22-5 *Effort for observation*

22.6.7 Critical Success Factors

Willingness of the stakeholders to cooperate

Observation results are only useful if the observed stakeholders are willing to share their knowledge with the observer. Stakeholders who are not willing to share their knowledge do not perform their activities in an authentic way. In addition, they may answer the questions of the observer incompletely or even incorrectly. This results in incorrect observation results and unusable requirements for the system.

Processing of results

Appropriate processing of the observation results (see Section 22.6.3) is necessary to use the results in the requirements engineering process. Observation results are not understandable for other stakeholders until they have been processed.

Objectivity of the observer

The quality of the observation results additionally depends on the objectivity of the observer. The observer should therefore document the results as objectively as possible.

Observability

Finally, the success of the technique strongly depends on how well the events, activities, and processes of interest can be observed, how much effort is involved in enabling the observation, and what amount of explanation is required from the stakeholders in order to obtain sufficient understanding of their activities. For instance, in the case of highly specialised tasks in a nuclear plant with few observable stakeholder activities, interviews or workshops may be better suited for requirements elicitation.

22.7 Questionnaires

Eliciting requirements by means of questionnaires (see [Oppenheim 1999; Bray 2002]) means that a stakeholder writes down his requirements for the system by himself. In contrast to an interview, the stakeholder may freely choose the point in time when he actually writes down the requirements within a set time frame.

Reflecting one's own ideas

From the psychology of learning it is known that writing down one's own ideas in a structured way supports reflecting on the ideas (see [Mietzel 2007]). For the elicitation of existing requirements this means that the stakeholder considers his own requirements, and, while writing down the requirements, reflects on and reconsiders them.

Questionnaires are well suited for eliciting an initial set of requirements or requirement sources, especially from a large number of stakeholders (see [Zowghi and Coulin 2005]).

22.7.1 Preparation

Defining the goal and selecting the stakeholders

First, the requirements engineers must explicitly define the goal of the questionnaire as well as the desired results. After a clear goal has been defined, the requirements engineers select the stakeholders who shall participate in the survey. Stakeholders from all four context facets should be involved.

Defining questions

Based on the goal and the desired results, the requirements engineers define the questions for the questionnaire. When defining the questions, the requirements engineers should take the capabilities and knowledge of the selected stakeholders into account. If the stakeholders are asked questions that do not relate to their area of expertise, they obviously cannot provide substantial answers. As in interviews, one can differentiate between open and closed questions (see Section 22.3.1).

Defining the documentation format for open questions

For open questions, the format in which the stakeholders shall document their answers must be defined. For this purpose, all documentation formats described in Part IV.a should be considered, such as textual documentation or model-based documentation. Solution-oriented models should be used only if the stakeholders are familiar with the corresponding modelling languages. Otherwise, the requirements engineers should ask for textual documentation (as far as possible) of the answers in order to avoid faulty or misleading answers caused by problems due to the use of modelling languages with which the stakeholders are not familiar.

Familiarity with the documentation format

If one or more stakeholders are not familiar with a documentation format that is mandatory for one or another reason, the stakeholders should be trained in the documentation format. Training is a reasonable option, for instance, if the stakeholders are employees of the client or contractor company and shall use the documentation format in their future work anyway. Alternatively, the answers can be documented using a different format and then transformed into the required format. However this requires additional effort and may lead to problems, for instance, if the desired documentation format does not permit documenting the information contained in the original answers. Further options are for the requirements engineers to support the stakeholders in documenting the requirements during a joint workshop (Section 22.4) or for the requirements engineers to conduct interviews (Section 22.3) and document the requirements based on the stakeholders' answers.

Defining the desired types of requirements

In addition to the documentation format, the requirements engineers should define the desired type(s) of requirements (e.g. goals, scenarios, solution-oriented requirements; see Part III) to be elicited. This helps to ensure that the answers contain the kind of information needed.

Defining response options for closed questions

If closed questions are used, the requirements engineers must define the possible response options and define whether the stakeholders should select only one option or multiple options. Also for closed questions, the stakeholders' familiarity with the documentation formats has to be considered. For example, if the response options are defined using solution-oriented requirements models, the stakeholders can only answer the questions correctly if they know the modelling language used to document the possible answers sufficiently well. Therefore, also in the case of closed questions, training of the stakeholders might be required.

Contact person

In addition, a contact person should be defined to answer the stakeholders' questions that may arise when they fill in the questionnaire. Such questions typically relate to the correct interpretation of the questionnaire, the options defined for closed questions, or the documentation formats defined for providing the answers.

Test persons

In order to discover issues with the questionnaire before sending it to the stakeholders, it is recommended that the questionnaire be filled in by two to three stakeholders who were not involved in designing it. The stakeholders performing this test should focus on detecting inconsistencies, ambiguities etc. rather than on providing useful answers. In other words, the purpose of the test is merely to identify and resolve any kind of issue with the questionnaire and thereby improve its quality.

22.7.2 Execution

Defining the time frame

The stakeholders must have an appropriate time frame to answer the questionnaire. If the time frame is too small and hence the stakeholders have little time to answer the questionnaire, they might document their requirements only superficially, if at all. In this case, the answers to the questionnaires may have little substance and hence not be useful. If the time frame is too long, some stakeholders may postpone answering the questionnaire and eventually forget to respond.

Contact person

The assigned contact person should be available during the entire time frame defined for responding to the questionnaire in order to answer the stakeholders' questions about the questionnaire and the expected results, should there be any.

Reminder before expiry of the time frame

The respondents should be kindly reminded to answer the questionnaire about 3–4 days before the set time frame expires. This can be done, for instance, by sending an email to the respondents. If a stakeholder has simply forgotten to respond, the questionnaire is called to his attention again, and the stakeholder is able to answer the questions in the remaining time.

Appreciation for participating

Answering the questions — especially open questions — results in a certain amount of work for the stakeholders. Therefore, it is recommended to thank the stakeholders for responding to the questionnaire. This motivates the stakeholders to respond to further enquiries and to continue participating in the system development.

22.7.3 Follow-up

Processing of the answers

During follow-up, the requirements engineer analyses the stakeholders' answers to the questionnaire. If the answers of a stakeholder are ambiguous or incomprehensible, the requirements engineer should check back with this stakeholder, if possible. During the analysis, the answers from the different participants are compared with each other and aggregated. Furthermore, it is recommended to inform the respondents about the results of the survey in order to keep them motivated to participate in further surveys.

Subsequent workshop

If open issues, inconsistencies, contradictions etc. are identified during the analysis of the responses to the questionnaire, these may be discussed and resolved in a joint workshop (see Section 22.4). In addition, a workshop is suitable for consolidating the elicited information and elaborating on the results.

22.7.4 Checklist for Applying the Technique

Hint 22-10 presents a checklist for the preparation, execution, and follow-up phases of requirements elicitation by means of questionnaires.

Hint 22-10: *Checklist for eliciting requirements by means of questionnaires*

!

Preparation:

- ❑ Define the goals and desired results.
- ❑ Select the stakeholders who shall answer the questionnaire.
- ❑ Define the questions for the questionnaire.
- ❑ In case of closed questions, define the response options.
- ❑ In case of open questions, define the documentation formats for the answers.
- ❑ Use solution-oriented requirements models only if the respondents are familiar with the corresponding modelling languages.
- ❑ If necessary, train the respondents in documenting requirements using the desired documentation formats.

Execution:

- ❑ Inform the stakeholders about the goal of the survey.
- ❑ Define an appropriate time period for answering the questions in the questionnaire.
- ❑ Provide contact persons to answer the stakeholders' enquiries.
- ❑ Express your gratitude to the stakeholders for their contributions.

Follow-up:

- ❑ Analyse the stakeholders' responses to the questions in the questionnaire.
- ❑ In case of ambiguous or incomprehensible answers, check back with the respondents, if possible.
- ❑ Communicate the results of analysing the questionnaires back to the respondents.
- ❑ Pay attention to conflicting requirements in the results.

22.7.5 Benefit for Requirements Elicitation

Identifying Relevant Requirement Sources

Suitable for identifying requirement sources

Questionnaires are well suited for identifying potential requirement sources. The requirements engineer simply has to include questions in the questionnaire that are suited for identifying requirement sources. These questions may be derived from our checklist for the identification of requirement sources (see Section 23.6.4), but should be more concrete, for instance, with regard to the specific domain.

Eliciting Existing Requirements

Questionnaires are well suited for eliciting an initial set of existing requirements from a large group of stakeholders quickly and easily. The stakeholders may be asked, for instance, to state their goals for the system to be developed. They may also be asked for scenarios in which the goals are satisfied with the help of the system, or for solution-oriented requirements (data, function, behaviour, quality, and constraints; see Sections 2.2 and 4.6).

Developing New and Innovative Requirements

Very limited suitability

Questionnaires are not very well suited for eliciting new and innovative requirements since they are typically filled in without interactions between different stakeholders. Still, when answering the questionnaire, the participants may document requirements that are, or appear to be, new and innovative to the requirements engineers. The requirements engineers may stimulate the documentation of such requirements by means of questions such as "Is there a feature you would like to be realised in the new system that no other system has?".

22.7.6 Effort

Effort mostly for the stakeholders

The elicitation of existing requirements using questionnaires requires effort from the respondents, in the first place. Answering open questions generally requires medium effort. For closed questions, the effort is low. In comparison, the effort required from the requirements engineer for preparing open questions is very low. However, as in the case of interviews, some diligence is necessary when writing up the questions. For instance, leading questions must be avoided (see Section 22.3). We estimate the effort for preparing closed questions as medium (in exceptional cases, e.g. with very detailed answers, as high).

Analysis effort

In the case of closed questions, the effort for analysing and processing the answers is low, since the answers can be evaluated by applying simple statistics. Analysing and processing results in the case of open questions generally requires medium effort, since the answers have to be evaluated qualitatively.

In total, low to medium effort

In total, we estimate the effort for eliciting requirements using questionnaires, compared with the total effort of the other elicitation techniques presented, as medium if exclusively open questions are used, and as low (or possibly even very low) if closed questions are used.

very high	high	medium	low	very low
		(✓)	✓	(✓)

Fig. 22-6 *Effort for requirements elicitation with questionnaires*

22.7.7 Critical Success Factors

Motivated stakeholders

Requirements elicitation by means of questionnaires requires stakeholders with a high degree of self-initiative. Therefore, motivated stakeholders who are willing to contribute to the development of the system are important. Communicating the goals and the desired results of applying the technique contributes positively to motivating the stakeholders.

Comprehensible questions

For both open and closed questions comprehensible and unambiguous phrasing is essential. If the respondent cannot understand a question, he needs to get back to the contact person in order to resolve the issue before answering the question. However, if a question is ambiguous, for instance, and the respondent is unaware of the ambiguity, he might misinterpret the question. A misinterpretation of the question leads to useless answers. If such misinterpretations are not discovered, incorrect requirements may be derived from the answers.

Clearly defined answers

To define the response options for a closed question the same criteria hold as for defining the questions. If the response options are ambiguous, the respondents may misunderstand the response options. Consequently, the given response options are likely to convey the wrong picture and lead to the derivation of incorrect requirements from the responses.

Training of stakeholders (if required)

If the stakeholders are not familiar with the documentation formats used, this may also lead to errors such as misinterpretations and, hence to answers conveying a distorted picture of the stakeholders' true requirements. In the case of open questions, insufficient familiarity with the requested documentation formats leads to "invalid" models of the system. This especially holds if conceptual models are requested as documentation formats. Therefore, training the respondents beforehand may be indispensable for successful application of this elicitation technique.

Selection of the right documentation format

Besides the stakeholders' motivation the selection of an adequate documentation format for the specific stakeholder also plays an important role. The selected documentation technique must correspond to the skills of the stakeholders. For example, a technical stakeholder is able to create solution-oriented requirements models (e.g. a statechart or a class model) more easily than a non-technical stakeholder.

22.8 Perspective-Based Reading

Perspective-based reading is a proven technique for assuring the quality of documents (see [Basili et al. 1996]).[3] During perspective-based reading, a requirements engineer or some other stakeholder (in the following, called the "reader") reads a document from a previously defined perspective, e.g. from the perspective of a user or from the perspective of a tester (see [Regnell et al. 2000]). When reading the document in this way, the reader can ignore all the details that are not relevant for the selected perspective. For instance, when reading a document from the perspective of a user, the reader may ignore technical details concerning the realisation of the system, i.e. technical information not directly related to using the system. Focussing on a specific perspective demonstrably leads to improved results of quality assurance activities (see [Laitenberger et al. 2000]). Since perspective-based reading is well suited for a goal-oriented analysis of existing documents, application of this technique for the elicitation of requirements from documents is recommended.

[3] In Part V, we take up the subject of perspective-based reading again and explain its application during requirements validation.

22.8.1 Preparation

Defining the goal and the desired results

First, the stakeholders define the goal of applying perspective-based reading to a document or a set of documents. The goal definition should characterise the desired results, for instance, by defining the desired types of requirements to be elicited.

Defining the perspectives

Based on the goal, the different perspectives for perspective-based reading are identified. In Section 22.8.5, we present examples of different perspectives for identifying requirement sources and for eliciting existing requirements by means of perspective-based reading.

Selecting the documents

The documents to be analysed by means of perspective-based reading are selected from the known requirement sources. The selection is made based on the goal and the defined perspectives. Examples of documents that can be analysed during requirements elicitation are stated in Section 6.2.1.

Alternative approach

Alternatively, the selection of the documents to be analysed can be performed, first, based on the defined elicitation goal. The perspectives are defined after the documents have been selected. This approach results in perspectives that are better aligned with the selected documents. However, this approach may also hide the fact that a relevant perspective is missing in the existing documents. For instance, if only technical documents are available, information on the usage perspective may be scarce in the documents even though the usage perspective is very important with regard to the elicitation goal.

Identifying and inviting the participants

After the documents and the perspectives have been selected, the requirements engineers identify the stakeholders who shall perform the perspective-based reading and document the results. The perspectives influence which stakeholders qualify for performing the perspective-based reading. For instance, if the perspective "data and data structures" has been identified, the requirements engineers should consider inviting a database analyst. If the perspective "safety requirements" has been identified, a safety expert should be invited and so on. The requirements engineers invite the stakeholders and, along with the invitation, inform the stakeholders about the goals, the desired results, and the rationale of the elicitation activity.

22.8.2 Execution

We distinguish two basic approaches for performing perspective-based reading:

- *Sequential reading*: During sequential reading, the reader reads the document from beginning to end from a specific perspective such as the perspective of a user or the perspective of a tester.

Selective reading

- *Top-down reading*: Reading a document top-down necessitates that the document has an appropriate structure. The structure of the document must support extraction of information that is relevant for the chosen perspective. Examples of appropriate structural elements are meaningful headings, a table of contents, index, list of figures, and list of tables. Instead of reading the document sequentially from the beginning to the end, the reader searches the structure for text passages that are relevant for the assigned perspective. In the table of contents, headings are browsed for indications of relevant content for the assigned perspective. Similarly, the index of a document is searched for relevant keywords.

Quality of the document structure

In the case of top-down reading, the quality of the document structure determines the quality of the results. For example, if an incomplete index serves as the basis for top-down reading, i.e. an index from which essential keywords of the document are missing, important text passages may be overlooked. As a consequence, these passages are not considered during requirements elicitation.

Ensuring traceability

In parallel to reading the document, the elicited requirements are documented. It is advisable to immediately record the relevant text passages that lead to the definition of a requirement. This traceability information supports validation of the elicited requirements and makes them traceable for other stakeholders (see Chapter 31).

22.8.3 Follow-up

Consolidation of results

During the follow-up phase, the elicited requirements are consolidated and transferred into the target documentation format, if necessary. Thorough recording of the elicited requirements during perspective-based reading can simplify the follow-up work. In addition, the results from the different perspectives should be aligned and integrated during the follow-up phase.

22.8.4 Checklist for Applying the Technique

Hint 22-11 presents a checklist for the preparation, execution, and follow-up phases of perspective-based reading.

!

Hint 22-11: *Checklist for perspective-based reading*

Preparation:

- ❑ Define goal(s) and desired results.
- ❑ Define the perspectives based on the goal.
- ❑ Select the documents to be analysed based on the defined goals and perspectives.
- ❑ Select the stakeholders for the different perspectives and inform them in due time.

Execution:

- ❑ Select an approach for reading the documents: either sequential reading or top-down reading.
- ❑ Establish traceability between text passages and elicited requirements.

Follow-up:

- ❑ Consolidate and integrate the elicitation results obtained by reading the documents from the different perspectives.
- ❑ Pay attention to potential conflicts in the elicited requirements and resolve them using one of the techniques described in Part IV.c (e.g. Win-Win approach).

22.8.5 Benefit for Requirements Elicitation

Identifying Relevant Requirement Sources

Perspective-based reading can be applied in order to identify requirement sources. In order to use perspective-based reading to elicit requirement sources, the requirements engineers need to define perspectives that focus on specific types of requirement sources (Hint 22-12). However, since there is typically no heading or index entry referring explicitly to requirement sources, extracting requirement sources from a document requires sequential reading.

!

Hint 22-12: *Perspectives for identifying requirement sources*

- ❑ Identify relevant stakeholders that are referred to in the document.
- ❑ Identify further, relevant documents that are referred to in the document.
- ❑ Identify relevant systems that are referred to in the document.

Eliciting Existing Requirements

Four context facets as perspectives

Perspective-based reading is very well suited to eliciting existing requirements from documents. In order to support the elicitation of existing requirements the requirements engineers can define perspectives based on the three types of requirements artefacts (goal, scenarios, and solution-oriented requirements) and/or on the four context facets. Hint 22-13 defines four generic perspectives based on the four context facets.

!

Hint 22-13: *Context facets as perspectives*

- ❑ *Subject perspective*: The subject perspective considers a document from the view of the subject facet. It thus focusses on the objects and events in the system context that are relevant for the system. The document is hence searched for objects (tangible as well as intangible) and events that the system must store or process. The document is also searched for aspects that influence the representation of the objects and events in the system (e.g. the accuracy of the representation).
- ❑ *Usage perspective*: The usage perspective considers a document from the viewpoint of the usage facet. This perspective focusses on the users and the usage workflows. The document is hence searched for requirements that are relevant for the user and the usage workflows of the system.
- ❑ *IT system perspective*: The IT system perspective considers a document from the view of the IT system facet. The document is hence searched for requirements pertaining to the hardware or software platform or to IT system strategies and policies.

(*to be continued*)

Hint 22-13 *(continued)*

- *Development perspective*: The development perspective considers a document from the view of the system developers. The document is hence searched for requirements that concern the system development process such as constraints regarding the development method and the development tools to be used.

Checklists

In order to support the reader, checklists may be defined for the selected perspectives based on the context facets (see Section 23.6).

Three kinds of requirements artefacts as perspectives

Another possibility for defining perspectives is to use the three types of requirements defined in our requirements engineering framework (see Chapter 4). Adopting such a perspective means reading a document with a focus either on goals, scenarios, or solution-oriented requirements. Hint 22-14 describes the three resulting perspectives.

!

Hint 22-14: *Goals, scenarios, and solution-oriented requirements as perspectives*

- *Identify goals*: The document is searched for goals that shall be satisfied by means of the system.
- *Identify scenarios*: The document is searched for scenarios the system must implement, fragments of such scenarios, or clues hinting at such scenarios.
- *Identify solution-oriented requirements*: The document is searched for solution-oriented requirements for the system, i.e. functions, data elements, behavioural elements, quality requirements and constraints, or clues hinting at such requirements.

The perspectives can be made more specific by choosing a context facet and a specific type of requirements. Furthermore, the perspectives can be refined to represent particular aspects of the respective facet. For example, a perspective may be defined that focusses on a particular type of system usage. This results in perspectives such as "identify usage goals" (goals and usage facet) or "identify maintenance scenarios" (scenarios and IT system facet restricted to the aspect "system maintenance"). How the perspectives are defined (broad or narrow) depends on the situation in the requirements engineering process and on the goals that the requirements engineers are pursuing in applying the elicitation technique.

Developing New and Innovative Requirements

Not sufficient

Perspective-based reading is generally not sufficient for developing new and innovative requirements. However, reading a document from a specific perspective can sometimes trigger new ideas which can then be discussed and further elaborated on, for instance, in a workshop (see Section 22.4) or a focus group (see Section 22.5).

22.8.6 Effort

	very high	high	medium	low	very low
Sequential reading		✓			
Top-down reading			✓		

Fig. 22-7 *Effort for perspective-based reading*

The effort required for perspective-based reading is influenced by the specific approach for performing perspective-based reading, i.e. sequential reading or top-down reading.

Sequential reading

The effort for sequential reading is generally high, since the entire document must be read from each perspective. However, sequential reading of the document reduces the risk of overlooking important requirements for the perspective which are contained in the document.

Top-down reading

The effort for top-down reading is lower compared with sequential reading, since only extracts of the document must be read. However, there is a risk of overlooking important requirements in the document, especially, if the quality of the document structure is low, for instance, because there are no headings or the headings are weak.

22.8.7 Critical Success Factors

Selection of perspectives and documents

The quality of the results of perspective-based reading depends essentially on the selection of the right perspectives for the document under consideration. Additionally, the selection of the right documents is decisive for the quality of the results.

Clearly defined perspectives

Experience shows that clearly defined perspectives influence the results very positively. The perspectives should therefore be defined clearly and with as little overlap as possible.

Good structure

For top-down reading, the structure of the document is very important. If there are doubts with regard to the quality of the structuring of a document, it is recommended to apply sequential reading in order to reduce the risk of overlooking important text passages.

Chapter 23
Assistance Techniques for Elicitation

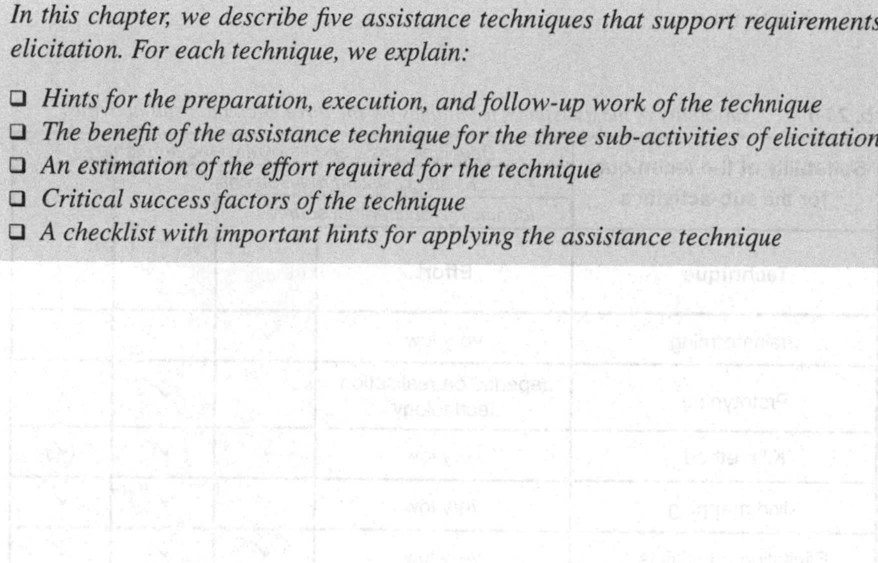

In this chapter, we describe five assistance techniques that support requirements elicitation. For each technique, we explain:

- *Hints for the preparation, execution, and follow-up work of the technique*
- *The benefit of the assistance technique for the three sub-activities of elicitation*
- *An estimation of the effort required for the technique*
- *Critical success factors of the technique*
- *A checklist with important hints for applying the assistance technique*

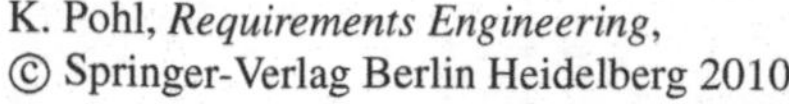

23.1 Evaluation of the Techniques

In this chapter, we describe the following assistance techniques for requirements elicitation:

- Brainstorming (see Section 23.2)
- Prototyping (see Section 23.3)
- KJ method (see Section 23.4)
- Mind mapping (see Section 23.5)
- Elicitation checklists (see Section 23.6)

The assistance techniques differ with regard to the required effort and their suitability for supporting each of the three sub-activities of requirements elicitation. Table 23-1 characterises the effort as well as the suitability of each technique for supporting the three sub-activities.

Tab. 23-1 *Suitability of the assistance techniques for the three elicitation sub-activities*

Suitability of the technique for the sub-activities Technique	Effort	*Identifying requirement sources*	*Eliciting existing requirements*	*Developing new and innovative requirements*
Brainstorming	very low	✓		✓
Prototyping	depends on realisation technology		✓	✓
KJ method	very low	✓	✓	(✓)
Mind mapping	very low	✓	✓	✓
Elicitation checklists	very low	✓	✓	✓

Use of the techniques in other requirements engineering activities

The assistance techniques presented in the following can partly be used in other requirements engineering activities; for instance, prototypes are also used in validation. However, the way in which the techniques are used can differ. We indicate these techniques in the respective chapters of the book and highlight the main differences regarding the way in which the techniques can be used in other requirements engineering activities (see e.g. Section 28.5).

23.2 Brainstorming

Brainstorming is commonly regarded as a creativity technique. The goal of brainstorming is to generate a large number of new ideas (see [Osborn 1948]). Brainstorming is performed with a group of stakeholders, for instance, during a workshop (see Section 22.4).

23.2.1 Preparation

Defining the goal/subject

For each brainstorming session, a clear goal must be defined. The goal is typically determined by a particular subject or problem (Example 23-1). During a brainstorming session, the stakeholders generate ideas related to the given subject or problem.

Determining the participants

The stakeholders included in a brainstorming session are selected from the known requirement sources according to the brainstorming goal or subject. Therein, all four context facets should be considered, unless the subject restricts the set of relevant context facets.

Fixing date and room

The room where the brainstorming takes place should be large enough to facilitate visualisation of the brainstorming results and allow for a seating arrangement where all participants can see each other.

Inviting participants

After the date for the brainstorming has been fixed and the room has been booked, the requirements engineers invite the selected participants and inform them about the goal and the rationales of the brainstorming. A brainstorming generally takes about 20–40 min.

E

Example 23-1: Goal of a brainstorming session

Which features/goals do you associate with the vision "accident-free driving"?

Providing visualisation media

In order to make the ideas of all participants visible to everybody during a brainstorming session, an appropriate visualisation medium must be available, such as a computer with a digital projector, a whiteboard, a flipchart, or a pin board and file cards.

Focussing by means of the four context facets

For requirements elicitation, the subject of the brainstorming can be additionally restricted using the four context facets. For instance, a brainstorming session can be restricted to a single facet.

Appointing a moderator and a minute-taker

The requirements engineers appoint a moderator who guides the brainstorming session. Additionally, a minute-taker is needed, who writes down the results during the brainstorming using a visualisation medium that is visible to all participants. During the brainstorming, the moderator and the minute-taker focus on their respective tasks and hence cannot participate in generating ideas.

23.2.2 Execution

Presentation of the subject

At the beginning of the brainstorming session, the moderator explains the subject and makes clear the goal of the brainstorming session to all participants. In addition, the participants' questions concerning the subject are answered and the rules for the brainstorming session are presented (see below).

Idea generation phase

Subsequently, the idea generation phase begins. Each participant expresses his/her ideas with regard to the subject. The minute-taker records all ideas and makes them visible to all participants.

Role of the moderator

Adhering to the brainstorming rules is essential for a successful brainstorming session. Therefore, the moderator should explain the rules at the beginning of the session and strictly enforce the rules during the brainstorming. If some participant breaks a rule, the moderator should address it immediately and remind the participants of the brainstorming rules.

Rules for performing brainstorming

In the following, we define seven rules for brainstorming (based on [Osborn 1948]). The rules are summed up in Hint 23-1:

Rule 1: quantity over quality

- *Rule 1: quantity over quality.* This rule supports attaining the brainstorming goal of generating as many ideas as possible in a session. Therein, the quality of the ideas does not matter. Generating a large number of ideas supports creativity, since the participants are provided with more associations on which they can build (see rule 2). For example, an idea that seems absurd to the majority can still stimulate the participants to improve on the idea, combine it with other ideas, and eventually lead to an innovative solution to the given problem.

Rule 2: free association desired

- *Rule 2: free association and visionary thinking are explicitly desired.* This rule shall motivate the participants to generate new ideas based on the present results and to give their imagination full scope. The participants shall express their ideas and thoughts freely and thereby stimulate other participants to develop new ideas and thoughts as well.

Rule 3: combining contents

- *Rule 3: taking on and combining expressed ideas is allowed and desired.* By taking on other participants' contributions, and developing and combining them, the participants of a brainstorming inspire each other and develop new ideas.

Rule 4: no criticism

- *Rule 4: criticism is forbidden.* This rule supports establishing a creative and non-coercive atmosphere. Criticism of ideas is prohibited and must be stopped by the moderator immediately. Criticism may inhibit the participants from generating further ideas. In addition, any discussion disturbs free association and thus the flow of idea generation. The discussion of ideas takes place after the generation of ideas has been completed.

Rule 5: clarification of ideas

- *Rule 5: questions for clarification are allowed.* If the participants have problems in understanding an idea, or if the idea is expressed ambiguously, it is important to let the originator of the idea explain it. Sufficient understanding of the other participants' ideas reduces misunderstandings and additionally promotes other participants' associations. Only ideas that are expressed sufficiently clearly can be documented unambiguously. If a participant is asked to clarify his idea, the minute-taker should record the key terms of the explanation.

Rule 6: overcoming initial deadlocks

- *Rule 6: do not abort the brainstorming at the first deadlock.* Almost every brainstorming session experiences a slack period (approximately 30–60 s of silence) in which the participants do not state new ideas. At this point, the moderator should not abort the brainstorming. Rather the slack period may be used as a short break. By expressing even a single new idea, the deadlock can be overcome and a new phase of idea generation is initiated. The moderator may also try to overcome the deadlock by producing new ideas and continuing the generation of ideas in this way. According to our experience, it is advisable to overcome at least two longer deadlock periods since, afterwards, often new, good ideas are generated.

Rule 7: natural end

- *Rule 7: the brainstorming shall come to a natural end.* The moderator should not terminate a productive brainstorming due to time restrictions, because this would signal to the participants that the time schedule is more important than their ideas. Typically, the natural end of a brainstorming is indicated by an increasing frequency of deadlocks that last increasingly long. Alternatively, the moderator may terminate the brainstorming during the third longer-lasting deadlock period.

23.2.3 Follow-up

A brainstorming generally results in a large number of ideas (see rule 1: quantity over quality). We recommend prioritising the ideas that have been generated during the brainstorming before the ideas are further processed. The following three categories can be used for prioritising the generated ideas:

Classifying ideas

- ❑ Category 1: directly usable ideas
- ❑ Category 2: ideas that need to be worked on to be usable
- ❑ Category 3: unusable ideas

The classification of the generated ideas into the three categories is performed by the group. Ideas assigned to the third category are immediately discarded.

Defining how to proceed

The group should define how to proceed with the ideas assigned to the first and the second category. Ideas assigned to the first category may, for instance, be elaborated on by different subgroups during a workshop (see Section 22.4). After all ideas assigned to the first category have been considered, the ideas assigned to the second category are processed.

Taking the minutes

The minutes of the brainstorming help to conserve the results of the brainstorming. Therefore, the minutes must document and, if necessary, also explain each generated idea from the first and the second category. Furthermore, the minutes should contain the procedures that have been agreed on for further processing of the generated ideas.

23.2.4 Checklist for Applying the Technique

Hint 23-1 presents a checklist for the preparation, execution, and follow-up phases of a brainstorming session.

!

Hint 23-1: *Checklist for brainstorming*

Preparation:

- ❑ Define the subject or problem.
- ❑ Select the stakeholders under consideration of the context facets.
- ❑ If required, focus the brainstorming on one context facet.
- ❑ Appoint a room and a time.
- ❑ Invite the participants.
- ❑ Provide visualisation media.
- ❑ Appoint a moderator and a minute-taker.

Execution – Brainstorming rules:

- ❑ Quantity over quality.
- ❑ Free association and visionary thinking are explicitly desired.
- ❑ Taking on and combining expressed ideas is allowed and desired.

(to be continued)

Hint 23-1 *(continued)*

- ❑ Criticising other participants' ideas is forbidden even if an idea seems to be absurd.
- ❑ Questions for clarification are allowed.
- ❑ Even at longer-lasting deadlocks do not abort immediately – overcome at least two longer-lasting deadlocks.
- ❑ Wait until the brainstorming comes to a natural end.

Follow-up:

- ❑ Assign each idea to a category.
- ❑ Discard unusable ideas.
- ❑ Define how to proceed with the usable ideas.
- ❑ Create the minutes to document the ideas and the procedures for further processing of the ideas.

23.2.5 Benefit for Requirements Elicitation

Identifying Relevant Requirement Sources

Simple and quick identification of requirement sources

Brainstorming is well suited for identifying potential requirement sources in a group quickly and with little effort. The subject of the brainstorming session is defined as a question such as "Which requirement sources should be considered for the system?" In order to further stimulate the identification of requirement sources during the brainstorming, it is advisable to focus on one of the four context facets (see Hint 23-2).

!

Hint 23-2: *Brainstorming for identifying requirement sources*

- ❑ *Subject facet*: Which requirement sources in the subject facet do you know?
- ❑ *Usage facet*: Which requirement sources in the usage facet do you know?
- ❑ *IT system facet*: Which requirement sources in the IT system facet do you know?
- ❑ *Development facet*: Which requirement sources in the development facet do you know?

Focus on stakeholders, documents, or systems

The brainstorming of potential requirement sources can alternatively or additionally be focussed by the three types of requirement sources. For example, one brainstorming session may be formed for the identification of documents and another one for the identification of stakeholders.

After the brainstorm, the group evaluates the relative relevance of each identified requirement source using the technique described in Section 21.4.

Eliciting Existing Requirements

Not suitable

A creativity technique such as brainstorming should generally be applied to support the invention of new requirements rather than for eliciting existing requirements.

To support the elicitation of existing requirements in a group we recommend, for instance, the KJ method (see Section 23.4).

Developing New and Innovative Requirements

Broad subject creates leeway for creativity

A brainstorm is very well suited for developing new ideas. At the beginning of the requirements engineering process, it is advisable to define a broad subject for brainstorming. At this stage, a brainstorming can be performed with a subject that is derived from the system vision (see Chapter 4). A broad subject facilitates the generation of many different ideas. If the subject is too narrow at the beginning of the requirements engineering process, many relevant ideas might not be expressed. A subject such as "Develop ideas for accident-free driving" that is based on the system vision facilitates generation of a substantially wider range of ideas than the more restricted subject "Develop ideas for keeping a safe following distance to vehicles driving ahead".

Narrow subjects support generation of solution ideas

If the requirements engineering process is already in an advanced stage, several narrower subjects may be selected for brainstorming sessions, such as the above example, "Develop ideas for keeping a safe following distance to vehicles driving ahead", in order to generate innovative ideas for realising a specific goal that refines the vision.

23.2.6 Effort

The effort for brainstorming can be estimated as very low. No substantial activities for the preparation or follow-up work of a brainstorming session are necessary. Additionally, the time required is very low.

very high	high	medium	low	very low
				✓

Fig. 23-1 *Effort for brainstorming*

23.2.7 Critical Success Factors

Observing the brainstorming rules

Strict adherence to the brainstorming rules is very important for the success of a brainstorming session. Therefore, the participants must understand and accept the rules. Additionally, the participants should understand and take in the subject or goal of the brainstorming session. It is advisable to pin up the subject in the brainstorming room where it is visible to everybody.

Size of the group influences creative performance

Research on brainstorming (see [Stroebe and Nijstad 2004]) suggests a correlation between the size of the group and the creative performance. Creative performance requires a person to access his long-term memory. This access is disturbed when a person listens to other persons' contributions. Since the number of expressed contributions increases with the size of the group, the time period for accessing long-term memory and hence also the creative performance is reduced. These considerations imply that it is advisable to keep the size of a group for a brainstorming to approximately 5–8 participants. [Stroebe and Nijstad 2004] even recommend groups of two.

Succinct description of ideas

In order to reduce the time for listening and hence the blocking of long-term memory, it is important that the ideas produced are expressed succinctly.

23.3 Prototyping

[Sommerville 2004] defines the term "prototype" as follows:

D

Definition 23-1: *Prototype*

"A prototype is an initial version of a software system which is used to demonstrate concepts, try out design options and, generally, to find out more about the problem and its possible solutions."

[Sommerville 2004]

Advantage: a prototype can be experienced

The main advantage of using prototypes in requirements engineering is that prototypes allow the stakeholders to experience the effects of their requirements. In contrast to abstract models and descriptions, prototypes can be touched and tried out. In this way, stakeholders obtain an understanding of the system and the effects of the implemented requirements more easily. [Robertson and Robertson 2006] emphasise that prototypes demonstrate the consequences of requirements to stakeholders. Instead of thinking abstractly about requirements and imagining the consequences, stakeholders experience the consequences of requirements by means of the prototype.

Advantage: alignment with the stakeholder's own expectations

Since a prototype can be directly experienced by the stakeholder, the stakeholder compares his/her own expectations with the properties of the prototype. Based on the differences between the stakeholder's own expectations and the experienced properties of the prototype, the stakeholder can define new requirements or change existing requirements.

Advantage: stimulation of new ideas for requirements

A prototype can stimulate stakeholders to define new requirements for the system. This pertains to requirements that have merely been forgotten so far, as well as to truly novel requirements (see [Alexander and Stevens 2002]).

The use of a prototype during requirements engineering is not restricted to requirements elicitation. Prototypes may also be used for validating requirements. In fact, it may sometimes be difficult to distinguish clearly between requirements elicitation and requirements validation when using prototypes. We explain the use of prototypes for requirements validation in Section 28.5.

23.3.1 Preparation

Deciding What Kind of Prototype to Use

Before developing a prototype, the stakeholders must decide what kind of prototype shall be developed. The kind of prototype has an essential influence on the effort required for its realisation. Prototypes can be distinguished based on their intended use and functionality.

Usage: throwaway vs. evolutionary prototype

Based on the criterion of their intended usage, prototypes are classified into throwaway prototypes and evolutionary prototypes (see [Sommerville 2004]). A throwaway prototype is no longer maintained after usage. Accordingly, the quality of the implementation is regarded as less important. In contrast, an evolutionary prototype is developed with the aim of incrementally extending and improving the prototype. Accordingly, a high importance is attached to its implementation quality. The architecture of an evolutionary prototype must support extensions and enhancements. This requires a significantly greater effort and is therefore more appropriate for usage after requirements elicitation.

Functionality: horizontal vs. vertical prototype

Based on the criterion of their functionality, prototypes are classified into horizontal prototypes and vertical prototypes (see [Lichter et al. 1993]). A horizontal prototype implements a functional layer of a system, such as the graphical user interface layer or the database layer. A vertical prototype implements an extract of the system functionality throughout all layers. It may for instance implement a specific usage scenario including the input of data, the processing of data, the storage of the data in the database, and the visualisation of the data in the graphical user interface.

For requirements elicitation, also paper prototypes or mock-ups can be used. Paper prototypes and mock-ups require less implementation effort than executable prototypes.

Paper prototypes

Paper prototypes are used, for instance, to demonstrate initial concepts of graphical user interfaces and thereby support the elicitation of additional requirements for the system. A paper prototype presents the user interface of the system by means of sketches and images which can be discussed with the stakeholders and are therefore especially useful during requirements elicitation.

Mock-up

A mock-up is a model of a system without any functionality. A mock-up can be realised either as a physical model or as a digital model (e.g. a 3D virtual model). Mock-ups are especially useful for supporting the elicitation of requirements for the physical appearance of the system and/or the user interface. For instance, a mock-up of the cockpit of a vehicle can be used for eliciting or clarifying requirements for the accessibility and the arrangement of the individual display and control elements in a car. The creation of a mock-up typically requires a certain amount of construction effort.

Developing usage scenarios

To provide stakeholders with easy access to the prototype, it is additionally recommended to develop usage scenarios for the prototype (see [Weidenhaupt et al. 1998]). These usage scenarios support both the development of the prototype as well as the elicitation of further requirements with the prototype. When presenting the prototype to the stakeholders, the usage scenarios are provided as tasks which the stakeholders shall perform with the prototype. By exemplarily executing the scenarios, the stakeholders are enabled to provide more profound feedback on the prototype, such as additional requirements or additional details about the requirements.

Developing the Prototype

Schematic vs. realistic prototypes

A prototype is not necessarily implemented using the same technologies as for the system to be developed. For the development of a mock-up or a paper prototype [Alexander and Stevens 2002] recommend to develop a schematic prototype, preferably, i.e. a prototype that is not too realistic. A prototype created after requirements elicitation which is overly realistic can mislead the stakeholders at the beginning of the project with regard to the actual status of the project. It may hence misdirect the stakeholders' expectations concerning the system. An overly realistic prototype leads to a narrow focus of the stakeholders with regard to possible realisations. Frequently, only suggestions for improving details of the prototype at hand are elicited, whereas necessary, important changes and alternative solutions are overlooked. In contrast, a schematic prototype encourages the stakeholders to question the design and the structure of the prototype.

23.3.2 Execution

Executing the usage scenarios

When experimenting with the prototype, the stakeholders' first step should be to execute the usage scenarios with the prototype.

Free usage of the prototype

After an introductory phase, the stakeholders must be given sufficient time to try out and examine the prototype at will.

Documenting the stakeholders' reactions

All reactions of the stakeholders during the use of the prototype provide valuable information and must therefore be documented appropriately. [Alexander and Stevens 2002] emphasise the importance of the stakeholders' first impression of the prototype and recommend using audio and video recording in order to record preferably all reactions of the stakeholders, such as their comments, facial expressions as well as the process of using the prototype. If audio and video recording is not possible, a second requirements engineer should observe and document the stakeholders' reactions.

Considering non-verbal reactions

Non-verbal reactions of the stakeholders are especially important. From non-verbal reactions one can derive how the prototype impacts on the stakeholders (see [Beyer and Holtzblatt 1998]). For example, the puzzled facial expression of a stakeholder during the examination of a user interface prototype indicates that the interface design might be too complex.

23.3.3 Follow-up

Analysis of the documented results

The follow-up work of a prototype demonstration consists of analysing the recorded results such as minutes as well as audio and video recordings.

23.3.4 Checklist for Applying the Technique

Hint 23-3 presents a checklist for the preparation, execution, and follow-up phases of using prototypes during requirements elicitation.

!

Hint 23-3: *Checklist for applying prototypes for elicitation*

Preparation:

- ❑ Decide whether the prototype shall be created during or after elicitation.
- ❑ Before creating the prototype, define usage scenarios for the prototype and decide which requirements shall be implemented in the prototype.
- ❑ Determine whether the prototype shall be realised as a software prototype, a paper prototype, or a mock-up.
- ❑ In case of a software prototype, define what kind of prototype to implement (throwaway vs. evolutionary, horizontal vs. vertical prototype)
- ❑ Identify a suitable implementation technology for the prototype (such as a tool environment for prototyping).
- ❑ Preferably use schematic prototypes as far as possible.

Execution:

- ❑ Let the stakeholders execute the usage scenarios with the prototype.
- ❑ Allot enough time for the stakeholders to try out the prototype.
- ❑ Capture the stakeholder's feedback during and after prototype usage.

Follow-up:

- ❑ Analyse the recorded results of the prototype demonstration.

23.3.5 Benefit for Requirements Elicitation

Identifying Relevant Requirement Sources

Not suitable

Prototyping is not suited for identifying requirement sources.

Eliciting Existing Requirements

Suitable

Prototyping is suited as an assistance technique for eliciting existing requirements in interviews and requirements workshops. Stakeholders get the opportunity to interact with the prototype and to experience the requirements for the system by interacting with the prototype. Subsequently, the requirements engineers ask questions about the prototype in an interview or the stakeholders discuss the prototype in a workshop. Hence, prototypes support communication among the stakeholders (see [Beyer and Holtzblatt 1998]).

Better comprehension of poorly understood requirements

Using prototypes supports the elicitation of poorly understood requirements (see [Sommerville and Sawyer 1997]). By means of prototypes, the stakeholders can experience how their requirements affect the system to be developed.

Developing New and Innovative Requirements

Partly suited (well suited)

Prototypes can support the development of new and innovative requirements. This especially holds for mock-ups and prototypes used in elicitation sessions. For instance, the stakeholders may create a paper prototype of the graphical user interface of a system to be developed during a workshop (see Section 22.4) or they may jointly build a mock-up of a new cockpit for a vehicle.

By jointly developing a prototype in a group, members of the group stimulate each other. This supports the development of new and innovative requirements. The development of a prototype may, for example, take place in the same way as a brainstorming session (see Section 23.2). Therein, a requirements engineer sketches a sequence of paper prototypes while the stakeholders generate new ideas for requirements. As in a brainstorming session, it is not allowed to criticise expressed ideas.

23.3.6 Effort

Low effort for paper prototypes

The effort for developing the prototype depends on what kind of prototype is developed (see Fig. 23-2). Paper prototypes can be developed with relatively low effort.

	very high	high	medium	low	very low
Paper prototype				✓	
Generated software prototype/mock-up				✓	(✓)
Development of software prototype/mock-up supported by tool			✓	(✓)	
Manually developed software prototype/mock-up	(✓)	✓			

Fig. 23-2 *Effort for prototyping*

High development effort for mock-ups and software prototypes

The realisation effort for mock-ups and software prototypes depends on the available realisation technology. We classify the effort for the manual realisation of a mock-up or software prototype for elicitation as high or, for complex systems, even as very high. If dedicated tool support is available, producing/developing the mock-up or prototype requires medium or low effort. If the mock-up or prototype can be produced or generated from an initial set of requirements, the effort is low or even very low.

23.3.7 Critical Success Factors

Selection of the requirements

The benefit of the prototype depends on the requirements that are selected for implementation in the prototype. Therein, the usage scenarios defined for the system play an important role.

Limitations of the prototype

For the success of a prototype it is important to point out its limitations. When a stakeholder who examines the prototype has wrong expectations, he/she may draw false conclusions from using the prototype.

23.4 KJ Method

Eliciting requirements or requirement sources from a group

The KJ method was originally developed by [Kawakita 1975] to support groups of stakeholders in developing new ideas. In requirements engineering, the method is used to elicit requirements and requirement sources from each participant of a group at the same time. Each participant sketches his/her ideas on a set of file cards. Each file card should contain the keywords characterising a single requirement (or requirement source). Subsequently, the cards are presented and grouped by subject. Eventually, the participants select the best ideas to be processed further.

When applying the KJ method, each participant has the possibility to write down his/her ideas independently of other participants. However, unlike brainstorming, the KJ method does not ensure that the participants stimulate each other with their ideas.

23.4.1 Preparation

Prior to eliciting requirements or requirement sources using the KJ method, the goal of the elicitation session must be defined clearly and unambiguously.

> **Example 23-2:** A goal for an elicitation session phrased as a question.
>
> "Which functionality should a car have to facilitate accident-free driving?"

Pin boards for visualisation

During the elicitation, the labelled cards have to be presented so that they are visible to all participants. For this purpose, a sufficient amount of pin boards and display boards must be provided.

Appointing a suitable room

The room in which the elicitation session takes place should be large enough to pin up all labelled cards on the pin boards or display boards so that they are visible to all participants.

Determining and inviting participants

According to the goal of the elicitation session, the requirements engineers select stakeholders from the known requirement sources. Therein, the requirements engineers have to consider all four context facets (if the context facets are not restricted by the subject). The selected participants are invited and informed about the goal and rationales of the elicitation activity. Generally, the elicitation session takes 30–60 min.

Providing cards and markers

A sufficient amount of cards (e.g. 5 × 7 inches or 4 × 6 inches in size) and markers and pens must be provided to perform the elicitation session. The provided pens and cards should allow the cards to be read from a large distance.

Sample card

As the readability of the cards is very important for the KJ method, a sample card should be provided as guidance for the participants on how to label the cards correctly (see Fig. 23-3).

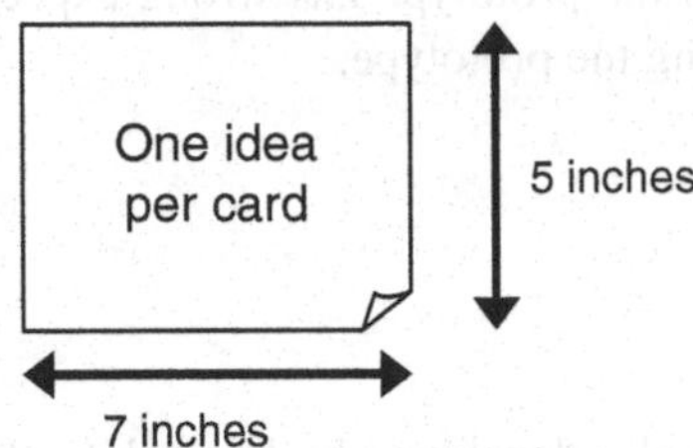

Fig. 23-3 *The sample card*

Rule: one idea per card

The sample card indicates that only one idea (requirement) shall be written on a card.

Determining a moderator

Furthermore, a moderator must be appointed for the elicitation session. The moderator has various tasks during the session (see below). However, he can also participate in writing cards himself. Additionally, a minute-taker is needed, who documents the participants' questions and answers concerning the labelled cards.

23.4.2 Execution

The elicitation session is divided into five phases: introduction, interrogation, presentation, explanation, and grouping.

Introduction

Explaining the goal

At the beginning, the moderator explains the goal of the elicitation session, such as identifying requirement sources or eliciting requirements concerning a specific aspect of the system. The goal should be expressed as a question which the participants shall answer when writing the cards. The participants are encouraged to ask questions in order to resolve ambiguities and clarify misunderstandings concerning the goal. The goal of the elicitation session is additionally written on a large card and pinned up at the top of the pin board so that it is visible for all participants.

Card Writing

Labelling the cards

After the introduction, the cards and markers are distributed to the participants. Each participant gets approximately the same number of cards. The participants are provided with a limited time period to write down their ideas regarding the given question. Generally, 10 min should be sufficient.

Presentation and Explanation

The moderator collects the written cards from the participants, reads out each card aloud, and pins it up on the pin board. The presentation of the cards on the pin board aims to allow all participants to additionally read the cards themselves. Initially, the cards are not sorted when being pinned up on the pin board. Figure 23-4 shows schematically the result of pinning up the written cards. If one pin board is not sufficient to present all cards, multiple pin boards are used.

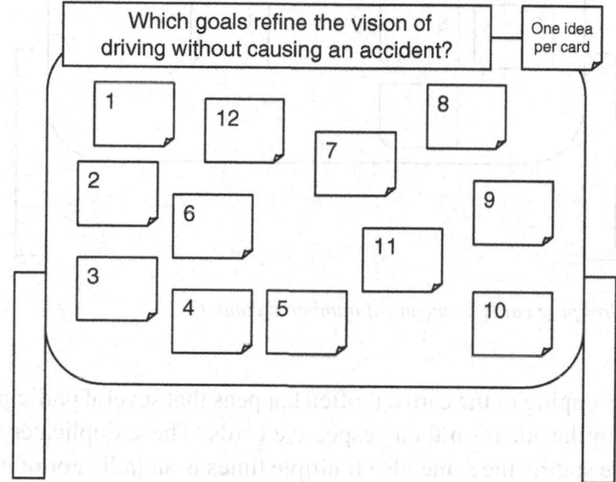

Fig. 23-4 *Typical presentation of the cards*

Numbering the cards

The cards are numbered sequentially, so that the minute-taker can note questions and explanations using the number of the card as a reference. The sequential numbering helps to unambiguously relate each note in the minutes to the corresponding card.

Clarifying the meaning of each card

After pinning up and reading the cards, the participants can ask clarification questions in order to resolve ambiguities. The author of the respective card answers the questions and may add further keywords to the card. Going through the unsorted cards sequentially is recommended.

Grouping

Sorting cards by subject

During this phase, the participants group the cards by subject. The moderator pins up the first card on a free pin board. We refer to this pin board also as the arrangement pin board. For each following card, the participants and the moderator check whether this card is related to another card that has already been pinned up. If this is the case, the considered card is pinned up beneath this card. Otherwise, the card is pinned up somewhere else on the board. To facilitate grouping we recommend preparing numbered columns on the arrangement pin board. The columns may also be assigned labels which indicate the subjects of the columns (as soon as the subjects are known). The cards are assigned to columns by calling out the number or label of the respective column. The result of the grouping is a set of columns where each column contains cards related to a common subject (see Fig. 23-5).

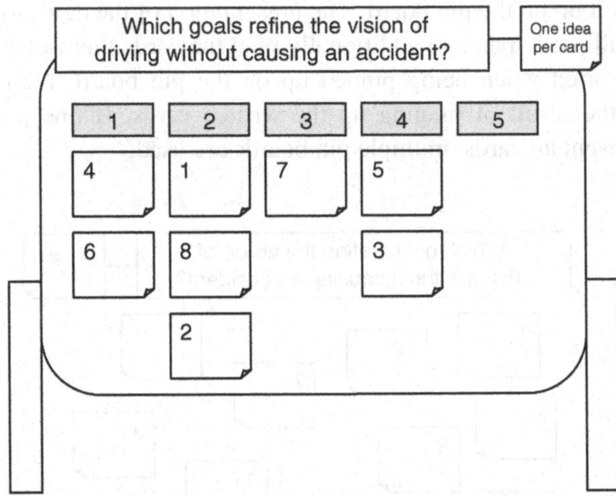

Fig. 23-5 *Grouping cards by means of numbered columns*

Double or similar cards

During the grouping of the cards, it often happens that several participants write the same idea or similar ideas on their respective cards. These duplicates should not be discarded, since stating the same idea multiple times is an indicator of its importance. Therefore, double cards are pinned up on top of each other during grouping.

Cards that are related to multiple subjects or columns are copied by the author of the card and pinned up in all columns to which they are related. Each copy should be tagged with the same number as the original, but should show a remark that identifies it as a copy.

Column headings

After all cards have been sorted by subject on the arrangement pin board, the participants assign a name to each column on the pin board. The columns may also be named while grouping the cards. In this case, a column name is defined as soon as the common subject of a set of cards in the column becomes evident. The column names additionally support grouping of the cards by subject.

Correlations between cards and groups

By assigning the cards to groups, relationships are established between the contents of the cards within each group as well as among different groups.

Relationship with card sorting

This last phase, in which the cards are assigned to columns, is a popular technique for knowledge acquisition called "card sorting" (see [Maiden et al. 1995; Maiden 2009]). Card sorting focusses on the way the stakeholders sort the cards and their rationale for doing so. During an open card sort, the stakeholders may define the categories themselves. During a closed card sort, the categories are predetermined.

23.4.3 Follow-up

Documenting the results

After the cards have been pinned up and sorted into groups, the results of the elicitation session are documented in an appropriate way. A simple way of recording the results is to take photos of the pin boards. Figure 23-6 shows photos of two different elicitation sessions. On the left-hand side, a presentation of unsorted cards is shown. On the right-hand side, the cards have been grouped, i.e. arranged into columns.

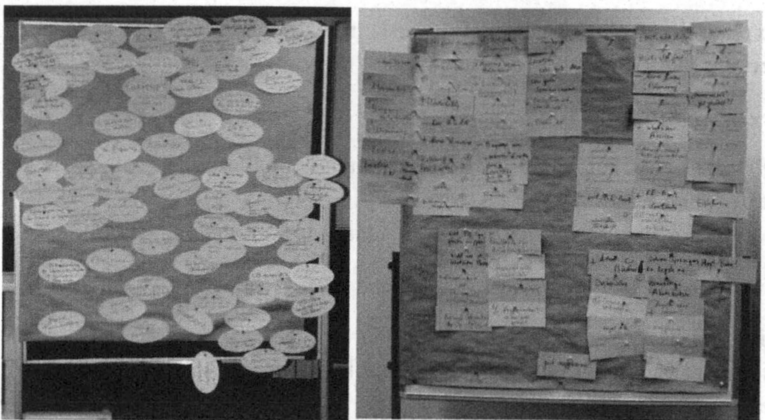

Fig. 23-6 *Documented results of an elicitation session using the KJ method*

Additionally, the explanations, questions, and answers documented in the minutes must be related to the cards. If the cards are numbered sequentially during the presentation and the same numbering is used to reference the cards in the minutes, the relation is clear.

Defining how the results are used

After grouping the cards, the participants must also define how to process the results. For example, the participants can determine the five most important groups of cards to be elaborated on. In order to determine these groups, the relevance assessment technique described in Section 21.4 can be used.

23.4.4 Checklist for Applying the Technique

Hint 23-4 presents a checklist for the preparation, execution, and follow-up phases of applying the KJ method for requirements elicitation.

!

Hint 23-4: *Checklist for the KJ method*

Preparation:

- ❑ Define the goal of the elicitation session.
- ❑ Appoint a room and a time.
- ❑ Select and invite the participants.
- ❑ Provide pin boards for visualisation and arrangement of the cards.
- ❑ Provide a sufficient amount of cards and markers.
- ❑ Create a sample card.
- ❑ Observe the rule of only one idea per card.
- ❑ Appoint a moderator.

(*to be continued*)

Hint 23-4 *(continued)*

Execution – Introduction:

- ❑ Explain the goal of the elicitation session to the participants.
- ❑ Present the rules and the sample card.

Execution – Interrogation:

- ❑ Distribute markers and an approximately equal number of cards to each participant.
- ❑ Let the participants write down their ideas (approximately 10 min).

Execution – Presentation and explanation:

- ❑ Pin up the labelled cards on the pin board.
- ❑ Number the unsorted cards sequentially and use the same numbering to reference the cards in the minutes.
- ❑ Let the participants explain and complement cards whose meaning is unclear or ambiguous.

Execution – Grouping:

- ❑ Let the participants group the cards by subject.
- ❑ Do not remove cards with double or similar ideas, but pin them up on top of each other instead.
- ❑ Let the participants define a heading for each group of cards.
- ❑ Let the participants analyse relationships among the cards within each group as well as among the groups.

Follow-up:

- ❑ Document the results of the elicitation session.
- ❑ Define together with the participants how the results shall be further processed.
- ❑ Distribute the minutes to the participants and collect their feedback on the minutes.

23.4.5 Benefit for Requirements Elicitation

Identifying Relevant Requirement Sources

Suitable

The KJ method is suited for identifying unknown requirement sources. If necessary, a separate round of card writing can be performed for each type of requirement source (stakeholders, documents, and systems). Hint 23-5 describes three possible questions for elicitation sessions during which the participants shall identify requirement sources.

!

Hint 23-5: *Enquiries for identifying requirement sources*

- *Identification of stakeholders*: Which stakeholders are relevant for the system?
- *Identification of important documents*: Which documents are relevant for the system?
- *Identification of important legacy systems*: Which legacy systems are relevant for the system?

Grouping according to the four context facets

After pinning up the cards, the identified requirement sources are grouped according to the four context facets. Each requirement source is thereby assigned to at least one context facet. After the grouping, the participants assess the relative relevance of the identified requirement sources using the technique presented in Section 21.4.

Eliciting Existing Requirements

Well suited

Generally, the KJ method is well suited for eliciting existing requirements. Existing goals can be elicited particularly well.

Developing New and Innovative Requirements

The KJ method is generally not well suited for developing new and innovative requirements.

Adapted procedure

However, a combination of the KJ method and brainstorming (see Section 23.2) can support the development of new and innovative requirements. For this purpose, when writing the cards, the participants pin up each card on the pin board immediately, i.e. they do not wait until the other participants have finished writing all their cards. Due to this modification of the procedure, the other participants can read each written card immediately, which stimulates the generation of further ideas. When applying this modified form of the KJ method, the brainstorming rules presented in Hint 23-1 (Page 455) must be observed.

23.4.6 Effort

The effort for an elicitation session with 8–10 participants can be estimated as very low. It does not require much preparation. The execution and follow-up phases of the KJ method also do not require much effort.

very high	high	medium	low	very low
				✓

Fig. 23-7 *Effort for the KJ method*

23.4.7 Critical Success Factors

Clearly defined goal

Similar to the other techniques, a clear goal must be defined and the participants must have a common understanding of this goal in order to successfully elicit the participants' ideas by means of the KJ method.

Size of the group

Additionally, the size of the group is a critical success factor. The larger the number of participants, the more effort is required to present and group the cards. According to our experience, at most 8–10 stakeholders should participate in an elicitation session.

Reducing effort in large groups

If an elicitation session shall be performed with more participants, the requirements engineers should divide the group into several sub-groups of, for example, 3–4 persons. Then, each sub-group is jointly assigned a number of cards on which the participants of this sub-group can write. In this way, the overall number of labelled cards and hence the effort for presenting and grouping the cards are reduced.

23.5 Mind Mapping

Overview

Mind maps allow the systematic presentation of information by means of text and graphics (see [Buzan and Buzan 2006]). In each mind map, there is one central subject. Other terms that are related to this subject are arranged around the central subject like branches of a tree. Each branch (i.e. term) can again be refined by further branches. Figure 23-8 shows an example of a mind map.

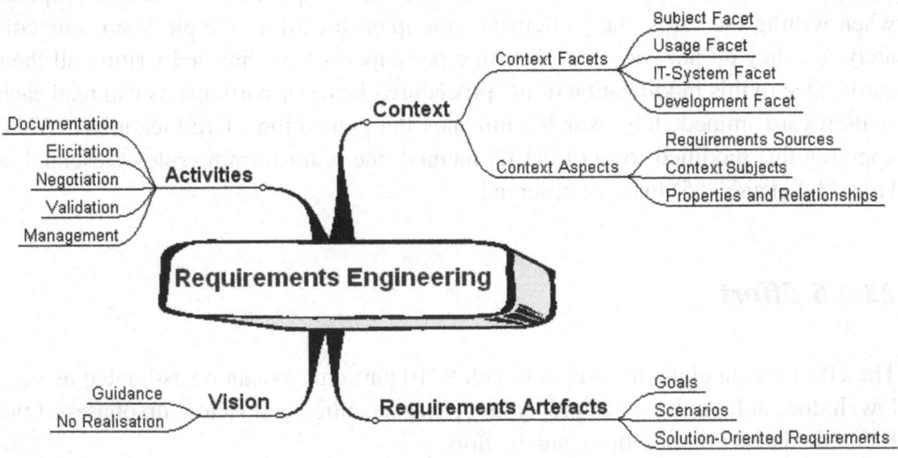

Fig. 23-8 *A mind map*[4]

Terms in a mind map need not necessarily be expressed using natural language but can also be represented by means of graphics (e.g. icons). In addition, branches can be supplemented by symbols, for example, in order to express their importance.

[4] All mind maps presented in this book were created with the Mindjet Mind-Manager.

The combination of textual information (subjects, headings, and keywords) and graphical information (branches and symbols) in a mind map stimulates the verbally oriented left hemisphere of the human brain as well as the spatially–visually dominated right hemisphere. This combined stimulation supports the brain in capturing, memorising, and organising information (see [Buzan and Buzan 2006]).

Combination of textual and graphical information

23.5.1 Preparation

Creating a mind map does not require much preparation. Mind maps are typically used in combination with other techniques (e.g. during a workshop) as a means of documentation. There are two ways to create a mind map:

- *Paper-based documentation*: This kind of documentation of a mind map can be created almost anywhere. For instance, a group can interactively create the mind map on a pin board. Shortcomings of this kind of documentation are the poor changeability and the limited further use of the mind map, e.g. in documents.
- *Software-based documentation*: Mind maps created using a software tool can be easily changed and distributed to all participants, e.g. via e-mail. Additionally, the mind maps can be easily transferred into other representation formats and embedded in presentations or other documents. If mind maps are created with a software tool, a technical infrastructure (laptop, projector, projection screen) must be provided to present the mind map so that it is visible to all group members.

23.5.2 Execution

The central subject of the mind map is written in the middle of the mind map clearly and precisely. Additionally, the subject may be visualised by a small picture or a sketch (see Fig. 23-9).

Central subject in the middle

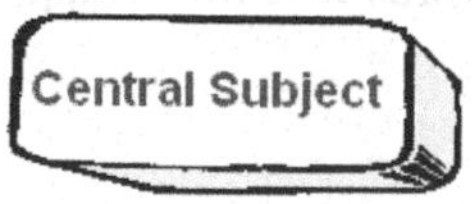

Fig. 23-9 *Visualising the central subject*

The headings of a mind map branch off from the central subject. They are shown as thick branches. The branches should be distributed evenly around the central subject. The font size of the headings should be smaller than the font size of the central subject.

From each heading, again branches originate which contain keywords related to the heading. The keywords should be presented in a font size that is smaller than the font size of the headings. Figure 23-10 shows schematically how headings refine the central subject and how keywords refine the headings.

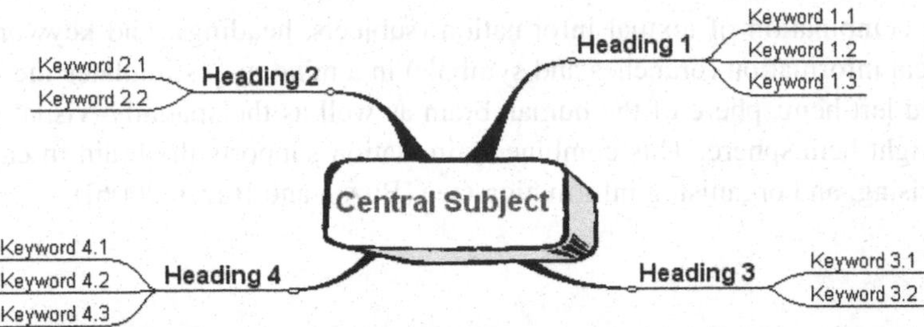

Fig. 23-10 *Refining headings by keywords*

Refining keywords

The keywords pertaining to a heading are further refined if necessary. The refinement of keywords can be nested arbitrarily deeply. However, one should stop at a nesting level of five or six, since it becomes difficult to read the mind map, otherwise.

Adding figures

Adding figures to text or replacing text by figures (see Fig. 23-11) supports making associations. However, if words are replaced by figures, a person who reads the mind map might misinterpret the figures.

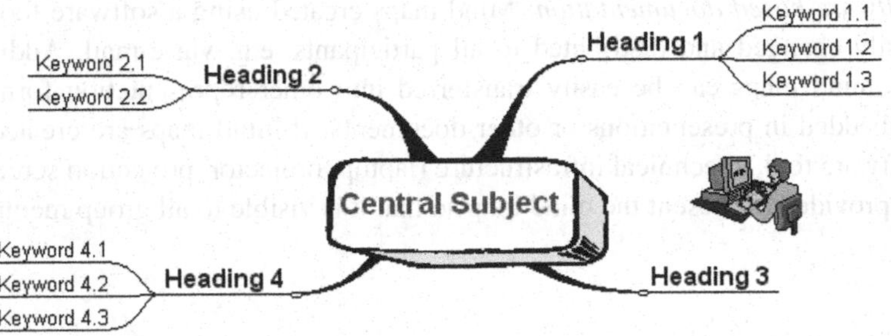

Fig. 23-11 *Adding figures to branches*

Links/ interconnections

In order to relate different branches (terms) in the mind map, links/ interconnections can be drawn between the branches. The links can be designed differently to distinguish, for instance, conflict and support relationships (see Section 7.4). Figure 23-12 shows how keywords in a mind map can be related to each other by means of arrows.

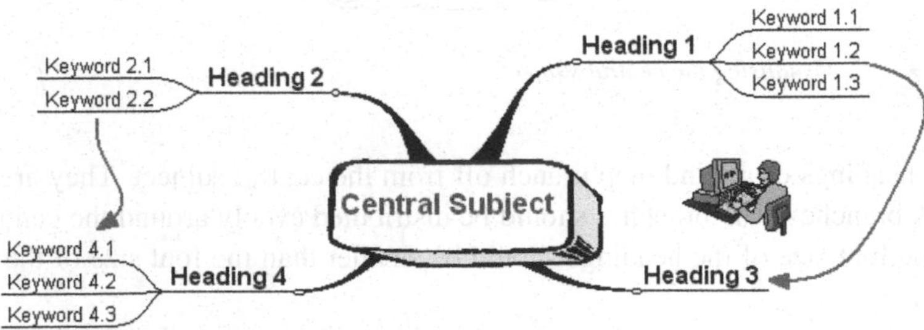

Fig. 23-12 *Links in a mind map*

Using colours

A coloured layout of the mind map supports the readability and memorability of the mind map. Colours may, for example, be used to point out important headings or keywords.

Mind maps are not static

A mind map is not a static document. While creating the mind map, new ideas and associations emerge which lead to a change of the mind map. If the mind map gets too large, a reorganisation of the mind map is necessary. For example, one branch can be divided into two or more branches. A branch can also be joined with another branch or placed at a different position in the tree. Therefore, software-based documentation of mind maps is recommended.

23.5.3 Follow-up

When a mind map is created on paper, the branches and keywords are often not arranged and presented in an ideal way. Therefore, such a mind map must be drawn anew after creating and/or adapting it in order to ensure a good presentation of the information.

Checking for ambiguous terms and structural flaws

Furthermore, it is advisable to check a mind map independently of the documentation format for ambiguities of the terms used. If necessary, the terms are adapted. In addition, the structure of the mind map should be checked for required reorganisations. Where needed, the mind map is reorganised.

23.5.4 Benefit for Requirements Elicitation

Suitable for all sub-activities

Mind maps are a means to visualise and document information in a structured way and can hence be used to support all three requirements elicitation sub-activities. A mind map can be used, for instance, during an interview in order to document and structure the facts being discussed. Mind maps can also be used for grouping the cards during an elicitation session based on the KJ method.

23.5.5 Effort

The effort for creating a mind map is not significantly larger than the effort needed for documenting the results of a group meeting using, for instance, a word-processing tool. We therefore estimate the effort of using mind maps as very low.

very high	high	medium	low	very low
				✓

Fig. 23-13 *Effort for mind mapping*

23.5.6 Critical Success Factors

Good structure and visualisation

Good structure of the tree and good visualisation contribute to the readability of the mind map and are essential for good organisation of facts in the mind map. The visualisation can be improved by deliberately using colours and symbols.

23.6 Elicitation Checklists

A checklist contains a number of items, documented as questions or statements, that are related to some issue. Checklists are very helpful when many aspects of a complex issue have to be considered and none of them should be forgotten. If new aspects are identified, e.g. while using a checklist, they are added to the checklist as checklist items to ensure their consideration in the future.

Checklists support all activities

During requirements engineering, checklists are also used for other activities besides requirements elicitation, e.g. validation (see Part V) or documentation (see Part IV.a). Checklists are also used successfully outside of requirements engineering, for example, for supporting maintenance work (e.g. in cars or planes).

23.6.1 Preparation

Adaptation or creation of a checklist

Prior to applying a checklist, the checklist must be created. For many subjects in requirements engineering, checklists already exist (see e.g. [Gottesdiener 2002; Kotonya and Sommerville 1997; Robertson and Robertson 2006]. When reusing an existing checklist, it may be necessary to adapt the checklist for the specific purpose. If a checklist needs to be created from scratch, the aspects for inclusion in the checklist may be elicited in a brainstorming session (see Section 23.2) or by applying the KJ method (see Section 23.4).

Subdividing long checklists

If a checklist contains a large number of items (i.e. questions or statements), it is advisable to subdivide the checklist into several checklists that are easier to manage.

23.6.2 Execution

Documenting suggestions for improvement

A checklist is applied by working through all the checklist items (i.e. questions or statements). If possible, the checklist items should be considered sequentially. If the requirements engineers identify new items when using the checklist or discover that some items in the checklist are defined incomprehensibly, they should document their findings for later use.

23.6.3 Follow-up

Improvement of the checklist

If potential improvements are identified when applying a checklist, the checklist should be revised under consideration of the identified suggestions for improvement.

If, for example, a missing question has been identified, this question should be added. If a question is ambiguous or incomprehensible, it should be reworded. For such cases, Hint 23-6 presents a checklist for improving checklists. Additional hints for improving checklists are presented in Section 29.1.

!

> **Hint 23-6:** *Checklist for improving checklists*
>
> - ❑ Are all statements in the checklist relevant for the considered issue?
> - ❑ Have any aspects been identified during the application of the checklist that should be included in the checklist?
> - ❑ Are there incomprehensible questions or statements in the checklist?
> - ❑ Are there any ambiguities?
> - ❑ Does the checklist contain redundant aspects?

23.6.4 Benefit for Requirements Elicitation

Identifying Relevant Requirement Sources

Suitable

Checklists are useful to support the identification of requirement sources. For this purpose, possible types of requirement sources are listed in a checklist. Such a checklist can be used, for instance, during an interview. For each type of requirement sources stated in the checklist, the interviewer asks the interviewee if he/she can think of a concrete requirement source in the context of the system to be developed. In the literature, a number of lists with requirement sources can be found (see e.g. [Lauesen 2002; Rupp 2004; Sommerville and Sawyer 1997]).

Generic checklists for identifying requirement sources

Hints 23-7, 23-8 and 23-9 present checklists for the identification of requirement sources (stakeholders, documents, and existing systems). Each checklist is divided into four categories by means of the four context facets. Some types of requirement sources are relevant for several facets and hence occur in multiple checklists. The types of requirement sources for each facet are listed in alphabetical order.

Adaptation of checklists

Generic checklists should be adapted before using them for specific domains such as automotive systems or information systems.

!

> **Hint 23-7:** *Checklist for identifying stakeholders*
>
> *Subject facet:*
>
> - ❑ Clients
> - ❑ Domain experts
> - ❑ Experts in the system environment
> - ❑ Legislation
> - ❑ Non-governmental organisations
> - ❑ Competitors to and opponents of the project, product, or system
> - ❑ Work council representatives
> - ❑ Standards-setting bodies
> - ❑ Etc.
>
> (*to be continued*)

Hint 23-7 (*continued*)

Usage facet:

- ☐ Experts in process optimisation and work ergonomics
- ☐ Legislation
- ☐ Managers of the client organisation
- ☐ Non-governmental organisations
- ☐ Persons indirectly affected by the system
- ☐ Project and product opponents of the system
- ☐ Purchasers of the system
- ☐ Sales and marketing persons for the system
- ☐ Security administrator
- ☐ Sponsors and other investors
- ☐ Standards-setting bodies
- ☐ System users
- ☐ Training personnel for the system
- ☐ Etc.

IT system facet:

- ☐ Experts in system integration
- ☐ Legislation
- ☐ Maintenance and service personnel for the system
- ☐ Producers of the system
- ☐ Project and product opponents of the system
- ☐ Persons Responsible for disposal of the system
- ☐ Person responsible for the IT strategy
- ☐ Standards-setting bodies
- ☐ Technical experts for the system
- ☐ Etc.

Development facet:

- ☐ Business partners of the client
- ☐ Controlling department of the client
- ☐ Designers of the system
- ☐ Developers of the system
- ☐ Legislation
- ☐ Managers of the organisation developing the system
- ☐ Persons responsible for research and development
- ☐ Programmers
- ☐ Sales and marketing representatives of the system
- ☐ Sponsors and other investors
- ☐ Standards-setting bodies
- ☐ Testers
- ☐ Etc.

!

Hint 23-8: *Checklist for identifying existing systems*

Subject facet:

- ❑ Predecessor systems that include representations of part of the subjects of the system to be developed
- ❑ Systems of competitors that include representations of part of the subjects of the system to be developed
- ❑ Systems that provide input or output to the system to be developed
- ❑ Etc.

Usage facet:

- ❑ Predecessor systems with similar mode of usage
- ❑ Systems of competitors with similar mode of usage
- ❑ Systems with similar or related functionality
- ❑ Etc.

IT system facet:

- ❑ Middleware systems
- ❑ Predecessor systems
- ❑ Systems with similar or related technical features
- ❑ Etc.

Development facet:

- ❑ Process management systems
- ❑ Process support systems
- ❑ Quality assurance systems
- ❑ Etc.

!

Hint 23-9: *Checklist for identifying documents*

Subject facet:

- ❑ Domain models of the subject domain
- ❑ Laws (existing and planned)
- ❑ Organisation-specific regulations concerning the subjects to be represented in the system
- ❑ Requirements documents of existing systems
- ❑ Standards (DIN, ISO, OMG, etc.)
- ❑ Technical literature from the context of the system
- ❑ Etc.

Usage facet:

- ❑ Business process models
- ❑ Failure reports of existing systems
- ❑ Laws (existing and planned)
- ❑ Manuals of existing systems

(to be continued)

Hint 23-9 (*continued*)

- ❑ Requirements documents of existing systems
- ❑ Standards (DIN, ISO, OMG, etc.)
- ❑ Technical literature from the context of the system
- ❑ Usage guidelines
- ❑ Etc.

IT system facet:

- ❑ Failure reports and failure correction reports
- ❑ Requirements documents of existing systems
- ❑ Technical literature from the context of the system
- ❑ Etc.

Development facet:

- ❑ Failure reports
- ❑ Interface documents
- ❑ IT strategy document
- ❑ Laws (existing and planned)
- ❑ Maintenance documents
- ❑ Organisation-specific development guidelines
- ❑ Process models
- ❑ Requirements documents of existing systems
- ❑ Standards (DIN, ISO, OMG, etc.)
- ❑ Etc.

Eliciting Existing Requirements

Suitable

Checklists are also suited for supporting the identification of existing requirements.

Domain-specific checklists are necessary

For the effective use of checklists during the elicitation of existing requirements, domain-specific checklists must be created. These checklists contain the aspects that are important for the system to be developed. The aspects should be structured according to the four context facets.

When creating a checklist to support the elicitation of existing requirements, all four context facets (subject, usage, IT-system and development) should be considered.

!

Hint 23-10: *Ensure that each context facet is considered:*

- ❑ Which requirements does the requirement source contain with regard to the subject facet?
- ❑ Which requirements does the requirement source contain with regard to the usage facet?
- ❑ Which requirements does the requirement source contain with regard to the IT system facet?
- ❑ Which requirements does the requirement source contain with regard to the development facet?

Developing New and Innovative Requirements

Suitable

Checklists are also suited for supporting the development of new and innovative requirements. The creative development of innovative requirements is, for example, supported by the so-called Osborn checklist (see [Osborn 1993]). The Osborn checklist contains simple questions that stimulate creativity with regard to a defined starting point (e.g. the vision of the system to be developed or an existing system; see Hint 23-11). The Osborn checklist can be used, for instance, in interviews, workshops, or brainstorming sessions.

!

Hint 23-11: *Osborn checklist*

The following questions support creativity with regard to a defined starting point:

- ❑ "*Put to other uses*? (New ways to use as is? Other uses if modified?)
- ❑ *Adapt*? (What else is like this? What other ideas does this suggest?)
- ❑ *Modify*? (Change meaning, color, motion, sound, odor, taste, form, shape? Other changes?)
- ❑ *Magnify*? (What to add? Greater frequency? Stronger? Larger? Plus ingredient? Multiply?)
- ❑ *Minify*? (What to subtract? Eliminate? Smaller? Lighter? Slower? Split up? Less frequent?)
- ❑ *Substitute*? (Who else instead? What else instead? Other place? Other time?)
- ❑ *Rearrange*? (Other layout? Other sequence? Change pace?)
- ❑ *Reverse*? (Opposites? Turn it backward? Turn it upside down? Turn it inside out?)
- ❑ *Combine*? (How about a blend, an assortment? Combine purposes? Combine ideas?)"

[Osborn 1993]

Example 23-3 shows an Osborn checklist applied to a navigation system with possible answers to selected questions.

Example 23-3: Osborn checklist for a navigation system

- ❑ *Put* navigation system *to other uses*?
  The navigation system can be used to guide the user during a sight-seeing tour of a city.
- ❑ *Adapt* the navigation system?
  The presentation of routes in the navigation system can be adapted.
- ❑ *Modify* the navigation system?
  The routes can be projected onto the windscreen.
- ❑ *Magnify* the navigation system?
  The navigation system can take control and act as an autopilot.
- ❑ *Reverse* the navigation system?
  The navigation system can learn the routes preferred by the driver.

(*to be continued*)

Example 23-3 (*continued*)

- ❑ *Combine* the navigation system?
  The navigation system can be combined with traffic information systems in order to take into consideration traffic congestion when route planning.

23.6.5 Effort

The effort for the initial creation of a checklist is low, because the checklist items can be identified using brainstorming or the KJ method. A checklist is typically used several times. The effort for creating the checklist must hence be calculated per application and is therefore nearly negligible.

very high	high	medium	low	very low
				✓

Fig. 23-14 *Effort for checklists*

Effort reduction

The effort for applying a checklist depends on the issue and the length of the checklist. According to our experience, a checklist not only increases the quality of the results but also reduces the effort required for performing the respective activity compared with performing the activity without the checklist.

Very low effort for improving the checklist

The effort required for improving a checklist is very low, if possible improvements of the checklist are documented during its application and the checklist is revised after each application.

23.6.6 Critical Success Factors

Quality of the questions

The quality of a checklist is essential for its successful application. The better the questions and statements in the checklist are aligned to the issue considered, the easier and more successful is the application of the checklist.

Unambiguous and comprehensible statements

If the questions and statements in a checklist are defined incomprehensibly or ambiguously, successful application of the checklist is impaired. Therefore, the questions and statements should be defined in a comprehensible and unambiguous way. In addition, the checklist should be checked for clarity and comprehensibility during each application.

Up-to-date questions

Another critical success factor is to keep the checklist up to date. If the checklist contains many questions that are out of date, no longer important, or important questions are missing, the stakeholders may disregard the checklist while performing the elicitation activity.

Recommended Literature for Part IV.b

Basic Reading

[Gottesdiener 2002] deals with organising and performing workshops for requirements elicitation. In addition to a sound presentation of the fundamentals of workshops, the author gives helpful advice for planning and performing workshops.

[Kotonya and Sommerville 1997] describe the elicitation of requirements and sketch elicitation techniques such as interviews and ethnographic studies.

[Leffingwell and Widrig 2000] describe the challenges of requirements elicitation and explain techniques such as prototyping and brainstorming.

[Oppenheim 1999] provides a comprehensive introduction to interviews and questionnaires. The book contains a number of practical hints for organising interviews and questionnaires.

Advanced Reading

[Buzan and Buzan 2006] explain the mind mapping technique and describe, by means of practical examples and exercises, how mind maps support creative work.

[Hammersley and Atkinson 2007] provide a comprehensive introduction to ethnographic research. The book deals with the planning, execution, and documentation of ethnographic research and hence goes beyond requirements engineering.

[Kuniavsky 2003] provides a comprehensive guide for conducting user-centred research and development. Among other things, focus groups are explained in this book.

[Maiden and Robertson 2005] describe the RESCUE approach for scenario-based requirements engineering. This approach comprises workshops, creativity techniques, as well as different types of use cases and different context modelling approaches.

[Marakas 2002] shows how groups of people collaboratively solve problems to arrive at decisions and ideas. He also discusses the groupthink effect.

[Sharp et al. 2007] describe a broad variety of techniques used in interaction and user-centred design such as card sorting, prototyping, and interviewing.

[Zowghi and Coulin 2005] provide a short overview of the state of the art of techniques, approaches, and tools for requirements elicitation.

Part IV.c
Negotiation

Overview Part IV.c – Negotiation

One goal of the requirements engineering process is to establish sufficient agreement among the stakeholders regarding the already known requirements for the system. The following four sub-activities described in this part of the book support achieving this goal:

- *Identifying conflicts*
- *Analysing conflicts*
- *Resolving conflicts*
- *Documenting conflict resolutions*

The sub-activities are mainly supported by the following techniques:

- *Win–Win approach*
- *Interaction matrix*

Classification Part IV.c Negotiation		Basic	Advanced
24	**Fundamentals of Requirements Negotiation**		
24.1	Goal of Requirements Negotiation	✓	
24.2	Requirements Negotiation: Definition	✓	
24.3	Use of Goals and Scenarios in Requirements Negotiation	✓	
25	**Conflict Management**		
25.1	Sub-activity: Identifying Conflicts	✓	
25.2	Sub-activity: Analysing Conflicts	✓	
25.3	Sub-activity: Resolving Conflicts	✓	
25.4	Sub-activity: Documenting Conflict Resolution		✓
26	**Negotiation Techniques**		
26.1	The Win–Win Approach		✓
26.2	Interaction Matrix	✓	

Chapter 24
Fundamentals of Requirements Negotiation

In this chapter, we outline:

- *The motivation for negotiating requirements*
- *The subject of requirements negotiation*
- *The benefits of goals and scenarios for negotiating requirements*

24.1 Goal of Requirements Negotiation

Stakeholder needs may conflict with each other

The system to be developed shall consider and realise preferably all the needs and wishes of the different stakeholders. Rarely are the stakeholders' needs and wishes free of conflicts. For example, the maintenance staff of an email system might demand that the incoming and outgoing messages are recorded in a log file in order to support fault analysis and, hence, system maintenance. In contrast, the users of the email system might demand high confidentiality of the exchanged messages and hence disapprove of the logging of messages.

Conflicts

The requirements engineers must hence check whether all stakeholders agree with the documented requirements. Negotiation in requirements engineering aims to achieve agreement among all stakeholders about the requirements and hence has to deal with conflicts about requirements. We define a conflict in requirements engineering as follows:

D

Definition 24-1: *Conflict (in requirements engineering)*

A conflict in requirements engineering exists, if the needs and wishes of different stakeholders (or groups of stakeholders) regarding the system contradict each other, or if some needs and wishes cannot be taken into account.

Examples of conflicts among different stakeholders about the requirements for a system are presented in Example 24-1.

E

Example 24-1: Simple examples of conflicts about requirements

A group of stakeholders demands the use of radar sensors for distance measurement. Another group of stakeholders asks, instead, for ultrasound sensors.

A stakeholder demands that safety-relevant information for the driver be displayed on a head-up display. Other stakeholders think this would detract the driver and hence reject this requirement.

Risks of unresolved conflicts

Unresolved conflicts compromise the acceptance of the system by the stakeholders. As a result of conflicts that are disregarded or even suppressed, some stakeholders may no longer support the development of the system, or the conflicts may even cause a failure of the development project (see e.g. [Easterbrook 1994]).

Regarding conflicts as an opportunity

Conflicts should not be regarded negatively in requirements engineering. They can serve as a source of new ideas and the development of innovative requirements (see e.g. [Gause und Weinberg 1989]).

Goal of the negotiation activity

Requirements negotiation is one of the three core activities of requirements engineering. The goal of requirements negotiation is to achieve progress in the agreement dimension (see Section 4.4) by identifying conflicts, analysing conflicts, and resolving the identified conflicts.

Involving the relevant stakeholders

To resolve conflicts in requirements engineering, the relevant stakeholders must be involved. In addition, software architects, developers, and testers should be trained so that they report detected conflicts to the requirements engineers. In other words, stakeholders such as architects, developers, or testers should not try to "resolve" the conflicts they have identified on their own, i.e. without involving the relevant stakeholders. The requirements engineers should thoroughly consider each conflict they detect or that is reported to them. They should resolve all reported conflicts jointly with the relevant stakeholders. Resolving conflicts about the requirements during requirements engineering generally leads to improved acceptance of the implemented system.

24.2 Requirements Negotiation: Definition

Based on the characterisation of requirements negotiation in Section 24.1, we define this core requirements engineering activity as follows:

D

Definition 24-2: *Requirements negotiation*

Requirements negotiation is one of the three core requirements engineering activities. The goal of the negotiation activity is to:

(1) Identify conflicts
(2) Analyse the cause of each conflict
(3) Resolve the conflicts by means of appropriate strategies
(4) Document the conflict resolution and the rationale

Four sub-activities

The attainment of the four sub-goals of the negotiation activity (Definition 24-2) is supported by the following four sub-activities, which are explained in Chapter 25:

- Identifying conflicts (see Section 25.1)
- Analysing conflicts (see Section 25.2)
- Resolving conflicts (see Section 25.3)
- Documenting conflict resolutions (see Section 25.4)

24.3 Use of Goals and Scenarios in Requirements Negotiation

Benefits of goals

The explicit definition of goals in the requirements engineering process supports the resolution of conflicts (see Section 25.3).

First, resolve conflicts at the goal level

Goals document the rationales of solution-oriented requirements. Many conflicts about solution-oriented requirements are in fact conflicts about the associated goals. Conflicts about the solution-oriented requirements are easier to resolve after the stakeholders have agreed on the associated goals. Therefore, conflicts should be identified, documented, analysed, and resolved at the goal level as far as possible (conflicts between goals are explained in Section 7.4). After resolving the conflicts at the goal level, the different, potentially conflicting realisations of the goals can be considered. Resolving conflicts at the goal level first has an essential advantage: Fundamental contradictions are resolved before the stakeholders go into technical details of the realisations of the goals.

Find creative solutions for conflicts at the goal level

When analysing a conflict at the level of solution-oriented requirements, the stakeholders are exposed to a large amount of details which may prove to be irrelevant for resolving the conflict. Hence it is typically much easier to find a solution to a conflict at the goal level rather than at the level of solution-oriented requirements. Identifying creative solutions for goal conflict resolution can be supported by means of alternative goal decompositions (see Section 7.3). If a goal G_1 is in conflict with one or multiple other goals, the stakeholders can try to identify alternative goals that satisfy the same super-goal as G_1. The identified goals denote alternatives to G_1. These alternatives are evaluated with regard to conflicts with the other, already defined goals. Subsequently, instead of realising G_1, an alternative that has fewer conflicts with the other goals can be chosen.

Support for decision-making

Furthermore, goals can be used to support decision-making when the stakeholders have to choose among different realisations. For instance, the stakeholders may choose a realisation that satisfies most of the defined goals (or the most important goals) and causes the fewest conflicts.

Benefits of scenarios

Scenarios support analysis of conflicts (see Section 25.2) as well as resolution of conflicts (see Section 25.3). Conflict analysis benefits from the use of scenarios: A scenario can clarify a conflict by describing an exemplary sequence of interactions in which the conflict occurs. The description of a situation exemplifying the conflict provides information that helps analyse the conflict and identify the cause of the conflict.

Concrete examples facilitate agreement

Conflict resolution also benefits from scenarios. The stakeholders can develop and discuss different scenarios in which the conflict is reduced or even completely avoided. Eventually, the stakeholders can evaluate the different scenarios and decide which scenario offers the best solution to the considered conflict and hence should be implemented.

Chapter 25
Conflict Management

In this chapter, we present the four sub-activities of conflict management:

- *Identifying conflicts*
- *Analysing conflicts*
- *Resolving conflicts*
- *Documenting conflict resolutions*

25.1 Sub-activity: Identifying Conflicts

Conflicts about requirements may surface during all requirements engineering activities (see [Easterbrook 1994]). Example 25-1 presents some situations in which conflicts about requirements are identified during different requirements engineering activities.

Example 25-1: Identifying conflicts in the different requirements engineering activities

- During the elicitation of requirements in a workshop, two stakeholders state requirements that contradict each other and hence cannot be realised together.
- When documenting requirements that have been elicited during interviews, the stakeholders detect a conflict between two requirements that originate from different interviews.
- In requirements management, a conflict occurs during the prioritisation of requirements. Two stakeholders have different opinions regarding the priority of a requirement.
- During requirements validation, a conflict occurs while the stakeholders check the specified requirements for correctness. One stakeholder considers a requirement to be correct, while another stakeholder objects to this requirement.
- During conflict resolution, a new conflict is identified.

Pay attention to conflicts during all requirements engineering activities

Conflicts do not always become obvious during the individual requirements engineering activities. For example, a stakeholder may not express his disapproval of a requirement immediately. Therefore, the requirements engineers should pay special attention during all requirements engineering activities to detecting and documenting (possibly latent) conflicts. In addition, similar conflicts should be consolidated in order to facilitate consideration of these conflicts jointly during conflict analysis and conflict resolution. Similarity among conflicts means, for instance, that the conflicts pertain to the same requirement or to the same system aspect.

Actively search for conflicts

In addition, the requirements engineers need to actively search for conflicts that have remained undetected during the other requirements engineering activities. For this purpose, the requirements engineers apply techniques that make conflicts explicit. For example, they can use the KJ method as a means of systematic conflict identification (see Section 23.4).

25.2 Sub-activity: Analysing Conflicts

Determining the conflict type

The goal of conflict analysis is to determine the conflict types of the identified conflicts. The further process of resolving the conflicts depends on the conflict types. In order to determine the conflict type, we suggest the following classification of conflicts according to [Moore 2003]:

- *Data conflict*: A data conflict is caused by a lack of information, by misinformation, or by different interpretations of an issue.
- *Interest conflict*: An interest conflict is caused by subjectively or objectively different interests or goals of stakeholders.
- *Value conflict*: A value conflict is caused by different criteria which stakeholders apply when evaluating an issue (e.g. cultural differences).
- *Relationship conflict*: A relationship conflict is caused by negative interpersonal behaviour among stakeholders (e.g. disrespect, insulting).
- *Structural conflict*: A structural conflict is caused by an unequal balance of power between stakeholders.

Relationship and structural conflicts are not considered

Relationship conflicts and structural conflicts are not further considered in this book. However, as relationships between stakeholders are important for requirements engineering, we refer to [Moore 2003; Masters and Albright 2002] for details on the management of relationship conflicts.

In Sections 25.2.1–25.2.3, we discuss three conflict types, namely data conflicts, interest conflicts, and value conflicts. In Section 25.2.4, we present a heuristic for determining the conflict type.

25.2.1 Data Conflict

Different interpretations due to incomplete or incorrect information

A data conflict about a requirement exists if stakeholders are wrongly or incompletely informed about the requirement or if stakeholders interpret the meaning of the requirement differently.

Example 25-2: Data conflict about requirements

The following requirement is defined for a car entertainment system:

R4: The DVD player shall be able to handle re-writeable CDs (CD-RW) and DVDs (DVD-RW).

A stakeholder disagrees with the requirement. In his opinion it does not make sense for a DVD player in the car to be able to write data onto CDs or DVDs.

The conflict in Example 25-2 results from the fact that the stakeholder interprets the requirement concerning the handling of rewritable CDs and DVDs such that the DVD player shall be able to write data on these media. To resolve the conflict, the stakeholders need to clarify that writing on these media is not part of the requirements for the DVD player.

25.2.2 Interest Conflict

Different goals

An interest conflict about the requirements for the system to be developed exists if the stakeholders' interests or goals with regard to the system contradict each other.

Example 25-3: Interest conflict about requirements

A stakeholder wants the car entertainment system to be equipped with MP3 functionality, an optional hard disk, and a USB interface in order to attract technology-oriented customers.

Another stakeholder wants the system to be equipped merely with standard CD player functionality and a radio. His goal is to reduce the costs in order to attract price-conscious customers.

25.2.3 Value Conflict

Different personal and cultural values

A value conflict about the requirements for the system to be developed exists if different stakeholders evaluate a requirement differently or each stakeholder considers the importance of the requirement differently. The evaluation of facts is affected by a number of factors such as experience in life and profession, education, training, personal ideals, culture, and religion.

The value conflict in Example 25-4 results from the fact that two stakeholders evaluate the importance of the OGG format[1] differently.

Example 25-4: Value conflict about requirements

A stakeholder demands that the DVD player of the car entertainment system shall support the OGG format in addition to the MP3 format.

Another stakeholder objects to this requirement since he thinks that supporting the OGG format is unimportant.

25.2.4 Heuristic for Conflict Analysis

An existing conflict can have several causes. In order to determine the conflict type, we recommend checking for data conflicts first, then for interest conflicts, and finally for value conflicts. The type of a conflict can be determined by the following three steps:

Conflict is based on misinterpretations or incorrect information

1. *Checking for a data conflict*: When checking for a data conflict, the requirements engineers must find out whether one or several stakeholders were misinformed or incompletely informed about the requirements. For this purpose, the requirements engineer can ask the stakeholders to write down their interpretation of the requirements. When the stakeholders write down their interpretation or

[1] The OGG format is a file compression format for audio data.

explain the requirements verbally, incorrect information as well as misinterpretation by the stakeholders can be detected. If this is the case, a data conflict exists.

2. *Checking for an interest conflict*: If no data conflict is detected or if a conflict still exists after resolving the data conflict, the requirements engineers check for an interest conflict. To do so, the requirements engineers must identify and bring together the interests of the conflicting parties. In addition, explicit documentation of the stakeholders' goals is suggested in order to support identification of interest conflicts. The requirements engineers hence ask each stakeholder to name his/her goals associated with the conflicting requirements. The elicitation of the stakeholders' goals can be supported by "why" questions. The requirements engineers document the identified goals of each stakeholder in a separate goal model. Subsequently, the different goal models are compared with one another. An interest conflict exists if conflicts are detected among the goals of the different stakeholders.

Conflict is based on different goals

3. *Checking for a value conflict*: If neither a data conflict nor an interest conflict is detected, or if a conflict still exists after resolving the existing data and interest conflicts, the requirements engineers check for a value conflict. This check consists of two steps. First, the requirements engineers must clarify the stakeholders' evaluation backgrounds, i.e. they have to find out why the stakeholders evaluate the requirements in the way they do. Subsequently, the requirements engineers must check whether the stakeholders' different evaluation backgrounds are the cause of the contradicting evaluations. If this is the case, a value conflict exists.

Conflict is based on different values

Hint 25-1 summarises the heuristic for conflict analysis.

!

Hint 25-1: *Heuristic for conflict analysis*

(1) Checking for a data conflict:

- Let the stakeholders explain the conflicting requirements.
- Does one of the explanations deviate from the actual requirement? If so, a data conflict exists.

(2) Asking for the stakeholders' interests:

- Ask the stakeholders for their goals with regard to the conflicting requirements.
- Check the resulting goals for contradictions. If there is a contradiction, an interest conflict exists.

(3) Clarifying the stakeholders' evaluation backgrounds:

- Ask the stakeholder why he/she evaluates the conflicting requirements in the way he/she does.
- Check the evaluation backgrounds of the different stakeholders for differences that may cause the detected conflict. If there is such a difference, a value conflict exists.

25.3 Sub-activity: Resolving Conflicts

Three strategies

To resolve a conflict, one of the following three basic strategies can be applied (see [Masters and Albright 2002]):

- *Negotiation*: The conflicting parties agree on a solution by means of negotiation (see Section 25.3.1).
- *Creative solution*: The original viewpoints of the conflicting parties are discarded and a new, creative solution is developed that harmonises the viewpoints of all conflicting parties (see Section 25.3.2).
- *Decision*: A higher authority makes a decision in favour of one conflicting party (see Section 25.3.3).

The three strategies are explained in Sections 25.3.1–25.3.3. Each strategy is illustrated by means of the conflict described in Example 25-5. In Section 25.3.4, we evaluate the three strategies with regard to their utility for resolving data, interest, and value conflicts.

Example 25-5: Exemplary conflict about requirements

The car safety system shall be equipped with radar technology in order to be able to monitor the traffic ahead of the car. There is a conflict among two groups of stakeholders regarding the distance up to which the radar sensor shall monitor the traffic in front of the car. One group demands 1,000 m; the other one demands 500 m.

25.3.1 Conflict Resolution through Negotiation

Exchange of arguments

The negotiation strategy aims to resolve a conflict by exchanging information, arguments, and opinions. In a dialogue, each conflicting party involved tries to convince the other parties that its own viewpoint is the right one.

Agreement upon a solution

The conflict is resolved if either the viewpoint of one of the conflicting parties is accepted by the other parties or the parties find a solution that ranges between the different viewpoints and is accepted by all parties as a compromise (see Fig. 25-1). Example 25-6 describes a possible resolution of the conflict presented in Example 25-5 by means of the negotiation strategy.

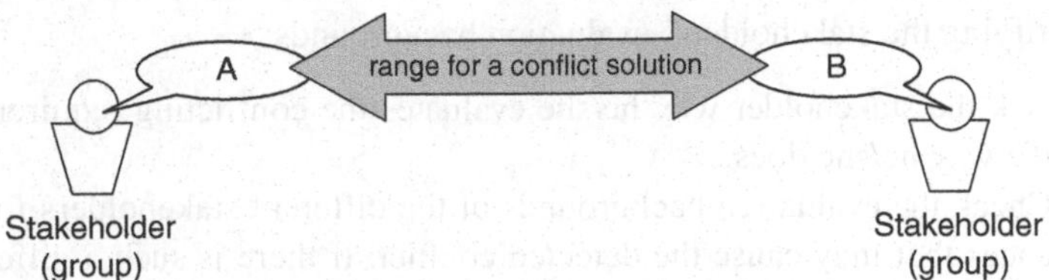

Fig. 25-1 *Conflict resolution through negotiation: each solution between the viewpoints A and B is possible*

Example 25-6: Conflict resolution through negotiation

The stakeholders resolve the conflict described in Example 25-5 using the negotiation strategy by agreeing on a detection range of 750 m.

Advantage

The advantage of a conflict resolution through negotiation is that the viewpoints of all conflicting parties are considered and a win–win situation is created (see Section 26.1).

Disadvantage

Resolving a conflict by means of negotiation can be a very time-consuming process. The duration generally depends on the conflicting parties and their willingness to find a compromise. In addition, the compromise may not be the best solution from an objective viewpoint.

25.3.2 Conflict Resolution through a Creative Solution

Discarding the old solutions

To resolve a conflict through a creative solution, the conflicting parties abandon their viewpoints in favour of a newly developed viewpoint that is acceptable to all conflicting parties.

Creative, novel solution

In contrast to the negotiation strategy, in the case of the creative solution a new solution is developed that is independent of the previous viewpoints (see Fig. 25-2). In order to support conflict resolution through a creative solution, creativity techniques such as brainstorming (see Section 23.2) are used. Example 25-7 describes a possible resolution of the conflict presented in Example 25-5 by means of a creative, new solution.

Fig. 25-2 *Conflict resolution through creative solution: A and B are abandoned; instead a new, creative solution is pursued*

Example 25-7: Creative, novel solution

The stakeholders resolve the conflict described in Example 25-5 by proposing a novel solution. By equipping the car with a laser sensor instead of a radar sensor the detection range is increased to 1,000 m without causing additional costs.

Advantage

Creative resolution of a conflict has the advantage that all conflicting parties come off as winners, since a solution is found that is acceptable to all parties.

Disadvantage

On the negative side, the development of a creative solution can be time consuming and impact on other requirements that are influenced by the solution.

25.3.3 Conflict Resolution through Decision

Complete agreement is rarely achievable

In general, the negotiation activity does not aim to achieve a complete agreement with respect to the requirements among all stakeholders. Resolving all conflicts by reaching an agreement among the stakeholders may, for example, be too costly in terms of required time and effort. In addition, there are also conflicts for which agreement can never be reached. In both cases, the conflict must be resolved in due time by a decision.

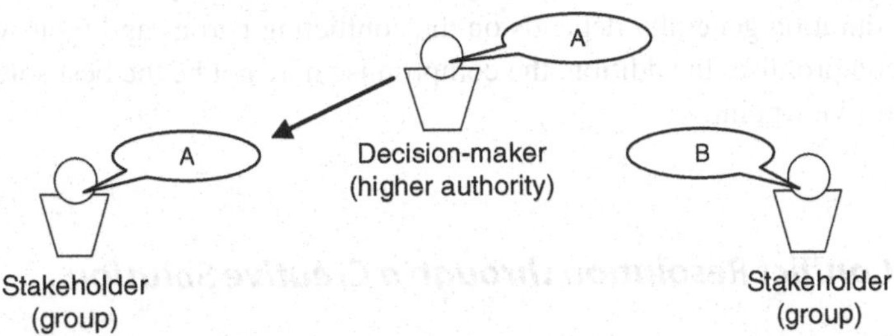

Fig. 25-3 *Conflict resolution through decision: a decision-maker decides in favour of viewpoint A*

Decision made by a higher authority

In the case of conflict resolution through a decision, the conflict is resolved by a decision-maker, i.e. a person or group who has the required decision-making authority. A decision-maker is generally a higher authority, e.g. a project leader or a representative of the client. Based on the present circumstances, the decision-maker decides which viewpoint shall be adopted for the system (see Fig. 25-3). Thereby, the decision-maker resolves the conflict. In some cases, the decision-maker may also be involved in the conflicting parties himself. Example 25-8 describes a possible resolution of the conflict presented in Example 25-5 by applying the decision strategy.

> **Example 25-8:** Conflict resolution by decision
>
> As the conflict in Example 25-5 exists between two groups of developers, the client is involved as a higher authority. The client decides that the detection range shall be 500 m.

Advantage

The advantage of resolving a conflict by a decision is that the conflict can be resolved quickly without consuming too many resources since long discussions do not take place.

Disadvantage

However, a conflict can only be resolved by a higher authority, if there is such an authority (which is not always the case). Furthermore, when a decision is made in favour of one viewpoint, the other viewpoint is ignored. This can negatively influence the motivation of the ignored, conflicting party. Hence resolving a conflict through negotiation or a creative solution should be preferred over resolving the conflict through a decision, if possible.

Voting

Another possibility to bring about a decision is to vote on the viewpoints of all involved stakeholders.

25.3.4 Evaluation of the Conflict Resolution Strategies

Depending on the type of the conflict, different conflict resolution strategies are suited. Table 25-1 presents an evaluation of the presented conflict resolution strategies.

Tab. 25-1 *Evaluation of the conflict resolution strategies*

	Negotiation	Creative solution	Decision
Data conflict	suitable	not suitable	not suitable
Interest conflict	suitable	conditionally suitable	suitable
Value conflict	conditionally suitable	suitable	conditionally suitable

In the following, we describe a procedure for each conflict type that allows the resolution of a conflict of this type using the presented strategies.

Resolving Data Conflicts

Negotiation strategy is well suited

Data conflicts should be resolved through negotiation. During negotiation, information exchange between the involved, conflicting parties takes place. Furthermore, the two conflicting parties may be provided with additional, relevant information. In this way, a data conflict can generally be resolved.

Creative solution strategy not suited

The strategy of resolving conflicts through a creative solution is not suited for data conflicts. A data conflict is based on the misinformation of stakeholders or on misinterpretation. The creative solution would therefore be based on incomplete or incorrect information.

Decision strategy not suited

The resolution of a data conflict through decision-making in favour of one conflicting party is not suited. Among other things, the decision could be made in favour of the wrong viewpoint due to missing information or a misunderstanding.

Resolving Interest Conflicts

Identifying common interests

In the case of an interest conflict, each conflicting party should explain its interests to the other parties in order to identify common interests.

Negotiation based on common interests

Based on the common interests, the parties should first try to resolve the conflict by applying the negotiation strategy. For this purpose, the conflicting parties negotiate towards a solution that considers the interests of each conflicting party as far as possible. Each conflicting interest and goal is considered separately during the negotiation. Between the conflicting parties, an agreement must be achieved about the question of which conflicting interests of one party are acceptable to the other parties. Thereby, each conflicting party should benefit from the resolution of the conflict (see Section 26.1).

Decision strategy for irresolvable parts of the problem

For aspects of the conflict that cannot be resolved by means of negotiation, bringing about a decision by a decision-maker is recommended. The decision strategy should also be applied when the conflicting parties are not willing to find a compromise at all.

Creative solution strategy only conditionally suited

The creative solution strategy is only conditionally suited for resolving interest conflicts, since the main problems are the different goals or interests. Hence, the different goals and interests have to be harmonised or substituted by new goals/interests before a creative solution can be found that is accepted to all parties.

Resolving Value Conflicts

Sensitivity required

In the case of value conflicts, the requirements engineers must act sensitively, since the conflict may offend the stakeholders' personal values.

Negotiation conditionally suited

Negotiation is only conditionally suitable as a strategy for resolving value conflicts, since values are often deeply rooted in the stakeholders' personality. These values cannot be easily changed or abandoned during a negotiation about the conflict.

Strive for a creative solution

Instead, in the case of a value conflict, the requirements engineers should strive for a creative solution. One example of a creative solution for a value conflict is to realise different variants of the system so that each stakeholder finds his or her values respected by some system variant. However, a creative solution to a value conflict should only be considered if the value conflict is of significant importance for the system and there are sufficient resources for implementing the solution.

Decision strategy in case of irresolvable value conflicts

If the values of the conflicting parties are irreconcilable, i.e. no party wants to amend its initial evaluation of the considered issue, the conflict should be resolved through a decision.

25.4 Sub-activity: Documenting Conflict Resolutions

During the requirements engineering process, the stakeholders identify a number of conflicts and, if possible, resolve them.

Documenting achieved resolutions of conflicts

Documentation of the achieved resolutions of conflicts is recommended in order to make them traceable for further requirements engineering activities. If conflict resolutions are not documented, the achieved solutions may be forgotten and conflicts that have already been resolved may recur. For instance, some stakeholder might ask for a requirement that is in conflict with another requirement and has therefore been discarded earlier during conflict resolution. Without appropriate documentation of conflict resolutions, the same conflicts may recur and hence need to be analysed and resolved anew each time.

Documenting central arguments

Documentation of achieved conflict resolutions together with the viewpoints of the conflicting parties and the pros and cons of each viewpoint is recommended.

Documenting revisions of conflict resolutions

If a conflict resolution is considered again and revised during the requirements engineering process, the revision of the conflict resolution must be documented as well.

Chapter 26
Negotiation Techniques

In this chapter, we present two negotiation techniques:

- *Win–Win approach*
- *Interaction matrices*

K. Pohl, *Requirements Engineering*,

26.1 The Win–Win Approach

The goal of the Win–Win approach is to make all stakeholders become winners. Boehm and Ross describe how the Win–Win approach is used for managing software projects (see [Boehm and Ross 1989]).

In the following, we describe relevant aspects of the Win–Win approach as a technique for requirements negotiation (see [Boehm et al. 1994; Boehm et al. 2001]), and in particular as a technique for conflict resolution. For all other aspects of the Win–Win approach, we refer to [Boehm and Ross 1989].

26.1.1 Possible Situations in the Win–Win Approach

The Win–Win approach differentiates three basic situations: win–lose, lose–lose, and win–win (see [Boehm and Ross 1989]).

Win-lose

If some stakeholders achieve their goals in a conflict at the expense of other stakeholders, this situation is referred to as a win–lose situation. Some stakeholders are the winners, other stakeholders are the losers of the conflict. Example 26-1 illustrates a win–lose situation.

Example 26-1: Win–lose situation

For the car safety system, stakeholder A proposes the function "monitoring the temperature of the brake discs". To realise this function, the stakeholders must abandon other functions of the car safety system, as the available resources are limited. Stakeholder A is the winner, since his function is realised. Other stakeholders whose functions are not realised as a consequence of realising this function are the losers.

Lose–lose

If no conflicting party achieves its goals in a conflict, this situation is referred to as a lose–lose situation. In this case, all involved parties are losers. Example 26-2 illustrates a lose–lose situation.

Example 26-2: Lose–lose situation

Stakeholder A tries to put through some function for the product to be developed against the resistance of another stakeholder B. In turn, stakeholder A rejects a function that stakeholder B wants to be implemented in the system. In the end, neither of the two functions is implemented, since the stakeholders are not able to resolve the conflict in time. Both stakeholders are losers.

Win–win

If all conflicting parties achieve their goals completely or partially in a conflict, the situation is referred to as a win–win situation, since all parties are winners. Example 26-3 illustrates a win–win situation. During conflict resolution, the stakeholders should always strive for a win–win situation.

Example 26-3: Win–win situation

Two stakeholders ask for system functions that exclude each other. During the negotiation about this conflict, the parties agree that two versions of the system shall be realised, each implementing one of the two sets of mutually exclusive functions. Both stakeholders are winners regarding this conflict.

26.1.2 Achieving a Win–Win Situation

In order to be able to achieve a win–win situation, the following steps are essential:

- *Understand how stakeholders want to win*: In order to create a win-win situation for all stakeholders, the requirements engineers must know what each stakeholder considers as a benefit for himself. The ability to put oneself in another stakeholder's place helps to understand what this stakeholder considers a benefit. According to [Boehm and Ross 1989], incorrect understanding of what the stakeholders consider as a benefit is an essential factor for not being able to achieve a win–win situation.
- *Raise adequate expectations*: Unrealistic expectations for the system to be developed hinder achievement of a win–win situation. For instance, a stakeholder who does not have a software engineering background may misjudge the difficulties related to realising the functionality that he asks for. Likewise, developers may misjudge the difficulties that stakeholders are confronted with during their everyday work with the system. In order to establish realistic expectations, the following principles should be observed:
  - Joint discussion about the stakeholders' expectations. In this way, wrong or unrealistic expectations are identified and altered, if necessary.
  - Putting oneself in the other stakeholders' place improves understanding of their viewpoints.
  - Expectations shall be defined based on objective criteria. Expectations shall be oriented towards experience (e.g. benchmarks, expert knowledge).

26.1.3 Win–Win Approach and Conflict Resolution Strategies

Resolution of a conflict by creating a win–win situation provides confidence among the stakeholders and also increases their willingness to make a compromise (see [Boehm and Ross 1989]).

Win–Win approach beneficial for negotiation and creative solution strategies

Therefore, if a conflict is resolved through negotiation or through a creative solution, all stakeholders should benefit from the resolution of the conflict. Mutual understanding of what the stakeholders consider as a benefit supports the negotiation and creative solution of conflicts. Common interests and values of the conflicting parties can be identified more easily. If the requirements engineers are able to scale down immoderate expectations for the system, unrealistic requirements are reduced, and consequently fewer conflicts arise. The Win–Win approach hence supports the negotiation strategy and the creative solution strategy for conflict resolution (see Section 25.3).

Decision creates win–lose situation

Resolving a conflict through a decision generally leads to a win–lose situation, since the decision is typically made in favour of a single viewpoint and hence privileges one party.

26.2 Interaction Matrix

Documentation and visualisation of known conflicts

An interaction matrix can be used for visualising and documenting overlapping requirements as well as conflicts about requirements (see [Kotonya and Sommerville 1997]).

Each cell in an interaction matrix represents a pair of requirements. The first row and the first column indicate which pair of requirements is represented by a specific cell (e.g. by using the unique identifier of each requirement as label). Table 26-1 shows a blank interaction matrix.

Tab. 26-1 *Blank interaction matrix*

	Requirement 1	Requirement 2	Requirement 3	Requirement 4
Requirement 1				
Requirement 2				
Requirement 3				
Requirement 4				

Filling in the fields of the matrix

Each cell of the interaction matrix describes the interaction between a specific pair of requirements. In order to fill in the matrix, all fields above the main diagonal are considered (the white fields in Tab. 26-1). Since conflict relationships are symmetric, the fields beneath the main diagonal are filled in symmetrically to the fields above the diagonal.

Values of the cells

If a conflict between two requirements exists, a "1" is written in the corresponding cell of the matrix. If two requirements overlap, this is documented by the entry "1,000". If the requirements are independent of each other, this is indicated by the entry "0". The main diagonal describes the relation of a requirement to itself and is filled in with the entry "0" by default.

Analysis

An interaction matrix is analysed by calculating the sum of values in each column. When the sum for a column is "0", the requirement represented by this column does not overlap or conflict with any other requirement. This holds, for example, for requirement 2 in Tab. 26-2.

Overlaps

The sum of a column divided by 1,000 (without remainder) equals the number of requirements that overlap with the considered requirement. For example, the sum of the column "requirement 3" in Tab. 26-2 divided by 1,000 equals 1 (without remainder), i.e. requirement 3 overlaps with one other requirement.

Conflicts

The remainder of the division of the sum of a column by 1,000 denotes the number of conflicts between the requirement in this column and other requirements. For instance, the remainder of dividing the sum of column 4 by 1,000 is 1. Hence, requirement 4 is in conflict with one other requirement.

Tab. 26-2 *Interaction matrix with identified conflicts and overlaps*

	Requirement 1	Requirement 2	Requirement 3	Requirement 4
Requirement 1	0	0	1	1
Requirement 2	0	0	0	0
Requirement 3	1	0	0	1,000
Requirement 4	1	0	1,000	0
Sum	2	0	1,001	1,001

Number of presentable requirements

Use of software such as a spreadsheet tool is recommended for creating interaction matrices. Even with tool support, the number of requirements that can be practically managed in an interaction matrix is limited to approximately 200 (see [Kotonya and Sommerville 1997]).

Not recommended for identification of conflicts

In addition to visualising and documenting overlaps and conflicts, interaction matrices can also be used for systematic identification of conflicts between requirements. For this purpose, the requirements are checked in pairs for potential conflicts. However, checking each pair of requirements for a potential conflict can be a very time-consuming process. Use of interaction matrices is therefore recommended only for documenting and visualising conflicts and not for identifying conflicts.

Recommended Literature for Part IV.c

Basic Reading

[Boehm and Ross 1989] describe an approach for managing software projects. An important part of this approach is the "Theory W", according to which each involved party should be made a winner (win–win situation).

[Kotonya and Sommerville 1997] discuss the negotiation of requirements in requirements engineering. Among other things, interaction matrices are introduced.

[Moore 2003] classifies conflicts by means of the types data conflict, interest conflict, value conflict, relationship conflict, and structural conflict. For each conflict type, possible resolution strategies are explained.

[Sutcliffe 2002b] provides an introduction to the management of conflicts in requirements engineering.

Advanced Reading

[Gause and Weinberg 1989] discuss the meaning of conflicts in requirements engineering and point out that conflicts should not only be regarded as a risk but also as an opportunity for requirements engineering.

[Masters and Albright 2002] explain the resolution of conflicts in general. The book goes beyond conflict management in requirements engineering. It provides a comprehensive introduction to conflict resolution, illustrated by many case studies and practical exercises.

Part V
Validation

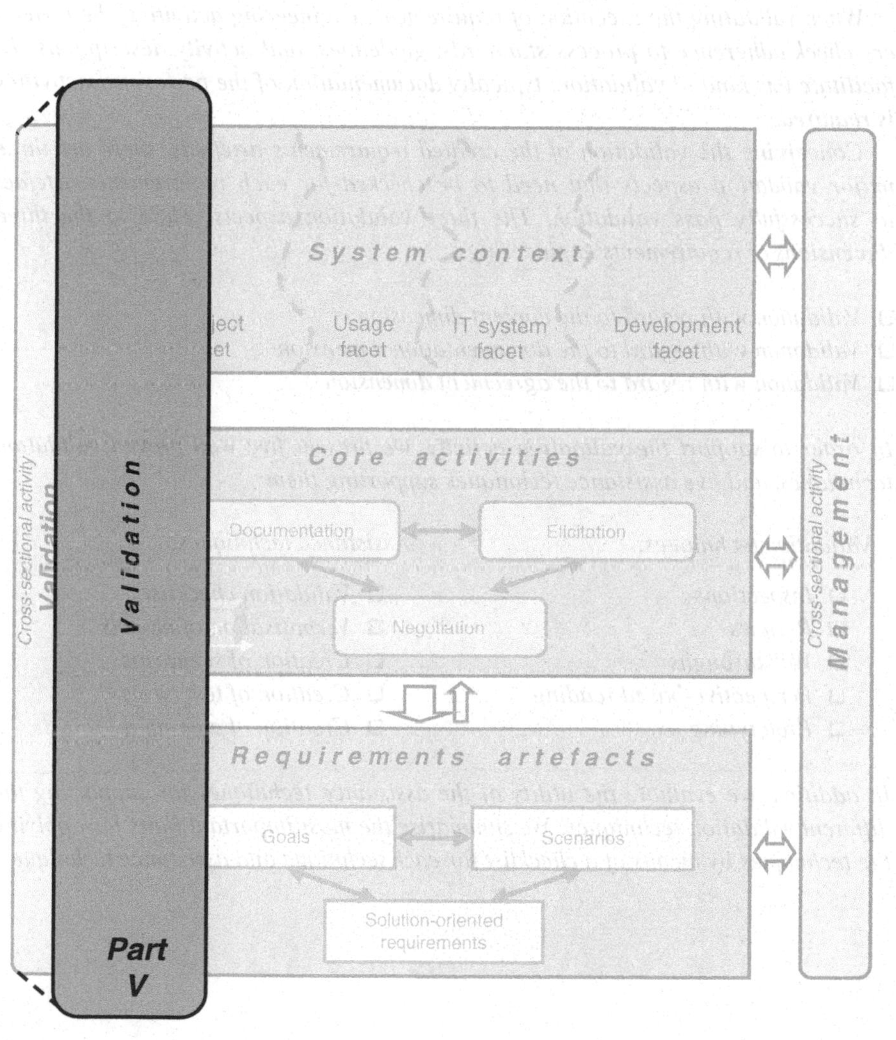

Overview Part V – Validation

The objectives of the cross-sectional activity validation can be defined based on our framework for requirements engineering:

- *Validating the consideration of the system context*
- *Validating the execution of requirements engineering activities*
- *Validating the created requirements artefacts*

When validating the consideration of the system context, the reviewers check whether all relevant context aspects in all four context facets have been considered adequately and documented correctly.

When validating the execution of requirements engineering activities, the reviewers check adherence to process standards, guidelines, and activity descriptions. To facilitate this kind of validation, typically documentation of the performed activities is required.

Concerning the validation of the created requirements artefacts, there are three major validation aspects that need to be checked for each requirements artefact to successfully pass validation. The three validation aspects relate to the three dimensions of requirements engineering:

- *Validation with regard to the content dimension*
- *Validation with regard to the documentation dimension*
- *Validation with regard to the agreement dimension*

In order to support the validation activity, we present five well-proven validation techniques, and five assistance techniques supporting them:

Validation techniques:

- *Inspections*
- *Reviews*
- *Walkthroughs*
- *Perspective-based reading*
- *Prototyping*

Assistance techniques:

- *Validation checklists*
- *Verbalisation of models*
- *Creation of scenarios*
- *Creation of test cases*
- *Creation of a manual*

In addition, we evaluate the utility of the assistance techniques for supporting the different validation techniques. We summarise the most important hints for applying the techniques by means of a checklist for each technique and assistance technique.

Classification Part V Validation	Basic	Advanced
27 Fundamentals of Requirements Validation		
27.1 Motivation and Goals	✓	
27.2 Validation vs. Verification	✓	
27.3 Sub-activity: Validating the Created Requirements Artefacts	✓	
27.4 Sub-activity: Validating the Consideration of the Context		✓
27.5 Sub-activity: Validating the Execution of Activities		✓
27.6 Capability Model for Validation	✓	
27.7 Goals and Scenarios in Validation		✓
27.8 Principles of Validation	✓	
28 Validation Techniques		
28.1 Inspections		✓
28.2 Desk-Checks	✓	
28.3 Walkthroughs	✓	
28.4 Comparison: Inspections, Desk-Checks, and Walkthroughs		✓
28.5 Validation Using Prototypes		✓
29 Assistance Techniques for Validation		
29.1 Validation Checklists	✓	
29.2 Perspective-Based Reading		✓
29.3 Creation of Artefacts		✓

Chapter 27
Fundamentals of Requirements Validation

In this chapter, we explain:

- *The main goals of the cross-cutting activity validation in requirements engineering*
- *The differentiation between validation and verification*
- *The three essential validation sub-activities:*
  - *Validation of the consideration of the context*
  - *Validation of the execution of activities*
  - *Validation of the created requirements artefacts*
- *Three major validation aspects for requirements artefacts that are derived from the three dimensions of requirements engineering*
- *A simple capability model of validation with three validation layers*
- *The advantages of goals and scenarios for requirements validation*
- *Six core principles of validation*

27.1 Motivation and Goals

Validation at defined points in time

Requirements artefacts result from a process during which elicitation, documentation, and negotiation activities are performed (see Section 30.5, where how the execution of requirements engineering activities can be managed is outlined). At defined points in time during the requirements engineering process, the quality of the requirements artefacts and other documented information (e.g. about the context) as well as the quality of the process itself need to be checked. To check the quality of requirements artefacts, these artefacts are communicated back to the stakeholders with the purpose of detecting deviations between the documented requirements and the stakeholders' true needs and wishes.

Validation of a requirements artefact

An important result of checking the quality of a requirements artefact is the decision of whether the checked artefact is released for use in further development activities or not (see Example 27-1 and Example 27-2). In order to avoid poor decisions based on subjective judgement, the decision about the release of a requirements artefact should be based on previously defined acceptance criteria (see Section 16.4).

Example 27-1: Release without revalidation

During the validation of a goal model for the car safety system, only minor deficiencies are found. The responsible stakeholders define the necessary corrections. After the corrections have been incorporated, the goal model is released without revalidation.

Example 27-2: No release, revalidation required

The validation of a statechart of a control device for a car safety system uncovers serious defects in this model. Therefore, the statechart is not released for use in further development activities. The stakeholders decide that, after the defects have been eliminated, revalidation of the statechart is required before it can be released.

27.1.1 Validation Goals

Three subgoals

Validation aims not only at checking requirements artefacts. Checking whether the right activities have been performed in the right way to produce the artefacts and whether the right inputs have been used to produce the artefacts is of equal importance to ensure a high quality of the requirements engineering process and the requirements artefacts. Consequently, the validation activity has three subgoals (see Fig. 27-1):

Checking requirements artefacts

- *Goal 1: checking whether the outputs of activities fulfil defined quality criteria.* Satisfying this goal of the validation activity means uncovering requirements defects by checking the created requirements artefacts. Some typical examples of defects in requirements artefacts are ambiguity, incompleteness, and contradictions. We define three major validation aspects (content, documentation, and agreement) that must be considered during validation before a requirements

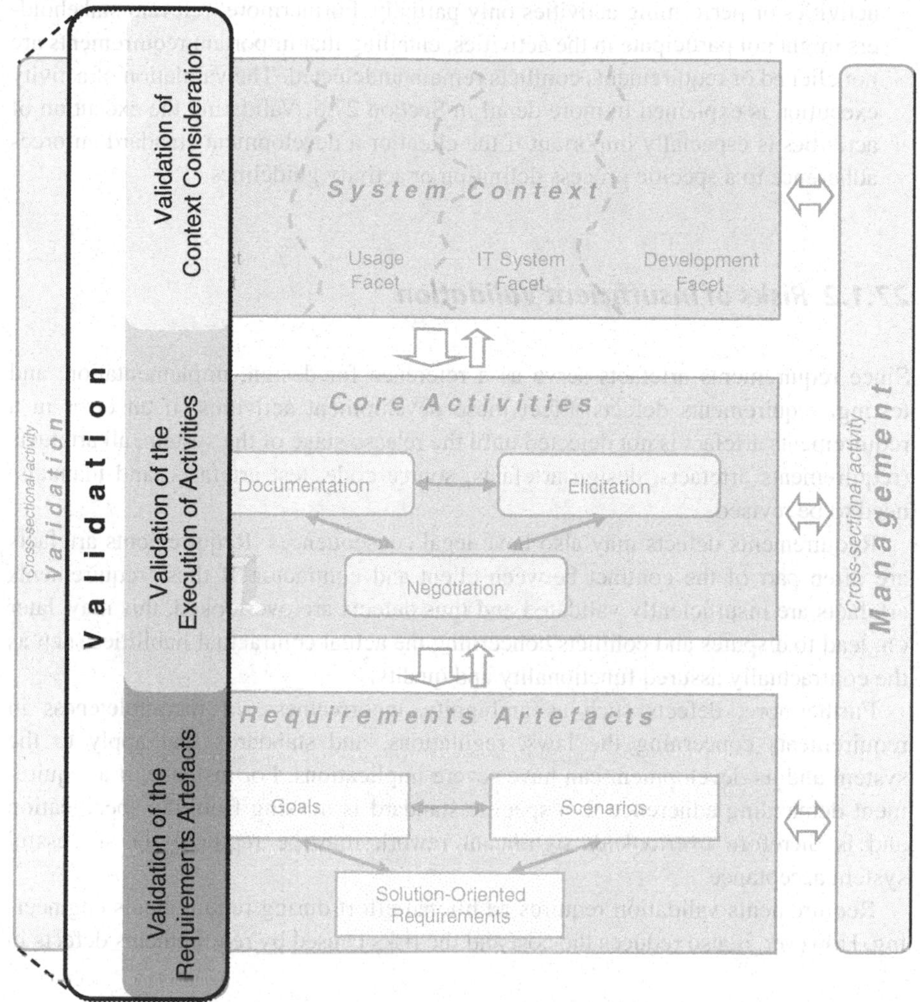

Fig. 27-1 *Cross-sectional activity: validation (left-hand side)*

artefact is released for use in other development activities. The validation of requirements artefacts is explained in more detail in Section 27.3.

Checking context consideration

- *Goal 2: checking whether the inputs of activities fulfil defined quality criteria.* The inputs for requirements engineering activities originate predominantly from the system context. If important context aspects are overlooked, if context information is insufficiently considered, or if the documented context information contains errors, this leads, in most cases, to errors in the requirements artefacts. Likewise, failing to involve relevant requirement sources may also lead to faulty (e.g. incomplete) requirements. The validation of context consideration is explained in more detail in Section 27.4.

Checking activity execution

- *Goal 3: checking whether the execution of activities adheres to process definitions and activity guidelines.* Errors in requirements often result from not adhering to prescribed processes and activity guidelines. For example, the requirements engineers might violate the defined guidelines by not using the relevant checklists for applying a specific technique or violate the process definition by omitting required activities or performing activities only partially. Furthermore, relevant stakeholders might not participate in the activities, entailing that important requirements are not elicited or requirements conflicts remain undetected. The validation of activity execution is explained in more detail in Section 27.5. Validating the execution of activities is especially important if the client or a development standard enforces adherence to a specific process definition or activity guidelines.

27.1.2 Risks of Insufficient Validation

Error propagation

Since requirements artefacts serve as a reference for design, implementation, and testing, requirements defects affect these development activities. If an error in a requirements artefact is not detected until the release stage of the system, all artefacts (requirements artefacts, design artefacts, source code, test artefacts, and manuals) need to be revised.

Legal issues due to requirements defects

Requirements defects may also have legal consequences. Requirements artefacts are often part of the contract between client and contractor. If these requirements artefacts are insufficiently validated and thus defects are overlooked, this may, later on, lead to disputes and conflicts concerning the actual contractual liabilities such as the contractually assured functionality and quality.

Furthermore, defects such as ambiguity, incorrectness, or incompleteness in requirements concerning the laws, regulations, and standards that apply to the system and its development can have severe implications. For instance, if a requirement demanding adherence to a specific standard is missing from the specification and is therefore overlooked, significant rework may be required for successful system acceptance.

Reduction of cost and risks in later phases

Requirements validation requires additional effort during requirements engineering. However, it also reduces the cost and the risks caused by requirements defects in

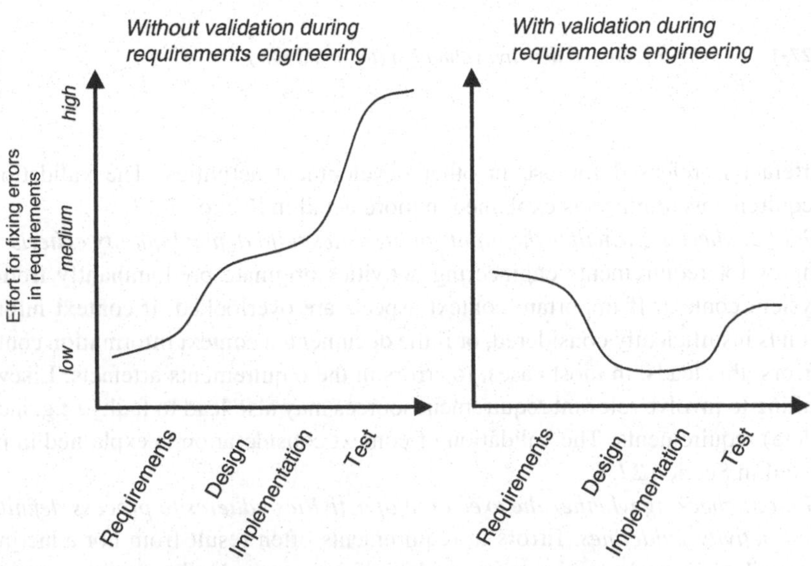

Fig. 27-2 *Coarse sketch of the progression of the effort needed to fix requirements defects*

later development phases. Fig. 27-2 sketches the qualitative progression of the effort to fix errors with and without adequate validation of the requirements artefacts during requirements engineering. Detecting and fixing errors in requirements artefacts early avoids defects having to be fixed in later development phases at significantly higher cost. The overall costs for fixing requirements defects demonstrably decrease, the earlier the defects are detected in the development process. Some additional details on the cost of correcting requirements defects in relation to the development phase in which the defects are detected can be found in Section 1.2.3 (see also [Boehm 1981; Baziuk 1995]).

27.2 Validation vs. Verification

Validation and verification are two important techniques for the analytical quality assurance of software artefacts. However, in the literature, the distinction between these two techniques is often vague and also differs from author to author. We first give an account of the difference between constructive and analytical quality assurance and then elaborate on the different notions of validation and verification that exist in the literature. Finally, we define the term "validation" for this book.

27.2.1 Constructive and Analytical Quality Assurance

Quality assurance is an essential part of any development process. There are two basic types of quality assurance (see [Liggesmeyer 2009]):

Avoiding errors during creation of artefacts

- *Constructive quality assurance*: Constructive quality assurance refers to the use of techniques aimed at the prevention of defects in development artefacts during the creation of these artefacts. Adhering to well-proven modelling rules when creating a data model is an example of constructive quality assurance.

Detecting errors in artefacts after their creation

- *Analytical quality assurance*: Analytical quality assurance refers to applying techniques for checking the quality of a development artefact after its creation. Having a review team check a data model for correctness and consistency is an example of performing analytical quality assurance.

Requirements validation is a specific kind of analytical quality assurance. Other examples of analytical quality assurance techniques are testing (see Chapter 37) and (formal) verification (see Section 27.2.2).

Note, however, that in practice, constructive and analytical quality assurance cannot be clearly distinguished in every case.

27.2.2 Definitions of Validation and Verification

Inconsistent use of terms

The term "validation" is used inconsistently, both in the literature and in practice. Often, the terms "validation" and "verification" are used more or less as synonyms.

Boehm's definition

A popular approach to distinguishing between validation and verification is that of [Boehm 1984]. Boehm defines the underlying questions of validation and verification as follows:

- *Validation*: Am I building the right system?
- *Verification*: Am I building the system right?

IEEE Standard 1012-2004: validation

The IEEE Standard 1012-2004 defines activities, inputs, and outputs of a life-cycle-spanning verification and validation process for software [IEEE Std 1012-2004]. In the IEEE standard, validation and verification are considered as closely connected sub-processes that cannot be clearly distinguished from each other.

Robertson and Robertson

[Robertson and Robertson 2006] define requirements validation as checking requirements with the goal of detecting errors such as ignored standards, ambiguities, and inconsistencies. The term "verification" is used exclusively to denote the formal (mathematical) proof of properties of a specification or program.

Dzida and Freitag

[Dzida and Freitag 1998] regard verification as "a synonym for correctness proving of software or specification" (which is identical to the notion of [Robertson and Robertson 2006]), whereas validation is characterised as "a synonym for appropriateness proving". In addition, [Dzida and Freitag 1998] characterise the answers to be provided by validation and verification:

- "For verification there are two basic types of results: correct and incorrect."
- "The two basic answers for validation are: appropriate and inappropriate. An inappropriate result reveals an 'error of the third kind'. Such an error occurs when the wrong question is asked or when the approach is wrong, or when the implemented system provides an output that nobody wants."

27.2.3 Use of the Term "Validation" in this Book

Requirements validation

Our definition of requirements validation is based on the validation goals defined in Section 27.1.1, i.e. the definition comprises the validation of inputs (context consideration), activity execution, and outputs (requirements artefacts) of all three core requirements engineering activities.

Definition 27-1: *Validation (in requirements engineering)*

Validation denotes checking whether inputs, performed activities, and created outputs (requirements artefacts) of the requirements engineering core activities fulfil defined quality criteria. Validation is performed by involving relevant stakeholders, other requirement sources (standards, laws, etc.) as well as external reviewers, if necessary.

Requirements verification

With regard to the differentiation between validation and verification, we adopt the view of Robertson and Robertson and Dzida and Freitag, respectively. We regard the task of requirements verification as checking the correctness of statements about a requirements model of the system. The result of verification is either the confirmation or the falsification of the statements. Verification allows stakeholders to formally prove desired and required properties and, from that, draw conclusions about properties of the system to be developed.

Main focus on validation

The main focus of this book lies on requirements validation. Prior to verifying statements about requirements artefacts, the question whether the right requirements have been defined must be answered. As long as this question is not answered, there is little value in verifying properties such as safety by means of formal methods. However, interested readers are referred to the website [FME 2009], which provides a good overview of methods for formal specification and verification.

Sections 27.3–27.5 elaborate on our definition of requirements validation (see Definition 27-1).

!

Hint 27-1: *Use of the terms "validation" and "verification"*

- ❑ When coming across the term "validation" or "verification", check which definition is meant.
- ❑ We recommend using the term "verification" exclusively in connection with formal (mathematical) proofs.

27.3 Sub-activity: Validating the Created Requirements Artefacts

Validation for content, documentation, and agreement

The objectives of validating the requirements artefacts, i.e. the outputs of the requirements engineering core activities, result from the three dimensions of requirements engineering (see Section 4.4):

- ❑ *Validation with regard to the content dimension*: Check whether all relevant requirements are known and understood to the required level of detail.
- ❑ *Validation with regard to the documentation dimension*: Check whether the requirements are documented according to the defined documentation and specification rules.
- ❑ *Validation with regard to the agreement dimension*: Check whether the stakeholders have reached agreement about the documented requirements. Check for each known conflict whether the conflict has been resolved. Also check whether there are conflicts that have not yet been identified.

All three objectives must be fulfilled

Each of these three objectives represents a major concern or aspect of requirements validation. As indicated in Fig. 27-3, each requirements artefact must be validated with regard to all three validation aspects in order to be able to decide about its acceptance or rejection. In the following, we explain each aspect and the quality criteria related to each aspect in detail. However, we do not mean to present an exhaustive list of quality criteria. In addition, in Section 30.5, we elaborate on the implications of the validation of requirements artefacts with regard to the three validation aspects for the planning of the further requirements engineering process.

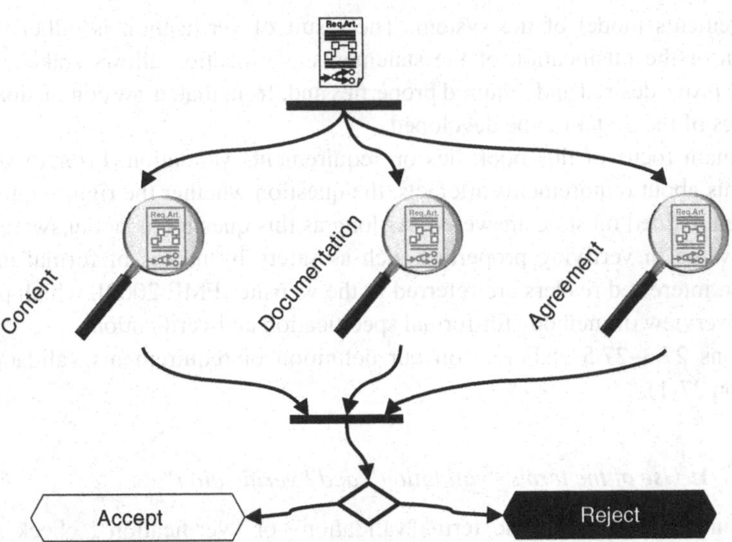

Fig. 27-3 *Three major validation aspects: achieved quality with regard to content, documentation, and agreement*

27.3.1 Validation in the Content Dimension

Performing requirements validation with regard to the content dimension means checking the requirements for deficiencies regarding their content, i.e. the quality of the information contained in the requirements artefacts. Defects in a requirements artefact concerning its content can lead to significant delays in subsequent development activities, as time has to be spent eliciting missing information and requirements as well as mitigating the problems caused by incorrect information. Furthermore, there is a risk of requirements defects creeping unnoticed into the architectural design, the implementation, and the test artefacts. Typical defects concerning the content of requirements artefacts are violations of quality criteria for requirements and/or requirements documents such as completeness, correctness, and consistency. Quality criteria for requirements and requirements documents are explained in Sections 16.3 and 17.3, respectively.

Validation criteria for the content dimension

To successfully pass a validation activity that focusses on the content dimension, it must be checked that the requirements artefacts satisfy the following criteria without serious deficiencies:

- *Completeness (artefact/document)*: Does the requirements artefact or document contain all relevant information and requirements?
- *Completeness (requirement)*: Does each requirement contain all the information that is needed according to the relevant reference model (e.g. the requirements template) or that is needed to perform the subsequent development activities?
- *Consistency*: Can the system meet all requirements together or are there requirements that contradict each other?
- *Correctness (requirement)*: Does the content of each requirement correspond to the actual stakeholder needs and wishes? Are all assumptions about the system context made when defining the requirements correct?

- *Correctness (requirements classification):* Has each requirement been assigned the right requirement type (e.g. goal, scenario, functional requirement, quality requirement, or constraint) and/or documented at the proper place, e.g. in the right document section?
- *Necessity*: Is each documented requirement needed to satisfy a defined and agreed goal?
- *No premature design decisions:* Is each requirement defined without premature design decisions or are there requirements that are biased (unnecessarily) towards a specific implementation?
- *Testability:* Have test or acceptance criteria been defined for each requirement which allow the realisation of the requirement to be checked? If not, is it possible to define test or acceptance criteria for each requirement based on the existing documentation?
- *Traceability*: Have all relevant traceability relationships been defined for each requirement (e.g. links to requirement sources)? Are the documented links correct?

27.3.2 Validation in the Documentation Dimension

With regard to the documentation dimension, the validation activity aims to check whether the documented requirements adhere to the documentation (or specification) rules and guidelines defined for the project (see Section 16.2). These documentation (or specification) rules comprise:

- General documentation rules and guidelines, i.e. rules and guidelines that apply to any kind of information documented in a requirements or supplementary document as well as rules and guidelines for the documents themselves such as general rules pertaining to the structure and layout of the documents
- Documentation/specification rules and guidelines for requirements documented in various formats. These include adherence to quality criteria of requirements and requirements documents such as readability and modifiability (see Sections 16.3 and 17.3) as well as rules and guidelines for specific documentation formats such as the rules for documenting goals (see Section 8.2) and scenarios (see Section 11.4) or the guidelines for documenting requirements using data, functional, and behavioural models outlined in Chapter 14.
- Organisation-specific documentation rules and guidelines which detail and/or extend the rules and guidelines mentioned above

Consequences of violating the documentation rules

The risks caused by requirements artefacts violating relevant documentation (or specification) rules and guidelines include:

- The requirements artefacts are unusable or incomprehensible for the stakeholders who have to read and interpret the requirements for a specific purpose.
- Development activities for which the requirements must be available in a specific documentation format cannot be performed.
- Other quality criteria of the requirements such as correctness and completeness cannot be checked due to the inappropriate documentation format.

Example 27-3 describes a situation in which a scheduled development activity cannot be performed due to an inappropriate documentation format of the requirements.

Example 27-3: Incorrect documentation format

According to the specification rules for safety-relevant vehicle systems, the behavioural requirements for these systems must be specified using state machine diagrams.

The project plan for a new vehicle safety system foresees that the behavioural requirements for this system will be checked for completeness and consistency before the specification is passed on to the developers. However, the behavioural requirements have been documented merely in natural language instead of state machine diagrams. Therefore, the planned check cannot be performed.

Validation criteria for the documentation dimension

To successfully pass a validation activity that focusses on the documentation dimension, the requirements artefacts need to be checked for the following kinds of errors and no significant deficiencies are allowed to occur:

- *Correct documentation format*: Does the requirements artefact have the prescribed documentation format?
- *Comprehensibility*: Are the documented requirements comprehensible in the given context (e.g. are all terms that are used in the requirements artefact clearly defined)?
- *Unambiguous documentation*: Does the documentation format of the requirements artefact allow for an unambiguous interpretation of the requirements or could ambiguities be avoided by using a different, more appropriate documentation format?
- *Compliance with documentation rules*: Does the requirements artefact adhere to the documentation (or specification) rules and guidelines?

27.3.3 Validation in the Agreement Dimension

During requirements engineering, requirements are negotiated with the involved stakeholders at different stages. However, it is not clear whether all relevant stakeholders agree with the final draft of the requirements artefacts or whether all detected conflicts have been resolved. The goal of the validation activity in the agreement dimension is to check whether all relevant stakeholders agree with the requirements (see Section 4.4).

Last opportunity for changes

During the requirements engineering process, the stakeholders continuously obtain additional knowledge about the system, its context, and the system requirements. This knowledge gain can cause some stakeholders to change their mind about the requirements that they have already agreed on earlier. Requirements validation often provides the last opportunity for stakeholders to suggest changes without affecting design and implementation artefacts.

Quality criteria neglect agreement dimension

The quality criteria for requirements that can be found in the literature insufficiently cover defect types that are related to the agreement dimension, if at all.

Definition of criteria for the agreement dimension

To successfully pass a validation activity that focusses on the agreement dimension, the requirements artefacts must be checked for the following kinds of defects and no significant deficiencies are allowed to occur:

- ❑ *Agreement*: Did the relevant stakeholders agree upon each requirement?
- ❑ *Agreement after modifications*: Has approval of the relevant stakeholders been obtained anew after a requirement was modified or after the context of a requirement changed?[1]
- ❑ *Checked for conflicts*: Have the requirements been checked for potential conflicts caused e.g. by conflicting goals?
- ❑ *Conflicts resolved*: Have all known conflicts been resolved for each requirement?[2]

27.4 Sub-activity: Validating the Consideration of the Context

Errors in context consideration lead to errors in requirements

Considering exclusively the requirements specification does not suffice to detect errors such as missing requirements, inappropriate documentation formats, or requirements that have not been agreed with the relevant stakeholders. Defects of these types often result from errors made when considering the system context. The major defect classes related to insufficient consideration of the context include:

- ❑ *Missing context information*: In this case, relevant context aspects have been overlooked during requirements definition. Consequently, important requirements have not been identified, or relevant aspects are missing in the documented requirements.
- ❑ *Incorrect context information*: In this case, the definition of a requirement is based on incorrect context information. For instance, the requirements engineers may have made wrong assumptions about the behaviour of an external system that interacts with the system to be developed. Furthermore, in the case of a business information system, the requirements might be based on out-of-date business process definitions, e.g. because the organisation did not update the process definitions or communicate the changes to the requirements engineers in some other way.
- ❑ *Insufficiently considered context information*: In this case, the relevant context aspects are known but have not been adequately considered when documenting the requirements. For example, the stakeholders might know about a legal regulation requiring the deletion of customer data after a specific period of time but have not defined a corresponding requirement for the system to be developed.
- ❑ *Incomplete requirement sources*: In this case, one or multiple requirement sources (in at least one of the four context facets) have not been considered. For example, if a relevant stakeholder has not been involved in the requirements engineering

[1] The validity of a requirement may also be affected if the context of the requirement (see Section 5.4) changes. For instance, a related goal or a business process may change and thereby invalidate the requirement.

[2] Unresolved conflicts should not be mistaken for requirements inconsistencies. Unresolved conflicts (with respect to the agreement dimension) can persist even if the requirements are consistent.

process, important requirements may be missing, and existing conflicts have probably not been identified. Such problems can only be detected by checking whether all relevant requirement sources have been included in the requirements engineering process (see Example 27-4). One goal of validation is therefore to check whether relevant sources have been considered at the appropriate point of time during requirements engineering. Furthermore, if a relevant source has not been considered during some requirements engineering activity, it is highly probable that other kinds of errors persist as well, such as missing context information.

Checking for appropriate consideration of the context aims to detect defects of the stated defect classes, i.e. defects that are related to insufficient consideration of the system context. In the following, we discuss characteristic questions for validating the consideration of the context with regard to the four context facets.

Example 27-4: Neglecting relevant requirement sources

A library system for pupils is developed without involving pupils of different ages in the requirements engineering process. As this relevant group of stakeholders is not involved, there is a high risk that important requirements of these stakeholders are not identified and hence also not documented. The resulting system may therefore not satisfy the needs of these stakeholders.

Such problems cannot be detected by checking the requirements specification itself but only by checking whether the context has been considered properly.

27.4.1 Subject Facet

Representation of objects with required quality

As explained in Sections 4.3 and 6.3 the system requires an appropriate representation of all relevant objects from the subject facet. This representation must have the required level of abstraction and the required quality. The appropriate representation of this information is a prerequisite for the system to be able to process the represented information according to the defined functional and quality requirements. For example, the system must capture the relevant objects with the required accuracy and observe the required updating intervals. The following questions support the detection of missing context information concerning the subject facet:

- ❑ Have all relevant objects been identified and documented?
- ❑ Have all identified objects been captured completely and correctly?
- ❑ Have all quality requirements for the representation of objects been captured (e.g. with the required accuracy and updating interval)?
- ❑ Have all relevant legal requirements for the representation of objects in the system (such as the protection of data privacy) been considered?
- ❑ Have all relevant requirement sources (stakeholders, documents, existing systems) been incorporated in the identification of the objects and their properties and relationships?

27.4.2 Usage Facet

Validation with regard to system usage

Requirements validation from the perspective of the usage facet has to ensure that the information about the intended ways of using the system, the relevant user groups and their preferred types of usage interfaces as well as the desired usage of the system by other systems is complete and correct. The system can only meet its objectives (i.e. satisfy the stakeholders' goals) if the interactions with the system are realised in a way that is appropriate for all persons using the system as well as other systems interacting with the system. The validation of the context consideration from the usage perspective involves asking the following questions:

- ❑ Have the desired interactions with the environment been captured completely and correctly, i.e. stimuli the system must detect and responses the system must produce?
- ❑ Have the quality requirements for the interaction with the environment been captured completely and correctly (e.g. desired performance, robustness against faulty operation and incorrect inputs, prevention of misuse)?
- ❑ Have the specifics of different user groups been taken into account (e.g. specific requirements for different cultures and countries)?
- ❑ Have the usage goals of the relevant stakeholders and the relevant systems been elicited completely and correctly?
- ❑ Have all other relevant requirement sources for the usage facet been involved, such as experts for human–machine–interfaces for the corresponding type of system?

27.4.3 IT System Facet

Validation with regard to IT system facet

Context aspects of the IT system facet must be considered so that the system can be successfully integrated into its IT system (or technical) environment. If the stakeholders do not have sufficient knowledge about the communication network to which the system will be connected or the resources that are provided by the technical environment, the system will either fail to work in its operational environment or it will operate with limited functionality and quality. Therefore, the questions to be considered during the validation of context consideration from the perspective of the IT system facet include:

- ❑ Have the relevant properties of the hardware and software components with which the system interacts or that belong to the underlying hardware and software platform of the system been captured completely and correctly?
- ❑ Have all required system interfaces and the relevant protocols at each interface been documented completely and correctly?
- ❑ Have all relevant IT strategies been considered appropriately (e.g. with regard to the use of upcoming or future technology)?
- ❑ Have all relevant IT policies such as installation, update, and backup policies been considered and documented?
- ❑ Have all relevant requirement sources of the IT system facet been involved in the requirements elicitation activities?

27.4.4 Development Facet

Validation with regard to development processes, methods, and tools

Context aspects of the development facet influence the development process of the system such as the methods and tools used to develop the system. Errors in the consideration of the development facet are hardly correctable afterwards, since adapting the development process or changing the development tools during the project requires considerable time, effort, and possibly also rework. Therefore, also the context aspects of the development facet should be validated early with the relevant stakeholders. During the validation of the context consideration from the perspective of the development facet, among other things, the following questions must be asked:

- ❑ Have all requirements pertaining to the languages (specification languages, programming languages, etc.) and development tools to be used been captured completely and correctly?
- ❑ Have the requirements for the development process and development standards, including the development rules and guidelines with which the project must comply, been captured completely and correctly?
- ❑ Have all development artefacts to be provided or exchanged, for instance between the client and the contractor, been identified?
- ❑ Have the targeted project duration and cost been checked for feasibility after all (essential) requirements have been agreed on?
- ❑ Have all relevant requirement sources of the development facet been considered?

!

Hint 27-2: *Use checklists to validate the consideration of the context with respect to each context facet*

- ❑ Support the validation of context consideration by using dedicated checklists for the four context facets (see Section 29.1).
- ❑ When defining a validation checklist for a specific context facet, include questions that support the detection of defects that are known to frequently occur during the consideration this facet (see Section 29.1).

27.5 Sub-activity: Validating the Execution of Activities

Trust in existing and future products

Verifying the execution of activities means checking whether each required requirements engineering activity has been performed and whether each activity has been performed properly. Compliance with an accepted and proven process definition increases confidence in the quality of the created development artefacts (in particular, if the relevant information about the execution of the development activities is documented in a checkable and traceable manner). For example, in the context of global outsourcing of software development activities, the introduction of CMM (Capability Maturity Model) and CMMI in contractor companies has contributed significantly to the acceptance of these companies [Carmel and Tjia 2005]. Validation of performed requirements engineering activities aims to detect unwanted and possibly critical deviations from the accepted and agreed development process. If the performed activities do not comply with the relevant process definition, this is an indication that the quality of the requirements artefacts may be impaired. Compliance with accepted process definitions is especially important in the development of safety-critical systems.

Detection of deviations

Development processes are defined (partly) in terms of task and activity descriptions. By validating performed activities against the process definitions, deviations from these definitions can be detected. If a deviation is detected, the stakeholders need to evaluate whether the deviation is critical and whether mitigation activities are needed.

Input for the management activity

Detected deviations from the process and activity descriptions are important inputs to managing the requirements engineering process. Hence, these findings need to be communicated to the project or process management activity. Within the management activity, the findings from validation are analysed. Based on the results of the analysis, the management activity may initiate a change of the process. For instance, additional elicitation, documentation, negotiation, or validation activities may be scheduled. The management activity of the requirements engineering process is described in Section 30.5.

The questions to be considered during the validation of the performed activities include:

- Has the execution of the activities been documented in the prescribed way?
- Have all activities that are required according to the process definition been performed?
- Have all inputs defined in each activity description been considered for the respective activity?
- Does the execution of each activity correspond to the rules and guidelines defined in the activity description?
- Have all outputs defined in each activity description been created?
- Have all stakeholders who are relevant for performing the respective activity been involved in the execution of the activity?

Suggestions for process improvement

The stakeholders involved should also think about ways of avoiding the detected problems in the future. If the same kind of deviations occurs regularly, this may be an indication that the process model must be revised.

27.6 Capability Model for Validation with Three Levels

Three levels of requirements validation

Introducing a process that considers all three validation sub-activities with all validation aspects described in Sections 27.3–27.5 in an organisation at once may be difficult or even unfeasible, for instance, due to time constraints. Therefore, a stepwise, incremental introduction of the different validation aspects is suggested, based on three levels of requirements validation defined for this purpose:

- Level 1 comprises the minimal validation aspects that each project should consider.
- Level 2 comprises the validation aspects for a standard validation, i.e. the validation aspects that should typically be achieved in a project. Level 2 includes the validation aspects defined at level 1.

- Level 3 describes validation aspects for projects in which the quality of the resulting requirements artefacts is of critical importance. Note that in such projects, in addition to the stated validation aspects, the use of (formal) specification and verification techniques is highly recommended or may even be mandatory. Level 3 includes the validation aspects of levels 1 and 2.

Assignment of the validation goals to the three levels

Table 27-1 outlines our assignment of the validation aspects to the three levels. The validation goals and the assignment to the levels should be adapted to organisation- and/or project-specific needs and constraints, i.e. the suggested validation goals should be complemented and refined, if necessary.

Tab. 27-1 *Three levels of validation*

Validation aspects	Levels		
	Level 1 Minimal validation	Level 2 Standard validation	Level 3 Advanced validation
CONTEXT CONSIDERATION			
Wrong context information		X	
Missing context information			X
Incomplete requirement sources		X	
Insufficiently considered context information			X
ARTEFACTS - CONTENT DIMENSION			
Requirements biased by a specific solution			X
Missing requirements	X		
Missing traceability information			X
Inconsistencies in requirements	X		
Incorrect requirements	X		
Untestable requirements		X	
Unnecessary requirements		X	
Incomplete requirements	X		
ARTEFACTS - DOCUMENTATION DIMENSION			
Requirements in the wrong documentation format	X		
Lacking comprehensibility	X		
Ambiguously documented requirements		X	
Broken documentation rules			X
ARTEFACTS - AGREEMENT DIMENSION			
Requirements not agreed	X		
Requirements not agreed anew after modification		X	
Unresolved conflicts	X		
Undetected conflicts			X
ACTIVITY EXECUTION			
All relevant stakeholders involved in activity execution	X		
All prescribed activities performed		X	
All prescribed outputs created		X	
Execution of the activities documented correctly		X	
All relevant inputs considered for each activity			X

27.7 Goals and Scenarios in Validation

In the following, we describe the benefits of using goals and scenarios during validation.

27.7.1 Benefits of Considering Goals

Validation of the defined goals with the relevant stakeholders as early as possible in the requirements engineering process is recommended. Since a goal is typically related to a number of other artefacts such as scenarios and solution-oriented requirements artefacts, defects in a goal can have substantial consequences for the development process. Later modification of a goal typically entails numerous changes in the other requirements artefacts. The longer a defect in a goal definition remains undetected, the larger is the amount of additional work needed to fix the defect.

Incomplete documentation of goals

If a relevant goal is overlooked, there is a risk that important usage scenarios as well as related functional and quality requirements will be omitted and therefore not included in the requirements specification. Possible causes for incomplete documentation of goals may lie in the communication between the stakeholders. For example, the client may presume that specific goals are known to the other stakeholders and hence not explicitly state these goals. However, if the other stakeholders are, in fact, not aware of these goals, these important goals do not become part of the specification. Another possible cause of incomplete documentation of goals is that relevant stakeholders (or other requirement sources) have not been involved in the goal definition process at all.

Unresolved conflicts among goals

The completeness of the documented goals is not the only critical success factor. The presence of unresolved or undetected conflicts about goals among the different stakeholders puts the stability of the requirements specification at risk. Revising a goal during conflict resolution necessitates revising all development artefacts that contribute to fulfilling that goal.

Advantages of goal validation

The validation of goals contributes to early detection of deficiencies and gaps in requirements. Hence, it helps to avoid serious errors in the resulting requirements specification. Since fixing errors in the detailed requirements generally requires much more resources than fixing errors early at the goal level, resources are saved.

Early validation of goals

Consequently, goals should be validated e.g. for agreement and completeness before the stakeholders develop detailed, solution-oriented requirements. In addition, the validation of goals itself requires less resources than the validation of solution-oriented requirements.

Supporting goal validation by scenarios

However, stakeholders often cannot decide to approve or reject a documented goal until they are provided with a concrete example of its realisation. Illustrating the satisfaction of goals by means of scenarios hence considerably supports goal validation. The interactions between goals and scenarios that are beneficial for goal validation are explained in Chapter 12.

!

Hint 27-3: *Avoid implicit goal conflicts*

The following procedure contributes to avoiding undocumented and hence also unresolved conflicts about goals:

- ❑ Document each goal stated by the stakeholders in a goal model, even if the goal obstructs or is in conflict with other goals (see Section 7.4).
- ❑ Document the identified goal conflict and goal obstruction dependencies in the goal model using the goal relationships described in Chapter 8.
- ❑ Check whether all known conflicts between the documented goals have been resolved. Document how the goal conflicts have been resolved (e.g. by decision; for details on conflict resolution, see Chapter 25).

27.7.2 Benefits of Considering Scenarios

Scenarios are well suited for validation

Since scenarios document concrete examples of system usage, they are well suited for supporting the validation of requirements by virtually all stakeholders. The stakeholders can go through a scenario step by step and thereby detect defects such as missing or faulty interactions. Therefore, scenarios are often created specifically for the purpose of validating solution-oriented requirements (see Section 29.3.2).

Validation from several perspectives

Scenarios allow the involvement of different stakeholders who validate the requirements from different perspectives. For example, system users can check whether they agree with the planned usage workflows or if the documented workflows need to be changed. Software architects can check, for example, whether the scenarios convey enough information to define an initial, coarse-grained system architecture. Testers can check whether the scenarios are suitable for deriving test cases.

Improved stakeholder involvement through context information

Scenarios put requirements in context, i.e. the requirements are presented along with context information (see Section 9.2). For instance, a scenario may be enriched by explanations of the processes that take place in the system context (see Section 10.6). The context information documented in the scenarios supports leveraging the stakeholders' expert knowledge about the system context during requirements validation. Furthermore, the documented context information itself is validated. In other words, scenarios provide natural support for validating the consideration of the context (Section 27.4). All in all, it is often easier for the stakeholders to check a scenario than to check a set of detailed, solution-oriented requirements artefacts which are decoupled both from the system context and from one another.

Combination with prototypes

In practice, scenarios are often used in combination with prototypes [Weidenhaupt et al. 1998]. After scenarios have been defined and validated with stakeholders with regard to completeness, correctness, and sufficient agreement, a prototype is developed based on the scenarios. The prototype enables the stakeholders to explore the scenarios interactively and detect thereby defects in the scenarios. In addition, misunderstandings and misinterpretations of the scenarios can be uncovered early with the help of prototypes. The use of prototypes during requirements validation is explained in Section 28.5.

Summarising, scenarios play an important role in each validation activity. The validation of requirements is hardly achievable without using scenarios.

27.8 Principles of Validation

In the following, we explain six important principles of requirements validation.

27.8.1 First Principle: Involving the Right Stakeholders

Choosing the validation team

For each aspect of a requirements artefact to be checked during validation, appropriate stakeholders must be involved. The choice of the stakeholders who form the validation team depends on the validation goal and the artefacts to be validated. The validation team should have the expertise to check the relevant aspects in the three dimensions as well as in the four context facets.

Responsibility for the three dimensions and the four context facets

Appointment of specific stakeholders as explicitly responsible for each of the three dimensions and each of the four context facets is recommended. The responsibility for several dimensions and/or several context facets may also be assigned to a single stakeholder, if necessary.

While forming a validation team, the reviewers' independence must be considered. Additionally, the advantages and disadvantages of internal and external validation (see below) should be taken into account. In the following, we elaborate on these two aspects.

Independence of Reviewers

The author of an artefact is not a suitable candidate for validating the artefact

Requirements artefacts should not be checked by a stakeholder who has been involved in their development (in the following this stakeholder is referred to as the author). When checking the artefact, the author interprets the information he reads against the background knowledge that he gained while creating the artefact. This background knowledge allows, for example, for correct interpretation of ambiguously or incompletely documented requirements. Hence, there is a risk that deficiencies in the artefacts remain undetected. For this reason, we recommend choosing stakeholders (as reviewers) who are familiar with the domain but do not know the development history of the requirements artefacts. Stakeholders who have not been involved in the development of an artefact can detect defects in that artefact more reliably.

The IEEE Standard 1012-2004 defines two additional factors for the independence of a reviewer (see [IEEE Std 1012-2004]):

Managerial independence

- *Managerial independence*: Managerial independence means that the persons responsible for validation can act independently of the developing organisation, i.e. they are not bound to instructions by the developing organisation.

Financial independence

- *Financial independence*: Financial independence means that the budget for validation is not managed by the developing organisation.

Internal vs. External Validation

Reviewers can be identified either within or outside the developing organisation. The identified reviewers are involved in the validation or commissioned to perform the validation. If the validation is performed by stakeholders from within the developing organisation it is called internal validation, otherwise it is called external validation. Note that the reviewers' independence (see previous section) needs to be ensured in both cases.

Company-internal validation

In internal validation, only stakeholders of the developing organisation are involved (or, in the case of large organisations, only stakeholders from the developing department or business unit). Internal validation is generally performed as a preliminary check of the requirements artefacts.

Definition 27-2: *Internal validation*

In internal validation, exclusively stakeholders from within the developing organisation are involved, or, in the case of large organisations, from within the developing department or business unit.

Shorter lead time and less effort

Internal validation can be realised with a shorter lead time and moderate preparation effort. Typically, company-internal regulations determine the group of persons who should be involved in the validation process. If standard validation techniques of the organisation are used, a significant part of the preparation time can be saved, as the stakeholders involved are familiar with the validation process and the document templates used.

Validation of intermediate results

Internal validation is well suited for checking intermediate results, such as checking whether an intermediate milestone has been achieved. The validation results generally remain in the developing organisation and are communicated to external stakeholders only in a filtered form, if at all.

External validation

In the case of external validation, stakeholders from outside the organisation are involved (or, in the case of large organisations, from outside the department or business unit). To conduct an external validation, for instance, an external domain expert may be appointed as a reviewer.

Definition 27-3: *External validation*

During external validation, stakeholders from outside the developing organisation (or department or business unit) judge the quality of the requirements artefacts.

Higher effort for external validation

In contrast to internal validation, external validation must be planned early in order to ensure that the required external stakeholders are available. The validation process is agreed between the developing organisation and the external stakeholders. The employees of the developing organisation may need some time to familiarise themselves with the procedures of the external stakeholders and/or the external stakeholders may need some time to become familiar with the organisation-specific procedures.

Disclosing the artefacts and the development process

By participating in the validation, the involved external stakeholders get a deep insight into the checked artefacts and, to a certain extent, into the development process.

High degree of completion necessary

Due to the greater effort required, external validation should only be performed for requirements artefacts that are mostly completed. Otherwise, when the external reviewers identify a defect, it is difficult to judge whether the author has committed an error or the detected defect arises from the low degree of completion.

Example 27-5: Internal and external validation

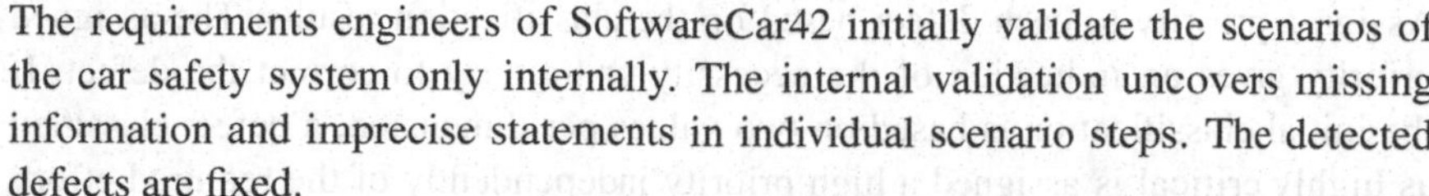

The requirements engineers of SoftwareCar42 initially validate the scenarios of the car safety system only internally. The internal validation uncovers missing information and imprecise statements in individual scenario steps. The detected defects are fixed.

Subsequently, validation is performed by an externally commissioned expert for automotive software. The expert's analysis of the scenarios reveals that the scenarios describe predominantly the normal workflows, whereas scenarios describing exception and error behaviour are missing.

27.8.2 Second Principle: Separating Defect Detection from Defect Correction

Defect detection in software testing

During validation, activities for defect detection should be clearly separated from activities for defect correction. The separation of defect detection and defect correction is a well-proven principle of software quality assurance and is especially applied in software testing. In software testing, defect detection comprises the execution of the software system or component with the goal of detecting defects. However, testers usually specialise in detecting defects, and therefore do not locate the causes of defects in the code or resolve software errors. Moreover, the first step after defect detection is to clarify whether a detected defect is indeed a defect or the specification used for testing is wrong. Only for confirmed defects does error correction takes place, i.e. the causes of the defects are located and the errors in the implementation are resolved.

Concentrating on error detection

In requirements engineering, the separation of defect detection and defect correction allows reviewers to initially concentrate mainly on the identification of requirements defects without having to think about possible corrections. Correction activities do not take place before the reviewers have gained a comprehensive picture of the defects and the defects have been confirmed. This has the advantage that the resources available for validation can be used in a purposeful manner (see Hint 27-4 and Fig. 27-4).

!

Hint 27-4: *Prioritisation of corrective actions*

Evaluate the identified and confirmed requirements defects with regard to their criticality (low, high) and required correction effort (low, high) as illustrated in Fig. 27-4. The criticality expresses the expected impact on the realisation of the system, and the effort expresses an estimation of the resources required to correct the error in the requirements artefacts. If a finer scale than two values per dimension is needed, the prioritisation scheme can be adapted accordingly. However, be aware that classifying the defects becomes increasingly complex with a more fine-grained scale.

(to be continued)

Hint 27-4 *(continued)*

Assign a priority to each defect based on the classification results. The assigned priority gives an indication of the necessity or urgency to correct the defect. If the initial classification is based on two values per dimension, a defect classified as highly critical is assigned a high priority independently of the required effort. Defects with low criticality and low estimated effort are assigned an intermediate priority. Defects with low criticality and high expected effort are assigned a low priority.

If the resources available do not suffice for removing all high-priority defects, increasing the allocated resources accordingly is advised. Correcting as many requirements defects as possible in an early stage is recommended, since error correction in subsequent development phases generally entails higher effort than early correction in requirements engineering.

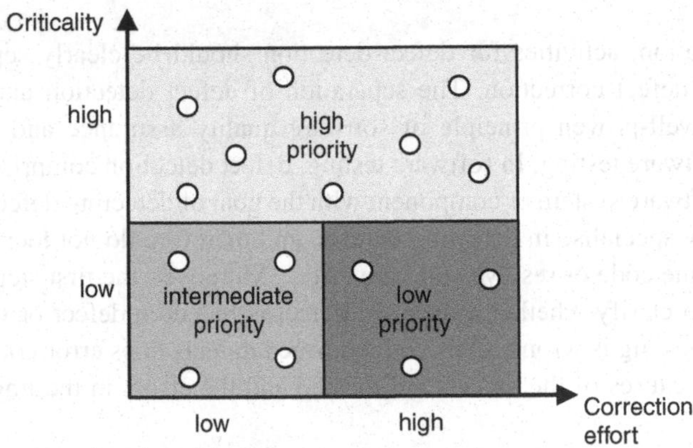

Fig. 27-4 *Priority of corrective actions depending on the effort and criticality of an error*

27.8.3 Third Principle: Leveraging Multiple Independent Views

Validation is greatly supported, if first multiple independent views are obtained which can then be consolidated in a systematic way. The purpose of consolidation is to detect differences between the different views obtained [Leite and Freeman 1991]. If, for instance, contradicting statements about the same subject are found in two or more views, this indicates that at least one view contains an error. This approach has proven useful in many disciplines, such as jurisdiction. In a trial, several witnesses describe the same facts, each from his/her own perspective. Based on the individual views, a more coherent overall picture is created, i.e. the views are consolidated.

Gaining independent views

Possibilities for obtaining multiple (more or less) independent views include:

- The reviewers validate the same set of artefacts separately from each other but from the same perspective. For instance, each reviewer might use the same checklist (such as a checklist focussing on the usage facet; see Section 29.1).

- The reviewers validate the same set of artefacts from different perspectives, for instance, by using different checklists where each checklist specialises on a different dimension (content dimension, agreement dimension, or documentation dimension) or on a different context facet (subject facet, usage facet, IT system facet, or development facet).
- The reviewers validate the same set of artefacts with different usage scenarios. For instance, each reviewer may check the same set of solution-oriented requirements artefacts against some usage scenario that was assigned specifically to this reviewer.
- The reviewers validate the same set of artefacts from different perspectives such as the perspective of the architect, the perspective of the tester, and the user perspective. To establish the perspectives, each reviewer may be asked to create development artefacts that are characteristic of the perspective assigned to him, i.e. architectural artefacts, test artefacts, or a (fragment of a) user manual (see Section 29.3).
- Each reviewer validates a different set of requirements artefacts or relationships between requirements artefacts. For instance, one reviewer might check the traceability relationships between goals and scenarios (see Example 27-6), while another reviewer checks the traceability relationships between scenarios and solution-oriented requirements. By collating the results for the different sets of artefacts, a broad overview of the quality of the requirements can be obtained. Thereby, for instance, systematic errors in the requirements engineering process can be uncovered.
- The reviewers validate different, yet interrelated types of requirements artefacts such as goals and scenarios with the aim of identifying differences between the artefact types such as conflicting statements about the same subject. The identified differences indicate requirements defects such as inconsistencies between different artefact types or incompleteness within one artefact type.

Consolidation of views

In addition, the possibilities for obtaining independent views described above can be combined in different ways (see Example 27-6). The selection of any one of these possibilities or some combination of them is made depending on the validation goal. The individual validation results that are obtained in this way must be consolidated afterwards. The consolidation can be performed either jointly by the validation team or by a requirements engineer. Conflicts between the individual views of the different stakeholders such as contradicting judgements regarding the same fact (see Section 25.2) should preferably be resolved immediately together with the stakeholders who participate in the validation.

Example 27-6: Views in the validation of goals and scenarios

During the development of a car safety system, the stakeholders have defined a goal model as well as associated scenarios that illustrate the satisfaction of the goals. In order to validate the goal model and the scenarios three groups are formed:

- The first group validates the goal model without considering the scenarios.
- The second group validates the scenarios without considering the goal model.

(to be continued)

Example 27-6 (*continued*)

- A third group validates the relationships between goals and scenarios. This group checks whether at least one scenario has been defined for each goal and whether each goal that is illustrated by some scenario is also contained in the goal model.

During validation, each group concentrates on a different aspect or view. Afterwards, the three groups consolidate their results, i.e. they bring together the detected defects in the goal model, in the scenarios, and in the relationships between goals and scenarios.

27.8.4 Fourth Principle: Use of Appropriate Documentation Formats

Strengths and weaknesses of different documentation formats

Not every documentation format is equally suited for supporting requirements validation with a specific stakeholder. For instance, use cases written in natural language are a suitable medium for validating requirements with representative system users. However, when validating requirements with system architects who prefer model-based requirements, use cases documented in natural language are inappropriate as a communication medium. The requirements engineers can change the documentation format of the requirements prior to or during requirements validation in order to exploit the strengths of a specific documentation format or to avoid weaknesses of the present documentation format. For example, natural language has the advantage of general comprehensibility and high expressiveness but also the disadvantage of ambiguity and weak support for presenting complex, interrelated facts in a structured manner. Hence, documenting requirements using natural language makes it difficult for a stakeholder who interprets the requirements to conceive from the text which objects are described and how the objects are related to each other. In contrast, visual models have their strengths in the structured representation of objects and relationships. However, models may be difficult to understand for stakeholders who are not trained in the corresponding modelling language. In addition, models have the disadvantage of limited expressiveness compared with natural language.

Improved detection of errors

Different documentation formats have different strengths and weaknesses. Therefore, transferring a requirements artefact from one documentation format into another prior to validating the artefact (see Example 27-7) can significantly ease defect detection and improve the defect detection rate. In addition, the change of the documentation format itself can already uncover some defects.

Example 27-7: Changing the documentation format for requirements validation

The requirements engineers of SoftwareCar42 plan to validate the requirements for a car safety system with a domain expert for automotive safety. Presently, the requirements are documented in natural language. In order to exploit the advantages that models have for requirements validation, the requirements engineers transfer the requirements into a model-based documentation format.

Consideration of stakeholder preferences

In addition to the individual strengths and weaknesses of the various documentation formats, also the preferences and knowledge of the stakeholders involved with regard to the different documentation formats can also be a strong argument for changing the documentation format. For instance, requirements validation must not be hindered by a documentation format that is incomprehensible to the stakeholders who shall validate the requirements. In order to facilitate validation by all relevant stakeholders, it may be necessary, for instance, to transfer natural language requirements into a model-based format or to verbalise a complex model, i.e. to transfer the model into a textual form which the stakeholders can understand more easily.

27.8.5 Fifth Principle: Creation of Development Artefacts during Validation

Creating architectural artefacts, test artefacts, or a manual based on the requirements

Creation of development artefacts during requirements validation aims to check how well the requirements artefacts are suited, for instance, as a basis for developing architectural artefacts, test artefacts, or a user manual. During validation, the development activities for creating the respective development artefacts are performed exemplarily. During the creation of these development artefacts, the reviewers deal intensively with the requirements artefacts for the system. In this way, defects in the requirements are generally found more reliably compared with just reading the requirements. However, this kind of validation also consumes more resources than validation performed without creating development artefacts.

27.8.6 Sixth Principle: Repeated Validation

Rechecking already released artefacts

A validation of requirements pertains to a specific point in time and the stakeholders' knowledge at this point in time. Since new knowledge is continuously gained during requirements engineering (as requirements engineering is also a learning process), the stakeholders' knowledge and understanding of the system evolve over time. Therewith, the stakeholders' requirements for the system may change as well. Consequently, a single validation and release of the requirements is no guarantee that the requirements are still valid at a later point in time. Especially in the following cases, already validated (and possibly released) requirements artefacts should be checked again at appropriate points in time:

- Long-term projects
- Very early validation of requirements
- Reuse of requirements artefacts
- Systems with a high degree of innovation
- Poorly understood domains
- High gain in knowledge during requirements engineering

!

Hint 27-5: *Validation principles*

- ❑ Ensure that relevant company-internal as well as relevant external stakeholders participate in validation.
- ❑ Pay attention to the reviewers' independence and appoint external, independent stakeholders, if necessary.
- ❑ Separate defect detection from the correction of the detected defects.
- ❑ Whenever possible, try to obtain independent views that can be integrated during requirements validation in order to detect defects more reliably.
- ❑ Consider changing the documentation format of the requirements into a format that matches the validation goal and the preferences of the stakeholders who actually perform the validation.
- ❑ If your validation approach generates poor results, try to support defect detection by creating development artefacts such as architectural artefacts, test artefacts, user manuals, or goals and scenarios during validation.
- ❑ Establish guidelines that clearly determine when or under what conditions an already released requirements artefact has to be validated again.

Chapter 28
Validation Techniques

In this chapter, we describe four techniques for validating requirements artefacts. For each technique, we outline:

- *Hints for the preparation, execution, and follow-up work*
- *The benefit of the technique for requirements validation*
- *An effort estimation*
- *Critical success factors*
- *A checklist with important hints for applying the technique*

We initially provide an overview of the sub-activities that have to be performed when preparing a validation activity regardless of the applied validation technique:

Clearly defined goal

- ❑ *Defining the validation goal*: The goal that is pursued by the validation should be clearly defined, communicated to the participants clearly, and agreed with the participants.

Coverage of the context facets

- ❑ *Identifying the required participants*: The participants are identified depending on the validation goal. In this way, the requirements engineers ensure that the participants have the domain knowledge that is required for the validation. Therein, it is important to pay attention to covering the four context facets so that each of the four facets is considered accordingly during the validation. If some facet is not represented by the participants, the validation team is likely to overlook some requirements defects that pertain to this facet.

Appropriate location

- ❑ *Choosing the location*: The location for the validation should be spacious enough and allow for an undisturbed validation meeting. If the validation shall be performed by several independent stakeholders or by groups of stakeholders, several rooms must be reserved. In addition, the required technical equipment should be provided such as whiteboards, flipcharts, or a digital projector.

Invitation of the participants

- ❑ *Inviting the participants*: The identified participants need to be invited in due time for the validation. The invitation should also inform the participants about the validation goal and the specific role of each participant. In addition, the participants should be provided with the background knowledge that is required for the validation.

!

Hint 28-1: *Checklist for preparing a validation activity*

- ❑ Define the validation goal.
- ❑ Identify the participants based on the validation goal.
- ❑ When selecting the participants, pay attention to covering the four context facets.
- ❑ Choose and reserve an appropriate location.
- ❑ Make sure that the required technical equipment is available.
- ❑ Invite the participants in due time.
- ❑ Let each participant confirm his participation.
- ❑ Remind the participants of the meeting shortly before the date.
- ❑ Communicate to each participant the validation goal and the participant's role in the validation activity.
- ❑ Provide relevant background knowledge in due time before the validation.

28.1 Inspections

Systematic examination of artefacts

The goal of (software) inspection is to detect defects in development artefacts. The systematic introduction of inspections for software artefacts can be traced back to Michael Fagan [Fagan 1976]. An important characteristic of an inspection is strict adherence to a defined process scheme. A detailed explanation of the inspection process can be found, for example, in [Gilb and Graham 1993].

Definition 28-1: *Inspection*

Inspection: A quality improvement process for written material. It consists of two dominant components; product (document itself) improvement and process improvement (of both document production and inspection).

[Gilb and Graham 1993]

D

Using goals and scenarios

Using goals and scenarios during the inspection process has the advantage that the stakeholders performing the inspection have better support in searching for defects. A specific inspection process for scenarios is suggested in [Leite et al. 2005].

In Fig. 28-1, the typical phases of an inspection are shown. We briefly characterise the goal of each inspection phase:

❶ *Planning*: briefing the inspection team
❷ *Overview*: presentation of the artefacts to be inspected
❸ *Defect detection*: identification of defects
❹ *Defect collection*: collection and consolidation of identified defects
❺ *Defect correction*: rework and resolution of detected defects
❻ *Follow-up*: checking the corrections made
❼ *Reflection*: collecting suggestions for process improvement

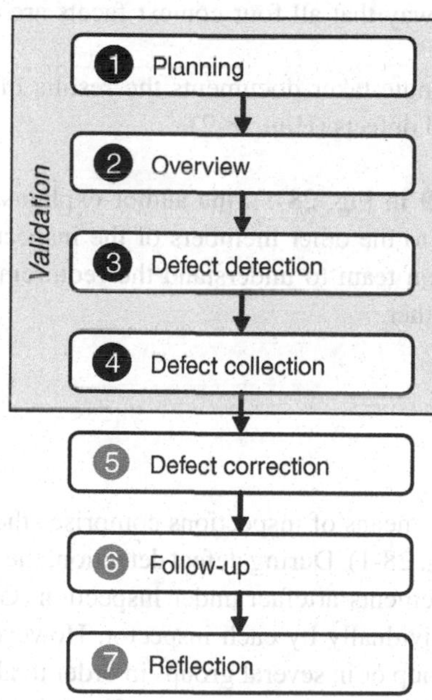

Fig. 28-1 *Inspection phases (based on [Laitenberger and DeBaud 2000])*

Refinement of phases ❶ to ❹

Only phases ❶ to ❹ support the identification of defects in requirements artefacts. Hence, these phases are the only focus of requirements validation (see Fig. 28-1). In the following, we explain these phases.

28.1.1 Preparation

❶ Planning

The preparation of a validation by means of inspections comprises the planning and overview phases. In the planning phase (❶ in Fig. 28-1), the following roles are assigned to the involved stakeholders:

- *Organiser*: The organiser is responsible for planning and monitoring the inspection process.
- *Moderator*: The moderator leads the inspection meeting and ensures that the participants adhere to the process scheme. The moderator should, in addition, provide for a balance between the (sometimes) contradicting interests of the author and the inspectors. Therefore, he should be as neutral and objective as possible. Consequently, a person who was not involved in the creation of the artefact to be inspected should be appointed as moderator.
- *Author*: The author created the artefact to be inspected. He explains the artefact to the inspectors in the overview phase and is responsible, later on, for correcting the detected defects.
- *Reader/presenter*: The reader presents the inspection material successively and guides the inspectors through the artefact under inspection. In order to focus the inspection on the requirements artefact itself and not on the interpretation of the author, it is advisable to select a neutral (independent) reader.
- *Inspectors*: The inspectors are responsible for detecting defects. They inform the other members of the inspection team about their findings. The inspectors should be selected in such a way that all four context facets are considered accordingly during the inspection.
- *Minute-taker*: The minute-taker documents the results of the inspection and, in particular, the detected defects (Hint 28-2).

❷ Overview

In the overview phase (❷ in Fig. 28-1), the author explains, in a first meeting, the artefacts to be inspected to the other members of the inspection team. The meeting shall enable the inspection team to understand the requirements artefacts and their relationships with each other.

28.1.2 Execution

❸ Defect detection

Performing validation by means of inspections comprises the defect detection phase of an inspection (❸ in Fig. 28-1). During defect detection, the inspectors detect potential defects in the requirements artefact under inspection. Generally, the search for defects is performed individually by each inspector. However, it is also possible to search for defects in a group or in several groups in order to allow for communication among the inspectors and hence achieve synergy effects during defect identification.

Scope for discretion during defect identification

During the identification of defects, there is some scope for discretion. It may be, for example, not obvious to an inspector whether an error of omission exists or the author has omitted some information intentionally. In order to reduce the scope for discretion and to avoid defect detection being left to chance, the inspectors need concrete guidelines such as checklists for performing the defect identification (see Chapter 29).

28.1.3 Follow-up

❹ Defect collection

The follow-up work after validation by means of inspections comprises the defect collection phase (❹ in Fig. 28-1). In this phase, the detected defects are collected, consolidated, and documented, including a classification of each defect and the agreed corrective actions.

Clarification of defects

Not each defect detected by the inspectors is necessarily an actual defect. It is also possible that the reason for identifying a defect is not an actual defect in the artefact itself but rather a wrong assumption of the inspector who has detected the defect. The detected defects are considered and discussed jointly by the validation team. If a defect reported by an inspector is not confirmed as an actual defect, this defect is eliminated from the list of defects. Questions regarding the reported defects should be clarified during defect collection. However, during defect collection, the participants are not allowed to discuss how the defects shall be corrected.

Documentation

Defect collection is accompanied by documentation activities. Each detected defect, the defined correction activities as well as important process parameters such as the duration of the defect detection and the number of defects detected are documented. Typically an appropriate form is used for this purpose during defect collection (see Hint 28-2). This documentation provides the basis for defect correction as well as process control and improvement.

!

Hint 28-2: *Documenting the inspection results*

Document the following information in an inspection protocol:

- ❑ Date and location of the inspection
- ❑ Stakeholders involved and their roles
- ❑ Requirements artefacts inspected with version numbers
- ❑ Checklists used and other supportive means
- ❑ Inspection result (release or no release)
- ❑ Relevant process parameters (e.g. duration, number of defects, etc.)
- ❑ Reference to the associated list of defects

Create a list of defects with the following information for each defect:

- ❑ Number/identifier of the defect
- ❑ Reference to the artefact that contains the defect
- ❑ Location of the defect in the artefact (e.g. page number)
- ❑ Classification of the defect (e.g. suggestion for improvement or critical defect)
- ❑ Broken rule or regulation (e.g. reference to a checklist)
- ❑ Description of the defect, if necessary.

28.1.4 Checklist for Applying the Technique

Hint 28-3 presents a checklist with important hints that should be considered when conducting an inspection.

!

Hint 28-3: *Checklist for conducting an inspection*

Preparation – Planning phase:

- ❑ Apply, initially, a well-proven process scheme for inspections. When you have gained experience, adapt the process to your needs.
- ❑ Assign the inspection roles described in the process scheme to the participants and let each participant become familiar with his role.
- ❑ Select a neutral moderator as well as a neutral reader, i.e. the author is not allowed to play the role of the moderator or the reader.

Preparation – Overview phase:

- ❑ Let the author present the requirements artefacts that shall be inspected to the other participants.
- ❑ Give the participants the opportunity to ask questions about the requirements artefacts.

Execution – Defect detection:

- ❑ Experiment with defect detection by individual inspectors vs. defect detection in groups in order to find out which way of detecting defects works best for your projects or your organisation.
- ❑ Provide templates or forms for documenting defects, decisions, and rationales.
- ❑ Make sure that the inspectors document all detected defects.
- ❑ Guide the defect detection by means of appropriate instructions, e.g. provided as checklists (see Chapter 29).

Follow-up – Defect collection:

- ❑ Let the reader present the inspected artefacts piece by piece, e.g. paragraph by paragraph.
- ❑ Make sure that all detected defects are collected and classified.
- ❑ Create your own defect class for conflicts about requirements (see Part IV.c).
- ❑ Pay attention to complete documentation of the results during defect collection (e.g. questions posed to the author as well as suggestions for improvement).

28.1.5 Benefit

Detailed checking of the artefacts

Inspections are suited for detailed checking of requirements artefacts. The reader presents the artefacts to be inspected piece by piece during defect collection. Several inspectors comment on each specific part of the artefact. Through this procedure, a high intensity of checking is achieved, i.e. each part of the artefact under inspection is checked in detail by several inspectors. A further advantage of inspections is that they can be applied to all kinds of documented requirements, i.e. to text, models, and combinations of text and models (see Part IV.a).

Check for achieved understanding (content dimension)

Inspections are well suited for checking the achieved understanding about the requirements for the system to be developed. Thus, for instance, clarification questions that are posed during the inspection should be noted. During defect correction, the artefacts should be adapted accordingly so that all open questions are answered.

Detailed checking of an artefact by several inspectors is, in addition, a good test of quality attributes pertaining to the documentation dimension (see Section 27.3), such as the suitability of the chosen documentation format for the stakeholders, the comprehensibility, and the inambiguity of the artefacts (see [Wiegers 2002]). For example, if the inspectors start a discussion on the correct interpretation of an artefact (e.g. a part of a model) and the author has to clarify the proper meaning of the artefact, this is a clear indication that the requirements are documented ambiguously.

Check for comprehensibility and inambiguity (documentation dimension)

If the inspection is performed by different stakeholders from all four context facets, the inspection is also a good check of the achieved agreement about the documented requirements. For example, if the inspectors discuss during the inspection meeting whether a requirement is relevant for the system or not, this is an indication of unresolved or undetected conflicts between the stakeholders. Detected conflicts should be documented explicitly and resolved during defect correction by means of the techniques presented in Part IV.c (e.g. the Win–Win approach).

Check for achieved agreement (agreement dimension)

28.1.6 Effort

The inspection of a requirements artefact requires medium to high effort. This effort is, for example, caused by the fact that several inspectors check the requirements artefact in detail. However, in contrast to validation with prototypes, the inspection process does not require any effort to create additional development artefacts.

Medium to high effort

very high	high	medium	low	very low
	✓	(✓)		

Fig. 28-2 *Effort for inspections*

28.1.7 Critical Success Factors

Considering the relatively high effort related to the introduction and regular conduction of inspections in a developing organisation, two prerequisites for the introduction of an inspection process must be given: management commitment and the inspection team members' willingness to learn and perform the tasks associated with the individual roles of an inspection team. Therein, an important aspect is how the stakeholders regard criticism and how the inspection team deals with criticism during an inspection:

Commitment of the organisation

- Inspectors should express their criticism in an adequate way.
- The author should take up the criticism in a constructive way to improve the quality of his work results.

The inspected artefacts themselves also influence the success of an inspection. The larger the extent of the inspected artefacts, the longer the time required for the inspection. If the extent of the inspection is too large, the inspectors might not be

Size and complexity of the inspected artefacts

able to check the artefacts with sufficient care and hence overlook important defects. The complexity of the artefact to be checked also impacts on the success of an inspection. With increasing complexity the number of detected defects decreases. For these reasons, it can be beneficial to reduce the complexity of a requirements artefact through appropriate consolidation prior to performing the inspection. For example, the structure of the artefacts to be inspected can be improved by using structuring means such as abstraction layers (see Sections 34.1 and 35.1) or the structuring of solution-oriented requirements by means of goals (see Section 12.1).

Artefacts matching the entry criteria

An artefact that shall be inspected should fulfil defined entry criteria with regard to the achievement of goals in the three dimensions documentation, content, and agreement (see Section 27.3). In particular, all obvious defects should already have been corrected. If these conditions hold, the inspection team is able to concentrate on the detection of nontrivial defects during the inspection.

Factors related to the inspectors

Finally, the inspectors themselves influence the success of the inspection. During the planning of the inspection, among other things, the following influencing factors must be considered:

- Number of inspectors
- Technical background of the inspectors
- Experience of the inspectors
- Coverage of the relevant aspects in the four context facets

Number and experience of the inspectors

If the number of inspectors is too small (in the extreme case, only one inspector), there is a high risk that defects will remain undetected, since a single person generally cannot cover all context facets in an appropriate way. In addition, the requirements engineers should ensure that at least some of the inspectors already have experience with inspecting requirements artefacts. If experienced inspectors are not available within the organisation, external experts should be appointed to train the inspection team members and, initially, support the inspection.

!

Hint 28-4: *Critical success factors for inspections*

Process and organisation:

- Strict adherence to a defined inspection process
- Acceptance of the role-specific tasks
- Management commitment
- Ability to deal with criticism in an adequate way

Artefacts:

- Size of the artefacts
- Complexity of the artefacts
- Entry quality of the artefacts regarding the three dimensions of content, documentation, and agreement

Selection of the inspection team members:

- Number of inspectors
- Coverage of the four context facets
- Experience of the inspectors

28.2 Desk-Checks

Validation by individual stakeholders

When validating requirements by means of a desk-check, the author of a requirements artefact distributes the artefact to a set of stakeholders (the reviewers) who check the artefact individually. Defect collection is conducted either by reporting the identified defects to the author (e.g. by returning the commented artefact to the author) or in a group session. If a group session is performed, the procedure is less strict than the group session of an inspection. For instance, the participants are allowed to discuss open issues. In addition, the extent of the artefacts to be checked is typically larger than in an inspection.

28.2.1 Preparation

Role assignment

The following roles participate in a desk-check (see Section 28.1 for the role descriptions):

- Author
- Reviewers

If a group session shall be performed for defect collection, additionally the following roles must be assigned:

- Reader/presenter
- Moderator
- Minute-taker

Moderator is reader at the same time

In addition, the roles of moderator and reader are often occupied by the same person. In the following, we assume that the moderator also presents the artefacts to be checked in addition to leading the group session.

The author selects the reviewers based on the validation goal and distributes the artefacts to be checked to them, possibly along with further review instructions (e.g. a checklist).

28.2.2 Execution

Defect detection

Each reviewer checks the artefacts that were assigned to him individually. Typically, each reviewer decides on his own how to check the artefact. However, review instructions e.g. in the form of a checklist may be provided by the author. During defect detection, each reviewer should document the identified defects in an appropriate way.

28.2.3 Follow-up

Defect collection

After each reviewer has checked the requirements artefact, the author collects and consolidates the defects and issues found by each reviewer. The reviewers communicate the detected defects and issues to the author either verbally or by passing on a document to the author (e.g. a commented version of the reviewed artefact). Optionally, a group session may be performed for defect collection.

Group session

If a group session is performed, the moderator presents the artefacts to be checked. By presenting the artefact in sections or page by page, the moderator gives the reviewers the opportunity to comment on each section or page. In contrast to an inspection, the participants of the group session are allowed to discuss open issues and suggest corrections. Typically, not all defects found by the reviewers can be addressed in the group session, since the participants must discuss a larger extent of requirements artefacts in the available period of time. The moderator must therefore pay attention to appropriately prioritising the defects stated by the reviewers, otherwise it may happen that minor defects are discussed in detail while critical defects are skipped due to a lack of time.

No follow-up check of the corrections

After defect collection, it is up to the author to correct the defects. Generally, a formal follow-up check of the corrections is not performed.

28.2.4 Checklist for Applying the Technique

Hint 28-5 presents a checklist of important hints to be considered when performing a desk-check.

!

Hint 28-5: *Checklist for conducting a desk-check*

Preparation:

- ❑ Distribute the requirements artefacts to the reviewers and provide them with sufficient background information.
- ❑ Provide the reviewers with hints for detecting defects, e.g. as checklists.
- ❑ Make clear how the reviewers shall document and report detected defects.

Execution:

- ❑ Each reviewer performs the defect detection individually.
- ❑ If necessary, remind the reviewers about reviewing the artefacts in due time.

Follow-up:

- ❑ Collect the detected defects from each reviewer either by exchanging documents or in a group session (see below).
- ❑ If necessary, prioritise the defects.
- ❑ Express your gratitude to the reviewers for their effort.

Follow-up – Group session (optional):

- ❑ Appoint a moderator, who leads the group session and presents the artefact section by section or page by page.
- ❑ Give the participants the opportunity to discuss the detected defects and to suggest corrections as appropriate.
- ❑ Document the identified conflicts about requirements and try to achieve agreement by means of the techniques described in Part IV.c (e.g. Win–Win approach).
- ❑ Appoint a minute-taker to ensure that the results of the group session are recorded.

28.2.5 Benefit

A desk-check allows the requirements engineer to obtain feedback on a requirements artefact from individual reviewers. If the desk check is combined with a group session for defect collection, it additionally allows:

- Discussion of open questions and issues
- Achievement of agreement about requirements
- Promotion of decisions about requirements

In contrast, the group session of an inspection focusses solely on defect collection, i.e. it does not provide the opportunity for discussion or conflict resolution.

28.2.6 Effort

Smaller relative effort than for an inspection

During a desk-check, typically a larger extent of requirements artefacts is checked than in an inspection. Consequently, the relative effort of a desk-check is smaller than the effort of an inspection. All in all, the effort of a desk-check can be estimated as medium.

Not recommended for critical artefacts

However, the defect detection rate of a desk-check (e.g. measured as the number of defects detected per hour) tends to be lower than the detection rate of an inspection. Therefore, for validating critical requirements artefacts, an inspection should be preferred over a desk-check, or a desk-check should be conducted only as a predecessor to an inspection.

very high	high	medium	low	very low
		✓		

Fig. 28-3 *Effort of a desk-check*

28.2.7 Critical Success Factors

Commitment of the participants

In contrast to inspections, where the process and hence the roles and tasks of the participants are specified in detail, desk-checks are less strict in terms of roles and tasks. Furthermore, if a group session is performed, the moderator of this session has additional tasks compared with an inspection. For instance, the moderator is also responsible for presenting the checked artefacts. Due to the less formal nature of a desk-check, the commitment of each individual participant is a very critical success factor. The reviewers' commitment becomes evident, for instance, from the intensity with which they conduct the defect detection and participate in group discussions. For a successful desk-check it is essential that the reviewers are willing to point out critical defects and issues in the requirements artefacts even if pointing out such issues possibly leads to controversial (but necessary) discussion and requires a substantial correction effort.

Coverage of the four context facets

Like in the case of inspections, selecting reviewers who sufficiently cover all four context facets is essential in order not to miss important aspects during defect detection. For instance, stakeholder groups such as clients, users, architects, database designers, testers, technical maintenance staff etc. should be appointed as reviewers at an appropriate stage of the requirements validation.

28.3 Walkthroughs

Abandonment of formal definitions

A walkthrough does not have a formally defined procedure and does not require a differentiated role assignment. This means that one typically abstains from formal definitions of the roles and the procedures during a walkthrough. Generally, the author presents some artefacts that he has selected himself to a group of stakeholders of his own choice. The motivation for performing a walkthrough is typically a mixture of the following aspects:

- ❑ Checking early whether an idea or a concept is feasible or not
- ❑ Obtaining the opinion and suggestions of other people
- ❑ Checking the approval of others and reaching an agreement

Contribution to validation

Walkthroughs should be an inherent part of all development activities. They also contribute to the validation of requirements artefacts to a limited extent, especially at the stage of idea generation and early drafts of a requirements artefact. Walkthroughs are also useful for involving stakeholders from different context facets early on in an informal manner with the aim of achieving agreement about the discussed requirements.

28.3.1 Preparation

Walkthrough initiated by the author

A walkthrough is initiated by the author of a requirements artefact. The author selects the participants and invites them to participate in the walkthrough. The selection of participants is often restricted to members of the project team. However, as mentioned above, in requirements engineering, it is important to involve stakeholders from all four context facets in the requirements validation right from the beginning. This especially holds, if the goal of the walkthrough is to check the stakeholders' agreement with a preliminary draft or sketch of a requirements artefact.

Artefact not distributed beforehand

Generally, the artefacts to be checked are not distributed beforehand. One reason for not distributing the artefact is that the artefact is typically in a provisional stage. Hence, understanding the artefact requires some amount of explanation by the author. Furthermore, similar to using prototypes for elicitation (see Section 23.3), the reaction of a stakeholder when being confronted with an artefact for the first time is very important for the requirements engineer who conducts the walkthrough [Alexander and Stevens 2002].

28.3.2 Execution

The author presents the artefact

During a walkthrough, the author himself presents a requirements artefact that he has created to a group of stakeholders. The author explains the artefact and points out critical spots on which he would like the stakeholders to comment. Since there is no formally imposed procedure for a walkthrough, the author decides freely how to perform the walkthrough. However, typically, the author pursues a validation goal and aligns the procedure of the walkthrough with this goal.

Documenting the feedback

Since the presented artefact is, in most cases, in a preliminary stage and there is no defined procedure, process parameters such as the duration of the walkthrough or the number of defects found are not recorded. Although it is not obligatory to take minutes during a walkthrough, we advise taking notes of the feedback, comments, and ideas stated by the stakeholders.

28.3.3 Follow-up

Incorporation of feedback is up to the author

The author is responsible for the further elaboration of the artefact after the walkthrough. It is hence up to the author to decide how to correct the uncovered deficiencies and how to incorporate the stakeholders' suggestions and requests into the requirements artefacts.

Follow-up validation activities

Typically, a walkthrough is followed by more formal validation activities in which the requirements artefact is examined in more detail to uncover defects that still persist in the artefact.

28.3.4 Checklist for Applying the Technique

Since walkthroughs are informal by definition, we abstain here from providing a detailed checklist. However, we summarise some important points in Hint 28-6 that should be considered when conducting a walkthrough.

!

Hint 28-6: *Hints for conducting a walkthrough*

- ❑ Use walkthroughs to validate requirements at an early stage.
- ❑ Define a clear goal for the walkthrough.
- ❑ Communicate the goal to the participants.
- ❑ If you are the author, present your artefact as objectively as possible.
- ❑ Address frankly deficiencies that you detected.
- ❑ Give the participants sufficient time to provide feedback.
- ❑ Pay special attention to comments made by the participants that indicate conflicts about requirements.

28.3.5 Benefit

Validation of ideas and sketches

A walkthrough is suited to validation of artefacts at an early stage (e.g. a new idea or a sketch) with the help of other stakeholders. A walkthrough supports communication and exchange of ideas within the development team as well as with external stakeholders who are involved in the walkthrough.

Promoting agreement

Another important aspect of a walkthrough is consolidation of different views on the requirements. By means of a walkthrough, agreement about fundamental properties of the system can be checked and promoted in an informal way and at an early stage.

28.3.6 Effort

Low effort

The effort required for planning and organising a walkthrough is very low. The effort required for performing a walkthrough is influenced by the number of participants and the extent of the presented material. All in all, the effort required for a walkthrough can be estimated as low (in exceptional cases as medium). A walkthrough occupies several people for about 1–3 h.

very high	high	medium	low	very low
		(✓)	✓	

Fig. 28-4 *Effort for walkthroughs*

28.3.7 Critical Success Factors

Clear goal

Due to the lack of a defined procedure, a concise and comprehensible definition of the validation goal is indispensable for a successful walkthrough. Only if the goal of the walkthrough is clear, can the author expect feedback that is helpful for further elaboration of the requirements artefact.

Involving stakeholders from different context facets

Furthermore, the coverage of the four context facets by the walkthrough participants has a decisive influence on the results of the walkthrough. Novel and unconventional ideas are often stated by stakeholders from other context facets than the facet representing the authors' own area of expertise. Furthermore, especially in the early stages of requirements engineering, it is important to reach agreement about key requirements with stakeholders from all context facets. In this regard, discussions with stakeholders from different context facets are particularly fruitful.

Comprehensible presentation of the artefact

The author should pay attention that the material presented is comprehensible for all stakeholders involved in the walkthrough and that the presentation has a clear focus which is aligned with the validation goal. Appropriate use of visualisations stimulates stakeholders' feedback further.

28.4 Comparison: Inspections, Desk-Checks, and Walkthroughs

Table 28-1 presents an overview of the essential differences between inspections, desk-checks, and walkthroughs. Therein, the indications of the required effort for each technique should be considered as rough estimations.

Tab. 28-1 *Essential differences between inspections, desk-checks, and walkthroughs*

	Inspection	Desk-check	Walkthrough
Goal	extensive search for defects in a manageable extent of requirements artefacts	less detailed check of a larger extent of artefacts including suggestions for corrections and decisions about requirements	feedback on early sketches of an artefact, elicitation of new ideas, agreement on requirements
Group session	yes, strict focus on defect collection	optional, for discussing open issues and achieving agreement	yes, for checking the presented artefact and providing feedback
Process	detailed process description, strict adherence	defined but flexible procedure	no predefined procedure
Defect correction	defect correction, follow-up check, process improvement	defect correction	up to the author
Effort for execution	medium to high	medium	low to medium
Benefit for validation	high	medium	low (yet good as preliminary validation at an early stage)

28.5 Validation Using Prototypes

Highly effective defect detection

Inspections, reviews, and walkthroughs support the validation of requirements documented in natural language as well as with conceptual models. However, both natural language and model-based requirements are relatively abstract compared with an actual system in use. Some requirements defects are very difficult to detect by inspecting or reviewing such abstractions of the system. For this reason, it is likely that some of the requirements defects are not detected until the stakeholders experience the implemented system by using it and working with it. However, at this time, it is very costly to remove requirements defects. The risk of overlooking important requirements defects is reduced when requirements are validated not only by reviewing requirements artefacts but also with the help of prototypes [Sommerville 2004; Young 2001]. Requirements defects that are hard to detect in the requirements artefacts may be quite easy to detect when experiencing and using a prototype. According to [Jones 2007], requirements validation using prototypes is even the most effective method for detecting requirements defects.

Recommendation: throw-away prototypes

A prototype for requirements validation allows the stakeholders to try out the requirements for the system and experience them thereby. As explained in Section 23.3, one can differentiate between throw-away prototypes and evolutionary prototypes. Jones points out that the effectiveness of throw-away prototypes during requirements validation is considerably higher than the effectiveness of evolutionary prototypes [Jones 2007].

Elicitation vs. validation

In the following, we explain the usage of prototypes as a means for requirements validation, as opposed to Section 23.3 where the elicitation of requirements using prototypes is explained. The validation of already known and documented requirements by means of a prototype typically also leads to the elicitation of further requirements. Therefore, despite the goals of using prototypes for elicitation or validation being different, in practice one cannot always clearly distinguish between these two uses of prototypes.

28.5.1 Preparation

Need for limiting the scope of the validation

During the preparation phase, the stakeholders select the requirements to be implemented in the prototype. The more realistic the impression of the system that the prototype conveys, the more significant the results of the validation (i.e. the acceptance or the rejection of requirements). This is contrary to the use of prototypes in requirements elicitation, where overly realistic prototypes should be avoided (see Section 23.3). However, due to resource limitations such as the effort for developing the prototype, the functionality and quality of a validation prototype need to be restricted compared with the functionality and quality of the actual system. Hence, part of the functional and quality requirements defined for the system are neglected when developing the prototype [Sommerville 2004] in favour of lower development effort and quicker availability of the prototype.

Goal- and scenario-based selection of requirements

The process of selecting the requirements to be implemented in the prototype can be supported by goals and scenarios (see Fig. 28-5). In the first step, the stakeholders select a subset of the goals that are defined for the system (see Fig. 28-5 top left-hand corner: "selected goals"). This subset encompasses the functional and quality goals that shall be validated by means of the prototype. As the number of goals is significantly smaller than the number of (detailed) requirements, goal-based selection can be accomplished in a shorter time. Therein, the selection of goals should be aligned with the validation goal (see Hint 28-1). Subsequently, the stakeholders select a subset of the scenarios that are related to the chosen goals. For instance, the stakeholders may select all main scenarios but only some of the exception scenarios, because implementing all exception scenarios would require too much effort. Note that a goal can only be validated if at least one scenario is selected in which the goal is achieved. Eventually, the requirements selected for the prototype implementation are those that are necessary to realise the selected goals and scenarios (see Fig. 28-5 at the bottom: requirements highlighted in black).

Benefit of goal- and scenario-based scope definition

Goal- and scenario-based selection of requirements for the prototype has the advantage that it helps to focus the prototype development on meaningful chunks of the entire set of requirements. The implemented prototype hence allows validation of coherent usage workflows including the intended added value of the usage workflows. In addition,scenarios support the consideration of different perspectives (e.g.

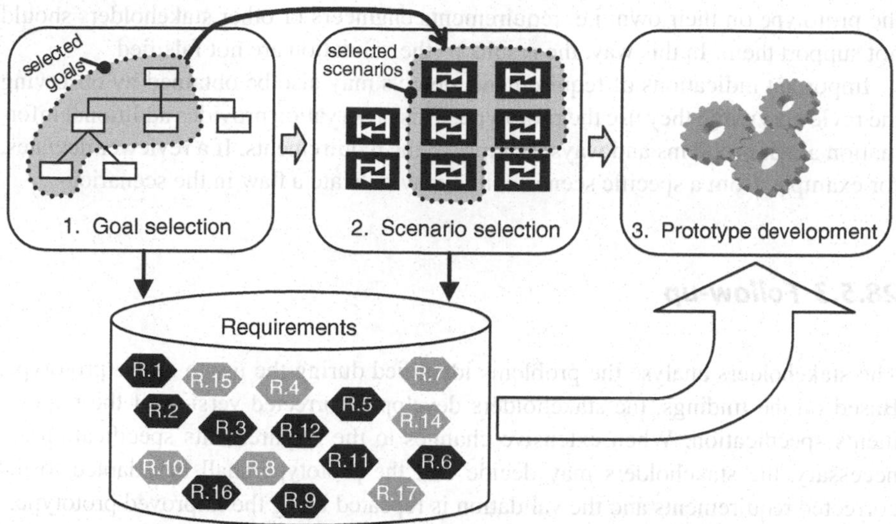

Fig. 28-5 *Goal- and scenario-based selection of requirements for prototype development*

those of managers, users, or software architects). Focussing on goals and scenarios avoids, furthermore, technical aspects from dominating the prototype development.

Guiding the experimentation with the prototype

When validating requirements by means of a prototype, it is not sufficient to let the stakeholders experiment with the prototype freely. The stakeholders may not be completely sure what they should actually validate and therefore perform the validation only partially. The stakeholders' attention can be drawn to the facts or aspects that need to be validated by means of usage scenarios. Usage scenarios document coherent workflows that the reviewers can execute with the prototype. The risk that the stakeholders validate only those requirements in which they are most interested is thereby reduced.

Checklists

In addition, the reviewers are provided with checklists that support detection of requirements defects when working with the prototype. The use of checklists in validation is explained in Section 29.1.

Beginners and experienced users

During requirements validation with a prototype, one must consider that users who use a system for the first time may have different needs than experienced users. Restricting validation to the perspective of inexperienced users leads to a bias in the validation results. In order to avoid this bias, the stakeholders should be selected and trained in a way that ensures that the group of experienced users is also represented.

Training of the stakeholders

Before the validation is performed, the requirements engineers must ensure that especially the reviewers who represent the group of experienced users are proficient in using the prototype. Therefore, the preparation phase of the validation comprises the creation of installation instructions, user manuals, and training material (for beginners and advanced users) as well as performing training courses for users.

28.5.2 Execution

Reviewers should not be influenced

The reviewers execute the usage scenarios provided to them, experiment with the prototype, and answer the questions contained in the checklist. The reviewers should use the prototype on their own, i.e. requirements engineers or other stakeholders should not support them. In this way, the results of the validation are not falsified.

Observation of system usage

Important indications of requirements defects may also be obtained by observing the reviewers while they use the prototype. This observation provides additional information about problems and ways to improve the requirements. If a reviewer deviates, for example, from a specific scenario, this may indicate a flaw in the scenario.

28.5.3 Follow-up

Analysis and defect correction

The stakeholders analyse the problems identified during the usage of the prototype. Based on the findings, the stakeholders develop a corrected version of the requirements specification. When extensive changes to the requirements specification are necessary, the stakeholders may decide that the prototype shall be adapted to the corrected requirements and the validation is repeated using the improved prototype.

28.5.4 Checklist for Applying the Technique

Hint 28-7 presents a checklist with important points that should be considered during requirements validation with prototypes.

!

Hint 28-7: *Checklist for requirements validation with prototypes*

Preparation of prototype development:

- ❑ Utilise goals and scenarios to support the selection of the requirements that shall be realised in the validation prototype.
- ❑ Check which functional and quality requirements can be omitted or weakened during prototype development.

Preparation of prototype usage:

- ❑ Prepare usage scenarios for the reviewers.
- ❑ Provide checklists for defect detection.
- ❑ Make sure that manuals and training material are created.
- ❑ While selecting the reviewers make sure that beginners as well as experienced users are represented.
- ❑ If necessary, train the reviewers in using the prototype.

Execution:

- ❑ Let the reviewers experiment with the prototype.
- ❑ Provide the reviewers with the usage scenarios and checklists.
- ❑ Make sure that the reviewers document all flaws and defects that they identify.
- ❑ Observe the reviewers while they experiment with the prototype. Document observed problems.
- ❑ Avoid influencing the reviewers while they work with the prototype.

(*to be continued*)

Hint 28-7 (*continued*)

Follow-up:

- ❑ Summarise the identified defects and analyse each defect.
- ❑ Compare the results of the individual reviewers in order to identify potential conflicts about requirements.
- ❑ If necessary, adapt the prototype after defect correction and repeat validation.

28.5.5 Benefit

Defect detection during prototype development

Defects in requirements artefacts may be detected during the development of a prototype itself, since incomplete and ambiguous requirements hinder the prototype development.

By checking the requirements using an executable prototype, deficiencies in the requirements become apparent that would otherwise not be detected until system test of the implemented system. The early detection of requirements defects demonstrably saves significant costs.

Proof of feasibility

A prototype increases the stakeholders' confidence in the success of the project. The requirements realised in the prototype are validated in detail so that there is no uncertainty for the stakeholders regarding the realisability of these requirements.

28.5.6 Effort

Necessity for a tool

Developing a prototype can require a high to very high effort. Therefore, the stakeholders should preferably use special tools or development environments for prototype development. In this way, the effort required can be significantly reduced. However, selecting and introducing an appropriate tool for prototype development in an organisation generally takes considerable effort. When tools are established and prototypes can be generated automatically, for example based on requirements models, the effort required for developing the prototype can even be low to very low. A rough estimation of the effort is illustrated in Fig. 28-6.

	very high	high	medium	low	very low
Prototype can be generated				✓	(✓)
Tool support during development			✓	(✓)	
Manually developed prototype	✓	(✓)			

Fig. 28-6 *Effort for validation with prototypes*

No replacement for system development

When stakeholders are provided with an executable prototype, they may misjudge the effort that is required for implementing the system. For the developing organisation the problem emerges of communicating to the client that considerable effort is still required for designing and implementing the system, i.e. that implementing the system is more than just making minor changes to the prototype.

28.5.7 Critical Success Factors

Effort

The most critical success factors are management commitment for investing in a prototype and the time required for implementing the prototype.

Quality of the review

Furthermore, developing a prototype does not in itself guarantee that the stakeholders review the requirements with sufficient care. For instance, a stakeholder might detect some undesired property but regard it as a flaw of the prototype and not as a requirements defect. Therefore, the success of the validation is also influenced by the quality of the documents that support validation (e.g. usage scenarios and checklists).

Level of detail of the prototype

Requirements can be validated with the prototype only to the level of detail at which they are implemented in the prototype. If the prototype implementation is very close to the actual system, fewer change requests can be expected when introducing the system later on. For example, if the prototype implements only the user interface but no coherent workflows, the requirements engineers can expect that the stakeholders will pose additional or changed requirements concerning the usage workflows when they use the system for the first time.

Chapter 29
Assistance Techniques for Validation

In this chapter, we describe six assistance techniques that support the validation of requirements. For each technique, we outline:

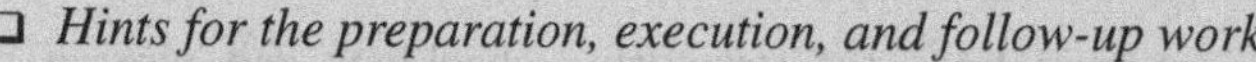

- *Hints for the preparation, execution, and follow-up work*
- *The benefit of the assistance technique for the validation sub-activities*
- *An effort estimation*
- *Critical success factors*
- *A checklist with important hints for applying the assistance technique*

29.1 Validation Checklists

Applicable with each validation technique

A checklist that is used for requirements validation such as an inspection checklist consists of questions that a reviewer shall consider during the validation of a requirements artefact. The questions support the validation team in detecting defects or deficiencies in this artefact. The use of checklists during validation is widespread in practice. Checklists can be applied to supplement each validation technique presented in Chapter 28, in particular inspections, desk-checks, and prototyping. The use of checklists in a walkthrough is less common. However, the author who initiates the walkthrough might use a checklist with questions he wants to ask the participants during the presentation of his artefact.

Phases, benefit, effort, critical success factors

In the following, we explain how checklists can be used in an effective way during requirements validation. We describe the preparation phase, the execution phase, and the follow-up phase of using checklists in validation. Subsequently, we provide a summary of the technique in the form of a checklist, highlight the benefit of the technique, provide a rough effort estimation, and name the critical success factors.

Guidelines for creating checklists

Additionally, we present guidelines for structuring checklists and writing up checklist questions in order to avoid typical mistakes during the use of checklists such as too many questions or too generic questions (see Section 29.1.8).

29.1.1 Preparation

Developing checklists

During the preparation phase, one or several checklists are created and distributed to the reviewers. There are different kinds of sources for identifying appropriate items for a validation checklist. Some of these sources are:

- The checklists used during requirements elicitation (Section 23.6)
- The validation principles presented in Section 27.8
- The requirements engineering framework (see Section 29.1.8)
- Rules that hold for the specific artefact such as the rules for documenting goals presented in Section 8.2 and the rules for documenting scenarios presented in Section 11.4
- Experience gained during requirements validation
- Defect statistics (see [Chernak 1996])

Example 29-1 describes a very simple example of deriving a question for a validation checklist from one of the above-mentioned sources.

Example 29-1: Deriving a checklist item for the validation of goals

In the context of a project, the rule is defined that each goal that is documented in the goal model must be associated with at least one main and one alternative scenario. Based on this rule, the following question is derived: "Is the goal associated with at least one main and one alternative scenario?" This question is integrated into the checklist that is used for validating goal models.

Short and concise checklists: less than one page

A checklist should comprise few questions so that the reviewer can use it during validation in an effective way. If a checklist contains a large number of questions, the reviewers must read the checklist repeatedly when performing the validation. This reduces the time that is left for actually reading the artefact and identifying defects. Therefore, the number of questions in a validation checklist should be sufficiently low, allowing the reviewers to keep all checklist items in mind when reading an artefact. [Gilb and Graham 1993] recommend that a checklist should not exceed one printed page, as it would be highly unpractical for the reviewers to have to browse multiple pages of a checklist when performing the validation. [Sommerville and Sawyer 1997] recommend that a checklist should comprise at most ten questions.

Multiple, narrowly focussed checklists

As a consequence, the requirements engineers who create the checklists should not simply collect all rules, quality criteria, and types of defects in a single checklist. Rather it is advisable to have different checklists for different validation goals (see Hint 28-1) and to use the checklists as appropriate for the situation. Guidelines that help to narrow down a checklist by focussing on one or a few selected topics are presented in Section 29.1.8.

Selecting, assigning and distributing the checklists

When preparing the validation activity (e.g. an inspection), the requirements engineers assign and distribute the checklists that are relevant for the validation goal to the validation team. Critical checklists should be distributed to several reviewers if possible.

29.1.2 Execution

Two modes of using the checklists

The reviewers check the artefacts assigned to them as described by the respective validation technique. In addition, they use the checklists provided to them. The organisers of the validation activity need to clarify in which of the following two ways the validation team should use the checklists:

Discretionary use

- *The checklist as a validation aid*: In this case, the checklist is regarded as an additional aid for detecting defects. The reviewer can use the checklist at his own discretion.

Compulsory use and documentation

- *Obligatory documentation*: In this case, the reviewer must provide detailed answers to all checklist questions for each requirements artefact or for each element of a requirements artefact to which the questions apply.

On the one hand, obligatory documentation of answers to each checklist question is more time-consuming. On the other hand, detailed documentation of each performed check and the results of each check are made available for later use, e.g. as proof of the performance of the validation. Furthermore, a statistical evaluation of the defects uncovered by each individual question is possible. This kind of data is essential for successive improvement of the checklists used. For instance, questions that do not prove effective in detecting defects can be rephrased or replaced by other questions.

29.1.3 Follow-up

Avoidance of decreasing checklist effectivity

When applying a requirements validation technique repeatedly, the reviewers' experience increases. The reviewers' ability to detect requirements defects and the requirements authors' ability to specify requirements improve, i.e. the authors try to avoid the reported types of defects as far as possible. Consequently, the questions of a checklist lose their effectiveness in supporting defect detection and must hence be refined or replaced by new questions.

Improving checklists

Consequently, during follow-up, the checklists themselves are checked for necessary improvements. The improvement of a checklist is based, for instance, on the statistics of defects uncovered by each checklist question [Gilb and Graham 1993]. The goal of this improvement is to adapt the checklists so that they always match the current situation in the project or the organisation, e.g. with regard to the requirements engineers' and reviewers' experience. By continuously evaluating and improving the checklist questions, the potential of the checklists to support the detection of defects is maintained or even enhanced over time.

!

Hint 29-1: *Improving a checklist*

- *Adding questions*: If the reviewers have detected some defects that cannot be assigned to any of the questions in the checklist, add an appropriate question to the checklist.
- *Eliminating questions depending on a relevance value*: Assign a relevance value to each checklist question (e.g. the value 3 as default). If the reviewers detect no or only few defects with the help of a specific question, the relevance value of the question is decreased. If the relevance value of a question becomes less than 1, eliminate the question from the checklist. If a question proves helpful, the relevance value is increased (e.g. up to a maximum value of 5).
- *Adaptation of questions*: If a reviewer has detected a defect that can be assigned to a question in the checklist but the question has not triggered the detection of the defect, rewrite the corresponding question.

29.1.4 Checklist for Applying the Technique

Hint 29-2 presents a checklist with important points for supporting requirements validation by means of checklists.

!

Hint 29-2: *Using checklists during validation*

Creating checklists:

- Create checklists for validation based on rules, experience, and defect statistics.
- Create different, specialised checklists for different validation goals.
- Checklists should not exceed one printed page.
- Structure and narrow down checklists with the help of the requirements engineering framework as described in Section 29.1.8.

(to be continued)

Hint 29-2 *(continued)*

Two usage modes:

- Provide checklists either as an auxiliary means or
- Ask the reviewers to provide detailed documentation of each check performed.

Establish a procedure for improving your checklists:

- Eliminate ineffective questions.
- Add missing questions.
- Rephrase incomprehensible questions.

29.1.5 Benefit

Each reviewer knows how to check the artefact

Checklists have repeatedly proven their worth in supporting validation. In particular, they support each member of a validation team in performing defect detection in a systematic and agreed way. With the help of checklists, each reviewer knows which questions to apply to check a requirements artefact according to the validation goal. The validation hence focusses on the questions contained in the checklist. The risk of omitting required checks is reduced if the validation team uses checklists.

Applicable for all three validation goals

By including appropriate questions in the checklist, all three validation goals presented in Section 27.1 can be enforced:

- *Checking of activity inputs*: The validation team has to check whether the system context has been considered properly, for instance whether all relevant requirement sources have been taken into account (see Section 27.4).
- *Checking of activity outputs*: The validation team has to check whether the resulting requirements artefacts match the defined quality criteria pertaining to one or multiple dimensions (content, documentation, and agreement; see Section 27.3).
- *Checking of activity execution*: The validation team has to check the process documentation, i.e. artefacts documenting the performance of requirements engineering activities. The team checks whether there are deviations from defined rules, guidelines, and process descriptions (see Section 27.5).

Used for validation and for elicitation

As stated in Section 23.6, checklists can be used not only to uncover requirements defects, but also to support the elicitation of new requirements and requirement sources. These two uses of checklists may be hard to distinguish in practice as the detection of an error of omission directly leads to the identification of additional requirements. However, when applying checklists, one should be aware of the purpose that the checklists are used for, i.e. for validating a final draft of a requirements artefact, or for eliciting new requirements.

29.1.6 Effort

No significant effort

The use of a checklist for requirements validation increases the validation effort only marginally. The reviewer merely has to familiarise himself with the checklist before performing the validation. Additional effort arises when the reviewer is asked to document the answers to each checklist question in detail. Therefore, we estimate the effort for the additional use of checklists as very low and the effort for detailed documentation as low.

Effort for maintaining the checklists

Checklists must be maintained and improved continuously in order to realise an added value for validation. If checklists are not continuously improved, their effectiveness in supporting defect detection decreases. Consequently, the reviewers' motivation to apply the checklists is reduced. The effort required for maintaining and improving checklists can be generally considered as very low.

very high	high	medium	low	very low
			(✓)	✓

Fig. 29-1 *Additional effort for the use of checklists*

Effort for eliminating false positives

One risk of using checklists is a possible increase in the number of false positives, i.e. uncovered defects which turn out, in fact, to be no defects. This is especially the case, if a checklist contains questions that are not relevant to the requirements artefact to which they are applied. Since these questions remain unanswered for the requirements artefact, the reviewer erroneously detects missing requirements due to the inappropriate checklist questions. During defect collection, false positives have to be filtered out, requiring some additional effort. However, this effort is generally low and can be avoided by choosing checklists or checklist questions effectively.

29.1.7 Critical Success Factors

Limiting the size of the checklists

Ideally, a checklist should contain only as many questions as a reviewer can keep in his mind during the search for defects. If a checklist contains too many items, successful use of the checklist is impaired. Hence, limiting the size of a checklist is essential for successful application of checklists. The size of a checklist can be reduced, e.g. by distributing the relevant questions between several checklists which are distributed to different reviewers (see Section 29.1.8).

Avoiding generic questions such as "Are the requirements complete?"

Besides the size of a checklist, also the abstraction level of the questions is a critical success factor. [Brykczynski 1999] has performed an extensive analysis of checklist questions, resulting in guidelines for the definition of appropriate checklist questions. One of the results is that overly generic questions should be avoided. If a checklist question is very generic, it is applicable to different requirements artefacts and to different types of systems without being changed. However, the benefit of generic questions for validation is very low. For example, the question "Are the requirements complete?" does not indicate what "complete" means or how a reviewer can identify missing or incomplete requirements.

Considering the stakeholders' background and experience

When using checklists, the requirements engineers should be aware of the different knowledge, preferences and levels of experience of the individual reviewers. For instance, if a stakeholder who represents the system users is given a validation checklist that was created for checking requirements from the viewpoint of a software architect, this stakeholder will have substantial difficulties in understanding and applying the checklist. For successful use of checklists it is hence advisable to select questions with respect to the expert knowledge and experience of the individual reviewers. The four context facets help to identify appropriate checklist questions for a stakeholder who belongs mainly to one of the facets.

29.1.8 Structuring Questions and Checklists

Typical mistakes during the creation of checklists

When creating checklists, two critical mistakes are frequently made:

- Too many questions in a checklist
- Too generic questions (such as "Is the requirement complete?")

Organisation of checklist questions

Both kinds of mistakes influence the successful application of checklists negatively. In the worst case, they lead to a state where stakeholders ignore the checklists instead of regarding them as an important aid for validation. However, when the requirements engineers try to avoid overly generic questions, they have to write specific questions with a narrow focus. However, focussing on specific questions leads to a significantly increased number of questions. Therefore, creating a checklist that includes a small number of questions and at the same time supports the validation goal by means of specific questions is a difficult task. To overcome this difficulty, maintaining a repository of validation questions structured according to defined criteria is recommended. Such a repository can be thought of as a collection of checklists for specific purposes from which entire checklists or individual checklist questions can be chosen as needed. In the following, we propose three (independent) structuring criteria to support the organisation and management of validation questions:

- *Artefact type*: Based on this criterion, the requirements engineers create and maintain separate checklists for goals, scenarios, and solution-oriented requirements. A more refined differentiation additionally considers the subtypes of each of these artefacts. With regard to scenarios, one can differentiate, for example, between positive and negative scenarios, or type A, type B, and type C scenarios (see Chapter 10). With regard to solution-oriented requirements one can differentiate between functional requirements, quality requirements, and constraints. Functional requirements can be further separated into the three perspectives function, data, and behaviour. Quality requirements can be further refined according to different quality properties. Thereby, for each type of requirements artefacts, a specific checklist is provided.
- *Dimension*: Based on this criterion, the requirements engineers create and maintain separate checklists for the documentation dimension, the content dimension, and the agreement dimension.
- *Context facet*: Based on this criterion, the requirements engineers create and maintain separate checklists for the subject facet, the usage facet, the IT system facet, and the development facet. Subsequently, aspects of each facet can be chosen to further differentiate the facet-specific checklists.

Using the criteria for writing checklist questions

These criteria do not only support the structuring of checklists but also help in writing questions for specific validation goals. By combining multiple criteria, the checklist questions can be made even more specific. An example is a checklist for scenarios that focusses on the usage facet, i.e. on usage scenarios. In the following, we explain each of the three criteria in detail.

Structuring Based on Artefact Types

Addressing the specifics of a particular type of artefact

Generic questions are applicable to different artefact types and hence do not consider the specifics of each individual artefact type. Therefore, generic questions cannot address specific constructs, rules, quality criteria, or typical kinds of defects that are characteristic of a specific artefact type. Defining specific questions for each artefact type that needs to be checked is therefore recommended. Thereby, at least the three types of requirements artefacts, i.e. goals, scenarios, and solution-oriented requirements (see Part III), should be differentiated.

Checklists for scenarios and entity-relationship models

The creation of checklists for a specific artefact type is illustrated in Example 29-2 for scenarios. An example of creating artefact-type-specific checklists for entity–relationship models, i.e. a subtype of solution-oriented requirements, can be found in [Wohlin and Aurum 2003].

Questions addressing the specific content of an artefact

Additionally, questions can also be written specifically for a specific model instance, for example, for a concrete scenario or a concrete data model. In this case, also the specific content of this instance can be addressed by the checklist questions.

Example 29-2: Exemplary questions for the validation of scenarios

- ❑ Do the actors of the scenario represent all relevant persons who shall use the system?
- ❑ Do the actors of the scenario represent all relevant systems that shall interact with the system to be developed?
- ❑ Is every actor that is documented in the scenario necessary for execution of the scenario?
- ❑ Does the scenario document the only permissible sequence of interactions, or are there also alternative sequences?
- ❑ Is the required reaction of the system defined for every interaction contained in the scenario even if the interaction takes place too early, too late or not at all?

Structuring Based on the Three Dimensions

Clarity regarding the dimension being checked

Checklist questions should be clear about which of the three dimensions, content, documentation, or agreement, they address, or which of the three dimensions is decisive for the requirements artefact to pass or fail the validation. If a validation checklist is not clear about the dimension, the reviewers might make their decisions focussing on different dimensions or even alternating between different dimensions according to their individual preferences. As a consequence, the validation goal might not be achieved (see Example 29-3).

Example 29-3: Missed validation goal

In collaboration with a customer, a requirements engineer creates 14 different usage scenarios for the car safety system. The requirements engineer assumes that important alternative and exception scenarios are missing (content dimension). Hence, he asks the responsible system architect to review the scenarios.

The system architect uses a standard checklist for scenarios during the review. The checklist contains questions such as "Are the scenarios complete?", "Are all interactions correct?". The system architect detects 40 defects in the scenarios.

An analysis of the detected defects reveals that 30% of the defects result from the system architect not agreeing with the specified scenarios (agreement dimension), 65% of the defects concern minor deviations from the documentation rules (documentation dimension), and only 5% of the defects concern missing alternative and exception scenarios, i.e. the content dimension. Presumably, the validation goal has been missed.

Specific checklist for each dimension

Structuring checklists based on the three dimensions directs the reviewers' attention to the desired dimension:

- *Checklist for the content dimension*: This checklist contains specific questions that support detecting failed goals in the content dimension. Hence it supports, for instance, detecting missing, incomplete, or incorrect requirements (see Section 27.3.1).
- *Checklist for the documentation dimension*: This checklist contains specific questions that support detecting failed goals in the documentation dimension such as incomprehensibly or ambiguously documented requirements as well as broken documentation rules (see Section 27.3.2).
- *Checklist for the agreement dimension*: This checklist contains specific questions that support detection of failed goals in the agreement dimension, such as unresolved conflicts or requirements that have not been agreed with relevant stakeholders (see Section 27.3.3).

References for validation questions

When creating a dimension-specific checklist, different sources or references may be used to identify relevant questions, such as the stakeholders' experience, rules, quality criteria, and statistics about frequently occurring kinds of defects. Examples of further references are:

- For the *content dimension*: reference models of a relevant sub-domain (e.g. a reference architecture for embedded control devices in a vehicle), domain-specific standards, existing documents (e.g. the text of a law), or legacy systems (see Example 29-4).
- For the *documentation dimension*: existing modelling guidelines, requirements attributes (see Section 18.3), documentation standards, or reference structures for requirements documents (see Section 18.1). Specifically for natural language requirements: rules for documenting goals and scenarios (see Sections 8.2 and 11.4) and the defects of natural language leading to different kinds of ambiguity (see Section 17.4.2 as well as Example 29-5).
- For the *agreement dimension*: decision and negotiation models such as the Win–Win approach (see Section 26.1) or a classification of conflict types (see Example 29-6).

Example 29-4: Creating a checklist for the content dimension

The stakeholders experiment with a legacy system in order to define questions for validating the requirements of the car safety system. They find out that, in the case of a failure of the communication bus, the legacy system gets into an undefined state and reboots. Based on this observation they write up the following question for the validation of the requirements:

- ❑ Is the system behaviour in case of a failure of the communication bus specified?

Example 29-5: Creating a checklist for the documentation dimension

In [Kamsties 2005], a model for frequently occurring kinds of ambiguities is presented. This model provides the basis for deriving checklist questions supporting the detection of ambiguities:

- ❑ Does the requirements artefact contain a term that has several meanings in the context of the development project?
- ❑ Does the requirements artefact contain a term that may stand for a class of objects as well as for a single object?
- ❑ Does the requirements artefact contain a term that may stand for a product as well as a process?
- ❑ Does the requirements artefact contain an expression that may describe a persistent as well as a volatile property of an object?
- ❑ Does the requirements artefact contain a logical construct that allows several interpretations?

Example 29-6: Creating a checklist for the agreement dimension

The requirements engineers of the car safety system create a checklist for validating goal achievement in the agreement dimension. Based on the Win–Win approach, they define questions that support detection of win–lose and lose–lose situations and hence contribute to achieving win–win situations:

- ❑ Does the specified property come up to your expectations? If no, how should the requirements for the system be changed in order to come up to your expectations?
- ❑ Could you imagine that there are groups of persons or organisations who do not agree with the specified property? How could these persons be satisfied in your opinion?

Structuring Based on the Four Context Facets

Specialisation of stakeholders

Each reviewer typically has a preference for a specific context facet, since he has expert knowledge or experience mainly in this facet of the context. A reviewer is able to deal with validation questions pertaining to his preferred context facet considerably better than generic questions about the quality of requirements or questions pertaining to other context facets. For example, a system user can typically contribute to validation of context aspects of the usage facet significantly better than to validation of context aspects of the IT system facet or the development facet. Structuring checklists according to the four context facets allows the validation questions contained in each checklist to be focussed on a specific context facet. Thereby, it is possible to take into account the expert knowledge of the individual reviewers when assigning and distributing validation checklists.

Uncovering presumed deficiencies with regard to a specific context facet

Furthermore, checklists that are differentiated according to the four context facets can be adapted to known or assumed deficiencies in a better way. For instance, the requirements engineers may know that the IT system facet has been considered insufficiently so far. Therefore, it is not clear whether the requirements are realisable in the given IT system environment (or with the given IT strategy) and whether all required system interfaces have been defined. In such a situation, a context-facet-specific checklist focussing on the IT system facet can be used to uncover deficiencies with respect to this facet and hence obtain an overview of the state of the requirements concerning this facet.

Addressing the type of context aspects to be examined

In principle, the questions for a context facet may pertain to one or more of the three types of context aspects: requirement sources, context objects, and their properties and relationships. If appropriate, a validation question should explicitly refer to the type of context aspect that shall be examined with the help of this question. Examples of the three types of context aspects for each context facet are presented in Chapter 6 (see also Section 23.6).

!

Hint 29-3: *Guidelines for structuring checklists*

General hints:

- ❑ Avoid checklists with too many questions.
- ❑ Avoid overly generic questions in validation checklists.
- ❑ Structure the checklists according to the three structuring criteria: artefact type, dimension, and context facet, or according to a combination of these criteria.
- ❑ Use checklists and questions that support achieving the set validation goal.

Checklists for the different artefact types:

- ❑ Use a separate checklist for each artefact type (goals, scenarios, and the different types of solution-oriented requirements).
- ❑ When creating a checklist, consider the specific elements of the artefact type as well as frequently occurring defects for this artefact type.
- ❑ If necessary, use the three dimensions as a second structuring means in order to subdivide an overly extensive checklist and to make generic questions more concrete.
- ❑ Use the four context facets as an additional structuring means, as appropriate, in order to subdivide overly extensive checklists and to make generic questions more concrete.

(*to be continued*)

Hint 29-3 *(continued)*

Checklists for the three dimensions:

- ❑ Use a separate checklist for each dimension (content, documentation, and agreement).
- ❑ Derive questions for the respective types of defects in each dimension. If necessary, create a separate checklist for each defect type.
- ❑ Use reference models pertaining to content, documentation, and agreement to support the definition of validation questions.

Checklists for the four context facets:

- ❑ Use a separate checklist for each context facet.
- ❑ Derive questions addressing the consideration of the relevant requirement sources in the four context facets.
- ❑ Derive questions addressing the relevant context objects in the four context facets.
- ❑ Assign checklists to reviewers based on their preferred context facet, i.e. the facet about which they have the best expert knowledge.
- ❑ Use context-specific checklists in order to focus the validation activity on the context facet where you presume the largest deficiencies occur.

29.2 Perspective-Based Reading

Validation from different perspectives

Applying perspective-based reading during requirements validation means checking the same set of artefacts from different perspectives, e.g. from the perspective of a customer, the perspective of a software architect, and the perspective of a tester (see [Basili et al. 1996]). During defect collection, the defects identified from the different perspectives are brought together.

Applicable to all validation techniques

Perspective-based reading can be applied in conjunction with inspections, desk-checks, and prototyping. During a walkthrough, systematic assignment of perspectives usually does not take place. Still, selection of participants with different perspectives, e.g. based on the four context facets (see Section 28.3), is recommended.

For each perspective, detailed instructions are provided to guide the reviewer in performing the validation from the specific perspective. Thus, each perspective is associated with specific reading instructions and specific validation questions. A reasonable way of providing the instructions to the validation team is to create a checklist for each perspective (see Section 29.1).

The perspectives most commonly used in perspective-based reading can be characterised as follows (see [Shull et al. 2000]):

- ❑ *Customer/user*: When adopting the perspective of a customer or user, the reviewer must check whether the requirements artefacts describe the functionality and quality desired by the customer or user.
- ❑ *Software architect*: When adopting the perspective of a software architect, the reviewer must check whether the requirements contain the information necessary

for developing the architecture. In addition to the required functionality, the architect is interested in the architectural drivers such as the required performance or the required portability.

- *Tester*: When adopting the perspective of a tester, the reviewer must check whether the requirements artefacts can be used as a basis for creating test artefacts (e.g. test cases). The tester is interested in using the requirements artefacts as a reference to identify test cases including the input data and the expected results of each test case as well as to determine the coverage of the requirements artefacts achieved by the identified test cases.

Further perspectives

Further perspectives for perspective-based reading can be derived easily from the four context facets, the three dimensions, and the three kinds of requirements artefacts. The perspectives can be identified similarly to the identification of checklist questions based on the four context facets, three dimensions, and three kinds of requirements artefacts (see Section 29.1.8).

Creation of artefacts for the perspectives

Perspective-based reading can be combined very well with the creation of artefacts (see Section 29.3). In this case, the reviewer who owns a particular perspective is additionally given the task of creating artefacts associated with the perspective. Table 29-1 lists the most important perspectives along with the artefacts that are characteristic of each perspective.

Tab. 29-1 *Assignment of development artefacts to the perspectives*

Perspective	Development artefact
Customer/user	Usage scenarios (Section 29.3.2) User manual (Section 29.3.4)
Tester	Test cases (Section 29.3.3)
Software architect	Design artefacts (high-level design)

29.2.1 Preparation

Inspection instructions and questions

The organisers assign each reviewer a perspective. They distribute to each reviewer the requirements artefact to be checked as well as the reading instructions and questions for the specific perspective. The reading instructions and questions support the detection of defects. In Example 29-7, exemplary questions for the perspective "tester" are presented.

Example 29-7: Exemplary questions for the perspective "tester"

- Are the requirements that are relevant for deriving test cases documented in a comprehensible way?
- Are the artefacts complete, or is important information missing? If so, which information that is relevant for test case derivation is missing?
- Is the information that is relevant for deriving test cases consistent, or are there contradictions?
- Is it possible to derive test data from the requirements artefacts?
- Does the artefact contain information that is useless for the tester?

29.2.2 Execution

Following the instructions and answering the questions

The perspective assigned to the reviewer determines how he performs the validation. During the validation, the reviewer follows the instructions of the perspective and answers the questions from the specific perspective. The instructions may prescribe how the reviewer shall read the artefact, i.e. which aspects he pays attention to when reading the artefact. The questions aim to support the detection of typical defects that are related to the perspective, such as missing or incomplete information with regard to a specific purpose (e.g. the creation of test cases or a draft of the architectural design).

Optional creation of artefacts

More thorough checking can be achieved if the reviewers not only read the artefact but also create (partial) artefacts corresponding to the perspectives assigned to them. For this purpose, the reading instructions need to be extended to guide the reviewers in creating the required artefacts.

29.2.3 Follow-up

Defect collection

The follow-up work after perspective-based reading comprises the analysis of the results of the different perspectives. The reviewers' answers to the questions from each perspective as well as the problems that occurred while following the reading instructions indicate deficiencies in the checked requirements artefact. The validation team consolidates the results of the individual perspectives and discusses the results in a group session, if appropriate.

Defect correction and follow-up check

The authors of the requirements artefacts correct the detected defects. Subsequently, a follow-up check of the corrections may be performed (see Section 28.1).

29.2.4 Checklist for Applying the Technique

Hint 29-4 presents a checklist with important points for supporting requirements validation by means of perspective-based reading.

!

Hint 29-4: *Checklist for perspective-based reading*

Preparation:

- ❑ Identify the perspectives that are relevant for the project.
- ❑ For each perspective, provide reading instructions and questions that support defect detection.
- ❑ Familiarise the reviewers with the perspectives assigned to them.
- ❑ Give the reviewers an overview of the system.

Execution:

- ❑ Ask the reviewers to follow the reading instructions and answer the questions belonging to their perspectives.

(*to be continued*)

Hint 29-4 *(continued)*

Follow-up:

- Make sure that all detected defects are consolidated and analysed.
- Identify conflicts about requirements between the individual perspectives and try to resolve them by means of the techniques described in Part IV.c.
- Provide the detected defects to the author as prescribed by the validation technique.
- Perform a follow-up check of the corrections, if applicable.
- Collect suggestions for improvement and optimise the reading instructions and questions for the different perspectives.
- Decide whether to extend or restrict the set of perspectives used for future applications of the technique.

29.2.5 Benefit

Practical support for reviewers

Perspective-based reading provides the reviewers with detailed, hands-on instructions for reading the requirements artefacts and for detecting defects associated with the particular perspective. The guidelines support stakeholders who have little experience in requirements validation, but also help to avoid experienced users performing the validation cursorily e.g. due to lack of time.

Artefact-usage-oriented validation

By means of perspective-based reading, the validation team checks whether the requirements artefact is suited for its different addressees or process users, i.e. the stakeholders who actually have to work with the requirements artefact. Typical addressees of a requirements artefact are customers, testers, software architects etc. Validation of requirements artefacts from the perspectives of these stakeholders enables early detection and removal of defects that inhibit the use of the requirements artefacts. Thereby, delays and errors caused by requirements artefacts that are inappropriate for their addressees are avoided.

More defects uncovered than without perspectives

During perspective-based reading, each inspector concentrates on a specific perspective. Perspective-based reading is based on the assumption that the reviewers find different defects by focussing on different perspectives and that, overall, more defects are detected in this way than by detecting defects without differentiated perspectives.

Standardisation and optimisation of the validation procedure

By providing detailed reading instructions and questions, a standard procedure for validation of requirements is established within the organisation. The documentation of the procedure and especially of the reading instructions supports the training of new employees. In addition, the documentation of the procedure allows for analysis as well as experience-based optimisation of the procedure.

29.2.6 Effort

Effort similar to an ordinary inspection

The effort for performing a validation technique with perspective-based reading is comparable to the effort that is required for an ordinary inspection. Each reviewer has to follow defined reading instructions and answer questions with regard to the perspective assigned to her. However, creating artefacts causes additional effort, if applied.

very high	high	medium	low	very low
	✓	(✓)		

Fig. 29-2 *Effort for perspective-based reading*

29.2.7 Critical Success Factors

Quality of the instructions and questions

The applicability of the instructions and questions provided for the individual perspectives is a critical success factor for perspective-based reading (see the success factors for applying checklists presented in Section 29.1). If the reviewer does not understand the instructions or the associated questions, for instance because he is not familiar with the assigned perspective, or if the instructions are not applicable to the requirements artefact at hand, a systematic validation is not possible.

Leveraging the participants' expertise during planning and follow-up

Furthermore, the reviewers might perceive the predefined, detailed instructions as cumbersome or obstructive to their work. They might also think that their expertise is undermined. Therefore, it is important to involve the reviewers already at an early planning stage of the validation and to make use of their expertise during the creation of the reading instructions and questions. After having performed the validation, the reviewers should also be provided with the possibility to evaluate the reading instructions and questions and to make suggestions for improvement.

29.3 Creation of Artefacts

Prerequisite: detailed requirements

Creating artefacts during validation means using the requirements to be checked as a reference for (partially) creating other development artefacts. However, a sufficient level of detail of the requirements artefacts is a prerequisite for creating other development artefacts such as usage scenarios, test cases, or a user manual.

Artefacts are primarily created to support validation

The chosen development artefacts (e.g. test cases) are primarily created for the purpose of validation. In order to keep the effort for creating the artefacts at an acceptable level, chosen quality criteria of the artefacts to be created may be alleviated or abandoned. For instance, test coverage criteria may be ignored when creating test cases for the purpose of requirements validation. Generally, the created artefact is discarded after performing the validation. Therefore, the effort for creating the artefacts should be reduced, for instance by suspending the traceability rules for these artefacts.

Reuse of the created artefacts as initial drafts

If significant effort is invested in creating a development artefact during requirements validation, it can still be reasonable to make further use of the artefact. For example, a user manual created for a validation based on prototypes can serve as a useful input for writing the final user manual for the system.

Validation support

The creation of artefacts supports requirements validation mainly in the following ways:

Defects uncovered during artefacts creation

- Already during the process of creation, deficiencies in the requirements artefact can be detected. For example, if the input required for a specific step of the creation process is missing, this is an indication of incomplete requirements.

- The created artefact makes the underlying requirements accessible to being validated more easily by specific stakeholders. For example, the requirements may be used as a reference for writing a user manual. This user manual contains only the information that is relevant for the users, i.e. it is stripped of irrelevant details and is written in a way that the users can understand. The user manual is hence suitable for being validated by system user representatives. As the user manual is based on the requirements artefacts, the results of the validation can be transferred to the original requirements artefacts.

Requirements made accessible for validation by specific stakeholders

Applicable in all validation techniques

The creation of artefacts can be applied as a supplement to the validation techniques presented in Chapter 28. Therein, the creation itself generally takes place prior to detecting defects by means of the chosen validation technique (e.g. an inspection). Furthermore, the creation of development artefacts of a specific type draws the reviewers' attention to the needs of the stakeholders who are normally responsible for creating this type of artefact. Therefore, perspective-based reading (see Section 29.2) and creating artefacts are quite often used in combination to support requirements validation.

Special case: validation with prototypes

When validating requirements using a prototype (see Section 28.5), the prototype is developed based on the requirements artefacts. Hence validation with prototypes is a special form of creating artefacts for requirements validation. Consequently, the above statements concerning the creation of artefacts hold for validation using prototypes as well.

In the following, we explain the following four creation activities:

- Verbalising models (Section 29.3.1)
- Creating scenarios (Section 29.3.2)
- Creating test cases (Section 29.3.3)
- Creating a user manual (Section 29.3.4)

29.3.1 Verbalisation of Models

Transforming models into natural language

The verbalisation of models denotes the transformation of formal or semi-formal requirements models into natural language. Therein, defects in the model may already be detected during verbalisation. However, the main purpose of this assistance technique is to facilitate validation of requirements models by stakeholders who are not familiar with the original, model-based documentation format. Verbalisation thus typically precedes a validation technique such as an inspection or a desk-check (see Chapter 28).

Preparation

Verbalisation rules

In order to verbalise a model in a systematic way, the stakeholders must define rules for how requirements artefacts should be transformed from their present formal or semi-formal documentation form into natural language. As a basis for the definition of the rules, the specification of the modelling language is considered. Based on the specification, one or multiple rules are defined for each model element. The concrete definition of the rules should, furthermore, take into account organisation- and project-specific extensions and interpretations of the language constructs. For instance, the organisation may have attached specific non-standard semantics to a common requirements modelling language.

Execution

Information must not be added, changed, or omitted

Verbalisation aims to leave the content of the artefact unchanged under the performed transformations. Therefore, information must not be added, changed, or omitted during the verbalisation process. The risk of adding information to a model during verbalisation is reduced when the verbalisation is performed by stakeholders who were not involved in creating the model.

Detecting requirements defects

The following exemplary situations make clear how verbalisation contributes to the detection of defects:

Comprehensibility and completeness

- If the author cannot write up a text for a model element, this is an indication that the model is not comprehensible or important information is missing.

Ambiguity

- If the author is not sure which of several possible interpretations of a model element or of a part of the model is correct, this is an indication of ambiguous requirements.

Resolution of defects and issues prior to validation

The author documents the defects detected during the verbalisation of the model as well as questions and problems that occurred. In order to finalise the verbalisation, the problems, questions, and defects must be resolved. In this way, better quality of the resulting verbalised artefact is achieved, which is beneficial for subsequent validation.

Tool support

Modelling tools generally have functions for generating documents from the models created with the tool. The main inputs for the generation procedure are the specific model instance, the textual documentation of the model instance contained in the model as well as a configurable document template. The generated document consists, among other things, of:

- Diagrams
- Tabular listings of model elements
- Detailed descriptions of the individual model elements (e.g. the attributes and relationships of each model element)
- Cross references

Advantages/ disadvantages of tool support

In principle it is possible to use the functionality for document generation from models for verbalisation. Tool-supported verbalisation allows, for example, for a simple check of whether all model elements have been verbalised, since model elements without textual documentation appear in the generated document and hence can easily be detected. However, [Sommerville and Sawyer 1997] point out that generated documents often do not exhibit the desired quality (e.g. readability) so that manual rework before validation is often necessary.

Follow-up

Validation of the verbalised form

The verbalised form of the requirements artefact is used to support a validation activity based on one of the techniques presented in Chapter 28, in particular an inspection or a desk-check. If the verbalised form was created in compliance with the rules stated above (no additional information etc.), the validation results can easily be transferred to the original model.

Checklist for Applying the Technique

Hint 29-5 presents a checklist with important points that should be considered during the verbalisation of models.

!

Hint 29-5: *Checklist for verbalising models*

Preparation:

- ❑ Define verbalisation rules for the modelling language used.
- ❑ When defining the rules, take into account domain- and project-specific peculiarities such as language extensions.
- ❑ Experiment with the verbalisation rules and optimise the rules when applying the technique repeatedly.

Execution:

- ❑ During verbalisation, do not add, change, or omit information.
- ❑ Perform the validation as prescribed by the procedure of the chosen validation technique (e.g. inspection or desk-check).

Follow-up:

- ❑ Transfer the validation results to the original requirements model.
- ❑ Decide whether the requirements changes should be integrated into the verbalisation or if the verbalisation can be discarded.

Benefit

Indications of requirements defects

Problems that occur during the verbalisation of a requirements model are indications of defects in the requirements (e.g. incompleteness, poor comprehensibility, or ambiguity).

Can be necessary for involving stakeholders

The main benefit of verbalisation is, however, that the requirements become accessible to stakeholders who cannot understand the original requirements model. Through verbalisation, the stakeholders are enabled to validate the model indirectly by validating its verbalised form.

Effort

Effort for introducing the technique

When introducing this assistance technique for the first time, some effort is needed to define appropriate verbalisation rules and train the authors who shall perform the verbalisation. The required effort depends on the complexity of the modelling language as well as the desired level of detail of the rules. Frequently, it is necessary to experiment with the rules for some time and rework them until a usable set of verbalisation rules is available.

Effort for performing the technique

The verbalisation of an extensive model may take several days. Therein, the training period for the author to become familiar with the details of the model (as regards its content) as well as the improvement of the comprehensibility and readability of the verbalised form must be taken into account. Therefore, we estimate the effort for performing this assistance technique as medium.

very high	high	medium	low	very low
		✓		

Fig. 29-3 *Effort for the verbalisation of models*

Verbalisation only as extension to the models

Two variants of this assistance technique can be applied in order to reduce the effort. The first variant is to use the verbalised form merely as an extension to the original requirements model, for example in order to support checking of critical contents.

Ad hoc verbalisation during a walkthrough

The second variant is to let the author of the requirements model perform the verbalisation ad hoc during the validation. However, this procedure is not suited for a detailed check, since, for example, the quality of the verbalisation cannot be assured. Therefore, we recommend the latter variant only in combination with walkthroughs (see Section 28.3).

Critical Success Factors

Comprehensibility of the verbalised form

Verbalising a model is only useful for validation if the verbalised form is readable and comprehensible for the stakeholders.

Compliance with the model

Since the verbalised form is used during validation as a substitute for the original model, the content of the model and the content of the text must agree as closely as possible.

29.3.2 Creating Scenarios

Scenarios for the usage, IT system, and subject facet

Generally, the creation of scenarios as an assistance technique for validation aims at validating the requirements from the usage perspective. However, scenarios can also be used to validate requirements from the IT system perspective (e.g. a software upgrade scenario) or from the subject perspective (e.g. scenarios describing the updating of information represented in the system).

Scenarios make it easier to involve both technical and non-technical stakeholders

Besides the possibility to detect requirements defects during the creation of scenarios, this assistance technique has further advantages for validation. In contrast to purely textual requirements and many solution-oriented models, scenarios are easily comprehensible to most stakeholders, in particular non-technical stakeholders. In addition, model-based scenarios can be animated, thereby increasing their readability as well as the stakeholders' motivation to participate in the validation. Furthermore, it is possible to let a larger group of (technical and non-technical) stakeholders validate the created scenarios e.g. in a group session (see [Alexander and Maiden 2004]). Due to their good comprehensibility, the created scenarios can simply be presented to the stakeholders, allowing the stakeholders to comment on the scenarios.

Preparation

When scenarios are created in the context of validation, the creators of the scenarios are at the same time the reviewers of the underlying requirements artefacts.

Reviewers create scenarios

In order to achieve comparability of the scenarios that are created by different authors or, respectively, different reviewers, the reviewers should be provided with a common scenario template. The scenario template used during validation may be based, for instance, on the scenario template presented in Section 11.2.2. However, the template is typically reduced, since some aspects may not be relevant or of little relevance for the set validation goal (see Hint 29-6).

Scenario template

The rules for documenting scenarios presented in Section 11.4 may be distributed, possibly in a reduced form, to the reviewers in order to provide additional guidance for creating the scenarios during validation.

Scenario authoring guidelines

!

Hint 29-6: *Deriving a scenario template for validation*

A validation activity has been scheduled with the goal of aligning the documented requirements with the desired usage workflows. To facilitate this validation goal, the reviewers shall create usage scenarios. The requirements engineers provide the reviewers with a reduced scenario template with the sections "identifier", "goal(s)", "precondition", "postcondition", and "scenario steps". If the validation goal would additionally include checking the consistency of the documented requirements, the requirements engineers might additionally include the section "relationship to other scenarios" in order to support detection of inconsistencies between different scenarios.

Execution

The reviewers create scenarios by applying the provided rules to the artefacts to be checked. During the creation of the scenarios, the reviewers document the defects they identify in the requirements. Therein, problems that occur during the creation of the scenarios hint at defects in the checked requirements. In addition, the search for defects can be supported by using checklists (see Section 29.1).

Checklists support the search for defects

The main results of scenario creation consist of the created scenarios and a list of defects identified in the original requirements.

List of defects in the original artefacts

Follow-up

Defects detected during scenario creation are analysed and corrected. The correction comprises both revision of the original requirements artefacts and revision of the created scenarios.

Defect correction after scenario creation

Subsequently, the revised scenarios must be validated by means of one of the validation techniques presented in Chapter 28, e.g. an inspection, a desk-check, or a prototype. Only subsequent validation of the scenarios allows for detecting defects such as incomplete or missing scenarios. Validation of the scenarios enables the requirements engineers to draw further conclusions about the quality of the requirements artefacts that were used as input to create the scenarios.

Necessity to validate the created scenarios

Involving additional stakeholders in the validation

If the scenario creation is performed in combination with perspective-based reading (see Section 29.2), each reviewer, after creating the scenarios, answers the specific questions that are associated with the reviewer's perspective (typically, scenarios are created and validated from the user perspective). However, generally, a larger group of stakeholders should validate the scenarios in addition to the reviewers who created the scenarios. This can be achieved easily, for instance, by conducting an inspection of the created scenarios with additional stakeholders.

Defect correction after scenario validation

The defects detected during the validation of the scenarios are indications of defects in the underlying requirements artefacts. These defects have to be analysed and corrected.

Checklist for Applying the Technique

Hint 29-7 presents a checklist with important points for supporting requirements validation by the creation of scenarios.

!

Hint 29-7: *Checklist for scenario creation*

Preparation:

- ❑ Provide the reviewers with all requirements artefacts that are relevant for creating the scenarios.
- ❑ Provide a (reduced) scenario template.
- ❑ Select only those sections of the scenario template presented in Section 11.2.2 that are relevant for the validation goal.
- ❑ Provide rules for documenting scenarios.
- ❑ Train the reviewers, if necessary.
- ❑ Provide checklists for detecting defects.

Execution:

- ❑ Ensure that the reviewers apply the rules for scenario creation correctly.
- ❑ Ensure that the reviewers document all detected defects.

Follow-up:

- ❑ Take care that both the original requirements artefacts as well as the created scenarios are corrected.
- ❑ Validate the created scenarios in a larger group of stakeholders by applying one of the techniques presented in Chapter 28.

Benefit

Detection of defects regarding the four context facets

The creation of scenarios allows for validation of the underlying requirements from the perspective of the subject facet, usage facet, IT system facet, and the development facet. Scenarios support the uncovering of missing or deficient context information concerning the respective context facet. As a consequence, also the defects in the requirements that are caused by incomplete or incorrect context information can be uncovered.

Defects can be detected firstly during scenario creation and secondly during the subsequent validation of the created scenarios by a larger group of stakeholders.

Validation of the created scenarios

Effort

Influencing factors

The effort for creating scenarios based on solution-oriented requirements depends on the extent of the scenarios to be created. It is hence influenced by the amount of requirements to be considered during scenario creation. Additionally, the effort is significantly influenced by the scenario template used, its adaptation (reduction) according to the validation goal and the rules provided for scenario creation.

Low to medium effort

All in all, the effort for the creation of scenarios can be estimated as low to medium. If the scenario template is reduced and the validation focusses on few requirements artefacts, the effort is low. Without a reduction of the template, or rather without an appropriate focus, medium effort is required.

very high	high	medium	low	very low
		(✓)	✓	

Fig. 29-4 *Effort for creating scenarios*

Critical Success Factors

Experience of the reviewers

Though the concept of scenarios can be understood quite easily, the creation of high-quality scenarios requires experience. Therefore, it is advisable that some of the reviewers have experience in scenario writing.

Quality of the artefacts

In addition, the input quality of the requirements artefacts is an important success factor. If the quality is not sufficient, for instance, if important information is missing, the creation of scenarios may be infeasible.

29.3.3 Creating Test Cases

Early defect detection through partially performing test case development activities

Creating test cases for supporting requirements validation means that the reviewers perform a part of the activities of requirements-based test case development. The goal is not to define test cases fully matching the quality criteria for test cases such as reusability, test automation, or specific coverage criteria such as branch coverage (see Chapter 37). Rather, test case development activities are performed only partially and with the aim of detecting defects in the requirements artefacts early in the development process.

Actual test activities require already validated and released requirements

However, the actual test activities that are performed e.g. as a part of system or software testing (see Chapter 37) also contribute to the validation of requirements artefacts. Especially, the test specification activities have a positive effect on the quality of the requirements. However, these test activities generally require that already validated and released requirements artefacts exist. This is a major difference from the (partial) creation of test cases as an assistance technique for requirements validation.

Example 29-8: Definition of test cases based on scenarios

During the validation of the car safety system, the reviewers create test cases based on the usage scenarios of the system. Therefore, the reviewers (a) derive the steps of the test case scenarios from the usage scenarios and (b) extend the resulting test cases with the following kinds of information:

- Steps for meeting the preconditions of a scenario
- Test data
- Evaluation steps

If a sub-activity of test case development cannot be performed, this is an indication of deficient requirements. For instance, if the permissible range of an input value is not specified in the requirements, it is hardly possible to derive the test data.

Preparation

Required documents

The preparation for the creation of test cases during validation comprises the provision of the following documents:

- An appropriate set of requirements artefacts
- A template for the test cases
- Instructions for how to create the test cases based on the given requirements artefacts

Step-by-step instructions

The provided instructions must explain the creation of test cases step by step. In order to enable the reviewers to create test cases, the instructions must describe comprehensibly, for instance, how the test data for a concrete test case shall be determined based on the provided requirements artefacts.

Selection of quality criteria for the test cases

During the definition of the instructions for the creation of test cases, one must consider that not all quality criteria that generally apply to test cases are relevant. Criteria such as the minimisation of the testing effort or the ability to automate the test cases are only relevant if one plans to really execute the test cases.

Checklists

The detection of requirements defects by means of creating test cases should be supported by appropriate checklists (see Section 29.1).

Execution

Creation of test cases and defect detection

The reviewers follow the instructions in order to create the test cases based on the provided requirements artefacts. In addition, the reviewers answer the questions provided in the validation checklists. The reviewers document the problems that occur as well as the defects detected during the creation of the test cases.

Follow-up

Analysis of defects

The stakeholders analyse the defects detected by the reviewers and define actions necessary for defect correction.

Additionally, the achieved quality of the created test cases can be checked. Deficiencies in the test cases originate either from incomplete creation (i.e. from the creation process) or from the underlying requirements artefacts. Hence, defects in the requirements artefacts may additionally be detected by validating the created test cases. The validation of the test cases can be performed in a similar way as validation of requirements, e.g. by applying a review technique (see Chapter 28).

Check of the created test cases

Checklist for Applying the Technique

Hint 29-8 presents a checklist with important points that should be considered when creating test cases for the purpose of requirements validation.

!

Hint 29-8: *Checklist for creating test cases*

Preparation:

- ❑ Collect all requirements artefacts that are needed as input for creating the test cases.
- ❑ Provide a template for the test cases.
- ❑ Provide detailed rules for deriving test cases from the requirements artefacts.
- ❑ Train the reviewers, if necessary.
- ❑ Provide checklists to support defect detection.

Execution:

- ❑ Ensure that the reviewers apply the rules for creating test cases correctly.
- ❑ Take care that the detected defects and issues are documented.

Follow-up:

- ❑ Ensure that the creator corrects the defects in the requirements artefacts that were detected during the creation of the test cases.
- ❑ Validate the created test cases in order to detect further requirements defects.
- ❑ If the created test cases shall be used as drafts for the actual test cases, the quality of the test cases must be thoroughly checked after the requirements have been validated and released.

Benefit

This assistance technique is well suited to checking functional requirements and specific quality requirements (e.g. performance requirements) for verifiability (see Section 16.3 for the definitions of requirements quality attributes).

Check for verifiability

In order to create test cases, the reviewers must read and understand the requirements artefact in detail. Thereby, defects such as lack of comprehensibility as well as ambiguity are detected. The creation of test cases is only possible if the requirements artefacts contain the information that is relevant from the test perspective.

Check for comprehensibility, unambiguousness, and completeness

It is possible to make further use of the created test cases later on when the actual test cases for the system are created. However, the test cases created during validation are generally not complete and do not satisfy the required quality criteria for production test cases.

Further use of the test cases

Effort

Application of this technique requires knowledge and experience in the creation of test cases. The reviewers therefore need to be adequately trained in test specification techniques. The effort for performing the technique can be estimated as medium. However, the effort strongly depends on the provided requirements artefacts as well as the expected extent and quality of the derived test cases.

very high	high	medium	low	very low
		✓		

Fig. 29-5 *Effort for creating test cases during requirements validation*

Critical Success Factors

Quality of the requirements artefacts

An important prerequisite for successfully creating test cases is sufficient entry quality of the requirements artefacts to be checked. It must be possible to extract test-relevant information from the requirements artefacts, at least to some degree.

Traceability between requirements and test cases

If the test cases shall be validated after their creation, comprehensible and good quality documentation of the test cases as well as documentation of the relationships between the test cases and the requirements artefacts are necessary. If a defect is detected during the validation of the test cases, the relationships between the test cases and the requirements artefacts allow the identification of faulty requirements artefacts from which the test cases have been derived.

Experience in test artefact creation

If the reviewers have experience in creating test cases, this has a positive influence on the results of the requirements validation by means of this assistance technique. The reviewers should therefore be trained in test case development to some extent.

29.3.4 Creating a User Manual

Relation to the requirements engineering process

User manual writing is generally a process of its own that takes place in conjunction with the system development process. In other words, unlike the creation of scenarios or test cases, user manual writing is strictly speaking not a system development activity. A user manual is often not written until the system development process has been completed. However, there are significant interrelations between the requirements and the user manual for a system. For example, both contain information about system functions and their use, e.g. in the form of scenarios.

Validation from the perspective of the end user

In this section, we describe how the creation of a user manual can be applied in a reasonable way to support the validation of requirements artefacts. In particular, the early availability of a (preliminary) user manual can support the validation of the requirements from the perspective of the end user. In order to support validation, a technical author should be appointed already during requirements engineering with the task of creating a user manual for the system based on the requirements artefacts (at least those that are considered to be sufficiently stable).

Preparation

Determining the structure

Before a user manual can be written, the structure of the manual must be agreed with the relevant stakeholders. For this purpose, a template or outline of the manual is created and discussed with the relevant stakeholders. An exemplary outline of a user manual is presented in Tab. 29-2.

Tab. 29-2 *Exemplary outline of a user manual*

1. Getting started	4.2 Function 2
2. User interface	4.3 …
3. Usage scenarios	5. Trouble shooting
3.1 Scenario 1	5.1 Problem 1
3.2 Scenario 2	5.2 Problem 2
3.3 …	6. Glossary
4. Functions	7. Index
4.1 Function 1	

Appointing a technical writer

The author of the user manual should have domain knowledge as well as experience in writing user manuals. One possibility is to commission an external technical writer who is familiar with the domain to write the manual.

Execution

Manual for the system to be developed

The technical writer creates the manual as if the system had already been realised (see [Berry et al. 2001]). Thereby, he considers preferably all requirements of an end user with regard to a high-quality user manual. The manual should, for example, contain the following elements:

- ❑ Overview figures that are easy to comprehend
- ❑ Instructions for frequently occurring problems (which are, for example, derived from exception and error scenarios)
- ❑ Pictures of a prototypical user interface

Identification of defects

The author documents open issues and problems that occur during the writing of the user manual, since each question and each problem may indicate a defect in the requirements. In order to support validation effectively, close interaction with the stakeholders of the requirements engineering process is necessary. For example, the questions and problems that have surfaced should be discussed regularly. Defects in the requirements that are detected during the creation of the manual can be corrected early in this way.

Up-to-date requirements artefacts

During the entire manual writing process, one must ensure that the author is provided with an up-to-date version of the requirements artefacts and informed about changes in the requirements artefacts.

Follow-up

Validation of the manual by end users

Eventually, the created user manual is validated. For this purpose, the requirements engineers can ask, for example, representative users to read and comment on the manual. For validation of the user manual, the desk-check technique described in Section 28.2 can be applied. In this way, the stakeholders get feedback on the requirements for the system to be developed from the perspective of the future end users. For instance, if a user identifies missing relevant system functionality in the manual, this can be an indication of a missing system goal.

Checklist for Applying the Technique

Hint 29-9 presents a checklist with important points that should be considered during the creation and validation of a user manual in the context of requirements validation.

!

Hint 29-9: *Checklist for creating a user manual*

Preparation:

- ❑ Create an outline of the user manual and discuss it with the relevant stakeholders.
- ❑ Identify and commission a technical writer who has experience in the application domain.
- ❑ Provide the writer with an overview of the requirements artefacts and give him the opportunity to ask clarification questions.

Execution:

- ❑ Ensure that the manual is written as if the system had already been implemented.
- ❑ Discuss questions and problems regularly with the technical writer.
- ❑ Arrange for the correction of deficiencies in the requirements that were identified during manual writing.
- ❑ Inform the manual writer about changes to requirements artefacts.

Follow-up:

- ❑ Validate the manual by involving representative end users.
- ❑ Arrange for the correction of the requirements artefacts as well as the user manual.

Benefit

Detection of defects during manual writing

The creation of the user manual allows for detection of a number of requirements defects, since the author intensively deals with the requirements artefacts (especially from the system usage perspective). If the author cannot write a relevant section of the user manual, this may indicate missing or incomplete requirements.

Further ways of using the manual

In addition to detecting requirements defects during manual writing, the created user manual can also be used for other purposes such as:

- Stakeholders from the usage facet can read the manual. Based on their feedback, conclusions about the quality of the underlying requirements can be drawn.
- A user manual is generally needed for requirements validation by means of a prototype (see Section 28.5).
- The early drafts of the manual can be incrementally elaborated to the final user manual.

Effort

The effort required for creating a user manual must be estimated as high, or even as very high, for example in the case of a large number of system functions and usage scenarios. A technical author generally needs several weeks or months to write a user manual. Therefore, a user manual should only be created if the requirements are sufficiently stable and of high quality.

very high	high	medium	low	very low
	✓			

Fig. 29-6 *Effort for creating a user manual*

Additional effort for the validation and evolution of the manual

Validating the manual requires additional effort. Furthermore, after releasing the requirements, the manual must be adapted and extended with design and realisation aspects. Again, this requires additional effort.

Critical Success Factors

Stable requirements

In order to be able to create a user manual, the parts of the requirements that are relevant for the users must be complete and stable to a large extent. They must also be documented with good quality. If major changes are applied to these requirements, significant parts of the user manual must be rewritten.

Support of the author

There is a risk that the draft of the user manual is not available in time. In order to reduce this risk, the stakeholders must ensure that the author is provided with all relevant information and informed about the relevant deadlines in due time.

Readability and comprehensibility

In order to support the validation effectively, the manual must exhibit good readability and comprehensibility. It must give the readers a realistic impression of the system to be developed even in the details. However, one should also communicate to the readers that they may still influence the requirements for the system through their comments.

Further ways of using the manual

In addition to detecting requirements defects during manual writing, the created user manual can also be used for other purposes such as:

- Stakeholders from the usage facet can read the manual. Based on their feedback, conclusions about the quality of the underlying requirements can be drawn.
- A user manual is generally needed for requirements validation by means of a prototype (see Section 26.3).
- The early drafts of the manual can be incrementally elaborated to the final user manual.

Effort

The effort required for creating a user manual must be estimated as high, or even as very high, for example in the case of a large number of system functions and usage scenarios. A technical author generally needs several weeks or months to write a user manual. Therefore, a user manual should only be created if the requirements are sufficiently stable and of high quality.

very low	low	medium	high	very high
			X	

Fig. 26-6 Effort for creating a user manual

Additional effort for the validation and evolution of the manual

Validating the manual requires additional effort. Furthermore, after releasing the requirements, the manual must be retained and extended with design and realisation aspects. Again, this requires additional effort.

Critical Success Factors

Stable requirements

In order to be able to create a user manual, the parts of the requirements that are relevant for the users must be complete and stable to a large extent. They must also be documented with good quality. If major changes are applied to these requirements, significant parts of the user manual must be rewritten.

Support of the author

There is a risk that the draft of the user manual is not available in time. In order to reduce this risk, the stakeholders must ensure that the author is provided with all relevant information and informed about the relevant deadlines in due time.

Readability and comprehensibility

In order to support the validation effectively, the manual must exhibit good readability and comprehensibility. It must give the readers a realistic impression of the system to be developed even in the details. However, one should also communicate to the readers that they may still influence the requirements for the system through their comments.

Recommended Literature for Part V

Basic Reading

[Shull et al. 2000] explain the advantages of perspective-based reading for the validation of requirements artefacts.

[Sommerville 2004] provides an introduction to the use of prototypes during the software development process. The author explains, among other things, the different techniques for prototype development, such as the use of rapid application development (RAD) environments.

[Sommerville and Sawyer 1997] provide guidelines for requirements validation. They explain the benefit of inspections and prototypes. Furthermore, the use of checklists and other assistance techniques for validation is described.

[Wiegers 2002] provides a comprehensive introduction to review techniques and review processes, including several hints for performing reviews.

Advanced Reading

[Bäumer et al. 1996] explain the concepts of user interface prototypes and present a case study on the use of user interface prototypes in nine industrial projects.

[Brykczynski 1999] analysed more than 100 checklists for the inspection of software artefacts. He provides a tabular overview of the analysed checklists as well as hints for appropriate and inappropriate checklist items.

[Fagan 1986] provides an overview of the inspection process, applications of inspections in practice as well as the factors that influence the success of inspections.

[Gilb and Graham 1993] explain inspection processes in detail and report extensively on the successful introduction of software inspections in several organisations. They emphasise the continuous improvement of the inspection process.

[Laitenberger and DeBaud 2000] present a rich taxonomy for inspection processes. They provide a comprehensive overview on existing inspection processes, reading techniques, the required

Part VI
Management

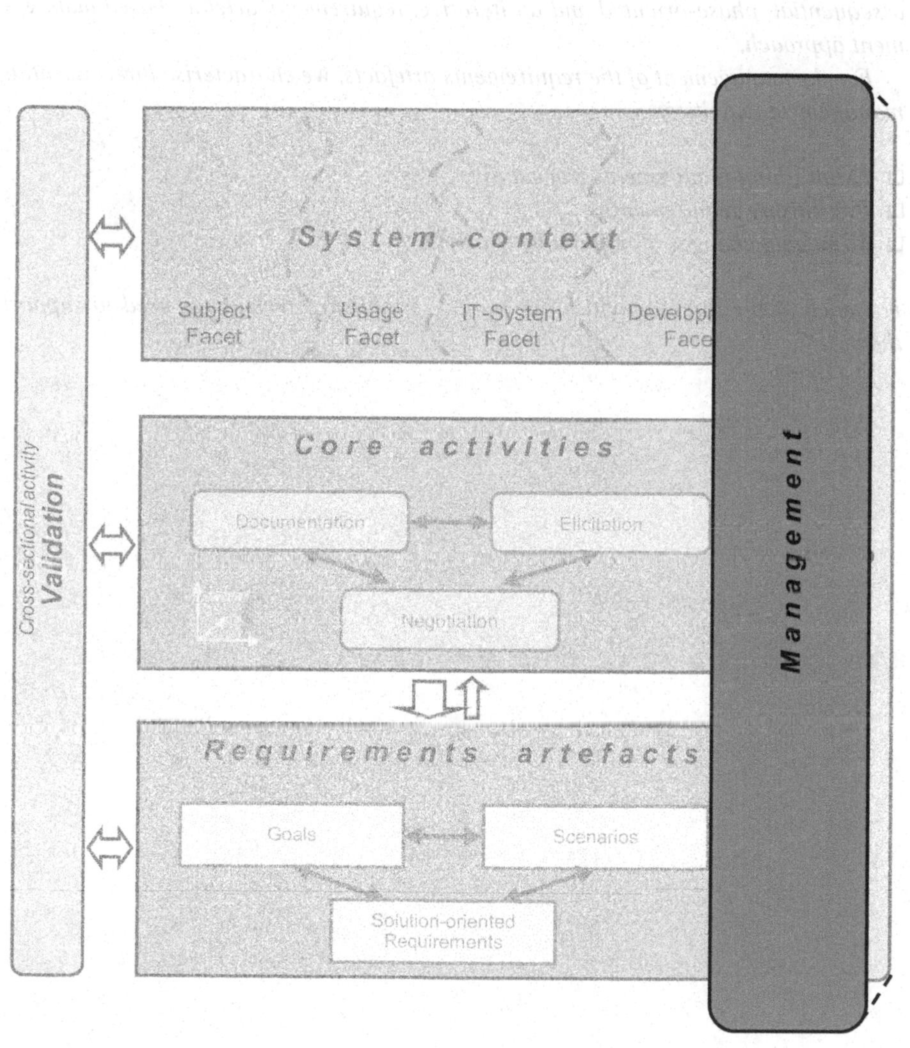

Overview Part VI – Management

According to our requirements engineering framework, management in requirements engineering has to consider three main aspects:

- *The identification and management of context changes*
- *The management of the requirements engineering activities*
- *The management of the requirements artefacts*

In this part of the book, we outline techniques for observing the system context. These techniques facilitate the identification of context changes. For management of the requirements engineering process and its activities, we differentiate between a sequential, phase-oriented and an iterative, requirements-artefact-based management approach.

For the management of the requirements artefacts, we characterise three essential management activities:

- *Establishing requirements traceability*
- *Prioritising requirements*
- *Managing changes of requirements artefacts*

For each of the three activities, we outline established techniques used to support them.

Classification Part VI Management		Basic	Advanced
30	**Fundamentals of Requirements Management**		
30.1	Goals of the Management Activity	✓	
30.2	Definition	✓	
30.3	Managing Requirements Artefacts	✓	
30.4	Observing the System Context		✓
30.5	Managing the Requirements Engineering Activities	✓	
31	**Requirements Traceability**		
31.1	Fundamentals of Traceability	✓	
31.2	Pre- and Post-traceability	✓	
31.3	Traceability Relationship		✓
31.4	Documenting Traceability	✓	
31.5	Presentation of Traceability	✓	
31.6	Project-Specific Traceability		✓
32	**Prioritising Requirements**		
32.1	Fundamentals of Requirements Prioritisation	✓	
32.2	Preparation Activities for Prioritisation	✓	
32.3	Techniques for Requirements Prioritisation		✓
33	**Change Management for Requirements**		
33.1	Configuration Management	✓	
33.2	Requirements Changes	✓	
33.3	Systematic Change Management		✓

Chapter 30
Fundamentals of Requirements Management

In this chapter, we characterise the goals of the management activity in the requirements engineering process and provide a definition of the management activity derived from our framework. We outline three essential management activities to be performed during requirements engineering:

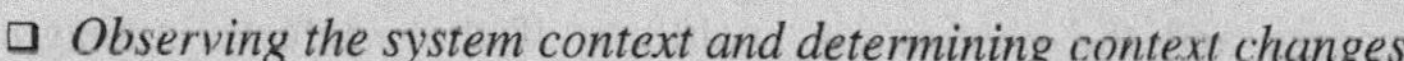

- *Observing the system context and determining context changes*
- *Managing the requirements engineering process and selecting the activities to be performed next*
- *Managing requirements artefacts, which includes, among other things, assigning attributes to requirements, establishing and managing requirements traceability, managing requirements changes, managing requirements configurations, and prioritising requirements.*

K. Pohl, *Requirements Engineering*,

30.1 Goals of the Management Activity

In the literature, the term "requirements management" refers to the management activity in the requirements engineering process. The term "requirements management" or, more precisely, "requirements engineering management" is unfortunately used differently. For example, [Leffingwell and Wirdrig 2000] regard requirements engineering as a part of requirements management. Other authors (e.g. [Kotonya and Sommerville 1997; Wiegers 1999]) consider the management of changes and associated activities as requirements management. Others again subsume parts of product and project management under the term "requirements management" (e.g. [Schienmann 2002]).

In principle, most of the definitions in requirements management literature are too restricted. As indicated by our requirements engineering framework (see Fig. 30-1), management in requirements engineering has a much broader scope and has to achieve at least three distinct goals:

Management of the artefacts

- *Managing requirements engineering artefacts*: The requirements artefacts documented during the requirements engineering process need to be properly managed. Given the typically large number of artefacts created during a requirements engineering process and the continuous evolution of the artefacts, managing requirements artefacts is a challenging task. To ease management, typically traceability between the requirements artefacts, their sources, and their use (e.g. refinement or realisation) is established. To support the evolution of the requirements, i.e. to allow for systematic integration of changes throughout the system lifecycle, a sophisticated change management process is required. In addition, the developing organisation must typically keep track of the evolution steps of each individual requirement over time. For this purpose, the requirements are put under version and configuration management.

Determine changes in the system context

- *Managing (observing) the system context*: The context in which the system is embedded in continuously changes throughout the system lifecycle. One goal of the management activity is therefore to observe the system context, detect relevant changes, and suggest appropriate activities in order to adjust the requirements engineering process and/or the requirements artefacts and thereby accommodate the context changes.

Management of the activities

- *Manage the requirements engineering process*: The main goal of this task is to define the requirements engineering activity (elicitation, documentation, negotiation, validation, etc.) to be executed next. Typically, at the beginning of a requirements engineering process a plan is developed which defines when, by whom and with which expected result the requirements engineering activities shall be executed. During the requirements engineering process, this plan needs to be continuously checked and, if required, revised in order to meet current challenges and to adjust the plan according to unforeseen events. For instance, an unexpected change in the context may require the execution of additional elicitation activities in order to analyse the context changes and adapt the requirements, if necessary. Such changes must be reflected in the actual work plan, i.e. the management process should continuously monitor the requirements engineering process and, if required, adjust the defined work plan.

Variability management

In the case of software product line development, in addition the variability of the requirements of the software product line must be managed (see Chapters 38 and 39 for details).

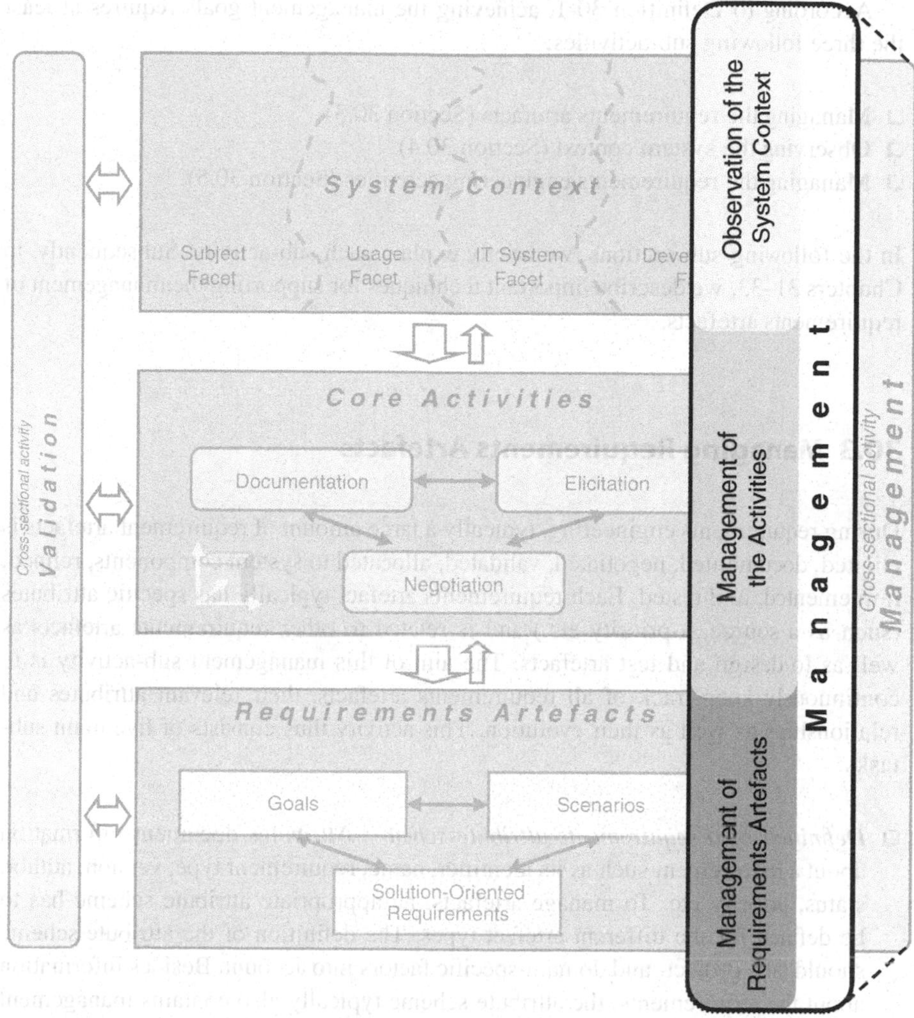

Fig. 30-1 *Cross-sectional activity: management (right-hand side)*

30.2 Definition

Based on the goals outlined in Section 30.1, we define the term "management in requirements engineering" as follows:

> **Definition 30-1:** *Management in requirements engineering*
>
> Management is one of the two cross-sectional requirements engineering activities. The goal of management in requirements engineering is to:
>
> (1) Observe the system context to detect context changes
> (2) Manage the execution of requirements engineering activities
> (3) Manage the requirements artefacts

D

Three sub-activities

According to Definition 30-1, achieving the management goals requires at least the three following sub-activities:

- Managing the requirements artefacts (Section 30.3)
- Observing the system context (Section 30.4)
- Managing the requirements engineering activities (Section 30.5)

In the following sub-sections, we briefly explain each sub-activity. Subsequently, in Chapters 31–33, we describe important techniques for supporting the management of requirements artefacts.

30.3 Managing Requirements Artefacts

Keep track of all requirements artefacts and their attributes, relationships, and evolution

During requirements engineering, typically a large amount of requirement artefacts is elicited, documented, negotiated, validated, allocated to system components, refined, implemented, and tested. Each requirements artefact typically has specific attributes (such as a source, a priority etc.) and is related to other requirements artefacts as well as to design and test artefacts. The aim of this management sub-activity is to continuously keep track of all requirements artefacts, their relevant attributes and relationships as well as their evolution. This activity thus consists of five main sub-tasks:

- *Definition of a requirements attribute scheme*: Attributes document information about a requirement such as its identifier, name, requirement type, version, author, status, priority etc. To manage artefacts, an appropriate attribute scheme has to be defined for the different artefact types. The definition of the attribute scheme should take project- and domain-specific factors into account. Besides information about the requirements, the attribute scheme typically also contains management attributes such as a unique identifier, a version number, or the priority of a requirement. When defining the attribute scheme, management should ensure that the right number of attributes is defined. If the number of attributes is very large, resources must be spent unnecessarily to define and fill in these attributes for all requirements artefacts. In contrast, if only very few attributes are defined, important information may be missing. In addition, the evolution of the attribute scheme as well as its content has to be managed. The fundamentals and techniques of defining an attribute scheme for requirements are explained in Chapter 18.
- *Requirements traceability*: A requirement is considered to be traceable when it can be traced to its origin (i.e. a requirement source or, in the case of a derived/refined requirement, a higher-level requirement) and to its refinement or realisation (i.e. the refinement by other requirements or the realisation by a design element). In addition, requirements should be related to quality assurance artefacts (e.g. test artefacts) which can be used to validate and/or verify the requirements. The fundamentals and techniques of requirements traceability are outlined in Chapter 31.
- *Requirements change management*: Requirements undergo changes throughout the entire development process. Requirements changes are caused, for example, by

changes in the system context (see Section 30.4) or by feedback from architectural design and testing. For instance, a requirements change is required if it turns out that a requirement (or a set of requirements) cannot be realised or tested. Change management for requirements should ensure that requirements changes are processed in a systematic way and that the changes are integrated consistently into the existing requirements artefacts. To support consistent integration of changes, change management utilises requirements traceability. The fundamentals and techniques of change management for requirements and their attributes are described in Chapter 33 (Sections 33.2–33.3).

- *Requirements configuration management*: Configuration management is based on version management. It manages the evolution of the requirements artefacts over time. A requirements version fixes the definition of a requirements artefact at a point in time. A configuration of requirements artefacts groups a set of different versions of requirements artefacts that are related to each other, e.g. different requirements artefacts which define the requirements for the entire system or a component. The fundamentals and techniques of configuration management for requirements are described in Section 33.1.
- *Requirements prioritisation*: Typically, not all documented requirements artefacts are equally important. In order to ensure that the available resources are used in a way that guarantees that each requirement is considered according to its (relative) importance, the documented requirements need to be prioritised. In addition to the prioritisation of requirements artefacts based on importance, other prioritisation criteria are also used such as risk, stability etc. Fundamentals of and techniques for prioritising requirements are presented in Chapter 32.

30.4 Observing the System Context

Goal: identification of context changes

The goal of this sub-activity is to identify changes in the context and estimate the impact of these changes. Changes in the system context must be addressed during requirements engineering. Detecting such context changes is a prerequisite for analysing these changes and for incorporating them into the requirements engineering process. Typical examples of context changes are:

- A new technology or a new competing product emerges
- A law or standard changes
- Evolution of stakeholder goals
- Involvement of additional stakeholders
- Change of an organisational policy
- Changes in the way that external actors (stakeholders or systems) use the system

30.4.1 Techniques for Context Observation

Changes in the context can be identified, among other things, by applying techniques used for environmental analysis in strategic management such as:

Systematic search for changes

- *Context scanning*: Context scanning denotes the systematic search for changes in the environment of the system that is performed periodically or on the occurrence of a special event. The scanned environment exceeds the context boundaries. It can include, for instance, the system context and the grey zone between the context and the (presumably) irrelevant environment (see Section 5.3). Details about scanning techniques for environmental analysis can be found in [Aguilar 1967; Day and Schoemaker 2005; Narayanan and Fahey 1987].

Tracking the evolution of the context

- *Context monitoring*: Context monitoring is based on continuous recording of the evolution of the context. It also includes tracking and interpretation of the context changes. Details on monitoring within environmental analysis can be found, for example, in [Narayanan and Fahey 1987].

Forecasting context changes

- *Context prognosis*: Context prognosis builds on the results of context scanning and/or context monitoring. It aims to gain information about the future development of the context based on knowledge about the current context and past changes of the context. Based on prognosis results, statements can be made about possible changes to the context in the future. Further details on context prognosis can be found, for example, in [Welge and Al-Laham 2007].

30.4.2 Structured Observation of the Context

Observation of the four context facets

Context changes can occur in each of the four context facets (the subject, the usage, the IT system, and the development facet). A major challenge for context observation is to detect and anticipate changes in all four context facets as early as possible. Since each context facet has its specific aspects, differentiation between the following is recommended:

- Observation of the subject facet
- Observation of the usage facet
- Observation of the IT system facet
- Observation of the development facet

Changes pertain to each type of context aspect

In principle, each type of context aspect (requirement sources, context objects, properties and relationships of context objects; see Section 6.2) can change. Changes in the context facet hence comprise:

- *Changes of requirement sources*: A new requirement source might appear in the context, which may result in new requirements surfacing or lead to changes in the documented requirements.
- *Changes of context objects*: A known context object can change or a new context object may become relevant for the system.
- *Changes in properties and relationships of the context objects*: The attributes of a context object or the relationships among different context objects may change.

Selection of observation techniques

An important aspect of the observation of the context is the selection of specific observation techniques for the context facets or the selected context aspects in the context facets. Context aspects critical to the success of the system (e.g. laws and regulations) should be observed using context monitoring. For less critical aspects, periodical scanning of the context should be generally sufficient.

Coordination of Context Observation with Project and Product Management

Relationships with project and product management

Besides in requirements engineering, context observation is also performed in product and project management. Project management must identify risks in connection with changes in the context and adapt, if necessary, the project plan as a result of the identified risks (for example, by reallocating resources). Product management must, for instance, observe the market with regard to existing and planned, competing systems.

Need for coordination

In requirements engineering, project management, and product management the context of the system should be observed from different perspectives. Since these perspectives are not completely disjoint, the observation of the context should be coordinated (see Example 30-1). If the stakeholders responsible for the management activities in requirements engineering detect changes in the system context they have to communicate the identified changes to the project management and, if applicable, also to product management.

Example 30-1: Coordination of context observation

In the SoftwareCar42 company, observation of the market with respect to competing systems is the responsibility of product management. Product managers inform the responsible requirements engineers about new systems or new system releases brought to the market by competitors. The requirements engineers analyse the properties of these systems in detail and provide a summary of their analysis results to the product managers.

30.5 Managing the Requirements Engineering Activities

Goal of this activity

For the requirements engineering process, no fixed sequence of activities can be defined that ensures the fulfilment of the goals of requirements engineering outlined in Section 4.4. The management of the requirements engineering activities therefore aims to monitor, control, and adjust the planned workflow of elicitation, documentation, negotiation, and validation activities. To achieve this, techniques known from project management are applied.

Phase-oriented approach vs. situative approach

We distinguish between two basic approaches for managing the requirements engineering activities: a phase-oriented approach and a situative approach. Whereas in the phase-oriented approach the same sequence of activities is applied to all requirements artefacts, the situative approach determines the activities to be executed next based on an assessment of the current status of the existing requirements artefacts. We elaborate on the two approaches in the following subsections.

30.5.1 Phase-Oriented Approach

Performing the activities sequentially

In the phase-oriented approach, the requirements engineering activities are embedded in a waterfall-based process model with feedback loops and are thus executed, in principle, in sequential order. The phase-oriented approach is applicable, for example, if the requirements for the system (or a subsystem) to be developed are, to a large extent, identical to the requirements of a previous project.

Feedback loops in the sequential order

Figure 30-2 depicts a phase-oriented model which defines a sequential order for executing the requirements engineering activities. As shown in the figure, this model includes the three core requirements engineering activities and the validation activity and defines the order of execution of these activities. Moreover, the model includes feedback loops which enable the stakeholders to decide, during the execution of an activity as well as at the end of an activity, if the current phase (activity) should be continued, the next phase should be entered, or a return to an earlier phase is required.

For instance, if during validation a major gap in a requirement (or set of requirements) is detected, the elicitation phase, the documentation phase, and the negotiation phase must be performed again (for a subset of the requirements artefacts) in order to close the detected gap.

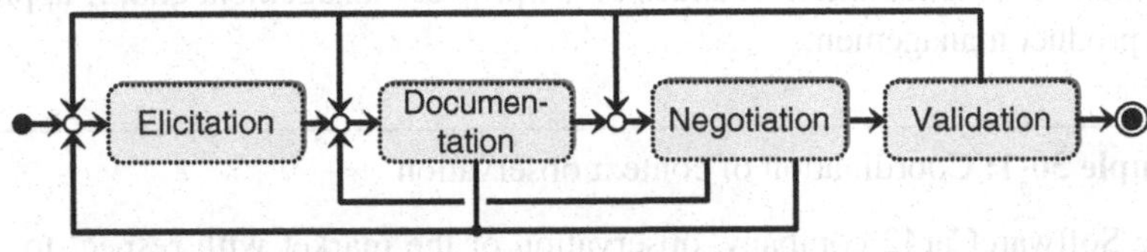

Fig. 30-2 *Sequence of phases including feedback loops*

Sequential Execution of the Four Activities

Elicitation

First, the stakeholders elicit the requirements that are relevant for the system. The main sources for the elicitation are the requirements documents from previous projects (note: the phase-oriented approach is only applicable if the requirements for the system are to a large extent identical to the requirements developed in past projects). Besides, new requirements can be elicited, for instance, with the help of goals and scenarios. During this phase, requirements management provides appropriate structures for recording the elicited requirements and for performing the activity. For instance, it provides the facilities for assigning the elicited requirements to individual requirements engineers. The elicitation phase ends when the stakeholders have established sufficient understanding of the requirements for the system, i.e. when all requirements for the system have been elicited.

Documentation and specification

After the elicitation phase has been completed, the requirements engineers document (specify) the requirements according to the project-specific rules (see Section 16.2). Following the project-specific documentation rules ensures that the requirements are specified in the appropriate formats needed to support further development activities. This phase ends when all elicited requirements are documented in the correct formats defined by the project-specific documentation and specification rules. If, during the documentation of the requirements, gaps in the elicited requirements are detected, the elicitation phase is entered again, e.g. after all known requirements have been documented.

Negotiation

After documenting the requirements, the requirements engineers check whether all relevant stakeholders agree with the documented requirements. If a conflict is detected, the conflict should be resolved. During conflict resolution, it might become clear that a previous phase (elicitation or documentation) should be re-executed in order to establish a better basis for negotiation. For example, if a conflict exists because a requirement source has been overlooked during elicitation, the elicitation activity should be performed again. Or, if the cause of a conflict is the use of an inappropriate documentation format, the documentation activity should be performed again. Prior to leaving the negotiation phase, agreement about all documented requirements should be checked.

Validation

After successfully completing the negotiation phase, the documented and agreed requirements are validated. The validation of the requirements artefacts considers the three validation aspects of content, documentation, and agreement (see Section 27.3). Validation is the last phase prior to release of the requirements. If defects are detected during validation, the elicitation, documentation, or negotiation phases are re-executed depending on the types of defects detected.

After all requirements have successfully passed the validation phase, the process ends. The sequential execution of the activities in the process outlined above is, of course, only possible for well-understood domains and systems, i.e. it is only possible if the majority of the requirements are already known and have been defined before.

In all other cases, the situative approach described in the next subsection is recommended. The phase-oriented approach is, for example, inappropriate whenever a (part of) the system should realise innovative solutions, or if there is no previous experience in developing very similar products.

30.5.2 Situative Approach

Evaluation and planning for a coherent set of artefacts

In contrast to the phase-oriented approach, in the situative approach, the decision regarding which activity is executed next is based on assessment of (a set of) requirements artefacts. In other words, the activity executed next depends on the status of the requirements artefacts (i.e. a single requirements artefact or a homogeneous subset of artefacts such as a set of system goals with associated interaction scenarios) and the current process situation.

Controlling the path through the three dimensions

The situative approach aims to determine the sequence of requirements engineering activities that leads to as favourable as possible a path through the three dimensions of content, agreement, and documentation. In other words, the situative approach aims to prevent the requirements engineers from performing activities that lead to little or no (real) progress. For instance, one should avoid a sequence of activities in which the stakeholders obtain only vague understanding of the requirements and reach little agreement about the requirements but put much effort into the documentation of the requirements (e.g. in order to satisfy the documentation and specification rules). Given the fact that there is only vague understanding and almost no agreement, the documentation effort is most likely wasted.

Evaluation of Requirements Artefacts

Evaluation with regard to three quality aspects

In order to determine the successor activity for a particular requirements artefact (or set of artefacts) in a specific project situation, application of the evaluation scheme presented in Tab. 30-1 is suggested. According to this scheme, the requirements artefacts are evaluated with regard to the three quality aspects (content, agreement, and documentation; see Section 27.3). For each requirements artefact (or set of artefacts), the stakeholders involved in the evaluation process assign one of the three values to each quality dimension:

- "+" – no deficiencies
- "0" – minor deficiencies
- "–" – major deficiencies

Key evaluation criteria

The evaluation criteria ("+", "0", "–") are specified more precisely in Tab. 30-1. To assess the current status of the requirements artefacts in a project, specification of the criteria in more detail by taking into account project- and product-specific characteristics is recommended. For example, more detailed criteria might be defined for assessing appropriate consideration of the context or conformance with specific documentation and specification goals. A more detailed definition of the criteria facilitates more precise evaluation.

Tab. 30-1 *Evaluation criteria for requirements artefacts*

	+	0	–
Content Sample criteria: (1) Completeness (2) Unambiguousness (3) Currentness	The artefact meets the defined criteria.	The artefact does not satisfy some of the defined criteria.	The artefact does not meet a significant part of the defined criteria.
Documentation/ specification Does the documentation/ specification of the requirement comply with the given documentation/ specification rules?	The artefact adheres to the defined documentation/ specification rules.	The artefact violates some of the defined documentation/ specification rules.	The artefact violates a significant number of the defined documentation/ specification rules.
Agreement	Agreement about the artefact is established, i.e. no unresolved, known conflict exists.	There are relevant, unresolved conflicts about the artefact.	There is no agreement about the artefact (either unknown status or significant open conflicts exist).

Basis for decision making

The evaluation scheme supports more objective evaluation of the current status of a requirements artefact. Nevertheless, the evaluation of a requirements artefact is influenced by the stakeholders' individual goals, preferences, and experiences. Therefore, if different stakeholders evaluate the same requirements artefact, the evaluation results often differ from each other. The product manager can, for example, approve the release of a requirements artefact while the requirements engineer suggests performing further elicitation activities. The evaluation scheme suggested in Tab. 30-1 helps in partially eliminating the personal preferences and thus supports the stakeholders' joint decision about the activity to be performed next.

Determining the Activity to Be Performed Next

Heuristics for determining the successor activity

Based on the evaluation of a requirements artefact (or set of artefacts) with respect to the three quality aspects (content, agreement, and documentation), a fairly objective selection of the activity to be executed next can be made. Table 30-2 suggests, for each triple of possible evaluation results, the activity to be executed next.

The suggestions in Tab. 30-2 were derived on the basis of the following rules:

1. If the requirements artefact has no obvious deficiencies in all three dimensions (content, documentation, and agreement), a validation activity is performed.
2. A significant deficiency in one dimension has a higher priority than a minor deficiency in another dimension.
3. A minor deficiency in one dimension has a higher priority than no deficiency in another dimension.
4. In case of equal evaluations in several dimensions, the content dimension has priority over the documentation dimension, and the documentation dimension has priority over the agreement dimension.

Tab. 30-2 *Determining the activity to be executed next based on the evaluation results*

Content	Documentation	Agreement	Subsequent Activity
+	–	–	Documentation
+	–	0	Documentation
+	–	+	Documentation
+	0	0	Documentation
+	0	+	Documentation
0	–	–	Documentation
0	–	0	Documentation
0	–	+	Documentation
–	–	–	Elicitation
–	–	0	Elicitation
–	–	+	Elicitation
–	+	–	Elicitation
–	+	0	Elicitation
–	+	+	Elicitation
–	0	–	Elicitation
–	0	0	Elicitation
–	0	+	Elicitation
0	+	0	Elicitation
0	+	+	Elicitation
0	0	0	Elicitation
0	0	+	Elicitation
+	+	–	Agreement
+	+	0	Agreement
+	0	–	Agreement
0	+	–	Agreement
0	0	–	Agreement
+	+	+	Validation

Rationale for the fourth rule

The fourth rule results from the consideration that eliciting additional content entails documentation and negotiation activities. Therefore, if in doubt about which activity to execute next, one should try to improve the understanding of the requirements, i.e. its content, first. If the documentation and agreement dimension have equal evaluations, the documentation dimension takes priority over the agreement dimension, since appropriate documentation supports the detection of conflicts. The detection of conflicts may even be infeasible if the requirements are not documented accordingly.

30.5.3 Comparison of Phase-Oriented and Situative Approach

Same sequence of activities applied to all requirements

The phase-oriented approach assumes that the requirements engineering activities are (basically) executed sequentially. Thus, at a specific point in time a single requirements engineering activity is performed. Flexibility is typically limited to the decision, how long this specific activity shall be performed and if a previously performed activity (phase) has to be re-executed. An evaluation with regard to all three quality aspects (content, agreement, and documentation) is only performed in the last phase, the validation activity.

Fine-grained planning of activities

In contrast to the phase-oriented approach, the situative approach facilitates considerably more flexible and fine-grained planning and execution of the requirements engineering activities. The situative approach considers individual requirements artefacts (or coherent sets of requirements artefacts) and defines, depending on the current situation, the activities to be executed next. An evaluation of the artefacts regarding the three quality aspects is performed whenever necessary. The situative approach thus supports a more iterative approach to developing the requirements artefacts for a system or subsystem.

The situative approach should be applied in case of frequent, rapid changes, when innovative requirements have to be developed and/or the stakeholders are unfamiliar with the system type or context. The situative approach typically leads to a slight increase of resource requirements for planning and coordinating the activities.

Chapter 31
Requirements Traceability

In this chapter, we describe:

- *The fundamentals of requirements traceability*
- *The importance of traceability for development projects*
- *The pre- and post-traceability of requirements*
- *Five classes of traceability relationship types with a total of 20 relationship types*
- *Different ways of visualising traceability information*
- *The necessity for and the fundamentals of project-specific traceability*

K. Pohl, *Requirements Engineering*,

31.1 Fundamentals of Traceability

An essential task of requirements management is to support the traceability of requirements throughout the entire development process.

The Term "Traceability"

Traceability of development artefacts

According to [IEEE Std 610.12-1990] traceability denotes, in general, the degree to which a relationship can be established between different development artefacts, especially artefacts having a predecessor–successor– or master–subordinate–relationship to one another.

Requirements traceability

A requirement is considered to be traceable if the origin of the requirement as well as its further use in the development process can be traced (see [IEEE Std 830-1998; Edwards and Howell 1992; Hamilton and Beeby 1991; Gotel and Finkelstein 1994; Pohl 1996b]). A prerequisite for the traceability of requirements throughout the development process is that each requirement has a unique identifier. We adopt the following definition of requirements traceability from [Gotel and Finkelstein 1994]:

D

Definition 31-1: *Requirements traceability*

"Requirements traceability refers to the ability to describe and follow the life of a requirement, in both a forwards and backwards direction (i.e. from its origins, through its development and specification, to its subsequent deployment and use, and through all periods of on-going refinement and iteration in any of these phases)."

[Gotel and Finkelstein 1994]

Motivation for Requirements Traceability

Recorded requirements traceability information supports various system development activities. For example, an impact analysis of a requirements change depends on the quality of the recorded traceability information. Table 31-1 provides some examples of the use of requirements traceability information in different system development activities (see, e.g., [Pohl 1996a; Ramesh 1998]).

Traceability as an indicator of the maturity of system development

The quality of the traceability information influences the quality of the system developed. Establishing a sophisticated traceability approach is therefore an important aspect of maturity models such as CMMI [CMMI 2006] or SPICE [Van Loon 2004; Hörmann et al. 2006].

Tab. 31-1 *Examples of using traceability information during system development*

Aspect	Use of traceability information
Verifiability and acceptance	Traceability supports the validation that a requirement was considered (correctly and completely) during the implementation of the system (see e.g. [Pinheiro and Goguen 1996]). Validating the (correct and complete) implementation of requirements supports the acceptance of the system, since it provides evidence that the stakeholders' requirements have been implemented in the system.
Gold plating	By using traceability information, functions or qualities of the system can be uncovered that were not specified in the requirements and, therefore, have no justification. The development and integration of such functions and qualities is referred to as gold plating. In the same way, requirements with no justification for their existence can be uncovered.
Change management	Traceability allows for analysing, in the case of a change, which other artefacts (e.g. requirements, components, or test cases) are affected by a change (see [Edwards and Howell 1992]). Furthermore, traceability information supports the prediction of the effort required for integrating the change.
Quality assurance, maintenance, and repair	Traceability facilitates the identification of the causes and the impact of errors, the identification of parts of the system affected by an error, and the prognosis of the effort required for correcting the error (see [Brown 1987]).
Re-engineering	Traceability supports the re-engineering of legacy systems by relating the functions of the legacy system to the requirements for the new system and by documenting which components of the new system realise these requirements.
Reuse	Traceability supports the reuse of development artefacts related to a requirement. When a (set of) requirement(s) is reused in the new system, the corresponding artefacts which realise this requirement(s) in the old system can be identified. These artefacts are potential reuse candidates and can be checked for whether they require adaptation or if they can be reused without adaptation.
Project traceability	Traceability information supports tracing the project and the current project status. Analysis of the recorded traceability information facilitates, for instance, determining which requirements have already been considered/implemented in the system architecture or which ones have even been implemented and tested.
Risk management	Traceability between requirements and other artefacts (e.g. components) supports risk management by facilitating the identification of development artefacts that are potentially affected by a risk or threat.
Accountability	Traceability information can be used to assign development effort to individual requirements. This enables, for example, determining the development effort of a specific stakeholder for a particular (set of) requirements artefacts (see e.g. [Cordes and Carver 1989]).
Process improvement	Traceability supports process improvement. Traceability information can be used to trace problems in the development process back to their causes. The planning and execution of improvement actions can thus be directed towards eliminating the actual causes of problems.

31.2 Pre- and Post-traceability of Requirements

As depicted in Fig. 31-1, we differentiate between requirements pre- and post-traceability (see [Gotel and Finkelstein 1994]).

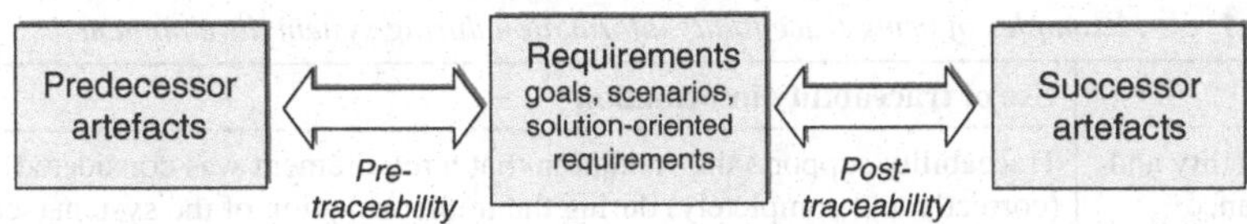

Fig. 31-1 *Pre- and post-traceability of requirements*

Predecessor and successor artefacts

Pre-traceability denotes the traceability of a requirements artefact to its predecessor artefacts. In other words, pre-traceability ensures the traceability of a requirement to its source or origin. Post-traceability denotes the traceability from a requirement to its successor artefacts, such as architectural components satisfying the requirement, the implementation of the requirement in the source code, or the test cases verifying the requirement. Post-traceability hence ensures the traceability from the requirements to, for example, design and implementation artefacts.

Extended Pre- and Post-traceability

Traceability among different types of requirements

Extended pre- and post-traceability structures the pre- and post-traceability of requirements into traceability among requirements artefacts and predecessor/successor artefacts and traceability among different types of requirements artefacts such as goals, scenarios, and solution-oriented requirements (see Fig. 31-2).

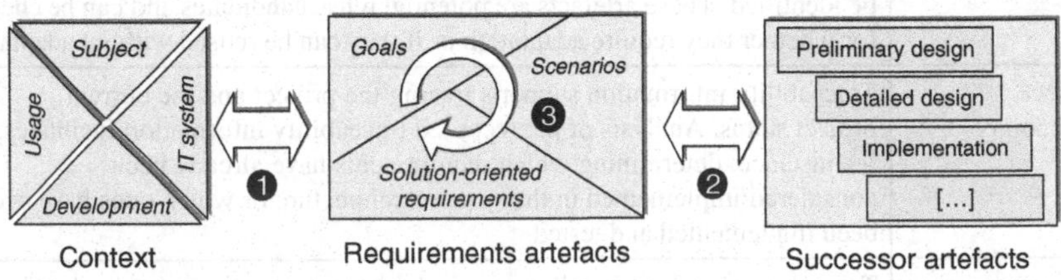

Fig. 31-2 *Extended pre- and post-traceability of requirements*

Traceability to context aspects

Pre-traceability of requirements (❶) comprises relationships from requirements artefacts (i.e. goals, scenarios, and solution-oriented requirements) to aspects in the four context facets. For example, it includes the traceability relationships from a requirements artefact to its source in one or more context facets (see Fig. 31-3 for an example).

Traceability to the realisation

Post-traceability of requirements (❷) comprises relationships between the requirements artefacts and their successor artefacts. For example, it includes traceability relationships between a requirements artefact and a class defined in the detailed design.

Traceability among requirements artefacts

In addition, extended pre- and post- traceability of requirements includes traceability among different requirements artefacts (❸), for example, between a goal and a set of scenarios that illustrate the satisfaction of the goal. Figure 31-4 depicts an example of traceability between different requirements artefacts as well as traceability between requirements and design artefacts.

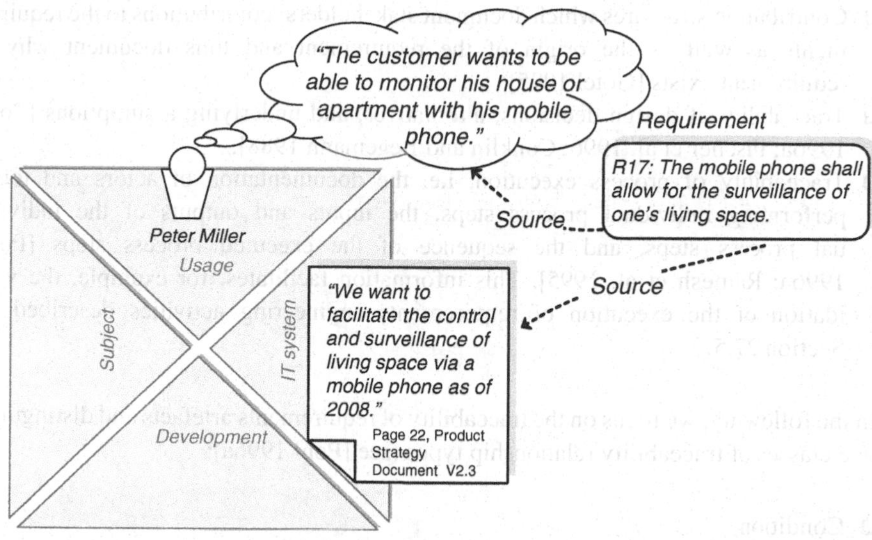

Fig. 31-3 *Example of pre-traceability of a requirement*

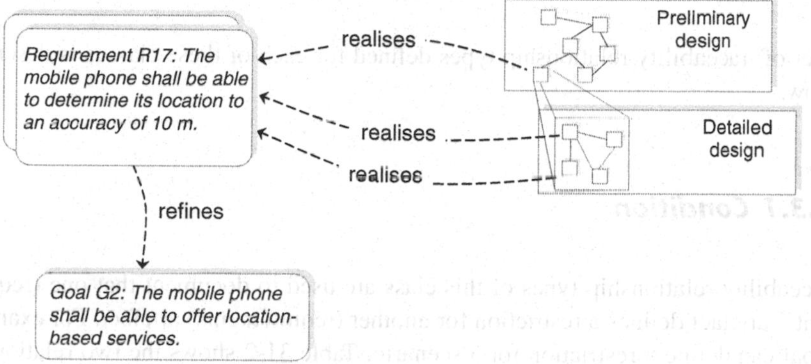

Fig. 31-4 *Example of post-traceability of requirements and traceability between requirements*

31.3 Traceability Relationship Types

Traceability information is often recorded in the form of traceability relationships. Between two development artefacts different types of traceability relationships (traceability links) can exist. For example, an artefact may refine another artefact, or an artefact may contradict another artefact.

In the literature, several suggestions for traceability relationship types have been made (see e.g. [Davis 1990; Gotel and Finkelstein 1994; Pohl 1996a; Thayer and Dorfmann 2000]). For example, one can distinguish between the following basic types of traceability (see [Dömges and Pohl 1998]):

- Traceability between requirements artefacts and successor artefacts such as derived requirements or architectural components [Pohl 1996a; Ramesh et al. 1995; Ramesh and Jarke 2001].

- Contribution structures which document stakeholders' contributions to the requirements as well as the origin of the requirement and thus document why a requirement exists [Gotel 1995].
- Traceability of design decisions, alternatives, and underlying assumptions [Pohl 1996a; Fischer et al. 1996; Conklin and Begemann 1988].
- Traceability of process execution, i.e. the documentation of actors and tools performing individual process steps, the inputs and outputs of the individual process steps, and the sequence of the executed process steps [Pohl 1996a; Ramesh et al. 1995]. This information facilitates, for example, the validation of the execution of requirements engineering activities described in Section 27.5.

Classes of traceability relationship types

In the following, we focus on the traceability of requirements artefacts and distinguish five classes of traceability relationship types (see [Pohl 1996a]:

- Condition
- Content
- Abstraction
- Evolution
- Miscellaneous

A set of traceability relationship types defined for each of these classes is described below.

31.3.1 Condition

Restriction of artefacts

Traceability relationship types of this class are used to document that one (requirements) artefact defines a restriction for another (requirements) artefact. For example, a goal can define a restriction for a scenario. Table 31-2 shows the two relationship types of the class "condition". The different relationship types are depicted in the column "relationship type" in Tab. 31-2. The column "description" contains a succinct description of each relationship type.

Tab. 31-2 *Traceability relationship types of the class "condition"*

Relationship type	Description
constraint	A relationship of this type from an artefact A to an artefact B documents that artefact A defines a constraint on artefact B. For example, a solution-oriented requirement can be constrained by another solution-oriented requirement.
precondition	A relationship of this type from an artefact A to an artefact B documents that artefact A defines a condition that must be fulfilled before artefact B can be realised. For example, the precondition for realising a functional requirement might be that the hardware meets a specific performance requirement.

31.3.2 Content

Dependencies between the contents of the artefacts

Traceability relationship types of this class are used to document dependencies between the content of the associated requirements artefacts or between requirements artefacts and other artefacts in the development process. A traceability relationship type of this class can be used, for example, to document a conflict relationship between two goals. For example, a conflict relationship can be introduced between two documented goals to document that satisfying one goal excludes the satisfaction of the other goal. Table 31-3 presents the four traceability relationship types of the class "content" and gives a brief description.

Tab. 31-3 *Traceability relationship types of the class "content"*

Relationship type	Description
similar	A relationship of this type documents that the two associated artefacts are similar in content.
compares	A relationship of this type between an artefact A_1 and a set of artefacts $A_2 \ldots A_n$ documents that A_1 represents the result of a comparison of the artefacts $A_2 \ldots A_n$.
contradicts	A relationship of this type between two artefacts documents that the two artefacts cannot be realised together. A "contradicts" relationship between two solution-oriented requirements thus indicates an inconsistency in the requirements artefacts.
conflicts	A relationship of this type from an artefact A to an artefact B documents that the realisation of A may hinder (but does not necessarily exclude) the realisation of B. In contrast to the "contradicts" relationship type, this relationship type does not hence (necessarily) document an inconsistency.

31.3.3 Abstraction

Abstraction dependencies between artefacts

This class comprises traceability relationship types that represent abstraction dependencies between requirements artefacts. Relationship types of this class can be used to document, for example, that a goal classifies a set of solution-oriented requirements or that an abstract scenario (e.g. a type scenario) is a generalisation of a set of more concrete scenarios (e.g. instance scenarios). Table 31-4 presents the three traceability relationship types of this class.

Tab. 31-4 *Traceability relationship types of the class "abstraction"*

Relationship type	Description
classifies	A relationship of this type between an artefact A and a set of artefacts $B_1 \ldots B_n$ documents that A classifies $B_1 \ldots B_n$.
aggregates	A relationship of this type documents that an artefact A is an aggregation of a set of other artefacts $B_1 \ldots B_n$.
generalises	A relationship of this type documents that an artefact is a generalisation of (one or) several other artefacts.

31.3.4 Evolution

Temporal relationships between artefacts

Traceability relationship types of this class document a kind of temporal relation between requirements artefacts or between requirements artefacts and other development artefacts. A relationship type of this class can document, for example, that a solution-oriented requirement is based on a scenario, or that an architectural component satisfies a set of requirements. Table 31-5 presents the five traceability relationship types of this class.

Tab. 31-5 *Traceability relationship types of the class "evolution"*

Relationship type	Description
replaces	A relationship of this type from an artefact A (e.g. a requirements artefact) to an artefact B documents that artefact B was replaced by artefact A.
satisfies	A relationship of this type from an artefact A to an artefact B documents that, if artefact A is realised in the system, artefact B is realised as well. The "satisfies" relationship type can be used, for instance, to relate a component to a requirement, thereby documenting that the requirement is realised by the component.
based_on	A relationship of this type from an artefact B to an artefact A documents that artefact A has influenced the definition of artefact B.
formalises	A relationship of this type from an artefact A to an artefact B documents that A is a formal documentation of the artefact B. A relationship of this type can be used, for instance, to relate a solution-oriented requirements model to a set of textual requirements.
refines	A relationship of this type from an artefact A to an artefact B documents that A refines B, i.e. artefact A defines the artefact B in more detail.
derived	A relationship of this type is used to document that a requirements artefact A was derived based on a (set of) other artefacts.

31.3.5 Miscellaneous

The class "miscellaneous" comprises additional traceability relationship types that can be defined between development artefacts. Traceability relationship types of this class document, for example, the fact that a scenario documents a concrete, exemplary interaction sequence for a dynamic aspect of a set of solution-oriented requirements. Table 31-6 presents the six traceability relationship types belonging to this class.

31.3.6 Traceability Relationship Types: Example

Figure 31-5 depicts some schematic examples of using the traceability relationship types explained in Sections 31.3.1–31.3.4 for documenting relationships between textual requirements fragments and model-based requirements artefacts.

Tab. 31-6 *Traceability relationship types of the class "miscellaneous"*

Relationship type	Description
example_of	A relationship of this type documents that an artefact contains exemplary aspects of a set of artefacts. For instance, an "example_of" relationship can be used to relate an interaction scenario to a set of solution-oriented requirements. This relationship documents that the scenario documents an exemplary sequence of interactions that a system implementing the solution-oriented requirements will support.
verifies	A relationship of this type is used to relate an artefact (e.g. a test artefact) to a requirements artefact. The former is used to verify or validate the requirements artefact.
rationale	A relationship of this type documents that one artefact documents the justification of another artefact. For instance, a "rationale" relationship can be used to relate a text fragment to a scenario, thereby documenting that the text fragment contains a justification for the existence of the scenario.
responsible_for	A relationship of this type documents that a stakeholder (or a role) is responsible for the associated artefact. Such a relationship can be used to document, for example, that a specific stakeholder is responsible for a specific requirements artefact.
background	A relationship of this type is used to assign "background information" to a requirements artefact. For example, a document containing a standard may be related to a solution-oriented requirement, thereby documenting that the standard must be considered during the specification or realisation of the requirement.
comment	A relationship of this type can be used to relate any kind of information to a requirements artefact. Use of this relationship type should be sparingly and really only if none of the other relationship types fits.

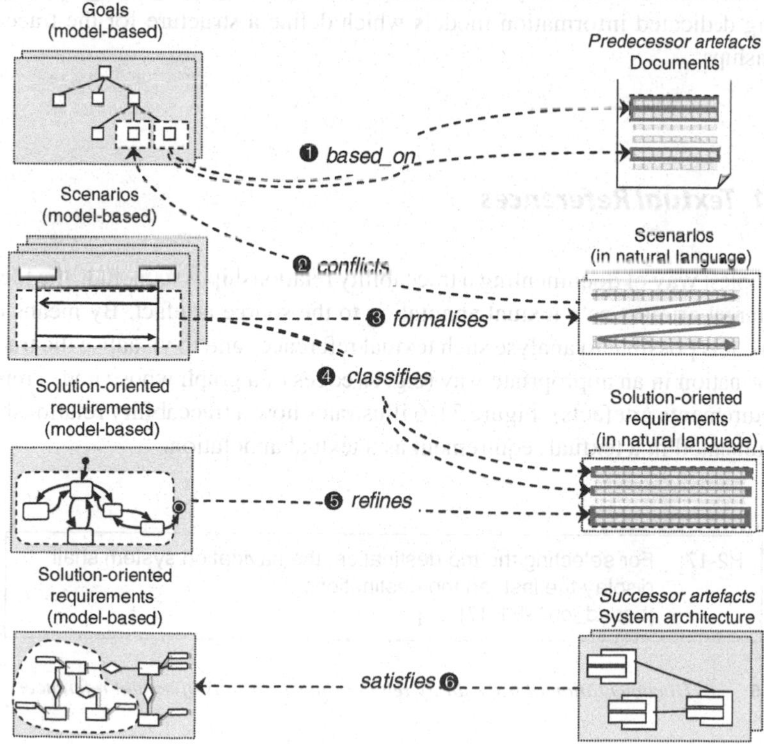

Fig. 31-5 *Examples of using the traceability relationships types*

The traceability relationships depicted in Fig. 31-5 are explained below:

❶ The traceability relationship with the label "based_on" documents that the associated goal is based on the text fragments of a predecessor artefact (e.g. fragments of the minutes of the interview).
❷ The traceability relationship with the label "conflicts" documents that a conflict between the textual scenario and the goal definition exists.
❸ The traceability relationship with the label "formalises" documents that the model-based scenario formalises the associated textual scenario.
❹ The two relationships labelled "classifies" between the model-based scenario and the associated textual, solution-oriented requirements document that the solution-oriented requirements are classified by the scenario.
❺ The traceability relationship labelled "refines" documents that the statechart (i.e. a model-based, solution-oriented requirement) refines the associated textual requirement.
❻ The traceability relationship labelled "satisfies" documents that the depicted fragment of the solution-oriented requirements model is realised if a specific component in the system architecture is realised.

31.4 Documenting Traceability Relationships

Traceability relationships can be documented in different ways. Besides the simple textual annotation, traceability relationships can be documented using hyperlinks or by using dedicated information models which define a structure for the traceability relationships.

31.4.1 Textual References

The simplest way of documenting a traceability relationship is to include the identifier of the target artefact as a textual annotation to the source artefact. By means of text analysis, it is possible to analyse such textual references and to visualise the traceability information in an appropriate way (e.g. as edges of a graph whose nodes represent the requirements artefacts). Figure 31-6 illustrates how a traceability relationship can be documented in a textual requirement as a textual annotation.

R2-17:	For selecting the trip destination, the navigation system shall display the last ten trip destinations. [based_on→R1-17] [...]

Fig. 31-6 *Documentation of traceability relationships by means of textual references*

31.4.2 Hyperlinks

Traceability relationships can also be documented by using hyperlinks. To document a traceability relationship, a hyperlink from the source artefact to the target artefact is created. Different types of traceability relationships can be documented by defining different hyperlink types. During traceability analysis, the hyperlinks may be visualised, for example, as edges of a graph.

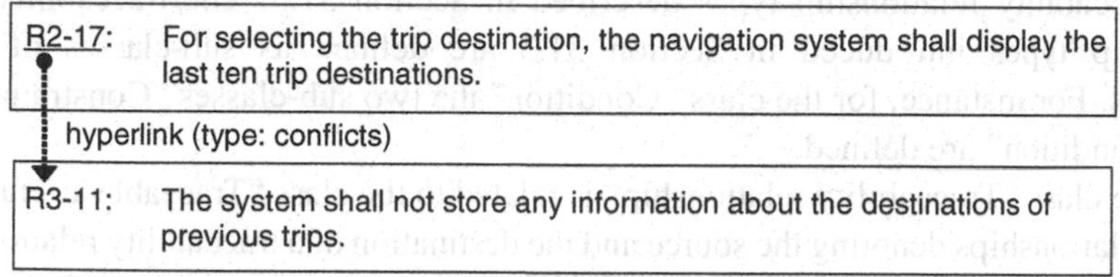

R2-17: For selecting the trip destination, the navigation system shall display the last ten trip destinations.
hyperlink (type: conflicts)
R3-11: The system shall not store any information about the destinations of previous trips.

Fig. 31-7 *Documentation of traceability relationships by means of hyperlinks*

31.4.3 Traceability Models

Traceability relationship types are used to relate different types of artefacts (see Section 31.3). Use of an information model to define and structure the traceability information and relationship types is recommended. Such a traceability information model defines, for a specific project, the traceability artefact types and the traceability relationship types between the artefact types to be used in this project. Furthermore, such a model can define cardinalities for the relationship types as well as specialisation relationships between different relationship types and artefact types. Figure 31-8 depicts a simplified example of a traceability information model.

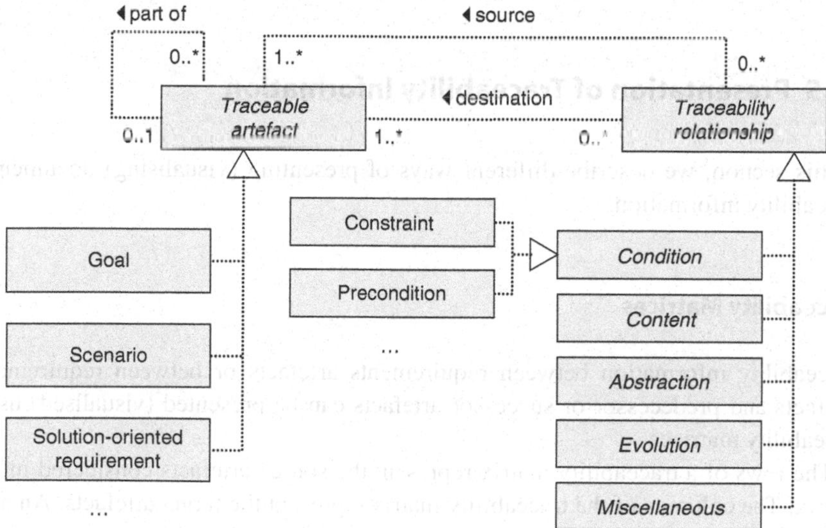

Fig. 31-8 *Simplified traceability information model*

Traceable artefacts

The information model shown in Fig. 31-8 defines an abstract class "Traceable artefact" specialised by various artefact types to be used in the project. Three specialisations are depicted in Fig. 31-8, namely "Goal", "Scenario", and "Solution-oriented requirement".

Traceability relationships

The class "Traceability relationship" is a super-class for all types of traceability relationships. It is specialised into the sub-classes "Condition", "Content", "Abstraction", "Evolution", and "Miscellaneous", denoting the different classes of traceability relationship types described in Section 31.3. The traceability relationship types introduced in Section 31.3 are defined as sub-classes of these classes. For instance, for the class "Condition" the two sub-classes "Constraint" and "Precondition" are defined.

Multiplicity of a traceability relationship

The class "Traceability relationship" is related to the class "Traceable artefact" by two relationships denoting the source and the destination of a traceability relationship. The cardinality defined in the model allows the definition of traceability relationships between sets of source artefacts and sets of destination artefacts. This can be restricted by defining more specific cardinality constraints for specific artefact types and/or traceability relationship types (see Chapter 20). For instance, a cardinality constraint could be defined which restricts all traceability relationship types defined between the class "Constraint" and the classes "Goal" or the class "Scenario" to a single instance of each class.

"Part-of" relationship between artefacts

Furthermore, the "part of" relationship of the class "Traceable artefact" enables the definition of part-of relationships between instances of the class "Traceable artefact". For instance, a class "Scenario step" and "Scenario" might be defined as sub-classes of "Traceable artefact". The class "Scenario step" might than be related to the class "Scenario" using the part-of relationship. Thereby, it would be possible to document that a scenario step is part of a scenario.

Development and use of a traceability model

In Section 31.6, we outline the creation of a project-specific traceability model based on project-specific usage strategies for traceability information and elaborate on the guidance to be provided for recording traceability information.

31.5 Presentation of Traceability Information

In this section, we describe different ways of presenting (visualising) documented traceability information.

Traceability Matrices

Traceability information between requirements artefacts or between requirements artefacts and predecessor or successor artefacts can be presented (visualised) using traceability matrices.

Traceability matrix for relationships of a single relationship type

The rows of a traceability matrix represent the source artefacts considered in this matrix. The columns of the traceability matrix represent the target artefacts. An artefact may be represented in the matrix, for instance, by its identifier. If a traceability relationship exists between the source artefact of row i and the target artefact of column j, cell (i, j) in the traceability matrix is marked. The type of traceability relationships documented in the matrix can be stated in the top left cell of the matrix. Figure 31-9 illustrates a simple traceability matrix for the traceability relationship type “satisfies”.

Target artefacts

Source artefacts

satisfies	Goal 1	Goal 2	Goal 3	Goal 4	Goal 5
Scenario 1	X				
Scenario 2				X	
Scenario 3					
Scenario 4			X		X
Scenario 5		X			

Traceability relationships

Fig. 31-9 *Traceability matrix for a single relationship type*

The traceability matrix in Fig. 31-9 documents “satisfies” relationships between scenarios and goals. A scenario is represented in a row of the traceability matrix, a goal in a column. An entry “×” in the matrix documents a traceability relationship of the type “satisfies” from a scenario to a goal; i.e. the existence of a “satisfies” relationship between a scenario i and a goal j is shown is depicted as a filled cell (i, j).

Traceability matrix for multiple relationship types

In addition, also different types of traceability relationships can be documented in a single matrix. Figure 31-10 illustrates such a traceability matrix. Instead of marks, the cells of the matrix contain the relationship types. For example, the “conflicts” relationship between “Scenario 2” and “Goal 2” is represented by the entry “conflicts” in column 2, row 2.

Target artefacts

Source artefacts

	Goal 1	Goal 2	Goal 3	Goal 4	Goal 5
Scenario 1	*satisfies*				
Scenario 2	*based_on*	*conflicts*		*satisfies*	
Scenario 3		*satisfies*			
Scenario 4	*conflicts*		*satisfies*		*satisfies*
Scenario 5		*satisfies*		*based_on*	

Fig. 31-10 *Traceability matrix for several relationship types*

In practice, due to the large number of requirements, the use of traceability matrices for visualising traceability information is limited.

Traceability Graphs

Traceability relationships as edges

In a traceability graph, the nodes represent artefacts and the edges represent traceability relationships between the artefacts. To distinguish different artefact types and/or different traceability relationship types, different types of nodes and edges can be introduced. Alternatively, an attribute can be assigned to each node and/or edge of the graph to denote the artefact or relationship types. Figure 31-11 illustrates the presentation of traceability information by means of a graph. In the traceability graph, a node type is defined for each type of requirements artefact (e.g. goal, scenario, solution-oriented requirement). In addition, three different relationship types, "based_on", "satisfies", and "example_of" (see Section 31.3), have been introduced.

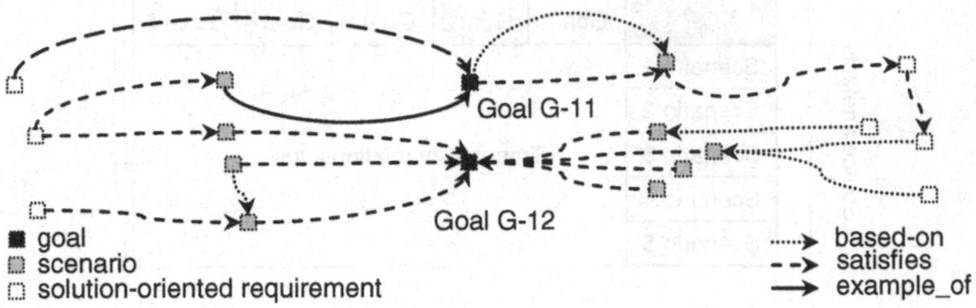

Fig. 31-11 *Representation of traceability information by means of traceability graphs*

Partial graphs

Based on the traceability graph, partial graphs may be derived. Such a graph can contain, for example, relationships of one specific type. Figure 31-12 depicts a partial graph derived from the graph in Fig. 31-11 that contains only the "satisfies" relationships between requirements artefacts.

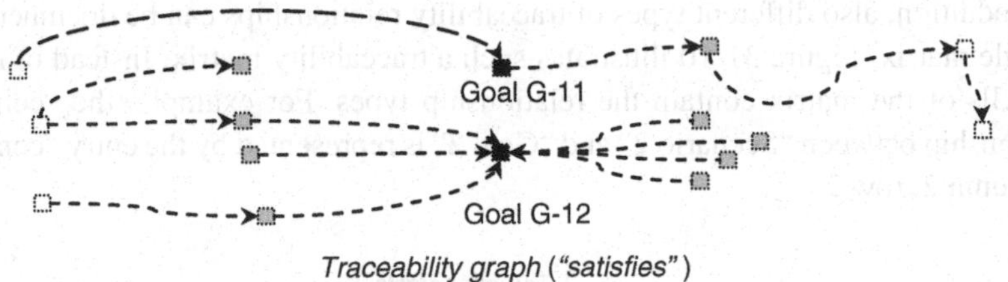

Fig. 31-12 *Partial graph derived from the graph in Fig. 31-11 showing "satisfies" relationships only*

Similarly, a specific artefact type (or set of concrete artefacts) can be used to derive a partial graph. For example, a sub-graph might show only the traceability relationships from Goal G-12 to all other artefacts.

Analysis of paths in a traceability graph

During traceability analysis, traceability graphs are often analysed along specific paths consisting of multiple nodes and edges. This kind of analysis reveals a path of artefacts (linked by traceability relationships) that logically belong together. Figure 31-13 shows a partial graph that has been derived from the graph in Fig. 31-11. This partial graph shows the traceability path for goal $G-12$ consisting of "satisfies" relationships.

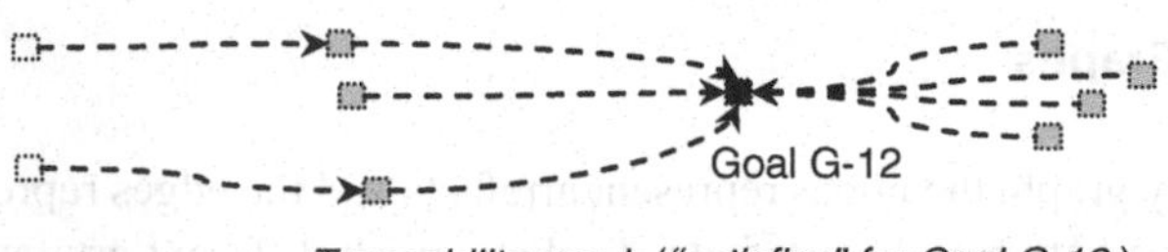

Fig. 31-13 *Traceability graph for goal G-12 consisting of "satisfies" relationships*

If relationships to predecessor artefacts (e.g. stakeholders and interview minutes) and successor artefacts (e.g. test cases and components) are also managed with the same tool, traceability graphs can be created for a requirements artefact which includes different artefact types. Even a complete traceability graph of the artefact over the entire lifecycle can be derived.

Common requirements management tools allow for choosing a search depth when creating traceability graphs. By choosing a depth of "1", only the immediate neighbours of an artefact are identified. If the depth is not restricted or a sufficiently large depth is chosen, the tool generates a complete traceability graph. Traceability paths are particularly important for change management. They are, among other things, the basis for impact analysis (see Chapter 33).

31.6 Project-Specific Traceability

Project-specific needs and constraints for recording traceability information

Recording and managing all traceability information that might potentially be of use in the further development process would require enormous resources. Recording all information is thus practically impossible. Therefore, for each project, a decision must be made regarding which traceability information should be recorded and maintained. This trade-off decision (which traceability information should be recorded and which information should not be recorded) has to take into account the resources (people, money, time) available for recording and managing traceability information. For recording and using traceability information, sophisticated strategies and guidelines should be provided in order to meet project-specific needs and constraints. In the majority of cases, the recording of traccability information without appropriate guidance leads to arbitrary accumulation of unstructured traceability information (see [Pohl et al. 1997; Dömges and Pohl 1998]).

Desired use determines the traceability information to be recorded

The project-specific traceability information to be recorded should be derived from the intended use of the traceability information and traceability constraints imposed by the organisation, the project, laws, the contract, standards or the like. For example, the customer might request that the developing organisation record the development effort needed to realise each customer requirement. This would require, among other things, an interrelation of each customer requirement with all the requirements and development artefacts derived from it as well as system maintenance artefacts such as change requests (see [Cordes and Carver 1989] for details). Furthermore, a certain law or standard could require that, for a safety-critical medical system, it must be possible to trace back each code fragment to the set of requirements realised by this code fragment.

31.6.1 Project-Specific Traceability Environment

Project-specific traceability environment

For defining and recording project-specific traceability information, different activities have to be performed. Figure 31-14 depicts a schematic structure of a so-called project-specific traceability environment which facilitates the definition, recording and use of project-specific traceability information.

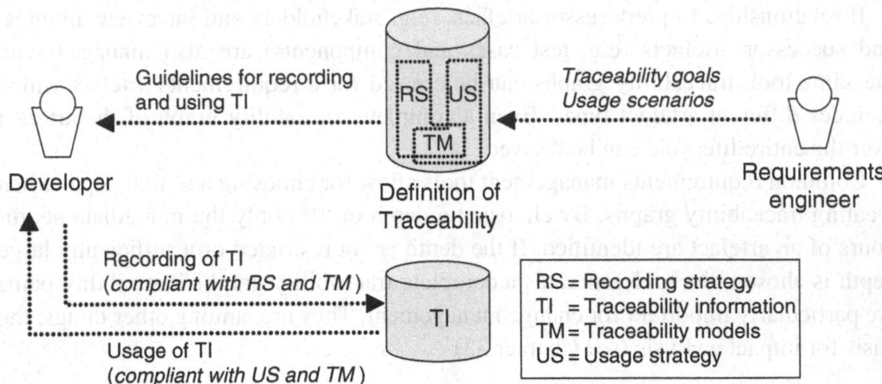

Fig. 31-14 *Scheme of a project-specific traceability environment (based on [Dömges and Pohl 1998])*

Traceability model (TM), recording strategy (RS), and usage strategy (US)

As illustrated in Fig. 31-14, the requirements engineer defines the project-specific traceability models (TM) as well as the strategies for recording (RS) and using (US) the traceability information during system development. The traceability information to be recorded (TM) is derived from the traceability usage strategies, i.e. for each type of traceability usage, the traceability information required for the particular usage is identified. The resulting traceability information required is then integrated into a coherent traceability model (TM).

Traceability information (TI)

During the development process, the members of the development team record the defined traceability information (TI) in compliance with the recording guidelines. The recorded traceability information (TI) is accessed within the development process according to the guidelines of the usage strategy. Similarly, the development team uses the defined traceability information according to the traceability usage guidelines (US).

Defining the project-specific traceability environment

To create a project-specific traceability environment, it is thus necessary to define the following elements:

- *Usage strategy*: The usage strategies define the intended use of traceability information during system development as well as during the whole lifecycle of the system. Each usage strategy requires a certain type of traceability information which is explicitly defined for each strategy. In other words, a usage strategy defines who should use which type of traceability information and when it should be used.
- *Traceability models*: The traceability models define the type of traceability information to be recorded. The type of information to be recorded is derived from the usage strategies defined for the project.
- *Recording strategy*: The recording strategy defines which type of traceability information has to be recorded for which activity and who is responsible for recording this type of information.

Goal- and scenario-based definition of project-specific traceability

Use of goals and scenarios to support the definition of project-specific traceability is recommended. Therefore, the stakeholders should first identify all relevant goals for recording traceability information. Subsequently, the stakeholders should define usage scenarios illustrating how the traceability goals are satisfied. The resulting traceability usage scenarios are analysed, among other things, in order to identify relevant types of traceability relationships. Example 31-1 illustrates the identification of traceability relationship types based on a usage scenario. The parts of the scenario that are relevant for the identification of traceability relationship types are underlined.

Example 31-1: Scenario-based definition of traceability

Traceability goal: The traceability environment shall facilitate the calculation of the development effort spent for each requirements artefact.

Usage scenario (simplified): The project manager selects the requirements artefact for which the actual development effort shall be determined using the requirements management (RM) tool. The RM tool identifies all classes that implement aspects of the selected requirements artefact. The RM tool calculates the total implementation effort of the identified classes by summing the implementation efforts of the individual classes. Subsequently, the RM tool identifies all test cases and change requests related to the selected requirements artefact. Based on the identified test cases, the RM tool calculates the total test and correction effort that can be attributed to the implementation of the selected requirements artefact. Based on the identified change requests, the RM tool identifies all changes to the selected requirements artefact and calculates the total effort for the adaptation of the associated components and classes. Finally, the RM tool calculates the actual development effort for the selected requirements artefact by summing the total implementation effort, the total test and correction effort, and the total adaptation effort determined for this artefact.

Required traceability relationship types:

- class – satisfies – requirement
- component – satisfies – requirement
- test case – verifies – requirement
- requirement – based_on – change request

In the following, we briefly explain the definition of project-specific usage strategies for traceability information (Section 31.6.2), the definition of a project-specific traceability model based on the usage strategies (Section 31.6.3), the definition of recording strategies to collect and record the required traceability information (Section 31.6.4) as well as guidance offered to the stakeholders for recording and using traceability information (Section 31.6.5).

31.6.2 Usage Strategies for Traceability Information

After defining the goals for using the traceability information (e.g. to support change requests), the stakeholders define usage scenarios describing in which situation traceability information should be used and how it should be used. The usage scenarios are then condensed into so-called usage strategies which define the intended use of traceability information during system development. Since the usage strategies lay the foundation for identifying the traceability information that needs to be recorded and maintained, usage strategies should be defined right at the beginning of the project. Moreover, if the usage strategies are defined later on, the traceability information recorded so far will most likely provide insufficient support for the intended usage strategies. A usage strategy should define (see [Dömges and Pohl 1996]):

- In which situation (When?)
- Which traceability information (What?) is used
- By whom, i.e. which role or agent (Who?)
- For performing which activity (For what?)

Example 31-2 shows the documentation of a single aspect of a usage strategy in natural language.

Example 31-2: Extract from a usage strategy

If a requirement is changed (When?), the requirements engineer who is responsible for the requirement (Who?) identifies which components are possibly affected by the requirements change in order to be able to estimate the effort for the integration of the requirements change. For the identification of the affected components (For what?) the recorded traceability information of the type "component – satisfies – requirement" (What?) is analysed.

Use of abstracted traceability information

Besides the recorded traceability information, abstractions (e.g. reduction, aggregation, or generalisation) derived from the recorded traceability information may also be used in a usage strategy. A simple example of an abstraction is the number of components that are affected by a requirements change. This information can be generated by aggregating the traceability relationships of type "component – satisfies – requirement".

31.6.3 Project-Specific Traceability Models

Definition of the traceability model

The traceability information required to fulfil the project-specific traceability usage strategies should be defined in a project-specific traceability information model.

For example, the usage strategy defined in Example 31-2 requires the recording of traceability relationships of the type "satisfies" between components and (solution-oriented) requirements. In addition, the strategy demands that, for each solution-oriented requirement, a responsible requirements engineer is assigned. Consequently this traceability information has to be defined in the project-specific traceability information model.

An excerpt of a project-specific traceability model which includes the information required for the usage strategy defined in Example 31-2 is depicted in Fig. 31-15.

Definition of traceability models based on a metamodel

A traceability metamodel defines the model elements to be used to define a project-specific traceability model. An example of a traceability metamodel can be found in [Ramesh et al. 1997]. A specific traceability model is created by instantiating the metamodel. The project-specific traceability models are thus instances of the traceability metamodel (see Section 19.5.2 for details on metamodels). Further

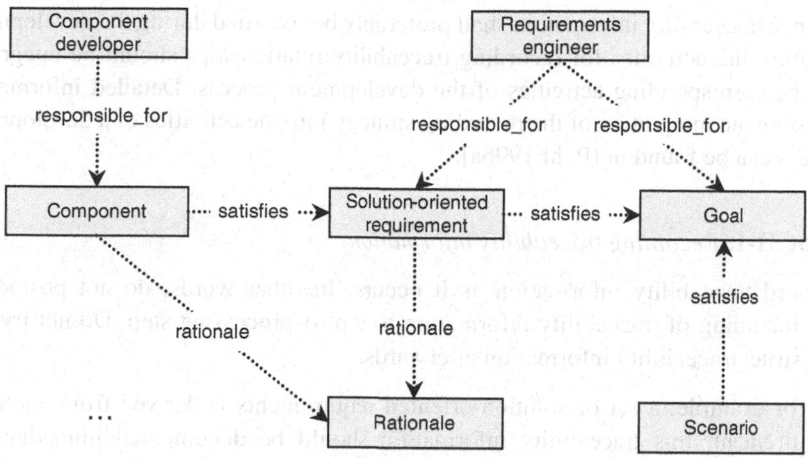

Fig. 31-15 *Simplified project-specific traceability model*

information about the project-specific definition of traceability models and the integration of the recording and usage of traceability information into process models can be found in [Pohl 1996a; Ramesh and Jarke 2001; Dömges and Pohl 1998].

31.6.4 Recording Strategies for Traceability Information

After defining the traceability information to be recorded and its structure (e.g. by means of a traceability model), project-specific strategies for recording the traceability information are defined depending on the objectives of the project and the available resources. A recording strategy determines (see [Dömges and Pohl 1998; Ramesh and Jarke 2001]):

- In which situation (When?)
- Which traceability information (What?) is recorded
- By whom, i.e. which role or agent (Who?)
- In which form (How?)

Documentation of the recording strategy

The different aspects of a recording strategy can be documented using natural language or using models (e.g. by means of an activity diagram or statechart). Example 31-3 shows the documentation of a single aspect of a recording strategy in natural language.

Example 31-3: Extract from a recording strategy

After a scenario has been documented (When?), the requirements engineer (Who?) responsible for this scenario documents the traceability relationship to the goal that is satisfied when executing the scenario (What?). The traceability relationship is recorded in the traceability module "scenarios × goals" using the traceability relationship type "scenario – satisfies – goal" (How?).

Integration of the recording strategy into existing process models

Since traceability information shall preferably be recorded during the development activities, the activities for recording traceability relationships should be integrated into the corresponding activities of the development process. Detailed information regarding the integration of the recording strategy into the activities of a development process can be found in [Pohl 1996a].

!

Hint 31-1: *Recording traceability information*

Record traceability information as it occurs. In other words, do not postpone the recording of traceability information to a post-processing step. Do not try to construct traceability information afterwards.

If, for example, a set of solution-oriented requirements is derived from another requirement, this traceability information should be documented immediately during the derivation.

If the information is recorded later, many aspects concerning the traceability information are no longer obvious, or documenting the traceability information is omitted because of other high-priority tasks.

31.6.5 Stakeholder Guidance

The project-specific traceability model and the project-specific recording and usage strategies lay the foundation for providing comprehensive guidance for recording and using traceability information within a development project. We distinguish two basic types of stakeholder guidance:

- ❑ Project-specific traceability handbook
- ❑ Process-integrated stakeholder guidance

Project-specific traceability handbook

The traceability information to be recorded (i.e. the traceability model) as well as the strategies for recording and using this information can be documented in a project-specific traceability handbook (see [Dömges and Pohl 1998]). In a training phase, the members of the development team first familiarise themselves with the traceability model and the recording and usage strategies defined in the handbook. During the development project, the team members apply the defined strategies. The traceability handbook then serves as a reference manual the team members can use to look up the relevant definitions while working on the project. However, using a project-specific traceability handbook does not guarantee that the traceability information is in fact recorded and used in compliance with the definitions.

Process-integrated traceability guidance

Ideally, a requirements engineering tool is available that supports process-integrated stakeholder guidance for recording and using traceability information (see [Pohl 1996a]). In this case, traceability information is recorded and used within the process steps (or development activities) executed in the process-integrated environment. Based on the traceability strategies, the process-integrated environment reminds the stakeholders about recording and using traceability information in the respective situations, i.e. the stakeholders are guided and supervised in recording and using the traceability information (see Fig. 31-16). Moreover, a large part of the traceability information can be derived from the execution of the process steps and can thus be automatically recorded by the environment (see [Pohl 1996a]).

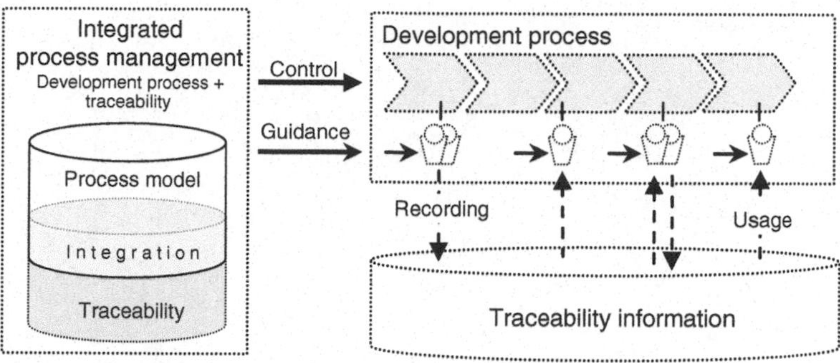

Fig. 31-16 *Process-integrated guidance of stakeholders (based on [Pohl 1996a])*

Example 31-4 illustrates the process-integrated guidance of a stakeholder based on a recording strategy for traceability information.

Example 31-4: Process-integrated guidance of stakeholders

Recording strategy: [...] For each goal bearing a high risk, decisions between alternative realisation possibilities shall be documented according to a predefined rationale structure. For each goal which bears a low risk, it is sufficient to record the corresponding decision in natural language.

Process-integrated guidance (documented as a scenario): During the development process, the stakeholder decides to choose one of several realisation possibilities for a high-risk goal. After documenting the realisation choice the requirements engineering tool executes the defined recording strategy and asks the stakeholder to document the rationale for this decision. Therefore it presents the predefined model to document the rationale. The stakeholder can decide whether to record this information right away or to create a task in his task list and record the information later on.

Detailed information regarding the process-integrated recording of traceability information can be found in [Pohl et al. 1996a].

Chapter 32
Prioritising Requirements

In this chapter, we describe:

- *The fundamentals of requirements prioritisation*
- *Four steps of requirements prioritisation*
- *Criteria for requirements prioritisation*
- *Five prioritisation techniques*
- *The selection and combination of prioritisation techniques*

32.1 Fundamentals of Requirements Prioritisation

Due to resource constraints and limitations (time, effort, people) typically not all requirements can be considered during system development with the same intensity and realised to the same degree. In order to ensure that the limited resources are used in a way that guarantees that as many important requirements as possible are realised as completely as possible, the documented requirements are typically prioritised. In other words, the requirements are classified into different priority classes which indicate the importance of a requirement depending on the prioritisation criteria.

We define the priority of a requirement as follows:

Definition 32-1: *Priority of a requirement*

The priority of a requirement documents the importance of the requirement with regard to one or several prioritisation criteria. The priority of a requirement may be determined either for each requirement in isolation or by pairwise comparison of requirements.

(Partial) ordering of the requirements

The result of the prioritisation is typically a (partial) ordering of the documented requirements with regard to the criteria considered during prioritisation (see Section 32.2.3). Each requirement is thus assigned to one priority class. Within the priority class no further ranking or order is defined.

Prioritisation in Requirements Engineering

Requirements are prioritised, for instance, to determine the order in which the requirements should be implemented, or to determine the order in which conflicts should be resolved during requirements negotiation. High-priority requirements are preferred over low-priority requirements in each of the requirements activities. For each of the five requirements engineering activities, the requirements can be prioritised as follows:

- *Elicitation*: During requirements elicitation, priorities can determine, for example, which requirements should be elaborated next or which requirement sources (e.g. stakeholders) should be considered first.
- *Documentation*: During requirements documentation, prioritisation can be used, for example, to determine an ordering in which the requirements shall be documented to satisfy the predefined documentation rules and formats.
- *Negotiation*: During negotiation, conflicting requirements can be prioritised, for example, with respect of their influence on the success of the project. The prioritisation can then be used to resolve the conflicts for the most important requirements first.
- *Validation*: In requirements validation, a prioritisation can be used, for example, to determine the order in which the requirements should be validated, to determine different intensities of validation for the requirements, or to define the order in which detected defects should be resolved.

- *Management*: Within management, prioritisation can be used, for example, for defining which change requests should be processed first, so that the most urgent changes are integrated first.

Prioritisation in release planning

In addition, requirements prioritisation is essential for many other activities, for example, in release planning. During release planning, the requirements documented for the system can be prioritised in order to define which requirements are implemented in the current system release and which ones are realised in later system releases.

32.2 Preparation Activities for Prioritisation

Four preparatory activities

Prioritisation of a set of requirements should always be directed by a clear goal and involve all relevant stakeholders (the customer, the project manager, the architect, the users, etc.). Therefore, the following four preparatory activities should be performed before defining the priorities for the requirements:

- Determine the stakeholders to be involved in the prioritisation of the requirements (see Section 32.2.1)
- Select the artefacts subject to the prioritisation (see Section 32.2.2)
- Define the prioritisation criteria for use (see Section 32.2.3)
- Select an appropriate prioritisation technique (see Section 32.2.4).

After completion of these activities, the priorities for the selected artefacts are defined, documented, and eventually checked for correctness.

32.2.1 Determining the Stakeholders

Goal- and criteria-based selection of stakeholders

To ensure that a prioritisation produces correct results, participation of all relevant stakeholders in the prioritisation process is important. The identification of the stakeholders to be involved in the prioritisation process is influenced, among other things, by the chosen prioritisation criteria.

Project and product managers

For instance, if one of the criteria is usability, a (group of) user(s) or user group representatives should be involved in the prioritisation activity. Or, if the prioritisation criterion is the strategic importance of a requirement for the market segment, the product manager should be involved in the prioritisation (see [Sommerville 2004]).

Building a team for performing the prioritisation

In general, at least one representative of the development team, one representative of the project management, one representative of the customer/users and one representative of the quality assurance team should be involved in the prioritisation of the requirements. These stakeholders have specific knowledge about the project context which must be considered during requirements prioritisation independently of the prioritisation criteria used. For example, the representative of the development team has specific knowledge about the technical restrictions and dependencies that are relevant for the realisation of requirements. The representative of the project management knows the project plan and project constraints (e.g. budget, personnel or time constraints). The representative of the customer or the users has detailed knowledge about the needs and wishes of the system users, and the representative of the quality assurance team has knowledge about the quality assurance and validation aspects.

32.2.2 Determining the Artefacts to Be Prioritised

Prioritise only artefacts of the same artefact type in one prioritisation activity

Three kinds of requirements artefacts can be differentiated (see Chapter 4), namely goals, scenarios, and solution-oriented requirements. For the latter, we further distinguish between data/structural, functional, and behavioural models. When selecting requirements artefacts for prioritisation, using only artefacts of the same artefact type is recommended, except if there is a very good reason for prioritising requirements of different types in one activity. For example, only goals or only behavioural requirements should be prioritised together.

Avoid prioritising requirements from different abstraction levels in one activity

Requirements (goals, scenarios, and solution-oriented requirements) are typically defined at different levels of abstraction (see Parts III and VII). According to several experiences, joint prioritisation of requirements defined at different abstraction levels often leads to erroneous prioritisation, since requirements at a higher abstraction level are typically assigned higher priorities by the stakeholders than corresponding requirements at a lower abstraction level (see [Yu 1995]).

For these reasons, prioritising (in the same prioritisation activity) only requirements artefacts of a single type that are, in addition, defined at an almost equal abstraction level is recommended. Determining which abstraction level is appropriate depends on the extent and complexity of the requirements (see [Berander and Andrews 2005]).

Prioritise high-level requirements, first

In practice, a proven strategy is to start with requirements artefacts at a high abstraction level such as goals. Requirements artefacts defined at lower levels of abstraction inherit the priorities of the higher-level requirements through the refinement relationships (e.g. from goals to sub-goals). If conflicts occur during the prioritisation of requirements, the related requirements at the lower abstraction level can be taken into account during the prioritisation. If the number of requirements to be prioritised is too large for the selected prioritisation technique (e.g. because the technique demands a pairwise comparison; see Section 32.3.6), the requirements may be divided into subsets and each subset may be prioritised individually. As an alternative, one may consider prioritising the requirements artefacts defined at a higher abstraction level first.

32.2.3 Selecting the Prioritisation Criteria

There are many possible criteria to be considered when prioritising requirements artefacts. For example, prioritisation can be used to determine the requirements to be realised next, or to determine the intensity of validation activities for requirements (e.g. with the values high, medium, and low intensity). In principle, the prioritisation goal indicates the criteria to be used for prioritising the requirements. Table 32-1 depicts a set of criteria which could be considered for prioritising requirements artefacts (see [Wiegers 1999; Lehtola et al. 2004; Berander and Andrews 2005]). Note that this table is not meant to be exhaustive.

Tab. 32-1 *Common criteria for the prioritisation of requirements artefacts*

Criterion	Explanation
Importance	The "importance" criterion of a requirement can consider different aspects, e.g. the urgency of implementing the requirement, the importance of the requirement for acceptance of the system, the importance of the requirement with regard to architectural design, or the strategic importance of the requirement with regard to the market position of the organisation.
Cost	The "cost" criterion refers to the financial resources that are needed to implement the requirement. These costs obviously depend on the complexity of the requirements artefact, the possible degree of reuse, or the extent of documentation and quality assurance activities associated with the requirement.
Damage	The "damage" criterion refers to the extent of the damage or disadvantage that would result from neglecting the requirement. The resulting damage can, for example, refer to contract penalties, to reduced sales potential of the system in the market or to loss of prestige.
Duration	The "duration" criterion refers to the time needed to realise the requirement. The duration explicitly considers possible parallelisation of development activities.
Risk	The "risk" criterion refers to the risk that is involved in realising the requirement. A risk is measured by the probability of its occurrence and the expected damage. When using the "risk" criterion, it is important to define as precisely as possible which risk is considered in the context of prioritisation, for example, the risk of exceeding the time schedule, the risk of not satisfying the customer, the risk of low system performance, or the risk of project failure.
Volatility	The "volatility" criterion refers to the probability of the requirement changing during the development process or system lifecycle. Requirements with high volatility typically increase the development cost, for instance, because the system architecture must be made flexible enough to accommodate future changes (see [Lauesen 2002; Sommerville 2004]). In addition, the effort required to integrate the changes may be considered. In this case, the combination of volatility and effort (i.e. the probability of a change and the expected "damage" caused by the change) defines a risk criterion.

Prioritisation based on one criterion

The simplest form of requirements prioritisation is prioritisation according to a single criterion. For example, requirements artefacts can be prioritised with regard to their importance for acceptance of the system. The effort required to perform a prioritisation according to a single criterion is typically low.

Prioritisation based on multiple criteria

If two or more criteria are considered during prioritisation, the required effort typically increases. For example, the prioritisation may be performed according to the criteria of importance and development cost. In this case, a specific requirement could have a very high importance but at the same time cause very high development cost. The final rank assigned to this requirement depends on how the two criteria of importance and development cost are weighted against each other. Such a weighting might depend on the available resources, the actual requirements ranked as "important" etc.

32.2.4 Selecting a Prioritisation Technique

Finally, the stakeholders must select the prioritisation techniques to be used for prioritising the selected requirements. Section 32.3 introduces different prioritisation techniques. Table 32-2 shows a coarse evaluation of the prioritisation techniques with regard to the prioritisation effort as well as the number and complexity of requirements to be prioritised.

Tab. 32-2 *Selection of prioritisation techniques*

Technique	Effort	Number and complexity of requirements: *Low number of requirements / low complexity of prioritisation*	*Large number of requirements / low complexity of prioritisation*	*Low number of requirements / high complexity of prioritisation*	*Large number of requirements / high complexity of prioritisation*
Ranking	low	★★★	★★★	★★	★
Top ten	very low	★★★	★★★	★★	★
One-criterion classification	low	★★★	★★	★★	★
Kano classification	low	★★	★★	★★★	★★
Wiegers' prioritisation matrix	medium	★	★	★★★	★★
Cost-value approach	high	★	★	★★★	★★

Estimation of effort required

The effort required for prioritisation using a specific prioritisation technique can generally be estimated only roughly. Among other things, the effort is influenced by the number of stakeholders involved, the degree of understanding of the requirements to be prioritised, the degree of agreement about the requirements, the prioritisation criteria used, and finally by the content defined in the requirements artefacts.

Prioritisation criteria supported

Besides the required effort, the prioritisation techniques presented in Tab. 32-2 and described in Section 32.3 differ in the underlying prioritisation criteria. The underlying prioritisation criteria of the prioritisation techniques can have a significant influence on the selection of a specific technique for a given prioritisation task.

32.3 Techniques for Requirements Prioritisation

Simple and advanced techniques

In most projects, simple ad hoc prioritisation techniques (e.g. ranking or classification) offer a pragmatic and, in many cases, sufficient approach for the prioritisation of requirements artefacts. If the ad hoc prioritisation gets too complex or if the risk associated with possibly wrong prioritisations is too high, sophisticated prioritisation techniques should be applied, e.g. techniques based on pairwise comparison.

Negotiation of priorities in the case of conflicts

Each prioritisation technique is (at least partially) based on the stakeholders' subjective judgements and evaluations. Conflicts concerning the priority of a requirements artefact (e.g. "How important is the requirement for the success of the system in the market?") should be resolved using negotiation techniques (see Chapter 26).

32.3.1 Ranking and Top-Ten Technique

Simple techniques for requirements prioritisation are, for example, the ad hoc ranking of requirements and the top-ten technique (see [Lauesen 2002]):

- *Ad hoc ranking*: When ad hoc ranking is applied, the requirements are ranked by individual stakeholders or by a group of stakeholders with regard to a chosen criterion such as risk.
- *Top-ten technique*: When the top-ten technique is applied a fixed number of requirements artefacts is selected (typically ten) as top-priority requirements artefacts. The selection is determined by a single selection criterion. Then, the selected requirements artefacts are ranked according to some criterion, for example, the importance of the requirements for the success of the system.

32.3.2 One-Criterion Classification

Prioritisation of requirements by classification according to IEEE Std 830-1998

A one-criterion classification prioritises requirements artefacts based on a single criterion. A common criterion for a single-criterion classification is the degree of necessity of a requirements artefact (see [IEEE Std 830-1998]). [IEEE Std 830-1998] suggests the following three priority classes for prioritisation with respect to the degree of necessity of a requirements artefact:

- *Essential*: Implies that the system will not be acceptable unless these requirements are fulfilled in an agreed manner.
- *Conditional*: Implies that these requirements artefacts would enhance the system, but would not make it unacceptable if they are absent.
- *Optional*: Implies a class of requirements artefacts that may or may not be worthwhile.

!

Hint 32-1: *Use of the IEEE classification (essential/ conditional/ optional)*

Practical experience shows that classification of requirements using the three priority classes essential/conditional/optional often results in an accumulation of requirements in the class "essential" while few requirements are assigned to the class "optional". Thus, application of the Kano classification is recommended in addition or even instead.

Using a different criterion

The approach for prioritising requirements artefacts presented above can also be used with a different prioritisation criterion. Possible prioritisation criteria are described in Section 32.2.3. After choosing the criterion (e.g. volatility), the stakeholders have to define a specific number of classes for this criterion (e.g. highly volatile, somewhat volatile, relatively stable, stable) together with a description of the characteristics that a requirement must have to be assigned to one of the defined classes (e.g. "relatively stable": the likelihood for a change is less than 10%).

If the requirements shall be prioritised using two or more criteria, a two- or *n*-criteria classification technique must be applied (see Section 32.3.4).

32.3.3 Kano Classification

[Kano et al. 1984] present an approach for classifying system features (or customer requirements) with regard to their effect on customer satisfaction. The evaluation and classification technique suggested by Kano is also well suited for prioritising requirements artefacts. The starting point of the Kano classification is the classification of system features (or requirements artefacts) into three classes (see [Walden 1993]):

- *Dissatisfier (also called a must-be requirement)*: A requirement is a dissatisfier if the system must realise this requirement to enable market entry.
- *Satisfier (also called a one-dimensional customer requirement)*: A requirement is a satisfier if the customers consciously demand the realisation of this requirement in the system. Satisfiers positively influence the degree of customer satisfaction, i.e. an increased amount of realised satisfiers generally results in increased customer satisfaction.
- *Delighter (also called an attractive requirement)*: A requirement is a delighter if the customers are not aware of this requirement or if they do not expect the realisation of the requirement in the system. Customer satisfaction increases disproportionately, if the system realises such a requirement.

Impact of requirements on the customer satisfaction

Figure 32-1 illustrates the impact of the level of fulfilment of dissatisfiers, satisfiers, and delighters on customer satisfaction (see [Kano et al. 1984]).

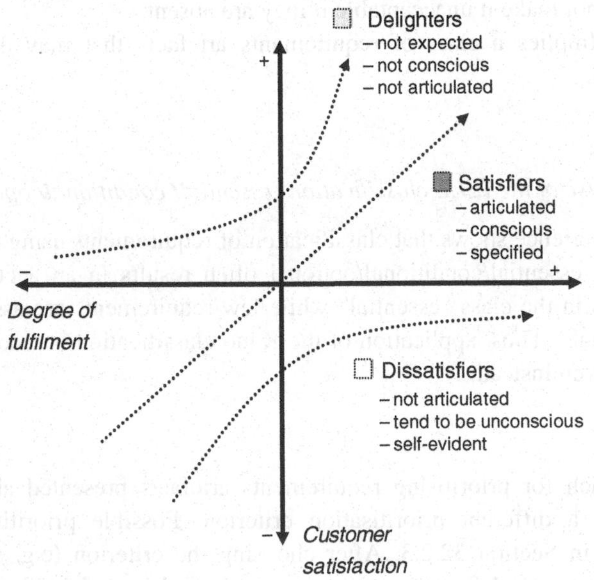

Fig. 32-1 *Effects of fulfilling different types of customer requirements on customer satisfaction*

Presence/absence of dissatisfiers

A high degree of fulfilment of requirements classified as dissatisfiers (must-be requirements) does not guarantee high customer satisfaction. However, a low degree of fulfilment of dissatisfiers considerably reduces customer satisfaction (see [Kano et al. 1984]).

Presence/absence of satisfiers

Customer satisfaction increases proportionally with the degree of fulfilment of requirements classified as satisfiers. A low degree of fulfilment of satisfiers reduces customer satisfaction, yet the effect is not as strong as in the case of dissatisfiers.

Presence/absence of delighters

The realisation of requirements classified as delighters leads to a disproportionately high increase in customer satisfaction. A low degree of fulfilment of delighters does not affect customer satisfaction negatively.

Over time, the classification of customer requirements according to the categories suggested by Kano evolves as illustrated in Fig. 32-2.

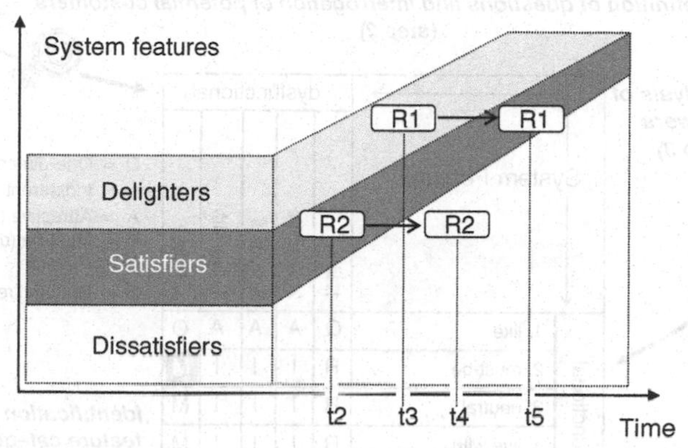

Fig. 32-2 *Change of requirements classification over time*

Evolution over time

As illustrated in Fig. 32-2, delighters (R1) become satisfiers and satisfiers (R2) become dissatisfiers over time. A delighter that initially fulfils a latent need of a customer and is maybe only offered in top-range products becomes a requested feature if, for example, the customers become well aware of the delighters and competitors on the market include the delighter in their products. For example, in the early 1990s the ABS system for car brakes was regarded as a delighter; nowadays it is almost a dissatisfier. Similarly, a satisfier becomes a dissatisfier over time. Details about the evolution of system features over time can be found in [Kano et al. 1984; Walden 1993].

Requirements classification according to Kano

The Kano approach suggests a systematic process for classifying system features (customer requirements):

- Step 1: Identify a set of system features to be classified.
- Step 2: Create a questionnaire containing a question for each system feature to determine how a potential customer would feel if (1) the feature is realised in the system (functional question) and (2) if the feature is not realised in the system (dysfunctional question).
- Step 3: Analyse the answers to the questionnaire and calculate the average values.
- Step 4: Identify the feature class of each system feature.

Figure 32-3 depicts a schematic process for classifying system features and associated requirements. After the system feature "integrated camera in the mobile phone" has been identified (step 1), the functional and the dysfunctional questions are defined and presented to potential customers, who answer the questions (step 2). After analysing the answers to the questionnaire (step 3), for each feature, the corresponding feature class is identified (step 4).

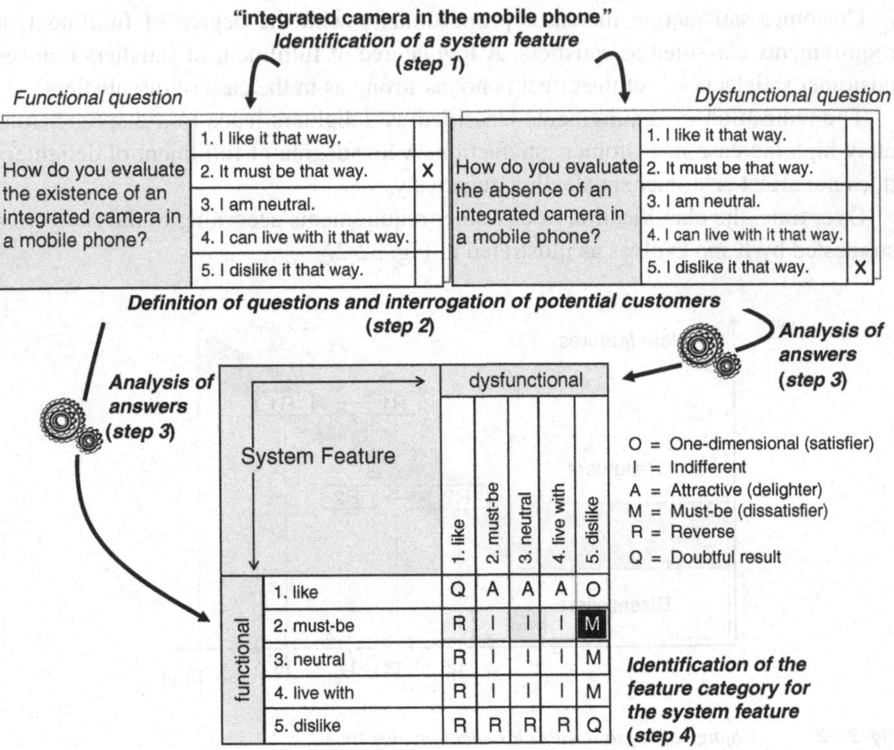

Fig. 32-3 *Schematic classification process according to Kano*

Alternatively, the classification may take place in a group session in which the relevant stakeholders are involved.

Requirements prioritisation based on the Kano classification

The classification of a system feature (or customer requirement) is inherited by the requirements artefacts that the system must realise in order to fulfil the system feature. Thereby, each requirements artefact is assigned to one of the priority classes "dissatisfiers", "satisfiers", or "delighters". The priorities can be used, for instance, in release planning in order to decide which requirements should be realised in which system release. In order to fulfil a specific system feature in a particular system release, all requirements associated with this feature must be realised in the corresponding release.

32.3.4 Two-Criteria Classification

Requirements prioritisation using two criteria

The one-criterion classification (see Section 32.3.2) can be extended to consider two or more prioritisation criteria. If two criteria are used and, for one criterion n classes are distinguished and for the other one m classes, the requirements artefacts to be prioritised can be classified into $n \times m$ priority classes. Figure 32-4 depicts possible priority classes of a two-criteria classification according to the criteria "urgency" and "risk regarding the acceptance of the system".

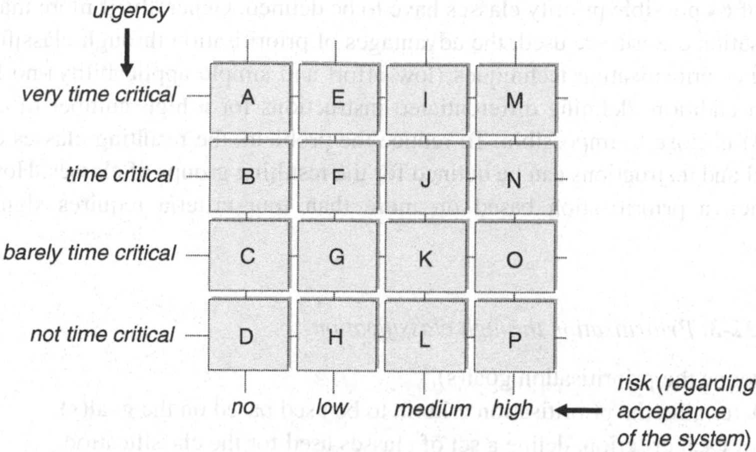

Fig. 32-4 *Example of two-criteria classification*

In the example depicted in Fig. 32-4, four prioritisation classes are defined for each prioritisation criterion. For the "urgency" criterion four classes are defined, namely "very time critical", "time critical", "barely time critical", and "not time critical". For the "risk" criterion, also four classes are defined, namely "high", "medium", "low", and "no". Each requirement to be prioritised is assigned to one of the classes of each criterion (i.e. in each dimension). The assignment of a requirement to a class can be performed ad hoc or, to some extent, analytically (e.g. risk score = probability of occurrence × extent of damage; "high risk": risk score > 100 etc.).

!

Hint 32-2: *Definition of the classes of a criterion*

When classifying requirements, stakeholders often assign the requirements preferably to the middle class. Moreover, classification often becomes unreasonably complicated if more than five classes are used. We therefore recommend defining four classes per criterion in order to avoid the "middle-class assignment" problem as well as too complicated a classification.

Definition of instructions for the priority classes

For each priority class, instructions are defined that determine how a requirements artefact assigned to this class should be treated. These instructions considerably support the stakeholders in their decision about the assignment of a requirement to a specific class. For instance, during release planning, a two-criteria prioritisation according to the scheme shown in Fig. 32-4 might be performed. Therein, for requirements artefacts categorised as "urgency: very time critical" and "risk: high" the following instruction is defined: "These requirements must be realised as early as possible depending on the available resources and they may only be realised by experienced developers."

Prioritisation of requirements using n-criteria

The two-criteria classification can be extended to an *n*-criteria classification (e.g. a four-criteria evaluation considering cost, urgency, risk, and loss). With an increasing number of criteria, the prioritisation of requirements requires more and more effort. If, for example, three criteria are used and four classes are defined for each criterion, a total of 64 possible priority classes have to be defined. Generally, if more than four prioritisation criteria are used, the advantages of prioritisation through classification over other prioritisation techniques (low effort and simple applicability) no longer hold. In addition, defining differentiated instructions for a high number of classes (e.g. 64) is close to impossible. To reduce the problem, the resulting classes can be grouped and instructions can be defined for the resulting groups of classes. However, even then a prioritisation based on more than four criteria requires significant effort.

!

Hint 32-3: *Prioritisation through classification*

(1) Define the prioritisation goal(s).
(2) Determine the prioritisation criteria to be used based on the goal(s).
(3) For each criterion, define a set of classes used for the classification.
(4) For each criterion and each class, define the characteristics that a requirement must have to be assigned to this class.
(5) For each priority class (i.e. each tuple of priorities for the different criteria), define instructions for how to deal with the requirements assigned to this priority class.
(6) Let the relevant stakeholders classify the requirements based on the defined criteria, classes, and instructions.

32.3.5 Wiegers' Prioritisation Matrix

An analytic process for the prioritisation of requirements was presented by [Wiegers 1999]. The prioritisation process considers four prioritisation criteria (see Section 32.2.3): benefit, penalty, cost, and risk. Requirements prioritisation is performed based on the assumption that the priority of a requirement is proportional to its benefit (if realised) and penalty (if not realised) and inversely proportional to the cost and the risk of the requirement.

Prioritisation matrix and process

The approach uses a prioritisation matrix to calculate the priorities of the requirements. The prioritisation process only leads to good results if the requirements to be prioritised are roughly defined at the same abstraction level and if no dependencies exist between the requirements. The process for calculating the requirements priorities using Wiegers' prioritisation matrix consists of nine steps:

- Step 1: Determine the weights of the four calculation parameters of benefit, penalty, cost, and risk. If the risk shall not be taken into account, the weight of this parameter is set to 0.
- Step 2: List all requirements to be prioritised in the prioritisation matrix.
- Step 3: Estimate the relative benefit of each requirement with regard to customer satisfaction or the achievement of business objectives. This value is documented for each requirement on a scale from 1 (lowest benefit) to 9 (highest benefit).
- Step 4: Estimate, for each requirement, the relative penalty that would occur, if the requirement were not realised in the system. The relative penalty is also measured on a scale from 1 (no penalty) to 9 (maximum penalty).

- Step 5: Calculate the value of each requirement based on the relative benefit (see step 3) and the relative penalty (see step 4) and the weights determined in step 1. The value of a requirement R_i results from applying the formula:

$$\text{Value}(R_i) = \text{Benefit}(R_i) \cdot \text{WeightBenefit} + \text{Penalty}(R_i) \cdot \text{WeightPenalty}$$

  After the value has been calculated for each requirement, the proportion of each value (value%) with respect to the sum of all values (i.e. the calculated total value), is determined.
- Step 6: Estimate, for each requirement, the relative cost related to the realisation of the requirement. The relative cost is recorded on a scale from 1 (low cost) to 9 (very high cost). Subsequently, for each requirement, the proportion of the cost (cost%) with respect to the calculated total cost is determined.
- Step 7: Estimate the relative risk of each requirement (e.g. with regard to technology, time planning, and market acceptance). The relative risk is recorded on a scale from 1 (no risk) to 9 (high risk). Subsequently, for each requirement, the proportion of the risk value (risk%) with respect to the calculated total risk is determined.
- Step 8: Calculate the individual requirements priorities based on the previously predicted and calculated values. The priority of a requirement R_i is calculated using the following formula:

$$\text{Priority}(R_i) = \frac{\text{Value\%}(R_i)}{\text{Cost\%}(R_i) \cdot \text{WeightCost} + \text{Risk\%}(R_i) \cdot \text{WeightRisk}}$$

- Step 9: Rank the requirements based on the calculated priority values in descending order. The requirements at the top of the list exhibit a promising relation between benefit/penalty and cost/risk. These requirements should therefore be considered first.

Structure of the prioritisation matrix

Figure 32-5 shows the structure of the prioritisation matrix and an exemplary calculation of requirement priorities using the matrix suggested by Wiegers.

Relative weight ①	2 (Weight Benefit)	1 (Weight Penalty)			1 (Weight Cost)		0,5 (Weight Risk)			
Requirement ②	Relative benefit	Relative penalty	Total	Value %	Relative cost	Cost %	Relative risk	Risk %	Priority	Rank
R1	5	3	13	16.8	2	13.3	1	9.1	0.941	1
R3	9	7	25	32.5	5	33.3	3	27.2	0.692	3
R3	5	7	17	22.1	3	20.0	2	18.2	0.759	2
R4	2	1	5	6.5	1	6.7	1	9.1	0.577	4
R5	4	9	17	22.1	4	26.7	4	36.4	0.489	5
Total	25	27	77	100	15	100	11	100		
	③	④	⑤			⑥	⑦		⑧	⑨

Fig. 32-5 *Exemplary calculation of priorities using Wiegers' matrix*

Determining the ranking of the requirements

The weights of the calculation parameters benefit (weight: 2), penalty (weight: 1), cost (weight: 1), and risk (weight: 0.5) lead to the priority values shown in the column "priority". Based on the priority values the ranks depicted in the column "rank" are assigned to the requirements.

32.3.6 Cost–Value Approach

Cost–value approach is based on AHP

The cost–value approach [Karlsson et al. 1997; Karlsson and Ryan 1997] is based on the Analytic Hierarchy Process (AHP), an approach for supporting decision-making proposed in [Saaty 1999]. The cost–value approach defines the following five steps for prioritising requirements:

- ❑ Step 1: The requirements engineers review the candidate requirements to ensure that the requirements are complete and clearly defined. *(Review of the requirements)*
- ❑ Step 2: Customers and users determine the relative value of each requirement using the pairwise comparison method of the Analytic Hierarchy Process (AHP). *(Relative value of each requirement)*
- ❑ Step 3: The relative cost of implementing each requirement is estimated by experienced software engineers using the pairwise comparison method of AHP. *(Relative cost of each requirement)*
- ❑ Step 4: The relative value and cost of each requirement is calculated using AHP. A cost–value diagram is created where the value is depicted on the *y*-axis and the cost is depicted on the *x*-axis. *(Cost-value diagram)*
- ❑ Step 5: The cost–value diagram is used by the stakeholders as a conceptual map for analysing and discussing the requirements. Based on the discussion, the requirements are prioritised and the decision regarding which requirements are implemented is made. *(Prioritisation of the requirements)*

Pairwise comparison

The pairwise comparison of the requirements applied in steps 2 and 3 can be briefly outlined as follows: Assuming there are n requirements to be prioritised, an $n \times n$ matrix is created. Each cell (i, j) of the matrix represents a pair of requirements (i.e. the pair consisting of requirement i and requirement j). For each pair of requirements, the stakeholders estimate the relative intensity (of cost or value) on a scale from 1 to 9. The semantics of the intensities of value are shown in Tab. 32-3.

Tab. 32-3 *Scale for a value-related pairwise comparison*

Relative intensity	Explanation
1	Of equal value – Two requirements are of equal value
3	Slightly more value – Experience slightly favours one requirement over another
5	Essential or strong value – Experience strongly favours one requirement over another
7	Very strong value – A requirement is strongly favoured and its dominance is demonstrated in practice
9	Extreme value – The evidence favouring one over another is of the highest possible order of affirmation
2, 4, 6, 8	Intermediate values between two adjacent judgments – When compromise is needed

Comparison matrix

For instance, if requirement R_2 is considered to have slightly more value than requirement R_3, the intensity value 3 (see Tab. 32-3) is entered in the matrix in the cell (R_2, R_3, see Tab. 32-4). In addition, the reciprocal intensity (1/3) is entered in cell (R_3, R_2). All cells on the main diagonal are filled with a 1, i.e. each requirement is considered to be of equal value compared with itself. The resulting matrix documents the relative intensity (with respect to value or cost) for each pair of requirements.

Tab. 32-4 *Comparison matrix*

	R_1	R_2	R_3
R_1	1	1/4	5
R_2	4	1	3
R_3	1/5	1/3	1

Estimation of relative cost/value of each requirement

To determine the total, relative value (or cost) of each requirement in AHP, the so-called principal eigenvector of the comparison matrix is determined. An easy way to obtain an estimation of the principal eigenvector is averaging over normalised columns (see [Karlsson and Ryan 1997]). First, each column of the matrix is normalised by dividing each cell by the sum of the values of the corresponding column. The principal eigenvector of the matrix is then estimated by calculating the average of each row. Therefore, the values in each row are summed, and the sum is divided by the number of requirements. The resulting vector defines the priority of each requirement regarding either cost or value.

For example, the priority vector of the comparison matrix shown in Tab. 32-4 is depicted in Tab. 32-5. In the example, requirement R_2 has the highest priority concerning the value of the requirements. The priority 0.58 of requirement R_2 means that R_2 represents 58% of the total value of all requirements. The priorities regarding cost are determined in the same way. However, for critical decisions, a more sophisticated (and more accurate) procedure for determining the principal eigenvector should be used (see [Saaty and Vargas 2001]).

Tab. 32-5 *Priority vector regarding the value of the requirements*

	R_1	R_2	R_3	Sum	Estimated priority vector
R_1	0.19	0.16	0.55	0.9	0.3
R_2	0.77	0.63	0.33	1.73	0.58
R_3	0.04	0.21	0.11	0.36	0.12

Cost–value diagram

After calculating the total relative value and the total relative cost of each requirement, the cost–value diagram is created. Figure 32-6 depicts the costs and values of an exemplary set of requirements (R_1 to R_8). Figure 32-6 also shows the resulting cost–value diagram for these requirements. In the example depicted in Fig. 32-6, the requirements R_1 and R_3 have a particularly high ratio of value to cost (cost–value ratio). If requirement R_3 is realised, already 26% of the total value of the requirements is achieved with only 9% of the total cost estimated to realise all requirements. The requirements R_4, R_5, R_6, and R_8 have a medium cost–value ratio that documents a balanced relation between cost and value. The requirements R_2 and R_7 have a low cost–value ratio. Compared with R_1 and R_3 these requirements have an adverse relation, since high relative cost is paired with low relative value. The realisation of

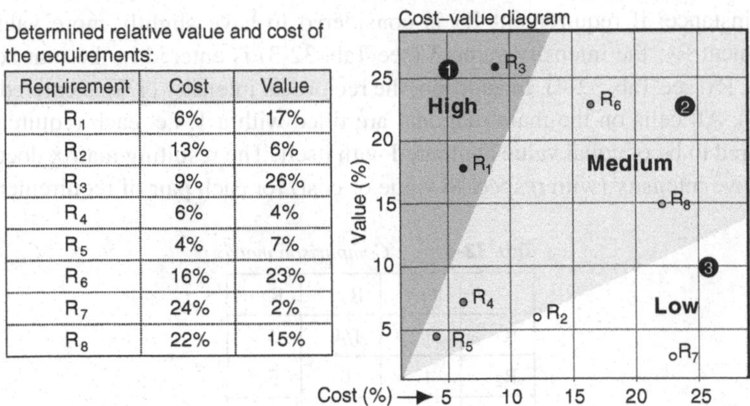

Determined relative value and cost of the requirements:

Requirement	Cost	Value
R_1	6%	17%
R_2	13%	6%
R_3	9%	26%
R_4	6%	4%
R_5	4%	7%
R_6	16%	23%
R_7	24%	2%
R_8	22%	15%

Fig. 32-6 *Exemplary cost–value diagram*

requirement R_7, for example, leads to the realisation of only 2% of the total value while it causes 24% of the total cost.

32.3.7 Combination of Prioritisation Techniques

Risk-based selection of a technique

In practice, often different prioritisation techniques are used complementarily when prioritising requirements (see [Lehtola and Kauppinen 2006]). For instance, the requirements may first be prioritised using an ad hoc technique. In a second step, the requirements for which the ad hoc classification implies a considerable risk of misclassification can be further prioritised using an analytic prioritisation technique (e.g. the cost–value approach).

The combination of different prioritisation techniques is especially appropriate if a large number of requirements have to be prioritised. During prioritisation in release management, the requirements may first be classified ad hoc with regard to their need for inclusion in the next release (e.g. "does not need to be included", "unsure if it should be included", "should be included", "must be included"). If all requirements classified as "must be included" are realised and there are still some resources left, the prioritisation matrix suggested by Wiegers may be applied to determine those requirements from the class "should be included" that shall be realised using the remaining resources.

Example of Combining Prioritisation Techniques

One popular approach often combined with other prioritisation techniques is the requirements triage (see [Davis 2003]). Originally, the requirements triage was developed especially for prioritisation within release planning. However, it can also be applied for other prioritisation tasks.

Goal of requirements triage

The requirements triage is adapted from the triage in medicine that was developed by a French physician during the Napoleonic wars (see [Simmons 2004]). The triage in medicine aims to classify casualties in order to use the available resources in an optimal way.

Classes in requirements triage

The requirements triage is based on a classification of requirements into three priority classes (see [Davis 1993]):

- Triage class I: The first class contains all requirements that must be realised in the next system release.
- Triage class II: This class contains all requirements which need not be realised in the next release.
- Triage class III: This class contains all requirements which, in principle, should be realised, but for which an analysis is required to determine which of them can be realised considering the available resources.

Prioritisation of triage class III requirements

In order to determine which requirements assigned to triage class III should be realised in the next release, the stakeholders typically prioritise these requirements using, for example, ad hoc techniques (e.g. ranking) or analytic prioritisation techniques (e.g. Wiegers' prioritisation matrix or the cost–value approach). [Davis 2003] suggests three simple strategies for determining which requirements of triage class III can be realised in consideration of the available resources:

- *Optimistic strategy*: This strategy assumes that all triage class III requirements can be realised in the next release. If the probability for this is too low, individual requirements are deferred to later releases until an acceptably low risk is obtained.
- *Pessimistic strategy*: This strategy assumes that no requirement can be realised in the next release. In this case, requirements are successively added to the current release until the risk is no longer considered to be acceptable.
- *Realistic strategy*: In this case, the stakeholders start with a specific set of requirements. Depending on the risk of whether the selected requirements can be realised in the next release, requirements are successively added or removed until an acceptable risk is achieved.

!

Hint 32-4: *Preparation of requirements prioritisation*

First identify the stakeholders to be involved in the prioritisation of requirements. To prepare the prioritisation itself, we suggest the following steps:

(1) Inform the stakeholders about the precise goals of the prioritisation, e.g. prioritisation of the requirements for planning the next two system releases.
(2) Determine the number of requirements to be prioritised.
(3) Select the prioritisation technique to be used (or set of techniques and the order in which they will be applied).
(4) Familiarise the stakeholders with the requirements. If the requirements are documented using a modelling language, explain the concepts of the modelling language. If the requirements have been documented using templates explain the slots of the templates to the stakeholders first.
(3) Explain the prioritisation technique to be used (e.g. classification). If the stakeholders are unfamiliar with the technique, use a simple example to explain the technique and train them in its usage.
(4) Define and communicate the meaning of the selected prioritisation criteria. If required, differentiate the selected criteria from other possible criteria.

Chapter 33
Change Management for Requirements

In this chapter, we outline:

- *The principles of configuration management in change management*
- *Causes of requirements changes and a template for documenting such changes*
- *The need for a systematic change management process and its key activities*
- *The role of the change control board*

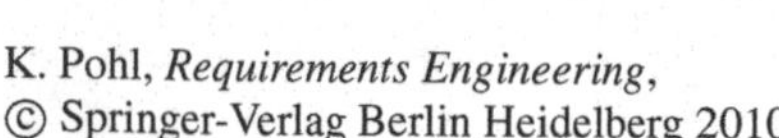

Throughout the system lifecycle, the requirements for the system may change. The task of change management in requirements engineering is to manage requirements changes and to ensure that each change is correctly implemented and traceable. Note, the implementation of a change is not the task of change management. In other words, change management analyses and decides about the changes and it controls the implementation of the changes, but it does not implement the changes.

33.1 Configuration Management

Two dimensions of configuration management

Configuration management can be characterised by two dimensions (see [Conradi and Westfechtel 1998]):

- *Product (artefact) dimension*: In the product dimension, configuration management considers artefacts of different types such as concrete goals, scenarios, and solution-oriented requirements.
- *Version dimension*: In the version dimension, version control (as part of configuration management) manages the different change states of the artefacts of the product dimension.

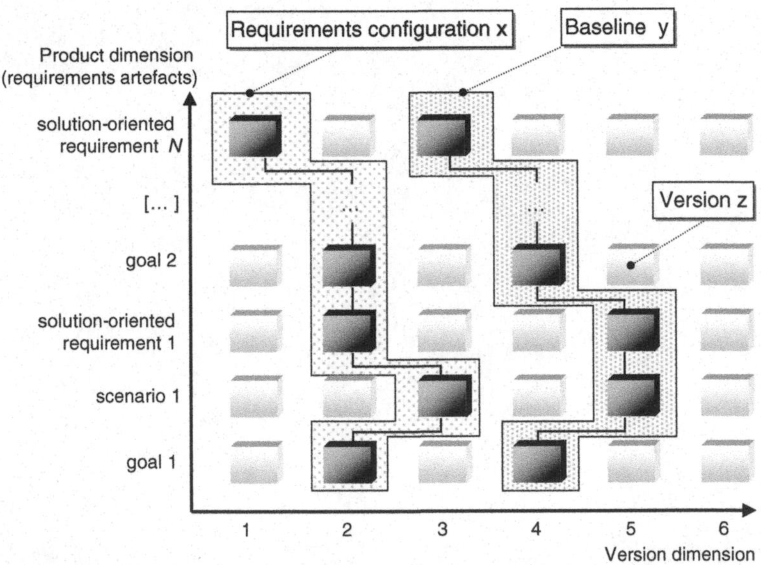

Fig. 33-1 *Requirements configurations (according to [Conradi and Westfechtel 1998])*

Figure 33-1 shows the two dimensions of configuration management. On the requirements axis, requirements artefacts of different types (i.e. goals, scenarios, and solution-oriented requirements) are considered. On the version axis, the different versions of each requirements artefact are considered. The terms "version", "configuration", and "baseline" used in Fig. 33-1 are explained in the following subsections.

33.1.1 Configuration Management Levels

Three levels of the configuration management of requirements artefacts

We distinguish between three configuration management levels for requirements artefacts:

- *Document level*: At this level, requirements documents are the smallest units to be considered in configuration management, i.e. configurations and versions of documents are created and managed.
- *Requirements artefact level*: At this level, requirements artefacts (e.g. goals, scenarios, solution-oriented requirements, and the relationships between the requirements artefacts) are the smallest units being managed, i.e. configurations and versions of individual requirements artefacts are created and managed.
- *Attribute level*: At this level, individual attributes of requirements artefacts (or set of attributes) are the smallest units considered in configuration management. Configuration management at the attribute level is typically not realised in practice due to the large amount and high complexity of the information.

33.1.2 Versions of Requirements Artefacts

Evolution of a requirements artefact in the three dimensions

A requirements artefact typically changes during requirements engineering, which can be explained along the three dimensions of requirements engineering (see Chapter 4). For example, a requirements artefact can be specified over time at increasing levels of detail (content dimension). Independently of that, each stakeholder may agree to a different extent with this requirement at different times; he may even revise his agreement (agreement dimension). Furthermore, the requirements artefact can be documented using different documentation formats (e.g. natural language or requirements models) and the documentation can vary over time with respect to compliance with different documentation and specification criteria (documentation dimension).

Requirements artefact versions

A version of a requirements artefact can be regarded as a defined state of a requirements artefact, i.e. a version of a requirements artefact freezes a particular state of a requirements artefact during the requirements engineering process.

Version and increment number

Each version of a requirements artefact is identified by a unique number. The unique numbering typically differentiates between the version number ("V-No.") and the increment number ("Incr-No."). For example, the identifier "3.12" indicates version 3 and increment 12 within version 3. In the case of a smaller change, the increment number is increased. In the case of a significant change, the version number is increased. Whenever the version number is increased, the increment number is reset to 0, i.e. each version starts with increment 0.

33.1.3 Configurations of Requirements Artefacts

A configuration of requirements artefacts comprises a set of related requirements artefacts, or more precisely, versions of requirements artefacts (see Fig. 33-1). A configuration of requirements artefacts has the following properties:

- *Consistency*: The versions of the requirements artefacts grouped together are consistent, i.e. the versions of the requirements artefacts included in the configuration are free of conflicts. For example, version 3.5 of requirements artefact 1 and version 3.9 of requirements artefact 5 are free of conflicts, or version 2.1 of scenario 13 refines version 5.4 of goal 8.
- *Unique identification (ID)*: A configuration has an identifier (ID) that identifies the configuration unambiguously.
- *Not changeable*: A configuration freezes a particular state. If any artefact that belongs to the configuration is changed, this results in a new artefact version which does not belong to the configuration. If this change should be included in a configuration, a new configuration has to be defined. In other words, changes of artefacts within a configuration are not allowed; the frozen state in a configuration cannot be modified. If necessary and appropriate, a new configuration can be created that includes the new artefact versions.
- *Basis for roll-back*: Configurations and their underlying artefact versions provide the basis for roll-back to previous states in the process. By roll-back to a former configuration (e.g. "requirements configuration *x*" in Fig. 33-1), a consistent state of the entire set of artefacts is restored, i.e. all changes performed after defining this configuration are eliminated. For example, such a roll-back can be required if changes to the requirements artefacts have led to inconsistencies which cannot be resolved by undoing individual changes.

33.1.4 Baselines of Requirements Artefacts

A requirements baseline is a selected configuration of requirements artefacts (see Fig. 33-1). The term "requirements baseline" refers to a configuration of stable requirements artefact versions. Typically a requirements baseline is realised in a particular system release. In contrast to an ordinary requirements configuration, a requirements baseline is typically visible to the customer.

Configuration vs. baseline

Since a requirements baseline is a specific requirements configuration, a baseline has all the above-mentioned properties of a requirements configuration. In addition, a baseline has the following properties:

- *Basis for the definition of system releases*: A requirements baseline typically defines the requirements artefacts that are realised in a system release, i.e. a version of the system delivered to the customer or made available to the market.
- *Visibility to the customer*: A requirements baseline is a requirements configuration that is typically visible to the customer.
- *Subject to change management*: The requirements contained in a requirements baseline cannot be changed arbitrarily. Typically, any change must first be approved in a change management process (see Sections 33.2 and 33.3). Note that, if a requirements artefact is changed, the new version of the artefact is not part of the baseline, i.e. a baseline is not changeable.

Use of requirements baselines in the development process

Requirements baselines support a number of important activities in the development process:

- *Basis for planning system releases*: Requirements baselines are configurations of "stable" requirements artefacts that are visible to the customer. Hence, baselines also serve as a basis for planning and defining systems releases.
- *Estimation of realisation effort*: A requirements baseline forms the basis for estimating the development effort required to realise a particular system release.
- *Comparison with competitors' products*: Requirements baselines are used for comparing the planned system release with competing systems on the market. Based on requirements baselines, the stakeholders compare the system features with the features offered by competing systems on the market at a specific time.

Requirements release vs. requirements baseline

In practice, the terms "requirements release" and "requirements baseline" are often used interchangeably.

33.2 Requirements Changes

Requirements change inevitably

Requirements change throughout the entire system lifecycle from "early" requirements engineering to system maintenance. Even if trying very hard, in many cases, requirements changes cannot be avoided.

Two main causes for changes

There are numerous causes for requirements changes. Among other things, one can distinguish between a change of a requirement that results from a problem encountered during system operation and a requirements change that results from a change in the system context (including the development of the system).

33.2.1 Problems Encountered During System Operation

Problems encountered during system operation can lead to requirements changes. For example, an inconsistency, a system error, or unsatisfactory system quality encountered during system operation (having its cause in the requirements and not in the realisation of the requirements) can lead to a requirements change. Example 33-1 illustrates such a change.

Example 33-1: Requirements change based on feedback from users

R-98: The navigation system shall calculate the estimated duration of a trip. To calculate the estimated duration of the trip, for motorways, an average speed of 120 km/h shall be used.

The feedback of many customers using the system clearly indicates that the estimated driving times are always too optimistic, i.e. in reality, a longer time is needed to reach the destination. To accommodate this feedback and to improve the system, requirement R-98 is changed. Now R-98 defines that the average speed on motorways shall be entered by the user of the system and can be changed by the user at any time.

33.2.2 Changes in the Context

Changes in the four context facets

Most requirements changes, however, stem from the system context and occur during the whole lifecycle of the system, including the development of the system itself. Examples of changes in the system context comprise the evolution of stakeholder needs, changes to laws, new technologies, additional products of competitors in the market as well as changes arising from problems encountered during system development (see Chapter 6).

Shift of the context boundaries

Changes in each of the context facets may result from changes in specific context aspects (e.g. changes in stakeholder needs and wishes or a new law which restricts the recording of personal data). In addition, an adaptation of the context boundaries (see Section 5.3) can cause such changes.

In the following, we provide some examples of contextual changes which lead to requirements changes for each of the four context facets (subject, usage, IT system, and development facet). A change can also have multiple causes, i.e. a change of a (set of) requirements artefact(s) can result from several changes in more than one context facet.

Changes in the Subject Facet

Changes of the objects represented in the system

Changes in the subject facet may result, for example, in the need to adapt the requirements artefacts defining the input or output data, i.e. the data provided as input to the system, stored, and processed by the system or provided as output by the system. Such changes may also affect the quality requirements defined for the system such as the data precision (see Section 6.3.1). Example 33-2 describes a change in the subject facet (here: precision of position data) that may require the adaptation of one or multiple requirements artefacts.

Example 33-2: Changes in the subject facet

The manufacturer of the digital roadmap that is used for the navigation system changes the format of the map data due to a newly introduced standard for storing geographic data. The new standard defines, among other things, new types of geographic objects. Consequently, the requirements artefacts of the navigation system related to reading and processing the map data must be adapted.

Changes in the Usage Facet

Changes of usage behaviour

Changes in the usage facet may cause changes to requirements concerning, for example, the usage of the system by stakeholders and other systems (see Section 6.3.2). For example, the interaction of the system with external actors (stakeholders or systems) may change, which requires an adaptation of the interaction patterns between the system and the external actors. Example 33-3 illustrates such a change in the usage facet that requires the adaptation of a (set of) requirements artefact(s).

> **Example 33-3:** Changes in the usage facet
>
> Clients demand that the navigation system additionally facilitates voice entry of the destination. Thus, requirements for speech recognition have to be defined and existing "input" requirements for the system have to be adjusted accordingly.

Changes in the IT System Facet

Changes of the technical environment

Changes in the IT system facet refer to the IT infrastructure or to the technical environment in which the system is embedded and executed (see Section 6.3.3). Changes in the IT system facet are in particular caused by technological progress and may also require changes and adjustments to the requirements artefacts. Example 33-4 describes a change in the IT system facet that may cause the adaptation of requirements artefacts.

> **Example 33-4:** Changes in the IT system facet
>
> The navigation system interacts with its technical environment (other electronic systems in the vehicle) via an in-vehicle network. The navigation system acquires the current speed and yaw rate of the vehicle via the network interface. As the car manufacturer decides to re-organise the in-vehicle network and use a new network standard, the requirements related to interactions of the navigation system with other electronic systems must be checked and adapted if necessary.

Changes in the Development Facet

Changes caused by development activities

The system development process also leads to changes to requirements artefacts. For instance, requirements changes may be required because it turns out during realisation that one or more requirement artefacts cannot be realised or contain inconsistencies, or a test activity (see Chapter 37) uncovers that some requirements cannot be tested. Example 33-5 describes a requirements inconsistency identified during the development process that leads to an adaptation of requirements artefacts.

> **Example 33-5:** Changes in the development facet
>
> R-17: In 98% of all cases, the system shall calculate and provide routing information to the destination in less than 1.3 s. Calculating and providing the routing information shall in no case take more than 2 s.
>
> R-34: The route calculated by the system shall in no case contain less than two waypoints per 10 km. For routes with a length of less than 10 km, one waypoint is sufficient.
>
> *(to be continued)*

Example 33-5 (*continued*)

During design, it becomes evident that the performance requirement R-17 and the precision requirement R-34 cannot be fulfilled at the same time, especially in the case of very long trips. This conflict prohibits realising the two requirements as originally specified and results in a change of the performance requirement R-17. Thus requirement R-34 is adjusted (not less than two waypoints per 10 km for trips <300 km; per 50 km for trips ≥300 km and ≤1,000 km; per 100km for trips >1,000 km.

!

Hint 33-1: *Analysis of context changes*

Make sure that context changes that were identified by management activities are checked for their impact on the requirements. If necessary, ask experts in the development team or domain experts to analyse possible impacts of an encountered context change.

33.3 Systematic Change Management

To deal with contextual, operational and requirements changes in general, a systematic change management process should be defined and established. A formal change management process is typically not required for early requirements engineering where requirements are elicited and gathered. However, for requirements belonging to a requirements baseline, a systematic change management process is a must.

In this section, we briefly elaborate on the role and tasks of a change control board (see Section 33.3.1), a template for documenting change requests (see Section 33.3.2), and the typical activities executed during a change management process (see Section 33.3.3).

33.3.1 Change Control Board

For deciding about requirements changes as well as the prioritisation of change integration, a change control board should be established. Especially in projects of a certain size, the constitution of a change control board as well as the definition of the responsibilities of the board is essential. However, even in small projects a formal change control board should be established. In extreme cases, a change control board could consist of just one representative of the client and one representative of project management or the development team. However, in each project it should be clearly defined who is responsible for deciding about change requests.

Tasks of the change control board

The change control board typically has the following responsibilities (based on [Wiegers 1999]), which are described in more detail in Section 33.3.3:

- *Classification of incoming change requests*: The change control board analyses each incoming change request and, based on the analysis, assigns the changes to different categories (e.g. corrective, adaptive, exceptional changes).

- *Effort estimation for change integration*: For each change request, the change control board estimates the effort required for integrating the change by conducting an impact analysis. If necessary, the effort estimation is commissioned to a third party.
- *Evaluation of change requests and decision-making*: The change control board evaluates the change requests, for example, with regard to the relation between effort and benefit. Based on the evaluation results, the change control board decides whether each change request is accepted or rejected.
- *Prioritisation of accepted change requests*: The change control board prioritises the change requests that have been accepted and assigns each request to a system release or a project in which the changes are to be integrated.

Stakeholders to be involved

Changes to the requirements artefacts should be agreed between the relevant stakeholders. It is thus important that, on the change control board, all relevant stakeholders and decision-makers are represented. Figure 33-2 depicts the members of a typical change control board, i.e. the stakeholder roles which should be represented on a change control board.

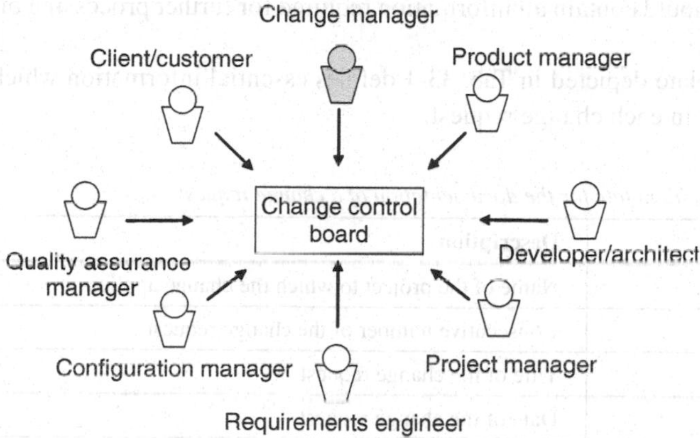

Fig. 33-2 *Possible composition of a change control board*

Change manager

The change control board is chaired by the change manager. In case of conflicts, the change manager tries to mediate between the parties involved. He is responsible for documenting the decisions made as well as for communicating the decisions and change integration activities to the corresponding stakeholders. Typically, the change manager is also responsible for monitoring change integration and reporting integration progress to the change control board. However, he may of course delegate parts of his responsibilities to other members of the change control board or other stakeholders.

!

Hint 33-2: *Composition of the change control board*

Take care that at least one stakeholder from each of the four context facets is part of the change control board. If you neglect a context facet, important aspects of this facet may not be considered during decision-making and, thus, wrong decisions might be taken which have to be adjusted later on.

(to be continued)

Hint 33-2 (*continued*)

When selecting the stakeholders for the change control board, take project specifics into account and introduce additional roles, or detail and/or specialise the roles depicted in Fig. 33-2.

In the case of a small project, you may even assign most of the roles to two or three stakeholders. However, we recommend that even in the case of small projects a systematic way of dealing with change requests is established. The change control board is a cornerstone of a systematic change process and should thus always be established.

33.3.2 Documenting Change Requests

Change requests for requirements artefacts should be documented in a way that supports decision-making by the change control board. Moreover, appropriate documentation should contain all information required for further processing of the change request.

The template depicted in Tab. 33-1 defines essential information which should be documented in each change request.

Tab. 33-1 *Template for the documentation of a change request*

Content	Description
Project name	Name of the project to which the change applies
Request no.	Consecutive number of the change request
Title	Title of the change request
Date	Date of the change request
Originator	Name of the originator
Origin	Origin of the change (e.g. marketing, management, customer, architectural design, and the context facet(s) from which the change originates)
Status	Current status of the change request (e.g. submitted, evaluated, rejected, to be integrated, verified, finalised)
Originator's priority	Priority of the change request (defined by the originator of the change)
Priority of realisation	Priority of the change request (defined by the change control board)
Verifier of the change	Name of the person responsible for verifying the change after its integration
Date of last update	Date of the last update of the change request
Release	Assignment to the release in which the change shall be integrated
Integration effort	Estimated effort required for change integration
Description of the change request	Textual description of the change request
Comments	Comments relating to the change request, e.g. from other stakeholders, the change control board, etc.

Management of change requests

The template for change requests shown in Tab. 33-1 defines the information that should be documented for each change request. Among other things, it contains information about the progress of processing the change request. For example, the "status" slot contains the current status of the change request or of the associated change. Since the information in the slots of a change request (such as the status) evolves during the change process, we recommend managing change requests in a (logically) centralised database providing access for all relevant stakeholders. Such a database shall ensure that all stakeholders obtain, at each point in time, the same, up-to-date information about the status and the content of a change request.

!

Hint 33-3: *Adaptation of the template for change requests*

The template for documenting change requests has to be adapted to match project- and organisation-specific needs. When adapting the template according to your specific needs, you might consider the attributes for requirements as well as the quality attributes described in Part IV.a.

33.3.3 Change Management Activities

Five kinds of changes

Change requests for requirements typically refer to requirements of an established requirements baseline (see Section 33.1.4). We differentiate five kinds of requirements change requests:

- *Integration of a new requirement*: A new requirement has been elicited and shall be integrated into the requirements baseline.
- *Removal of an existing requirement*: An existing requirements artefact is invalid and shall therefore be removed from the requirements baseline.
- *Extension of an existing requirement*: An existing requirement shall be extended by particular aspects, e.g. attributes neglected so far. These extensions shall be integrated into the requirements baseline.
- *Reduction of an existing requirement*: Some aspects of a requirement shall be removed. For example, particular inputs shall not be processed any more or outputs shall be omitted.
- *Change of an existing requirement*: A requirement is changed in a way that can be classified neither as a single extension nor as a reduction and the change has to be integrated into the requirements baseline. Such a change can, for example, modify the assignment of the output values to the input values of a function.

In order to be able to cope with requirements changes throughout the entire lifecycle of a system, establishing a change process that canalises and manages the changes is essential. A typical change management process comprises the canalisation of incoming change requests, the analysis of the changes (and their impact), and the decision regarding whether the change is integrated into a system release or rejected. If the change is integrated, the change management process also monitors the integration of the change. Figure 33-3 illustrates a simplified, generic process for requirements change management.

In the following, we describe the steps depicted in Fig. 33-3.

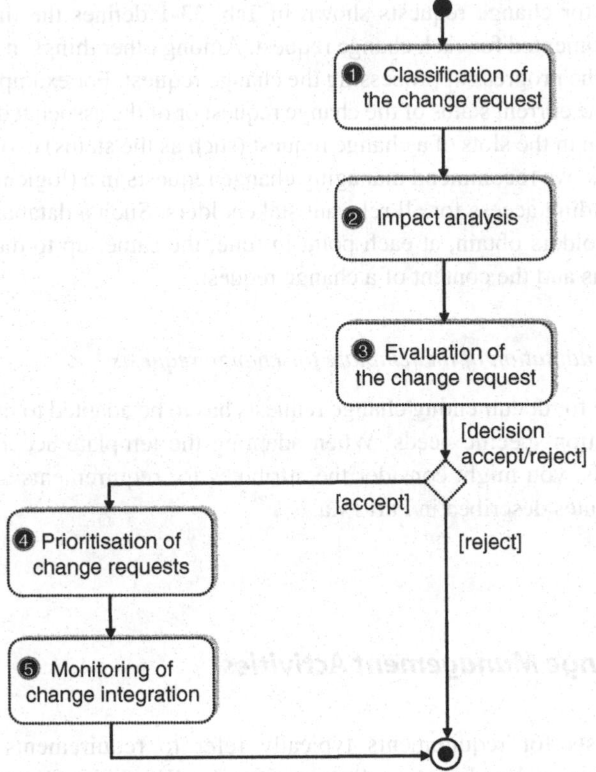

Fig. 33-3 *Process for requirements change management*

❶ Classification of Incoming Change Requests

Early classification of change requests: advantages

To process an incoming change request, the change request is first classified either by the change manager or the entire change control board (see Fig. 33-3). The early classification of change requests has several advantages. For example, depending on the classification of a change request, different processes can be executed to handle the change request. In addition, as a strategic decision an individual budget can be assigned to the different types of change requests. For example, a rule might be defined that at most 30% of the budget available for change integration shall be used for category A, 50% shall be used for category B, and the remaining 20% shall be used for category C.

We recommend assigning each change request to one of the following three categories:

- *Corrective change*: A change request is assigned to this category if the main cause of the change request is a system error or erroneous behaviour encountered during operation and if at least one requirements artefact is responsible for this error.
- *Adaptive change*: A change request is assigned to this category if the requirements artefacts must be adapted to integrate the change request.
- *Exceptional change (so-called hot fixes)*: A change request is assigned to this category if this change is absolutely necessary and must be integrated immediately. In other words, exceptional changes are typically handled in a different way, i.e. they do not pass the normal change integration process.

Processing exceptional changes

Exceptional change requests can be prioritised by the change manager or the change control board. Typically, the change manager suggests a prioritisation and presents his suggestion to the change control board for discussion and adaptation, if necessary.

Exceptional changes do not pass through the typical change management steps for corrective and adaptive changes described in the following. They are handled as exceptions and integrated as soon as possible. The changes requested by an exceptional change request may be corrective or adaptive.

❷ Impact Analysis

Effort estimation for a change request

As illustrated in Fig. 33-3, an impact analysis is performed after the change requests have been initially classified. The impact analysis aims to estimate the effort required to integrate a change request. The effort is not only caused by the adaptation of the requirements artefact that is affected by the change request. It also comprises the effort required for the realisation of the change request, i.e. it also includes the adaptation of, for example, the system architecture, the implementation, the integration as well as the effort for re-testing the system due to the integration of the change. A result of the impact analysis can be the conclusion that the change request requires restructuring of the overall system architecture or parts of the implementation (refactoring). In such cases, the integration of the change obviously requires significant effort.

Identification of affected artefacts

To estimate the effort, all requirements affected by the change request are identified. For each identified requirement, the successor artefacts (components, test cases, user manuals etc.) which might have to be adapted as well are identified. Subsequently, for each affected artefact, the effort for the integration of the change is estimated and the overall effort required is determined. The impact analysis can be performed by the change control board itself or by a third party.

Use of traceability information

The requirements and successor artefacts affected by a change request can be identified automatically by means of recorded traceability information. The prerequisite is, however, that the traceability relationships have been recorded reliably and managed correctly (Section 31.6). As outlined above, based on the requirement(s) referenced in the change request, all other requirements that might be affected by the change request can be identified using the traceability relationships. Subsequently, post-traceability information is used to identify the successor artefacts that might need to be changed (see Section 31.2). Figure 33-4 illustrates the use of traceability information during impact analysis.

Determining the total effort for integrating a change

As illustrated in Fig. 33-4, the change request for the requirement can lead to a number of further modifications of different system development artefacts. In order to be able to estimate the total effort required to integrate all the modifications caused by the change request, the efforts required in each development phase are estimated. The final estimate of the overall effort required is calculated as the sum of the effort required in each phase, sometimes multiplied by an overall uncertainty factor defined based on experience, which could be specific to the type of change request.

Figure 33-5 illustrates the estimation of the overall effort required to realise a change request based on the recorded traceability information. In order to estimate the required overall effort, the estimated partial efforts presented in Fig. 33-5 are summed.

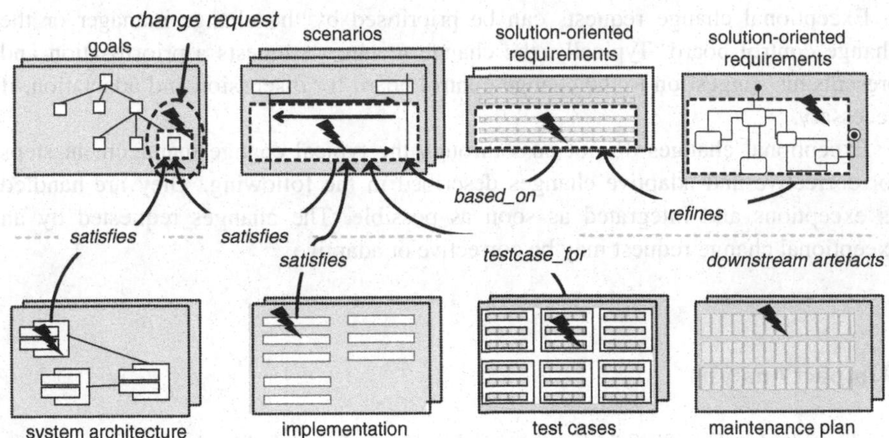

Fig. 33-4 *Use of traceability information during impact analysis*

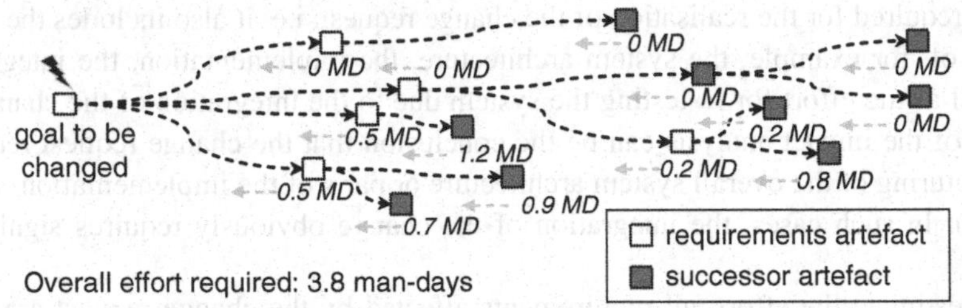

Fig. 33-5 *Effort estimation using traceability information*

Inquiring experts

If no traceability information is available or the recorded traceability information is incomplete, domain experts or experts from the development team can be involved to determine potentially affected development assets and to estimate the effort required to adjust these assets. Even if the traceability information appears to be complete, we suggest involving experts to determine the artefacts potentially affected by the change request.

❸ Evaluation of the Change Request

Cost-benefit evaluation

Based on the effort estimation obtained from the impact analysis, the change control board evaluates the cost and the benefits of realising a change request. In other words, for each change request the costs required to realise the change request are related to the benefits obtained from realising the change request. Benefits might be, for example, an improvement in market position, avoidance of loss of prestige, or contract fulfilment and thus the avoidance of contractual penalties. Based on this evaluation, the change control board decides whether the change request is finally accepted or rejected. If there are different opinions, negotiation and mediation techniques may be used in order to reach a consensus.

!

Hint 33-4: *Rejection of a change request*

If the change control board decides to reject a change request, the rejection including the reasons for rejecting the request should be communicated to the originator of the request as well as to all stakeholders involved.

❹ Prioritisation of Change Requests

Prioritisation of accepted changes

If a change request is accepted, the change control board prioritises the approved change requests. For prioritisation one or several of the prioritisation techniques presented in Chapter 32 can be used depending on the amount and the criticality of the change requests to be prioritised.

Based on the prioritisation, the change requests are bundled and assigned to a change project or to a system release to realise the change requests. The bundling or grouping of the change requests takes into account the priorities and existing dependency relationships between the change requests or between the artefacts affected by the changes. The requirements triage classification technique is a popular approach used for bundling/grouping of the change requests (see Section 32.3.7). Applying the triage classification facilitates good use of the available resources and ensures that the "most important" change requests are realised as early as possible in a system release.

❺ Monitoring of Change Integration

The change control board is not responsible for the realisation of the change requests. However, the change control board monitors the realisation of the change requests and the resulting integration of the changes. It tracks the status of each change request during its realisation and keeps the originator of the change request informed about the current status.

Recommended Literature for Part VI

Basic Reading

[Dahlstedt and Persson 2005] provide an overview of the application of requirements traceability in practice and discuss current research problems. In this contribution, the metamodel-based organisation of requirements traceability as well as specific traceability types are presented. Furthermore, the authors describe the benefits of requirements traceability for different requirements engineering activities.

[Leffingwell and Widrig 2000] provide a profound insight into the different activities of requirements management and explain the interrelations and dependencies between configuration management, change management, and traceability.

[Pohl 1996a] proposes a detailed approach for recording and using traceability information. The recording and use of traceability information is integrated into the process centred execution environment which facilitates the partially automated recording and use of traceability information. Moreover, essential traceability relationship types are defined and the principles of and detailed approach for metamodel-based recording of traceability information are introduced.

[Wiegers 1999] describes, among other things, different aspects of requirements management such as different techniques for requirements prioritisation (in particular, Wiegers' prioritisation matrix) as well as configuration and change management. Furthermore, the fundamentals of requirements traceability are explained.

Advanced Reading

[Dömges and Pohl 1998] outline the project- and organisation-specific organisation of requirements traceability and the integration of documentation and use of traceability information into process-centred tool environments.

[Jönsson and Lindvall 2005] discuss general aspects of change management within requirements engineering and explain the organisation of and process for change management as well as different techniques for impact analysis in development processes.

[Lehtola et al. 2004] provide an overview of important aspects of requirements prioritisation and describe established prioritisation techniques. In addition, the authors discuss various difficulties encountered when prioritising requirements in development projects.

[Ramesh and Jarke 2001] define traceability relationship types between different versions of requirements and software artefacts. The proposed traceability relationship types were determined based on comprehensive practice studies.

Part VII
COSMOD-RE: the Goal- and Scenario-Based RE Method

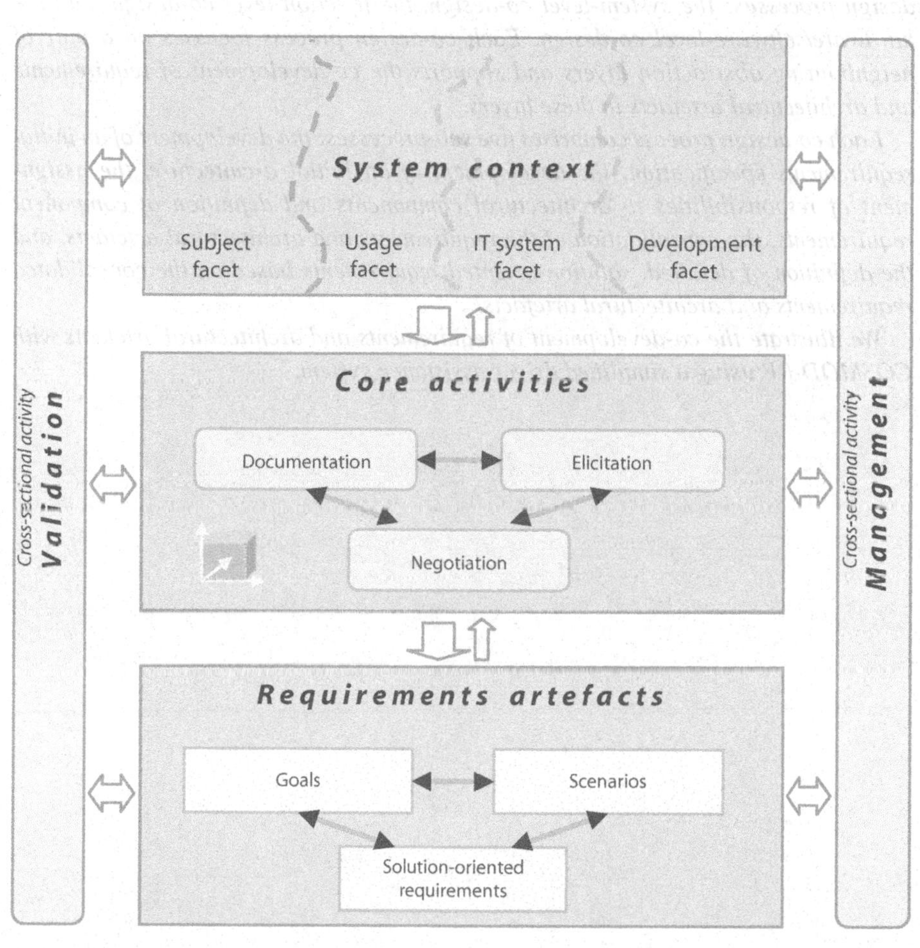

COSMOD-RE - the Goal- and Scenario-Based RE Method

Part VII

Software Product Lines and Requirements-Based Testing

Part VIII

Overview of Part VII – The COSMOD-RE Method

In this part of the book, we describe our COSMOD-RE method. COSMOD-RE supports the intertwined development of requirements and architectural artefacts for software-intensive embedded systems.

The COSMOD-RE method employs a hierarchy of four abstraction layers, in order to support management of a high system complexity. The highest layer considers the embedding of the system into its operational environment. The other layers focus on the logical decomposition of the system, the hardware/software partitioning of the system, and the deployment of the system to a hardware/software platform.

The COSMOD-RE method defines requirements artefacts (goals, scenarios, and solution-oriented requirements) and architectural artefacts for each abstraction layer and structures the development process of these artefacts into three co-design processes: the system-level co-design, the function-level co-design, and the hardware/software-level co-design. Each co-design process focusses on a pair of neighbouring abstraction layers and supports the co-development of requirements and architectural artefacts in these layers.

Each co-design process comprises five sub-processes: the development of an initial requirements specification, the development of an initial architecture, the assignment of responsibilities to architectural components and definition of component requirements, the consolidation of the requirements and architectural artefacts, and the definition of detailed, solution-oriented requirements based on the consolidated requirements and architectural artefacts.

We illustrate the co-development of requirements and architectural artefacts with COSMOD-RE using a simplified driver assistance system.

Classification Part VII COSMOD-RE - the Goal- and Scenario-Based RE Method		Basic	Advanced
34	**Fundamentals**		
34.1	Abstraction Layers		✓
34.2	Co-development of Requirements and Architectural Artefacts		✓
35	**The COSMOD-RE Method**		
35.1	The Four COSMOD-RE Abstraction Layers		✓
35.2	The Four COSMOD-RE Artefact Types		✓
35.3	COSMOD-RE Co-design Processes		✓
35.4	The Five Sub-processes of Each Co-design Process		✓
36	**Applying COSMOD-RE: an Example**		
36.1	Developing Initial Goals and Scenarios (SP_1)		✓
36.2	Developing an Initial Architecture (SP_2)		✓
36.3	Developing Component Goals and Scenarios (SP_3)		✓
36.4	Consolidating Requirements and Architectural Artefacts (SP_4)		✓
36.5	Specifying the Detailed System Requirements (SP_5)		✓

Chapter 34
Fundamentals

In this chapter, we outline the cornerstones of the COSMOD-RE method:

- *The need to specify requirements and architectural artefacts for software-intensive systems at multiple abstraction layers*
- *The mutual influences among requirements and architectural artefacts which call for co-development of both types of artefacts.*

When developing the requirements and architectural artefacts for complex, software-intensive systems, requirements engineers and developers face at least the following two key challenges:

Requirements at different levels of granularity

- *Managing the complexity of the requirements and architectural artefacts*: Customer and market needs demand that many software-intensive systems have to realise an increasingly large number of functions with many interrelations between the functions. The architecture that realises these functions is typically highly distributed. It consists of a large number of interacting components that are connected via one or several networks. The requirements for such systems are defined at different levels of granularity and detail, from high-level user requirements to detailed technical requirements. For instance, requirements in the automotive domain have to be defined for the vehicle itself, for the different vehicle systems (the light system, the braking system etc.), for individual control units (e.g. the engine control unit) as well as for individual software and hardware components. A well-proven concept for structuring and managing the requirements at different levels of granularity (as well as the respective architectural artefacts) is to use abstraction layers. Therefore, a cornerstone of the COSMOD-RE method is a hierarchy of clearly defined abstraction layers. We explain the advantages of using abstraction layers and outline the related issues in Section 34.1.

Requirements are influenced by architectural decisions

- *Dealing with the mutual influences between the requirements and architectural artefacts*: As outlined in Section 2.3 developing the requirements and the architecture is no simple, one-way process. Obviously, the requirements influence the definition of the architecture. On the other hand, design patterns and architectural design decisions influence the definition of requirements. The architectural design may reveal that the realisation of specific requirements is impossible, but it may also empower the realisation of entirely new requirements not envisioned before. In addition, the refinement of high-level requirements into detailed (implementable and testable) requirements is strongly influenced by architectural decisions. The strong, mutual influences between requirements and architectural artefacts demand appropriate support from the development method used to define the requirements and the architecture of the system. As its second cornerstone, the COSMOD-RE method thus supports the intertwined co-development of requirements and architectural artefacts. We motivate the need to support the co-development of requirements and architecture in Section 34.2.

34.1 Abstraction Layers

Advantages of using abstraction layers

The use of abstraction layers is a well-proven means for problem-solving and, in particular, for dealing with and managing the complexity of software-intensive systems (see e.g. [Leveson 2000]). The advantages of using abstraction layers to structure a problem or solution space include:

Divide-and-conquer strategy

- *Hierarchical decomposition*: When using abstraction layers to define requirements and architectural artefacts, a software-intensive system is decomposed into different levels of abstraction, i.e. the abstraction layers define a decomposition hierarchy. Figure 34-1 depicts an example of such a decomposition hierarchy.

The topmost layer, the system layer, defines the system to be developed. At this layer, the system is viewed as a black-box. At the subsystem layer, this system is decomposed into several subsystems, and the individual subsystems are specified in detail. At the lowest layer shown in Fig. 34-1, the component layer, the subsystems are decomposed into components such as mechanics, hydraulics, and software. Clearly, specifying the behaviour of a component (e.g. the requirements for the brake software) is a simpler task than specifying the behaviour of the entire vehicle at the same level of detail.

- *Separation of concerns*: Different concerns about the overall system can be assigned to different abstraction layers. Thereby, the different concerns are separated. If needed, each concern can thus be defined, accessed, and modified more conveniently and more easily. For instance, in the hierarchy depicted in Fig. 34-1, the system layer is concerned with the externally visible system functions and the interactions between the system and its environment. In contrast, the functions of individual subsystems or the interactions between the individual subsystems are not considered at the system layer. Furthermore, as the subsystem layer is concerned with logical subsystems, the problem of decomposing the system into subsystems is separated from the problem of decomposing the individual subsystems into hardware (mechanics, hydraulics, electronics etc.) and software.

Clearly separated concerns

- *Categorisation of requirements*: The clear decomposition of the system resulting from the use of abstraction layers facilitates the categorisation of requirements. Depending on the content and scope of a requirement, this requirement is assigned to a specific abstraction layer. For example, requirements pertaining to system usage (by persons or other systems) are typically assigned to the system layer, whereas requirements pertaining to individual hardware or software components are assigned to the (hardware/software) components layer. Moreover, the abstraction layers support the development of detailed requirements based on the requirements defined at a higher abstraction layer. For example, a requirement defined at the system layer typically leads to the definition of a number of requirements at the subsystem layer. Example 34-1 illustrates the definition of detailed requirements at lower abstraction layers.

Requirements assigned to abstraction layers

- *Requirements stability*: Requirements (and, partly, architectural solutions) at higher abstraction layers are defined independently of their technical realisation e.g. by hardware and software components. Since requirements defined at the system layer are fairly independent of the technical solution, they are typically not affected by changes in the technical realisation, i.e. changes at the components layer. The effects of the abstraction layers are hence similar to the positive effects of the differentiation between the "essence of a system" (technology-independent requirements) and the "incarnation of a system" (technology-dependent requirements) in Essential Systems Analysis (see Sections 3.2 and 14.2.2). The definition of almost technology-independent requirements at the higher abstraction layers also supports the reuse of these requirements for different technical solutions. For instance, the essential functionality of a brake system defined at the system layer does not change very much even if the brake mechanics defined at the lower abstraction layer changes significantly.

Essence separated from incarnation at the next abstraction layer

- *Traceability and rationales*: Requirements defined at lower abstraction layers can be related (e.g. by means of "refines" relationships; see Section 31.3) to requirements defined at higher abstraction layers. Thereby, the requirements defined at the lower abstraction layers can be traced back to higher-level requirements. The

Requirements traceability across abstraction layers

requirements defined at higher abstraction layers thus provide rationales for the requirements defined at the lower abstraction layers. Among other things, this improves the traceability of the requirements (see Section 31.1) and contributes to their comprehensibility.

Similar benefits for architectural artefacts

For architectural artefacts, the use of abstraction layers offers similar or, in part, the same advantages as for requirements artefacts.

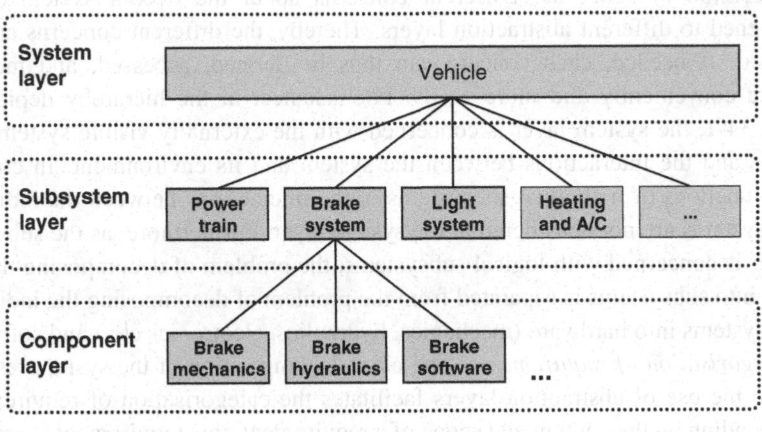

Fig. 34-1 *Example of a hierarchy of abstraction layers*

E

Example 34-1: Defining requirements at different abstraction layers

At the system layer, an interface requirement may be defined as follows:
R2 (Vehicle): The driver shall be able to switch on the ambient light manually.

At the subsystem layer, to realise the system requirement (R2), several requirements for the different subsystems are defined, such as:

R2.1 (Light system): If the driver operates the 'Ambient' button on the user interface of the light system, the light system shall activate the ambient light.

R2.2 (…) …

At the lowest layer, the requirements for the different components of the light system are defined to realise the subsystem requirements:

R2.1.1 (Door control unit): If the driver operates the 'Ambient' button on the light panel, the door control unit shall send the message LIGHT_AMB_ON to the roof control unit.

R2.1.2 (Roof control unit): If the roof control unit receives the message LIGHT_AMB_ON, it shall output the signal 'high' at the digital output DIG_IO_AMB.

R2.2.1 (…) …

Activities related to the use of abstraction layers

Structuring the specification of a software-intensive embedded system into multiple abstraction layers demands systematic support for the transitions between the different abstraction layers. For instance, the following activities should be supported:

- The assignment of known requirements to abstraction layers
- Ensuring that the requirements (both natural language requirements as well as requirements models) at each abstraction layer are defined independently of the solutions at the lower abstraction layers
- The definition of requirements at a lower abstraction layer based on the requirements defined at a higher abstraction layer (and an initial, architectural solution)
- Checking the consistency between the requirements defined at the different abstraction layers
- The recording and use of traceability links between requirements across different abstraction layers as well as between requirements and architectural artefacts.

Abstraction layers in COSMOD-RE

In summary: Using clearly defined abstraction layers when developing and documenting requirements and architectural artefacts for software-intensive systems offers significant advantages. A cornerstone of COSMOD-RE is hence a decomposition hierarchy based on clearly defined abstraction layers. In Chapter 35, we introduce the abstraction layers of the COSMOD-RE method and sketch the support COSMOD-RE offers for defining the requirements and architectural artefacts for software-intensive systems.

34.2 Co-development of Requirements and Architectural Artefacts

Architectural design influences the definition of detailed requirements

When developing requirements and architectural artefacts for a complex software-intensive system the stakeholders have to accomplish two different but closely related tasks (see e.g. [Harel and Pnueli 1985]):

- *Detailing of the requirements*: The stakeholders have to detail the high-level requirements. The level of detail of the requirements must be sufficient to facilitate the implementation of the system and the quality assurance of all developed artefacts.
- *Decomposition of the system*: The stakeholders have to decompose the overall system into a set of interacting parts (subsystems or components). The stakeholders thus have to define a detailed architecture which satisfies the defined (detailed) requirements.

Mutual influences between requirements and architecture

Clearly, the requirements influence and partially determine the architecture. However, design decisions (e.g. the choice of a specific architectural solution for the system) strongly influence the definition of detailed (implementable and testable) requirements based on the specified high-level requirements. The development of the detailed requirements is thus clearly influenced by the design choices taken. Furthermore, an innovative, new architectural solution can even lead to entirely new requirements and thus also influence requirements defined at a higher level of abstraction. For instance, the development of a braking system architecture able to detect imminent interlocking of the wheels facilitates the development of an "anti-lock braking" feature. In such a case, the new architectural solution may lead to the definition of an entirely new vehicle requirement.

Intertwined and (partly) parallel development

The strong, mutual influence between requirements and architectural artefacts demands that a development method supports the tightly intertwined co-development of requirements and architectural artefacts. We elaborate on the need for supporting the co-development of requirements and architectural artefacts in the next sections.

34.2.1 Architectural Influence on Requirements

During the development of a cruise-control system, the requirements engineers have elicited the following requirement:

> *R1: The system shall ensure that the vehicle maintains a safe distance to the vehicle ahead.*

Investigating design options

Clearly, requirement R1 does not define enough details for starting the development of the system. The requirements engineers must hence develop and specify more detailed requirements based on requirement R1. As illustrated by the following example, the choice of a particular architecture (design solution) significantly influences the development of the detailed requirements.

Tab. 34-1 *Example properties for two different design solutions*

Property	Design solution: Radar	Design solution: Laser
Detection range	10–150 m	5 mm to 250 m
Speed range	30–250 km/h	0–130 km/h
Cost	$350	$650
Enabled additional requirements	Adaptive cruise control Emergency brake assistant	Adaptive cruise control Parking aid

The choice of a specific design or architectural solution is typically influenced by quality properties such as performance, accuracy, safety, reliability, physical properties such as size, weight, and energy consumption, or economic properties such as production cost. Table 34-1 presents some properties for two different design solutions for the realisation of requirement R1. In addition to satisfying the initial requirement(s), the design solution chosen may facilitate the fulfilment of additional functional and/or quality requirements not considered before. Examples of such additional requirements are listed in the row "Enabled additional requirements" in Tab. 34-1.

Influence of Design Decisions on the Definition of Detailed Requirements: Two Examples

In the following we illustrate the influence of different design solutions on the definition of a set of detailed requirements based on the high-level requirement R1. One design solution uses a distance sensor to determine the distance to the vehicles ahead. The other design solution determines the distance to the vehicles ahead based on the exchange of movement data via inter-vehicle communication.

Solution concept "distance sensor"

The design solution which uses a distance sensor is depicted in Fig. 34-2. The system architecture consists of a distance sensor and a processing unit. The distance sensor measures the distance to objects in front of the vehicle. The processing unit processes the sensor data, tracks relevant objects ahead, and controls the speed of the vehicle by interacting with the engine control system and the brake control system.

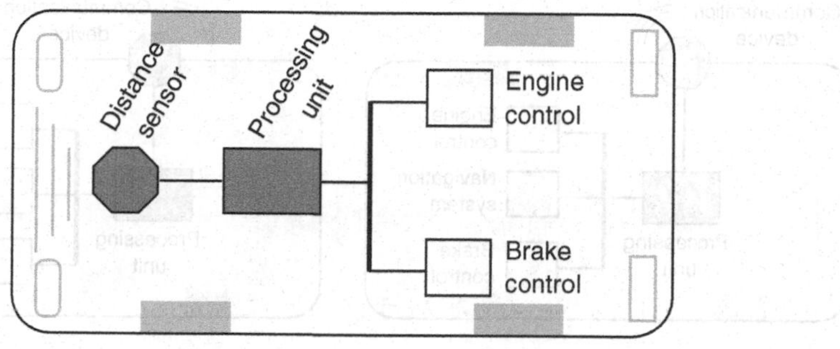

Fig. 34-2 *Solution concept based on distance sensor*

Detailed requirements for the "distance sensor" solution

Based on this solution, the following requirements are defined for the distance sensor and the processing unit to satisfy the requirement R1:

R1.1a: *The distance sensor shall measure the distance, angle, and speed of objects ahead.*

R1.2a: *The distance sensor shall perform at least 20 measurement cycles per second.*

R1.3a: *The distance sensor shall provide access to the measured data through its interface.*

R1.4a: *The processing unit shall read the measured data from the distance sensor.*

R1.5a: *The processing unit shall track the speed and distance of each relevant object within a range of at least 150 m.*

R1.6a: *The processing unit shall use the engine control system and the brake control system to adjust the speed of the vehicle.*

Solution concept "exchange of vehicle movement data"

The second design solution (see Fig. 34-3) is based on the exchange of speed and position data between the vehicles through an inter-vehicle communication network. The communication network allows a vehicle to interact with other vehicles in the vicinity. Each vehicle is equipped with a network device and a processing unit responsible for exchanging movement data with other vehicles, keeping track of the other vehicles, and controlling the speed of the vehicle.

Detailed requirements for the "exchange of movement data" solution

Based on this solution, the following requirements are defined to satisfy requirement R1:

R1.1b: *The network device must allow exchange of data with other vehicles within a range of at least 250 m.*

R1.2b: *The processing unit shall acquire the speed and position of the vehicle from the navigation system.*

R1.3b: *The processing unit shall send the speed and position to other vehicles via the network device.*

R1.4b: *The processing unit shall acquire the speed and position data of other vehicles via the network device.*

R1.5b: *The processing unit shall track the speed and distance of each relevant object within a range of at least 150 m (same as R1.5a).*

R1.6b: *The processing unit shall use the engine control system and the brake control system to adapt the speed of the vehicle (same as R1.6a).*

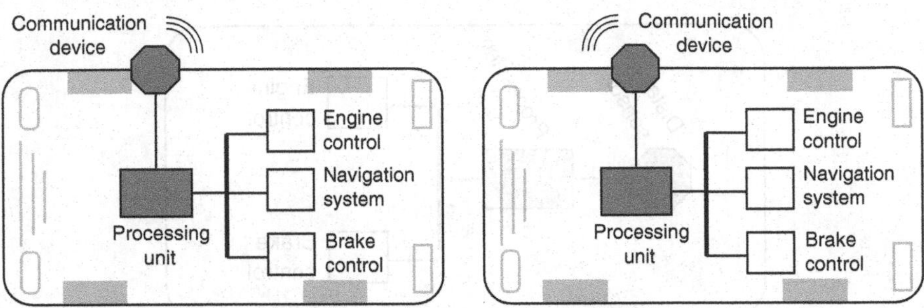

Fig. 34-3 *Solution concept based on inter-vehicle communication*

Need for Support of the Intertwined Development of Requirements and Architecture

Implicit design decisions during requirements engineering

The above example illustrates that architectural design decisions influence the definition of detailed requirements. Thus requirements engineering and architectural design processes are inherently intertwined. Surprisingly, existing development methods do not foster the intertwined development of requirements and architecture. Defining detailed requirements without systematic exploration of possible design options leads to the danger that important design decisions are made implicitly. In other words, detailed requirements often hide the implicit and explicit design decisions and assumptions made by the stakeholders during the definition of the detailed requirements. This often rules out other, perhaps better design solutions, as illustrated in Example 34-2.

Example 34-2: Implicit design decisions in requirements artefacts

A vehicle manufacturer defines the following requirement for a driver assistance system:

R2.3: The system shall read the data from the ultrasound sensor every 100 ms.

This requirement is based on the design decision (or assumption) that the driver assistance system uses an ultrasound sensor for distance measurement. Other design alternatives such as the use of a radar sensor or a video sensor are ruled out by this requirement even if they are cheaper to realise, lead to lower maintenance costs, or facilitate higher quality.

Required support from development methods

In order to avoid such problems a development method should foster and systematically support the intertwined development of requirements and architectural artefacts and should facilitate:

- The concurrent and tightly intertwined co-development of requirements and solution concepts
- Clearly separated documentation of requirements and solution concepts, design decisions, and the system structures resulting from these decisions
- An appropriate interrelation of requirements and architectural artefacts to support the co-development of both artefacts

34.2.2 Co-design Processes

Co-development of requirements and architectural artefacts

Co-design processes support the concurrent development of different development artefacts. In this part, we focus on co-design processes that support the tightly intertwined co-development of requirements and architectural artefacts. The requirements artefacts developed in a co-design process comprise goals, scenarios, and solution-oriented requirements. The architectural artefacts comprise the decomposition of the system into components, the interfaces of these components, and the connections between these components. To document the structural artefacts of the architecture, typically an architectural description language (ADL) is used (see e.g. [Medvidovic and Taylor 2000]).

Co-design processes and abstraction layers

As outlined in Section 34.1, software-intensive systems can be structured according to a hierarchy of abstraction layers. Each abstraction layer includes both requirements and architectural artefacts. Figure 34-4 schematically depicts the definition of requirements and architectural artefacts at different abstraction layers. Within each abstraction layer, the architecture must satisfy the requirements defined at this layer. In addition, the requirements defined at a lower abstraction layer must satisfy

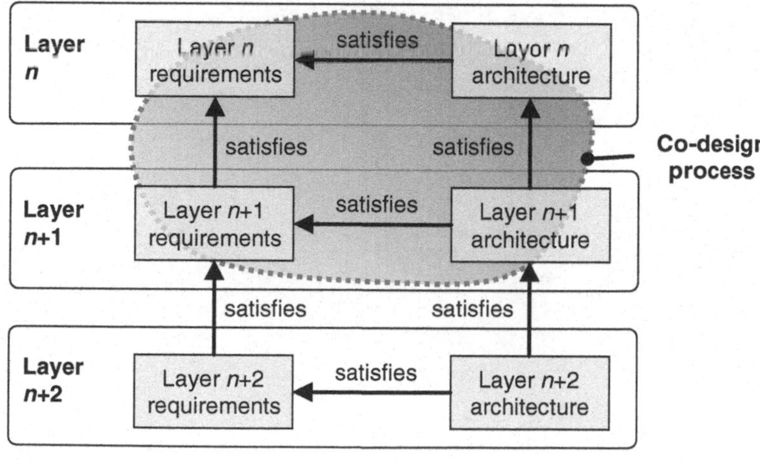

Fig. 34-4 *Co-design processes and abstraction layers*

the requirements defined at the higher abstraction layer. The architecture at a lower abstraction layer satisfies the architecture defined at the higher abstraction layer.

Scope of a co-design process

The definition of the detailed requirements at layer $n + 1$ (see Fig. 34-4) is obviously influenced by the requirements defined at layer n. In addition, as elaborated above, the requirements defined at layer $n + 1$ influence the definition of the architectural artefacts at layer $n + 1$ and vice versa. As a consequence, the activity supporting the definition of the requirements at layer $n + 1$ has to take into account the requirements artefacts defined at layer n as well as the architecture artefacts defined at layer $n + 1$. A co-design process must therefore consider at least two neighbouring abstraction layers, as indicated by the area labelled "Co-design process" in Fig. 34-4. In Section 35.3, we outline the co-design processes of the COSMOD-RE method which facilitate the consideration of two neighbouring abstraction layers when defining requirements and architectural artefacts.

Iterative development

A co-design process as depicted schematically in Fig. 34-4 is typically performed iteratively. The requirements and architectural artefacts developed in iteration k can be extended, refined, or modified in each subsequent iteration $k + i$. Consequently, the requirements and architectural artefacts developed in an earlier iteration influence the requirements and architectural artefacts in later iterations.

Chapter 35
The COSMOD-RE Method

COSMOD-RE supports the co-development of requirements and architectural artefacts for software-intensive embedded systems at multiple layers of abstraction. In this chapter, we introduce the key building blocks of our COSMOD-RE method, namely:

- *The four abstraction layers of COSMOD-RE*
- *The four types of development artefacts defined at each abstraction layer (goals, scenarios, solution-oriented requirements, and architectural artefacts)*
- *The three co-design processes for developing the requirements and architectural artefacts. Each sub-process consists of five sub-processes.*

Overview of the COSMOD-RE Method

Three building blocks of the method

The main goal of COSMOD-RE (sCenario- and gOal-based System development MethOD)[1] *is to support the intertwined co-development of requirements and architectural artefacts for software-intensive embedded systems. COSMOD-RE consists of three main building blocks (see Fig. 35-1):*

Hierarchy of four abstraction layers

- ❑ *The four COSMOD-RE abstraction layers: The abstraction hierarchy of the COSMOD-RE method consists of four abstraction layers: the system layer, the functional decomposition layer, the hardware/software partitioning layer, and the deployment layer. The four abstraction layers are explained in Section 35.1.*

Four basic artefact types at each layer

- ❑ *The four COSMOD-RE artefact types: At each abstraction layer, the COSMOD-RE method differentiates between four types of development artefacts: goals, scenarios, solution-oriented requirements, and architectural artefacts. The four artefact types are described in Section 35.2.*

Three co-design processes and five sub-processes

- ❑ *The three COSMOD-RE co-development processes: COSMOD-RE provides three co-design processes: the system-level co-design, the function-level co-design, and the hardware/software-level co-design process. Each of the three co-design processes focusses on two neighbouring abstraction layers (Section 35.3) and consists of five sub-processes (Section 35.4).*

[1] This chapter describes the current version of the COSMOD-RE method, which builds on its predecessor version described in [Pohl and Sikora 2005; Pohl and Sikora 2007; Pohl 2008].

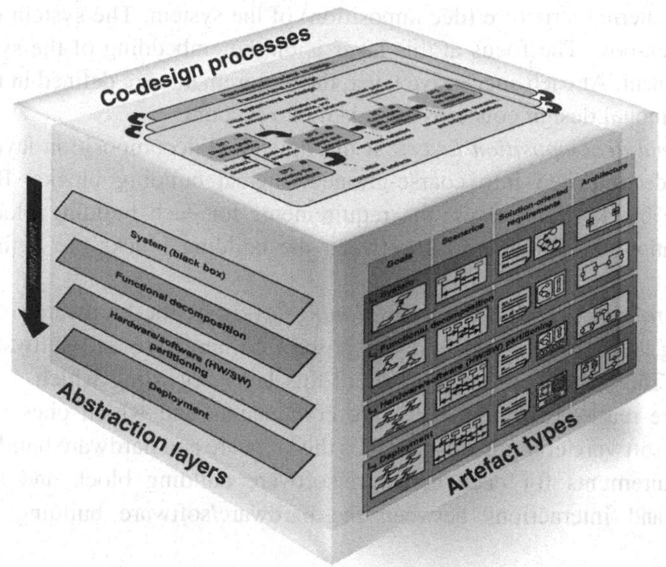

Fig. 35-1 *Main building-blocks of the COSMOD-RE method*

35.1 The Four COSMOD-RE Abstraction Layers

The COSMOD-RE method is based on a hierarchy of four abstraction layers. Each abstraction layer has a well-defined focus and defines a specific viewpoint on the system. At each abstraction layer, requirements and architectural artefacts are defined.

Characteristics and scope of requirements and architectural artefacts at each layer

We provide an overview of the four abstraction layers (Section 35.1.1) and describe each abstraction layer in the subsequent sections in more detail (Sections 35.1.2–35.1.5). To illustrate the essential characteristics and scope of the requirements artefacts defined at each abstraction layer we use simplified behavioural requirements models (a subset of the requirements artefacts typically defined at each layer). To illustrate the essential characteristics and the scope of the architectural artefacts defined at each abstraction layer we use simplified, structural architecture models.

The different types of requirements and architectural artefacts used in the COSMOD-RE method are explained in more detail in Section 35.2.

35.1.1 Overview

Separation of concerns

Figure 35-2 depicts the four abstraction layers of COSMOD-RE. From the topmost layer to the bottom layer, each abstraction layer defines requirements and architectural artefacts at an increasing level of detail:

Embedding of the system, technology-independent specification

- ❑ *System layer*: The system layer (highest abstraction layer) defines requirements and architectural artefacts fairly independently of the implementation technology and the internal structure (decomposition) of the system. The system is regarded as a black-box. The focus at this layer is on the embedding of the system in its environment. At each successive layer, the requirements are defined in more detail and additional design concerns are taken into account.

Logical building blocks

- *Functional decomposition layer*: At the functional decomposition layer, the system is decomposed into coarse-grained, logical building blocks. Besides the building blocks themselves, the requirements for each building block and the interrelations and interactions between the building blocks are defined at this layer.

Hardware and software building blocks

- *Hardware/software (HW/SW) partitioning layer*: At the hardware/software partitioning layer, the system is decomposed into hardware and software building blocks. Thus, the decision is made at this layer regarding which system properties are realised through hardware components and which ones are realised through software components. Besides the software and hardware building blocks, the requirements for each hardware/software building block and the interrelations and interactions between the hardware/software building blocks are defined.

Deployment to a hardware/software platform

- *Deployment layer*: At the deployment layer, the deployment of the system into the hardware and software platform (network of physical units) is defined. The definition of the deployment includes the decision regarding which software component is executed on which physical unit.

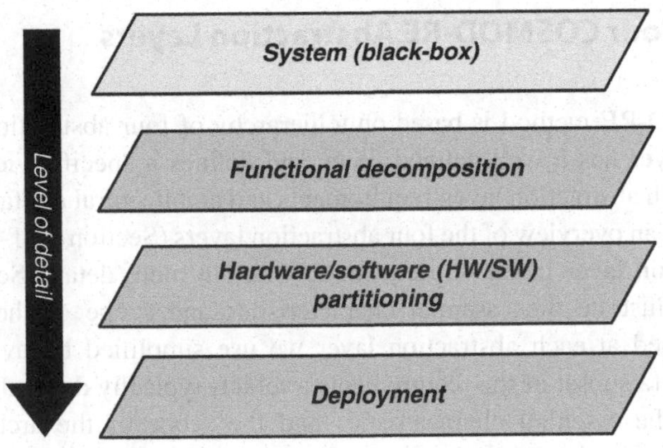

Fig. 35-2 *COSMOD-RE abstraction layers (based on [Pohl and Sikora 2007])*

Top-down development not enforced

Although COSMOD-RE promotes a hierarchy of four abstraction layers, the COSMOD-RE method neither imposes nor enforces a top-down development process. A strict top-down development process would require that requirements and architectural artefacts are first defined exclusively at the system layer and then detailed at the functional decomposition layer etc.

Top-down, middle-out, and bottom-up development

In contrast, COSMOD-RE supports the co-development of requirements and architectural artefacts across the abstraction layers as described in Section 35.3. Moreover, COSMOD-RE supports the top-down, bottom-up as well as the middle-out development and alignment of requirements and architectural artefacts (see Fig. 35-3).

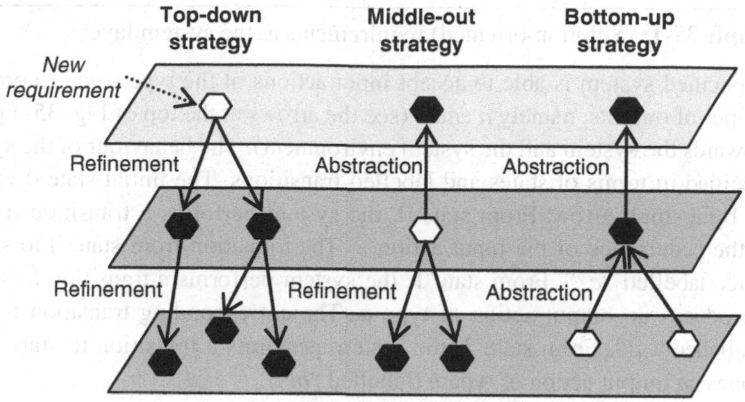

Fig. 35-3 *Top-down, bottom-up, and middle-out strategies*

35.1.2 System Layer

System as a black-box

The system layer defines the embedding of the system in its environment, the interactions between the system and its environment, and the externally visible system properties (pertaining to functionality and quality). The system itself is regarded as a black-box.

System Requirements

Goals, scenarios, and solution-oriented requirements

The interactions between the system and its environment are defined in terms of scenarios. The high-level objectives or properties of the system are defined in terms of goals. Detailed requirements at the system layer such as the externally visible behaviour of the system are specified using solution-oriented requirements models (e.g. UML state machine diagrams). Figure 35-4 shows a simplified example of a solution-oriented requirements model at the system layer. The model defines the system behaviour using the notation of interface automata described in [Alfaro and Henzinger 2001]. The model is explained in Example 35-1.

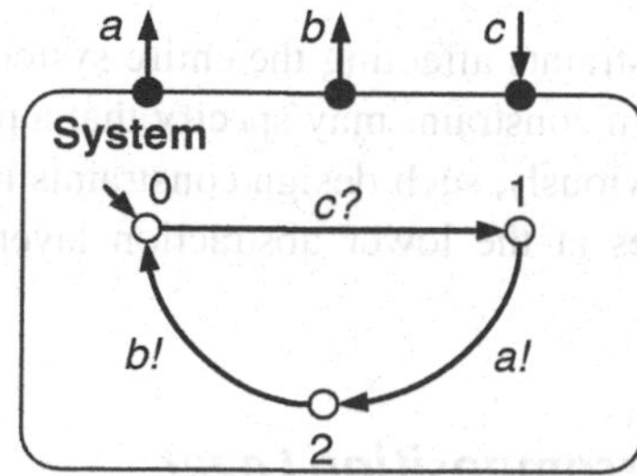

Fig. 35-4 *A system as a single component interacting with its environment*

Example 35-1: (Solution-oriented) requirements at the system layer

The specified system is able to accept input actions of the type *c* and to produce two types of outputs, namely *a* and *b* (see the arrows at the top of Fig. 35-4 pointing towards the system and the system environment). The behaviour of the system is specified in terms of states and labelled transitions. The initial state 0 is indicated by a small arrow. From state 0, the system performs a transition to state 1 on the occurrence of the input action *c*. The transition from state 0 to state 1 is hence labelled "*c?*". From state 1, the system performs a transition to state 2 and produces an output action of type *a*. The corresponding transition to state 2 is labelled "*a!*". From state 2, the system performs a transition to state 0 and produces an output action of type *b* (labelled "*b!*").

System Architecture (System Interfaces)

System interfaces

At the system layer, the system is regarded as a single black-box that interacts with its environment through defined interfaces (see Fig. 35-5). The system interfaces defined at the system layer specify the embedding of the system into its environment. These interfaces are defined independently of a technical solution. To support the understanding of the system and its interactions with the environment, external systems and actors should be included in the architectural model. In the simplified model depicted in Fig. 35-5, a brake system with two input interfaces and one output interface is defined. A typical brake system comprises mechanics, hydraulics, electronics, and software components. Due to the black-box view at the system layer all those details are hidden and only the abstract interfaces of the brake system are defined at the system layer.

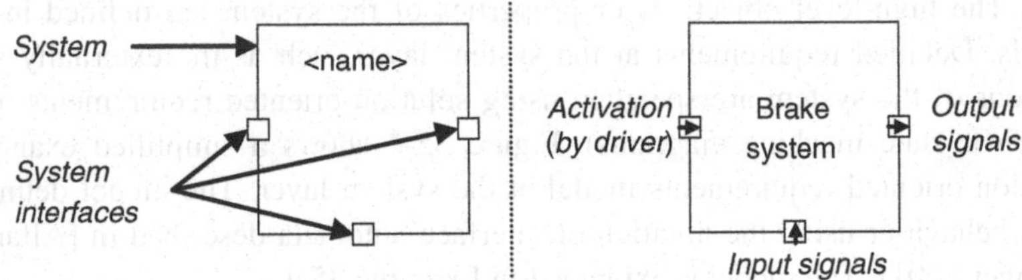

Fig. 35-5 *Black-box view of the system at the system layer*

Documentation of design constraints

In addition, design constraints affecting the entire system can be specified at this layer. For instance, a design constraint may specify that a particular reference architecture has to be used. Obviously, such design constraints impose severe restrictions on possible design choices at the lower abstraction layers and hence need to be explicitly documented.

35.1.3 Functional Decomposition Layer

Functional components

The main concern of the second layer is the functional decomposition of the system. At this layer, the system is decomposed into logical building blocks or components. Each logical component defined at this layer represents a unit of coherent functionality and is hence called a "functional component".

Technology-independent decomposition

The requirements and architectural artefacts defined at the functional decomposition layer are defined independently of a particular implementation technology, like in Essential Systems Analysis (see Section 3.2). For example, the system functionality is defined independently of a hardware/software partitioning. The artefacts defined at this layer thus remain (relatively) stable even if the implementation technology at lower abstraction layers changes. Moreover, the technology-independent definition supports the reuse of the requirements and architectural artefacts across system boundaries.

Requirements for Functional Components

Requirements for each functional component

At the functional decomposition layer, requirements (goals, scenarios, and solution-oriented requirements) are defined for each functional component. When defining the requirements for the functional components the system requirements defined at the level above are considered. However, also new requirements for a functional component can be elicited and defined at this layer. Figure 35-6 depicts simplified solution-oriented requirements models for the two logical components FC1 and FC2. More precisely, the figure depicts simplified behavioural requirements models for the two interacting, functional components FC1 and FC2. The models are explained in Example 35-2.

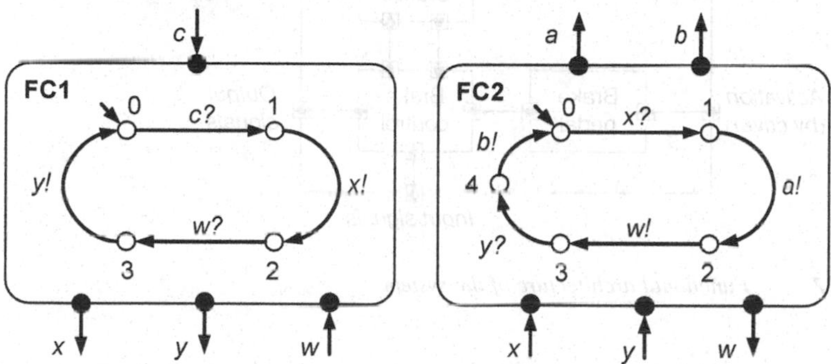

Fig. 35-6 *Simplified behavioural requirements model for the functional components FC1 and FC2*

Example 35-2: Solution-oriented requirements at the functional decomposition layer

The models shown in Fig. 35-6 specify the desired behaviour of the two functional components FC1 and FC2. The functional components interact with external actors as well as with each other. FC1 is able to process inputs of type *c*, while FC2 produces outputs of types *a* and *b*. The system-internal interactions among the two functional components are defined as shared transitions of the corresponding automata. For instance, if the automaton FC1 is in state 1 and the automaton FC2 is in state 0, the output action "*x!*" of automaton FC1 and the input action "*x?*" of the automaton FC2 are performed synchronously.

Logical (Functional) Architecture

Coarse-grained logical architecture

The architectural artefacts at this level define the logical components of the system, logical interfaces, and logical connections between the components (see Fig. 35-7). The architecture thus abstracts from any differentiation between hardware and software components as well as from physical devices, physical interfaces, and physical communication networks (e.g. busses). Thus, the functional (logical) architecture defines a structure for the problem and is, besides the requirements, a key input for defining a more concrete system architecture at the hardware and software partitioning layer.

Simplified example

In the simplified example shown in Fig. 35-7, three logical components of a brake system are shown: "Brake pedal", "Brake control", and "Wheel brakes". The component names denote functions and should not be mistaken for specific implementation technologies such as a mechanic brake pedal. The functional component "Brake pedal" empowers the driver to control the deceleration of the car. The brake pedal might be realised purely by means of mechanical components or as a smart brake pedal that facilitates advanced braking functions such as configurable braking behaviour or a brake assistant through software. Depending on the technology used for the brake pedal the logical connection between the brake pedal and the brake control would be realised in different ways.

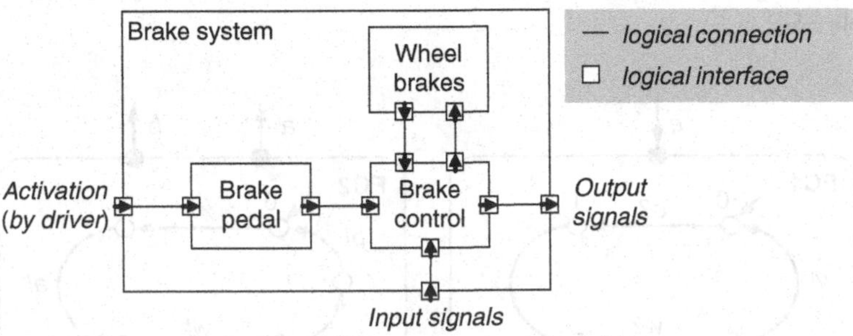

Fig. 35-7 *Functional architecture of the system*

Quality requirements

In addition to the functional (logical) architecture, quality requirements should be defined for the architecture at this layer. Examples of quality requirements are the adaptability of the system functionality or the reusability of the functional components.

35.1.4 Hardware/Software Partitioning Layer

Definition of hardware and software components

The partitioning of the system functionality into hardware and software components and the requirements for these components are defined at the hardware/software partitioning layer. Obviously, hardware and software components of an embedded system closely interact. For example, the software typically interacts with peripheral devices such as sensors and actuators, display and control elements, or network interface components. Thus, the hardware/software interfaces (in terms of both interface requirements and a coarse-grained interface design) are defined at the hardware/software partitioning layer.

Hardware and Software Requirements

Requirements for HW and SW components

The requirements at the hardware/software partitioning layer are defined based on the requirements specified at the functional decomposition layer and are associated to the hardware and software components defined at this layer. In addition, additional requirements are elicited and defined which depend on the chosen decomposition of the system into hardware and software components.

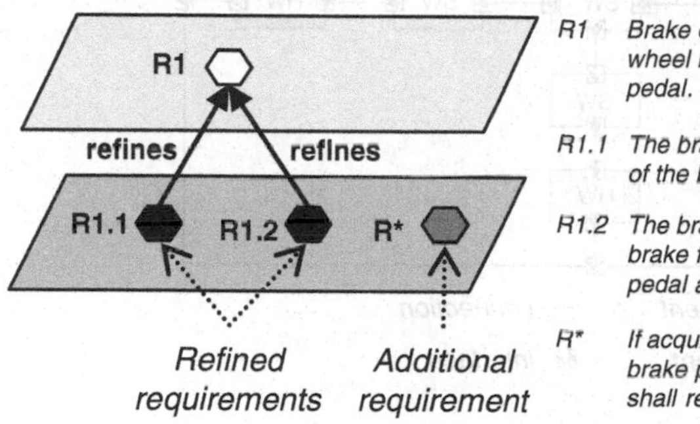

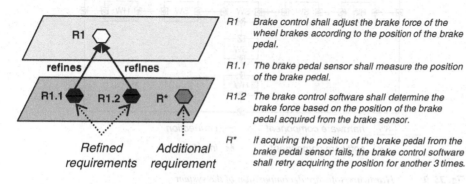

R1 *Brake control shall adjust the brake force of the wheel brakes according to the position of the brake pedal.*

R1.1 *The brake pedal sensor shall measure the position of the brake pedal.*

R1.2 *The brake control software shall determine the brake force based on the position of the brake pedal acquired from the brake sensor.*

*R** *If acquiring the position of the brake pedal from the brake pedal sensor fails, the brake control software shall retry acquiring the position for another 3 times.*

Fig. 35-8 *Example of a new requirement defined at a lower abstraction layer*

Figure 35-8 depicts an example of requirements defined at the hardware/software partitioning layer. Besides the detailing of R1 by the requirements R1.1 and R1.2, a new requirement R* has been defined. This requirement results from the partitioning of the functional component "Brake control" into hardware and software components. The requirement R* is added, because the stakeholder assumes that reading data from the brake pedal sensor occasionally fails, yet the failure is very unlikely to occur more than three times consecutively. This requirement hence does not follow from detailing R1, but from the specific hardware/software partitioning and the associated technology chosen at this layer.

Architectural Hardware and Software Components

Hardware and software components and their interactions

The decomposition of the system considered at the hardware/software partitioning layer defines a coarse-grained architecture consisting of hardware and software components, their interfaces, and connectors defining communication channels between hardware and software components (see Fig. 35-9). When defining this architecture, typically quality requirements such as performance and cost are taken into account.

At this layer, only hardware and software components needed for realising the functional components defined at the functional decomposition layer are defined. The software components typically include the application software required for the system. The hardware components typically include peripheral components such as sensors and actuators.

Hardware/software platform is not considered

Hardware and software components that belong to the underlying hardware and software platform of the system such as the operating system, standard device drivers, processing units etc. are not defined at the hardware/software partitioning layer.

No assignment to physical units

Furthermore, no assignment of the hardware and software components to physical units (e.g. electronic control units) is made at the hardware/software partitioning layer.

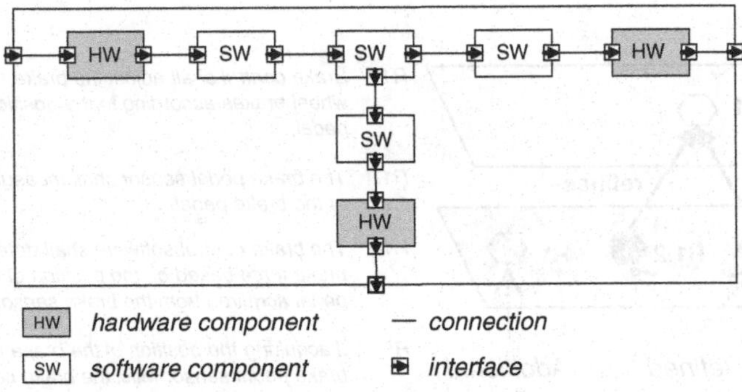

Fig. 35-9 *Hardware/software decomposition of the system*

35.1.5 Deployment Layer

Adjusting requirements for the specific hardware/software platform

At the deployment layer, the requirements and architectural artefacts defined at the hardware/software partitioning layer are clustered to form physical units such as electronic control units of a vehicle or aircraft. Figure 35-10 illustrates such a clustering. The system depicted in the figure is a distributed system consisting of two electronic control units (ECU 1 and ECU 2). Each ECU is equipped with an operating system (RTOS1 and RTOS2). The components “SW 1” and “Sensor 1” have been assigned (deployed) to ECU 1, and the components “SW 2”, “SW 3”, and “Actuator 1” have been assigned to ECU 2. The connection between “SW 1” and “SW 2” is realised by a communication bus linking ECU 1 and ECU 2.

New or existing system topology

Depending on the type of project, one of the following three cases may apply:

- The hardware and software components are deployed to an existing topology of physical units which is predefined and remains unchanged.
- An existing topology of physical units is modified during the deployment. For example, a new control unit may be added.
- An entirely new topology of physical units is created and thus no predefined topology is used.

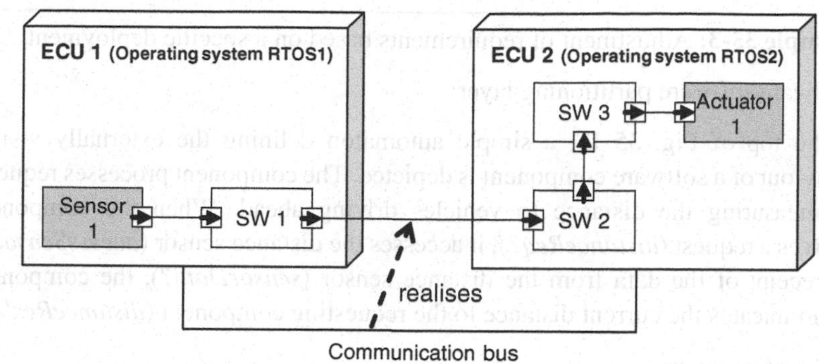

Fig. 35-10 *Example deployment of HW and SW components to physical units*

Adjustment of requirements

The deployment of the software and hardware components to the topology of physical units can require refinement and adjustment of the requirements defined at the hardware/software partitioning layer. For instance, it might be necessary to alter a requirement due to the specific properties of a concrete hardware component belonging to the hardware/software platform (such as available computation time, memory, and network bandwidth). Also, an adjustment of the hardware and software components may be required.

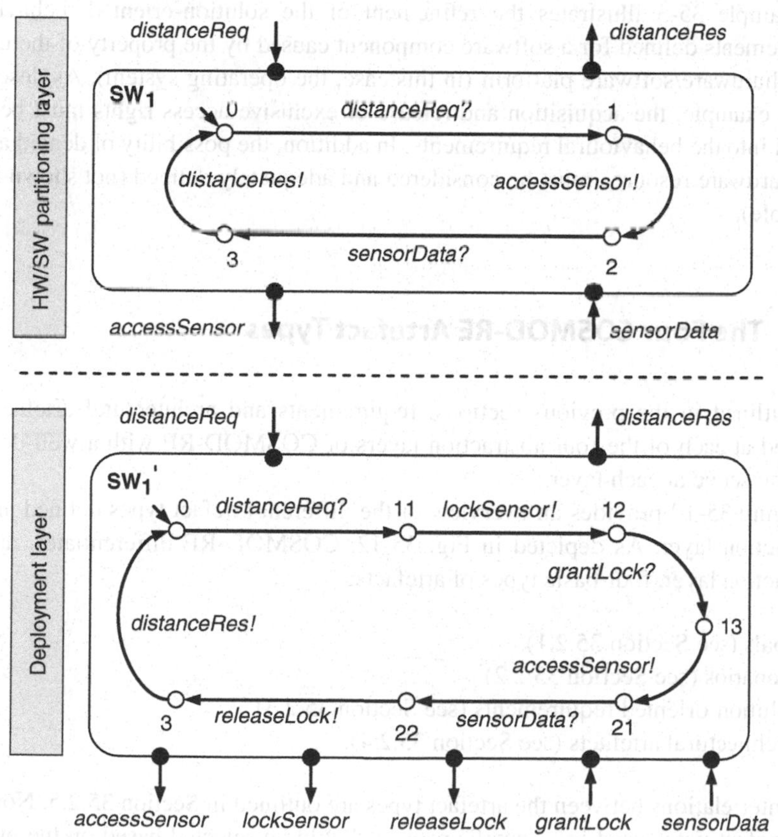

Fig. 35-11 *Refinement of the requirements for a software component based on the hardware/software deployment*

Example 35-3: Adjustment of requirements based on a specific deployment

Hardware/software partitioning layer:

At the top of Fig. 35-11, a simple automaton defining the externally visible behaviour of a software component is depicted. The component processes requests for measuring the distance to vehicles driving ahead. When the component receives a request (*distanceReq?*), it accesses the distance sensor (*accessSensor!*). On receipt of the data from the distance sensor (*sensorData?*), the component communicates the current distance to the requesting component (*distanceRes!*).

Deployment layer:

At the bottom of Fig. 35-11, a refined automaton is depicted. This refinement takes into account the specifics of the hardware/software platform (e.g. the operating system). When the component receives a request, it must first acquire a lock (*lock-Sensor!*) in order to access the sensor (*grantLock?*). After accessing the sensor, the component must release the lock (*releaseLock!*).

Example of adjusting requirements

For example, the operating system of "ECU 1" (see Fig. 35-10) may demand that the software component "SW 1" acquires exclusive access to "Sensor 1" before it can read the data from this sensor. This is not considered in the requirements for "SW 1" until the component is deployed to "ECU 1".

Example 35-3 illustrates the refinement of the solution-oriented, behavioural requirements defined for a software component caused by the property of the underlying hardware/software platform (in this case, the operating system). As described in the example, the acquisition and release of exclusive access rights must be integrated into the behavioural requirements. In addition, the possibility of denied access to a hardware resource must be considered and adequately defined (not shown in the example).

35.2 The Four COSMOD-RE Artefact Types

As outlined in the previous sections, requirements and architectural artefacts are defined at each of the four abstraction layers of COSMOD-RE with a well-defined, specific scope at each layer.

Figure 35-12 provides an overview of the different artefact types defined at each abstraction layer. As depicted in Fig. 35-12, COSMOD-RE differentiates, at each abstraction layer, four basic types of artefacts:

- ❑ Goals (see Section 35.2.1)
- ❑ Scenarios (see Section 35.2.2)
- ❑ Solution-oriented requirements (see Section 35.2.3)
- ❑ Architectural artefacts (see Section 35.2.4).

The interrelations between the artefact types are outlined in Section 35.2.5. Note that the artefact types used in a specific project should be selected based on the project-specific needs. In other words, not all artefacts must be used within a project or at each abstraction layer.

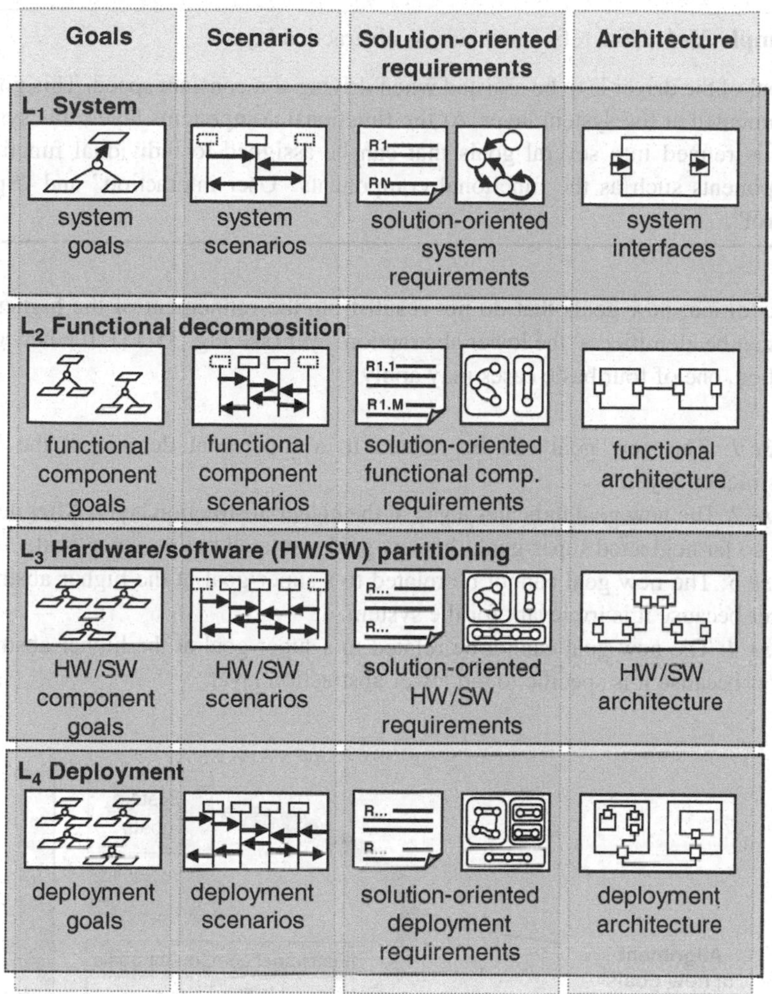

Fig. 35-12 *Overview of the artefact types defined at the abstraction layers of COSMOD-RE*

35.2.1 Goals

From system goals to component goals

In this section, we elaborate on the development of goals at the four abstraction layers of COSMOD-RE introduced in Section 35.1 (see Part III.a. for a detailed description of the principles of goals and their usage in requirements engineering).

In COSMOD-RE, goals are defined at each of the four abstraction layers. For example, an overall system goal is defined at the system layer, whereas a specific goal for a hardware component is defined at the hardware/software partitioning layer. During the transition from a higher abstraction layer to a lower abstraction layer, the goals for the components at the lower abstraction layer are defined taking into account the goals defined at the higher abstraction layer (see Example 35-4).

> **Example 35-4:** Goal refinement across abstraction layers
>
> A goal of the driver is to be assisted when driving at a constant speed. This goal is documented at the system layer. At the functional components layer, this system goal is refined into several goals that can be assigned to individual functional components such as the functional components "User interaction" and "Speed control".

Identification of new goals at lower abstraction layers

In addition, new goals that do not result from the refinement of the higher-level goals can be identified at the lower abstraction layer (see Fig. 35-13). If a new goal is identified, one of four basic cases may apply:

- *Case 1*: The new goal can be related to a super-goal defined at the higher abstraction layer.
- *Case 2*: The new goal indicates a gap at the higher abstraction layer. After defining the so far neglected super-goal, the new goal is related to this super-goal.
- *Case 3*: The new goal cannot be related to a super-goal at the higher abstraction layer because it is irrelevant for the system.
- *Case 4*: The new goal cannot be related to a super-goal at the higher abstraction layer because it is specific to the lower abstraction layer.

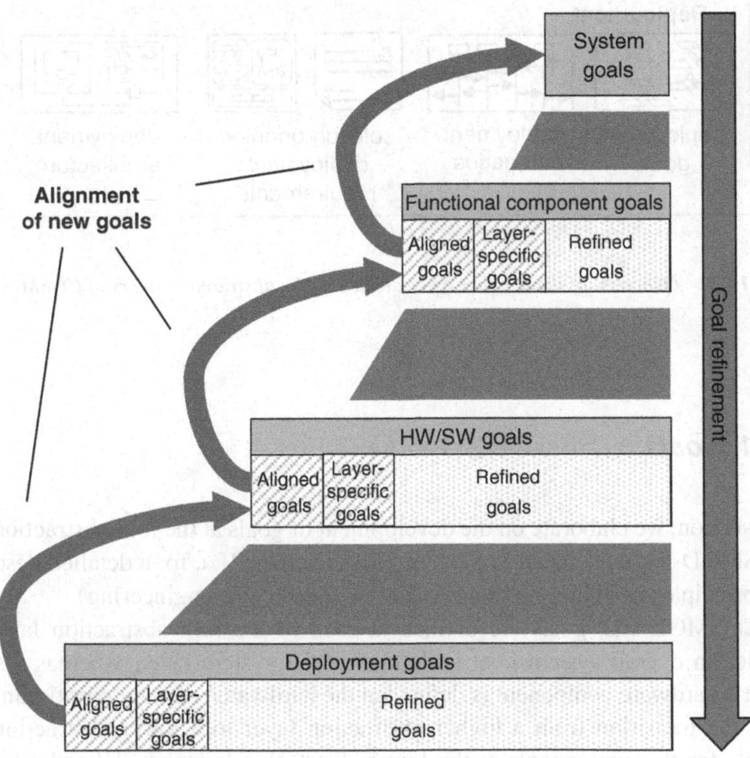

Fig. 35-13 *Goal refinement (top down) and alignment (bottom up) across the four abstraction layers*

Alignment of goals with the higher abstraction layer

If possible, the new goals identified at the lower abstraction layer should be aligned with the goals defined at the layer above (see "aligned goals" in Fig. 35-13). This is accomplished either, by adding a relationship to an existing goal (case 1) by adding or modifying a goal at the higher abstraction layer (case 2), or by discarding the goal at the lower abstraction layer (case 3).

Layer-specific goals

However, there are also abstraction layer-specific goals (case 4). Such goals are relevant for the system but cannot be related to a super-goal at the higher abstraction layer because defining a corresponding super-goal at the higher abstraction layer would be out of scope for this layer. For example, technology-specific goals which depend on the chosen technology should only be defined at the abstraction layer where the technology choice is manifested (see Example 35-5). Similarly, goals that depend on a particular system decomposition should be defined only at the layer where the decomposition is defined (see Example 35-6).

Example 35-5: Layer-specific goals

The used real-time operating system (RTOS) is known to provide functions that consume a large amount of memory due to an inefficient implementation. Hence, at the deployment layer, the goal is defined to only use functions that make efficient use of memory.

Example 35-6: Decomposition-related goals

A functional component defined at the functional decomposition layer is realised by two software components at the hardware/software components layer that interact with each other. The stakeholders define a new goal at the hardware/software components layer pertaining to the quality of the communication between the two software components. This goal has no obvious relationship to any goal defined at the functional decomposition layer because it is specific to the decomposition of the functional component into two software components.

Figure 35-13 illustrates the refinement of goals across the abstraction layers, the definition of new goals, and the (partial) alignment of new goals with the goals defined at the higher abstraction layers.

Solution-independent specification of goals

Restrictions concerning the desired solution (e.g. imposed by the client, a law, the technical infrastructure or the like) should be defined as explicit design constraints and not hidden in goal definitions. Therefore, a goal defined at a specific abstraction layer should not prescribe a specific solution such as a specific architecture or a specific decomposition at the abstraction layers below. For example, a goal defined at the system layer should not prescribe a specific functional decomposition, hardware/software partitioning, or deployment but rather document the actual intention. In Example 35-7, a goal that, in fact, defines a solution is redefined in order to clarify the intention behind the design solution initially required. If needed, the solution space can be restricted by defining design constraints and relating the design constraints to the goal. Over time, even if the design constraints change, the goal will most likely not change.

Example 35-7: Avoiding restrictions of the solution in goals

Goal definition imposing a design solution:

"G12: The system shall consist of two separate electronic control units."

Revised goal definition clarifying the intention:

"G12: An error during the execution of the comfort-related functions must not affect the execution of the safety-related functions."

The revised goal definition gives the designers freedom to find other design solutions. For instance, the designers might come up with a solution that satisfies the goal by using one electronic control unit with two independent processors.

System Goals

Functionality and quality of the system

System goals pertain to the functionality and quality that the system offers to its external actors (humans and other systems). For instance, a system goal can define the intended use of the system by an external actor. An example for a driver-assistant system would be the goal: "The driver shall be able to adjust the desired speed."

A system goal should contribute to the overall system vision. The system vision is thus typically refined into a set of system goals. Documenting system goals in a goal model using extended AND/OR-trees (see Section 8.4) or the notation provided by the KAOS framework (see Section 8.6) is recommended. In addition, each goal should be defined in more detail using a goal template such as the one introduced in Section 8.1.

Goal responsibility

A goal defined at the system layer can be assigned to the system or to an external actor. By assigning a goal to the system, the system becomes responsible for satisfying the goal. In order to be able to satisfy a goal assigned to the system, the goal must be defined using "variables" that the system can monitor or control via its interfaces (see [Van Lamsweerde 2009]).

Functional Component Goals

Refinement of terminal system goals

The goals defined at the system layer as leaves of the goal tree (called terminal goals) are refined at the functional decomposition layer into more fine-grained goals. A goal resulting from the refinement can be assigned to a functional component. By relating a goal to a specific functional component this component is made responsible for satisfying the goal.

Satisfaction of system goals

During the refinement of the terminal system goal, the stakeholders must ensure that, if all goals resulting from the refinement are satisfied, the terminal system goal is satisfied as well.

Alignment of system goals and functional component goals

In addition to the refinement, the stakeholders elicit and document new functional component goals which have no relationship to a system goal (see Page 690). If a new functional component goal is identified, the four cases outlined above apply: To identify which of the four cases applies, the requirements engineer should check whether the newly identified goal refines a system goal (case 1). If this is the case, the requirements engineer has to relate this goal to the corresponding system goal. If a new functional component goal cannot be related to a system goal, the requirements engineers should validate if the goal is actually needed (cases 2 and 4), or if the goal should be discarded (case 3). Therefore, the requirements engineer should ensure that the functional component goal really represents needed functionality or needed quality properties. If so, the functional component goal either leads to an adaptation of the goals at the system layer (a new system goal is identified) or existing system goals are adapted (case 2), or the goal is marked as a layer-specific goal (case 4).

Hardware/Software Component Goals

Refinement of terminal functional-component goals

The terminal goals defined at the functional decomposition layer are refined at the hardware/software partitioning layer into sub-goals which are assigned to individual hardware or software components. The goals defined at the hardware/software partitioning layer must satisfy the defined functional component goals.

New goals at the hardware/software partitioning layer

In addition, (as outlined above) new goals can be elicited for each hardware and software component. The new goals should be aligned with the goals defined at the functional decomposition layer. If a relevant hardware/software component goal cannot be related to a functional component goal, it is marked as a layer-specific goal and thus represents a goal that is specific to the chosen hardware/software partitioning or the chosen technology.

Deployment Goals

Platform-specific goal refinement

When a hardware/software component is assigned to a specific physical unit, the operating environment for the hardware/software component is fixed. As a consequence, it may be necessary to refine the goals defined at the hardware/software layer for this component under consideration of the operating environment or the hardware/software platform. The resulting goals are defined as platform-specific goals at the deployment layer.

Like at the other abstraction layers, also new goals can be defined at the deployment layer. Some of these goals may be specific to the layer and hence not refine any goal defined at the hardware/software partitioning layer.

35.2.2 Scenarios

In this section, we outline the development of scenarios at the four abstraction layers defined by the COSMOD-RE method (for a detailed description of the basic concepts of scenarios in requirements engineering, we refer to Part III.b).

Interaction scenarios and system-internal scenarios

COSMOD-RE employs interaction scenarios (see Definition 10-5, Page 158) at the system layer and system-internal scenarios (see Definition 10-4, Page 157) at the lower abstraction layers. Interaction scenarios enable the description and analysis of the interactions that take place between the system and its external actors, whereas system-internal scenarios define interactions among the components of the system. System-internal scenarios can be used at the three lower layers, for instance, to support the identification of relationships between components or even to identify the components themselves.

Refinement of a scenario

Figure 35-14 illustrates the principles of developing scenarios across the four abstraction layers. System scenarios which define the interactions of the system with its environment are successively refined at the lower abstraction layers. When a scenario is refined, the instance (lifeline) representing the system is decomposed into a set of components, e.g. functional components at the functional decomposition layer or hardware/software components at the hardware/software partitioning layer. In the refined scenario, in addition to the interactions already defined in the scenario at the higher abstraction layer, interactions are added between the instances that result from the decomposition. These new interactions are required to fulfil the scenario defined at the higher abstraction layer.

A scenario can be refined by multiple scenarios

The scenario at the higher abstraction layer can be refined into one or more scenarios at a lower abstraction layer. For instance, there may be different ways of satisfying a system scenario by a sequence of system-internal interactions. In such a case, at the lower abstraction layer, one main scenario and several alternative scenarios are defined when refining the system scenario.

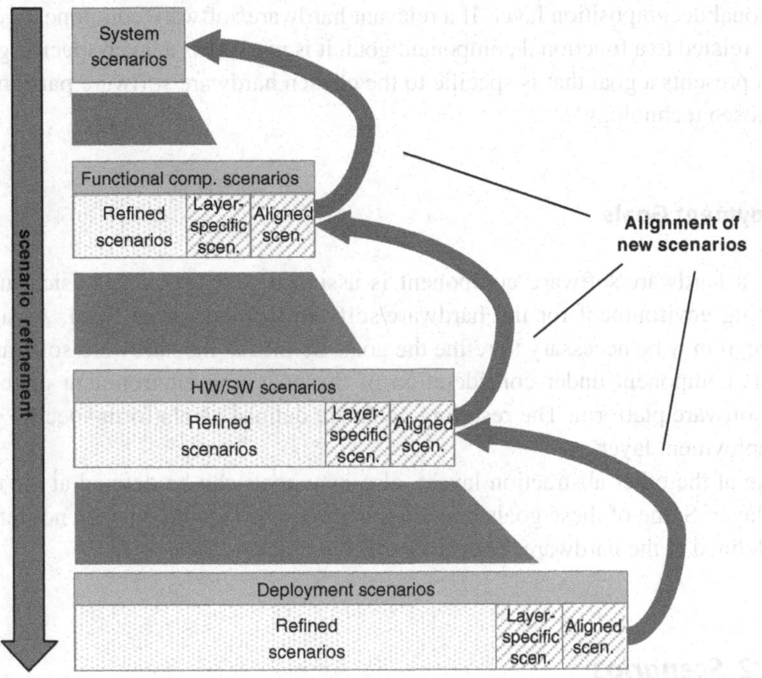

Fig. 35-14 *Scenario refinement (top down) and consolidation (bottom up) across the four abstraction layers*

New scenarios and interactions

In addition to refining the scenarios defined at the higher abstraction layers, additional interactions (for instance, with the environment) as well as entirely new scenarios can be identified at the lower abstraction layers. If a new scenario is identified at a lower abstraction layer, one of the following cases may apply:

- *First case*: The new scenario can be related to a scenario that is already defined at the higher abstraction layer (by a "refines" relationship).

- *Second case*: The new scenario indicates a missing scenario at the higher abstraction layer. After defining the missing scenario, the two scenarios are related to each other by a "refines" relationship.
- *Third case*: The new scenario cannot be related to a scenario at the higher abstraction layer because the scenario is irrelevant for the system.
- *Fourth case*: The new scenario cannot be related to a scenario at the higher abstraction layer because it is specific to the lower abstraction layer.

Alignment of scenarios across abstraction layers

The new scenarios and interactions identified at the lower abstraction layer should, wherever possible, be aligned with the scenarios defined at the higher abstraction layers (see "aligned scenarios" in Fig. 35-14). This is accomplished either by adding a relationship to an existing scenario (first case), by adding or modifying a scenario at the higher abstraction layer (second case), or by discarding the scenario at the lower abstraction layer (third case).

Layer-specific scenarios

However, the architectural refinement across the layers can also require the definition of entirely new scenarios which have no relationship to the scenarios defined at the layer above (fourth case). For instance, at the hardware/software layer, additional scenarios may be defined that are required for managing the hardware but are not in the scope of the higher abstraction layers (see Example 35-8). In other words, these scenarios do not have a meaningful abstraction at the higher abstraction layer, for instance, because they are purely technology specific. Such scenarios are defined as layer-specific scenarios (see Fig. 35-14).

Example 35-8: Layer-specific scenarios

An actuator defined at the hardware/software partitioning layer needs to be calibrated every *n* activations. The stakeholders define a scenario to document the requirements for the calibration (such as checking the number of activations, performing the calibration, and resetting the number of activations). At the abstraction layer above (the functional decomposition layer) the calibration scenario has no meaningful counterpart, since the calibration of a hardware component is not a meaningful concept at this abstraction layer or is merely an internal process of a single functional component.

System Scenarios

Avoiding premature design decisions

System scenarios are defined at the system layer and focus on the interactions between the system and its external actors. System-internal actions are not defined at the system layer in order to avoid premature design decisions as well as unnecessary design constraints.

Template- and model-based documentation

We recommend eliciting a set of initial system scenarios and documenting these scenarios by means of a use case template (see Section 35.4.2 for a description of the template used in COSMOD-RE). The documented scenarios should then be specified using sequence diagrams (see Section 11.5). Specifying scenarios with sequence diagrams directs the focus on the actors in the scenarios and their interactions. Moreover, the documentation of scenarios using sequence diagrams significantly facilitates the refinement of the scenarios at the lower abstraction layers.

Positive and negative scenarios

Note that scenarios should be used to specify both required sequences of interactions as well as unwanted or prohibited sequences of interactions. In other words, positive scenarios should be used to define the required sequences of interactions, and negative scenarios to define undesired or prohibited sequences of interactions (see Section 10.2).

Technology-independent actors and interactions

The definition of external actors has a decisive impact on the scenarios at the system layer. The external actors should be chosen in such a way that all essential interactions of the system can be captured and, at the same time, technical details of the interactions are omitted. For instance, the actors and interactions defined at the system layer should abstract from the technical details of specific, peripheral hardware components such as sensors and actuators.

Functional Component Scenarios

Logical interactions between functional components

Functional component scenarios are system-internal scenarios that focus on the logical interactions between functional components. Since functional component scenarios are defined at a logical level, the interactions are defined independently of their potential realisation, for instance, through the exchange of messages via a network and/or a set of method calls.

Refined and layer-specific scenarios

Functional component scenarios are defined based on the interaction scenarios defined at the system layer. The resulting functional component scenarios define the interactions between the functional components required to realise the interactions of the system with the external actors, i.e. the system scenarios. In addition, new, layer-specific scenarios can be defined at the functional components layer.

Avoid defining control structures in scenarios

A functional component scenario should represent an exemplary, linear course of interactions between the functional components. Keeping the functional component scenarios simple (at least in the first place), e.g. by avoiding branches and loops within the scenarios, is hence recommended. If a functional component scenario actually defines the control structure of an algorithm, this scenario might be biased by a specific solution. In such a case, the requirements engineers should try to identify the actual requirements and then to define the scenario with fewer branches, loops etc.

Hardware/Software Scenarios

Interactions between hardware and software components

Hardware/software scenarios focus on the interactions between hardware and software components such as application software components, sensors, actuators, computing devices, network components, human–machine interface devices etc.

Refined and layer-specific scenarios

Hardware/software scenarios can be developed based on the functional component scenarios. In addition, typically hardware/software scenarios need to be defined that do not follow from a functional component scenario but are specific to the hardware/software layer (see Example 35-8).

Deployment Scenarios

Deployment scenarios define the interactions between hardware and software components that have been deployed to a specific hardware/software platform. They define both local interactions within individual, physical units of the hardware/software platform as well as remote interactions between different physical units. When defining the scenarios, the specifics of the hardware/software platform are taken into account such as the operating system or the type(s) of communication network(s) used.

Deployment-specific refinement of interactions

When developing a deployment scenario based on an already defined hardware/software scenario, an interaction defined in the hardware/software scenario can result, for instance, in a local interaction within a physical unit or a sequence of messages that are exchanged between different physical units via a network. The interactions defined at the hardware/software partitioning layer may also need to be refined in order to accommodate specifics of the hardware/software infrastructure. For instance, it may be necessary to refine an interaction due to the specifics of the operating system running on a physical unit or the specifics of the network connecting a set of physical units.

Deployment-specific scenarios

In addition to the deployment scenarios that are based on hardware/software scenarios, new scenarios may be defined at the deployment layer which are specific to the deployment itself (see Example 35-9).

Example 35-9: Layer-specific scenario at the deployment layer

The topology to which the hardware and software components of the system are deployed includes a specific network. To ensure the correct functioning of this network, the physical nodes connected to it are required to exchange management messages. The stakeholders document the requirements related to this exchange of messages using a set of deployment scenarios. These scenarios are not directly related to any scenario at the hardware/software partitioning layer, i.e. they are purely specific to the chosen deployment.

35.2.3 Solution-Oriented Requirements

Documentation using natural language or solution-oriented models

At each abstraction layer detailed, solution-oriented requirements are specified. Detailed requirements comprise functional requirements such as functions, data, and behaviour as well as quality requirements such as performance, safety, or security requirements and constraints. The solution-oriented requirements can be specified using natural language (see Chapter 16) as well as using solution-oriented requirements models such as data flow models, class models, or state models (see Chapter 14).

Granularity and scope depend on the abstraction layer

The granularity and scope of a solution-oriented requirements artefact depend on the abstraction layer at which the requirements artefact is defined. Functional and quality requirements that affect the entire system are defined at the system layer. Requirements pertaining to individual functional components are defined at the functional decomposition layer. Requirements for the hardware and software components are defined at the hardware/software partitioning layer. At the deployment layer, the requirements for the physical units are defined based on the hardware and software component requirements defined at the layer above.

Illustration of the concept using behavioural requirements

Below, we illustrate the definition of solution-oriented requirements at the four abstraction layers. For reasons of simplicity, we focus mainly on behavioural requirements. The basic concepts outlined below can, however, be easily adapted to all other types of solution-oriented requirements.

External and internal behaviour

The behavioural requirements at a specific abstraction layer define the externally visible behaviour of the system (system layer), a functional component (functional decomposition layer), a hardware or software component (hardware/software partitioning layer), or a physical unit or network (deployment layer).

Behavioural specification in architectural artefacts

Note that the realisation of the required behaviour can be specified using architectural artefacts. In contrast to the behavioural requirements artefacts, the architectural artefacts are not restricted to the external behaviour at the respective layer, i.e. they may additionally define the internal behaviour of the system, functional component, hardware/software component, or physical unit or network.

System Requirements

Externally visible system behaviour

The behavioural requirements at the system layer define the externally visible behaviour of the system, i.e. the required behaviour of the system at its interfaces. These requirements essentially define how the system reacts to events and which responses the system provides to the external actors.

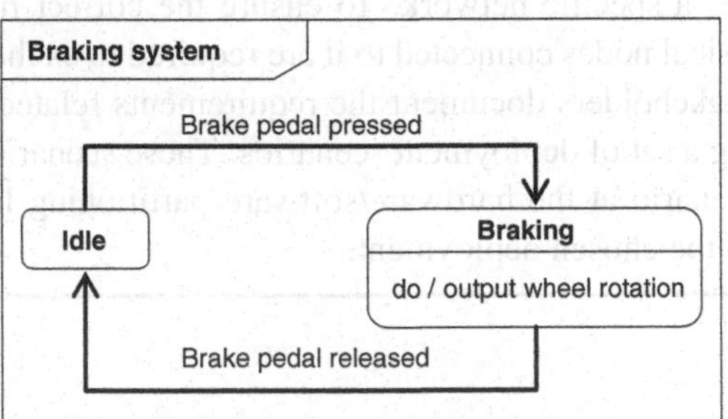

Fig. 35-15 *Example of a behavioural model at the system layer*

Behavioural model of the system

The model of the required behaviour at this layer comprises the main inputs, the main outputs, and the major states of the system. The model is hence very coarse grained, i.e. at the system layer, no internal details of the system are defined in order to avoid premature design decisions. The behavioural requirements model at the system layer should therefore not include definitions of internal system behaviour such as internal events or internal actions. In contrast, a behavioural, architectural model at the system layer may also define system-internal behaviour. A very simple example of a behavioural requirements model is depicted in Fig. 35-15.

Functional Component Requirements

A functional component can interact with the system environment as well as with other functional components. At the functional decomposition layer, the behavioural requirements for each functional component are defined.

Documentation using state machines

Defining the behavioural requirements using automata or state machines is recommended. If state machines are used to define the behaviour of each functional component, the behavioural requirements specification at the functional decomposition layer consists of a set of communicating state machines (see Fig. 35-6 for an example of communicating automata). Interactions between functional components are represented by shared transitions of the corresponding state machines (see Example 35-1).

Externally visible behaviour of each functional component

Each state machine should specify the externally visible behaviour of an individual functional component, i.e. the behaviour that can be observed by external actors and/or by other functional components. Capturing the major inputs and outputs as well as the major states of each functional component, is therefore recommended when documenting behavioural requirements at the functional components layer. In other words, the state machines should not define the internal behaviour of the functional components. If a state machine is overly complex, this may be an indication that the stakeholders have defined internal details of the functional component instead of focussing on the externally visible behaviour.

Reducing the complexity of a state machine

If a state machine becomes very complex even though it focusses on the externally visible behaviour of the functional component, the stakeholders should decompose the functional component into several functional components and define the behavioural requirements for the sub-components. Thereby, the complexity of the state machine as well as the complexity of the functional component itself is reduced.

Hardware/Software Requirements

Behavioural requirements for each HW/SW component

A hardware or software component can interact with other hardware or software components as well as with the system environment. At the hardware/software partitioning layer, the behavioural requirements for each individual hardware and software component are defined. Therefore, for each software and hardware component, a model of the externally visible behaviour of this component is defined (see Section 35.2.4 for an example). Focussing on the externally visible behaviour of the hardware and software components aims to avoid premature design decisions. Again, the behavioural requirements can be documented using automata or state machines. Together, the behavioural models of the software and hardware components form a network of communicating automata (state machines).

Reducing complexity at the HW/SW layer

Note that, to reduce the complexity, only specific types of software and hardware components are defined at the hardware/software partitioning layer (see Section 35.1.4). Hardware and software components that are part of the hardware/software platform are not considered at this layer.

Deployment Requirements

At the deployment layer, the behavioural requirements for the physical units are defined. This is achieved by assigning the hardware and software components defined at the hardware/software partitioning layer together with the associated requirements to the physical units and refining the requirements based on the assignment to physical units.

Refinement of requirements due to the deployment

For instance, two interacting software components SW_1 and SW_2 may be deployed to two different physical units connected via a network. In this case, the interactions between the two software components SW_1 and SW_2 (defined by their behavioural requirements at the hardware/software partitioning layer) must be adapted in order to take into account the distribution of the components and the communication via a network. Most likely, the network employs a specific communication protocol which the components SW_1 and SW_2 must observe. As a consequence the behavioural requirements defined for SW_1 and SW_2 need to be refined at the deployment layer. Similarly, the software infrastructure (i.e. the operating system, device drivers etc.) of the physical unit to which a specific software component is deployed may necessitate a refinement of the behavioural requirements (see Example 35-3).

35.2.4 Architectural Artefacts

The COSMOD-RE method employs structural architectural models (see e.g. [Hofmeister et al. 1999; Kruchten 1995]) in order to document the decomposition of the system across the four abstraction layers. In addition, the internal behaviour of the architectural components at each layer can be defined in detail using state machines. In this section, we focus on the structural part of the architectural models used in COSMOD-RE.

Structural architectural models at the four abstraction layers

The structural architectural model consists of components, interfaces, and connectors. The components possess defined interfaces and are linked to one another by means of connectors. As described in Section 35.1, each of the four abstraction layers has a certain focus and scope and thus considers a specific kind of system decomposition. In the following, we sketch the scope of the structural architecture models at each abstraction layer.

System Interfaces

Embedding of the system

The structural architecture model at the system layer focusses on the embedding of the system into its operational environment. For this purpose, the system is modelled as a single black-box component, i.e. the system is not decomposed into sub-components. The interfaces of this single component define the locations of the interactions between the system and its environment, i.e. between the system and the external actors (humans or systems).

Logical system interfaces

A complex software-intensive system typically needs several different types of interfaces such as human–machine interfaces, network interfaces as well as interfaces the system uses to monitor and control variables in the environment. The interfaces defined in the architectural model at the system layer are logical interfaces, i.e. they realise logical (essential) interactions between the system and its environment. A logical or essential interaction represents the exchange of information, events, energy, or material. For each interface, the kinds of interactions (e.g. functions, services) offered by the interface to the environment are defined.

Functional Architecture

Logical decomposition is independent of the implementation technology

The functional system architecture defines a decomposition of the system into a set of logical, functional components. A logical, functional component represents a coherent fragment of the system functionality. It is defined independently from the technology (such as software, digital hardware, mechanics, hydraulics etc.) used to realise this functionality, i.e. the functional architectural model should be (as far as possible) technology free. Thus, the functional architecture defines a logical, essential architectural model of the system.

Logical interfaces and connectors

A functional component has well-defined interfaces through which it can interact with other functional components and/or external actors (persons and systems). A connector represents a logical connection between two or more components. It thus interrelates functional components. Via a connector, and the corresponding interfaces assigned to this connector, the functional components exchange data and/or control signals.

Hierarchical decomposition of components and connectors

Functional components and connectors may be hierarchically decomposed into sub-components and sub-connectors. This facilitates the definition of a coarse-grained functional architecture and its later decomposition into more detailed functional components. However, as the decomposition is conducted within the functional decomposition layer, the resulting sub-components and sub-connectors must still be defined independently from the realisation technology (e.g. digital hardware or software). In other words, the sub-components and their interfaces as well as the sub-connectors should be technology free.

Hardware/Software Architecture

Components, interfaces, and connectors at the HW/SW partitioning layer

The (structural) architecture model at the hardware/software partitioning layer defines the decomposition of the system into hardware and software components. The hardware components defined at this layer represent, for instance, displays, controls, sensors, and actuators. The software components defined at this layer partition the application software. Hardware/software connectors represent connections between hardware and software components such as a communication network or a communication bus. Therein, an entire network or bus is typically defined as a single connector, i.e. the details of the network are hidden at this abstraction layer.

Hiding technical details

In order to further reduce the complexity of the models at the hardware/software partitioning layer, detailed technical aspects should not be defined at this layer. For example, components that belong to the infrastructure (e.g. the operating system of a physical unit) should not be considered when defining the architectural model at this layer. Moreover, the assignment of hardware and software components to physical units (deployment) is not considered at this layer.

1-to-n vs. n-to-m mapping between functional and HW/SW components

Note that there is not necessarily a simple 1-to-*n* mapping (nor a 1-to-1 mapping) between the functional decomposition at the layer above and the hardware/software architecture defined at this layer. In other words, a functional component can be realised by several hardware and/or software components. Vice versa, a hardware or software component can realise the functionality of more than just one functional component defined at the functional decomposition layer. Therefore, an *n*-to-*m* mapping between the functional and the hardware/software components can exist. Such *n*-to-*m* mappings are required, for instance, if the functional decomposition is performed based on entirely different design criteria than the hardware/software decomposition. Nevertheless, one can decide to forbid an *n*-to-*m* mapping and thus enforce a 1-to-*n* mapping between functional components and the hardware/software components. This typically results in a significantly simpler transition from the functional decomposition layer to the hardware/software partitioning layer.

Deployment Architecture

System topology and hardware/software platform

At the deployment layer, the hardware and software components defined at the hardware/software partitioning layer are assigned to physical units. These physical units have (physical) interfaces and are connected to each other via (physical) communication channels. The resulting configuration of physical units, their interfaces, and communication channels is called the system topology. Each physical unit has its own software infrastructure consisting e.g. of an operating system and device drivers. The system topology and the software infrastructures of the physical units form the hardware/software platform of the system.

Deployment of the hardware and software components

The hardware and software components defined at the layer above are deployed to the hardware/software platform defined at the deployment layer. If two hardware/software components are related by a connector at the hardware/software partitioning layer and these components are assigned to different physical units, the connector must be mapped to a physical connection between the physical units. The relationships between the hardware/software architecture and the deployment architecture must be documented accordingly. In addition, the rationales for the deployment decisions made should be documented as well.

n-to-m mapping of HW/SW components to physical units

Each component defined at the hardware/software partitioning layer must be assigned to one or more physical units defined at the deployment layer. Vice versa, to each physical unit, one or multiple software and hardware components can be assigned. Consequently, in principle, an *n*-to-*m* mapping between the hardware/software components defined at the hardware/software partitioning layer and the physical units defined at the deployment layer is possible.

Realisation of an n-to-m mapping

If a software component is deployed to two or more physical units, this means that the software component is distributed across these physical units. In such a case, requirements must be defined making clear how the architecture shall realise the mapping. For instance, some kind of middleware may be needed to support the distributed execution of the software component, and the physical units need to be connected by communication channels.

Restriction to an n-to-1 mapping

Like at the higher abstraction layers, the stakeholders can decide to forbid an *n*-to-*m* mapping between hardware/software components and physical units in order to facilitate simpler transitions between the abstraction layers. However, as a consequence of such a restriction, the need arises to further decompose the components at the hardware/software layer so that each hardware/software component can be assigned to exactly one physical unit. Thus, the hardware/software architecture is strongly influenced by the deployment architecture, i.e. the separation of concerns is not maintained any more.

35.2.5 Interrelations between the Artefacts

In this section, we point out the major interrelations between the artefacts described in the previous sections.

Interrelations between Goals and Scenarios

Exploiting the benefits of goal–scenario–coupling

Each (terminal) goal defined at a specific layer must be associated with at least one scenario at this layer which concretises the goal. For instance, each (terminal) goal defined at the hardware/software partitioning layer should be related to at least one hardware/software component scenario. Vice versa, each scenario at a specific abstraction layer must be associated with at least one goal at this layer which is satisfied by executing the scenario. The benefits of goal–scenario–coupling are described in Section 12.3. Among other things, at each abstraction layer, the goals defined at this layer can be used to support the elicitation as well as the validation of the scenarios at this layer and vice versa. For instance, the elicitation and validation of functional component scenarios can be supported by the defined functional component goals.

Interrelations between Goals/Scenarios and Solution-Oriented Requirements

Basis for defining detailed, solution-oriented requirements

Scenarios together with their associated goals facilitate the identification and definition of solution-oriented requirements at each of the four abstraction layers. Typically, several (detailed) solution-oriented requirements can be derived from each goal and its associated scenarios. For instance, hardware/software scenarios together with the associated hardware/software goals facilitate the elicitation and definition of the solution-oriented hardware/software requirements.

Validation of solution-oriented requirements using goals and scenarios

In addition, goals and scenarios can be used to validate the solution-oriented requirements at each abstraction layer. The solution-oriented requirements should satisfy the goals and scenarios defined at the respective abstraction layer. Forbidden, negative scenarios (see Section 10.2) should be excluded by the solution-oriented requirements. For instance, the scenarios defined at the system layer can be used to validate the behavioural requirements model of the system and ensure that (forbidden) negative system scenarios are excluded by the solution-oriented system requirements defined in the behavioural model.

Interrelations between Goals and Architecture

Intertwining of goal decomposition and system decomposition

The decomposition of goals is intertwined with the decomposition of the system components. For example, the decomposition of system goals into functional component goals is influenced by the decomposition of the system into functional components and vice versa. Similarly, the definition of hardware/software component goals is intertwined with the partitioning of the system into hardware and software components.

Alternative goal refinements for exploring architectural alternatives

During the decomposition of goals and architecture, the stakeholders can use OR-decomposition relationships to denote alternative decompositions of goals that are related to different decompositions of the system. For instance, at the deployment layer, goal models can be used to support the exploration of and the reasoning about different possible assignments of the hardware and software components to the physical units of the hardware/software platform.

Architecture evaluation using goals

In addition, the goals defined at each abstraction layer support architectural evaluation. For instance, the defined hardware/software goals can be used to validate a draft of the high-level hardware/software architecture.

Interrelations between Scenarios and Architecture

Scenarios support architectural design

Scenarios support the design of the system architecture at the different abstraction layers. At each layer, the identification and definition of the components, their interfaces, and their connections can be supported by defining scenarios at this layer. Vice versa, the (draft) architecture defined at a specific abstraction layer influences the definition of the scenarios at this abstraction layer. For instance, at the functional decomposition layer, the system architect may suggest an initial functional architecture (i.e. functional components, interfaces, and connectors) based on the requirements defined at the system layer. Using this initial functional architecture, system scenarios can be refined into functional component scenarios.

Validating and improving the architecture using scenarios

Scenarios can also be used to explore, validate, and improve architectural drafts. For instance, the stakeholders may define hardware/software scenarios in order to explore and evaluate several alternative hardware/software design solutions.

Hence, at each layer, the definition of the scenarios is typically intertwined with the development of the architecture.

35.3 COSMOD-RE Co-design Processes

COSMOD-RE provides three distinct co-design processes which structure the development process across the four abstraction layers defined in Section 35.1. We provide an overview of the three co-design processes in Section 35.3.1 and outline each co-design process in Sections 35.3.2–35.3.4. The interrelations between the co-design processes are described in Section 35.3.5.

35.3.1 Overview

Co-development of requirements and architecture

Each of the three co-design processes focusses mainly on two abstraction layers. For instance, the system co-design process focusses on the development of the artefacts at the system layer and the artefacts at the functional decomposition layer. In addition, each co-design processes partially overlaps with another co-design-process with regard to a specific abstraction layer (see Section 35.3.5). The goals of the three co-design processes can be briefly characterised as follows:

- *System-level co-design* (see Section 35.3.2): The main goal of this co-design process is to develop the system requirements along with an initial functional decomposition of the system.
- *Function-level co-design* (see Section 35.3.3): The scope of this co-design process is the definition of the functional component requirements and an initial hardware/software partitioning.
- *Hardware/software-level co-design* (see Section 35.3.4): This co-design process mainly aims at defining the hardware/software requirements along with an initial deployment of the hardware/software components to the hardware/software platform.

Intertwining of requirements and architecture

Each co-design process supports the intertwined development of requirements and architectural artefacts. For instance, by co-developing system requirements and the functional architecture, the system co-design process supports the intertwined development of the system requirements and the functional architecture (see Section 34.2). The relationship between COSMOD-RE artefact types and the three co-design processes is depicted in Fig. 35-16 on Page 707.

Sequential execution of the co-design processes

The stakeholders may iterate the system co-design process until they achieve satisfactory results at the upper two abstraction layers, and then initiate the function-level co-design process, or they might follow a more iterative approach and switch between the two co-design processes more frequently. In a similar manner, the stakeholders can switch more or less frequently between the function-level and the hardware/software-level co-design processes.

Parallel execution of the co-design processes

If the co-design processes are performed by different teams, departments, or organisations, the different co-design processes may be performed (partly) in parallel. For instance, if partial results of the system-level co-design process are available, the function-level co-design process can be initiated based on these partial results. Since, at this time, the system-level co-design process has not been completed yet, the two co-design processes are performed in parallel. Furthermore, multiple instances of the function-level co-design process can be performed in parallel. After the high-level, functional architecture has been defined in the system-level co-design process, multiple instances of the function-level co-design process can be initiated, each instance focussing on a different functional component.

35.3.2 System-Level Co-design

Goal and key results

The goal of the system-level co-design process is to co-develop requirements artefacts at the system layer and architectural artefacts at the functional decomposition layer (see Fig. 35-16). The key results of the system-level co-design process thus comprise all system-layer artefact types as well as partial artefacts of the functional decomposition layer. The system-layer artefacts comprise system goals, system scenarios, solution-oriented system requirements as well as the system interfaces. The partial artefacts of the functional decomposition layer comprise an initial set of functional component goals and functional component scenarios as well as an initial functional architecture. All stated artefact types are described in detail in Section 35.2.

Definition of solution-oriented system requirements

When defining the solution-oriented system requirements, the system goals and system scenarios as well as the initial artefacts of the functional decomposition layer developed during system-level co-design are taken into account. At the time when the solution-oriented system requirements are defined, the system goals and system scenarios have already been aligned with the (initial) functional architecture (see Section 35.4). Note, however, that the artefacts defined at the functional decomposition layer are considered merely as initial or preliminary artefacts as they must be completed and further elaborated in the function-level co-design process.

35.3.3 Function-Level Co-design

Goal and input

The goal of the function-level co-design process is to co-develop requirements artefacts at the functional decomposition layer and architectural artefacts at the hardware/software partitioning layer (see Fig. 35-16). When the function-level co-design process is initiated, an initial functional architecture along with initial functional component goals and initial functional component scenarios are available from the system-level co-design process. These artefacts are extended and adapted during function-level co-design. For instance, the stakeholders may define additional goals and scenarios for the functional components or elaborate on the functional architecture. Note that these extensions and adaptations may affect the system-layer artefacts and hence trigger the execution of the system-level co-design process to integrate the required adaptations.

Key results

The results of the function-level co-design process at the functional decomposition layer are the revised and complemented functional-component goals and scenarios, the solution-oriented functional-component requirements, and a revised functional architecture. At the hardware/software partitioning layer, initial, preliminary hardware/software goals and scenarios as well as an initial hardware/software architecture are developed.

35.3.4 Hardware/Software-Level Co-design

Goal and input

The goal of the hardware/software-level co-design process is to co-develop requirements artefacts at the hardware/software layer and architectural artefacts at the deployment layer. When the hardware/software-level co-design process is initiated, at least partial hardware/software goals and scenarios and an initial hardware/software architecture are available. These artefacts are adapted and extended during hardware/software-level co-design.

Key results

The key results of this co-design process are the adapted and extended hardware/software goals and scenarios, the solution-oriented hardware/software requirements defined for each hardware and software component as well as an initial, preliminary deployment of the hardware and software components to the physical units of the (existing or envisioned) hardware/software platform.

Solution-oriented deployment requirements

After the deployment goals and scenarios have become sufficiently stable by iterating the hardware/software-level co-design process, the solution-oriented deployment requirements can be defined based on the deployment goals and scenarios. At that time, the deployment goals and scenarios have been aligned with the deployment architecture. However, it may still be necessary to revise the deployment architecture after defining the solution-oriented deployment requirements.

35.3.5 Overlaps between the Co-design Processes

Reasons for the overlaps

Figure 35-16 depicts the artefact types defined in Section 35.2 and relates them to the three co-design processes outlined above. For each co-design process, the artefacts created or changed are depicted. As highlighted in the figure some overlaps between neighbouring co-design processes exist. For instance, the goals, scenarios, and architectural artefacts defined at the functional decomposition layer are subjects of the system-level co-design process as well as the function-level co-design process. The reason for this overlap is that the output of one co-design process obviously serves as input for the next co-design process. For example, the goals, scenarios, and architecture defined at the functional decomposition layer are the input (the problem definition) for the function-level co-design process. Moreover, due to the co-development, the artefacts defined at the functional decomposition layer evolve while the solution at the hardware/software partitioning layer is established.

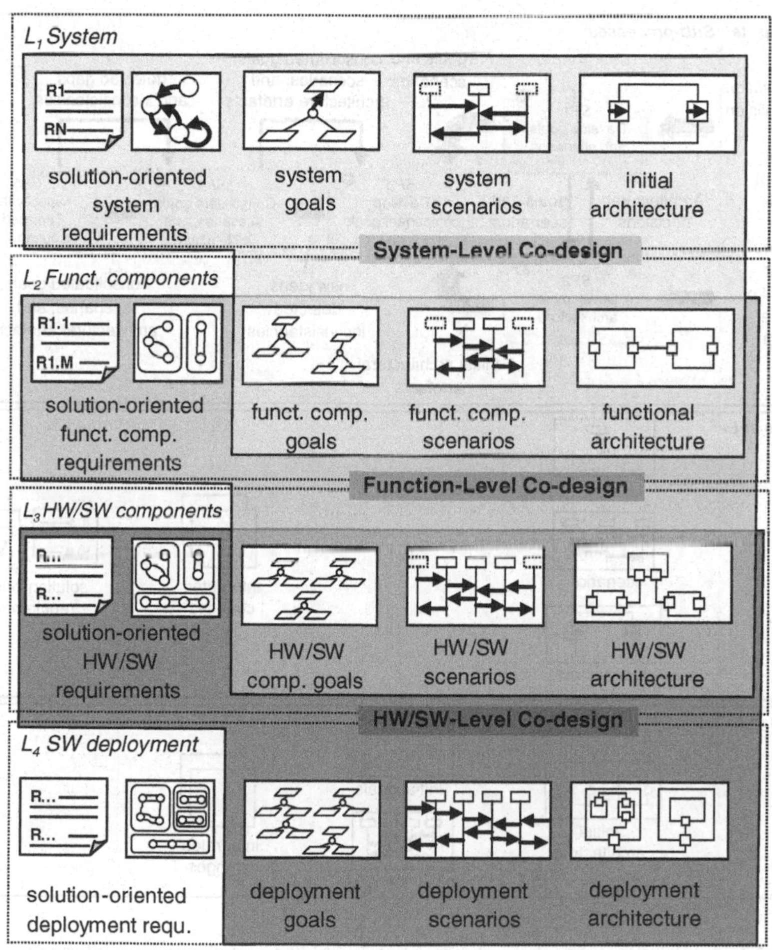

Fig. 35-16 *COSMOD-RE artefact types and the three co-design processes*

35.4 The Five Sub-processes of Each Co-design Process

COSMOD-RE provides five interrelated sub-processes for each co-design process and thereby structures the co-development of requirements and architectural artefacts in each co-development process (see Section 34.2). Section 35.4.1 provides an overview of the sub-processes. The individual sub-processes are described in more detail in Sections 35.4.2–35.4.6. In Chapter 36, we provide a comprehensive example that illustrates the execution of the five sub-processes.

35.4.1 Overview

Figure 35-17 shows an overview of the five sub-processes and the main information flows between them.

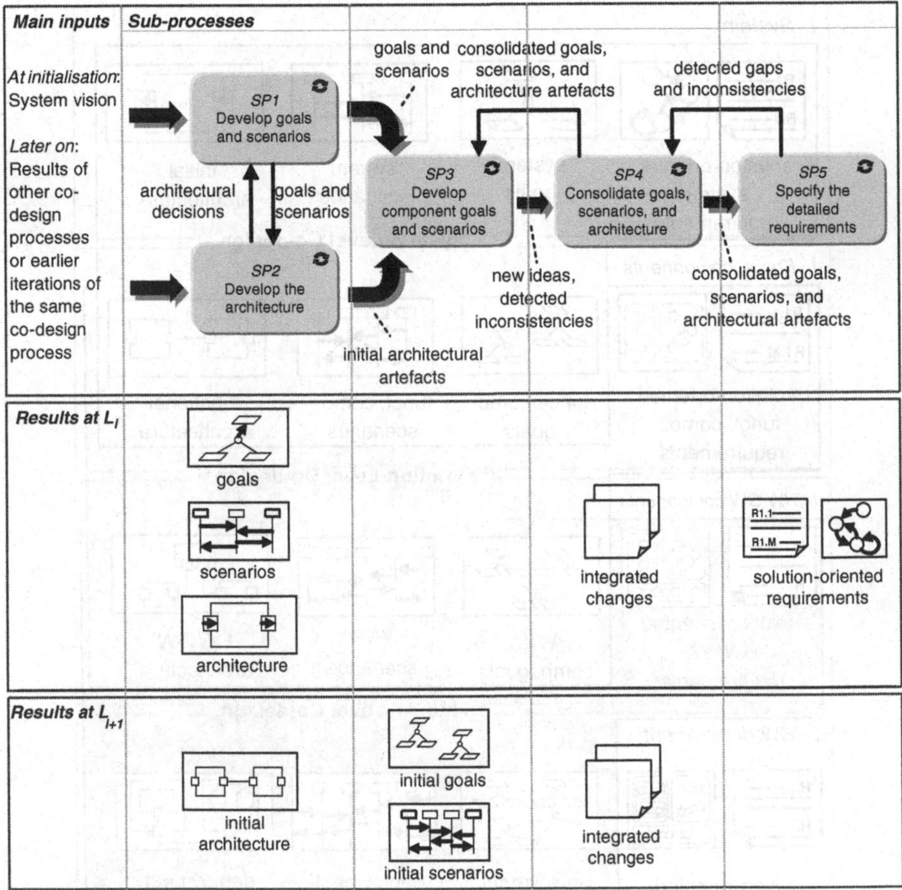

Fig. 35-17 *Overview of the sub-processes including inputs, main information flows, and key results*

- Sub-process SP_1 supports the development of initial goals and scenarios at the layer L_i.
- Sub-process SP_2 supports the development of initial architectural artefacts at the layer L_{i+1}. Sub-processes SP_1 and SP_2 can be performed in an intertwined manner or, partly, in parallel.
- In sub-process SP_3 the goals and scenarios for the architectural components at layer L_{i+1} are defined based on the goals and scenarios defined at layer L_i and the initial architecture defined at layer L_{i+1}. Therein, the responsibilities for satisfying the goals and scenarios at layer L_{i+1} are assigned to the architectural components and inconsistencies between the goals, scenarios, and architecture are identified.
- Sub-process SP_4 is responsible for reconciling the requirements and the architecture at the two neighbouring layers L_i and L_{i+1}. It results in corrections and changes applied to the requirements artefacts and the architectural artefacts at both layers.
- In sub-process SP_5, the detailed (solution-oriented) requirements at layer L_i are specified based on the results obtained from the other sub-processes.

Generic procedure for each co-design process

The five sub-processes embody a generic procedure which can be applied at different abstraction layers, i.e. to the system as a whole, to individual functional components, or to individual hardware/software components. In other words, this procedure is applicable in each co-design process presented in Section 35.3. We characterise each sub-processes and sketch the interworking of the five sub-processes in the following subsections. When describing the five sub-processes, we focus on the execution of the five sub-processes within the system-level co-design process.

35.4.2 Developing Initial Goals and Scenarios (SP_1)

Goal, input, and output

The goal of this sub-process is to develop initial goals and initial scenarios for the system. At process initialisation the main inputs to this sub-process are typically the system vision and the stakeholders' experience and knowledge about similar systems. Later on during the process, already defined goals and scenarios are available as input. The output is a set of (new or extended) system usage scenarios and system goals (see Fig. 35-17). The system goals represent the key properties of the system that are needed to fulfil the system vision. The system (usage) scenarios document exemplary sequences of interactions between the system and its external actors which lead to the satisfaction of the system goals.

Elicitation of system goals and scenarios

System goals and system scenarios are elicited by involving the relevant stakeholders such as product managers, customers as well as other requirement sources. The identification of requirement sources can be accomplished by the technique presented in Section 21.4. During the elicitation of system goals and scenarios, the requirements engineers have to identify the relevant external actors (humans and other systems), the goals of each actor, the relevant actor–system–relationships, the required system inputs and outputs as well as the required quality properties of the actor–system–interactions. The elicitation of system goals and system scenarios can be supported by applying the elicitation techniques described in Part IV.b.

Documentation of goals and scenarios

The system goals and scenarios are documented using the techniques explained in Chapters 8 (documentation of goals) and 11 (documentation of scenarios). We recommend documenting each goal and each scenario using an appropriate template.

Therein, logically related scenarios should be grouped into use cases, and each use case should be related to one or several goals. When documenting the goals and use cases, the rules for documenting goals described in Section 8.2 and the rules for documenting scenarios described in Section 11.4 should be observed. The templates we use in COSMOD-RE for documenting goals and scenarios are explained below.

Iterative development of goals and scenarios

As explained in Section 12.3, the development of goals and scenarios is an iterative process, in which scenarios initiate, for instance, the definition of new goals, and goals initiate the definition of new scenarios. The process of eliciting and documenting goals and scenarios should be continued until a sufficiently stable set of goals and scenarios is attained.

Model-based specification of goals and scenarios

Goals and scenarios that are sufficiently stable should be specified using appropriate models. The model-based specification of goals and scenarios helps to uncover errors in the template-based documentation. Furthermore, the models ease the definition of goals and scenarios for the next abstraction layer in sub-process SP_3 as well as the consolidation of goals and scenarios across different abstraction layers in sub-process SP_4.

Goals and their relationships should be documented using a goal modelling language such as an extended AND/OR goal graph or a KAOS goal model (see Chapter 8). Each use case scenario should be documented using a modelling language such as message sequence charts or UML2/SysML sequence diagrams (see Section 11.5). In addition, one or more use case diagrams should be created to provide an overview of the system use cases.

Goal Template

The goal template used in COSMOD-RE has been defined based on the goal template presented in Section 8.1. The goal template is shown in Tab. 35-1.

Tab. 35-1 *Goal template applied in the COSMOD-RE method*

Goal [ID]	[Short name of the goal]
Abstraction layer	[Name of the abstraction layer at which this goal is defined]
Scope	[Name of the system or component for which this goal has been defined]
Goal category	[Soft goal or hard goal]
Goal description	[Precise description of the goal in natural language]
Goal responsibility	[Name of the agent responsible for satisfying this goal]
Super-goals	[References to goals that are refined by this goal and the type of refinement]
Sub-goals	[References to goals that refine this goal and the type of refinement]
Conflicting goals	[References to goals that are in conflict with this goal]
Related scenarios	[References to scenarios documenting the satisfaction of this goal]

Slots of the goal template

The first slot below the name of the goal denotes the *abstraction layer* at which this goal is defined, i.e. system layer, functional decomposition layer, hardware/software partitioning layer or deployment layer. The next slot documents the *scope* of the goal. At the system layer, the scope is the system itself. However, at lower abstraction layers the scope can be limited to a specific functional component or hardware/software component. The *goal category* documents whether the goal is a hard goal or a soft goal (see Section 8.6). The *goal description* provides an as precise as possible definition of the goal in natural language. The *goal responsibility* defines the agent responsible for satisfying the goal. At the system layer, the responsibility for satisfying a goal can be assigned either to the system or an external actor. At the lower abstraction layers, the responsibility can be assigned to architectural elements such as functional components or hardware/software components. The last four slots document relationships to other goals and to scenarios.

Use Case Template

The use case template employed in COSMOD-RE has been defined based on the template presented in Section 11.2. The use case template is depicted in Tab. 35-2.

Tab. 35-2 *Use case template applied in the COSMOD-RE method*

Use case [ID]	[Short name of the use case]	
Abstraction layer	[Name of the abstraction layer at which the use case is defined]	
Scope	[Name of the system or component whose interactions are documented in this use case]	
Primary actor	[Name of the actor whose goal(s) shall be satisfied by executing this use case]	
Secondary actors	[Other actors, i.e. persons, systems, components, devices etc. involved in this use case.]	
Input and output variables	❑ *Input*: [Names of external variables whose values are measured or read during the execution of this use case.] ❑ *Output*: [Names of external variables whose values are changed or influenced during the execution of this use case.]	
Related goals	[References to the goals that shall be satisfied by executing this use case.]	
Preconditions	[Conditions on the system/component or its environment that must hold before the use case can be executed.]	
Success guarantee	[Conditions on the system / component or its environment that are guaranteed to hold after the use case has been completed successfully.]	
Minimal guarantee	[Conditions on the system / component or its environment that are guaranteed to hold after any execution of this use case, both, in case of success and in case of failure.]	
Extension points	[Locations, i.e. steps of the use case scenarios, at which this use case is extended by other use cases or includes other use cases.]	
Trigger	[Event that initiates the use case, e.g. a system event, time event, or external event.]	
Main scenario	Step	Action
	…	…
Alternative scenarios	Step	Action
	…	…
Failure scenarios	Step	Action
	…	…
Technology and data variation	[Descriptions of realisation alternatives for performing individual steps of the use case scenarios.]	
Special requirements	[Descriptions of quality requirements and constraints for individual steps of the use case scenarios or the entire use case.]	

Abstraction layer and scope

Since a use case can be documented at different abstraction layers, the first slot below the name slot denotes the *abstraction layer* of the use case. The *scope* of a use case at the system layer is typically the system itself. At lower abstraction layers the scope of a use case may be limited to a specific functional component or hardware/software component. The abstraction layer and scope of a use case influence the interactions that are defined by the use case scenarios. At the system layer, the scenarios document interactions between the system and the external actors. A scenario at a lower abstraction layer can document, for instance, the interactions of a functional component with external actors and other system components. In this case, the scope of the use case is the stated functional component.

Primary actor, secondary actors, and input/output variables

Like an ordinary use case template, the template shown in Tab. 35-2 defines the primary actor and the secondary actors of the use case. However, an embedded system not only interacts with tangible actors such as humans and other system, but also with variables, e.g. variables of the physical environment such as speed, temperature etc. The use case template has therefore been extended by a slot for *input and output variables*.

Related goals

The slot *related goals* documents the relationships of the use case to goals which are concretised by the use case, i.e. goals that shall be satisfied by executing the use case. Typically, the identifier of the associated goal is included in this slot. For better readability, the name of the goal can be stated as well.

Preconditions, guarantees, trigger, and scenarios

The slots *preconditions, success guarantee, minimal guarantee, extension points*, and *trigger* are standard slots that are quite common in use case modelling. The template distinguishes three types of scenarios: *main scenario, alternative scenarios*, and *failure scenarios. Technology and data variation* The slot *technology and data variation* can be used to define alternative realisations of a scenario step. For instance, a step in which a driver unlocks the car can be realised by turning the key, by using a remote control, or by keyless go.

Special requirements

The slot *special requirements* defines additional requirements with regard to the use case scenario such as quality requirements or constraints.

35.4.3 Developing an Initial Architecture (SP_2)

Goal, input, and output

The goal of this sub-process is to develop an initial architecture for the intended system. For this purpose, the sub-process explores and evaluates possible architectural solutions (i.e. system concepts). Therein, the stakeholders involved in SP_2 typically differ from those involved in SP_1. The inputs to this sub-process include the system vision, the known requirements (goals and scenarios), and existing/known system concepts. The output of the sub-processes is a solution concept consisting mainly of a coarse-grained and possibly partial architecture (see Fig. 35-17 on Page 708).

Design of the architecture

The architectural design created in the system-level co-design process consists of two parts: the system interfaces (i.e. the embedding of the system into its operational environment) and an initial, coarse-grained functional architecture of the system. When defining the system interfaces, the known system scenarios should be considered since, by documenting the interactions with external actors, the scenarios indicate required system interfaces. The functional architecture should reflect the chosen system concept. Typically, several system concepts have to be explored in order to define the functional architecture. The exploration of different system concepts should take into account the known quality goals (e.g. safety goals) influencing the functional architecture. The functional architecture should be defined in a way that supports the further structuring and detailing of the problem. It should therefore abstract from solution details.

Documentation of the architecture

During the early design stages, box-and-line diagrams are generally sufficient for documenting the different candidate architectures. After the system architects have selected a candidate architecture, documenting this architecture using an architecture description language (ADL) is recommended. The chosen language should support the modelling of components, interfaces, and connectors. In addition to the architecture itself, the design decisions and rationales should also be documented and related to the elements of the architecture.

35.4.4 Developing Component Goals and Scenarios (SP_3)

Goal, input, and output

This sub-process aims to obtain initial requirements for each functional component defined in the functional architecture in order to be able to detect mismatches between the (system) requirements and the functional architecture. The inputs for SP_3 are the results of the sub-processes SP_1 and SP_2, i.e. the defined system goals and system scenarios, and the initial, functional architecture (see Fig. 35-17 on Page 708). Sub-process SP_3 consists of mainly three activities that are performed iteratively:

- *Responsibility assignment*: This activity assigns the responsibilities for the system goals and scenario steps to architectural elements. Therein, for a system goal or scenario, a unique responsibility assignment is typically not possible.
- *Refinement*: To facilitate a unique responsibility assignment of goals and scenarios to architectural elements, this activity defines goals and scenarios for the individual architectural elements based on the goals and scenarios defined at a higher abstraction layer.
- *Comparison*: This activity identifies differences between the requirements (goals and scenarios) and the architecture in order to improve consistency and develop new ideas.

Responsibility assignment

During responsibility assignment, the stakeholders identify the architectural elements that are needed to realise a specific goal or a specific scenario and relate the goal or scenario to the identified architectural elements.

Definition of detailed goals and scenarios

In most cases, the responsibility for satisfying a goal or scenario defined at the system layer cannot be assigned to an individual architectural element defined at the functional components layer. To facilitate a unique responsibility assignment, initial goals and scenarios for the individual functional components must be defined based on the goals and scenarios defined for the system. Therein, the traceability of the functional component goals to the system goals and the traceability of the functional component scenarios to the system scenarios need to be ensured.

Comparison

The comparison of the requirements (i.e. the refined goals and scenarios) and the architecture has the following two main objectives:

- Validate whether the architecture supports the system goals and scenarios sufficiently well.
- Identify new ideas for system goals and system scenarios based on the proposed system architecture.

Comparison leads to additional insights

The comparison of the requirements and the architecture reveals goals and scenarios that are not accounted for by the architecture as well as architectural solutions that empower, for instance, new kinds of system usage. Hence, the comparison of the requirements and the architecture facilitates additional insights about both the envisioned requirements and the envisioned architecture. The results of the sub-process include ideas for new goals and scenarios as well as ideas for new design solutions. Furthermore, this sub-process detects inconsistencies between the requirements artefacts and the architectural artefacts (system interfaces and functional architecture).

Goal Refinement

Developing component goals by goal refinement

Goal refinement aims to identify sub-goals at the functional components layer that satisfy the terminal system goals and can, in addition, be assigned to individual functional components defined in the (initial) functional architecture. To identify the functional component goals, the stakeholders should focus on a specific, terminal system goal and perform the following steps iteratively:

- *Step 1*: Identify the functional components that are needed to satisfy the considered goal.
- *Step 2*: If multiple components must cooperate in order to satisfy the considered goal, decompose the goal into sub-goals each of which can be satisfied by fewer functional components.
- *Step 3*: Relate the sub-goals resulting from step 2 to the super-goal by an AND-decomposition relationship. Continue with step 2 for each sub-goal until the each resulting sub-goal can be uniquely assigned to some functional component.

Consolidation of the refined goals

The process outlined above is performed for each terminal system goal. Therein, if the sub-goals of two or more terminal system goals overlap, the respective sub-goals should be merged.

Responsibility assignment

Goal refinement results in sub-goals that can be assigned to individual functional components defined in the functional architecture. Through the responsibility assignment of goals to architectural components, each architectural component is assigned a set of responsibilities expressed by the goals.

Detection of problems in goals and architecture

The assignment of goals to components helps reveal potential problems with the goal model and the architecture model. For instance, the following cases may occur:

- The refinement results in a relevant goal cannot be assigned to any component. This case indicates that either a component is missing or the goal is unnecessary.
- After all system goals have been refined, some components have no assigned goals. This case indicates that either one or multiple goals are missing or the components are unnecessary.
- A single component is responsible for realising all or most sub-goals. This case indicates that the component is a “hot-spot” that will probably cause difficulties during implementation and testing. The architects should consider changing the design (e.g. splitting the component into several components) and/or reassigning the responsibilities.

- A goal has been assigned to a component, yet the component cannot fully satisfy the goal. In this case, the requirements engineers and architects should jointly analyse which changes of the architecture and the requirements are necessary to facilitate a responsibility assignment that allows for satisfying the goal. For instance, additional interfaces and connections or a decomposition and reassignment of the goal might be needed.

Documentation of problems and suggestions

Throughout this sub-process, the stakeholders document the detected problems, suggested extensions and changes as well as ideas concerning the goal model and the architecture model.

Identification of additional goals

During the refinement, responsibility assignment, and comparison, the stakeholders may identify additional goals at the functional components layer which do not result from the refinement of system goals. These goals should be documented for further use. Note, however, that additional goals for each individual functional component (not necessarily resulting from goal refinement) are identified systematically during function-level co-design. In other words, as outlined in Section 35.3.5, there is an overlap between the system-level and the function-level co-design processes regarding the definition of functional-component goals.

Scenario Refinement

Developing component scenarios by scenario refinement

The refinement of a system scenario can be accomplished by the following steps:

- *Step 1*: Identify the functional components that are responsible for realising the considered system scenario. Decompose the instance representing the system in the system scenario into the identified set of functional components.
- *Step 2*: Assign each scenario step (i.e. each system–actortinteraction) defined in the system scenario to a functional component.
- *Step 3*: Complete the refinement by adding the required, system-internal interactions between the functional components.

Consolidation of the refined scenarios

The process outlined above is performed for each system scenario. During the refinement it may turn out that the refined scenarios have some overlaps, i.e. redundant sequences of steps. These overlaps should be eliminated by restructuring and consolidating the refined scenarios. For instance, "include" and "extend" relationships can be used to reduce redundancy among the functional component scenarios.

Responsibility assignment

The responsibility assignment is performed in steps 1 and 2. In step 1, a coarse-grained assignment is performed, i.e. entire scenarios are assigned to sets of architectural components. Step 2 assigns responsibilities at a more fine-grained level, i.e. individual scenario steps are assigned to individual components. If, in step 2, a scenario step cannot be uniquely assigned to a functional component, either the scenario step must be refined or the architecture needs to be adapted. If a scenario step (i.e. a system–actor–interaction) is refined at the functional decomposition layer, it becomes more difficult to ensure consistency between the system scenario and its associated functional component scenario. It is hence advisable to adapt the system scenario as well in such a case.

Refinement relationships

The resulting functional component scenario documents the interactions between the functional components that are needed to realise the interactions between the system and its environment. The resulting functional component scenario is hence a refinement of the system scenario. This fact is documented by a refinement relationship from the functional component scenario to the system scenario.

Possible results of the comparison

The refinement of system scenarios supports the detection of deficiencies both in the initial scenarios and in the initial architecture. For instance, the following cases indicate required changes to the scenarios or the architecture:

- A component defined in the architecture has no interactions with other components or the environment. This case indicates that either the component is unnecessary or that relevant scenarios, interactions in some scenario, and/or component interfaces have not been considered yet.
- Two or multiple components are connected to each other according to the architecture model, yet none of the scenarios defines an interaction between these components. This case hints at unnecessary interfaces and connections in the architecture or at missing scenarios or interactions.
- A component is required to interact with another component, yet, according to the architecture model, the components are not connected to each other. This case hints at missing interfaces and connections in the architecture or unnecessary scenarios or interactions.

Documentation of problems and suggestions

Throughout this sub-process, the stakeholders document the identified problems, suggestions, and ideas concerning the scenarios and the architecture.

Identification of additional scenarios

During the refinement of scenarios, the stakeholders may identify additional scenarios that do not result from the refinement of system scenarios. In particular, by considering the architecture, the stakeholders typically identify many alternative and failure scenarios that are not evident at the system layer. The stakeholders should document the additional scenarios and thereby complement the set of functional component scenarios resulting from the refinement. Note, however, that in the function-level co-design process, scenarios for each functional component are identified systematically. This is achieved, for instance, by considering the input and output actions of each functional component. The overlap between the system-level and the function-level co-design processes concerning the definition of functional component scenarios is explained in Section 35.3.5.

35.4.5 Consolidating Requirements and Architectural Artefacts (SP_4)

Goal, input, and output

The main goal of this sub-process is to reconcile the requirements and the architecture based on the results of the comparison performed in sub-process SP_3. The results of the comparison drive the consolidation of the requirements and the architecture (see Fig. 35-17 on Page 708). The output of this sub-process is a consolidated set of goals and scenarios as well as architectural artefacts.

Consolidation activities

In sub-process SP_4, mainly the following, essential activities are performed:

- Consolidation and prioritisation of the proposed changes
- Adaptation of the goals, scenarios, and architecture

In the following, we briefly outline these activities.

Consolidation and Prioritisation of the Proposed Changes

Resolving contradictions

Prior to adapting the goals, scenarios, and architectural artefacts an evaluation and analysis of the problems, suggestions, and ideas resulting from SP_3 must be performed. For instance, the suggestions resulting from goal refinement and the suggestions resulting from scenario refinement (see Section 35.3) can include contradictions which must be resolved.

Approving the proposed changes

Furthermore, it is advisable to classify the proposed changes into two classes and deal with each proposed change according to its class:

- ❑ Changes that must be negotiated with stakeholders
- ❑ Changes that can be integrated without negotiation

Changes that should be assigned to the first class are, for instance, extensions and reductions of the initial requirements and modifications of the architecture. Such changes must typically be negotiated with the relevant stakeholders. Conflicts that arise while negotiating the changes with the stakeholders need to be resolved. Changes assigned to the second class are typically minor corrections and improvements of the documentation.

Prioritisation and cost-value analysis

If the amount of proposed (and approved) changes is large, assigning a priority to each change by applying one or more of the prioritisation techniques described in Chapter 32 is recommended. For significant changes, a cost–value analysis should be performed where each (major) change is prioritised with regard to its contribution to the overall system vision and its impact on the (development and/or production) costs. Based on the assigned priorities, a subset of the proposed changes is selected for integration into the requirements and architectural artefacts.

Adaptation of the Goals, Scenarios, and Architecture

Consistent adaption within each abstraction layer

Each approved change is integrated into the goals, scenarios, and architecture. The stakeholders should pay attention to integrating each change consistently into all artefacts affected by the change. For instance, changes applied to the system goals, in addition, need to be incorporated into the system scenarios. If a new goal is added, the stakeholders must ensure that at least one scenario is defined that documents the satisfaction of this goal. The new goal must, in addition, be related to the architectural model in order to define the responsibility for this goal.

Consistent adaptation across layers

Each change to the system goals, the system scenarios, or the system interfaces (i.e. the artefacts at the system layer) entails further changes at the functional decomposition layer. Vice versa, changes applied, initially, to the artefacts at the functional decomposition layer may lead to changes at the system layer if they affect an aspect of the system layer. For instance, if a new goal is defined at the functional decomposition layer, this may entail the definition of an additional system goal that is the super-goal of this new goal. However, the new goal defined at the functional decomposition layer may also be specific to this layer, i.e. have no super-goal at the system layer.

Adaptation of the artefact relationships

Furthermore, the relationships between the different artefacts must be adapted consistently within each abstraction layer as well as across the abstraction layers.

Iteration of the sub-processes SP_3 and SP_4

Although the integration of changes in this sub-process aims to achieve a consistent overall specification, the changes performed may still lead to new inconsistencies both between the artefacts of the individual layers as well as across layers that are not immediately obvious. In addition, the integration of changes is likely to trigger additional ideas and insights concerning the envisioned requirements and architecture. Hence, after each major revision of the requirements and architecture in sub-process SP_4, sub-process SP_3 should be re-executed with the results of sub-process SP_4 as inputs. This facilitates the detection of further or newly introduced inconsistencies as well as the generation of additional ideas. The iteration of the two sub-processes continues until the artefacts are sufficiently aligned and stable.

35.4.6 Specifying the Detailed System Requirements (SP_5)

Goal, input, and output

The goal of this sub-process is to define the solution-oriented system requirements based on the system goals, system scenarios, and the functional decomposition developed and aligned in the sub-processes SP_1 to SP_4 (see Fig. 35-17 on Page 708). The input to this sub-process includes goals, scenarios, and architectural artefacts that have reached sufficient stability from iterating the sub-processes SP_3 and SP_4. The results of the sub-process are detailed (solution-oriented) system requirements (i.e. functional requirements, quality requirements, and constraints) that are documented as textual requirements and/or by means of models. The detailed system requirements are the basis for further development activities such as the function-level co-design process.

Basis for the elaboration of the architecture

The sub-process SP_5 should make sure that the system requirements conform to the system goals and system scenarios and, in addition, all architecturally relevant requirements as well as design constraints are considered in the system requirements specification. If these conditions are fulfilled, the system requirements can be used to guide and support the further development of the artefacts at the lower abstraction layers. Note that the functional architecture needs to be reconsidered after the system requirements have been defined. However, the necessary adjustments tend to be local, since the key decisions concerning the requirements and the architecture have already been made during the execution of sub-processes SP_1 to SP_4.

Choosing an appropriate amount of details

The solution-oriented requirements are typically more detailed than the system goals and scenarios but contain less technical details than the functional component goals and scenarios. Hence, the stakeholders need to carefully choose the details that are included in the solution-oriented requirements at the system layer.

Chapter 36
Applying COSMOD-RE: an Example

In this chapter, we illustrate the application of the COSMOD-RE method to a driver assistance system. We sketch the main activities and artefacts of the system-level co-design process. Our example is based on the adaptive cruise control (ACC) system presented in [Bosch 2003]. For illustration purposes, the example uses a simplified version of the ACC system.

In the following, we use a simplified cruise control system to illustrate the system-level co-design process and the five sub-processes executed in this process.

36.1 Developing Initial Goals and Scenarios (SP_1)

In sub-process SP_1 of the system-level co-design process, initial goals and scenarios for the system are developed (see Section 35.4.2).

System Goals

Decomposition of the system vision into high-level system goals

In Fig. 36-1, an excerpt of the goal model for the ACC system is shown. The model has been documented using the KAOS goal modelling language described in Section 8.6. The model documents a set of goals defined at the system layer and the relationships between these goals. At the top of the model the system vision "Develop innovative adaptive cruise control system" is depicted as a super-goal. To refine the system vision, two system goals have been defined and related to the system vision by an AND-decomposition relationship: "Maintain set speed" and "Maintain safety distance to vehicle ahead". Note that, in the model, only the names of the goals are shown. In addition, each goal has a description that explains the goal in more detail.

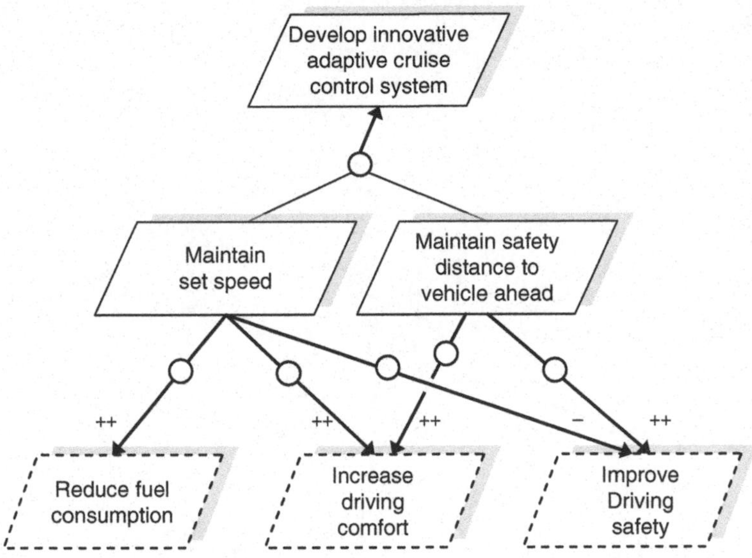

Fig. 36-1 *Excerpt of the goal model for the ACC system*

Goals and relationships in the example

The model also depicts the contributions of the goal "Maintain set speed" and the goal "Maintain safety distance to vehicle ahead" to three different quality goals (modelled as soft goals in Fig. 36-1). The three soft goals "Reduce fuel consumption", "Increase driving comfort", and "Improve driving safety" represent important qualities in the automotive domain and therefore also need to be considered during the development of the ACC system. The goal "Maintain set speed" contributes positively to the quality goals "Reduce fuel consumption" (e.g. because unnecessary acceleration and deceleration is avoided) and "Increase driving comfort" (because the driver is freed from the task of controlling the speed of the car e.g. during long trips). However, the contribution to the goal "Improve driving safety" is (slightly) negative, because, in certain situations, for instance, the danger of rear-end collisions may be increased. The goal "Maintain safety distance to vehicle ahead" contributes positively to the quality goals "Improve driving safety" and "Increase driving comfort".

Detailed description of each goal

Each goal shown in Fig. 36-1 is described in detail using the goal template depicted in Tab. 35-1. Table 36-1 shows the template-based description of the goal "Maintain set speed". Note that the slot "related scenarios" is filled in after an initial set of scenarios has been identified.

Tab. 36-1 *Description of the goal "Maintain set speed"*

Goal G2	**"Maintain set speed"**
Abstraction layer	System layer
Scope	ACC system
Goal category	Hard goal
Goal description	When the ACC system is active, it shall maintain the speed set by the driver until the system is deactivated, and allow the driver to adjust the set speed.
Goal responsibility	ACC system
Super-goals	G1 – Adaptive cruise control (AND-decomposition)
Sub-goals	—
Conflicting goals	—
Related scenarios	to be defined

Elicitation of system scenarios based on the goals

After defining this initial set of goals and documenting each goal using the goal template depicted in Tab. 35-1, system scenarios are developed to illustrate the satisfaction of these goals. Furthermore, the development of scenarios can lead to the identification of additional goals or the refinement of the identified system goals.

System Scenarios

Use case model

The initial set of scenarios (use cases) elicited for the ACC system based on the initial system goals is depicted in Fig. 36-2. The use case diagram in Fig. 36-2 shows the system boundary of the ACC system, the external actors, the initial set of use cases, and the relationships between external actors and use cases.

External actors

During the development of the scenarios, the following four external actors have been identified for the ACC system by analysing the initial system goals and the system context:

- *Driver*: The main purpose of the ACC system is to satisfy the goals of the driver. The driver is hence the primary actor of all use cases shown in Fig. 36-2.
- *Vehicle ahead*: The ACC system must obviously be aware of the distance to the vehicle ahead in order to be able to satisfy the goal "Maintain safety distance to vehicle ahead". Hence the vehicle ahead is modelled as an external actor of the system.
- *Engine*: The ACC system must interact with the engine in order to be able to satisfy the goals "Maintain set speed" and "Maintain safety distance to vehicle ahead", i.e. to maintain or increase the driving speed.

- *Brakes*: The ACC system must interact with the brakes in order to be able to satisfy the goal "Maintain safety distance to vehicle ahead", i.e. to reduce the driving speed.

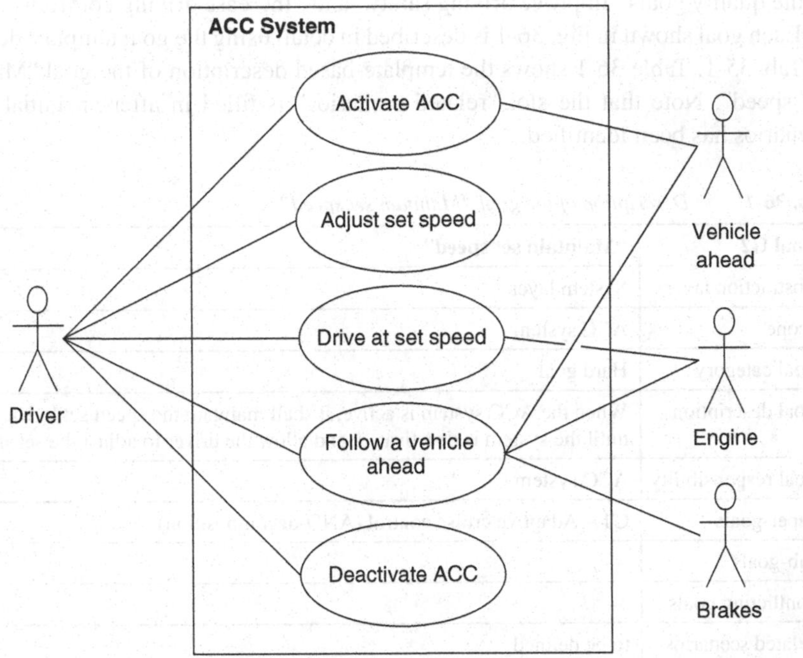

Fig. 36-2 *Use case diagram for the ACC system*

Use cases

The satisfaction of the system goals defined for the ACC system is illustrated by means of the following use cases defining the required interactions between the ACC system and its external actors:

- *Activate ACC*: This use case comprises a set of scenarios documenting different ways of activating the ACC system.
- *Adjust set speed*: This use case comprises a set of scenarios documenting different ways of adjusting the speed that the ACC system shall maintain.
- *Drive at set speed*: This use case illustrates how the ACC system achieves the goal "Maintain set speed" by interacting with the driver and the engine.
- *Follow a vehicle ahead*: This use case illustrates how the ACC system achieves the goal "Maintain safety distance to vehicle ahead" by interacting with the driver, the vehicle ahead, the engine, and the brakes.
- *Deactivate ACC*: This use case comprises a set of scenarios documenting different ways of deactivating the ACC system.

Detailed descriptions of the use cases
Use cases

After eliciting an initial set of use cases, each use case is defined in detail using the use case template shown in Tab. 35-2 (see Tables 36-2 and 36-3). For instance, the detailed description of use case "Activate ACC" is shown in Tab. 36-2. The use

Tab. 36-2 *Description of the use case "Activate ACC"*

Use case UC1	"Activate ACC"	
Abstraction layer	System layer	
Scope	ACC system	
Primary actor	Driver	
Secondary actors	Vehicle ahead	
Input and output variables	❑ *Input*: current speed ❑ *Output*: —	
Related goals	Maintain set speed	
Preconditions	ACC is inactive	
Success guarantee	Set speed is displayed to the driver	
Minimal guarantee	—	
Extension points	—	
Trigger	Initiated by the driver	
Main scenario	Step	Action
	1	The driver activates the system with the current speed as the set speed.
	2	The system validates that the current speed is in the permissible range (if the validation fails, the use case terminates; see step 3b).
	3	The system validates that no vehicle is within the minimum safety distance (if the validation fails, the use case terminates; see step 4c).
	4	The system displays the set speed to the driver.
Alternative scenarios	Step	Action
	1a	The driver activates the system with the stored speed as the set speed.
	2a	The use case continues with step 3
Failure scenarios	Step	Action
	3b	The use case terminates.
	4c	The use case terminates.
Technology and data variation	—	
Special requirements	Step 2: To activate the ACC, the current speed must be within the range of 30 to 200 km/h.	

case defines a main scenario, an alternative scenario, and two failure scenarios. If the use case is executed successfully, the ACC system is activated and the set speed is displayed to the driver. If one of the failure scenarios is executed, the ACC system is inactive after the execution.

Use case "Follow a vehicle ahead"

Table 36-3 shows the detailed description of the use case "Follow a vehicle ahead". To reduce complexity, only the main scenario of this use case has been defined, initially.

Tab. 36-3 *Description of the use case "Follow a vehicle ahead"*

Use case UC4	"Follow a vehicle ahead"	
Abstraction layer	System layer	
Scope	ACC system	
Primary actor	Driver	
Secondary actors	Engine, brakes	
Input and output variables	❑ *Input*: current speed ❑ *Output*: engine torque, braking rate	
Related goals	Maintain safety distance to vehicle ahead	
Preconditions	ACC is active	
Success guarantee	The vehicle drives at a safe following distance to the vehicle ahead.	
Minimal guarantee	—	
Extension points	—	
Trigger	The system detects an object ahead.	
Main scenario	Step	Action
	1	The system validates that the distance to the object ahead is within the relevant detection range.
	2	The system notifies the driver about the detection of a relevant object ahead.
	3	The system acquires the current speed in order to determine the required deceleration.
	4	The system reduces the engine torque.
	5	The system actuates the brakes.
Alternative scenarios	Step	Action
	—	—
Failure scenarios	Step	Action
	—	—
Technology and data variation	—	
Special requirements	—	

36.2 Developing an Initial Architecture (SP_2)

In sub-process SP_2 of the system-level co-design process, the system interfaces and the initial functional architecture of the system are defined (see Section 35.4.3).

System Interfaces

Use of goals and scenarios

The system interfaces defined in this sub-process are logical locations at which the system exchanges information, energy, or material with its environment (see

Section 35.2.4). To define the system interfaces, among other things, the system goals and system scenarios (i.e. the system use cases) are analysed. Each system interface is typically required either to satisfy a system goal or to realise an interaction defined in a scenario. In addition, system interfaces can be identified by considering the external actors of the system. By analysing the goals, scenarios, and actors defined in Section 36.1, the following system interfaces have been identified for the ACC system:

- *Input from driver*: The input from the driver comprises, for instance, the activation of the system and the increase and decrease of the set speed.
- *Output to driver*: The output to the driver includes, among other things, displaying the set speed and notifying the driver about the detection of relevant objects ahead.
- *Distance to vehicles ahead*: Via this input interface, the ACC system determines the distance to the vehicle ahead as well as the speed of this vehicle.
- *Current speed*: Through this input interface, the ACC system acquires the current speed of the vehicle.
- *Output to engine*: The ACC system uses this interface in order to adjust the engine torque when accelerating or decelerating.
- *Output to brakes*: Via this interface, the ACC system operates the brakes.

Documentation of the system interfaces

Figure 36-3 depicts the system interfaces of the ACC system using an architecture description language. Note that, in addition to this model, the architectural artefacts at the system layer also include a description of each system interface as well as the rationales for defining each interface.

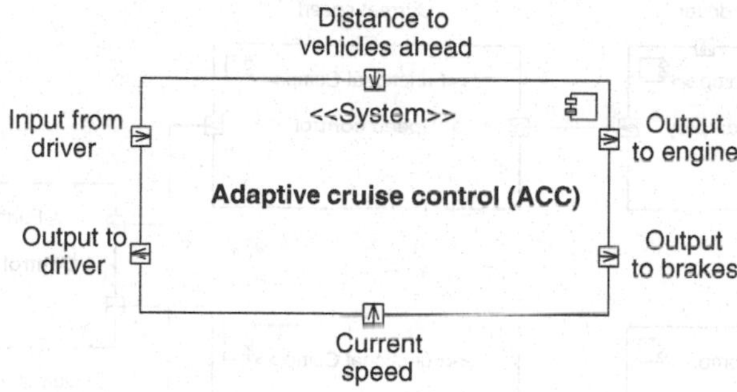

Fig. 36-3 *Initial definition of the system interfaces at the system layer*

Functional Architecture

Identification of components and their connections

The functional architecture defines the essential, functional (logical) components of the system as well as the logical interfaces and logical connections of these components. An initial functional architecture for the ACC system can be derived based on the known functionality (i.e. the services) that the ACC system must offer at its interfaces. Preliminary connections between the components can be defined based on the mutual dependencies between the components. However, these connections need to be checked and adapted, for instance, with the help of functional component goals and scenarios. The preliminary functional architecture comprises the following functional components:

- *Operation and display*: This component is responsible for detecting the inputs from the driver and for displaying outputs to the driver. When the system is activated, this component informs the "Speed control" and "Distance control" components about the activation.
- *Object detection*: This component is responsible for detecting relevant objects in front of the vehicle and estimating their distance and speed. It communicates the detected distance and speed of a relevant vehicle ahead to the "Distance control" component.
- *Speed control*: This component is responsible for controlling the vehicle speed in case no relevant object ahead has been detected (i.e. for driving at a constant speed). For this purpose, the component gets the current speed of the vehicle as input.
- *Distance control*: This component is responsible for controlling the speed of the vehicle when following a relevant vehicle ahead.
- *Control mode selection*: This component is responsible for determining the required engine torque and the required braking rate based on the input from the components "Speed control" and "Distance control".

The external interfaces of the system (see Fig. 36-3) are assigned to the individual functional components. Figure 36-4 depicts the resulting, preliminary functional architecture of the ACC system.

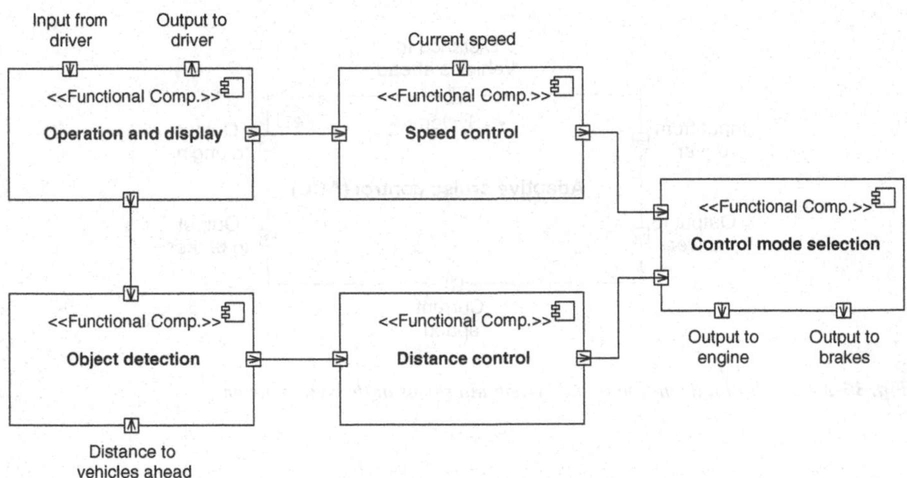

Fig. 36-4 *Preliminary functional architecture of the ACC system*

36.3 Developing Component Goals and Scenarios (SP_3)

Suggestion of changes to the goals, scenarios, and architecture

In this sub-process of the system-level co-design process initial goals and scenarios at the functional decomposition layer are defined based on the system goals, the system scenarios, and the initial, functional architecture. Through the assignment of the functional component goals and scenarios to the elements of the functional architecture, the stakeholders detect inconsistencies and propose changes to the goals, scenarios, and architecture (see Section 35.4.4).

Functional Component Goals

Refinement of the system goal "Maintain safety distance"

Figure 36-5 depicts the refinement of the system goal "maintain safety distance to vehicle ahead" (see Fig. 36-1) based on the functional architecture shown in Fig. 36-4. The process for refining system goals based on an initial functional architecture is outlined in Section 35.4.4. First, the system goal is refined into the two sub-goals "detect vehicle driving ahead" and "adapt speed to detected vehicle ahead". As both sub-goals must be satisfied to satisfy the system goal "maintain safety distance to vehicle ahead", the sub-goals are related to the super-goal by an AND-decomposition relationship. The stakeholders recognise that the responsibilities for realising these sub-goals cannot be uniquely assigned to the defined functional components. For instance, to satisfy the goal "adapt speed to vehicle ahead", the functional components "distance control" and "control mode selection" have to cooperate. Hence, the goal cannot be assigned uniquely to one of these functional components. Therefore, the sub-goals resulting from the first refinement need to be refined again.

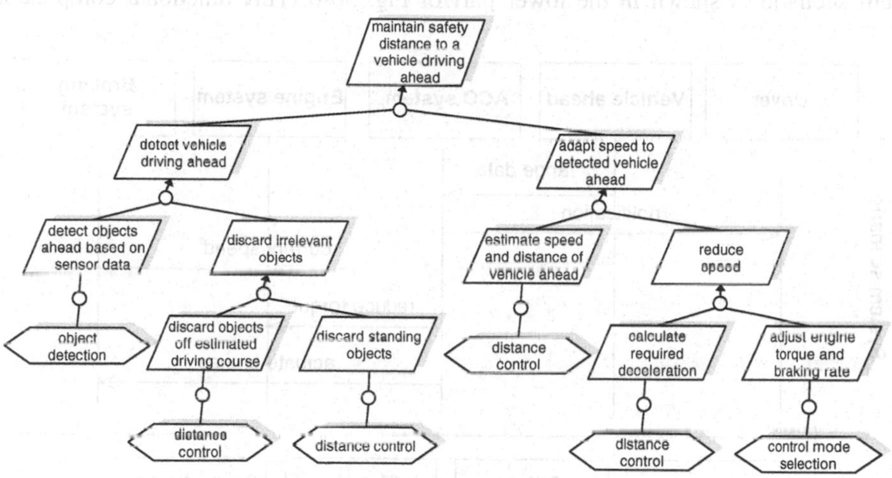

Fig. 36-5 *Refinement of the system goal "Keep safety distance to a vehicle driving ahead"*

Refinement of the sub-goal "Detect vehicle driving ahead"

The sub-goal "detect vehicle driving ahead" is refined into the sub-goals "detect objects ahead based on sensor data" and "discard irrelevant objects". The sub-goal "detect objects ahead based on sensor data" can be directly assigned to the functional component "object detection", i.e. the functional component is made responsible for satisfying this goal. Concerning the sub-goal "discard irrelevant objects" the stakeholders are unsure whether it can be assigned uniquely to a functional component. The stakeholders hence decide to refine this sub-goal again. The refinement results in the two sub-goals "discard objects off estimated driving course" and "discard standing objects", which are both assigned to the functional component "distance control". In a similar way, the goal "adapt speed to detected vehicle ahead" is refined, and the sub-goals are assigned to functional components.

Decomposition of a functional component

Based on the results of the refinement and responsibility assignment, the stakeholders suggest extensions and changes to the goal model and the architecture model. For instance, it is apparent from Fig. 36-5 that the component "distance control" is responsible for at least four (out of six) terminal functional component goals. The stakeholders interpret this as an indicator of high complexity of this component and suggest that the component be split into two separate components.

Identification of new goals

Furthermore, the component "operation and display" has no assigned goals. The stakeholders hence suggest the definition of two additional goals: "inform the driver about relevant events" and "allow the driver to activate/deactivate the system".

Functional Component Scenarios

Refinement of the scenario "Follow a vehicle ahead"

Figure 36-6 illustrates the refinement of the system use case "Follow vehicle ahead" (see Tab. 36-3) based on the architecture presented in Fig. 36-4. The process for refining system scenarios based on an initial functional architecture is outlined in Section 35.4.4. Prior to refining a use case, we recommend transferring the use case scenarios into sequence diagrams or message sequence charts (this is typically done already in sub-process SP_1).

The upper part of Fig. 36-6 shows the main scenario of the use case "Follow a vehicle ahead" documented as a message sequence chart. The refinement of the system scenario is shown in the lower part of Fig. 36-6. This functional component

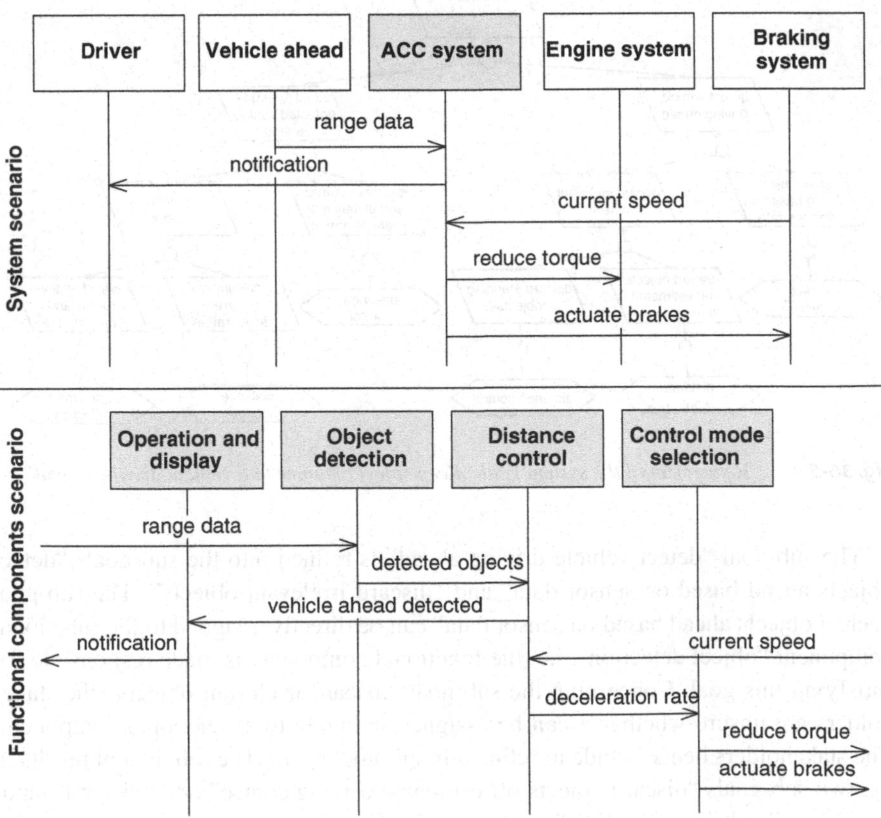

Fig. 36-6 *Refinement of the system scenario "Follow a vehicle ahead"*

scenario documents the interactions between the functional components that are needed to realise the interactions between the system and its environment. The interactions with the external actors are also shown in the refined scenario. However, due to space limitations, we have omitted the external actors themselves.

Identification of a new failure scenario

Based on the results of the refinement and responsibility assignment, the stakeholders suggest extensions and changes to the scenarios and the functional architecture (and possibly also the system interfaces). For instance, the stakeholders recognise that the interaction step labelled "deceleration rate" between the components "Distance control" and "Control mode selection" (see Fig. 36-6) may cause a failure. If the required deceleration rate exceeds a given bound, the system fails and must pass over the control to the driver. Hence, the stakeholders suggest defining a new failure scenario that documents the passing over of control to the driver. Due to the required interaction with the driver, the additional scenario not only affects the functional decomposition layer but also the system layer.

Identification of a new connection

By analysing the interactions among the functional components defined in the functional component scenarios, the stakeholders detect, for instance, that an interaction is needed between the "Distance control" component and the "Operation and display" component. If the "Distance control" component detects a relevant vehicle ahead, it must inform the "Operation and display" component (see the arrow labelled "vehicle ahead detected" in Fig. 36-6), which in turn signals the detection of a relevant vehicle to the driver. The stakeholders hence suggest adding the required interfaces and connections for this interaction to the architectural model.

36.4 Consolidating Requirements and Architectural Artefacts (SP_4)

Approval and consistent integration of changes

In this sub-process, the stakeholders evaluate, consolidate, and prioritise the changes proposed in sub-process SP_3. The approved changes are consistently integrated into the goals, scenarios, and architecture models, both at the system layer and at the functional decomposition layer (see Section 35.4.5).

Adaptation of Goals and Scenarios

Adaptation of the system goals

Based on the proposed changes (see Section 36.3), the initial system goals are extended by the goal "Interact with the driver". This goal is further decomposed into the two sub-goals "Inform the driver about relevant events" and "Allow the driver to activate/deactivate the system". In addition, two relationships from the new sub-goals to the soft goal "Improve driving safety" are included in the goal model, documenting that informing the driver about relevant events and allowing him to deactivate the system at any time contributes positively to driving safety. Figure 36-7 shows the revised system goal model of the ACC system.

In addition, template-based descriptions of the new goals are created and the descriptions of the existing goals are adapted if needed. Furthermore, the changes applied to the system goals may also affect other artefacts such as the system scenarios, functional component goals, and the functional architecture. These artefacts are adapted accordingly.

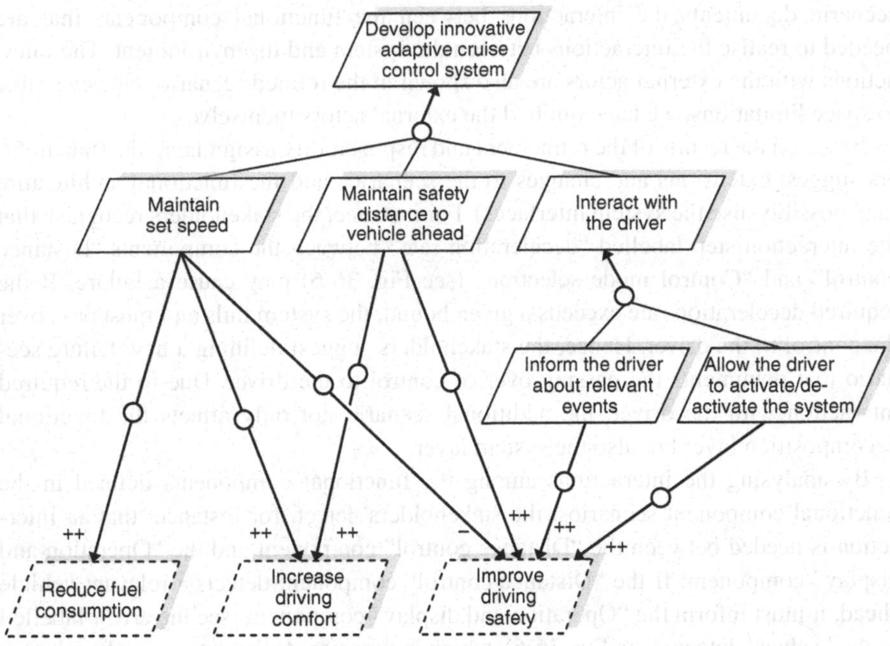

Fig. 36-7 *Revised goal model for the ACC system*

Adaptation of the system scenarios

The refinement of the system scenarios based on the functional architecture revealed an important gap in the system scenarios (see Section 36.3). Therefore, as suggested in sub-process SP_3, an additional scenario "Pass over control to driver" is defined. This new scenario is included as a failure scenario in the use cases "Follow a vehicle ahead" and "Drive at set speed". Table 36-4 contains the description of the new scenario.

Adaptation of the Architecture

New component "Object selection"

The definition and analysis of functional component goals and functional component scenarios in sub-process SP_3 have also revealed some deficiencies of the initial, functional architecture (see Section 36.3). The stakeholders suggested, for instance, to split the functionality of the component "Distance control" due to the estimated high complexity of this component. Hence, a new functional component, "Object selection", is included in the functional architecture. The new component is responsible for determining relevant objects based on the input from the "Object detection" component. The functional component goals "Discard standing objects" and "Discard objects off estimated driving course" are assigned to the new component.

New interface "Steering angle"

Additionally, the stakeholders detect that, to satisfy the goal "Discard objects off estimated driving course", the component "Object selection" must be able to predict the driving course. Therefore, the component requires an additional interface "Steering angle". Since the system interfaces are affected by this change, the change is also propagated to the architecture model defined at the system layer.

Tab. 36-4 *Additional use case "Pass over control to driver"*

Use case UC6	"Pass over control to driver"	
Abstraction layer	System layer	
Scope	ACC system	
Primary actor	Driver	
Secondary actors	—	
Input and output variables	❑ *Input*: — ❑ *Output*: —	
Related goals	Inform driver about relevant events	
Preconditions	ACC is active	
Success guarantee	The system is inactive and the driver takes over control.	
Minimal guarantee	—	
Extension points	—	
Trigger	Defined by the including use case.	
Main scenario	Step	Action
	1	The system notifies the driver about the passing over of control.
	2	The system stops transmitting the required engine torque to the engine system.
	3	The system stops transmitting the required braking rate to the braking system.
	4	The system signals its deactivation to the driver.
Alternative scenarios	Step	Action
	—	—
Failure scenarios	Step	Action
Technology and data variation	—	
Special requirements	Step 1: The driver must be warned by an optical and an acoustic warning signal.	

Additional connection between "Control mode selection" and "Operation and display"

Furthermore, the stakeholders define an additional connection between the component "Control mode selection" and the component "Operation and display". This connection is required to allow the component "Control mode selection" to inform the driver about the passing over of control to the driver, i.e. to realise the new scenario "Pass over control to driver".

The resulting, revised functional architecture is shown in Fig. 36-8.

Rejection of a suggested, additional connection

The suggested, additional connection between the components "Distance control" and "Operation and display" (see Section 36.3) required for informing the driver about the detection of a relevant vehicle ahead has been rejected by the stakeholders. The stakeholders have decided that "Distance control" shall inform "Control mode selection" and then "Control mode selection" shall inform "Operation and display" about the detection of a relevant vehicle ahead.

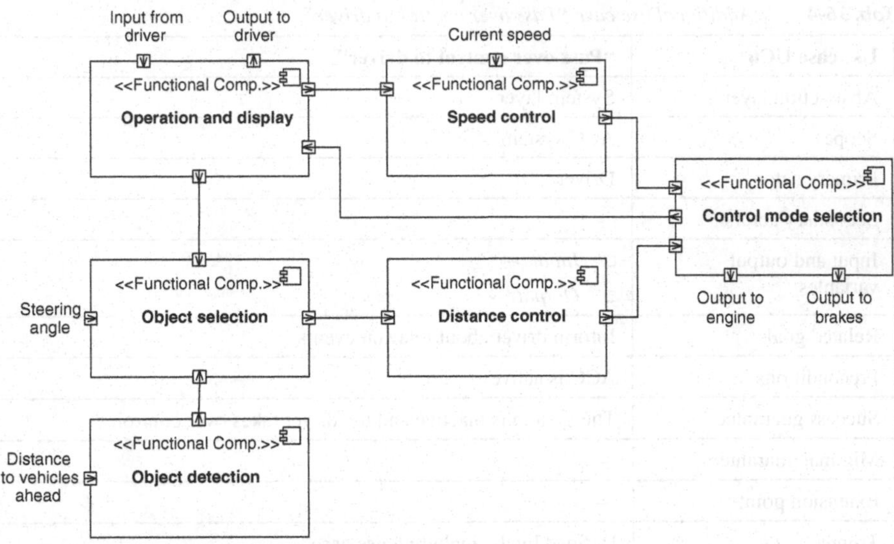

Fig. 36-8 *Revised functional architecture of the ACC system*

36.5 Specifying the Detailed System Requirements (SP_5)

Solution-oriented requirements

In this sub-process of the system-level co-design process, the detailed solution-oriented requirements for the system are defined after the system goals, system scenarios, and the functional architecture have been consolidated and hence reached sufficient stability (see Section 35.4.6). In the following, we illustrate the definition of solution-oriented, behavioural requirements.

Influence of the functional decomposition

Clearly, the system goals and system scenarios influence the solution-oriented requirements because the solution-oriented requirements must satisfy the goals and scenarios. However, the functional decomposition of the system also affects the solution-oriented requirements in many different ways:

- The system goals and system scenarios have already been aligned with the functional architecture. During this alignment, for instance, the scenario "Pass over control to driver" has been identified. In this way, the architecture indirectly influences the solution-oriented requirements through its influence on the goals and scenarios.
- When defining solution-oriented, behavioural requirements, the functional architecture may ease the identification of the states and events of the system that must be specified in the behavioural model. For instance, the state "Maintaining set speed" depicted in Fig. 36-9 is closely related to the functional component "Speed control": When in the state "Maintaining set speed", the system behaviour is mainly determined by the "Speed control" component.

Required system behaviour

Figure 36-9 shows a simple example of a state machine (see Section 14.3) documenting solution-oriented, behavioural requirements for the ACC system. This model has been defined based on the goals and scenarios defined for the ACC system as well as the functional architecture of the ACC system. In the following, we illustrate how the state machine satisfies two system scenarios defined for the ACC system.

Satisfaction of the scenario "Activate ACC"

When the ACC system is in the state "ACC inactive", the driver can activate the system. On activation, the system checks that the activation conditions are met and changes to the state "ACC active". During this transition, the system switches on the display which shows, among other things, the set speed to the driver. Thereby, the scenario "Activate ACC" (see Tab. 36-2) is satisfied.

Satisfaction of the scenario "Follow a vehicle ahead"

By default, on entering the state "ACC active", the ACC system enters the "Maintaining set speed" sub-state. If, while in this sub-state, the system detects a relevant object ahead (event "Object detected", the system informs the driver about this event (action "Object display on") and changes either to the state "Maintaining set distance" or to the state "Passing over control". If the required deceleration is below the specified maximum (condition "deceleration < maxValue"), the system changes to the state "Maintaining set distance". In this state, the system adjusts the engine torque as well as the braking rate in order to maintain the desired minimum distance to the vehicle ahead (activity "do / control torque and braking rate"). Thereby, the system scenario "Follow a vehicle ahead" (see Tab. 36-3) is satisfied. Furthermore, by the transition from the state "Maintaining set speed" to the state "Passing over control" the failure scenario "Pass over control to driver" (see Tab. 36-4) is satisfied.

Behavioural requirements not complete

Note that the state machine depicted in Fig. 36-9 is only an excerpt, i.e. it does not include all behavioural requirements for the ACC system and also omits some details of the specified behavioural requirements.

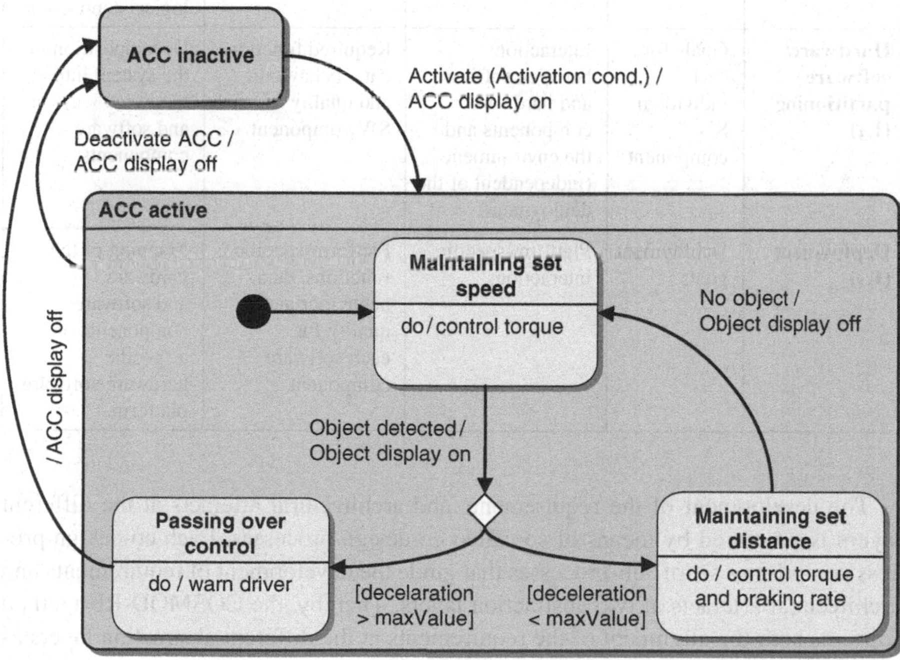

Fig. 36-9 *Example of a state machine defining the behavioural requirements for the ACC system (excerpt)*

36.6 Summary

Complex software-intensive systems require sophisticated approaches for developing and structuring requirements at different levels of granularity and detail, from high-level requirements (related e.g. to company and product strategies) to detailed technical requirements (e.g. for individual software components). The COSMOD-RE method suggests a hierarchy of four, essential abstraction layers for structuring a system along with the requirements for this system. Each abstraction layer deals with different concerns of the system and defines requirements in terms of goals, scenarios, and solution-oriented requirements artefacts. In addition, to clarify the scope of the requirements at each abstraction layer and to support the transitions between the layers, structural architectural models are used. Table 36-5 briefly characterises the COSMOD-RE artefact types at each of the COSMOD-RE abstraction layers.

Tab. 36-5 *Brief characterisation of the COSMOD-RE artefacts*

Layer	Goals	Scenarios	Solution-oriented requirements	Structural architecture
System layer (L_1)	System goals	Interactions between the system and external actors	Required functions, data, behaviour, and quality of the system	System interfaces
Functional decomposition (L_2)	Goals for each individual functional component	Interactions between the functional components of the system and the environment	Required functions, data, behaviour, and quality for each functional component	Functional decomposition of the system including logical building blocks, interfaces and logical connections
Hardware/ software partitioning (L_3)	Goals for each individual SW component	Interactions between software and hardware components and the environment (independent of the deployment)	Required functions, data, behaviour, and quality for each SW component	Decomposition of the system into hardware and software components
Deployment (L_4)	Deployment goals	Platform-specific interactions	Platform-specific functions, data, behaviour and quality for each software component	Mapping of the hardware and software components onto a specific hardware/software platform

The development of the requirements and architectural artefacts at the different layers is structured by means of so-called co-design processes. Each co-design process comprises a set of sub-processes that guide the development of requirements and architectural artefacts at two abstraction layers. Thereby, the COSMOD-RE method supports both the alignment of the requirements at the different abstraction layers as well as the alignment of the requirements with the system architecture.

Part VIII
Software Product Lines and Requirements-Based Testing

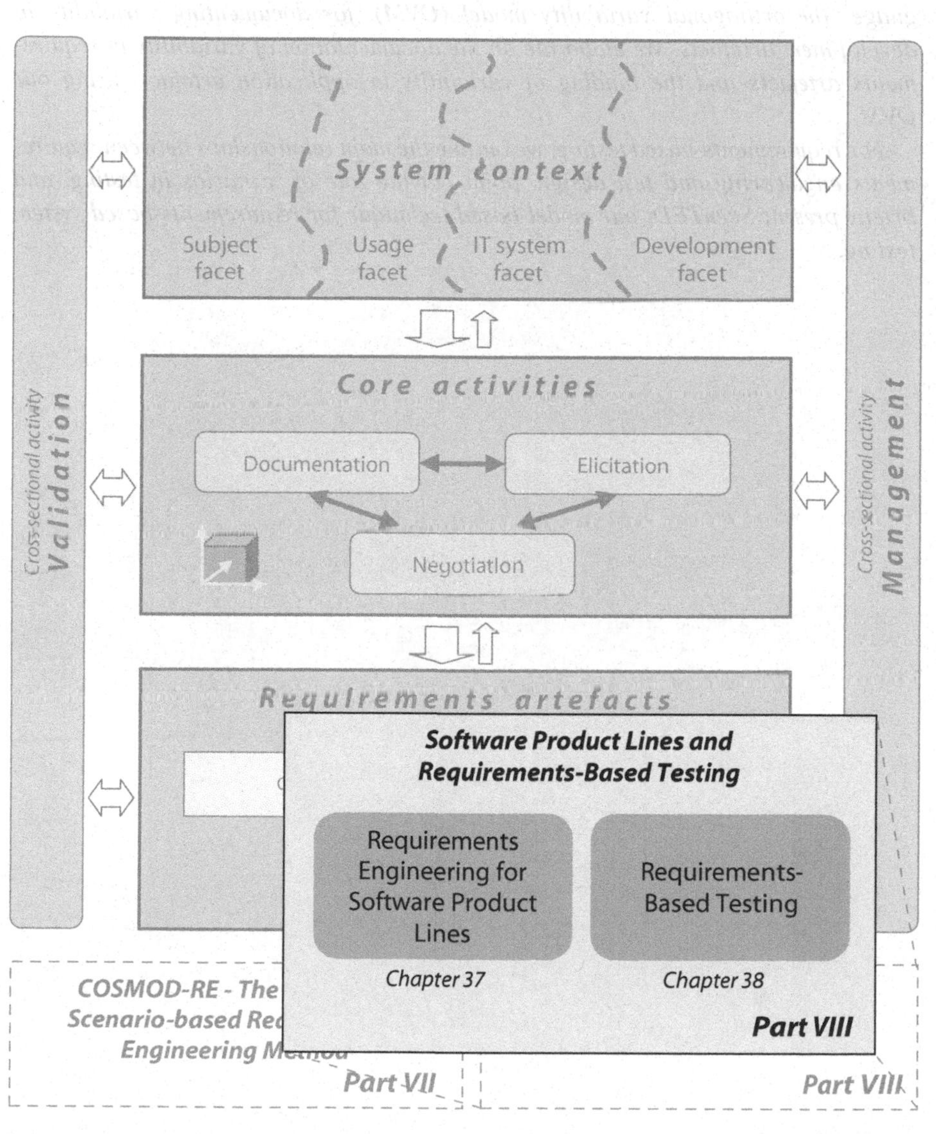

Overview of Part VIII – Software Product Lines and Requirements-Based Testing

In this part of the book, we outline the application of our framework and the associated foundations, principles, and techniques in two different settings:

- *Software product line engineering*
- *Requirements-based testing*

For software product line engineering, we outline the core concepts of product line engineering: the separation between domain engineering and application engineering and the need for sophisticated variability management. To support variability management in software product line engineering, we introduce our modelling language, the orthogonal variability model (OVM), for documenting variability in development artefacts. We elaborate on the documentation of variability in requirements artefacts and the binding of variability in application artefacts using our OVM.

For requirements-based testing, we outline the main relationships between requirements engineering and test design, point out the role of scenarios in testing, and briefly present ScenTED, our model-based technique for requirements-based system testing.

Classification Part VIII Software Product Lines and Requirements-Based Testing	Basic	Advanced
37 Requirements Engineering for Software Product Lines		
37.1 Core Concepts of Product Line Engineering	✓	
37.2 Challenges for Requirements Engineering in Software Product Line Engineering	✓	
37.3 Documenting Variability	✓	
37.4 Domain Requirements Engineering		✓
37.5 Application Requirements Engineering		✓
38 Requirements-Based Testing: the ScenTED Approach		
38.1 Motivation	✓	
38.2 Main Concepts behind Testing	✓	
38.3 The Role of Scenarios in Testing		✓
38.4 Requirements-Based Definition of Test Cases		✓
38.5 The ScenTED Approach		✓

Chapter 37
Requirements Engineering for Software Product Lines

In this chapter, we describe:

- *The core concepts of product line engineering: the separation of domain and application engineering and the consideration and management of product line variability*
- *A modelling language for documenting the variability of a product line and its application for documenting variability in goals, scenarios, and solution-oriented requirements*
- *Specific tasks for the different requirements engineering activities in domain and application requirements engineering*

Goal of software product line engineering

Software product line engineering is a reuse-driven development paradigm that aims to develop a set of similar high-quality products at reasonable cost and within a short time to market (see [Clements and Northrop 2001; Van der Linden 2002; Pohl et al. 2005]).

Examples of successful software product lines

The success of product lines has been demonstrated by various industrial examples. In [Pohl et al. 2005] several product line cases are described including product lines of Hewlett-Packard, Robert Bosch GmbH, Siemens AG Medical Solutions, and MARKET MAKER Software AG. For instance, MARKET MAKER could cut the development times for new products by 50% and the development costs by 70% (see [SPL 2009]) by introducing product line engineering.

In this chapter, we first introduce the core concepts of product line engineering. Then we focus on requirements engineering for software product lines. We outline the challenges of requirements engineering for product lines and present important concepts of requirements engineering for product lines.

37.1 Core Concepts of Product Line Engineering

Clements and Northrop define a software product line as follows:

D

Definition 37-1: *Software product line*

"A software product line is a set of software-intensive systems sharing a common, managed set of features that satisfy the specific needs of a particular market segment or mission and that are developed from a common set of core assets in a prescribed way."

[Clements and Northrop 2001]

Product line engineering differs from single system engineering mainly through the following two core concepts (see [Pohl et al. 2005]):

- *Two development processes*: In product line engineering, the two development processes of domain and application engineering are distinguished. These two processes are presented in Section 37.1.1.
- *Variability*: The variability of a product line describes its ability to vary, i.e. the changeability of the product line and its elements in order to develop different systems[1] in the product line. The concept of variability is explained in Section 37.1.2.

[1] In the following, when the term "system" is used in this chapter, a system is meant that has been realised or will be realised based on a product line.

37.1.1 Domain and Application Engineering

Two development processes

Product line engineering consists of two distinct development processes (see e.g. [Weiss and Lai 1999]) with different objectives:

- *Domain engineering*: The goal of domain engineering is the development of reusable domain artefacts[2] for the product line that can be reused for the development of different systems.
- *Application engineering*: The goal of application engineering is the development of individual systems of the product line by reusing the domain artefacts developed in domain engineering. For each system of the product line, a separate application engineering process is performed.

Activities in domain and application engineering

Domain and application engineering cover all activities that are known from single system engineering, such as requirements engineering, design, implementation, and testing (see Fig. 37-1). Domain engineering additionally requires a product management activity that defines the context and scope for the product line, major required system properties, and first drafts of required variations of the systems in the product line.

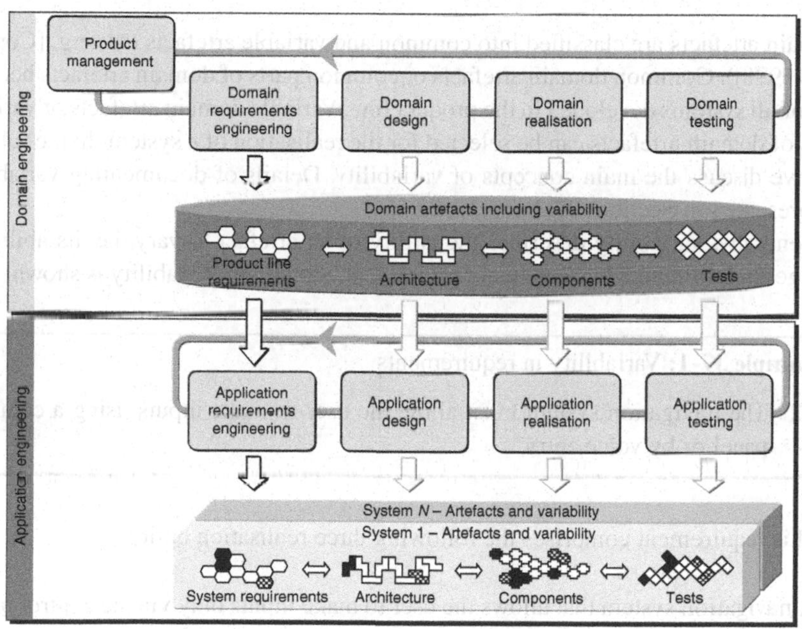

Fig. 37-1 *Framework for software product line engineering [Pohl et al. 2005]*

Feedback loops

The individual activities of domain and application engineering are performed iteratively and provide feedback to one another. There are also feedback loops between domain and application engineering. For instance, a reused component from domain

[2] Artefacts comprise all documented (partial) results of a software development process such as requirements, design artefacts, components, and test cases.

engineering may be adapted in application engineering and the adapted component may be passed on to domain engineering in order to make the adaptations available to the entire product line.

Requirements engineering for product lines

Requirements engineering is a central activity in domain and application engineering. In domain requirements engineering, the domain requirements are defined. Domain requirements comprise common and variable requirements of the product line and are used during domain engineering as the basis for the development of further reusable artefacts. The success of a product line largely depends on the domain requirements, since successful reuse of artefacts in application engineering can only be realised, if adequate artefacts have been developed during domain engineering (based on the domain requirements). In application requirements engineering, the requirements for individual products of the product line are defined by reusing the domain requirements of the product line.

Focus of this chapter: requirements engineering

In this chapter, we explain the processes of domain requirements engineering (Section 37.4) and application requirements engineering (Section 37.5). The descriptions of the other sub-processes can be found in [Pohl et al. 2005].

37.1.2 Variability

Common and variable domain artefacts

Domain artefacts are classified into common and variable artefacts (see e.g. [Coplien et al. 1998]). Common domain artefacts or common parts of domain artefacts become part of all systems developed in the product line. Variable domain artefacts or variable parts of domain artefacts can be selected for the realisation of a system. In the following, we discuss the main concepts of variability. Details of documenting variability are presented in Sections 37.3 and 37.4.2.

Generally, variability describes the ability of an artefact to vary, i.e. its ability to change. In Example 37-1, a textual requirement containing variability is shown.

Example 37-1: Variability in requirements

R12: The navigation system must allow the user to make inputs using a control panel or by voice entry.

Possible realisations of the requirement

This requirement comprises the following three realisation options:

- A navigation system that allows the user to make inputs only via the control panel.
- A navigation system that allows the user to make inputs only via voice entry.
- A navigation system that allows the user to make inputs via a control panel and by voice entry.

The requirement in Example 37-1 does not clearly specify which of these three options are, in fact, asked for. The conjunction “or” in the requirement can be interpreted as a logical “or” or as an exclusive “or”. In the former case, all three options would be valid; in the latter case, only the first and second options apply. Furthermore, it is not clear, whether only one system is asked for, or two or three different systems, each realising a different option.

Variation points and variants

In the following, we describe important concepts for explicit and unambiguous documentation of product line variability. A variation point in a product line can be defined as follows:

Definition 37-2: *Variation point*

A variation point represents an aspect of a product line that varies among the different systems of the product line.

In Example 37-1, the input modality of the user interface of the navigation system can vary. Hence, in this example, the variation point "input modality of the user interface" would be defined. A variant in a product line can be defined as follows:

Definition 37-3: *Variant*

A variant represents a specific incarnation of a variable aspect that a system in a product line can have.

Orthogonal variability model

In Example 37-1, the two options "input via control panel" and "input via voice entry" would be defined as variants of the variation point "input modality of the user interface". Variation points and variants are two important modelling constructs of the orthogonal variability model (OVM). Using the OVM is recommended for explicitly, unambiguously documenting the variability of a product line (see Section 37.3).

Documentation of variability is key for successful reuse

The explicit consideration and documentation of the variability of the product line is an essential prerequisite for the success of a product line:

- In domain engineering the explicit consideration and documentation of variability supports the identification of possible variable aspects and fosters explicit decisions about which aspects shall be variable in the product line (variation points) and which options shall exist for each variable aspect (variants). Then, the explicitly documented variability supports requirements engineers, architects, designers, and testers in realising the defined variation points and variants in the development artefacts that are created in domain engineering.
- In application engineering, the explicit documentation of variability in terms of variation points and variants supports system development since it makes the necessary decisions and decision options explicit. For instance, the documented variation points and variants can be used to communicate the variability of the product line to the customer and to document the customer's choices regarding the specific system.

37.2 Challenges for Requirements Engineering in Software Product Line Engineering

The separation of the two development processes and the need to define and manage product line variability lead to several challenges for requirements engineering in software product line engineering. We outline the major challenges by reconsidering the main building blocks of our requirements engineering framework (see Chapter 4):

Common and variable context aspects

- *Context*: The context of a software product line comprises the context aspects of all systems of the product line. Therein, some context aspects are common to all systems, while others are relevant only for specific systems of the product line. Identifying which context aspects are common and which are variable is an important prerequisite for defining the product line variability. In addition, to define the required variation points and variants, also the possible future evolution of the context must be taken into account, such as the emergence of new technologies or new user groups.

Specialised requirements engineering activities

- *Activities*: The separation of domain engineering and application engineering leads to a specialisation of the core and cross-sectional requirements engineering activities in domain requirements engineering and application requirements engineering:
  - *Domain requirements engineering* aims at eliciting, documenting, negotiating, validating, and managing common and variable requirements for the product line.
  - *Application requirements engineering* aims at eliciting, documenting, negotiating, validating, and managing the requirements for each specific system of the product line. Therein, application requirements engineering reuses the requirements artefacts developed in domain requirements as far as possible.

Domain and application requirements

- *Artefacts*: Due to the separation between domain artefacts and application artefacts in product line engineering, the following two kinds of requirements artefacts must be developed and managed:
  - *Domain requirements artefacts* are created in domain requirements engineering. These artefacts define the goals, scenarios, functional requirements, quality requirements, and constraints for the entire product line. Hence, the domain requirements artefacts contain all common and variable requirements that can be reused in application engineering.
  - *Application requirements artefacts* are created in application requirements engineering for each specific system. When defining the requirements for a specific system, the application requirements engineers reuse, as far as possible, the existing domain requirements artefacts. All common requirements and a subset of the variable requirements (i.e. those requirements that have been chosen for the specific system) are included in the application requirements artefacts. In addition, it may be necessary to develop application-specific requirements artefacts to satisfy customer needs (see [Halmans et al. 2008]).

Section 37.3 elaborates on the explicit documentation of product line variability using the orthogonal variability model. The documentation of variability in requirements artefacts is outlined in Section 37.4.2. In Section 37.4, the core and cross-sectional requirements engineering activities in domain requirements engineering are outlined. Section 37.5 focusses on the requirements engineering activities in application requirements engineering.

37.3 Documenting Variability

Tabular documentation

Exclusively textual documentation of variability is not advisable due to the ambiguity of natural language (as demonstrated by the example in Section 37.1.2). Tables allow documentation of variability in a structured manner and help to reduce ambiguity. Table 37-1 shows an extract of a tabular documentation of variability. Each row in the table defines either a variation point or a variant. The columns document the properties (ID and type) and dependencies of the variation points and variants. The different types of dependencies, i.e. variability dependencies, "requires" and "excludes" constraint dependencies, and artefact dependencies are explained below.

Tab. 37-1 *Tabular documentation of variability*

ID	VP type	Variation point/ variant	Variability dependency	"Requires" constraint dependency	"Excludes" constraint dependency	Artefact dependency
VP-1	mand.	comfort functionality		VP-3		
V-1.1		circum-navigating traffic blocks	opt.	V-5.1		Req-T-1.1
VP-2	opt.	recording of traffic blocks				
V-2.1		manual	alternative [1..2]		V-10.4, V-22.1	Req-T-2.1, Req-T-2.2
V-2.2		automatic				Req-T-3.1

Separate variability model

Tabular documentation of variability is well suited for listing the variation points and variants of a product line. In order to support, for instance, communication about variability with stakeholders, documenting variability using a separate variability model is recommended. Figure 37-2 shows a simple example of a variability model along with a set of domain requirements that are related to the variants defined in the variability model.

In the following, we elaborate on our orthogonal variability model (OVM). The OVM was introduced in [Pohl et al. 2005] to support explicit documentation of

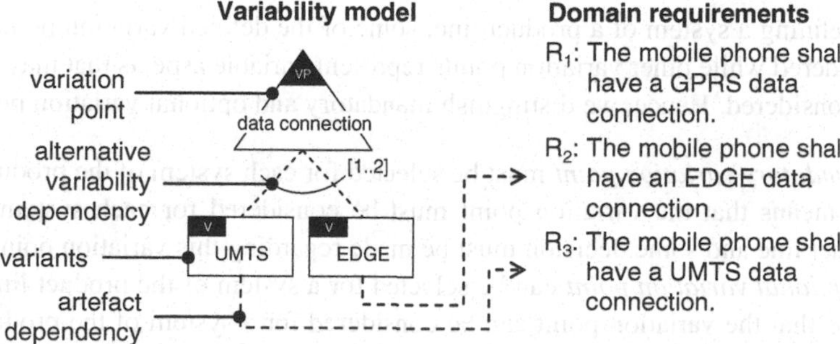

Fig. 37-2 *Simple example of a variability model*

product line variability. The advantages of documenting product line variability using a dedicated, conceptual model include:

Communicating variation points and variants

- *Improved communication*: Explicit documentation of variation points and variants supports communication about variability with different stakeholders. Through explicit documentation, it is possible, for example, to communicate to a customer which variants can be selected at which variation points of the product line in order to define a specific system.

Variability makes decisions transparent

- *Decision support*: The explicit documentation of variability leads to more careful decisions of the stakeholders regarding the introduction of variability in development artefacts as well as a conscious choice of the location (in a domain artefact) at which the variability is introduced. Furthermore, the explicit documentation of variation points and variants allows for documenting the rationales for introducing variability. In other words, the originator of a variation point is forced to state the rationale for introducing variability in a specific domain artefact.

Relationships between requirements and variants become traceable

- *Traceability*: The explicit documentation of product line variability supports the traceability of requirements and other development artefacts to variants and variation points. For instance, the stakeholders can document which requirements, design, implementation, and test artefacts are influenced by a variant.

In the following subsections, we describe the individual modelling constructs of our orthogonal variability model.

37.3.1 Variation Points and Variants

Visibility of variation points

Two essential modelling constructs of the orthogonal variability model are variation points (Definition 37-2) and variants (Definition 37-3). A variation point can be either external or internal (see [Pohl et al. 2005]):

- *External variation point*: An external variation point is visible to stakeholders who are interested mainly in the externally observable properties (functionality and quality) of a system of the product line, such as customers or users.
- *Internal variation point*: An internal variation point is visible mainly to stakeholders who develop a system of the product line such as application designers, developers, and testers. Customers do not have to take internal variability into account when defining a system.

Necessity of variation points

When defining a system of a product line, some of the defined variation points must be considered while other variation points represent variable aspects that may or may not be considered. Hence, we distinguish mandatory and optional variation points:

- A *mandatory variation point* must be selected for each system of the product line. This means that the variation point must be considered for each system of the product line and some decision must be made regarding this variation point.
- An *optional variation point* can be selected for a system of the product line. This means that the variation point can be considered for a system of the product line and a decision can be made, but does not have to be made regarding this variation point.

Graphical notation of variation points

In the graphical notation of the OVM, a variation point is represented by a triangle with the label "VP" at the top (see Fig. 37-3). Within the triangle, the name of the variation point is shown. Variation points with a black-filled top are external variation points. Internal variation points are represented by triangles with a white top. In case of mandatory variation points, the triangle is drawn with a solid line. In case of optional variation points, the triangle is drawn with a dashed line. Figure 37-3 depicts the four possible kinds of variation points.

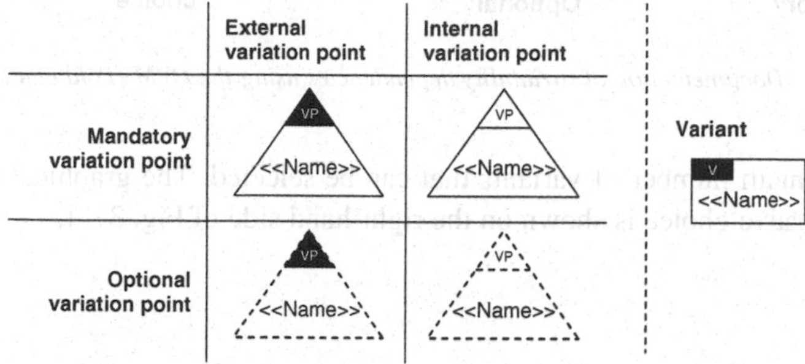

Fig. 37-3 *Documentation of variation points and variants using the OVM [Pohl et al. 2005]*

Graphical notation of a variant

Variants are shown as white rectangles with a small black rectangle in the top left-hand corner labelled "V". Within the white rectangle, the name of the variant is shown (see right-hand side of Fig. 37-3).

37.3.2 Variability Dependencies

Types of variability dependencies

To document relationships between variation points and variants, the OVM offers the so-called variability dependency. The variability dependency documents important information about the permissible choices of variants at a specific variation point. The OVM supports the following types of variability dependencies:

Mandatory variants

- *Mandatory*: A mandatory variability dependency between a variation point and a variant documents that this variant must always be selected if the variation point is selected. A mandatory variability dependency is drawn as a continuous line (see left-hand side of Fig. 37-4).

Optional variants

- *Optional*: An optional variability dependency between a variation point and a variant documents that, if the variation point is selected, this variant can be selected but does not have to be selected. An optional variability dependency is drawn using a dashed line (see the variability dependency shown in the middle of Fig. 37-4).

Choice of a defined number of variants

- *Alternative choice*: An alternative choice defines a grouping of optional variability dependencies. An alternative choice comprises at least two variants that are related to a variation point by optional variability dependencies. The alternative choice defines, in addition, the permissible number of variants to be selected. For this purpose, the OVM uses the [min..max] notation: "min" defines the minimum number of variants that must be selected for the alternative choice, "max" defines

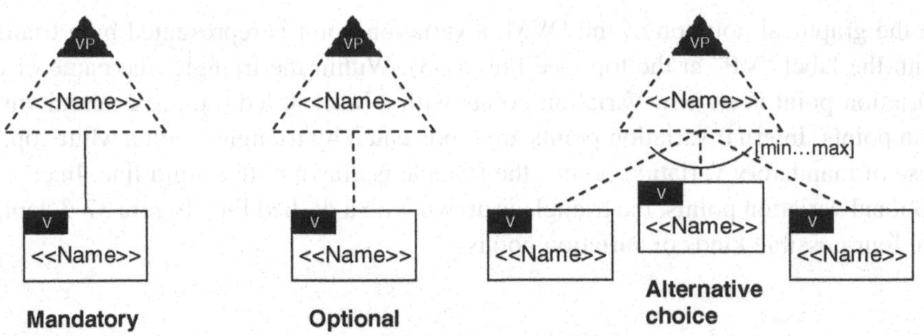

Fig. 37-4 *Documentation of variability dependencies using the OVM [Pohl et al. 2005]*

the maximum number of variants that can be selected. The graphical notation of the alternative choice is shown on the right-hand side of Fig. 37-4.

37.3.3 Constraint Dependencies

Types of constraint dependencies

The selection made at one variation point may affect the available choices at another variation point. To document such relationships, the OVM offers the constraint dependency. The following types of constraint dependencies can be documented using the OVM:

- *Variation point requires variation point*: This dependency documents that the consideration of one variation point requires the consideration of another variation point, i.e. variability dependencies of the required variation point must also be fulfilled.
- *Variation point excludes variation point*: This dependency documents that the consideration of one variation point excludes the consideration of another variation point, i.e. at the excluded variation point, variants must not be selected.
- *Variant requires variation point*: This dependency documents that, through the selection of a variant, the consideration of another variation point is required, i.e. at the required variation point, variants must also be selected.
- *Variant excludes variation point*: This dependency documents that, through the selection of a variant, the consideration of a variation point is excluded, i.e. at the excluded variation point, variants must not be selected.
- *Variant requires variant*: This dependency documents that, in the case that a specific variant is selected, another variant must also be selected.
- *Variant excludes variant*: This dependency documents that, in the case that a specific variant is selected, the selection of another variant is excluded.

Graphical notation for constraint dependencies

In the OVM, "requires" dependencies are documented as dashed arrows from the source variant or variation point to the target variant or variation point (i.e. the required model element). Additionally, the type of the "requires" relationship is indicated in the arrow (i.e. VP requires VP, V requires VP, or V requires V).

"Excludes" dependency is symmetric

"Excludes" dependencies are documented as dashed double-headed arrows (see Fig. 37-5). For the "excludes" dependency, a double-headed arrow is used because the "excludes" dependency is symmetric, i.e. the exclusion of a model element B by a model element A also implies the exclusion of A by B. In other words, an "excludes" dependency between two variants A and B means that A and B can never be selected together. This does not hold for the "requires" dependency. When a model element B requires a model element A, this does not mean that A also requires B.

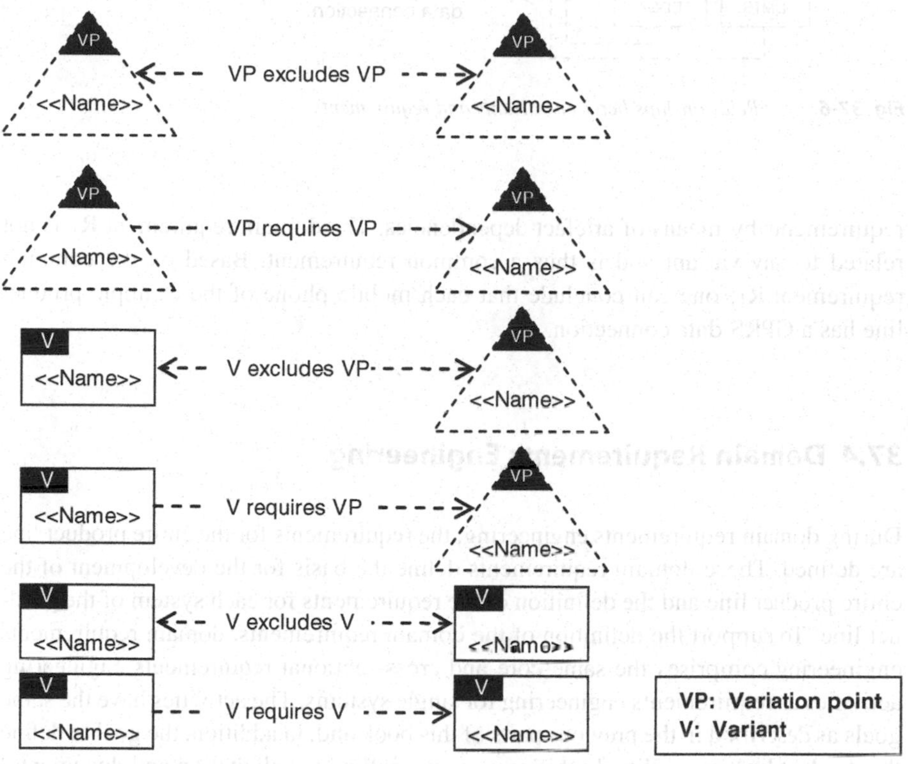

Fig. 37-5 *Documentation of constraint dependencies [Pohl et al. 2005]*

37.3.4 Artefact Dependency

Common and variable requirements

To document variability in development artefacts such as requirements, architectural, implementation, and test artefacts the OVM provides the artefact dependency. An artefact dependency relates a development artefact (or part of it) to a variant defined in the variability model. By relating a development artefact (or a part of it) to a variant, this artefact is defined as a variable artefact and thus becomes selectable. Artefacts that are not related to a variant are considered to be common artefacts of the product line.

Example of using artefact dependencies

Figure 37-6 depicts a mandatory variation point with two alternative variants (left-hand side) as well as an extract of a domain requirements specification (right-hand side). The domain requirements specify requirements for a mobile phone product line. The variability model documents that the data connection of the mobile phone is a variation point and that either UMTS or EDGE or both can be selected for data connection. The variants UMTS and EDGE are related to the corresponding domain

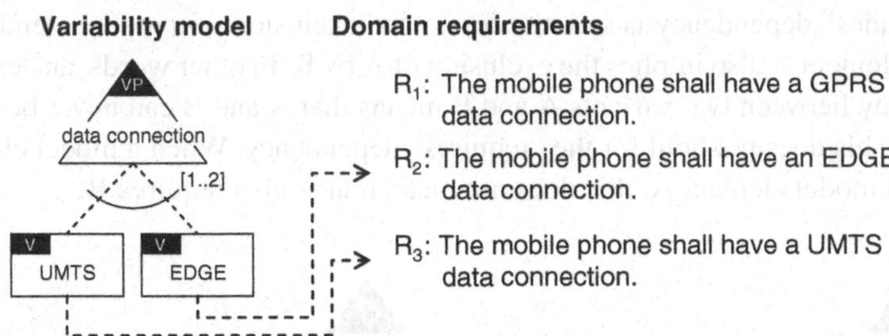

Fig. 37-6 *Relationships between variants and requirements*

requirements by means of artefact dependencies. The domain requirement R_1 is not related to any variant and is thus a common requirement. Based on the common requirement R_1, one can conclude that each mobile phone of the example product line has a GPRS data connection.

37.4 Domain Requirements Engineering

Definition of the domain requirements

During domain requirements engineering, the requirements for the entire product line are defined. These domain requirements define the basis for the development of the entire product line and the definition of the requirements for each system of the product line. To support the definition of the domain requirements, domain requirements engineering comprises the same core and cross-sectional requirements engineering activities as requirements engineering for single systems. The activities have the same goals as described in the previous parts of this book and, in addition, the goal to define the product line variability. In this section, we outline the elicitation and documentation of product line variability as well as the validation of requirements in the presence of variability.

More details on domain requirements engineering activities can be found in [Pohl et al. 2005].

37.4.1 Elicitation of Requirements Variability

Requirement sources

For the elicitation of requirements in domain engineering and the identification of variation points and variants, domain requirements engineers make use of all requirement sources presented in Section 6.2 and Chapter 21. In particular, domain requirements engineers analyse already existing systems in the scope of the product line in order to identify variation points and variants for the product line.

Commonality and variability analysis

During the elicitation of domain requirements from stakeholders such as domain experts or system architects, variability can be identified, for instance, by directly asking the stakeholders for required variation points and variants. When eliciting product line requirements from customers or (representative) users, first the requirements of each customer or each user are elicited. Then, a commonality and variability analysis is performed to identify required variation points and variants (see [Pohl et al. 2005]). A commonality and variability analysis can also be applied to requirements elicited from different documents (e.g. different standards) or from different systems (existing systems in the scope of the product line). The inputs and outputs of the commonality and variability analysis are depicted schematically in Fig. 37-7. Besides the requirements from different sources, also different prioritisations of the (same set of) requirements can be used as input for a commonality and variability analysis (see [Pohl et al. 2005]).

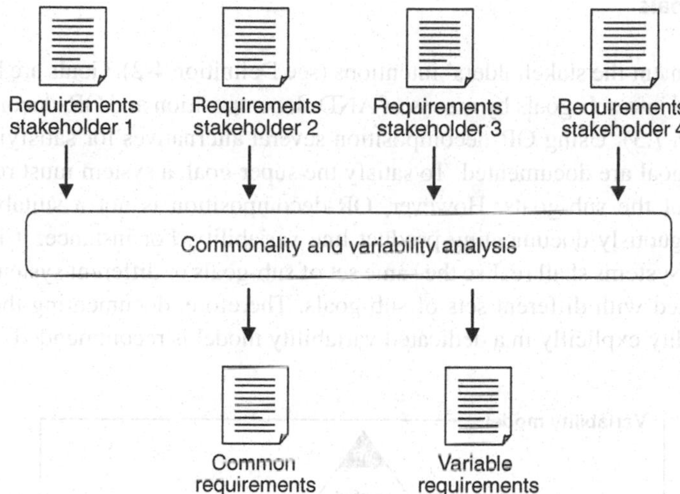

Fig. 37-7 *Inputs and outputs of a commonality and variability analysis*

Common and variable domain requirements

As an essential result of the commonality and variability analysis, the domain requirements are classified into common and variable domain requirements:

- *Common (domain) requirements*: A common requirement has to be fulfilled by all systems of the product line.
- *Variable (domain) requirements*: A variable requirement can be selected for a system. The system has to fulfil the variable requirement only if the requirement is selected for the specific system. The selection of a variable requirement typically entails the selection of variable design, implementation, and test artefacts that are related to this requirement.

Requirements variability

The variable requirements define the possible differences among the systems of the product line. Variable requirements are typically defined because of the different requirements that exist in the market (in case of market-driven development) or because the systems of the product line shall be supplied to different customers with (partly) different requirements for their system.

37.4.2 Documentation of Domain Requirements

The variability in the domain requirements artefacts of a product line can be documented using the orthogonal variability model (see Section 37.3). In this section, we describe exemplarily how the orthogonal variability model supports the documentation of variability in the requirements artefacts presented in Part III. We hence focus on the documentation of variable domain goals, domain scenarios, and solution-oriented domain requirements. For a detailed introduction to the documentation of domain requirements for product lines, we refer to [Pohl et al. 2005].

Domain Goals

Goals document the stakeholders' intentions (see Definition 4-2). Goals are hierarchically refined into sub-goals by means of AND-decomposition and OR-decomposition (see Section 7.3). Using OR-decomposition several alternatives for satisfying a specific super-goal are documented. To satisfy the super-goal, a system must realise one or several of the sub-goals. However, OR-decomposition is not a suitable means for unambiguously documenting product line variability. For instance, it is unclear whether all systems shall realise the same set of sub-goals or different system variants are associated with different sets of sub-goals. Therefore, documenting the product line variability explicitly in a dedicated variability model is recommended.

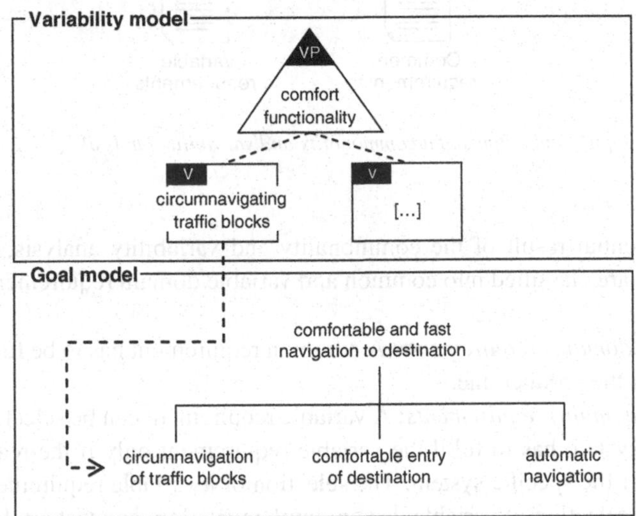

Fig. 37-8 *Simple example of documenting variability in a domain goal model*

Examples of common and variable goals

Figure 37-8 contains excerpts of a domain goal model (bottom) and a variability model (top) for a product line of navigation systems. For the systems of this product line, the circumnavigation of traffic blocks is defined as an optional functionality. This is documented by the variation point "comfort functionality" and the optional variant "circumnavigating traffic blocks". This variant is related to the domain goal "circumnavigation of traffic blocks" by an artefact dependency (see Section 37.4.2).

In this way, the goal "circumnavigation of traffic blocks" is defined as a variable goal that must be satisfied only when the associated variant is selected. The goals "comfortable entry of destination" and "automatic navigation" are not related to variants. Therefore, these goals are common, i.e. each system of the product line must satisfy these two goals. Note that if, the variant "circumnavigating traffic blocks" is not selected for system, this system only partly satisfies the super-goal "comfortable and fast navigation to destination".

Support for elicitation of additional variability

The documentation of goals can lead to the elicitation of additional product line variability. For instance, if a conflict dependency between two goals (see Definition 7-4) is documented, this may indicate the need to introduce additional variation points and variants: If the conflicting intentions cannot be satisfied by the same system, each intention might be satisfiable by a different system variant.

Domain Scenarios

Scenarios document exemplary interaction sequences that illustrate goal satisfaction or the failure to satisfy one or several goals; see Definition 4-3. In domain requirements engineering, entire scenarios, parts of scenarios, or individual scenario steps may be defined as variable.

Documenting domain scenarios by means of use case diagrams

For instance, to define an entire use case as variable, this use case is related to a specific variant defined in the variability model. If a use case is not related to a variant, it is a common use case for the product line.

Figure 37-9 depicts the documentation of a variable domain use case in a use case diagram of a navigation systems product line. The use case "transfer from mobile

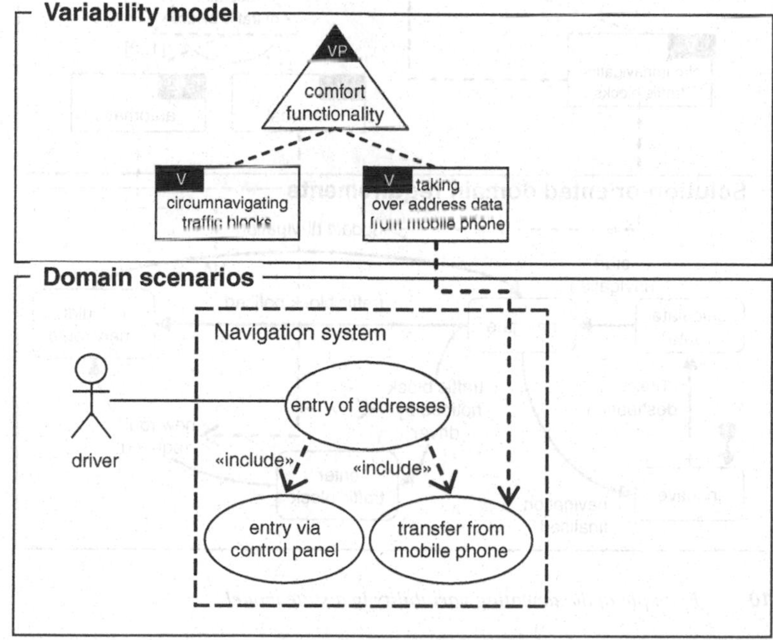

Fig. 37-9 *Example of documenting variability in domain scenarios*

phone" is related to the variant "taking over address data from mobile phone" defined in the variability model of the product line. This use case is hence defined as variable for this product line and is only realised in systems for which the corresponding variant is selected. In contrast, the use case "entry via control panel" is a common use case, i.e. each navigation system of the product line allows entry of the address data using the control panel.

For more details on the documentation of variability in scenarios, we refer to [Pohl et al. 2005].

Solution-Oriented Domain Requirements

Solution-oriented requirements specify the detailed requirements (data, function, and behaviour) needed for the realisation and testing of the system. In domain requirements engineering, entire solution-oriented requirements artefacts, parts of these artefacts, or individual elements of these artefacts (e.g. individual functions) can be defined as variable.

Common and variable transitions

Figure 37-10 depicts a statechart (see Section 14.3) documenting behavioural requirements for a product line of navigation systems. Some of the transitions defined in this statechart are related to variants defined in the variability model of the product line and are hence variable. The transitions that are not related to any variant are common to all systems of the product line.

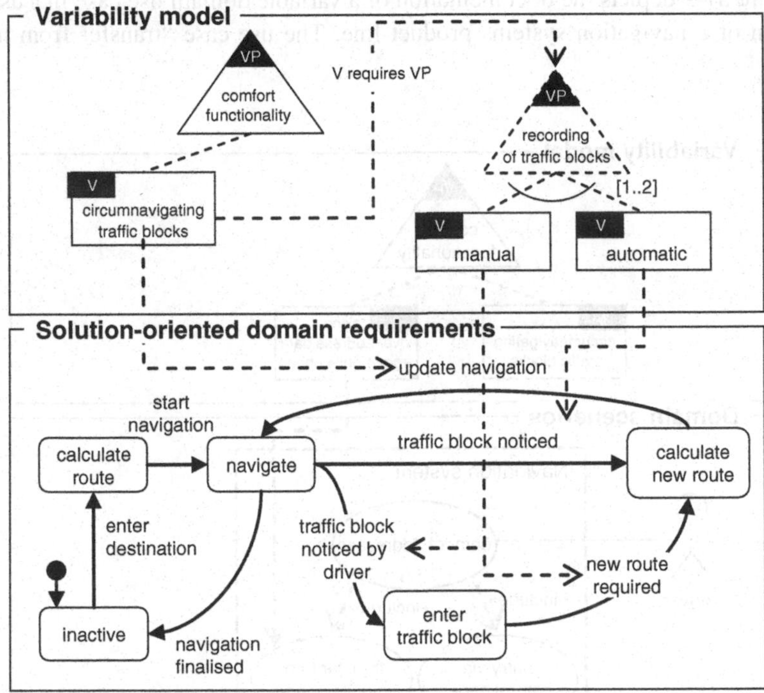

Fig. 37-10 *Example of documenting variability in a state model*

Common and variable states

Whether a state in a domain statechart of a product line is common or variable depends on the incoming and outgoing transitions of this state. If a state is related only to variable transitions, this state is variable and only becomes part of a system, if at least one of the variable, incoming or outgoing transitions is selected. If a state has at least one common transition, this state is also common, since there is at least one incoming or outgoing transition related to this state that is part of all systems of the product line. Consequently, if a state is related to common and variable transitions, this state is a common state. In the statechart depicted in Fig. 37-10, the states "inactive", "calculate route", and "navigate" are common because each of these states has at least one common, incoming or outgoing transition. The state "enter traffic block" is variable because it has only variable transitions. If the variant "manual" of the variation point "recording of traffic blocks" is not selected for a system, the state "enter traffic block" with its two variable transitions are not realised in this system.

For more details on the documentation of variability in solution-oriented requirements artefacts, we refer to [Pohl et al. 2005].

37.4.3 Validation in the Presence of Variability

Intended inconsistencies

The elicited and documented requirements variability must be considered during requirements validation in domain requirements engineering because some quality criteria need to be checked differently due to the presence of variability. In particular, domain requirements artefacts include intended inconsistencies (see [Savolainen and Kuusela 2001; Lauenroth and Pohl 2007; Lauenroth 2009]). These inconsistencies must not be considered as requirements defects as long as it is ensured that only consistent subsets of the domain requirements artefacts are selected for a system (see Example 37-2).

Example 37-2: Consistency of domain requirements

Figure 37-11 shows a simplified statechart that is related to a variability model. This statechart documents the possible activation behaviours of a product line of navigation systems. For the variant "automatically", the navigation system shall be in the "active" mode after turning on the ignition (see ❶). For the variant "manually", the navigation system shall be in stand-by mode after turning on the ignition (see ❷). If this statechart defined the requirements for a single system, the requirements would be inconsistent because the system cannot change to both the "active" and the "stand-by" mode, when it is in the "inactive" mode and the ignition is turned on. However, in the product line case, the statechart is consistent because each of the two transitions is associated with a variant, and the two variants are defined as alternatives (see ❸), i.e. for each system, only one of the two variants and thus only one of the two transitions can be selected.

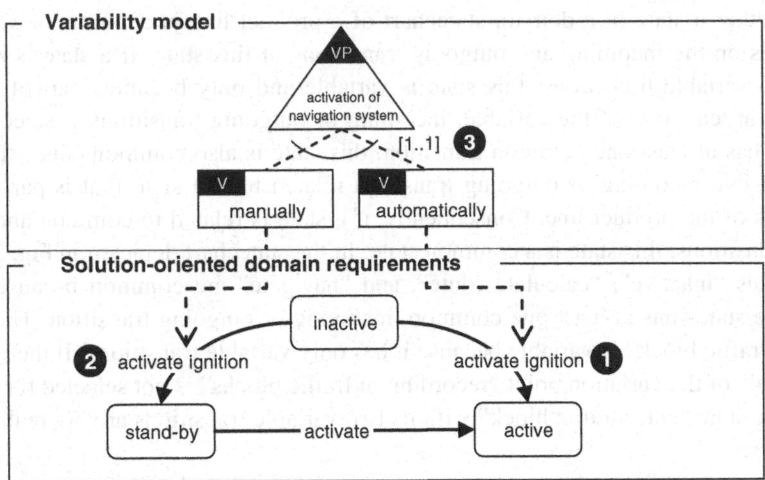

Fig. 37-11 *Example of consistency checking during validation of domain requirements*

37.5 Application Requirements Engineering

Binding of variability

The objective of application requirements engineering is to define the requirements for a specific application of the product line. Therein, the domain requirements artefacts including the defined variation points and variants are exploited, as far as possible, in order to define the application requirements. Compared with requirements engineering for single systems, application requirements engineering must accomplish two additional tasks, the binding of the defined variability and the documentation of the variability binding.

37.5.1 Binding the Variability

Making decisions about variation points and variants

When developing application requirements artefacts, the common domain requirements and the variable requirements are considered. For the variable domain requirements, the requirements engineers must communicate the available variability to the customer. Supporting the communication of the variability to the customer by means of the orthogonal variability model is recommended. Using this model, the customer can be informed about the variable aspects of the product line (variation points) and the available options for each variable aspect (variants). The orthogonal variability model can also be used to document customer choices (see Section 37.5.2). Choosing specific variation points and variants and rejecting other variation points and variants is called "binding the variability". The variability of the product line is bound completely if, for each variation point and each variant, a decision has been made regarding whether this variation point or variant is selected or rejected for the specific system.

Changes and extensions of domain artefacts

As far as possible, the application requirements are defined by reusing domain requirements artefacts. In practice, it is rarely the case that all application requirements can be defined purely by reusing domain requirements artefacts. Hence, for most systems, a certain amount of application-specific requirements need to be defined. Furthermore, to satisfy the application-specific requirements, other application-specific artefacts must be developed such as application-specific components, test cases etc.

Categories of application requirements

Consequently, each application requirement can be assigned to one of the following three categories:

1. *Application requirements defined by reusing domain requirements artefacts*: In this case, the expectations of the customer can be satisfied by reusing common and/or variable domain requirements artefacts.
2. *Application requirements defined by partly adapting the domain requirements artefacts*: In this case, the domain requirements artefacts only partly satisfy the customer's expectations and therefore must be adapted to define the application requirements.
3. *Application requirements artefacts developed anew*: In this case, the available domain requirements artefacts cannot be reused for defining the application requirements.

For the application requirements of the first category (application requirements defined by reusing domain requirements artefacts), the variability binding needs to be documented in order to record the choices made during application requirements engineering for further application engineering activities and the maintenance of the system. The documentation of application-specific requirement is considered in [Halmans 2007; Halmans et al. 2008].

37.5.2 Documenting the Variability Binding

Documentation of the selected variability in a selection model

We suggest documenting the choices made concerning the binding of variability for a specific system using a so-called selection model. The selection model is based on the variability model of the product line, yet it contains only the variants that are selected for the specific system. Figure 37-12 depicts the transition from the variability model of a product line to a selection model of a specific system.

Derivation of application requirements from domain requirements

Figure 37-13 depicts the concept of defining application requirements artefacts by reusing (common and variable) domain requirements artefacts. All common parts of the domain requirements artefact as well as the variable parts that are related to a selected variant become part of the application requirements artefact. Figure 37-13 shows the derivation of an application requirements artefact based on a domain requirements artefact.

Example

In the variability model at the top of Fig. 37-13, the variants "circumnavigating traffic blocks" and "automatic" have been selected (as highlighted in the figure). The variant "manual" (depicted in grey) has been rejected. All transitions in the statechart at the bottom of Fig. 37-13 that are related to the variant "manual" are also shown in grey, since these transitions and the related state "enter traffic block" do not become part of the statechart for this specific system.

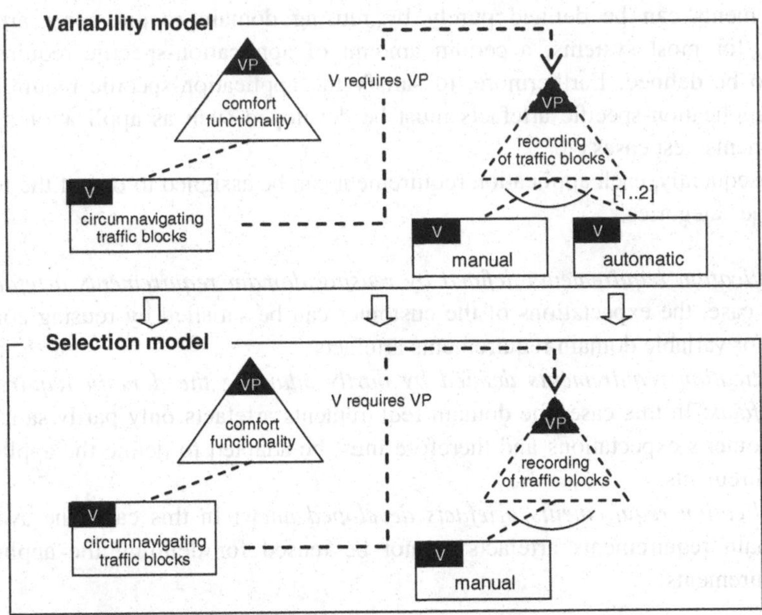

Fig. 37-12 *Example of a selection model*

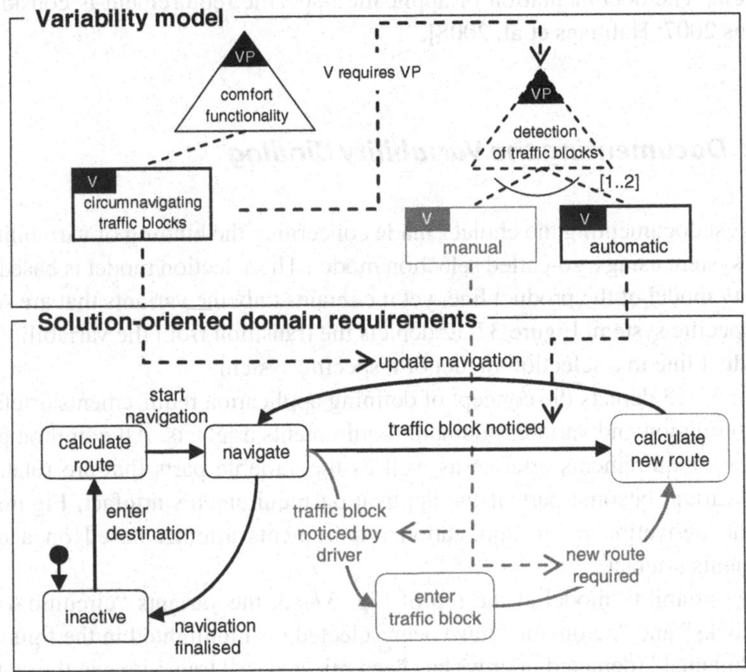

Fig. 37-13 *Definition of an application requirements artefact based on a domain requirements artefact and the selection model*

37.6 Summary

Requirements engineering in software product line engineering differs from requirements engineering for single systems in mainly two essential aspects: the separation of domain and application requirements engineering and the definition and binding of variability during requirements engineering. The variability of a product line is essential for the success of the product line, since the available variability strongly influences which systems can be developed based on the product line according to customer wishes. Hence, a central task of domain requirements engineering is to elicit, document, and validate the required variability (Section 37.4). During application requirements engineering, the available variability is communicated to the customer in order to bind the variation points and variants needed for the specific system. To acknowledge the central role of variability in software product line engineering we have proposed a separate model documenting the variability of a product line (Section 37.3) as well as its binding in each specific application (Section 37.5).

Chapter 38
Requirements-Based Testing: the ScenTED Approach

In this chapter, we describe:

- *The interrelations between requirements engineering and testing*
- *Main concepts behind testing*
- *The role of scenarios in testing*
- *Different approaches for requirements-based testing*
- *The key concepts of ScenTED, our model-based technique for requirements-based system testing*
- *An example application of ScenTED*

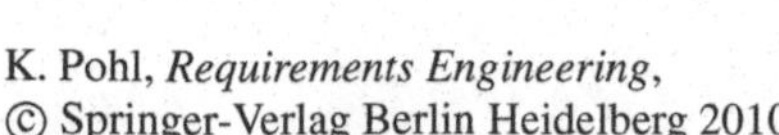

38.1 Motivation

Testing aims to execute a software-intensive system or parts of the system in a controlled environment and under controlled circumstances in order to detect deviations from the specification and to check whether the system satisfies the defined acceptance criteria (see Section 16.4). Deviation of the observed output of the system from its expected output indicates a fault (also known as a defect or bug) in the design or implementation, provided that the requirements specification is correct.

Core activities of testing

The two core activities of testing are test-case definition and test execution. To execute tests, the system (or parts of it) must be available. However, test cases can be defined prior to implementing the system or its components. Consequently, test-case definition and requirements engineering may be performed in parallel, i.e. early on in the development process.

Benefits of specifying tests early

Defining test cases can reveal defects in the specification that is used as the reference for testing. Hence, defining test cases has a positive effect on the quality of the requirements artefacts. Testers have a different view on the requirements compared with other stakeholders. They can therefore detect defects in the requirements artefacts which were overlooked by those other stakeholders. This positive effect (see also [Pretschner et al. 2005]) is also exploited during perspective-based reading from the perspective of the tester (see Section 29.2) and during requirements validation supported by the creation of test artefacts (see Section 29.3).

Synergies between requirements engineering and testing

Thus, there is a reciprocal, positive relationship between the activities of requirements engineering and testing (see [Graham 2002]). On the one hand, a complete, consistent, and readable requirements specification (see also Section 17.3) supports test-case definition. On the other hand, performing test activities, particularly defining test cases, provides valuable information for the improvement of the requirements specification.

38.2 Main Concepts behind Testing

In the following, we introduce the main concepts behind testing software-intensive systems that are relevant for requirements-based testing.

38.2.1 Test Activities

Test-case definition and test execution

As introduced above, the two key activities[3] during testing software-intensive systems are:

- *Test-case definition*: During test-case definition, testers define which properties of the system to be tested shall be checked and how they shall be checked. The result of this activity is a set of test cases (see Section 38.2.2).
- *Test execution*: During test execution, the system is executed for each previously defined test case, and the deviation of the observed output from the expected output (as specified in the test cases) is evaluated.

[3] Other test activities are, for instance, test planning and test implementation (see [Spillner et al. 2007]).

Software test

In the literature as well as in practice, the term "test" is often used synonymously with the term "test execution". We follow this use and characterise the term "software test" as follows:

Definition 38-1: *Software test*

A software test denotes the systematic execution of a software unit (in this context called the test object) with the aim of detecting failures.

Based on [Spillner et al. 2007; Myers 2001]

Failures and faults

A failure denotes a deviation between the expected output (defined during test-case definition) and the output observed during test execution. The causes of such failures are faults in the test object (see e.g. [Spillner et al. 2007]). Examples of faults are wrongly initialised variables or wrongly defined exit conditions for loops. Strictly speaking, the identification of faults is not a task of testing but is done during debugging.

38.2.2 Test Case

A test case specifies the information required for the test execution. We define the term "test case" as follows:

Definition 38-2: *Test case*

A test case comprises the preconditions required for test execution, the set of inputs and expected outputs, test instructions (how inputs are passed to the test object and how outputs are read from the test object) as well as the expected postconditions.

Based on [Spillner et al. 2007]

Possible results of test execution

By means of the specified outputs and postconditions of a test case, it is possible to check whether the test object has passed or failed the executed test. A test is considered to be passed when the observed output corresponds to the specified output and the postconditions are true. If this is not the case, the test is considered to have failed.

Hint 38-1: *Limitations of testing*

Generally, the test object can never be completely checked by testing. In the case of non-trivial systems, the number of possible inputs and outputs of the test object becomes so large that they can no longer be tested with a justifiable effort.

Even in the case of a simple calculator with the basic arithmetic operation "multiplication of natural numbers" and a valid range of inputs from 0 to 999.999, one billion combinations of input values are possible, which would have to be tested for a complete test.

(to be continued)

Hint 38-1 (*continued*)

As a consequence, a set of test cases must be selected from the set of all possible test cases. (In the course of this chapter, we will present possible criteria for the selection of test cases.)

Since a test object can never be checked completely by testing, testing cannot guarantee that the test object is free from faults. This is already reflected in Definition 38-1.

38.2.3 Test Levels

Test-case definition and test execution are typically structured into several test levels (see e.g. [Liggesmeyer 2009; Spillner et al. 2007; Graham 2002]). In Fig. 38-1, coarse-grained test levels are depicted roughly following the V-model of Boehm (see [Boehm 1979]).

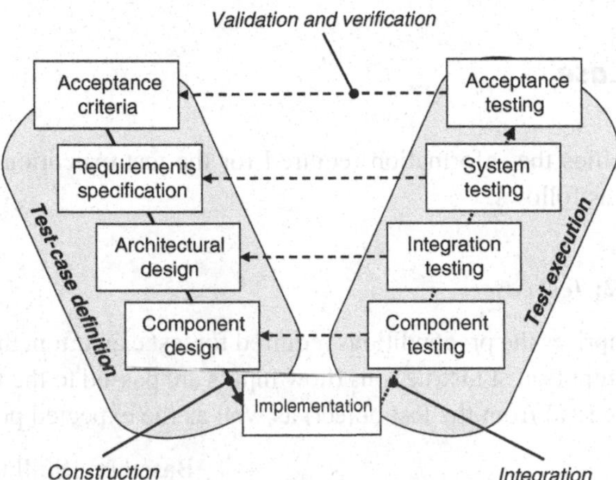

Fig. 38-1 *Test levels and test activities (based on [Graham 2002])*

The left-hand side of the "V" shown in Fig. 38-1 represents the typical development activities for a software-intensive system, or rather the artefacts created during these activities. Each development activity is related to a test activity on the right-hand side of the "V". During the development activities (on the left-hand side), the test artefacts of a particular test level should be created (test-case definition). Those test cases are used during the test activities on the right-hand side of the "V" for executing the tests at the various testing levels.

Component testing

The test execution begins at the lowest level of the V-model with so-called component testing. During component testing, each component (or each module or class) is tested (preferably) in isolation. Thereby, failures that occur during the execution of individual components can be detected.

Integration testing

After the integration of components into subsystems or after the integration of smaller subsystems into larger subsystems, integration testing is performed on the integrated subsystem. The objective is to detect failures in the interactions that take place between the components or subsystems. The tests shall detect, for example, whether only those interactions specified during design take place and that no undesired interactions occur.

System testing

Once the complete system has been integrated, system testing is performed. Thereby, testers check whether deviations exist between the behaviour of the system and its requirements (documented in the requirements specification).

Acceptance testing

Acceptance testing aims at checking, among other things, whether the services on which client and contractor agreed are provided. Acceptance testing comprises different individual tests, including the following (see e.g. [Spillner et al. 2007]):

- *Field test*: During the field test, a pre-release version of the software-intensive system is tested under realistic conditions.
- *User acceptance test*: During a user acceptance test, the acceptance of the system by different users is tested.
- *Test for acceptance according to the contract*: During the test for contractual acceptance, the customer decides on the basis of the test results whether he regards that services agreed upon in the contract are provided. This test is based on the explicitly documented acceptance criteria (see Section 16.4).

38.2.4 Test-Case Definition

Artefact-based classification

Approaches to test-case definition are generally classified according to the kind of artefact that is used as a basis for identifying the test cases (called the test reference). According to [Spillner et al. 2007; Myers 2004; Liggesmeyer 2009], the two most important kinds of approaches for test-case definition are:

- *Code-based testing*: During code-based testing, the structure of the program code serves as a test reference. For example, test inputs are determined in such a way that each instruction in the program code is executed at least once during test execution. The expected outputs are determined based on the specification of the test object. Code-based tests are so-called white-box tests, since the definition of the test cases relies on the internal structure (the implementation) of the test objects.
- *Specification-based testing*: During specification-based testing, the test cases (including the test input and expected output) are identified on the basis of the test object's specification. The specification-based test is a so-called black-box test, since the internal structure (the implementation) of the test objects is not considered during test-case definition. In Section 38.4, requirements-based testing is introduced as a special form of specification-based testing.

Advantages/disadvantages

These two kinds of approaches for test-case definition have different implications with regard to the following two characteristics:

- *Applicability to test levels*: Source-code-based testing is suited for component testing and to some extent for integration testing (see [Liggesmeyer 2009]). Specification-based testing is applicable to all test levels. During component testing, the component specification (from design) is used as a basis for identifying the test cases, during integration testing the design documentation is used, during system testing the requirements specification is used, and during acceptance testing the acceptance criteria are used.

- *Coverage of the test object during testing*: Code-based testing has the advantage that the complete source code of the system can be covered, since the source code of the system is known during test-case definition. Thus, faults in the whole source code can be detected. This is generally not possible when specification-based testing is applied, since the realisation of the system specification, i.e. the source code, is not considered for test-case definition. A requirement can, for example, be realised by several alternative code blocks which are executed depending on the system state. Without knowledge of the source code, it can thus not be guaranteed that test cases which test all these code blocks, i.e. system states, are derived. Inversely, specification-based testing has the advantage that the whole specification can be covered during testing and one can therefore detect, for example, the missing implementation of a requirement. During a code-based test, no such test case would be created and this fault would thus not be detected.

38.3 The Role of Scenarios in Testing

Test cases contain scenarios

A test case is executed by passing the input specified in the test case to the test object and reading the results provided as output by the test object. Thus, the execution of a test case comprises a sequence of interactions between elements in the context of the test object (e.g. users or testers) and the test object (see Example 38-1). During test-case definition, the corresponding interactions can thus be defined by means of scenarios at different levels of abstraction.

Example 38-1: Calculator: interactions during an addition

The test case "addition" with inputs 40 and 2 and specified output 42 implies the following scenario:

(1) System asks for the first summand. (output)
(2) User enters 40. (input)
(3) System asks for the second summand. (output)
(4) User enters 2. (input)
(5) System outputs 42. (output)

38.3.1 Instance and Type Scenarios

Instance scenarios during test execution

The execution of a test case can be described in the form of an instance scenario (see Section 10.5). The data that is passed to the test object and the output of the test object are concrete instances. For instance, in Example 38-1 in step 5 of the scenario, the number "42" is expected as an output of the test object. The actors involved in the test execution are also concrete, since the test is executed by a concrete person on a concrete test object.

So-called test-case scenarios abstract from concrete instances, e.g. inputs and expected outputs (see Example 38-2) and thus provide a means to describe sets of instance scenarios. The term "test-case scenario", which will be used in the remainder of this section, is defined as follows:

Test-case scenarios abstract from the test execution

Definition 38-3: *Test-case scenario*

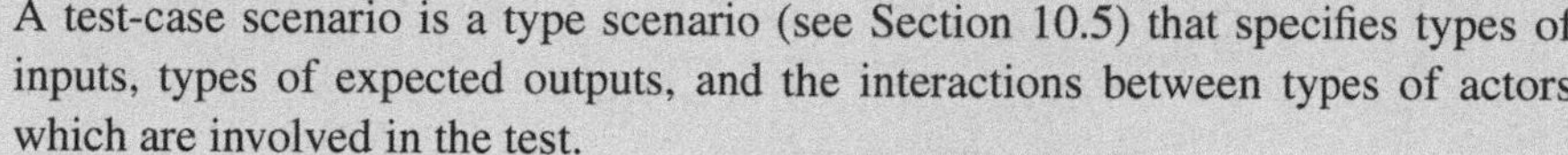

A test-case scenario is a type scenario (see Section 10.5) that specifies types of inputs, types of expected outputs, and the interactions between types of actors which are involved in the test.

Example 38-2: Calculator: test-case scenario for addition

(1) System asks for the first summand.
(2) User enters a number.
(3) System asks for the second summand.
(4) User enters a number.
(5) System outputs the result of the addition.

38.3.2 Test Levels and Kinds of Scenarios

Depending on the test level (see Section 38.2), a test-case scenario is a system-internal, an interaction, or a context scenario (see Section 10.6). In Fig. 38-2, the correlation between the test levels and the kinds of test-case scenarios is illustrated:

Type A scenarios

- *System-internal scenarios*: The test-case scenarios of component testing are system-internal scenarios, since the individual components of the system are tested. The test-case scenarios of integration testing are also system-internal scenarios, since the interactions between components or subsystems are tested.

Type B scenarios

- *Interaction scenarios*: The test-case scenarios of system testing are interaction scenarios, since the expected interactions between the users and the system or between the system and other systems are specified in the system test-case scenarios.

Type C scenarios

- *Context scenarios*: During acceptance testing, also context scenarios play a role (see Section 38.2.3). For example, during a field test, the software-intensive system is tested by selected users under realistic conditions, i.e. the system is tested in the context of its actual use. If test-case scenarios are specified for the field test, context information must also be considered and documented in the test-case scenarios (e.g. interactions which take place in the context and influence the interaction with the system).

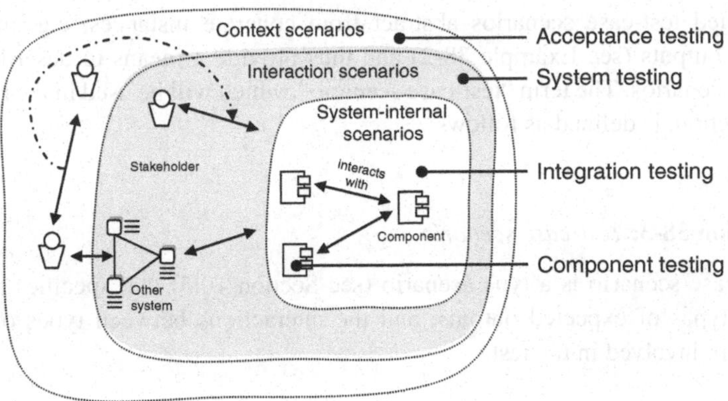

Fig. 38-2 *Test levels and kinds of scenarios*

38.4 Requirements-Based Definition of Test Cases

Advantages of requirements-based testing

The main focus of the following sections is the requirements-based definition of test cases for system and acceptance testing, i.e. on deriving test cases from requirements artefacts. A requirements-based system and acceptance test provides the following advantages:

- The system properties which are relevant for the customer or user are documented in requirements artefacts. Requirements artefacts are thus an excellent basis for the derivation of test cases, since in this way the test cases relate to the system properties that are significant for customers and users.
- Since test cases are derived for all specified requirements, missing or erroneous realisations of the specified requirements can be detected during test execution.
- Undetected faults in the requirements artefacts can be detected during the derivation of test cases from requirements artefacts.

Approaches for the derivation of test cases

Existing approaches for deriving test cases from requirements artefacts can be classified into two main groups:[4]

- Direct derivation of test cases from requirements artefacts
- Model-based test case derivation, during which the test cases are derived from a so-called test model

38.4.1 Direct Derivation of Test Cases from Requirements Artefacts

When deriving test cases directly from requirements artefacts, the test cases are derived without constructing preliminary artefacts.

Experience-based selection of test cases

Since a complete test is not possible (see Hint 38-1), a number of representative test cases must be selected. In practice, this step is often performed based on experience in

[4] Other authors (see e.g. [Allmann et al. 2005]) suggest a more fine-grained classification, which is not relevant for the further discussions in this chapter.

the case of textual requirements (see [Allmann et al. 2005]). However, this approach is not systematic and thus important test cases might be overlooked (see also [Pretschner et al. 2005]).

Equivalence classes

Test cases can be determined systematically, for example, by means of equivalence class partitioning (see e.g. [Liggesmeyer 2009; Myers 2004; Spillner et al. 2007]). During equivalence class partitioning, the possible system inputs and outputs defined in the requirements specification are classified into so-called equivalence classes. Thereby, it is assumed that all values that belong to the same equivalence class lead to the same test result (i.e. pass or fail). When determining test cases by means of equivalence class partitioning, at least one representative from each equivalence class is selected to define test inputs or outputs (see Example 38-3).

E

Example 38-3: Calculator: equivalence classes for multiplication

Equivalence classes for "multiplication" are [greater than zero], [less than zero], and [equal to zero] for the multiplicand and the multiplier. A test case would be determined from the following representatives, for example:

- Multiplicand = 100 [greater than zero]
- Multiplier = −5 [less than zero]

Test-case derivation from requirements scenarios

A different approach for requirements-based, systematic definition of test cases consists of using the scenarios from requirements engineering (see Part III.b) as a starting point (see [Allmann et al. 2005]). In this approach, requirements scenarios can be used as test-case scenarios (see Section 38.3) and, based on these test-case scenarios, test cases can be derived. Test cases are derived by defining concrete inputs (and preconditions), expected outputs (and postconditions), and test instructions (see Definition 38-2, Page 763). The advantage of deriving test cases based on scenarios over the other approaches is that the focus lies on the main interactions between the users and the system.

Advantage of direct derivation of test cases

The direct derivation of test cases from requirements artefacts provides the advantage that no additional notation or documents have to be introduced (for the documentation of intermediary artefacts). Furthermore, all requirements artefacts can be used as a starting point, since the used artefacts do not have to be formalised or interpretable by tools.

Disadvantages of direct derivation

In the case of textual requirements, however, the derivation of the test cases is often not performed systematically (see above). During the derivation of test cases from requirements scenarios, the quality of the test also strongly depends on the completeness of the requirements specification. This is a problem, as requirements scenarios are generally not created with the objective of defining the system behaviour completely. This shortcoming is addressed by model-based test-case derivation.

38.4.2 Model-Based Test-Case Derivation

Test model

During model-based test-case derivation, a so-called test model serves as the basis for systematically deriving test cases (see e.g. [Pretschner et al. 2005]). The following two initial situations may be distinguished during model-based testing:

- *Model-based solution-oriented requirements exist*: If model-based solution-oriented requirements were created during requirements engineering (see Chapter 14), they can be used as a test model provided that they are at a level of detail that is sufficient for test purposes. For use as a test model, especially state machines (e.g. in the form of UML state machine diagrams, see Section 14.3) and flow diagrams (e.g. in the form of UML activity diagrams, see Section 11.6) are suited.
- *Model-based solution-oriented requirements do not exist*: If model-based solution-oriented requirements do not exist, a test model is created based on the existing requirements artefacts for the sole purpose of supporting testing. For this test model, again state machines and flow diagrams can serve as suitable documentation techniques.

Selection of test cases according to test coverage criteria

Each path through a test model represents a test-case scenario (see Example 38-4). By selecting paths systematically, a subset of all possible test-case scenarios can be identified for the test. Table 38-1 shows a selection of possible criteria (so-called coverage criteria) which can be used for identifying the test-case scenarios based on a test model. The quality of the test is not only influenced by the selected test coverage criterion, but can also be controlled by defining the percentage to which the criterion shall be fulfilled.

Tab. 38-1 *Examples of coverage criteria for different kinds of test models (based on [Liggesmeyer 2009; Spillner et al. 2007])*

Coverage criterion	***Definition***
State machine	
State coverage	*Number of tested states ÷ number of all states*
Transition coverage	*Number of tested transitions ÷ number of all transitions*
Event coverage	*Number of tested events ÷ number of all events*
Flow diagram	
Activity coverage	*Number of tested activities ÷ number of all activities*
Branch coverage	*Number of tested edges ÷ number of all edges*
Path coverage	*Number of tested paths through the test model ÷ number of all possible paths through the test model*

Example 38-4: Derivation of test-case scenarios from a test model

Figure 38-3 shows a simple example of a test model in the form of a state machine diagram. For the selection of the test-case scenarios (right-hand side of Fig. 38-3), the transition coverage criterion was used. The objective of the test-case derivation in this case was to achieve transition coverage of 100%.

This is achieved by executing two test-case scenarios: scenario ❶ with the transitions (a, c) and scenario ❷ with the transitions (b, e, f, b, d). Alternatively, the scenarios (b, e, f, a, c) and (b, d) could also have been selected to achieve transition coverage of 100%.

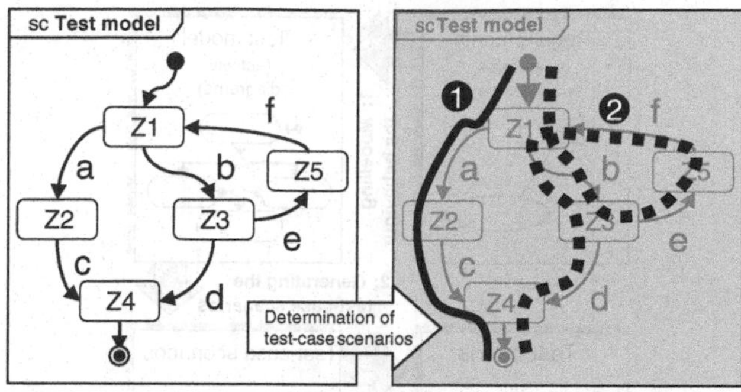

Fig. 38-3 *Test model and test-case scenarios for transition coverage of 100%*

Automatic generation of test cases

If modelling languages with precisely defined syntax and semantics (e.g. state charts) are used for the documentation of the test models, test-case scenarios and—depending on the level of detail—also test cases may be derived automatically from the test models (see [Pretschner et al. 2005]).

38.5 The ScenTED Approach

The ScenTED approach (Scenario-based TEst-case Derivation) is a technique for requirements- and model-based system testing (see [Reuys et al. 2005a; Reuys et al. 2005b; Kamsties et al. 2004; Pohl et al. 2005]). We have developed ScenTED in the context of the European EUREKA research projects ESAPS, CAFÉ, and FAMILIES [Van der Linden 2002] and applied it successfully in industrial projects [Goetz et al. 2005; Reuys et al. 2005a; Reuys et al. 2005b].

Application areas of the ScenTED technique

ScenTED was designed for testing in software product line engineering (see Chapter 37 and [Pohl and Metzger 2006; Pohl et al. 2005]). However, ScenTED has also proven to be applicable for testing single systems. For this purpose, we assume that we test a product line with a single product, i.e. we assume a product line without variability (see Chapter 37 and [Pohl et al. 2005]).

Main activities

In Fig. 38-4, the main activities of the ScenTED technique are sketched. These are:

- *Modelling the behaviour*: On the basis of use cases and their scenarios (see Section 10.8), the complete system behaviour is modelled in a test model. For documentation of the test model, the ScenTED technique uses UML 2 activity diagrams (see Section 11.6).
- *Generating test-case scenarios*: Based on the test model, test-case scenarios are generated by applying the branch coverage criterion (see Tab. 38-1).
- *Determining the test data*: The test-case scenarios are complemented with concrete test inputs and expected outputs, thus leading to concrete test cases.

!

Hint 38-2: *Use of model-based solution-oriented requirements for ScenTED*

When model-based solution-oriented requirements in the form of activity diagrams already exist as an output of requirements engineering, the ScenTED technique can directly start with the second step (generating test-case scenarios).

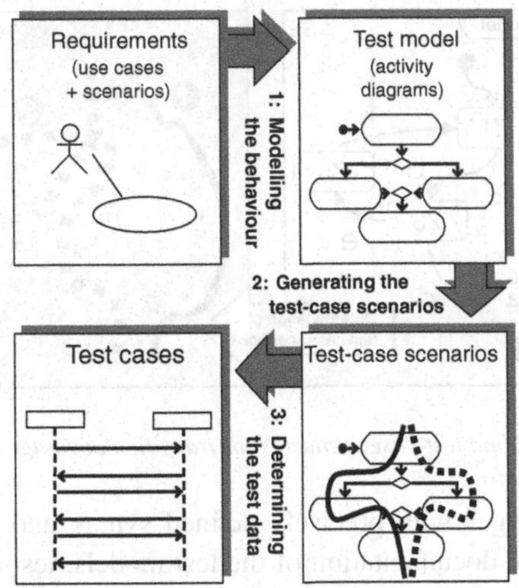

Fig. 38-4 *Main activities of the ScenTED technique*

Traceability between requirements artefacts and test cases

One significant benefit that is achieved by applying the ScenTED technique to derive test cases from use cases is that traceability links are established between the use cases and test cases. This traceability between the artefacts allows the determination of whether a use case is covered by test cases to the desired extent. In Fig. 38-5, the relationships between the relevant artefacts are depicted. A use case contains one or several use case scenarios (see Section 10.8). Based on the use case scenarios, the test model is developed. The individual test-case scenarios are identified on the basis of the test model. Finally, test cases are derived from the test-case scenarios.

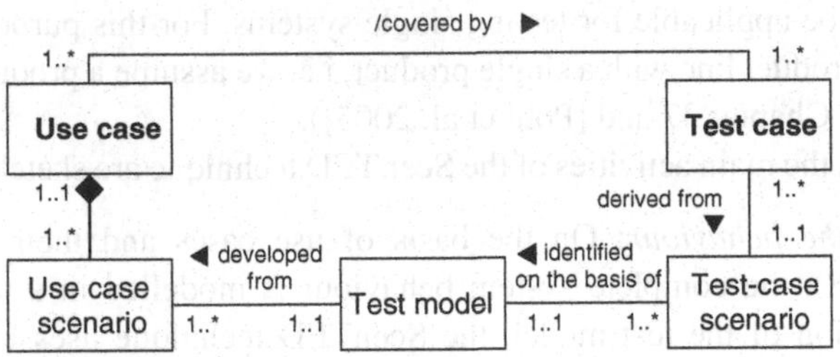

Fig. 38-5 *Relationships between use cases and test cases in ScenTED*

38.5.1 Modelling the System Behaviour in a Test Model

Based on the use cases, the complete behaviour of the system is described in a test model. The UML 2 activity diagrams used in ScenTED for documentation of the test model are particularly well suited for describing main, alternative, and exception scenarios and their relationships in a common model (see Section 11.6). In Example 38-5, creation of a test model on the basis of a use case is illustrated.

!

Hint 38-3: *Development of the test model in ScenTED*

Systematic construction of the test model can be achieved by performing the following steps:

(1) *Transfer the main scenario of the use case into an initial activity diagram*: Each interaction described in the main scenario is modelled as an activity in the activity diagram. First, activity partitions (see Section 11.6) are created for the system and the actors. Afterwards, the activities are assigned to the activity partitions.

(2) *Complement the test model with alternative scenarios*: For each alternative scenario, the activity diagram is complemented with further activities. To model the beginning of the alternative scenario in the activity diagram, a decision node with corresponding conditions is inserted (see Section 11.6). After the last activity of the alternative scenario, a merge node is inserted into the activity diagram.

(3) *Complement the test model with exception scenarios*: Finally, exception scenarios are also modelled in the same way as the test model was complemented with alternative scenarios. After the last activity of the exception scenario, either a merge node or a final node is inserted into the test model. The latter case is the typical one, since exception scenarios describe situations in which the goal of the use case is not achieved.

E

Example 38-5: Development of a test model for the navigation system example

In Tab. 38-2, the use case "navigation to destination" of a car navigation system is presented. This use case shall serve as a starting point for the derivation of system test cases with the ScenTED technique. Figure 38-6 shows the test model that was derived from the scenarios described in the use case "navigation to destination".

Tab. 38-2 *Use case "navigation to destination"*

Use case: Navigation to destination
Goal: Automatic navigation to destination
Primary actor: Driver
Result: Display of the route to the destination
Main scenario: 1. The driver starts the navigation system. 2. The system determines the current position of the car using GPS. 3. The system asks for the desired destination. 4. The driver keys in the destination. 5. The system calculates the route. 6. The system displays the route.

Tab. 38-2 *(continued)*

Alternative scenarios:
2a. The navigation system cannot determine the current position.
- 2a1. The system asks the driver to enter the position manually.
- 2a2. The driver enters the current position manually.
- 2a3. Scenario is continued with 3.

4a. Voice entry of the destination.
- 4a1. The driver names the destination.
- 4a2. The system interprets the voice entry.
- 4a3. Scenario is continued with 5.

5a. The destination was not found.
- 5a1. The system outputs a message.
- 5a2. Scenario is continued with 3.

Exception scenarios:
5b. The destination exists but the map is not available.
- 5b1. The system outputs an error message.
- 5b2. The system shuts down.

38.5.2 Generating Test-Case Scenarios

To generate test-case scenarios, paths through the test model are automatically identified in ScenTED by following the branch coverage criterion. The objective is to achieve branch coverage of 100%.

Branch coverage criterion

We chose the branch coverage criterion for the ScenTED technique as a compromise between maximum coverage and adequate test effort. The activity coverage criterion (see Tab. 38-1) has turned out to be too weak, while the path coverage criterion leads to an unmanageably large number of test-case scenarios in the case of large systems (see [Reuys et al. 2005b]). Example 38-6 illustrates the definition of test-case scenarios.

Example 38-6: Generation of test-case scenarios for the navigation system example

In Fig. 38-7, the two test-case scenarios generated by ScenTED for the test model in Fig. 38-6 are shown. These two scenarios cover all edges of the activity diagram and, hence, branch coverage of 100% is achieved.

In Fig. 38-8 scenario ❶ from Fig. 38-7 is shown as a UML sequence diagram.

38.5.3 Determining the Test Data

Determination of the inputs and specified outputs

Based on the generated test-case scenarios, test cases are derived. Therefore, a test-case scenario is complemented with concrete test input and expected outputs (and, if necessary, with pre- and postconditions). Example 38-7 illustrates this step.

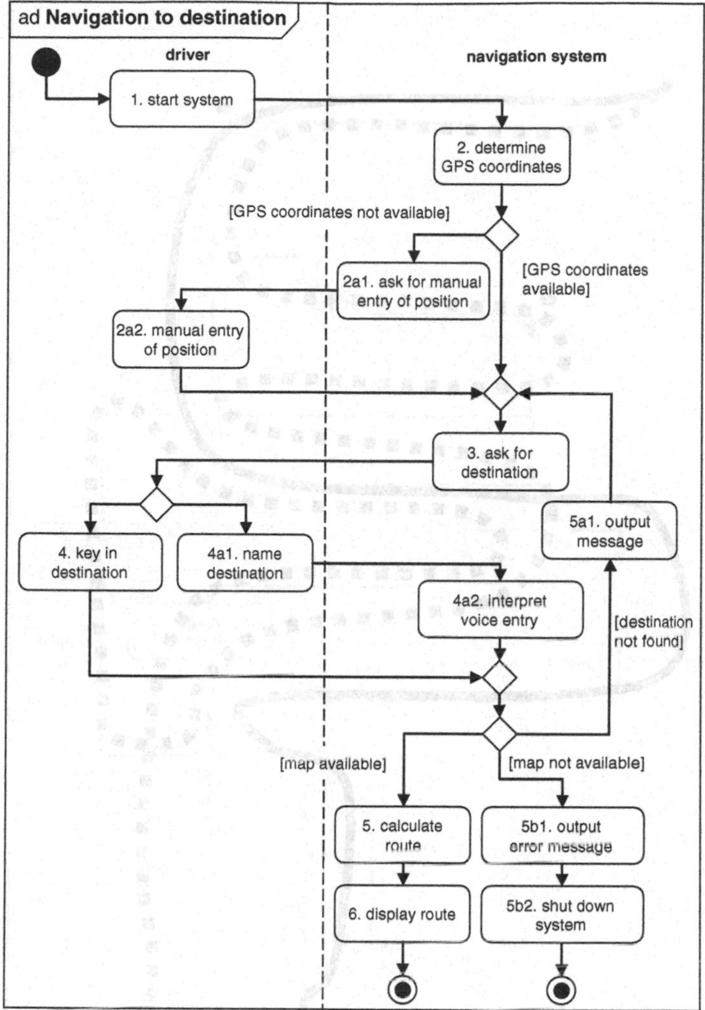

Fig. 38-6 *Test model for the use case "navigation to destination"*

Example 38-7: Derivation of test cases for the navigation system example

Figure 38-9 shows the test-case scenario ❶ complemented with concrete test inputs and expected outputs. This test case represents only one of several possible test cases, e.g., "Munich", "Stuttgart", and "Hamburg" would also have been possible destinations to serve as inputs.

Automating test data determination

In practical settings the description of the activities and conditions in the activity diagrams are often not detailed and formalised enough to automatically determine the test data (i.e. test inputs and expected outputs). The examples in this section illustrate this issue. In ScenTED, this activity is therefore performed manually by the testers. However, when sufficiently precise and formal models are available, this step can be automated by tools (see e.g. [Pretschner et al. 2005]).

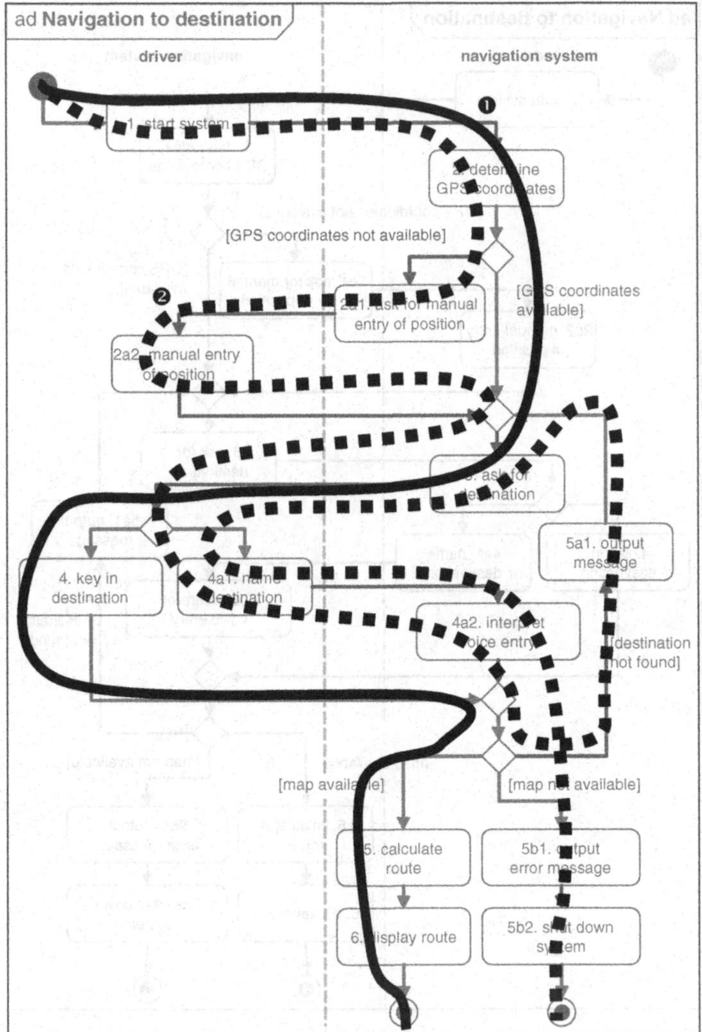

Fig. 38-7 *Test-case scenarios for the test model shown in Fig. 38-6*

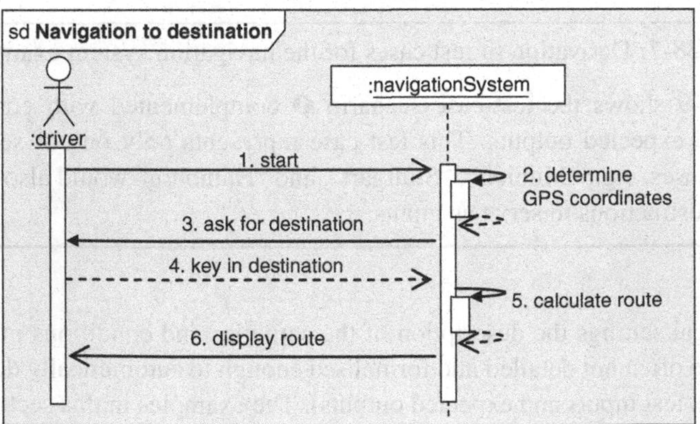

Fig. 38-8 *Test-case scenario ❶ from Fig. 38-7 as a sequence diagram*

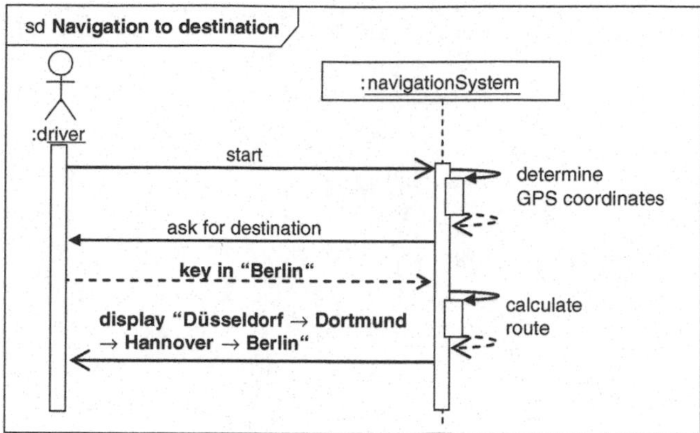

Fig. 38-9 *Possible test case for the test-case scenario from Fig. 38-8*

38.6 Summary

In requirements-based testing, requirements artefacts are used as the main inputs for defining the test cases for detecting errors in the implemented system. The advantages of requirements-based testing include the early availability of the test cases (the test cases are available even before the system is implemented) and the positive effects of test-case definition on the quality of the requirements artefacts. Since the execution of a test case comprises a sequence of interactions between the test object and some actors in the environment of the test object, test cases are typically defined by means of scenarios (so-called test-case scenarios). The ScenTED approach supports the derivation of test-case scenarios based on a set of scenarios defined during requirements engineering. To derive the test-case scenarios, first the required behaviour of the system is defined in a test model (an activity diagram). Then, the test-case scenarios are derived from the test model based on a (model) coverage criterion. The ScenTED approach can be applied to single systems as well as to software product lines.

Appendix

Glossary

A

Abstract syntax The abstract syntax of a language defines the abstract language constructs of this language and rules for combining them without prescribing a specific notation for the abstract language constructs.
See: Concrete syntax

Acceptance criterion An acceptance criterion defines a rule for checking a development artefact during a formal acceptance test of the system. To pass the acceptance test successfully, the artefact must fulfil all defined acceptance criteria.

Alternative scenario An alternative scenario documents a sequence of interactions that can be executed instead of a main scenario and results in the satisfaction of the goals associated with the main scenario.
See: Main scenario.

Ambiguous requirement A documented requirement is ambiguous, if different stakeholders with approximately the same knowledge about the system and its context interpret the requirement differently.
See: Lexical ambiguity, semantic ambiguity, syntactic ambiguity

Analysis of the desired state During the analysis of the desired state, potential improvements to be realised by a new system are identified based on the current-state model of the current system.
See: Current-state model

AND/OR graph (AND/OR goal graph) An AND/OR goal graph is a directed, acyclic graph with nodes that represent goals and edges that represent AND-decomposition relationships and OR-decomposition relationships between the goals.
See: AND/OR tree, goal model

AND/OR tree (AND/OR goal tree) An AND/OR goal tree consists of nodes that represent goals and directed edges that represent AND-decomposition and OR-decomposition relationships between the goals. Each node (except the root node) is related to exactly one super-goal.
See: AND/OR graph, goal model

Application requirements engineering Application engineering is one of the two development processes of product line engineering. During application engineering, development with reuse is pursued, i.e. the artefacts from domain engineering are reused to realise different systems of the product line.
See: Domain requirements engineering

Attribute scheme An attribute scheme defines the attributes for a particular requirement type. For each attribute, the attribute scheme defines a unique attribute name, the semantics of the attribute, its range of values, and the semantics of the values.
See: Requirements attribute

B

Baseline *See: Requirements baseline*

Behavioural perspective The focus of the behavioural perspective is to define the overall behaviour of the system. Within this perspective, the external stimuli that the system receives and the

reactions of the system as well as the relationship between stimuli and reactions are defined. In addition, the possible states (or modes) the system can be in and the allowed transitions between the states (as reactions to stimuli) are defined.
See: Data perspective, functional perspective

C

Change management (in requirements engineering) Change management in requirements engineering analyses and decides about requirements changes and controls the implementation of the changes, but does not implement the changes.

Checklist A checklist contains a number of items, documented as questions or statements, that are related to some issue.

Conceptual model A conceptual model is an abstract (partial) documentation of an existing or conceived (i.e. future) reality.

Conceptual modelling language A conceptual modelling language is defined by an abstract syntax, the semantics of the modelling constructs of the language, and a notation for the modelling constructs.
See: Abstract syntax, concrete syntax, semantics

Concrete syntax The concrete syntax of a language establishes a relationship between the (abstract) language constructs of the abstract syntax and the concrete (often graphical) representations of these constructs.
See: Abstract syntax

Configuration of requirements artefacts A configuration of requirements artefacts comprises a set of related requirements artefacts, or more precisely, versions of requirements artefacts.

Conflict A conflict in requirements engineering exists, if the needs and wishes of different stakeholders (or groups of stakeholders) regarding the system contradict each other, or if some needs and wishes cannot be taken into account.
See: Negotiation

Constraint A constraint is an organisational or technological requirement that restricts the way in which the system shall be developed.
(Based on: [Robertson and Robertson 2006])

Context *See: System context*

Context aspect Context aspects are material and immaterial objects of the system context such as people, technical systems, non-technical systems, processes, or physical laws.
See: System context, context object

Context boundary The context boundary separates the relevant part of the system environment from the irrelevant part. In other words, it separates the system context from the irrelevant environment which contains all those aspects that do not need to be considered during system development.
See: System boundary, system context

Context facet The system context is structured into four context facets which have to be considered for each software-intensive system during requirements engineering: the subject facet, usage facet, IT system facet, and development facet.
See: System context, subject facet, usage facet, IT system facet, development facet

Context object Context objects are either immaterial or material objects or persons which exist in the system context and need to be considered when defining the requirements for the system.
See: Context aspect, system context

Context of a requirement The context of a requirement consists of context aspects in the system context and of other requirements which are associated with the considered requirement.

Context scenario A context scenario documents the direct interactions between the system and its actors as well as additional context information that is relevant for the system usage or the system itself, e.g. interactions among the actors as well as the indirect users of the system.
(Based on [Pohl and Haumer 1997])
See: Interaction scenario, system-internal scenario

Continuous requirements engineering Continuous requirements engineering is an activity which spans the entire system lifecycle and even extends across projects and products. We differentiate two quality levels of continuous requirements engineering: requirements engineering as a cross-lifecycle activity and requirements engineering as a cross-project and cross-product activity.

See: Requirements engineering as a cross-lifecycle activity, requirements engineering as a cross-project and cross-product activity

Controlled language A controlled language defines, for a specific domain, a restricted natural language grammar (syntax) and a set of terms (including the semantics of the terms) to be used within the restricted grammar to document statements about the domain.

Current-state analysis During the analysis of the current state, existing systems and processes are analysed, and the identified and collected requirements are documented in a current-state model.
See: Analysis of the desired state

Current-state model A current state model documents the current state of a system. Current state models reflect the current situation and provide a basis for the analysis and identification of possible improvements of a system.
See: Desired-state model

D

Data conflict (about requirements) A data conflict about a requirement exists if stakeholders are wrongly or incompletely informed about the requirement or if stakeholders interpret the meaning of the requirement differently.
See: Interest conflict, value conflict

Data perspective The data perspective focusses on defining the data/information to be managed by the software-intensive system. In the data perspective, static aspects of the data are considered and defined such as the entities, relationships between entities, attributes, and attribute types relevant for the system.
See: Functional perspective, behavioural perspective

Descriptive scenario A descriptive scenario describes a process or workflow for the purpose of understanding its operations, involved agents, triggering events etc. (see [Rolland et al. 1998a]).
See: Explanatory scenario, exploratory scenario

Desired-state model The desired-state model results from adapting the current-state model by integrating the improvements identified during the analysis of the desired state into the current-state model. The desired-state model thus defines the requirements for the new system.
See: Current-state model

Development facet The development facet comprises all aspects of the context concerning the development process of the system, e.g. process guidelines and constraints, development tools, quality assurance methods.
See: Subject facet, context facet, usage facet, IT-system facet

Direct observation During direct observation, the observer watches the stakeholders while they are performing a particular task, analyses their activities, and asks questions.
(Source: [Bray 2002])
See: Ethnographic observation

Documentation (of requirements) Documentation is one of the three core requirements engineering activities. The focus of the documentation activity is the documentation and specification of the elicited requirements according to the defined documentation and specification rules. In addition, other important types of information such as rationale or decisions must be documented.
See: Elicitation, negotiation

Domain requirements engineering Domain engineering is one of the two development processes of product line engineering. During domain engineering, development for reuse is pursued, i.e. artefacts are developed proactively that can be used for the development of systems of the product line.
See: Application requirements engineering

E

Elicitation (of requirements) Requirements elicitation is one of the three core requirements engineering activities. The goal of the elicitation activity is to:

(1) Identify relevant requirement sources
(2) Elicit existing requirements from the identified sources
(3) Develop new and innovative requirements.

See: Documentation, negotiation

Essence of a system The essence of a system is the complete set of true requirements for the system.

A true requirement is a feature or capability that a system must possess in order to fulfil its purpose, regardless of how the system is implemented.
(Source: [McMenamin and Palmer 1984])
See: Incarnation of a system

Essential Systems Analysis Essential Systems Analysis [McMenamin and Palmer 1988] extends and improves the Structured Analysis method of DeMarco. It differentiates between the essence and the incarnation of a system.
See: Structured Analysis, essence of a system, incarnation of a system

Ethnographic observation During ethnographic observation, the observer spends a long period of time with the stakeholders to learn and understand actively their way of working and their procedures.
(Source: [Kotonya and Sommerville 1997])
See: Direct observation

Exception scenario An exception scenario documents a sequence of interactions that is executed instead of the interactions documented in another scenario (main, alternative, or exception scenario) when an exceptional event occurs. As a consequence, one or multiple goals associated with the original scenario cannot be satisfied.
See: Alternative scenario, main scenario

Explanatory scenario An explanatory scenario is created to explain a goal, an alternative solution, or a sequence of interactions. It comprises arguments, rationales, and alternative views of the stakeholders.
See: Descriptive scenario, exploratory scenario

Exploratory interview An exploratory interview is a conversation by means of which the interviewer elicits information about the opinion or view of the interviewee with respect to some issue. The interview is based on a list of prepared questions. The interviewer may deviate from the prepared questions. The results of such an interview are qualitative.
See: Interview, standardised interview, unstructured interview

Exploratory scenario An exploratory scenario is created to explore and evaluate possible alternative solutions in order to support the selection of one of them.
See: Descriptive scenario, explanatory scenario

External validation During an external validation, stakeholders from outside the developing organisation (or department or business unit) judge the quality of the requirements artefacts.

F

Failure (in testing) A failure is a deviation between the expected outputs and the outputs actually observed during the execution of a test object. A failure is caused by a fault (defect) in the tested artefact.
(Based on [Spillner et al. 2007])
See: Fault

Fault (in testing) A fault is a defect in an artefact. It may, for example, be caused by an error or mistake of a person.
(Based on [Spillner et al. 2007])
See: Failure

Functional perspective The functional perspective typically defines the processes (functions) to be provided by the system, the manipulation of the data in each process, and the input–output relationships (information flows) among the processes.
See: Data perspective, behavioural perspective

Functional requirement Functional requirements are statements of services the system should provide, how the system should react to particular inputs and how the system should behave in particular situations. In some cases, the functional requirements may also state what the system should not do.
(Source: [Sommerville 2007])
See: Non-functional requirement, quality requirement

G

Glossary A glossary is a collection of technical terms that are part of a language (terminology). A glossary defines the specific meaning of each of these terms. A glossary can additionally contain references to related terms as well as examples that explain the terms.

Goal A goal is an intention with regard to the objectives, properties, or use of the system.

Goal model A goal model is a conceptual model that documents goals, their decomposition into sub-goals, and existing goal dependencies.
See: AND/OR tree, AND/OR graph, conceptual model

H

Homonym A homonym is a word that has different meanings in different contexts despite being spelled in the same way.
See: Lexical ambiguity, synonym

I

Incarnation of a system The sum of people, wires, paper clips, carbon paper, pencils, typewriters, computer terminals, office furniture, file cabinets, offices, telephones, CPUs, and so forth that are used to implement the essential activities and memory of a system are called its incarnation.
(Source: [McMenamin and Palmer 1984])
See: Essence of a system

Information model An information model is an abstract representation of the structure of information in a considered universe of discourse. Information models are defined using a conceptual modelling language.
See: Model, conceptual model, universe of discourse

Inspection A quality improvement process for written material. It consists of two dominant components: product (document itself) improvement and process improvement (of both document production and inspection).
(Source: [Gilb and Graham 1993])

Instance scenario An instance scenario describes a concrete sequence of interactions between concrete actors.
See: Type scenario

Interaction scenario An interaction scenario documents interactions between the system and its actors (i.e. persons and systems in the context of the system).
(Based on [Pohl and Haumer 1997])
See: System-internal scenario, context scenario

Interest conflict (about requirements) An interest conflict about the requirements for the system to be developed exists if the stakeholders' interests or goals with regard to the system contradict each other.
See: Data conflict, value conflict

Internal validation In internal validation, exclusively stakeholders from within the developing organisation are involved, or, in the case of large organisations, from within the developing department or business unit.

Interview An interview is a conversation in which an interviewer questions one or several interviewees (stakeholders) about requirements for the new system.
See: Exploratory interview, standardised interview, unstructured interview

IT system facet The IT system facet comprises all aspects of the operational and technical environment in which the system is deployed. In addition, the IT system facet deals with IT strategies and policies such as the policy to use only software components that have passed a specific certification.
See: Development facet, subject facet, usage facet

L

Lexical ambiguity Lexical ambiguity occurs when (1) a word has the same meaning as at least one other word or when (2) a word has different meanings in different contexts despite being spelled in the same way.
See: Homonym, synonym, syntactic ambiguity, semantic ambiguity

M

Main scenario A main scenario documents the sequence of interactions that is executed normally in order to satisfy a specific set of goals.
See: Alternative scenario, exception scenario

Management (in requirements engineering) Management is one of the two cross-sectional requirements engineering activities. The goal of management in requirements engineering is to:

(1) Observe the system context to detect context changes
(2) Manage the execution of requirements engineering activities
(3) Manage the requirements artefacts

See: Validation

Meta-model of a modelling language A meta-model is a conceptual model that defines a modelling language.
See: Conceptual model

Misuse scenario A misuse scenario documents a sequence of interactions in which a hostile actor uses the system against the stakeholders' intention.
See: Negative scenario, positive scenario

Mock-up A mock-up is a model of a system without any functionality.
See: Prototype

Model A model is an abstract representation of information about the universe of discourse for a specific purpose.
See: Model-based requirement

Model-based requirement Model-based requirements are requirements documented in requirements models.
See: Natural language requirement

N

Natural language requirement A natural language requirement is a requirement that is documented using natural language.
See: Model-based requirement

Negative scenario A negative scenario documents a sequence of interactions that fails to satisfy a goal or set of goals associated with the scenario. A negative scenario can be either allowed or forbidden.
See: Positive scenario, misuse scenario

Negotiation (about requirements) Requirements negotiation is one of the three core requirements engineering activities. The goal of the negotiation activity is to:

(1) Identify conflicts
(2) Analyse the cause of each conflict
(3) Resolve the conflicts by means of appropriate strategies
(4) Document the conflict resolution and the rationales

See: Documentation, elicitation

Non-functional requirement A non-functional requirement is either an underspecified functional requirement or a quality requirement.
See: Underspecified requirement, quality requirement

P

Paper prototype A paper prototype presents the graphical user interface of the system to be developed by means of sketches and images.
See: Prototype, mock-up

Perspective-based reading Perspective-based reading is a proven technique for assessing the quality of documents. During perspective-based reading, the reader reads a document from a previously defined perspective, e.g. from the perspective of a user or tester.

Positive scenario A positive scenario documents a sequence of interactions that satisfies a goal or a set of goals associated with the scenario.
See: Negative scenario

Post-traceability Post-traceability denotes the traceability from a requirement to its successor artefacts such as architectural components satisfying the requirement, the implementation of the requirement in the source code, or the test cases verifying the requirement.
See: Traceability, pre-traceability

Pragmatic quality The pragmatic quality of a conceptual model describes how well the representation of information of the universe of discourse in the model is suited for the specific use.

Pragmatics The pragmatics deals with effects that the interpretation of representations (symbols) has on the behaviour of the interpreting actor.
See: Semantics

Pre-traceability Pre-traceability denotes the traceability of a requirements artefact to its predecessor artefacts, i.e. to its source or origin.
See: Traceability, post-traceability

Priority of a requirement The priority of a requirement documents the importance of the requirement with regard to one or several prioritisation criteria. The priority of a requirement may be determined either for each requirement in isolation or by pairwise comparison of requirements.

Prototype A prototype is an initial version of a software system which is used to demonstrate concepts, try out design options and, generally, to find out more about the problem and its possible solutions.
(Source: [Sommerville 2004])

Q

Quality requirement A quality requirement defines a quality property of the entire system or of a system component, service, or function.
See: Functional requirement, non-functional requirement

R

Referential ambiguity Referential ambiguity occurs if a word or phrase in a sentence refers to an object, and there are different interpretations regarding what that object is.
See: Lexical ambiguity, semantic ambiguity, syntactical ambiguity

Release A release is a requirements configuration that is composed for the delivery of a system.
See: Requirements configuration

Requirement A requirement is:

(1) A condition or capability needed by a user to solve a problem or achieve an objective
(2) A condition or capability that must be met or possessed by a system or system component to satisfy a contract, standard, specification, or other formally imposed documents
(3) A documented representation of a condition or capability as in (1) or (2)

(Source: [IEEE Std 610.12-1990])

Requirements artefact A requirements artefact is a documented requirement.
See: Goal, scenario, solution-oriented requirement

Requirements attribute A requirements attribute is defined by the attribute name, the associated semantics of the attribute, the range of values defined for the attribute, and the semantics of these values.
See: Attribute scheme

Requirements baseline A requirements baseline is a selected configuration of requirements artefacts. The term requirements baseline refers to a configuration of stable requirements artefact versions. Typically, a requirements baseline is realised in a particular system release.
See: Configuration of requirements artefacts, version of a requirements artefact

Requirements document In a requirements document, the requirements for the system to be developed are defined.
See: Requirements specification, documentation

Requirements engineering Requirements engineering is a cooperative, iterative, and incremental process which aims to ensure that:

(1) All relevant requirements are explicitly known and understood at the required level of detail.
(2) Sufficient agreement about the system requirements is achieved between the stakeholders involved.
(3) All requirements are documented and specified in compliance with the relevant documentation/specification formats and rules.

Requirements engineering as a cross-lifecycle activity Requirements engineering is performed throughout the entire development process of a product/system.
See: Continuous requirements engineering

Requirements engineering as a cross-project and cross-product activity Requirements engineering is not only performed throughout the entire development process of a product but is executed across multiple project and product developments.
See: Continuous requirements engineering

Requirements model Requirements models are conceptual models that document requirements (goals, scenarios, and solution-oriented requirements).
See: Conceptual model

Requirement source Requirement sources are the origins of the requirements defined for the system (e.g. stakeholders, existing documentations, existing systems)
See: Stakeholder

Requirements specification (document) A requirements specification is a document that contains specified requirements, i.e. requirements that comply with defined specification rules and guidelines.
See: Specification of requirements

Requirements traceability *See: Traceability*

S

Scenario A scenario describes a concrete example of satisfying or failing to satisfy a goal (or set of goals). It thereby provides more detail about one or several goals. A scenario typically defines a sequence of interaction steps executed to satisfy the goal and relates these interaction steps to the system context.
See: Goal

Semantic ambiguity Semantic ambiguity occurs when a sentence has more than one interpretation in the specific context, even if it contains no lexical or syntactic ambiguity.
See: Lexical ambiguity, syntactic ambiguity

Semantic quality The semantic quality of a conceptual model states the extent to which information defined in the conceptual model corresponds to the artefacts of the universe of discourse. The semantic quality of a conceptual model can be determined by means of two characteristics: the validity of the model and the completeness of the model.

Semantics The semantics of a language define the meaning of the language constructs (i.e. the meaning of the symbols and their combinations).
See: Syntax, pragmatics

Software requirements specification The software requirements specification details the software requirements defined in the system requirements specification.
See: System requirements specification

Software test A software test denotes the systematic execution of a software unit (also called test object) with the aim of detecting failures.
(Based on [Spillner et al. 2007; Myers 2001])
See: Failure

Solution-oriented requirement Solution-oriented requirements define the data perspective, the functional perspective, and the behavioural perspective on a software-intensive system. Furthermore, solution-oriented requirements comprise (solution-oriented) quality requirements and (solution-oriented) constraints.
See: Data perspective, functional perspective, behavioural perspective, quality requirement, constraint

Specification of requirements
See: Requirements specification

SRS Software requirements specification

Stakeholder (in requirements engineering) A stakeholder is either a person or an organisation that has a potential interest in the system to be developed. A stakeholder typically has their own requirements for the system. A person can represent the interest of different stakeholders (people and/or organisations), i.e. a stakeholder can have more than one role and represent more than one stakeholder.
(Based on [Robertson and Robertson 2006])

Standardised interview During a standardised interview, the interviewer asks an interviewee prepared questions concerning an issue of interest. Independently of the answers given, the interviewer does not deviate from the prepared questions.
See: Explorative interview, unstructured interview, interview

Structured Analysis Structured Analysis is a method for systems analysis in which the functions of the new system take centre stage. The functions are described using hierarchical data flow diagrams, the static structure of the data is described using a data dictionary and the behaviour of elementary functions is described using mini specifications.
See: Essential Systems Analysis

Subject facet The subject facet comprises the objects and events in the context that are relevant for the system. In other words, these objects and events must be represented in the system. The subject facet also comprises aspects that influence the representation of information in the system (e.g. data privacy laws disallowing the storage of certain types of data).
See: Development facet, IT system facet, usage facet

Synonym A synonym is a word that has the same meaning as at least one other word.
See: Homonym, lexical ambiguity

Syntactic ambiguity Syntactic ambiguity occurs if there are at least two valid syntax trees that can be assigned to the same sentence, and for each assignable syntax tree, the sentence has a different meaning. (Source: [Hirst 1987]).
See: Syntax tree, semantic ambiguity, lexical ambiguity

Syntactic quality The syntactic quality of a conceptual model refers to the language constructs (representations) used in the model or, more precisely, to the adherence to syntactic rules. The syntactic quality of a conceptual model is thus a measure of compliance with the syntactic rules defined for the modelling language.

Syntactic requirements pattern A syntactic requirements pattern defines a syntactic structure for documenting requirements in natural language and defines the meaning of each part of the syntactic structure.

Syntax The syntax of a language defines the atomic language constructs (atomic symbols or representations) and the valid combinations of these constructs.
See: Abstract syntax, concrete syntax, pragmatics, semantics

Syntax tree A syntax tree denotes the grammatical structure of a sentence.

SysRS System requirements specification

System boundary The system boundary separates the system to be developed from the system context. The system boundary separates the parts that belong to the system and can hence be changed during the development process from the parts of the system context that cannot be changed during the development process.
See: Context boundary, system context

System context The system context is the part of the system environment relevant for defining, understanding, and interpreting the system requirements. The system context consists of the four context facets: the subject facet, the usage facet, the IT system facet, and the development facet.
See: Context of a requirement, context aspect, context facet, context boundary, system boundary

System requirements specification The system requirements specification defines the requirements for the system hardware and software as well as necessary relationships between hardware and software.
See: Software requirements specification

System-internal scenario A system-internal scenario documents only system-internal interactions, i.e. a sequence of interactions among different parts of a system.
(Based on [Pohl and Haumer 1997])
See: Interaction scenario, context scenario

System vision
See: Vision

Systems analysis The term "systems analysis" subsumes different approaches that define requirements for a new system based on the analysis of existing systems or processes.
See: Essential Systems Analysis

T

Test case A test case comprises the preconditions required for test execution, the set of inputs and expected outputs, test instructions (how inputs are passed to the test object and how outputs are read from the test object) as well as the expected postconditions.
See: Software test

Test-case scenario A test-case scenario is a type of scenario that specifies types of inputs, types of expected outputs, and the interactions between types of actors which are involved in the test.
See: Type scenario

Textual requirement
See: Natural language requirement

Traceability (of a requirement) Requirements traceability refers to the ability to describe and follow the life of a requirement, in both a forwards and backwards direction (i.e. from its origins, through its development and specification, to its subsequent deployment and use, and through all periods of on-going refinement and iteration in any of these phases).
(Source: [Gotel and Finkelstein 1994])
See: Pre-traceability, post-traceability

Type scenario A type scenario abstracts from the concrete actors, inputs, and outputs of a specific sequence of interactions. Type scenarios describe interactions by means of types of inputs and outputs.

Type A scenario
See: System-internal scenario

Type B scenario
See: Interaction scenario

Type C scenario
See: Context scenario

U

Unambiguous requirement A documented requirement is unambiguous, if all stakeholders with approximately the same knowledge about the system and its context interpret the requirement in the same way.
See: Ambiguous requirement

Underspecified requirement If details about a requirement are not documented, different stakeholders can assume different details and thereby interpret the requirement in a different way. Thus, underspecified requirements must be refined and detailed during requirements engineering.
See: Non-functional requirement

Universe of discourse The universe of discourse comprises any part or aspect of the existing or conceived reality under consideration.

Usage facet The usage facet is the part of the system context that comprises all aspects concerning the system usage by people and other systems.
See: Development facet, subject facet, IT-system facet

Use case The specification of sequences of actions, including variant sequences and error sequences, that a system, subsystem, or class can perform by interacting with outside objects to provide a service of value. (Source: [Rumbaugh et al. 2005])
See: Alternative scenario, exception scenario, main scenario

Use case scenario A use case scenario is a valid sequence of interactions that results from the main, alternative, and exception scenarios defined for the use case and leads to a defined termination of the use case. Therein, termination means that the use case scenario either leads to the satisfaction of the goals associated with the use case or to a defined abort.

Unstructured interview Unstructured interviews do not make use of a prepared question catalogue. The interviewer freely asks broad questions and allows the interviewee to lead the conversation in a direction at his own discretion.
See: Interview, standardised interview, exploratory interview

V

Validation (in requirements engineering) Validation denotes checking whether inputs, performed activities, and created outputs (requirements artefacts) of the requirements engineering core activities fulfil defined quality criteria. Validation is performed by involving relevant stakeholders, other requirement sources (standards, laws, etc.) as well as external reviewers, if necessary.
See: Management

Value conflict (about requirements) A value conflict about the requirements for the system to be developed exists if different stakeholders evaluate a requirement differently or each stakeholder considers the importance of the requirement differently.
See: Interest conflict, data conflict

Variability Variability describes the ability of an object to vary, i.e. its ability to change. In product line engineering, variability in the domain artefacts is defined with the goal of realising different products in the product line through variation (i.e. through modification) of the domain artefacts.
(Based on [Clements and Northrop 2001; Pohl et al. 2005]).

Version of a requirements artefact A version of a requirements artefact can be regarded as a defined state of a requirements artefact, i.e. a version of a requirements artefact freezes a particular state of a requirements artefact during the requirements engineering process.

Vision The system vision describes a significant desired change of the current reality.

Literature

A

[Aguilar 1967] F. Aguilar: Scanning the Business Environment. Macmillan, New York, 1967.

[Alexander 2003] I. Alexander: Misuse Cases: Use Cases with Hostile Intent. IEEE Software, Vol. 20, No. 1, IEEE Computer Society, Los Alamitos, 2003, pp. 58–66.

[Alexander and Maiden 2004] I. Alexander, N. Maiden (Eds.): Scenarios, Stories, Use Cases – Through the Systems Development Life-Cycle. Wiley, Chichester, 2004.

[Alexander and Stevens 2002] I. Alexander, R. Stevens: Writing Better Requirements. Addison-Wesley, Boston, 2002.

[Alfaro and Henzinger 2001] L. de Alfaro, T. A. Henzinger: Interface Automata. In: Proceedings of the 8th European Software Engineering Conference (ESEC) held jointly with the 9th ACM SIGSOFT International Symposium on Foundations of Software Engineering (SIGSOFT FSE), 2001, pp. 109–120.

[Allmann et al. 2005] C. Allmann, C. Denger, T. Olsson: Analysis of Requirements-Based Test Case Creation Techniques. IESE-Report No. 046.05/E, Version 1.0, June 2005. Fraunhofer-Institute for Experimental Software Engineering IESE, Kaiserslautern, 2005.

[Alur and Dill 1994] R. Alur, D. L. Dill: A Theory of Timed Automata. Theoretical Computer Science, Vol. 126, No.2, 1994, pp. 183–235.

[Antón 1996] A. I. Antón: Goal-Based Requirements Analysis. In: Proceedings of the 2nd International Conference on Requirements Engineering (ICRE '96), IEEE Computer Society, Washington, DC, USA, 1996, pp. 136–144.

[Antón and Potts 1998] A. I. Antón, C. Potts: The Use of Goals to Surface Requirements for Evolving Systems. In: Proceedings of the 20th International Conference on Software Engineering (ICSE'98), IEEE Computer Society, Washington, DC, USA, 1998, pp. 157–166.

[Antón et al. 1994] A. I. Anton, W. M. Mc Cracken, C. Potts: Goal Decomposition and Scenario Analysis in Business Process Reengineering. In: Proceedings of 6th International Conference on Advanced Information Systems Engineering (CAiSE'94), Springer, Berlin, Heidelberg, New York, 1994, pp. 94–104.

[Antón et al. 2000] A. I. Antón, J. Dempster, D. Siege: Deriving Goals from a Use Case Based Requirements Specification for an Electronic Commerce System. In: Proceedings of 6th International Workshop on Requirements Engineering – Foundation for Software Quality (REFSQ'00), Essener Informatik Berichte, Essen, 2000, pp. 10–19.

[Armour and Miller 2001] F. Armour, G. Miller: Advanced Use Case Modeling – Software Systems. Addison-Wesley, Boston, 2001.

[Autosar 2009] AUTOSAR, Automotive Open System Architecture, *http://www.autosar.org*; accessed on 12/10/2009.

B

[Bandler and Grinder 1975] R. Bandler, J. Grinder: The Structure of Magic I – A Book about Language and Therapy, Science and Behavior Books, Palo Alto, California, 1975.

[Basili et al. 1996] V. Basili, S. Green, O. Laitenberger, F. Lanubile, F. Shull, S. Sörumsgard, M. Zelkowitz: The Empirical Investigation of Perspective-Based Reading. Empirical Software Engineering, Vol. 1, No. 2, Springer Netherlands, 1996, pp. 133–144.

[Bass et al. 2003] L. Bass, P. Clements, R. Kazman: Software Architecture in Practice. 2nd edition, Addison-Wesley, SEI Series in Software Engineering, Boston, 2003.

[Batory 2005] D. Batory: Feature Models, Grammars, and Propositional Formulas. In: Proceedings of the International Software Product Line Conference (SPLC), 2005, pp. 7–20.

[Bäumer et al. 1996] D. Bäumer, W. Bischofberger, H. Lichter, H. Züllighoven: User Interface Prototyping – Concepts, Tools, and Experience. In: Proceedings of the 18th International Conference on Software Engineering (ICSE'96), IEEE Computer Society Press, Los Alamitos, 1996, pp. 532–541.

[Baumgarten 1996] B. Baumgarten: Petri-Netze – Grundlagen und Anwendungen. 2nd edition, Spektrum Akademischer Verlag, Heidelberg, 1996.

[Baziuk 1995] W. Baziuk: BNR/NORTEL – Path to Improve Product Quality, Reliability and Customer Satisfaction. In: Proceedings of the 6th International Symposium on Software Reliability Engineering, IEEE Computer Society Press, Los Alamitos, 1995, pp. 256–262.

[Beck and Andres 2004] K. Beck, C. Andres: Extreme Programming Explained: Embrace Change. 2nd edition, Addison-Wesley, Amsterdam, 2004.

[Benner et al. 1993] K. M. Benner, M. S. Feather, W. L. Johnson, L. A. Zorman: Utilizing Scenarios in the Software Development Process. In: C. Rolland, N. Prakash, B. Pernici (Eds.): Proceedings of the IFIP WG 8.1 Working Conference on Information System Development Process, North-Holland, Amsterdam, 1993, pp. 117–134.

[Berander and Andrews 2005] P. Berander, A. Andrews: Requirements Prioritization. In: A. Aurum, C. Wohlin (Eds.): Engineering and Managing Software Requirements. Springer, Berlin, Heidelberg, 2005, pp. 69–94.

[Berry et al. 2001] D. M. Berry, K. Daudjee, J. Dong, M. A. Nelson, T. Nelson: User's Manual as a Requirements Specification. Technical Report CS 2001-17, University of Waterloo, 2001.

[Berry et al. 2003] D. M. Berry, E. Kamsties, M. M. Krieger: From Contract Drafting to Software Specification – Linguistic Sources of Ambiguity – A Handbook, 2003, *http://se.uwaterloo.ca/~dberry/handbook/ambiguityHandbook.pdf*, accessed on 09/09/2009.

[Beyer and Holtzblatt 1998] H. Beyer, K. Holtzblatt: Contextual Design – Defining Customer-Centered Systems. Morgan Kaufmann, San Fransisco, 1998.

[Birk et al. 2003] A. Birk, G. Heller, I. John, K. Schmid, K. Von der Maßen, K. Müller: Product Line Engineering – The State of the Practice. IEEE Software, Vol. 20, No. 5, IEEE Press, Los Alamitos, 2003, pp. 52–60.

[Bittner and Spence 2003] K. Bittner, I. Spence: Use Case Modeling. Addison-Wesley, Boston, 2003.

[BMEcat 2009] BMEcat – eBusiness Standardization Committee, *http://www.bmecat.org*; accessed on 09/09/2009.

[Böckle et al. 2004] G. Böckle, P. Knauber, K. Pohl, K. Schmid (Eds.): Software-Produktlinien – Methoden, Einführung und Praxis. dpunkt.verlag, Heidelberg, 2004.

[Boehm 1979] B. Boehm: Guidelines for Verifying and Validating Software Requirements and Design Specification. In: Proceedings of the European Conference on Applied Information Technology of the International Federation for Information Processing (Euro IFIP), North Holland, 1979, pp. 711–719.

[Boehm 1981] B. Boehm: Software Engineering Economics. Prentice Hall, New Jersey, 1981.

[Boehm 1984] B. Boehm: Verifying and Validating Software Requirements and Design Specifications. IEEE Software, Vol. 1, No. 1, IEEE Press, Los Alamitos, 1984, pp. 75–88.

[Boehm and Basili 2001] B. Boehm, B. Basili: Software Defect Reduction Top 10 List. IEEE Computer, Vol. 34, No. 1, IEEE Computer Society, Los Alamitos, 2001, pp. 135–137.

[Boehm and Ross 1989] B. Boehm, R. Ross: Theory-W Software Project Management – Principles and Examples. IEEE Transactions on Software Engineering, Vol. 15, No. 7, 1989, pp. 902–916.

[Boehm et al. 1994] B. Boehm, P. Bose, E. Horowitz, M. Lee: Software Requirements as Negotiated Win Conditions. In: Proceedings of the 1st International Conference on Requirements Engineering (ICRE'94), IEEE Computer Society Press, Los Alamitos, 1994, pp. 74–83.

[Boehm et al. 2001] B. Boehm, P. Grünbacher B. Briggs: EasyWinWin – Developing Groupware for Requirements Negotiation – Lessons Learned. IEEE Software, Vol. 18, No. 3, IEEE Press, Los Alamitos, 2001, pp. 46–55.

[Boman et al. 1997] M. Boman, J. A. Bubenko Jr, P. Johannesson, B. Wangler: Conceptual Modelling. Prentice-Hall International Series in Computer Science, Prentice Hall, London, New York, 1997.

[Booch 1994] G. Booch: Object-Oriented Analysis and Design with Applications. Benjamin/Cummings, Redwood City, 1994 (new edition available: Addison-Wesley, 2007).

[Borgida et al. 1985] A. Borgida, S. Greenspan, J. Mylopoulos: Knowledge Representation as the Basis for Requirements Specifications. IEEE Computer, Vol. 18, No. 4, 1985, pp. 82–91.

[Bosch 2003] Robert Bosch GmbH: ACC Adaptive Cruise Control. The Bosch Yellow Jackets, Edition 2003.

[Bray 2002] I. K. Bray: An Introduction to Requirements Engineering. Addison-Wesley, Reading, 2002.

[Brown 1987] B. J. Brown: Assurance of Software Quality – SEI Curriculum Model SEI-CM-7-1.1 (Preliminary). Carnegie Mellon University, SEI, Pittsburgh, 1987.

[Brykczynski 1999] B. Brykczynski: A Survey of Software Inspection Checklists. ACM SIGSOFT Software Engineering Notes, Vol. 24, No. 1, 1999, pp. 82–89.

[Bubenko et al. 1994] J. Bubenko, C. Rolland, P. Loucopoulos, V. de Antónellis: Facilitating "Fuzzy to Formal" Requirements Modelling. In: Proceedings of the 1st International Conference on Requirements Engineering (ICRE'94), IEEE Computer Society Press, Los Alamitos, 1994, pp. 154–158.

[Buzan and Buzan 2006] T. Buzan, B. Buzan: The Mind Map Book – Full Illustrated Edition. BBC Active, 2006.

C

[Campbell 1992] R. L. Campbell: Will the Real Scenario Please Stand Up? ACM SIGCHI Bulletin, Vol. 24, No. 2, 1992, pp. 6–8.

[CAN 2009] CAN in Automation (CiA); Controller Area Network (CAN). *http://www.can-cia.org/index.php?id=170*; accessed on 09/09/2009.

[Carmel and Tjia 2005] E. Carmel, P. Tjia: Offshoring Information Technology – Sourcing and Outsourcing to a Global Workforce. Cambridge University Press, Cambridge, 2005.

[Carroll 1995] J. M. Carroll: The Scenario Perspective on System Development. In: J. M. Carroll (Ed.): Scenario-Based Design – Envisioning Work and Technology in System Development. Wiley, New York, 1995, pp. 1–17.

[Carroll 2000] J. M Carroll (Ed.): Making Use – Scenario-Based Design of Human Computer Interactions. MIT Press, Cambridge, 2000.

[Chen 1976] P. Chen: The Entity–Relationship Specification – Toward a Unified View of Date. ACM Transactions on Database Systems, Vol. 1, No. 1, 1976, pp. 9–38.

[Chernak 1996] Y. Chernak: A Statistical Approach to the Inspection Checklist Formal Synthesis and Improvement. IEEE Transactions on Software Engineering, Vol. 22, No. 12, 1996, pp. 866–874.

[Chrissis et al. 2006] M. B. Chrissis, M. Konrad, S. Shrum: CMMI® – Guidelines for Process Integration and Product Improvement. 2nd edition, Addison-Wesley, Boston, 2006.

[Chung et al. 1996] L. Chung, B. A. Nixon, E. Yu: Dealing with Change – An Approach using Non-Functional Requirements. Requirements Engineering, Vol. 1, No. 4, Springer, Berlin, Heidelberg, 1996, pp. 238–259.

[Chung et al. 1999] L. Chung, B. A. Nixon, E. Yu, J. Mylopoulos: Non-functional Requirements in Software Engineering, Kluwer Academic Publishers, Boston, 1999.

[Clements and Northrop 2001] P. Clements, L. Northrop: Software Product Lines – Practices and Patterns. 3rd edition, Addison-Wesley, Boston, 2001.

[Clements et al. 2002] P. Clements, R. Kazman, M. Klein: Evaluating Software Architectures – Methods and Case Studies. Addison-Wesley, Boston, 2002.

[CMMI 2006] Software Engineering Institute: CMMI for Development, Version 1.2 – Improving Processes for Better Products. CMU/SEI-2006-TR-008, Carnegie Mellon University, Pittsburgh, 2006.

[Cockburn 1997] A. Cockburn: Structuring Use Cases with Goals. Journal of Object-Oriented Programming, Sep-Oct 1997 & Nov-Dec 1997.

[Cockburn 2001] A. Cockburn: Writing Effective Use Cases. Addison-Wesley, Boston, 2001.

[Cockburn 2006] A. Cockburn: Agile Software Development – The Cooperative Game. 2nd edition, Addison Wesley, Boston, 2006.

[Codd 1970] E. F. Codd: A Relational Model for Large Shared Data Banks. Communications of the ACM, Vol. 13, No. 6, 1970, pp. 377–387.

[Cohn 2009] R. C. Cohn: Von der Psychoanalyse zur Themenzentrierten Interaktion. 15th edition, Klett-Cotta, Stuttgart, 2009.

[Conklin and Begemann 1988] J. Conklin, M. Begemann: gIBIS – A Hypertext Tool for Exploratory Policy Discussion. ACM Transactions on Office Information Systems, Vol. 6, No. 4, 1988, pp. 303–331.

[Conradi and Westfechtel 1998] R. Conradi, B. Westfechtel: Version Models for Software Configuration Management. ACM Computing Surveys, Vol. 30, No. 2, pp. 232–282.

[Coplien et al. 1998] J. Coplien, D. Hoffman, D. Weiss: Commonality and Variability in Software Engineering. IEEE Software, Vol. 15, No. 6, IEEE Press, Los Alamitos, 1998, pp. 37–45.

[Cordes and Carver 1989] D. W. Cordes, D. L. Carver: Evaluation Method for User Requirements Documents. Information and Software Technology, Vol. 31, No. 4, 1989, pp. 181–188.

D

[Dahlstedt and Persson 2005] A. G. Dahlstedt, A. Persson: Requirements Interdependencies – State of the Art and Future Challenges. In: A. Aurum, C. Wohlin (Eds.): Engineering and Managing Software Requirements, Springer, Berlin, Heidelberg, 2005, pp. 95–116.

[Dardenne 1993] A. Dardenne: On the Use of Scenarios in Requirements Acquisition. Technical Report CIS-TR-93-17, Department of Computer and Information Science, University of Oregon, Eugene, 1993.

[Dardenne et al. 1991] A. Dardenne, S. Fickas, A. van Lamsweerde: Goal-Directed Concept Acquisition in Requirements Elicitation. In: Proceedings of the 6th International Workshop on Software Specification and Design, IEEE Computer Society Press, Los Alamitos, 1991, pp. 14–21.

[Dardenne et al. 1993] A. Dardenne, A. van Lamsweerde, S. Fickas: Goal-Directed Requirements Acquisition. Science of Computer Programming, Vol. 20, No. 1-2, Elsevier Science, Amsterdam, 1993, pp. 3–50.

[Davis 1990] A. M. Davis: The Analysis and Specification of Systems and Software Requirements. In: M. Dorfman, R. Thayer (Eds.): Tutorial: Systems and Software Requirements Engineering, IEEE Computer Society Press, Los Alamitos, 1990, pp. 119–144.

[Davis 1993] A. M. Davis: Software Requirements – Objects, Functions, and States. 2nd edition, Prentice Hall, Englewood Cliffs, New Jersey, 1993.

[Davis 2003] A. Davis: The Art of Requirements Triage. IEEE Computer, Vol. 36, No. 3, 2003, pp. 42–29.

[Day and Schoemaker 2005] G. S. Day, P. J. H. Schoemaker: Scanning the Periphery. Harvard Business Review, November 2005, pp. 135–148.

[DeMarco 1978] T. DeMarco: Structured Analysis and System Specification. Prentice Hall, Englewoods Cliffs, New Jersey, 1978.

[DIN 69901-5 2009] Deutsches Institut für Normung e.V.: DIN 69901-5 – Projektmanagement – Projektmanagementsysteme – Teil5: Begriffe. Beuth-Verlag, 2009.

[Dömges and Pohl 1998] R. Dömges, K. Pohl: Adapting Traceability Environments to Project-Specific Needs. Communications of the ACM, Vol. 41, No. 12, 1998, pp. 54–62.

[Dudley 2000] B. Dudley (Ed.): The Greatest Speeches of President John F. Kennedy. Titan, West Vancouver, 2000.

[Dzida and Freitag 1998] W. Dzida, R. Freitag: Making Use of Scenarios for Validating Analysis and Design. IEEE Transactions on Software Engineering, Vol. 24, No. 12, 1998, pp. 1182–1196.

E

[Eason 1988] K. Eason: Information Technology and Organisational Change. Taylor & Francis, London, 1988.

[Easterbrook 1994] S. Easterbrook: Resolving Requirements Conflicts with Computer-Supported Negotiation. In: M. Jirotka, J. Goguen (Eds.): Requirements Engineering – Social and Technical Issues, Academic Press, London, 1994, pp. 41–65.

[Ebert 2008] C. Ebert: Systematisches Requirements Management – Anforderungen ermitteln, spezifizieren, analysieren und verfolgen. 2nd edition, dpunkt.verlag, Heidelberg, 2008.

[Edwards and Howell 1992] M. Edwards, S. Howell: A Methodology for Requirements Specification and Traceability for Large Real-Time Complex Systems. Technical Report, Naval Surface Warfare Center, Dahlgren, 1992.

[Elmasri and Navathe 2006] R. Elmasri, S. B. Navathe: Fundamentals of Database Systems. 5th edition, Addison-Wesley, 2006.

[Erickson 1995] T. Erickson: Notes on Design Practice – Stories and Prototypes as Catalysts for Communication. In: J. M. Caroll (Ed.): Scenario-Based Design – Envisioning Work and Technology in System Development, Wiley, New York, 1995.

[ESI 1996] European Software Institute: European User Survey Analysis. Technical Report, ESI-1996-TR95104, 1996.

F

[Fagan 1976] M. E. Fagan: Design and Code Inspections to Reduce Errors in Program Development. IBM Systems Journal, Vol. 15, No. 3, 1976, pp. 258–287.

[Fagan 1986] M. E. Fagan: Advances in Software Inspections. IEEE Transactions on Software Engineering, Vol. SE-12, No. 7, 1986, pp. 744–751.

[Falkenberg et al. 1998] E. D. Falkenberg, W. Hesse, P. Lindgreen, B. E. Nilsson, J. L. Han Oei, C. Rolland, R. K. Stamper, F. J. M. Van Assche, A. A. Verrijn-Stuart, K. Voss: A Framework of Information System Concepts – The FRISCO Report. IFIP Report, 1998.

[FAST 2004] Mercer Management Consulting, Fraunhofer-Institut für Produktionstechnik und Automatisierung (IPA), Fraunhofer-Institut für Materialfluss und Logistik (IML): Future Automotive Industry Structure (FAST) 2015 – die neue Arbeitsteilung in der Automobilindustrie. Verband der Automobilindustrie (VDA), Heinrich Druck + Medien GmbH, Frankfurt, 2004.

[Finkelstein and Dowell 1996] A. Finkelstein, J. Dowell: A Comedy of Errors – The London Ambulance Service Case Study. In: Proceedings of the 8th International Workshop on Software Specifications & Design, IEEE Computer Society Press, Los Alamitos, 1996, pp. 2–4.

[Fischer et al. 1996] G. Fischer, A. C. Lemke, R. McCall, A. I. Morch: Making Argumentation Serve Design. In: T. P. Moran, J. M. Caroll (Eds.): Design Rationale – Concepts, Techniques, and Use, Erlbaum, Mahwah, 1996, pp. 267–293.

[FlexRay 2009] FlexRay Consortium, 2009, *http://www.flexray.com*; accessed on 09/09/2009.

[FME 2009] Formal Methods Europe, *http://www.fmeurope.org*; accessed on 09/09/2009.

[Frege 1923] G. Frege: Compound Thoughts. In: B. McGuiness (Ed.): Collected Papers on Mathematics, Logic, and Philosophy. Blackwell, Oxford, 1984, pp. 390–406.

[Friedenthal et al. 2008] S. Friedenthal, A. Moore, R. Steiner: A Practical Guide to SysML – The Systems Modeling Language. The MK/OMG Press, Burlington, 2008.

G

[Gane and Sarson 1977] C. Gane, T. Sarson: Structured Systems Analysis – Tools and Techniques. Prentice Hall, 1977.

[Gause 2005] D. C. Gause: Why Context Matters – And What Can We Do about It? IEEE Software, Vol. 22, No. 5, IEEE Press, Los Alamitos, 2005, pp. 13–15.

[Gause and Weinberg 1989] D. C. Gause, M. Weinberg: Exploring Requirements – Quality before Design. Dorset House, New York, 1989.

[Gilb and Graham 1993] T. Gilb, D. Graham: Software Inspection. Addison-Wesley, 1993.

[Glass and Holyoak 1986] A. L. Glass, K. J. Holyoak: Cognition. 2nd edition, Random House, New York, 1986.

[Goetz et al. 2005] H. Goetz, E. Kamsties, J. Neumann, K. Pohl, S. Reis, A. Reuys, J. Weingärtner: Testing a Product Line of Radiology Systems at Siemens. In: Proceedings of the 5th Conference on Software Validation for Healthcare (CSVHC 2005), SQS, 2005.

[Gotel 1995] O. Gotel: Contribution Structures for Requirements Traceability. PhD. Thesis, Imperial College of Science, Technology, and Medicine, University of London, 1995.

[Gotel and Finkelstein 1994] O. Gotel, A. Finkelstein: An Analysis of the Requirements Traceability Problem. In: Proceedings of the First IEEE International Conference on Requirements Engineering (ICRE'94), IEEE Computer Society Press, Los Alamitos, 1994, pp. 94–101.

[Gottesdiener 2002] E. Gottesdiener: Requirements by Collaboration – Workshops for Defining Needs. Addison-Wesley, Reading, 2002.

[Gough et al. 1995] P. A. Gough, F. T. Fodemski, S. A. Higgins, S. J. Ray: Scenarios – An Industrial Case Study and Hypermedia Enhancements. In: Proceedings of the 2nd IEEE International Symposium on Requirements Engineering (RE'95), IEEE Computer Society Press, Los Alamitos, 1995, pp. 10–17.

[Graham 2002] D. Graham: Requirements and Testing – Seven Missing-Link Myths. IEEE Software, Vol. 19, No. 5, IEEE Press, Los Alamitos, 2002, pp. 15–17.

[Greenspan 1984] S. J. Greenspan: Requirements Modeling – A Knowledge Representation Approach to Software Requirements Definition. Ph.D. Thesis, Dept. of Computer Science, University of Toronto, Toronto, 1984.

[GRL 2009] Goal-oriented Requirements Language (GRL): GRL Ontology. *http://www.cs.toronto.edu/km/GRL*; accessed on 09/09/2009.

[Gunter et al. 2000] C. A. Gunter, E. L. Gunter, M. Jackson, P. Zave: A Reference Model for Requirements and Specifications. IEEE Software, Vol. 17, No. 3, IEEE Press, Los Alamitos, 2000, pp. 37–43.

H

[Hall et al. 2002] T. Hall, S. Beecham, A. Rainer: Requirements Problems in Twelve Companies – An Empirical Analysis. In: Proceedings of the 6th International Conference on Empirical Assessment and Evaluation in Software Engineering (EASE 2002), Keele University, 2002.

[Halmans and Pohl 2003] G. Halmans, K. Pohl: Communicating the Variability of a Software-Product Family to Customers. Software and Systems Modeling, Vol. 2, No. 1, Springer, Berlin, Heidelberg, 2003, pp. 15–36.

[Halmans 2007] G. Halmans: Ein Ansatz zur Unterstützung der Ableitung einer Applikationsanforderungsspezifikation mit Integration spezifischer Applikationsanforderungen (in German). Doctoral Thesis. Logos, Berlin, 2007.

[Halmans et al. 2008] G. Halmans, K. Pohl, E. Sikora: Documenting Application-Specific Adaptations in Software Product Line Engineering. In: Proceedings of the 20th International Conference on Advanced Information Systems Engineering (CAiSE 2008), LNCS 5074, Springer, 2008, pp. 109–123.

[Hamilton and Beeby 1991] V. L. Hamilton, M. L. Beeby: Issues of Traceability in Integrating Tools. In: Proceedings of the IEE Colloquium on Tools and Techniques for Maintaining Traceability During Design, IEE (Institution of Electrical Engineers), London, 1991, pp. 4/1-4/3.

[Hammersley and Atkinson 2007] M. Hammersley, P. Atkinson: Ethnography – Principles in Practice. 3rd edition, Routledge, London, 2007.

[Hammond et al. 2001] J. Hammond, R. Rawlings, A. Hall: Will It Work? In: Proceedings of the 5th IEEE International Symposium on Requirements Engineering (RE'01), IEEE Computer Society Press, Los Alamitos, 2001, pp. 102–109.

[Harel 1987] D. Harel: Statecharts – A Visual Formalism for Complex Systems. Science of Computer Programming, Vol. 8, No. 3, 1987, pp. 231–274.

[Harel and Gery 1996] D. Harel, E. Gery: Executable Object Modeling with Statecharts. In: Proceedings of the 18th International Conference on Software Engineering (ICSE'96), IEEE Computer Society Press, Los Alamitos, 1996, pp. 246–257.

[Hartshorne and Weiss 1931] C. Hartshorne, P. Weiss (Eds.): Collected Papers of Charles Sanders Peirce. Harvard University Press, Cambridge, 1931.

[Hatley and Pirbhai 1988] D. J. Hatley, I. A. Pirbhai: Strategies for Real Time System Specification. Dorset House, New York, 1988.

[Hatley et al. 2000] D. Hatley, P. Hruschka, I. Pirbhai: Process for System Architecture and Requirements Engineering. Dorset House, New York, 2000.

[Haumer et al. 1998] P. Haumer, K. Pohl, K. Weidenhaupt: Requirements Elicitation and Validation with Real World Scenes. IEEE Transactions on Software Engineering, Vol. 24, No. 12, 1998, pp. 1036–1054.

[Haumer et al. 1999] P. Haumer, P. Heymans, M. Jarke, K. Pohl: Bridging the Gap Between Past and Future in RE – A Scenario-Based Approach. In: Proceedings of the 4th IEEE International Symposium on Requirements Engineering (RE'99), IEEE Computer Society Press, Los Alamitos, 1999, pp. 66–73.

[Haumer et al. 2000] P. Haumer, M. Jarke, K. Pohl, K. Weidenhaupt: Improving Reviews of Conceptual Models by Extended Traceability to Captured System Usage. Interacting with Computers Journal, Vol. 13, No. 1, Elsevier Science, 2000.

[Hebb 1949] D. O. Hebb: The Organization of Behaviour. Wiley, New York, 1949 (new edition available: Lawrence Erlbaum, 2002).

[Highsmith 1999] J. A. Highsmith: Adaptive Software Development. Dorset House, New York, 1999.

[Hirst 1987] G. Hirst: Semantic Interpretation and the Resolution of Ambiguity. Cambridge University Press, Cambridge, 1987.

[Hofmeister et al. 1999] C. Hofmeister, R. Nord, D. Soni: Applied Software Architecture. Addison-Wesley, Reading, 1999.

[Holbrook 1990] H. Holbrook: A Scenario-Based Methodology for Conducting Requirements Elicitation. ACM SIGSOFT, Vol. 15, No. 1, 1990, pp. 95–104.

[Holmqvist et al. 1996] B. Holmqvist, P. B. Andersen, H. Klein, R. Posner (Eds.): Signs of Work – Semiosis and Information Processing in Organisations. De Gruyter, Berlin, 1996.

[Honsig 2005] M. Honsig: Mit Vollgas in die Krise. Technology Review No. 5/2005, Heise Zeitschriften Verlag, Hannover, 2005.

[Hopcroft et al. 2007] J. Hopcroft, R. Motwani, J. Ullman: Introduction to Automata Theory, Languages, and Computation. 3rd edition, Pearson, Boston, MA, 2007.

[Hörmann et al. 2006] K. Hörmann, L. Dittmann, B. Hindel, M. Müller: SPICE in der Praxis – Interpretationshilfe für Anwender und Assessoren. dpunkt.verlag, Heidelberg, 2006.

[Huffman 1954] D. A. Huffman: The Synthesis of Sequential Switching Circuits. Journal of the Franklin Institute, Vol. 257, No. 3-4, 1954, pp. 161–190.

I

[IEEE Std 610.12-1990] Institute of Electrical and Electronics Engineers: IEEE Standard Glossary of Software Engineering Terminology (IEEE Std 610.12-1990). IEEE, New York, 1990.

[IEEE Std 830-1998] Institute of Electrical and Electronics Engineers: IEEE Recommended Practice for Software Requirements Specifications (IEEE Std 830-1998). IEEE Computer Society, New York, 1998.

[IEEE Std 1012-2004] Institute of Electrical and Electronics Engineers: IEEE Standard for Software Verification and Validation (IEEE Std 1012-2004). IEEE Computer Society, New York, 2005.

[IEEE Std 1233-1998] Institute of Electrical and Electronics Engineers: IEEE Guide for Developing System Requirements Specifications (ANSI/IEEE Std 1233-1998). IEEE Computer Society, New York, 1998.

[ISO Std 9000] International Organization for Standardization: ISO/IEC 9000:2005 Quality Management Systems – Fundamentals and Vocabulary, 2005.

[ISO/IEC Std 9075] ISO/IEC: Information Technology – Standards Series for Structured Query Language (SQL), ISO/IEC International Standard 9075, 2003.

[ISO/IEC Std 10027] ISO/IEC: Information Technology – Information Resource Dictionary Systems (IRDS)-Framework. ISO/IEC Intl. Standard 10027, 1990.

[ITU 1998] International Telecommunication Union (ITU-T): Recommendation Z.120 Annex B (04/98) – Formal Semantics of Message Sequence Charts. Genf, 1998.

[ITU 1999] International Telecommunication Union (ITU-T): Recommendation Z.120 (11/99) – Message Sequence Chart (MSC). Geneva, 1999.

[ITU 2004] International Telecommunication Union (ITU): ITU-T Recommendation Z.120 – Message Sequence Chart (MSC). Geneva, 2004.

J

[Jackson 1995] M. Jackson: Software Requirements and Specification – A Lexicon of Practice, Principles and Prejudices. ACM/Addison-Wesley, New York, 1995.

[Jacobson et al. 1992] I. Jacobson, M. Christerson, P. Jonsson, G. Oevergaard: Object-Oriented Software Engineering – A Use Case Driven Approach. Addison-Wesley, Reading, 1992.

[Janis 1982] I. L. Janis: Groupthink: Psychological Studies of Policy Decisions and Fiascoes. 2nd edition, Houghton-Mifflin, Boston, 1982.

[Jarke and Pohl 1993] M. Jarke, K. Pohl: Establishing Visions in Context – Towards a Model of Requirements Processes. In: Proceedings of the 14th International Conference on Information Systems, 1993, pp. 23–34.

[Jarke and Pohl 1994] M. Jarke, K. Pohl: Requirements Engineering in the Year 2001 – (Virtually) Managing a Changing Reality. Software Engineering Journal, Vol. 9, No. 6, 1994, pp. 257–266.

[John and Muthig 2002] I. John D. Muthig: Modeling Variability with Use Cases. IESE-Report, No. 063.02/E, Fraunhofer IESE, Kaiserslautern, 2002.

[Jones 2007] T. C. Jones: Estimating Software Costs. 2nd edition, McGraw-Hill, New York, 2007.

[Jönsson and Lindvall 2005] P. Jönsson, M. Lindvall: Impact Analysis. In: A. Aurum, C. Wohlin (Eds.): Engineering and Managing Software Requirements. Springer, Berlin, Heidelberg, 2005, pp. 117–142.

K

[Kamlah and Lorenzen 1996] W. Kamlah, P. Lorenzen (Eds.): Logische Propädeutik, 3rd edition, Metzler, Stuttgart, 1996.

[Kamsties 2001] E. Kamsties: Surfacing Ambiguity in Natural Language Requirements. Ph.D. Thesis, Department of Computer Sciences, University of Kaiserslautern, Kaiserslautern, 2001.

[Kamsties 2005] E. Kamsties: Understanding Ambiguity in Requirements Engineering. In: A. Aurum, C. Wohlin (Eds.): Engineering and Managing Software Requirements. Springer, Berlin, Heidelberg, 2005, pp. 245–266.

[Kamsties et al. 2004] E. Kamsties, K. Pohl, S. Reis, A. Reuys: Anforderungsbasiertes Testen. In: G. Böckle, P. Knauber, K. Pohl, K. Schmid (Eds.): Software-Produktlinien – Methoden, Einführung und Praxis. dpunkt.verlag, Heidelberg, 2004, pp. 119–136.

[Kang et al. 1990] K. Kang, S. Cohen, J. Hess, W. Nowak, S. Peterson: Feature-Oriented Domain Analysis (FODA) – Feasibility Study. Technical Report CMU/SEI-90-TR-21, Software Engineering Institute (SEI), Carnegie Mellon University, Pittsburgh, 1990.

[Kano et al. 1984] N. Kano, S. Tsuji, N. Seraku, F. Takahashi: Attractive Quality and Must-Be Quality (in Japanese). Journal of the Japanese Society for Quality Control, Vol. 14, No. 2, 1984, pp. 147–156.

[Karat and Bennett 1991] J. Karat, J. L. Bennett: Using Scenarios in Design Meetings – A Case Study. In: J. Karat (Ed.): Taking Software Design Seriously – Practical Techniques for Human–Computer Interaction Design, Academic, Boston, 1991.

[Karlsson and Ryan 1997] J. Karlsson, K. Ryan: A Cost–Value Approach for Prioritizing Requirements. IEEE Software, Vol. 14, No. 5, IEEE Press, Los Alamitos, 1997, pp. 67–74.

[Karlsson et al. 1997] J. Karlsson, S. Olsson, K. Ryan: Improved Practical Support for Large-Scale Requirements Prioritising. Requirements Engineering, Vol. 2, No. 1, Springer, London, 1997, pp. 51–60.

[Kavakli 1999] E. Kavakli: Goal-Driven Requirements Engineering – Modelling and Guidance. Ph.D. Thesis, University of Manchester, Institute of Science and Technology, Manchester, 1999.

[Kawakita 1975] J. Kawakita: The KJ Method – A Scientific Approach to Problem Solving. Technical Report, Kawakita Research Institute, Tokyo, 1975.

[Kosslyn 1988] S. M. Kosslyn: Imagery in Learning. In: M. Gazzaniga (Ed.): Perspectives in Memory Research, The MIT Press, Cambridge, 1988.

[Kotonya and Sommerville 1997] G. Kotonya, I. Sommerville: Requirements Engineering – Processes and Techniques. Wiley, Chichester, 1997.

[Kovitz 1998] B. Kovitz: Practical Software Requirements – A Manual of Content and Style. Manning, Greenwich, 1998.

[Krogstie et al. 1995] J. Krogstie, O. I. Lindland, G. Sindre: Defining Quality Aspects for Conceptual Models. In: Proceedings of the IFIP8.1 Working Conference on Information Systems Concepts – Towards a Consolidation of Views, Chapman & Hall, London, 1995.

[Kruchten 1995] P. Kruchten: The 4+1 View Model of Architecture. IEEE Software, Vol. 12, No. 6, IEEE Press, Los Alamitos, 1995, pp. 42–50.

[Kruchten 2003] P. Kruchten: The Rational Unified Process – An Introduction. 3rd edition, Addison-Wesley, Reading, 2003.

[Kulak and Guiney 2003] D. Kulak, E. Guiney: Use Cases – Requirements in Context. 2nd edition, Addison-Wesley, Reading, 2003.

[Kuniavsky 2003] M. Kuniavsky: Observing the User Experience – A Practitioner's Guide to User Research, Morgan Kaufmann, San Francisco, 2003.

L

[Laitenberger and DeBaud 2000] O. Laitenberger, J.-M. DeBaud: An Encompassing Life Cycle Centric Survey of Software Inspection. Journal of Systems and Software, Vol. 50, No. 1, 2000, pp. 5–31.

[Laitenberger et al. 2000] O. Laitenberger, C. Atkinson, M. Schlick, K. El Emam: An Experimental Comparison of Reading Techniques for Fault Detection in UML Design Documents. Journal of Systems and Software, Vol. 53, No. 2, 2000, pp. 183–204.

[Larman 2004] C. Larman: Applying UML and Patterns – An Introduction to Object-Oriented Analysis and Design and Iterative Development. 3rd edition, Prentice Hall, Upper Saddle River, 2004.

[Lauenroth 2009] K. Lauenroth: Konsistenzprüfung von Domänenanforderungsspezifikationen (in German). Doctoral Thesis, Logos, Berlin, 2009.

[Lauenroth and Pohl 2007] K. Lauenroth, K. Pohl: Towards Automated Consistency Checks of Product Line Requirements Specifications. In: Proceedings of the 22nd IEEE/ACM International Conference on Automated Software Engineering, ACM, 2007, pp. 373–376.

[Lauesen 2002] S. Lauesen: Software Requirements – Styles and Techniques, Addison-Wesley, London, 2002.

[Leffingwell and Widrig 2000] D. Leffingwell, D. Widrig: Managing Software Requirements – A Unified Approach. Addison-Wesley, Reading, 2000.

[Lehtola and Kauppinen 2006] L. Lehtola, M. Kauppinen: Suitability of Requirements Prioritization Methods for Market-Driven Software Product Development. Software Process – Improvement and Practice, Vol. 11, No. 1, 2006, pp. 7–19.

[Lehtola et al. 2004] L. Lehtola, M. Kauppinen, S. Kujala: Requirements Prioritization Challenges in Practice. In: Proceedings of the 5th International Conference on Product Focused Software Process Improvement (PROFES'04), Springer, Berlin, Heidelberg, New York, 2004, pp. 497–508.

[Leite and Freeman 1991] J. C. S. P. Leite, P. A. Freeman: Requirements Validation through Viewpoint Resolution. IEEE Transactions on Software Engineering, Vol. 17, No. 12, 1991, pp. 1253–1269.

[Leite et al. 1997] J. C. S. P. Leite, G. Rossi, F. Balaguer, V. Maiorane, G. Kaplan, G. Hadad, A. Oliveros: Enhancing a Requirements Baseline with Scenarios. In: Proceedings of 3rd International Symposium on Requirements Engineering (RE'97), IEEE Computer Society Press, Los Alamitos, 1997.

[Leite et al. 2005] J. C. S. P. Leite, J. H. Doorn, G. D. S. Hadad, G. N. Kaplan: Scenario Inspections. Requirements Engineering, Vol. 10, No. 1, Springer, Berlin, Heidelberg, 2005, pp. 1–21.

[Lichter et al. 1993] H. Lichter, M. Schneider-Hufschmidt, H. Züllighoven: Prototyping in Industrial Software Projects – Bridging the Gap between Theory and Practice. In: Proceedings of the 15th International Conference on Software Engineering (ICSE'93), IEEE Computer Society Press, Los Alamitos, 1993, pp. 328–338.

[Liggesmeyer 2009] P. Liggesmeyer: Software-Qualität – Testen, Analysieren und Verifizieren von Software. 2nd edition, Spektrum Akademischer Verlag, Heidelberg, 2009.

[LIN 2009] LIN – Local Interconnect Network, 2009, *http://www.lin-subbus.org*; accessed on 09/09/2009.

[Lindland et al. 1994] O. I. Lindland, G. Sindre, A. Sølverg: Understanding Quality in Conceptual Modelling. IEEE Software, Vol. 11, No. 2, IEEE Press, Los Alamitos, 1994, pp. 42–49.

[Lorenzen 1973] P. Lorenzen: Semantisch normierte Orthosprachen. In: F. Kambartel, J. Mittelstraß, (Eds.): Zum Normativen Fundament der Wissenschaft, Athenäum, Frankfurt, 1973, pp. 231–249.

[Loucopoulos 1994] P. Loucopoulos: The f3 (from fuzzy to formal) View on Requirements Engineering. Ingénierie des Systémes d'Information, Vol. 2, No. 6, 1994, pp. 639–655.

M

[Machado et al. 2005] R. J. Machado, I. Ramos, J. M. Fernandes: Specification of Requirements Models. In: A. Aurum, C. Wohlin (Ed.): Engineering and Managing Software Requirements. Springer, Berlin, Heidelberg, 2005, pp. 47–68.

[Maiden 2009] N. Maiden: Card Sorts to Acquire Requirements. IEEE Software, Vol. 26, No. 3, 2009, pp. 85–86.

[Maiden and Robertson 2005] N. Maiden, S. Robertson: Integrating Creativity into Requirements Processes – Experiences with an Air Traffic Management System. In: Proceedings of the 13th IEEE International Conference on Requirements Engineering (RE'05), IEEE Computer Society Press, Los Alamitos, 2005, pp. 105–116.

[Maiden et al. 1995] N. A. M. Maiden, P. Mistry, A. G. Sutcliffe: How People Categorise Requirements for Reuse: a Natural Approach. In: Proceedings of the 2nd IEEE Symposium on Requirements Engineering, IEEE Computer Society, Los Alamitos, 1995, pp. 148–155.

[Maier and Rechtin 2009] M. W. Maier, E. Rechtin: The Art of Systems Architecting, 3rd edition, CRC Press, New York, 2009.

[Marakas 2002] G.M. Marakas: Decision Support Systems in the 21st Century. 2nd edition, Prentice Hall, New Jersey, 2002.

[Martin 1989] J. Martin: Information Engineering, Book I – Introduction. Prentice Hall, Englewood Cliffs, 1989.

[Masters and Albright 2002] M. Masters, R. Albright: The Complete Guide to Conflict Resolution in the Workplace. American Management Association, New York, 2002.

[McAdams et al. 2006] D. McAdams, R. Josselson, A. Lieblich (Eds.): Identity and Story – Creating Self in Narrative (Narrative Study of Lives). American Psychological Association (APA), Washington, 2006.

[McCall et al. 1977] J. A. McCall, P. K. Richards, G. F. Walters: Factors in Software Quality – Concepts and Definitions of Software Quality. Technical Report No. RADC-TR-77-369, Volume I (of III). General Electric Company, November 1977.

[McDermott and Fox 1999] J. McDermott, C. Fox: Using Abuse Case Models for Security Requirements Analysis. In: Proceedings of the 15th Annual Computer Security Applications Conference (ACSAC '99), 1999, pp. 55–64.

[McMenamin and Palmer 1984] S. M. McMenamin, J. F. Palmer: Essential Systems Analysis. Prentice Hall, London, 1984.

[Mealy 1955] G. H. Mealy: A Method for Synthesizing Sequential Circuits. Bell System Technical Journal, Vol. 34, No. 5, 1955, pp. 1045–1079.

[Medvidovic and Taylor 2000] N. Medvidovic, R. N. Taylor: A Classification and Comparison Framework for Software Architecture Description Languages. IEEE Transactions on Software Engineering, Vol. 26, No. 1, 2000, pp. 70–93.

[Mietzel 2007] G. Mietzel: Pädagogische Psychologie des Lernens und Lehrens. 8th edition, Hogrefe-Verlag, Göttingen, 2007.

[Miller et al. 2008] J. A. Miller, R. Ferrari, N. H. Madhavji: Architectural Effects on Requirements Decisions: An Exploratory Study. In: Proceedings of the Seventh Working IEEE/IFIP Conference on Software Architecture (WICSA 2008), IEEE Computer Society, Washington, 2008, pp. 231–240.

[Mills 1959] C. W. Mills: The Sociological Imagination. Oxford University Press, New York, 1959 (new edition available: Oxford University Press, 2000).

[Möller 1996] K.-H. Möller: Ausgangsdaten für Qualitätsmetriken – Eine Fundgrube für Analysen. In: C. Ebert, R. Dumke (Ed.): Software-Metriken in der Praxis, Springer, Berlin, 1996, pp. 105–116.

[Moore 1956] E. F. Moore: Gedanken-Experiments on Sequential Machines. In: C. Shannon, J. McCarthy (Eds.): Automata Studies, Princeton University Press, Princeton, 1956, pp. 129–153.

[Moore 2003] C. Moore: The Mediation Process – Practical Strategies for Resolving Conflicts. 3rd edition, Jossey-Bass, San Francisco, 2003.

[Morris 1946] C. Morris: Signs, Language and Behaviour. Prentice Hall, New York, 1946.

[MOST 2009] MOST (Media Oriented Systems Transport) Cooperation: *http://www.mostcooperation.com*; accessed on 10/09/2009.

[Myers 2004] G. Myers; revised and updated by T. Badgett, T. Thomas, C. Sandler: The Art of Software Testing. 2nd edition, Wiley, Hoboken, New Jersey, 2004.

[Mylopoulos et al. 1990] J. Mylopoulos, A. Borgida, M. Jarke, M. Koubarakis: Telos – Representing Knowledge about Information Systems. ACM Transactions on Information Systems (TOIS), Vol. 8, No. 4, 1990, pp. 325–362.

[Mylopoulos et al. 1999] J. Mylopoulos, K. L. Chung, E. Yu: From Object-Oriented to Goal-Oriented Requirements Analysis. Communications of the ACM, Vol. 42, No. 1, ACM Press, 1999, pp. 1–37.

N

[Narayanan and Fahey 1987] V. K. Narayanan, L. Fahey: Environmental Analysis for Strategy Formulation. In: W. R. King, D. J. Cleland (Eds.): Strategic Planning and Management Handbook. Van Nostrand, New York, 1987, pp. 141–176.

[Nardi 1992] B. A. Nardi: The Use of Scenarios in Design. SIGCHI Bulletin, Vol. 24, No. 4, October 1992.

[Nuseibeh 2001] B. Nuseibeh: Weaving Together Requirements and Architectures. IEEE Computer, Vol. 34, No. 3, IEEE Computer Society, Los Alamitos, 2001, pp. 115–117.

[Nuseibeh et al. 1994] B. Nuseibeh, J. Kramer, A. Finkelstein: A Framework for Expressing the Relationship between Multiple Views in Requirements Specification. IEEE Transactions on Software Engineering, Vol. 2, No. 10, 1994, pp. 760–773.

O

[Oberweis 1996] A. Oberweis: Modellierung und Ausführung von Workflows mit Petri-Netzen. Teubner-Verlag, Leipzig, 1996.

[Ogden and Richards 1923] C. K. Ogden, I. A. Richards: The Meaning of Meaning – A Study of the Influence of Language upon Thought and of the Science of Symbolism. Routledge & Kegan, London, 1923 (new edition available: Harcourt Brace Jovanovich, 1989).

[OMG 2005] Object Management Group: UML Profile for Schedulability, Performance, and Time Specification. Version 1.1. *http://www.omg.org/cgi-bin/doc?formal/2005-01-02*; accessed on 29/10/2009.

[OMG 2008a] Object Management Group: OMG Systems Modeling Language (OMG SysML). Version 1.1. *http://www.omg.org/spec/SysML/1.1/PDF/*; accessed on 29/10/2009.

[OMG 2008b] Object Management Group: UML Profile for Modeling Quality of Service and Fault Tolerance Characteristics and Mechanisms Specification. Version 1.1. *http://www.omg.org/spec/QFTP/1.1/PDF/*; accessed on 29/10/2009.

[OMG 2009a] Object Management Group: OMG Unified Modeling Language™ (OMG UML), Infrastructure. Version 2.2. *http://www.omg.org/spec/UML/2.2/Infrastructure/*; accessed on 11/01/2010.

[OMG 2009b] Object Management Group: OMG Unified Modeling Language™ (OMG UML), Superstructure. Version 2.2. *http://www.omg.org/spec/UML/2.2/Superstructure/*; accessed on 29/10/2009.

[Oppenheim 2000] A. N. Oppenheim: Questionnaire Design, Interviewing and Attitude Measurement. 2nd edition, Leicester University Press, 2000.

[Ortner 1997] E. Ortner: Methodenneutraler Fachentwurf. Teubner, Stuttgart, 1997.

[Osborn 1948] A. F. Osborn: Your Creative Power – How to Use Imagination. Charles Scribner's Sons, New York, 1948.

[Osborn 1993] A. F. Osborn: Applied Imagination – Principles and Procedures of Creative Problem-Solving. 3rd edition, Creative Education Foundation, New York, 1993.

[OSEK/VDX 2009] OSEK/VDX Portal (OSEK: Offene Systeme und deren Schnittstellen für die Elektronik im Kraftfahrzeug – Open Systems and the Corresponding Interfaces for Automotive Electronics), (VDX – Vehicle Distributed eXecutive): *http://www.osek-vdx.org*; accessed on 10/09/2009.

P

[Parnas and Madey 1995] D. L. Parnas, J. Madey: Functional Documents for Computer Systems. Science of Computer Programming, Vol. 25, No. 1, Elsevier North-Holland, Amsterdam, 1995, pp. 41–61.

[Pinheiro and Goguen 1996] F. A. C. Pinheiro, J. Goguen: An Object-Oriented Tool for Tracing Requirements. IEEE Software, Vol. 13, No. 2, IEEE Press, Los Alamitos, 1996, pp. 52–64.

[Pohl 1994] K. Pohl: The Three Dimensions of Requirements Engineering – A Framework and its Applications. Information Systems, Vol. 19, No. 3, Elsevier, 1994, pp. 243–258.

[Pohl 1996a] K. Pohl: Process-Centered Requirements Engineering. Wiley, Research Studies, Advanced Software Development Series, Taunton, Somerset, 1996.

[Pohl 1996b] K. Pohl: PRO-ART – Enabling Requirements Pre-Traceability. In: Proceedings of the 2nd International Conference on Requirements Engineering (ICRE '96), IEEE Computer Society Press, Los Alamitos, 1996, pp. 76–84.

[Pohl 1997] K. Pohl: Requirements Engineering. In: A. Kent, J. Williams, C. M. Hall (Eds.): Encyclopedia of Computer Science and Technology, Vol. 36. M. Dekker, New York, 1997, pp. 345–386.

[Pohl 1999] K. Pohl: Continuous Documentation of Information Systems Requirements. Habilitation, RWTH Aachen, November, 1999.

[Pohl and Haumer 1997] K. Pohl, P. Haumer: Modelling Contextual Information about Scenarios. In: Proceedings of the 3rd International Workshop on Requirements Engineering – Foundation for Software Quality (REFSQ'97), Presses Universitaires de Namur, Namur, 1997.

[Pohl and Metzger 2006] K. Pohl, A. Metzger: Software Product Line Testing – Principles and Potential Solutions. Communications of the ACM, Vol. 49, No. 12, ACM Press, New York, 2006.

[Pohl and Sikora 2005] K. Pohl, E. Sikora: Requirements Engineering für eingebettete Software. In: P. Liggesmeyer, D. Rombach (Eds.): Software Engineering eingebetteter Systeme, Spektrum Akademischer Verlag, Heidelberg, 2005.

[Pohl and Sikora 2007] K. Pohl, E. Sikora: COSMOD-RE: Supporting the Co-design of Requirements and Architectural Artifacts. In: Proceedings of the 15th IEEE International Requirements EngineeringConference (RE 2007), IEEE Computer Society Press, Los Alamitos, 2007, pp. 258–261.

[Pohl 2008] K. Pohl: Requirements Engineering – Grundlagen, Prinzipien, Techniken. dpunkt, Heidelberg, 2008.

[Pohl et al. 1997] K. Pohl, R. Dömges, M. Jarke: Towards Method-Driven Trace Capture. In: Proceedings of the 9th International Conference on Advanced Information System Engineering (CAiSE'97), Springer, Berlin, Heidelberg, New York, 1997, pp. 103–116.

[Pohl et al. 2005] K. Pohl, G. Böckle, F. van der Linden: Software Product Line Engineering – Foundations, Principles, and Techniques. Springer, Berlin, Heidelberg, 2005.

[Polanyi 1958] M. Polanyi: Personal Knowledge. University of Chicago Press, Chicago, 1958 (new edition available: University of Chicago Press, 1974).

[Potts 1995] C. Potts: Using Schematic Scenarios to Understand User Needs. In: Proceedings of the ACM Symposium on Designing Interactive Systems – Processes, Practices, Methods and Techniques (DIS'95), ACM, New York, 1995, pp. 247–266.

[Potts 1997] C. Potts: Fitness for Use – The Systems Quality that Matters Most. In: Proceedings of the 3rd International Workshop on Requirements Engineering – Foundations for Software Quality (REFSQ'97), Presses Universitaires de Namur, Namur, 1997, pp. 15–18.

[Potts 1999] C. Potts: ScenIC – A Strategy for Inquiry-Driven Requirements Determination. In: Proceedings of the 4th IEEE International Symposium on Requirements Engineering (RE'99), IEEE Computer Society Press, Los Alamitos, 1999, pp. 58–65.

[Potts et al. 1994] C. Potts, K. Takahashi, A. I. Antón: Inquiry-Based Requirements Analysis. IEEE Software, Vol. 11, No. 2, IEEE Press, Los Alamitos, 1994, pp. 21–32.

[Pretschner et al. 2005] A. Pretschner, W. Prenninger, S. Wagner, C. Kühnel, M. Baumgartner, B. Sostawa, R. Zölch, T. Stauner: One Evaluation of Model-Based Testing and its Automation. In: Proceedings 27th International Conference on Software Engineering (ICSE'05), ACM Press, 2005, pp. 392–401.

[Price and Shanks 2005] R. Price, G. Shanks: A Semiotic Information Quality Framework – Development and Comparative Analysis. Journal of Information Technology, Vol. 20, No. 2, Palgrave Macmillan, 2005, pp. 88–102.

R

[Ramesh 1998] B. Ramesh: Factors Influencing Requirements Traceability Practice. Communications of the ACM, Vol. 41, No. 12, ACM Press, 1998, pp. 37–44.

[Ramesh and Jarke 2001] B. Ramesh, M. Jarke: Toward Reference Models for Requirements Traceability. IEEE Transactions on Software Engineering, Vol. 27, No. 1, IEEE Press, 2001, pp. 58–93.

[Ramesh et al. 1995] B. Ramesh, C. Strubbs, T. Powers, M. Edwards: Implementing Requirements Traceability – A Case Study. In: Proceedings of the 2nd International Symposium on Requirements Engineering (RE'95), IEEE Computer Society Press, Los Alamitos, 1995, pp. 176–192.

[Ramesh et al. 1997] B. Ramesh, C. Stubbs, T. Powers, M. Edwards: Requirements Traceability – Theory and Practice. Annals of Software Engineering, Vol. 3, Springer, Berlin, Heidelberg, 1997, pp. 397–415.

[Rausch und Broy 2007] A. Rausch, M. Broy: Das V-Modell XT – Grundlagen, Erfahrungen, Werkzeuge. dpunkt.verlag, Heidelberg, 2007.

[Regnell et al. 1996] B. Regnell, M. Andersson, J. Bergstrand: A Hierarchical Use Case Model with Graphical Representation. In: Proceedings of the 2nd IEEE International Symposium of Computer-Based Systems (ECBS'96), IEEE Computer Society Press, Los Alamitos, 1996, pp. 270–277.

[Regnell et al. 2000] B. Regnell, P. Runeson, T. Thelin: Are the Perspectives Really Different? – Further Experimentation on Scenario-Based Reading of Requirements. Empirical Software Engineering, Vol. 5, No. 4, Kluwer Academic, Hingham, 2000, pp. 331–356.

[Reisig 1986] W. Reisig: Petrinetze – Eine Einführung. Springer, Berlin, Heidelberg, New York, 1986. English version: W. Reisig: Petri Nets – An Introduction. Springer, 1994.

[Reuys et al. 2005a] A. Reuys, E. Kamsties, K. Pohl, S. Reis: Model-Based System Testing of Software Product Families. In: Proceedings 17th Conference on Advanced Information Systems Engineering (CAiSE 2005), Springer, Heidelberg, 2005, pp. 519–534.

[Reuys et al. 2005b] A. Reuys, E. Kamsties, K. Pohl, S. Reis: Szenario-basierter Systemtest von Software-Produktfamilien. In: Informatik – Forschung und Entwicklung, Vol. 20, No. 1-2, Springer, Berlin, Heidelberg, 2005, pp. 33–44.

[Robertson and Robertson 2006] S. Robertson, J. Robertson: Mastering the Requirements Process. 2nd edition, Addison-Wesley, Amsterdam, 2006.

[Rolland and Proix 1992] C. Rolland, C. Proix: A Natural Language Approach for Requirements Engineering. In: Proceedings of the 4th International Conference on Advanced Information Systems Engineering (CAiSE'92), Springer, Berlin, Heidelberg, 1992, pp. 257–277.

[Rolland and Salinesi 2005] C. Rolland, C. Salinesi: Modeling Goals and Reasoning with Them. In: A. Aurum, C. Wohlin (Eds.): Engineering and Managing Software Requirements. Springer, Berlin, Heidelberg, 2005, pp. 189–217.

[Rolland et al. 1998a] C. Rolland, C. Ben Achour, C. Cauvet, J. Ralyt, A. Sutcliffe, N. Maiden, M. Jarke, P. Haumer, K. Pohl, E. Dubois, P. Heymans: A Proposal for a Scenario Classification Framework. Requirements Engineering Journal, Vol. 3, No. 1, Springer, Berlin, Heidelberg, 1998, pp. 23–47.

[Rolland et al. 1998b] C. Rolland, C. Souveyet, C. Ben Achour: Guiding Goal Modelling Using Scenarios. IEEE Transactions on Software Engineering, Vol. 24, No. 12, pp. 1055–1071.

[Rolland et al. 1999] C. Rolland, G. Grosz, R. Kla: Experience with Goal–Scenario Coupling. In: Proceedings of the 4th IEEE International Symposium on Requirements Engineering (RE'99), IEEE Computer Society Press, Los Alamitos, pp. 74–81.

[Ross and Schoman 1977] D. T. Ross, K. E. Schoman: Structured Analysis for Requirements Definition. IEEE Transactions on Software Engineering, Vol. 3, No. 1, 1977, pp. 6–15.

[Rosson and Carroll 1993] M. B. Rosson, J. M. Carroll: Integrating Scenario Evolution with Application Development. IBM Research Report RC 19290, 1993.

[Royce 1987] W. W. Royce: Managing the Development of Large Software Systems. In: Proceedings of the 9th International Conference on Software Engineering (ICSE'87), IEEE Computer Society Press, Los Alamitos, 1987, pp. 328–338.

[Rumbaugh et al. 1991] J. Rumbaugh, M. Blaha, W. Premerlani, F. Eddy, W. Lorensen: Object-Oriented Modeling and Design. Prentice Hall, Upper Saddle River, 1991 (new edition available: Prentice Hall, 2004).

[Rumbaugh et al. 2005] J. Rumbaugh, I. Jacobson, G. Booch: The Unified Modeling Language Reference Manual. 2nd edition, Addison-Wesley, Boston, 2005.

[Rupp 2009] C. Rupp, Sophist Group: Requirements-Engineering und –Management. 5th edition, Hanser, München, Wien, 2009.

[Rupp and Goetz 2000] C. Rupp, R. Goetz: Linguistic Methods of Requirements-Engineering (NLP). In: Proceedings of the European Software Process Improvement Conference (EuroSPI'00), 2000.

S

[Saaty 1999] T. L. Saaty: Decision Making for Leaders – The Analytical Hierarchy Process. 3rd edition, McGraw-Hill, New York, 1999.

[Saaty and Vargas 2001] T. L. Saaty, L. G. Vargas: Models, Methods, Concepts and Application of the Analytic Hierarchy Process. Kluwer Academic, 2001.

[Salinesi 2004] C. Salinesi: Authoring Use Cases. In: I. F. Alexander, N. Maiden (Eds.): Scenarios, Stories, Use Cases – Through the Systems Development Life-Cycle, Wiley, Chichester, 2004.

[Schienmann 2002] B. Schienmann: Kontinuierliches Anforderungsmanagement – Prozesse, Techniken, Werkzeuge. Addison-Wesley, Munich, 2002.

[Schobbens et al. 2006] P. Schobbens, P. Heymans, J.-C. Trigaux, Y. Bontemps: Feature Diagrams: a Survey and a Formal Semantics. In: Proceedings of the 14th IEEE International Requirements Engineering Conference (RE'06), IEEE Computer Society, Washington, 2006, pp. 136–145.

[Schulz von Thun 2005] F. Schulz von Thun: Miteinander reden 1–3. Rowohlt Tb., Hamburg, 2005.

[Schwaber und Beedle 2001] K. Schwaber, M. Beedle: Agile Software Development with Scrum. Prentice Hall, Upper Saddle River, 2001.

[Seidewitz 2003] E. Seidewitz: What Models Mean. IEEE Software, Vol. 20, No. 5, IEEE Press, Los Alamitos, 2003, pp. 26–32.

[Sharp et al. 2007] H. Sharp, Y. Rogers, J. Preece: Interaction Design: Beyond Human–Computer Interaction. 2nd edition, John Wiley & Sons, West Sussex, 2007.

[Shull et al. 2000] F. Shull, I. Rus, V. Basili: How Perspective-Based Reading Can Improve Requirements Inspections. IEEE Computer, Vol. 33, No. 7, 2000, pp. 73–79.

[Simmons 2004] E. Simmons: Requirements Triage – What Can We Learn from a "Medical" Approach? IEEE Software, Vol. 21, No. 4, IEEE Press, Los Alamitos, 2004, pp. 86–88.

[Simon 1996] H. A. Simon: The Sciences of the Artificial. 3rd edition, MIT Press, Cambridge, 1996.

[Sindre and Opdahl 2001] G. Sindre, A. L. Opdahl: Capturing Security Requirements through Misuse Cases. In: Proceedings of the 14th Norwegian Informatics Conference (NIK'01), 2001, pp. 219–230.

[Sindre and Opdahl 2005] G. Sindre, A. L. Opdahl: Eliciting Security Requirements with Misuse Cases. Requirements Engineering, Vol. 10, No. 1, Springer, Berlin, Heidelberg, 2005, pp. 34–44.

[Sinnema et al. 2004] M. Sinnema, S. Deelstra, J. Nijhuis, J. Bosch: COVAMOF – A Framework for Modeling Variability in Software Product Lines. In: Proceedings of the 3rd International Conference on Software Product Lines (SPLC 2004), Lecture Notes in Computer Science, Vol. 3154, Springer, Berlin, Heidelberg, 2004, pp. 197–213.

[Savolainen and Kuusela 2001] J. Savolainen, J. Kuusela: Consistency Management of Product Line Requirements. In: Proceedings of the 5th International Symposium on Requirements Engineering (RE'01), IEEE Computer Society, 2001, pp. 40–47.

[Sommerville 2007] I. Sommerville: Software Engineering. 8th edition, Addison-Wesley, Boston, 2007.

[Sommerville and Sawyer 1997] I. Sommerville, P. Sawyer: Requirements Engineering – A Good Practice Guide. Wiley, Chichester, 2000.

[Spillner et al. 2007] A. Spillner, T. Linz, H. Schaefer: Software Testing Foundations. 2nd edition, Rocky Nook, Santa Barbara, CA, 2007.

[SPL 2009] Software Product Lines: *http://www.softwareproductlines.com*; accessed on 10/09/2009.

[Stachowiak 1973] H. Stachowiak: Allgemeine Modelltheorie. Springer, Wien, 1973.

[Stapleton 1997] J. Stapleton: DSDM – Dynamic System Development Method: The Method in Practice. Addison-Wesley, London, 1997.

[Starke 2008] G. Starke: Effektive Software-Architekturen – Ein praktischer Leitfaden. 3rd edition, Hanser, Munich, 2008.

[Stricker et al. 2009] V. Stricker, A. Heuer, J. M. Zaha, K. Pohl, S. de Panfilis: Agreeing Upon SOA Terminology – Lessons Learned. In: G. Tselentis, J. Domingue, A. Galis, A. Gavras, D. Hausheer, S. Krco, V. Lotz, T. Zahariadis: Towards the Future Internet – A European Research Perspective. IOS Press, Amsterdam, 2009, pp. 345–354.

[Stroebe and Nijstad 2004] W. Stroebe, B. A. Nijstad: Warum Brainstorming in Gruppen Kreativität vermindert – Eine kognitive Theorie der Leistungsverluste beim Brainstorming. Psychologische Rundschau, Vol. 54, No. 1, 2004, pp. 2–10.

[Sutcliffe 2002a] A. Sutcliffe: The Domain Theory – Patterns for Knowledge and Software Reuse. L. Erlbaum, Mahwah, 2002.

[Sutcliffe 2002b] A. Sutcliffe: User-Centred Requirements Engineering – Theory and Practice. Springer, London, 2002.

[Sutcliffe et al. 1998] A. Sutcliffe, N. Maiden, S. Minocha, M. Darrel: Supporting Scenario-Based Requirements Engineering. IEEE Transactions on Software Engineering, Vol. 24, No. 12, 1998, pp. 1072–1088.

T

[Teorey et al. 1986] T. J. Teorey, D. Yang, J. P. Fry: A Logical Design Methodology for Relational Databases using the Extended Entity–Relationship Model. ACM Computing Surveys, Vol. 18, No. 2, 1986, pp. 197–222.

[Thayer and Dorfman 2000] H. Thayer, M. Dorfman: Software Requirements Engineering. 2nd edition, IEEE Computer Society Press, Los Alamitos, 2000.

[The Standish Group 1995] The Standish Group Report: CHAOS. The Standish Group, 1995.

[The Standish Group 2009] The Standish Group. *http://standishgroup.com*; accessed on 10/09/2009.

[Tselentis et al. 2009] G. Tselentis, J. Domingue, A. Galis, A. Gavras, D. Hausheer, S. Krco, V. Lotz, T. Zahariadis: Towards the Future Internet - A European Research Perspective. IOS Press, Amsterdam, 2009.

V

[Van der Linden 2002] F. van der Linden: Software Product Families in Europe – The ESAPS and CAFÉ Projects. IEEE Software, Vol. 19, No. 4, IEEE Press, Los Alamitos, 2002, pp. 41–49.

[Van der Vlist 2002] E. van der Vlist: XML Schema. O'Reilly, Cambridge, 2002.

[Van Lamsweerde 2001] A. van Lamsweerde: Goal-Oriented Requirements Engineering – A Guided Tour. In: Proceedings of the 5th IEEE International Symposium on Requirements Engineering (RE'01), IEEE Computer Society Press, Los Alamitos, 2001, pp. 249–263.

[Van Lamsweerde 2009] A. van Lamsweerde: Requirements Engineering: From System Goals to UML Models to Software Specifications. Wiley, West Sussex, 2009.

[Van Lamsweerde et al. 1991] A. van Lamsweerde, A. Dardenne, B. Delcourt, F. Dubisy: The KAOS Project – Knowledge Acquisition in Automated Specification of Software. In: Proceedings of AAAI Spring Symposium Series, Stanford University, American Association for Artificial Intelligence, 1991, pp. 69–82.

[Van Lamsweerde and Letier 2000] A. van Lamsweerde, E. Letier: Handling Obstacles in Goal-Oriented Requirements Engineering. IEEE Transactions on Software Engineering, Vol. 26, No. 10, IEEE Press, 2000, pp. 978–1005.

[Van Lamsweerde and Willemet 1998] A. van Lamsweerde, L. Willemet: Inferring Declarative Requirements Specifications from Operational Scenarios. IEEE Transactions on Software Engineering, Vol. 24, No. 12, IEEE Press, 1998, pp. 1089–1114.

[Van Loon 2004] H. van Loon: Process Assessment and ISO/IEC 15504 – A Reference Book. Springer, Berlin, Heidelberg, New York, 2004.

[VDA 2003] Verband der Automobilindustrie (VDA): HAWK 2015 – Herausforderung Automobile Wertschöpfungskette. Henrich Druck + Medien, 2003.

[VDI/VDE 1991] Verein Deutscher Ingenieure e.V., Verband der Elektrotechnik Elektronik Informationstechnik e.V.: Lastenheft/Pflichtenheft für den Einsatz von Automatisierungssystemen. VDI/VDE 3694, 1991.

[V-Modell 2006] V-Modell® 97 – Development Standard for IT Systems of the Federal Republic of Germany, May 2006. *http://v-modell.iabg.de*; accessed on 28/10/2009.

[V-Modell 2009] V-Modell® XT, Version 1.3, February 2009. *http://v-modell.iabg.de/dmdocuments/V-Modell-XT-Gesamt-Englisch-V1.3.pdf*; accessed on 28/10/2009.

[Von der Beeck 1994] M. von der Beeck: A Comparison of Statecharts Variants. In: Proceedings of the Formal Techniques in Real-Time and Fault-Tolerant Systems (FTRTFT 94), Springer, Berlin, Heidelberg, New York, 1994.

[Vossen 2008] G. Vossen: Datenmodelle, Datenbanksprachen und Datenbankmanagementsysteme. 5th edition, Oldenbourg, Munich, 2008.

W

[Walden 1993] D. Walden (Ed.): Kano's Methods for Understanding Customer-defined Quality. Center for Quality of Management Journal, Special Issue, Vol. 2, No. 4, 1993.

[Ward and Mellor 1985] P. Ward, S. Mellor: Structured Development of Real-Time Systems – Introduction and Tools. Vol. 1. Prentice Hall, Upper Saddle River, 1985.

[Wedekind 1979] H. Wedekind: Eine Methodologie zur Konstruktion des Konzeptionellen Schemas. In: Band zur Tagung „Datenbanktechnologie" des German Chapters of the ACM, Bad Nauheim, Teubner, Stuttgart, 1979, pp. 65–79.

[Weidenhaupt et al. 1998] K. Weidenhaupt, K. Pohl, M. Jarke, P. Haumer: Scenario Usage in System Development – A Report on Current Practice. IEEE Software, Vol. 15, No. 2, IEEE Press, Los Alamitos, pp. 24–45.

[Weinberg 1978] V. Weinberg: Structured Analysis. Yourdon, New York, 1978.

[Weiss and Lai 1999] D. Weiss, C. Lai: Software Product-Line Engineering – A Family-Based Software Development Process. Addison-Wesley, Reading, 1999.

[Welge and Al-Laham 2007] M. K. Welge, A. Al-Laham: Strategisches Management – Grundlagen, Prozesse, Implementierung. 5th edition, Gabler, Wiesbaden, 2007.

[Wiegers 2003] K. E. Wiegers: Software Requirements. 2nd edition, Microsoft Press, Redmond, 2003.

[Wiegers 2002] K. E. Wiegers: Peer Reviews in Software – A Practical Guide. Addison-Wesley, Boston, 2002.

[Wieringa 1998] R. Wieringa: A Survey of Structured and Object-Oriented Software Specification Methods and Techniques. ACM Computing Surveys, Volume 30, No. 4, 1998, pp. 459–527.

[Wieringa 2003] R. Wieringa: Design Methods for Reactive Systems – Yourdon, Statemate, and the UML. Morgan Kaufmann, San Francisco, 2003.

[Wittgenstein 1963] L. Wittgenstein: Tractatus logico-philosophicus. Suhrkamp, Frankfurt, 1963.

[Wohlin and Aurum 2003] C. Wohlin, A. Aurum: An Evaluation of Checklist-Based Reading for Entity–Relationship Diagrams. In: Proceedings of the 9th International Software Metrics Symposium (METRICS'03), IEEE Computer Society Press, Los Alamitos, 2003, pp. 286–297.

[Wright 1992] P. Wright: What's in a Scenario. SIGCHI Bulletin, Vol. 24, No. 4, October 1992, pp. 11–12.

Y

[Young 2001] R. R. Young: Effective Requirements Practices. Addison-Wesley, Boston, 2001.

[Young 2004] R. R. Young: The Requirements Engineering Handbook. Artech House, Boston, 2004.

[Yourdon 1989] E. Yourdon: Modern Structured Analysis. Prentice Hall, Englewood Cliffs, 1989.

[Yourdon 2006] E. Yourdon: Just Enough Structured Analysis. Ed Yourdon, 2006, *http://www.yourdon.com/jesa/pdf/JESA_euddntbc.pdf*; accessed on 11/11/2009.

[Yu 1993] E. Yu: An Organisational Modelling Framework for Multiperspective Information System Design. In: J. Mylopoulos et al. (Eds.): Requirements Engineering 1993 – Selected Papers, Tech Report DKBS-TR-92-2, Department of Computer Science, University of Toronto, Toronto, 1993, pp. 66–86.

[Yu 1995] E. Yu: Modelling Strategic Relationships for Process Reengineering. Ph.D. Thesis, Department of Computer Science, University of Toronto, Toronto, 1995.

[Yu 1997] E. Yu: Towards Modeling and Reasoning Support for Early-phase Requirements Engineering. In: Proceedings of the 3rd International Symposium on Requirements Engineering (RE'97), IEEE Computer Society Press, Los Alamitos, 1997.

[Yu and Mylopoulos 1994] E. Yu, J. Mylopoulos: Understanding "Why" in Software Process Modelling, Analysis, and Design. In: Proceedings of the 16th International Conference on Software Engineering (ICSE'94), IEEE Computer Society Press, Los Alamitos, 1994, pp. 159–168.

[Yue 1987] K. Yue: What Does It Mean to Say that a Specification is Complete? In: Proceedings of the 4th International Workshop on Software Specification and Design (IWSSD-4), 1987.

Z

[Zowghi and Coulin 2005] D. Zowghi, C. Coulin: Requirements Elicitation – A Survey of Techniques, Approaches and Tools. In: A. Aurum, C. Wohlin (Eds.): Engineering and Managing Software Requirements. Springer, Berlin, Heidelberg, New York, 2005, pp. 19–46.

Index

Printed in the United States
By Bookmasters